Last Poems, 1821–1850

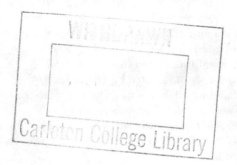

The Cornell Wordsworth

General Editor: Stephen Parrish
Associate Editor: Mark L. Reed
Assistant Editor: James A. Butler

Coordinating Editor: Jared Curtis

Advisory Editors: M. H. Abrams, Geoffrey Hartman, Jonathan Wordsworth

---

Early Poems and Fragments, 1785–1797, edited by Carol Landon and Jared Curtis
An Evening Walk, edited by James Averill
Descriptive Sketches, edited by Eric Birdsall
The Salisbury Plain Poems, edited by Stephen Gill
The Borderers, edited by Robert Osborn
The Ruined Cottage and *The Pedlar*, edited by James Butler
Lyrical Ballads, and Other Poems, 1797–1800, edited by James Butler and Karen Green
Peter Bell, edited by John Jordan
The Prelude, 1798–1799, edited by Stephen Parrish
Home at Grasmere, edited by Beth Darlington
The Thirteen-Book *Prelude*, edited by Mark L. Reed
Poems, in Two Volumes, and Other Poems, 1800–1807, edited by Jared Curtis
Benjamin the Waggoner, edited by Paul F. Betz
The Tuft of Primroses, with Other Late Poems for *The Recluse*, edited by Joseph Kishel
The White Doe of Rylstone, edited by Kristine Dugas
Shorter Poems, 1807–1820, edited by Carl Ketcham
Translations of Chaucer and Virgil, edited by Bruce E. Graver
The Fourteen-Book *Prelude*, edited by W. J. B. Owen
Last Poems, 1821–1850, edited by Jared Curtis

Last Poems, 1821–1850

by William Wordsworth

Edited by

Jared Curtis

with Associate Editors

Apryl Lea Denny-Ferris
Jillian Heydt-Stevenson

CORNELL UNIVERSITY PRESS

ITHACA AND LONDON

PUBLICATION OF THIS BOOK WAS ASSISTED BY GRANTS FROM THE PROGRAM FOR EDITIONS AND THE PUBLICATIONS PROGRAM OF THE NATIONAL ENDOWMENT FOR THE HUMANITIES, AN INDEPENDENT FEDERAL AGENCY.

First published 1999 by Cornell University Press.

Printed in the United States of America.

Cornell University Press strives to use environmentally responsible suppliers and materials to the fullest extent possible in the publishing of its books. Such materials include vegetable-based, low-VOC inks and acid-free papers that are recycled, totally chlorine-free, or partly composed of nonwood fibers. Books that bear the logo of the FSC (Forest Stewardship Council) use paper taken from forests that have been inspected and certified as meeting the highest standards for environmental and social responsibility. For further information, visit our web site at www.cornellpress.cornell.edu.

Library of Congress Cataloging-in-Publication Data

Wordsworth, William, 1770–1850.
[Poems. Selections]
Last poems, 1821–1850 / by William Wordsworth ; edited by Jared Curtis, with associate editors Apryl Lea Denny-Ferris, Jillian Heydt-Stevenson.
p. cm. — (The Cornell Wordsworth)
Includes index.
ISBN 0-8014-3625-7 (cloth)
I. Curtis, Jared R., 1936– . II. Denny-Ferris, Apryl Lea. III. Heydt-Stevenson, Jillian.
IV. Title. V. Series: Wordsworth, William, 1770–1850. Selections. 1975.
PR5853.C8 1999
821'.7–dc21 99-30685

Cloth Printing 10 9 8 7 6 5 4 3 2 1

The Cornell Wordsworth

The individual volumes of the Cornell Wordsworth series, some devoted to long poems, some to collections of shorter poems, have had two common aims. The first has been to bring the early Wordsworth into view. Wordsworth's practice of leaving his poems unpublished for years after their completion, and his lifelong habit of revision—Ernest de Selincourt called it "obsessive"—have obscured the original, often thought the best, versions of his work. These original versions are normally presented in the form of clean, continuous "reading texts" from which all layers of later revision have been stripped away. In volumes that cover the work of Wordsworth's middle and later years, bringing the "early Wordsworth" into view means simply presenting as "reading texts," wherever possible, the earliest finished versions of the poems, not the latest revised versions.

The second aim of the series is to provide, for the first time, a complete and accurate record of variant readings, from Wordsworth's earliest drafts down to the final lifetime (or first posthumous) publication. The most important manuscripts are shown in full transcription; for the most complex and interesting transcriptions, photographs of the manuscript pages are also provided. Besides the transcriptions and the photographs, on which draft revisions may be seen, and an *apparatus criticus* in which printed variants are collected, a third device for the study of revisions is adopted: when two versions of a work match sufficiently well, they are arrayed so that the steps by which one was converted into the other become visible.

Volumes in the series are unnumbered, but upon publication their titles are inserted into the list of volumes in print in the order in which the works were written. A more detailed introduction to the series may be found in the first volume published, *The Salisbury Plain Poems*, edited by Stephen Gill.

S. M. Parrish

Ithaca, New York

Contents

Part II: Notes and Nonverbal Variants

Part III
Selected Transcriptions and Photographic Reproductions

Preface

Wordsworth's poems from the period 1821 to 1850 presented in this edition must be considered in the context of what is omitted. Longer works, composed much earlier but thoroughly revised during this later period—*Guilt and Sorrow*, the fourteen-book *Prelude*, and *The Borderers*—have already appeared in The Cornell Wordsworth series. The translation of Virgil's *Aeneid* and modernizations of Chaucerian poems that Wordsworth produced after 1820 are likewise available in a separate volume in the series. And the various sonnet series and "tours," important works in their own right, are being edited together in a single volume. What this volume offers, then, is necessarily only a portion of the poet's output during the last three decades of his life. It is nonetheless a substantial portion, featuring such poems as *On the Power of Sound*, the sequence of Evening Voluntaries, a large number of sonnets that were not included in any sequence, and Wordsworth's tributes to the dead, like those to Sir George Beaumont, James Hogg, Charles Lamb, Owen Lloyd, and Robert Southey. The poems contained in this volume display a wide range of verse forms (with exclusions already mentioned), including examples from most of the "classes" and types that Wordsworth himself used to organize his oeuvre, and of poems best described as efforts to push the envelope of form, to bend and shape it in new ways. Chronologically arranged, the poems explore themes both perennial and topical as Wordsworth endeavored to make sense of a rapidly changing world by exploring the past, the present, and the links between them.

Preparation of this volume, as of all volumes in this series, was made possible by the Trustees of The Wordsworth Trust, Grasmere, who generously gave access to manuscripts and books in the Wordsworth Library at Grasmere and authorized the publication of manuscript material. We are grateful as well for the access and able assistance provided to us by keepers of Wordsworth manuscripts in other libraries and archives. For permission to cite from and reproduce this far-flung body of materials we are indebted to private collectors and both private and public institutions. We owe special thanks to private collectors Paul F. Betz (McLean, Va.), Leslie Holden (Chichester, U.K.), Mark L. Reed (Chapel Hill, N.C.), Arthur Sale (Cambridge, U.K.), and John Spedding (Mirehouse, Keswick, U.K.). We have been granted permission to cite from and in some instances to reproduce selected portions of manuscripts by the governing bodies of the following libraries and institutions (arranged alphabetically by country and name of library or institution). Specific manuscripts and their locations are listed in the Manuscript Census.

Australia: State Library of Victoria, Melbourne.

Canada: E. J. Pratt Library, Victoria University Libraries, Toronto.

Ireland: The Board of Trinity College, Dublin.

New Zealand: Rare English Collection, Special Printed Collections, Alexander Turnbull Library, Wellington.

United Kingdom: Bristol City Council on behalf of Bristol Reference Library; British Library, London; Special Collections, Edinburgh University Library; the Syndics of the Fitzwilliam Museum, Cambridge; Keswick Museum and Art Gallery, Cumbria; the Lowther Family Trusts for materials on loan to the Cumbria Record Office, Carlisle; the Royal Collection, the Royal Library, Windsor Castle; the Trustees of Rydal Mount, Ambleside, Cumbria; John Rylands University Library of Manchester; the Master and Fellows of St. John's College, Cambridge; Dr. Williams's Library, London.

United States: Amherst College Library; Beinecke Rare Book and Manuscript Library, Yale University; James Fraser Gluck Manuscript and Autograph Collection, Buffalo and Erie County Public Library; Rare Book and Manuscript Library, Columbia University; Division of Rare Books and Manuscript Collections, Cornell University Library; Dartmouth College Library; Houghton Library, Harvard University; Historical Society of Pennsylvania, Philadelphia; Huntington Library, San Marino, California; Manuscript Division of the Library of Congress; Lilly Library, Indiana University; the Henry W. and Albert A. Berg Collection of English and American Literature and the Gilbert Holland Montague Collection of Historic Autographs, Manuscripts and Archives Division, New York Public Library, Astor, Lenox and Tilden Foundations; Pierpont Morgan Library, New York; Robert H. Taylor Collection, Department of Rare Books and Special Collections and General Manuscripts Collection, Princeton University Libraries; the Treasure Room, McCabe Library, Swarthmore College, Swarthmore, Pennsylvania; Kenneth Spencer Research Library, University of Kansas Libraries; English Literary Authors Collection, Special Collections Library, University of Michigan; Harry Ransom Humanities Research Center, The University of Texas at Austin; Tracy W. MacGregor Library, Special Collections Department, University of Virginia; Margaret Clapp Library, Wellesley College, Wellesley, Massachusetts.

My associate editors, Jillian Heydt-Stevenson, of the University of Colorado, Boulder, and Apryl Lea Denny-Ferris, of Viterbo College, La Crosse, Wisconsin, have been primarily responsible for the initial record of variants collected at the Wordsworth Library in Grasmere; I am grateful, too, for their vigilance in checking details and striving for accuracy throughout. Financial assistance for the project has been provided by a grant from the Program for Editions of the National Endowment for the Humanities, an independent grant-making agency of the federal government to support research, education, and public programs in the humanities. Librarians and staff in the departments of Interlibrary Loans and Special Collections, W. A. C. Bennett Library, Simon Fraser University, have been creatively and tirelessly helpful. Jeffrey C. Robinson of the University of Colorado, Boulder, assisted in the early stages of research. To our great benefit Mark L. Reed shared his invaluable analyses of some of the more complex manuscript recensions in the Wordsworth Library and his extensive knowledge of the history of Wordsworth's publications. The assistance given so generously by many other scholars has helped smooth our way. Chief among them are our fellow editors Paul F. Betz, James Butler, Bruce Graver, Karen Green, Geoffrey Jackson, Michael C. Jaye, and Stephen Parrish; Carol Landon has led by example through her rigorous scholarship and intense interest in matters Wordsworthian. Others who have contributed their expertise and time are Alan Bewell, Jeffrey Cowton, David Garcia, Geoffrey Little, and Duncan Wu. No less a gift has been the kind encouragement and unstinting support of Ida Curtis over the years devoted to this task.

JARED CURTIS

Vancouver, British Columbia

Abbreviations

At the end of the Editorial Procedure the reader will find short forms of citation used in transcriptions, those employed to record textual variants and lifetime editions in the *apparatus criticus* and notes, and those used to indicate Wordsworth's classifications of his poems. The Manuscript Census lists short forms of citation for manuscripts.

AFR	Alexis François Rio.
BF	Barron Field.
BL	British Library.
Blanshard	Frances Blanshard, *Portraits of Wordsworth* (London, 1959).
Borderers	*The Borderers* (the poem).
Borderers (Osborn)	*"The Borderers" by William Wordsworth,* ed. Robert Osborn (Ithaca, 1982).
BRH	Benjamin Robert Haydon.
CCl	Catherine Clarkson.
Chalmers	*The Works of the English Poets from Chaucer to Cowper,* ed. Alexander Chalmers (21 vols.; London, 1810).
Chronology: MY	Mark L. Reed, *Wordsworth: The Chronology of the Middle Years, 1800–1815* (Cambridge, Mass., 1975).
CL	Charles Lamb.
Curry	*New Letters of Robert Southey,* ed. Kenneth Curry (2 vols.; New York and London, 1965).
CW	Christopher Wordsworth, the poet's brother.
CW, Jr.	Christopher Wordsworth, Jr.
DC	Dove Cottage.
DC1	Proof pages of the pamphlet form of "To a good Man of most dear memory."
DC MS.	Dove Cottage manuscript.
Dora W	Dora Wordsworth.
DQ	Dora (Wordsworth) Quillinan.
DW	Dorothy Wordsworth.
Early Poems, 1785–1797	*Early Poems and Fragments, 1785–1797, by William Wordsworth,* ed. Carol Landon and Jared Curtis (Ithaca, 1997).
EdeS	Ernest de Selincourt, or his note(s) in his five-volume edition of Wordsworth's *Poetical Works* (see the abbreviation *PW* below).
EEH	Elizabeth (Ebba) Hutchinson.
EFO	Elizabeth Frances Ogle.

1847 Bell	*Ode, on the Installation of His Royal Highness Prince Albert as Chancellor of the University of Cambridge, by William Wordsworth, Poet Laureate* (London: George Bell, Fleet Street, [1847]).
1847 M&P	*Ode, Performed in the Senate-House, Cambridge, on the Sixth of July, M.DCCC.XLVII. at the First Commencement after The Installation of His Royal Highness the Prince Albert, Chancellor of the University. Written by William Wordsworth, Esq.; and Set to Music by Thomas Attwood Walmisley, M.A., Mus. Prof. Cantab.* (Cambridge: Metcalfe and Palmer, 1847).
EM	Edward Moxon.
EMS	Edith May Southey.
EQ	Edward Quillinan.
ES	*Ecclesiastical Sketches by William Wordsworth* (London, 1822).
EY	*The Letters of William and Dorothy Wordsworth: The Early Years, 1787–1805*, ed. Ernest de Selincourt (2d ed., rev. Chester L. Shaver; Oxford, 1967).
FMR	Frederic Mansel Reynolds, editor of *The Keepsake.*
FNW	*The Fenwick Notes of William Wordsworth*, ed. Jared Curtis (London, 1993).
14-Bk Prelude	*The Fourteen-Book "Prelude" by William Wordsworth*, ed. W. J. B. Owen (Ithaca, 1985).
Halliday	F. E. Halliday, *Wordsworth and His World* (New York, 1970).
HCR	Henry Crabb Robinson.
HCR Books	*Henry Crabb Robinson on Books and their Writers*, ed. Edith J. Morley (3 vols.; London, 1838; rpt. New York, 1967)
HCR Correspondence	*The Correspondence of Henry Crabb Robinson with the Wordsworth Circle*, ed. Edith J. Morley (2 vols.; Oxford, 1927).
Healey	George Harris Healey, *The Cornell Wordsworth Collection* (Ithaca, 1957).
Holland & Everett	John Holland and James Everett, *Memoirs of the Life and Writings of James Montgomery* (7 vols.; London: Longman, Brown, Green, and Longmans, 1854–1856).
HR	Henry Reed.
IF	Isabella Fenwick, or note(s) dictated to her by Wordsworth in 1843 (see *FNW* above).
JC	John Carter, Wordsworth's secretary at Rydal Mount.
JK	John Kenyon.
JOH	John O. Hayden's notes in his edition of *William Wordsworth, Poems* (2 vols.; Harmondsworth: Penguin, 1977).
JS	James Stanger.
JSmith	Juliet Smith.
JTC	John Taylor Coleridge.
JW_1	John Wordsworth, Wordsworth's brother.
JW_2	John Wordsworth, Wordsworth's son.
JW_3	John Wordsworth, Wordsworth's nephew.
JWP	Jane Wallas Penfold (see *Madeira*, below).
Knight	William Knight, or his note(s).
Lady B	Lady Beaumont.
Lamb Letters	*The Letters of Charles Lamb*, ed. with a "Sketch of his Life" by Thomas Noon Talfourd (London, 1837).
LB, 1797–1800	*"Lyrical Ballads," and Other Poems, 1797–1800, by William Wordsworth*, ed. James Butler and Karen Green (Ithaca, 1992).
LG	*Literary Gazette and Journal of Belles Lettres, Arts, Science, &c.* (London).

LY, I, II, III, IV	*The Letters of William and Dorothy Wordsworth: The Later Years, 1821–1853*, ed. Ernest de Selincourt (4 vols.; 2d ed., rev., arranged, and ed. Alan G. Hill; Oxford, 1978, 1979, 1982, 1988). Roman numerals refer to parts.
Madeira	Jane Wallas Penfold, *Madeira: Flowers, Fruits and Ferns* (London, 1845).
Memoirs	Christopher Wordsworth, Jr., *Memoirs of William Wordsworth* (2 vols.; London, 1851).
MJJ	Maria Jane Jewsbury.
MMH	Mary Monkhouse Hutchinson, MW's cousin, married to MW's brother Thomas.
MP	*The Morning Post* (London).
MW	Mary Wordsworth.
MWL	*The Letters of Mary Wordsworth, 1800–1855*, ed. Mary Burton (Oxford, 1958).
MY, I, II	*The Letters of William and Dorothy Wordsworth: The Middle Years, 1806–1820*, ed. Ernest de Selincourt (2 vols.; 2d ed.; Part I, 1806–1811, rev. Mary Moorman, Oxford, 1969; Part II, 1812–1820, rev. Mary Moorman and Alan G. Hill, Oxford, 1970). Roman numerals refer to parts.
NMM	*New Monthly Magazine* (London).
NYPL	New York Public Library.
PELY	*Poems, Chiefly of Early and Late Years* (1842). Cited thus in editor's notes.
Poems, 1800–1807	*"Poems, in Two Volumes," and Other Poems, 1800–1807*, ed. Jared Curtis (Ithaca, 1983; corr. 1990).
Poems, 1807–1820	*Shorter Poems, 1807–1820, by William Wordsworth*, ed. Carl H. Ketcham (Ithaca, 1989).
Prelude	The poem, cited from the AB-stage text in *The Thirteen-Book "Prelude," by William Wordsworth*, ed. Mark L. Reed (2 vols.; Ithaca, 1991).
Prose	*The Prose Works of William Wordsworth*, ed. W. J. B. Owen and Jane Smyser (3 vols.; Oxford, 1974).
Prose (Grosart)	*Prose Works of William Wordsworth*, ed. Alexander B. Grosart (3 vols.; London, 1876).
PW	*The Poetical Works of William Wordsworth*, ed. Ernest de Selincourt and Helen Darbishire (5 vols.; Oxford, 1940–1949; rev. 1952–1959).
PW, 18—	The edition of Wordsworth's *Poetical Works* published in the year given.
PW Knight 1889	*The Poetical Works of William Wordsworth*, ed. William Knight (11 vols.; London, 1882–1889).
PW Knight 1896	*The Poetical Works of William Wordsworth*, ed. William Knight (8 vols.; London and New York, 1896).
RMM	Richard Monckton Milnes.
Rotha Q	Rotha Quillinan.
RS	Robert Southey.
SCML	*Memoir and Letters of Sara Coleridge*, ed. E. Coleridge (2 vols.; London: Henry S. King, 1873).
SH	Sara Hutchinson, MW's sister.
SH_2	Sara Hutchinson, MW's niece, daughter of MMH.
Shaver, *MLN*	Chester L. Shaver, "Wordsworth on Byron: An Unpublished Letter to Southey," *Modern Language Notes*, 75 (1960): 488–490.
SHL	*The Letters of Sara Hutchinson, from 1800 to 1835*, ed. Kathleen Coburn (Toronto, 1954).

Sir GB	Sir George Beaumont.
SNL	*The Letters of William and Dorothy Wordsworth: A Supplement of New Letters*, ed. Alan G. Hill (Oxford, 1993).
STC	Samuel Taylor Coleridge.
TA	Thomas Arnold.
TAW	Thomas Attwood Walmisley.
TBB	Thomas Bridges Barrett.
TH	Thomas Hutchinson, Mary Wordsworth's brother.
TM	Thomas Monkhouse.
TNT	Thomas Noon Talfourd.
Tuft	*"The Tuft of Primroses" with Other Late Poems for "The Recluse,"* ed. Joseph F. Kishel (Ithaca, 1986).
WC	*The Wordsworth Circle* (Philadelphia).
WL	Wordsworth Library, Grasmere.
WL Letters	Original letters in the Wordsworth Library, Grasmere.
WPN	*Wordsworth's Pocket Notebook*, ed. George Harris Healey (Ithaca, 1942).
WRH	William Rowan Hamilton.
WW	William Wordsworth.
WW, Jr.	William Wordsworth, the poet's son.
YR, 18–	*Yarrow Revisited, and Other Poems* (London, 1835, 1836, 1839).

Manuscript Census

Short forms of citation for the manuscripts that bear directly on the texts in this edition are listed below in alphabetical order, with letters grouped together under *L* and alphabetized by the letter writer's last name, then listed chronologically. Each entry is followed by a description of the source, the type and size of paper (the horizontal measurement followed by the vertical), and any watermarks or other distinguishing features; by the current location, where appropriate; and by the names of the users or transcribers and the occasions and dates of use. Most abbreviations will be found in the list on pp. xxi–xxiv, above. Short forms of citation for Wordsworth's classes and groups of poems ("Italy 1837" for "Memorials of a Tour in Italy 1837," for example) and for lifetime editions and other publications are listed in Editorial Procedure (pp. 15–17, below).

Amherst MS. WW's copy, revised, of *Decay of Piety,* on the verso of a singleton, inlaid with fourteen other sonnets (most from *Ecclesiastical Sketches*) in a copy of *ES,* 1822. The sheet is of brownish wove stock measuring 18.0 by 11.3 cm. On the recto is MW's copy of "Illustration" ("The Virgin Mountain, wearing like a Queen," *ES,* II, xxxiii). (See Cornelius Howard Patton, *The Amherst Wordsworth Collection: A Descriptive Bibliography* [Amherst, Mass.: Trustees of Amherst College, 1936], p. 66. See also the description of Cornell MS. 2, below.) Amherst College Library.

Barlow MS. (copy) A copy of a version of "Prithee gentle Lady list," partly transcribed by WW for Fanny Barlow on December 21, 1826. Reported by Knight (*PW*Knight 1896), who also printed a footnote to the text, "*Composed,* and in part transcribed, for Fanny Barlow, by her affectionate Friend, Wm. Wordsworth. Rydal Mount, *Shortest Day,* 1826." Knight's own note reads, "These lines were written for Miss Fanny Barlow of Middlethorpe Hall, York. She was first married to the Rev. E. Trafford Leigh, and afterwards to Dr. Eason Wilkinson of Manchester." The manuscript has not been traced.

Berg MS. 1 MW's copy of ll. 38–131 of "To a good Man of most dear memory" on a bifolium of creamy white wove stock measuring 23.0 by 18.8 cm. and countermarked R TURNER / 1834. The sheet is embossed on upper left in a circular device, "LONDON / [*crown*] / SUPERFINE." It was sent by WW to TNT on January 13, 1836; the address panel is postmarked January 14, 1836. Henry W. and Albert A. Berg Collection of English and American Literature, NYPL, Astor, Lenox and Tilden Foundations.

Berg MS. 2 WW's copy of *Extempore Effusion upon the Death of James Hogg,* dated "Park Street May 29th—36." On creamy white wove stock measuring 22.7 by 18.6 cm. and countermarked J GREEN & SON / 1836. Henry W. and Albert A. Berg Collection of English and American Literature, NYPL, Astor, Lenox and Tilden Foundations.

Berg MS. 3 WW's copy, signed and dated August 24, 1840, of the last five lines of "Soft as a cloud is yon blue Ridge—the Mere" on a singleton of creamy white wove stock measuring 13.5 by 17.6 cm. and countermarked [J] WHATMAN / TURKEY MILL / 1838. Henry W. and Albert A. Berg Collection of English and American Literature, NYPL, Astor, Lenox and Tilden Foundations.

Berg MS. 4 Dora W's copy of *Sonnet on the Projected Kendal and Windermere Railway* on a single sheet of creamy white wove stock measuring 22.8 by 18.0 cm. It is signed and dated by WW "Rydal Mount / Oct. 12—1844." Similarity of readings suggests that this is the copy sent to the editor of *MP.* Henry W. and Albert A. Berg Collection of English and American Literature, NYPL, Astor, Lenox and Tilden Foundations.

Berg MS. 5 BRH's copy, with his corrections, of *On a Portrait of the Duke of Wellington, upon the Field of Waterloo, by Haydon.* Though described by George Healey and others as holograph, the manuscript has readings WW later rejected as never his own words, and closely resembles the copy in the Haydon Family Clipping Book described below (Haydon MS.). Like the latter, Berg MS. 5 is probably one of several that BRH prepared to send to newspapers, but he gave this one, instead, as a signed note indicates, to his apprentice. It is on a singleton of blue-tinted laid paper measuring 22.8 by 18.7 cm. and countermarked 1838; chain lines occur at intervals of 2.7 cm. Henry W. and Albert A. Berg Collection of English and American Literature, NYPL, Astor, Lenox and Tilden Foundations.

Berg MS. 6 WW's copy of *Written in an Album* ("Small service is true service while it lasts") on a singleton of creamy wove stock measuring 11.4 by 18.0 cm., folded twice as for an enclosure in a letter. WW has signed and dated it "Rydal Mount / 8th June 1846." Henry W. and Albert A. Berg Collection of English and American Literature, NYPL, Astor, Lenox and Tilden Foundations.

Betz MS. 1 Two gatherings of Dora W's copies of poems by WW and others, tied together with red ribbon. Probably a gift from Dora W to one of her Hutchinson or Monkhouse cousins. The paper is countermarked W WEATHERLEY / 1826 and measures 17.8 by 12.5 cm.; a gathering of three folded sheets contains RS's "The

March to Moscow" in Dora W's hand and a section of sonnets by WW that is headed by Dora W "Stage Coach Inspirations." Relevant materials present in this section are her copies of *Filial Piety; A Tradition of Darley Dale, Derbyshire; A Gravestone upon the Floor in the Cloisters of Worcester Cathedral; Roman Antiqities Discovered, at Bishopstone, Herefordshire;* and *To* ——— ("'Wait, prithee, wait!' this answer Lesbia threw"). The manuscript is discussed and the poems transcribed in Paul F. Betz, "Locating Unrecorded Wordsworth Manuscripts, with Some Examples," *WC* (1997): 106–109. Paul F. Betz Collection.

Betz MS. 2 WW's copy of *With a Small Present* (here titled *To a female Friend with a small Present*) on a slip of white wove stock measuring 8.2 by 18.1 cm., cut from a larger sheet. Stains of adhesive show that it has been extracted from an album. The number "3" is written in ink at the upper right in an unidentified hand. Paul F. Betz Collection.

Betz MS. 3 WW's copy of *Upon the sight of the Portrait of a female Friend* on a single sheet of white wove stock measuring 13.1 by 18.6 cm., cut from a larger sheet that was at some time folded in eight. Paul F. Betz Collection.

Betz MS. 4 Dora W's copies of *The Norman Boy* and *Sequel to The Norman Boy* on a bifolium and a singleton of wove stock measuring 25.1 by 20.2 cm. Both sheets are embossed within a circular device, "LONDON / [*crown*] / SUPERFINE"; both were at the same time folded in six as for the post. Paul F. Betz Collection.

Betz MS. 5 WW's copy of *Sonnet on the Projected Kendal and Windermere Railway* on a single sheet of laid paper measuring 9.2 by 11.2 cm. with chain lines running vertically at intervals of 2.4 cm. The sheet is sewn to the verso of the title page of a copy of *Poems,* 1845, beneath a note "Autograph, sent by Miss Cririe of Rydal Cottage August 1853. See page 217 [i.e., the page on which the sonnet is printed]." The note was apparently written by one of the owners of the book who inscribed it on the front paste-down, "Eliza M. and Georgina Lyon Jan[y.] 20[th.] 1847." Paul F. Betz Collection.

BL MS. 1 MW's copy of the first two stanzas (ll. 1–16) of *Gold and Silver Fishes, in a Vase* on a slip of paper once inserted in Ashley 2262 (see the entry below for MS. 1835/40). The faded blue-tinted sheet measures 18.4 by 11.3 cm. The figures "36" and "146" (revised from "147") appear at the top; a single line is struck through the whole sheet, which at one stage was folded, perhaps for the post. Ashley "A" Series VI, fol. 34, BL.

BL MS. 2 WW's fair copy of *A Night Thought* on a singleton of wove stock measuring 23.0 by 18.6 cm. and watermarked J WHATMAN / TURKEY MILL / 1829. WW signed the copy at Upper Grosvenor Street, the home of Mr. and Mrs. John Marshall, and dated it June 12, 1836. The verso is blank. Ashley 4643, BL.

BL MS. 3 Fragment of a letter from WW to Dora W, February–March 1838 (*LY,*

III, 524–525). Cut away from DC MS. 144, the fragment is of wove stock (gray) and measures approximately 12.6 by 18.7 cm. The sheet when whole measured approximately 22.9 cm. high. Contains ll. 1–8 and a fragment of l. 9 of "Oh what a Wreck! how changed in mien and speech!" Ashley "A" Series XII, fol. 103, BL.

BL MS. 4 MW's copy of "Hark! 'tis the Thrush, undaunted, undeprest" (with "If with old love of you, dear Hills! I share" [titled *Composed on May-Morning, 1838* in *Sonnets*, 1838] on the recto) and *Composed on the Same Morning* ("Life with yon Lambs, like day, is just begun") on the verso of a singleton of wove stock, once bifoliate, measuring 25.0 by 20.2 cm. In 1845 "If with old love" was added to the sequence Italy 1837. The fragment is addressed by MW to "Mrs. Clarkson / Playford Hall" and postmarked May 11, 1838. Add MS. 41186, fol. 35, BL.

BL MS. 5 (copy) A photocopy of an exported manuscript; the original is untraced. WW's copy of the last six lines of *Elegiac Stanzas. 1824* on a single sheet, approximately 16.0 by 20.0 cm. Inscribed below the text of the poem: "W[m] Wordsworth / Lowther Castle / Nov[b] 13—1839." Exported MS., RP2519(ii), BL.

BL MS. 6 WW's correspondence with JTC between November and the end of December 1843 regarding WW's verse memorial to RS, *Inscription for a Monument in Crosthwaite Church, in the Vale of Keswick.* The documents begin on folio 168 and run through folio 176 of BL Add MS. 47553. One of these documents is a copy of the privately printed letterpress circular of the poem (fol. 173); individual autograph manuscripts are listed below:

fol. 168 EQ's transcription, sent to JTC near the end of November 1843, of the earliest surviving version of WW's verse memorial to RS, here titled *Sacred to the Memory of Robert Southey*. . . . The text occupies the recto of a single sheet of wove stock measuring 22.6 by 18.3 cm.

fols. 169–170 WW to JTC, December 2, 1843. A bifolium of wove stock measuring 20.2 by 12.6 cm., countermarked J WHATMAN / TURKEY MILL, and containing WW's revisions of the inscription in fol. 168 and of a subsequent—but now missing—alteration (WW mentions having earlier used the word "prematurely" which "must not be retained"; but the word does not appear in fol. 168). Ll. 11–12 are given twice in the letter.

fols. 171–172 WW to JTC, December 6, 1843. A bifolium of wove stock measuring 18.4 by 11.4 cm. and containing WW's draft for and fair copy of an additional couplet to open the poem and revisions to other lines in the inscription.

fols. 174–175 WW to JTC, December 23, 1843. A bifolium of wove stock, measuring 17.6 by 11.7 cm. and countermarked J GREEN / 1842. WW defended his choice of word in l. 1 and proposed revisions to two further lines of the inscription.

fol. 176 WW to JTC, December ?, 1843 (but after December 23). A singleton of wove stock measuring 11.3 by 18.4 cm. and containing WW's revisions to the last two and a half lines of the inscription. Perhaps this slip of paper was enclosed with one of the previous two letters, but it may have been sent independently.

BL MS. 7 WW's copy of the final stanza of *To*——— ("Let other Bards of Angels sing") on a singleton of wove stock measuring 21.8 by 19.1 cm. and embossed within a circular device, "VICTORIA / [*crown*] / CROWN." It is signed and dated at Rydal Mount, March 12, 1844. Add MS. 37725, fol. 10, BL.

BL MS. 8 MW's copy of WW's *Sonnet on the Projected Kendal and Windermere Railway*, signed by WW, on a singleton of wove stock measuring 12.5 by 20.1 that was once folded in four to accompany a letter sent to William Gladstone dated October 15, 1844. Add MS. 44361, fol. 278, BL.

Cardiff Facsimile A lithographic facsimile of WW's copy of "When Severn's sweeping Flood had overthrown." Two examples are known, one owned by Paul F. Betz, the other by John Windsor. While strictly not a "manuscript," the facsimile replicates what was certainly a genuine holograph copy now lost. Both examples have been examined; the one selected as the basis for the reading text is in the Paul F. Betz Collection.

Catalogue Facsimile An entry in a sale catalogue lists WW's copy of ll. 9–16 of *To*——— ("Let other Bards of Angels sing") signed and dated October 1, 1826. The original manuscript has not been traced.

Coatalen MS. (copy) A photocopy of WW's transcription of *The Poet and the Caged Turtledove* and *To the Author's Portrait.* Both poems are signed and dated by WW October 3, 1832. Owned by Mrs. A. H. Coatalen, Pangbourne, Berkshire, in the 1970s. Original not traced.

Cornell MS. 1 SH's copy of *To the Lady*———. *On Seeing the Foundation Preparing for the Erection of*——— *Chapel, Westmoreland* on a bifolium of laid paper measuring 32.0 by 20.6 cm. and countermarked CLARKE / & / HORSINGTON / 1821 with chain lines at intervals of 2.6 cm. This may be the manuscript of the nine-stanza version that WW sent Lord Lonsdale, a possibility suggested by the formal label, "Wordsworth on / Rydal Chapel," supplied by MW on the center panel of the outside leaf. If so, SH prepared her copy on paper stock different from that used for the letter enclosing it, a common practice. Healey, 2279; Division of Rare Books and Manuscript Collections, Cornell University Library.

Cornell MS. 2 A copy of "Not Love, nor War, nor the tumultuous swell" in a homemade notebook of copies of sonnets from *Ecclesiastical Sketches* in the hand of JK, including some fragments and poems transferred elsewhere. This appears to be JK's copy of holograph manuscripts at Amherst College Library and The Pierpont Morgan Library and is of no textual value except in recording poems missing from the holograph manuscripts; "Not Love, nor War, nor the tumultuous swell," on 14^r, is one of these. There are twenty-nine leaves measuring 21.6

by 16.8 cm.; leaves 1, 6–15, 20–29 are of laid paper with chain lines 2.6 cm. apart and leaves 2–5, 16–19 are of wove stock. Leaves 2^{v}–29^{r} are numbered "1–55." Healey, 2278; Division of Rare Books and Manuscript Collections, Cornell University Library.

Cornell MS. 3 A notebook with imitation-leather covers and repaired leather backstrip; it measures 22.8 by 18.5 cm. and has brown endpapers. Early extracts, replacements of leaves, and modern repairs obscure the original collation, which was perhaps entirely of eights with the outer two leaves being employed as lining for the free endpapers. Sixty leaves remain whole. The first page is inscribed by Dora W "To Emma Ayling / A Memorial of love & affection / from / Dora Wordsworth / Rydal Mount / July $7^{\underline{th}}$ 1824." Poems included in the notebook that are relevant to this edition are *To the Lady ———. On Seeing the Foundation Preparing for the Erection of ——— Chapel, Westmoreland* (Dora W's hand; inscribed by her "Rydal Mount / July $6^{\underline{th}}$ 1824"), three copies of "Why, Minstrel, these untuneful murmurings—" (an imperfect copy and two complete, all beginning "What ails thy Harp, O minstrel, that it rings," in two different hands, both unidentified), and *Installation Ode* (EQ's hand). For a list of most of the WW contents see Healey, 2558; not listed there are *Installation Ode* and a four-line quotation from *Personal Talk.* Division of Rare Books and Manuscript Collections, Cornell University Library.

Cornell MS. 4 Dora W's copy of *On Seeing a Needlecase in the Form of a Harp, the Work of E. M. S.* on a bifolium of white wove stock countermarked G & R TURNER and measuring 18.5 by 11.3 cm. "Wm Wordsworth" is inscribed beneath the text by the copyist. The sheet was at some time folded in three, probably for enclosure. Healey, 2281; Division of Rare Books and Manuscript Collections, Cornell University Library.

Cornell MS. 5 Dora W's copy of *A Grave-stone upon the Floor in the Cloisters of Worcester Cathedral,* which she has inscribed "Wm Wordsworth / Jan^{ry} 1828 / (Written by Dora, Daughter of Wm Wordsworth)" on a sheet of wove bifolium measuring 18.3 by 11.6 cm. and embossed within a circular device, "SUPERFINE / [*star or wheel*] / BATH," at the upper left corner of the first leaf. The bifolium is attached to 28^{v} of the Cottle Notebook (described in Healey, 2797; Healey transcribed the date in Dora W's hand as "1825" but the final digit is an "8"). The title in the manuscript reads ". . . Floor of the Cloisters. . . ." Division of Rare Books and Manuscript Collections, Cornell University Library.

Cornell MS. 6 DW's copy of ll. 1–43 and WW's pencil draft of ll. 97–99 of *On the Power of Sound* on a singleton of laid paper measuring 20.3 by 16.3 cm. and watermarked G C & Co; chain lines are 2.6 cm. apart. Healey, 2283; Division of Rare Books and Manuscript Collections, Cornell University Library.

Cornell MS. 7 Dora W's fair copy of *The Poet and the Caged Turtledove* on a biofolium of wove stock measuring 20.1 by 12.6 cm., folded as for a letter. An accompanying note states that the poem was sent to G. H. Gordon, and was removed from his copy of *PW*, 1832. Division of Rare Books and Manuscript Collections, Cornell University Library.

Cornell MS. 8 Dora W's copy of "Why art thou silent! Is thy love a plant" on a bifolium of wove stock measuring 23.5 by 19.3 cm. For the inscription see the headnote to the poem (p. 214); the sheet is folded and was sent as a letter addressed to "Christopher Wordsworth Esqre, Trin: Coll:, Cambridge." Division of Rare Books and Manuscript Collections, Cornell University Library.

Cornell MS. 9 MW's copy of the sonnet version of *Love Lies Bleeding* on 35^{v}, 36^{r} of a notebook written in MW's and WW's hands containing thirty poems "composed or suggested during a tour of Scotland, in the summer of 1833"; most appeared in *Yarrow Revisited, and Other Poems*, 1835. The notebook, bound in red paper boards, is the *Kendal Almanac* for 1819 and was probably in use during WW's and MW's tour of 1833, but also later, perhaps until the end of 1835. It measures 12.5 by 7.1 cm. and is 0.6 cm. thick and contains 84 pages. The paper is wove stock measuring 12.5 by 7.1 cm. (See Healey, 2285, for a list of contents.) Division of Rare Books and Manuscript Collections, Cornell University Library.

Cornell MS. 10 MW's copy of "Hark! 'tis the Thrush, undaunted, undeprest," signed by WW and dated from Rydal Mount, Easter Sunday, 1838, on a bifolium of bluish wove stock countermarked J WHATMAN / 1835 and measuring 22.7 by 18.6 cm. The sheet was folded in six as a letter and on the outer panel WW has written "Mary Spring Rice / from / Wm Wordsworth." Healey, 2286; Division of Rare Books and Manuscript Collections, Cornell University Library.

Cornell MS. 11 Dora W's copy of *The Cuckoo-clock* on a single leaf of wove stock measuring 22.5 by 18.7 cm. Folded in six as if for an enclosure. Division of Rare Books and Manuscript Collections, Cornell University Library.

Cornell MS. 12 A copy of *The Westmoreland Girl. To My Grandchildren* (here titled simply *To my Grand children*) in an unidentified hand, dated from Rydal Mount, June 6, 1845, signed by WW, on a bifolium of wove stock measuring 20.3 by 12.2 cm. and watermarked J WHATMAN / 1843. This copy is the one WW enclosed in WW to HR, July 1, 1845 (Healey, 2503); the fold size of the poem manuscript fits exactly in the folded letter. On the poem manuscript is a pencil annotation, "July—45," at the upper right corner. Healey, 2293; Division of Rare Books and Manuscript Collections, Cornell University Library.

Cornell MS. 13 MW's fair copy, untitled, of *Written upon a fly leaf in the Copy of the Author's Poems which was sent to her Majesty Queen Victoria.* The manuscript is a bifolium of white wove stock measuring 23.0 by 18.8 cm. and countermarked CANSELL / 1845. It is dated "Cloisters Westminster April 15th 1847" and signed "Mary Wordsworth / William Wordsworth"—not an indication that she contributed some of the verses, but an example of the occasional practice of WW's copyists, when making fair copies of his poems as gifts, of inscribing their own name as well as the poet's. Healey, 2294; Division of Rare Books and Manuscript Collections, Cornell University Library.

DC1 MS. Revisions of "To a good Man of most dear memory" entered by MW on proof pages (DC1) of EM's private printing of the pamphlet form, February 1836. WL.

DC MS. 89 Described in *Tuft* (pp. 72–73) and *Poems, 1807–1820* (p. xxvii). A folio volume bound in calf containing 201 leaves and 25 stubs. The contents include poems that were composed from about 1820 onward, transcribed in various hands. On 48r is a prose tribute, in IF's hand, to RS (relevant perhaps to WW's two poems on RS); in several lists WW detailed possible "Arrangements of [his] Miscellaneous Sonnets." Most of the poems were transcribed in a single fair copy, a few in more than one copy; and for several there are draftings and revisions entered where space was available. Only the poems relevant to this edition are listed (in order of appearance, even if just a few words or lines were entered), each followed by an indication of the hand in the fair copy. Revisions are mostly in WW's hand. *Airey-Force Valley* (Dora W); *Sequel to The Norman Boy* (Dora W); *The Cuckoo-clock* (MW); "These Vales were saddened with no common gloom" (here titled *Epitaph for Mrs. Quillinan*; MW); *Written upon a fly leaf in the Copy of the Author's Poems which was sent to her Majesty Queen Victoria* (MW); "The unremitting voice of nightly streams" (here beginning "The unremitting voice of mountain streams"; WW); *On the Power of Sound* (WW's draft, Dora W's fair copy); *The Triad* (WW); *Presentiments* (WW); "Lyre! though such power do in thy magic live" (Dora W and MW's fair copies, WW's drafts); *To the Lady ———. On Seeing the Foundation Preparing for the Erection of ——— Chapel, Westmoreland* (two stubs, MW); *On the Same Occasion* ("When in the antique age of bow and spear," MW); *Poor Robin* (here "Ragged Robin"; MW); "Why, Minstrel, these tuneful murmurings—" (here "What ails thy Harp O minstrel that it rings"; MW); *Filial Piety* (DW); *A Tradition of Darley Dale, Derbyshire* (DW); *Roman Antiquities Discovered, at Bishopstone, Herefordshire* (stub; WW); *To ———* ("'Wait, prithee, wait!' this answer Lesbia threw"; here titled *To Ellen Loveday Walker*, DW); "Miss not the occasion" (motto to *To Ellen Loveday Walker*, DW); *On a Portrait of the Duke of Wellington, upon the Field of Waterloo, by Haydon* (Dora W); "A volant tribe of Bards on earth are found" (WW); "Go back to antique Ages, if thine eyes" (WW, a second copy by DW); "Just vengeance dost thou crave for rights invaded" (WW, a second copy by MW); *Retirement* (WW); "Fair Prime of life! were it enough to gild" (WW); *Decay of Piety* (WW, a second copy by MW); "Her only Pilot the soft breeze the Boat" (WW, a second copy by MW); "Not Love, nor War, nor the tumultuous swell" (MW).

DC MS. 100 A bifolium of wove stock, 24.7 by 19.8 cm., countermarked C WILMOTT / 1824, containing SH's fair copy, with her corrections, of *To the Lady ———. On Seeing the Foundation Preparing for the Erection of ——— Chapel, Westmoreland.*

DC MS. 101A Described in *Translations* (p. xx). At the back of DW's fair copy of books 1–4 of Virgil's *Aeneid*, are MW's copy, with WW's revisions, of "What month can rival thee sweet May" (here titled *Vernal Stanzas*; see the first reading text of May Odes) and DW's two copies of *Rural Illusions* (A and B in the *apparatus criticus*), with WW's revisions, on the final three leaves of the notebook (60–62), once torn out and then replaced. Paper type and remaining stubs make it certain that 61–62 belong at the end of the notebook of MS. 101A; they have been restored to this position from an incorrect placement in DC MS. 106 (see below).

DC MS. 103 Dora W's fair copy, revised by WW, of *Cenotaph* ("By vain affections unenthralled") on a singleton of laid paper measuring 20.2 by 25 cm., watermarked with the top of a crowned medallion and with chain lines 2.6 cm. apart. WW has added a note to the last line.

DC MS. 106 A collection of poems composed between 1826 and 1835, mostly incorporated in *Yarrow Revisited, and Other Poems*, 1835, chiefly in DW's hand, some in Dora W's and MW's hands, with revisions and drafts by WW. It consists mainly of a handmade notebook of bifolia, with occasional singletons, measuring 18.7 by 11.4/5 cm. The collection also includes five additional leaves of similar size, one a singleton, the others two bifolia gathered as a four but unstitched. All are preserved loose within a cardboard wrapper covered with marbled paper and lined with white wove paper, measuring 20.7 by 13.4 cm. The leaves are sewn in gatherings of varying combinations of singletons and bifolia; present in all are 82 leaves, including six stubs. The wrapper lining at rear has also been used for entry of draft. One bifolium (25, 26) is of blue-tinted wove stock. The outer bifiolium of the two that are gathered as a four but unstitched is of cream-colored wove stock without watermark, as is the one singleton that is not part of the notebook. The rest of the sheets are of cream-colored wove stock watermarked G & R TURNER / 1829. On 6^r and 12^v WW has penciled figures that appear to count the lines of sixteen sonnets (twice) and several longer poems, probably in an effort to gauge the length of the planned volume. MS. 106 seems to have been drawn up chiefly after WW and Dora W returned from their 1831 visit to Scotland on October 17. There can be no doubt, then, that MS. 106 postdates the preparation of MS. 107, which does not contain poems composed during this tour. When DW's list of contents for MS. 106 was compiled (on leaf 7), presumably after entry of poems in the manuscript was virtually complete, four of the poems listed had already been published in *The Keepsake* for 1829 and one in *The Casket* for the same year (both publications appeared in 1830). By January 19, 1832, WW had sent Longman copy for the revised four-volume collected edition, which was to appear in July, superseding the five-volume edition of 1827. As decisions were made concerning the inclusion of additional material previously intended for the new collection and already entered in DC MS. 106, it is possible that further copy was sent to Longmans between January and the end of June, by which time printing had started. The five poems already published in the annuals mentioned, along with two others, were transferred to the 1832 edition; there is some physical evidence of this in the notebook, which now lacks the pages carrying five of the seven poems in question, numbered 47 and 143 through 154, although they had been present when the list was drawn up. It would seem to follow from these considerations that all the poems listed in the contents were composed probably by January 19, 1832, and certainly by late June, the latest date by which the list had been made.

Five leaves in the front that were not part of the original collection contain, on the singleton, MW's list headed "Arrangement as directed by last proofs," followed by the names of groups of poems and single titles in the order of the contents of *Yarrow Revisited, and Other Poems* from "Sonnets, 1833" to the end of the volume (two poems are abbreviated "Janey & Sequel" and three short poems are indicated by the epithet "Smalls": the list is thus complete); on the gathering of four are DW's copy, with WW's revisions, of *To ———* (here titled *To Ellen Loveday Walker*, "'Wait, prithee, wait!' this answer Lesbia threw"), and below it WW's pencil drafting for the same poem; Dora W's copy, with WW's revisions, of *To the Author's Portrait;* MW's copy of *Lines Written in the Album of the Countess of ———. Nov. 5, 1834;* and WW's copy of "The Sun, that seemed so mildly to retire" (later *On a High Part of the Coast of Cumberland Easter Sunday, April 7. The Author's Sixty-third Birthday*). The sewn-up section of the notebook, the main recension, contains copies of the following poems relevant to this edition; the hand in the fair copy of each poem is indicated in parentheses; revisions are mainly in WW's hand: *On the Power of Sound* (DW); *A Grave-stone upon the Floor of Worcester Cathedral* (DW); *A Tradition of Darley Dale, Derbyshire* (DW); "Desponding Father! mark this altered bough" (here titled *Sonnet;* DW); *Filial Piety* (DW); *Ode to May* (later split to form *Ode, Composed on May Morning* and *To May;* DW); *Presentiments* (DW); *St. Catherine of Ledbury* (DW); *Roman Antiquities Discovered, at Bishopstone, Herefordshire* (DW); "Why art thou silent! Is thy love a plant" (DW); "Four fiery steeds impatient of the rein" (DW's two fair copies); *The Poet and the Caged Turtledove* (DW); *Elegiac Musings in the Grounds of Coleorton Hall, the Seat of the late Sir George Beaumont, Bart.* (title here begins *Supposed to be written in . . .* ; DW); *Gold and Silver Fishes, in a Vase* (here untitled; DW); *Inscription Intended for a Stone in the Grounds of Rydal Mount* (DW); *To a Friend* ("Those breathing tokens of your kind regard," DW; later divided into *Liberty* and *Humanity*); *Rural Illusions* (DW); *A Jewish Family* (DW); *The Primrose of the Rock* (untitled; DW); *The Armenian Lady's Love* (DW); *The Russian Fugitive* (DW); "Chatsworth! thy stately mansion, and the pride" (DW); *Inscription* ("The massy Ways, carried across these Heights," DW; here titled *Inscription Intended to be placed on the door of the further Gravel Terrace if we had quitted Rydal Mount*); *The Egyptian Maid; or, The Romance of the Water Lily* (DW); *Epitaph* ("By a blest Husband guided, Mary came"; DW). Inside the back cover WW has written two lines in pencil of *On the Power of Sound,* and two in pencil and in ink of *Humanity. (Written in the year 1829.);* MW entered ten lines of *The Redbreast. (Suggested in a Westmoreland Cottage.),* to which WW added four lines of revision.

DC MS. 107 A collection of copies and drafts of poems mostly incorporated into *Yarrow Revisited, and Other Poems,* 1835, chiefly in Dora W's hand, with some in MW's and DW's hands, and with revisions and drafts by WW. It consists of a large gathering (1–68) never finally stitched together but formed by an obviously deliberate process of inserting smaller gatherings of varying construction within two outer bifolia (1, 68; 2, 67), followed by a sequence of bifolia and singletons (69–114, including one stub) most of which have been at some time stitched together, followed by a bifolium (114, 115) apparently never systematically attached to either of the previous sets of leaves. The first set of leaves measures 20.3/6 by 13.0/3 cm., the second measures 19.2 by 12.8 cm., and the concluding bifolium measures 20.7 by 13.2 cm. The paper of the first set is normally of creamy white wove stock, some watermarked H & McM / 1823 under a three-feathers device, some J Whatman / 1825, and one bifolium J Budgen / 1823. One smaller internal gathering is of a blue-tinted wove stock with watermark C Wilmot / 1827. The second set, with the exception of one leaf obviously a late insert, is apparently entirely of J Budgen / 1823 sheets. The concluding bifolium is of a blue-tinted paper watermarked JX / 1813. The collection is preserved loose in the outer binding—half leather, with marbled-paper-covered boards—of a notebook from which the bound sheets have been extracted. On the front cover is pasted a paper label inscribed, in the hand of JC, "Russian Fugitive / Armenian Lady's Love / &c. / Egyptian Maid / Sound / &c." The paper of the paste-downs on the inner boards, although revealing no watermark, appears to match that of the concluding bifolium 114, 115, which is perhaps a survival from the original binding. The evidence of content and textual variants suggests that DC MS. 107 was in use and virtually complete before DW began transcribing copy for MS. 106; that is, by the time WW and Dora W left for their visit to Scotland in September and October 1831. The poems in this manuscript that are relevant to this edition are listed below in order of first appearance (even if only a few lines were entered). Most of them were transcribed in a single fair copy, a few in more than one copy; and for several there are draftings and revisions entered where space was available. The hand in the fair copy of each poem is indicated in parentheses; revisions are mainly in WW's hand: *The Egyptian Maid; or, The Romance of the Water Lily* (Dora W, WW's pencil draft; a second copy by Dora W); *The Primrose of the Rock* (MW; a second copy by WW; a third copy by Dora W; WW's pencil drafts); "Why art thou Silent? Is thy love a plant" (WW's copy, deleted; Dora W's copy, titled *Sonnet* by WW); *St. Catherine of Ledbury* (WW); "Four fiery steeds impatient of the rein" (here titled *Sonnet*; WW); *Roman Antiquities Discovered, at Bishopstone, Herefordshire* (here titled *Sonnet*; WW); *The Poet and the Caged Turtledove* (here titled *The Poet and the Dove*; two copies by Dora W); *This Lawn, &c.* (WW; a second copy by MW, drafts by WW); *A Jewish Family* (here titled *The Jewish Child;* Dora W's fair copy, revisions by MW and WW; a second copy by Dora W); *The Russian Fugitive* (Dora W's fair copy, revisions by MW and WW; a second copy by Dora W and MW; a third copy by Dora W; WW's pencil drafts); *Elegiac Musings in the Ground, of Coleorton Hall, the Seat of the late Sir George Beaumont, Bart.* (title here begins *Supposed to be written in* . . . ; DW); *Epitaph* ("By a blest Husband guided, Mary came"; WW); "Chatsworth! thy stately mansion, and the pride" (here titled *Composed on my solitary equestrian journey through Derbyshire after visiting Chatsworth*; DW); *Liberty. (Sequel to the Above.)* (WW); *Ode to May* (DW; the poem was later split to form *Ode, Composed on May Morning* and *To May*); *Gold and Silver Fishes, in a Vase* (here untitled; DW); *Inscription Intended for a Stone in the Grounds of Rydal Mount* (untitled, WW); *Presentiments* (Dora W and DW's fair copy); *To B. R. Haydon, Esq. on seeing his Picture of Napoleon Buonaparte on the Island of St. Helena* (here titled *Sonnet To R B. Haydon Esq*[re]*. Composed on seeing his Picture of Napoleon Buonaparte on the Island of S*[t] *Helena*; DW); "Desponding Father! mark this altered bough" (here titled *Sonnet;* WW); *Vernal Stanzas* (later incorporated into *To May;* Dora W); *The Triad* (WW); *Ode to May* (later enlarged and divided into *To May* and *Ode, Composed on May Morning;* MW); *Rural Illusions* (here *Innocent Illusions;* MW's fair copy with WW's revisions); *The Armenian Lady's Love* (MW; a second copy by Dora W; WW's pencil drafts); *Filial Piety* (DW); *The Warning. A Sequel to the Foregoing. March, 1833* (WW); "Chatsworth! thy stately mansion, and the pride" (WW); *Ode, Composed on May Morning* (WW); *On the Power of Sound* (Dora W).

DC MS. 108 A handmade notebook of laid paper made up of three gatherings, the first and last of two bifolia, the second of one bifolium and a singleton (there are two paste-overs). The folded leaves measure 15.1 by 18.8 (gatherings 1 and 2) and 15.1 by 18.3 cm. (gathering 3). They are watermarked with a crowned and quartered medallion bearing two horses and rampant lion above and a conch and a rearing horse below, countermarked WP / 1815 (the same paper and markings as DC MSS. 88 and 116). SH's fair copy of *The Triad* (here titled *The Promise*), beginning "Shew me the noblest Youth of present time," is found on leaves 1^r–7^r with paste-overs on 3^r (10.9 by 14.1 cm.), 5^v (2.6 by 14.1 cm.); the first paste-over covers and contains lines which were canceled and later used for the opening stanza of *On the Power of Sound* (the first reading text, based on DC MS. 131). SH's fair copy of *The Wishing-gate* is on 8^r–10^r; and her fair copy of *The Gleaner* (untitled) follows on 10^r–11^r.

DC MS. 109 A hand-sewn packet containing Dora W's copy of *The Egyptian Maid; or, The Romance of the Water Lily*, here given a facetious title, "The Egyptian Maid or The Romance of Don Juan The water Lilly by Silly Billy Sen[r]." It is made up of seven bifolia and four singletons; two of the latter were used as paste-overs and one as a tipped-in leaf; the fourth is a loose insert. All sheets but the second paste-over and the insert are of creamy laid paper measuring approximately 18.8 by 14.1/15.0 cm. with chain lines at intervals of 2.5/6 cm. The first paste-over, the tipped-in leaf, and the seven bifolia are watermarked with a crowned and quartered shield and countermarked WP / 1815. The second paste-over is of creamy wove stock measuring 6.55 by 15.3 cm. The bifolia were used first in loose form; the stanzas were revised and renumbered and one bifolium (12, 13), containing a version of stanzas 2 through 8, was partly canceled and the remainder used for additional stanzas. One singleton, half of a bifolium, was stuck with wax to the top inner corner of the bifolium 11, 14 as a way of keeping these revised addenda in place. The recto of the first leaf (1^r), left blank for some reason, was inscribed with revised stanzas 2 through 5 and the two paste-overs were added to accommodate further revisions. All the sheets were then sewn tightly together as a packet of fourteen leaves. After the sewing up a full sheet of the laid paper type was used as a singleton, measuring 26.0 by 18.6 cm. approximately (the bottom is torn off). This leaf bears further revisions by Dora

W and WW and was loosely inserted between the paste-over originally attached to 11^{v} and the next leaf (12). The stanza numbers, original and revised, are probably WW's.

DC MS. 112 This loose assembly of manuscripts is made up of lots 406, 407, and 408 of a Sotheby sale; the date of sale is unknown. Lot 406 is a letter from WW to DW (dated August 5, 1829, at Penrith on the address panel) containing WW's fair copy of *Rural Illusions,* here untitled. The lower third of the second leaf of the bifolium has been cut away (probably for WW's signature, now lacking), but the "three little copies of verses" that WW was sending to DW to "amuse" her remain intact on the recto of the first leaf. It is of creamy white laid paper measuring 23.5 by 18.8 cm. with chain lines at intervals of 2.5/6 cm. and countermarked [G]REEN & SON / 1825.

Lot 407 is WW's fair copy of a three-stanza version of *This Lawn, &c.* (here titled *Suggested by our new Lawn*) on a singleton of creamy white paper countermarked G WILMOT / 1828 and measuring 18.7 by 17.2 cm.

Lot 408 is WW's fair copy of a four-stanza version of *To May* (titled *Composed or rather suggested in the Valley of Newlands—1829*) on a singleton measuring 20.2 by 18.7 cm. that was torn from a sheet of embossed creamy white wove stock.

DC MS. 113 Dora W's fair copy of *Gold and Silver Fishes, in a Vase* on three pages of a bifoliate sheet of creamy white wove stock measuring 18.0 by 11.2 cm. and countermarked J GODDING / 1828. Below the last line Dora W has written "Wm Wordsworth / Rydal Mount / Nov^{b} 1829—"; the fourth page is addressed "Mr Wordsworth / Bremen" (that is, WW, Jr., who was living at Bremen in the fall of 1829).

DC MS. 114 A homemade packet containing DW's fair copy, with WW's pencil and ink revisions, as well as some revisions in ink entered by MW, of *To a Friend* (later divided into two poems, *Liberty* and *Humanity*); DW's unrevised fair copy of *Inscription Intended for a Stone in the Grounds of Rydal Mount*; and WW's fair copy of *To B. R. Haydon, Esq. on seeing his Picture of Napoleon Buonaparte on the Island of St. Helena.* WW has also entered pencil draft for ll. 13–18 of *Epitaph* ("By a blest Husband guided, Mary came"). The packet comprises three bifolia (with thirteen paste-overs) arranged in a gathering of two that is sewn to a single bifolium. The blue-tinged laid paper measures (approximately) 20.5 by 16.1 cm. with chain lines running horizontally at intervals of 2.6 cm. and is watermarked with a crowned medallion bearing a seated Britannia and countermarked J WHATMAN / TURKEY MILL / 1828. On the verso of the last leaf, with the leaf reversed, Dora W has written "Epistle to Sir GB. / Gold & Silver Fishes"; the latter poem (published in 1835) is addressed to MJJ and the former is addressed to Sir George Beaumont (published in 1842), but no portion of either poem is found in the packet. One full-sized leaf, of the same paper as the packet, was used for the expansion of *To a Friend* and pasted over the original text on 3^{r}; subsequently nine other (and smaller) pieces of paper of various types were similarly attached to this first paste-over to accommodate further revisions. Leaves 2 and 5 have one and two paste-overs, respectively, which, like those on leaf 3, were introduced to maintain the semblance of a fair copy of the poem.

DC MS. 115 A small quarto notebook, hand-stitched and unbound, containing DW's fair copy of four poems and one stanza of a fifth from the period 1830–1835. It is constructed of two gatherings, each of two gilt-edged sheets, sewn together to form eight leaves; the leaves, of laid paper, measure 18.2 by 11.3 cm. and are countermarked J GREEN & SON. The first recto is inscribed (perhaps by Gordon Graham Wordsworth, WW's grandson), "Turtle Dove / Airy Force / Bruges / Jewish Family." The poems in MS. 115 that are relevant to this edition are *The Poet and the Caged Turtledove, A Jewish Family*, and *On the Power of Sound.* Despite the title's presence in the list on the first page, the text of *Airey-Force Valley* is not present.

DC MS. 116 Nine large folio sheets of blue-tinted laid paper measuring 18.6/8 by 30.1/3 cm.; watermarked with a crowned and quartered medallion bearing animal figures and a harp; countermarked WP / 1815; chain lines 2.5 cm. apart (see the entries for DC MSS. 108 and 109, above). Stab holes in the fold suggest the bifolia were once sewn up as a notebook. The manuscript contains Dora W's fair copies of *Aira Force, or Sir Eglamore & Elva* ("'Tis sweet to stand by Lyulph's Tower"; published as *The Somnambulist*); *The Poet and the Caged Turtledove* (here titled *The Poet and the Dove*); and *The Russian Fugitive* (here titled *Ina, or The Lodge in the Forest, A Russian Tale*).

DC MS. 120 Described in *Early Poems, 1785–1797*, p. 345. DW's "Commonplace Book" containing copies of poems, letters, and other prose writings by DW and others. Relevant to this edition are DW's copy of an early version of WW's sonnet "Chatsworth! thy stately mansion, and the pride"; her copy of WW's *Inscription Intended for a Stone in the Grounds of Rydal Mount* (here untitled), dated June 26, 1830, and recopied August 2, 1832; and her copy of a shortened version of *Elegiac Musings in the Grounds of Coleorton Hall, the Seat of the Late Sir George Beaumont, Bart.*

DC MS. 128 A notebook of 60 leaves, first used for fair copies of poems eventually published in *Yarrow Revisited, and Other Poems*, 1835. Most of these copies are in the hand of Dora W; some are in the hand of MW; and one ("They called Thee merry England in old time") is in the hand of HCR. WW and the two family copyists have revised extensively throughout. The notebook originally consisted of a single gathering of at least 56 leaves. Three of the original leaves remain only as stubs, and four supplementary leaves have been stitched in. The original leaves are of heavy cream-colored wove stock measuring 18.4 by 10.8/11.3 cm. and watermarked in script WL & Co. The stitched-in leaves, 12, 13 (a bifolium) and 24 and 26 (singletons), are of a lighter-weight wove stock. The notebook is bound in a cardboard wrapper covered in red leather and lined with wove paper like that of the gathered sheets. On the front cover is an inscription, in the hand of JC, "Tour. 1833." The poems in the manuscript relevant to this edition are listed below in order of first appearance (even if only a few lines were entered). Most of them were transcribed in a single fair copy, and for several there are draftings and revisions entered where space was available. The hand in the fair copy of each poem listed is indicated in parentheses; revisions are mainly in WW's hand: *A Wren's Nest* (here untitled; WW's draft; MW's fair copy); "The Sun, that seemed so mildly to retire" (here titled *Sea Side/Moresby;* Dora W); *(By the Sea-side.)*, here titled *Composed by the Seaside At Moresby After a Storm* (Dora W); "The leaves that rustled on this oak-crowned hill" (an early version beginning "Grave Creature whether while the Moon shines bright"; MW); *Love Lies Bleeding* (Dora W); *Twilight* (later split into "The leaves that rustled on this oak-crowned hill" and "Not in the lucid intervals of life"; MW); "The sun has long been set" (an expanded version beginning "The Labourer wont to rise with early light"; MW); "Calm is the fragrant air, and loth to lose" (MW); *(By the Side of Rydal Mere.)*, here untitled (MW); *Written in an Album* (untitled; Dora W); "Soft as a cloud is yon blue Ridge—the Mere" (here beginning "The dewy Evening has withdrawn"; Dora W's fair copy, WW's draft).

DC MS. 129 WW's revised fair copy of *(By the Sea-side.)* on a fragment of laid paper, approximately 15.0 by 13.0 cm.; countermarked 1827; horizontal chain lines 2.5/6 cm. apart. Lines 13–20 of the poem have been cut away. Probably transcribed during or shortly after WW's visit to JW_2 at Moresby in April 1833.

DC MS. 130 Two bifolia sewn up as a booklet and with it a single additional sheet, containing Dora W's fair copies of *Lines Suggested by a Portrait from the Pencil of F. Stone* and *The Foregoing Subject Resumed.* The booklet containing *Lines* (leaves 1–4) is of laid paper, 15.8 by 30.6 cm.; it is watermarked with a crowned medallion bearing a seated Britannia and countermarked HARRIS & [?] / 1833 and has horizontal chain lines 2.6 cm. apart. The single sheet (leaf 5) is of wove stock, 12.75 by 20.3 cm., countermarked J WHA[TMAN] / 18[?]; it contains a revised and expanded ending of *Lines Suggested by a Portrait* and *The Foregoing Subject Resumed.* A pencil note in MW's hand identifies "Wilkie" as the "British Painter." An ink note in SH's hand on 4^v reads "1834. / Rydal. Poem by Wordsworth / on Mima's Portrait by Stone. / transcribed by Dora." Some entries in the text are by MW and WW.

DC MS. 131 Nine gatherings of different papers and sizes sewn and tied together as one collection housed in a leather-and-board portfolio that measures roughly 12.5 by 19.6 cm. The collection contains SH's and Dora W's fair copies of poems, some of which appeared in *Yarrow Revisited, and Other Poems,* 1835; the transcription of *The Egyptian Maid; or, The Romance of the Water Lily,* at least, includes fair copy of what is only late revision of fair copy in MS. 107. MS. 131 seems to have been a collection of "keeping copies" and commonplace entries that was not used in the development of the 1835 volume. The first gathering was originally of ten gilt-edged leaves (now eight leaves and two stubs) of wove stock, 11.3 by 17.9 cm., and countermarked BATH / 1815. The second gathering is of four silver-edged leaves of wove stock, 11.4 by 18.75 cm., countermarked G & R TURNER / 1829. The third, fourth, and fifth, each with four leaves of wove stock, 11.6 by 19.15 cm., are sewn up together. The sixth gathering is of fourteen leaves of the same paper as the first gathering (containing SH's fair copies of several poems by "R[obert] H[errick]" and others). The seventh gathering of 16 gilt-edged leaves of wove stock, 11.25 (outer bifolium) and 11.1 (inner bifolium) by 18.1 cm., countermarked G & R TURNER / 1826 (including SH's fair copies of several poems by EQ on 43^r–46^v). The eighth gathering is of four leaves of wove stock, 11.7 by 18.9 cm. Next is a single bifolium of wove stock, 11.5 by 18.8 cm., countermarked G & R TURNER / 1827, followed by a second bifolium of wove stock identical with the first bifolium, but without a countermark, and a third bifolium of blue-tinted wove stock, 11.25 by 18.45 cm.

The poems relevant to this edition appear in the manuscript in the following order; all but the last three are in the hand of SH: *To the Lady ———. On Seeing the Foundation Preparing for the Erection of ——— Chapel, Westmoreland; On the Same Occasion* ("When in the antique age of bow and spear"); *Decay of Piety; The Infant M—— M——; To Rotha Q——; The Armenian Lady's Love; The Egyptian Maid; or, The Romance of the Water Lily;* "These Vales were saddened with no common gloom"; *On the Power of Sound; The Russian Fugitive; The Poet and the Caged Turtledove; The Wishing-gate* (Dora W); *The Gleaner* (Dora W); and *A Jewish Family* (Dora W).

DC MS. 133 A miscellaneous collection of various types and sizes of paper, most of which had once been sewn up in one or more homemade collections but are now loose, apparently gathered up by the Wordsworths from other manuscripts during the preparation of copy for *Yarrow Revisited, and Other Poems,* 1835. Some of the sheets were deposited here from DC MS. 134 when no longer needed there. The paper that makes up the collection is too various to describe in detail. The largest section, containing stanzas from the "May poems," is made up of leaves cut or torn from MS. 134 (see the census entry below). MS. 133 contains materials and drafts of poems in the hands of MW and Dora W, with WW's drafts and revisions throughout. One poem is copied on a half-sheet of wove stock that contains part of a letter addressed to WW at Rydal and is postmarked Cambridge, October 24, 1832; another sheet, bearing the countermark B CLEMENTS / 1833, is similarly addressed and is dated "London May twenty five 1834" (postmarked the next day); and a third, addressed to "Mrs. Luff," is dated January 3, 1834. Most of the work of copying was probably done between January and June 1834. The poems relevant to this edition appear in the manuscript in the following order; the hand in the fair copy of each poem is indicated in parentheses; revisions are mainly in WW's hand: *Devotional Incitements* (Dora W); *The Redbreast. (Suggested in a Westmoreland Cottage.)* (MW); *Ode, Composed on May Morning* (Dora W); and *To May* (Dora W).

DC MS. 134 A collection mainly of bifolia, typically around 18.5 by 15.3 cm., containing copies in the hand of Dora W, written to be gathered by twos, of what became poems published in 1835 in *Yarrow Revisited, and Other Poems.* Dora used a stock of laid paper with chain lines 2.5 cm. apart containing a crowned quartered shield watermark and countermark 1827. Patterns of stab holes used for stitching indicate that it was at some point sewn together in at least two sets. Most of what survives belongs to a first section once stitched through four fairly evenly spaced stab holes. As this section contains work published in *PW*, 1832, it probably largely dates by January 1832. Altogether there are 31 bifolia (two with stubs) and two single sheets of laid paper. The poems relevant to this edition appear in the following order: *The Poet and the Caged Turtledove*; *Gold and Silver Fishes, in a Vase*; *Ode, Composed on May Morning*; *Presentiments*; *This Lawn, &c.*; *Inscription Intended for a Stone in the Grounds of Rydal Mount*; *A Jewish Family*; *Rural Illusions*; *A Tradition of Darley Dale, Derbyshire*; *On the Power of Sound*; *The Primrose of the Rock*; *The Armenian Lady's Love*; *The Russian Fugitive*; *The Egyptian Maid; or, The Romance of the Water Lily*; *To the Author's Portrait* (here titled *To my own Portrait*); "The Sun, that seemed so mildly to retire" (later titled *On a High Part of the Coast of Cumberland Easter Sunday, April 7*).

DC MS. 135 An amalgamation of manuscripts of individual pieces or small collections prepared separately and obviously at different times. Apparently sent to the printer of *Yarrow Revisited, and Other Poems*, 1835, in five groupings of materials—which, because of the variety of degrees of certainty possible about the way they may have been stitched or otherwise combined, are referred to here as packets, of which the first three were numbered together by the printer as a unit. The fifth and last, consisting of the Postscript, had not yet been sent to the printer when DC MS. 138 proof of signature P was read by the Wordsworths (printer Owen Rees's note on that gathering that he will write to ask for the general title indicates that the leaf containing the general title and dedication was sent by the Wordsworths later also). A few supplementary manuscripts are present, and are apparently materials sent after the main collections of manuscripts with which their contents are associated (as is shown both by the content of the published volume and by the intrinsic character of the supplementary manuscripts). The manuscripts of some materials present in the published volume appear to have been lost. The date of the dedication manuscript, December 11, 1834, is probably an indication of the date of the last-written portion of the manuscript.

The manuscript as a physical body appears to have been organized by the Wordsworths with much internal revision and reconstruction in process, and sent off or at least put up in separate packets with unnoticed defects in order and numbering that they discovered, and sent instructions correcting, subsequently. The Wordsworths also added poems—and the manuscripts of the poems—to the materials originally sent off. And they also rearranged materials (in addition to materials at first mistakenly arranged) subsequently. The contents and ordering of the volume were in flux throughout preparation; and to identify a particular state of contents or ordering of the poems as reflecting consistently and in detail a settled conception of the entire organization of the volume would be misleading. The paper, of various types and sizes, may be summarized thus: the main stock consists of two types of blue-tinged laid paper, 21.0 by 15.8 cm., with chain lines at intervals of 2.5/6 cm.; one is watermarked with a seated Britannia in a crowned medallion and countermarked HARRIS / & / TREMLETT / 1833; the other is watermarked with a quartered crowned shield and countermarked 1827; attached sheets, additions, and the final section bearing the endnotes are cream-colored wove stock of varying thickness and size.

The poems and the various notes are in the hands of MW and Dora W, with revisions by WW; for the most part the running titles were inserted by MW. Those poems that are relevant to this edition appear in the manuscript in the following order: *The Egyptian Maid; or, The Romance of the Water Lily* (MW); *Inscription* ("The massy Ways, carried across these Heights"; Dora W); *Elegiac Musings in the Grounds of Coleorton Hall, the Seat of the Late Sir George Beaumont, Bart.* (here *Inscription Composed in the Grounds of Coleorton Hall;* Dora W); *Epitaph* ("By a blest Husband guided, Mary came"; Dora W); *The Armenian Lady's Love* (Dora W); *The Primrose of the Rock* (Dora W); *Presentiments* (Dora W); *The Poet and the Caged Turtledove* (Dora W); *Roman Antiquities Discovered, at Bishopstone, Herefordshire* (Dora W); *St. Catherine of Ledbury* (Dora W); *The Russian Fugitive* (MW); "Why art thou silent! Is thy love a plant" (Dora W); *To B. R. Haydon, Esq. on seeing his Picture of Napoleon Buonaparte on the Island of St. Helena* (Dora W); "Four fiery steeds impatient of the rein" (Dora W); *To the Author's Portrait* (MW); *Gold and Silver Fishes, in a Vase* (Dora W); *Liberty. (Sequel to the Above.)* (Dora W); "Calm is the fragrant air, and loth to lose" (Dora W); "Not in the lucid intervals of life" (Dora W); "The leaves that rustled on this oak-crowned hill" (Dora W); "The Sun, that seemed so mildly to retire" (later titled *On a High Part of the Coast of Cumberland Easter Sunday, April 7;* Dora W); *(By the Side of Rydal Mere.)* (Dora W); "Soft as a cloud is yon blue Ridge—the Mere" (Dora W); *(By the Sea-side.)* (Dora W); "The sun has long been set" (MW); "Throned in the Sun's descending car" (MW); *The Labourer's Noon-day Hymn* (MW); *Devotional Incitements* (WW); *A Wren's Nest* (Dora W); *To———, Upon the Birth of her First-born Child, March, 1833* (Dora W); *To———* ("'Wait, prithee, wait!' this answer Lesbia threw"; MW); *The Redbreast. (Suggested in a Westmoreland Cottage.)* (MW); *Rural Illusions* (DW); *This Lawn, &c.* (DW); *Thought on the Seasons* (Dora W and MW); *The Warning, A Sequel to the Foregoing* (MW); "If this great world of joy and pain" (MW); *Humanity. (Written in the Year 1829.)* (MW); *Lines Suggested by a Portrait from the Pencil of F. Stone* (Dora W); *On the Power of Sound* (MW's title and argument, Dora W); *The Foregoing Subject Resumed* (here designated "Part 2d" of *Lines Suggested by a Portrait from the Pencil of F. Stone*, MW); *Lines Written in the Album of———; Nov. 5, 1834* (MW).

DC MS. 137 An incomplete set of corrected proof pages of *Yarrow Revisited, and Other Poems*, 1835; signatures: B (pp. 3–24), D (49–72), E (73–96), F (97–120), G (123–142), H (145–168), L(a) (217–238), M(a) (241–264), N(a) (265–288), O(a) (295–308), and second states L(b) (217– 240), M(b) (241–264), N(b) (265–288), O(b) (291–310), plus one manuscript leaf bound in at 308/309. Besides the printer's markings, revisions are entered in the proof by MW and WW. Dates entered by the printer on gatherings B–L, first state, indicate that these gatherings were completed between September 5 and October 23, 1834. The rest, M–O, and revised states of L–O, were completed between late October and around December 29, 1834. The revised states were called for by WW's decision, after October 23, to rearrange the poems in these gatherings and to introduce new material, and by the printer's confusion over WW's instructions about reordering.

Signature O(b) contains a manuscript leaf. A single sheet of cream wove stock measuring 18.6 by 12.2 cm. contains MW's copy of *The Foregoing Subject Resumed* that was attached to the page proofs of *Lines Suggested by a Portrait from the Pencil of F. Stone.* The writing of the printer's note on O(b) 291 ("7 hours") runs partly onto the folded-back stub of the manuscript leaf that is bound in at 308/309; so, certainly, the manuscript leaf had been sewn into, and was part of, the gathering on which the printer made his notation. Probably what had happened was that the printer, worried when he received the latest revision of materials for *Lines Suggested by a Portrait from the Pencil of F. Stone* with its new manuscript, and not bothering to set small corrections, produced a mockup (now MS. 137 O[b]), incorporating the manuscript for *The Foregoing Subject Resumed,* in order to confirm the poet's intentions before setting *The Foregoing Subject Resumed* possibly somehow wrongly; and on that gathering the printer noted the number of hours expended on both of the O gatherings. The Wordsworths then received and corrected the mockup, MS. 137 O(b), largely duplicating there the revisions they had already entered in MS. 138 O(aa) (including the page number revision; see below) but adding a few small corrections to *Humanity. (Written in the Year 1829.)* and some major revision—including the pool-of-Bethesda simile drawn from "Part 2d"—at the conclusion of *Lines Suggested by a Portrait from the Pencil of F. Stone.* Individual poems are not listed here; where possible, the handwriting of corrections to individual poems is identified in the *apparatus criticus.*

DC MS. 138 A second incomplete set of corrected proof pages of *Yarrow Revisited, and Other Poems,* 1835; signatures: H (pp. 145–168), I (169–192), K (193–216), N (265–288), O(aa) (295–308), O(bb) (291–310), P (315–322). Besides the printer's markings, revisions are entered in the proof by MW and WW. The printer's completion date survives only on signature K, October 22, 1834. This gathering is of just the same stage as gathering L(a) of MS. 137, which properly belongs in MS. 138. Signature N was apparently printed in part to settle the order of the poems. Signature O(aa) is a complete twelve, commencing with a fly-title for *Rural Illusions.* It sets out the poems according to the instructions with *Humanity, Lines Suggested by a Portrait from the Pencil of F. Stone,* and *On the Power of Sound* at the end, and incorporates the corrections in M(a) in the first two of these poems. The gathering was done up after instructions on sequence were received and to that extent executed. Its page numbering overshoots by only two the final numbering. The difference in pagination is caused by the presence of a fly-title for *Rural Illusions* (as the first page); the leaf concerned was later removed on WW's instructions written in O(bb) as well as in MS. 137 O(b), reducing the page numbers of what followed by 2. The page numbering indicates that the preceding portions of the book must by the time of this proof have been in practically final order and form. The Wordsworths received O(aa) and corrected it, adding major changes at the end of *Lines Suggested by a Portrait from the Pencil of F. Stone* that altered it into a two-part poem, and adding a manuscript (a single sheet of cream wove stock measuring 18.5 by 11.6 cm. [at one time included as a supplementary leaf in MS. 135—the indicative stitch holes are present in the leaf and at the foot of the proof leaf]) that contained the largely new second part (some of which came from the end of the poem as first completed and printed), and adding a note about RS to follow the second part. Before the Wordsworths received back from the printer the new proof that was to have been produced by this revision, they sent off further revisions revoking the two-part *Lines Suggested by a Portrait from the Pencil of F. Stone* and adding the poem (substantially from the previous "2nd part") titled *The Foregoing Subject Resumed,* written out by MW in longhand. Individual poems are not listed here; where possible, the handwriting of corrections to individual poems is identified in the *apparatus criticus.*

DC MS. 139 Dora W's fair copy of *Airey-Force Valley,* untitled, dated "September 1836," on a bifolium of cream-colored wove stock measuring 20.0 by 12.5 cm. and countermarked C ANSELL / 1834.

DC MS. 140 This commercially prepared notebook served as WW's passport, bound in marbled boards and measuring 16.9 by 11 cm.; it is composed of a single gathering of 38 leaves and 6 stubs of ruled wove stock. The passport portion (2^r–14^r) is dated April 11, 1837, to July 28, 1837. On 14^v–15^r is a note by Robert Percival Graves dated "19th February." The notebook was used by WW for drafts and fair copies of the following poems, often running the text of a single poem over to the next page; because of the crowding of text, leaf numbers are given for each poem; the hand in the fair copy or draft of each poem is indicated in parentheses; revisions are mainly in WW's hand: on 15^v–16^r *Composed on May-Morning, 1838* ("If with old love of you, dear Hills! I share"; later titled *Composed at Rydal on May Morning, 1838;* MW); on 16^v–17^r *Composed on the Same Morning* ("Life with yon Lambs, like day, is just begun"; here beginning "Does joy approach? they feel the coming tide"; later titled *Composed on a May Morning, 1838;* WW); on 17^r *Composed on the Same Morning* (MW); on 17^v–18^r *Composed on May-Morning, 1838* ("If with old love . . . "; WW); on 18^r "Hark! 'tis the Thrush, undaunted, undepressed" (here beginning "Hark! tis the thrush the Sun low in the west"; MW); on 19^r *Composed on the Same Morning* (here beginning "Life with yon Mountain lambs is just begun"; MW); on 20^r a third draft, dated May 1, 1838, of *Composed on May-Morning, 1838* ("If with old love . . . "; MW); on 20^v *A Plea for Authors. May, 1838* (WW); on 21^r *A Plea for Authors. May, 1838* (WW), and another draft by WW of the same poem on 22^r–21^v (with the notebook reversed); on 22^v *Composed on the Same Morning* ("Life with yon Lambs . . . "; WW); on 23^r *A Poet to his Grandchild. (Sequel to the foregoing.)* (MW); on 31^v *Inscription Intended for a Stone in the Grounds of Rydal Mount* (here titled *Inscription on a Rock at Rydal Mount;* MW); on 32^v *At Dover* ("From the pier's head, musing—and with increase"; WW) with two unidentified hexameter lines above, in MW's hand:

> Tho' cheered with wildwood growths flowers set with care
> Mid gardens trim and bright each kind to catch and fix.

Folios 33–36 are stubs with fragments of lines showing (the notebook was reversed and used from back to front); 37–41 (transcribed in reverse order) hold a copy in an unidentified hand of *The Antique Sepulchre* "by Mrs. Hemans"; 42 is blank; 43–44 hold a copy in an unidentified hand of DW's letter to Edward Ferguson, her physician and cousin, October 8, 1837. The notebook was employed for literary purposes from around August 1837 through May 1838.

DC MS. 143 A half-leather-bound notebook with marbled boards, inscribed on the cover by JC, "Various Sonnets / & Poems / Scotch Tour / Italian Tour." It was in use in early 1841 while WW was preparing for the publication of *PELY*, 1842. An entry by Dora W near the end of the notebook (118^r^) is dated "Febr^y^ 25th. 1841" (Dora left home on March 4). The notebook contains 129 leaves (including 20 stubs) in 12 surviving gatherings of varying size, though originally there were probably 13 gatherings of which most were 16s. The original notebook leaves are of wove stock and measure 16.6/7 by 20.0 cm. and are watermarked RR 1803; many leaves were cut out, some restored, others pasted on and entirely over other leaves. Several sheets of different paper were inserted, including a gathering of blue-tinted laid paper watermarked with a crowned Britannia medallion and countermarked EHC / 1838; for accounts of the notebook in this state see the descriptions in several volumes of The Cornell Wordsworth: *SPP; Poems, 1800–1807; Tuft;* and *Poems, 1807–1820.*

The notebook has since been restored, however; the leaves have been separated, foliated, and rebound; stubs have been preserved but not counted in the foliation (see *LB, 1797–1800*). The original gatherings cannot be everywhere determined, partly because of depredations by the Wordsworths in their use of the notebook and partly because of the recent restorations. A portion has largely consecutive numbering of leaves, by MW, running from 15 through 103 with some gaps, but leaves had almost certainly been removed even before her numbering. One or more stubs, or the placement of one or more stubs, reflect conjecture by the restorer. One case in which the restorer undoubtedly altered the original binding occurs in what is, as restored, the first gathering. This gathering is at present an "eight" consisting of one stub followed by seven whole leaves, all of them at some time disjunct and, as indicated by pinholes, removed from the notebook and kept separately. The third-from-last and last leaves of the gathering are numbered 15 and 17, and the stub now 1 is conjunct, in the restoration, with 17. The present gathering of eight appears an improbable reconstruction in that it assumes that MW's numbering sequence leading to 17 did not in fact include fully seventeen leaves.

MS. 151 (printer's copy) contains 14 leaves (one a stub) obviously removed from this section of MS. 143. Uncertainties respecting the original binding are in all so numerous that foliation must rest on some other basis: while the sometime presence of missing leaves can be posited frequently with confidence, the specific number missing can be determined surely only in some cases. A numbering of the leaves that actually survive, in the probable order of their original gathering, seems by default the most practical, and is used for purposes of the present edition. Leaves eventually transferred to MS. 151 are taken into account. An unnumbered loose sheet kept with the notebook contains MW's copy of stanzas of *Guilt and Sorrow,* and is of blue-tinted paper of the same type and bearing the same countermark ("1838") as those at 94–107. Pinholes indicate that it was at one time attached to another sheet, perhaps one of the leaves of *Guilt and Sorrow* transcription that the Wordsworths removed from the manuscript (stubs 60–61). However, as no evidence confirms its placement, it is numbered "A1." Most of the poems in the notebook are in the hand of MW, a few are in the hand of Dora W and possibly IF, a version of "Let more ambitious Poets take the heart" is in an unidentified hand, and throughout are drafts, revisions, and copies in WW's hand.

The poems in the manuscript relevant to this edition are listed below in order of first appearance (even if only a few lines were entered). Most of them were transcribed in a single fair copy, several in multiple copies, and for many there are draftings and revisions entered where space was available; the hand in the fair copy of each poem is indicated in parentheses; revisions are mainly in WW's hand. The poems are: *On the Banks of a Rocky Stream* (here untitled; WW); *To an Octogenarian* (WW; two copies, one deleted); "Let more ambitious Poets take the heart" (here "Let more ambitious Poets strive to take"; WW); *Farewell Lines* (MW, a second copy by WW); *Composed by the Sea-shore* (lacking ll. 1–5; MW); "I know an aged Man constrained to dwell" (WW); *Poor Robin* (MW); *At the Grave of Burns. 1803* (MW); *Thoughts Suggested the Day Following on the Banks of Nith, near the Poet's Residence* (here titled *Suggested the following day on . . .* ; MW); *Love Lies Bleeding* (MW); *Companion to the Foregoing* (MW); "The unremitting voice of nightly streams" (here beginning "The unremitting voice of mountain streams" and titled *Introduction to the Somnambulist*; MW, further drafts by WW); *The Norman Boy* (MW); *Sequel to The Norman Boy* (here titled *The Poet's dream / Sequel to the Norman Boy*; MW, WW's title); *The Cuckoo-clock* (a copy in an unknown hand, a second copy by MW); "Intent on gathering wool from hedge and brake" (here beginning "Ambition—can she tame Distress and Grief"; WW, a second copy by MW); *A Night Thought* (MW); *With a Small Present* (MW); *Suggested by a Picture of the Bird of Paradise* (MW); "Lyre! though such power do in thy magic live" (MW); "Though the bold wings of Poesy affect" (here titled *Sonnet;* MW); "Lo! where she stands fixed in a saint-like trance" (MW); *The Widow on Windermere side* (MW); "The Star that comes at close of day to shine" (MW); *Upon a Portrait* ("We gaze, not sad to think that we must die"; here titled *Upon a Portrait of a Friend;* MW); *To a Painter* (here untitled, "All praise the Likeness by thy skill pourtrayed"; MW); *On the Same Subject* (here titled *Continued;* "Though I beheld at first with blank surprise"; MW); *To Lucca Giordano* (here titled *Upon a Picture brought from Italy by my Son, which, together with its Companions now hangs at Rydal Mount;* WW); *Illustrated Books and Newspapers* (WW); "Why should we weep or mourn, Angelic boy" (MW); "Where lies the truth? has Man in wisdom's creed" (WW's draft and fair copy); "Who but is pleased to watch the moon on high" (WW's two copies); "The Crescent-moon, the Star of Love" (WW); *The Westmoreland Girl. To my Grandchildren* (here titled simply *To My Grandchildren / Rydal May 1845*; MW).

Of the two copies of *The Cuckoo-clock,* copy B is the first in the notebook, though placed there after copy A was entered; B is a single sheet of wove stock measuring 18.9 by 22.8 cm.; the handwriting has not been identified. Now pasted in at the stitching of the notebook, it was originally a free sheet folded three times, as for a letter. This copy closely corresponds to the readings found in Cornell MS. 11, while these two copies differ from others.

DC MS. 144 Fragment of a letter from WW to Dora W, February–March 1838 (*LY*, III, 524–525). Cut away from BL Ashley A.5141 (see the entry above for BL MS. 3), the fragment is of wove stock (gray) and measures approximately 10.3 by 18.8 cm. When whole the sheet measured approximately 22.9 cm. high. On the verso is the portion of the letter including "Said Secrecy to Cowardice and Fraud" (later included in Poems Dedicated to Liberty and Order; see the note to the reading text of *Protest against the Ballot. 1838*); part of ll. 10–11 and all of ll. 12–14 of "Oh what a Wreck! how changed in mien and speech!" are on the recto. The piece of this fragment bearing WW's signature was cut away and has not been traced; on the other side the missing piece also bore parts of ll. 9–11 of "Oh what a Wreck!"

DC MS. 146 MW's fair copy of *On a Portrait of the Duke of Wellington, upon the Field of Waterloo, by Haydon* on a single sheet of laid paper measuring 11.4 by 18.1 cm.; it bears part of a watermark of a crowned shield. Inscribed on the verso by EC are the words "Be so good as to give the enclosed to M[rs]. Hutchinson—and M[r]. Carter—." The recipients were Mrs. Mary (Monkhouse) Hutchinson, MW's sister-in-law, who was staying at Rydal Mount in August 1841, and JC, WW's secretary. EC (Mrs. Elizabeth Cookson of Ambleside, a long-time friend of the Wordsworths) was sometimes pressed into service as a copyist of WW's poems (*LY*, III, 691 and note).

DC MS. 147 MW's fair copies of "Private Memorials not to be printed"; the first five are numbered: 1, "Lo! where she stands fixed in a saint-like trance"; 2, "The star that comes at close of day to shine"; 3, "We gaze, not sad to think that we must die" (here "We gaze—nor grieve to think . . . "); 4, *To a Painter* ("All praise the Likeness by thy skill portrayed"); 5, *On the Same Subject* ("Though I beheld at first with blank surprise"); "Oh what a Wreck! how changed in mien and speech" (here titled *To R.S.* and beginning "God's will ordained that piteous blight should reach"); *Valedictory Sonnet* (here titled *Concluding Sonnet*). Once sewn up as a notebook, the sheets are made up of two singletons and a bifolium; they are of the same cream-colored wove stock and measure 23.0 by 18.9 cm.

DC MS. 150 WW's fair copy of *A Jewish Family* on a bifoliate sheet of wove stock embossed with a crown within a rectangle (1.3 by 1.7 cm.). The folded sheet measures 22.8 by 18.7 cm. WW's signature and his inscription, "Transcribed / October / 8th / Rydal Mount 1842," are entered below the last line on the second leaf.

DC MS. 151 A collection of manuscripts, transcribed by various hands and on various kinds of paper, used in preparation of *PELY*, 1842. The materials of DC

MS. 151 may be divided according to original function into three classes, each of which suggests its own internal logic of ordering. WW began work toward a collective volume of early and late poems in early 1841. The principal manuscript result of that work was a large number of fair copies by MW of earlier and recent poems in DC MS. 143. Few of the poetic manuscripts in DC MS. 151 seem likely to date before late July 1841, when, after returning from a long trip, WW appears to have embarked on a prolonged endeavor of writing out new manuscripts of poems then available in DC MS. 143, and still other works, for reasons that probably included: (1) convenience in arranging and rearranging materials as he developed the plan of final order of the projected volume, (2) need for legible fair copies of works that he had revised heavily (most such revision being work of 1841), and (3) preparation of printer's copy. This work continued into early 1842. The logistical plan of the late 1841–early 1842 work appears to have included use principally of two kinds of paper: (1) bifolium sheets of cream wove paper, 23.0 by 18.8, embossed superfine, and (2) bifolium sheets of blue wove paper, without watermark, measuring 20.2 by 25.0 cm., except for one section (114–121) where they measure 12.6 by 20.0 cm. In general, (1) was used for copies for home use and record keeping, and (2) was used for printer's copy, but some of each became employed for the other purpose, and many other papers were used incidentally, especially for the home manuscripts. For the purposes of refoliation MS. 151 is divided in three sections, with foliation prefaced by the numbers 1., 2., and 3., respectively: the first section is of manuscripts retained at home, the second of printer's copies actually sent, and the third of printer's proofs. The second and third groups stand in sequences that were in general the result of careful intrinsic ordering or the necessary result of the process of printing. The printer's manuscript has stitch holes, notes by the scribes, and numberings by the printer that indicate that the manuscript was sent off mostly in large and small packets comprising (1) 1–28 (28^v concludes "More M.S. tomorrow"); (2) 29–38 (39–40, containing *At Vallombrosa* and *Among the Ruins of a Convent in the Apennines,* appear to have been attached to these but removed from them, and the two poems from each other, and sent finally attached to the next packet); (3) 39–77; (4) 80–107; (5) a small batch, 109–111; (6) 113–122; and (7) 123–126 (notes). (Of the missing numbered leaves the status of 78–79 with respect to packets sent is uncertain; 108 was probably sent off separately; and 112 and 127 were sent off separately.) The first group of manuscripts was never put into a finished and secured physical sequence. Some of its sheets were used for poems or prose items that stood widely separated in the volume as published, and many having first been used for fair copy were used for later draft work without any final fair copy of the results having been prepared for keeping and, in the case of poems in series, without clear designation of the series numbers of the poems. In the absence of a clearly formed intrinsic ordering, the ordering of the published book appears the most sensible basis for a general listing.

Poems relevant to this edition appear in MS. 151 in the following order; the hand in each is indicated in parentheses; the revisions are mainly by WW.

The poems found in section 1 are: "Lyre! though such power do in thy magic live" (MW); *Airey-Force Valley* (MW); *At the Grave of Burns. 1803* (MW); *Thoughts*

Suggested the Day Following on the Banks of Nith, near the Poet's Residence (MW); *A Night Thought* (MW); *Farewell Lines* (MW); *Love Lies Bleeding* (MW); *Companion to the Foregoing* (MW); *Suggested by a Picture of the Bird of Paradise* (MW); *Prelude* ("In desultory walk through orchard grounds"; WW); *Poor Robin* (MW); *The Wishing-gate Destroyed* (SH_2); *The Widow on Windermere Side* (MW); "The most alluring clouds that mount the sky" (WW); *On a Portrait of the Duke of Wellington, upon the Field of Waterloo, by Haydon* (MW); *With a Small Present* (MW); "The Crescent-moon, the Star of Love" (MW); "Intent on gathering wool from hedge and brake" (MW); "When Severn's sweeping Flood had overthrown" (WW).

Poems in section 2 are: *At the Grave of Burns. 1803* (IF); *Thoughts Suggested the Day Following on the Banks of Nith, near the Poet's Residence* (IF); *Upon Perusing the Foregoing Epistle Thirty Years after its Composition* (refers to *Epistle to Sir George Beaumont*; Dora W); *Airey-Force Valley* (Dora W); *A Night Thought* (Dora W); *Farewell Lines* (MW); *Love Lies Bleeding* (EC); *Companion to the Foregoing* (Dora W and EC); *Suggested by a Picture of the Bird of Paradise* (EC); *Composed by the Sea-shore* (MW); *The Norman Boy* (MW); *Sequel to The Norman Boy* (MW); *Poor Robin* (EC); *The Cuckoo-clock* (MW); *The Wishing-gate Destroyed* (EC); *The Widow on Windermere Side* (EC); "The most alluring clouds that mount the sky" (MW); "*A Poet!*—He hath put his heart to school" (MW); *On a Portrait of the Duke of Wellington, upon the Field of Waterloo, by Haydon* (IF); "Lo! where she stands fixed in a saint-like trance" (MW); *To a Painter* (MW); *On the Same Subject* (MW).

Section 3 is made up of leaves of proof of *PELY*, revised by MW, WW, and JC. All pages except the first two are numbered in the proof, and the numbers in all instances, except for the first leaf, correspond with those of the volume as published, and with their basic content. The first leaf is unnumbered; the equivalent pages in *PELY* were [*ix*] and *x*. All leaves other than the first are given by printed page number, in a form like "p. 33." In the case of the first leaf, the numbers assigned are based on the equivalents in the volume as published. Gatherings represented are D, M, P, Q, and R. D is represented by the first five leaves of an octavo gathering, of which the first two are signed D and D2, and of which the first three are disjunct from their conjugates, which are not present, the only intact bifolium being that of leaves 4 and 5. M is a complete eight (first two leaves signed M, M2), as are P (first two leaves signed P, P2), Q (signature is cut away from first leaf, second signed Q2), and R (first two leaves signed R, R2). A slip formerly attached to p. 228 ($Q2^v$) is now free but for convenience is designated as a paste-over. Individual poems are not listed here; where possible, the handwriting of corrections to individual poems is identified in the *apparatus criticus.*

DC MS. 154 Described in *Poems, 1800–1807*, p. xxvi. Covers, endpapers, and end matter of *PW*, 1840, vol. II, with revisions to a few poems and a list by WW of proposed categories "Morning Voluntaries, Noon and Evening Voluntaries" with appropriate poems for each. *The Primrose of the Rock* is among the poems revised.

DC MS. 155 A small paper-covered ledger notebook—subsequently dismembered—containing MW's copy of *The Westmoreland Girl. To my Grandchildren* (titled here simply *To my Grandchildren*), with WW's revisions. The poem was entered on leaves 1–4, 5^v–7, bottom to top across each opening. MW's copy, revised by WW, of a portion of *Grace Darling* was entered on 5^r, which was then pasted over 4^v, hiding the *Grace Darling* lines and the discarded version of ll. 49–52, 57–60 of *The Westmoreland Girl*. The seven surviving leaves are of wove stock measuring 15.3 by approximately 12.2 cm.; the cover, of the same size, is of marbled paper. On the inside of the cover, to which the first leaf had once been pasted, is WW's inscription "Wm Wordsworth, bought at Workington July 24th 1835," followed by several names and addresses.

DC MS. 156 Covers, endpapers, and one leaf of end matter for *PW*, 1840, Vol. I. On the verso of the back endpaper is MW's copy, revised, and below it WW's revisions, of "Yes! thou art fair, yet be not moved." WW recopied his revision of ll. 9–12 on the recto of the back endpaper. Also on this endpaper are WW's revisions for *The Longest Day. Addressed To*——— (see *Poems, 1807–1820*, pp. xxix, 245–247), *The Prioress' Tale* (l. 173), and the Latin motto from Eusebius for *Anecdote for Fathers* (see *LB, 1797–1800*). There is no writing on the two leaves of front endpapers.

DC MS. 157 Corrected proofs and manuscript additions for WW's pamphlet *Kendal and Windermere Railway. Two Letters Re-printed from the Morning Post*. The proof pages are addressed to Mssrs Branthwaite, Printers, Kendal, and postmarked January 1, 1845. The pamphlet was ready on January 23, 1845, when WW began distributing copies, and was available for sale to the public February 2, 1845 (*Prose*, III, 333–334). The revisions and corrections are mostly in the hand of EQ, with some notes and marginal corrections by WW and perhaps some by HCR (see *Prose*, III, 335–336). *Sonnet on the Projected Kendal and Windermere Railway* is on p. [3]; the text of "Proud were ye, Mountains, when, in times of old" is uncorrected but was subsequently altered before the pamphlet was issued.

DC MS. 158 WW's aborted copy of ll. 1–3 of *Decay of Piety* on a fragment of wove stock measuring 11.0 by 18.3 cm. DQ has added an explanatory note: "Written by the Poet Wordsworth by desire of his daughter for a friend in Portugal & discarded for faults, Jany 1st 1846—Rydal Mount."

DC MS. 159 WW's signed copy, on an ornately embossed leaf of heavy white stock measuring 28.4 by 23.0 cm., torn from an album or similar bound notebook, of *To*——— ("Look at the fate of summer Flowers"), dated at Rydal Mount, "April 14th 1849."

DC MS. 160 WW's copy of "Camoëns, he the accomplished and the good," the sestet of a sonnet by Tasso ("Vasco, le cui felici ardite antenne"), on the verso of a single half-sheet of wove stock measuring 22.5 by 18.6 cm. On the recto EQ has transcribed the Italian text of the sonnet and a literal prose version, first in Italian and then in English. EdeS reported (*PW*, IV, 372) that the manuscript was "sold at Sotheby's in December 1896."

DC MS. 162 WW's drafts for *At Furness Abbey* ("Here, where, of havoc tired and rash undoing"); ll. 1–8 on one side and ll. 1–10 on the other of a singleton of wove stock that measures 9.0 by 16.9 cm.

DC MS. 165 Dora W's copy of *A Poet to his Grandchild. (Sequel to the foregoing.)*—revised by WW and then canceled—on the recto, and WW's fresh copy on the verso, of part of a half-sheet of creamy white wove stock, measuring 16.7 by 18.7 cm. and countermarked J WHATMAN / TURKEY MILL / 1835. The top portion of the half-sheet, now missing, once contained MW's copy of *A Plea for Authors. May, 1838*, one line of which remains on the surviving piece.

DC MS. 176 Dora W's copy of *To the Rev. Christopher Wordsworth, D.D. Master of Harrow School, After the perusal of his Theophilus Anglicanus, recently published* on a single sheet of cream-colored wove stock measuring 19.8 by 12.1 cm. Below the text Dora has inscribed "William Wordsworth / Rydal Mount / Dec[r] 11th 1843." Notes in a different and later hand identify WW as "friend" of Francis Atkinson Faber, Fellow of Magdalen College, Oxford, to whom the transcription was probably a gift. Faber, older brother of WW's friend Frederick William Faber, introduced himself to WW in April 1839, when he wrote to ask whether WW would accept an honorary degree from Oxford University (WLMS/A/Faber, F. A./1; see *LY*, III, 689n, and the entry for Michigan MS., below).

Dora Harrison's Album (copy) A small autograph album, described as having been presented to "Dora Harrison, Wordsworth's cousin from her friend Mary Dickinson, December 1834." The album is quarto, 6.7 by 8.5 cm., with autograph verses on 14 pages and the remainder of the pages blank; bound in original blind stamped morocco, with the spine lettered "Forget me not" in gilt. WW entered his autograph verse "Fairy skill"; the album also contains autograph verses by Frederick William Faber, Hartley Coleridge, and EQ and signatures of RS, Agnes Strickland, and others. The manuscript has not been traced; the description is drawn from item 47 in Catalogue 200 of Dawsons of Pall Mall (1969).

Dr. Williams's Library MS. WW's draft of *To the Moon. (Composed by the Sea-side,—on the Coast of Cumberland.)* on a singleton of wove stock measuring 22.8 by 18.4 cm. Incorporated in this draft is a version of the first five lines of *To the Moon. (Rydal)*. HCR Papers, Bundle I, II 33; Dr. Williams's Library.

EdeS MS. 1 A manuscript of "Let other Bards of Angels sing" recorded by EdeS (*PW*, II, 35). The original is untraced.

EdeS MS. 2 A manuscript of "Ere with cold beads of midnight dew" recorded by EdeS (*PW*, II, 31). The original is untraced.

Field Album An album belonging to Mrs. Field. BF asked WW to write in his wife's album in a letter of December 24, 1828; WW had done so by January 19, 1829, when he returned the album to BF with a letter (*LY*, II, 6 and note).

According to EdeS, who saw the album or a record of it, it contains WW's transcription of *Written in Mrs. Field's Album Opposite a Pen-and-Ink Sketch in the Manner of a Rembrandt Etching done by Edmund Field* ("That gloomy cave, that gothic nich"; *PW*, IV, 387, 479). BF's letters are in WL; the album is untraced.

Fitzwilliam MS. WW's fair copy of *The Poet and the Caged Turtledove* on two sides of a single sheet of wove stock measuring 22.9 by 18.8 cm. and bearing the watermark G & R TURNER / 1828. WW inscribed his copy "Rydal Mount Wm Wordsworth / 21st Jan^ry^ 1832." Fitzwilliam Museum, Cambridge.

Fleming Album (copy) WW's copy of ll. 49–54 of *Elegiac Stanzas. 1824*, signed and dated Rydal Mount, April 26, 1841, on an oblong octavo page affixed to an album leaf. The album, in green morocco, with boards detached, in which these lines are mounted belonged to members of the Fleming family and includes transcripts of other poems by WW and evocations of the Lake District. This description and the record of variants in the *apparatus criticus* to the poem are based on entry 696 of Sotheby's catalogue of a sale held July 22–23, 1982; the album is untraced.

Gluck MS. WW's copy of "If this great world of joy and pain" on a sheet of wove stock that measures 22.9 by 18.3 cm. and bears a floral form in the center and a circular embossment in the upper left-hand corner with the text "SUPERFINE / POST"; below the text WW has inscribed "Wm Wordsworth / Rydal Mount / 29th July—1840." The sheet is mounted in an album of miscellaneous autographs and manuscripts. Accompanying the manuscript is a letter, dated Kendal, July 29, 1840, to Rev. E. E. Lester, an American minister, from Mary Caroline Braithwaite: "Dear Sir: You are indeed honored! I never knew Wordsworth [to] write so much before. It is unusual for him, as his eyesight is very defective, and the exertion is painful to him. No doubt you will justly appreciate the favour. I rejoice to send you so gratifying an autograph as it is just what you wished but which I did not dare to hope for. . . . I think it would gratify Wordsworth if you were to acknowledge the receipt of the Autograph and if you like you might say you had ventured to take a piece of the Stone he has celebrated. My Conscience rather smites me for being accessory to it." The "Stone" referred to in the letter is probably the one commemorated in *Inscription Intended for a Stone in the Grounds of Rydal Mount* (see above). James Fraser Gluck Manuscript and Autograph Collection, Buffalo and Erie County Public Library, Buffalo, New York.

Graves MS. (copy) WW's revision of ll. 40–47 of "To a good Man of most dear memory" pasted in a copy of the Moxon private printing in early 1836 and given to Robert Percival Graves. The contents were reported by Edward Dowden in the fifth volume of his edition of WW's *PW* in 1893. Graves's printed copy is in the Henry W. and Albert A. Berg Collection of English and American Literature, NYPL, but the manuscript is untraced.

Haydon MS. BRH's copy of *On a Portrait of the Duke of Wellington, upon the Field* *of Waterloo, by Haydon.* The single sheet of laid paper was once folded as a letter; it measures 19.2 by 20.3 cm. with chain lines running vertically. It is watermarked with Britannia inside a roundel. At least one line, probably the title, has been torn from the head of the sheet and a strip 3–5 cm. high has been torn from the foot, apparently not affecting the text. The text of this sonnet, including the inscription with "signature" in full, "William Wordsworth," and the title entered at the foot are all in BRH's hand. Readings that WW gave in his letters to BRH, September 11 and 23, suggest that BRH made this copy between his receipt of the two letters (*LY*, IV, 111, 121). Haydon Family Clipping Book, MS D42:125, Kenneth Spencer Research Library, University of Kansas.

Hoare Album A brown leather-bound notebook with a metal clasp originally containing 192 leaves, of which five are now stubs, plus three free endpapers at each end. Two of the front free endpapers have been removed; and three leaves have been inserted. The inside cover is inscribed: "Sarah Hoare / The Heath" and "Ellen Pryor" below. There are a few paste-ons, and a number of blank pages; pages are numbered in ink from 1 to 466, followed by two unnumbered pages of "Contents." Leaves measure 21.9 by 17.9 cm. and are ruled lightly with lines 0.9 cm. apart; the watermark is W THOMAS / 1820. Contents include copies of some Byron, a good deal of Crabbe, Barbauld, and others, most in one hand, presumably Sarah Hoare's. One poem, "The Death of Cyrus," is attributed in pencil to John Wordsworth (WW's son or his nephew) or CW, Jr., and signed "Winton 1822." The page numbered 143 contains a four-line poem entered by STC, "To a generous Economist," and beneath the poem his signature and date, "27 Decr 1830." The page numbered 174 (87^r^) has a seven-line fragment in WW's autograph: "Time flies—it is his melancholy task . . . " (*Excursion*), signed and dated at Hampstead Heath, July 1, 1836. Other WW poems are *November, 1836* ("Even so for me a Vision sanctified") on p. 176; *Inscription for a Monument in Crosthwaite Church, in the Vale of Keswick* (transcribed from the first broadside circular) on pp. 191–192; "Young England—what is then become of Old" on p. 209; and *The Cuckoo-clock* on pp. 227–229. The first two of these copies were made by Sarah Hoare; autographs of the others have not been identified. A note below the title of *The Cucko-clock* indicates that the version in the album was copied from an earlier copy, "Found it [*error for* in] an old portfolio belonging to Mrs Hoare written by Mr Wordsworth on his 70th birthday April 7—1840"; as the differences between the Album copy and the Cornell copy are slight, the latter may be the original given to Mrs. Hoare by WW. Arthur Sale Collection, Magdalene College, Cambridge.

Houghton MS. 1 WW's copy, revised, of *To* ——— ("'Wait, prithee, wait!' this answer Lesbia threw") on the verso of a single sheet of wove stock measuring 25.2 by 20.1 cm. and watermarked J GREEN & SON / 1826. On the recto is his copy of *Filial Piety*, with his note at the foot, "Given to Edith Southey / by / Wm Wordsworth / Brinsop Court / near Hereford / Jan^ry^ 1828." bMS Eng 327 (3), Houghton Library, Harvard University.

Houghton MS. 2 Dora W's copy of the expanded version of *Extempore Effusion upon the Death of James Hogg* in WW's letter to Robert Percival Graves, mid-December 1835 (*LY*, III, 139). The sheet is a bifolium of white wove stock measuring 23.0 by 18.7 cm. Houghton Library, Harvard University.

Houghton MS. 3 WW's copy, revised, of "The Star that comes at close of day to shine" on a single sheet of wove stock measuring 18.6 by 11.3 cm. bearing the watermark [J WHA]TMAN / [18]37. The leaf was numbered 3 at upper left in an entry apparently at or near the time of the writing of the text. In this manuscript the sonnet is titled *To——— on her Departure from A——— Feb^ry^ 1840* and inscribed "Wm Wordsworth / Rydal Mount / Feb^ry^." bMS Eng 327 (5), Houghton Library, Harvard University.

Houghton MS. 4 WW's fair copy of "Glad sight wherever new with old," dated November 29, 1843, transcribed for Alexander B. Grosart, who later edited and published *The Prose Works of William Wordsworth* (3 vols.; London, 1876). It is transcribed on a singleton of blue-tinted wove stock measuring 20.4 by 17.9 cm. (the sheet is pasted to a slightly larger album page). WW inscribed the sheet, "Mss. / Wm Wordsworth. — / Rydal Mount / 29th Nov^br^ 1843 / Transcribed at the request / of / Alex. B. Grosart [Grosart *revised from* Glossert]"; the notation "Mss." above the signature probably indicates that the poem was an unpublished one drawn from WW's store of manuscripts. bMS Eng 327(6), Houghton Library, Harvard University.

Houghton MS. 5 WW's copy of "Wansfell! this Household has a favoured lot" and "While beams of orient light shoot wide and high." Both poems are copied on the recto of a singleton of wove stock measuring approximately 25.4 by 20.0 cm.; the sheet is now pasted to a piece of cardboard. "Transcribed for his Friend Sergeant Talfourd. Oct. 1844 Rydal Mount." MS. Lowell 3, Houghton Library, Harvard University.

Huntington MS. 1 WW's copy of *The Gleaner* on a bifolium of wove stock measuring 18.6 by 11.3 cm. when folded. The paper is watermarked BATH 1825 below an ornate set of initials, "B [?] P." WW copied the poem on the recto and verso of the first leaf, but in place of a title providing a note, "Title to be supplied by Mr Reynolds" (FMR); above the note, probably in FMR's hand, is written "The Country Girl." FMR was the proprietor of *The Keepsake,* in which the poem appeared in 1829 under the title, apparently supplied by FMR, *The Country Girl.* On the verso of the second leaf (the recto is blank), WW has addressed the sheet to "Mr Reynolds." HM2093, Huntington Library.

Huntington MS. 2 WW to EM, November 20, 1835. A bifolium of laid paper measuring 30.9 by 19.2 cm., with chain lines running vertically at intervals of 2.45 cm.; watermarked with a crowned medallion containing a seated Britannia and countermarked RW & H / NICHOLS / 1828. WW's letter, in MW's hand, fills the first leaf; on 2^r^ is MW's copy of WW's Lamb *Epitaph* ("To the dear memory of a frail good Man") and on 2^v her copy of CL's poem *To Dora W. on being asked by her Father to write here* ("An Album is a Banquet: from the store"). The verso of the second leaf is stamped "Kendal Penny Post" and postmarked November 23, 1835; it is addressed by MW. HM22091, Huntington Library.

Huntington MS. 3 WW to EM, November 23, 1835. Letter containing WW's instructions to EM regarding WW's Lamb *Epitaph* ("To the dear memory of a frail good Man"), adding three lines and deleting two, on a sheet of wove stock measuring 18.6 by 11.8 cm. It is in the handwriting of EEH and MW, and is dated "Rydal Mount—No[vr] 23rd 1835" by EEH and signed by WW. The address is by MW. The letter is stamped "T:P / St. James's St" and postmarked November 25, 1835. HM6874, Huntington Library.

Huntington MS. 4 WW to EM, November 24, 1835. A bifolium of laid paper measuring 31.7 by 20.7 cm., with chain lines running vertically at intervals of 2.6 cm.; watermarked with a crowned medallion containing a seated Britannia and countermarked HARRIS / & / TREMLETT / 1833. EEH and MW's fair copy of WW's Lamb *Epitaph* ("To the dear memory of a frail good Man") is on the first leaf, recto and verso (MW copied the final sixteen lines); WW's letter, in his own hand, is on both sides of the second, dated by MW simply "Tuesday" (November 24, 1835). The letter is stamped "Kendal Penny Post" and postmarked November 26, 1835; 2^v is addressed by MW. HM22092, Huntington Library.

Huntington MS. 5 WW to EM, December 6, 1835. Letter containing WW's corrections of the early version of *Extempore Effusion upon the Death of James Hogg.* The sheet of wove stock, measuring 18.7 by 11.4/7 cm., is written in MW's hand, except for WW's signature. It is watermarked R TURNER / 1834. There are no postmarks. HM22093, Huntington Library.

Huntington MS. 6 WW to EM, mid-December 1835. Letter containing WW's corrections to first printed version of his Lamb *Epitaph* ("To the dear memory of a frail good Man"). The sheet of wove stock, measuring 18.6 by 11.6 cm., is written in MW's hand, except for WW's signature. There are no postmarks. HM22094, Huntington Library.

Huntington MS. 7 WW to EM, February 8, 1836. Letter containing WW's further corrections to his Lamb monody, "To a good Man of most dear memory." A bifolium of wove stock measuring 18.7 by 11.5 cm., with an accompanying slip, apparently a postscript, at some time stitched or pinned to the bifolium (now glued to it); the slip measures 4.5 by 18.6 cm. The letter is in WW's hand throughout and has two postmarks, "T. [?] / Southamp[?]" and the date, February 10, 1836. HM22098, Huntington Library.

Huntington MS. 8 WW to EM, ?February 12, 1836. Letter containing WW's further corrections to his Lamb monody, "To a good Man of most dear memory." A sheet of wove stock measuring 18.7 by 11.8 cm. when folded, it is in WW's hand.

There are no postmarks (for the dating of this letter see pp. 293–294). HM22088, Huntington Library.

Huntington MS. 9 WW to EM, March 17, 1836. Letter containing WW's corrections to the printed version of his Lamb monody, "To a good Man of most dear memory." A bifolium of wove stock measuring 18.4 by 11.8 cm. and a single leaf of the same dimensions and paper; the letter is in WW's hand, with the complimentary closing in MW's hand; the date was added by EM. The bifolium is embossed with a crowned circular ornament containing a daisy-like blossom and possibly some lettering. Frederick Locker, who later owned the manuscript, wrote "4 Jan 36" (the date adopted in error in *LY*; see p. 292, below). There are no postmarks. HM22095, Huntington Library.

Huntington MS. 10 A single sheet of laid paper measuring 21.4 by 17.9 cm. with chain lines running horizontally at intervals of 2.6/7 cm.; the sheet is countermarked BELLOWS. On the recto BRH inscribed a fair copy in ink of *On a Portrait of the Duke of Wellington, upon the Field of Waterloo, by Haydon.* On the verso, in an unknown hand, heavily deleted in ink, is a name, perhaps "Thomas Clarkson." It is probable that this is one of the copies sent by BRH to the newspapers in mid-September 1840. HM12313, Huntington Library.

Huntington MS. 11 A bifolium of wove stock measuring 23.0 by 20.0 cm. The sheet contains WW's fair copy of *The Wishing-gate Destroyed,* which he has signed and dated August 29, 1841, at the foot of 4^v. HM1270, Huntington Library.

Huntington MS. 12 A set of loose pages, [1]–4, torn from the privately printed pamphlet of *Grace Darling.* The leaves are of wove stock and measure 16.3 by 10.1 cm. WW has corrected the text of *Grace Darling* as though for reprinting, not only by entering ink revisions between the lines and in the margins, but also by deleting the running heads and printer's colophon, probably in preparation for its inclusion in *Poems,* 1845. The number 16 has been entered by JC above the drop title, assigning its place in the sequence of Miscellaneous Poems in *Poems,* 1845. The colophon, on the fourth page, reads "[Not Published.] / Carlisle: Printed at the Office of Charles Thurnam."

With the manuscript, on different paper, is an engraving of "Grace Darling," on the verso of which is pasted a fragment of a title page [?] which reads "GRACE DARLING. / London: Ackermann & Co Strand Dickinson Bond St Newcastle, Carrie and Bowman. / Printed by C. Hullmandel." Following the manuscript in the album is a holograph note on a separate sheet of paper: "Mr. James Sinclair, Agent to Lloyds Berwick-upon-Tweed begs to present you with my handwriting"; it is signed G. H. Darling and dated "Longstone Light House / Sept. 3d. 1839." This manuscript, the engraving, and several other manuscripts are bound in an album once belonging to Frederick Locker titled "William Wordsworth. / Poems and Letters. / MSS." Some of the manuscripts contained in it, but certainly not this one, may have belonged at one time to CL, to judge from a pencil note at the top of the title page of the album, "Lamb's Copy." HM2092, Huntington Library.

Keswick MS. SH's copy of *The Triad* and *The Wishing-gate* with WW's revisions and a printer's markings ("81 G"). Laid paper with a portion of watermark visible (small cross) and countermarked JOSEPH COLES / 1818. Five leaves apparently once part of a single large folio sheet. Three of the separate leaves are now sewn into a small booklet and two others are loose. The leaves average 20.0 by 11.0 cm. Chain lines run horizontally at intervals of 2.6 cm. The manuscript is described briefly by Mary Ellen Priestley in "The Southey Collection in the Fitz Park Museum, Keswick, Cumbria," *WC* 9 (1980): 63, item 533. The manuscript is not "proof"—as suggested by Priestley—but may have been used, at least for *The Triad*, as printer's copy for *The Keepsake*, 1829. Southey Collection, KESMG 249, Keswick Museum and Art Gallery, Cumbria.

Knight MS. A manuscript copy of "When Philoctetes in the Lemnian Isle," untraced (reported in *PW* Knight 1896; see also *PW*, III, 433). Knight recorded the "original title" as "Suggested by the same Incident"—i.e., the incident of "Strange visitation! at *Jemima's* lip"; the latter sonnet very probably was copied in the same manuscript.

Laing MS. A single sheet approximately 22.5 by 9.0 cm. The sheet contains a copy of *Thoughts Suggested the Day Following on the Banks of Nith, near the Poet's Residence.* It also contains copies of *Fancy and Tradition* and "'There!' said a Stripling, pointing with meet pride" (published in the sequences Yarrow Revisited and Tour 1833 respectively). Laing Bequest, Edinburgh University Library.

Letters, arranged alphabetically by author, then chronologically:

SH to MMH, December 13, 1826. SH's copy, on 2^r of her letter to MMH, of WW's sonnet *To S. H.* The bifolium is of creamy white laid paper measuring 25.5 by 20.4 cm. with chain lines 2.3/4 cm. apart; it is countermarked J GREEN & SON / 1824. WL.

TAW to WW, May 3, 1847. TAW's letter requesting changes in the wording of the *Installation Ode.* Letters, A/Walmisley/1–4, WL.

CW, Jr., to CW, January 2, 1834. CW, Jr.'s copy of WW's *(By the Sea-side.)* and his sonnet *To a Friend. (On the Banks of the Derwent.)* ("Pastor and Patriot!—at whose bidding rise"; here titled *To the Rev John Wordsworth*; published in the sequence Tour 1833). The bifolium is of white wove stock watermarked C WILMOT / 1829 and measuring 22.7 by 18.6 cm. Division of Rare Books and Manuscript Collections, Cornell University Library.

Dora W to EQ, May 11, 1824. Dora W's copy of "First Floweret of the year is that which shows," here titled, probably by Dora W herself, *In the first Page of an Album by one whose handwriting is wretchedly bad,* on a bifolium of creamy white wove stock measuring 23.3 by 18.8 cm. Dora W's Letters, WL.

Dora W to MJJ, November or December 1829. Dora W's copy of the third stanza of *Gold and Silver Fishes, in a Vase* on a bifoliate sheet of wove stock measuring 18.7 by 11.3 cm. and watermarked J LAV[?E]NDER / 1826. The letter reads, in part, "Father sends his best thanks for your lively Poem and a third stanza to his Poem after 'peace among yourselves' read 'Type of a sunny human breast,'" followed by ll. 19–23 of the poem. The rest of her letter makes it clear that the fish were MJJ's gift to Dora W. Hall Series, Dreer Collection, VIII, 309–310; Historical Society of Pennsylvania.

Dora W to EQ, December 19, 1829. Dora W's copy of *Gold and Silver Fishes, in a Vase*, as well as her references to *On the Power of Sound* and *The Primrose of the Rock*; 2r, 2v, 3r; postmarked December 19, 1829. The letter is written on a singleton and a bifolium of blue-tinted wove stock measuring 22.9 by 18.9 cm. and watermarked TW & BB / 1822. Dora W's Letters, WL.

Dora W to ?, January 18, 1830. Dora W's copy of "Why art thou silent! Is thy love a plant" on a single sheet of cream wove stock measuring 23.5 by 19.5 cm., folded to be inserted in a letter, and marked by her on the address panel "Sonnet to be sent to Chris: Wordsworth"; her note below the text on 1r reads "I mean to send this to Chris: on Valentine's day—he would not tell me the name of his Mona Love & I have found her out through Aunt Joanna." This copy is "signed" with the name "Kate Barker" and dated "Athol St / Douglas / Mona / Janry 18th 1830," probably the date of the letter to an unknown correspondent. Dora W's Letters, WL.

Dora W to EQ, October 3, 1832. Dora W's copy of *To the Author's Portrait* on the recto of the second leaf of a bifolium of creamy white stock measuring 22.9 by 18.6 cm. Dora W's Letters, WL.

Dora W to EQ, February 20, 1834. Dora W's copy of *Love Lies Bleeding*, on 2r of a bifolium of blue-tinted wove stock measuring 25.9 by 20.6 cm. and watermarked J WHATMAN / 1832 / G & D. Dora W's Letters, WL.

Dora W to Rotha Q, July 19, 1834. Dora W's copy of the quatrain *Written in an Album* ("Small service is true service while it lasts"). The poem is on 1v of the second of two bifolia of blue-tinted wove stock measuring 18.5 by 11.5 cm. A larger bifolium of the same paper concludes the letter. Dora W's Letters, WL.

Dora W to EQ, June 1–2, 1835. Dora W's copies, accompanying her letter, of *Love Lies Bleeding* (untitled) and *Companion to the Foregoing* (here titled *Upon the same subject*), on a bifolium of blue-tinted wove stock, measuring 25.5 by 20.5 cm. and watermarked J WHATMAN 1831. Dora W's Letters, WL.

Dora W to IF, ?April 1, 1840. Above Dora's letter, dated only "Wednesday night" from "The Heath Hampstead," is her note headed "Amendments for Cuckoo

Clock"; with it, on a separate sheet, are her copies of *To a Painter* ("All praise the Likeness by thy skill pourtrayed") and *On the Same Subject* ("With disappointment strange I first beheld")—the two sonnets, here untitled, on Margaret Gillies's portrait of MW. Each leaf is a single half-sheet of wove stock measuring 11.2 by 18.5 cm. Dora W's Letters, WL.

DW to CCl, October 24, 1821. DW's copy, on 2ᵛ of her letter to CCl, of WW's and SH's parody, "Queen and Negress chaste and fair." The letter is a bifolium of laid paper measuring 21.9 by 18.1 cm. and watermarked STACEY WISE & C[?] / 1818, with chain lines at intervals of 2.4 cm. Add MS. 36997, fols. 189–192, BL.

DW to HCR, December 21, 1822. DW's copy of WW's "By Moscow self-devoted to a blaze," in her letter to HCR. The sonnet is copied on 2ᵛ of a bifolium of laid paper measuring 21.8 by 18.1 cm. and countermarked STACEY WISE & C[?] / 1818 with chain lines at intervals of 2.35 cm. HCR correspondence, 1818–1826, fols. 86–87; Dr. Williams's Library.

DW to HCR, December 13, 1824. DW's copy of *The Infant M—— M——* and *To Rotha Q——* in her letter on a bifolium of wove stock measuring 24.8 by 20.0 cm. and countermarked C WILMOT / 1821. HCR correspondence, 1818–1826, fol. 115; Dr. Williams's Library.

DW, MW, and WW to CW, Jr., late March 1836. WW's corrections to ll. 34–35 and 40–47 of an early version of the private printing of WW's Lamb monody, "To a good Man of most dear memory." See *LY*, III, 192–193. The manuscript is untraced.

MW to EQ, November 29, 1822. MW's copy of "These Vales were saddened with no common gloom" on a bifolium of creamy white wove stock measuring 24.6 by 20.0 cm. with a watermark C WILMOT / 1821. MW's Letters, WL.

MW to TM, December 3, 1822. MW's copy of "These Vales were saddened with no common gloom" in her letter on a bifolium of creamy white wove stock measuring 23.1 by 18.6 cm. and watermarked K CHILTON MILL / 1810. MW's Letters, WL.

MW to Lady B, February 5, 1823. MW's copy of *To the Lady ——. On Seeing the Foundation Preparing for the Erection of —— Chapel, Westmoreland* on 1ʳ–2ʳ of a bifolium of blue-tinted laid paper watermarked with a seated Britannia in a crowned medallion and countermarked JOSEPH COLES / 1818 and measuring 32.5 by 20.1 cm. Chain lines appear at intervals of 2.5 cm. Coleorton Papers, MS. MA1581 (Wordsworth), Pierpont Morgan Library.

MW to EQ, December 18, 1824. MW's letter to EQ contains a revision to l. 6 of *The Infant M—— M——* on 1ᵛ of a bifolium of creamy white wove stock measuring 23.0 by 18.8 cm. MW's Letters, WL.

MW to Lady B, February 25, 1825. MW's copies of *A Flower Garden*; *Elegiac Stanzas. 1824*; and *Cenotaph* ("By vain affections unenthralled"); with the letter is a sheet containing second copies by MW of *Cenotaph* and *Elegiac Stanzas*. The letter, with its transcriptions of the three poems, is on a bifolium of blue-tinted laid paper watermarked with a seated Britannia in a crowned shield and countermarked J & T JELLYMAN / 1821. In the letter MW corrects l. 26 of *Elegiac Stanzas* and mentions its additional final stanza previously sent. The letter (pt. 1) is not dated and there are no dated postmarks. With the letter is a singleton (pt. 2) bearing the two second copies; it is of the same stock as the letter, showing the same countermark. Coleorton papers, MS. MA1581 (Wordsworth) 38, pts. 1 and 2; Pierpont Morgan Library.

MW to Lady B, December 9, 1825. MW's copy of an early version of *To* ——— ("Such age how beautiful! O Lady bright"—here beginning "Lady, what delicate graces may unite") on 2^{v} of a bifolium of blue-tinted laid paper watermarked with a hunting horn in a crowned device and measuring 23.0 by 18.6 cm. with chain lines 2.4 cm. apart. Coleorton Papers, MS. MA1581 (Wordsworth), 40; Pierpont Morgan Library.

MW and WW to JK, July 25, 1826. SH's copy of "Once I could hail (howe'er serene the sky)" on the recto and verso of the second leaf of the letter, which is on a bifoliate sheet of laid paper measuring 23.3 by 18.5 cm. with chain lines 2.3 cm. apart; it is countermarked PINE & DAVIS / 1823. Robert H. Taylor Collection (49850), Rare Books and Special Collections, Princeton University Libraries.

MW to HCR, November 1 or December 19, 1836. MW's copy of WW's epigram, *On an Event in Col: Evans's redoubted performances in Spain*, on a singleton of wove stock addressed to HCR. This postscript was part of a longer letter written on November 1, 1836 (or perhaps enclosed with MW's letter to HCR, December 19, 1836). The sheet measures 22.9 by 18.5 cm. HCR correspondence, 1836–1837, fol. 72; Dr. Williams's Library.

MW to TH & MMH, April 18, 1838. MW's copy of "Hark! 'tis the Thrush, undaunted, undeprest" in her letter on a bifolium of blue-tinted wove stock measuring 23.0 by 18.4 cm. and countermarked J WHATMAN / 1833. MW's Letters, WL.

MW to IF, April 10, 1840. MW's copy of revisions to "The Star that comes at close of day to shine" and her fair copy, corrected by WW, of the last stanza of *The Cuckoo-clock*, on 2^{r} and 2^{v} of the letter, which is dated only "10 April." Also on 2^{v} is MW's copy of "John the Baptist" (*Before the Picture of the Baptist, by Raphael, in the Gallery at Florence*, published in the sequence Italy 1837). The bifolium is of wove stock and measures 23.3 by 18.8 cm. MW's Letters, WL.

MW to IF, November–early December 1841. MW's letter contains her transcription of revisions to *The Norman Boy* and *Sequel to The Norman Boy* and is accompanied by her copies of the two poems, with corrections in her hand. The manuscript containing copies of the two poems was probably given to IF or sent with an earlier letter that does not survive; but it has been kept with the letter containing the revisions for obvious reasons. The letter, with its revisions, is on a single sheet of blue-gray tinted wove stock measuring 25 by 20 cm. and is embossed on upper left in a circular device, "LONDON / [*crown*] / SUPERFINE." The sheet is folded twice, as for the post. (See WL MS. 2, below, for a description of the copies of the two poems.) MW's Letters, WL.

WW to RS, late December 1821. WW's copies of his four epigrams on Byron's *Cain* on the verso of his letter to RS. Epigrams i and ii were first published in *PW* (Knight, 1896); the full letter was published by Chester L. Shaver in 1960 (Shaver, *MLN*; see also *LY*, I, 101–102). The original manuscript was offered for sale by Simon Finch Rare Books, Catalogue 35 (1998), item 145 (see the notes to the epigrams, pp. 419–420, below).

WW to Lord Lonsdale, January 25, 1823. DW's copy of ll. 21–30 of *To the Lady ———. On Seeing the Foundation Preparing for the Erection of ——— Chapel, Westmoreland* in WW's letter, supplementing the copy of the poem that WW sent to Lord Lonsdale the day before and enclosing "A corrected Copy . . . of the whole" (neither this full copy nor the one sent on January 24 has been traced). The stanza appears on 2^r of a bifolium of laid paper measuring 18.1 by 11.0 cm. and watermarked with a hunting horn in a crowned medallion over the date 1818. Chain lines appear at intervals of 2.4 cm. D/LONS/L1/2/55, Lowther Papers on loan to Cumbria County Council (Cumbria Record Office, Carlisle).

WW to Sir GB, September 20, 1824. MW's copy of *To the Lady E. B. and the Hon. Miss P.* and *To the Torrent at the Devil's Bridge, North Wales* on a bifolium of creamy white laid paper measuring 32.4 by 20.2 cm. with chain lines at intervals of 2.6 cm. The paper is watermarked with a crowned shield with a seated Britannia and countermarked E SMITH / 1822. WL.

WW to TBB, November 19, 1824. MW's copy of *To Rotha Q———* and *The Infant M——M——*, in WW's letter to TBB (a relation of EQ's first wife) of November 19, 1824, with WW's request that the verses be passed on to EQ. The poems appear on 2^r of a bifolium of wove stock measuring 24.9 by 19.6 cm. and countermarked C WILMOT / 1821. Historical Society of Pennsylvania.

WW to CW, January 4, 1825. DW's copy of *To the Torrent at the Devil's Bridge, North Wales* on 2^v of a bifolium of creamy white wove stock measuring 23.0 by 18.8 cm. WL.

WW to MW and Dora W, March 1828. WW's revisions to an unrecovered early version of *The Triad* in his letter to MW and Dora W. The revisions appear on 2^r and 2^v of a bifolium of wove stock measuring 22.9 by 18.7 cm. and countermarked G & R TURNER / 1826. Ashley 4641, fols. 1–2; BL.

WW to BF, April 16, 1828. Described in *Poems, 1800–1807*, p. xxxi. The letter contains WW's revisions to several poems, including *To the Lady ———. On Seeing the Foundation Preparing for the Erection of ——— Chapel, Westmoreland.* Rylands English MS. 355/226, John Rylands University Library of Manchester.

WW to DW, November 8, 1830. WW's copy of "Chatsworth! thy stately mansion, and the pride" on 2ʳ of a bifolium of creamy white laid paper measuring 31.9 by 20.0 cm. with chain lines at intervals of 2.6 cm.; the sheet is watermarked with a seated Britannia in a crowned shield and countermarked RUSH & TURNER / 1827. WL.

WW to BRH, June 11, 1831. MW's copy, with corrections by DW, and signed by WW, of *To B. R. Haydon, Esq. on seeing his Picture of Napoleon Buonaparte on the Island of St. Helena,* on 1ʳ of a bifolium of blue-tinted wove stock measuring 22.8 by 18.7 cm. and watermarked FELLOWS / 1827. The sonnet was copied on the sheet first and WW's letter, also in MW's hand, follows on the verso. The text of the letter is in *LY*, II, 396–397, derived from Knight's edition of Wordsworth family letters, but neither the poem nor its variants are recorded there. John Spedding Collection, Mirehouse, Keswick.

WW and DW to WRH (and Eliza Hamilton), June 13, 1831. DW's copy of *To B. R. Haydon, Esq. on seeing his Picture of Napoleon Buonaparte on the Island of St. Helena* enclosed in their letter to the Hamiltons (see *LY*, II, 399). The original of the letter is untraced, but it was offered for sale with "Property of the Descendants of Sir William Rowan Hamilton" on July 22, 1983; a part of the letter was reproduced in the sale catalogue (of which only proof pages survive, with the seller unidentified). The copy of the sonnet appears to replicate the copy sent to BRH two days earlier, but only the first seven and a half lines, which are not entirely legible, are reproduced in the catalogue.

WW to JK, September 9, 1831. MW's copy of *Inscription Intended for a Stone in the Grounds of Rydal Mount* in WW's letter to JK; the poem is on the second leaf of a bifolium of creamy wove stock that measures 23.0 by 18.4 cm. The letter is addressed to "John Kenyon Esqʳᵉ. / St Leonards / near Hastings" and is postmarked September 13, 1831. William Knight first printed it in *Transactions of the Wordsworth Society*, no. 6 (Meeting of May 10, 1884), p. 101. WL.

WW and MW to EQ, November 14, 1831. MW's copies of *Gold and Silver Fishes, in a Vase* and *On the Departure of Sir Walter Scott from Abbotsford, for Naples* (here titled *To Sir Walter Scott on his quitting Abbotsford for Naples* (published in the sequence Yarrow Revisited) on 2ʳ of a bifolium of creamy white wove stock measuring 38.8 by 24.0 cm. and watermarked with an emblem of the Prince of Wales feathers above the initials J M M. The first part of the letter is from Rotha Q to her father and sister. WL.

WW to TA, September 19, 1832. WW's copy of *To the Author's Portrait* at the end of his letter to TA. The letter is in private hands; it was first published by Cecil Lang in *The Arnoldian* 15.3 (1989–1990): 5–7.

WW to JSmith, November 28, 1832. WW's copy of *To the Author's Portrait* on a single sheet of white or cream paper measuring 23.0 by 19.0 cm. The sheet is pasted to a heavier sheet of paper, making it impossible to identify any paper markings. Lilly Library, Indiana University.

WW, DW, and Dora W to JW$_3$, December 5, 1832. WW's copy of "For Lubbock vote—no legislative Hack" and "If this great world of joy and pain" in a letter to his nephew. The poems appear on 1^r and 2^v of a bifoliate sheet of wove stock measuring 23.0 by 18.6 cm. Add MS. 46136, fol. 72; BL.

WW to JW$_3$, December 7, 1832. WW's copy of "For Lubbock vote—no legislative Hack," "Now that Astrology is out of date," *Question and Answer*, and *Thought on the Seasons* (here titled *A Thought upon the Seasons*) in his letter to his nephew. The poems appear on 2^r and 2^v of a bifoliate sheet of laid paper measuring 23.2 by 19.1 cm. with chain lines 2.4 cm. apart. It is countermarked GW / 1828; it was dated "7th Dec^{br}" at Lowther Castle and postmarked the next day at Penrith. Add MS. 46136, fol. 74; BL.

WW to HCR, May 5, 1833. WW's copy of *To the Utilitarians* on 2^v of his letter to HCR (see *LY*, II, 608–610). The sheet of laid paper is bifoliate. The first leaf has been torn or cut away at the foot, obliterating some of the text (see Morley, *HCR Correspondence*, I, 237–238), and measures 24.5 by 18.6 cm.; the second leaf measures 30.3 by 18.3 cm. Chain lines are at intervals of 2.5 cm.; the sheet is watermarked with a lion and horse rampant in a crowned shield and countermarked 1827. HCR Correspondence, 1832–1833, fol. 117; Dr. Williams's Library.

WW to JK, December 31, 1833. MW's copy of ll. 26–37 of *Devotional Incitements* in WW's letter to JK, a single bifoliate sheet of creamy wove stock 23.0 by 18.6 cm., with the poem transcribed on 2^r. The sheet is embossed within a circle "LONDON / [*crown*] / SUPERFINE" at the upper left of the first recto. bMS AM 1622(210), Houghton Library, Harvard University.

WW to Joshua Watson, October 5, 1835. MW's copy of *Airey-Force Valley* on the second leaf of WW's letter to Watson; on a bifoliate sheet of wove stock measuring 23.1 by 18.7 cm. and watermarked R TURNER / 1831. See John Edwin Wells, "Wordsworth and Church Building: 'Airey-Force Valley,'" *Modern Language Review* 35 (1940): 350–354. Swarthmore College Library.

WW to HCR, August 16, 1836. WW's quotation of ll. 138–140 of *The Triad* in a postscript to his letter to HCR; the letter is in MW's hand, the postcript in WW's. The bifolium of wove stock measures 23.0 by 18.6 cm. HCR correspondence, 1836–1837, fol. 150; Dr. Williams's Library.

WW to HCR, March 26, 1838. WW's copy of "Said red-ribbon'd Evans" in his letter to HCR. It appears on 2ᵛ of a bifoliate sheet of wove stock measuring 23.1 by 18.8 cm. HCR annotated the letter with the date March 26, 1836, but the incident referred to in the poem, as well as other references in the letter, can be dated 1838. HCR correspondence, 1836–1837, fol. 110; Dr. Williams's Library.

WW to TNT, April 18, 1838. WW's copy of "Hark! 'tis the Thrush, undaunted, undeprest" on a singleton of blue-tinted wove stock countermarked J WHATMAN / 1835 and measuring 23.0 by 18.5 cm. The first part of the letter to TNT (up to the copy of the poem) is at Cornell (Healey, 2434), the rest, described here, is in the Berg Collection. WW dated the poem "Easter Sunday" (that is, April 8, 1838); the letter was postmarked at Kendal on April 18, 1838. Henry W. and Albert A. Berg Collection of English and American Literature, NYPL, Astor, Lenox and Tilden Foundations.

WW to TNT, June 14, 1838. WW's copy of *A Poet to his Grandchild. (Sequel to the foregoing.)* in his undated letter to TNT written on a sheet and a bifolium of white or cream wove stock measuring 25.0 by 20.5 cm. The letter was probably written on June 14, 1838, and was postmarked on June 17 at Kendal and June 19 in London. Lilly Library, Indiana University.

WW to Sarah Coles Stevenson, December 24, 1838. The letter is written on a bifolium of blue-tinted wove stock countermarked J WHATMAN / 1835 and measuring 22.7 by 18.5 cm. when folded (probably the same stock as WW to TNT, April 18, 1838). On 1ʳ is WW's copy of the final six lines of *Humanity. (Written in the Year 1829.)*; on 2ʳ is WW's note, "Mʳ. Wordsworth hopes that the Autograph is not sent too late for Mʳˢ. Stephenson's purpose.— / Rydal Mount / Dec 24ᵗʰ 1838"; see *LY*, III, 652. Stevenson Family Papers, vol. 10 (1838–1839), fols. 27603 and 27604, Library of Congress.

WW to HR, December 23, 1839. MW's copy of *Thoughts Suggested the Day Following on the Banks of Nith, near the Poet's Residence* in WW's letter on a bifolium of white wove stock measuring 23.0 by 18.7 and countermarked J WHATMAN / TURKEY MILL / 1836. A cover with the letter is postmarked Ambleside, December 24, 1839, and December 25, 1839 (London). WW and HR correspondence; Division of Rare Books and Manuscript Collections, Cornell University Library.

WW to Lord Monteagle, December 30, 1839. WW's copy of ll. 49–54 of *Elegiac Stanzas. 1824* on 2ᵛ of a bifolium of wove stock measuring 18.2 by 11.2 cm. and countermarked J WHATMAN / 1837. Healey, 2443; Division of Rare Books and Manuscript Collections, Cornell University Library.

WW and MW to IF, March 24, 1840. MW's fair copy of *The Cuckoo-clock*, on 2ʳ and 2ᵛ of the letter, which is dated only "Tuesday night." March 24 is the most likely date. The bifolium is of wove stock and measures 22.8 by 18.5 cm. WL.

WW to EFO, May 22, 1840. MW's copy of *The Norman Boy*, untitled, in a letter in her hand, with a note by WW, on a bifolium of wove stock measuring, when folded, 22.9 by 18.8 cm., without watermark. Addressed to Miss Ogle, Cholmondeley Cottage, Richmond, Surrey. MW's copy of *The Norman Boy* is dated "Rydal Mount / May 20th 1840"; the accompanying envelope is postmarked May 22, 1840. WW's note reads: "The state of my eyes, which are subject to inflammation causes me to employ an amanuensis which you will excuse as also the interlations which always become more or less necessary when one dictates." WL.

WW to BRH, September 4, 1840. MW's transcription of WW's corrections to *On a Portrait of the Duke of Wellington, upon the Field of Waterloo, by Haydon* on a bifolium of white wove paper measuring 18.5 by 11.5 cm. Robert H. Taylor Collection (49850), Rare Books and Special Collections, Princeton University Libraries.

WW to BRH, September 7, 1840. Dora W's transcription of WW's corrections to *On a Portrait of the Duke of Wellington, upon the Field of Waterloo, by Haydon* on a bifolium of white wove paper measuring 11.5 by 9.5 cm. Robert H. Taylor Collection (49850), Rare Books and Special Collections, Princeton University Libraries.

WW to BRH, September 10, 1840. MW's transcription of WW's corrections to *On a Portrait of the Duke of Wellington, upon the Field of Waterloo, by Haydon* on a bifolium of white wove paper measuring 17.8 by 11.0 cm. Robert H. Taylor Collection (49850), Rare Books and Special Collections, Princeton University Libraries.

WW to BRH, September 11 (a), 1840. MW's transcription of WW's corrections to *On a Portrait of the Duke of Wellington, upon the Field of Waterloo, by Haydon* on a bifolium of white wove paper measuring 18.7 by 11.5 cm. and watermarked J W[ ]TMAN / TU[ ]Y MILL / 1833. Robert H. Taylor Collection (49850), Rare Books and Special Collections, Princeton University Libraries.

WW to BRH, September 11 (b), 1840. MW's transcription of WW's corrections to *On a Portrait of the Duke of Wellington, upon the Field of Waterloo, by Haydon* on a bifolium of white wove paper measuring 18.3 by 11.5 cm. and watermarked J GREEN & SON / 1829. Robert H. Taylor Collection (49850), Rare Books and Special Collections, Princeton University Libraries.

WW to HR, September 14, 1840. WW included *On a Portrait of the Duke of Wellington, upon the Field of Waterloo, by Haydon* in his letter to HR, with the remark, "I send you a Sonnet composed the other day while I was climbing our Mountain—Helvellyn." The sheet is a bifolium of wove paper. It measures 25.0 by 19.8 cm. and is embossed in the upper left corner of the first page. The autograph of the text of the sonnet is MW's for the first nine lines and the first two words of the tenth, and thereafter WW's. WW and HR correspondence; Division of Rare Books and Manuscript Collections, Cornell University Library.

WW to IF, September 14, 1840. WW's correction of l. 10 of *On a Portrait of the Duke of Wellington, upon the Field of Waterloo, by Haydon.* The letter is on two half-sheets of wove stock measuring 22.8 by 18.6 cm. It was postmarked at Penrith and dated September 14, 1840. WL.

WW to BRH, September 23, 1840. WW's corrections to *On a Portrait of the Duke of Wellington, upon the Field of Waterloo, by Haydon* in his letter on a bifolium of white wove paper measuring 18.7 by 11.5 cm. and watermarked J WHATMAN / TURKEY MILL / 1833. Robert H. Taylor Collection (49850), Rare Books and Special Collections, Princeton University Libraries.

WW to RMM, September 25, 1840. WW's corrections to ll. 2, 4, and 10 of the newspaper version of his *On a Portrait of the Duke of Wellington, upon the Field of Waterloo, by Haydon* in his letter on a bifolium of blue-tinted wove stock measuring 23.3 by 19.0 cm. Tinker 2326, Beinecke Rare Book and Manuscript Library, Yale University.

WW to BRH, October 24, 1840. WW's acknowledgment, in his own hand, of receipt of the *Literary Gazette* issue in which BRH placed *On a Portrait of the Duke of Wellington, upon the Field of Waterloo, by Haydon.* WW makes two corrections to the text. The bifolium of wove stock measures 12.5 by 10.1 cm. and is signed and dated "Sat: 24th"; BRH has added "1840" and deleted a sentence or two relating to his proposed visit to the Lakes. HM27488, Huntington Library.

WW to HCR, October 27, 1840. WW's emendation of ll. 9–11 of "The Sonnet upon the Duke's Picture" (*On a Portrait of the Duke of Wellington, upon the Field of Waterloo, by Haydon*) on the verso of the second leaf of this letter to HCR. WW comments that the poem "was printed very incorrectly, in all the newspapers in which I saw it. It was in one passage altered by myself after I sent it to you" (*LY*, IV, 133). The bifoliate sheet of laid paper measures 18.3 by 11.9 cm. The sheet has chain lines running vertically at intervals of 2.4 cm. and is countermarked 1832. John James Masquerier Album, fol. 34 (Mesquerier, a painter [d. 1855], was an acquaintance of HCR), Dr. Williams's Library.

WW to AFR, May 11, 1842. A copy, probably in the hand of SH_2, and signed by WW, of *The Eagle and the Dove*; it is written on the recto of a single sheet of wove stock measuring 23.0 by 19.1 cm. and watermarked G WILMOT / 1834. The sheet is addressed on the verso to "Mon^{r} / Monsieur Rio / 36bis rue du Bac / Paris" (Alexis François Rio) and postmarked May 11, 1842 (London), and May 13, 1842 (Calais). Healey, 2289; Division of Rare Books and Manuscript Collections, Cornell University Library.

WW to EFO, November 15, 1842. WW's copy of six new lines, to follow l. 72, of *Sequel to The Norman Boy*, in a letter written in response to objections by EFO about the poem. The bifolium of blue-tinted wove stock measures 20.0 by 12.6 cm.; the lines of verse appear on 1^{v} and 2^{r}, written across the two pages. The accompanying envelope was postmarked at Ambleside, November 16, 1842 (see *LY*, IV, 722, where the letter is assigned incorrectly to 1845). (Uncat) Wordsworth, Bienecke Rare Book and Manuscript Library, Yale University.

WW to JS, early January 1844. WW's repetition of his alteration of l. 14 of *Inscription for a Monument in Crosthwaite Church, in the Vale of Keswick* to read "Could private feelings meet in holier rest," and direction to instruct the "sculptor" to inscribe it thus (*LY*, IV, 515–516; the letter is in private hands and has not been reexamined).

WW to CW, Jr., January 16, 1844. WW's revisions for *Inscription for a Monument in Crosthwaite Church, in the Vale of Keswick*, and revision of l. 2 of his sonnet *To the Rev. Christopher Wordsworth, D.D. Master of Harrow School, After the perusal of his Theophilus Anglicanus, recently published*, in a letter on a bifolium and a singleton measuring 18.1 by 11.5 cm. The bifolium is blue-tinted wove stock countermarked WHATMAN / 18[?]1. The singleton is blue-tinted laid paper with chain marks at intervals of 2.4 cm., countermarked C W[?]. Add MS. 46136, fols. 126–129; BL.

WW to HCR, February 5, 1844. MW's transcription of WW's revision of the final two lines of *Inscription for a Monument in Crosthwaite Church, in the Vale of Keswick* in WW's letter to HCR. The letter is made up of two bifolia of wove stock that measure 20.2 by 12.5 cm. HCR correspondence, 1844, fols. 10b, 11a; Dr. Williams's Library.

WW to HCR, February 2, 1845. WW's correction of the first line only of *Sonnet on the Projected Kendal and Windermere Railway* in his letter to HCR on a bifolium of wove stock measuring 12.5 by 10.1 cm. HCR correspondence, 1845, fol. 16b; Dr. Williams's Library.

WW to HR, July 31, 1845. WW's copy of two stanzas (ll. 53–56, 89–92) of *The Westmoreland Girl*[,] *To my Grandchildren*, July 31, 1845, in a letter written on a bifolium of white wove stock measuring 18.1 by 11.2 cm. Healey, 2504; Division of Rare Books and Manuscript Collections, Cornell University Library.

WW to CW, Jr., around January 10, 1846. WW's initialed copy of "Why should we weep or mourn, Angelic boy," on 2^r of a bifolium of wove stock measuring 22.7 by 18.7 cm. Add MS. 46136, fol. 138; BL.

WW to HR, January 23, 1846. MW's fair copy in WW's letter to HR of two sonnets, "Why should we weep or mourn, Angelic boy," and "Where lies the truth? has Man in wisdom's creed." The sonnets are copied each side of the address panel on 2^v of a bifolium of wove stock measuring 23.1 by 18.6 cm. Healey, 2292; Division of Rare Books and Manuscript Collections, Cornell University Library.

WW to TAW, May 5, 1847. WW's revision of "path" to "lore" in l. 47 of the *Installation Ode* in his letter to the composer of the music for his ode. The original letter has not been traced; see *LY*, IV, 846.

Lilly MS. 1 WW's copy of *To the Author's Portrait*, signed and dated October 3, 1832, has been mounted and framed; part of a watermark is visible (ONDS) on a bifolium of white or cream paper measuring approximately 18.5 by 11.5 cm. The word "ditto" has been entered above the word "Portrait" in an unidentified hand. Lilly Library, Indiana University.

Lilly MS. 2 WW's copy of ll. 1–43 of *Elegiac Musings in the Grounds of Coleorton Hall, the Seat of Sir George Beaumont, Bart.* on a singleton of white wove paper measuring 22.7 by 18.5 cm.; the sheet is watermarked R TASSELL / 1830; a second sheet that presumably bore the remaining lines has not been found. Lilly Library, Indiana University.

Lilly MS. 3 WW's fair copy of ll. 5b–11 of *Lines Suggested by a Portrait from the Pencil of F. Stone* on a single sheet of white or cream wove stock measuring 15.5 by 19 cm. The date 1835 is written in ink in the lower right-hand corner but is probably not contemporary with WW's entry of the text. The sheet was once pasted to a smaller piece of paper containing WW's signature and a brief note; the two pieces of paper have since been separated. Lilly Library, Indiana University.

Lilly MSS. 4 and 5 MS. 4 contains WW's drafts for "So fair, so sweet, withal so sensitive," beginning "Would that the little flowers were born to live" and titled *Suggested upon Loughrigg Fell;* it is a single sheet of white or cream wove stock measuring 18.5 by 14.25 cm. and watermarked with two small circles, each about 1 cm. in diameter, about 0.75 cm. apart, with a crown in the center of the circles. MS. 5 contains a fair copy of the poem, with the same title, and beginning "So fair, so sweet, withal so sensitive"; it is a single sheet of white or cream wove stock measuring 20.0 by 12.5 cm. MS. 5 is signed by WW, with his note "Transcribed for Esther Morris Aug[st] 1844," but the copyist's hand has not been identified. The sheet was at one time pasted to another sheet or a leaf in an album but has since been removed. Lilly Library, Indiana University.

Lonsdale Album Album of 136 leaves once belonging to Lady Lonsdale. WW inscribed *To a Sky-lark* ("Ethereal Minstrel! Pilgrim of the sky!") on 33[r] (item "20" in the album), dating it at Lowther Castle, October 2, 1826. MS Vault, Lonsdale; Beinecke Rare Book and Manuscript Library, Yale University.

Lutwidge Family MS. MW's copy of four lines of verse beginning "He who defers his work from day to day" on a bifolium of cream-colored wove stock measuring 18.3 by 11.0 cm. Inscribed below by WW, "W[m] Wordsworth / Rydal Mount / 17 April 1833." The rest of the sheet is blank. WLMS/Lutwidge/56; WL.

MS. 1827/28 A copy of *PW*, 1827, in which WW entered revisions to *To the Lady ———. On Seeing the Foundation Preparing for the Erection of ——— Chapel,*

Westmoreland (IV, 257–262), probably around or shortly after the time of his letter to BF, April 16, 1828. Beinecke Rare Book and Manuscript Library, Yale University.

MS. 1827/32C An annotated set of *PW*, 1827, in which WW, in pencil, and MW, in ink, entered alternate readings and revisions that were in part adopted in *PW*, 1832. Volume four contains MW's ink transcription of two stanzas of *To the Lady ———. On Seeing the Foundation Preparing for the Erection of ——— Chapel, Westmoreland* (p. 259). There are also revisions to *Michael*, *The Excursion*, and several shorter poems throughout the five-volume set. The set, inscribed by WW's son "From J. Wordsworth, Curate of Whitwick, to his kind Friends M^{r}. and M^{rs}. Merewether. Whitwick Vicarage June 18th 1829," is uniformly bound with *Yarrow Revisited and Other Poems* (1835) and the posthumous second edition of *The Prelude* (1851). The latter two volumes are not annotated, apart from an inscription, "From the Author," in an unknown hand in pencil in the *Yarrow* volume. Division of Rare Books and Manuscript Collections, Cornell University Library.

MS. 1827/32L Described, as "MS. 1827/40," in *Poems, 1800–1807* (Curtis), p. xxxiv: "WW's copy of 1827 *Poetical Works*, vol. 2 of which was used to enter revisions adopted, in part, in the 1840 edition of *Poetical Works*." The poems thus revised are "Yes, it was the mountain Echo" (p. 164; MW's hand), *To a Sky-lark* ("Ethereal Minstrel! Pilgrim of the sky!" p. 165; possibly Dora W's hand), and *French Revolution* (p. 168; MW's hand; an excerpt from *The Prelude* first published in *The Friend*, October 26, 1809; see *Prelude*, X, 689–727). All revisions were in fact adopted in 1832. Lilly Library, Indiana University.

MS. 1831JH Copies of three Evening Voluntaries in a copy of *Selections from the Poems of William Wordsworth, Esq., Chiefly for the Use of Schools and Young Persons* (London: Edward Moxon, 1831), presented to the Hutchinson family at Brinsop. The volume was inscribed "To the Children at / Brinsop / from / their affectionate Uncle / Wm Wordsworth." The holograph copies include "Calm is the fragrant air, and loth to lose" (on flyleaf facing title page, in pencil in WW's hand); "Not in the lucid intervals of life" (on flyleaf facing the advertisements, in ink in SH's or DW's hand); and "The Sun, that seemed so mildly to retire"; on flyleaf facing the endboard, in pencil in WW's hand). John Alban Finch examined the volume when it was owned by Joanna Hutchinson and recorded variants in the transcribed texts (notebook 15, WL). The volume itself has not been located.

MS. 1832/36 Revisions and drafts in the copy of *PW*, 1832, that WW used in August 1836 in preparation for the edition of 1836. Much of the added material is in WW's hand, some in the hands of MW, Dora W, JC, and EQ. A large part of those corrected leaves served as printer's copy. On some pages there are marks that look like deletions of text, but they were made by the Wordsworth household or by the printer to indicate the new layout and placement in the 1836 edition.

(See Jared Curtis, "The Wellesley Copy of Wordsworth's Poetical Works, 1832," *Harvard Library Bulletin*, 28 [January 1980], 5–15.) The printer marked changes in punctuation and capitalization, probably before sending the loose gatherings to WW; MW or WW made a few additional changes of this type. The set is bound for "S. M. Samuel" by Riviere 1893 in brown morocco with gilt lettering and decorations, in the same style as other similarly signed bindings of annotated copies of printed works; they include MS. 1835/36, MS. 1842P, the Turnbull MS. (see the entries for these three manuscripts, below), and an interleaved copy of *PW*, 1836, at Princeton University Library. The English Poetry Collection, Wellesley College Library.

MS. 1835/36 WW's copy of *Yarrow Revisited, and Other Poems*, 1835, with revisions for most of the poems in the volume, entered probably between November 1836 and January 1837 by MW, WW, and the printer when the fifth volume of *Poetical Works*, 1836–1837, was in preparation. Substantive revisions are mostly in MW's hand, with a few in WW's. The printer marked changes in punctuation and capitalization, probably before sending loose gatherings to WW; MW or WW made a few additional changes of this kind. The volume is bound for "S. M. Samuel" by Riviere 1893 in deep crimson levant morocco decorated with bees and roses (see the entry for MS. 1832/36, above). Ashley 2262, BL.

MS. 1835B A copy of *Yarrow Revisited, and Other Poems*, 1835, inscribed by WW to T. Hamilton (author of *Cyril Thornton*), in which MW has entered corrections to *The Egyptian Maid; or, The Romance of the Water Lily* (pp. 47, 48) and *Inscription Intended for a Stone in the Grounds of Rydal Mount* (p. 85). Henry W. and Albert A. Berg Collection of English and American Literature, NYPL, Astor, Lenox and Tilden Foundations.

MS. 1835Col A copy of *Yarrow Revisited, and Other Poems*, 1835, inscribed on the half title "From the Author." WW has entered corrections to *The Trossachs* (p. 13; published in the sequence Yarrow Revisited); *The Egyptian Maid; or, The Romance of the Water Lily* (pp. 47, 48); *Ode, Composed on May Morning* (p. 70); *Inscription Intended for a Stone in the Grounds of Rydal Mount* (p. 85); *A Jewish Family. (In a small valley opposite St. Goar, upon the Rhine.)* (p. 89); *Devotional Incitements* (p. 92); and *The Primrose of the Rock* (p. 108). Rare Book and Manuscript Library, Butler Library, Columbia University.

MS. 1836/45 WW's revisions and additional verse entries in the copy of *PW*, 1836, that he used when preparing the editions of 1840 and 1845. Almost all of the revisions for 1840 are in the hand of JC; those for 1845 were dictated to MW, Dora W, or EQ, or written out by WW himself. Evidence indicates that this copy, or part of it, was probably made up of unused sheets from an early uncorrected state of the 1836 edition. The sheets appear to have been marked by the printer, who chiefly made changes from upper- to lowercase, when the 1840 edition was being prepared. Several poems that are not present in printed form in these volumes were entered by hand between 1840 and 1845. Those relevant to this edition are WW's copy of "Come gentle Sleep, Death's image tho' thou art" and EQ's copies of the two versions of "Grateful is Sleep" on the front flyleaves of Vol. I; WW's copies of "What heavenly smiles! O Lady mine" on the end flyleaf of Vol. I and p. [xii] of Vol. IV; WW's copy of "Forth from a jutting ridge, around whose base" on pp. 302–303 of Vol. II; WW's copy of ll. 9–14 of "While beams of orient light shoot wide and high" on p. [353] of Vol. II; MW's fair copy, revised by WW, of "Glad sight wherever new with old" in Vol. III, p. [356] (probably entered between January 1842 and mid-November 1845); Dora W's fair copy, revised by WW, and WW's drafts of *To a Lady, in answer to a request that I would write her a poem upon some drawings that she had made of flowers in the island of Madeira* in Vol. III, the fair copy—probably the earliest entry—on pp. [358–359], WW's later draft of ll. 4, 11–13, 24 on the opening flyleaf, and WW's draft of ll. 12–20 on p. [356]; and EQ's copy, revised by WW, of "So fair, so sweet, withal so sensitive," on the opening flyleaves of Vol. V (probably entered in August 1844). The Royal Collection, the Royal Library, Windsor Castle.

MS. 1838/40 WW's revisions in the copy of *Sonnets*, 1838, that he used during preparation of the edition of *PW*, 1840, and later editions. The revisions of printed texts are by MW, JC, or WW himself. Texts of several new sonnets were added: WW's fair copy, dated December 31, 1842, and later deleted in pencil, of "Glad sight wherever new with old"—in this earliest version, "Look up, look round, let things unfold"; this entry appears below MW's copy of "Wansfell! this Household has a favoured lot" on p. [478]; MW's fair copy, revised by WW, of the same sonnet appears on p. [xii], and another fair copy by MW on p. [478]; WW's drafts and fair copy of "While beams of orient light shoot wide and high" appear on pp. iv, 1, 2, 3. *ED. 8.W8915.838s, Houghton Library, Harvard University.

MS. 1842P Page proofs—corrected probably by WW—of *PELY*, 1842. They represent a later proof state than that of section 3 of DC MS. 151 (see above). There are print variants and corrections for the following poems relevant to this edition: "Though the bold wings of Poesy affect" (p. 43), "Lyre! though such power do in thy magic live" (pp. 45–46), *At the Grave of Burns. 1803* (pp. 52–55), *Thoughts Suggested the Day Following on the Banks of Nith, near the Poet's Residence* (pp. 56–58), *A Night Thought* (p. 79), *Farewell Lines* (pp. 80–81), *Love Lies Bleeding* (pp. 82–83), *Companion to the Foregoing* (pp. 83–84), *Suggested by a Picture of the Bird of Paradise* (pp. 89–90), "*A Poet!*—He hath put his heart to school" (p. 215), "The most alluring clouds that mount the sky" (p. 216), *On the Same Subject* [as *To a Painter*] (p. 225), and *To a Redbreast—(In Sickness)* (p. 229). The volume is bound for "S. M. Samuel" by Riviere 1893 (see MS. 1832/36, above). Tracy W. McGregor Collection, Alderman Library, University of Virginia.

MS. 1842WC A copy of *PELY*, 1842, which is inscribed by WW: "To / His beloved Friend / Isabella Fenwick / from / William Wordsworth / Rydal Mount / 17th April / 1842." On p. 46 IF has entered a revision to l. 27 of "Lyre! though such power do in thy magic live." On pp. 138–139, in an unidentified hand, and on the verso of the rear free endpaper, possibly in the hand of EQ, there are various pencil notes concerning the ordering of WW's five translations from Michaelangelo, "Yes! hope may with my strong desire keep pace," "No mortal object did these eyes behold," "The prayers I make will then be sweet indeed" (all three in Miscellaneous Sonnets; see *Poems, 1800–1807*, pp. 143–145), "Rapt above earth by power of one fair face," and "Eternal Lord! eased of a cumbrous load" (both in the sequence Italy 1837). The intended reordering is not clear; the position of each sonnet was never altered by WW. Widener Collection, Houghton Library, Harvard University.

MS. 1845D A copy of *Poems*, 1845, inscribed and signed by WW "Rydal Mount. 17th Decr 1845" and by MW to "Dora Quillinan from her Mother . . . July 30th. 1846"; it is annotated in EQ's hand in both pencil and ink. EQ's copy of *To Lucca Giordano* appears on p. 360; EQ's copies of *On the Banks of a Rocky Stream* and "How beautiful the Queen of Night, on high" appear on p. 415 ("Transcribed from M^{r}. Wordsworth's Autograph in his own copy of this edition of his works. E.Q. Rydal—Sep^{br}. 3. 1849."); MW's copy of "Why should we weep or mourn, Angelic boy" appears on p. 535. Copy 2, WL.

MS. 1845RL WW's fair copy, untitled, of *Written upon a fly leaf in the Copy of the Author's Poems which was sent to her Majesty Queen Victoria*, inscribed on an opening flyleaf of *Poems*, 1845, which he sent to the Queen early in January 1846. It is inscribed "Your Majesty's devoted Subject and Servant William Wordsworth 9th Jan^{ry} 1846." The poem was first published by Alexander B. Grosart in *Prose* (Grosart) in 1876, I, v–vi; his text seems to be based on the Royal Library copy but in l. 21 he follows the reading found in DC MS. 89 and in Cornell MS. 13. The Royal Collection, the Royal Library, Windsor Castle.

MS. 1845W WW's copy of *Poems*, 1845, inscribed by him and dated "7th April—1844 / Rydal Mount." A sheet tipped in at the front has MW's copies of two sonnets from the sequence Tour 1833, "Why stand we gazing on the sparkling Brine" (1^{r}) and "A Youth too certain of his power to wade" (1^{v}) and bears the date 1826 in pencil and two notes: MW's note to WW, Jr., "You are not to give, or suffer, a copy of these to be taken. Have you heard from your friends at Dunolly Castle? Your Father cannot transcribe Mrs H's this morning" and WW, Jr.'s note "These two Sonnets are in my Mother's handwriting / W.W. of Carlisle 1832." At the end of Evening Voluntaries, on p. 360, MW entered a transcription of *To Lucca Giordano* (here untitled); on p. 415 are MW's copy, over WW's erased and mostly illegible pencil, of *On the Banks of a Rocky Stream*, and below this WW's copy of "How beautiful the Queen of night, on high"; on p. 429 is MW's copy of ll. 37–44 of *The Cuckoo-clock*; and on p. 443 is WW's copy of "Why should we weep or mourn, Angelic boy" (here titled *On the death of my Grandson*). Probably entered at a later time are several of WRH's annotations and corrections to the printed text, principally on p. 127 (pencil date of *The Poet and the Caged Turtledove* altered from 1830 to 1829), p. 133 (pencil correction to *The Waggoner*), p. 212 (ink note to *To Rotha Q———*, giving the date of her death), p. 213 (ink correction to "Oker" in *A Tradition of Oken Hill in Darley Dale, Derbyshire*), p. 217 (ink date 1832 below *At Furness Abbey* ["Here, where, of havoc tired and rash undoing"]), p. 373, the addition to "A little onward lend thy guiding hand" of the title, in pencil, "To Dora.—," and on the back flyleaf ink corrections to two lines of *A Fact, and an Imagination* (readings found in the 1850 *PW;* for the last two poems see *Poems, 1807–1820,* pp. 223–225, 210–212). Pencil corrections, perhaps in the hand of Gordon Graham Wordsworth, WW's grandson, appear on the front endpaper, and on pp. 177, 251, 414, all corresponding to the text in *PW,* 1850. Copy 1, WL.

Mary Smith Album The album of Mary Proctor Smith, WW's cousin, who visited Rydal Mount in 1834 and whose home in London WW visited in May 1836, before setting off for the continent. WW's fair copy of *A Night Thought* on a bifoliate sheet of wove stock measuring 28.6 by 23.1 cm.; the countermark J WHATMAN / TURKEY MILL / 1832 appears on a cognate sheet in the same gathering with MW's copy of the final six lines of *Humanity. (Written in the Year 1829.)* on 1r of a bifolium of wove stock (MW's note at the foot reads, "Transcribed by M.W. Rydal Mount, Sepr 3d 1836"); SH's copy of "These Vales were saddened with no common gloom" (here titled *To the memory of Jemima Anne D. Quillinan,* on laid paper, measuring 23.0 by 19.1 cm. and bearing the countermark 1822, with chain lines at intervals of 2.4 cm. Paul F. Betz Collection.

Melbourne MS. WW's copy of ll. 79–91 of *Lines Suggested by a Portrait from the Pencil of F. Stone,* signed and dated February 22, 1836 (after *YR,* 1835, but before *PW,* 1836), on a singleton of white wove stock measuring 23.1 by 19.3 cm. The text differs only in accidentals from the published form. See Geoffrey Little, *Bulletin of the Bibliographical Society of Australia and New Zealand* 10.4 (1986): 134–138 (includes photograph). State Library of Victoria, Melbourne, Australia.

Michigan MS. WW's holograph copy of "Wansfell! this Household has a favoured lot," "While beams of orient light shoot wide and high," and "Is then no nook of English ground secure," on a singleton of wove stock measuring 25.5 by 20.5 cm. Below "Is then no nook" is inscribed "Octbr 12th 1844 Facit indignatio Wm Wordsworth" and, on the verso, below "While beams" is inscribed "Wm Wordsworth Octbr 1844." On the recto, with the sheet reversed, the initials "WW" are inscribed in ink in an unknown hand. The three sonnets were copied out for Francis Atkinson Faber (see the entry for DC MS. 176, above). Eng. Lit., Special Collections Library, University of Michigan.

Monkhouse Album An album belonging to Mary Elizabeth Monkhouse, the daughter of MW's cousin TM. Three entries are relevant to this edition. *Extract from the Strangers book Station Winandermere, On seeing the above* appears in two copies, one by Dora W (MS. A) and one by SH (MS. B). MS. A is a bifolium of yellowish wove stock of which the second leaf has been cut away, leaving a stub; the intact leaf measures 20.0 by 12.5 cm., and has three stab holes near the fold; in MS. A there are pencil notations in a later hand (probably not WW's) beneath the title ("by W. W.") and below the last line ("W. W."). MS. B is also a bifolium, cut away in the same fashion as MS. A, of white wove paper; it measures 22.8 by

18.4 cm. A single copy of *On Seeing a Needlecase in the Form of a Harp, the Work of E. M. S.*, in SH's hand, appears on a bifolium of laid paper measuring 23.1 by 18.8 cm. and countermarked PINE & DAVIS / 1823. Chain lines appear at intervals of 2.8 cm. Beneath the text SH has inscribed "W. Wordsworth." Paul F. Betz Collection.

Monkhouse Album (copy) Facsimiles of three leaves, apparently once part of an album belonging to Mary Elizabeth Monkhouse: a copy of *The Infant M—— M——* in a tiny unidentified hand; Dora W's fair copy of *On a Portrait of the Duke of Wellington, upon the Field of Waterloo, by Haydon*; and WW's transcription of the last five lines of "Soft as a cloud is yon blue Ridge—the Mere," which he inscribed "W[m] Wordsworth / Transcribed for Mary Elizabeth Monkhouse/Rydal Mount / Aug[st] 16th 1840.—" The album of Mary Elizabeth Monkhouse that is in Paul F. Betz's collection does not contain these entries. Photocopies of the three manuscripts are held by Cornell University Library. The originals are untraced, but John Finch recorded the lines from "Soft as a cloud is yon blue Ridge—the Mere" (notebook 14, WL; see also the entries for MS. 1831JH and Monkhouse MS. [copy]).

Monkhouse MS. (copy) Copies of WW's poems made by Dora W and SH were described by John Alban Finch in a survey he made of WW manuscripts; these records are now among his papers at the Wordsworth Library. When Finch saw the manuscripts, they belonged to Joanna Hutchinson (see also the entries for MS. 1831JH and Monkhouse Album [copy]), but their present location has not been discovered. Finch noted Dora W's copy of *Gold and Silver Fishes, in a Vase*, inscribed (probably by her) "W[m] Wordsworth / for WW J[r] from DW J[r] / Rydal Mount / Dec[r] 1829" on a sheet of white wove stock measuring 18.5 by 24.2 cm. and countermarked J GOLDING / 1828; the sheet was folded once top to bottom, and then in three with "Mrs Hutchinson" inscribed on the center panel. Finch also described a sewn-up gathering of two sheets of white stock embossed on the inner left corner with a crown and "BATH"; the folded sheets measure 18.0 by 10.12 cm. A small picture of a young girl has been pasted to 1[v] over the initials "M. E. M." The sonnet *The Infant M—— M——* is in SH's hand on 2[r], where it is titled *Mary Elizabeth Monkhouse*; under the title SH has added the words "By Mr Wordsworth" in pencil and below the text the date in ink "Nov[r] 15th 1824." On 2[v] is SH's copy of *To Rotha Q———*, here titled *Rotha Quillinan*. Finch notebook 14, WL.

Montague MS. WW's copy of "Scorn not the Sonnet; Critic, you have frowned" on 1[r] of a bifolium of wove stock measuring 22.9 by 18.5 cm. At the foot WW inscribed it "William Wordsworth / Rydal Mount / Written for / M[rs] Dunlop—"; the rest of the sheet is blank. The sheet is accompanied by a letter of June 6, 1830, from WW to [?John Wilson Croker] supporting EQ's candidacy for the Atheneum (see *SNL*, p. 205 and note, where the recipient is conjectured to be Croker or Thomas Moore; see also *LY*, II, 279 and note). Gilbert Holland Montague Collection of Historic Autographs, Box 12, Manuscripts and Archives Division,

NYPL, Astor, Lenox and Tilden Foundations.

Monument, in St. Kentigern's Church, Crosthwaite, near Keswick On the side of the monument facing the altar is a white marble stone engraved with WW's *Inscription for a Monument in Crosthwaite Church, in the Vale of Keswick* and installed in the church in April 1844. L. 14 reads "find a holier nest" despite the wish that WW expressed to JS that the sculptor be instructed to engrave "meet for holier rest"; ll. 17–18 have been reengraved where the surface of the marble has been scraped clean.

Morgan MS. 1 A copy, possibly in the hand of MW, of *A Flower Garden* on a bifolium of creamy white stock watermarked RUSE & TURNER / 1824 and measuring 22.8 by 18.9 cm. MS. MA2012, 2. Pierpont Morgan Library.

Morgan MS. 2 DW's copy of *Incident at Brugès* (published in the sequence Continent 1820) and *A Jewish Family. (In a small valley opposite St. Goar, upon the Rhine.)* on a bifolium of creamy white wove stock measuring 18.1 by 11.2 cm. The paper is the same as that of Morgan MS. 4 (MA2012, 4), with the same squarish embossment at the upper left but without the countermark (see Morgan MS. 4, below). DW's note suggests that the bifolium accompanied a letter. Coleorton Papers, MS. MA1581 (Wordsworth), 52; Pierpont Morgan Library.

Morgan MS. 3 A copy, perhaps by Bertha Southey, of *On Seeing a Needlecase in the Form of a Harp, the Work of E. M. S.* on a bifolium of creamy white wove stock countermarked J GREEN & SONS / 1827 and measuring 18.0 by 11.1 cm. Coleorton Papers, MS. R–V 12 D, Pierpont Morgan Library.

Morgan MS. 4 DW's copy of *The Poet and the Caged Turtledove* on the first recto of a bifolium of creamy white wove stock countermarked SIMMONS / 1827 and measuring 18.1 by 11.2 cm. At upper left of the sheet is an indecipherable embossment, near-square with rounded corners. The bifolium was folded in three by DW, who wrote on the center outside panel "Twenty minutes' Exercise." MS. MA2012, 4, Pierpont Morgan Library.

Morgan MS. 5 WW's copy of ll. 1–6 of "Throned in the Sun's descending car" on a singleton of creamy white wove stock countermarked G H / 180[?] and measuring 20.4 by 13. 9 cm. Below WW's copy he inscribed it "[Transcribed *revised from* transcribed] by Wm Wordsworth." Pasted to a loose album page (numbered 12), the sheet is labeled "Lines written for my Father's Album by W Wordsworth." The album leaf is like another such leaf in the same collection that is identified as from JK's album. Gordon Ray Collection, MS. MA4500W, Pierpont Morgan Library.

O'Callaghan Album Red leather binding with paper covers measuring 18.3 by 11.0 cm.; the paper is watermarked RUSE & TURNER / 1817. WW entered "First Floweret of the year is that which shows" on the front flyleaf of the album, which once belonged to the Hon. George O'Callaghan (see note to the poem). The first page has been removed, cut neatly down the margin, with parts of initial characters visible, suggesting perhaps that the poem was first written on this leaf, then reentered on the inside flyleaf (so as literally to be first) and the redundant leaf removed. Below the last line WW inscribed "Wm Wordsworth / Whitehaven Castle / 1st Oct^br^ 1823—" (In her copy of the poem Dora W's title disparaging WW's handwriting [Dora W to EQ, May 11, 1824] appears to confirm this interpretation; perhaps she recalled that WW's first entry in the album was botched and for that reason recopied.) Besides sketches in ink and color, the following poems are present: "Lines written for the Lonsdale's Album in Oct 1821 by R Southey" (in an unidentified hand), dated 1821; "To Chearfulness" by "Mrs. Carlyle"; and a ballad, "'How d'ye do' and 'Goodbye,'" dated April 15, 1826. Leslie Holden Collection.

Pocket Notebook The notebook was described by George Harris Healey in *WPN*: "a large red-leather wallet, lined with leather, and provided with inside compartments. In the middle, fastened in place by a green ribbon, lies the notebook. Its paper wrappers are of double thickness, and are decorated only with an over-all watered-silk design impressed into the outer layer. Sewn to these covers are 28 pages, each measuring 6 3/4 by 3 1/2 inches. The stock is a wove paper, thin but of good quality, without watermark. Counting the inside covers, the book consists of 30 pages, of which 24 are written upon. The lack of conjugates for two leaves indicates that at least so many have been torn out" (pp. 1–2). The notebook was in use as a record, partly in WW's hand but mostly in an unidentified hand, of WW's appointments from May 12 to June 20, 1839. Probably around the same time or shortly after, WW entered drafts and fragments of several poems (pp. 2–5). A photograph of one page that shows WW's draft for "Art, Nature, Love here claim united praise" appears as frontispiece in *WPN*. Dr. Richard Hall, the owner of the notebook when Healey first examined it, published excerpts and a photographic facsimile of an opening that shows WW's early draft for *At Furness Abbey* ("Here, where, of havoc tired and rash undoing") in *The Chimes* (Rome, Ga.) 40 (December 1927): 5–9, and, earlier, an account without photographic illustration in *The Seminary Magazine* (Louisville, Ky.) 12 (December 1898): 113–117. The notebook has not been located.

Princeton MS. 1 MW's fair copy of *Upon Seeing a Coloured Drawing of the Bird of Paradise in an Album* on a single sheet of wove stock measuring 19.5 by 12.3 cm. A light printer's casting-off mark was struck through the text on each side of the sheet. MW added the date 1835 below the text. General Manuscripts (24811), Rare Books and Special Collections, Princeton University Libraries.

Princeton MS. 2 MW's copy, prepared for the printer, of *To the Moon. (Composed by the Sea-side,—on the Coast of Cumberland.)*, on creamy white wove stock measuring 19.2 by 15.9 cm. The running head "Evening Voluntaries" appears at the top of each of the four pages of text; the poem is numbered 10 at head and dated 1835 at the end. Some of the revisions appear to be in the hand of JC, some in a hand of someone in the printer's office. Only the revisions we can confidently ascribe to JC are so marked in the *apparatus criticus*. General Manuscripts (24811), Rare Books and Special Collections, Princeton University Libraries.

Princeton MS. 3 MW's fair copy, prepared for the printer, of *To the Moon. (Rydal.)* on a bifoliate sheet of creamy white wove stock that is countermarked H N & F / 1835. The sheet is folded once to measure 19.0 by 15.6 cm. The text on all four sides has been struck through with the printer's casting-off marks. MW has entered the running head "Evening Voluntaries" at the top of each page. The poem is twice numbered 11 at the head, and below the last line is the date 1835. General Manuscripts (24811), Rare Books and Special Collections, Princeton University Libraries.

Princeton MS. 4 WW's draft of seven lines of *Extempore Effusion upon the Death of James Hogg* on an irregularly shaped piece of creamy white wove stock. The height varies from 11.0 to 10.4 cm. and the width from 14.0 to 16.5 cm. Along the top edge are illegible fragments of letters from the preceding line. On the recto is WW's transcription of ll. 59–60 and a revisionary stanza from *Thoughts Suggested the Day Following on the Banks of Nith, near the Poet's Residence.* Beneath the latter is inscribed by the sometime owner B. B. Thatcher, "Given to me this day, Oct 23, 1837, by Mr Wordsworth at Rydal Mt. [?Inn] at Grasmere Vale." Robert H. Taylor Collection (49847), Rare Books and Special Collections, Princeton University Libraries.

Princeton MS. 5 MW's copy of *On a Portrait of the Duke of Wellington, upon the Field of Waterloo, by Haydon* on a sheet of creamy white wove stock that measures 23.1 by 19.9 cm. WW has added his own signature. Revisions are in BRH's hand at WW's direction (see notes to the poem). Now shelved separately, the manuscript was originally sent with a letter from WW to BRH, September 2, 1840. Robert H. Taylor Collection (49850), Rare Books and Special Collections, Princeton University Libraries.

Princeton MS. 6 WW's copy of *Epitaph in the Chapel-yard of Langdale, Westmoreland* on two sides of the first leaf of a bifolium of wove stock. The folded sheet measures 23.0 by 18.5 cm. and is inscribed "Wm Wordsworth / Transcribed / for / Lady Farquhar. / Elleray / 7th August / 1841—" (that is, at Elleray, Windermere, the home of John Wilson). General Manuscripts (24812), Rare Books and Special Collections, Princeton University Libraries.

Princeton MS. 7 WW's holograph transcription, with revisions, of "While beams of orient light shoot wide and high," on a single sheet of wove stock measuring 23.0 by 18.5 cm. and inscribed "Front of Rydal Mount, Jan^ry^ 1st 1843." On the recto is WW's holograph transcription, "Wansfell! this Household has a favoured lot," which is inscribed, "Transcribed for his dear Friend, Mrs Arnold, Jan^ry^ 5th, 1843." The paper is folded into six sections, with the direction "Mrs Arnold" written under the "While beams" drafts; adhesive along one edge of the sheet indicates that it was at some time mounted in an album. Robert H. Taylor Collection (49847), Rare Books and Special Collections, Princeton University Libraries.

Quaritch MS. (copy) Bernard Quaritch Catalogue 898 (1970) listed a "holograph fair copy by the Author of his poem 'Sonnet on the Projected Kendal and Windermere Railway'" (item 51). This untraced copy, as reported in the catalogue entry, is titled and signed without a date or place, as in BL MS. 8, and in l. 6 verbally resembles BL MS. 8 and Michigan MS.; but the copy appears to be unique in several of its nonverbal readings.

Ransom MS. WW's signed fair copy of "Hark! 'tis the Thrush, undaunted, undeprest," which he dated "Rydal Mount / Easter Sunday Evening / 1838" and annotated "transcribed for his young / Friend, Miss Roughsedge / by the Author / WW." The poem is transcribed on a singleton of white wove paper, measuring 25.1 by 23.0 cm. The sheet was at some time folded horizontally across the middle and then folded in three to make it the size of a small envelope. The left edge is rough, indicating that the sheet has been torn from a bifolium. Harry Ransom Humanities Research Center, The University of Texas at Austin.

Reed MS. WW's signed copy of "How rich that forehead's calm expanse" on a singleton of wove stock measuring 22.6 by 16.8 cm. and countermarked C WILMOT / 1824. Mark L. Reed Collection.

Rendell MS. Item 181 in Catalogue 55 (Winter 1970–1971) of Kenneth W. Rendell, Inc. (Somerville, Mass.) listed an "Autograph Manuscript Signed, one page, oblong, octavo, Rydal Mount, December 24, 1835" and included a facsimile of *Written in an Album* ("Small service is true service while it lasts") in WW's hand. The manuscript has not been traced.

RHT MS. MW's revision of the Lamb monody "To a good Man of most dear memory" in a copy of the early pamphlet form (see the editor's headnote to this poem, pp. 293–296, below) that was set up by the printer in January 1836. Robert H. Taylor Collection, Rare Books and Special Collections, Princeton University Libraries.

Rotha Q's Album This album bound in red morocco is made up of 76 leaves of creamy white wove stock; it belonged to Rotha Q (1821–1876) from about 1831. WW made two entries, "Rotha! my Spiritual Child! this head was grey," on 3^r, and *Written in an Album* ("Small service is true service while it lasts") on 37^r. The first is dated May 13, 1831, and the second July 3, 1834. There are entries by numerous writers and artists, among them Matthew Arnold, Joanna Baillie, STC, George Crabbe, Felicia Dorothea Hemans, Leigh Hunt, CL, Letitia Elizabeth Landon, Harriet Martineau, Samuel Rogers, RS, and Alfred Tennyson, and a pencil portrait of a young woman by Frank Stone that he dated February 18, 1833. WLMS 11/57. WL.

Rydal Mount MS. WW's fair copy of *On a Portrait of the Duke of Wellington, upon the Field of Waterloo, by Haydon.* There is no title; it is signed "Wm Wordsworth" and a note in WW's hand reads, "Transcribed by the author / Nov^{br} 1 [?7]th 1840." The single sheet is of cream wove stock that measures approximately 25.0 by 19.0 cm. The manuscript, now mounted and framed, was originally fastened to the back of an engraving of BRH's picture, also at Rydal Mount, that is inscribed "B. R. Haydon to William Wordsworth 1840. with affection and gratitude." Rydal Mount Trust.

St. John's MS. Dora W's copy of *To the Author's Portrait,* signed by WW, on a single sheet of paper 23.0 by 18.7 cm., mounted and framed. Reproduced in Wise, *Two Lake Poets* (1927), xx–xxi, and *The Eagle* (St. John's College Magazine) 14 (1887), 252, and 54 (1951), 130. St. John's College Library, Cambridge.

Southey Album 1 Album bound in red leather with a metal locking clasp and lettered on the front cover in gold leaf EDITH SOUTHEY / 1820. The album contains 113 leaves of wove stock watermarked J WHATMAN / TURKEY MILLS / 1818 and measuring 25.2 by approximately 20.5 cm. It was given to Bristol Central Library by Miss E. A. Boult. Poems and drawings by many hands appear in the album (there is one drawing by Constable). Dora W and EMS were staying with the Thomas Hutchinsons at Brinsop Court when WW and MW visited there from mid-December 1827 to January 9, 1828 (*LY,* I, 570), at which time the several poems of WW's were transcribed into the album, including the following ones relevant to this edition: *A Tradition of Darley Dale, Derbyshire* (MW); *A Gravestone upon the Floor in the Cloisters of Worcester Cathedral* (inscribed "Wm Wordsworth—/ Dora Wordsworth 1828."; Dora W); and *Filial Piety* (inscribed "William Wordsworth / Mary Hutchinson / Brinsop Court Feb^{ry} 5th 1828"; MMH). Poems by others include: RS, "Little Beck in green & gold," *The March to Moscow;* Hartley Coleridge, "Ah! woe betide, my bonny Bride," *A Brother's Love to his Sister,* and *To Wordsworth;* STC, *Constancy to an Ideal Object;* DW, "Fair Edith of the Classic Hill" and its *Continuation* (several copies); CL, *Christian Names of Women.* SR91, Bristol Reference Library, Central Library, County of Avon.

Southey Album 2 A maroon leather album kept by RS's family, with entries by EMS, MW, and (principally) Herbert Hill, Bertha Southey's husband. EMS's copy of "Prithee gentle Lady list" appears on a singleton of wove stock once folded in five horizontally. The sheet measures 12.5 by 4.8 cm. It is attached to an album page along with another singleton bearing her copy of "The Lady whom you here behold"; this sheet is also of wove stock but measures 9.4 by 5.6 cm.; it has no fold lines. Written on the album page beneath the two pasted-on singletons is Herbert Hill's note concerning the two poems (see the note to the first poem). MW's copy of "Why should we weep or mourn, Angelic boy" appears on a singleton of wove stock measuring 10.2 by 15.7 cm.; the sheet is attached to an album page. Herbert Hill's note reads "Sonnet by Mr. Wordsworth on the death of his Grandson Edward Wordsworth Written January 1846"; and below, "The Handwriting is Mrs. Wordsworth's." Herbert Hill's copy of *Extempore Effusion upon the Death of*

James Hogg (here titled *Extempore Effusion upon reading in the Newcastle Journal / the notice of the Death of the Poet James Hogg / by W. Wordsworth Decr 1835*) appears on two leaves of the album, the first a singleton, surviving from a bifolium, of brownish-white wove stock, the second on the verso of the second leaf of a bifolium of white wove stock, watermarked [?]ADE / 1824; both measure 22.2 by 18.0 cm. Hill's copy probably derives from the one printed in the *Newcastle Journal*, which it closely resembles, though it possibly derives from the Yale or Berg copies, or from a similar transcription by the Wordsworth household. Hill's copy of "Wouldst Thou be gathered to Christ's chosen flock" appears on a singleton of wove stock measuring 22.4 by 18.2 cm. A note by Hill locates the stone "in the meadow below the garden" (that is, in Dora's Field, below Rydal Mount). Though it is most probable that Hill transcribed the verses from the rock, he may have had access to a manuscript copy. This album is described in *Poems, 1807–1820*, pp. xxix–xxx, as the "Hill" album. Paul F. Betz Collection.

Southey Album 3 A miscellaneous group of manuscripts associated with Robert Southey that have been mounted in a letter album, including WW's copy of a prose epitaph "To the Memory of Robert Southey" on a singleton of bluish-white wove stock measuring 20.5 by 12.6 cm. A copy of this early version of the prose epitaph was sent to JTC shortly before November 30, 1843 (see the editor's headnote to *Inscription for a Monument in Crosthwaite Church, in the Vale of Keswick*, p. 379). WL MS A/Southey/29. In the same album is a copy of the early state of the broadside circular (designated 1a) of *Inscription for a Monument in Crosthwaite Church, in the Vale of Keswick* (WL MS A/Southey/28). WL.

Swarthmore MS. 1 WW's couplet "Thus far I write to please my Friend," signed and dated at Rydal Mount, September 7, 1822, on a singleton of wove stock measuring 6.4 by 17.1 cm. See James A. Butler, "Wordsworth in Philadelphia Area Libraries, 1787–1850," *WC*, 4 (1973), 58. Swarthmore College Library.

Swarthmore MS. 2 WW's fair copy of *Written in an Album* ("Small service is true service while it lasts") on a single sheet of wove stock 19.9 and 16.1 cm. The leaf shows evidence of having been torn from an album (three edges are gilt). Swarthmore College Library.

Swarthmore MS. 3 WW's copy of *Cenotaph* (1^r) and *Epitaph in the Chapel-yard of Langdale, Westmoreland* (1^v) on a single sheet of wove stock that measures 22.9 by 18.6 cm. It is watermarked J WHATMAN / TURKEY MILL / 1838 and appears to be the sheet sent with WW's letter to CW on August 11, 1841, or one sent shortly after. WW's note reads, "You may have seen these Lines [*Cenotaph*] when you [?] at Coleorton but I send them as a Companion to those upon dear Owen." Swarthmore College Library.

Tablet, in St. Oswald's Church, Grasmere, Cumbria "These Vales were saddened with no common gloom," engraved on a monument to the memory of Jemima Quillinan, first wife of EQ, on the south wall of the church. Mrs. Quillinan died May 22, 1822; the monument was fashioned by Francis Legatt Chantrey, who completed it by February 1, 1824 (see *LY*, I, 249).

Ticknor MS. MW's copy of *To the Rev. Christopher Wordsworth, D.D. Master of Harrow School, After the perusal of his Theophilus Anglicanus, recently published* on the flyleaf preceding the title page of *Theophilus Anglicanus* by CW, Jr. (3d ed.; London, 1845). MW has also signed WW's name at the foot. Ticknor Collection, Val/825W89/X3, Dartmouth College Library.

Tombstone, at Chapel Stile, Langdale, Cumbria Cut on the stone marking the grave of Owen Lloyd (1803–1841) is WW's *Epitaph in the Chapel-yard of Langdale, Westmoreland.* The stone has subsided into the ground, partly obscuring the last line of text.

Trinity MS. A bifolium that has on 1ʳ a sonnet by Hartley Coleridge, signed "Hartley Coleridge" ("A new years day! Time was that I was glad"). Notes at the bottom, in ink, show that the whole bifolium is copied from one or more original transcripts: "Written throughout by / Hartley Coleridge Written Jany 1 1840 / at Calgarth." On 1^v are two columns, each containing one WW sonnet. At left is a copy of "While beams of orient light shoot wide and high" (here titled *Ambleside*) signed "Wm Wordsworth—/Jany 1, 1843./Leamington." Underneath the text an inscription reads "Transcribed but signed Wm Wordsworth /JTCH." In the right column is "Wansfell! this Household has a favoured lot," again signed "Wm Wordsworth—/ Dec. 24. 1842." with inscription beneath reading "Transcribed but signed Wm Wordsworth /JTCH." On 2^r is another Hartley Coleridge sonnet, "Could I but harmonize one happy thought." The transcriber had difficulty reading the original, and queried several words. Signature is "Hartley Coleridge" and underneath the inscription is inscribed "Written throughout by / Hartley Coleridge / Query. '<u>Base</u> <u>Born</u> <u>Allan</u>' 2 '<u>Lines</u>' /J.T.C.H." (referring to queries opposite lines 12 and 14 of the text). On 2^v of the bifolium is WW's *Upon a Portrait* (here titled *Upon the sight of a Portrait of a Female Friend painted by Margaret Gillies*); the signature is "Wm Wordsworth / Rydal Mount / New Years Day / 1840" and, beneath, an inscription reads "This is in Wordsworths handwriting throughout—" A slip of paper (TCD 3144/53) clipped to the main manuscript (TCD 3144/54) reads: "The pedigree of the poems is this / they were written by Wordsworth / & Hartly Coleridge when staying / at my Grand Mothers Mrs C. M. Ricketts / house who was a friend of theirs, the / poem in my copy was written under / the same circumstances for Miss L. / [?] Taylor who was a daughter of / my Grand Mother by her first / marriage to Col. Taylor." Mrs. Ricketts and her daughters, Anna and Ellen, lived at Leamington Spa, where they often received the Wordsworths as guests. TCD 3144/53–54, Trinity College Library, Dublin.

Turnbull MS. WW's drafts in pencil and ink, with revisions and corrections also entered by MW, on a copy of the privately printed Lamb monody "To a good Man of most dear memory" (an early state of this pamphlet; see the editor's headnote, pp. 293–296). F. M. Todd reported that Helen Darbishire thought none of the several hands belonged to WW, MW, or Dora W, but some entries are almost certainly by MW and WW; fair copy on a paste-over and on a tipped-in sheet is in JC's hand. Interlinear and marginal entries are designated as "MS. 1" while JC's fair copy is "MS. 2." Bound for S. M. Samuel in 1893 (see the entry for MS. 1832/36, above), the pamphlet contains pp. [1]–7, a folded sheet tipped in to face p. [1] and a folded slip of paper glued to p. 2. The pages of print are of wove stock and measure 20.5 by 14.0 cm. The sheet facing p. [1] is laid paper measuring 16.0 by 19.4 cm. and countermarked 1827. The chain lines of the sheet run horizontally at intervals of 2.5 cm. For an account of the handwriting and the stages of revision see F. M. Todd, "Wordsworth's Monody on Lamb: Another Copy," *Modern Language Review,* 50 (1955), 48–50. Alexander Turnbull Library, National Library of New Zealand.

Victoria MS. 1 WW's fair copy (with two stanzas deleted) of *The Wishing-gate* on a bifolium of creamy white stock measuring 17.0 by 13.5 cm. A note in the hand of Emily Trevenen is entered at the foot of the fourth page: "Wordsworth original of this given to me by his Daughter Dora 1829—E T." Coleridge Collection, SMS F5.54, E. J. Pratt Library, Victoria University Libraries, Toronto.

Victoria MS. 2 A copy in an unidentified hand of ll. 1–28 of *Extempore Effusion upon the Death of James Hogg* on green-gray laid paper measuring 18.0 by 16.0 cm. and countermarked HARRIS / & / TREMLETT / 1834. Chain lines appear at intervals of 2.6 cm. The sheet is folded twice as though for enclosure in a letter and is irregular at the foot and on the right edge, having been cut with scissors or a knife. "Wordsworth" has been added, in the same hand, in the margin beside l. 28. Coleridge Collection, LT 82, E. J. Pratt Library, Victoria University Libraries, Toronto.

Victoria MS. 3 WW's two-line epigram attached to two lines of the old song "Sigh no more Ladies, sigh no more." Inscribed and signed by WW on a single sheet of blue-tinted laid paper measuring 12.0 by 18.0 cm. (torn from a larger sheet). Part of a countermark is visible: & DAVIS. Coleridge Collection, SMS F5.55, E. J. Pratt Library, Victoria University Libraries, Toronto.

Victoria MS. 4 WW's fair copy of *At Furness Abbey* ("Here, where, of havoc tired and rash undoing") on a single sheet of blue-tinted wove stock measuring about 20.0 by 20.5 cm. Coleridge Collection, SMS F5.52, E. J. Pratt Library, Victoria University Libraries, Toronto.

WL MS. 1 Dora W's Portuguese Sketchbook. It contains her copy of *The Westmoreland Girl. To my Grandchildren* (titled here simply *Stanzas to my Grand-Children*) on the recto of the last leaf and the verso of the penultimate leaf of this commercially prepared sketchbook in paper boards (15.4 by 23.0 cm.). Beneath the end of "Stanzas" is her copy of *At Furness Abbey* ("Well have yon Railway Labourers to THIS ground," here beginning "Behold the Labourers on the chosen ground" and titled *Sonnet / Rail-way Labourers at Furness Abbey*—), which she inscribed "W. W." She dated the transcription of both poems July 2, 1845, at Foz, Portugal. The paper is wove stock measuring 14.5 by 22.3 cm. GRMDC: B52, WL.

WL MS. 2 MW's copies of *The Norman Boy* and *Sequel to The Norman Boy*, with corrections in her hand, and two revised stanzas of *Sequel* in an unidentified hand. The copies were given or sent to IF, probably shortly before the letter from MW to IF, November–early December 1841, in which MW sent revisions to both poems (see the entry above for a description of the letter). The manuscript consists of a bifolia and a single sheet of paper similar to the single sheet used for MW's letter: blue-gray tinted wove stock measuring 25 by 20 cm. and, on the first page only, embossed on upper left in a circular device, "LONDON / [*crown*] / SUPERFINE." *The Norman Boy* appears on 1^r–1^v, *Sequel* on 2^r–3^r. The revised stanzas, probably copied—as MW suggested in her letter—by one of IF's nieces, appear on 3^v. MW's Letters, WL.

Yale MS. 1 WW's copy of *A Grave-stone upon the Floor in the Cloisters of Worcester Cathedral* on a singleton of creamy brown wove stock measuring 22.7 by 18.4 cm. MS. Vault (uncat) Wordsworth, Beinecke Rare Book and Manuscript Library, Yale University.

Yale MS. 2 DW's copy of an early version of *The Primrose of the Rock* on two sheets of creamy white wove stock measuring 13.2 by approximately 12.0 cm.; the sheets were apparently torn from a small notebook. The title here is *Written in March 1829 on seeing a Primrose-tuft of flowers flourishing in the chink of a rock in which that Primrose-tuft had been seen by us to flourish for twenty nine seasons*; it is signed "M.S.— W. Wordsworth / Copied by D Wordsworth Senr / [?Santer] Green / August 28th 1829." MS. Vault (uncat) Wordsworth, Beinecke Rare Book and Manuscript Library, Yale University.

Yale MS. 3 WW's copy, dated August 1, 1831, of *To B. R. Haydon, Esq. on seeing his Picture of Napoleon Buonaparte on the Island of St. Helena* on a bifolium of creamy white wove stock measuring 23.0 by 18.7 cm. The verso of the first leaf and the second leaf are blank. Tinker 2317, Beinecke Rare Book and Manuscript Library, Yale University.

Yale MS. 4 WW to John Hernaman (editor of the *Newcastle Journal*), November 30, 1835; MW's copy, signed by WW, on 2^r–2^v of ll. 1–28 of *Extempore Effusion upon the Death of James Hogg* on a bifolium of creamy white wove stock measuring 22.5 by 18.7 cm. and watermarked B TURNER / 1834. Intended for publication in *Newcastle Journal* in this seven-stanza form. Tinker 2318 and 2321, Beinecke Rare Book and Manuscript Library, Yale University.

Yale MS. 5 WW to John Hernaman (editor of the *Newcastle Journal*), December 1, 1835; MW's copy of ll. 28–44 of *Extempore Effusion upon the Death of James Hogg* on a bifolium of creamy white wove stock measuring 22.5 by 18.2 cm.; a supplement and correction for Yale MS. 4. Intended for publication in the *Newcastle Journal.* Tinker 2322, Beinecke Rare Book and Manuscript Library, Yale University.

Yale MS. 6 WW's draft for "Lo! where she stands fixed in a saint-like trance" on a singleton of bluish white wove stock measuring 24.9 by 20.0 cm. and countermarked J WHATMAN / 1838. The sheet was originally used as an envelope: it had been folded in six and addressed in pencil on the outer side "Wm Wordsworth Esq." MS. Vault (uncat) Wordsworth, Beinecke Rare Book and Manuscript Library, Yale University.

Yale MS. 7 WW's copy of *A Plea for Authors. May, 1838* on a singleton of creamy white wove stock measuring 18.7 by 15.6 cm. The sheet was once folded in six as if for the post. On the verso is his copy of "'Tis He, whose yester-evening's proud disdain" and his note above the sonnet "Here follows a 2nd Thrush." MS. Vault (uncat) Wordsworth, Beinecke Rare Book and Manuscript Library, Yale University.

Yale MS. 8 WW's draft of stanzas 1–4, 6, and the first line of stanza 5 of *The Wishing-gate Destroyed* on a bifolium of blue-tinted wove stock, once folded in four and measuring 24.9 by 20.0 cm. The second leaf is blank. MS. Vault (uncat) Wordsworth, Beinecke Rare Book and Manuscript Library, Yale University.

Yale MS. 9 A copy, possibly by MMH, of *Sonnet on the Projected Kendal and Windermere Railway* on 1^v of what is now a single sheet of white wove stock (torn from a bifoliate sheet or from an album); it measures 22.1 by 18.5 cm, countermarked J WHATMAN / 1843. MMH (ll. 1–3) and EC (ll. 4–14) have entered a copy of "So fair, so sweet, withal so sensitive" on 1^r. MS. Vault (uncat) Wordsworth, Beinecke Rare Book and Manuscript Library, Yale University.

Yale MS. 10 EQ's copy of *Written upon a fly leaf in the Copy of the Author's Poems which was sent to her Majesty Queen Victoria* (here untitled) on a singleton of blue-tinted wove stock measuring 22.6 by 18.1 cm. MS. Vault (uncat) Wordsworth, Beinecke Rare Book and Manuscript Library, Yale University.

Yale Sonnets MS. IF's copies of nine sonnets first published in an appendix in *Sonnets,* 1838, and here prepared in printer's copy for *PELY,* 1842. With the exception of the first and fifth leaves, the paper is blue-tinted wove stock measuring 12.5 by 20.2 cm., and pinholes in all ten leaves indicate that they were sewn up as a packet. The first leaf is a scrap of creamy white wove stock measuring 7.2 by approximately 18.7 cm. The fifth leaf is creamy white stock measuring approximately 12.5 by 18.7 cm. The sonnets relevant to this edition are *Composed on the Same Morning* (later titled *Composed on a May Morning, 1838* ["Life with yon Lambs, like day is just begun"]); *To the Planet Venus, upon its Approximation (as an Evening Star) to the Earth, January 1838*; "Hark! 'tis the Thrush, undaunted, undeprest"; "'Tis He whose yester-evening's high disdain"; "Oh what a Wreck! how changed in mien and speech!"; *A Plea for Authors. May, 1838.* The first leaf bears MW's instructions to the printer, "(To the Printer, these to follow, having been previously Published)"; and also bears further instructions in MW's hand in the left margin, "note to stand at the head of the first Sonnet"; and also bears her copy of the note, "The Sonnets that follow, having been published in [in *revised from* an] an appendix to one, and a comparatively, small Ed: of the Author's Poems, they are here reprinted, a liberty as it is presumed that will not be objected to [that will not be objected to *revised from* will be agreeable to the Purchasers of this Volume]." The rectos of each leaf bearing a sonnet are numbered 1 to 9, by IF or MW. In the right margin of the second leaf MW has added an instruction "To the Printer / See the back of these Sonnets for their Title." The printer has marked some of the rectos lightly with a pencil "x," probably to indicate that the poem had been set. Paper types, paper size, and the several handwritings all suggest that these half-sheets were once part of the printer's copy of *PELY* (DC MS. 151). MS. Vault (uncat) Wordsworth, Beinecke Rare Book and Manuscript Library, Yale University.

Last Poems, 1821–1850

Introduction

The first poem included in this volume was written in January 1821 and the last was completed in April 1847.[1] In this period Wordsworth composed or substantially revised and prepared for publication several large works not included here. The late reworkings of *Guilt and Sorrow, The Borderers, The Prelude,* and poems for *The Recluse* are omitted, as is new composition in the form of several sonnet series and itinerary poems, including *River Duddon; Memorials of a Tour on the Continent, 1820; Ecclesiastical Sketches, 1822; Yarrow Revisited; Sonnets, 1833, Composed During a Tour; Memorials of a Tour in Italy; Sonnets Upon the Punishment of Death;* and *Sonnets Dedicated to Liberty and Order.* What remain are roughly two hundred poems of surprising variety in form and content and in degrees of intensity and ambition.

In *Lyrical Ballads* in 1798 Wordsworth attempted to transform taste by experimenting with traditional or well-established forms such as the ballad and the loco-descriptive poem. Though the results seem less startling than the experiments of 1798, some of the poems he composed after 1820 can be described in similar terms. In the immensely popular genre of romance verse narrative of the late 1820s Wordsworth composed three poems, *The Russian Fugitive, The Egyptian Maid,* and *The Armenian Lady's Love.* Though the three long verse tales differ widely from one another in content and atmosphere, in them Wordsworth combined the excitement of exotic places and past times with a high moral sense of virtue in an attempt to curb the excesses he associated with the form, especially in such productions as the wildly popular *Lalla Rookh* (1817) by Thomas Moore and *The Giaour* by Lord Byron (1813). Wordsworth's Arthurian tale and two Eastern tales press the romance narrative into use as an emblematic story of loyalty, generosity, charity, and courage. In all three poems Wordsworth

[1]The latest poem in *Poems, 1807–1820* is the sonnet titled *June, 1820.* WW was preparing copy for the printer of *Poetical Works* (1820) when he composed it; it was the last one to be inserted in that edition. The hiatus between this date and January 1821, when *Decay of Piety* was composed, is explained by WW's undertaking a continental tour, which he began in July and completed in November 1820. He then remained in London for several weeks before returning to Rydal Mount around December 23. The composing he did while traveling was related either to *Memorials of a Tour on the Continent, 1820* or to *Ecclesiastical Sketches* (1822); this material will be included in Geoffrey Jackson's forthcoming volume of the Cornell Wordsworth, *Sonnet Series and Itinerary Poems.* Though no fresh composition can be dated after April 1847, WW continued to oversee the revision, arrangement, and publication of his poems through the edition of 1849–1850.

casts in somber hues Moore's exotic—and erotic—imagery of the Orient and counters Byron's ironic deconstruction of virtue and courage as social values in the scandalous and scornful *Don Juan* (1819–1824).[2]

Both before and long after the preparation of *Lyrical Ballads* Wordsworth employed various dramatic voices and viewpoints to unsettle the reader's preconceptions about narrative, producing verse tales in widely different but equally complex and allusive styles. A swift survey might include the credulous sexton who narrates the two early ballads of the 1790s, *The Greyhound Ballad* and *The Three Graves*; the garrulous and superstitious sea captain who tells the story of *The Thorn*; the uneasy poet who narrates his encounter with the leech-gatherer in *Resolution and Independence;* the "dramatized ejaculations" of *Ode. The Morning of the Day Appointed for a General Thanksgiving. January 18, 1816,* and *Ode. 1815* (*MY*, II, 324); the sentimental and paternalistic magus of *The Norman Boy* and *Sequel to The Norman Boy;* and the curmudgeonly moralist of *The Warning.* In 1816 Wordsworth praised Robert Burns's ability to "avail himself of his own character and situation in society, to construct out of them a poetic self,—introduced as a dramatic personage—for the purpose of inspiriting his incidents, diversifying his pictures, recommending his opinions, and giving point to his sentiments" (*Letter to a Friend of Robert Burns, Prose,* III, 125). With greater variety but in much the same way, and even in poems less obviously uttered by a fictional voice, Wordsworth constructed a poetic self whose speaking could disturb the surface of the reader's consciousness, so that the light of perception is refracted in new and revealing ways.

In this span of thirty years Wordsworth wrote hundreds of sonnets, a form he had been exploring extensively since early 1802. As some of the early sonnets themselves attest, composing sonnets brought Wordsworth relief from creative drought, release of energy from intense effort on other composition, or the expression of pent-up emotions or outraged feelings: he summarized these uses by surveying the work of classic sonneteers in a sonnet published in 1827:

Scorn not the Sonnet; Critic, you have frowned,
Mindless of its just honours;—with this Key
Shakspeare unlocked his heart; the melody
Of this small Lute gave ease to Petrarch's wound;
A thousand times this Pipe did Tasso sound;
Camöens soothed with it an Exile's grief;
The Sonnet glittered a gay myrtle Leaf
Amid the cypress with which Dante crowned
His visionary brow: a glow-worm Lamp,
It cheered mild Spenser, called from Faery-land
To struggle through dark ways; and when a damp
Fell round the path of Milton, in his hand
The Thing became a Trumpet, whence he blew
Soul-animating strains—alas, too few!

Wordsworth found his own uses, of course, notably recasting Miltonic form in

[2]See WW's canceled note to *At the Grave of Burns. 1803* and *Thoughts Suggested the Day Following on the Banks of Nith, Near the Poet's Residence,* pp. 471–475 below.

sonnets expressing his own views on social and political matters. But the possibilities are not exhausted by this tribute to past achievements. Wordsworth's efforts include a valentine, several epitaphs, tributes to ill or departed loved ones and friends, an encapsulation of a friend's childhood experience, treatment of local legends and stories, and observations on stars, moon, clouds, and the surrounding landscape, all in sonnet form.

Most of the sonnets of this period were composed in series, or ultimately included in them—sequences of sonnets and sometimes other verse forms written in response to the scenes and emotions called up by his recollection of a journey, or composed in a sustained discourse on a public issue or theme. The major works of this kind are treated elsewhere in The Cornell Wordsworth in the forthcoming *Sonnet Series and Itinerary Poems, 1819–1850*, but included here is the shortest such sequence, *The Widow on Windermere Side*, which began as a pair of sonnets and was extended to three before publication in 1842. The main complement of sonnets, however, is made up of single efforts, "Produced as lonely Nature or the strife / That animates the scenes of public life / Inspired" ("In these brief Records, by the Muses' art").

On occasion the sonnet's "crowded room" imposed limitations that the addition of more sonnets could not overcome. What may have seemed to Wordsworth at first well-suited to the brevity and compression of a sonnet could demand more than that form allowed. One such example is the series of Evening Voluntaries, which had its beginning in a single sonnet, *Twilight by the side of Grasmere Lake* (see p. 248). Wordsworth no sooner submitted the sonnet to Dora Wordsworth to be fair-copied into his notebook (DC MS. 128) than he began adding couplets below it, first in pencil, then in ink, expanding these evening descriptions and reflections, now entirely in couplets after a brief experiment in tetrameter, until the material grew beyond the limits of even one poem. As the couplets mounted up, Wordsworth composed them into five separate poems that seem to grow out of the mood and manner of the original sonnet. Adding to this total two poems inspired by a visit to the Cumbrian coast, a lyric composed thirty years earlier, and a cento of recent date, Wordsworth published a group of nine Evening Voluntaries in 1835. The history of this sequence can be traced in the introductory note, reading texts, notes, photographs, transcriptions, and Appendix III (pp. 235–251, 456–458, 740–757, and 841).

In two instances the manuscript record reveals Wordsworth producing a single long composition that he later divided into two separate poems. In the spring of 1826 he composed *Vernal Stanzas* in three stanzas and an untitled poem in four stanzas beginning "What month can rival thee sweet May?" Mary Wordsworth copied both versions into the notebook currently in use (DC MS. 107). But on blank pages in the same notebook Wordsworth soon developed this material into the ten-stanza poem *Ode to May*. Then, in a different manuscript (DC MS. 133), he expanded and revised *Ode to May* by entering more than thirty stanzas, some of them duplicates, before settling, through rearranging and revising these stanzas, on two poems, the eight-stanza *Ode, Composed on May Morning* and the twelve-stanza *To May* (see the editor's headnote to the May odes, pp. 65–67, and the photographs and transcriptions from MS. 133, pp. 620–655). In the second example, in response to a gift of goldfish by Maria Jane Jewsbury in 1829, Wordsworth first composed *Gold and Silver Fishes, in a Vase,* and then attempted a ruminative and wide-ranging sequel called *To a Friend* that grew to more than 200 lines. On Mary Wordsworth's suggestion that this lengthy production was really two poems, the poet split the work into more or less equal parts to form *Liberty. (A Sequel to the Above.)*, still the "sequel" to *Gold and Silver Fishes, in a Vase,* and *Humanity. (Written in the Year 1829)*, reconceived to stand alone as a meditation on society's tendency to dehumanize mankind. There are other examples of Wordsworth's reshaping material for publication, also from the 1835 volume. In early proof stages Wordsworth initially intended "Rural Illusions" as the title for a group of three poems, comprising what are now *Rural Illusions, This Lawn, &c,* and *Thought on the Seasons,* but before final proof was returned he altered the arrangement so that each poem stood alone without a common title. And again in an early set of proofs he indicated that *Lines Suggested by a Portrait from the Pencil of F. Stone* was to incorporate additional verses that formed *The Foregoing Subject Resumed* when published.

Evolution of one set of verses into something quite different is revealed in the manuscripts associated with the composition of *On the Power of Sound.* The germ of the poem seems to have been a short passage in an early version of *The Triad,* a mythopoeic tribute to three young women, the poet's daughter and two of her friends. Revised, then deleted from *The Triad,* this section of sixteen lines then formed the opening stanza of the first version of *On the Power of Sound* (see the "Text of MS. 131," pp. 113–115, and the photographs and transcriptions on pp. 680–693). In the much expanded published version of *On the Power of Sound* of 1835 Wordsworth placed these lines in an emphatic position near the close of the poem (as the twelfth of fourteen stanzas; see the editor's headnote, p. 112).

Early in his career Wordsworth was drawn to the elegy and the epitaph as modes of expression (see *Early Poems, 1785–1797* for numerous examples among his juvenile poems). If we accept the Lucy poems as elegies, Wordsworth may be said to have found a place for at least one elegy or epitaph in nearly every collection from 1798 onward. The collected poems from 1815 assembled these "Epitaphs and Elegiac Pieces"—eleven of them (including epitaphs translated from Chiabrera)—in a separate class, the contents of which grew in number as the years wore on and as Wordsworth felt called upon to honor departed friends and fellow poets (see "Wordsworth's Arrangements and Classifications of His Poems, 1807–1820: Manuscript Lists and Contents of Editions," Appendix II of *Poems, 1807–1820,* pp. 608–631). The accretion of elegies and epitaphs accelerated through the last thirty years of his life until, in the final lifetime edition of 1849–1850, the total number of poems in this class reached twenty-six. Of the many examples of this intensely private yet resolutely public form in this volume the poems composed on the death of Charles Lamb and the memorial verses to Robert Southey, along with the assembled manuscript evidence concerning them, reveal a compositional process shaped by negotiation as well as by inspiration. In the fall of 1835 Wordsworth accepted Mary Lamb's request that he compose an epitaph for her brother Charles, but he could not express his thoughts in small enough space for the poem to serve as an inscription (*LY,* III,

122). The "Epitaph" form of the poem (in two versions) extended to a little over thirty lines, but, still unsatisfied, Wordsworth pressed on to compose a monody of more than 130 lines in tribute to Lamb. Along the way he consulted with Mary herself, with his own family and friends, and with friends of Lamb to refine and embellish his record of his "silent and invisible Friend" (l. 108; see the editor's headnote, pp. 291–296, and the notes to the three reading texts for details of these "negotiations"). With *Inscription for a Monument in Crosthwaite Church, in the Vale of Keswick,* his tribute to Robert Southey, Wordsworth engaged to produce an inscription appropriate for the monument that Southey's friends proposed to place in Crosthwaite Church. Though manuscripts of the poem itself are not extensive, the record of Wordsworth's correspondence with John Taylor Coleridge and James Stanger, two principals in the drive to establish the memorial, shows the surprising extent to which the community participated in the composition of the poem (see the editor's headnote, pp. 379–384).

Collaboration of other kinds can be found among the poems in this volume. In several instances Wordsworth accepted suggestions for poems, often from complete strangers, producing what he liked to call "stories and . . . incidents" (*LY*, I, 692) from tales told by others. Examples of this genre are "'Wait, prithee, wait!' this answer Lesbia threw"; *Filial Piety; A Tradition of Darley Dale, Derbyshire; The Norman Boy* and its sequel; *To a Lady;* and *Grace Darling*—the last poem an imaginative recreation of a dramatic sea rescue that had been reported at length in local and national newspapers. Wordsworth's sonnet *A Grave-stone upon the Floor in the Cloisters of Worcester Cathedral* may have been composed in friendly contest with Francis Wrangham, his fellow undergraduate at Cambridge and collaborator in composing the *Imitation of Juvenal* in 1797, after their chance meeting and discussion of the gravestone in Worcester in 1828 (see p. 437; see also *Early Poems, 1785–1797,* pp. 788–795). Perhaps the earliest collaborative project during this period was the inscription in St. Oswald's Church, Grasmere, that honored Edward Quillinan's first wife, Jemima. "These Vales were saddened with no common gloom" was rewritten by Wordsworth from a draft by Quillinan in November 1822. The last such project and probably the last poetry Wordsworth composed was *The Installation Ode* in 1847. Wordsworth reluctantly consented to write the lyrics of an ode to be performed at the installation of Prince Albert as chancellor of Cambridge University, but the final illness and death of his daughter Dora forced the poet to rely heavily upon his son-in-law, Edward Quillinan, to plan the poem, and, it seems likely, to prepare a rough draft. Correspondence reveals that Wordsworth himself took responsibility for the work, undertaking to revise the wording to accommodate the demands of the music being composed, though he clearly took little pleasure in the task or in the result (see the editor's headnote, pp. 407–410; the first edition [Cambridge, 1847] was published anonymously, but subsequent editions, apparently unauthorized, appeared with ever more elaborate acknowledgment of the author).

Finally, a few words may be said of Wordsworth's publishing ventures between 1821 and 1850. During this period he authorized more than thirty publications of his works in single- and multiple-volume format, in verse and in prose. The occasion of reissuing works, like the many editions of *The Excursion* and the collected poems, involved Wordsworth in revision and addition of poems, and for some works, notably the editions of collected poems of 1836–1837 and 1845, he undertook very extensive alteration of the text (see the *apparatus criticus* to poems published before these dates).

Two volumes, both collections of new or unpublished poems, are of particular interest here. The first, published by Longman, Rees, Orme, Brown, Green, & Longman in 1835, was *Yarrow Revisited, and Other Poems*, and the second was *Poems, Chiefly of Early and Late Years*, published by Edward Moxon in 1842.[3] Each in its way epitomizes the work of the last three decades of Wordsworth's career. Both volumes "revisit" the past as a means of assessing the present and imagining a future. The earlier volume does so by featuring *Yarrow Revisited* and its sequence of poems based on a tour covering ground in large part familiar to the poet-traveler from earlier tours of Scotland and in varying degrees echoing the forms and language of poems produced from the experiences of the earlier tours and at the same time noting differences and changes, "foretaste[s] of winter" when "every day brought with it tidings new / Of rash change, ominous for the public weal" (ll. 27–29 of *Apology* from the series Yarrow Revisited). And in subtle ways the other poems of his maturity in the 1835 volume echo and play against earlier poems on similar themes, often with an enhanced sense of loss or of the value in remembered bonds. "The Sun has long been set," one of the Evening Voluntaries, was lifted virtually unchanged (after an unsuccessful attempt to alter it) from "Moods of my own Mind," a group of poems published in *Poems, in Two Volumes* in 1807, and *Rural Illusions* and *The Primrose of the Rock* recall the several bird and flower poems of the spring of 1802, also published in 1807. But in an "after-lay" to the latter poem Wordsworth sets aside the mood of longing typical of the early lyrics and comes to regard the "myriads of bright flowers" as "types beneficent" to help make "each soul a separate heaven, / A court for Deity." *On the Power of Sound* echoes the language of the Intimations *Ode* of 1802–1804, reconstituting its record of loss and recompense as a song in praise of "the Word, that shall not pass away." Though there is a somber strain through much of the verse in this volume, in *Humanity* and *The Warning*, for example, the overall spirit is captured in the closing lines of the sequel to *Lines on a Portrait from the Pencil of F. Stone.* Here Wordsworth mused that the "enduring quiet" of a work of art can "gently raise / A household small and sensitive" to a

> salutary sense of awe,
> Or sacred wonder, growing with the power
> Of meditation that attempts to weigh,
> In faithful scales, things and their opposites. (ll. 24–27)

On the whole darker in mood than the 1835 volume, *Poems, Chiefly of Early and Late Years* is also a kind of revisitation. In its title the volume recalls Robert Burns's *Poems, chiefly in the Scottish Dialect* (Kilmarnock, 1786) and it includes in the first section two tributes to Burns, *At the Grave of Burns, 1803* and *Thoughts on the Banks of Nith, on the Day Following*, both written in a stanza form often employed

[3]See Appendix I (p. 833) for a listing of the contents of these volumes.

by Burns and the first poem conceived and partly written when Wordsworth visited Burns country in August 1803 during his tour of Scotland with Dorothy Wordsworth (see *Poems, 1800–1807*, pp. 534–535). Wordsworth's volume also recaptures—and reshapes—the past more directly, as already noted, by presenting two works that he composed in the 1790s and thoroughly revised before their publication in 1842, *Guilt and Sorrow* and *The Borderers.* Among the shorter "early" poems included in the volume, in order of their appearance, are *The Forsaken,* a survival from manuscripts preserved when Wordsworth was preparing materials to send to the printer of *Poems, in Two Volumes* in 1807; *Address to the Scholars of the Village School of ——, 1798,* his reworking of the Matthew elegies he had composed in 1798 (see *LB, 1797–1800*, pp. 297–302, 807–808); *Elegiac Verses, in Memory of John Wordsworth,* composed in 1805; *At Applethwaite, near Keswick,* composed in 1804 but held back until after the death of Sir George Beaumont, whose gift of the property at Applethwaite the sonnet commemorates (for this and the previous poem see *Poems, 1800–1807*, pp. 614–616, 532–533); *Epistle to Sir G. H. Beaumont, Bart.*, Wordsworth's extended tribute to his friend first composed in 1811 (see *Poems, 1807–1820*, pp. 80–95); and *Address to the Clouds* and *Maternal Grief,* blank verse pieces, dating from 1808 and 1813 respectively, that are associated with composition for *The Recluse* (for the first see *Tuft*, pp. 61–71; *Maternal Grief* will appear in Michael C. Jaye's edition of *The Excursion*). Each in its own way shows the poet searching out the means to "nourish the hope that memory lacks not power / To keep the treasure unimpaired" while at once and steadily aware that this is a "Vain thought" since "joy and rest" are "lodged in the bosom of eternal things" (ll. 90–94 of *Address to the Clouds*).

In keeping with Wordsworth's desire to enhance the sale of his books, Moxon printed the third edition of *Yarrow Revisited, and Other Poems* (1839) in a format that would permit its being bound to match the bindings of the 1832 *Poetical Works,* even though the first edition of *Poetical Works,* published by Moxon in 1836, had incorporated the contents of the *Yarrow Revisited* volume into the set. A similar arrangement was made with Moxon in 1842 so that *Poems, Chiefly of Early and Late Years* could be bound to match the multivolume *Poetical Works* of 1836, 1840, 1841, and 1843. It was then included, with some alterations, as volume six (of seven) in the reissues of 1846 and 1849, while in the one-volume 1845 *Poems* (and its reissues in 1847 and 1849) and in the *Poetical Works* of 1849–1850 the contents of the 1842 volume were distributed among the various classes and groups, finding their places in Wordsworth's career-long scheme to form the body of his work into a unified whole. But these two volumes were not Wordsworth's only publishing ventures during this period. Encouraged by Moxon in 1838 to gather up all of his sonnets in a separate publication, in that year Wordsworth published his volume of *Sonnets.*[4]

In addition to these major undertakings during these years Wordsworth published several circulars and pamphlets that contained one or more poems edited here; examples are the pamphlet *Kendal and Windermere Railway* (containing two sonnets), the privately printed pamphlets of the monody on the death of

[4]See Appendix II (p. 839) for an account of late additions to *Sonnets.*

Lamb ("To a good Man of most dear memory"), *Grace Darling*, and *Inscription for a Monument in Crosthwaite Church, in the Vale of Keswick.* He contributed to several annuals, notably Joanna Baillie's *A Collection of Poems* (1823), *The Casket* (published by John Murrary in 1829), Frederic Mansel Reynolds's *The Keepsake* (1829), *The Winter's Wreath* (1828), and Lord Northampton's *The Tribute* (1837). He also authorized two selections from his works to be made by others, intended for sale at a modest price. Joseph Hine edited *Selections from the Poems of William Wordsworth, Esq. Chiefly for the use of Schools and Young Persons,* published by Moxon in 1831. Henry Gough, undermaster of St. Bees School, obtained permission for what was to be a similarly unpretentious collection in 1842, but without Wordsworth's knowledge he turned the project over to James Burns, who brought out *Select Pieces from the Poems of Wordsworth* in 1843 in an elaborately illustrated form intended for monied purchasers. Moxon instantly commandeered the enterprise, ensuring that the main profit would come to the poet and himself; and in 1847 he republished the book for Wordsworth over his own imprint.[5]

The poetry of Wordsworth's later years has not ranked high in the world's opinion. The poet left himself open to this ranking through his attention in his early poetry to memory as a means of recovering a full sense of self and his resulting emphasis on the experiences of youth and their significance in mental and spiritual development. Coleridge's enthusiasm for—and his reservations about—the poetry Wordsworth composed between 1797–1798 (when the poems of *Lyrical Ballads* were written) and 1817 (when *Biographia Literaria* appeared) led naturally to the view, expressed first by his daughter, Sara Coleridge, that the poetry composed after that point did not measure up (see her letters to Aubrey de Vere in *SCML*, vol. II). In his influential selective edition of Wordsworth's poems (1879) Matthew Arnold developed this view into a virtual canon that has cast a long shadow over critical response to Wordsworth's lifetime production. But just as the union of passion and intellect—what attracts readers to Wordsworth in the first place—is evident in work composed before *Lyrical Ballads,* so it continues to be evident in the poetry of the years following the publication of *Poems, in Two Volumes* in 1807. The poems of the period 1821–1850 (for those of the intervening period see *Poems, 1807–1820*), individually and collectively, have complex histories, and Wordsworth was deeply absorbed in their production and expended much thought and energy in their revision. The history of a large portion of this relatively unstudied creative enterprise has here been made ready for exploration.

[5]See Mark L. Reed, "Wordsworth's Surprisingly Pictured Page: *Select Pieces*," *Book Collector* 46.1 (1997): 69–91, for an account of *Select Pieces from the Poems of Wordsworth* as first published by Burns and then by Moxon.

Editorial Procedure

This edition presents the earliest completed form of each of Wordsworth's shorter poems composed between 1820 and 1850, together with all variant readings in manuscripts of these poems over which Wordsworth exercised some influence and in all editions over which he had some control—that is, most English editions that appeared in his lifetime—and periodical publications that he authorized. Excluded are those poems that have been edited in other volumes in this series: *The Salisbury Plain Poems of William Wordsworth,* edited by Stephen Gill (Ithaca, 1975); *"The Borderers" by William Wordsworth,* edited by Robert Osborn (Ithaca, 1982); *The Fourteen-Book "Prelude" by William Wordsworth,* edited by W. J. B. Owen (Ithaca, 1985); *Translations of Chaucer and Virgil by William Wordsworth,* edited by Bruce E. Graver (Ithaca, 1998); and the forthcoming *Sonnet Series and Intinerary Poems by William Wordsworth,* edited by Geoffrey Jackson.

As in *The Shorter Poems of William Wordsworth, 1807–1820,* edited by Carl H. Ketcham (Ithaca, 1989), the arrangement of these earliest texts is intended to show the sequence in which Wordsworth "met and dealt with the challenges of his developing interests." When possible, then, we have ordered the poems according to what appears to be the earliest probable date when composition on each was begun. Poems for which we know only the latest probable date of composition are placed under that date. In this chronological presentation we have made an exception of the group of poems that eventually made up the first publication of the series of Evening Voluntaries. These poems flowed initially from a single impetus, a sonnet composed in 1833, and were developed as a group or sequence over the course of two years; to show the close relation they bear to one another we have placed the nine poems at the earliest probable time of the initial sonnet's composition and arranged them in the sequence of their first published appearance rather than their probable order of composition. For most of the poems we give the rationale for dating in the notes (pp. 417–506); for poems with more than one reading text and those with involved histories of composition or publication we discuss the date and other relevant matters in a headnote to the reading texts.

We present each poem in a reading text from which all revisions and variant readings have been stripped away. The reading text is ordinarily the first form of the poem published under Wordsworth's supervision; we occasionally provide an alternate reading text, more rarely two or three, for a poem that reached temporary completion in an early manuscript or periodical publication; and we present a few reading texts drawn from the earliest, or only, manuscript of poems that Wordsworth never published. Unless we have indicated otherwise, spelling, punctuation, paragraphing, and capitalization of the reading texts, and, where possible, the typography of their titles, agree with the sources on which they are based, with the exception of ampersands, which we have silently expanded to "and." The degree of punctuation in manuscripts varies widely; in a few cases the copyist has punctuated very lightly or not at all. We have rarely emended reading texts, whether based on manuscripts or print, altering only what are clearly copyist's or printer's errors and occasionally supplying punctuation where sense requires it; all such emendations are noted in the *apparatus criticus* beneath the poems. A fly-title page that is present in lifetime printings and that bears the title of an individual poem is noted but not set as a separate page. We have added editorial line numbers in the margins of reading texts.

Each poem is accompanied by an *apparatus criticus* headed by the date of composition, lists of manuscripts and printings, the source of the reading text, and the poem's classification by Wordsworth. After the heading "*published in,*" the year of an edition followed by a short dash indicates that all subsequent collective editions (exclusive of selective editions published in 1831, 1834, 1835, 1836, 1838, 1839, 1842, and 1847) contain the poem in question; if a selective edition contains the poem, it is cited. After the heading "*found in,*" manuscripts listed are original documents or records of originals that are now untraced and contain full or partial records of the poem. Details about content, handwriting, source, and other related matters for each manuscript appear in the Manuscript Census (pp. xxv–lxxxv); any supplementary information appears in the editor's notes to the poem. In the case of manuscripts written into printed editions, "*found in*" means that the poem is either present in the printed edition and accompanied by autograph revisions in a particular copy of that edition, entered by Wordsworth or authorized by him (e.g., MS. 1832/36), or is present there only as an autograph copy or draft (e.g., MS. 1831JH). The *apparatus* proper shows—unless the "*found in*" or "*published in*" list indicates otherwise—all verbal variants from the reading text, both in listed manuscripts that led up to it and followed it and in indicated editions. A short dash following the year of an edition (or of a book in which autograph revisions appear) shows that those subsequent editions listed in the "*published in*" entry repeat the reading cited. The word "*so*" in this *apparatus* signals that the base text has been emended; in such instances, the emendation will almost always have been drawn from another authorial text, which the *apparatus* will indicate, as in the following example:

13 wing'd *so MS. 134, 1836–* winged *all other MSS., 1835*

Here we have emended the base text of *The Egyptian Maid* (1835) to agree with MS. 134, the reading of which is repeated in all editions from 1836 onward. We also employ "*so*" in the *apparatus* to signal that a subsequent manuscript repeats the first one cited, as in this example:

11 time-worn face, for he such seed] Face time-worn—But he such seed *Berg MS. 5, so WW to BRH but rev to text*

In this instance, drawn from *On a Portrait of the Duke of Wellington, upon the Field of Waterloo, by Haydon,* the reading in the Berg MS. differs from the reading text, and the letter ("WW to BRH") repeats that reading; *but rev to text* means that WW to BRH has been revised to match the reading text.

When material is entered after the last line of a poem, we cite the final line number, followed by a slash ("14/"), and record the additional matter and its source. Material inserted or intended to be inserted within the text of a poem is recorded at the point of insertion ("24/25").

Capital letters in parentheses following a manuscript name—as in "MS. 107 (A)"—designate the several copies of a poem within a single manuscript. Occasionally we employ subscript numerals—as in "Amherst $MS._2$—to indicate the primary and secondary level of composition within a single copy of the text on the same page of a manuscript.

In order to avoid overloading the *apparatus* we have listed nonverbal variants separately—with the exceptions of those reported with editorial emendations and those embedded in verbal variants—in Part II. Such variants exclude the substitution of "and" for the ampersand and vice versa, and single-letter miswritings corrected by the copyists. The means used to indicate verse paragraph breaks, changes from single to double quotation marks, and changes in the typefaces and arrangements of titles, subtitles, and prose headnotes or endnotes are not reported unless it seems probable that Wordsworth authorized such changes. When manuscripts are particularly complex or pose other special concerns, we present them in Part III in full transcription, with facing photographs, rather than in an *apparatus.*

In the transcriptions in Part III, the aim is to show with reasonable typographic accuracy everything in the manuscript that can be helpful to a study of the poem's development. Even false starts and corrected letters can sometimes indicate the writer's intentions, and they are recorded; simple reinforcement of letters, however, is not. We treat punctuation in all manuscripts as original or "base text" punctuation except in obvious cases of addition, particularly where different punctuation marks are clearly distinguishable, or where one mark has clearly been converted to another, or where punctuation has been added together with verbal revision. Passages in Wordsworth's hand are in roman type, those in other hands in italic, though identification of hands must sometimes be conjectural, especially for scattered words or parts of words. Doubled-back lines are shown approximately as they appear in the manuscript. Revisions appear in reduced type—single words or parts of lines positioned as nearly as possible as they appear in the manuscript, entire lines emphasized by indentation. Material written over erasure and enclosed by a screen is not, however, reduced, since the screen itself signals a revision. Deletion of blocks of lines by large X's or other marks, where their purpose can be clearly understood from the facing photographs, is not shown in transcription; however, horizontal cross-out lines and slashes that delete single letters are reproduced, since they frequently enable the reader to follow the sequence of smaller-scale revisions. We omit the words of irrelevant material on the same page as the poem being reproduced even though they may be visible in the photograph. Unless otherwise noted, the numbering of leaves counts stubs, but not pasted-down endpapers; numbers assigned to stubs and leaves thus include both in the consecutive count (i.e., stub 35, leaf 36, stub 37). We identify pasted-over revision slips editorially by adding the suffix "P" to the manuscript number, and, if necessary, "P1" and "P2" to identify first and second paste-overs. Editorial line numbers in the left-hand margins identify lines of the base text. Line numbers and occasionally titles in brackets on the right indicate correspondence between lines of transcription and those of the reading text or texts. Lines of revision are not normally numbered, but in both transcriptions and *apparatus criticus,* line numbers are occasionally assigned serially by page or passage in the right-hand margin to make possible reference to lines not in the base-text sequence or in the reading text. Occasionally, when the passage is complex but brief, we have placed transcriptions in the verbal *apparatus.* Here we do not represent revisionary text in reduced type.

To avoid unnecessary elaboration in the *apparatus* and notes, quotations from manuscripts or printed books normally appear in roman type. In untranscribed manuscripts that precede the date of first book publication, revisions should be understood to be in the hand of the copyist (identified in the Manuscript Census) unless individual *apparatus* entries indicate otherwise. Revisions in those untranscribed manuscripts that postdate the first book publication of a poem are assumed to be the author's, in his own hand, or made at his direction.

The following abbreviations are used in the *apparatus criticus:*

alt	Alternate reading; original not deleted.
apos	Apostrophe.
cap, caps	Capital, capitals.
DC	Dove Cottage (*i.e.,* the archive of The Wordsworth Trust).
del	Reading deleted.
eras	Erased, erasure.
exclam	Exclamation point.
illeg	Illegible.
ital	Italics.
MS., MSS.	Manuscript, manuscripts. Followed by a number (not a date or number-letter combination), a shortened reference to a Dove Cottage manuscript or manuscripts.
om	Reading omitted.
orig	First reading, originally.
para	Indentation, usually beginning a prose or verse paragraph; or a marking indicating indentation.
punct	Punctuation (excluding apostrophes and hyphens).
quot, quots	Quotation mark, quotation marks.
rev	Revised; revision; revised by (with initials). (The original may be canceled in any of various ways, including deletion, erasure, overwriting, or blotting, but will be given if legible.)

The following symbols are used in transcriptions and the *apparatus criticus;* the first two also appear in reading texts:

[ ]	Blank, defacement, tear, or trimmed-off word in the manuscript.
[?last]	Conjectural reading, or missing word supplied editorially in a reading text.
[? ?]	Illegible words; each question mark represents one word.
[~~? ?~~]	Deleted and illegible word or words.
ha{d / ve}	An overwriting: original reading, "have," converted to "had" by the writing of "d" on top of "ve."
s}	A short addition, sometimes only a mark of punctuation.
that more	Words written over a totally illegible erasure.
{that more / wh wa}	Words written over a legible or partly legible erasure.

In reports of variants in lifetime printings and in the editor's notes, the following short forms of citation are used (the dates in the first column indicate editions in the main series of collected works while those in the second indicate selections or individual works):

1827		*The Poetical Works of William Wordsworth* (5 vols.; London, 1827).
	1831	*Selections from the Poems of William Wordsworth, Esq.*, ed. Joseph Hine (London, 1831).
1832		*The Poetical Works of William Wordsworth* (4 vols.; London, 1832).
	1834	*Selections from the Poems of William Wordsworth, Esq.*, ed. Joseph Hine (London, 1834).
	1835	*Yarrow Revisited, and Other Poems* (London, 1835).
	1836YR	*Yarrow Revisited, and Other Poems* (2d ed., London, 1836). Reset with various alterations.
1836		*The Poetical Works of William Wordsworth* (6 vols.; London, 1836–1837). Reissued in stereotype, with various alterations, 1840, 1841, 1843, 1846, and 1849.
	1838	*The Sonnets of William Wordsworth* (London, 1838).
	1839	*Yarrow Revisited, and Other Poems* (3d ed., reset; London, 1839).
1840		*The Poetical Works of William Wordsworth* (6 vols.; London, 1840). The revised stereotype reissue of *1836*.
1841		The revised stereotype reissue of *1840*.
	1842	*Poems, Chiefly of Early and Late Years* (London, 1842).
1843		The revised stereotype reissue of *1841*.
1845		*The Poems of William Wordsworth* (London, 1845). Reissued in stereotype, with minor alterations, 1847 and 1849.
1846		*The Poetical Works of William Wordsworth* (7 vols.; London, 1846). Another stereotype reissue of the six volumes of *1836*, incorporating further alterations, with an additional volume incorporating much of *Poems, Chiefly of Early and Late Years*, 1842; reissued, again with a few alterations, 1849.
1847		The revised stereotype of *1845*.

1847 Cambridge	*Ode, Performed in the Senate-House, Cambridge, on the Sixth of July, M.DCCC.XLVII. at the First Commencement after The Installation of His Royal Highness the Prince Albert, Chancellor of the University* (Cambridge: Cambridge University Press, 1847).
1847M	*Select Pieces from the Poems of William Wordsworth,* published by Edward Moxon (London, 1847).
1849	The revised stereotype reissue of 1846.
1849P	The revised stereotype reissue of 1847.
1850	*The Poetical Works of William Wordsworth* (6 vols.; London, 1849–1850).

In the *apparatus criticus,* a citation of each volume in the list above implies its reissues as well, unless otherwise noted, as follows:

1831 implies *1834*
1835 implies *1836YR, 1839*
1836 implies *1840, 1841, 1843*
1840 implies *1841, 1843*
1841 implies *1843*
1845 implies *1847, 1849P*
1846 implies *1849*
1847 implies *1849P*

Wordsworth approved the concept of *Select Pieces* (London: James Burns, 1843; see *LY,* IV, 504–505, 509–510), but the editor and publisher in the end combined several states of the text into a jumbled form that Wordsworth could not have approved. With one exception made for *The Labourer's Noon-day Hymn* (see the note to that poem), the variants in the 1843 *Select Pieces* are excluded.

Wordsworth published several broadsides and pamphlets that presented texts of single poems or included one or more poems along with other matter.

BL Pamphlet	*Poems on the Loss and Re-building of St. Mary's Church, Cardiff. By William Wordsworth. James Montgomery. Thomas William Booker. John Dix* (Cardiff: W. Bird, 1842).
Broadside 1	*Inscription for a Monument in Crosthwaite Church, in the Vale of Keswick,* the first broadside, soon after December 20, 1843.
Broadside 2	*Inscription for a Monument in Crosthwaite Church, in the Vale of Keswick,* the second broadside, a lithograph, probably soon after February 5, 1844.
Cardiff Facsimile	"When Severn's sweeping Flood had overthrown," a lithographic facsimile of Wordsworth's holograph copy, published in 1842.
CL1	"To the dear memory of a frail good Man," the first issue of the long version (London: Moxon, 1836).
CL2	"To the dear memory of a frail good Man," the second issue of the long version (London: Moxon, 1836).
Darling	*Grace Darling* (Carlisle: Charles Thurnam, 1843).
Epitaph	*Epitaph,* "To the dear memory of a frail good Man," without imprint, but published in London by Moxon in 1835.

Kendal & 1 — *Kendal and Windermere Railway. Two Letters Re-printed from the Morning Post*, the first issue (Kendal and London, January 1845).

Kendal & 2 — *Kendal and Windermere Railway. Two Letters Re-printed from the Morning Post*, the second issue (Kendal and London, January 1845).

Wordsworth contributed several poems to annuals and other publications:

Atheneum	*Atheneum*, December 12, 1835 (No. 424, p. 930).
Baillie	*A Collection of Poems, Chiefly Manuscript, and from Living Authors*, ed. Joanna Baillie (London: Longman, Hurst, Rees, Orme, and Brown, 1823).
Casket	*The Casket, a Miscellany, Consisting of Unpublished Poems* (London: John Murray, 1829).
Chouannerie	Alexis François Rio, *La Petite Chouannerie, ou Histoire d'un Collège breton sous l'Empire* (Paris: Olivier Fulgence, 1842).
Keepsake	*The Keepsake for MDCCCXXIX*, ed. Frederic Mansel Reynolds (London: Hurst, Chance, and Co. and R. Jennings, [1829]).
Madeira	Jane Wallas Penfold, *Madeira Flowers, Fruits and Ferns* (London: Reeve Brothers, 1845).
MP	*Morning Post*, October 16 and December 20, 1844.
Newcastle Journal	*Newcastle Journal*, December 5, 1835 (p. 3).
NMM	*New Monthly Magazine*, July 1, 1831 (vol. 32, no. 127, p. 26).
Tribute	*The Tribute: A Collection of Miscellaneous Unpublished Poems, by Various Authors*, ed. Lord Northampton (London: John Murray, 1837).
Winter's Wreath	*The Winter's Wreath, a Collection of Original Contributions in Prose and Verse* (London: George B. Whittaker and J. Hatchard & Son; Liverpool: George Smith, 1828).

Wordsworth divided his poems into classes in the collective editions from the 1815 *Poems* onward, but not—with a few minor exceptions noted in the text—in the selective editions of 1831, 1834, and 1847. And in the two collections of new poems that he published in 1835 and 1842 he created some new classes that he incorporated into subsequent collective editions. These classes are given in this edition at the beginning of each poem's verbal *apparatus* and are used in brief references elsewhere. Designations for classes cited in this edition and the varying titles given to each by Wordsworth, with their dates, follow below.

Affections	Poems Founded on the Affections. *1815–*
Childhood	Poems Referring to the Period of Childhood. *1815– but* Poems Referring to Childhood and Early Youth. *1820*
Continent 1820	Memorials of a Tour on the Continent, 1820. *1822, 1827, 1845–* Memorials . . . Continent. *1832, 1836 (included in* Itinerary Sonnets; *see below)*
Ecclesiastical Sketches [. . . Sonnets]	Ecclesiastical Sketches. *1822, 1827* Ecclesiastical Sketches in a Series of Sonnets. *1832* Ecclesiastical Sonnets. In Series. *1836–, 1838*
Epitaphs	Epitaphs and Elegiac Poems *1815–1832* Epitaphs and Elegiac Pieces. *1836–*
Evening Voluntaries	Evening Voluntaries. *1835–*

Fancy	Poems of the Fancy. *1815–*
Imagination	Poems of the Imagination. *1815–*
Inscriptions	Inscriptions. *1815–*
Italy 1837	Memorials of a Tour in Italy. *1842, 1846, 1849* Memorials . . . Italy, 1837. *1845, 1850*
Itinerary Sonnets	Itinerary Sonnets. *1838–1843, 1849*
Juvenile Pieces	Juvenile Pieces. *1815–1843* Poems Written in Youth. *1845–*
Liberty	Sonnets Dedicated to Liberty. *1807–1843, 1846, 1849 but* Sonnets . . . Liberty, with Lyrical Pieces Interspersed, and Thanksgiving Ode. *1827 Contents* Political Sonnets. *1838* Poems Dedicated to National Independence and Liberty. *1845, 1850*
Liberty and Order	Sonnets Dedicated to Liberty and Order. *1845, 1850*
Miscellaneous Pieces	Miscellaneous Pieces, Referring Chiefly to Recent Public Events. *1816* (In *Thanksgiving Ode, January 18, 1816. With Other Short Pieces, Chiefly Referring to Recent Public Events*)
Miscellaneous Poems	Miscellaneous Poems. *1845, 1850*
Miscellaneous Sonnets	Miscellaneous Sonnets. *1807–* An appendix (otherwise untitled) was added to *1838* and this group, with some omissions and additions, became a separate group of Miscellaneous Sonnets in *1842, 1846, 1849;* in *1846* and *1849P* there were two such groups, the second deriving from *1838.* In *1815* the group was in two parts; a third part was added in *1845*. Sonnets in this group based on *1838* were distributed variously in this new Part III and elsewhere.
Moods of My Own Mind	*1807*
Naming of Places	Poems on the Naming of Places. *1800–*
Old Age	Poems Referring to the Period of Old Age. *1815–*
Punishment of Death	Sonnets Upon the Punishment of Death. *1842, 1845–*
River Duddon	The River Duddon. *1820RD, 1827–1843, 1846, 1849* The River Duddon, A Series of Sonnets Published in 1820 *1820* The River Duddon. A Series of Sonnets *1845, 1850*
Scotland 1803	Memorials of a Tour in Scotland, 1803. *1807–1827, 1845–* Memorials . . . Scotland. 1803 *1836–1843, 1846, 1849*
Scotland 1814	Memorials of a Tour in Scotland, 1814. *1827, 1832, 1845–* Memorials . . . Scotland. 1814 *1836–1843, 1846, 1849*
Sentiment and Reflection	Poems Proceeding from Sentiment and Reflection. *1815* Poems of Sentiment and Reflection. *1820–*
Tour 1833	Sonnets Composed or Suggested During a Tour in Scotland, in the Summer of 1833. *1835, 1836–1843* Poems, Composed or Suggested During a Tour, in the Summer of 1833. *1845–*
Yarrow Revisited	Yarrow Revisited, And Other Poems, Composed (Two Excepted) During a Tour in Scotland, and on the English Border, in the Autumn of 1831. *1835, 1836–* Memorials of a Tour in Scotland, 1831 *appears in running heads 1845, 1847, 1849P*

PART I

Reading Texts

DECAY OF PIETY.

Oft have I seen, ere Time had ploughed my cheek,
Matrons and Sires—who, punctual to the call
Of their loved Church, on Fast or Festival
Through the long year the House of Prayer would seek:
By Christmas snows, by visitation bleak
Of Easter winds, unscared, from Hut or Hall
They came to lowly bench or sculptured Stall,
But with one fervour of devotion meek.
I see the places where they once were known,
And ask, surrounded even by kneeling crowds,
Is ancient Piety for ever flown?
Alas! even then they seemed like fleecy clouds

---

composed after January 17, 1821, but probably by March 12 or a few weeks later; certainly by November 24, 1821

found in Amherst MS.; DC MSS. 89, 131, 158

published in *1827–, 1838*

classed Miscellaneous Sonnets *1827–, 1838*

reading text *1827*

title *lacking Amherst MS.*

1 Ere riddling care had touchd my youthful cheek *alt*
Oft have I seen ere Time had ploughed *alt*
Oft have I seen ere time had ploughed my cheek *alt*
~~[?Some]~~ have ~~some~~ I seen *alt*
~~Once~~ *alt*
A gleam of Joy upon ~~my~~ furrowed cheek *Amherst MS.₁*
Of Time
have I seen ere ~~Woe~~ had ploughd my cheek *alt Amherst MS.₂*
Time *rev from* care *MS. 89* care *MS. 131*

2 Matrons and Sires *rev from* Mark of those *Amherst MS.*

3 on *rev from* in *Amherst MS.*

4 High converse in the House of prayer *rev to* Through the long year the House of God *Amherst MS.*

5 Such my Youth saw by blush of Ember weak *rev to*
By christmas snow or visitation bleak *Amherst MS.₁*
By Cristmas snow by blush of Ember weak *alt Amherst MS.₂*

6 Of Easter winds] Or christmas snow *rev to* By Easter rain *alt* [?] Easter winds *Amherst MS.* winds *rev from* rains *MS. 89*

8 fervour] spirit *alt* fervour *Amherst MS.*

9 see *rev from* seek *Amherst MS.*

12–14 *MS. 89 pencil alt:*
they seemed, like fleecy clouds
Lingering {the
~~Struggling~~ amid {a western sky, to have won
Their pensive light from a departed sun

That, struggling through the western sky, have won
Their pensive light from a departed sun!

"Not Love, nor War, nor the tumultuous swell"

Not Love, nor War, nor the tumultuous swell
Of civil conflict, nor the wrecks of change,
Nor Duty struggling with afflictions strange,
Not these alone inspire the tuneful shell;
But where untroubled peace and concord dwell,
There also is the Muse not loth to range,
Watching the blue smoke of the elmy grange,
Skyward ascending from the twilight dell.
Meek aspirations please her, lone endeavour,
And sage content, and placid melancholy;
She loves to gaze upon a crystal river,
Diaphanous, because it travels slowly;
Soft is the music that would charm for ever;
The flower of sweetest smell is shy and lowly.

---

13 the *MW rev to* a *MS. 89* a *MS. 131* struggling] straggling *MS. 131* have] had *Amherst MS., MS. 131*

14 Their *rev to* A *rev to* Their *MS. 89* A *MS. 131* pensive light *inserted above illeg del Amherst MS.* a departed] the depart[ ] *MS. 89* the departing *MS. 131*

---

composed after January 17, 1821, but probably by March 12 or a few weeks later; certainly by November 24, 1821; revised in 1827

found in Cornell MS. 2, DC MS. 89

published in Baillie (1823); *1827–, 1831, 1838*

classed Miscellaneous Sonnets *1827–, 1831, 1838*

reading text *1827*

title Sonnet. *Baillie*

1–2 And must we having left behind the swell
Of war and conflict and the wrecks of change *Cornell MS. 2*

1 nor] not *1832–, 1838*

2 conflict] conflicts *Baillie* nor *MW rev from* and *MS. 89*

3 Nor] And *MS. 89, Baillie*

4–5 Henceforth to silence doom the chorded shell
Unworthy thought! Where peace and concord dwell *Cornell MS. 2*

7 Watching *MW rev from* She loves *MS. 89* She loves the blue smoke from the elmy [*alt* chimney] grange *Cornell MS. 2*
Watching the twilight smoke of cot or grange, *1836–; so 1838 but* cot] hut

8 the twilight] a woody *1836–, 1838*

9 Meek] Mute *Cornell MS. 2* Meets *rev to* Meek *MS. 89* please] soothe *Cornell MS. 2*

10 placid] quiet *Cornell MS. 2*

11 Her eyes delight to brood upon a river *Cornell MS. 2; so MS. 89 but* Her eye delights *and line rev to text*

12 travels *rev from* [?moves] *Cornell MS. 2*

13 charm] please *MS. 89; Baillie*

RECOLLECTION OF THE PORTRAIT OF KING HENRY EIGHTH, TRINITY LODGE, CAMBRIDGE.

THE imperial Stature, the colossal stride,
Are yet before me; yet do I behold
The broad full visage, chest of amplest mould,
The vestments 'broidered with barbaric pride:
And lo! a poniard, at the Monarch's side,
Hangs ready to be grasped in sympathy
With the keen threatenings of that fulgent eye,
Below the white-rimmed bonnet, far descried.
Who trembles now at thy capricious mood?
Mid those surrounding worthies, haughty King!
We rather think, with grateful mind sedate,
How Providence educeth, from the spring
Of lawless will, unlooked-for streams of good,
Which neither force shall check, nor time abate.

[Translation of the Sestet of a Sonnet by Tasso]

Camoëns, he the accomplished and the good,
Gave to thy Fame a more illustrious flight
Than that brave vessel though she sailed so far,
Through him her course along the austral flood
Is known to all beneath the polar star
Through him the antipodes in thy name delight.

---

composed probably between about March 1821 or May 1824 and April 1827
published in *1827—, 1831, 1838*
classed Miscellaneous Sonnets *1827—, 1831, 1838*
reading text *1827*

---

composed perhaps in July–August 1821 but before late 1849
found in DC MS. 160
published in *The Academy*, January 2, 1897
reading text DC MS. 160
1 Camoëns] Camoens *MS. 160*
6 *no punct MS. 160*

"A volant Tribe of Bards on earth are found"

A VOLANT Tribe of Bards on earth are found,
Who, while the flattering Zephyrs round them play,
On "coignes of vantage" hang their nests of clay;
How quickly from that aery hold unbound,
Dust for oblivion! To the solid ground
Of nature trusts the Mind that builds for aye;
Convinced that there, there only, she can lay
Secure foundations. As the year runs round,
Apart she toils within the chosen ring;
While the stars shine, or while day's purple eye
Is gently closing with the flowers of spring;
Where even the motion of an Angel's wing
Would interrupt the intense tranquillity
Of silent hills, and more than silent sky.

"Queen and Negress chaste and fair!"

Queen and Negress chaste and fair!
  Christophe now is laid asleep
Seated in a British Chair
State in humbler manner keep
  Shine for Clarkson's pure delight
  Negro Princess, ebon bright!

---

composed perhaps around but by October 2, 1821, revised by early July 1822 and again by late January 1827
found in DC MS. 89
published in Baillie (1823); *1827–, 1831, 1838*
classed Miscellaneous Sonnets *1827–, 1831, 1838*
reading text *1827*
title Sonnet. *Baillie*
4–9 Work cunningly devis'd, and seeming sound;
But quickly from its airy hold unbound
By its own weight, or wash'd, or blown away
With silent imperceptible decay.
If man must build, admit him to thy ground,
O Truth!—to work within the eternal ring, *Baillie*
5 To *rev from* on *MS. 89*   solid *rev from* common *MS. 89*
6 trusts *rev from* rests *MS. 89*
8 year runs] years run *MS. 89*
9 toils rev from [?turns] *MS. 89*
10 While] When *Baillie*
12 Where] When *Baillie*
14 hills] Hills *rev from* [?Fields] *MS. 89*

---

composed October 21, 1821
found in DW to CCl, October 24, 1821
published in *Letters of the Wordsworth Family,* ed. William Knight (3 vols.; London, 1907)
reading text DW to CCl, October 24, 1821

Lay thy Diadem apart
  Pomp has been a sad Deceiver
Through thy Champion's faithful heart
Joy be poured, and thou the Giver
  Thou that mak'st a day of night
  Sable Princess, ebon bright!

Let not "Wilby's" holy shade
  Interpose at Envy's call,
Hayti's shining Queen was made
To illumine Playford Hall
  Bless it then with constant light
  Negress excellently bright!

[Epigrams on Byron's *Cain*]

i. "Critics, right honourable Bard! decree"

Critics, right honourable Bard! decree
Laurels to some, a nightshade wreath to thee,
Whose Muse a sure though late revenge hath ta'en
Of harmless Abel's death by murdering Cain.

ii.
On Cain a Mystery dedicated to Sir Walter Scott

A German Haggis—from Receipt
Of him who cook'd "The death of Abel"
And sent "warm–reeking rich" and sweet
From Venice to Sir Walter's table.

iii.
After reading a luscious scene of the above— The Wonder explained

What! Adam's eldest Son in this sweet strain!
Yes—did you never hear of Sugar-Cain?

---

9 Champion's] Champions *DW to CCl*
15 Hayti's] Haytis *DW to CCl*

---

composed probably late December 1821
found in WW to RS, late December 1821
published in *PW* Knight 1896 ("i" and "ii" only) and Shaver, *MLN*. (See also pp. 419–420, below.)
reading text Shaver's transcription (see entry for "published in," above)
i. 1 right *rev from* like *WW to RS*
ii. 2 cook'd *rev from* cooked *WW to RS*
iii. *title* After *rev from* On *WW to RS*

iv.

On a Nursery piece of the same, by a Scottish Bard—

Dont wake little Enoch,
Or he'll give you a wee knock!
For the pretty sweet Lad
As he lies in his Cradle
Is more like to his Dad
Than a Spoon to a Ladle.

"Thus far I write to please my Friend"

Thus far I write to please my Friend;
And now to please myself I end.

"By Moscow self–devoted to a blaze"

By Moscow self–devoted to a blaze
Of dreadful sacrifice; by Russian blood
Lavished in fight with desperate hardihood;
The unfeeling Elements no claim shall raise
To rob our Human–nature of just praise
For what she did and suffered. Pledges sure
Of a deliverance absolute and pure
She gave, if Faith might tread the beaten ways
Of Providence. But now did the Most High
Exalt his still small Voice;—to quell that Host

---

iv. 5 his Dad *rev from* [?kick] *WW to RS*

---

composed probably on September 7, 1822
found in Swarthmore MS. 1
published in *WC*, 4 (1973), 58.
reading text Swarthmore MS. 1

---

composed around November–December 1822, but by December 21
found in DW to HCR, December 21, 1822
published in *1827–, 1838*
classed Liberty *1827–*
reading text *1827*

1 By self-devoted Moscow—by the blaze *DW to HCR*
2 dreadful] that dread *DW to HCR*
4 unfeeling] impassive *rev from* impassioned *DW to HCR*
5 just] her *DW to HCR*
6 Enough was done & suffered to insure *DW to HCR*
7 Of a] Final *DW to HCR*
8 Enough for faith, tracking the beaten ways *DW to HCR*
10 to quell that Host] his wrath unshroud, *DW to HCR*

Gathered his Power, a manifest Ally;
He whose heaped waves confounded the proud boast
Of Pharaoh, said to Famine, Snow, and Frost,
Finish the strife by deadliest Victory!

"These Vales were saddened with no common gloom"

In the Burial-ground of this Church are deposited the Remains of Jemima A. D. second daughter of Sir Egerton Brydges Bart—of Lee Priory, Kent—who departed this life at Rydal May 25th 1822 Ag: 28 years. This memorial is erected by her afflicted husband Edwd Quillinan

These Vales were saddened with no common gloom
When good Jemima perished in her bloom;
When (such the awful will of heaven) she died
By flames breathed on her from her own fire-side.
On Earth we dimly see, and but in part

11–14 And lay his justice bare to mortal eye;
He who, of yore, by miracle [miracle *rev from* miracles] spake aloud
As openly that purpose here avow'd,
Which only madness ventures to defy. *DW to HCR*

---

composed November 28, 1822
found in DC MS. 89 (A) and (B), both on 47^{r}; DC MS. 131; MW to EQ, November 29, 1822; MW to TM, December 3, 1822; Mary Smith Album; Tablet (St. Oswald's Church, Grasmere, 1824)
published in *PW* Knight 1896
reading text DC MS. 89 (B)
headnote Jemima A. D.] Jemima A. B. *and* years.] years *and* by] by by *MS. 89 (B)* *epigraph lacking MW to TM* Mr. Quillinan's Sketch for his Wife's Epitaph (to be erected in Grasmere Church *MS. 89 (A)* Epitaph *MS. 131* IN THE BURIAL GROUND / OF THIS CHURCH ARE DEPOSITED THE REMAINS OF / JEMIMA ANNE DEBORAH / SECOND DAUGHTER OF / SIR EGERTON BRYDGES, OF DENTON COURT, KENT, BART / SHE DEPARTED THIS LIFE AT THE IVY COTTAGE, RYDAL, / MAY 25TH 1822, AGED 28 YEARS. / THIS MEMORIAL IS ERECTED BY HER HUSBAND EDWARD QUILLINAN. *Tablet* To the memory of Jemima Anne D. Quillinan / Daughter of Sir Egerton Brydges Bart. & wife of Edwd Quillinan Esqre —Died at Rydal May 25th 1822— *Mary Smith Album* *MW to EQ as MS 89 (B) but* Jemima Anne Deborah, . . . Brydges, of Lee Priory Kent, Bart. She departed . . . Aged . . . Husband
1–16 *EQ's "Sketch" (as recorded by MW):*
The good Jemima perished in her bloom;
Her hapless fate o'erspread these vales with gloom.
The good, the kind, the lovely & the meek,
Might have fit Epitaph could feelings speak.
If woods could tell or marble could [marble could *alt* monuments] record
How treasures lost are by the heart deplored,
No name by grief's fond eloquence adorned
[Would more than Quillinan's *rev to* More than Jemima's would] be prais'd and mourn'd.
The tender virtues of her blameless life
Bright in the Daughter, brighter in the Wife,
And in the cheerful Mother brightest shone;
[~~? ? ? ? ? ? ? ? ?~~]
That light is past to heaven—the will of God be done! *MS. 89 (A); so WW rev in MW to EQ but ll. 1–2 omitted and* marble could] monuments adorn'd *rev from* adorned chearful
4 from *rev from* by *MW to EQ*

We know, yet Faith sustains the sorrowing heart;
And she, the pure, the patient and the meek,
Might have fit Epitaph could feelings speak;
If words could tell and monuments record,
How treasures lost are inwardly deplored,
No name by grief's fond eloquence adorn'd,
More than Jemima's would be praised and mourn'd;
The tender virtues of her blameless life,
Bright in the Daughter, brighter in the Wife,
And in the cheerful Mother brightest shone:
That light hath past away—the will of God be done!

TO THE LADY———,

ON SEEING THE FOUNDATION PREPARING FOR THE ERECTION OF ——— CHAPEL, WESTMORELAND.

BLEST is this Isle—our native Land;
Where battlement and moated gate
Are objects only for the hand
Of hoary Time to decorate;
Where shady hamlet, town that breathes
Its busy smoke in social wreaths,
No rampart's stern defence require,
Nought but the heaven-directed Spire,
And steeple Tower (with pealing bells
Far heard)—our only Citadels.

---

7 pure,] pure *rev from* good *MS. 89 (B)* good, *Mary Smith Album*
10 lost] lost, *MS. 89 (B)* inwardly] by the heart *MS. 131* by the *rev to* inwardly *MW to EQ* by the [?soul] *rev to* inwardly *MW to TM*
16 hath] is *Mary Smith Album*

---

composed eight-stanza version around but by December 21, 1822; a stanza added January 25, 1823, and another perhaps soon after but before December 1824; revised 1832
found in DC MSS. 100 and 131; WW to Lord Lonsdale, January 25, 1823; MW to Lady B, February 5, 1823; Cornell MSS. 1 and 3; WW to BF, April 16, 1828; MS. 1827/28; MS. 1827/32C: MS. 1832/36 (JC)
published in *1827–, 1847M*
classed Sentiment and Reflection *1827–1843, 1846* Miscellaneous Poems *1845, 1850*
reading text *1827*
title To the Lady le Fleming / Composed upon seeing the Foundation preparing for the / erection of a Chapel in the Village of Rydal / Jan^{ry} —— 1823 *with dash added MS. 100; Cornell MS. 1 as rev MS. 100 but* Rydal, *and* Jan^{ry} 1823— *Cornell MS. 3 as MS. 100 but* chapel *and* village *and* 1823. *MW to Lady B as MS. 100 but no dash; MS. 131 as MS. 100 but* Rydal. Jany 24 1823
TO THE LADY FLEMING, ON SEEING THE FOUNDATION PREPARING FOR THE ERECTION OF RYDAL CHAPEL, WESTMORELAND. *1840–*
stanza numbers I. . . . X. *1836–*
6 busy] tranquil *MSS. 100, 131, MW to Lady B, Cornell MSS. 1, 3* social] silver *MSS. 100, 131, MW to Lady B, Cornell MSS. 1, 3*
9 And] Or *MW to Lady B, Cornell MS. 3, MS. 131*

O Lady! from a noble line
Of Chieftains sprung, who stoutly bore
The spear, yet gave to works divine
A bounteous help in days of yore,
(As records mouldering in the Dell
Of Nightshade* haply yet may tell)
Thee kindred aspirations moved
To build, within a Vale beloved,
For Him upon whose high behests
All peace depends, all safety rests.

Well may the Villagers rejoice!
Nor heat, nor cold, nor weary ways,
Will be a hindrance to the voice
That would unite in prayer and praise;
More duly shall wild-wandering Youth
Receive the curb of sacred truth,
Shall tottering Age, bent earthward, hear
The Promise, with uplifted ear;
And all shall welcome the new ray
Imparted to their Sabbath-day.

Even Strangers, slackening here their pace,
Shall hail this work of pious care,

*Bekangs Ghyll—or the Vale of Nightshade—in which stands St. Mary's Abbey, in Low Furness.

---

13 *line inserted MW to Lady B*
15 records] records* *Cornell MS. 1, MW to Lady B*
16 *no asterisk MSS. 100, 131, Cornell MSS. 1, 3, MW to Lady B*
note lacking Cornell MS. 3 Vale] dell *MS. 1832/36–* At Furness Abbey *MW to Lady B, so Cornell MS. 1, but* Abbey—
17 Thee *rev in pencil from* The *Cornell MS. 1*
21–30 *lacking MS. 100; added but transposed with ll. 31–40 WW to Lord Lonsdale; MW to Lady B, MS. 131 as WW to Lord Lonsdale rev; WW to BF, Cornell MSS. 1, 3, MS. 1827/28, MS. 1827/32C, 1832– transpose these lines with ll. 31–40*
22 heat, nor cold,] storms, henceforth, *WW to Lord Lonsdale* Storms henceforth, *Cornell MS. 1* storms henceforth, *Cornell MS. 3, MW to Lady B, MS. 131*
23 Will] Shall *WW to Lord Lonsdale, Cornell MSS. 1, 3, MW to Lady B, MS. 131* hindrance] hinderance *WW to Lord Lonsdale, MW to Lady B, Cornell MS. 1, 3, MS. 131, 1832–1843, 1846*
27 The Aged shall be free to hear *WW to Lord Lonsdale, Cornell MS. 1, MW to Lady B, MS. 131; but* aged *Cornell MS. 1*
The sick, and Aged, free to hear *Cornell MS. 3*
28 The Promise, caught with steadfast ear; *WW to Lord Lonsdale*
The Promise, shall have comfort near, *Cornell MS. 3*
31–40 *WW to BF, Cornell MSS. 1, 3, MS. 1827/28, MS. 1827/32C, 1832– transpose these lines with ll. 21–30*
31–32 How fondly will the woods embrace
This Daughter of thy pious care *MSS. 100, 131, WW to BF, Cornell MS. 1, MS. 1827/32C; Cornell MS. 3 as MS. 100 but* daughter *MW to Lady B, 1832 as MS. 100 but* care, *MS. 1827/28 as MS. 100 but* care *rev in pencil to* care, *MS. 1832/36– as 1832 but* daughter
32 hail *corrected from* bless *1827 errata page*
33 its] her *MSS. 100, 131, WW to BF, Cornell MSS. 1, 3* its *rev in pencil to* her *MS. 1827/28* her *1832–*

Lifting its front with modest grace
To make a fair recess more fair;
And to exalt the passing hour;
Or soothe it, with a healing power
Drawn from the Sacrifice fulfilled,
Before this rugged soil was tilled,
Or human habitation rose
To interrupt the deep repose!

Nor yet the corner stone is laid
With solemn rite; but Fancy sees
The tower time-stricken, and in shade
Embosomed of coeval trees;
Hears, o'er the lake, the warning clock
As it shall sound with gentle shock
At evening, when the ground beneath
Is ruffled o'er with cells of Death;
Where happy Generations lie,
Here tutored for Eternity.

Lives there a Man whose sole delights
Are trivial pomp and city noise,
Hardening a heart that loathes or slights
What every natural heart enjoys?
Who never caught a noon-tide dream
From murmur of a running stream;
Could strip, for aught the prospect yields
To him, their verdure from the fields;
And take the radiance from the clouds
In which the Sun his setting shrouds.

36–38 With saintly thoughts on Him whose power
The circuit of these mountains filled,
Ere the primæval soil was tilled, *MS. 100*

38 this] that *Cornell MS. 3*

41–46 Nor deem the Poets hope misplaced
His fancy cheated that can see
A Shade upon the Structure cast
Of Time's pathetic sanctity;
Can hear the monitory clock
Sound oer the Lake with gentle shock *WW to BF; MS. 1827/28 as WW to BF but* Poet's . . . misplac'd . . . shade . . . times . . . lake *MS. 1827/32C1 as MS. 1827/28 but* misplaced . . . time's
Nor deem the Poet's hope misplaced,
His fancy cheated—that can see
A shade upon the future cast,
Of Time's [time's *MS. 1832/36–*] pathetic sanctity;
Can hear the monitory clock
Sound o'er the lake with gentle shock *MS. 1827/32C2, 1832–*

41–50 *lacking MSS. 100, 131, MW to Lady B, Cornell MSS. 1, 3*

55 noon-tide] soothing *MSS. 100, 131, MW to Lady B, Cornell MS. 1* waking *Cornell MS. 3*

59 clouds *rev from illeg word Cornell MS. 1*

A Soul so pitiably forlorn,
If such do on this earth abide,
May season apathy with scorn,
May turn indifference to pride,
And still be not unblest—compared
With him who grovels, self-debarred
From all that lies within the scope
Of holy faith and Christian hope;
Or, shipwrecked, kindles on the coast
False fires, that others may be lost.

Alas! that such perverted zeal
Should spread on Britain's favoured ground!
That public order, private weal,
Should e'er have felt or feared a wound
From champions of the desperate law
Which from their own blind hearts they draw;
Who tempt their reason to deny
God, whom their passions dare defy,
And boast that *they alone* are free
Who reach this dire extremity!

But turn we from these "bold bad" men;
The way, mild Lady! that hath led

61–70 Fields—sunset clouds—and sky of morn
Opening in spendor deep and wide—
That wordling may renounce with scorn,
And in his chosen seat abide;
A Spirit not unblest—compared
With One who fosters disregard
For all that lies within the scope
Of holy faith and christian hope;
Yea strives that lustre to bedim
For Others, which has failed for him. *last two lines rev to*
Yea strives for Others to bedim
The glorious light too pure for Him *MS. 100*
64 pride] Pride *rev from* [?scorn] *Cornell MS. 1*
66 With one who fosters disregard *Cornell MS. 1; so MW to Lady B, MS. 131, Cornell MS. 3 but* One
67 From] For *Cornell MSS. 1, 3, MW to Lady B, MS. 131*
69–70 Yea strives for others to bedim
The glorious light too pure for him. *Cornell MSS. 1, 3; MW to Lady B as Cornell MS. 1 but* for others *rev from* [?faith]*; MS. 131 as Cornell MS. 1 but* Others *and* him! *1832 as Cornell MS. 1 but* Yea, *and* Light *so MS. 1832/36, 1836–1843 but* light
71 perverted *rev from* distempered *MS. 100*
72 favoured] happy *MSS. 100, 131, MW to Lady B, Cornell MSS. 1, 3*
74 feared *rev from* fe[?] *MS. 100*
75–76 From impious Anarchists [impious Anarchists *rev from* reckless, lawless Men] who plot
To make their own the general lot; *MS. 100*
From Scoffers leagued in desperate plot
To make their own the general lot; *Cornell MS. 1, MW to Lady B, MS. 131*
78 dare] do *MSS. 100, 131, WW to Lady B, Cornell MSS. 1, 3*
80 this] that *MS. 100*
82 hath *rev from* had *MW to Lady B*

Down to their "dark opprobrious den,"
Is all too rough for Thee to tread.
Softly as morning vapours glide
Through Mosedale-cove from Carrock's side,
Should move the tenour of *his* song
Who means to Charity no wrong;
Whose offering gladly would accord
With this day's work, in thought and word.

Heaven prosper it! may peace, and love,
And hope, and consolation, fall,
Through its meek influence, from above,
And penetrate the hearts of all;
All who, around the hallowed Fane,
Shall sojourn in this fair domain;
Grateful to Thee, while service pure,
And ancient ordinance, shall endure,
For opportunity bestowed
To kneel together, and adore their God.

ON THE SAME OCCASION.

Oh! gather whencesoe'er ye safely may
The help which slackening Piety requires;
Nor deem that he perforce must go astray
Who treads upon the footmarks of his Sires.

Our churches, invariably perhaps, stand east and west, but *why* is by few persons *exactly* known; nor, that the degree of deviation from due east often noticeable in the ancient

---

85 Soft as the morning mists that glide *MS. 100*
86 Through] Down *1832–* Mosedale-cove] Rydal cove *MSS. 100, 131; MW to Lady B* Rydal grove [grove *rev from* ?groo] *Cornell MS. 1* Rydal Cove *Cornell MS. 3* Mosedale-cove *rev in pencil to* Rydal-cove *MS. 1827/28* Rydal-cove *1832–* Carrock's] Fairfield's *MS. 100, MW to Lady B, Cornell MSS. 1, 3, MS. 131, 1832–* Carrock's *rev in pencil to* Fairfield's *MS. 1827/28*
87 move] be *MSS. 100, 131* tenour] motion *MS. 100*
93 meek] mild *MS. 131*
95 the] this *MS. 100*

---

composed probably around late January to mid-February 1823
found in DC MSS. 89 and 131, MS. 1832/36
published in *1827–, 1847M*
classed Sentiment and Reflection *1827–1836, 1846* Miscellaneous Poems *1845, 1850*
reading text *1827*
title ON] Upon *MSS. 89, 131*
epigraph *inserted MS. 89 (see l. 20/21 below); lacking MS. 131*
headnote *lacking MSS. 89, 131; printed at foot of page 1847M*

ones was determined, in each particular case, by the point in the horizon, at which the sun rose upon the day of the Saint to whom the church was dedicated. These observances of our Ancestors, and the causes of them, are the subject of the following stanzas.

WHEN in the antique age of bow and spear
And feudal rapine clothed with iron mail,
Came Ministers of peace, intent to rear
The mother Church in yon sequestered vale;

Then, to her Patron Saint a previous rite
Resounded with deep swell and solemn close,
Through unremitting vigils of the night,
Till from his couch the wished-for Sun uprose.

He rose, and straight—as by divine command,
They who had waited for that sign to trace
Their work's foundation, gave with careful hand
To the high Altar its determined place;

Mindful of Him who in the Orient born
There lived, and on the cross his life resigned,
And who, from out the regions of the Morn,
Issuing in pomp, shall come to judge Mankind.

So taught *their* creed;—nor failed the eastern sky,
Mid these more awful feelings, to infuse
The sweet and natural hopes that shall not die
Long as the Sun his gladsome course renews.

For us hath such prelusive vigil ceased;
Yet still we plant, like men of elder days,
Our Christian Altar faithful to the East,
Whence the tall window drinks the morning rays;

---

4 mother Church in] Church that hallows *MSS. 89, 131*
5 her] the *MSS. 89, 131*
8 his *rev from* the *MS. 89*
9 Straight, as if urged by a divine command, *MS. 89; so MS. 131 but* Straight,] Straight
10 had] have *MS. 131*
14 *rev from* There lived and there a bitter death did find *MS. 89*
18 Mid] With *MSS. 89, 131*
19 The *rev from* These *MS. 89*
20 gladsome *rev from* vital *MS. 89*
20/21 Oh! gather whencesoe'er ye safely may
The help which slackening Piety requires!
Nor deem that he perforce [perforce *rev from* perchance] must go astray
Who treads upon the footmarks of his Sires? *MS. 89, with WW's punct and marginal note:* to be printed in Italics as a Motto
22 days *rev from* time *MS. 89*

That obvious emblem giving to the eye
Of meek devotion, which erewhile it gave,
That symbol of the dayspring from on high,
Triumphant o'er the darkness of the grave.

MEMORY.

A PEN—to register; a key—
That winds through secret wards;
Are well assigned to Memory
By allegoric Bards.

As aptly, also, might be given
A Pencil to her hand;
That, softening objects, sometimes even
Outstrips the heart's demand;

That smooths foregone distress, the lines
Of lingering care subdues,
Long-vanished happiness refines,
And clothes in brighter hues:

Yet, like a tool of Fancy, works
Those Spectres to dilate
That startle Conscience, as she lurks
Within her lonely seat.

O! that our lives, which flee so fast,
In purity were such,
That not an image of the past
Should fear that pencil's touch!

Retirement then might hourly look
Upon a soothing scene,

25–28 *rev from*
That emblem yielding as it fronts the source
Of light restored which heretofore it gave [gave *rev from illeg word*]
Of dust enkindled—and thy mouldered corse
O Man! resurgent from the gloomy grave *MS. 89*

---

composed 1823
found in MS. 1832/36 (MW)
published in *1827–, Winter's Wreath (1828)*
classed Sentiment and Reflection *1827–*
reading text *1827*

5 As aptly, also,] And not inaptly *Winter's Wreath*

Age steal to his allotted nook,
Contented and serene;

With heart as calm as Lakes that sleep,
In frosty moonlight glistening;
Or mountain Rivers, where they creep
Along a channel smooth and deep,
To their own far-off murmurs listening.

"First Floweret of the year is that which shows"

First Floweret of the year is that which shows
Its rival whiteness mid surrounding snows;
To guide the shining company of heaven,
Brightest as first appears the star of Even;
Upon imperial brows the richest gem
Stands ever foremost in the diadem;
How, then, could mortal so unfit engage
To take his station in this leading page,
For others marshal with his *pen* the way
Which shall be trod in many a future day!
Why was not some fair Lady call'd to write
Dear words—for Memory characters of light—
Lines which enraptur'd Fancy might explore
And half create her image?—but no more;
Strangers! forgive the deed, an unsought task,
For what you look on, Friendship deigned to ask.

"How rich that forehead's calm expanse!"

How rich that forehead's calm expanse!
How bright that Heaven-directed glance!

---

composed probably around October 1, 1823
found in Dora W to EQ, May 11, 1824; O'Callaghan Album
published in *PW*, IV (1958)
reading text O'Callaghan Album
title In the first Page of an Album by one whose handwriting is wretchedly bad *Dora W to EQ*
1 Floweret] flowret *Dora W to EQ*
9 marshal] martial *Dora W to EQ*
14 half] thence, *Dora W to EQ*

---

composed probably around mid-February to mid-March 1824
found in Reed MS., MS. 1832/36
published in *1827–*
classed Affections *1827–*
reading text *1827*
title Contemplation— *Reed MS.*

—Waft her to Glory, wingèd Powers,
Ere Sorrow be renewed,
And intercourse with mortal hours
Bring back a humbler mood!
So looked Cecilia when she drew
An Angel from his station;
So looked—not ceasing to pursue
Her tuneful adoration!

But hand and voice alike are still;
No sound *here* sweeps away the will
That gave it birth;—in service meek
One upright arm sustains the cheek,
And one across the bosom lies—
That rose, and now forgets to rise,
Subdued by breathless harmonies
Of meditative feeling;
Mute strains from worlds beyond the skies,
Through the pure light of female eyes
Their sanctity revealing!

A FLOWER GARDEN.

TELL me, ye Zephyrs! that unfold,
While fluttering o'er this gay Recess,
Pinions that fanned the teeming mould
Of Eden's blissful wilderness,
Did only softly-stealing Hours
There close the peaceful lives of flowers?

Say, when the *moving* Creatures saw
All kinds commingled without fear,
Prevailed a like indulgent law

---

3 wingèd *so Reed MS., MS. 1832/36–* winged *1827–1832*
17 breathless] inward *Reed MS.*
18 meditative *rev from* meditating *Reed MS.*

---

composed perhaps mid-February to mid-March 1824 but completed by February 25, 1825
published in *1827–*
found in MW to Lady B, February 25, 1825; Morgan MS. 1; MS. 1832/36 (WW?); MS. 1836/45 (JC)
classed Fancy *1827–*
reading text *1827*
title A flower garden. *MW to Lady B* On a flower Garden at Coleorton *Morgan MS. 1* A FLOWER GARDEN, AT COLEORTON HALL, LEICESTERSHIRE. *1836–, but* GARDEN,] GARDEN. *1850*
stanza numbers 1 . . . 9 *MW to Lady B, Morgan MS. 1*
6 peaceful *rev from* life of *MW to Lady B*
9 law *rev from* fear *Morgan MS. 1*

For the still Growths that prosper here?
Did wanton Fawn and Kid forbear
The half-blown Rose, the Lily spare?

Or peeped they often from their beds
And prematurely disappeared,
Devoured like pleasure ere it spreads
A bosom to the Sun endeared?
If such their harsh untimely doom,
It falls not *here* on bud or bloom.

All Summer long the happy Eve
Of this fair Spot her flowers may bind,
Nor e'er, with ruffled fancy, grieve,
From the next glance she casts, to find
That love for little Things by Fate
Is rendered vain as love for great.

Yet, where the guardian Fence is wound,
So subtly is the eye beguiled
It sees not nor suspects a Bound,
No more than in some forest wild;
Free as the light in semblance—crost
Only by art in nature lost.

And, though the jealous turf refuse
By random footsteps to be prest,
And feeds on never-sullied dews,
Ye, gentle breezes from the West,
With all the ministers of Hope,
Are tempted to this sunny slope!

And hither throngs of Birds resort;
Some, inmates lodged in shady nests,
Some, perched on stems of stately port
That nod to welcome transient guests;
While Hare and Leveret, seen at play,
Appear not more shut out than they.

---

12 spare *rev from* [?fair] *MW to Lady B*
26 is the eye] are our eyes *1836–*
27 It sees not nor suspects] We see not nor suspect *1836–*
29 The sight is free as air—or crost *1836–*
31 And,] What *MW to Lady B, Morgan MS. 1*
32 footsteps] footstep *MW to Lady B, Morgan MS. 1*
33 feeds] feed *1836–* feed *rev to* feeds *rev to* feed *MS. 1836/45*
35 With] And *MW to Lady B* With *rev in pencil from* And *Morgan MS. 1*

Apt emblem (for reproof of pride)
This delicate Enclosure shows
Of modest kindness, that would hide
The firm protection she bestows;
Of manners, like its viewless fence,
Ensuring peace to innocence.

Thus spake the moral Muse—her wing
Abruptly spreading to depart,
She left that farewell offering,
Memento for some docile heart;
That may respect the good old Age
When Fancy was Truth's willing Page;
And Truth would skim the flowery glade,
Though entering but as Fancy's Shade.

TO ———.

LET other Bards of Angels sing,
Bright Suns without a spot;
But thou art no such perfect Thing;
Rejoice that thou art not!

Such if thou wert in all men's view,
A universal show,
What would my Fancy have to do,
My Feelings to bestow?

The world denies that Thou art fair;
So, Mary, let it be
If nought in loveliness compare
With what thou art to me.

---

51 that] this *MW to Lady B, Morgan MS. 1*

---

composed probably late spring or summer 1824
found in BL MS. 7; EdeS MS. 1; Catalogue Facsimile; MS. 1832/36 (MW)
published in *1827–*
classed Affections *1827–*
reading text *1827*
5–8 *lacking 1845–*
9 The World is slow to call thee fair *Catalogue Facsimile*
Heed not tho' none should call thee fair; *1832–*

True beauty dwells in deep retreats,
  Whose veil is unremoved
Till heart with heart in concord beats,
  And the Lover is beloved.

TO ———.

Look at the fate of summer Flowers,
Which blow at daybreak, droop ere even-song;
And, grieved for their brief date, confess that ours,
Measured by what we are and ought to be,
Measured by all that trembling we foresee,
  Is not so long!

If human Life do pass away,
Perishing yet more swiftly than the Flower,
Whose frail existence is but of a day;
What space hath Virgin's Beauty to disclose
Her sweets, and triumph o'er the breathing Rose?
  Not even an hour!

The deepest grove whose foliage hid
The happiest Lovers Arcady might boast,
Could not the entrance of this thought forbid:
O be thou wise as they, soul-gifted Maid!
Nor rate too high what must so quickly fade,
  So soon be lost.

Then shall Love teach some virtuous Youth
"To draw out of the Object of his eyes,"
The whilst on Thee they gaze in simple truth,
Hues more exalted, "a refinèd Form,"
That dreads not age, nor suffers from the worm,
    And never dies.

---

13 dwells] lurks *EdeS MS. 1*
15 concord] concert *Catalogue Facsimile*
16 Till lovers are beloved *EdeS MS. 1*

---

composed probably sometime in late spring or summer 1824
found in DC MS. 159; MS. 1832/36 (MW)
published in *1827–*
classed Affections *1827–*
reading text *1827*
5 trembling *inserted MS. 159*
9 If we are creatures of a *winter's* day; *MS. 1832/36–*
21 whilst] while *MS. 1832/36–*

TO ROTHA Q———

Rotha, my Spiritual Child! this head was grey
When at the sacred Font for Thee I stood;
Pledged till thou reach the verge of womanhood,
And shalt become thy own sufficient stay:
Too late, I feel, sweet Orphan! was the day
For stedfast hope the contract to fulfil;
Yet shall my blessing hover o'er thee still,
Embodied in the music of this Lay,
Breathed forth beside the peaceful mountain Stream*
Whose murmur soothed thy languid Mother's ear
After her throes, this Stream of name more dear
Since thou dost bear it,—a memorial theme
For others; for thy future self a spell
To summon fancies out of Time's dark cell.

*The River Rotha, that flows into Windermere from the Lakes of Grasmere and Rydal.

---

composed between late April and mid-November 1824
found in DC MS. 131; WW to TBB, November 19, 1824; DW to HCR, December 13, 1824; Rotha Q's Album; Monkhouse MS. (copy)
published in *1827–, 1831, 1838*
classed Miscellaneous Sonnets *1827–, 1831, 1838*
reading text *1827*
title *lacking Rotha Q's Album* To Rotha Quillinan *MS. 131, WW to TBB, DW to HCR* Rotha Quillinan *Monkhouse MS. (copy)*
3 till] 'till *Rotha Q's Album* *no comma MS. 131* reach *so all MSS., 1827 errata page, 1832–* reached *1827, 1831* verge] age *Monkhouse MS. (copy)*
9 beside *inserted WW to TBB* *note lacking MS. 131, WW to TBB, DW to HCR, Rotha Q's Album, Monkhouse MS. (copy)*
10 murmur] murmurs *MS. 131, DW to HCR*
11–12 After her throes; whose name is thine to bear
Hanging around thee—a memorial theme *MS. 131; WW to TBB as MS. 131 but* name] Name *DW to HCR as WW to TBB but* throes;] throes, name] Name bear] bear, thee—] Thee *Monkhouse MS. (copy) as MS. 131 but* throes. whose
13 thy future self *rev from* thy self *MS. 131*

COMPOSED AMONG THE RUINS OF A CASTLE IN NORTH WALES.

THROUGH shattered galleries, 'mid roofless halls,
Wandering with timid footstep oft betrayed,
The Stranger sighs, nor scruples to upbraid
Old Time, though He, gentlest among the Thralls
Of Destiny, upon these wounds hath laid
His lenient touches, soft as light that falls,
From the wan Moon, upon the Towers and Walls,
Light deepening the profoundest sleep of shade.
Relic of Kings! Wreck of forgotten Wars,
To winds abandoned and the prying Stars,
Time *loves* Thee! at his call the Seasons twine
Luxuriant wreaths around thy forehead hoar;
And, though past pomp no changes can restore,
A soothing recompense, his gift, is Thine!

TO THE LADY E. B. AND THE HON. MISS P.
COMPOSED IN THE GROUNDS OF PLASS NEWIDD, NEAR LLANGOLLIN, 1824.

A STREAM, to mingle with your favourite Dee,
Along the VALE OF MEDITATION flows;
So styled by those fierce Britons, pleased to see
In Nature's face the expression of repose;
Or haply there some pious Hermit chose
To live and die, the peace of Heaven his aim;
To whom the wild sequestered region owes,
At this late day, its sanctifying name.
GLYN CAFAILLGAROCH, in the Cambrian tongue,
In ours the *Vale of Friendship*, let *this* spot
Be named; where, faithful to a low-roofed Cot,
On Deva's banks, ye have abode so long;

---

composed probably around September 1824
published in *1827–, 1838*
classed Miscellaneous Sonnets *1827–, 1838*
reading text *1827*
2 footstep] footsteps *1836–, 1838*

---

composed September 9, 1824
found in WW to Sir GB, September 20, 1824
published in *1827–, 1838*
classed Miscellaneous Sonnets *1827–, 1838*
reading text *1827*
title *lacking WW to Sir GB*
3 styled] named *WW to Sir GB*
10 the *rev from* [?a] *WW to Sir GB*

Sisters in love—a love allowed to climb,
Even on this Earth, above the reach of Time!

TO THE TORRENT AT THE DEVIL'S BRIDGE, NORTH WALES.

How art thou named? In search of what strange land
From what huge height, descending? Can such force
Of waters issue from a British source,
Or hath not Pindus fed Thee, where the band
Of Patriots scoop their freedom out, with hand
Desperate as thine? Or come the incessant shocks
From that young Stream, that smites the throbbing rocks
Of Viamala? There I seem to stand,
As in Life's Morn; permitted to behold,
From the dread chasm, woods climbing above woods
In pomp that fades not, everlasting snows,
And skies that ne'er relinquish their repose;
Such power possess the Family of floods
Over the minds of Poets, young or old!

TO ———.

O DEARER far than light and life are dear,
Full oft our human foresight I deplore;
Trembling, through my unworthiness, with fear
That friends, by death disjoined, may meet no more!

---

composed September 14, 1824
found in WW to Sir GB, September 20, 1824; WW to CW, January 4, 1825
published in *1827–, 1838*
classed Miscellaneous Sonnets *1827–, 1838*
reading text *1827*
title *lacking WW to Sir GB* Sonnet, composed in the Chasm of the Devil's Bridge, after a Flood *WW to CW* To the Torrent at the Devil's Bridge, North Wales. 1824. *1836–, 1838, but* Wales.] Wales *1840–1849*
9 Morn;] morn, *rev from* morning *WW to CW*
10–11 High oer the yawning fissure piny woods,
And sun-bright lawns, and everlasting snows, *WW to Sir GB; so WW to CW but l. 10* oer . . . fissure] o'er . . . fissure,
13 power] sway *WW to Sir GB, WW to CW*

---

composed probably between about September 20, 1824, and late February 1825
found in MS. 1832/36 (MW, except date)
published in *1827–*
classed Affections *1827–*
reading text *1827*

Misgivings, hard to vanquish or control,
Mix with the day, and cross the hour of rest;
While all the future, for thy purer soul,
With "sober certainties" of love is blest.

If a faint sigh, not meant for human ear,
Tell that these words thy humbleness offend,
Cherish me still—else faltering in the rear
Of a steep march; uphold me to the end.

Peace settles where the Intellect is meek,
And Love is dutiful in thought and deed;
Through Thee communion with that Love I seek;
The faith Heaven strengthens where *he* moulds the creed.

THE CONTRAST.

WITHIN her gilded cage confined,
I saw a dazzling Belle,
A Parrot of that famous kind
Whose name is NON-PAREIL.

Like beads of glossy jet her eyes;
And, smoothed by Nature's skill,
With pearl or gleaming agate vies
Her finely-curvèd bill.

Her plumy Mantle's living hues
In mass opposed to mass,
Outshine the splendour that imbues
The robes of pictured glass.

---

9 If . . . sigh] That sigh of thine *MS. 1832/36–*
10 Tell] Tells *MS. 1832/36–*
11 Cherish me still] Yet bear me up *MS. 1832/36–*
12 uphold] support *MS. 1832/36–*

---

composed around but by September 27, 1824
found in MS. 1832/36; MS. 1836/45 (?WW)
published in *1827–*
classed Fancy *1827–*
reading text *1827*
title THE CONTRAST. THE PARROT AND THE WREN. *1832–, but* CONTRAST, *1836–1843* CONTRAST: *in pencil MS. 1836/45*
part *above l. 1* I. *above l. 29* II. *and half-rule om 1832–*
8 finely-curvèd *so MS. 1832/36–* finely-curved *1827–1832*

And, sooth to say, an apter Mate
Did never tempt the choice
Of feathered Thing most delicate
In figure and in voice.

But, exiled from Australian Bowers,
And singleness her lot,
She trills her song with tutored powers,
Or mocks each casual note.

No more of pity for regrets
With which she may have striven!
Now but in wantonness she frets,
Or spite, if cause be given;

Arch, volatile, a sportive Bird
By social glee inspired;
Ambitious to be seen or heard,
And pleased to be admired!

This moss-lined shed, green, soft, and dry,
Harbours a self-contented Wren,
Not shunning man's abode, though shy,
Almost as thought itself, of human ken.

Strange places, coverts unendeared
She never tried; the very nest
In which this Child of Spring was reared,
Is warmed, thro' winter, by her feathery breast.

To the bleak winds she sometimes gives
A slender unexpected strain;
That tells the Hermitess still lives,
Though she appear not, and be sought in vain.

Say, Dora! tell me by yon placid Moon,
If called to choose between the favoured pair,
Which would you be,—the Bird of the Saloon,
By Lady fingers tended with nice care,
Caressed, applauded, upon dainties fed,
Or Nature's DARKLING of this mossy Shed?

---

39 That tells] Proof that *1836–*

THE INFANT M——— M———.

Unquiet Childhood here by special grace
Forgets her nature, opening like a flower
That neither feeds nor wastes its vital power
In painful struggles. Months each other chase,
And nought untunes that Infant's voice; a trace
Of fretful temper sullies not her cheek;
Prompt, lively, self-sufficing, yet so meek
That one enrapt with gazing on her face,
(Which even the placid innocence of Death
Could scarcely make more placid, Heaven more bright,)
Might learn to picture, for the eye of faith,
The Virgin, as she shone with kindred light;
A Nursling couched upon her Mother's knee,
Beneath some shady Palm of Galilee.

---

composed between November 12 and December 13, 1824
found in WW to TBB, November 19, 1824; Monkhouse MS. (copy); Monkhouse Album (copy); DC MS. 131; DW to HCR, December 13, 1824; MW to EQ, December 18, 1824
published in *1827–, 1838*
classed Miscellaneous Sonnets *1827–, 1838*
reading text *1827*
title Mary Monkhouse *WW to TBB, MS. 131, DW to HCR* Mary Monkhouse Sonnet *MW to EQ* Mary Elizabeth Monkhouse *Monkhouse MS. (copy)* Mary Monkhouse — W. Wordsworth *Monkhouse Album (copy)*
3 power] powers *MS. 131*
5 a] no *1836–, 1838*
6 sullies not *rev from* ne'er *MS. 131, MW to EQ* bedews ne'er bedews *WW to TBB, Monkhouse Album (copy)* not her] her pure *1836–, 1838*
8 enrapt with] who has been *WW to TBB* enrapt by *MS. 131, Monkhouse MS. (copy), Monkhouse MS. (copy)*
10 more *inserted Monkhouse MS. (copy)*
11 Might see in no unholy mood of faith *WW to TBB, so Monkhouse Album (copy) but* see] see,
14 shady] spreading *MS. 131*

CENOTAPH.

In affectionate remembrance of Frances Fermor, whose remains are deposited in the church of Claines, near Worcester, this stone is erected by her sister, Dame Margaret, wife of Sir George Beaumont, Bart., who, feeling not less than the love of a brother for the deceased, commends this memorial to the care of his heirs and successors in the possession of this place.

By vain affections unenthralled,
Though resolute when duty called
To meet the world's broad eye,
Pure as the holiest cloistered nun
That ever feared the tempting sun,
Did Fermor live and die.

This Tablet, hallowed by her name,
One heart-relieving tear may claim;
But if the pensive gloom
Of fond regret be still thy choice,
Exalt thy spirit, hear the voice
Of Jesus from her tomb!

"I AM THE WAY, THE TRUTH, AND THE LIFE."

---

composed between mid-December 1824 and early February 1825
found in MW to Lady B, February 25, 1825 (copies A and B); DC MS. 103; Swarthmore MS. 3
published in *1842, 1845–*
classed Epitaphs *1845–*
reading text *1842*
title *lacking MS. 103* Inscription in the Church of Coleorton* *with* in the Church *over illeg erasure MW to Lady B (A)* The Inscription *MW to Lady B (B)*
headnote *lacking MW to Lady B*
7 Tablet, hallowed by] sacred stone that bears *alt* Tablet hallowed by *MS. 103*
This sacred stone that bears her Name *over illeg eras MW to Lady B (A)*
This Cenotaph [Cenotaph *MW alt* sacred stone] that bears her name, *MW to Lady B (B)*
9 *over illeg eras MW to Lady B (A)*
10 *over illeg eras MW to Lady B (A)* fond *over illeg eras MW to Lady B (B)*
11 Exalt thy Spirit, *over illeg eras MW to Lady B (A)*

ELEGIAC STANZAS.
1824.

O for a dirge! But why complain?
Ask rather a triumphal strain
When FERMOR's race is run;
A garland of immortal boughs
To bind around the Christian's brows,
Whose glorious work is done.

We pay a high and holy debt;
No tears of passionate regret
Shall stain this votive lay;
Ill-worthy, Beaumont! were the grief
That flings itself on wild relief
When Saints have passed away.

Sad doom, at Sorrow's shrine to kneel,
For ever covetous to feel,
And impotent to bear:
Such once was hers—to think and think
On severed love, and only sink
From anguish to despair!

But nature to its inmost part
Had Faith refined, and to her heart
A peaceful cradle given;
Calm as the dew-drop's, free to rest
Within a breeze-fanned rose's breast
Till it exhales to heaven.

Was ever Spirit that could bend
So graciously?—that could descend,

---

composed between mid-December 1824 and early February 1825
found in MW to Lady B, February 25, 1825 (copies A and B); Fleming Album (ll. 49–54); MS. 1832/36 (MW); MS. 1836/45; BL MS. 5 (ll. 49–54); WW to Lord Monteagle, December 30, 1839 (ll. 49–54)
published in *1827–*
classed Epitaphs *1827–*
reading text *1827*
title To Sir George Beaumont Bart. *MW to Lady B (A)* To Sir Geo H. Beaumont Bart. *MW to Lady B (B)* ELEGIAC STANZAS. (ADDRESSED TO SIR G. H. B. UPON THE DEATH OF HIS SISTER-IN-LAW.) 1824. *1836–*
5 bind] twine *MW to Lady B, 1845–*
13 kneel *rev from* [?feel] *MW to Lady B (B)*
14 covetous *over illeg eras MW to Lady B (B)*
16 hers *over illeg eras MW to Lady B (A)*
17 On] Of *MW to Lady B*
17–18 *over illeg eras MW to Lady B (A)*
18 despair *rev from illeg eras MW to Lady B (B)*
20 Had Faith] Faith had *MS. 1832/36–*
26 graciously *rev from* [?courteously] *MW to Lady B (A)*

Another's need to suit,
So promptly from her lofty throne?—
In works of love, in these alone,
How restless, how minute!

Pale was her hue; yet mortal cheek
Ne'er kindled with a livelier streak
When aught had suffered wrong,—
When aught that breathes had felt a wound;
Such look the Oppressor might confound,
However proud and strong.

But hushed be every thought that springs
From out the bitterness of things;
Her quiet is secure;
No thorns can pierce her tender feet,
Whose life was, like the violet sweet,
As climbing jasmine, pure;—

As snowdrop on an infant's grave,
Or lily heaving with the wave
That feeds it and defends;
As Vesper, ere the star hath kissed
The mountain top, or breathed the mist
That from the vale ascends.

Thou takest not away, O Death!
Thou strik'st—and absence perisheth,
Indifference is no more;
The future brightens on our sight;
For on the past hath fallen a light
That tempts us to adore.

---

31 yet] but *MW to Lady B*

41 like *rev from* as *MW to Lady B (A)*

43 As] Or *MS. 1832/36, 1836* As *in pencil MS. 1836/45* As *1840–*

49–54 *lacking MW to Lady B (A)*

50 strik'st—and absence *rev to* strikest—absence *rev to* strikest, absence *MS. 1836/45* strikest, absence *rev to* strikest—absence *WW to Lord Monteagle* strikest—absence *BL MS. 5, Fleming Album, 1840–* perisheth *over illeg eras MW to Lady B (B)* vanisheth *Fleming Album*

52 on our sight;] —a sad Light *BL MS. 5*

53 For on] From *BL MS. 5*

"Why, Minstrel, these untuneful murmurings—"

Ernest de Selincourt suggested a composition date for "Why, Minstrel, these untuneful murmurings" of 1826, which he adduced from its proximity to other poems in DC MS. 89 and its first publication in 1827 (*PW*, III, 421). A more likely date is around but by July 8, 1824. Three copies of the poem in an unidentified hand appear in a commonplace book (Cornell MS. 3) that Dora Wordsworth inscribed to Emma Ayling on July 7, 1824; the second and third copies of the sonnet are inscribed (not by Wordsworth) "Wm Wordsworth / Rydal Mount: July 8th 1824." "Why, Minstrel" was probably revised extensively in December 1826 or early January 1827 when the Wordsworths were preparing copy for the 1827 edition of *Poetical Works*. The first reading text below is drawn from the earliest version in MS. 89, the second from the edition of 1827.

[Text of MS. 89 (A)]

"What ails thy Harp O Minstrel that it rings
With such discordant measures?" He replied,
"Think gentle Knight how far from Shannon's side
We wander, and forgive the tuneless strings."
A simple answer! but to memory clings

---

composed around but by July 8, 1824
found in DC MS. 89 (A) 217^{v}, (B) 116^{r}; Cornell MS. 3 (A) 5^{v}, (B) 6^{v}, (C) 9^{v}
reading text DC MS. 89 (A)

1–5 What ails thy Harp, O minstrel
That it rings bereft of all sweet concord?
He replied "think Gentle Knight how far from Shannons side we wander
And forgive its tuneless strings"
A simple answer but even so, forth springs *rev in pencil to*
What ails thy Harp, O minstrel
That it rings
Bereft of all sweet concord?
He replied
"Think Gentle Knight how far from Shannons side we wander
And forgive its tuneless strings,"
A simple answer but even so, forth springs *MS. 89 (A_2)*

2 *alt* Bereft of all sweet concord? He replied *MS. 89 (A_2); MS. 89 (B) and Cornell MS. 3 (A, B, C) as alt but* "Bereft . . . replied: *Cornell MS. 3 (B, C) and* concord?" *Cornell MS. 3 (B)* concord." *Cornell MS. 3 (C)*

4 the *rev to* its *MS. 89 (A_1)* its *MS. 89 (B)*

5 to memory clings] even forth springs *MS. 89 (B)* even so forth springs *Cornell MS. 3 (B), so (C) but* so] so,

The unaffected language of the heart;
Which, suffering in herself, bestows a part
Of her own nature upon lifeless things.—
From the bare neck of Innocence recoils
The axe—the sword of Valour sickens, when
Summoned to stain its edge in civil broils;
Droops in the mourner's hand the silent pen;
And the poor Irish harp feels Sympathy
With its sad lord, "far from his own Countree."

[Text of 1827]

"Why, Minstrel, these untuneful murmurings—
Dull, flagging notes that with each other jar?"
"Think, gentle Lady, of a Harp so far

6–11 *rev to*
The language in which natural hearts confide
Aided by urgent Fancy to divide
Their own emotions with insensate things.
From the submissive neck of unoffending Men [unoffending Men *rev to* guiltless men]
Stretched on the block the glittering axe recoils
The sword of Valour shrinks from civil broils, *MS. 89 (A)*
From the Castalian Fountain of the heart
The poetry of life, and all that art
Divine of Words quickening insensate things.
From the submissive neck of guiltless Men,
Stretched on the block the lifted Axe recoils;
The Sword of Valour shrinks from civil broils; *MS. 89 (B); so Cornell MS. 3 (B, C) but l. 6* fountain *(B, C)* heart] heart *(B)* heart, *(C)* *ll. 7–8* art / Divine of Words] art divine / Of words, *(C)* *l. 7* Poetry *(B, C)* *l. 8* words, . . . things— *(B)* *l. 9* neck] necks *(B, C)* *l. 10* block, . . . axe *(B, C)* lifted] th'uplifted *(C)* *l. 11* valour *(B)*
From the Castalian fountain of the Heart, the poetry of life,
And all that art divine of words quick'ning insensate things.
From the submissive necks of guiltless men,
Stretch'd on the Block, the lifted axe recoils,
The sword of Valor shrinks from civil broils, *Cornell MS. 3 (A)*

9 bare *rev from* fair *MS. 89 (A)*

11 stain *rev from* stay *MS. 89 (A)*

12 in] from *Cornell MS. 3 (A, B, C)*

13–14 *rev to*
And the poor harp reluctant [reluctant *alt* distemper'd] music yields
To its sad lord, "far from his native fields." *MS. 89 (A)*
And the poor Harp distempered music yields
To its sad Lord, far from his own Country [own Country *rev to* native fields.] *MS. 89 (B); Cornell MS. 3 (A–C) as rev MS. 89 (B) but* distemper'd *(A, C)* distemper's *(B_2)* distemper'd *(C)* Harp, *(B)* fields— *(A, C)*

14 *no period MS. 89 (A)*

---

composed begun in 1824, revised by early January 1827
found in Cornell MS. 3 (B_2), MS. 1838/40
published in *1827–, 1838*
classed Miscellaneous Sonnets *1827–, 1838*
reading text *1827*

From its own Country, and forgive the strings."
A simple answer! but even so forth springs,
From the Castalian fountain of the heart,
The Poetry of Life, and all that Art
Divine of words quickening insensate Things.
From the submissive necks of guiltless Men
Stretched on the block, the glittering axe recoils;
Sun, Moon, and Stars, all struggle in the toils
Of mortal sympathy; what wonder then
If the poor Harp distempered music yields
To its sad Lord, far from his native Fields?

A MORNING EXERCISE.

Fancy, who leads the pastimes of the glad,
Full oft is pleased a wayward dart to throw;
Sending sad shadows after things not sad,
Peopling the harmless fields with signs of woe:
Beneath her sway, a simple forest cry
Becomes an echo of Man's misery.

Blithe Ravens croak of death; and when the Owl
Tries his two voices for a favourite strain—
Tu-whit—Tu-whoo! the unsuspecting fowl
Forebodes mishap, or seems but to complain;
Fancy, intent to harass and annoy,
Can thus pervert the evidence of joy.

Through border wilds where naked Indians stray,
Myriads of notes attest her subtle skill;
A feathered Task-master cried, "WORK AWAY!"
And, in thy iteration, "WHIP POOR WILL*,"

*See Waterton's Wanderings in South America.

11–14 *Cornell MS. 3 (B_2) as text but l. 13* That the poor Harp, distemper's music yields
12 mortal *alt* human *MS. 1838/40*
13 If] That *1836–, 1838*

---

composed possibly in 1825 or 1828
found in MS. 1832/36
published in *1832–*
classed Fancy *1832–*
reading text *1832*

11–14 "Why, Minstrel, these untuneful murmurings—": For nonverbal differences from reading text in Cornell MS. 3 (B_2), see Nonverbal Variants.

Is heard the Spirit of a toil-worn Slave,
Lashed out of life, not quiet in the grave!

What wonder? at her bidding, ancient lays
Steeped in dire griefs the voice of Philomel;
And that fleet Messenger of summer days,
The Swallow, twittered subject to like spell;
But ne'er could Fancy bend the buoyant Lark
To melancholy service—hark! O hark!

The daisy sleeps upon the dewy lawn,
Not lifting yet the head that evening bowed;
But *He* is risen, a later star of dawn,
Glittering and twinkling near yon rosy cloud;
Bright gem instinct with music, vocal spark;
The happiest Bird that sprang out of the Ark!

Hail, blest above all kinds!—Supremely skilled
Restless with fixed to balance, high with low,
Thou leav'st the Halcyon free her hopes to build
On such forbearance as the deep may show;
Perpetual flight, unchecked by earthly ties,
Leavest to the wandering Bird of Paradise.

Faithful, though swift as lightning, the meek Dove;
Yet more hath Nature reconciled in thee;
So constant with thy downward eye of love,
Yet, in aerial singleness, so free;
So humble, yet so ready to rejoice
In power of wing and never-wearied voice!

How would it please old Ocean to partake,
With Sailors longing for a breeze in vain,
The harmony that thou best lovest to make
Where earth resembles most his blank domain!

---

20 griefs] grief *1836–*
36 Leavest] Leav'st *MS. 1832/36–*
42/43 To the last point of vision, and beyond,
Mount, daring warbler!—that love-prompted strain,
('Twixt thee and thine a never-failing bond)
Thrills not the less the bosom of the plain:
Yet might'st thou seem, proud privilege! to sing
All independent of the leafy spring. *1845–*
45 lovest] lov'st *MS. 1832/36*
The harmony thy notes most gladly make *1836–*
46 blank] own *1836–*

Urania's self might welcome with pleased ear
These matins mounting towards her native sphere.

Chanter by Heaven attracted, whom no bars
To day-light known deter from that pursuit,
'Tis well that some sage instinct, when the stars
Come forth at evening, keeps Thee still and mute;
For not an eyelid could to sleep incline
Were thou among them singing as they shine!

TO A SKY-LARK.

ETHEREAL Minstrel! Pilgrim of the sky!
Dost thou despise the earth where cares abound?
Or, while the wings aspire, are heart and eye
Both with thy nest upon the dewy ground?
Thy nest which thou canst drop into at will,
Those quivering wings composed, that music still!

To the last point of vision, and beyond,
Mount, daring Warbler! that love-prompted strain,
('Twixt thee and thine a never-failing bond)
Thrills not the less the bosom of the plain:
Yet might'st thou seem, proud privilege! to sing
All independent of the leafy spring.

Leave to the Nightingale her shady wood;
A privacy of glorious light is thine;
Whence thou dost pour upon the world a flood
Of harmony, with rapture more divine;
Type of the wise who soar, but never roam;
True to the kindred points of Heaven and Home!

---

composed probably around spring 1825 but before October 2, 1826
found in Lonsdale Album; MS. 1827/32L; MS. 1832/36
published in *1827–, Winter's Wreath (1828), 1831*
classed Imagination *1827–; not classed in 1831*
reading text *1827*
7–12 *om 1845–*
14 privacy of glorious *rev from* glorious privacy of *Lonsdale Album*
16 rapture] instinct *Lonsdale Album, MS. 1827/32L–*

"While they, her Playmates once, light-hearted tread"

WHILE they, her Playmates once, light-hearted tread
The mountain turf and river's flowery marge;
Or float with music in the festal barge;
Rein the proud steed, or through the dance are led;
Is Anna doomed to press a weary bed—
Till oft her guardian Angel, to some Charge
More urgent called, will stretch his wings at large,
And Friends too rarely prop the languid head.
Yet Genius is no feeble comforter:
The presence even of a stuffed Owl for her
Can cheat the time; sending her fancy out
To ivied castles and to moonlight skies,
Though he can neither stir a plume, nor shout,
Nor veil, with restless film, his staring eyes.

To ——— ("Such age how beautiful! O Lady bright")

Mary Wordsworth included an early version of *To* ——— ("Such age how beautiful! O Lady bright") in her letter to Lady Beaumont, December 9, 1825. This 1825 version is followed by the one Wordsworth published in 1827.

[Text of MW to Lady B, December 9, 1825]

Lady, what delicate graces may unite
In age—so often comfortless and bleak!
Though from thy unenfeebled eye-balls break
Those saintly emanations of delight,
A snow-drop let me name thee; pure, chaste, white,
Too pure for flesh and blood; with smooth, blanch'd cheek,

---

composed probably around May–August 1825, but before January 1827
published in *1827–, 1831, 1838*
classed Miscellaneous Sonnets *1827–, 1831, 1838*
reading text *1827*
1 While they, who once were Anna's Playmates, tread *1832*
While Anna's peers and early playmates tread, *1836–, 1838*
2 In freedom, mountain-turf and river's marge; *1836–, 1838*
5 Is Anna doomed] Her doom it is *1832–, 1838*
9 Yet, helped by Genius—untired comforter, *1836–, 1838*

---

composed around but by December 9, 1825
found in MW to Lady B, December 9, 1825
reading text MW to Lady B, December 9, 1825
1 what *rev from* whose *MW to Lady B*

And head that droops because the soul is meek
And not that Time presses with weary weight.
Hope, Love, and Joy are with thee fresh as fair;
A Child of Winter prompting thoughts that climb
From desolation towards the genial prime:
Or like the Moon, conquering the misty air
And filling more and more with chrystal light
As pensive evening deepens into night.

[Text of 1827]

TO ———

SUCH age how beautiful! O Lady bright,
Whose mortal lineaments seem all refined
By favouring Nature and a saintly Mind
To something purer and more exquisite
Than flesh and blood; whene'er thou meet'st my sight,
When I behold thy blanched unwithered cheek,
Thy temples fringed with locks of gleaming white,
And head that droops because the soul is meek,
Thee with the welcome Snowdrop I compare;
That Child of Winter, prompting thoughts that climb
From desolation tow'rds the genial prime;
Or with the Moon conquering earth's misty air,
And filling more and more with crystal light
As pensive Evening deepens into night.

---

13 light] light. *MW to Lady B*
14 night.] night *MW to Lady B*

---

composed between December 9, 1825, and January 1827
published in *1827–, 1831, 1838*
classed Miscellaneous Sonnets *1827–, 1831, 1838*
reading text *1827*
title To ———, In Her Seventieth Year. *1832–, 1838*
11 tow'rds] toward *1832–, 1838*

"Ere with cold beads of midnight dew"

Ere with cold beads of midnight dew
  Had mingled tears of thine,
I grieved, fond Youth! that thou shouldst sue
  To haughty Geraldine.

Immoveable by generous sighs,
  She glories in a train
Who drag, beneath our native skies,
  An Oriental Chain.

Pine not like them with arms across,
  Forgetting in thy care
How the fast-rooted trees can toss
  Their branches in mid air.

The humblest Rivulet will take
  Its own wild liberties;
And, every day, the imprisoned Lake
  Is flowing in the breeze.

Then, crouch no more on suppliant knee,
  But scorn with scorn outbrave;
A Briton, even in love, should be
  A subject, not a slave!

---

composed probably 1826
found in EdeS MS. 2; MS. 1832/36 (JC)
published in *1827–*
classed Affections *1827–*
reading text *1827*

3 fond] lost *EdeS MS. 2*
5–6 No care hath she for generous sighs / But *EdeS MS. 2*
9–16 The humblest rill thro' bush and brake
Meanders here and there;
The rooted trees are free to shake
Their leafy boughs in air. *EdeS MS. 2*
17 suppliant] faultering *EdeS MS. 2*
19 Briton *so 1827 errata page, 1832–* Britain *1827*

INSCRIPTION.

THE massy Ways, carried across these Heights
By Roman Perseverance, are destroyed,
Or hidden under ground, like sleeping worms.
How venture then to hope that Time will spare
This humble Walk? Yet on the mountain's side
A Poet's hand first shaped it; and the steps
Of that same Bard, repeated to and fro
At morn, at noon, and under moonlight skies,
Through the vicissitudes of many a year,
Forbade the weeds to creep o'er its grey line.
No longer, scattering to the heedless winds
The vocal raptures of fresh poesy,
Shall he frequent these precincts; locked no more
In earnest converse with beloved Friends,
Here will he gather stores of ready bliss,
As from the beds and borders of a garden
Choice flowers are gathered! But, if Power may spring
Out of a farewell yearning favoured more
Than kindred wishes mated suitably
With vain regrets, the Exile would consign
This Walk, his loved possession, to the care
Of those pure Minds that reverence the Muse.

---

composed between January and October 1826, but probably by July
found in DC MSS. 106, 135, 137
published in *1835, 1836–*
classed Inscriptions *1836–*
reading text *1835*
title *omitted 1836–*
1 carried across *written over illeg eras MS. 106*
5 mountain's *rev in pencil to* mountain *MS. 106*
10–14 *written over illeg eras MS. 106*
13 Shall] Will *alt in pencil* Shall *MS. 106*
15 will *rev from* may *MS. 106*
17 Choice *rev written over illeg erasure MS. 106*
21 loved] heart- *MS. 106* heart *rev to* loved *MS. 135*

"Strange visitation! at *Jemima's* lip"

STRANGE visitation! at *Jemima's* lip
Thus hadst thou pecked, wild Redbreast! Love might say,
A half-blown rose had tempted thee to sip
Its glistening dews; but hallowed is the clay
Which the Muse warms; and I, whose head is grey,
Am not unworthy of thy fellowship;
Nor could I let one thought—one motion—slip
That might thy sylvan confidence betray.
For are we not all His, without whose care
Vouchsafed no sparrow falleth to the ground?
Who gives his Angels wings to speed through air,
And rolls the planets through the blue profound;
Then peck or perch, fond Flutterer! nor forbear
To trust a Poet in still vision bound.

---

composed around 1826 but by early January 1827, certainly by April 1827
found in MS. 1838/40; MS. 1836/45 (JC)
published in *1827–, 1838*
classed Miscellaneous Sonnets *1827–, 1838*
reading text *1827*
title In the Woods of Rydal. *1836–, 1838*
1–2 Wild Redbreast! hadst thou at Jemima's lip
Pecked, as at mine, thus boldly, Love might say, *1836–, 1838*
10 Vouchsafed *so 1832, 1838, 1840–, MS. 1836/45* Vouchsafed, *1827, 1836*
14 vision] musings *1836–, 1838*

"When Philoctetes in the Lemnian Isle"

WHEN Philoctetes in the Lemnian Isle
Lay couched;—upon that breathless Monument,
On him, or on his fearful bow unbent,
Some wild Bird oft might settle, and beguile
The rigid features of a transient smile,
Disperse the tear, or to the sigh give vent,
Slackening the pains of ruthless banishment
From home affections, and heroic toil.
Nor doubt that spiritual Creatures round us move,
Griefs to allay that Reason cannot heal;
And very Reptiles have sufficed to prove
To fettered Wretchedness, that no Bastile
Is deep enough to exclude the light of love,
Though Man for Brother Man has ceased to feel.

RETIREMENT.

IF the whole weight of what we think and feel,
Save only far as thought and feeling blend

---

composed around 1826 but perhaps between about late January and late April 1827
found in Knight MS.
published in *1827–, 1831, 1838*
classed Miscellaneous Sonnets *1827–, 1831, 1838*
reading text *1827*
title Suggested by the same Incident *Knight MS.*
2–11 Reclined with shaggy forehead earthward bent,
Lay silent like a weed-grown Monument,
Such Friend, for such brief moment as a smile
Asks to be born and die in, might beguile
The wounded Chief of pining discontent
From home affections, and heroic toil.
Seen or unseen, beneath us, or above,
Are Powers that soften anguish, if not heal;
And toads and spirders have sufficed to prove *Knight MS.*
2–3 Like a Form sculptured on a monument
Lay couched; on him or his dread bow unbent *1836–, 1838*
8 From his lov'd home, and from heroic toil. *1836–, 1838*
9 Nor doubt] And trust *1836–, 1838*
10 that] which *1836–, 1838*
11 And very Reptiles] Yea, veriest reptiles *1836–, 1838*

---

composed probably after late February 1826, perhaps around April or May
found in DC MS. 89
published in *1827–, 1831, 1838*
classed Miscellaneous Sonnets *1827–, 1831, 1838*
reading text *1827*
title *lacking MS. 89*
2 blend] tend *MS. 89*

With action, were as nothing, patriot Friend!
From thy remonstrance would be no appeal;
But to promote and fortify the weal
Of our own Being, is her paramount end;
A truth which they alone shall comprehend
Who shun the mischief which they cannot heal.
Peace in these feverish times is sovereign bliss;
Here, with no thirst but what the stream can slake,
And startled only by the rustling brake,
Cool air I breathe; while the unincumbered Mind,
By some weak aims at services assigned
To gentle Natures, thanks not Heaven amiss.

"Fair Prime of life! were it enough to gild"

Fair Prime of life! were it enough to gild
With ready sunbeams every straggling shower;
And, if an unexpected cloud should lower,
Swiftly thereon a rainbow arch to build
For Fancy's errands,—then, from fields half-tilled
Gathering green weeds to mix with poppy flower,
Thee might thy Minions crown, and chant thy power,
Unpitied by the wise, all censure stilled.
Ah! show that worthier honours are thy due;
Fair Prime of Life! arouse the deeper heart;

---

3 With] To *MS. 89* patriot] then O *alt* patriot *MS. 89*
6 her] its *MS. 89*
12 the . . . Mind,] services assigned *rev to* the unincumbered mind *MS. 89*
14 gentle *alt* [?humbler] *MS. 89*

---

composed probably early in 1826, perhaps by mid-February
found in DC MS. 89
published in *1827–, 1831, 1838*
classed Miscellaneous Sonnets *1827–, 1831, 1838*
reading text *1827*

2 The homeliest surface of the present hour *rev in pencil to*
With flying touch the surface of each hour *alt in ink as text MS. 89*
3 With dazzling touch, or, if a cloud should lower, *rev in pencil to*
Or, if an unexpected cloud should lower, *rev to text MS. 89*
6 green] bright *rev to* fresh *alt* green *MS. 89*
7 power] powers *MS. 89*
8 the] thy *MS. 89*
10 arouse *rev from* rouse *MS. 89*

Confirm the Spirit glorying to pursue
Some path of steep ascent and lofty aim;
And, if there be a joy that slights the claim
Of grateful memory, bid that joy depart.

"Go back to antique Ages, if thine eyes"

The first reading text of "Go back to antique Ages, if thine eyes" is based on Mary Wordsworth's fair copy on 217^{v} of DC MS. 89 (version A). Wordsworth's revisions to this version are recorded in the *apparatus.* Below this revised fair copy in MS. 89 and along the margins of the same page are the poet's draftings toward the complete version that was entered above. There is also some erased pencil draft beneath the sonnet *Retirement.* The second reading text is based on the 1827 printing with variants from the versions in MS. 89 (B and C) that anticipate the 1827 text. The position of these entries in the manuscript relative to other entries suggests a date after mid-February 1826, but probably by April or May (see the note to *Retirement*, p. 430, below).

[Text of MS. 89 (A)]

Go back to early ages if thou prize
A Talk with Fear or Folly face to face
Would'st meet the idolatries that still have place
Within man's heart, exposed without disguise;
There, see the Tower of Babel heavenward rise;

---

11 Inflame with emulation to pursue *rev in pencil and ink to text MS. 89*
12 steep *rev in pencil to* [?pure] *MS. 89*

---

composed probably after mid-February 1826, perhaps around April or May
found in DC MS. 89 (A) 218^{v}
reading text DC MS. 89 (A_1)

1–4 *rev to* Go back to antique ages that [that *alt in pencil* if] thine eyes
By outward help more easily may [may *rev in pencil to* would] trace
The internal Spirit that still holds her place
Prompting the world's audacious vanities *MS. 89 (A_1)*

3 Would'st] Wouldst *MS. 89 (A_1)*

See the photograph and transcription of "Go back to early ages if thou prize," DC MS. 89 (A_2), 218^{v}, pp. 618–619.

The Pyramid extend its monstrous base,
For some Aspirant of our short-lived Race
Anxious an aery name to immortalise.
Others behold who mid night's darkest hours
Have cast their hopes upon infernal powers
Trusting that while the elements are wrapp'd
With spell and clamorous ritual—better mute
They from the sickly turmoil may extract
The petty thing they crave the obnoxious law uproot.

[Text of 1827]

Go back to antique Ages, if thine eyes
The genuine mien and character would trace
Of the rash Spirit that still holds her place,
Prompting the World's audacious vanities!
See, at her call, the Tower of Babel rise;
The Pyramid extend its monstrous base,
For some Aspirant of our short-lived race,
Anxious an aery name to immortalize.

---

8 aery *alt* guilty *MS. 89 (A_1)*
9 mid night's darkest *rev to* in night's murkiest *MS. 89 (A_1)*
11 wrapp'd *rev in pencil to* rack'd *MS. 89 (A_1)*
12 clamorous ritual *alt* ritual clamorous *MS. 89 (A_1)*
14 petty *del in pencil MS. 89 (A_1)* obnoxious law *alt* impediments *MS. 89 (A_1)*

---

composed probably around early 1826, perhaps by mid-February
found in DC MS. 89 (B) 216^{r}, (C) 215^{v}
published in *1827–, 1838*
classed Liberty *1827–*
reading text *1827*
title Sonnets *MS. 89 (C)*
1 if thine eyes] ere disguise *alt* if thine eyes *MS. 89 (B)*
2 Was thought of—ere a mask concealed the face *rev in pencil to*
Was studied—art meddled with the face *alt*
The Genuine mien and character would *MS. 89 (B)*
4 audacious *alt* [?prize] [?] *del MS. 89 (B)*
5 Then see—the Tower of Babel heavenward rise *rev to*
See, at her call the Tower of Babel rise *rev to*
Then, at her call, see Babel heavenward rise *MS. 89 (B)*
See, at her call,] Go back, and see *1836–, 1838*

There, too, ere wiles and politic dispute
Gave specious colouring to aim and act,
See the first mighty Hunter leave the brute
To chase mankind, with men in armies packed
For his field-pastime, high and absolute,
While, to dislodge his game, cities are sacked!

"Just vengeance dost thou crave for rights invaded"

This sonnet, probably composed in 1826 and surviving in three drafts in Wordsworth's hand in DC MS. 89, was never published by the poet. The first reading text, the earliest version, is based on the text as first entered on 218^{r}. The second is based on the version, also in Wordsworth's hand, on 215^{v}, where there may be some doubt as to the poet's latest choices among many alternate lines and phrases (see the notes to ll. 1, 3, 5 in text of MS. 89, version C). The readings in the intervening version on 217^{v}, with fair copy in Mary Wordsworth's hand, heavily revised by Wordsworth, are reported in the *apparatus* to the first reading text. Alternate draftings for ll. 10–12 at the foot and in the margin of 215^{v}, probably entered after the revisions to the version of the sonnet on the same page, are reported in the *apparatus* to the second reading text.

[Text of MS. 89 (A)]

Just vengeance dost thou crave for rights invaded,
Lo while before Minerva's altar quake
The conscious Tyrants like a glistening snake

9–14 See the first mighty Hunter in pursuit
Of men by armies of his Fellows back'd
See those who while the elements are rack'd
With spell and clamorous ritual better mute
Hope from the sickly turmoil to extract
The thing they crave, the obnoxious law uproot *with alt below in pencil:*
See the first mighty Hunter leave the brute
For higher prey [?enjoy] not to extract
[~~? ? ? ? ?~~]
Behold him [?pressing] on to hot pursuit
[?Of] [? ? ?] [?sack'd]
[? ? ? ?] *rev in pencil and ink to text MS. 89 (B)*

10 colouring *inserted* aim *rev from illeg wd MS. 89 (C)*

---

composed probably in 1826, after February 18
found in DC MS. 89 (A) 218^{r}, (B) 217^{v}
published in *PW*, III (1946)
reading text DC MS. 89 (A)

1 dost thou crave *alt* craves thy Soul *MS. 89 (A)* craves thy soul *rev to* craves the Soul *rev to* dost thou crave *rev to* craves thy Soul *MS. 89 (B)*

9–14 Nonverbal differences from the 1827 text of "Go back to antique Ages, if thine eyes" in MS. 89 (B) are reported as belonging to MS. 89 (B_2) in Nonverbal Variants

Forth leaps the Sword erewhile with mirtles braided,
O tis a dark delight by fancy aided
The hush'd design of Brutus to partake,
To muse with Tell beside the guardian Lake
Till from that rocky couch with pine oershaded
He starts and grasps his deadly carabine;
There to participate the draught divine
Of Liberty that like a liquid fountain
Refresh'd Pelayo on that illustrious mountain
So lived the Swede within the hollow mine
When every hope but his was parch'd and shrunk and faded.

[Text of MS. 89 (C)]

Are States oppress'd afflicted and degraded
Lo! while before Minerva's altar quake
The concious Tyrants, like a vengeful snake
Leaps forth the Sword that lurk'd with myrtles braided!
Thence to the Capitol by Fancy aided

---

4 leaps the Sword erewhile with *alt in pencil* springs the sword that lurkd w *MS. 89 (A)* springs the sword that lurked by *MS. 89 (B)*

5 O tis a dark delight *rev to* Thence may she wing her flight *MS. 89 (A)*
Thence may she wing his [his *rev to* her] flight, by fancy aided, *rev to*
Thence the [the *rev to* thy] Spirit fly, full long degraded; *rev to*
Thence to the Capitol full long degraded; *MS. 89 (B)*
Thence may the Patriot fly, by fancy aided *alt* Thence may the Spirit fly *alt* Thence mayst thou urge thy flight, *all del MS. 89 (B)*

6 hush'd] hushed *alt* august *del MS. 89 (B)*

7 To *alt* Or *MS. 89 (A)* Or *MS. 89 (B)* the *rev from* his *MS. 89 (B)*
rev to Or watch the Hero of the Helvetian Lake *MS. 89 (B)*

8 that *rev from* this *MS. 89 (B)*

10 There to participate *rev to* Thence hurry to partake *rev to* Thus shall his thirst forgo *MS. 89 (A)* Nor shall her [her *rev to* our *rev to* her *rev to* this *rev to* his *rev to* thy] thirst forgo *MS. 89 (B)*

11 like a liquid fountain *rev in transcr from* on the illustrious mountain *MS. 89 (A)* that] which *MS. 89 (B)*

12 Refresh'd] Refreshd *MS. 89 (A)* Refreshed *MS. 89 (B)*

13 So lived *alt in pencil* Sustained *MS. 89 (A)* Swede] Sweed *MS. 89 (A)*
alt The Swed within the Dalecarlian mine *alt in pencil* Or share in your ~~black~~ dark cave *MS. 89 (A); MS. 89 (B) as first alt but* Sweede

14 his *rev in pencil and ink from* [?theirs] *MS. 89 (A)* his *MS. 89 (B)* parch'd] parchd *MS. 89 (A)* faded. *so MS. 89 (B)* faded *MS. 89 (A)* parched, and shrunk, and faded. *(with punct added) rev to* shrunk, and faded. *MS. 89 (B)*

---

composed probably in 1826, after February 18
found in DC MS. 89 (C) 215^{v}
reading text DC MS. 89 (C)

1, 6, 12 *no apos MS. 89 (C)*

1 Just vengeance claims thy Soul for rights invaded *alt* Shall vengeance [vengeance *rev to* Vengeance] sleep if Freedom be invaded.? *alt as text MS. 89 (C)*

2 while *rev from* when *MS. 89 (C)*

3 vengeful *rev from* glistening *MS. 89 (C)*

4 with *rev from* by *MS. 89 (C)*

5 by Fancy aided] by Fancey aided *rev from* full long degraded *MS. 89 (C)*

The hush'd design of Brutus to partake
Or watch the Hero of the Helvetian Lake
'Till from that rocky couch with pine oershaded
He starts and grasps his deadly Carabine
Nor let thy thirst forego the draught divine
Of Liberty which like a liquid Fountain
Refresh'd Pelayo on the illustrious mountain;
The Swede within the Dalecarlian mine
When every hope but his was shrunk and faded

May Odes

Manuscripts in the Wordsworth Library reveal that two poems addressed to May and published together in 1835 as *Ode, Composed on May Morning* and *To May* had their origin as the single three-stanza poem *Vernal Stanzas*, the fair copy of which in DC MS. 107 (version A on 57^{v}–58^{r}) was crossed out and another version, untitled, in four stanzas, was copied in MS. 107 (version B on 58^{v}–59^{r}, the basis for the first reading text). A fair copy of the second version was entered in DC MS. 112; and, with a new first stanza, it was copied in MS. 101A, where Wordsworth revised it and added a fifth stanza. At about this point, though the compositional sequence is uncertain, he drafted four new stanzas on the verso of a discarded leaf of Mary Wordsworth's fair copy of "This Lawn, a carpet all alive," marking the top of the page with three penciled crosses perhaps to indicate his intention to insert the new stanzas in another copy of the shorter version that has not been preserved (see the photograph and transcription of MS. 107, version C, on 82^{v}, 83^{v}, pp. 620–621). By some such process Wordsworth eventually expanded the poem to ten stanzas, the earliest extant version of which is found in MS. 107 (version D, on 41^{v}–44^{r}, the basis for the second reading text), and a fair copy of the revised version D was recorded in MS. 106 (these two copies both by DW). In MS. 133, a kind of workbook of materials intended for *Yarrow Revisited, and Other Poems,*

---

8 that *rev from* this *MS. 89 (C)*
10 let . . . draught *written above undeleted* shall . . . cup *MS. 89 (C)*
10–12 Shrinkst thou from these
{Deemst a breach of law divine
{Th thou such deeds ~~unsanctiond—be it thine~~
Then bids thee seek
Let Freedom ~~guide thee to~~ that ~~purer~~ fountain
{s
That cha{tned Pelayo on the illustrious Mountain
Then haste with Freedom *all del MS. 89 (C)*
~~Recoilst thou from such deeds? then be it thine~~
speed
~~To haste~~ with Freedom
Bold retribution, but by law divine *MS. 89 (C)*
11 *written above undeleted* Which fill'd by Freedom from her sacred Fountain *MS. 89 (C)*
14 every *rev from* ho *MS. 89 (C)* shrunk and faded *rev from* crushd [crushd *rev to* parchd] and faded *but* parch'd *undeleted MS. 89 (C)*

1835, a total of twenty full stanzas and segments of two others are entered on a sequence of leaves and paste-overs. At first Wordsworth at least provisionally regarded this work in MS. 133 as one long poem to May (see pp. 622–649); but the twenty-odd stanzas were finally distributed between two separate poems, one to be titled, on publication in 1835, *Ode, Composed on May Morning*, and the other, *To May*. The section of manuscript containing these poems is missing from the surviving printer's copy for *Yarrow Revisited, and Other Poems* (MS. 135), but revised proofs do appear in MS. 137. In the preparation of printer's copy (MS. 135) three leaves from MS. 133 were moved, one to MS. 134 and two to MS. 135 (see the transcriptions, pp. 650–655).

The table below attempts to summarize the progress of the poems through the various manuscript versions. The stanza numbers of the poems as published are listed in the left-hand column and their occurrence and order in the manuscripts appear in the columns to the right. An asterisk indicates the presence of more than one version of that stanza; parentheses around a second number indicate its standing before revision. The multiple versions in MS. 133, as explained above, are really a single sequence (with some duplicates) that Wordsworth subsequently reordered by renumbering stanzas and pasting sheets over canceled stanzas; these sheets have now been lifted, so that we can see what is beneath. In two instances stanzas were entered directly over earlier stanza entries in the space between lines, whether as substitution or addition is not clear.

ODE	107A	107B	112	101	107C	107D	106	133A	133B	133C	133D
1								1		1	
2	1	1	1			1*	1	3	1	2*	
3					3	5*	5	4	9	3	
4					4	6*	6	5	10	4*	
5					2	4*	4	6	4	5	
6								7		6*	
7								8(9)		7	
8						10	10	9(8)	14	8*	
MAY											
1											1
2				2		2	2		2		2
3					1	3*	3	2	3		3
4											4
5											5
6									5		6(4)
7									6		7(5)
8									7		8
9				1				10	8		9
10	2	2	2	3(2)		7*	7	11	11		10
11		3	3	4(3)		8*	8	12	12		11
12	3	4	4	5(4)		9*	9	13	13		12

The difficulties inherent in representing this complex evolution in an *apparatus* to the published poems should be apparent. To bring into focus the main stages of composition, we print two of the early versions as texts of MS. 107, B and D, where each seems to have attained a "final" state, both versions having been fair-copied elsewhere. Related manuscript versions are reported in the notes to these reading texts or in photographs and transcriptions. The massive expansion and reworking of this material in MS. 133 does not reach a final form as a single long poem, precluding the derivation of a reading text from it. However, to make it possible to view the long version in its entirety it is represented by a full set of transcriptions and photographs. Finally the two poems as published in 1835 appear as the third and fourth reading texts, though strictly speaking they are now separate poems, the notes to which record the variants in corrected proofs and subsequent printings.

Vernal Stanzas was probably begun around May 1826, added to as either one or two poems around spring 1829—but by November 15, 1830 (WW to WRH, November 26, 1830, where the poet refers to "New stanzas" composed while riding through Lancashire; see *LY*, II, 353)—and completed as two poems by mid-September 1834 (one of the proof pages bearing corrections to *To May* is dated September 24, 1834). In the Fenwick note Wordsworth identified the third and fourth stanzas of "What month can rival thee, sweet May"—see the "Text of MS. 107 (B)," below—as the starting point for composition, though the earliest version, *Vernal Stanzas*, lacks the first of these; he later positioned them as the final stanzas of *To May* (ll. 81–95).

[Text of MS. 107 (B)]

What month can rival thee sweet May?
Tempering the year's extremes
And scattering lustres o'er noon-day
Like morning's pearly gleams
   While mellow warble, lively trill

---

composed probably begun around May 1826, added to around May 1829 but by November 15, 1830
found in DC MS. 107 (A) 56^{v}–57^{r}, (B) 57^{v}–58^{r}; DC MSS. 112, 101A
reading text DC MS. 107 (B)
title Vernal Stanzas *MS. 107 (A); lacking MSS. 107 (B), 101A* Composed ~~in the~~ or rather suggested in the valley of Newlands – 1829 *MS. 112*
stanza numbers 1, 2 *etc. MS. 112*
1 *rev to* All Nature welcomes Thee blithe May, *MS. 101A*
1–3 Hail gladsome Spirit! whose mild sway
Tempers the year's extremes,
And breathes a freshness o'er noon day *MS. 107 (A), with* noon *rev from* to
2 year's] years *MS. 107* (B)
3 lustres] freshness *MS. 112* o'er] oer *MSS. 107 (B), 112*
4 morning's] mornings *MSS. 107 (B), 112*

The tremulous heart excite
And hums the balmy air—to still
The balance of delight.

The streams that April could not check
Are patient of thy rule,
Gurgling in foamy water-break
Loitering in glassy pool
  By thee, thee only, could be sent
Such gentle mists as glide,
Curling with unconfirmed intent
On that green mountain's side.

How delicate a leafy Veil
To grace the house of God
Hast thou renew'd in this deep dale
By few but Shepherds trod
  And lowly huts, near beaten ways
No sooner stand attired
In thy fresh wreaths than they for praise
Peep forth and are admired.

Season of fancy and of hope
Permit not for one hour

---

6 excite *rev from* [?re]cite *MS. 107 (B)*
7 And a soothing hum prevails—to still *MS. 107 (A)*
8/9 Delicious odors, music sweet
Too sweet to pass away
O for a deathless song to greet
This bless'd return—a lay
That when a thousand years are told
Should praise thee, genial Power
Through summer heat—autumnal cold
And winter's dreariest hour *WW inserted MS. 101A*
9–12 *del in pencil MS. 101A*
9–16 Thine is the concert, May! and sent
By thee yon vapors glide,
Curling with unconfirmed intent
Along the mountain side:
The streams, that April could not check,
Are patient of thy rule,
Gurgling in foamy water-break,
Loitering in glassy pool. *MS. 107 (A)*
14 as *rev from* that *MS. 107 (B)*
15 intent *over illeg eras MS. 101A*
16 mountain's] mountains *MS. 107* (B)
17–24 *lacking MS. 107 (A)*
17 Veil *WW rev from* Vale *MS. 107 (B)*
18 To grace *WW alt* Half hides *MS. 101A*
19 Hast thou renew'd *WW alt* Thy net work worn *MS. 101A* dale *rev from* Dale *MS. 107 (B)*
20 Shepherds *rev from* Shepherd's *MS. 107 (B)*
21 And lowly *rev from* In lonely *MS. 107 (B)* While lowly *MS. 112* And lowly *WW rev to* And lowliest *MS. 101A*

A blossom from thy crown to drop
Nor add to it a flower
  So perfect now is that fine touch
Of self-restraining art
The modest charm of not too much
Part seen, imagined part.

[Text of MS. 107 (D)]

Ode to May

All Nature welcomes thee, blithe May,
Tempering the Year's extremes,
And scattering lustres o'er noonday,
Like morning's pearly gleams,
While mellow warble, sprightly trill
The tremulous heart excite,
And hums the balmy air, to still
The balance of delight!

Delicious odours, music sweet,
Too sweet to pass away
Oh for a deathless song to greet
This blest return—a lay
That when a thousand years are told
Should praise thee, genial Power!
Through summer heat, autumnal cold,
And Winter's dreariest hour!

Earth, Sea thy presence feel—nor less,
If yon ethereal blue
With its soft smile the truth express
The Heavens have felt it too.
The inmost heart of man, if glad,
Partakes a livelier chear;
And eyes that cannot but be sad
Let fall a brightened tear.

---

composed probably between November 1830 and mid-September 1834
found in DC MS. 107 (C) 82r, 83v, (D) 40v–43r; DC MS. 106
reading text DC MS. 107 (D)
5 sprightly *rev from* lively *MS. 107 (D)*
9 *illeg del after* music *MS. 107 (D)*
12 This] Thy *alt in pencil* This *MS. 106*
15 *rev from* Through summer's heat and winter's cold, *MS. 107 (D), but* heat,] heat
19 its *rev from* her *though ink blot obscures both readings MS. 107 (D)*

See the photograph and transcription of DC MS. 107 (C) 82v, 83v on pp. 620–621.

Cloud-piercing Peak, and desart Heath
Instinctive tribute pay
Nor wants the dim-lit cave a wreath
To honour Thee, sweet May;
But most some little favorite nook
That our own hands have drest
Upon thy train delights to look,
And seems to love thee best.

Time was, when courtly Youths and Maids
At blush of dawn would rise,
And wander forth in forest glades
Thy birth to solemnize.
Though mute the song—to grace the rite,
Untouch'd the hawthorn bough,
Thy Spirit triumphs o'er the Slight:
Man changes but not thou.

Thy feathered Lieges bill and wings
In love's disport employ,
Warm'd by thy influence, creeping things
Awake to silent joy.
Queen art thou still for each gay plant
Where the slim wild deer roves
And serv'd in depths where fishes haunt
Their own mysterious groves

Lo! Streams that April could not check
Are patient of thy rule,
Gurgling in foamy water-break,
Loitering in glassy pool;
By thee, thee only, could be sent
Such gentle mists as glide,
Curling with unconfirm'd intent
On that green mountain's side.

---

25 desart *rev from* distant *MS. 107 (D)*
33 Youths and Maids *rev from* Youth and Maid *MS. 107 (D)*
42 love's] loves *MS. 107 (D)* employ, *rev to* employ *MS. 107 (D)*
50 of *rev from* at *MS. 106*

How delicate the leafy veil
Through which the House of God
Gleams mid the peace of this deep dale,
By few but shepherds trod!
The lowliest huts near beaten Ways
No sooner stand attired
In thy fresh wreaths than they for praise
Peep forth, and are admired.

Season of fancy, and of hope,
Permit not for one hour
A blossom from thy crown to drop,
Nor add to it a flower!
So perfect now is that fine touch
Of self-restraining art,
The modest charm of not too much,
—Part seen imagined part.

Hush feeble Lyre weak words refuse
The service to prolong
To yon exulting Thrush, the Muse
Entrusts the unfinish'd song
His voice shall chaunt in accents clear
Throughout the live long day,
Till the first silver star appear,
The sovereignty of May!

57–58 How from a leafy net-work veil
Through which the House of God *rev to*
How softly through her veil
Of leaves the House of God *rev in pencil to text MS. 107 (D_1)*
alt With Nun-like beauty through a veil *MS. 107 (D_1)*
[?How a] leafy viel [viel *rev to* veil] *rev to*
How a delicate a leafy veil *MS. 107 (D_2)*
How delicate the leafy veil
Which for the House of God*MS. 107 (D_3)*

59 Through [?a] season ịn this deep dale *MS. 107 (D_4)*

60 shepherds *rev from* shepherd *MS. 107 (D)*

61 The] And *rev to* Even *rev to* E'en *MS. 106*

73 *rev from* O listen! if weak words refuse *rev from* Here cease—let words refuse *rev from* Here cease—let words, weak words *MS. 107 (D)*

73–76 *del draft:*
O listen! if weak words
Spirit of love if words refuse
The service
To yon exulting thrush the Muse
Will trust the *MS. 107 (D)*

76 Entrusts *rev from* Will trust *rev from* Entrusts *MS. 107 (D)* unfinish'd] imperfect *rev to* unfinisd *MS. 107 (D)*

77 His *alt in pencil* This *MS. 106* accents *rev in pencil from* accent *MS. 106*

[Text of 1835]

ODE,

COMPOSED ON MAY MORNING.

While from the purpling east departs
  The Star that led the dawn,
Blithe Flora from her couch upstarts,
  For May is on the lawn.
A quickening hope, a freshening glee,
  Foreran the expected Power,
Whose first-drawn breath, from bush and tree,
  Shakes off that pearly shower.

All Nature welcomes Her whose sway,
  Tempers the year's extremes;
Who scattereth lusters o'er noon-day,
  Like morning's dewy gleams;
While mellow warble, sprightly trill,
  The tremulous heart excite;
And hums the balmy air to still
  The balance of delight.

Time was, blest Power! when Youths and Maids
  At peep of dawn would rise,
And wander forth, in forest glades
  Thy birth to solemnize.
Though mute the song—to grace the rite
  Untouched the hawthorn bough,
Thy Spirit triumphs o'er the slight;
  Man changes, but not Thou!

Thy feathered Lieges bill and wings
  In love's disport employ;
Warmed by thy influence, creeping Things
  Awake to silent joy:
Queen art thou still for each gay Plant
  Where the slim wild Deer roves;

---

composed probably completed as a separate poem around mid-July to mid-September 1834
found in DC MSS. 133; 134; 137 (MW and WW); MS. 1835/36
published in *1835, 1836–, 1847M*
classed Sentiment and Reflection *1836–*
reading text *1835*
stanza numbers 1, 2 . . . 8 *del MS. 137*
23 o'er *so 1836–, 1839* e'er *1835*

See the photographs and transcriptions of DC MSS. 133, 15r–21v, and 134, 13r on pp. 622–651.

And served in depths where Fishes haunt
Their own mysterious groves.

Cloud-piercing Peak, and trackless Heath,
Instinctive homage pay;
Nor wants the dim-lit Cave a wreath
To honour Thee, sweet May!
Where Cities fanned by thy brisk airs
Behold a smokeless sky,
Their puniest Flower-pot-nursling dares
To open a bright eye.

And if, on this thy natal morn,
The Pole, from which thy name
Hath not departed, stands forlorn
Of song and dance and game,
Still from the village-green a vow
Aspires to thee addrest,
Wherever peace is on the brow,
Or love within the breast.

Yes! where Love nestles thou canst teach
The soul to love the more;
Hearts also shall thy lessons reach
That never loved before.
Stript is the haughty One of pride,
The bashful freed from fear,
While rising, like the ocean-tide,
In flows the joyous year.

Hush, feeble lyre! weak words, refuse
The service to prolong!
To yon exulting Thrush the Muse
Intrusts the imperfect song;
His voice shall chant, in accents clear,
Throughout the live-long day,
Till the first silver Star appear,
The sovereignty of May.

59 yon *rev from* you *MS. 137*

[Text of 1835]

TO MAY.

THOUGH many suns have risen and set
  Since thou, blithe May, wert born,
And Bards, who hailed thee, may forget
  Thy gifts, thy beauty scorn;
There are who to a birthday strain
  Confine not harp and voice,
But evermore throughout thy reign
  Are grateful and rejoice!

Delicious odours! music sweet,
  Too sweet to pass away!
Oh for a deathless song to meet
  The soul's desire—a lay
That, when a thousand years are told,
  Should praise thee, genial Power!
Through summer heat, autumnal cold,
  And winter's dreariest hour.

Earth, Sea, thy presence feel—nor less,
  If yon ethereal blue
With its soft smile the truth express,
  The Heavens have felt it too.
The inmost heart of man if glad
  Partakes a livelier cheer;
And eyes that cannot but be sad
  Let fall a brightened tear.

Since thy return, through days and weeks
  Of hope that grew by stealth,
How many wan and faded cheeks
  Have kindled into health!
The Old, by thee revived, have said,

---

composed probably completed as a separate poem around mid-July to mid-September 1834
found in DC MSS. 133, 134, 135, 137; MS. 1835/36
published in *1835, 1836–, 1847M*
classed Sentiment and Reflection *1836–*
reading text *1835*
stanza numbers 1, 2 . . . 12 *del MS. 137*
7 evermore *rev from* even more *MS. 137*
17 nor *rev from* not *MS. 137*

See the photographs and transcriptions of DC MSS. 133, 15^r–21^v; 134, 13^r; and 135, 23^r, 23^v on pp. 622–655.

"Another year is ours;"
And wayworn Wanderers, poorly fed,
Have smiled upon thy flowers.

Who tripping lisps a merry song
Amid his playful peers?
The tender Infant who was long
A prisoner of fond fears;
But now, when every sharp-edged blast
Is quiet in its sheath,
His Mother leaves him free to taste
Earth's sweetness in thy breath.

Thy help is with the Weed that creeps
Along the humblest ground;
No Cliff so bare but on its steeps
Thy favours may be found;
But most on some peculiar nook
That our own hands have drest,
Thou and thy train are proud to look,
And seem to love it best.

And yet how pleased we wander forth
When May is whispering, "Come!
Choose from the bowers of virgin earth
The happiest for your home;
Heaven's bounteous love through me is spread
From sunshine, clouds, winds, waves,
Drops on the mouldering turret's head,
And on your turf-clad graves!"

Such greeting heard, away with sighs
For lilies that must fade,
Or "the rathe primrose as it dies
Forsaken" in the shade!
Vernal fruitions and desires
Are linked in endless chase;
While, as one kindly growth retires,
Another takes its place.

And what if thou, sweet May, hast known
Mishap by worm and blight;
If expectations newly blown
Have perished in thy sight;
If loves and joys, while up they sprung,

---

61 Vernal *rev from* Rural *MS. 137*

Were caught as in a snare;
Such is the lot of all the young,
However bright and fair.

Lo! Streams that April could not check
Are patient of thy rule;
Gurgling in foamy water-break,
Loitering in glassy pool:
By thee, thee only, could be sent
Such gentle Mists as glide,
Curling with unconfirmed intent,
On that green mountain's side.

How delicate the leafy veil
Through which yon House of God
Gleams 'mid the peace of this deep dale
By few but shepherds trod!
And lowly Huts, near beaten ways,
No sooner stand attired
In thy fresh wreaths, than they for praise
Peep forth, and are admired.

Season of fancy and of hope,
Permit not for one hour
A blossom from thy crown to drop,
Nor add to it a flower!
Keep, lovely May, as if by touch
Of self-restraining art,
This modest charm of not too much,
Part seen, imagined part!

"Once I could hail (howe'er serene the sky)"

"Late, late yestreen I saw the new moone
Wi' the auld moone in hir arme."
Ballad of Sir Patrick Spence, Percy's Reliques.

Once I could hail (howe'er serene the sky)
The Moon re-entering her monthly round,
No faculty yet given me to espy

---

composed July 25, 1826
found in MW and WW to JK, July 25, 1826; MS. 1832/36 (JC)
published in *1827–*
classed Epitaphs *1836* Miscellaneous Poems *1845, 1850*
reading text *1827*
epigraph *lacking MW and WW to JK*

The dusky Shape within her arms imbound,
That thin memento of effulgence lost
Which some have named her Predecessor's Ghost.

Young, like the Crescent that above me shone,
Nought I perceived within it dull or dim;
All that appeared was suitable to One
Whose fancy had a thousand fields to skim;
To expectations spreading with wild growth,
And hope that kept with me her plighted troth.

I saw (ambition quickening at the view)
A silver boat launched on a boundless flood;
A pearly crest, like Dian's when it threw
Its brightest splendour round a leafy wood;
But not a hint from under-ground, no sign
Fit for the glimmering brow of Proserpine.

Or was it Dian's self that seemed to move
Before me? nothing blemished the fair sight;
On her I looked whom jocund Fairies love,
Cynthia, who puts the *little* stars to flight,
And by that thinning magnifies the great,
For exaltation of her sovereign state.

And when I learned to mark the spectral Shape
As each new Moon obeyed the call of Time,
If gloom fell on me, swift was my escape;
Such happy privilege hath Life's gay Prime,
To see or not to see, as best may please
A buoyant Spirit, and a heart at ease.

Now, dazzling Stranger! when thou meet'st my glance,
Thy dark Associate ever I discern;
Emblem of thoughts too eager to advance
While I salute my joys, thoughts sad or stern;
Shades of past bliss, or phantoms that to gain
Their fill of promised lustre wait in vain.

So changes mortal Life with fleeting years;
A mournful change, should Reason fail to bring
The timely insight that can temper fears,
And from vicissitude remove its sting;

---

25 I learned to mark] aloft I marked *MW and WW to JK*
27 *rev from* From its dominion fleet was my escape; *MW and WW to JK*
28 hath *rev from* of *MW and WW to JK*
29 or *rev from* and *MW and WW to JK*
30 bouyant [bouyant *rev from* daring] Spirit, or *MW and WW to JK*

While Faith aspires to seats in that Domain
Where joys are perfect, neither wax nor wane.

"The Lady whom you here behold"

The Lady whom you here behold
Was once Pigmalion's Wife
He made her first from marble cold
And Venus gave her life.

When fate remov'd her from his arms
Thro' sundry Forms she pass'd
And conquering hearts by various charms
This shape she took at last.

We caught her, true tho' strange th' account
Among a troop of Fairies
Who nightly frisk on our green Mount
And practise strange vagaries.

Her raiment then was scant, so we
Bestowed some pains upon her
Part for the sake of decency
And part to do her honor.

But as no doubt 'twas for her sins
We found her in such plight
She shall do penance stuck with pins
And serve you day and night.

TO ———.

HAPPY the feeling from the bosom thrown
In perfect shape whose beauty Time shall spare

---

composed probably around December 1826
found in Southey Album 2
published in *PW*, IV (1947)
reading text Southey Album 2
19 penance] pennance *Southey Album 2*
20 *no punct Southey Album 2*

---

composed probably around December 1826 or January 1827
found in MS. 1836/45
published in *1827–, 1838*
classed Miscellaneous Sonnets *1827–, 1838*
reading text *1827*
title Dedication. To ———. *1836–* Dedication. *1838*

Though a breath made it, like a bubble blown
For summer pastime into wanton air;
Happy the thought best likened to a stone
Of the sea-beach, when, polished with nice care,
Veins it discovers exquisite and rare,
Which for the loss of that moist gleam atone
That tempted first to gather it. O chief
Of Friends! such feelings if I here present,
Such thoughts, with others mixed less fortunate;
Then smile into my heart a fond belief
That Thou, if not with partial joy elate,
Receiv'st the gift for more than mild content!

TO S. H.

Excuse is needless when with love sincere
Of occupation, not by fashion led,
Thou turn'st the Wheel that slept with dust o'erspread;
My nerves from no such murmur shrink,—tho' near,
Soft as the Dorhawk's to a distant ear,
When twilight shades bedim the mountain's head.
She who was feigned to spin our vital thread
Might smile, O Lady! on a task once dear
To household virtues. Venerable Art,

---

8 that . . . gleam] those . . . gleams *1838*
9–11 That here,
O chief of Friends! such feelings I present,
To thy regard, with thoughts so fortunate,
Were a vain notion; but the hope is dear, *1836–*
If here,
O Friend! such feelings sometimes I present
To thy regard, with thoughts so fortunate,
Then let a hope spring up my heart to cheer *1838*
14 Receiv'st] Receivest *1832*
Wilt smile upon this gift with more than mild content! *1836–; so 1838 but* Gift

---

composed December 12, 1826; completed probably around January 1827
found in SH to MMH, December 13, 1826; MS. 1838/40 (JC); MS. 1836/45 (MW)
published in *1827–, 1838*
classed Miscellaneous Sonnets *1827–, 1838*
reading text *1827*
title Sonnet / To a Lady "apologizing for her Spinning wheel." (the noise rather) *SH to MMH*
2 not by fashion] by caprice not *SH to MMH*
3 that slept] erewhile *SH to MMH*
6 bedim] darken *1836–, 1838*
7 She who was feigned] Even She who toils *MS. 1838/40, 1840–* Even she who toiled *rev to* Even she who toils *rev to* She who was feigned *rev to* Even she who toils *MS. 1836/45*
8 once] so *SH to MMH*
Might smile on work, O Lady, once so dear *1836–, 1838*

Torn from the Poor! yet will kind Heaven protect
Its own, not left without a guiding chart,
If Rulers, trusting with undue respect
To proud discoveries of the Intellect,
Sanction the pillage of man's ancient heart.

"Prithee gentle Lady list"

Prithee gentle Lady list
To a small Ventriloquist
I whose pretty voice you hear
From this paper speaking clear
Have a mother, once a Statue!
I thus boldly looking at you
Do the name of Paphus bear
Fam'd Pygmalion's son and heir
By that wondrous marble wife
That from Venus took her life
Cupid's nephew then am I
Nor unskilled his darts to ply
But from him I crav'd no warrant
Coming thus to seek my parent
Not equipp'd with bow and quiver
Her by menace to deliver
But resolv'd with filial care
Her captivity to share
Hence while on your Toilet she
Is doom'd a Pincushion to be
By her side I'll take my place
As a humble Needlecase
Furnish'd too with dainty thread

---

10 will] shall *1836–, 1838*
11–12 Its own; though Rulers, with undue respect,
Trusting to crowded factory and mart *1836–, 1838*
12 Rulers, trusting] States, reposing *SH to MMH*
13 To] And *1836–, 1838*
14 Sanction] Heed not *1836–, 1838* heart] hearth *SH to MMH*

---

composed probably around December 1826 but by December 21
found in Southey Album 2; Barlow MS. (copy)
published in *PW* Knight 1896
reading text Southey Album 2
1–2 *lacking Barlow MS.*
4 Lady (you will think it queer), *Barlow MS.*
8 Pygmalion's] Pigmalions *Southey Album 2*
11 Cupid's] Cupids *Southey Album 2*
23 Furnish'd] Furnishd *Southey Album 2*

For a Sempstress thorough bred
Then let both be kindly treated
Till the Term for which she's fated
Durance to sustain be over
So will I ensure a Lover
Lady! to your heart's content
But on harshness are you bent?
Bitterly shall you repent
When to Cyprus back I go
And take up my Uncle's bow.

CONCLUSION.

TO ———

If these brief Records, by the Muses' art
Produced as lonely Nature or the strife
That animates the scenes of public life
Inspired, may in thy leisure claim a part;
And if these Transcripts of the private heart
Have gained a sanction from thy falling tears,
Then I repent not: but my soul hath fears
Breathed from eternity; for as a dart
Cleaves the blank air, Life flies: now every day
Is but a glimmering spoke in the swift wheel
Of the revolving week. Away, away,
All fitful cares, all transitory zeal;
So timely Grace the immortal wing may heal,
And honour rest upon the senseless clay.

29 heart's] hearts *Southey Album 2*

composed probably around January but certainly by April 1827
found in MS. 1838/40; MS. 1836/45 (JC)
published in *1827–, 1831, 1838*
classed Miscellaneous Sonnets *1827–, 1831, 1838*
reading text *1827*
6 thy falling *alt* some [?start]ing *del MS. 1838/40*

"Scorn not the Sonnet; Critic, you have frowned"

SCORN not the Sonnet; Critic, you have frowned,
Mindless of its just honours;—with this Key
Shakspeare unlocked his heart; the melody
Of this small Lute gave ease to Petrarch's wound;
A thousand times this Pipe did Tasso sound;
Camöens soothed with it an Exile's grief;
The Sonnet glittered a gay myrtle Leaf
Amid the cypress with which Dante crowned
His visionary brow: a glow-worm Lamp,
It cheered mild Spenser, called from Faery-land
To struggle through dark ways; and when a damp
Fell round the path of Milton, in his hand
The Thing became a Trumpet, whence he blew
Soul-animating strains—alas, too few!

"There is a pleasure in poetic pains"

THERE is a pleasure in poetic pains
Which only Poets know;—'twas rightly said;
Whom could the Muses else allure to tread
Their smoothest paths, to wear their lightest chains?
When happiest Fancy has inspired the Strains,
How oft the malice of one luckless word
Pursues the Enthusiast to the social board,
Haunts him belated on the silent plains!
Yet he repines not, if his thought stand clear
At last of hindrance and obscurity,
Fresh as the Star that crowns the brow of Morn;
Bright, speckless as a softly-moulded tear
The moment it has left the Virgin's eye,
Or rain-drop lingering on the pointed Thorn.

---

composed probably around January but certainly by April 1827
found in Montague MS.
published in *1827–, 1831, 1838*
classed Miscellaneous Sonnets *1827–, 1831, 1831*
reading text *1827*

6 Camöens soothed with it] With it Camoens soothed *with* it *inserted Montague MS.; so 1836–, 1838, but* Camöens

---

composed between about late January and late April 1827
published in *1827–, 1831, 1838*
classed Miscellaneous Sonnets *1827–, 1831, 1838*
reading text *1827*

TO THE CUCKOO.

Not the whole warbling grove in concert heard
When sunshine follows shower, the breast can thrill
Like the first summons, Cuckoo! of thy bill,
With its twin notes inseparably paired.
The Captive, 'mid damp vaults unsunned, unaired,
Measuring the periods of his lonely doom,
That cry can reach; and to the sick man's room
Sends gladness, by no languid smile declared.
The lordly Eagle-race through hostile search
May perish; time may come when never more
The wilderness shall hear the Lion roar;
But, long as Cock shall crow from household perch
To rouse the dawn, soft gales shall speed thy wing,
And thy erratic voice be faithful to the Spring!

"In my mind's eye a Temple, like a cloud"

In my mind's eye a Temple, like a cloud
Slowly surmounting some invidious hill,
Rose out of darkness: the bright Work stood still,
And might of its own beauty have been proud,
But it was fashioned and to God was vowed
By virtues that diffused, in every part,
Spirit divine through forms of human art:
Faith had her arch—her arch, when winds blow loud,
Into the consciousness of safety thrilled;
And Love her towers of dread foundation laid
Under the grave of things; Hope had her spire
Star-high, and pointing still to something higher;
Trembling I gazed, but heard a voice—it said,
Hell-gates are powerless Phantoms when *we* build.

---

composed between about late January and late April 1827
published in *1827–, 1831, 1838*
classed Miscellaneous Sonnets *1827–, 1831, 1838*
reading text *1827*

---

composed between about late January and late April 1827
found in MS. 1836/45 (JC)
published in *1827–, 1831, 1838*
classed Miscellaneous Sonnets *1827–, 1831, 1838*
reading text *1827*

ON SEEING A NEEDLECASE IN THE FORM OF A HARP, THE WORK OF E. M. S.

Frowns are on every Muse's face,
  Reproaches from their lips are sent,
That mimickry should thus disgrace
  The noble Instrument.

A very Harp in all but size!
  Needles for strings in apt gradation!
Minerva's self would stigmatize
  The unclassic profanation.

Even her *own* Needle that subdued
  Arachne's rival spirit,
Though wrought in Vulcan's happiest mood,
  Like station could not merit.

And this, too, from the Laureate's Child,
  A living Lord of melody!
How will her Sire be reconciled
  To the refined indignity?

I spake, when whispered a low voice,
  "Bard! moderate your ire;
"Spirits of all degrees rejoice
  "In presence of the Lyre.

"The Minstrels of Pygmean bands,
  "Dwarf Genii, moonlight-loving Fays,
"Have shells to fit their tiny hands
  "And suit their slender lays.

"Some, still more delicate of ear,
  "Have lutes (believe my words)
"Whose framework is of gossamer,
  "While sunbeams are the chords.

"Gay Sylphs this Miniature will court,

---

composed March or early April 1827
found in Cornell MS. 4; Morgan MS. 3; Monkhouse Album; MS. 1832/36 (MW)
classed Fancy *1827–*
reading text *1827*
title E. M. S.] Edith May Southey *Cornell MS. 4, Morgan MS. 3* Edith May Southey: *Monkhouse Album*
6 Needles for strings] With Needles strung *Cornell MS. 4* With needles strung *Monkhouse Album*
12 Like station] Such honour *1845–*

"Made vocal by their brushing wings,
"And sullen Gnomes will learn to sport
"Around its polished strings;

"Whence strains to love-sick Maiden dear,
"While in her lonely Bower she tries
"To cheat the thought she cannot cheer,
"By fanciful embroideries.

"Trust, angry Bard! a knowing Sprite,
"Nor think the Harp her lot deplores;
"Though mid the stars the Lyre shines bright,
"Love *stoops* as fondly as he soars."

"Her only Pilot the soft breeze the Boat"

HER only Pilot the soft breeze the Boat
Lingers, but Fancy is well satisfied;
With keen-eyed Hope, with Memory, at her side,
And the glad Muse at liberty to note
All that to each is precious, as we float
Gently along; regardless who shall chide
If the Heavens smile, and leave us free to glide,
Happy Associates breathing air remote
From trivial cares. But, Fancy and the Muse,
Why have I crowded this small Bark with you
And others of your kind, Ideal Crew!
While here sits One whose brightness owes its hues

---

30 brushing *inserted Monkhouse Album*
39 shines] shine *1832–*
40 he] she *Cornell MS. 4, Monkhouse Album, Morgan MS. 3*

---

composed around April 1827
found in DC MS. 89
published in *1827–, 1838*
classed Miscellaneous Sonnets *1827–, 1838*
reading text *1827*

1 *rev from* The Stream hath widened to a Lake, *but* the soft *rev from* a soft *MS. 89*
3 With undisturbed remembrance [remembrance *rev to* Remembrance] *rev to* With spritely Hope, with Memory, *with* spritely *rev in pencil to* bright eyed *alt in pencil* keen eyed *MS. 89*
5 All that is prized by either *rev to* All that to each is grateful *MS. 89*
6 regardless *rev from* not caring *MS. 89*
7 *rev from* If they be free to halt and free *MS. 89*
8 Happy Associates *rev from* In social converse, *MS. 89*
9 trivial cares *rev from* present Strife *MS. 89*
10 crowded *so MS. 89, 1836–, 1838* crowded, *1827–1832*
11 kind] tribe *MS. 89*
12 its] it *1827, but errata page rev to text* owes its hues] [?] *MS. 89*

To flesh and blood; no Goddess from above,
No fleeting Spirit, but my own true Love?

Farewell Lines

Farewell Lines was written, as Wordsworth told Isabella Fenwick, for "Charles Lamb and his Sister who had retired from the throngs of London to comparative solitude in the village of Enfield Hert[ds]." The Lambs moved to Chase Side in September 1827, and—after a sojourn in London—Wordsworth visited them there on August 10, 1828. He probably composed the twenty-two-line version of the poem shortly after his visit (see ll. 7–8 of the "Text of MS. 143" and *LY*, I, 626). As with other such "private memorials," Wordsworth withheld the poem from publication until after the death of its recipient.

[Text of MS. 143]

"High bliss is only for a higher state,"
But surely, if severe affliction borne
With patience merit the reward of peace—
Peace they deserve; and may the good which here
Has been accorded, never be withdrawn,
Nor for our life's best promises renounced.
Most soothing was it for a welcome Friend
Fresh from the crowded City, to behold
That lonely union, privacy so deep
Such calm employments, such entire content!
So, when the rain is over, the storm laid,
A pair of Herons sometimes may be seen,
Upon a rocky islet, side by side
Drying their feathers in the sun, at ease;
In Lake and Mountain I again behold
Those happy Creatures thus by Nature paired;
Even as your presence led my thoughts to them
They in their quiet haunts, tho', of such power
Unconscious, will not fail to pay the debt,
And, mid a thousand Images of peace
Concord and love in Heaven or Earth perceived,
Will send a thankful spirit back to you.

---

13 To] True *rev to* Its *MS. 89*

---

composed between September 1827 and August 1828 but probably shortly after August 10, 1828
found in DC MS. 143
reading text DC MS. 143

See the photographs and transcription of *Farewell Lines*, DC MS. 143, 19^r, 19^v, pp. 656–659.

[Text of 1842]

FAREWELL LINES.

"HIGH bliss is only for a higher state,"
But, surely, if severe afflictions borne
With patience merit the reward of peace,
Peace ye deserve; and may the solid good,
Sought by a wise though late exchange, and here
With bounteous hand beneath a cottage-roof
To you accorded, never be withdrawn,
Nor for the world's best promises renounced.
Most soothing was it for a welcome friend,
Fresh from the crowded city, to behold
That lonely union, privacy so deep,
Such calm employments, such entire content.
So, when the rain is over, the storm laid,
A pair of herons oft-times have I seen,
Upon a rocky islet, side by side,
Drying their feathers in the sun, at ease;
And so, when night with grateful gloom had fallen,
Two glowworms in such nearness that they shared,
As seemed, their soft self-satisfying light,
Each with the other, on the dewy ground,
Where He that made them blesses their repose.

---

composed between September 1827 and August 1828; revised and expanded around December 1841 to February 1842
found in DC MSS. 151.1, 151.2; MS. 1842P
published in *1842, 1845–*
classed Affections *1845, 1850*
reading text *1842*
title *lacking MS. 151.1* Farewell lines addressed to friends in retirement. *MS. 151.2; so MS. 1842P (in caps) rev to text*

2 severe afflictions *rev from* affliction *MS. 151.2* severe affliction *MS. 151.1*
4 ye *rev from* they *MS. 151.1*

ye solid good ~~to you~~
4, 6–7 Peace ~~they~~ deserve; & may the ^ ~~good which here~~
~~To you~~
Beneath your ^ lowly cottage roof ~~,~~
With plenteous hand
~~Has been accorded~~, never be withdrawn,
To you accorded never *MS. 151.1*

5 *inserted MS. 151.2*
6 bounteous . . . a *rev from* plenteous . . . your *MS. 151.2*
8 Nor for the world's] Nor for our life's *rev to* Be for the worlds *MS. 151.1*
9 for *rev from* to *MS. 151.2*
12 employments *rev from* enjoyments *MS. 151.1*
13 the rain *rev from* to rain *MS. 151.2*
14 oft-times . . . seen *rev from* sometimes may be seen *MS. 151.1*
17 so *inserted MS. 151.1* hath *rev to* had *MS. 151.1*

See the photographs and transcription of DC MSS. 151.1, 47v and 151.2, 19v on pp. 660–663.

When wandering among lakes and hills I note,
Once more, those creatures thus by nature paired,
And guarded in their tranquil state of life,
Even, as your happy presence to my mind
Their union brought, will they repay the debt,
And send a thankful spirit back to you,
With hope that we, dear Friends! shall meet again.

Extract from the Strangers book
Station Winandermere

"Lord & Lady Darlington, Lady Vane, Miss
"Taylor & Cap[n] Stamp pronounce this Lake
"superior to Lac de Geneve, Lago de Como,
"Lago Maggiore, L'Eau de Zurick, Loch Lomond
"Loch Ketterine or the Lakes of Killarney"—

On seeing the above

My Lord and Lady Darlington
I would not speak in snarling tone
Nor to you good Lady Vane
Would I give one moment's pain
Nor Miss Taylor Captain Stamp
Would I your flights of *memory* cramp
Yet having spent a summer's day
On the green margin of Loch Tay
And doubled (prospects ever bettering)
The mazy reaches of Loch Ketterine
And more than once been free at Luss
Loch Lomond's beauties to discuss
And *wish'd* at least to hear the blarney
Of the sly boatmen of Killarney
And dipt my hand in dancing wave
Of "Eau de Zurich Lac Genêve"
And bow'd to many a Major Domo
On stately terraces of Como
And seen the Simplon's forehead hoary
Reclinèd on Lago Maggiore

---

composed between mid-September 1827 and September 1829
found in Monkhouse Album (A) and (B)
published in *PW* Knight 1889, vol. 10
reading text Monkhouse Album (A)
title book / Station Winandermere] at the Station Windermere *MS. B*
4 one] a *Monkhouse Album (B)*
8 green margin] margin *Monkhouse Album (B)*
11 And] Had *Monkhouse Album (B)*

At breathless eventide at rest
On the broad water's placid breast
I, not insensible Heaven knows
To the charms this station shows,
Must tell you Cap^{n} Lord and Ladies,
For honest truth one Poet's trade is,
That your praise appears to me
Folly's own Hyperbole—!

"Four fiery steeds impatient of the rein"

Four fiery steeds impatient of the rein
Whirled us o'er sunless ground beneath a sky
As void of sunshine, when, from that wide Plain,
Clear tops of far-off Mountains we descry,
Like a Sierra of cerulean Spain,
All light and lustre. Did no heart reply?
Yes, there was One;—for One, asunder fly
The thousand links of that ethereal chain;
And green vales open out, with grove and field,
And the fair front of many a happy Home;
Such tempting spots as into vision come

---

22 water's] waters *Monkhouse Album (A, B)*

---

composed perhaps around December 11, 1827, but by January 24, 1828
found in DC MSS. 107, 106 (A) 33^{v}, (B) 33^{v}P^{v}; 135; 137 (MW); 138 (MW)
published in *1835, 1836–, 1838*
classed Miscellaneous Sonnets *1836–, 1838*
reading text *1835*
title Sonnet *MS. 107*
9 grove *alt* [?brooks] *del MS. 106 (A)*
10 fair front] bright looks *MS. 107* bright looks *alt in pencil and ink* fair front *MS. 106 (A)*
11–14 Such tempting spots such scnes [scnes *rev to* Scnes] of [of *rev to* on *rev to* for] peaceful life
As shape themselves and into vision come
While tented Sodiers sick of earthly strife
Gaze on the sun [sun *rev to* Moon] by parting clouds revealed. *MS. 107*
Such tempting spots, such scenes for peaceful life
As shape themselves, and into vision come
While tented Soldiers, sick of earthly strife,
Gaze on the [?sun] [?sun *rev to* moon] by parting clouds revealed *rev to*
Such tempting spots, as into vision come
While Soldiers weary of the Arms they wield,
And sick at heart of strifeful Christendom,
Gaze on the moon, by parting clouds revealed. *MS. 106 (A)*

While Soldiers, of the weapons that they wield
Weary, and sick of strifeful Christendom,
Gaze on the moon by parting clouds revealed.

ROMAN ANTIQUITIES DISCOVERED,
AT BISHOPSTONE, HEREFORDSHIRE.

While poring Antiquarians search the ground
Upturned with curious pains, the Bard, a Seer,
Takes fire:—The men that have been reappear;
Romans for travel girt, for business gowned,
And some recline on couches, myrtle-crowned,
In festal glee: why not? For fresh and clear,
As if its hues were of the passing year,
Dawns this time-buried pavement. From that mound
Hoards may come forth of Trajans, Maximins,
Shrunk into coins with all their warlike toil:
Or a fierce impress issues with its foil
Of tenderness—the Wolf, whose suckling Twins
The unlettered Ploughboy pities when he wins
The casual treasure from the furrowed soil.

12–13 While Soldiers, weary of the Arms they wield, [wield, *rev to* wield] *MS. 137*
And sick at heart of strifeful Christendom, *MSS. 106 (B), 135, 137; MS. 138 as MS. 137 but rev to text*
12 of the weapons that] weary of the arms *1836–, 1838, 1839*
13 Weary, and sick] And sick at heart *MS. 106 (B), 1836–, 1838, 1839*

---

composed probably between December 11, 1827, and January 24, 1828
found in DC MSS. 107, 106, 135; Betz MS. 1; DC MS. 137 (MW)
published in *1835, 1836–, 1838*
classed Miscellaneous Sonnets *1836–, 1838*
reading text *1835*
title *lacking MS. 106* Sonnet *MS. 107* Composed on / The site of a Roman Villa—Herefordshire *Betz MS. 1* ROMAN . . . HEREFORDSHIRE. *MW rev from* ROMAN ANTIQUITIES DISCOVERED. *MS. 137* Roman antiquities discovered *MW added MS. 135*
1–3 Let Antiquarians soberly expound
Pampering minute regards—The Poet here
Takes fire; before—around him reappear *Betz MS. 1*
1 poring] curious MS. 107 peering *rev to* poring [?*with* patient *in pencil, eras*] *MS. 106* search] turn *MS. 107*
2 Pampering minute regards, [the Poet here *rev to* the Bard—a Seer *rev to*] The Bard a Seer *MS. 107* pains *rev from* [?care] *MS. 135*
5 myrtle *rev in pencil from* marble *Betz MS. 1*
6 In *rev from* W *MS. 107*
8–9 Da{wns / wn} this time-buried pavement;~~and~~ that mound [From that ~~moun~~]
Hoards may come ~~hoards of~~ forth
~~Yields of its Others~~ [of] Trajans Ma{x / sc}imins *MS. 107*
10 Shrunk *rev from* Shrink *MS. 107*
11 a] that *Betz MS. 1* issues *rev to* issue *MS. 107* issue *MS. 106, Betz MS. 1*

ST. CATHERINE OF LEDBURY.

WHEN human touch, as monkish books attest,
Nor was applied nor could be, Ledbury bells
Broke forth in concert flung adown the dells,
And upward, high as Malvern's cloudy crest;
Sweet tones, and caught by a noble Lady blest
To rapture! Mabel listened at the side
Of her loved Mistress: soon the music died,
And Catherine said, "Here I set up my rest."
Warned in a dream, the Wanderer long had sought
A home that by such miracle of sound
Must be revealed:—she heard it now, or felt
The deep, deep joy of a confiding thought;
And there, a saintly Anchoress she dwelt
Till she exchanged for heaven that happy ground.

To——— ("'Wait, prithee, wait!' this answer Lesbia threw")

Wordsworth probably composed the sonnet *To*——— ("'Wait, prithee, wait!' this answer Lesbia threw") while visiting at Brinsop Court in December 1827 and January 1828. It seems likely that he included it among the sonnets sent to Frederic Mansel Reynolds for publication in *The Keepsake* (1829), but it did not appear there (see the note to *St. Catherine of Ledbury*, p. 435, below).

Ellen Loveday Walker, so identified in DC MS. 89 and Dora Wordsworth's copy of the poem in Betz MS. 1, was the daughter of the rector of Brinsop. The earliest

---

composed between December 11, 1827, and January 25, 1828
found in DC MSS. 89, 107 (A) 16^{v} and (B) 25^{r}; 106; 135; 137 (MW)
published in *1835, 1836–, 1838*
classed Miscellaneous Sonnets *1836–, 1838*
reading text *1835*
title Sonnet *etc MS. 107 (B) untitled MS. 107 (A)*
1 monkish *rev from* monki[?s] *MS. 107 (B)*
2 Ledbury] Lethbury *MS. 107 (A)*
3 flung adown the dells,] proof that Miracles *alt* flung adown the dells [dells *rev to* Dells] *(pen over pencil) MS. 107 (A)*
4 To serve a holy purpose had not ceas'd *rev in pencil to* And high as [?cloudy] Malverns rocky etc *alt in pencil* upward high [?as] Malverns *rev to* And upward high as Malverns cloudy crest, *alt in pencil* [*illeg word rev to* And] upwards [upwards *rev to* upward], high as Malverns cloudy crest *MS. 107 (A)* cloudy *rev from* rocky *MS. 107 (B)*
5 a noble Lady] One who listen'd *MS. 107 (A)*
6 Mabel *alt* The Maid *MS. 107 (A)*
8 "Here] 'Here *rev from* [?t]here *MS. 107 (A)*
10 that *rev from* [?which] *MS. 107 (B)* which *MS. 107 (A)* by . . . sound] by such wondrous sound *rev in pencil to* by like [?miracle] [?] [?wondrous] *rev to* by like miracle of sound *MS. 107 (A)*
11 Must] Might *alt* Must *pen over pencil MS. 107 (A)* felt *rev from* caught *MS. 107 (A)*
13 saintly] sainted *MS. 107 (A)* Anchoress] hermitess *rev to* Hermitess *alt* Anchoress *MS. 107 (A)*

See the photograph and transcription of *St. Catherine of Ledbury*, DC MS. 89, 118^{r}, pp. 664–665.

form of "Wait, prithee, wait," found in Houghton MS. 1, differs substantially from the version published in 1835; it lacks the motto and has, in its unrevised form, nine lines that differ from the published version. The underlying text in MS. 89 forms the basis for the first reading text with an *apparatus* showing Wordsworth's revisions in MS. 89 and the details from Houghton MS. 1 and from Betz MS. 1. The motto first appears in MS. 89, where Dorothy Wordsworth added it at the foot of the page beneath a copy of *St. Catherine of Ledbury*, probably because she had no room for it above her copy of "To Ellen Loveday Walker," but without indicating the epigraph's proper placement. The second reading text is based on the 1835 printing, with all other variants appended to it.

[Text of MS. 89]

To Ellen Loveday Walker

[Miss not the occasion; by the forelock take
That Power of Powers, the never-halting Time
Lest a mere moment's putting-off should make
Mischance almost as heavy as a crime.]

"Wait, prithee wait!" are words which Lesbia threw
Forth to her Dove, and sate—all further heed
Suspended, while her joyous fingers flew
Across the Harp, with soul-engrossing speed;
But when her thoughts were from the thraldom freed
Of her own pastime, Lesbia rose and drew
Tow'rd the shut casement, where the Favorite, true
To habits and affections or through need
Of shelter, had sought entrance. O the shriek
Sent from that voice, so lately to a strain
Of harmony attuned—the terror, pain,

---

composed between December 11, 1827, and around January 24, 1828
found in Houghton MS. 1, DC MS. 89, Betz MS. 1
reading text DC MS. 89
title To Ellen Loveday Walker] *untitled Houghton MS. 1* To *rev to* On *MS. 89* An incident/which occur'd to Ellen Loveday Walker *Betz MS. 1*
epigraph lacking Houghton MS. 1, Betz MS. 1; added by DW at foot of page MS. 89
1 which] that *Houghton MS. 1* are words which *rev to* said *rev to* this answer *MS. 89*
2 and sate—all *rev to* and took no *MS. 89*
3 Suspended, while her joyous *rev to* Her eye was busy while her *MS. 89*
5 *rev to* But from that bondage when her thoughts were freed *MS. 89*
6 Of her own pastime, Lesbia [Lesbia *rev to* up she] rose and drew *rev to* Promptly she rose and tow'rd the casement drew *MS. 89*
7 *rev to* From thence [From thence *rev to* Whence] the poor unregarded favourite true *MS. 89* the *rev from* her *Houghton MS. 1*
8–9 *rev to*
To [To *rev from* ?For] old affections had been heard to plead
With flapping wing for entrance.—O the shriek *MS. 89*
8 through *over eras Betz MS. 1*
10 Sent from that *rev to* Sent from Lesbias *rev to* Lesbias [?softer] *rev to text MS. 89*

And self-reproach! for from aloft a kite
Pounced, and the Dove, which from its ruthless beak
She could not rescue, perish'd in her sight.

[Text of 1835]

TO ———.

[Miss not the occasion; by the forelock take
That subtile Power, the never-halting Time,
Lest a mere moment's putting-off should make
Mischance almost as heavy as a crime.]

"WAIT, prithee, wait!" this answer Lesbia threw
Forth to her Dove, and took no further heed;
Her eye was busy, while her fingers flew
Across the harp, with soul-engrossing speed;
But from that bondage when her thoughts were freed
She rose, and toward the close-shut casement drew,
Whence the poor unregarded Favorite, true
To old affections, had been heard to plead
With flapping wing for entrance. What a shriek
Forced from that voice so lately tuned to a strain
Of harmony!—a shriek of terror, pain,

---

12 from aloft a *rev from* when aloft the *Houghton MS. 1*
13 Pouncing [Pouncing *rev to* Pouncd] with ruthless talons, ravenous beak, *alt* Pouncd with . . . ravenous *as text Houghton MS. 1*
14 On the poor Dove, devoured it in her sight.— *rev to*
She cannot rescue perish'd, in her sight *Houghton MS. 1*
She cannot rescue, perished in her sight. *Betz MS. 1*

---

composed after late January 1828; revised before publication in 1835
found in DC MSS. 106; 135; 137 (A) and (B), both on p. 237 (MW); 138
published in *1835, 1836–, 1838*
classed Miscellaneous Sonnets *1836–, 1838*
reading text *1835*
title To ——.] To Ellen Loveday Walker. *MS. 106*
epigraph subtile Power] Power of Powers *MS. 106*
3 eye was busy *DW rev to* song resuming *del in pencil MS. 106*
5 But from that *DW rev to* From that sweet *WW reinstated* But *in pencil without del* sweet *MS. 106*
6 Promptly she rose, and tow'rd the casement drew *MS. 106* drew, *over illeg eras MS. 135*
7 true *over illeg eras MS. 135*
9 What a *rev in pencil from* Oh! the *MS. 106*
10 Sent from that [that *rev to* a] voice, so lately to a strain *MS. 106*
10–14 From lips that breathed so lately a soft strain
Of harmony—for from aloft a kite
Pounced and the maidens Dove which from its beak
She could not rescue that had sought in vain
Timely protection perishd in her sight *alt in pencil MS. 106*
11 Of harmony attuned—the terror, pain, *MS. 106*

And self-reproach!—for, from aloft, a Kite
Pounced, and the Dove, which from its ruthless beak
She could not rescue, perished in her sight!

FILIAL PIETY.

UNTOUCHED through all severity of cold,
Inviolate, whate'er the cottage hearth
Might need for comfort, or for festal mirth,
That Pile of Turf is half a century old:
Yes, Traveller! fifty winters have been told
Since suddenly the dart of death went forth
'Gainst him who raised it,—his last work on earth;

---

12 *DW entered the words* And self-reproach *at the end of l. 11 then del MS. 106*
13 the Dove *DW rev from* from aloft *MS. 106*

---

composed between around December 13, 1827, and January 9, 1828
found in Houghton MS. 1; Southey Album 1; DC MSS. 89, 107, 106; Betz MS. 1
published in *Casket* (1829), *1832–*, *1838*
classed Miscellaneous Sonnets *1832–*, *1838*
reading text *1832*
title *lacking Houghton MS. 1* Filial Piety or the turf Pile between Ormskirk and Preston Lancashire *Southey Album 1* [Stagecoach Inspirations by an Outside Passenger. *del*] / N° 1 / Filial Piety[; or / The Turf Pile between Ormskirk and Preston. *del*] *MS. 89* Sonnet / Filial Piety. *MS. 107* THE PEAT STACK. / SONNET. *Casket* Filial Piety or the Turf Pile between Ormskirk & Preston—Lancashire *Betz MS. 1* FILIAL PIETY. (On the Way-side between Preston and Liverpool.) *1836– but 1845, 1849, 1850* Wayside
epigraph The traveller, who has had frequent occasion to pass the high road between Ormskirk and Preston in Lancashire, may have noticed for many years a pile of turf for fuel, of unvarying dimensions during the winter and summer season. The following lines record its history. *Casket*
1 Untouched] Sacred, *1838* cold *rev from* pain *MS. 107*

Thence by his Son more prized than aught which gold
Could purchase—watched, preserved by his own hands,
That, faithful to the Structure, still repair
Its waste.—Though crumbling with each breath of air,
In annual renovation thus it stands—
Rude Mausoleum! but wrens nestle there,
And red-breasts warble when sweet sounds are rare.

A GRAVE-STONE UPON THE FLOOR IN THE CLOISTERS OF WORCESTER CATHEDRAL.

"*Miserrimus!*" and neither name nor date,
Prayer, text, or symbol, graven upon the stone;
Nought but that word assigned to the unknown,
That solitary word—to separate
From all, and cast a cloud around the fate

8–10 Thence to the Son endear'd; by such strong hold
Link'd to his Fathers memory that his hands
Preserv'd the Fabric, and do still repair *Houghton MS. 1; so Betz MS. 1 and Southey Album 1 but* endear'd] endeared Fathers] Father's Fabric] fabric *Southey Album 1 only* *MS. 89 as Houghton MS. 1 but* the Son *rev to* his Son by] —by Link'd to *rev to* Link'd with Fathers] Father's Thence to his Son endeared; *alt* Dear therefore to the [the *rev to* his] Son *MS. 107 as MS. 89 rev but no dash and* fabric,] fabric
Thence to the son endear'd, by such strong hold
Link'd to his father's memory, that his hands
Preserved the fabric, and do still repair *Casket*
~~to~~ ~~prized which [?]~~
Thence by his Son [more prized than aught which gold *over eras*]
{Could purchase — watched, preserved by his} own hands.
{Watchd preserved thus [? ?]}
{That faithful to the Structures still
{Pleased with [?] structures [?] repair *MS. 106*
That faithful to the structures
{still
{the
Could purchase—watchd, preserved
{prompt
Blessed is [?the]{[?]
still repair *pencil draft MS. 106*
Thence has it, with the Son, so strong a hold
Upon his Father's memory, that his hands,
Through reverence, touch it only to repair *1836–, 1838*

11 breath *inserted MS. 89*

---

composed between around December 15, 1827, and January 9, 1828
found in Yale MS. 1; Cornell MS. 5; Southey Album 1; DC MS. 106; Betz MS. 1
published in *Keepsake* (1829); *1832–, 1838*
classed Miscellaneous Sonnets *1832–, 1838*
reading text *1832*
title *untitled Yale MS. 4* Sonnet./W. Wordsworth./A Gravestone . . . Cathedral. *Keepsake* UPON] On *Cornell MS. 2, Southey Album 1, MS. 106, Betz MS. 1* IN] of *Cornell MS. 5, Betz MS. 1* CATHEDRAL.] Cathedral / Sonnet. *MS. 106*
2 or] nor *Yale MS. 1, Cornell MS. 5, Southey Album 1, Betz MS. 1*
5 From] from *written first at end of l. 4, then deleted Yale MS. 1*

Of him who lies beneath. Most wretched one,
Who chose his Epitaph? Himself alone
Could thus have dared the grave to agitate,
And claim, among the dead, this awful crown;
Nor doubt that He marked also for his own,
Close to these cloistral steps a burial-place,
That every foot might fall with heavier tread,
Trampling upon his vileness. Stranger, pass
Softly!—To save the contrite, Jesus bled.

THE WISHING-GATE.

In the vale of Grasmere, by the side of the high-way, leading to Ambleside, is a gate, which, time out of mind, has been called the wishing-gate, from a belief that wishes formed or indulged there have a favourable issue.

Hope rules a land for ever green:
All powers that serve the bright-eyed Queen
Are confident and gay;
Clouds at her bidding disappear;
Points she to aught?—the bliss draws near,
And Fancy smooths the way.

Not such the land of wishes—there
Dwell fruitless day-dreams, lawless prayer,
And thoughts with things at strife;
Yet how forlorn should *ye* depart,
Ye superstitions of the *heart*,
How poor were human life!

---

11 these . . . a *rev from* this . . . his *Yale MS. 1*
14/ Finis *Betz MS. 1*

---

composed probably early in 1828, certainly by early March
found in Victoria MS. 1; Keswick MS.; DC MSS. 108, 131, 151.1; MS. 1832/36 (MW)
published in *Keepsake* (1829), *1832–*
classed Sentiment and Reflection *1832* Imagination *1836–*
reading text *1832*
title The Wishing-gate. / By W. Wordsworth. *Keepsake*
headnote *lacking Victoria MS. 1, MSS. 108, 131* the high-way,] the public road *rev to* the High-way *Keswick MS.* the old high-way *1836–*
stanza numbers 2, 3 *only in MS. 131*
12/13 Whence but from You, misdeem'd of Powers!
The Faith that in auspicious Hours
Builds castles out of air?
Bodings unsanction'd by the Will
Flow from your [?visionary] skill,
And teach us to [?have care]. *del Victoria MS. 1*

When magic lore abjured its might,
Ye did not forfeit one dear right,
One tender claim abate;
Witness this symbol of your sway,
Surviving near the public way,
The rustic Wishing-gate!

Inquire not if the faery race
Shed kindly influence on the place,
Ere northward they retired;
If here a warrior left a spell,
Panting for glory as he fell;
Or here a saint expired.

Enough that all around is fair,
Composed with Nature's finest care,
And in her fondest love;
Peace to embosom and content,
To overawe the turbulent,
The selfish to reprove.

Yea! even the Stranger from afar,
Reclining on this moss-grown bar,
Unknowing, and unknown,
The infection of the ground partakes,
Longing for his Belov'd—who makes
All happiness her own.

Then why should conscious Spirits fear
The mystic stirrings that are here,
The ancient faith disclaim?
The local Genius ne'er befriends
Desires whose course in folly ends,
Whose just reward is shame.

---

19 Inquire *rev to* I ask *Victoria MS. 1*
31–36 *inserted Victoria MS. 1*
31 Yea!] Yes, *Victoria MS. 1* Yes! *MSS. 108, 131, Keswick MS., Keepsake*
36 own *rev from illeg word Victoria MS. 1*
42/43 On, with his favour Ye who skim
Oer life in boat of gallant trim,
Equipp'd with oar and sail;
Who sparing not the Rower's arm
Solicit, though a blameless charm
The [?succour] of the gale! *del Victoria MS. 1*

Smile if thou wilt, but not in scorn,
If some, by ceaseless pains outworn,
Here crave an easier lot;
If some have thirsted to renew
A broken vow, or bind a true,
With firmer, holier knot.

And not in vain, when thoughts are cast
Upon the irrevocable past,
Some penitent sincere
May for a worthier future sigh,
While trickles from his downcast eye
No unavailing tear.

The Worldling, pining to be freed
From turmoil, who would turn or speed
The current of his fate,
Might stop before this favoured scene,
At Nature's call, nor blush to lean
Upon the Wishing-gate.

The Sage, who feels how blind, how weak
Is man, though loth such help to *seek,*
Yet, passing, here might pause,
And yearn for insight to allay
Misgiving, while the crimson day
In quietness withdraws;

Or when the church-clock's knell profound
To Time's first step across the bound
Of midnight makes reply;
Time pressing on with starry crest,
To filial sleep upon the breast
Of dread eternity!

---

44 If *rev to* That *MS. 1832/36*
45 an easier *rev from* a happier *Victoria MS. 1, MS. 108*
50 Upon . . . irrevocable *alt* On guilt . . . irrevocably *del Victoria MS. 1*
53 from his *inserted MS. 131*
58 Might stop *rev from* [?May cease] *Victoria MS. 1* this *over illeg eras MS. 108*
64 yearn] thirst *MS. 1832/36–*
65 Misgiving *rev in pencil and ink from* Misgivings *Keswick MS.*

A TRADITION OF DARLEY DALE, DERBYSHIRE.

'TIS said that to the brow of yon fair hill
Two Brothers clomb, and, turning face from face,
Nor one look more exchanging, grief to still
Or feed, each planted on that lofty place
A chosen Tree; then, eager to fulfil
Their courses, like two new-born rivers, they
In opposite directions urged their way
Down from the far-seen mount. No blast might kill
Or blight that fond memorial;—the trees grew,
And now entwine their arms; but ne'er again
Embraced those Brothers upon earth's wide plain;
Nor aught of mutual joy or sorrow knew
Until their spirits mingled in the sea
That to itself takes all—Eternity.

"The unremitting voice of nightly streams"

The title given to "The unremitting voice of nightly streams" in a late draft (DC MS. 143, 41ᵛ), "Introduction to the Somnambulist," recalls the early drafts of 1828 but confirms only that in the early 1840s Wordsworth wanted to introduce the one poem with the other. The link is suggestive. *The Somnambulist* (composed 1826–1828) features a knight who, imagining he has caused the madness and death of his beloved, "built a cell" and "In hermits' weeds repose he found . . . Beside the torrent dwelling—bound / By one deep heart-controlling sound" (ll. 147–152). In drafts of "The unremitting voice" in DC MS. 89 there are references to a knight and a hermit, and the theme of the poem has similarities with the opening stanza of *The Somnambulist* (see the transcription of "The unremitting voice" on p. 671); in both poems the sound from a distant and secluded stream speaks to the "spirit" of the listener.

A similar confluence of knight, hermit, and cell occurs in *Effusion in the Pleasure-ground on the Banks of the Bran, near Dunkeld*, ll. 46–73, a passage Wordsworth seems to refer to in the margin opposite the draft for ll. 1–11 of "The unremitting voice" in MS. 89, 91ᵛ (B), where he has written "The Hermits Cell nr. Knaresboro." He received the inspiration for the *Effusion*—and presumably

---

composed probably in early 1828, but by March
found in DC MSS. 89, 106, 134; MS. 1845W; Southey Album 1; Betz MS. 1
published in *Keepsake* (1829), *1832–*, *1838*
classed Miscellaneous Sonnets *1832–*, *1838*
reading text *1832*
title Tradition of Darley-dale / Derbyshire *Southey Album 1, Betz MS. 1, Keepsake* A Tradition of Oken Hill in Darley Dale, Derbyshire. *1836–, 1838, but* Oken] Oker *MS. 1845W, 1850*
3 look] word *MSS. 106, 134*
11 Embraced *inserted MS. 106* those] these those *rev from* Those *MS. 106*

composed part of it—in 1814 during a tour of Scotland (see *Poems, 1807–1820,* pp. 526–527); but though he published *Memorials of a Tour in Scotland, 1814,* in the 1820 *Poems,* he did not include *Effusion* in the sequence until he published the five-volume *Poetical Works* in 1827. In the note published with the poem in 1827 he identified "St. Robert's cell" (l. 55) as situated "On the banks of the Nid, near Knaresborough," in Yorkshire, a place he had visited, probably more than once, between 1788 and 1806 (*Chronology: MY,* p. 63). In these lines Wordsworth compares the undignified memorial to Ossian at Dunkeld with the "Effigies" of the Knight in St. Robert's Chapel near Knaresborough. The Knight, drawing his sword from its "dull sheath," guards the Hermit's "cell"—

> his loved retreat,
> Where altar-stone and rock-hewn seat
> Still hint that quiet rest is found,
> Even by the *Living,* under ground.
> [ll. 64–67]

Moreover, just preceding "The unremitting voice" in MS. 89, and probably entered first, is a fair copy in the handwriting of Dora Wordsworth and John Carter of *Composed when a probability existed of our being obliged to quit Rydal Mount as a Residence.* Written in 1826, the more developed version of the poem addressed the spring behind Rydal Mount with the lines:

> Thou . . . hast cheared a simple board
> With beverage pure as ever fixed the choice
> Of Hermit dubious where to scoop his cell.
> [ll. 11–14; *Tuft,* p. 77]

There is evidence that "The unremitting voice" may date from 1828 in the placement of drafts of this poem on the same page with the 1828 draft of stanza 12 of *On the Power of Sound.* Both placement and handwriting suggest that "The unremitting voice" was added shortly after the lines from *On the Power of Sound* (see the full-page photographs of MS. 89, 91^v–92^r, on pp. 666–667). In the *Power of Sound* entry both the shade of ink used and the thickness of stroke match those of the draft of "The unremitting voice" that lies nearest to it. The phrase "heart-controlling sound" from *The Somnambulist* occurs in some of these drafts of "The unremitting voice," while the word "controlling" is found in the stanza from *On the Power of Sound* and is used in the same way (that is, the power of sounds from nature subdue, or "control," the passions). Similarly, the first two lines of the draft on MS. 89, 91^v (version B), "The unsuspended voice of mountain streams / Tires not the day nor wastes in night its powers," are verbally close to the opening lines of stanza 2 from the first reading text of *On the Power of Sound,* "The headlong streams and fountains / Tire not the day, nor waste by night their powers" (alteration of the second line of *Sound* in the final version obscured the parallel). Jeffrey C. Robinson has noted the links among the three poems in his article "The Power of Sound: 'The Unremitting Voice of Nightly Streams'" in *WC* 23 (1992): 176–179.

Finally, the lines that may be draft for *The Triad* were added in the margin of leaf 92^r of MS. 89 after the first two versions of "The unremitting voice" were entered, and on the same page with that stanza from *On the Power of Sound* which originally appeared among drafts for *The Triad.* This proximity suggests that while working on this page (92^r) Wordsworth may still have associated this *On the Power of Sound* stanza with *The Triad,* which he was composing in 1828. And if so, then the likely date for all of this work is 1828.

Not published until the revised stereotype edition of 1846, "The unremitting voice of nightly streams" (where Wordsworth dated it 1846) seems likely, then, to have been first drafted in 1828 (in five versions in MS. 89), composed in a version near its final form in 1840–1842 (MS. 143), and revised before publication in 1846. The two earliest drafts, on 92^r of MS. 89, present an unfinished poem of thirteen or fourteen lines. Soon after entering this form of the poem Wordsworth expanded it to seventeen lines (91^v), developing the section concerning the "hermit" as "knight," and thus appearing deliberately to link the poem to *The Somnambulist.* The first reading text, representing the most developed stage of this version, is based on the draft at the top of 91^v of MS. 89.

Wordsworth seems to have put the poem aside until the early 1840s: it appears in three new drafts in MS. 143 (on 41^v, 42^r, 42^v, and 43^v) that were entered on pages of existing fair copies of two poems, *The Norman Boy*—read to Henry Crabb Robinson in January 1841—and its *Sequel,* both of which were composed in 1840–1841 and published in 1842. The first of these drafts (41^v–42^r), titled "Introduction to the Somnambulist," is similar to the latest version of the poem in MS. 89 (the third on 91^v). In the two later drafts in MS. 143, having dropped the link to *The Somnambulist,* Wordsworth moved toward the first published version of "The unremitting voice" as it appeared in the *Poetical Works* of 1846. Accordingly, the second reading text is based on this published version.

We provide photographs and transcriptions of the entries in MS. 89 (excluding the draft drawn on for the first reading text) and two of the three copies in MS. 143 (excluding the latest, which replicates the 1846 text). Variants from MS. 89, 92^r (version A) are appended to the first reading text and those from MS. 143, 43^v, appear in the *apparatus* for the second reading text. The first two facing photographs for this poem (pp. 666–667, below) reproduce the opening in MS. 89 where drafts of "The unremitting voice" may be seen in relation to one another and to the material from *On the Power of Sound* and the lines associated with *The Triad.*

[Text of MS. 89 (C)]

The unremitting voice of mountain streams
That calls the breeze to modulate its powers
If neither soothing to the worm that gleams
Through dusky grass—the small birds hushed in bowers
Nor unto silent leaves and drowsy flowers
(Yet who what is shall measure by what seems
  To be or not to be
Or tax high heav'n with prodigality,)
That voice it has been known to mix with sleep
And regulate the notions of our dreams
Once for event how strange a Knight full well
Had learned, who scoop'd into a cell
A rock impending from a shaggy steep
  That he in hermits weeds might dwell
  Forever bound
To one deep solemn heart-controlling sound
Why let these words to courteous Listeners tell.

[Text of 1846]

THE unremitting voice of nightly streams
That wastes so oft, we think, its tuneful powers,
If neither soothing to the worm that gleams

---

composed probably in 1828
found in DC MS. 89 (A–E) 91^{v}, 92^{r}
reading text DC MS. 89 (C)
1 unremitting *alt* neer suspended *MS. 89 (C)*
2 That calls *rev from* Calls on *MS. 89 (C)*
4 Through] Throgh *MS. 89 (C)* hushed in *rev from* in their *MS. 89 (C)*
9 voice] voce been] been to *MS. 89 (C)*
10 our dreams *rev from* a dream *MS. 89 (C)*
12 scoop'd *alt* hewed *MS. 89 (C)*
13 from *rev from* on shaggy *rev from* shall *MS. 89 (C)*
16 heart-controlling *rev from* [?]eart controlling *MS. 89 (C)*
17 courteous *rev from* simple *MS. 89 (C)*

---

composed probably early 1828 and revised in the early 1840s but by early July 1846
found in DC MS. 143 (A) 41^{v}–42^{r}, (B) 42^{v}, and (C) 43^{v}
published in *1846, 1850*
classed Sentiment and Reflection *1846, 1850*
reading text *1846*
~~The unremitting Voice of nightly~~
The unremitting {V nightly streams
1 ~~The nightly~~ voice of ~~Streams~~ *MS. 143 (C)*

See the photographs and transcriptions of DC MS. 89 (A–D), 91^{v}, 92^{r} on pp. 668–673 and those of DC MS. 143 (A), 41^{v}–42^{r} and (B), 42^{v} on pp. 674–679.

Through dewy grass, nor small birds hushed in bowers,
Nor unto silent leaves and drowsy flowers,—
That voice of unpretending harmony
(For who what is shall measure by what seems
To be, or not to be,
Or tax high Heaven with prodigality?)
Wants not a healing influence that can creep
Into the human breast, and mix with sleep
To regulate the motion of our dreams
For kindly issues—as through every clime
Was felt near murmuring brooks in earliest time;
As at this day, the rudest swains who dwell
Where torrents roar, or hear the tinkling knell
Of water-breaks, with grateful heart could tell.

THE GLEANER.

(SUGGESTED BY A PICTURE.)

THAT happy gleam of vernal eyes,
Those locks from summer's golden skies,
    That o'er thy brow are shed;
That cheek—a kindling of the morn,
That lip—a rose-bud from the thorn,
    I saw;—and Fancy sped
To scenes Arcadian, whispering, through soft air,
Of bliss that grows without a care,
Of happiness that never flies—
How can it where love never dies?
Of promise whispering, where no blight

---

4 nor *rev from* or *MS. 143 (C)*
5 drowsy *alt (twice)* folded *MS. 143 (C)*
6 voice of *del, reinstated MS. 143 (C); see note to l. 9/10 below*
9/10 That voice of night's still hours *inserted, then del MS. 143 (C)*
12 motion of our *rev to* weary Sufferer[?]s *MS. 143 (C)*

---

composed around but by early March 1828
found in DC MSS. 108, 131; Huntington MS. 1; MS. 1832/36 (MW)
published in *Keepsake* (1829), *1832–*
classed Sentiment and Reflection *1832–*
reading text *1832*
title *lacking MS. 108* The Gleaner *with* Gleaner *added in pencil MS. 131* The Country Girl. *Huntington MS. 1, Keepsake*
1 gleam] smile *MS. 108*
2 locks] looks *MS. 108*
8 a care] care *Huntington MS. 1*
9 Of] And *MS. 1832/36–* happiness] loveliness *MS. 108* flies] flies *rev from* dies *MS. 131*
11 Of promise whispering] Whispering of promise *MS. 1832/36–*

Can reach the innocent delight;
Where pity, to the mind conveyed
In pleasure, is the darkest shade
That Time, unwrinkled Grandsire, flings
From his smoothly-gliding wings.

What mortal form, what earthly face,
Inspired the pencil, lines to trace,
And mingle colours, that should breed
Such rapture, nor want power to feed;
For had thy charge been idle flowers,
Fair Damsel, o'er my captive mind,
To truth and sober reason blind,
'Mid that soft air, those long-lost bowers,
The sweet illusion might have hung, for hours.

—Thanks to this tell-tale sheaf of corn,
That touchingly bespeaks thee born
Life's daily tasks with them to share
Who, whether from their lowly bed
They rise, or rest the weary head,
Ponder the blessing they entreat
From Heaven, and *feel* what they repeat,
While they give utterance to the prayer
That asks for daily bread.

---

12 Can reach *rev from* Comes to *Huntington MS. 1*
13 mind] heart *MS. 108*
19 should breed] could breathe *rev to* could breed *MS. 108*
20 power] skill *MS. 108*
26 this] that *MS. 108* this *rev from* that *Huntington MS. 1*
27 That] Which *MS. 108*
30 or *rev from* nor *Huntington MS. 1*
31 Ponder] Do weigh *MSS. 108, 131, Huntington MS. 1, Keepsake*

THE TRIAD.

SHOW me the noblest Youth of present time,
Whose trembling fancy would to love give birth;
Some God or Hero, from the Olympian clime
Returned, to seek a Consort upon earth;
Or, in no doubtful prospect, let me see
The brightest star of ages yet to be,
And I will mate and match him blissfully.

I will not fetch a Naiad from a flood
Pure as herself—(song lacks not mightier power)
Nor leaf-crowned Dryad from a pathless wood,
Nor Sea-nymph glistening from her coral bower;
Mere Mortals bodied forth in vision still,
Shall with Mount Ida's triple lustre fill
The chaster coverts of a British hill.

"Appear!—obey my lyre's command!
Come, like the Graces, hand in hand!
For ye, though not by birth allied,
Are Sisters in the bond of love;
And not the boldest tongue of envious pride
In you those interweavings could reprove
Which They, the progeny of Jove,
Learnt from the tuneful spheres that glide
In endless union earth and sea above."—
—I speak in vain,—the pines have hushed their waving:

---

composed March 1828
found in DC MSS. 108, 107 (ll. 153–160, 167); WW to MW and Dora W, March 1828; Keswick MS.; WW to HCR, August 16, 1836; MS. 1832/36 (MW); MS. 1836/45 (JC)
published in *Keepsake* (1829), *1832–*
classed Imagination *1832–*
reading text *1832*
title The Promise *MS. 108, WW to MW & Dora W* The Promise *rev to* The Triad / By W. Wordsworth. *Keswick MS.; Keepsake as rev Keswick MS.*
3–5 Or Demi God, if from the Olympian clime
The immortalized return to visit earth,
Here seeking what heaven wants—or let me see *MS. 108, so Keswick MS. but* earth] Earth *and all rev to text*
8 fetch a] draw the *MS. 108* fetch the *Keswick MS., Keepsake*
19–21 Nor shall the tongue of envious pride
Presume those interweavings to reprove
In you, which that fair progeny of Jove, [Jove, *alt* Jove] *MS. 1832/36; 1836– as orig MS. 1832/36*
22 Learnt *rev in pencil to* Learn'd *MS. 108* Learned *1836–*
24 speak] sing *1836–*

For the photograph and transcription of DC MS. 108, 3r see pp. 680–683.

A peerless Youth expectant at my side,
Breathless as they, with unabated craving
Looks to the earth, and to the vacant air;
And, with a wandering eye that seems to chide,
Asks of the clouds what Occupants they hide:—
But why solicit more than sight could bear,
By casting on a moment all we dare?
Invoke we those bright Beings one by one,
And what was boldly promised, truly shall be done.

"Fear not this constraining measure!
Drawn by a poetic spell,
Lucida! from domes of pleasure,
Or from cottage-sprinkled dell,
Come to regions solitary,
Where the eagle builds her aery,
Above the hermit's long-forsaken cell!"
—She comes!—behold
That Figure, like a ship with silver sail!
Nearer she draws—a breeze uplifts her veil—
Upon her coming wait
As pure a sunshine and as soft a gale
As e'er, on herbage covering earthly mould,
Tempted the bird of Juno to unfold
His richest splendour, when his veering gait
And every motion of his starry train
Seem governed by a strain
Of music, audible to him alone.—
O Lady, worthy of earth's proudest throne!
Nor less, by excellence of nature, fit
Beside an unambitious hearth to sit
Domestic queen, where grandeur is unknown;
What living man could fear
The worst of Fortune's malice, wert thou near,
Humbling that lily stem, thy sceptre meek,
That its fair flowers may brush from off his cheek
The too, too happy tear?
——Queen and handmaid lowly!

---

25 A peerless Youth expectant *over erased* I speak in vain the *MS. 108*
34 this] a *rev to* this *rev to* a *MS. 1832/36* a *1836–*
35 Yielding to a gentle spell, *MS. 1832/36*
—Yielding to this gentle spell, *1836–*
42 silver] snow-white *1845–*
56–60 *inserted WW to MW & Dora W*
56 could] would *WW to MW & Dora W*
58 lily stem] lily-branch *WW to MW & Dora W*
59 To brush from off his cheek *WW to MW & Dora W* brush from off] from *1845–*
60 The too,] Brush the *1845–*

Whose skill can speed the day with lively cares,
And banish melancholy
By all that mind invents or hand prepares;
O thou, against whose lip, without its smile,
And in its silence even, no heart is proof;
Whose goodness, sinking deep, would reconcile
The softest Nursling of a gorgeous palace
To the bare life beneath the hawthorn roof
Of Sherwood's archer, or in caves of Wallace—
Who that hath seen thy beauty could content
His soul with but a *glimpse* of heavenly day?
Who that hath loved thee, but would lay
His strong hand on the wind, if it were bent
To take thee in thy Majesty away?
—Pass onward (even the glancing deer
Till we depart intrude not here;)
That mossy slope, o'er which the woodbine throws
A canopy, is smoothed for thy repose!"

Glad moment is it when the throng
Of warblers in full concert strong
Strive, and not vainly strive, to rout
The lagging shower, and force coy Phœbus out,
Met by the rainbow's form divine,
Issuing from her cloudy shrine;—
So may the thrillings of the lyre

---

79 repose!" *so 1836–* repose. *MS. 108* repose! *1832*
80–100 Like notes of Birds that, after showers,
In April [April *rev from* april] concert try their powers,
And with a tumult and a rout
Of warbling force coy Phoebus out,
Or bid some dark cloud's bosom show
That Form divine, the many-colour'd Bow,
Ev'n so the thrillings of the Lyre
Prevail to farther our desire,
While to these shades a Nymph I call,
The youngest of the lovely Three;—
With glowing cheek, from pastimes virginal
Behold her hastening to the tents
Of Nature and the lonely elements!
And as if wishful to disarm
Or to repay the tuneful Charm,
She bears the stringed Lute of old Romance &c *WW to MW & Dora W*
80 *rev from* With rapturous notes the vernal throng *MS. 108*

79/80 See the transcription of MS. 108, pp. 681, 683.

Prevail to further our desire,
While to these shades a Nymph I call,
The youngest of the lovely Three.—
"Come, if the notes thine ear may pierce;
Submissive to the might of verse,
By none more deeply felt than thee!"
—I sang; and lo! from pastimes virginal
She hastens to the tents
Of nature, and the lonely elements.
Air sparkles round her with a dazzling sheen,
And mark her glowing cheek, her vesture green!
And, as if wishful to disarm
Or to repay the potent charm,
She bears the stringèd lute of old romance,
That cheered the trellised arbour's privacy,
And soothed war-wearied knights in raftered hall.
How light her air! how delicate her glee!
So tripped the Muse, inventress of the dance;
So, truant in waste woods, the blithe Euphrosyne!

But the ringlets of that head
Why are they ungarlanded?
Why bedeck her temples less
Than the simplest shepherdess?
Is it not a brow inviting
Choicest flowers that ever breathed,
Which the myrtle would delight in
With Idalian rose enwreathed?

---

88 these shades] these Shades *alt* this glade *MS. 108* a Nymph I call *rev from* I call a Nymph *MS. 108*

88–92 While to these shades a sister Nymph I call.

"Come, if the notes thine ear may pierce,
Come, youngest of the lovely three,
Submissive to the might of verse
And the dear voice of harmony,
By none more deeply felt than Thee!" *1836– but* three] Three *MS. 1836/45 (pencil), 1845–*

90 "Come, with a shooting Star's velocity!" *rev to*
"Come if these notes thine ear may pierce!" *MS. 108*
thine *rev from* thy *Keswick MS.*

91–92 *inserted MS. 108*

94 *rev from* With glowing cheek she hastens to the tents *MS. 108*

96–97 *inserted MS. 108*

97 And] But *MS. 108, Keswick MS., Keepsake, 1836–*

102 raftered hall *over illeg eras MS. 108*

103 How vivid, yet how delicate, her glee! *1836–*

105 waste *rev from* wild *MS. 108* blithe *alt* blythe *over illeg eras MS. 108*

111 flowers] Flower *MS. 108*

113 Idalian *Rev from* happy *WW to MW & Dora W*

But her humility is well content
With *one* wild floweret (call it not forlorn)
FLOWER OF THE WINDS, beneath her bosom worn;
Yet is it more for love than ornament.

Open, ye thickets! let her fly,
Swift as a Thracian Nymph o'er field and height!
For She, to all but those who love Her shy,
Would gladly vanish from a Stranger's sight;
Though where she is beloved, and loves, as free
As bird that rifles blossoms on a tree,
Turning them inside out with arch audacity.

Alas! how little can a moment show
Of an eye where feeling plays
In ten thousand dewy rays;
A face o'er which a thousand shadows go!
—She stops—is fastened to that rivulet's side;
And there (while, with sedater mien,
O'er timid waters that have scarcely left
Their birth-place in the rocky cleft
She bends) at leisure may be seen
Features to old ideal grace allied,
Amid their smiles and dimples dignified—
Fit countenance for the soul of primal truth,
The bland composure of eternal youth!

What more changeful than the sea?
But over his great tides
Fidelity presides;
And this light-hearted Maiden constant is as he.—
High is her aim as heaven above,
And wide as ether her good-will,
And, like the lowly reed, her love

---

117 Yet is it more] Yet more *1836–*
122–123 Though where she is beloved and loves,
Light as the wheeling buttefly she moves;
Her happy spirit as a bird is free,
That rifles blossoms on a tree, *1836–*
122 is beloved *rev from* knows, is loved *MS. 108*
136–137 *rev from*
A face clear mirror of the ingennuous soul
Where not a thought stands single
But all things intermingle
To make a very wonder of the whole *MS. 108*
136 Fit *rev from* A *MS. 108*
139 But] Yet *WW to HCR*
143 Œther her good will *over illeg eras MS. 108*
144 lowly] lowliest *Keswick MS.*

Can drink its nurture from the scantiest rill;
Insight as keen as frosty star
Is to *her* charity no bar,
Nor interrupts her frolic graces
When she is, far from these wild places,
Encircled by familiar faces.

O the charm that manners draw,
Nature, from thy genuine law!
If from what her hand would do,
Her voice would utter, there ensue
Aught untoward or unfit,
She, in benign affections pure,
In self-forgetfulness secure,
Sheds round the transient harm or vague mischance
A light unknown to tutored elegance:
Her's is not a cheek shame-stricken,
But her blushes are joy-flushes—
And the fault (if fault it be)
Only ministers to quicken
Laughter-loving gaiety,
And kindle sportive wit—
Leaving this Daughter of the mountains free
As if she knew that Oberon king of Faery
Had crossed her purpose with some quaint vagary,
And heard his viewless bands
Over their mirthful triumph clapping hands.

"Last of the Three, though eldest born,
Reveal thyself, like pensive morn,
Touched by the skylark's earliest note,
Ere humbler gladness be afloat.

---

145 Can drink *rev from* [?] drinks *MS. 108*

152/153 Through benign affections pure,
In the slight of self secure; *MS. 108; so Keswick MS. but* affections—pure, self-secure; *Keepsake as Keswick MS. but* self-secure,

152 thy] the *1836* thy *in pencil MS. 1836/45*

154–159 Or tongue utter, there ensue
Aught untoward or unfit,
Transient mischief, vague mischance,
Shunned by guarded elegance, *MS. 108, Keswick MS.; so Keepsake but* Shunn'd

154 Her] Or *rev from* [?Her] *MS. 107* there] aught *1845–*

155 Aught untoward] Untoward *1845–*

163–166 Only ministers to quicken
Sallies of instinctive wit;
Unchk'd in laughter-loving gaiety,
In all the motions of her spirit, free *WW to MW & Dora W; so ll. 163–166 in MS. 108 under paste-over but* Unchk'd] Unchecked *and all rev to text*

167 king of] the *MS. 108, Keswick MS., Keepsake*

But whether in the semblance drest
Of dawn—or eve, fair vision of the west,
Come with each anxious hope subdued
By woman's gentle fortitude,
Each grief, through meekness, settling into rest.
—Or I would hail thee when some high-wrought page
Of a closed volume lingering in thy hand
Has raised thy spirit to a peaceful stand
Among the glories of a happier age."

—Her brow hath opened on me—see it there,
Brightening the umbrage of her hair;
So gleams the crescent moon, that loves
To be descried through shady groves.
—Tenderest bloom is on her cheek;
Wish not for a richer streak—
Nor dread the depth of meditative eye;
But let thy love, upon that azure field
Of thoughtfulness and beauty, yield
Its homage offered up in purity.—
What would'st thou more? In sunny glade
Or under leaves of thickest shade,
Was such a stillness e'er diffused
Since earth grew calm while angels mused?
Softly she treads, as if her foot were loth
To crush the mountain dew-drops, soon to melt
On the flower's breast; as if she felt
That flowers themselves, whate'er their hue,
With all their fragrance, all their glistening,
Call to the heart for inward listening;
And though for bridal wreaths and tokens true
Welcomed wisely—though a growth
Which the careless shepherd sleeps on,
As fitly spring from turf the mourner weeps on,
And without wrong are cropped the marble tomb to strew.
The charm is over; the mute phantoms gone,

---

175 semblance *rev from* attraction *alt* attire *MS. 108*
176 Of morn or eve ere darkness steals upon the west *rev to*
Of morn or eve ere twilight dims the west *rev to*
Of Dayspring, or the Twilight of the West, *rev to text MS. 108*
182 peaceful] fearless *MS. 108, Keswick MS.*
186 So gleams *rev from* Like the *MS. 108*
187 descried *rev from* espied *MS. 108*
190 the *rev from* that *MS. 108*
200 flower's] flowers' *Keepsake*
208 tomb *over illeg eras MS. 108*

Nor will return—but droop not, favoured Youth;
The apparition that before thee shone
Obeyed a summons covetous of truth.
From these wild rocks thy footsteps I will guide
To bowers in which thy fortune may be tried,
And one of the bright Three become thy happy Bride!

On the Power of Sound

In a letter to George Huntley Gordon, December 15, 1828, Wordsworth said that "during the last week" he had written "some stanzas on the Power of Sound" (*LY*, I, 689). The trip to Ireland when the eagle was sighted (text of 1835, ll. 199–201) took place in September and early October 1829. The nucleus for *On the Power of Sound* was probably the seven lines on "a world together bound / By sight dependant upon sound"—later revised to sixteen lines resembling the first stanza of the DC MS. 131 text of *On the Power of Sound*—that appear between lines 79 and 80 of *The Triad* (DC MS. 108). This latter poem was composed early in 1828, certainly by early March (*LY*, I, 590–591; see the notes to *The Triad*, p. 438). Thus the probable date of composition of the early version extends from March 1828 at least through December of that year. The lines on the eagle, however, were not composed until after October 1829. These lines and the rest of the work toward the published version were composed and revised between November 1829 and March 1835, though most of the new composition took place before July 24, 1834, when copy was sent to the printer (*LY*, II, 724–725). There seems to have been a delay of about three months between the printing of first proofs for *Yarrow Revisited, and Other Poems* around November–December 1834 and the book's distribution in April 1835 (*LY*, II, 747; III, 39).

There are many surviving manuscripts. The earliest work for *On the Power of Sound* appears in MS. 89 and a fair copy of the six-stanza poem, part of which is present in MS. 89, was entered in MS. 131, which is the basis for the first reading text (part of another fair copy appears in MS. 115). Line numbers in brackets in the right margin of the first reading text refer to the corresponding lines in the second reading text.

Wordsworth may have continued work on the poem in MS. 89 (there are drafts toward ll. 172–176 of the 1835 text; and stanza 6 of the text of MS. 131 is renumbered 7, suggesting another stanza was to be inserted earlier in the poem). But the next full copy, in MS. 107, is of the expanded version in fourteen stanzas. MS. 106 contains a revised copy based on the version in MS. 107, and the copy in MS. 134 and a single surviving sheet of another copy (Cornell MS. 6) both seem to have been based on the revised version in MS. 106. MS. 135, apparently based on MS. 134, is the copy sent to the printer; MSS. 137 and 138 contain various stages of corrected proofs of the poem and in them Wordsworth revised the title of the poem. The 1835 printing is the basis for the second reading text.

---

215 happy] joyful *MS. 108* joyful *rev to* happy *Keswick MS.*

[Text of MS. 131]

On the Power of Sound

"That Strain I heard was of a higher mood"

There is a world of Spirit, [177–192]
By tones and numbers guided and controll'd,
And glorious privilege have they who merit
Initiation in that mystery old.
The Heavens, whose aspect makes our minds as still
As they themselves appear to be
Innumerable voices fill
With everlasting harmony.
The towering Headlands crown'd with mist,
Their feet among the billows, know
That Ocean is a mighty harmonist:—
Thy pinions universal Air!
Ever waving to and fro,
Are Delegates of harmony and bear
Strains that support the seasons in their round;
Even winter loves a dirge-like sound.

The headlong streams and fountains [17–32]
Tire not the day, nor waste by night their powers,
Cheering the wakeful Tent, and Syrian mountains
They lull, perchance, ten-thousand thousand flowers.

---

composed probably around March–December 15, 1828
found in DC MSS. 131, 108; DC MS. 89 (A) 94^{r} (ll. 1–16), (B) 102^{v} (ll. 1–40), 104^{r}, 105^{v}, 107^{r} (ll. 80–95); DC MSS. 115, 106
reading text DC MS. 131
title lacking MS. 89 except 105^{v} *(see transcriptions).*
motto inserted (without quotation marks) by WW MS. 89 (B) Strain] strain *MS. 115*
stanza numbers –, 2, 3, *etc. MS. 89 (B)*
2 Whose motions by fit [fit *rev from* ?fair] music are controlled *MS. 89 (A)*
3 And glorious is their privilege who merit *rev to* And glorious [glorious *rev from* a high] privilege it is to merit *MS. 89 (A)*
5 our *rev from* own *MS. 89 (B)* minds] mind *MS. 89 (A)*
10 know *rev from* show *MS. 89 (A)*
13 Ever waving] For ever [ever *rev from* ?e'er] moving *MS. 89 (A)*
19 and] mid *MS. 89 (B)*

For photographs and transcriptions of DC MSS. 108, 3^{r}, $3^{r}P1^{r}$; 89, 104^{r}, 105^{v}, 107^{r}; and 106, 10^{v}, $10^{v}P1^{r}$ see pp. 680–693.
Margin numbers in brackets refer to the corresponding lines in the text of 1835.

That roar—the hungry Lion's—"*here I am*"
How fearful to the Desart wide!
That bleat, how tender, of the Dam,
Calling a Straggler to her side!
Shout Cuckoo! let the vernal soul
Go with thee to the frozen Zone;
Toll from thy loftiest perch, lone Bell-Bird, toll!
At the still hour to mercy dear,
Mercy from her golden throne
Listening to the Nun's soft sigh of holy fear,
The sailor's prayer breathed from a darkening sea,
The widow's cottage lullaby.

Ye voices, and ye shadows, [33–48]
And images of voice—to hound and horn
Flung back by woods, and rock-besprinkled meadows,
And in the clear crystalline sky re-born,
On with your pastime!—till the Church tower bells
A greeting give of measured glee,
And milder echoes from their cells
Repeat the bridal symphony.
Then, or far earlier, let me rove
The mountain side if mists be gone
And from aloft look down into a cove
Frequented by a scattered quire,
Nymph-like Milk maids, one by one,
Chanting or warbling each to her desire
A strange wild concert, matchless by nice art,
A stream—as if from one full heart.

How oft along thy mazes [81–96]
Spirit of Sound! have dangerous passions trod.
Thou! thro' whom the Temple rings with praises,
And blackening clouds in thunder speak of God,
Betray not by a charm of sense
Thy youthful votaries resign'd
To a voluptuous influence
That taints the purer better mind;
But lead sick fancy to the Harp
That hath in noble tasks been tried;
And if the virtuous feel a pang too sharp

---

28 the still *WW alt in pencil* eve—the *MS. 89 (B)*
30 soft sigh *WW alt* faint sob *MS. 89 (B)* of *rev from* and *MS. 89 (B)*
31 The *WW rev in pencil to* To *MS. 89 (B)*
32 The *WW rev in pencil then ink to* Or *MS. 89 (B)* widow's] widows *MS. 131*
35 woods] words *MS. 89 (B) (copyist's slip)*
36 re-born *WW rev from* are born *MS. 89 (B)*

For patience, steal the pang away,
Melt the gloom of Suicide;
And let some mood of thine in firm array
Knit every feeling which the thoughtful need
To triumph in some glorious deed.

For terror, love, or pity, [161–176]
Vast is the compass and the swell of notes
From Babe's first cry to voice of regal city
Rolling a solemn sea-like bass that floats
Far as the woodlands, with the thrill to blend
Of that sweet songstress whose love-tale
Might tempt an Angel to descend,
While passing o'er the moonlight vale!
What skill in soul-affecting scheme
Of moral music shall unite
Those viewless powers more fleeting than a dream,
Shall bind those wanderers thro' loose air
In the precious chains of sight
That laboured minstrelsies thro' ages wear?
Shall frame a balance fit the truth to tell
Of the unsubstantial, ponder'd well!

A Voice to Light gave being [209–224]
To changeful Time and Man his Chronicler,
A Voice shall finish doubt and dim foreseeing,
And sweep away Life's visionary stir
The Trumpet (we the puny sons of Pride
Arm at its blast for ruthless wars)
To archangelic lips applied,
The grave shall open, quench the stars.
O Silence! are Man's noisy years
No more than moments of thy Life?
Is Harmony, blest Queen of smiles and tears
Awakened thro' a world of dust
Smoothly, or in rapturous strife,
Thy destined Bond slave? No—but where the trust?
Not in the Earth or Heaven (how fleet are they)
But in the *Word* that shall not pass away.

---

82 Chronicler] Chronicles *MS. 131 (copyist's slip)*
88 grave] grove *MS. 131 (copyist's slip)*
96/ W.W. *MS. 131*

65–66 SH entered the two lines as one in MS. 131.

[Text of 1835]

fly-title

STANZAS

ON

THE POWER OF SOUND.

ARGUMENT.

The Ear addressed, as occupied by a spiritual functionary, in communion with sounds, individual, or combined in studied harmony.—Sources and effects of those sounds (to the close of 6th Stanza).—The power of music, whence proceeding, exemplified in the idiot.—Origin of music, and its effect in early ages—how produced (to the middle of 10th Stanza).—The mind recalled to sounds acting casually and severally.—Wish uttered (11th Stanza) that these could be united into a scheme or system for moral interests and intellectual contemplation.—(Stanza 12th.) The Pythagorean theory of numbers and music, with their supposed power over the motions of the universe—imaginations consonant with such a theory.—Wish expressed (in 11th Stanza) realised, in some degree, by the representation of all sounds under the form of thanksgiving to the Creator.—(Last Stanza) the destruction of earth and the planetary system—the survival of audible harmony, and its support in the Divine Nature, as revealed in Holy Writ.

composed from November 1829 to July 24, 1834; revised through March 1835

found in DC MSS. 107 and 106; Cornell MS. 6; DC MSS. 134; 135; 137 (A) pp. 267–280 (first set corrected by MW, JC), (B) pp. 267–280 (second set corrected by WW), (C) pp. 309–310; DC MS. 138 (A) pp. 309–312, (B) pp. 309—322; MS. 1835/36 (MW); MS. 1836/45 (JC)

published in *1835, 1836–*

classed Imagination *1836–*

reading text *1835*

fly-title *lacking MSS. 107, 106, 134, 1836–* Ode. *MS. 135* STANZAS / ON THE POWER OF SOUND. *rev from* ODE / ON THE POWER OF SOUND. *MS. 137 (C); MSS. 137 (A, B), 138 (A) as orig MS. 137 (C)*

argument *lacking MSS. 107, 106, 134, Cornell MS. 6; placed below title 1836–*

title ARGUMENT.] Argument *MS. 135*

3–5 The power ~~of the harmony~~ of music, [~~and~~ whence proceeding, ~~or~~ *inserted*] exemplified in [the *inserted*] idiot. [idiots *rev from* Idiots;] ~~and chiefly through its relation to the order of the universe—~~ Origin of music, and its effect [effect *rev from* results] in early ages—how produced—(to the middle of 10th Stanz). *MS. 135*

6 A wish *rev to* Wish *MS. 135*

7 interests] interest *MS. 135*

9 (Stan: 12th) *rev from* which introduces Stan: 12th *MS. 135* theory *rev from* system *MS. 135*

10 imaginations *rev from* imagination *MS. 137 (B)* imagination *MSS. 135, 137 (A), 138 (A)*

For photographs and transcriptions of DC MS. 106, 10^{v}, 10^{v}P1^{r} see pp. 692–693.

In several manuscripts the copyists employed running heads, abbreviating the title to "The Power of Sound" (MSS. 135, 137, 138).

ON THE POWER OF SOUND.

1.

THY functions are etherial,
As if within thee dwelt a glancing Mind,
Organ of Vision! And a Spirit aerial
Informs the cell of hearing, dark and blind;
Intricate labyrinth, more dread for thought
To enter than oracular cave;
Strict passage, through which sighs are brought,
And whispers, for the heart, their slave;
And shrieks, that revel in abuse
Of shivering flesh; and warbled air,
Whose piercing sweetness can unloose
The chains of frenzy, or entice a smile
Into the ambush of despair;
Hosannas pealing down the long-drawn aisle,
And requiems answered by the pulse that beats
Devoutly, in life's last retreats!

2.

The headlong Streams and Fountains
Serve Thee, Invisible Spirit, with untired powers;
Cheering the wakeful Tent on Syrian mountains,
They lull perchance ten thousand thousand flowers.
That roar, the prowling Lion's *Here I am,*
How fearful to the desert wide!
That bleat, how tender! of the Dam
Calling a straggler to her side.
Shout, Cuckoo! let the vernal soul
Go with thee to the frozen zone;
Toll from thy loftiest perch, lone Bell-bird, toll!
At the still hour to Mercy dear,
Mercy from her twilight throne

---

title *lacking Cornell MS. 6* Ode / On the Power of Sound *MSS. 106, 107 (WW's pencil), 134* Ode / On the Power of Sound *rev from* The Power of Sound *MS. 135* ODE / ON THE POWER OF SOUND. *MSS. 137 (A, B), 138 (A)* ON THE POWER OF SOUND. *rev from* ODE / ON THE POWER OF SOUND. *MSS. 137 (C), 138 (B)*

stanza numbers I, II . . . *1836–; first stanza unnumbered MSS. 107, 134, 135; no stanza numbers 1839*

4 Informs *rev from* Inform'd *Cornell MS. 6*

12 chains *rev from* chain *Cornell MS. 6*

15 And] Mid *MS. 134*

20 flowers] fountains *rev to* flowers *rev to* fountains *rev to* flowers *MS. 135*

21 prowling] hungry *DW rev to* famish'd *Cornell MS. 6*

29 twilight *rev from* pensive *MS. 107* pensive *Cornell MS. 6*

Listening to Nun's faint sob of holy fear,
To Sailor's prayer breathed from a darkening sea,
Or Widow's cottage lullaby.

3.

Ye Voices, and ye Shadows,
And Images of voice—to hound and horn
From rocky steep and rock-bestudded meadows
Flung back, and, in the sky's blue caves, reborn,
On with your pastime! till the church-tower bells
A greeting give of *measured* glee;
And milder echoes from their cells
Repeat the bridal symphony.
Then, or far earlier, let us rove
Where mists are breaking up or gone,
And from aloft look down into a cove
Besprinkled with a careless quire,
Happy Milk-maids, one by one
Scattering a ditty each to her desire,
A liquid concert matchless by nice Art,
A stream as if from one full heart.

4.

Blest be the song that brightens
The blind Man's gloom, exalts the Veteran's mirth;
Unscorned the Peasant's whistling breath, that lightens
His duteous toil of furrowing the green earth.
For the tired Slave, Song lifts the languid oar,
And bids it aptly fall, with chime
That beautifies the fairest shore,

---

30 sob] throb *1836–*
34 Images] image *MS. 107*
35 bestudded *WW rev from* besprinkled *MS. 134*
35–36 Flung back from rocky steep o'er lake and meadows
And in the clear crystalline sky re-born [re-born *rev from* reborn] , *MS. 107; so Cornell MS. 6 but* meadow *and* reborn,
Musical discord from the woods
Flung back and in [? ?] sky [?] *pencil draft, eras MS. 106*
41 us] me *MSS. 107, Cornell MS. 6* rove *over illeg eras Cornell MS. 6*
42 Some pastoral hill if mists be gone, *MS. 107; so Cornell MS. 6, MSS. 106, 134 but* hill] hill, *MS. 135 as Cornell MS. 6 but rev to text*
43 aloft] its brow *MSS. 106, 107, 134* its brow *rev to* some hill *MS. 135* some hill *MS. 137 (A); so MS. 137 (B), WW rev to* aloft
Cornell MS. 6 ends with the words And from aloft look etc. etc.
46 Scattering *rev from* Muttering *MS. 137*
53 the languid *rev from* his languid *MS. 107* oar *rev from* air *MS. 106*

33–36 For MS. 106 readings see transcriptions, p. 693.

And mitigates the harshest clime.
Yon Pilgrims see—in lagging file
They move; but soon the appointed way
A choral *Ave Marie* shall beguile,
And to their hope the distant shrine
Glisten with a livelier ray:
Nor friendless He, the Prisoner of the Mine,
Who from the well-spring of his own clear breast
Can draw, and sing his griefs to rest.

5.

When civic renovation
Dawns on a kingdom, and for needful haste
Best eloquence avails not, Inspiration
Mounts with a tune, that travels like a blast
Piping through cave and battlemented tower;
Then starts the Sluggard, pleased to meet
That voice of Freedom, in its power
Of promises, shrill, wild, and sweet!
Who, from a martial *pageant*, spreads
Incitements of a battle-day,
Thrilling the unweaponed crowd with plumeless heads;
Even She whose Lydian airs inspire
Peaceful striving, gentle play
Of timid hope and innocent desire
Shot from the dancing Graces, as they move
Fanned by the plausive wings of Love.

6.

How oft along thy mazes,
Regent of Sound, have dangerous Passions trod!
O Thou, through whom the Temple rings with praises,
And blackening clouds in thunder speak of God,
Betray not by the cozenage of sense
Thy Votaries, wooingly resigned
To a voluptuous influence
That taints the purer, better mind;
But lead sick Fancy to a harp
That hath in noble tasks been tried;

---

60 And *rev in pencil to* Then *MS. 107*
61 Glisten *rev in pencil to* Glistens *MS. 107* Glistens *rev to* Glisten *MS. 106*
64 sing *rev from* [?pray] *MS. 135*
64/65 *Two lines of WW's illeg pencil erased MS. 106*
72 wild *rev from* [?m]ild] *above rev* wild *penciled* w *erased MS. 106*
76 inspire *WW rev from* are pure *MS. 107* *line inserted MSS. 107, 106*
90 tasks *WW rev in pencil from* deeds *MS. 107*

And, if the Virtuous feel a pang too sharp,
Soothe it into patience,—stay
The uplifted arm of Suicide;
And let some mood of thine in firm array
Knit every thought the impending issue needs,
Ere Martyr burns, or Patriot bleeds!

7.

As Conscience, to the centre
Of Being, smites with irresistible pain,
So shall a solemn cadence, if it enter
The mouldy vaults of the dull Idiot's brain,
Transmute him to a wretch from quiet hurled—
Convulsed as by a jarring din;
And then aghast, as at the world
Of reason partially let in
By concords winding with a sway
Terrible for sense and soul!
Or, awed he weeps, struggling to quell dismay.
Point not these mysteries to an Art
Lodged above the starry pole;
Pure modulations flowing from the heart
Of divine Love, where Wisdom, Beauty, Truth
With Order dwell, in endless youth?

8.

Oblivion may not cover
All treasures hoarded by the Miser, Time.
Orphean Insight! Truth's undaunted Lover,
To the first leagues of tutored passion climb,
When Music deigned within this grosser sphere
Her subtle essence to enfold,
And Voice and Shell drew forth a tear
Softer than Nature's self could mould.
Yet *strenuous* was the infant Age:
Art, daring because souls could feel,
Stirred nowhere but an urgent equipage
Of rapt imagination sped her march

---

93 uplifted] lifted *MS. 107*
97–99 *WW has written ll. 97–99 in pencil at the top of the first recto of Cornell MS. 6*
101 to a *rev from* from a *MS. 134*
103 then *WW rev from* now *MS. 135* now *MSS. 107, 106, 134*
107 Or, awed *rev to* Oer awed, *MS. 106* struggling *MW inserted MS. 107*
118 enfold] unfold *1839*
124 rapt *rev from* [?rash] *MS. 135*

Through the realms of woe and weal:
Hell to the lyre bowed low; the upper arch
Rejoiced that clamorous spell and magic verse
Her wan disasters could disperse.

9.

The GIFT to King Amphion
That walled a city with its melody
Was for belief no dream; thy skill, Arion!
Could humanise the creatures of the sea,
Where men were monsters. A last grace he craves,
Leave for one chant;— the dulcet sound
Steals from the deck o'er willing waves,
And listening Dolphins gather round.
Self-cast, as with a desperate course,
'Mid that strange audience, he bestrides
A proud One docile as a managed horse;
And singing, while the accordant hand
Sweeps his harp, the Master rides;
So shall he touch at length a friendly strand,
And he, with his Preserver, shine star-bright
In memory, through silent night.

10.

The pipe of Pan, to Shepherds
Couched in the shadow of Menalian Pines,
Was passing sweet; the eyeballs of the Leopards,
That in high triumph drew the Lord of vines,
How did they sparkle to the cymbal's clang!
While Fauns and Satyrs beat the ground
In cadence,—and Silenus swang
This way and that, with wild-flowers crowned.
To life, to *life* give back thine Ear:
Ye who are longing to be rid
Of Fable, though to truth subservient, hear
The little sprinkling of cold earth that fell
Echoed from the coffin lid;

---

125 the *MW inserted MS. 107*
126 arch *rev in pencil and ink from* air *MS. 107*
134 dulcet *rev from* dullest *MS. 106*
149 the *rev from* thei *MS. 134* cymbal's] cymbals' *MS. 106* cymbals *rev in pencil to* cymbal's *MS. 107*
152 wild-flowers] wild flowers *rev in pencil from* roses *MS. 107*
153/154 [?Know] [?] *in pencil MS. 134*
153–158 *transposed by printer to ll. 144/145, rev to text MS. 137 (B)*

The Convict's summons in the steeple knell;
"The vain distress-gun," from a leeward shore,
Repeated—heard, and heard no more!

11.

For terror, joy, or pity,
Vast is the compass, and the swell of notes:
From the Babe's first cry to voice of regal City,
Rolling a solemn sea-like bass, that floats
Far as the woodlands—with the trill to blend
Of that shy Songstress, whose love-tale
Might tempt an Angel to descend,
While hovering o'er the moonlight vale.
O for some soul-affecting scheme
Of *moral* music, to unite
Wanderers whose portion is the faintest dream
Of memory!—O that they might stoop to bear
Chains, such precious chains of sight
As laboured minstrelsies through ages wear!
O for a balance fit the truth to tell
Of the Unsubstantial, pondered well!

12.

By one pervading Spirit
Of tones and numbers all things are controlled,
As Sages taught, where faith was found to merit
Initiation in that mystery old.
The Heavens, whose aspect makes our minds as still
As they themselves *appear* to be,
Innumerable voices fill
With everlasting harmony;

---

158 steeple] steeple's *1836–* knell; *so 1845, 1850* knell, *MSS. 107, 106, 135, 137 (A), 138* knell *MS. 134* knell, *rev to* knell. *MS. 137 (B)* knell. *1835, 1836* knell: *in pencil MS. 1836/45*

159 *note added at page foot:* "Her vain distress-guns hear." Coleridge *MS. 137 (A); so MS. 138 but* —COLERIDGE *then asterisks and entire note del*

165 trill] thrill *MS. 137* trill *rev from* thrill *MSS. 135, 138*

166 shy *WW rev in pencil from* sweet *MS. 107*

169–171 Ye wandering utterances has earth no scheme
[Of *rev to*] Its scale of moral music to unite
Your powers—that live but in the faintest dreams *MS. 1835/36, with l. 171 rev by WW to* Powers that survive but in the faintest dream
Ye wandering Utterances, has earth no scheme,
No scale of moral music—to unite
Powers that survive but in the faintest dream *1836–; 1839*

171 is *inserted MS. 135*

172 they] ye *MS. 1835/36–; 1839*

179 where *MW rev from* when *MS. 107*

The towering Headlands, crowned with mist,
Their feet among the billows, know
That Ocean is a mighty harmonist;
Thy pinions, universal Air,
Ever waving to and fro,
Are delegates of harmony, and bear
Strains that support the Seasons in their round;
Stern Winter loves a dirge-like sound.

13.

Break forth into thanksgiving,
Ye banded Instruments of wind and chords;
Unite, to magnify the Ever-living,
Your inarticulate notes with the voice of words!
Nor hushed be service from the lowing mead,
Nor mute the forest hum of noon;
Thou too be heard, lone Eagle! freed
From snowy peak and cloud, attune
Thy hungry barkings to the hymn
Of joy, that from her utmost walls
The six-days' Work, by flaming Seraphim,
Transmits to Heaven! As Deep to Deep
Shouting through one valley calls,
All worlds, all natures, mood and measure keep
For praise and ceaseless gratulation, poured
Into the ear of God, their Lord!

14.

A Voice to Light gave Being;
To Time, and Man his earth-born Chronicler;
A Voice shall finish doubt and dim foreseeing,
And sweep away life's visionary stir;
The Trumpet (we, intoxicate with pride,
Arm at its blast for deadly wars)
To archangelic lips applied,
The grave shall open, quench the stars.
O Silence! are Man's noisy years
No more than moments of thy life?
Is Harmony, blest Queen of smiles and tears,
With her smooth tones and discords just,

---

189 waving *rev from* wavering *MS. 134*
196 notes] note *MW inserted and WW rev in pencil to* notes *MS. 107* the *inserted in pencil MSS. 106, 134; lacking MS. 107*
210 *WW rev in pencil from* To changeful Time, and Man his Chronicler; *MS. 107*
218 thy *rev from* the *MS. 134*

Tempered into rapturous strife,
Thy destined Bond-slave? No! though Earth be dust
And vanish, though the Heavens dissolve, her stay
Is in the WORD, that shall not pass away.

The Egyptian Maid; or, The Romance of the Water Lily

Wordsworth assigned *The Egyptian Maid; or, The Romance of the Water Lily* to 1830 in editions from 1836 and in the *Yarrow Revisited* issued in 1839. However, the poem was probably composed between November 18 and 25, 1828; Wordsworth told George Huntley Gordon on November 25 that he had "just concluded a kind of romance"; in a letter written the same day Mary Wordsworth told Edward Quillinan that it was written "within the last 8 days" and Wordsworth himself added that "it rose out of my mind like an exhalation" (*LY*, I, 663, 665–667). In the headnote to his poem Wordsworth cites a nineteenth-century edition of Sir Thomas Malory's *Le Morte d'Arthur* as the source for the "names and persons" in his story, stating that the rest was his own invention (see the note to the reading text). The climactic incident of Wordsworth's poem, a sleeping maiden roused from a deep sleep by a worthy knight and intended husband, is not in Malory; but the popular tale *Briar Rose* by Jacob and Wilhelm Grimm may have suggested it. In an early English translation of the Grimms' tale, a spell is cast upon Rose-Bud, who falls into a deep sleep and is awakened by the prince's kiss (*German Popular Stories, Translated from the kinder und hans Märchen,* translated anonymously by Edgar Taylor [London, 1825], pp. 51–57). An awakening touch or kiss is also a feature of late eighteenth- and early nineteenth-century English adaptations of Charles Perrault's *La Belle au bois dormant* (usually translated as "The Sleeping Beauty in the Wood") and is common to many renditions in pantomime; the sleeping maiden awakened by the successful performance of a test by her rescuer-lover can be traced back at least to the story of Brynhild in the *Volsunga Saga* (noticed by the Grimms, as translated by Taylor in *German Popular Stories,* p. 222).

The first reading text is that of 1835; the second presents an early version of the chorus from DC MS. 109.

[Text of 1835]

---

fly-title

THE EGYPTIAN MAID;

OR,

THE ROMANCE OF THE WATER LILY.

224/ The end *MS. 135* THE END. *MS. 138*

[For the name and persons in the following poem, see the "History of the renowned Prince Arthur and his Knights of the Round Table;" for the rest the Author is answerable; only it may be proper to add, that the Lotus, with the bust of the goddess appearing to rise out of the full-blown flower, was suggested by the beautiful work of ancient art, once included among the Townley Marbles, and now in the British Museum.]

THE EGYPTIAN MAID;

OR,

THE ROMANCE OF THE WATER LILY.

WHILE Merlin paced the Cornish sands,
Forth-looking toward the Rocks of Scilly,
The pleased Enchanter was aware
Of a bright Ship that seemed to hang in air,
Yet was she work of mortal hands,
And took from men her name—THE WATER LILY.

Soft was the wind, that landward blew;
And, as the Moon, o'er some dark hill ascendant,
Grows from a little edge of light
To a full orb, this Pinnace bright,

---

composed November 20–28, 1828
found in DC MS. 107 (A) 1^{r}, 4^{r}–14^{r}, (B) 14^{v}–15^{r} (pencil), (C) 68^{r}, ll. 279–281 (pencil), 91^{r}–100^{v}, (D) 119^{r}, l. 159 (pencil); DC MSS. 106; 109; 131; 134; 135; 137 (MW); MS. 1835B; MS. 1835Col
published in *1835, 1836–*
classed Imagination *1845, 1850*
reading text *1835*
fly-title *lacking MSS. 107, 106, 109, 131, 134, 135; om 1836–, but headnote preserved below title*
title The Egyptian Maid or / The [The *rev from* A] Romance / of / [Don Juan *Dora W inserted* /] The Water Lily [Lily *rev from* Lilly] / [by / Silly Billy Senr *Dora W inserted*] *MS. 109*
stanza numbers 3 *(WW)*, 6 . . . 20, 22 . . . 56 , 1 . . . 8 *(Dora W and WW) MS. 107 (A)* 1 . . . 59, 1 . . . 8 *MSS. 107 (C), 106* 6 . . . 44 *with some renumbering MS. 109* 1 . . . 59, 1 . . . 8 *MS. 131* 2, . . . 59 *with some omissions*, 1 . . . 8 *MS. 134*
headnote *lacking MSS. 107, 106, 109, 131, 134; del MS. 135* name] Names *MS. 135 del* full-blown flower, was suggested by] flower, is described from *MS. 135*
1–30 *lacking MS. 135*
5 mortal *rev from* human *MS. 109*
7 wind,] breeze, *MSS. 107 (A)* breeze *MS. 109* blew *rev from* ble[?] *MS. 109*
8 dark] black *MSS. 107 (A), 109, 131*
9 edge *rev from* orb *MS. 109*

Became, as nearer to the Coast she drew,
More glorious, with spread sail and streaming pendant.

Upon this wingèd Shape so fair
Sage Merlin gazed with admiration:
Her lineaments, thought he, surpass
Aught that was ever shown in magic glass;
Was ever built with patient care;
Or, at a touch, set forth with wondrous transformation.

Now, though a Mechanist, whose skill
Shames the degenerate grasp of modern science,
Grave Merlin (and belike the more
For practising occult and perilous lore)
Was subject to a freakish will
That sapped good thoughts, or scared them with defiance.

11–12 Became . . . / . . . pendant. *so 1835 errata page, MS. 1835B, MS. 1835Col, 1836–*
As nearer to the coast she drew,
Appear'd more glorious, with spred Sail and Pendant. *MS. 107 (A); so MS. 134, 1835 but* Coast Appeared . . . spread sail . . . pendant.

12 spread] out-spread *MS. 131*

13–15 Thought Merlin, surely Thing [Thing *rev from* thing] so fair
Must be renown'd through many a nation;
The simple lineaments surpass *MS. 109*

13 wingèd *so MS. 134, 1836YR, 1836–, 1839* winged *all other MSS., 1835*

16 shown] seen *rev to* shewn *MS. 109*

17 Was . . . care; *so 1835 errata page, MS. 1835B, MS. 1835Col, 1836YR, 1836–, 1839*
For wonder built with patient [patient *rev to* subtl] care, *MS. 109*
In patience built with subtle care; *MS. 134, 1835*

18 As clothed with life by sudden transformation. *rev to*
Or shaped anew by instant transformation. *MS. 109*
set forth with wondrous] produced by happiest *1836YR, 1836–, 1839*

19–24 But he whose humblest feats of skill
Shame the degenerate grasp of modern Science
Thy reply theatrical, belike [belike *over illeg wd*] the more
For tampering in occult and perilous lore
Was subject to a freak[?ish] will
That sapped good thoughts or scared them with defiance *pencil, all but l. 19 del in ink MS. 107 (A)*

19–24 *lacking MS. 109*

19 Now *alt* But *MS. 107 (B)* whose] of *MSS. 107 (B_1), 131*

20 Whose least effect [effect *rev from* effects] w^{d} startle modern science *MS. 107 (B); so MS. 131 but* w^{d}] might science] science,

22 practising] practicing *rev from* tampering with *MS. 107 (B)* tampering with *MS. 131*

Provoked to envious spleen, he cast
An altered look upon the advancing Stranger
Whom he had hailed with joy, and cried,
"My Art shall help to tame her pride—"
Anon the breeze became a blast,
And the waves rose, and sky portended danger.

With thrilling word, and potent sign
Traced on the beach, his work the Sorcerer urges;
The clouds in blacker clouds are lost,
Like spiteful Fiends that vanish, crossed
By Fiends of aspect more malign;
And the winds roused the Deep with fiercer scourges.

But worthy of the name she bore
Was this Sea-flower, this buoyant Galley;
Supreme in loveliness and grace

25–27 Dire envy followed all too fast;
And he who to the unconscious stranger
Had giv'n a joyful welcome, cried, *line rev to* Whom he had hailed with joy and cried,
WW alt in pencil:
Provoked to envious spleen he cast
A sullen look upon the dazzling [*alt* winged] shape *MS. 107 (A)*
a sullen look
Full soon ~~by every strand~~ he cast
Upon the bright
~~An altered look upon the~~ unconscious stranger
~~Whom~~ he had hailed with joy and cried
OR
And sullen
All soon an ~~altered~~ look he cast
the
Whom the bright ^ unconscious stranger
Whom
[?] he had hailed with joy and cried *MS. 107 (B)*
And soon a sullen look he cast
Upon the bright unconscious Stranger
Whom he had hailed with joy and cried *rev to text except* advancing] unconscious *MS. 107 (C)*
So envy followed all too fast;
And he, who to the unconscious stranger
Had given a joyful welcome, cried, *MS. 109*
Full soon a sullen look he cast
Upon the bright unconscious Stranger
Whom he had hailed with joy, and cried *MS. 131*

25 Provoked *rev to* And soon *alt* Provoked *MS. 107 (B2)*

26 A sullen look upon the approaching stranger *MS. 107 (B2)*
An altered *alt* A frownin[g] *MS. 106* advancing] unconscious *alt in pencil and ink* approaching *MS. 106* glorious *MS. 134*

29 Anon *rev from* [?Erewhile] *MS. 109*

30 waves *Dora W rev from* deep *MS. 107 (A)* deep *MS. 109* Sea *MS. 131* portended] foreboded *MS. 109*

31–36 *lacking MS. 109*

35 malign *over illeg word MS. 135*

37 *entered after l. 30 then del MS. 131*

39 and *Dora W rev from* in *MS. 107 (A)* in *MS. 109*

Of motion, whether in the embrace
Of trusty anchorage, or scudding o'er
The main flood roughened into hill and valley.

Behold, how wantonly she laves
Her sides, the Wizard's craft confounding;
Like something out of Ocean sprung
To be for ever fresh and young,
Breasts the sea-flashes, and huge waves
Top-gallant high, rebounding and rebounding!

But Ocean under magic heaves,
And cannot spare the Thing he cherished:
Ah! what avails that She was fair,
Luminous, blithe, and debonair?
The storm has stripped her of her leaves;
The Lily floats no longer!—She hath perished.

Grieve for her,—She deserves no less;
So like, yet so unlike, a living Creature!
No heart had she, no busy brain;
Though loved, she could not love again;
Though pitied, *feel* her own distress;
Nor aught that troubles us, the fools of Nature.

---

40 Of motion, and the power [power *rev to* pride] of place, *MS. 109*
Of motion, and the pride of place; *Dora W rev to*
Of motion, whether rocked within the'embrace *MS. 107 (A); MS. 131 as rev MS. 109* *MS. 107 (C) as rev MS. 107 (A) but* rocked] rock'd *MS. 106 as rev MS. 107 (A) but* Of motion *and no apos in inserted MS. 134*

41 Whether at anchor rock'd, or scudding o'er *MS. 109; so MS. 131 but* rock'd] rocked *MS. 107 (A) as MS. 109 but no comma and Dora W rev to*
Of some protecting bay or scudding o'er *Dora W rev to text*

42 The main flood *rev from* Wide waters *MS. 107 (A)* Wide waters *MS. 109* Wide waters, *MS. 131*

43 laves *rev from* leaves *MS. 109*

44 Her sides *rev from* The gale *MS. 109*

47 sea-flashes *rev from* sea-flushes *MS. 135*

49 Ocean *del MS. 107 (A)* magic *rev from* ma[?]ic *MS. 135*

54 hath] has *MS. 109*

55 Grieve *rev from* Grieve not *MS. 107 (C)*

56 Though but a visionary Creature; *MS. 109; so MS. 131 but* Though] Tho' *and* Creature] creature *MS. 107 (A) as MS. 109 but Dora W rev to* So like—yet so unlike—a living Creature;

58 could not love] could love *(?copyist's slip) MS. 107 (A)*

Yet is there cause for gushing tears;
So richly was this Galley laden;
A fairer than Herself she bore,
And, in her struggles, cast ashore;
A lovely One, who nothing hears
Of wind or wave—a meek and guileless Maiden.

Into a cave had Merlin fled
From mischief, caused by spells himself had muttered;
And, while repentant all too late,
In moody posture there he sate,
He heard a voice, and saw, with half-raised head,
A Visitant by whom these words were uttered:

---

61 there *rev from* their *MS. 135*
62 So *Dora W rev from* For *?WW rev from* So *MS. 107 (A)*
64 struggles,] struggle *MSS. 107 (A), 109*
65–66 One mightier far than all the Seers
And Sorcerers of earth—a guiless Maiden. *rev to*
One frail and feeble but than Seers
And Sorcerers mightier far—a guiless Maiden. *rev to*
A lovely one who nothing hears of this wild roar *rev to*
A lovely One who nothing hears
Of this wild roar *rev to*
A lovely One who nothing hears
Of wind and wave, a meek and guiless Maiden *MS. 109*
65 lovely] lonely *MS. 131*
66 or . . . guileless] and . . . guiltless *MS. 131*
67–72 "Bestrew with dust thy hoary head!
Such were the words to Merlin uttered [uttered *rev to* utter'd]
While as repentant all too late
Within a Cave the Sorcerer sate,
Whither for shelter he had fled
From mischief wrought by spells himself had muttered [muttered *rev to* mutter'd] *MS. 109, stanza rev to text but l. 68* From *rev from* By *l. 72* A *rev from* The were *inserted*
67 had *rev from* hath *MS. 131*
68 From *rev from* By *MS. 131*
72 uttered:] muttered— *rev to* uttered— *MS. 131*

"On Christian service this frail Bark
Sailed" (hear me, Merlin!) "under high protection,
Though on her prow a sign of heathen power
Was carved—a Goddess with a Lily flower,
The old Egyptian's emblematic mark
Of joy immortal and of pure affection.

"Her course was for the British strand,
Her freight it was a Damsel peerless;
God reigns above, and Spirits strong
May gather to avenge this wrong
Done to the Princess, and her Land
Which she in duty left, though sad not cheerless.

73–78 "Rash Mortal! know that this frail Bark
"Sail'd westward under high protection;
"And on her prow a sign of power
"Was carv'd—the Egyptian Lily-flower
"The Lily, emblematic mark
"Of joy immortal, and of pure affection *Dora W rev to*
"Rash Mortal! know that this frail Bark
"Sail'd westward under high protection;
On Christian service tho' she bore
Carved on her prow the [the *rev to* a] heathen sign of power
The [?] Egyptian Lilly *Dora rev to*
"Rash Mortal! know that this frail Bark
On Christian service sailed with high protection
Sailed Merlin hear me under high protection *Dora rev to*
On Christian service this frail Bark
Sailed,—hear me Merlin under high protection
Tho' on her prow a sign of heathen power
Was carved the [the *rev to* a] Goddess with her lily flower
The old Egyptian's emblematic mark
Of joy immortal and of pure affection. *MS. 107 (A)*
The Voice [Voice *rev from* voice] continued, "This [This *rev from* this] fair Bark
"Steered westward under high protection;
"And on her prow a sign of power
"Was carv'd—the Egyptian lily- [lily- *rev from* lilly-] flower;
"The lily [lily *rev from* lilly], emblematic mark
"Of joy immortal and of pure affection. *MS. 109 but l. 73 rev to* "Rash Mortal! know that this fair Bark
"Rash Mortal know that this fair bark
Steered westward under high protection
On Christian service tho' she bore
Carved on her prow a heathen sign of power
The Egyptian Lily emblematic mark
Of joy immortal, and of pure affection. *MS. 131*

76 a Lily] her Lily *MSS. 106, 134*

79 was *inserted MS. 109*

80 Damsel peerless; *rev from* peerless Damsel *MS. 135*

81 *rev from* "Gods are there, Merlin,! Spirits strong, *MS. 109 but see nonverbal list*

82 *rev from* Who will not overlook the wrong *MS. 109*

84 though sad] sad but *1836–, 1839* not] and *MS. 131*

"And to Caerleon's loftiest tower
Soon will the Knights of Arthur's Table
A cry of lamentation send;
And all will weep who there attend,
To grace that Stranger's bridal hour,
For whom the sea was made unnavigable.

"Shame! should a Child of Royal Line
Die through the blindness of thy malice:"
Thus to the Necromancer spake
Nina, the Lady of the Lake,
A gentle Sorceress, and benign,
Who ne'er embittered any good man's chalice.

"What boots," continued she, "to mourn?
To expiate thy sin endeavour!
From the bleak isle where she is laid,
Fetched by our art, the Egyptian Maid
May yet to Arthur's court be borne
Cold as she is, ere life be fled for ever.

"My pearly Boat, a shining Light,
That brought me down that sunless river,
Will bear me on from wave to wave,
And back with her to this sea-cave;
Then Merlin! for a rapid flight
Through air to thee my charge will I deliver.

---

85 Caerleon's] Tintaggel's *MSS. 107 (A), 109* Tintaggels *MSS. 107 (C)* Tintaggel's *alt* Caerleons *in pencil MS. 106* Tintaggios *MS. 131*   tower *rev from* towers *MS. 109*

85–87 *over miscopied and erased ll. 91–93 MS. 107 (C)*

86 will *rev from* with *MS. 109*

88 weep *alt in pencil* grieve *MS. 134*

89 that *rev from* the *MS. 109*

90 sea was *rev from* seas were *MS. 134*

91 a *rev from* this *MS. 109*

100–102 Our Art shall [shall *rev to* must]fetch the Egyptian Maid
Who may to [to *rev to* unto *del*] Arthur's court be born[?e], *Dora W rev to text (but no commas) MS. 107 (A)*
Myself shall [shall *rev to* will] fetch the Egyptian Maid
Hence by degree [degree *rev to* degrees] cause to be born
To Arthur's court ere life be fled for ever. *rev to*
Our art must [must *rev to* may *rev to* shall] fetch the Egyptian Maid
Who might [might *rev from* may *rev from* must] to Arthur's Court be [be *rev from* she [?]] born,
Cold as she is, ere life be fled for ever. *MS. 109; MS. 131 as rev MS. 109 but* born] borne *and* ere *rev from* th

103 pearly *inserted MS. 109*   a *rev from* that *MS. 109*

104 that *rev from* this *MS. 137* this *MSS. 107 (A, C), 106, 131, 134*

107 Then *rev from* [?Wh]en *MS. 107 (A)* Thence, *MS. 109*—Whence *MS. 131*

108 to thee my charge] my charge to Thee *MS. 131*

"The very swiftest of thy Cars
Must, when my part is done, be ready;
Meanwhile, for further guidance, look
Into thy own prophetic book;
And, if that fail, consult the Stars
To learn thy course; farewell! be prompt and steady."

This scarcely spoken, she again
Was seated in her gleaming Shallop,
That, o'er the yet-distempered Deep,
Pursued its way with bird-like sweep,
Or like a steed, without a rein,
Urged o'er the wilderness in sportive gallop.

Soon did the gentle Nina reach
That Isle without a house or haven;
Landing, she found not what she sought,
Nor saw of wreck or ruin aught
But a carved Lotus cast upon the shore
By the fierce waves, a flower in marble graven.

Sad relique, but how fair the while!
For gently each from each retreating
With backward curve, the leaves revealed
The bosom half, and half concealed,
Of a Divinity, that seemed to smile
On Nina as she passed, with hopeful greeting.

---

110 part is *rev from* best be *MS. 109*

114 learn] know *MSS. 107 (A, C), 106, 131, 134* and] be *MSS. 107 (A), 109*

117 That, *rev in pencil from* Which, *MS. 107 (C)* Which, *MSS. 107 (A), 109* Which *MS. 131*

118 bird-like] cloud like *rev to* bird like *MS. 107 (A)* cloud like *MS. 109* cloud-like *MS. 131*

123 Landing, she found not what] There landing—Found she whom *MSS. 107 (A, C)* There landing, —found [found *rev from* Found] she whom *MSS. 106, 109 but comma added in pencil MS. 106; MS. 134 as rev MS. 106* There landing, <u>found</u> She what *MS. 131*

124 Nor saw] No—nor *MSS. 107 (A, C), 106, 131, 134* No—not *MS. 109*

125 cast upon *rev from* on *MS. 109* shore] beach, *MSS. 107 (A, C), 106, 109, 131, 134* beach *1836–, 1839*

126 And in its cup a Goddess daintily engraven. *MSS. 107 (A, C); so MS. 106 but* in *rev from* on *MS. 109 as MS. 107 but* daintily engraven *rev from* exquisitely graven *MSS. 131, 134 as MS. 107 but* in *rev from* on *MS. 134 and no period MSS. 131, 134*

127–129 This symbol cast upon the Isle
Round which the wild waves yet were beating
Had Leaves which sloping back revealed *Dora W rev to*
This symbol (not unnamed erewhile)
Had Leaves which each from each retreating
And gently sloping back revealed *WW rev to text MS. 109*$_1$

127 relique, *rev from* reliques! *MS. 109*$_2$

129 *pencil draft:* with backward curve with the same backward curve / [?which] *MS. 109*$_1$

131 a] the *MSS. 107 (A, C), 106, 109, 131, 134* smile *rev from* smi[?] *MS. 109*$_2$

No quest was hers of vague desire,
Of tortured hope and purpose shaken;
Following the margin of a bay,
She spied the lonely Cast-away,
Unmarred, unstripped of her attire,
But with closed eyes,—of breath and bloom forsaken.

Then Nina, stooping down, embraced,
With tenderness and mild emotion,
The Damsel, in that trance embound;
And, while she raised her from the ground,
And in the pearly shallop placed,
Sleep fell upon the air, and stilled the ocean.

The turmoil hushed, celestial springs
Of music opened, and there came a blending
Of fragrance, underived from earth,
With gleams that owed not to the Sun their birth,
And that soft rustling of invisible wings
Which Angels make, on works of love descending.

And Nina heard a sweeter voice
Than if the Goddess of the Flower had spoken:
"Thou hast achieved, fair Dame! what none
Less pure in spirit could have done;
Go, in thy enterprise rejoice!
Air, earth, sea, sky, and heaven, success betoken."

---

136 lonely] lovely *MS. 107 (C)*
137 *lacking MS. 131*
138 bloom *rev from* gloom *MS. 109*
140 *rev from* With all the strength her arms c[d] muster *MS. 109*
141 trance embound] trance em-bound *WW rev from* slumber bound *MS. 109*
143 the] her *MSS. 109, 131*
144 *rev from* The sea forgot to roar the wind to bluster. *MS. 109*
the air *rev from* her air *MS. 134*
145 *WW inserted line in pencil, adding a row of crosses above and the words* see end note. *MS. 107 (A)*
145–150 *lacking MSS. 107 (A), 109*
146 *rev from* As peace returned, the sacred springs *MS. 107 (B)* music *rev from* mercy *rev from* pity *MS. 107 (B)*
149 And *rev from* With *MS. 107 (B)*
151 sweeter *Dora W rev from* heavenly *MS. 107 (A)* heavenly *MS. 109*
152 Than *Dora W rev from* As *MS. 107 (A)* As *MS. 109*
154 Less pure in spirit *rev from* Of soul less gentle *MS. 107 (A)* Of soul less gentle *MSS. 109; so MS. 131 but* Of] "Of
156 Air, sky [and *inserted*] earth, and sea, success betoken. *MS. 109; MS. 107 (A) as rev MS. 109 but* sky] sky, *then line rev to text (but no quot)*
"Air sky and earth sea success betoken."— *MS. 131*

So cheered she left that Island bleak,
A bare rock of the Scilly cluster;
And, as they traversed the smooth brine,
The self-illumined Brigantine
Shed, on the Slumberer's cold wan cheek
And pallid brow, a melancholy lustre.

Fleet was their course, and when they came
To the dim cavern, whence the river
Issued into the salt-sea flood,
Merlin, as fixed in thought he stood,
Was thus accosted by the Dame:
"Behold to thee my Charge I now deliver!

---

157 So cheered she left *rev from* So with good heart *(WW pencil, Dora W ink) MS. 107 (A)* So with good heart *MSS. 109, 131*

158 A bare *rev from* The *MS. 109*

159 They skimmed the sea the heaving brine *in pencil MS. 107 (D)* They left; and, as they skimm'd the brine, *MS. 109; so MS. 107 (A) rev to text; MS. 131 as MS. 109 but* left; and,] left, and skimm'd the brine,] skimmed the Brine

161 cold wan] wan *MS. 131*

163 their *rev from* there *MS. 134*

164 whence *rev from* where *MS. 109*

165 Issued] Issues *MSS. 107 (A), 109, 131*

168 to thee my Charge *rev from* my Charge to thee *MS. 109*

"But where attends thy chariot—where?"
Quoth Merlin, "Even as I was bidden,
So have I done; as trusty as thy barge
My vehicle shall prove—O precious Charge!
If this be sleep, how soft! if death, how fair!
Much have my books disclosed, but the end is hidden."

169–174 *Dora W's fair copy in MS. 107 (A), revised in pencil (WW) and ink (Dora W):*
attends thy Chariot
"But where ~~thy book,~~^~~thy Dragons~~ where?"
Quoth Merlin, "even as I was bidden,
~~my books have given~~ ~~The Princess now is given~~
"So ~~for the Princess~~ have I done; ~~my way~~
A light to guide me with my charge sweet heaven
~~In trust to me my way is marked—sweet heaven~~
"~~Is clear before me through this day~~
If this be sleep how soft, if Death how fair
"(~~Sweet Heavens how fair the Slumberer is, how fair~~)
I go in hope ~~the end from~~
"~~I go in hope though much from me is hidden.~~"
I go in hope thoug
~~Bright hopes conduct~~ me tho' the end be is hidden
~~the course is~~
So have I done, a light is given
To guide me willing charge—sweet heaven *MS. 107 (A)*
So have I done, a light is given
To guide me with my charge—sweet Heaven
If this be Sleep how soft, if Death how fair
I go in hope though the end from me is hidden. *MS. 107 (C)*
If this be sleep, how soft! Light of my Books
I go in hope, but the end from me is hidden *rev to*
If this be sleep, how soft! if death how fair
Light have [have *rev from* of] my Books bestowed but the end is hidden *l. 174 rev to*
My Books point out our course but the end is hidden *rev to*
My Books have spoken but the end is hidden *rev to*
Much have my Books spoken [spoken *rev from* revealed] but the end is hidden *all above rev by paste-over to text MS. 106*

169 attends thy chariot—] thy book, thy Dragons *MS. 109* thy Book?—Thy Dragons *MS. 131*

171–172 *alt in pencil eras:* My [?vehicle] will prove as trusty as thy Barge *MS. 106*
So for the Princess have I done; my way
[My way is *del*] "Is clear before me thro' [thro' *rev from* for] this day *MS. 109; MS. 131 as rev MS. 109 but* have I] I have

172, 174 *WW's pencil draft:* my books have given / a light to guide me with my Charge / Hopeful I go / I go though the end *MS. 107 (A)*

172 shall] will *MS.* 106_1

173–174 "('Sweet heavens how fair the slumberer is, how fair')
"And good I hope for [future *del*] things from me [from me *inserted*] yet hidden!" *MS. 109*
"(Sweet heavens how fair the Slumberer is how fair!)
"I go in hope tho' much to me is hidden." *MS. 131*

173 if death how fair *rev from* Light [Light *rev from* light] of my Books bestowed *MS.* 106_1

174 *rev from* [?Bright] hopes [?conduct me tho the end is] hidden *MS.* 106_1*; but also WW and DW canceled drafts:*
Light of [of *rev to* have] my Books bestowed but [?]
My Books point out [point out *rev to* have shown] our course but the end is hidden
Much have my Books revealed

He spake, and gliding into view
Forth from the grotto's dimmest chamber
Came two mute Swans, whose plumes of dusky white
Changed, as the pair approached the light,
Drawing an ebon car, their hue
(Like clouds of sunset) into lucid amber.

Once more did gentle Nina lift
The Princess, passive to all changes:
The car received her; then up-went
Into the ethereal element
The Birds with progress smooth and swift
As thought, when through bright regions memory ranges.

Sage Merlin, at the Slumberer's side,
Instructs the Swans their way to measure;
And soon Caerleon's towers appeared,
And notes of minstrelsy were heard
From rich pavilions spreading wide,
For some high day of long-expected pleasure.

175–180 *rev from*
The Enchanter spake his words were true
And from the Grotto's dimest chamber
Appeared two swans of dusky white
Which took, as they approached the light
With the trim Chariot which they drew,
A hue not snowy but of lucid amber *MS. 109 but see nonverbals*

176 dimmest] inmost *MS. 131*

180 lucid] liquid *MS. 131*

183 then *rev from* and *MS. 109*

187 Sage *rev from* And *MS. 109*

188 Swans *rev from* Birds *MS. 109*

189 Caerleon's] Tintaggel's *MSS. 107 (A), 131* Tintaggels *MS. 107 (C)* Tintaggel's *alt* Caerleons *MS. 106* Tintaggal's *rev to* Tintaggel's *MS. 109*

190–191 *rev from* Through curling smoke and notes were heard
Of minstrelsy and pomps decried *MS. 109*

181–188 In MS. 134_1 MW entered these lines a second time in error, then deleted them.

Awe-stricken stood both Knights and Dames
Ere on firm ground the car alighted;
Eftsoons astonishment was past,
For in that face they saw the last
Last lingering look of clay, that tames
All pride, by which all happiness is blighted.

Said Merlin, "Mighty King, fair Lords,
Away with feast and tilt and tourney!
Ye saw, throughout this Royal House,
Ye heard, a rocking marvellous
Of turrets, and a clash of swords
Self-shaken, as I closed my airy journey.

"Lo! by a destiny well known
To mortals, joy is turned to sorrow;
This is the wished-for Bride, the Maid
Of Egypt, from a rock conveyed
Where she by shipwreck had been thrown;
Ill sight! but grief may vanish ere the morrow."

193–198 All stood the dames
~~And~~ wonder-stricken ~~were~~
Oh dole and pity for the Dames [193]
And Warriors when the car alighted [194]
Eftsoons Eftsoons
Soon
When their astonishment was past [195]
[?While] face
{in ~~face [?look] face a look of~~ face they saw the last
And {on that ~~death-like face they~~ ^ cast [196]
Last lingering look of clay
~~A look full well assured,~~ that tames [197]
All pride by which all happiness is blighted [198]
~~[?face of death]~~
in margin And gathering round the bier [?] *all del, all revs in pencil except ll. 196–197 MS. 109*$_1$

193 stood *rev from* st[?an]d *MS. 107 (A)* were *MSS. 109, 131*

194 Ere *rev in pencil and ink from* But *MS. 109*$_2$

195 Eftsoons *rev in pencil and ink from* [?But] soon *MS. 109*$_2$

199–204 *lacking MS. 109*$_1$

202 rocking *rev from* shutting *MS. 107 (A)* shutting *MSS. 109, 131*

203 turrets] door and window *rev to* Turrets *MS. 107 (A)* door and window *MS. 109* door and window, *MS. 131*

204 airy] weary *MS. 131*

205 Said Merlin [*rev in pencil to* Look [?look] by a lot *MS. 109*$_1$
Lo!— *written over eras pencil* Look look— *MS. 109*$_2$

207 wished-for] look'd for *alt* wish'd for *MS. 109*$_1$ look'd for *rev to* wish'd for *MS. 109*$_2$

208 Of Egypt *rev from* [?She who] *MS. 107 (C)*

209 Where she by shipwreck had been thrown] Whither [Whither *rev to* Whereon] by shipwreck she was thrown *MS. 109*$_1$ shipwreck] Shepherds *MS. 131*

210 sight!] Night!— *MS. 131* ere] on *MS. 131* morrow."] morning *alt in pencil* morrow *MS. 134*

"Though vast thy power, thy words are weak,"
Exclaimed the King, "a mockery hateful;
Dutiful Child! her lot how hard!
Is this her piety's reward?
Those watery locks, that bloodless cheek!
O winds without remorse! O shore ungrateful!

"Rich robes are fretted by the moth;
Towers, temples, fall by stroke of thunder;
Will that, or deeper thoughts, abate
A Father's sorrow for her fate?
He will repent him of his troth;
His brain will burn, his stout heart split asunder.

"Alas! and I have caused this woe;
For, when my prowess from invading Neighbours
Had freed his Realm, he plighted word
That he would turn to Christ our Lord,
And his dear Daughter on a Knight bestow
Whom I should choose for love and matchless labours.

"Her birth was heathen, but a fence
Of holy Angels round her hovered;
A Lady added to my court
So fair, of such divine report

211–212 King Arthur cried thy words are weak
A bitter mockery and hateful *rev to*
"Tho' vast thy power thy words are weak"
King Athur said, "a mockery hateful; *MS. 109*
pencil draft:
Though vast thy power thy words are weak
~~Thou~~
Thy powers and thy words are weak
King Arthur [?said] *MS. 109*
212 Exclaimed the King,] King Arthur said *MSS. 107 (A, C), 106, 131, 134* King Arthur said, *MSS. 135, 137*
213 her lot how hard! *rev from* how hard her lot *MS. 135*
215 bloodless] bloomless *MS. 131*
216 shore *rev from* shores *MS. 109*
219 deeper *Dora W rev from* better *MS. 107 (A)* better *MSS. 109, 131*
222 stout heart] heart will *MS. 131*
223 Alas! and I have *rev from* Alas! and have I *MS. 131, MS. 135* Alas, and I have *rev to* And I have *alt* I—none else have *orig reinstated MS. 106*
224 invading *rev from* intruding *MS. 137*
227–228 And his dear Daughter would bestow
On knight that I might [that I might *rev to* whom I should] chuse for worth and worthiest labours. *MS. 109*
"And his dear Daughter would bestow
"On Knight that I might chuse for worth and worthiest labours. *Dora W rev to text but* love] worth *MS. 107 (A); MS. 131 as orig MS. 107 (A) but* Knight . . . labours] knight . . . labors
228 love] worth *MS. 107 (C)*
229 Her birth was heathen, *rev from* Half heathen was she *MS. 109*

And worship, seemed a recompence
For fifty kingdoms by my sword recovered.

"Ask not for whom, O champions true!
She was reserved by me her life's betrayer;
She who was meant to be a bride
Is now a corse; then put aside
Vain thoughts, and speed ye, with observance due
Of Christian rites, in Christian ground to lay her."

"The tomb," said Merlin, "may not close
Upon her yet, earth hide her beauty;
Not froward to thy sovereign will
Esteem me, Liege! if I, whose skill
Wafted her hither, interpose
To check this pious haste of erring duty.

"My books command me to lay bare
The secret thou art bent on keeping;
Here must a high attest be given,
What Bridegroom was for her ordained by Heaven;
And in my glass significants there are
Of things that may to gladness turn this weeping.

"For this, approaching, One by One,
Thy Knights must touch the cold hand of the Virgin;

---

233 seemed] seems *rev to* seem'd *MS. 109*

235 "Ask not, my knights, for which of you *MS. 107 (A); MS. 107 (C) as (A) but rev in pencil and ink to text; MS. 131 as MS. 107 (A)*
And you [*rev in pencil and ink to* Ask not,] my knights, for which of you *MS. 109*

236 She was ordained demand of no soothsayer *rev in pencil and ink to text but* lifes betrayer *(pencil)* Life's betrayer; *(ink) MS. 109*

238/239 Pomps jewels, spousal pageantry *del MS. 109*

239 Vain thoughts *inserted in pencil and ink MS. 109* ye,] you *MS. 131*

241 "may *rev in pencil and ink from* must *MS. 109*

245 interpose *inserted MS. 109* interpose *rev in pencil from* interfere *MS. 134*

246 To *rev from* Interpose to *MS. 109*

247 *line entered after l. 234 then del MS. 131*
command *rev from* instruct *MS. 109*$_1$ me *rev from illeg wd MS. 106*

248 The *rev from* A *MS. 109*$_1$

249–252 It must be shewn by surer sign
Than act, intent, or word of thine
What Bridegroom should for her the ring prepare
And haply whether she be dead or sleeping *rev to*
Clear attestation must be given
What Bridegroom was for her design'd by heaven
Who should for her the spousal ring prepare
And haply whether she be dead or sleepeth *rev to text MS. 109*$_1$

253 For this *rev from* Thy Knights *MS. 109*$_1$

254 Thy Knights must . . . the *rev from* Must . . . the royal *MS. 109*$_1$

So, for the favoured One, the Flower may bloom
Once more; but, if unchangeable her doom,
If life departed be for ever gone,
Some blest assurance, from this cloud emerging,

May teach him to bewail his loss;
Not with a grief that, like a vapour, rises
And melts; but grief devout that shall endure,
And a perpetual growth secure
Of purposes which no false thought shall cross,
A harvest of high hopes and noble enterprises."

"So be it," said the King;—"anon,
Here, where the Princess lies, begin the trial;
Knights each in order as ye stand
Step forth."—To touch the pallid hand
Sir Agravaine advanced; no sign he won
From Heaven or Earth;—Sir Kaye had like denial.

255–258 So in the favor'd One behoof
Will truth be known perhaps by vital proof;
But if the life indeed be gone,
And from this silent gloom be no emerging *rev to text but l.* 258 Some *rev from* A *and* cloud *rev from* gloom *MS. 107 (A)*
So for the favord one this flower pale
May bloom fair—at most if that proof fail
[?By] some assurance from this gloom emerging
Those after thoughts to mourn his loss *alt*
So for the favord One this flower may bloom
Once more *alt*
So for the favord One this flower may bloom
Once more [or *del*] if unchangeable her doom
Some blest assurance from this cloud [?emerg]ing
Shall teach to bewail her loss *pencil draft MS. 107 (A)*
So in the favor'd One's behoof
Will [Will *rev from* Till] truth be known perhaps by vital proof;
But if [indeed *del*] the Life indeed be gone,
And from this darksome cloud [darksome cloud *rev to* silent gloom] be no emerging, *MS. 109; MS. 131 as rev MS. 109 but opening quots in each line and l.* 255 One's *rev from* one's *l.* 256 known] known, *l.* 257 gone,] gone

256 unchangeable *rev from* unchanged *MS. 106*

258 cloud emerging, *so MSS. 107 (C), 106; 1835_2, 1836–, 1839* cloud emerging *MS. 134* cloud, emerging, *rev to* cloud, emerging *MS. 137; 1835, 1836YR as MS. 137 rev*

259 Then One at least shall mourn her loss *MS. 109; so MS. 107 (A) rev to text; MS. 131 as MS. 109 but* "Then One, . . . least, . . . loss,

261 And melts, but in the heart endures *rev to* And melts, but grief [that *del*] devout that doth endure *MS. 109* but . . . endure, *rev from* but from devout [? ? ?] *MS. 106* shall *rev from* will *rev from* doth *rev from* shall *MS. 107 (A)* doth *MS. 131*

262 secure *rev from* secures *MS. 109*

263 false thought *alt in pencil* [?senti]ment *MS. 107 (A)* shall *rev to* will *MS. 107 (A)*

264 high *rev from* great *MS. 107 (A)* high *rev to* great *MS. 109* great *MS. 131*

267 Knights *rev from* Let *MS. 109* in *rev from* [?an] *MS. 107 (C)* ye *rev from* you *MS. 134*

268 pallid] clay-cold *MSS. 109, 131*

269 Agravaine] Kay *alt in pencil* Agravaine *MS. 107 (A)* Kay *MSS. 109, 131*

270 Kaye *rev in pencil from* Tor *MS. 107 (A)* Sir . . . denial] Sir Bors encountered denial *rev to* Sir Tor had like denial *MS. 109; MS. 131 as rev MS. 109*

Abashed, Sir Dinas turned away;
Even for Sir Percival was no disclosure;
Though he, devoutest of all Champions, ere
He reached that ebon car, the bier
Whereon diffused like snow the Damsel lay,
Full thrice had crossed himself in meek composure.

270/271 Sir Gawaine touched and next in place
Sir Launcelot tired Slave [Slave *rev from* slave] of vain contrision
Before he touched Queen Guinevre lookd sad
Next came his son the youth Sir Gallahad
[He gazed he paused and [gazes *del*] stood gazing on the face *rev to*]
He paused and conned [conned *rev from* read] the features [features *rev from* Featuring] of the face
Which he had met before in midnight vision

Sir Gallahad with trembling hand
Touch'd and those birds far famed thro' loves dominions
The Swans in triumph clappd their wings
And their necks played involved in rings
Like sinless snakes in Eden's happy land
Mine is she said the knight, again they shook their pinions *del MS. 109*

271–300 *first expansion of the "trial" scene:*

2

When Sir
Sir Dinas and Sir Delamere
Approachd the Car
~~Advanced~~ with step undaunted
withdrew
When they ~~retired~~ abashed Sir Gawaine, mail'd
For Tournament his beaver ~~veil'd~~ vail'd
And softly touched but to his princely cheer
And high expentancy no sign was granted.

3

Next
Then disencumbered of his harp
Came one endeared to thousands as a Brother
His fruitless touch Sir Tristram nothing rued
{The
{To fair Izonda he had sued
In
~~With~~ love too true with pangs too shar
{o
In wood and wilderness with love to{ sharp
{,
From hope too distant{ not to dread another

4

Not so Sir Launcelot from Heaven's grace
A sign he craved tired slave of vain contrision
was passing
The guilty Guenevre ~~look'd~~ glad
~~hope~~
When his ~~touch~~ failed his Son Sir Galahad
touch
Came next and stood entranced with that still face
Whose features he had seen in midnight vision *all del MS. 109*

271–276, 277–282 *stanzas transposed in MSS. 109, 131*

275 like snow *DW inserted MS. 106*

276 thrice . . . meek] twice . . . much *MS. 131*

Imagine (but ye Saints! who can?)
How in still air the balance trembled;
The wishes, peradventure the despites
That overcame some not ungenerous Knights;
And all the thoughts that lengthened out a span
Of time to Lords and Ladies thus assembled.

What patient confidence was here!
And there how many bosoms panted!
While drawing toward the Car Sir Gawaine, mailed
For tournament, his Beaver vailed,
And softly touched; but, to his princely cheer
And high expectancy, no sign was granted.

277–282 Imagine, he who will or can,
How in still air the balance trembled
As to the proof advanced the knights
The hopes, the fears, the wishes the despites
And all the thoughts that lengthened out a span
Of Time to Lords and Ladies there assembled. *del, reentered by WW, rev, below l. 276 MS. 107 (A)*

WW's ink draft:
ye Saints!
~~Ah think~~—Imagine but who can?
While ~~yet [?]~~ trembles yet
as it
How ~~in still air,~~ the balance ^ trembled, *rev to*
~~wishes peradventure~~ the
~~The fears~~; ~~the wishes~~ haply the despites
The perturbations haply the despite
That overcame some not ungenerous Knights
ever ~~glimpses of [?joy] joy~~
And ~~all the lightenings of glad hope that ran~~
Through the ~~hush'd~~ minds of Ladies there assembled
~~And all the thoughts that crowd like a span~~
~~Of time for Lords and Ladies there assembled~~ *MS. 107 (A)*
Imagine, he who will or can,
How in still air the balance [balance *rev from* Barons] trembled
The hopes, the fears, the wishes the despites
As to the proof advanced the knights
And all the thoughts that lengthened out a span
Of Time to Lords and Ladies there [there *alt* on that [?ring]] assembled *MS. 109, but ll. 279, 280 transposed; MS. 131 as rev MS. 109 (excluding transposition) but l. 277* who will *rev from* who can *l. 278* trembled, *l. 279* wishes,

277 but *rev from illeg wd MS. 106* ye *rev from* the *MS. 107 (C)*

279 *rev from* The perturbation haply the despites *MS. 107 (A)* peradventure *alt* haply *MS. 106*

282 thus *rev from* there *MS. 137* there *MS. 106*

283–284 *WW's pencil draft:* with fear
How many bosoms panted

284 how *rev in pencil from* too *MS. 107 (C)* panted *rev from* trembled *pencil draft MS. 109*

284/285 The moment *pencil draft MS. 109*

285 While . . . toward] When . . . towards *rev to* While . . . tow'rd *MS. 109*

286 his *rev from* with *MS. 109* he *MS. 131*

Next, disencumbered of his harp,
Sir Tristram, dear to thousands as a brother,
Came to proof, nor grieved that there ensued
No change;—the fair Izonda he had wooed
With love too true, a love with pangs too sharp,
From hope too distant, not to dread another.

Not so Sir Launcelot;—from Heaven's grace
A sign he craved, tired slave of vain contrition;
The royal Guinever looked passing glad
When his touch failed.—Next came Sir Galahad;
He paused, and stood entranced by that still face
Whose features he had seen in noontide vision.

289–294 *Dora W's fair copy, WW's revisions:*
~~Yet, at Sir Tristrams touch no change~~
~~came disburthen'd of~~
Next, ~~disencumbered~~ of his harp,
Sir Tristram dear to
~~Came One endeared~~ to thousands as a brother;
*~~Yet, though Sir Tristram touch'd no change ensued~~
~~His vain attempt Sir Tristram nothing rued~~;
~~Nor grieved he—fair Isonda he had woo'd~~
~~The fair Isonda he had sued~~
With
~~In~~ love too true, a love with pangs too sharp,
From hope too distant, not to dread another.—
*Came to the proof,—nor grieved though there ensued
No change—the fair Isonda he had woo'd *MS. 107 (A)*
Next, disencumbered of his harp,
Came One [One *rev from* one] endeared to thousands as a brother;
His vain attempt Sir Tristram nothing rued;
The fair Izonda he had sued
In love too true, a love with pangs too sharp,
From hope too distant—[*dash del*] not to dread another. *MS. 109; MS. 131 as rev MS. 109 but l. 289* Next, . . . harp] Next . . . Harp *l. 292* Izonda . . . sued] Isonda . . . sued, *l. 293* a love *om*

291 to] to the *MS. 134*

296 contrition; *rev from* cont[?en]ion; *MS. 107 (C)* contention— *MS. 131*

297–299 *Dora W's fair copy, WW's revisions:*
The Guenever
His royal Paramour was passing glad
~~To see the vain attempt~~ ~~next came~~ next came
When his touch fail'd;—~~his Son~~ Sir Galahad,
In ~~He paus'd and~~
~~Came next~~, and stood entranced by that still face
~~Came here~~ *MS. 107 (A)*
His royal Paramour was passing glad
When ~~his~~ touch fail'd;—his Son, Sir Galahad [Galahad *rev from* Gallahad],
Came next, and stood entranced with [with *alt* by] that still face *MS. 109; MS. 131 as rev MS. 109 but l. 297* The royal Genevere *and* passing glad *rev from* glad *l. 298 no ital* *l. 299* next, . . . with that still face] next . . . by that still face,

300 Whose . . . noontide *rev from* What . . . midnight *MS. 109*

For late, as near a murmuring stream
He rested 'mid an arbour green and shady,
Nina, the good Enchantress, shed
A light around his mossy bed;
And, at her call, a waking dream
Prefigured to his sense the Egyptian Lady.

Now, while his bright-haired front he bowed,
And stood, far-kenned by mantle furred with ermine,
As o'er the insensate Body hung
The enrapt, the beautiful, the young,
Belief sank deep into the crowd
That he the solemn issue would determine.

Nor deem it strange; the Youth had worn
That very mantle on a day of glory,
The day when he achieved that matchless feat,
The marvel of the PERILOUS SEAT,
Which whosoe'er approached of strength was shorn,
Though King or Knight the most renowned in story.

He touched with hesitating hand,
And lo! those Birds, far-famed through Love's dominions,

301–318 *inserted MS. 109*
301–302 For, while [For, while *rev to* Once, as] beside a murmuring stream
He slept within an arbour green and shady *MS. 109₁; MS. 131 as orig MS. 109₁ but* For late, as by . . .
301 near] by *MS. 131*
305–306 And to his sense revealed the Egyptian Lady. *rev to*
And a preparatory dream
That to [*etc.*] *MS. 109₁*
307–308 *rev from* While o'er that face his head he bowed
Far-kennd by mantle furr'd with richest ermine *MS. 109*
309 As *rev from* as *rev from* While *MS. 107 (A)* While *MSS. 109, 131* insensate *rev from* senseless *MS. 109*
311 sank] struck *MSS. 107 (A, C), 109* sunk *MSS. 106, 131*
312 the *over illeg eras MS. 106*
313 Nor deem it strange;] Nor deem it strange *rev from* What wonder; [; *rev to* !] for *MS. 109* worn *rev from* won *MS. 137* won *MSS. 107 (C), 106, 134*
315 The day when *rev to* When *MS. 106* that matchless feat *rev from* the feat *MS. 107 (A)* the feat *MS. 131*
When he the memorable feat *rev to* The day when he achiev'd the feat *MS. 109*
316 The marvel *rev from* Accomplished, *MS. 109*
317 strength *rev from* sense *MS. 106*
That none had ere [ere *rev to* e'er] approach'd of strength unshorn, *rev to*
That whosoee'r approached of strength was shorn *MS. 107 (A)*
Which [Which *rev to* That] none had ere approached of strength unshorn *MS. 109; so MS. 131 but* Which] That of] with
318 Though . . . or] Nor . . . nor *rev to* Or . . . or *MS. 107 (A)* Or . . . or *MSS. 107 (C), 106* Or [*pencil alt* Though] . . . or *MS. 134* Nor . . . nor *MSS. 109, 131* King] King *rev from* Knight *MS. 107 (C)* the most renowned] how ere renown'd *rev to* how ever famed *alt* the most renown'd *MS. 109*
320 through] tho *rev in pencil to* thro *MS. 134*

The Swans, in triumph clap their wings;
And their necks play, involved in rings,
Like sinless snakes in Eden's happy land;—
"Mine is she," cried the Knight;—again they clapped their pinions.

"Mine was she—mine she is, though dead,
And to her name my soul shall cleave in sorrow;"
Whereat, a tender twilight streak
Of colour dawned upon the Damsel's cheek;
And her lips, quickening with uncertain red,
Seemed from each other a faint warmth to borrow.

Deep was the awe, the rapture high,
Of love emboldened, hope with dread entwining,
When, to the mouth, relenting Death
Allowed a soft and flower-like breath,
Precursor to a timid sigh,
To lifted eyelids, and a doubtful shining.

In silence did King Arthur gaze
Upon the signs that pass away or tarry;
In silence watched the gentle strife
Of Nature leading back to life;
Then eased his Soul at length by praise
Of God, and Heaven's pure Queen—the blissful Mary.

Then said he, "Take her to thy heart
Sir Galahad! a treasure that God giveth,
Bound by indissoluble ties to thee
Through mortal change and immortality;
Be happy and unenvied, thou who art
A goodly Knight that hath no Peer that liveth!"

---

321 clap *rev from* clappd *MS. 109*, clapped *MSS. 106, 134*
322 And *rev from* Like *MS. 131 (miscopied l. 323)*
324 is *rev from* was *MS. 106* pinions.] wings *MS. 131*
326 shall] will *MSS. 107 (A), 109, 131*
327 Whereat *rev from* He paused *MS. 109*
329–330 *Dora W's fair copy and rev:*
~~her pale lips were faintly tinged with red~~
And ~~to her lips returned the faintest red~~
~~vague hue which each from other seemed to borrow~~
~~That cold was ever known from warmth to borrow~~ *Dora W rev to text MS. 107 (A)*
And to her lip returned [returned *rev from* return'd] the faintest red
That cold was ever known from warmth to borrow. *MS. 109*
329 quickening] quivering *MS. 131 ("X" in left margin, perhaps to mark variant)*
340 leading *rev from* bleading *(probably printer's error) MS. 137*
341 Soul] heart *MS. 131* his Soul at length] at length his heart *MS. 109* at length his soul *MS. 107 (C); MS. 107 (A) as MS. 109 but* heart *rev to* soul
345 ties *rev from* tie *MS. 107 (A)* tie *MSS. 109, 131*
348 A goodly] goodly *1836YR* Knight that *rev from* Knight who *MS. 106* that *rev in pencil from* who *MS. 134*

Not long the Nuptials were delayed;
And sage tradition still rehearses
The pomp the glory of that hour
When toward the Altar from her bower
King Arthur led the Egyptian Maid,
And Angels carolled these far-echoed verses;—

Who shrinks not from alliance
Of evil with good Powers,
To God proclaims defiance,
And mocks whom he adores.

A Ship to Christ devoted
From the Land of Nile did go;
Alas! the bright Ship floated,
An Idol at her Prow.

By magic domination,
The Heaven-permitted vent
Of purblind mortal passion,
Was wrought her punishment.

The Flower, the Form within it,
What served they in her need?
Her port she could not win it,
Nor from mishap be freed.

The tempest overcame her,
And she was seen no more;
But gently gently blame her,
She cast a Pearl ashore.

---

349 Nuptials] spousals *rev to* nuptials *MS. 109*
354 *rev from* And Angels sung far heard these [spousal *inserted*] verses *MS. 109*
360 From the *rev from* From *MS. 107 (A)* From *MS.* 109_2
361 the *rev from* a *MS.* 109_2 ship *inserted MS.* 109_2
363–366 Just Heaven for her vexation
Permitted Arts abuse *line rev to* Permitting strange abuse
By [By *WW rev in pencil to* Through] momentary passion
Was [Was *rev to* Were] winds and waves let loose *MS.* 109_2
366 her *rev from* the *MS.* 109_4
367–370 *lacking MS.* 109_2*; entered in margin then del MS.* 109_3
367 the] and *MS.* 109_3
368 in] at *MS.* 109_3
370 But from the storm be freed *MS.* 109_3
371 The tempest] Wild mischief *MS.* 109_2
374 She cast a Pearl] A Pearl, she cast *MS. 107 (A), so MSS. 107 (C) and 106 but no comma; MSS. 109, 131 as MS. 107 (C); MS. 134 as MS. 107 (C) but rev in pencil to text*

355–386 See the second reading text of Chorus on the following page.

The Maid to Jesu hearkened,
And kept to him her faith,
Till sense in death was darkened,
Or sleep akin to death.

But Angels round her pillow
Kept watch, a viewless band;
And, billow favouring billow,
She reached the destined strand.

Blest Pair! whate'er befall you,
Your faith in Him approve
Who from frail earth can call you,
To bowers of endless love!

[Text of MS. 109: Chorus only]

Who places his reliance
On good and evil powers
To God proclaims defiance
   And mocks whom he adores

A Ship to Christ devoted
Across the sea did go
Alas she gaily floated
   An Idol at her Prow

---

375 Jesu *rev from* Jesus *MS. 109*$_2$ Jesus *MS. 131*
379–382 The bare rock was her pillow
But Seraphs were at hand
To speed her o'er the [?billow]
For wedlock's holy band [*line rev to* On to this happy land] *rev to text MS. 107 (A)*
From rocky pillow lifted
She to this happy land
Across the Deep was wafted
For wedlocks holy band *MS. 131*
381 favouring *rev from* favour[?ed] *MS. 107 (A)*
383 befall] betide *MS. 131*
386/ Rydal Mount. / Nov: 1828 *MS. 107 (A)* The End. *MS. 106* W. Wordsworth / The End of Egypt: Maid *MS. 131*

---

composed November 20–28, 1828
found in DC MS. 109$_1$
1–16 *del MS. 109*$_1$
1–4 *rev to 1835 text*
3 *written over eras* Who hopes *MS. 109*$_1$
6 Across the sea *rev to* Across the Nile *rev to* From land of Nile *MS. 109*$_1$

379–382 For MS. 109 readings see the alternate reading text of Chorus and its *apparatus*.

Hence demons overcame her
And she was seen no more
But gently, gently blame her
  She cast a pearl ashore

The Maid to Jesu harkened
And kept to him her faith
Till sense in death was darkened
  Or counterfeits of death

The base rock was her pillow,
But Seraphs were at hand,
To help her o'er the billow
  For wedlock's holy band.

Blest pair, what e'er befal you;
Confide in him alone
Who at the last will call you
  To sing before his throne.

A JEWISH FAMILY.

(IN A SMALL VALLEY OPPOSITE ST. GOAR, UPON THE RHINE.)

GENIUS of Raphael! if thy wings
  Might bear thee to this glen,

---

9 demons *rev to* mischief *MS. 109₁*
16 counterfeits of *rev to* sleep akin to *MS. 109₁*
18 Seraphs] Seraphas *MS. 109₁*
19 help *rev to* speed *MS. 109₁*
21 Blest pair, . . . befal] Blest pair! . . . befall *rev from* Blesst pair, . . . befal *MS. 109₁* e'er] e're *MS. 109₁*
22–24 Your faith in him approve
Who from frail earth will call you
To bowers of endless love *alt MS. 109₁*
22 alone *rev from* alone, *alt* above *MS. 109₁*
23 at the last *rev to* to the bowers *MS. 109₁*
24 *rev to* Of everlasting love *MS. 109₁*

---

composed between November 29 and December 19, 1828
found in DC MSS. 107 (A) 28ʳ–29ʳ, (B) 71ᵛ–72ʳ; 106; 115; 131; 134; 137 (MW); 150; Morgan MS. 2; MS. 1835Col; MS. 1835/36
published in 1835, 1836–
classed Imagination *MS. 1835/36–*
reading text 1835
title lacking MS. 107 (B) The Jewish Child *rev to text MS. 107 (A)* A Jewish [?Child] [?Child *rev to* Family]. *MS. 106* A Jewish Family, met with in a Dingle near the Rhine. *Morgan MS. 2* A Jewish Family—In a Dingle near the Rhine *MS. 115* A Jewish Family / In the Swiss Valley (near the Rhine) *MS. 131* A Jewish Family. *with subtitle added by MW* (In a small valley opposite St. Goar, / upon the Rhine.) *MS. 137*
stanza numbers II . . . VI *MS. 107 (B)* 2 . . . 6 *MSS. 107 (B), 131, 134* 1 . . . 6 *MS. 106, Morgan MS. 2, MS. 115; so MS. 137 but rev to text*

With faithful memory left of things
  To pencil dear and pen,
Thou wouldst forego the neighbouring Rhine,
  And all his majesty,
A studious forehead to incline
  O'er this poor family.

The Mother—her thou must have seen,
  In spirit, ere she came
To dwell these rifted rocks between,
  Or found on earth a name;
An image, too, of that sweet Boy,
  Thy inspirations give:
Of playfulness, and love, and joy,
  Predestined here to live.

Downcast, or shooting glances far,
  How beautiful his eyes,
That blend the nature of the star
  With that of summer skies!
I speak as if of sense beguiled;
  Uncounted months are gone,
Yet am I with the Jewish Child,
  That exquisite Saint John.

I see the dark brown curls, the brow,
  The smooth transparent skin,
Refined, as with intent to show
  The holiness within;
The grace of parting Infancy
  By blushes yet untamed;
Age faithful to the mother's knee,
  Nor of her arms ashamed.

---

3 With memory left of shapes and things *Morgan MS. 2, MSS. 115, 131; so MS. 107 (A) rev to text*
5–8 *rev from*
  Thy studious Forehead would incline
  O'er this poor family
  And thou forget the neighbouring Rhine
  And all his majesty. *MS. 107 (A)*
8 O'er] On *MS. 115*
12 on *so all MSS., 1836–* no *1835*
13 An image *rev from* A dawning *MS. 107 (A)* that] this *MSS. 107, 106, Morgan MS. 2, MS. 115, 131*
14 Thy inspirations *rev from* Might dream or vision *MS. 107*
15 Of *rev from* In *rev from* For *MS. 107 (A)* In *MSS. 115, 131*
16 *rev from* Which yet in colours live. *MS. 107 (A)*
17 far *rev from* fair *MS. 106*
19 star *rev from* stars *MS. 137*
29 parting] lingering *MS. 131*

Two lovely Sisters, still and sweet
  As flowers, stand side by side;
Their soul–subduing looks might cheat
  The Christian of his pride:
Such beauty hath the Eternal poured
  Upon them not forlorn,
Though of a lineage once abhorred,
  Nor yet redeemed from scorn.

Mysterious safeguard, that, in spite
  Of poverty and wrong,
Doth here preserve a living light,
  From Hebrew fountains sprung;
That gives this ragged group to cast
  Around the dell a gleam
Of Palestine, of glory past,
  And proud Jerusalem!

33–34 Fair Creatures! in this lone retreat
By happy chance espied *rev to*
Two elder Innocents as sweet
Stand gazing side by side *rev to*
Two lovely Sisters, still and sweet
As flowers, stood [stood *rev to* stand] side by side *MS. 107 (A)*
Two [?elder Innocents] as sweet *alt* A sister flower [?as fresh] as sweet
Stand gazing side by side *erased pencil MS. 107 (A)*
Fair creatures, in this lone retreat
By happy chance espied *Morgan MS. 2; so MSS. 115, 131 but* espied] espied, *MSS. 115, 131, and* creatures] Creatures *MS. 131*

35 Their *rev from* Your *MS. 107 (A)* Your *Morgan MS. 2, MSS. 115, 131* looks *rev from* look *MS. 137* look *MS. 134*

37 hath] has *Morgan MS. 2, MSS. 115, 131* *illeg erased pencil above* Eternal pour'd *MS. 107 (A)*

38 them] them *rev from* you *MS. 107 (A)* you— *Morgan MS. 2* you— *MSS. 115, 131*

41 Mysterious safeguard *rev from* Strange mystery— *MS. 107 (A)* spite *rev from* despite *MS. 107 (A)*

45 That *alt pencil eras* And *MS. 107 (A)*

48/ The End *Morgan MS. 2*

THE POET AND THE CAGED TURTLEDOVE.

As often as I murmur here
My half-formed melodies,
Straight from her osier mansion near,
The Turtledove replies:
Though silent as a leaf before,
The captive promptly coos;
Is it to teach her own soft lore,
Or second my weak Muse?

I rather think, the gentle Dove
Is murmuring a reproof,
Displeased that I from lays of love
Have dared to keep aloof;
That I, a Bard of hill and dale,
Have caroll'd, fancy free,
As if nor dove, nor nightingale,
Had heart or voice for me.

If such thy meaning, O forbear,
Sweet Bird! to do me wrong;
Love, blessed Love, is every where
The spirit of my song:
'Mid grove, and by the calm fireside,
Love animates my lyre;
That coo again!—'tis not to chide,
I feel, but to inspire.

---

composed between November 29 and December 19, 1828

found in DC MSS. 107 (A, 26^{v}–27^{r}, (B) 114^{v}–115^{r}; 106; 115; 116; 131; 134; 135; 137 (MW); Morgan MS. 4; Cornell MS. 7; Fitzwilliam Museum MS.; Coatalen MS. (copy); MS. 1835/36

published in 1835, 1836–

classed Fancy *1836–*

reading text 1835

title lacking MS. 131, Coatalen MS. The Poet and the Dove *MSS. 107, 116; so MSS. 106, 135 but both rev to text* "Twenty minutes exercise upon the Terrace last night" (at the beginning of December) "but the scene within doors. *MS. 115* Twenty minutes' Exercise *Morgan MS. 4_1* Twenty minutes' exercise upon the Terrace last night, but the Scene within-doors. *Morgan MS. 4_2*

stanza numbers 1, 2, 3 *MSS. 107 (A), 115, Morgan MS. 4, Cornell MS. 7; roman numerals MS. 107 (B)* (II *and* III *only); MS. 137 as MS. 107 (A) but full stop after each number then all del*

3 her] her *rev from* his *MSS. 107 (A), 131* his *MSS. 115, 116, Morgan MS. 4, Cornell MS. 7*

7 her] his *MSS. 131, Morgan MS. 4* lore *rev from* love *MS. 106*

16 voice *rev from* verse *MS. 131*

20 spirit] subject *Coatalen MS.*

21 'Mid grove] Mid grove *rev from* In field *MS. 107 (A)* the] this *MS. 107, 115, 116; Cornell MS. 7, Coatalen MS.*

24 I feel, but *rev from* But *MS. 135*

24/ finis *MS. 107 (A)* The End *Morgan MS. 4* W.W. *MS. 131* Wm Wordsworth / Rydal Mount / 21st Jan^{ry} 1832 *Fitzwilliam MS.* Wm Wordsworth / Rydal Mount / October 3^{d}—1832— *Coatalen MS.*

---

7 In MS. 106 the original word— "love"—was probably the copyist's error.

Written in Mrs. Field's Album Opposite a Pen-and-ink Sketch in the Manner of a Rembrandt Etching done by Edmund Field

That gloomy cave, that gothic nich,
Those trees that forward lean
As if enamoured of the brook—
How soothing is the scene!

No witchery of inky words
Can such illusions yield;
Yet all (ye Landscape Poets blush!)
Was penned by Edmund Field.

---

fly-title

THE

RUSSIAN FUGITIVE.

[Peter Henry Bruce, having given in his entertaining Memoirs the substance of the following Tale, affirms, that, besides the concurring reports of others, he had the story from the Lady's own mouth.

The Lady Catherine, mentioned towards the close, was the famous Catherine, then bearing that name as the acknowledged Wife of Peter the Great.]

---

composed late December 1828 to mid-January 1829
found in Mrs. Field's Album, untraced
published in *PW*, IV (1947, 1958)
reading text *PW*, IV (1958)

---

composed probably after November 1828 but by January 29, 1829; revised before publication
found in DC MSS. 107 (A) 29^{v}–37^{v}, 54^{r}–55^{r}, (B) 102^{r}–113^{v}, (C) 119^{v}; 106; 116; 131; 134; 135; 137 (MW); MS. 1836/45 (WW, with nonverbal revs by JC)
published in *1835, 1836–*
classed *unclassed MS. 1835/36–1843, 1846, 1849* Miscellaneous Poems *1845, 1850*
reading text *1835*
fly-title *lacking MSS. 107 (A), 116, 131, 134, 135, 137; 1836–, 1839* FUGITIVE.] Fugitive / in / Four Parts. *MSS. 107 (B), 106*
headnote *lacking MSS. 131, 134, 135, 137; transferred to end notes 1845, 1850* *first para* entertaining] interesting *MS. 116* the following] this *1845, 1850* reports *rev from* testaments *MS. 107 (A)* *second para* was *rev to* is *MS. 116* is *MS. 1835/36–, 1839* then *del MS. 116* name *rev in pencil to* title *MS. 107 (A)* acknowledged *alt in pencil from* unacknowledged *MS. 107 (A)* unacknowledged *rev to* then unacknowledged *MS. 116*

THE RUSSIAN FUGITIVE.

PART I.

1.

ENOUGH of rose-bud lips, and eyes
  Like harebells bathed in dew,
Of cheek that with carnation vies,
  And veins of violet hue;
Earth wants not beauty that may scorn
  A likening to frail flowers;
Yea, to the stars, if they were born
  For seasons and for hours.

2.

Through Moscow's gates, with gold unbarred,
  Stepped one at dead of night,
Whom such high beauty could not guard
  From meditated blight;
By stealth she passed, and fled as fast
  As doth the hunted fawn,
Nor stopped, till in the dappling east
  Appeared unwelcome dawn.

---

title *inserted in pencil MS. 107 (A), in ink MS. 131* Ina, / or / The Lodge in the Forest, / A Russian Tale. *MS. 116*

part title THE RUSSIAN FUGITIVE. PART I.] The Russian Fugitive. *MS. 106 lacking MSS. 107 (B), 116* Part 1st *MSS. 107 (A), 135* First Part *MS. 131*

stanza numbers *del MS. 1835/36–; lacking 1836–, 1839*

1 eyes] eye *MS. 131*

2 dew *over illeg eras MS. 116*

5 wants . . . may scorn] lacks . . . will bear *MS. 131*

6 A *rev from* [?The] *MS. 107 (A)* No *MS. 131*

7–8 More lofty is its character
 More lasting are its powers *MS. 131*

7 Yea [Yea *rev in pencil and ink from* And] to the Stars themselves if born, *over illeg eras MS. 107 (A); MS. 107 (B) as rev (A)* Yea to the stars themselves,— [*comma, dash rev from exclam*] if born *MS. 106; so MS. 116 but* themselves, if *MS. 134 as MS. 106 but no punct, then rev to text* Yea, to the stars themselves, if born *in pencil MS. 1836/45*

8–16 *lacking (page cut away) MS. 134*

8 *over illeg eras MS. 107 (A)*

9 Moscow's *rev from* Moscow *MS. 135* Moscow *MSS. 107 (A), 106, 116* with *rev to* by *MS. 116*

14 hunted *rev from* haunted *MS. 107 (B)*

16 unwelcome] the unwelcome *MS. 131*

7–8 An ink cross was entered to the right of these lines in MS. 131.

3.

Seven days she lurked in brake and field,
  Seven nights her course renewed,
Sustained by what her scrip might yield,
  Or berries of the wood;
At length, in darkness travelling on,
  When lowly doors were shut,
The haven of her hope she won,
  Her Foster-mother's hut.

4.

"To put your love to dangerous proof
  I come," said she, "from far;
For I have left my Father's roof,
  In terror of the Czar."
No answer did the Matron give,
  No second look she cast;
She hung upon the Fugitive,
  Embracing and embraced.

5.

She led her Lady to a seat
  Beside the glimmering fire,
Bathed duteously her wayworn feet,
  Prevented each desire:
The cricket chirped, the house-dog dozed,
  And on that simple bed,
Where she in childhood had reposed,
  Now rests her weary head.

6.

When she, whose couch had been the sod,
  Whose curtain pine or thorn,
Had breathed a sigh of thanks to God,
  Who comforts the forlorn;
While over her the Matron bent

---

17 and] or *MSS. 107 (B), 116, 131* and *rev to* or *MS. 106*
29 Matron *rev from* Mother *MS. 137* Mother *MS. 135*
31 She] But *MS. 1835/36–, 1839*
33 her] the *MS. 1835/36–, 1839*
39 she in childhood] as a Child she *MSS. 107, 134* as a child, she *MS. 106; so MS. 116 but no comma* as a Child, she *MS. 131* as a Child she *rev to* She in Childhood *MS. 135*
40 Now] There *MS. 131* Now *rev from* She *MS. 135*

Sleep sealed her eyes, and stole
Feeling from limbs with travel spent,
And trouble from the soul.

7.

Refreshed, the Wanderer rose at morn,
And soon again was dight
In those unworthy vestments worn
Through long and perilous flight;
And "O beloved Nurse," she said,
"My thanks with silent tears
Have unto Heaven and You been paid:
Now listen to my fears!

8.

"Have you forgot"—and here she smiled—
"The babbling flatteries
You lavished on me when a child
Disporting round your knees?
I was your lambkin, and your bird,
Your star, your gem, your flower;
Light words, that were more lightly heard
In many a cloudless hour!

9.

"The blossom you so fondly praised
Is come to bitter fruit;
A mighty One upon me gazed;
I spurned his lawless suit,
And must be hidden from his wrath:

---

48 the] her *MSS. 107 (A), 116*
45–48 Upon her lids with travel spent
Sleep dropped and gently stole
(While over her the Matron bent)
Into her dreamless soul. *MS. 131*
51 In *rev from* With *MS. 135* With *MSS. 107, 106, 116,131*
53 said *rev from* cried *MS. 116*
54 "My *so MSS. 107, 116, 131, 135; 1836–, 1836YR, 1839* My *rev to* "My *MS. 116* My *1835*
57 forgot] forget *(?copyist's slip) MS. 106*
60 round] on *MS. 131* knees? *rev from* knee? *MS. 116* knee? *MS. 107* knee *MSS. 106, 134*
65 "The *so MSS. 107, 116, 1836–, 1836YR, 1839* The *MSS. 106, 131, 134, 135; 1835* The *in pencil MS. 1836/45*
69 must be hidden *rev from MS. 106* I must hide me *MSS. 107, 116, 131*

45–48 An ink cross was entered to the right of these lines in MS. 131.

You, Foster-father dear,
Will guide me in my forward path;
I may not tarry here!

10.

"I cannot bring to utter woe
Your proved fidelity."—
"Dear Child, sweet Mistress, say not so!
For you we both would die."
"Nay, nay, I come with semblance feigned
And cheek embrowned by art;
Yet, being inwardly unstained,
With courage will depart."

11.

"But whither would you, could you, flee?
A poor Man's counsel take;
The Holy Virgin gives to me
A thought for your dear sake;
Rest shielded by our Lady's grace;
And soon shall you be led
Forth to a safe abiding-place,
Where never foot doth tread."

THE RUSSIAN FUGITIVE.

PART II.

1.

THE Dwelling of this faithful pair
In a straggling village stood,

---

70 Foster-father] Foster-mother *MSS. 106, 134, 137* Foster Mother *MS. 135*
71 in] on *MSS. 107, 116, 131*
73–88 *lacking MS. 131*
73 "I *so MS. 116; 1836–, 1836YR, 1839* I *1835* I *in pencil MS. 1836/45*
76 would] could *MSS. 107, 116*
77 come *rev from* came *MS. 137* came *MSS. 107, 106, 116, 135*
82 counsel] counsel's *MS. 135*
85 Rest *rev from* Best *(printer's error) MS. 137*
88/89 *part title:* THE RUSSIAN FUGITIVE. PART II.] Part II *MS. 107* Second Part. *MS. 106; so MS. 134 but no punct; lacking MS. 116* Part second *MS. 131* 2[d] Part *MS. 135* PART II. *1836–, 1839*
90 In *rev from* I *MS. 107 (B)*

For One who breathed unquiet air
  A dangerous neighbourhood;
But wide around lay forest ground
  With thickets rough and blind;
And pine-trees made a heavy shade
  Impervious to the wind.

2.

And there, sequestered from the sight,
  Was spread a treacherous swamp,
On which the noonday sun shed light
  As from a lonely lamp;
And midway in the unsafe morass,
  A single Island rose
Of firm dry ground, with healthful grass
  Adorned, and shady boughs.

3.

The Woodman knew, for such the craft
  This Russian Vassal plied,
That never fowler's gun, nor shaft
  Of archer, there was tried;
A sanctuary seemed the spot
  From all intrusion free;
And there he planned an artful Cot
  For perfect secrecy.

4.

With earnest pains unchecked by dread
  Of Power's far-stretching hand,
The bold good Man his labour sped
  At nature's pure command;

---

93 lay] was *MS. 131*
95 pine *rev from illeg eras MS. 106*
98 Was spread] Spread many *MS. 131*
99 noonday] mid-day *MS. 131*
100 And out of one, a broad morass, *MS. 131*
101 unsafe *rev from* safe *MS. 137* safe *MS. 135*
104 Adorned, and] Adorned with *MS. 131*
105 the craft *rev from* his craft *MS. 135*
109–112 That no one ventured to the spot
Belike from age to age,
And there he planned a sylvan cot [cot *rev to* Cot]
A lurking Hermitage. *MS. 131*
109 A sanctuary seem'd *over illeg eras MS. 107 (A)*
113 earnest pains] tender care *MS. 131*

Heart-soothed, and busy as a wren,
  While, in a hollow nook,
She moulds her sight-eluding den
  Above a murmuring brook.

5.

His task accomplished to his mind,
  The twain ere break of day
Creep forth, and through the forest wind
  Their solitary way;
Few words they speak, nor dare to slack
  Their pace from mile to mile,
Till they have crossed the quaking marsh,
  And reached the lonely Isle.

6.

The sun above the pine-trees showed
  A bright and cheerful face;
And Ina looked for her abode,
  The promised hiding-place;
She sought in vain, the Woodman smiled;
  No threshold could be seen,
Nor roof, nor window; all seemed wild
  As it had ever been.

7.

Advancing, you might guess an hour,
  The front with such nice care
Is masked, "if house it be or bower,"
  But in they entered are;

---

120 a] the *MS. 131*
121 *rev from* His task perform'd his wishes crown'd *MS. 107 (A)*
When all was finished to his mind, *MS. 131*
122 The twain] The Twain *rev from* Forth crept *MS. 107 (A)* Abroad *MS. 131*
123 Creep forth *rev from* The Pair, *and* wind *rev from* wound *MS. 107 (A)*
They thro' the houseless forest wind *MS. 131*
125 speak, *rev from* spake *MSS. 107 (A), 116* dare *rev from* dared *MS. 107 (A)*
127 have *rev from* had *MS. 107 (A)*
133 sought] looked *MS. 131*
135 seemed] was *MS. 131*
137 Advancing,] Approaching— *MS. 131*
138–139 *rev from*
As will the Builder's care
Whether it were a house or bower; *MS. 107 (A)*
So nice the Builder's care,
Whether it were a house or bower; *MS. 131*
139 be *rev from* were *MS. 116*

As shaggy as were wall and roof
  With branches intertwined,
So smooth was all within, air-proof,
  And delicately lined.

8.

And hearth was there, and maple dish,
  And cups in seemly rows,
And couch—all ready to a wish
  For nurture or repose;
And Heaven doth to her virtue grant
  That here she may abide
In solitude, with every want
  By cautious love supplied.

9.

No Queen, before a shouting crowd,
  Led on in bridal state,
E'er struggled with a heart so proud,
  Entering her palace gate;
Rejoiced to bid the world farewell,
  No saintly Anchoress
E'er took possession of her cell
  With deeper thankfulness.

10.

"Father of all, upon thy care
  And mercy am I thrown;
Be thou my safeguard!"—such her prayer
  When she was left alone,
Kneeling amid the wilderness
  When joy had passed away,
And smiles, fond efforts of distress
  To hide what they betray!

---

141 wall] walls *MS. 131*
143–144 So smooth was all within, and delicately lined. *MS. 131*
148 or] and *MS. 131*
150 here] there *1850*
154 bridal] pride and *MS. 131*
155 E'er *rev from* Ever *MS. 106*
157–159 *over illeg eras MS. 107 (A)*
162 am I] I am *MS. 131*
167 fond efforts *rev in pencil and ink from* the sunshine *MS. 106* the sunshine *alt in pencil as text MS. 107 (A)* the sunshine *MSS. 107 (B), 116, 131*
168 *rev from* That hide yet more betray. *MS. 106; MS. 107 (A) as orig 106 but* hide— *alt in pencil to text but no punct; MS. 107 (B) as orig 106 but no punct; MS. 116 as orig 106; MS. 131 as 116 but* hide,

11.

The prayer is heard, the Saints have seen,
  Diffused through form and face,
Resolves devotedly serene;
  That monumental grace
Of Faith, which doth all passions tame
  That Reason *should* control;
And shows in the untrembling frame
  A statue of the soul.

THE RUSSIAN FUGITIVE.

PART III.

1.

'Tɪs sung in ancient minstrelsy
  That Phœbus wont to wear
"The leaves of any pleasant tree
  Around his golden hair,"*
Till Daphne, desperate with pursuit
  Of his imperious love,
At her own prayer transformed, took root,
  A laurel in the grove.

2.

Then did the Penitent adorn
  His brow with laurel green;
And 'mid his bright locks never shorn
  No meaner leaf was seen;
And Poets sage, through every age,
  About their temples wound
The bay; and Conquerors thanked the Gods,

---

169 The] Her *MSS. 107 (A), 116, 131* "Her *MS. 107 (B)*
172–173 Exalting lowly grace;
A Faith which does all passions tame *MS. 116; so MS. 107 (A) rev in pencil and ink to text but* Faith,] faith *pencil* Faith *ink and* which doth] that Does *pencil; MS. 131 as MS. 116 but* does] doth tame] tame,
176/177 *part title:* THE RUSSIAN FUGITIVE. PART III.] Part III. *MS. 107* PART III. *1836–, 1839* Third Part. *MS. 106; so MS. 134 but no punct; lacking MS. 116* Part Third *MS. 131* 3[d] Part *MS. 135*
177 'Tis] 'T is *MSS. 135, 137, 1835, 1836YR*
180 *note lacking MSS. 107, 106, 116, 131, 134; 1836–, 1839*
181 desperate with pursuit *rev from* flying from the suit *MS. 107 (A); MS. 131 as orig MS. 107 (A)*

With laurel chaplets crowned.

3.

Into the mists of fabling Time
So far runs back the praise
Of Beauty, that disdains to climb
Along forbidden ways;
That scorns temptation; power defies
Where mutual love is not;
And to the tomb for rescue flies
When life would be a blot.

4.

To this fair Votaress, a fate
More mild doth Heaven ordain
Upon her Island desolate;
And words, not breathed in vain,
Might tell what intercourse she found,
Her silence to endear;
What birds she tamed, what flowers the ground
Sent forth her peace to cheer.

5.

To one mute Presence, above all,
Her soothed affections clung,
A picture on the Cabin wall
By Russian usage hung—
The Mother-maid, whose countenance bright
With love abridged the day;
And, communed with by taper light,
Chased spectral fears away.

6.

And oft, as either Guardian came,
The joy in that retreat

---

192 laurel chaplets *rev from* laurels chaplet [chaplet *rev to* Chaplets] *MS. 107 (B)*
193 mists *rev from* depths *rev from* midst *MS. 135*
202 mild *rev from* wild *(printer's error) MS. 137*
204–205 *rev from* Nor were it labour vain
To tell what Company she found *MS. 107 (A); MS. 131 as orig MS. 107 (A) but* company
209–216 *MW's pencil addition (see nonverbal variants below), then inserted in ink MS. 107 (A); these lines lacking MS. 131*
211 the] her *MSS. 107 (A), 116*
217 And oft,] And, oft *(affecting the sense) MSS. 107, 106, 116* And oft *MS. 131*

Might any common friendship shame,
So high their hearts would beat;
And to the lone Recluse, whate'er
They brought, each visiting
Was like the crowding of the year
With a new burst of spring.

7.

But, when she of her Parents thought,
The pang was hard to bear;
And, if with all things not enwrought,
That trouble still is near.
Before her flight she had not dared
Their constancy to prove,
Too much the heroic Daughter feared
The weakness of their love.

8.

Dark is the Past to them, and dark
The Future still must be,
Till pitying Saints conduct her bark
Into a safer sea—
Or gentle Nature close her eyes,
And set her Spirit free
From the altar of this sacrifice,
In vestal purity.

9.

Yet, when above the forest-glooms
The white swans southward passed,
High as the pitch of their swift plumes
Her fancy rode the blast;
And bore her tow'rd the fields of France,
Her Father's native land,
To mingle in the rustic dance,
The happiest of the band!

---

219 Might] Would *MS. 131* shame *rev from* tame *MS. 134*
231 *rev from* Too much she feared heroic Daughter *MS. 131*
241 forest-glooms] forest gloom *MS. 131*
243 swift *rev from illeg eras MS. 106*
245 tow'rd] towards *MS. 131* fields *rev from* field *MS. 137* groves *MS. 131*
247 in] with *MSS. 107 (A), 116, 131*

10.

Of those belovèd fields she oft
  Had heard her Father tell
In phrase that now with echoes soft
  Haunted her lonely Cell;
She saw the hereditary bowers,
  She heard the ancestral stream;
The Kremlin and its haughty towers
  Forgotten like a dream!

THE RUSSIAN FUGITIVE.

PART IV.

1.

THE ever-changing Moon had traced
  Twelve times her monthly round,
When through the unfrequented Waste
  Was heard a startling sound;
A shout thrice sent from one who chased
  At speed a wounded Deer,
Bounding through branches interlaced,
  And where the wood was clear.

2.

The fainting Creature took the marsh,
  And toward the Island fled,
While plovers screamed with tumult harsh
  Above his antlered head;
This, Ina saw; and, pale with fear,
  Shrunk to her citadel;
The desperate Deer rushed on, and near
  The tangled covert fell.

---

249 belovèd *so MS. 1835/36–, 1839* beloved *MSS. prior to publication, 1835, 1836YR*
252 lonely *rev in pencil and ink from* lowly *MS. 106* lowly *MSS. 107, 116*
256/257 *part title:* THE RUSSIAN FUGITIVE. PART IV.] Part IV. *MS. 107* PART IV. *1836–, 1839* Fourth Part. *MS. 106; so MS. 134 but no punct; lacking MS. 116* Fourth Part *MS. 131* The Russian Fugitive / 4th Part *MS. 135*
259 Waste] waste *rev in pencil from* place *MS. 107 (B)*
269–272 Affrighted Ina saw, and heard,
And shrunk into her Cell;
The desperate Deer rush'd on, and near
To her dark threshold fell. *MS. 131*

3.

Across the marsh, the game in view,
The Hunter followed fast,
Nor paused, till o'er the Stag he blew
A death-proclaiming blast;
Then, resting on her upright mind,
Came forth the Maid—"In me
Behold," she said, "a stricken Hind
Pursued by destiny!

4.

"From your deportment, Sir! I deem
That you have worn a sword,
And will not hold in light esteem
A suffering woman's word;
There is my covert, there perchance
I might have lain concealed,
My fortunes hid, my countenance
Not even to you revealed.

5.

"Tears might be shed, and I might pray,
Crouching and terrified,
That what has been unveiled to day,
You would in mystery hide;
But I will not defile with dust
The knee that bends to adore
The God in heaven;—attend, be just:
This ask I, and no more!

6.

"I speak not of the winter's cold,
For summer's heat exchanged,

---

273 the game] his game *MSS. 107, 116, 131*
279 Hind] hind *rev from* deer *MS. 116*
281 "From *so MSS. 107, 116; 1836–, 1836YR, 1839* From *1835* From *in pencil MS. 1836/45*
282 worn] borne *MS. 131*
286 might] could *MSS. 107 (A), 106, 116, 131, 134*
287 fortunes] fortune *MS. 131*
289–320 *lacking MS. 137*
289 "Tears *so 1836–, 1836YR, 1839* Tears *1835* Tears *in pencil MS. 1836/45*
291 has] hath *MS. 131*
297 "I *so 1836–, 1836YR, 1839* I *1835* I *in pencil MS. 1836/45*
298 summer's] summers *MSS. 107 (B), 134* summer *MS. 131*

While I have lodged in this rough hold,
From social life estranged;
Nor yet of trouble and alarms:
High Heaven is my defence;
And every season has soft arms
For injured Innocence.

7.

"From Moscow to the Wilderness
It was my choice to come,
Lest virtue should be harbourless,
And honour want a home;
And happy were I, if the Czar
Retain his lawless will,
To end life here like this poor Deer,
Or a Lamb on a green hill."

8.

"Are you the Maid," the Stranger cried,
"From Gallic Parents sprung,
Whose vanishing was rumoured wide,
Sad theme for every tongue;
Who foiled an Emperor's eager quest?
You, Lady, forced to wear
These rude habiliments, and rest
Your head in this dark lair!"

---

300 estranged *over illeg eras MS. 135*
303 has] hath *MS. 131*
305 "From *so 1836–, 1836YR, 1839* From *1835* From *in pencil MS. 1836/45*
306 choice] chance *MS. 131*
310 his *rev from miswritten* her *MSS. 107 (B), 106*
318–320 You, Lady in this humble wild
Disguised, and here so long
Hovel'd under heath and reeds
The barren trees among *rev to*
Who foil'd an Emperor's eager quest
Disguised, and forc'd to wear
That servile garb's disguise, and rest
Your head in this rough lair! *MS. 107 (A), then rev to text but no punct*
You Lady! in those humble weeds
Disguised, and here so long
Hovel'd under heath and reeds
The barren trees among?"— *MS. 131*
319 These *rev from* Those *MS. 116* rest *rev from* wear *MS. 134*
320 this *rev to* that *MS. 116*

9.

But wonder, pity, soon were quelled;
  And in her face and mien
The soul's pure brightness he beheld
  Without a veil between:
He loved, he hoped,—a holy flame
  Kindled 'mid rapturous tears;
The passion of a moment came
  As on the wings of years.

10.

"Such bounty is no gift of chance,"
  Exclaimed he; "righteous Heaven,
Preparing your deliverance,
  To me the charge hath given.
The Czar full oft in words and deeds
  Is stormy and self-willed;
But, when the Lady Catherine pleads,
  His violence is stilled.

11.

"Leave open to my wish the course,
  And I to her will go;
From that humane and heavenly source,
  Good, only good, can flow."
Faint sanction given, the Cavalier
  Was eager to depart,
Though question followed question, dear
  To the Maiden's filial heart.

---

321 were *rev from* was *MS. 135*
337–338 Her will I seek—along my course
In confidence I go; *MS. 131*
337 "Leave] Leave *MSS. 106, 135, MS. 1835/36, MS. 1836/45 in pencil*
341–344 A sanction [?given] the Cavalier
Departed—grievd that he
So ill [?cd] answer questions dear
To filial Piety— *pencil draft MS. 107 (C)*
This said, the gallant Cavalier
Withdrew ere full reply
Was made to crowding questions, dear
To filial piety. *MS. 131*
342–344 Recounted all he knew
The sufferer's filial heart to cheer
Then hastily withdrew *MS. 107 (A); so MS. 116 but l. 342* knew, *l. 343* cheer; *l. 344* withdrew.
MS. 107 (A) then rev to text but l. 342 depart,] depart *l. 343* Though] Tho' *l. 344* heart.] heart

12.

Light was his step,—his hopes, more light,
Kept pace with his desires;
And the third morning gave him sight
Of Moscow's glittering spires.
He sued:—heart-smitten by the wrong,
To the lorn Fugitive
The Emperor sent a pledge as strong
As sovereign power could give.

13.

O more than mighty change! If e'er
Amazement rose to pain,
And over-joy produced a fear
Of something void and vain,
'Twas when the Parents, who had mourned
So long the lost as dead,
Beheld their only Child returned,
The household floor to tread.

14.

Soon gratitude gave way to love
Within the Maiden's breast:
Delivered and Deliverer move
In bridal garments drest;
Meek Catherine had her own reward;
The Czar bestowed a dower;
And universal Moscow shared
The triumph of that hour.

345–347 But soon that cloud departed
Hope quickend his desires
And the third morning *pencil draft MS. 107 (C)*

347 third] fifth *MS. 1835/36–, 1839*

348 glittering] golden *MS. 131*

355 over-joy] joy's excess *MS. 1835/36–, 1839*

358 as] and *MS. 131*

359 returned,] return *MS. 131*

364–376 *lacking MS. 107 (B)*

15.

Flowers strewed the ground; the nuptial feast
  Was held with costly state;
And there, 'mid many a noble Guest,
  The Foster-parents sate;
Encouraged by the imperial eye,
  They shrank not into shade;
Great was their bliss, the honour high
  To them and nature paid!

The Primrose of the Rock

Sara Coleridge, born on December 23, 1802, wrote of Dorothy Wordsworth that "She told us once a pretty story of a primrose, I think, which she spied by the way-side when she went to see me soon after my birth, though that was at Christmas, and how this same primrose was still blooming when she went back to Grasmere" (*SCML*, I, 20). The rock became a favorite spot: in 1802 Dorothy first called it "Glow-worm Rock" and noted its tuft of primroses in her journal (April 24, 1802), and in 1808 Wordsworth composed a long blank verse poem, never completed, called *The Tuft of Primroses* (see *Tuft*, pp. 39–56). Wordsworth assigned the date 1831 to *The Primrose of the Rock* in MS. 1835/36, in editions from 1836, and in the Fenwick note of 1843. But Dorothy Wordsworth supplied the correct date in her copy of the much shorter version of the poem, elaborately titled *Written in March 1829 on seeing a Primrose-tuft of flowers flourishing in the chink of a rock in which that Primrose-tuft had been seen by us to flourish for twenty nine seasons*, which she dated August 28, 1829. Wordsworth must have been working on this version of *The Primrose of the Rock* about the same time as *Rural Illusions* (composed between about April and August 5, 1829) and *This Lawn, &c.* (composed probably between about April and September 1829); all three poems show both proximity and textual overlaps in DC MS. 107, as well as confluence of tone and subject matter. The first reading text is based on Dorothy's copy, which is among manuscripts in the Beinecke Rare Book and Manuscript Library at Yale.

The manuscripts in which the revised form of the poem appears were in use over a period of several years, 1828–1835; however, the presence of this form in MS. 106, which was not in use after Wordsworth's tour of Scotland in the fall of 1831, establishes that year as a convincing end date, but the much-revised state of the poem in MS. 107 suggests that he was at work on it for some time, probably

---

369–372 Truth rules the Song; nor deem it care
Too humble to relate
That, at the spousal feast, the pair
Of rustic Guardians sate; *MS. 107 (A_1) rev in pencil and ink to text (see Nonverbal Variants); MS. 131 as orig MS. 107 (A_1) but* Truth] Faith Song;] song, That, . . . pair,] That . . . Pair

374 shrank] shrunk *MSS. 107 (A), 116, 131, 135*

376/ Finis— *MS. 107 (A); so MS. 134 but no dash* The End *MS. 106* W. Wordsworth *MS. 131*

beginning shortly after Dorothy Wordsworth made her fair copy (Yale MS. 2)—that is, around September 1829.

Wordsworth's dissatisfaction with the effort represented by version A of MS. 107 is evident from his extensive drafting and redrafting of the poem in that manuscript. MS. 107 is a small notebook, much amplified by insertions, in which various copyists entered fair copies of poems, many showing one or more layers of revision by Wordsworth that were eventually included in *Yarrow Revisited, and Other Poems* in 1835 (for discussion of the several manuscript recensions leading up to this publication, see the Manuscript Census for MSS. 106, 133, 134, 135). In MS. 107 the evolution of the poem toward its final two-part structure can be traced.

This form of the poem is represented by the second reading text, based on the 1835 printing in *Yarrow Revsited, and Other Poems,* and appended to it is an *apparatus* of related manuscript variants and later printed readings. Photographs and transcriptions of all the draft work in MS. 107 (version A—related to B, on which the first reading text is based; and versions B, C, D, and G—related to *Ode to May,* the second reading text) appear on pages 694–717; a photograph and transcription of E appear on pages 720–721 among materials for *Rural Illusions.* Those leaves of MS. 107 that are designated as belonging to B, E, and G, contain various preliminary drafts of lines 25–54; C and D give differing versions of the concluding five stanzas (D appears to be earlier than C, though it follows C in the manuscript, and both are heavily deleted); and F, Dora Wordsworth's fair copy, provides a complete text of the two-part poem, though it lacks a title (variant readings in F are to be found in the *apparatus* to the second reading text).

[Text of Yale MS. 2]

Written in March 1829 on seeing a
Primrose-tuft of flowers flourishing in
the chink of a rock in which that
Primrose-tuft had been seen by us
to flourish for twenty nine seasons.

1

A Rock there is whose homely front
   The passing Traveller slights
Yet there the glow-worms hang their lamps

---

composed March to August 28, 1829
found in Yale MS. 2; DC MS. 107 (A) 3^r–3^v and 4^r–5^r
reading text Yale MS. 2
title Primrose *rev by eras from* [?] Primrose *Yale MS.* chink] [?same *eras*] chink *Yale MS. 2*

See the photographs and transcriptions of DC MS. 107 (A), 3^r, 3^v on pp. 694–697.

Like stars, at various heights;
And one coy Primrose to that Rock
The vernal breeze invites.

2

What hideous warfare hath been wag'd
What kingdoms overthrown
Since first I spied this Primrose tuft
And mark'd it for my own,
A lasting link in Nature's chain
From highest Heaven let down.

3

The flowers still faithful to their stems
Their fellowship renew;
The stems are faithful to the root
That worketh out of view
And to the rock the root adheres
In every fibre true.

4

Close clings to earth the living rock,
Though threatening still to fall;
The earth is constant to her sphere,
And God upholds them all.
So blooms this lonely plant, nor dreads
Her annual funeral.

5

And shall not we, earth's noblest growth,
The reasoning Sons of Men,
From the dark winter in the grave
Rise up, and breathe again,
And for eternal summer change
Our threescore years and ten?

6

Parent of all things! more forlorn
Than flower that withereth,
More abject than the worm is man
Without that eye of faith
Which guides the Pious, piercing thro'
The mystery of death.

[Text of 1835]

THE PRIMROSE OF THE ROCK.

A Rock there is whose homely front
The passing Traveller slights;
Yet there the Glow-worms hang their lamps,
Like stars, at various heights;
And one coy Primrose to that Rock
The vernal breeze invites.

What hideous warfare hath been waged,
What kingdoms overthrown,
Since first I spied that Primrose-tuft
And marked it for my own;
A lasting link in Nature's chain
From highest Heaven let down!

The Flowers, still faithful to the stems,
Their fellowship renew;
The stems are faithful to the root,
That worketh out of view;
And to the rock the root adheres
In every fibre true.

Close clings to earth the living rock,
Though threatening still to fall;
The earth is constant to her sphere;
And God upholds them all:
So blooms this lonely Plant, nor dreads
Her annual funeral.

* * * * * * * * *

---

composed Probably between September 1829 and November 1831

found in DC MS. 107 (B) 1^{r}–2^{v}, (C) 21^{v}–22^{r}, (D) 22^{v}–23^{r}, (E) 59^{r}, (F) 114^{r}–115^{r}, (G) 118^{r}–119^{r}; DC MSS. 106, 134, 135, 137, 154; MS. 1835Col; MS. 1835/36; MS. 1836/45 (MW)

published in *1835, 1836–*

classed Imagination *MS. 1835/36–*

reading text *1835*

title *lacking MSS. 107 (F), 106, 134* The Primrose Rock *MS. 135* The Primrose Rock *MW rev to* The Primrose on [on *rev to* of] the Rock *MS. 137*

stanza numbers II, III *in first part (first and fourth stanzas unnumbered),* II *to* V *in second part (first stanza unnumbered) MS. 107 (F)* 2–4 *and* 1–5 *MS. 106* 2–4 *and* 3–5 *MS. 134* 1–4 *and* 1–5 *MS. 137 but del*

1 homely *over illeg eras MS. 106* lonely *rev to* homely *MS. 154* lonely *1836, 1840* homely *MS. 1836/45*

20 threatening *rev from* threatning *MSS. 135, 137* threatning *MSS. 107 (F), 134*

See the photographs and transcriptions of DC MS. 107 (B) 1^{r}–2^{v}, (C) 21^{v}–22^{r}, (D) 22^{v}–23^{r}, and (G) 118^{r}–119^{r}, pp. 698–717; for DC MS. 107 (E), see pp. 720–721.

Here closed the meditative Strain;
  But air breathed soft that day,
The hoary mountain-heights were cheered,
  The sunny vale looked gay;
And to the Primrose of the Rock
  I gave this after-lay.

I sang, Let myraids of bright flowers,
  Like Thee, in field and grove
Revive unenvied,—mightier far
  Than tremblings that reprove
Our vernal tendencies to hope
  Is God's redeeming love:

That love which changed, for wan disease,
  For sorrow that had bent
O'er hopeless dust, for withered age,
  Their moral element,
And turned the thistles of a curse
  To types beneficent.

Sin-blighted though we are, we too,
  The reasoning Sons of Men,
From one oblivious winter called
  Shall rise, and breathe again;
And in eternal summer lose
  Our threescore years and ten.

To humbleness of heart descends
  This prescience from on high,
The faith that elevates the Just,
  Before and when they die;
And makes each soul a separate heaven,
  A court for Deity.

---

25 the *rev from* this *MS. 134*
31 sang *rev from* sung *MSS. 135, 137*
35 tendency *rev to* tendencies *MS. 134*
36 Is *so 1835 errata page, MS. 1835Col, 1836YR, 1836–* In *MS. 137, 1835 (printer's error)*
38 For] And *rev to* for *MS. 107 (B)*   had *rev in pencil from* hath *MS. 107 (F)*
39 for] and *rev to* from *MS. 107 (B)*   age *over illeg word MS. 135*
40–42 *rev from* Their moral element; and turned the thistles
    Of a curse to types beneficent *MS. 107 (B)*
43 We also shall revive we too *MS. 107 (F)*

THE ARMENIAN LADY'S LOVE.

[The subject of the following poem is from the Orlandus of the author's friend, Kenelm Henry Digby; and the liberty is taken of inscribing it to him as an acknowledgment, however unworthy, of pleasure and instruction derived from his numerous and valuable writings, illustrative of the piety and chivalry of the olden time.]

1.

YOU have heard "a Spanish Lady
  How she wooed an English Man;"*
Hear now of a fair Armenian,
  Daughter of the proud Soldàn;
How she loved a Christian Slave, and told her pain
By word, look, deed, with hope that he might love again.

2.

"Pluck that rose, it moves my liking,"
  Said she, lifting up her veil;
"Pluck it for me, gentle Gardener,
  Ere it wither and grow pale."
"Princess fair, I till the ground, but may not take
From twig or bed an humbler flower, even for your sake."

*See, in Percy's Reliques, that fine old ballad, "The Spanish Lady's Love;" from which Poem the form of stanza, as suitable to dialogue, is adopted.

---

composed probably between mid-March 1829 and late spring 1830
found in DC MSS. 107 (A) 62^{r}–68^{r}, 119^{v}, (B, 74^{r}–88^{r}; 106; 131; 134; 135; 137; MS. 1835/36 (MW)
published in *1835, 1836–*
classed Affections *MS. 1835/36–*
reading text *1835*
stanza numbers 1., 2., . . . 26.] I., II., . . . XXVI. *1836–*
headnote *lacking MSS. 107, 106, 131, 134, 135* the piety *rev from* piety *MS. 137*
note to l. 2 *lacking MSS. 107, 106, 131, 134* *See [that fine old poem called ballad *del*] in Percy's [Colle *del*] Reliques that fine old ballad "The Spanish Lady's Love." *MS. 135; MS. 137 as rev MS. 135 then rev to text but* Love;" . . . stanza . . . dialogue] Love," . . . Stanza . . . Dialogue . . . adopted *1836YR, 1839 as 1835 but* Poem] poem

11 but] and *MS. 131*

12 an humbler *rev from* a humble *MS. 135* a humbler *rev in pencil from* a meaner *MS. 107 (A)* a humbler *MS. 107 (B)* the meanest *MS. 131*

5–6 . . . 156 The fifth and sixth lines of each stanza were transcribed as four lines in MSS. 107, 106, 134 (see note on p. 447), following the pattern 4, 3, 4, 3, 4, 3, 4, 3 and producing an eight-line stanza form.

3.

"Grieved am I, submissive Christian!
To behold thy captive state;
Women, in your land, may pity
(May they not?) the unfortunate."
"Yes, kind Lady! otherwise Man could not bear
Life, which to every one that breathes is full of care."

4.

"Worse than idle is compassion
If it end in tears and sighs;
Thee from bondage would I rescue
And from vile indignities;
Nurtured, as thy mien bespeaks, in high degree,
Look up—and help a hand that longs to set thee free."

5.

"Lady, dread the wish, nor venture
In such peril to engage;
Think how it would stir against you
Your most loving Father's rage:
Sad deliverance would it be, and yoked with shame,
Should troubles overflow on her from whom it came."

6.

"Generous Frank! the just in effort
Are of inward peace secure;
Hardships for the brave encountered,
Even the feeblest may endure:
If Almighty Grace through me thy chains unbind,
My Father for slave's work may seek a slave in mind."

---

13 Christian!] Stranger; *rev to* Christian; *MS. 107 (A)*
14 thy *rev from* your *rev from* thy *MS. 135*
15 Women *rev from* Woman *MS. 107 (A)*
20 end *rev from* ends *MSS. 135, 137*
22 from *rev from illeg word MS. 135*
24 thee *rev from* three *(?copyist's slip) MS. 134*
29 yoked *rev from illeg word MS. 107 (A)* clogged *MS. 131*
33 for *rev from* from *MS. 106* from *eras MS. 107 (B)*
34 feeblest *rev in pencil and ink from* weakest *MS. 107 (A)* weakest *MS. 131*
35 *rev in pencil and ink from* If with Gods good help thy chains / I may unbind *MS. 107 (A), so MS. 131 but* God's
36 seek *rev from* find *MS. 134*

7.

"Princess, at this burst of goodness,
  My long-frozen heart grows warm!"
"Yet you make all courage fruitless,
  Me to save from chance of harm:
Leading such Companion I that gilded Dome,
Yon Minarets, would gladly leave for his worst home."

8.

"Feeling tunes your voice, fair Princess!
  And your brow is free from scorn,
Else these words would come like mockery,
  Sharper than the pointed thorn."
"Whence the undeserved mistrust? Too wide apart
Our faith hath been,—O would that eyes could see the heart!"

---

39 *rev in pencil to* make all courage not then fruitless *rev to text MS. 107 (A)* fruitless] useless *MS. 131*

40 of *inserted in pencil MS. 107 (A)*

42 Yon *rev from* These *MS. 107 (A)* 'These *MS. 131*

45 these] those *MS. 107*

47–48 *alt* Whence such [such *rev from* this] [?queryings] / Venal suspicion and [?chill]
alt Words or [or *rev from* and] looks and [and *alt* are] from one source / too wide apart *MS. 107 (A)*

47 the] such *MS. 131*

48 hath] has *MS. 107 (A)*

48/49 Weak am I and inexperienc'd,
Yet {But *in pencil*] my reason shrinks from trust
In a [a *alt in pencil* an] law to man remorseless
And to womankind unjust
I hope for me a fairer course which thou canst do
How readily if to thyself, thyself be true.

Embryo of divine endowments *line rev to* Embryo of celestial promise
Heaven that opend out the rose
By [By *rev in pencil to* With] his breath will in due season
Gently thy sweet bed unclose
Or by miracle will work:" and is it none
That I a Princess thus should plead nor thou not be won *line rev to* That I a timid maid this boldness have put on *first stanza in pencil and ink, second in ink, all del MS. 107 (A)*
pencil draft And to woman kind,—unjust
Help [?] a [a *rev to* your] fairer course which thou canst do
How readily if to thy self thyself be true
ink draft That I a Princess thus shall beplea, nor thou be won *rev to* That I a timid Maid this [this *rev to* such] boldness have put on. *MS. 107 (A); see ll. 79–84 below*

9.

"Tempt me not, I pray; my doom is
These base implements to wield;
Rusty Lance, I ne'er shall grasp thee,
Ne'er assoil my cobwebb'd shield!
Never see my native land, nor castle towers,
Nor Her who thinking of me there counts widowed hours."

10.

"Prisoner! pardon youthful fancies;
Wedded? If you *can*, say no!—
Blessed is and be your Consort;
Hopes I cherished let them go!
Handmaid's privilege would leave my purpose free,
Without another link to my felicity."

11.

"Wedded love with loyal Christians,
Lady, is a mystery rare;
Body, heart, and soul in union,
Make one being of a pair."
"Humble love in me would look for no return,
Soft as a guiding star that cheers, but cannot burn."

12.

"Gracious Allah! by such title
Do I dare to thank the God,
Him who thus exalts thy spirit,
Flower of an unchristian sod!
Or hast thou put off wings which thou in heaven dost wear?
What have I seen, and heard, or dreamt? where am I? where?"

13.

Here broke off the dangerous converse:
Less impassioned words might tell
How the Pair escaped together,

61–66, 67–72 *stanzas transposed then rev to text MS. 107 (A)*
64 one] a *MS. 131*
65 look *rev from* [?peer] *MS. 106*
66 but] And *MS. 107* and *MS. 131*
72 and *rev from* or *MS. 135*
74 might *rev from* may *MSS. 134, 135* may *MSS. 107, 106, 131*

Tears not wanting, nor a knell
Of sorrow in her heart while through her Father's door,
And from her narrow world, she passed for evermore.

14.

But affections higher, holier,
Urged her steps; she shrunk from trust
In a sensual creed that trampled
Woman's birthright into dust.
Little be the wonder then, the blame be none,
If she, a timid Maid, hath put such boldness on.

15.

Judge both Fugitives with knowledge:
In those old romantic days
Mighty were the soul's commandments
To support, restrain, or raise.
Foes might hang upon their path, snakes rustle near,
But nothing from their inward selves had they to fear.

---

77 in *rev in pencil from* from *MS. 106* through *rev in pencil from* from *MS. 106* from *MSS. 107, 131*

79–84 *lacking MSS. 107 (A_1), 131; WW's pencil draft in MS. 107 (A_1):*
~~Soon the~~ grief was hushd by reason
Reason that had shrunk from trust
In a law [law *alt* creed] ~~to man~~ to man remorseless
And to womankind unjust *MS. 107 (A_2)*
WW rev in ink (on 119^v) to
Soon that grief was hushd by reason
Reason that had shrunk from trust
In a law to man remorseless
And to woman-kind unjust
Little be the wonder then, the blame be none
[If a she *del*] That she a timid Maid hath put such boldness on *MS. 107 (A_2)*
WW's pencil and ink:
But affections higher holier
Urged her steps—she shrunk from trust
~~In a creed to man remorseless~~ [?stet]
~~And to woman kind unjust~~
Little be the wonder then/the blame be none
If she a timid Maid hath put such boldness on. *MS. 107 (A_3), rev in pencil and ink to text*

84 on] none *(?copyist's slip) MS. 134*

85 both *rev from* the *MS. 107 (A)* the *MS. 131*

86 old romantic *rev from* unperverted *MS. 107 (A_1)* un-perverted *MS. 107 (A_2)* unperverted *MS. 131*
alt in pencil Proof abounds that in [?those] days *MS. 107 (A)*

88 To support,] To support *rev from* Whether to *MS. 107 (A)* Whether to *MS. 131*

89 upon] on *MS. 131* path,] track— *MSS. 107 (A), 131* near *del in error MS. 135, lacking MS. 137 but inserted*

16.

Thought infirm ne'er came between them,
Whether printing desert sands
With accordant steps, or gathering
Forest-fruit with social hands;
Or whispering like two reeds that in the cold moonbeam
Bend with the breeze their heads, beside a crystal stream.

17.

On a friendly deck reposing
They at length for Venice steer;
There, when they had closed their voyage,
One, who daily on the Pier
Watched for tidings from the East, beheld his Lord,
Fell down and clasped his knees for joy, not uttering word.

18.

Mutual was the sudden transport;
Breathless questions followed fast,
Years contracting to a moment,
Each word greedier than the last;
"Hie thee to the Countess, Friend! return with speed,
And of this Stranger speak by whom her Lord was freed.

19.

"Say that I, who might have languished,
Drooped and pined till life was spent,
Now before the gates of Stolberg
My Deliverer would present
For a crowning recompence, the precious grace
Of her who in my heart still holds her ancient place.

---

91 ne'er came] came neer *MS. 131*
94 social *rev from* mingled *MS. 107 (A)* mingled *MS. 131*
97–101 Hills they crossed—then broad seas measured
Steadily as ship could steer
And while in the port of Venice
They were landing on the pier,
One, who there for tidings watched, beheld his Lord *MS. 131*
97 friendly *alt* shady *del MS. 107 (A)* deck] Boat *rev to* Deck *MS. 107 (A)*
99 There *rev from* And *MS. 107 (A)*
106 last *rev from* past *MS. 107 (A)*
113 grace *rev from* gift *MS. 107 (B)*

20.

"Make it known that my Companion
Is of royal Eastern blood,
Thirsting after all perfection,
Innocent, and meek, and good,
Though with misbelievers bred; but that dark night
Will Holy Church disperse by beams of Gospel Light."

21.

Swiftly went that grey-haired Servant,
Soon returned a trusty Page
Charged with greetings, benedictions,
Thanks and praises, each a gage
For a sunny thought to cheer the Stranger's way,
Her virtuous scruples to remove, her fears allay.

22.

Fancy (while, to banners floating
High on Stolberg's Castle walls,
Deafening noise of welcome mounted,
Trumpets, Drums, and Atabals,)
The devout embraces still, while such tears fell
As made a meeting seem most like a dear farewell.

23.

Through a haze of human nature,
Glorified by heavenly light,
Looked the beautiful Deliverer
On that overpowering sight,
While across her virgin cheek pure blushes strayed,
For every tender sacrifice her heart had made.

---

120 *alt in pencil* Already hath given way to beams of heavenly [heavenly *rev to* Gospel] light *MS. 107 (A)*

127–132 And how blest the Reunited
While beneath their castle walls,
Runs a deafening noise of welcome!— [welcome!— *WW rev from* welcome,]
Blest, though every tear that falls
Doth in its silence of past sorrow tell,
And makes a meeting seem most like a dear farewell. *MS. 1835/36 (MW); so 1836–, 1839 but* Reunited, castle-walls, *1836YR as 1836 but* And how] And, how castle-walls,] Castle walls welcome!—] welcome; though] tho'

128 on] oer *MS. 107 (A)*

133 nature *over illeg eras MS. 107 (A)*

24.

On the ground the weeping Countess
  Knelt, and kissed the Stranger's hand;
Act of soul-devoted homage,
  Pledge of an eternal band:
Nor did aught of future days that kiss belie,
Which, with a generous shout, the crowd did ratify.

25.

Constant to the fair Armenian,
  Gentle pleasures round her moved,
Like a tutelary Spirit
  Reverenced, like a Sister, loved.
Christian meekness smoothed for all the path of life,
Who, loving most, should wiseliest love, their only strife.

26.

Mute Memento of that union
  In a Saxon Church survives,
Where a cross-legged Knight lies sculptured
  As between two wedded Wives—
Figures with armorial signs of race and birth,
And the vain rank the Pilgrims bore while yet on earth.

---

140 Knelt,] Dropped *MS. 131*
141 soul-devoted] self-devoted *MS. 131*
143 kiss *rev in pencil and ink from* bliss *MS. 107 (B)*
145 fair] mild *MS. 131*
149 smoothed *rev in pencil from* soothed *MS. 106*
Concord blessd for each and all / Their daily life *rev to*
Blest by God above, all liv'd / A happy life *rev to text MS. 107 (A)*
Blest by God above all lived a happy life *MS. 131*
150 Whose rule of heart should wisest be / Their only strife *MS. 107; so MS. 106 but* strife. *MS. 131 as MS. 106 but* their *MS. 134 as MS. 107 but* heart] life *MS. 135 as MS. 134 but rev from two lines to one*
Whose rule of life should wisest be their only strife. *rev to text MS. 137*
151 that] this *MS. 131*

RURAL ILLUSIONS.

1.

SYLPH was it? or a Bird more bright
  Than those of fabulous stock?
A second darted by;—and lo!
  Another of the flock,
Through sunshine flitting from the bough
  To nestle in the rock.
Transient deception! a gay freak
  Of April's mimicries!
Those brilliant Strangers, hailed with joy
  Among the budding trees,
Proved last year's leaves, pushed from the spray
  To frolic on the breeze.

---

composed between about April and August 5, 1829
found in DC MSS. 101A (A) 61^{r}, 62^{v}, (B) 62^{r}; 107 (A) 58^{v}–59^{r}, (B) 59^{v}–60^{v}; 112; 106; 134; 135 (A) $108^{r}1P^{v}$–$108^{r}2P^{r}$ (ll. 25–30 and other fragments), (B) 107^{r}–107^{v}; 137; 138; MS. 1835/36 (MW)
published in *1835, 1836–*
classed Fancy *1836–*
reading text *1835*
title *lacking MS. 112*
stanza numbers *WW numbered first* 2 *and second* 1 *adding the annotation* Begin here *then revised figures to* 1 *and* 2 *respectively and deleted the annotation in MS. 107 (B); number for first stanza del then reinstated,* "2" *and* "3" *inserted by MW in MS. 137;* "2" *and* "3" *inserted by MW in MS. 138; lacking 1836–, but* I, II . . . *1839*
1 a Bird *rev from* Bird *MS. 112* Bird more bright *rev in pencil and ink from* dazzling Bird *rev from* dazzling bird *MS. 107 (B)*
2 *rev from* Sprung from a foreign stock *MS. 107 (B)*
3 second *rev from* brighter *MS. 107 (B)*
7–8 Soon was the pride of fancy tamed
Conjecture set at ease, *MS. 107 (B); so MS. 101A (A) but* tamed] tamed, *MS. 112 as MS. 107 (B) but* fancy] Fancy tamed *rev to* tam'd *rev to* tam'd,
MSS. 107 (B) then rev in ink over pencil to
Illusion gay!— it passed away
Those sportive companies *so MS. 101A (A) but* gay— . . . away, *MS. 135 (B) as rev MS. 107 (B) but* gay— . . . away! *then MW rev MS. 135 (B) to*
Transient deception! a mere feat
Of April's mimicries! *then rev to text*
Transient [Transient *rev to* —Transient] deception, a gay freak
Of April's mimicries! *MS. 106*
9 Those] The *MSS. 101A, 112* The *rev to* Of *MSS. 107 (B), 101A (A)* Of *rev to* Those *MS. 135 (B)* brilliant *rev from* dazzling *MS. 112*
12 on *rev from* in *MS. 106*

See the photographs and transcription of DC MS. 107 (A), 58^{v}–59^{r} on pp. 718–721.

2.

Maternal Flora! show thy face,
  And let thy hand be seen
Which sprinkles here these tiny flowers,
  That, as they touch the green,
Take root (so seems it) and look up
  In honour of their Queen.
Yet, sooth, those little starry specks,
  That not in vain aspired
To be confounded with live growths,
  Most dainty, most admired,
Were only blossoms dropped from twigs
  Of their own offspring tired.

3.

Not such the World's illusive shows;
  Her wingless flutterings,

---

14 thy] that *MS. 101A (B), MS. 112* that *rev to* thy *MSS. 107 (B), 101A (A)* seen *so all MSS., 1836–* seen *ital 1835, 1836YR, 1839*

15 Here sprinkling softly full-blown flowers *MS. 101A (B); so MS. 112 but* full grown flowers, [flowers *rev from* Flowers] *MSS. 107 (B), 101A (A) as MS. 101A (B) but* full-blown *rev to* tiny
Here [*alt* Thy hand Here] sprinkling (full-blown) flowers *(parens and underlining added) MS. 134*
Here softly [softly *rev to* tiny *del*] sprinkling tiny [tiny *rev to* tiny full-blown] flowers, *MS. 135 (B)*
Here sprinkling tiny full-blown flowers *MS. 106; so MSS. 137, 138 but* flowers,
Thy hand here sprinkling tiny flowers, *MS. 1835/36–*

19 *rev from* Bold words yet sooth those starry specks *MS. 107 (B)*

19–24 *inserted MS. 101A (A)*

25 shows; *defaced by wax MS. 135 (A)*

25–36 *lacking MS. 101A (B)*

25–30, 31–36 *order reversed MS. 112*

25–30 *lacking MS. 101A (A); WW added in pencil MS. 135 (A)*
Vain heart of man to thy false shows
No fond remembrance clings
When withered joys by time cast off
Make sport—as if on wings
And blooms of hope tho' shed to earth
Would pass for thriving things *rev to*
                from
Vain world ~~to~~ thy illusive shews
    light amusement
If ~~pleasure sometimes~~ springs
                of ~~mimic~~ joy
~~Yet the~~ shed blooms that mimic flowers
  ~~Tho~~ Pride's
~~And~~ wingless flutterings,
  Smile as we may
~~That in thy walks~~, for after-thought,
    [?mela]
Are but unwelcome things. *rev to*
          ~~mid~~
Vain world from thy etherial shows

[*cont. on facing page*]

Her blossoms which, though shed, outbrave
  The Floweret as it springs,
For the Undeceived, smile as they may,
  Are melancholy things:
But gentle Nature plays her part
  With ever-varying wiles,
And transient feignings with plain truth
  So well she reconciles,
That those fond Idlers most are pleased
  Whom oftenest she beguiles.

25–30 [*cont.*]
    If ~~Whereer~~ If casual ~~pleasure~~ pastime
  ~~Though~~ light amusement springs
          offspring that mimic
  Shed blooms that mimic growing flowers
    Pride's
  And wingless flutterings, ~~to the undeceivd~~
    To the undeceivd
          { they
  ^Smile as { he may. ~~for after thoughts~~
      melancholy
  Are ~~but unwelcome~~ things. *rev to text then del MS. 107 (B)*

29 For] To *MS. 112*

29–30 *alt* Smile as we may, for after thoughts
    Are but unwelcome things?? *del MS. 107 (B)*

31 But] So *rev to* Thus *MS. 107 (B)* Thus *MSS. 101A (A), 112* Thus *rev to* But *MS. 135 (A)*

32 ever-varying *rev from* ever varying *MS. 107 (B)*   wiles,] wiles *MS. 107 (B)*

33 feignings with plain *rev from* semblance with the *MS. 107 (B)*

35 *rev from* That they most love to be deceived *rev from* That undeceived we are not grieved *MS. 107 (B)*

36 *rev from* Repent not of our smiles *MS. 107 (B)*

29–30 The second question mark at the end of these alternate lines may query their insertion.

This Lawn, &c.

Wordsworth assigned *This Lawn, &c.* to 1829 in MS. 1835/36 and editions from 1836. A more precise date between about April and September 1829, around the same time as *Rural Illusions* (see the note to this poem, pp. 448–449, below), may be inferred from the position of *This Lawn, &c.* in DC MS. 107, since drafts for the two poems are intertwined. The earliest version of *This Lawn, &c.*, on which the first reading text is based, is on 62^{r} of MS. 107 in Wordsworth's hand (see "Text of MS. 107 (A)," below). He revised it and recopied the first stanza on the verso before deleting all the text on the recto. The other full and continuous version in MS. 107, on 28^{r}–28^{v}, shares some readings with that on 62^{r} but was then revised toward the published version. Entries in MS. 107 on 83^{r} and 118^{r} supply versions of stanzas 2 and 3, respectively. The version in Dorothy Wordsworth's hand in MS. 106, comprising only lines 1–12, has independent readings; the sheet bearing its third stanza was used by Wordsworth for a copy of "Chatsworth" and moved to MS. 107, still bearing the uncanceled final stanza of *This Lawn, &c.* (leaf 83 in MS. 107).

At the time Wordsworth was preparing his poems for the press, *This Lawn, &c.* bore the title "Bustle and Stillness," but he deleted this title and subsequently intended the title *Rural Illusions* ("Sylph was it? or a Bird more bright") to include *This Lawn, &c.* as a second "illusion," but the repeated title and its subtitle "II" were revised to "This Lawn, &c." in proof (MSS. 137, 138) and the poem was titled thus in 1835 (see "Text of 1835," below). The uncharacteristically abbreviated title, *This Lawn, &c.*, was dropped in 1836.

[Text of MS. 107 (A)]

This carpeting that Nature weaves
Of shadows flung from newborn leaves
    To dance amid a press
Of sunshine is a type of thee
Too busy World a simile
    For strenuous idleness.

Less quick the stir on summer seas
Where to the billows tide and breeze

---

composed probably between about April and September 1829
found in DC MS. 107 (A) 61^{r}
reading text DC MS. 107 (A)
1–2 *rev to* Vain World! this Lawn that seems alive
With shadows flung from leaves to strive *MS. 107 (A)*
3 To *alt* In *MS. 107 (A)*
4 is *rev to* yields *and* a type *alt* a hint *MS. 107 (A)*
5 *rev to* Thy profitless activity *MS. 107 (A)*
6 For *alt* And *MS. 107 (A)*
6/7 *WW entered* 2 *but no other stanza numbers MS. 107 (A)*
8 Where *alt in pencil* When[?ce] *MS. 107 (A)*

Forbid a moment's rest
The bustle in a martial sky
When aery [knights] prick forth to try
Whose spear is tempered best.

Yet spite of all this eager strife
And ceaseless play, that genuine life
That serves the steadfast hours
Is in the grass beneath that grows
Unheeded and the mute repose
Of sweetly breathing flowers.

[Text of 1835]

THIS LAWN, &c.

THIS Lawn, a carpet all alive
With shadows flung from leaves—to strive
In dance, amid a press
Of sunshine—an apt emblem yields
Of Worldlings revelling in the fields
Of strenuous idleness;

Less quick the stir when tide and breeze
Encounter, and to narrow seas

---

9 moment's] moments *MS. 107 (A)*
10 bustle *alt* conflict *MS. 107 (A)*
alt The medley less when boreal lights *MS. 107 (A)*
11 [knights] *supplied from alt line MS. 107 (A)*
alt Stream through the sky like aery knights *MS. 107 (A)*
12 Whose . . . best. *rev to* To feats of arms addrest *MS. 107 (A)*
14 And . . . that *rev to* This . . . the *MS. 107 (A)*

---

composed probably between about April and September 1829
found in DC MS. 107 (B) 61^{v}, rev ll. 1–6 of (A); (C) 27^{r}–27^{v}; (D) 82^{r}, stanza 3 only; (E) 118^{r}, pencil, stanza 2 only; DC MSS. 101A; 112; 134; 135; 137; 138 (MW); MS. 1835/36
published in *1835, 1836–*
classed Sentiment and Reflection *1836–*
reading text *1835*
title *lacking MSS. 107, 101A, 1836–* Suggested by our new Lawn *MS. 112* Bustle and Stillness *del MS. 135* Rural Illusions / II *rev to* This Lawn &c *MSS. 137, 138*
4 emblem *rev in pencil to* lesson *rev to* emblem *MS. 107 (B)* lesson *MS. 112*
5 Worldlings revelling *rev from* worldling revellers *MS. 135* worldling reveler *rev to* worldling revellers *MS. 107 (B)* worldling revellers *rev to* worldling Revellers *MS. 107 (C)* worlding revellers *MSS. 106, 134* worlding Revelers *MS. 112*
7–8 Less quick the stir on summer seas
When with billows tide and breeze *MS. 107 (E)*
Less quick the stir of [of *rev to* on] summer flowers [flowers *rev to* seas]
When [*rev to* Where] to the billows sun and breeze *MS. 112*

Forbid a moment's rest;
The medley less when boreal Lights
Glance to and fro like aery Sprites
To feats of arms addrest!

Yet, spite of all this eager strife,
This ceaseless play, the genuine life
That serves the steadfast hours,
Is in the grass beneath, that grows
Unheeded, and the mute repose
Of sweetly-breathing flowers.

Presentiments

The earliest version of *Presentiments,* in three stanzas with a fourth sketched below, appears in DC MS. 89. Wordsworth entered the title "Presentiments" and the three stanzas from MS. 89 on the verso of leaf 69 in MS. 107 and, with apparently the same ink and form of entry, added a new first stanza on 70[r], inserted numbers above the four stanzas showing their arrangement, and deleted the title. The underlying text of this four-stanza poem in MS. 107 (version A) is the basis for the first reading text, with variants cited from MS. 89 and version A in MS. 107. Elsewhere in MS. 107 three copies of an expanded version lead on to the eventual 76-line poem of the text of 1835. Wordsworth marked B, the earliest of these, in pencil, "A more correct Copy elsewhere." Copies in other manuscripts show only minor variants from D, the most fully developed version in MS. 107. The position of drafts of *Presentiments* in MS. 107 in proximity to datable poems suggests that Wordsworth may have begun it around the same time as *Rural Illusions,* in August 1829.

9 Forbid *rev by eras from* Forbids *MS. 134*
10–12 The bustle of a martial sky
When "aery Knights prick forth"—to try
Whose spear is temper'd best. *MS. 112*
11 Stream through the sky like aery knights *MS. 107 (E)* Sprites] Knights *MS. 107 (C)*

[Text of MS. 107 (A)]

1

Presentiments!—they judge not right
Who deem that all which shrinks from light
Is false and merits shame
If that poor Pleader Common Sense
Fail you, go deeper for defense
Remembering your high name.

2

Whence but from you, misdeem'd of Powers
The Faith that in auspicious hours
Builds Castles, not of air;
Bodings unsanctioned by the Will
Flow from your visionary skill
And teach us to beware.

3

What though some subtle Foes to good
Work near you in our human blood
And mischief intertwine
With benefit which ye infuse
This hides not from the thoughtful Muse
Your origin divine.

---

composed probably between August 1829 and the end of 1830
found in DC MSS. 89, 107 (A) 68^{v}–69^{r}
reading text DC MS. 107 (A)
title Poem *MS. 89* Presentiments. *entered then del above what became second stanza MS. 107 (A)*
1–6 *lacking MS. 89; inserted and stanzas numbered from* 1 *accordingly MS. 107 (A)*
1 Presentiments *rev in pencil to* PRESENTIMENTS *MS. 107 (A)*
2 shrinks from *rev in pencil to* dreads the *MS. 107 (A)*
3 *alt in pencil* Retire through fear *MS. 107 (A)*
4 poor *rev in pencil to* cold *MS. 107 (A)*
6 Remembering *rev in pencil to* Nor blush for *MS. 107 (A)*
7–8 *alt MS. 107 (A) as 1835, ll. 19–20, but no pnct and marked to follow l. 18*
7 from *inserted MS. 89* Whence but from *rev to* From you, from you *MS. 107 (A)* Powers *rev from* powers *MS. 107 (A)*
8 Faith *alt* From Faith *MS. 107 (A)*
10 Will *rev from* will *MS. 107 (A)*
15 And *rev from* Thus *MS. 89*
16 benefit] benefits *MS. 89*
17 not *inserted MS. 107 (A)*

4

Alas for Man upon whose eye
Hangs such a world of mystery,
Whose freedom's but a chain
To struggle with should he affect
Your divinations to reject,
Your Alchemy disdain.

[Text of 1835]

PRESENTIMENTS.

PRESENTIMENTS! they judge not right
Who deem that ye from open light
  Retire in fear of shame;
All *heaven-born* Instincts shun the touch
Of vulgar sense, and, being such,
  Such privilege ye claim.

---

19 for *rev to* if *MS. 89* Man *rev from* a man *MS. 107 (A)*
22 To struggle with] to struggle with *rev from* With which he struggles *rev from* He struggles with *MS. 89*
23 divinations] divination *alt* astrology *full line alt* Your bold and starry wisdom *MS. 89* reject,] reject *MS. 107 (A)*
24/ *additional drafts in MS. 89:*

Nor frown on those who while they skim
Lifes stream in boat of gallant trim
If [~~?dreary~~] [?weary] calm prevail

Nor frown upon the gay
~~Nor frown upon the~~ gay
~~And grant~~
~~Nor hide your~~ smile to those who skim
  Lifes stream
Our life in boat of galla~~u~~nt trim
  Equipp'd with oar & sail
Who sparing not the Rowers arm
    through
Solicit, ~~by~~ a blameless charm
The service of the Gale.

---

composed probably between August 1829 and the end of 1830
found in DC MSS. 107 (B) 45^{r}–46^{v}, (C) 47^{r}–49^{r}, (D) 49^{v}–51^{r}, (E) 69^{r}; 106; 134; 135; MS. 1835/36; MS. 1836/45 (JC)
published in *1835, 1836–*
classed Imagination *MS. 1835/36–*
reading text *1835*
title *lacking MS. 107 (E)* Presentiments To DW. *MS. 134*
stanza numbers II . . . IX *MS. 107 (B)* 1 . . . 15 *MS. 107 (D)* 2 . . . 12 *MS. 135* 1. . . . 13. *del MS. 137*
2 ye *rev from* you *MS. 107 (C)*

The tear whose source I could not guess,
The deep sigh that seemed fatherless,
  Were mine in early days;
And now, unforced by Time to part
With Fancy, I obey my heart,
  And venture on your praise.

What though some busy Foes to good,
Too potent over nerve and blood,
  Lurk near you, and combine
To taint the health which ye infuse,
This hides not from the moral Muse
  Your origin divine.

How oft from you, derided Powers!
Comes Faith that in auspicious hours
  Builds castles, not of air;
Bodings unsanctioned by the will
Flow from your visionary skill,
  And teach us to beware.

The bosom-weight, your stubborn gift,
That no philosophy can lift,
  Shall vanish, if ye please,
Like morning mist; and, where it lay,
The spirits at your bidding play
  In gaiety and ease.

---

10 now *rev in pencil from* so *MS. 107 (E)* Time] age *MSS. 107 (B, C), 106* Age *MS. 107 (D)* time *rev in pencil to* age *MS. 107 (E)* age *rev to* time *MS. 134*

11 obey *rev in pencil from* I will *MS. 107 (E)*

13–18 *placed as stanza* VIII *after l. 60 in fair copy, then marked for insertion after l. 12 MS. 107 (B)*

13–14 What though some subtle foes to good
Lurk near you in our human blood *rev to*
What though some enemies to good
Too potent over human [*alt* nerve and] blood *MS. 107 (B); WW rev to text and inserted after l. 12 in MS. 107 (B) to mark both revision and transfer of ll. 13–18.*

13 busy foes to good *added in pencil MS. 107 (C)*

15–16 *rev from* And mischief intertwine
With benefits which ye infuse *MS. 107 (B)*

15 Lurk near you *alt* This mischief *MS. 107 (B)*

16 health *rev from* hearth *MS. 107 (D)* infuse] inspire *alt* infuse *MS. 107 (C)*

17 moral] thoughtful *rev to* moral *rev to* artfull *MS. 107 (B)*

26 That *rev from* What *MS. 107 (B)*

28 it *rev from* ye *MS. 107 (D)*

Star-guided Contemplations move
Through space, though calm, not raised above
  Prognostics that ye rule;
The naked Indian of the Wild,
And haply, too, the cradled Child,
  Are pupils of your school.

But who can fathom your intents,
Number their signs or instruments?
  A rainbow, a sunbeam,
A subtle smell that Spring unbinds,
Dead pause abrupt of midnight winds,
  An echo, or a dream.

The laughter of the Christmas hearth

31–36 *lacking MS. 107 (B); so MS. 107 (C) fair copy; in MS. 107 (D) placed to follow unpublished stanza between ll. 48/49 then marked to follow l. 30*
  The Sage whose contemplations move
      breathes not rais'd
~~Star-guided is not raised~~ above
The province where ye rule
  This naked Indian of the Wild
~~Apart in reasons [?frontal] Cell~~
~~Where oft unveil'd~~ ideas dwell
  And haply too the cradled child
~~Ere these Ye live and move~~
  Are pupils of your school *ink draft MS. 107 (C) (but ink draft marked to follow unpublished stanza between ll. 48/49; see below)*
  The Sage whose contemplations move
Most firmly breathes not raised above
That province where ye rule;
[?The] naked Indian of the wild
And haply too the cradled child
Are pupils of your School— *pencil draft MS. 107 (C)*
The Sage, whose contemplations move
Star-guided, breathes not rais'd above
The province where ye rule; *rest as text MS. 107 (C) (but marked as stanza* 9 *to follow stanza between ll. 48/49; see below)*

31–32 The Sage, whose contemplations move
Star-guided, breathes not raised above *rev to*
Newtonian contemplations move
Star-guided, are they raised above *MS. 107 (D), so 106 but* move *rev from* move, *and* guided, *rev to* guided;
MS. 134 as rev MS. 107 (D) but no punct, then rev in pencil and ink to text

33 Prognostics that] The province where *MSS. 107 (D), 106*

37–39 But who shall search that inner school
Whence ye can mark your twofold rule
Even by a weather gleam, *alt*
But who can fathom your intents
Number their signs and [and *rev to* or] instruments
A star—a weather-gleam, *MS. 107 (B)*

38 or *rev from* and *MS. 107 (D)*

39 *rev from* A Star—a weather-gleam— *MS. 107 (C)*

40 A subtle] By a sweet *alt* A subtle *MS. 107 (B)*

43 Christmas *alt* social *del MS. 107 (B)*

With sighs of self-exhausted mirth
  Ye feelingly reprove;
And daily, in the conscious breast,
Your visitations are a test
  And exercise of love.

When some great change gives boundless scope
To an exulting Nation's hope,
  Oft, startled and made wise
By your low-breathed interpretings,
The simply-meek foretaste the springs
  Of bitter contraries.

Ye daunt the proud array of War,
Pervade the lonely Ocean far
  As sail hath been unfurled;
For Dancers in the festive hall
What ghastly Partners hath your call
  Fetched from the shadowy world!

---

44 With . . . of] By . . . from *MS. 107 (B)*
48/49 Ye [*rev to* They] fill with tears the Mother's eyes
While in soft calm her Infant lies
Asleep upon her knee;
Ah! why this sadness? let [let *rev to* Let] her trace
Prognostics in that quiet face
Of happy destiny. *MS. 107 (C); MS. 107 (D) as rev 107 (C) but* knee;] knee *then stanza del WW inserted*
49–54 When some great change a transport spreads
That maddens even experienced heads
  The simply meek made wise
By your low breathd interpretings
The [*rev to* With] fear and grief foretaste the springs
  Of bitter contraries. *MS. 107 (B) with penultimate line rev to* With drooping [heart *del*] soul foretaste the springs
When public change a transport springs
That seizes even experienced heads *rev to*
When one [one *rev to* some] great chan[ge] gives boundless scope
To an exulting Nation's hope *rest as text MS. 107 (C)*
58 For Maidens dancing in gay Halls *rev to* For Dancers in the festive Hall *MS. 107 (D)*
58–60 Unboastful ministers of faith,
Ye flutter through the shades of death
  To seek a brighter world *MS. 107 (B); so MS. 107 (C) but* Faith, *and* world. *then MS. 107 (C) rev to*
Not softly [Not softly *rev to* Ye merrily] peal the festive bell *rev to*
And [And *rev from* ?To] ghastly Partners at your call
Come from the shadowy world. *MS. 107 (C) but WW's marginal note* The other sta *(see below)*
Ye mingle mid the festive balls [balls *rev to* ball]
And ghastly Partners at your call
Are from the shadowy world *rev to*
For Maidens dancing in gay halls
What ghastly Partners hear [hear *alt* ?heed] your calls
Fetched from the shadowy world *MS. 107 (C)*
59 hath . . . call *rev from* have . . . calls *MS. 107 (D)*
60/61 *stanza number rev from* 11 *to* 13 *MS. 107 (C)*

'Tis said, that warnings ye dispense,
Emboldened by a keener sense;
  That men have lived for whom,
With dread precision, ye made clear
The hour that in a distant year
  Should knell them to the tomb.

Unwelcome Insight! Yet there are
Blest times when mystery is laid bare,
  Truth shows a glorious face,
While on that Isthmus which commands
The councils of both worlds she stands,
  Sage Spirits! by your grace.

God, who instructs the Brutes to scent
All changes of the element,
  Whose wisdom fixed the scale
Of Natures, for our wants provides
By higher, sometimes humbler, guides,
  When lights of Reason fail.

61–72 *lacking from fair copy MS. 107 (B)*
61–62 *WW's drafts:*
Tis said that knowledge ye dispense
With yet a loftie *alt*
Tis said that sometimes ye dispense
Knowledge with lofty confidence *alt*
Such knowledge sometimes ye dispense
Tis said, with lofty confidence *all del*
Tis said that from a bolder [from a bolder *rev to* through a finer] sense
Ye drew a loftier confidence *with last line rev to* Your intimations ye dispense *MS. 107* (B_1)
Tis said, that [?even] [?even *rev to* often *rev to* sometimes] ye dispense
Your knowledge through a bolder sense *MS. 107* (B_2)
Tis said that through a bolder sense
Your intimations ye dispense *MS. 107* (B_3)
62 keener *rev from* finer *MS. 107 (C)*
63 men *rev from* man *MS. 134*
64 With *rev from* That *MS. 107 (B)* precision *rev from* [?de]cision *MS. 106*
65 hour *alt* day *del MS. 107 (B)*
66 Should *rev from* Would *MS. 107 (B)* the *rev from* their *MSS. 107 (C, D)*
66/67 *stanza number rev from* 12 *to* 14 *MS. 107 (C)*
67–72 *no fair copy but WW's draft:*
Alas for man upon whose eye
Hangs such a cloud of mystery
  ~~sometimes ere his race~~
~~Yet oft—a little space~~
  ~~high~~ Each, on that Istmus
~~On a firm~~ Isthmus that commands
The concils of both worlds he stands
Sage Spirits! by your grace *MS. 107 (B)*
70 which *rev to* that *rev in pencil to* which *MS. 107 (D)*
72 by] lay *uncorrected printer's error MS. 137*
72/73 *stanza number rev from* 13 *to* 15 *MS. 107 (C)*
75 Whose *rev from* [?Where] *MS. 134*
76 Natures] natures *rev in pencil from* nature *MS. 107 (B)* Nature *MS. 107 (C)*
77 sometimes *alt* or by *MS. 107 (B)*

GOLD AND SILVER FISHES,
IN A VASE.

THE soaring Lark is blest as proud
  When at Heaven's gate she sings;
The roving Bee proclaims aloud
  Her flight by vocal wings;
While Ye, in lasting durance pent,
  Your silent lives employ
For something "more than dull content
  Though haply less than joy."

Yet might your glassy prison seem
  A place where joy is known,
Where golden flash and silver gleam
  Have meanings of their own;
While, high and low, and all about,
  Your motions, glittering Elves!
Ye weave—no danger from without,
  And peace among yourselves.

Type of a sunny human breast
  Is your transparent Cell;
Where Fear is but a transient Guest,
  No sullen Humours dwell;
Where, sensitive of every ray
  That smites this tiny sea,
Your scaly panoplies repay
  The loan with usury.

---

composed around November but before December 19, 1829

found in DC MSS. 107, 106, 113, 135, 137, 138; Dora W to MJJ, November or December, 1829; Dora W to EQ, December 19, 1829; Monkhouse MS. (copy); WW and MW to EQ, November 14, 1831; BL MS. 1 (ll. 1–16); MS. 1835/36; MS. 1835/36 (MW)

published in *1835, 1836–*

classed Sentiment and Reflection *1836–* Miscellaneous Poems *1845, 1850*

reading text *1835*

title *lacking MSS. 107, 106, WW and MW to EQ* To our Gold and Silver Fish *MS. 113* Gold [Gold *rev from* gold] and Silver Fish. / in a Vase. *MS. 135* Fishes *rev from* Fish *MS. 137*

epigraph "O mutis quoque piscibus
"Donatura cycni, si libeat sonum!" *MS. 113, Dora W to EQ, Monkhouse MS. (copy)*

stanza numbers 1 . . . 7 *WW and MW to EQ*

3 roving] roaming *WW and MW to EQ*

4 Her] His *Monkhouse MS. (copy)* by] with *MS. 113, Dora W to EQ*

11 golden] silent *MS. 113*

13 high and low,] low and high, *MS. 113, Dora W to EQ* low and high *Monkhouse MS. (copy)*

19 but a transient] not a lingering *Dora W to EQ, Monkhouse MS. (copy)* Guest] Guess *printer's error 1836YR*

22 smites] strikes *Dora W to EQ*

23 repay *rev from* display *MS. 107*

How beautiful! Yet none knows why
  This ever-graceful change,
Renewed—renewed incessantly—
  Within your quiet range.
Is it that ye with conscious skill
  For mutual pleasure glide;
And sometimes, not without your will,
  Are dwarfed, or magnified?

Fays—Genii of gigantic size—
  And now, in twilight dim,
Clustering like constellated Eyes
  In wings of Cherubim,
When they abate their fiery glare:
  Whate'er your forms express,
Whate'er ye seem, whate'er ye are,
  All leads to gentleness.

Cold though your nature be, 'tis pure;
  Your birthright is a fence
From all that haughtier kinds endure
  Through tyranny of sense.
Ah! not alone by colours bright
  Are Ye to Heaven allied,
When, like essential Forms of light,
  Ye mingle, or divide.

For day-dreams soft as e'er beguiled
  Day-thoughts while limbs repose;
For moonlight fascinations mild
  Your gift, ere shutters close;
Accept, mute Captives! thanks and praise;
  And may this tribute prove

---

25 Yet] and *MS. 113, Dora W to EQ, Monkhouse MS. (copy)*
26 ever-graceful *rev from* [?ever-varying] *MS. 106* ever-varying *MS. 107* graceful *ink over pencil over illeg eras WW and MW to EQ*
34 And now] Or Ye *MS. 1835/36*
34–35 And now when air is dim
Lustrous [Lustrous *rev from* Lusterous] as regal gems—or eyes *MS. 113*
And now when air is dim
Lustrous as regal gems, or eyes *Dora W to EQ, Monkhouse MS. (copy)*
35 Clustering] Cluster *MS. 1835/36*
36 wings] wheels *MS. 113, Dora W to EQ, Monkhouse MS. (copy)*
37 When the fierce orbs abate their glare;— *MS. 1835/36–, 1839*
38 *line inserted MS. 135* forms] shapes *MSS. 107, 106, WW and MW to EQ*
41–48 *lacking MS. 113*
41 though] if *Dora W to EQ, Monkhouse MS. (copy)*
45 alone *rev from* in vain *MS. 107*
48 or] and *Dora W to EQ, Monkhouse MS. (copy)*
53 Accept,] Receive *MS. 113, Dora W to EQ* Receive, *Monkhouse MS. (copy)* mute *rev from* meek *MSS. 107, 106, WW and MW to EQ* praise; *rev from* praises, *MS. 135*

That gentle admirations raise
Delight resembling love.

To a Friend, Liberty, and *Humanity*

The earliest surviving composition toward *Liberty. (Sequel to the Above.)*—that is, sequel to *Gold and SilverFishes, in a Vase*—and *Humanity. (Written in 1829.)* is found in a unified composition, *To a Friend.* Wordsworth entered drafts toward *To a Friend* on the four final sides of a gathering containing fair copies of several shorter poems in DC MS. 107 (see the headnote to *The Primrose of the Rock*, third paragraph, and the entry for DC MS. 107 in the Manuscript Census). Dorothy Wordsworth's earliest fair copy of *To a Friend* in 202 lines, found in MS. 114, was probably made in 1829. This copy was extensively revised, and in its revised state was probably the source for later copies (mentioned below).

Line numbers in MS. 114, probably entered by Wordsworth, show that before the poem was expanded by about 40 lines, it had reached a stable phase of just over 200 lines. This underlying text, for the most part exclusive of Wordsworth's pencil revisions and his and Dorothy's ink revisions and additions, has been recovered to produce the text of *To a Friend* given below. But within a relatively short period, Wordsworth added more than 40 lines to the poem and revised the line numbering (all in MS. 114) to reflect the state of the text as it then stood. This added material, written on smaller sheets carefully pasted to the fair copy, is reported in the *apparatus* to *To a Friend.* The "Friend" of the title was Maria Jane Jewsbury, who had given the Wordsworths the goldfish in 1829, an occasion Wordsworth had initially marked by writing *Gold and Silver Fishes, in a Vase* in November and December of that year. The opening line of *To a Friend,* "Those breathing tokens of your kind regard" (also the opening line of *Liberty*), alludes again to this gift.

At least two more fair copies of *To a Friend* were made. Dorothy Wordsworth's copy in MS. 106 preserves the expanded state to be found in MS. 114; Wordsworth entered revisions in pencil in this MS. 106 copy, some of which were written over in ink. Wordsworth said in his Fenwick note to *Humanity* (see the note on p. 450) that Mary Wordsworth "complained" that the poem was "unwieldly and ill proportioned," and he accordingly divided it into two poems, *Liberty* and *Humanity.* He placed *Liberty* to follow *Gold and Silver Fishes* and to precede *Evening Voluntaries,* and he moved *Humanity* to a section of miscellaneous poems near the end of *Yarrow Revisited, and Other Poems* (see these poems edited above and below). Mary Wordsworth's marginal notations in MS. 106 confirm her part in the division of *To a Friend.*

A third fair copy of *To a Friend* was made by Dora Wordsworth on paper bearing the countermark 1827 and must have been prepared around the same time as MSS. 114 and 106, probably early in 1830. A complete copy no longer exists but can be partly reconstructed from sheets later used for the printer's copy of *Yarrow Revisited, and Other Poems.* Moreover, there is some evidence to suggest that Dora's copy of *To a Friend* was given a place in the arrangement of poems for *Yarrow*

Revisited, and Other Poems: in the printer's copy, MS. 135, the poem follows *Gold and Silver Fishes* on the same sheet with the title *To a Friend, The Gold and Silver Fish being removed to a Pool in the Pleasure-Ground of Rydal-mount.*

At the end of William and Mary Wordsworth's letter to Edward Quillinan of around November 14, but by November 20, 1831, Dora Wordsworth transcribed *Gold and Silver Fishes, in a Vase* and *On the Departure of Sir Walter Scott from Abbotsford, for Naples* (here titled *To Walter Scott on his quitting Abbotsford for Naples*), adding in a note that the "second fish poem is at least 250 lines long" (WL MS; *LY*, II, 450–452, prints the letter but not the note). The length of the sequel to *Gold and Silver Fishes, in a Vase* at this stage confirms that Dora refers to *To a Friend* rather than to *Liberty. (Sequel to the Above.)*. So the poem seems to have stood for several years until the Wordsworths began to prepare copy for *Yarrow Revisited, and Other Poems* to send to the printer in the latter half of 1835.

Sometime between July and December 1835, the third fair copy, the one transcribed by Dora on the 1827 paper, was pulled apart and combined with sheets freshly copied by Mary Wordsworth (who also entered revisions to the title and text) to produce the two separate poems that were actually sent to the printer, probably by November. The canceled portions of these 1827 sheets bearing Dora's copy of *To a Friend* (struck out or covered over because the lines were not wanted in that place in the new configuration) are reported in the *apparatus* to *To a Friend,* since they represent the continuation of the compositional history of that poem. However, the text of the "new" poems produced (the text that is not canceled) is reported in the appropriate *apparatus* to *Liberty* or *Humanity.*

[Text of MS. 114]

To a Friend

Those breathing tokens of your kind regard,
(Suspect not, Anna, that their fate is hard;
Not soon does aught to which mild fancies cling
In lonely spots become a slighted thing)
Those silent Inmates now no longer share,
Nor need, I trust, our hospitable care.
—Removed in kindness from their glassy Cell
To the fresh waters of a living Well

---

composed between December 1829 and November 14–20, 1831
found in DC MSS. 107 (A) 40^r (2 ll.), (B) 52^r, (C) 52^v, (D) 53^r, (E) 53^v; 114; 106; 135 (A) 52^v–56^v, 119^v (canceled portions of printer's copy that survive from the early version; includes the end-note)
reading text DC MS. 114
title *rev in pencil to* Addressed To a Friend. *MS. 114* To a friend, / The Gold and Silver fish [fish *rev to* Fish] being removed / To a Pool in the Garden [Garden *rev to* Pleasure-Ground of Rydal-mount] *MS. 135 (A)*
7 their *rev in pencil and ink from* the *MS. 114*
8 living Well *rev to* favourite *orig reading reinstated MS. 114*

See the photographs and transcriptions of DC MS. 107 (B), 52^r, (C), 52^v, (D), 53^r, and (E), 53^v on pp. 722–729.

That spreads into an elfin pool opaque
Of which close boughs a glimmering mirror make
On whose smooth breast with dimples light and small
The fly may settle, leaf or blossom fall,
Hailstones, and big drops of the thunder shower:
There swims, but how obscured! the *golden* Power;
That from his bauble prison used to cast
Gleams by the richest jewel unsurpass'd
And there, a darkling Gnome in sullen robe,
The *silver* Tenant of the crystal globe;
Dissevered both from all the mysteries
Of hue and altering shape that charmed all eyes.
—They pined, perhaps, they languished—while they shone;
And if not so, what matters beauty gone,
And admiration lost by change of place,
That brings to the inward creature no disgrace;
But, if the change restore his birthright, then,
Whate'er the difference, boundless is the gain.
Who can divine what impulses from God
Reach the caged lark within a town abode
From his poor inch or two of daisied sod?
O yield him back his privilege;—no sea
Swells like the bosom of a man set free;
A wilderness is rich with liberty.
Roll on ye spouting Whales, who die, or keep
Your independence in the fathomless Deep!
Spread, tiny Nautilus, the living sail,
Dive at thy choice, or brave the freshening gale!
If unreproved the ambitious Eagle mount
Sunward, to seek the daylight in her fount,
Bays, gulphs, and Ocean's Indian width shall be,
Till the world perishes, a field for thee

What, though dislodged by purer faith, no more
White-vested Priests the hallowed Oak adore,
Nor Seer nor Judge consult the Stone of Power!

---

13 *rev to* In that live pool within that living bower *orig reading reinstated MS. 114*

14 There swims, *rev to* Swims there *MS. 114*

17 *rev in pencil to* near him like a sullen Gnome *rev in ink to* And near him darkling like a sullen Gnome *MS. 114; MS. 106 as rev MS. 114 but* him] him,

18 globe; *rev in pencil and ink to* dome; *MS. 114* dome— *MS. 106*

31 free; *rev in pencil from* free *MS. 114* free; *MS. 106*

41–102 *WW marked for del MS. 106*

41 dislodged by purer faith, *rev in pencil and ink to* in depth of shadowy woods *MSS. 106, 135 (A_1; see note)*

42 White-vested *pencil alt* The Druid *and* the hallowed *pencil alt* his spreading *MS. 114* hallowed *rev to* [?] *rev in pencil and ink to* central *MS. 106* central *MS. 135 (A_1)*

42–43 No more the druid Priest the hallowed Oak adores *MS. 135 (A_2)*

Yet, for the Initiate, rocks and whispering trees
Do still perform mysterious offices;
And still in beast and bird a function dwells
That, while we look and listen, sometimes tells
Upon the heart in more authentic guise
Than Oracles, or wingèd Auguries,
Spake to the science of the ancient Wise.
Not uninspired appear their simplest ways,
Their voice ascends symbolical of praise,
Of hymns which blessèd spirits make and hear;
And to fallen Man their innocence is dear.
Where martyrs stand, or soar, in hues pourtrayed
That, if a wish might save them, ne'er would fade
The unspotted lily, the victorious palm
Shed round the altar a celestial calm;
There, too, behold the Lamb and guileless Dove
Press'd, in the tenderness of virgin love,
To saintly bosoms.—Glorious is the blending
Of right affections, climbing, or descending
Along the scale of things with ceaseless cares
Alternate, carrying holy thoughts and prayers
Up to the sovereign seat of the Most High;
Descending to the worm in charity;
Like those good angels whom a dream of night
Shewed to the Patriarch; not in banded flight
But, treading, while he slept, the pendant stairs
Earthward and heavenward; radiant Messengers

---

52 voice ascends *rev in pencil and ink to* voices mount *MS. 135 (A_2)*
53 Of hymns which blessèd *rev in pencil and ink to* To mix with hymns that *MS. 135 (A_2)*
54/55 Enraptured Art draws from those sacred springs
Streams that reflect the poetry of things *inserted MS. 135 (A_2)*
55 martyrs stand or soar *rev to* Christian Martyr's stand *MS. 135 (A_2)*
56–57 That [ ] a wish avail that would not fade,
[ ] the Lily the victorious palm *rev in pencil and ink to*
That might a wish avail would never fade
Borne in their hands the Lily and the Palm *MS. 106; so MS. 135 (A_2) but* avail] avail,
57–59 When round the altar breathes celestial calm
From spotless lily and victorious palm
By martyrs born that soar in hues pourtrayed
That if a wish could save them neer should fade
There the meek Lamb beh[ ] and guileless Dove *alt MS. 114*
57 lily] lilly *MS. 114* The unspotted . . . the *pencil alt* And spotless . . . and *MS. 114*
58 That round the altar shed celestial calm *rev in pencil and ink to text MS. 106*
59 *pencil alt* There the meek Lamb behold and guileless Dove *MS. 114* There *rev from* Here *MS. 106*
63 *rev to* As an authentic scale *rev to* Along the scale of light and life with cares *rev to* In a perpetual exercise of cares— *all del MS. 135 (A_2)*
68–69 Gave in the Field of Luz to Jacob's sight
All, while he slept, treading the pendant stairs *pencil and ink over illeg eras MS. 106*

56–59 Damage to this and several following leaves of MS. 114 obscures the text.

That with a perfect will, in one accord
Of strict obedience, served the Almighty Lord,
And with untired humility forbore
The ready service of the wings they wore.

What a fair world were ours for verse to paint
If Power could live at ease with self-restraint,
And Policy bow down before the sense
Of the great Vision,—faith in providence,—
Merciful over all existence, just
To the least particle of sentient dust!
Then Genius, shunning fellowship with pride,
Would braid his golden locks at Wisdom's side,
Love ebb and flow untroubled by caprice;
And not alone harsh Tyranny would cease,
But unoffending creatures find release
From qualified Oppression, whose defence
Rests on a hollow plea of recompence;
Thought-tempered wrongs, for each humane respect
Oft worse to bear, or deadlier in effect:
Witness those glances of indignant scorn
From some high-minded Slave impelled to spurn
The kindness that would make him less forlorn:
Or, if the soul to bondage be subdued,
His look of pitable gratitude!
Alas! for thee, bright Galaxy of Isles
Where day departs in pomp, returns with smiles
To greet the flowers and fruitage of a Land,
(As the sun mounts) by sea-born breezes fanned,

---

77 Opinion bow before the naked sense *MSS. 114 (2^{v}P), 106*
79 existence *pencil alt* his Creatures *MS. 106*
80/81 Then would be closed that restless oblique eye
That looks for evil like a treacherous spy;
Disputes would then relax like stormy winds
That into breezes sink; and ardent minds
By discipline endeavour to grow meek
As Truth herself—whom they profess to seek *MS. 114 (2^{v}P); so MS. 106 but* winds] winds, *and above this entry (repeated in margin), in pencil:*
And fixing by immutable decrees
Seed time and harvest for his purposes *MS. 106*
83 ebb and *over illeg eras MS. 106*
84 *rev in pencil to* And not alone would bold faced Tyranny cease, *MS. 106*
89 Oft worse *rev from* Now hard *MS. 114*
91 impelled *rev in pencil and ink from* compelled *MS. 114*

A land whose azure mountain-tops are seats
For Gods in Council whose green Vales—retreats
Fit for the shades of Heroes, mingling there,
To breathe Elysian peace in upper air.

102/103 Alas, for favoured Countries nearer home,
Realms to which personal slavery may not come,
For "merry England's" self! (the gallant name
By outward looks, at least, she still may claim)
For her, whose floors, whose streets, whose hardy soil *MS. 114 (3^{r}P1, 3^{r}P9^{v}); MS. 114 (3^{r}P2) revises the last line*
Yet do her floors, her streets, her kindly soil *and continues*
Groan underneath a weight of abject toil,
For the poor Many measured out by rules
Fetched with cupidity from heartless schools,
That to an idol, falsely styled "the Wealth
~~Of Nations" sa~~[ ]
Body, and mind [ ]
Is ever urging on [ ]
Of sleepless labour, 'mid whose dizzy wheels
The power least prized is that which thinks and feels,
[—Then for the pastimes of this delicate age, *line inserted*]
And all the heavy or light vassalage, *MS. 114 (3^{r}P2)*
Body and mind and soul—a thirst so keen
Is ever urging on the vast machine
Of sleepless labour, 'mid whose dizzy wheels
The power least prized is that which thinks and feels
—Then for the pastimes of this delicate age [age *rev to* Age]
And all the heavy or light vassalage *MS. 114 (3^{r}P3); so MS. 106 but* labour] Labour power] Power pastimes *underscored in pencil* age] Age, heavy . . . vassalage] heavy, . . . vassalage,
Which, for their sakes we fasten, as may suit
Our varying moods, on human kind or brute
'Twere well in little as in great to pause
Lest [*rev from* Less] Fancy trifle with eternal laws.
There are who dread to violate the grace
The lowliest herb possesses in its place,
Nor [*rev in pencil from* To] shorten the sweet life too fugitive *last three lines alt in pencil:*
[There are to whom the garden and the field
Perpetual lessons of forbearance yield
Who would not lightly violate the grace]
Which nothing less than Infinite Power could give. *MS. 114 (3^{r}P2); MS. 114 (3^{r}P4) revises to*
There are to whom the garden and the field
Perpetual lessons of forbearance yield
Who would not lightly violate the grace
The lowliest herb possesses in its place,
Nor shorten the sweet life, too fugitive,
Which nothing less than Infinite Power could give *MS. 114 (3^{r}P4); MS. 106 as rev MS. 114 (3^{r}P4) but* sakes] sakes, brute] brute; little] little, There] —There yield] yield, herb *rev in pencil and ink to* flower give] give. sakes] sakes, brute] brute; little . . . great] little, . . . great,
The first lines of the addition, through ~~Of Nations" sa~~[ ] *then revised on P5–P10 thus*
Though cold as winter, gloomy as the grave,
Stone walls a Prisoner make, but not a Slave:—
Shall man for lucre shackle guiltless man?
[~~?Garrot~~] him with stripes?—endure the sight who can [*alt in pencil* Let those endure the monstrous sight who can]
Turn [*rev to* —Turn *MS. 114 (3^{r}P7)*] we to shores that brook not such foul shame [shame *rev in pencil from* ?crime]

While, musing, here I sit in shadow cool,
And watch (by glimpses caught) in this calm pool,
Among reflected boughs of leafy trees,

To "merry England's" [England's *rev to* England *MS. 114 (3^rP6–P7)*] self [self *rev in pencil to* hour] (the gallant name
By outward shews, [looks *MS. 114 (3^rP6)* looks, *MS. 114 (3^rP7)*] at least, she still may claim)
Yet do her floors, her streets, her kindly soil
Groan underneath a weight of abject [abject *alt in pencil* slavish] toil. *MS. 114 (3^rP5)*
Tho' cold as winter, gloomy as the grave,
Stone walls a Prisoner make, but not a Slave.
Shall Man assume a property in Man,
Lay on the moral Will [Will *rev from* will] a withering ban?
~~/ Turn we to Shores that brook not the foul shame,~~ [?show tha]
~~To "merry England" turn,—the gallant name,~~
~~By outward looks at least, she still may claim.~~ *(3-line del in pencil)*
Yet as if distance flung, to cheat her view,
O'er crime and misery a softening hue
The usurpation which her laws reject
At home—abroad they cease not to protect.
And, though by Slaves untrod, her jealous soil
Groans underneath a weight of slavish toil,
For the poor Many measured out by rules
Fetched with cupidity from heartless Schools [Schools *rev from* schools];
That to an Idol, falsely styled "the wealth
Of Nations" [ ] a People's health *MS. 114 (3^rP8)*
~~Yet sophistry, than air more subtle, flings~~
~~Illusive colours over distant things;~~
The usurpation which our laws reject
At home,—abroad they cease not to protect
~~And, though by~~ slaves untrod, our native soil
Groans underneath a weight of slavish toil,
For the poor Many measured out by rules
Fetched with cupidity from heartless Schools; *(punct added in pencil))*
That to an Idol, falsely styles the "Wealth
Of Nations" sacrifice a People's health,— *MS. 114 (3^rP9)*
Though cold as winter, gloomy as the grave~~xx~~,
Stone walls a prisoner make; but not a Slave,
Shall Man assume a property in Man,
Lay on the moral will a withering ban?
Shame that our laws at distance should protect
Enormities which they at home reject
Slaves cannot breathe in England, yet her soil [*WW and MW expanded last line to*
Slaves cannot breath in England, a proud boast
And yet a mockery, if from coast to coast
Though fettered slave be none, her floors and soil]
Groans underneath a weight of slavish toil
For the poor Many measured out by rules
Fetched with cupidity from heartless Schools
That to an Idol, falsely styled, the "Wealth
Of Nations" sacrifice a People's health— *MS. 114 (3^rP10), but ll. [3–4] entered first in pencil (but no comma) in margin of 2^v and ll. [8–9], in ink, in margin of 3^r; MS. 106 as finally rev MS. 114 but [1]* Though *rev to* Tho' *to create paragraph break* grave] grave, *[2]* make; . . . Slave,] make, . . . slave. *[3]* Man . . . Man] man . . . man *[4]* will] Will *[5]* laws] Laws protect *rev in pencil to* protect, *[7]* England,] England— boast] boast, *[8]* if *rev in pencil to* if, coast . . . coast] coast . . . coast, *[7–8] alt in pencil to* A slave the very moment that he lands / Unconscious is he, with liberty shakes hands *[9]* fettered *underscored in pencil* slave] Slave *[10]* Groans] Groan slavish *pencil alt* servile *[12]* Schools] Schools, *[13]* styled,] called the "Wealth *rev to* "the Wealth

Those mute Companions, as they sport at ease,
Enlivened, braced by hardy luxuries
I ask what warrant fixed them (like a spell
Of witchcraft fixed them) in the glassy Cell
To wheel with languid motion round and round,
Beautiful, yet in a mournful durance bound.
Their peace, perhaps, our lightest foot-fall marr'd,
On their quick sense our sweetest music jarr'd;
And whither could they dart if seized with fear?
No sheltering stone, no tangled root was near;
When fire or taper ceased to cheer the room
They wore away the night in starless gloom;
And when the sun first dawned upon the streams,
How faint their portion of his vital beams.
Thus, and unable to complain, they fared
While not one joy of ours by them was shared.

  Is there a cherished Bird (I venture now
To snatch a sprig from Chaucer's reverend brow)
Is there a brilliant Fondling of the cage,
Though sure of plaudits on his costly stage,
Though fed with dainties from the snow-white hand
Of a kind mistress, fairest of the land,
But gladly would escape, and, if need were,
Scatter the colours from the plumes that bear
The emancipated Captive through blithe air
Into strange woods, where he at large may live
On best or worst, which they and nature give?
The beetle loves his unpretending track,
The snail the house he carries on his back,
The far-fetched worm with pleasure would disown
The bed we give him, though of softest down;
A noble instinct, in all Kinds the same,—
All ranks—what Sovereign, worthy of the name
If doomed to breathe against his lawful will
An element that flatters him, to kill,
But would rejoice to barter outward shew
For the least boon that freedom can bestow?
But most the Bard is true to inborn right,
Lark of the dawn, and Philomel of night,

---

106 *rev to* By glimpses caught while sporting at their ease *del MS. 135 (A_3)*
109 glassy *rev to* crystal *del MS. 135 (A_3)*
111 mournful *rev from* piteous *MS. 114*
131 live *rev from* [?thrive] *MS. 114*

143–144 Apparently to enlarge on the poet's "inborn right," WW began and then abandoned a simile, "[?As when]" in MS. 107 (A_2).

Exults in freedom, can with rapture vouch
For the dear blessings of a lowly couch,
A natural meal, days, months from Nature's hand,
Time, place, and business all at his command.
Who bends to happier duties, who more wise
Than the industrious Poet, taught to prize
Above all grandeur a pure life, uncross'd
By cares in which simplicity is lost?
That life, the flowery path that winds by stealth
Which Horace needed for his spirit's health,
Sighed for, in heart and genius overcome
By noise, and strife, and questions wearisome
And the vain splendours of Imperial Rome.
Let easy mirth his social hour inspire,
And fiction animate his sportive lyre
Attuned to verse that, crowning light distress
With garlands, cheats her into happiness!
—Give *me* the humblest note of those sad strains
Drawn forth by pressure of his gilded chains,
As a chance sunbeam from his memory fell
Upon the Sabine farm he loved so well,
Or when the prattle of Bandusia's Spring
Haunted his ear, he only listening!
He, proud to please, above all rivals, fit
To win the palm of gaiety and wit;
He, doubt not, with involuntary dread
Shrinking from each new favour to be shed
By the World's Ruler, on his laurel'd head!

In a deep vision's intellectual scene,
Such earnest longings, and regrets as keen
Depressed the melancholy Cowley, laid
Under a fancied Yew-tree's luckless shade,
A doleful bower for penitential song,
Where Man and Muse complained of mutual wrong
While Cam's ideal current glided by,
And antique Towers nodded their foreheads high,
Citadels dear to studious privacy.
But Fortune, who had long been used to sport
With this tried Servant of a heartless Court,

---

153 that *rev to* which *MS. 106*
155 in heart and genius *alt in pencil* by endless hurry *MS. 114*
156 questions *rev in pencil and ink from illeg word MS. 114*
158 hour] hours *MS. 106*
163 gilded *rev from* golden *MS. 114*
172 laurel'd *rev from* [?honour'd] *MS. 114* honoured *MS. 106*
178 Man and Muse *rev from* Muse and Man *MS. 114*
183 heartless *alt in pencil* thankless *MS. 114* thankless *MSS. 114 (5ʳP1), 106*

Relenting, met his wishes, and to you
The *remnant* of his days, at least, was true
You, whom, howe'er neglected, he loved best
You, Muses, books, fields, liberty, and rest.
Thrice happy they, who, fixing hope and aim
On the humanity of peaceful fame,
Enter betimes with more than martial fire
The generous course; aspire, and still aspire;
Forewarned by voices heeded, *not* too late,
Stifle the contradictions of their fate;
And to one purpose cleave, their Being's god-like mate.

Thus, gifted Friend, but with the placid brow
That woman ne'er should forfeit keep *thy* vow;
With modest scorn reject what e'er would blind
The ethereal eyesight, cramp the wingèd mind
Then, with a blessing granted from above
To every act, word, look and thought of love,
Life's book for Thee may lie unclosed till age
Shall with a thankful tear bedrop its latest page.

187/188 Whose was the voice that filled the air, that spake
From the deep forest, from the wide-spread lake,
From heaven's blue depth above the mountain's head,
And from my heart, not dulled by age, it said *rev in pencil and ink to*
Whose was that voice [voice *rev to* voice, *rev to* voice] that like a Trumpet spake-
From lawn and woodland, from the gleaming lake,
From the blue sky above the mountain's head,
Spake to my heart, unchilled by age? It said
"[Thrice . . .] *inserted then del MS. 114 (5ʳP1)*

188 they *rev from* thee *MS. 114*

192 Forewarned by voices] Upheld by warnings *MSS. 114 (5ʳP2), 106*

197 what e'er] whate'er *MS. 106*

200 look and thought] thought and look *MS. 106*

202 tear *rev from* heart *MS. 106*

[Text of 1835]

LIBERTY.

(SEQUEL TO THE ABOVE.)

[Addressed to a Friend; the Gold and Silver Fishes having been removed to a pool in the pleasure-ground of Rydal Mount.]

"The liberty of a people consists in being governed by laws which they have made for themselves, under whatever form it be of government. The liberty of a private man, in being master of his own time and actions, as far as may consist with the laws of God and of his country. Of this latter we are here to discourse." Cowley.

THOSE breathing Tokens of your kind regard,
(Suspect not, Anna, that their fate is hard;
Not soon does aught to which mild fancies cling,
In lonely spots, become a slighted thing;)
Those silent Inmates now no longer share,
Nor do they need, our hospitable care,
Removed in kindness from their glassy Cell
To the fresh waters of a living Well;
That spreads into an elfin pool opaque
Of which close boughs a glimmering mirror make,
On whose smooth breast with dimples light and small
The fly may settle, leaf or blossom fall.
—*There* swims, of blazing sun and beating shower

---

composed as *To a Friend* in December 1829, as a separate poem between November 20, 1831, and around November 1835
found in DC MSS. 135, 137, 138; MS. 1835/36 (MW); MS. 1836/45 (JC)
published in *1835, 1836–*
classed Sentiment and Reflection *1836, 1846* Miscellaneous Poems *1845, 1850*
reading text *1835*
title To a friend, / the Gold and Silver fish being removed / To a Pool in the Garden. *rev to* Liberty, (sequel to the above). / Addressed to a Friend, / The Gold and Silver Fish being removed / To a Pool in the Pleasure-Ground of Rydal-Mount *MS. 135* LIBERTY. (SEQUEL TO THE PRECEDING.) *1850* Liberty. *rev to* Personal Liberty *MS. 137* Personal Liberty. *rev to* Liberty. *MS. 138*
headnote *incorporated in title MS. 135* Fishes having been *rev from* Fish being *MS. 137*
epigraph *lacking MS. 135* consists] consist *MS. 137* whatever] whatsoever *MS. 137* of his] his *1836YR* —Cowley.] Cowley, on Liberty *placed in footnote MS. 137* Cowley *rev to headnote from position as footnote* Cowley, on Liberty. *MS. 138*
1 Those *rev from* These *MS. 135*
6 do they need, *rev from* need, I trust, *MS. 135*
9–12 An elfin pool so sheltered that its rest
No winds disturb; the mirror of whose breast
Is smooth as clear, save where with dimples small
A fly may settle, or a blossom fall. *1845–*
12 leaf or] or the *MS. 1835/36, 1836–1843, 1839*
13 Hailstones and big drops of the thunder shower *rev to*
There canopied from sun and beathing shower *rev to*
Fearless of ~~noonti~~ blazing sun and beating shower *rev to text MS. 135*

See the photograph and transcription of DC MS. 107, 40[r] on pp. 730–731.

Fearless (but how obscured!) the golden Power,
That from his bauble prison used to cast
Gleams by the richest jewel unsurpast;
And near him, darkling like a sullen Gnome,
The silver Tenant of the crystal dome;
Dissevered both from all the mysteries
Of hue and altering shape that charmed all eyes.
They pined, perhaps, they languished while they shone;
And, if not so, what matters beauty gone
And admiration lost, by change of place
That brings to the inward Creature no disgrace?
But if the change restore his birthright, then,
Whate'er the difference, boundless is the gain.
Who can divine what impulses from God
Reach the caged Lark, within a town-abode,
From his poor inch or two of daisied sod?
O yield him back his privilege! No sea
Swells like the bosom of a man set free;
A wilderness is rich with liberty.
Roll on, ye spouting Whales, who die or keep
Your independence in the fathomless Deep!
Spread, tiny Nautilus, the living sail;
Dive, at thy choice, or brave the freshening gale!
If unreproved the ambitious Eagle mount
Sunward to seek the daylight in its fount,
Bays, gulfs, and Ocean's Indian width, shall be,
Till the world perishes, a field for thee!

While musing here I sit in shadow cool,
And watch these mute Companions, in the pool,
Among reflected boughs of leafy trees,
By glimpses caught—disporting at their ease—
Enlivened, braced, by hardy luxuries,
I ask what warrant fixed them (like a spell
Of witchcraft fixed them) in the crystal Cell;
To wheel with languid motion round and round,
Beautiful, yet in a mournful durance bound.
Their peace, perhaps, our lightest footfall marred;
On their quick sense our sweetest music jarred;
And whither could they dart, if seized with fear?

---

14 *rev from* There swims but how obscured! the golden Power, *MS. 135*
21 Alas! they pined, they languished while they shone; *1845–*
28 Reach the *rev from* Reached *MS. 135*
36 freshening *rev from* freshing *MS. 135*
38 its *rev from* her *MS. 135*
44 disporting *rev from* while sporting *MS. 135*
47 crystal *rev from* glassy *MS. 135*
49 in a] in *MS. 1835/36–, 1839*

No sheltering stone, no tangled root was near.
When fire or taper ceased to cheer the room,
They wore away the night in starless gloom;
And, when the sun first dawned upon the streams,
How faint their portion of his vital beams!
Thus, and unable to complain, they fared,
While not one joy of ours by them was shared.

Is there a cherished Bird (I venture now
To snatch a sprig from Chaucer's reverend brow)—
Is there a brilliant Fondling of the cage,
Though sure of plaudits on his costly stage,
Though fed with dainties from the snow-white hand
Of a kind Mistress, fairest of the land,
But gladly would escape; and, if need were,
Scatter the colours from the plumes that bear
The emancipated captive through blithe air
Into strange woods, where he at large may live
On best or worst which they and Nature give?
The Beetle loves his unpretending track,
The Snail the house he carries on his back:
The far-fetched Worm with pleasure would disown
The bed we give him, though of softest down;
A noble instinct; in all Kinds the same,
All Ranks! What Sovereign, worthy of the name,
If doomed to breathe against his lawful will
An element that flatters him—to kill,
But would rejoice to barter outward show
For the least boon that freedom can bestow?

But most the Bard is true to inborn right,
Lark of the dawn, and Philomel of night,
Exults in freedom, can with rapture vouch
For the dear blessings of a lowly couch,
A natural meal—days, months, from Nature's hand;
Time, place, and business, all at his command!
Who bends to happier duties, who more wise
Than the industrious Poet, taught to prize,
Above all grandeur, a pure life uncrossed
By cares in which simplicity is lost?
That life—the flowery path which winds by stealth,
Which Horace needed for his spirit's health;
Sighed for, in heart and genius, overcome
By noise, and strife, and questions wearisome,
And the vain splendours of Imperial Rome?

---

85 hand; *rev from* hands, *MS. 137* hands, *MS. 135* hand; *rev from* hands; *MS. 138*
91 which] that *MS. 1835/36–, 1839*

Let easy mirth his social hours inspire,
And fiction animate his sportive lyre,
Attuned to verse that crowning light Distress
With garlands cheats her into happiness;
Give *me* the humblest note of those sad strains
Drawn forth by pressure of his gilded chains,
As a chance sunbeam from his memory fell
Upon the Sabine Farm he loved so well;
Or when the prattle of Bandusia's spring
Haunted his ear—he only listening—
He proud to please, above all rivals, fit
To win the palm of gaiety and wit;
He, doubt not, with involuntary dread,
Shrinking from each new favour to be shed,
By the World's Ruler, on his honoured head!

In a deep vision's intellectual scene,
Such earnest longings and regrets as keen
Depressed the melancholy Cowley, laid
Under a fancied yew-tree's luckless shade;
A doleful bower for penitential song,
Where Man and Muse complained of mutual wrong;
While Cam's ideal current glided by,
And antique Towers nodded their foreheads high,
Citadels dear to studious privacy.
But Fortune, who had long been used to sport
With this tried Servant of a thankless Court,
Relenting met his wishes; and to You
The *remnant* of his days at least was true;
You, whom, though long deserted, he loved best;
You, Muses, Books, Fields, Liberty, and Rest!
But happier they who, fixing hope and aim
On the humanities of peaceful fame,
Enter *betimes* with more than martial fire
The generous course, aspire, and still aspire;
Upheld by warnings heeded not too late

---

104 Or *rev from* As *MS. 137*
124 though long deserted *rev from* howeer neglected *MS. 135*
126 But happier *rev from* Thrice happy *MS. 138* Thrice happy *MSS. 135, 137*—Far happier *MS. 1835/36* Far happier *1836–, 1839*
127 humanities *rev from* humanity *MS. 137* humanity *MS. 135*

Stifle the contradictions of their fate,
And to one purpose cleave, their Being's godlike mate!

Thus, gifted Friend, but with the placid brow
That Woman ne'er should forfeit, keep *thy* vow;
With modest scorn reject whate'er would blind
The ethereal eyesight, cramp the wingèd mind!
Then, with a blessing granted from above
To every act, word, thought, and look of love,
Life's book for Thee may lie unclosed, till age
Shall with a thankful tear bedrop its latest page.*

*There is now, alas! no possibility of the anticipation, with which the above Epistle concludes, being realised: nor were the verses ever seen by the Individual for whom they were intended. She accompanied her husband, the Rev. Wm. Fletcher, to India, and died of cholera, at the age of thirty-two or thirty-three years, on her way from Shalapore to Bombay, deeply lamented by all who knew her.

Her enthusiasm was ardent, her piety steadfast; and her great talents would have enabled her to be eminently useful in the difficult path of life to which she had been called. The opinion she entertained of her own performances, given to the world under her maiden name, Jewsbury, was modest and humble, and, indeed, far below their merits; as is often the case with those who are making trial of their powers with a hope to discover what they are best fitted for. In one quality, viz., quickness in the motions of her mind, she was in the author's estimation unequalled.

---

136 wingèd *so MS. 135; 1836–, 1836YR, 1839* winged *MSS. 137, 138*

138 and *rev from* or *MS. 135*

note to l. 140, last sentence was . . . unequaled] had, within the range of the Author's acquaintance, no equal *MS. 1835/36–, 1839*

[Text of 1835]

HUMANITY.

(WRITTEN IN THE YEAR 1829.)

Not from his fellows only man may learn
Rights to compare and duties to discern:
All creatures and all objects, in degree,
Are friends and patrons of humanity.—MS.

[The Rocking-stones, alluded to in the beginning of the following verses, are supposed to have been used, by our British ancestors, both for judicial and religious purposes. Such stones are not uncommonly found, at this day, both in Great Britain and in Ireland.]

WHAT though the Accused, upon his own appeal
To righteous Gods when Man has ceased to feel,
Or at a doubting Judge's stern command,
Before the STONE OF POWER no longer stand—
To take his sentence from the balanced Block,
As, at his touch, it rocks, or seems to rock;
Though, in the depths of sunless groves, no more
The Druid-priest the hallowed Oak adore;
Yet, for the Initiate, rocks and whispering trees
Do still perform mysterious offices!
And still in beast and bird a function dwells,
That, while we look and listen, sometimes tells
Upon the heart, in more authentic guise
Than Oracles, or wingèd Auguries,
Spake to the Science of the ancient wise.
Not uninspired appear their simplest ways;

---

composed as *To a Friend* in December 1829, as a separate poem between November 20, 1831, and around November 1835

found in DC MSS. 135; 137 (MW and WW); 138 (A) pp. 297–302, (B) pp. 295–300 (MW); MS. 1835/36 (MW); MS. 1836/45; Mary Smith Album; WW to Sarah Coles Stevenson, December 24, 1838

published in *1835, 1836–*

classed Sentiment and Reflection *MS. 1835/36–*

reading text *1835*

title HUMANITY. (WRITTEN IN THE YEAR 1829.)] Humanity written a few years ago *rev to* Humanity (written in the year 1830) *MS. 135* HUMANITY. *MS. 1835/36–, 1839*

epigraph *added MS. 135 (by MW) except* objects] Objects humanity.—] humanity. MS.] M.S *4 ll. of epigraph transferred to follow l. 101 in MS. 1835/36–, 1839 (see below)*

headnote verses,] verses *rev from* poem *MS. 135* supposed to have been used,] supposed to have been used *rev from* supposed *MS. 135* ancestors,] Ancesters *rev to* Ancestors *MS. 135* both in Great Britain and in Ireland *rev from* there is a remarkable one upon a Moorland [Moorland *rev from* moorland] Eminence over looking the Vale of the Nid in Yorkshire *MS. 135*

8 No more the Druid Priest the hallowed Oak adores *MS. 135,*

11–15 And functions dwell in beast and bird that sway
The reasoning mind, or with the fancy play,
Inviting, at all seasons, ears and eyes
To watch for undelusive auguries: *MS. 1835/36; so 1836–, 1839 but* auguries:—

Their voices mount symbolical of praise—
To mix with hymns that Spirits make and hear;
And to fallen Man their innocence is dear.
Enraptured Art draws from those sacred springs
Streams that reflect the poetry of things!
Where Christian Martyrs stand in hues portrayed,
That, might a wish avail, would never fade,
Borne in their hands the Lily and the Palm
Shed round the Altar a celestial calm;
There, too, behold the Lamb and guileless Dove
Prest in the tenderness of virgin love
To saintly bosoms!—Glorious is the blending
Of right Affections, climbing or descending
Along a scale of light and life, with cares
Alternate; carrying holy thoughts and prayers
Up to the sovereign seat of the Most High;
Descending to the worm in charity;*
Like those good Angels whom a dream of night
Gave, in the Field of Luz, to Jacob's sight;
All, while *he* slept, treading the pendent stairs
Earthward or heavenward, radiant Messengers,
That, with a perfect will in one accord
Of strict obedience, served the Almighty Lord;
And with untired humility forbore
The ready service of the wings they wore.

What a fair World were ours for Verse to paint,
If Power could live at ease with self-restraint!

*The author is indebted, here, to a passage in one of Mr. Digby's valuable works.

---

17 Their voices mount *rev from* Their voice ascends *with alt in pencil in WW's hand* [Then?] so blest with perfect *MS.* 135_1

18 *Rev from* Of hymns which blessed Spirits make and hear *with alt in pencil in WW's hand* Let [?] [?] [?] *MS.* 135_1

20 *Line added in revision with alt in pencil in WW's hand* [?] studying Art *MS.* 135_1

21 *Line added in revision MS.* 135_1

22 Christian Martyr's stand *rev from illeg. MS.* 135_1 hues *rev from illeg word MS.* 135_2

24 Borne] Born *MS.* 135_2

27 Prest *rev from* Pressed *MS.* 135_2 Pressed, *MS.* 135_1

30 Along the scale of light and life with cares *rev from*
Along the scale of Truth with ceaseless cares *rev from*
To a harmonious reverse of cares *rev from*
In a perpetual reverse of cares *rev from*
[As?] [T?] an authentic scale with ceaseless cares *rev from*
Along the scale of things with ceaseless cares *MS.* 135_1

33 *footnote added in revision MS.* 135_2*; lacking asterisk, note moved to end of volume 1836–, 1839*

37 or *rev from* and *MS. 135*

39 served] serve *1845, 1850*

41 To speed their errand by the wings they wore. *MS. 1835/36–, 1836YR, 1839*

Opinion bow before the naked sense
Of the greatest Vision,—faith in Providence;
Merciful over all existence, just
To the least particle of sentient dust;
And, fixing by immutable decrees,
Seedtime and harvest for his purposes!
Then would be closed the restless oblique eye
That looks for evil like a treacherous spy;
Disputes would then relax, like stormy winds
That into breezes sink; impetuous Minds
By discipline endeavour to grow meek
As Truth herself, whom they profess to seek.
Then Genius, shunning fellowship with Pride,
Would braid his golden locks at Wisdom's side;
Love ebb and flow untroubled by caprice;
And not alone *harsh* tyranny would cease,
But unoffending creatures find release
From *qualified* oppression, whose defence
Rests on a hollow plea of recompence;
Thought-tempered wrongs, for each humane respect
Oft worse to bear, or deadlier in effect.
Witness those glances of indignant scorn
From some high-minded Slave, impelled to spurn
The kindness that would make him less forlorn;
Or, if the soul to bondage be subdued,
His look of pitable gratitude!

Alas for thee, bright Galaxy of Isles,
Where day departs in pomp, returns with smiles—
To greet the flowers and fruitage of a land,
As the sun mounts, by sea-born breezes fanned;
A land whose azure mountain-tops are seats
For Gods in council, whose green vales, Retreats
Fit for the Shades of Heroes, mingling there
To breathe Elysian peace in upper air.

Though cold as winter, gloomy as the grave,
Stone-walls a Prisoner make, but not a Slave.

---

46 existence] his creatures *MS. 1836/45 (in pencil), 1840–*
46–47 Compationate to all that suffer, just
In the end to every creature born of dust *in pencil MS. 1836/45*
48 And] But *MS. 1836/45 (in pencil), 1840–*
48–49 *inserted MS. 135*
51 evil] evil, *with comma added in pencil MS. 135*
53 impetuous *rev from* and headstrong *rev by WW in pencil from* and ardent *MS. 135*
68 to] to be *1836YR*
71 Where] Whose *1836–, 1839*
76 Shades *rev from* shadows *MS. 135*
78 Though] Tho' *MS. 138*

Shall Man assume a property in Man?
Lay on the moral Will a withering ban?
Shame that our laws at distance should protect
Enormities, which they at home reject!
"Slaves cannot breathe in England"—a proud boast!
And yet a mockery! if, from coast to coast,
Though *fettered* slave be none, her floors and soil
Groan underneath a weight of slavish toil,
For the poor Many, measured out by rules
Fetched with cupidity from heartless schools,
That to an Idol, falsely called "the Wealth
Of Nations," sacrifice a People's health,
Body and mind and soul; a thirst so keen
Is ever urging on the vast machine
Of sleepless Labour, 'mid whose dizzy wheels
The Power least prized is that which thinks and feels.

Then, for the pastimes of this delicate age,
And all the heavy or light vassalage
Which for their sakes we fasten, as may suit
Our varying moods, on human kind or brute,
'Twere well in little, as in great, to pause,
Lest Fancy trifle with eternal laws.
There are to whom even garden, grove, and field,
Perpetual lessons of forbearance yield;
Who would not lightly violate the grace
The lowliest flower possesses in its place;
Nor shorten the sweet life, too fugitive,
Which nothing less than Infinite Power could give.

---

82 should] still *1836–, 1839*
84 a proud] empty *MS. 1835/36* yet that *1836–, 1839*
85 And yet a . . . if,] Insulting . . . when *MS. 1835/36* Is but a . . . when *1836–, 1839*
90 an Idol, falsely] monstrous Idol, *MS. 1836/45*
92–93 The weal of body mind and soul; so keen
a thirst is ever urging on the vast machine *alt MS. 1836/45*
93 Is] It *1836YR*
100 'Twere *so 1836–, 1839* Twere *MS. 135* 'T were *1835*
101/102 Not from his fellows only man may learn
Rights to compare and duties to discern!
All creatures and all objects, in degree,
Are friends and patrons of humanity. *MS. 1835/36–; 1839 as 1836 but* degree,] degree
102 even] even *rev from* the *MS. 135* the *MS. 1835/36–, WW to Sarah Coles Stevenson, 1839* grove, and *rev from* and the *del in pencil MS. 135*
102–105 *inserted MS. 135*

"Why art thou silent! Is thy love a plant"

Wordsworth initially composed "Why art thou silent! Is thy love a plant" in three quatrains with an interlocking rhyme scheme but deleted this version in DC MS. 107 (on 2[r]; the basis for the first reading text). Preserved in the same manuscript, but not part of the original notebook, is a copy of the sonnet version that Dora Wordsworth transcribed and signed "Kate Barker / Atholl S[t] / Douglas / Mona"—perhaps a preparatory copy for the one she sent as a valentine to her cousin Christopher Wordsworth, Jr., inscribing it "Kate Barker / ---- Your true Valentine / Athol St / Douglas – Mona. / Feb:[y] 14th 1830" (Cornell MS. 8). Dora commented in a letter to an unknown correspondent to whom she also sent the poem, "I mean to send this to Chris: on Valentine's day—he would not tell me the name of his Mona Love & I have found her out through Aunt Joanna—"; this copy she also inscribed "Kate Barker" of Douglas but dated it "Jan[y] 18th 1830." Mary Wordsworth's sister Joanna lived with their brother Henry on the Isle of Man (Douglas is its capital city and chief seaport), where Christopher had spent a holiday. The text providing the sonnet version is that of 1835.

[Text of MS. 107 (A)]

Why art thou silent?—is thy love a plant
Of such weak fibre that the treacherous air
Of absence withers what was once so fair,
Yet have my thoughts been true and vigilant
As would my hand have been with every grant
(Had fate allow'd) of anxious anxious care,
A poor abandon'd heart once proud to hold
A thousand tender pleasures thine and mine
That soft warm heart is now more dreary-cold
Than a linnet's nest fill'd with unmelting snow
Mid its own bush of leafless eglantine—
Speak—and all other dues will I forgo.

---

composed around early January 1830
found in DC MS. 107 (A) 1[r]
reading text MS. 107 (A)
1 silent *rev from* Silent *MS. 107 (A)*
5 As *rev from* And *MS. 107 (A)*
7 A *rev from* My *MS. 107* abandon'd] abandond *MS. 107 (A)*
8 pleasures] pleasure *MS. 107 (A)*
10 linnets . . . filld *MS. 107 (A)* unmelting *rev from* un[?]ting *MS. 107 (A)*
11 Mid its own *rev from* Amid a *MS. 107 (A)*
12 forego.] forego *MS. 107 (A)*

[Text of 1835]

WHY art thou silent! Is thy love a plant
Of such weak fibre that the treacherous air
Of absence withers what was once so fair?
Is there no debt to pay, no boon to grant?
Yet have my thoughts for thee been vigilant
(As would my deeds have been) with hourly care,
The mind's least generous wish a mendicant
For nought but what thy happiness could spare.
Speak, though this soft warm heart, once free to hold
A thousand tender pleasures, thine and mine,
Be left more desolate, more dreary cold
Than a forsaken bird's-nest filled with snow
'Mid its own bush of leafless eglantine;
Speak, that my torturing doubts their end may know!

---

composed January 18, 1830
found in DC MSS. 107 (B) 21[r]; 106; 135; 137 (MW); 138 (MW); Dora W to ?, January 18, 1830; Cornell MS. 8; MS. 1838/40 (MW)
published in *1835, 1836–, 1838*
classed Miscellaneous Sonnets *1836–, 1838*
reading text *1835*
title Sonnet *MS. 107 (B)*
1 thy *inserted Dora W to ?*
3 was] seem'd *rev from* [?seems] *Dora W to ?* seem'd *Cornell MS. 8*
6 *rev to* Bound to thy service with incessant care, *MS. 1838/40*
Bound to thy service with unceasing care, *1845–*
7 a *rev from* and *MS. 107 (B)*
11 more dreary] and dreary *MS. 107 (B), Dora W to ?, Cornell MS. 8*
12 Than a Linnet's nest filled with unmelting snow *MS. 106, Dora W to ?, Cornell MS. 8; so MS. 107 (B) but* linnet's *and so MS. 135 but* linnet's *rev to* last year's
Than a last year's nest filled with unmelting snow *MS. 137; so MS. 138, rev to text*
14 torturing *rev from illeg word MS. 135*

Inscription Intended for a Stone in the Grounds of Rydal Mount

In his letter to John Kenyon, after a playful account of a dance held at Rydal Mount, Wordsworth explained, "... Mary shall transcribe for you a serious Stanza or two, intended for an Inscription in a part of the grounds of Rydal Mount with which you are not acquainted, a field adjoining our Garden which I purchased two or three years ago"—actually six years previous. "Under the shade of some Pollard Oaks, and on a green Terrace in that field, we have lived no small part of the long bright days of the summer gone by; and in a hazel nook of this favourite piece of ground is a Stone, for which I wrote one day the following serious Inscription, you will forgive its Egotism" (*LY*, II, 426).

The date of composition of the first reading text is June 26, 1830, a date supplied by Dorothy in the copies of the *Inscription Intended for a Stone* that she made among copies of her own poems and other items in her commonplace book (DC MS. 120). Of the published version Wordsworth said it was "engraven, during my absence in Italy, upon a brass plate inserted in the stone" (*FNW*, p. 29). The stone was fitted with a metal plate bearing the inscription while Wordsworth was traveling with Henry Crabb Robinson in Italy between March and September 1837. The inscription on the stone is dated 1830, and Wordsworth assigned this date to the poem in editions from 1836. But the revised nine-line version was probably produced nearer the date of Wordsworth's letter to Kenyon quoted above. Final revisions to the poem, now titled *Inscription Intended for a Stone in the Grounds of Rydal Mount*, took place on proof pages of *Yarrow Revisited, and Other Poems* early in 1835.

[Text of MS. 120 (B)]

26th June 1830 Dictated by W. Wordsworth
to D Wordsworth Senr

In this fair Vale hath many a Tree
At Wordsworth's suit been spared:
The builder touched this old grey STONE—
'Twas rescued by the Bard—

---

composed June 26, 1830
found in DC MSS. 120 (A) 89^v, (B) 77a^r; 107 (A) 45^v, (B), 48^r
reading text DC MS. 120 (B)
title *lacking MSS. 120, 107*
headnote 26 June 1830—Sunday Evening—dictated by William Wordsworth to D Wordsworth Senr— — *MS. 120 (A)*

3–4 *rev from* And from the Builders hand this stone
Was rescued by the Bard— *MS. 120 (A)*
rev from He sav d this [this *rev from* the] old grey stone that pleas'd
The grove frequenting Bard; *MS. 107 (A)*
~~His wish preserv'd~~ He also sav d
His pleading saved this old grey Stone
That pleasd the musing Bard *MS. 107 (B)*

Long may it last!—and here, perchance,
The good and tender-hearted
May heave a gentle sigh for him,
As one of the Departed.

[Text of 1835]

INSCRIPTION

INTENDED FOR A STONE IN THE GROUNDS OF RYDAL MOUNT.

In these fair Vales hath many a Tree
  At Wordsworth's suit been spared;
And from the Builder's hand this Stone,
For some rude beauty of its own,
  Was rescued by the Bard:
So let it rest,—and time will come
  When here the tender-hearted
May heave a gentle sigh for him,
  As one of the departed.

---

5 Long *rev from illeg word MS. 107 (A)* perchance] perhaps *alt* perchance *MS. 107 (A)*

---

composed around and certainly by early September 1831, revised by March 1835
found in DC MSS. 106; 114; 134; 137 (MW); WW to JK, September 9, 1831; MS. 1835B; MS. 1835Col; MS. 1836/45
published in *1835, 1836–*
classed Inscriptions *1836–*
reading text *1835*
title Inscription. *MSS. 106, 114; lacking WW to JK* Inscription for a Stone *MS. 134* Intended for a Stone in the Grounds of Rydal Mount. *1836, 1846; title del MS. 1836/45; lacking Rydal Mount Stone, 1845, 1850*
6–7 Long may it rest in peace!—and here,
Perchance, the tender-hearted *MSS. 106, 137; so MS. 114 but* Perchance,] Perchance *so MS. 134 but* peace!—and] peace and *and* Perchance,] Perchance *so WW to JK but* peace! and *and* Perchance,] Perchance
To let it rest in peace; and here
(Heaven knows how soon) the tender-hearted *1835; 1835 errata page and MSS. 1835B, 1835Col rev to text; 1836YR, 1836– as text*
8 May] Will *MSS. 106, 114, 134, 137, WW to JK* him *rev in pencil to* them *MS. 114*

ELEGIAC MUSINGS

IN THE GROUNDS OF COLEORTON HALL, THE SEAT OF THE LATE SIR GEORGE BEAUMONT, BART.

[In these grounds stands the Parish Church, wherein is a mural monument, the Inscription upon which, in deference to the earnest request of the deceased, is confined to name, dates, and these words:—"Enter not into judgment with thy servant, O LORD!"]

WITH copious eulogy in prose or rhyme
Graven on the tomb we struggle against Time,
Alas, how feebly! but our feelings rise
And still we struggle when a good man dies:
Such offering BEAUMONT dreaded and forbade,
A spirit meek in self-abasement clad.
Yet *here* at least, though few have numbered days
That shunned so modestly the light of praise,
His graceful manners, and the temperate ray
Of that arch fancy which would round him play,
Brightening a converse never known to swerve
From courtesy and delicate reserve;
That sense—the bland philosophy of life
Which checked discussion ere it warmed to strife;
Those fine accomplishments, and varied powers,
Might have their record among sylvan bowers.

---

composed around November 6–8, 1830
found in Lilly MS. 2; DC MSS. 107; 106; 120; 135; 137 (MW); MS. 1835/36 (MW)
published in *1835, 1836–*
classed Epitaphs *1836–*
reading text *1835*
title *lacking Lilly MS. 2*

Supposed to be written in the Grounds / of Coleorton Hall, Leicestershire, / the Seat of late Sir Geo H. Beaumont, Bar^{t}. *MS. 107; so MS. 106 but* Sir George Beaumont, Bart

Supposed to be written [written *rev to* Composed] in the Grounds of Coleorton Hall, the Seat of the Late Sir G. B. [Sir G. B. *MW alt* Sir George Beaumont] Bart *MS. 135* ELEGIAC MUSINGS IN *rev from* Lines Composed in *rev from* Inscription Composed in *MS. 137* GEORGE] G. H. *1836–*

For a Monument to be placed in the grounds / of Coleorton Hall Leicestershire to the Memory of / the late Sir George Howland Beaumont. *MS. 120*

headnote *lacking Lilly MS. 2, MS. 120* monument, the Inscription upon] monument bearing an Inscription *1836–* name, dates,] name and dates— *MSS. 107, 106* thy] the *MS. 107* the *rev to* thy *MS. 106* *opening and closing brackets present in 1836YR, 1839; closing bracket only 1835; both brackets lacking MSS. 107, 106, 120, 135, 137, 1836–*

1 or *so Lilly MS. 2, MSS. 107, 106, 120, 135; MS. 1835/36–* and *MS. 137, 1835, 1836YR, 1839*
3 how *rev from* our *Lilly MS. 2*
4 when *rev from* if *MS. 107*
5 offering] tribute *MS. 120*
10 which] that *Lilly MS. 2, MSS. 107, 120*
11 converse] Fancy *rev to* Converse *MS. 107*
12 From nicest points of delicate reserve; *MS. 120*
15 Those] His *MS. 120* fine] high *alt* fine *Lilly MS. 2* rare *MS. 1835/36–, 1839*
16 Might] Shall *MS. 120*

---

headnote In MS. 120 DW's footnote conveys similar information; see editor's note, p. 452.

—Oh, fled for ever! vanished like a blast
That shook the leaves in myriads as it passed;
Gone from this world of earth, air, sea, and sky,
From all its spirit-moving imagery,
Intensely studied with a Painter's eye,
A Poet's heart; and, for congenial view,
Portrayed with happiest pencil, not untrue
To common recognitions while the line
Flowed in a course of sympathy divine—
Oh! severed too abruptly from delights
That all the seasons shared with equal rights—
Rapt in the grace of undismantled age,
From soul-felt music, and the treasured page,
Lit by that evening lamp which loved to shed
Its mellow lustre round thy honoured head,
While Friends beheld thee give with eye, voice, mien,

---

17 —Oh fled forever! vanished] O vanished too abruptly *Lilly MS. 2, so MS. 120 but*—Oh] Oh!
19–23 Gone from that Nature whence thy Genius drew
Ideal beauty, for a pencil true *MS. 120*
20 From] Through *Lilly MS. 2* *line inserted Lilly MS. 2*
22 congenial *rev from* the general *Lilly MS. 2*
24 common *rev from* humbler *Lilly MS. 2*
25–26 Bear with our frailty (once the like was Thine
That craves for such regrets a lasting shrine [shrine *rev in pencil to* shrine.] *two ll. inserted then del MS. 135; see also ll. 34/35 below*
26 O fled for ever from serene delights *Lilly MS. 2, MS. 120* Dissevered, too abruptly, *MS. 1835/36 (WW)*
27 which] that *MS. 120*
28 Rapt *rev from* [?Apt] *MS. 107*
30 Which] That *MS. 120*
32–33 *inserted Lilly MS. 2, MS. 107*
32 with eye, voice, mien *rev from* by voice and mien *MS. 135* by voice and mien *Lilly MS. 2, MSS. 107, 106, 120*

More than theatric force to Shakspeare's scene—
Rebuke us not!—The mandate is obeyed
That said, "Let praise be mute where I am laid;"
The holier deprecation, given in trust
To the cold Marble, waits upon thy dust;
Yet have we found how slowly genuine grief
From *silent* admiration wins relief.
Too long abashed thy Name is like a Rose
That doth "within itself its sweetness close;"
A drooping Daisy changed into a cup
In which her bright-eyed beauty is shut up.

---

33 *rev from* More than theatric force *rev to* And heart the very life *alt*
And warmth theatric force *rev to* And warmth the very life *del MS. 135*
34 The humble mandate strictly is obeyed
Bear with our frailty (once the like was thine)
That craves for such regrets a lasting shrine
Rebuke us not *alt ink over pencil, del MS. 135*
–}
}if thy Spirit [~~?by~~] ~~art~~ may
{'st {—
Oh if thou hear{ me{ ~~and ^ art free to know~~
Aught of these bowers and whence their
in our pleasures flow;
If things ^ remembrance held so dear,
And thoughts & projects fondly cherished here,
To thy exalted ~~Spirit~~ only seen
Nature
Time's vanities, light fragments of earth's
dream
Rebuke us not *MS. 1835/36*
If thou hast heard me—if thy Spirit know
Aught of these bowers and whence their pleasures flow;
If things in our remembrance held so dear,
And thoughts and projects fondly cherished here,
To thy exalted nature only seem
Time's vanities, light fragments of earth's dream— *1836–, 1839*
34–38 —Rebuke us not if thus on earth we strive
To keep some shadows of a skill alive
That could not be conceal'd where thou wert known:
Thy virtues, He must judge, and he alone
The God upon whose mercy they are thrown. *MS. 120*
38 found how] learned that *Lilly MS. 2*
too
~~Full long~~ ~~Thy name~~ ~~full~~ long thy name
40 ~~Thy name,~~ abash'd, is like a ~~hooded~~ rose *Lilly MS. 2*
41 itself its *rev in pencil to* herself her *MS. 107*
42–43 Or bright-eyed daisy timidly shut up
~~With~~ In the strait prison of its own green cup. *Lilly MS. 2*

Within these Groves, where still are flitting by
Shades of the Past, oft noticed with a sigh,
Shall stand a votive Tablet, haply free,
When towers and temples fall, to speak of Thee!
If sculptured emblems of our mortal doom
Recall not there the wisdom of the Tomb,
Green ivy, risen from out the cheerful earth,
Shall fringe the lettered stone; and herbs spring forth,
Whose fragrance, by soft dews and rain unbound,
Shall penetrate the heart without a wound;
While truth and love their purposes fulfil,
Commemorating genius, talent, skill,
That could not lie concealed where Thou wert known;
Thy virtues *He* must judge, and *He* alone,
The God upon whose mercy they are thrown.

"Chatsworth! thy stately mansion, and the pride"

CHATSWORTH! thy stately mansion, and the pride
Of thy domain, strange contrast do present
To house and home in many a craggy rent
Of the wild Peak; where new–born waters glide
Through fields whose thrifty Occupants abide
As in a dear and chosen banishment,
With every semblance of entire content;
So kind is simple Nature, fairly tried!

44–58 *lacking Lilly MS. 2*
51 Shall] Will *MS. 1835/36 (WW), so 1836–*
52 dews and rain] rains and dews *MS. 107*

---

composed November 7 to 8, 1830, revised by March 1835
found in WW to DW, November 8, 1830; DC MSS. 107 (A) 82[r], (B) 40[r]; 106; 120; 137 (MW)
published in *1835, 1836–, 1838*
classed Miscellaneous Sonnets *1836–, 1838*
reading text *1835*
title Sonnet Novb[r] 6th *MS. 107 (A)* Composed on my [solitary equestrian *inserted*] journey through Derbyshire after visiting Chatsworth. *MS. 107 (B)* 1830. *1836–, 1838*
1 stately] splendid *MS. 107 (B)*
1–5 Chatsworth! thy Park, and Mansion spreading wide
And towering high, strange contrast do present
To the [poor *del*] plain treasures of that craggy Rent
Which late I saw, where Wey's blue waters glide;
A Dell whose [native *del*] native Occupants abide *WW to DW*
1–3 Chatsworth how [how *rev from* a most] strange a [a *inserted*] contrast doth the pride
Of thy domain to House and Home present
In many a [v *del*] dell profound and craggy Rent *rev in pencil to text MS. 107 (A); MS. 120 as in-line rev 107 but* Chatsworth! house and home rent
5 thrifty *rev from* crafty *MS. 106*
7 *rev from* With [?narrow] prospect yet in calm content; *WW to DW*

Yet He whose heart in childhood gave her troth
To pastoral dales, thin set with modest farms,
May learn, if judgement strengthen with his growth,
That, not for Fancy only, pomp hath charms;
And, strenuous to protect from lawless harms
The extremes of favoured life, may honour both.

TO B. R. HAYDON, ESQ. ON SEEING HIS PICTURE OF NAPOLEON BUONAPARTE ON THE ISLAND OF ST. HELENA.

HAYDON! let worthier judges praise the skill
Here by thy pencil shown in truth of lines
And charm of colours; *I* applaud those signs
Of thought, that give the true poetic thrill;
That unencumbered whole of blank and still,
Sky without cloud—ocean without a wave;
And the one Man that laboured to enslave
The World, sole-standing high on the bare hill—
Back turned, arms folded, the unapparent face
Tinged, we may fancy, in this dreary place
With light reflected from the invisible sun
Set like his fortunes; but not set for aye
Like them. The unguilty Power pursues his way,
And before *him* doth dawn perpetual run.

---

9 heart] youth *MS. 107 (B)* gave *rev from* pledg *MS. 107 (A)*
13 strenuous to protect] diligent to guard *WW to DW, MS. 120* diligent to guard *alt* zealous [zealous *alt* sedulous *alt* strenuous] to protect *rev to* strenuous to protect *MS. 107 (A)*

---

composed June 11, 1831
found in DC MSS. 107, 114, 135; WW to BRH, June 11, 1831; WW and DW to WRH, June 13, 1831; Yale MS. 3; Morgan MS. 6
published in *NMM*, July 1, 1831 (vol. 32, no. 127, p. 26); *1832–, 1838*
classed Miscellaneous Sonnets *1832–, 1838*
reading text *1832*
title B. R.] R. B. *1832* HAYDON, ESQ.] Haydon, *1836–, 1838* Sonnet— / To R. B. Haydon Esq[re]—. Composed on [on *rev from* after] seeing his Picture of Napoleon Buonaparte on the Island of S[t] Helena. *MS. 107* Sonnet / To R. B. Haydon Esq[re] / Composed on seeing his Picture of Buonaparte / on the Island of St. Helena. *WW to BRH* To R. B. Haydon Esq[r] / on seeing his Picture of/Bonaparte in the Island / of St Helena *Yale MS. 3* SONNET, BY WILLIAM WORDSWORTH. / To B. R. Haydon. Composed on seeing his Picture of Napoleon musing at St. Helena. *NMM*
7 that] who *MS. 114*
8 *rev from* Sole-standing high on the bare hill— *WW to BRH*
high on the bare hill *rev from* on the rocky hill *MS. 107*
9 With arms close folded and averted face *DW rev to*
Arms knit back turn'd the unapparent *rev to text MS. 107*
Arms knit—Back turned—the unapparent Face *alt MS. 107; WW to BRH as MS. 107 alt but* face
10 we *rev from* you *MS. 107* may] might *Yale MS.* this] that *MS. 107, Yale MS. 3* dreary] dismal *Yale MS. 3* place *rev from illeg word MS. 107*
13 them.] thine— *MS. 114* his *rev to* her *MS. 114*
14 *rev from* And dawn perpetual doth before him run. *del MS. 107*
14/ Saturday—June 11th *WW to BRH* Saturday, June 11th, 1831. *NMM*

Epitaph ("By a blest Husband guided, Mary came")

Wordsworth's ink drafts approximating lines 13–18 of *Epitaph* appear below the revised fair copy of *Elegiac Musings* ("With copious eulogy in prose or rhyme") in MS. 107 (39^{r}–40^{v}), though not clearly part of the latter poem, and in pencil drafts in MSS. 107 (44^{v}) and 114 (5^{v}), in isolation, without any hint of placement. The phrase "[?Mis] trust us not" in the pencil draft in MS. 107 (44^{v}) seems to echo "Berate us not" (l. 34) in *Elegiac Musings in the Grounds of Coleorton Hall, the Seat of the Late Sir George Beaumont, Bart.*, suggesting that WW thought of adding these lines to his elegy to Beaumont, though the phrase may be an early transition to line 19 in *Epitaph*, "Bear with Him—judge *Him* gently. . . ." It is possible, at least, that the passage in MS. 107 was composed as early as November–December 1830, when *Elegiac Musings in the Grounds of Coleorton Hall, the Seat of the Late Sir George Beaumont, Bart.* was reaching completion.

In late June 1831, however, Wordsworth made use of these lines for an *Epitaph* for Mary Elizabeth (Carleton) Vernon, a young woman, as he explained in the Fenwick note, who was raised "in the neighbourhood of Ambleside." A few years after her marriage she apparently revisited her old home. The names "Mrs. Vernon" and "The Rector" from Bromsgrove are entered in the Rydal Mount Visitor's Book for 1830 (begun in that year, the book is now in the Wordsworth Library, Grasmere). Mary Elizabeth Vernon was born in 1804, the same year as the birth of Wordsworth's daughter Dora, and died at Hanbury on June 12, 1831. A version of the *Epitaph* was inscribed on a tablet in St. Mary's Church at Sprawley, near Hanbury. The readings from the tablet are recorded in the notes to the reading text.

EPITAPH.

By a blest Husband guided, Mary came
From nearest kindred, * * * * * * her new name;
She came, though meek of soul, in seemly pride
Of happiness and hope, a youthful Bride.
O dread reverse! if aught *be* so, which proves
That God will chasten whom he dearly loves.
Faith bore her up through pains in mercy given,
And troubles that were each a step to Heaven:

---

composed probably composed shortly after June 12, 1830, but by December 1834
found in DC MSS. 107 (A) 39^{v}, (B) 40^{r}, (C) 43^{v}; 106; 114 (ll. 13–18 only); 135; MS. 1835/36; Tablet (in St. Mary's Church, Shrawley, Worcs.)
published in *1835, 1836–*
classed Epitaphs *MS. 1835/36–*
reading text *1835*
title *untitled MSS. 107, 114; omitted 1836–* Epitaph. / Sacred to the Memory of Mary &c &c *MS. 106*
2 ****** *rev from* V—r—n *rev from* Vernon *MS. 135; MS. 1835/36–, 1839* <u>Vernon</u> *MS. 106*

See the photographs and transcription of DC MS. 107, 39^{v}, 40^{r}, on pp. 730–731.

Two Babes were laid in earth before she died;
A third now slumbers at the Mother's side;
Its Sister-twin survives, whose smiles afford
A trembling solace to her widowed Lord.

Reader! if to thy bosom cling the pain
Of recent sorrow combated in vain;
Or if thy cherished grief have failed to thwart
Time still intent on his insidious part,
Lulling the Mourner's best good thoughts asleep,
Pilfering regrets we would, but cannot, keep;
Bear with Him—judge *Him* gently who makes known
His bitter loss by this memorial Stone;
And pray that in his faithful breast the grace
Of resignation find a hallowed place.

Devotional Incitements

The first reading text is based on Mary Wordsworth's fair copy of just 29 lines, apparently a complete poem, on a single sheet of paper in DC MS. 133. She drew a line under line 29 and commenced copying another poem. Wordsworth then revised her copy. When he wrote to John Kenyon on December 31, 1833, the poem had been expanded, for it contains MW's copy of lines 26–37 of the full version of *Devotional Incitements* (though still untitled in this letter version), which Wordsworth said he composed "about 18 months ago." MS. 135, the printer's copy for *Yarrow Revisited, and Other Poems*, 1835, contains a single page of draft for lines 54/55, 5–8, and 15–16, all of it canceled in ink. The first reading text is based on the copy in MS. 133; the second is that of 1835.

13–18 If thou blest Spirit eer did[?] feel the pain
Of recent sorrow combatted in vain
learn thwart
Or ~~know~~ how difficult it is to [—?—]
Time still intent on his insidious part
mourners
Lulling the Mourners best good thoughts asleep
Stealing the pain she would but cannot keep—
[?Mis]trust us not *WW's pencil MS. 107 (C)*
or strives to know
If thou blest Spirit eer has known the pain
Of recent sorrow combating in vain
Or know how difficult is to thwart
Time still intent on his insidious part
Lulling the Mourners best good thoughts asleep
Pilfering the sorrow we would but cannot keep *WW's pencil MS. 114*

18–22 *lacking MS. 135*

[Text of MS. 133]

Cast off your bonds awake arise
So speaks mid pomp of sacrifice
The iterated summons loud
Not wasted on the attendant crowd
Nor wholly lost upon the throng
Hurrying the busy streets along.

Yet ever thro' the year renewed
In undisturbed vicissitude
Of Seasons balancing their flight
On the swift wings of day and night
Tho' all the sanctities combined
By Art to unsensualize the mind
The solemn Rites the awful Forms
Founder amid fanatic storms
Tho' Priests are from their Altars thrust
And Temples levelled with the dust
Yet still, untouched by varying creeds
Mistakes, mischances and misdeeds
Where flowerbreathed Incense to the skies
Is wafted in mute harmonies
And ground fresh cloven by the plough
Is fragrant with a humbler vow
Where birds and brooks from leafy dells
Chime forth unwearied Canticles
And fuming mists enlarge and spread
The glory of the Sun's bright head
There Nature keeps a heavenly door
Wide open for the scattered Poor
Whether they sow or reap the fields—

---

composed probably begun around June 1832
found in DC MS. 133
reading text DC MS. 133
2 *alt* Repleads [*rev from* Repeats] the urgent sacrifice *MS. 133*
3 The *rev to* With *MS. 133* *alt* With silent summons as with loud *MS. 133*
6/7 Through [*rev from* Of] Cities hallowed by these calls
Repeated at fixd intervals *MS. 133*
alt But Interval [Interval *rev from* interval] fix'd at birth *MS. 133*
alt in margin Through cities by those ritual calls
Shouted at fixd intervals
alt in margin Streets hallowed by these [these *rev to* those] ritual calls *MS. 133*
7 Yet ever thro'] Yet still throughout *alt MS. 133*
15 are *rev to* be *del MS. 133*
17 Yet still, untouched *alt* Well unrepressed undeterrd *alt* Still un[?shakable] *MS. 133*
27 There *rev from* Their *alt* Doth *MS. 133*

In l. 15 we adopt the original "are"; the word was revised to "be" and "be" was deleted, though "are" was not reinstated.

[Text of 1835]

DEVOTIONAL INCITEMENTS.

"Not to the earth confined,
"Ascend to heaven."

WHERE will they stop, those breathing Powers,
The Spirits of the new-born flowers?
They wander with the breeze, they wind
Where'er the streams a passage find;
Up from their native ground they rise
In mute aërial harmonies;
From humble violet modest thyme
Exhaled, the essential odours climb,
As if no space below the sky
Their subtle flight could satisfy:
Heaven will not tax our thoughts with pride
If like ambition be *their* guide.

Roused by this kindliest of May-showers,
The spirit-quickener of the flowers,
That with moist virtue softly cleaves
The buds, and freshens the young leaves,
The Birds pour forth their souls in notes
Of rapture from a thousand throats,
Here checked by too impetuous haste,
While there the music runs to waste,
With bounty more and more enlarged,
Till the whole air is overcharged;
Give ear, O Man! to their appeal
And thirst for no inferior zeal,
Thou, who canst *think*, as well as feel.

Mount from the earth; aspire! aspire!
So pleads the town's cathedral choir,
In strains that from their solemn height

---

composed probably begun around June 1832, perhaps revised around November–December 1833; revised and title added around November–December 1834

found in WW to JK, December 31, 1833; DC MSS. 135; 137 (MW); MS. 1836/45 (MW); MS. 1835Col; MS. 1835/36 (MW)

published in *1835, 1836–*

classed Imagination *MS. 1835/36–*

reading text *1835*

title *inserted MS. 137*

8 Exhaled,] Aloft *MS. 135*

15 moist *rev from* its *MS. 135*

16 freshens *rev from* [?quiets] *MS. 135*

Sink, to attain a loftier flight;
While incense from the altar breathes
Rich fragrance in embodied wreaths;
Or, flung from swinging censer, shrouds
The taper lights, and curls in clouds
Around angelic Forms, the still
Creation of the painter's skill,
That on the service wait concealed
One moment, and the next revealed.
—Cast off your bonds, awake, arise,
And for no transient ecstasies!
What else can mean the visual plea
Of still or moving imagery?
The iterated summons loud,
Not wasted on the attendant crowd,
Nor wholly lost upon the throng
Hurrying the busy streets along?

Alas! the sanctities combined
By art to unsensualise the mind,
Decay and languish; or, as creeds
And humours change, are spurned like weeds:
The solemn rites, the awful forms,
Founder amid fanatic storms;
The priests are from their altars thrust,
The temples levelled with the dust:
Yet evermore, through years renewed
In undisturbed vicissitude
Of seasons balancing their flight
On the swift wings of day and night,
Kind Nature keeps a heavenly door
Wide open for the scattered Poor.
Where flower-breathed incense to the skies
Is wafted in mute harmonies;
And ground fresh cloven by the plough

---

29 Sink *rev from* Sing *MS. 137*
30 *rev from* While fragrance in embodied [in embodied *over illeg eras*] *WW to JK*
37 revealed *rev from* unvealed *WW to JK*
46–55 Rejoice ye cities in these calls *alt* Citis, art thankful for the call
Repeated at fix'd intervals
Yet hamlet and each lonely seat [seat *rev to* cot]
Rejoice in your still happier lot
For ever through the year renewed
With undisturbed *MS. 135*
50–53 The priests are from their altars thrust,
Temples are levelled with the dust;
And solemn rites and awful forms
Founder amid fantastic storms; *MS. 1835/36; so 1836–, 1839 but* thrust; *and* storms.
54 Yet *rev from* But *MS. 137*
59 scattered *rev from* rustic *MS. 137*

Is fragrant with a humbler vow;
Where birds and brooks from leafy dells
Chime forth unwearied canticles,
And vapours magnify and spread
The glory of the sun's bright head;
Still constant in her worship, still
Conforming to the almighty Will,
Whether men sow or reap the fields,
Her admonitions Nature yields;
That not by bread alone we live,
Or what a hand of flesh can give;
That every day should leave some part
Free for a sabbath of the heart;
So shall the seventh be truly blest,
From morn to eve, with hallowed rest.

TO THE AUTHOR'S PORTRAIT.

[Painted at Rydal Mount, by W. Pickersgill, Esq., for St. John's College, Cambridge.]

Go, faithful Portrait! and where long hath knelt
Margaret, the saintly Foundress, take thy place;
And, if Time spare the colours for the grace
Which to the work surpassing skill hath dealt,
Thou, on thy rock reclined, though Kingdoms melt

63/64 *MW entered l. 68 and* Conf *(l. 69) here, without punct, then del MS. 1835/36*
69 almighty] eternal *MS. 1835/36–, 1839*
71 Divine admonishment She yields, *MS. 1835/36–,1836*
Divine monition Nature yields, *MS. 1836/45, 1845–*

---

composed around but by September 19, 1832
found in DC MSS. 106; 134; 135; 137 (MW); 138 (MW); WW to TA, September 19, 1832; Dora W to EQ, October 3, 1832; Coatalen MS. (copy); Lilly MS. 1; WW to JSmith, November 28, 1832; St. John's MS.; MS. 1836/45 (JC)
published in *1835, 1836–, 1838*
classed Miscellaneous Sonnets *1836–, 1838*
reading text *1835*
title *lacking MS. 106, WW to TA, Coatalen MS., Lilly MS. 1, WW to JSmith* To my own Portrait *over illeg eras MS. 134* To my Portrait *Dora W to EQ, St. John's MS.* To my own Portrait, *rev to* To the Author's Portrait, *MS. 135*
headnote *lacking MS. 106, WW to TA, Coatalen MS., Lilly MS. 1, WW to JSmith* painted, at Rydal Mount, by [by *rev from* at] the request of the Mas^{r} and Fellows of St. John's [Coll. *del*] Cambridge and to be placed in their College. *inserted as continuation of title MS. 134* Painted at Rydal Mount by Pickersgill for St Johns College Cambridge *Dora W to EQ* Painted by Pickersgill at Rydal-Mount / For S^{t}. John's College Cambridge *St. John's MS.* at Rydal Mount; by the Request of the Mas^{r}. and Fellows of St. John's [College, Cambridge *inserted*] and to be placed in their College *rev to* Painted at Rydal Mount by W. Pickersgill Esq, for St John's College, Cambridge. *as continuation of title MS. 135*
1 Go faithful *over illeg eras MS. 135* hath] has *WW to JSmith, Lilly MS. 1*
4 dealt *over illeg eras MS. 134*
5 reclined *rev from* reclining *MS. 134*

And States be torn up by the roots, wilt seem
To breathe in rural peace, to hear the stream,
To think and feel as once the Poet felt.
Whate'er thy fate, those features have not grown
Unrecognised through many a household tear,
More prompt more glad to fall than drops of dew
By morning shed around a flower half blown;
Tears of delight, that testified how true
To life thou art, and, in thy truth, how dear!

Poems Written in Response to the Reform Movement, December 1832

Wordsworth wrote four poems in response to the elections of December 1832, when reform of Parliamentary elections and of Church governance were much at issue. Of the four only "If this great world of joy and pain" was published, not in the *Cambridge Intelligencer,* where all four were originally intended to appear, but in *Yarrow Revisited, and Other Poems* in 1835. Wordsworth opposed the Whig candidates in these elections because, as he put it to his nephew John Wordsworth, to whom he sent the poems, "a thoroughpaced Whig whatever may be his intentions, will prove in conduct a Revolutionist" *(LY,* II, 569). John William Lubbock, the target of the three epigrams, stood as a candidate to represent Cambridge University in Parliament and was opposed by Charles Manners-Sutton (Speaker of the House at dissolution) and Henry Goulburn. Manners-Sutton and Goulbourn were returned without opposition when Lubbock retired before the polls closed on December 14 (*LY,* II, 568n).

The texts of the first, third, and fourth poems are based on the letters to John Wordsworth; that of the second is based on the 1835 publication.

6–7 Before the breath of Change, unchanged, wilt seem
Green [Green *rev to* (Green] hills in sight, and listening to the Stream [Stream *rev to* Stream)] *all rev to*
In the hot crucible of Change, wilt seem
To breathe in rural peace to hear the Stream, *MS. 106*
Before the breath of Change, unchanged wilt seem,
Green hills in sight, and listening to the Stream, *WW to TA*

6 In the hot crucible of Change wilt seem *rev to*
And States be shaken to [shaken to *rev from* torn up by] the roots, wilt seem *MS. 134*
And States be shaken to the roots, wilt seem *rev to text MS. 135*

7 In the hot crucible of change, wilt seem *Coatalen MS., so Lilly MS. 1, Dora W to EQ, WW to JSmith, St. John's MS. but* change] Change

10 through] by *Lilly MS. 1* household *rev from* starting *MSS. 134, 135* falling *rev to* starting *WW to TA* starting *MS. 106, Coatalen MS., Lilly MS. 1, Dora W to EQ, WW to JSmith, St. John's MS.*

11 dew *rev from* due *MS. 134*

14/ Wm Wordsworth / October 3^{d} 1832. *Coatalen MS.* Wm Wordsworth / Oct^{br} 3^{d} 1832— *Lilly MS. 1* Wm Wordsworth *St. John's MS.*

[Poems Written in Response to the Reform Movement, December 1832]

i. "For Lubbock vote—no legislative Hack"

[Text of WW, DW, and Dora W to JW_3, December 5, 1832]

For Lubbock vote—no legislative Hack
The dupe of History—that "old almanack";
The Sage has read the *stars* with skill so true
The Almanack he'll follow, must be *new.*

[Text of WW to JW_3, December 7, 1832]

For Lubbock vote—no legislative Hack
The dupe of History—that old Almanack!
The Sage has read the Stars with skill so true
That Men may trust him, and be certain, too,
The almanack He'll follow must be *new.*

ii. "If this great world of joy and pain"

If this great world of joy and pain
  Revolve in one sure track;
If Freedom, set, will rise again,
  And Virtue, flown, come back;
Woe to the purblind crew who fill
  The heart with each day's care;
Nor gain, from past or future, skill
  To bear, and to forbear!

---

composed around but by December 5, 1832
found in WW, DW and Dora W to JW_3, December 5, 1832

---

composed a few days before December 7, 1832, when WW revised it
found in WW to JW_3, December 7, 1832
5 new.] new *WW to JW_3*

---

composed around but by December 7, 1832
found in DC MSS. 134; 135; 137 (A) p. 248 (MW), (B) p. 248 (MW); WW, DW, and Dora W to JW_3, December 5, 1832; MS. 1835/36; Gluck MS.
published in *1835, 1836–*
classed Sentiment and Reflection *1836–*
reading text *1835*
title Addressed to Revolunists of all classes *inserted WW, DW, and Dora W to JW_3*
3–4 If what has set, will rise again;
And what is flown, come back; *WW, DW, and Dora W to JW_3; so MS. 133 but no punct*
5 who] that *WW, DW, and Dora W to JW_3*
7 gain . . . or] learn . . . and *WW, DW, and Dora W to JW_3*

iii. "Now that Astrology is out of date"

Now that Astrology is out of date,
What have the Stars to do with Church and State?
In Parliament should Lubbock go astray,
Twould be an odd excuse for Friends to say,
"He's wondrous knowing in *The Milky Way*!"

iv.
Question and Answer.

"Can Lubbock fail to make a good M.P,
A Whig so clever in Astronomy?"
"*Baillie*, a Brother-sage, went forth as keen
Of change—for what reward?—the Guillotine:
Not Newton's Genius could have saved his head
From falling by the "Mouvement" he had led."

THOUGHT ON THE SEASONS.

FLATTERED with promise of escape
  From every hurtful blast,
Spring takes, O sprightly May! thy shape,
  Her loveliest and her last.

Less fair is summer riding high
  In fierce solstitial power,

---

composed around but by December 7, 1832
found in WW to JW_3, December 7, 1832
reading text WW to JW_3, December 7, 1832

---

composed December 6, 1832
found in WW to JW_3, December 7, 1832
reading text WW to JW_3, December 7, 1832

---

composed probably between December 1 and 6, revised around December 28, 1832
found in WW to JW_3, December 7, 1832; DC MSS. 135; 137; 138(A) p. 292, (B) p. 294 (MW); MS. 1835/36
published in *1835, 1836–*
classed Sentiment and Reflection *1836–*
reading text *1835*
title *lacking MS. 135* A Thought upon the Seasons *WW to JW_3* III. *rev to* Thought on the Seasons *MS. 138 (A)* Thought] Thoughts *1850*
stanza numbers 1 *and* 2 *only WW to JW_3*
2 hurtful] harmful *WW to JW_3*
3 sprightly] genial *WW to JW_3*
3–4 *rev from* Spring takes, o sprightly May!
Thy shape her loveliest and her last. *MS. 135*
6 fierce solstitial] full meridian *WW to JW_3*

Less fair than when a lenient sky
  Brings on her parting hour.

When earth repays with golden sheaves
  The labours of the plough,
And ripening fruits and forest leaves
  All brighten on the bough,

What pensive beauty autumn shows,
  Before she hears the sound
Of winter rushing in, to close
  The emblematic round!

Such be our Spring, our Summer such;
  So may our Autumn blend
With hoary Winter, and Life touch,
  Through heaven-born hope, her end!

A WREN'S NEST.

AMONG the dwellings framed by birds
  In field or forest with nice care,
Is none that with the little Wren's
  In snugness may compare.

No door the tenement requires,
  And seldom needs a laboured roof;
Yet is it to the fiercest sun
  Impervious and storm-proof.

So warm, so beautiful withal,
  In perfect fitness for its aim,

---

9 earth repays] fields repay *WW to* JW_3
10 labours] labour *WW to* JW_3
11 ripening fruits and *rev from* fruits are reddening *MS. 135* daily, fruits and *WW to* JW_3
12 All brighten *rev from* All brightening *MS. 135* Are brightening *WW to* JW_3
13 What pensive *rev from* What *MS. 135* What pomp what *WW to* JW_3

---

composed probably March–May 1833
found in DC MSS. 128, 135, 138; MS. 1835/36
published in *1835, 1836–*
classed Fancy *1836–*
reading text *1835*
1 framed *alt* built *MS. 135*

See the photographs and transcriptions of *A Wren's Nest,* DC MS. 128, inside front cover, 1^r–2^r, pp. 732–739.

That to the Kind by special grace
  Their instinct surely came.

And when for their abodes they seek
  An opportune recess,
The Hermit has no finer eye
  For shadowy quietness.

These find, 'mid ivied Abbey walls,
  A canopy in some still nook;
Others are pent-housed by a brae
  That overhangs a brook.

There to the brooding Bird her Mate
  Warbles by fits his low clear song;
And by the busy Streamlet both
  Are sung to all day long.

Or in sequestered lanes they build,
  Where, till the flitting Bird's return,
Her eggs within the nest repose,
  Like relics in an urn.

But still, where general choice is good,
  There is a better and a best;
And, among fairest objects, some
  Are fairer than the rest;

This, one of those small Builders proved
  In a green covert, where, from out
The forehead of a pollard oak,
  The leafy antlers sprout;

For She who planned the mossy Lodge,
  Mistrusting her evasive skill,
Had to a Primrose looked for aid
  Her wishes to fulfil.

High on the trunk's projecting brow,
  And fixed an infant's span above
The budding flowers, peeped forth the nest
  The prettiest of the grove!

The treasure proudly did I show
  To some whose minds without disdain

---

19 brae *rev from* wall *MS. 138*

Can turn to little things, but once
  Looked up for it in vain:

'Tis gone—a ruthless Spoiler's prey,
  Who heeds not beauty, love, or song,
'Tis gone! (so seemed it) and we grieved
  Indignant at the wrong.

Just three days after, passing by
  In clearer light the moss-built cell
I saw, espied its shaded mouth,
  And felt that all was well.

The Primrose for a veil had spread
  The largest of her upright leaves;
And thus, for purposes benign,
  A simple Flower deceives.

Concealed from friends who might disturb
  Thy quiet with no ill intent,
Secure from evil eyes and hands
  On barbarous plunder bent,

Rest, mother-bird! and when thy young
  Take flight, and thou art free to roam,
When withered is the guardian flower,
  And empty thy late home,

Think how ye prospered, thou and thine,
  Amid the unviolated grove
Housed near the growing primrose tuft
  In foresight, or in love.

49, 51 'Tis *so 1839, 1845–* 'T is *MSS. 135, 138; 1835–1843 (except 1839)*

Evening Voluntaries

The evening reverie in verse, a long-established tradition in English poetry, was given a central place by Milton's much imitated *Il Penseroso*, companion to his "morning poem," *L'Allegro*. Among Wordsworth's earliest poems are several in this mode: *Beauty and Moonlight, A Winter's Evening—Fragment of an Ode to winter*, four evening sonnets, and some fragments recording the sounds heard "by waterside at night." This subgenre, as adapted by Thomas Gray, James Thomson, and others, offered a loco-descriptive content and elegiac tone that appealed to the young poet, who ambitiously attempted sustained versions of it in *The Vale of Esthwaite* (1787) and *An Evening Walk* (1788–1792). His enthusiasm for it was tempered by other interests over the ensuing years but never waned. In his maturity Wordsworth wrote in this strain most frequently in short lyrics and sonnets: "The sun has long been set" and "It is a beauteous Evening, calm and free," both written in 1802, and a half-dozen others composed before 1820, notably the more extended lyric *Ode, Composed upon an Evening of Extraordinary Splendor and Beauty*, begun in 1817 and published in the *River Duddon* volume in 1820.

In 1834 Wordsworth composed the sonnet *Twilight by the side of Grasmere Lake* with an unusual rhyme scheme: an octet of four couplets followed by a sestet of two triplets (see Evening Voluntaries, the first alternate reading text, p. 248, below). Mary Wordsworth entered a fair copy of the poem, with its title, in a red-leather notebook in use initially for fair copies of new material during preparations for the publication of *Yarrow Revisited, and Other Poems*, 1835. Very soon Wordsworth took over the notebook and began revising and expanding this "effusion" into a much longer poem, using the same pentameter line, but mainly in couplets. As the couplets multiplied, Mary and Dora Wordsworth entered them more or less continuously over seven pages of the notebook, and Wordsworth revised and added to them here and on the inside back cover. At the time of entry and first revision the verses seem to have been an undifferentiated stream (represented in this volume by the photographs and transcriptions from DC MS. 128 on pp. 740–757). Details of when and in what circumstances the idea for a group of evening "voluntaries" occurred to Wordsworth are not recorded, but the mass of couplets entered in the notebook contained the seeds of several poems and out of it emerged Evening Voluntaries I through V.

Wordsworth worked on these five poems and two others, in this manuscript and several others, until they were published as "Evening Voluntaries"—with their own separate fly-title—in *Yarrow Revisited* in late 1835. Very near the time of publication he added two more, one recovered from *Poems, in Two Volumes* ("The sun has long been set," mentioned above) and the other a cento assembled from poems by earlier practitioners of the genre, Mark Akenside, James Thomson, and James Beattie. Although the date of composition of these nine poems does not correspond to their placement in the series, we have elected to preserve their published order and to retain their integrity as a group, instead of dispersing them among other poems in strict adherence to chronology. In a sense we are treating the 1835 set of "Evening Voluntaries" as a single composition, to emphasize the ground shared by the poems it contains and to reveal more fully their interrelations.

Wordsworth added seven poems to the 1835 set of Evening Voluntaries in subsequent editions of his poems. These we have placed in the main chronological listing: *Composed by the Sea-shore,* written in 1833, first published in 1842, and added to the series in 1845 (p. 251); *To the Moon. (Composed by the Sea-side,—on the Coast of Cumberland.)* and *To the Moon. (Rydal.),* written in 1835, added to the series in 1836–1837 (pp. 286–290); "The Crescent-moon, the Star of Love," composed in 1842, added to the series in 1845 (pp. 354–355); and three sonnets written in 1846 and added to the series in 1850, *To Lucca Giordano,* "Who but is pleased to watch the moon on high," and "Where lies the truth? has Man in wisdom's creed" (pp. 403–405). *Ode, Composed upon an Evening of Extraordinary Splendor and Beauty* (1817), mentioned above, was inserted in Evening Voluntaries in the reissue of *Yarrow Revisited, and Other Poems* in 1836 (and 1839) and then moved from Poems of Imagination to Evening Voluntaries in collected editions from 1836 (see *Poems, 1807–1820,* pp. 255–260). The contents and arrangement of Evening Voluntaries in the final lifetime edition are displayed in Appendix III (p. 841).

In 1843 Wordsworth, in the Fenwick note to *Ode, Composed upon an Evening of Extraordinary Splendor and Beauty,* singled out some "morning impressions" that "might be read with mutual benefit in connection with these Evening Voluntaries." However, though Dora Wordsworth had reported to Edward Quillinan in June 1835 that her father was working on "a series of 'Morning Voluntaries,'" and Wordsworth himself began compiling a list of candidates for inclusion around 1840–1845, he never published such a series (for the reference to Dora's letter see the editor's headnote to *Love Lies Bleeding*; see also *FNW,* pp. 56, 161; Wordsworth's list is in DC MS. 154).

The texts for Evening Voluntary VII, "The sun has long been set" (first composed in 1802 and published in 1807), are drawn from the late configurations of this poem in MS. 128 and the published version of 1835. Alternate reading texts drawn from apparently stable, if provisional, texts in MS. 128 follow Evening Voluntary IX.

---

fly-title

EVENING VOLUNTARIES.

The fly-title is found only in the proof states (DC MSS. 137 and 138) and the editions of *Yarrow Revisited, and Other Poems* (1835, 1836, 1839). It was dropped in collected editions from 1836. See alternate reading texts of "The Labourer wont to rise at break of day" and *Twilight by the side of Grasmere Lake* (pp. 246, 248–249), and photographs and transcription of DC MS. 128, 54^{v}–57^{r} (pp. 740–751).

EVENING VOLUNTARIES.

I.

Calm is the fragrant air, and loth to lose
Day's grateful warmth, tho' moist with falling dews.
Look for the stars, you'll say that there are none;
Look up a second time, and, one by one,
You mark them twinkling out with silvery light,
And wonder how they could elude the sight.
The birds, of late so noisy in their bowers,
Warbled a while with faint and fainter powers,
But now are silent as the dim-seen flowers:
Nor does the Village Church-clock's iron tone
The time's and season's influence disown;
Nine beats distinctly to each other bound
In drowsy sequence; how unlike the sound
That, in rough winter, oft inflicts a fear
On fireside Listeners, doubting what they hear!
The Shepherd, bent on rising with the sun,
Had closed his door before the day was done,
And now with thankful heart to bed doth creep,
And join his little Children in their sleep.
The Bat, lured forth where trees the lane o'ershade,
Flits and reflits along the close arcade;
Far-heard the Dor-hawk chases the white Moth
With burring note, which Industry and Sloth
Might both be pleased with, for it suits them both.
Wheels and the tread of hoofs are heard no more;
One Boat there was, but it will touch the shore
With the next dipping of its slackened oar;
Faint sound, that, for the gayest of the gay,
Might give to serious thought a moment's sway,
As a last token of Man's toilsome day!

---

composed probably around April 1833
found in DC MSS. 128; 135; 137 (MW); 138; MS. 1831JH; MS. 1835/36 (MW)
published in *1835, 1836–*
classed Evening Voluntaries *1835, 1836–*
reading text *1835*
2 moist *over eras MS. 135*
3 for] to *MS. 1831JH*
9 But *rev from* And *MS. 135*
19 join] joins *MS. 1835/36–, 1839*
22 Far-heard the] The busy *MS. 1835/36–, 1839*
24/25 A stream is heard—I see it not, but know
By its soft music whence the waters flow; *MS. 1835/36; so 1836–, 1839 but* flow:
25–28 *om MS. 1831JH*

II.

Not in the lucid intervals of life
That come but as a curse to Party-strife;
Not in some hour when Pleasure with a sigh
Of langour puts his rosy garland by;
Not in the breathing-times of that poor Slave
Who daily piles up wealth in Mammon's cave,
Is Nature felt, or can be; nor do words,
Which practised Talent readily affords,
Prove that her hand has touched responsive chords;
Nor has her gentle beauty power to move
With genuine rapture and with fervent love
The soul of Genius, if he dares to take
Life's rule from passion craved for passion's sake;
Untaught that meekness is the cherished bent
Of all the truly Great and all the Innocent.
But who *is* innocent? By grace divine,
Not otherwise, O Nature! we are thine,
Through good and evil thine, in just degree
Of rational and manly sympathy.
To all that Earth from pensive hearts is stealing,
And Heaven is now to gladdened eyes revealing,
Add every charm the Universe can show
Through every change its aspects undergo,
Care may be respited, but not repealed;
No perfect cure grows on the bounded field.
Vain is the pleasure, a false calm the peace,
If He, through whom alone our conflicts cease,
Our virtuous hopes without relapse advance,
Come not to speed the Soul's deliverance;
To the distempered Intellect refuse
His gracious help, or give what we abuse.

---

composed probably between April 1833 and early 1834
found in DC MSS. 128; 135; 137 (MW); 138; MS. 1831JH; MS. 1835/36
published in *1835, 1836–*
classed Evening Voluntaries *1835, 1836–*
reading text *1835*

3–4 *lacking MS. 1831JH*
5 breathing-times *rev from* breathing time *MS. 137* breathing time *MS. 1831JH, MS. 135*
6 piles] heaps *MS. 1831JH*
12 dares] dare *1836–*
29 speed *rev from* speak *MSS. 135, 137*
31 give *rev from* gives *MS. 137* gives *MS. 135*

With "Not in the lucid intervals of life" compare alternate reading texts 2 and 3, *Twilight* ("Advancing slowly from the faded west") and "Alas for them who crave impassioned strife" (pp. 249–250) and photographs and transcriptions of DC MS. 128, 58r and inside back cover (pp. 752–753, 756–757).

III.

(By the Side of Rydal Mere.)

The Linnet's warble, sinking towards a close,
Hints to the Thrush 'tis time for their repose;
The shrill-voiced Thrush is heedless, and again
The Monitor revives his own sweet strain;
But both will soon be mastered, and the copse
Be left as silent as the mountain-tops,
Ere some commanding Star dismiss to rest
The throng of Rooks, that now, from twig or nest,
(After a steady flight on home-bound wings,
And a last game of mazy hoverings
Around their ancient grove) with cawing noise
Disturb the liquid music's equipoise.
O Nightingale! Who ever heard thy song
Might here be moved, till Fancy grows so strong
That listening sense is pardonably cheated
Where wood or stream by thee was never greeted.
Surely, from fairest spots of favoured lands,
Were not some gifts withheld by jealous hands,
This hour of deepening darkness here would be,
As a fresh morning for new harmony;
And Lays as prompt would hail the dawn of night;
A *dawn* she has both beautiful and bright,
When the East kindles with the full moon's light.

Wanderer by spring with gradual progress led,
For sway profoundly felt as widely spread;
To king, to peasant, to rough sailor, dear,
And to the soldier's trumpet-wearied ear;

---

composed probably between April 1833 and early 1834
found in DC MSS. 128; 135; 138; MS. 1835/36 (MW)
published in *1835, 1836–*
classed Evening Voluntaries *1835, 1836–*
reading text *1835*
title *lacking MSS. 135, 138*
2 'tis *so MSS. 128, 135, 138, 1836–, 1839* 't is *1835*
19 would] could *MS. 138*
23/24 Not like the rising sun's impatient glow
Dazzling the mountains, but an overflow
Of solemn splendour, in mutation slow. *MS. 1835/36–, 1839; so 1836YR but* sun's] Sun's *and* splendour] Splendour

---

With *(By the Side of Rydal Mere.)* compare alternate reading text 4, "The dewy evening has withdrawn," on pp. 250–251, and photographs and transcriptions of DC MS. 128, 57^{r}, 58^{v}, and inside back cover on pp. 750–757.

How welcome wouldst thou be to this green Vale
Fairer than Tempe! Yet, sweet Nightingale!
From the warm breeze that bears thee on alight
At will, and stay thy migratory flight;
Build, at thy choice, or sing, by pool or fount,
Who shall complain, or call thee to account?
The wisest, happiest, of our kind are they
That ever walk content with Nature's way,
God's goodness measuring bounty as it may;
For whom the gravest thought of what they miss,
Chastening the fulness of a present bliss,
Is with that wholesome office satisfied,
While unrepining sadness is allied
In thankful bosoms to a modest pride.

IV.

Soft as a cloud is yon blue Ridge—the Mere
Seems firm as solid crystal, breathless, clear,
And motionless; and, to the gazer's eye,
Deeper than Ocean, in the immensity
Of its vague mountains and unreal sky!
But, from the process in that still retreat,
Turn to minuter changes at our feet;
Observe how dewy Twilight has withdrawn
The crowd of daisies from the shaven lawn,
And has restored to view its tender green,
That, while the sun rode high, was lost beneath their dazzling sheen.
—An emblem this of what the sober Hour
Can do for minds disposed to feel its power!
Thus oft, when we in vain have wish'd away
The petty pleasures of the garish day,

---

38 present *rev from* loving *MS. 137* loving *MS. 135*

---

composed probably between April 1833 and early 1834
found in DC MSS. 128; 135; 138 (MW); Monkhouse Album (copy) (ll. 22–26); Berg MS. 3 (ll. 22–26); MS. 1835/36
published in *1835, 1836–*
classed Evening Voluntaries *1835, 1836–*
reading text *1835*
11 *rev from* Lost, while the sun rode high, beneath their dazzling sheen. *MS. 135*
14 Oft, when we've wished, in vain have wished away *MS. 135; so MS. 138 but* wish'd *then line rev to text*

See the photographs and transcriptions of "Soft as a cloud is yon blue Ridge—the Mere," DC MS. 128, 58r, 58v and inside back cover, pp. 752–757.

Meek Eve shuts up the whole usurping host
(Unbashful dwarfs each glittering at his post)
And leaves the disencumbered spirit free
To reassume a staid simplicity.
'Tis well—but what are helps of time and place,
When wisdom stands in need of nature's grace;
Why do good thoughts, invoked or not, descend,
Like Angels from their bowers, our virtues to befriend;
If yet To-morrow, unbelied, may say,
"I come to open out, for fresh display,
The elastic vanities of yesterday?"

V.

THE leaves that rustled on this oak-crowned hill,
And sky that danced among those leaves, are still;
Rest smooths the way for sleep; in field and bower
Soft shades and dews have shed their blended power
On drooping eyelid and the closing flower;
Sound is there none at which the faintest heart
Might leap, the weakest nerve of superstition start;
Save when the Owlet's unexpected scream
Pierces the ethereal vault; and 'mid the gleam
Of unsubstantial imagery—the dream,
From the hushed vale's realities, transferred

16–17 Unbashful dwarfs each glittering at his post,
Meek Eventide shuts up the whole usurping host, *MS. 135; so MS. 138, rev to text*
21 need *rev in pencil from* needs *MS. 135*

---

composed probably between April 1833 and January 1835.
found in DC MSS. 128, 135, 138; MS. 1835/36
published in *1835, 1836–*
classed Evening Voluntaries *1835, 1836–*
reading text *1835*
1–5 Advancing slowly from the faded west
Sleep treads away prepared for him by Rest [Rest *rev from* rest]
Ceased is the rustling on this oak crowned hill
The sky that danced among the leaves is still *MS. 128, couplets reversed, then rev to text*
2 And . . . leaves *rev from* The . . . hills *MS. 128*
3 and] or *alt* and *MS. 128*
5 eyelid] eyelids *MS. 128*
7 Might *rev from* Could *MS. 128* superstition] fancy *alt* superstition *MS. 128*
from [?evng] on ~~wou~~ screa unexpected
8–10 Save when at intervals the owlets scream
Pierces the etherial vault; and in the dream
The glimmering image and the fading gleam *MS. 128*

With "The leaves that rustled on this oak-crowned hill" compare the alternate reading text *Twilight* on p. 249 and the photograph and transcription of DC MS. 128, 57[r] on pp. 750–751.

To the still lake, the imaginative Bird
Seems, 'mid inverted mountains, not unheard.

Grave Creature! whether, while the moon shines bright
On thy wings opened wide for smoothest flight,
Thou art discovered in a roofless tower,
Rising from what may once have been a Lady's bower:
Or spied where thou sit'st moping in thy mew
At the dim centre of a churchyard yew;
Or, from a rifted crag or ivy tod
Deep in a forest, thy secure abode,
Thou giv'st, for pastime's sake, by shriek or shout,
A puzzling notice of thy whereabout;
May the night never come, the day be seen,
When I shall scorn thy voice or mock thy mien!
In classic ages men perceived a soul
Of sapience in thy aspect, headless Owl!
Thee Athens reverenced in the studious grove;
And, near the golden sceptre grasped by Jove,
His Eagle's favourite perch, while round him sate
The Gods revolving the decrees of Fate,
Thou, too, wert present at Minerva's side—
Hark to that second larum! far and wide
The elements have heard, and rock and cave replied.

14–20 Grave Creature whether at some lucky hour
Thou art encountered in a moon-lit tower
In which may once have been a Lady's bower
Or in a glimmering Barn where thou dost chuse
(Wishing the Sun good speed) to mope & muse
Or watch for food; or from an ivy tod *MS. 128, then rev to text but* may] might *and* for *rev from* of *MS. 128*

18 sit'st] sits *MS. 135* sit'st *rev from* sitst *MS. 138* sitt'st *1836–, 1839*

22 giv'st *rev from* givest *MS. 135* givest *rev from* gives *MS. 128* by *over illeg word MS. 135*

23/24 Or hast been robbed of liberty and joy
The drooping Captive of a thoughtless boy *MS. 128*

24 the day] nor day *MS. 1835/36–, 1839*

25 scorn *rev from illeg word MS. 135*

28 the *rev from* thy *MS. 135*

In l. 17 of MS. 128 the word "bower" was deleted, apparently by accident.

VI.

THE Sun, that seemed so mildly to retire,
Flung back from distant climes a streaming fire,
Whose blaze is now subdued to tender gleams,
Prelude of night's approach with soothing dreams.
Look round;—of all the clouds not one is moving;
'Tis the still hour of thinking, feeling, loving.
Silent, and stedfast as the vaulted sky,
The boundless plain of waters seems to lie:—
Comes that low sound from breezes rustling o'er
The grass-crowned headland that conceals the shore!
No 'tis the earth-voice of the mighty sea,
Whispering how meek and gentle he *can* be!

Thou Power supreme! who, arming to rebuke
Offenders, dost put off the gracious look,
And clothe thyself with terrors like the flood
Of ocean roused into his fiercest mood,

---

composed April 7, 1833
found in DC MSS. 106 (A) 4[v], (B) inside back cover; 128; 134; 135; 138; MS. 1831JH; MS. 1835/36
published in *1835, 1836–*
classed Evening Voluntaries *1835, 1836–*
reading text *1835*
title *lacking MS. 1831JH* Sea Side / Moresby *MS. 128* By the Seaside [Seaside *rev from* Sea-side]. *MS. 135* (BY THE SEA-SIDE) *rev to text MS. 138* (On a high part of the Coast of Cumberland) *WW rev to* On a high part of the Coast of Cumberland. Easter Sunday, April 7. The Author's 63rd Birthday *MS. 1835/36* ON A HIGH PART OF THE COAST OF CUMBERLAND. Easter Sunday, April 7. THE AUTHOR'S SIXTY-THIRD BIRTH-DAY. *1836–*
2 distant] other *MS. 106 (A)*
3 is now *inserted MS. 106 (A)*
5 Look round;—of] Of *MS. 1831JH*
7 vaulted sky] Dome *rev to* dome *rev to* concave sky *MS. 106 (A)*
8–9 Silent and steadfast as the clouds and sky
The supine world of waters seem to lie *MS. 106 (B)*
8 boundless plain of waters] illimitable ocean *alt* bound plain of waters *MS. 106 (A)*
9 sound *rev from* voice *MS. 134* voice *MS. 106 (A)*
10 The cliff high raised above the unseen shore *MS. 106 (A); so MS. 134; so MS. 128 but* cliff-high *then rev to text*
11 No 'tis] No 't is *1835* No; 't is *MS. 1835/36* No; 'tis *1836–, 1836YR, 1839* mighty *rev from* [?darkning] *MS. 106 (A)*
13 —Father! who when thy justice must rebuke *MS. 106 (A); MS. 134 as MS. 106 (A) but* Father, *and* Justice *and* must *then line rev to*
Dread Power of Powers who arming to rebuke
MS. 128 as rev MS. 134, then rev to text
14 Offenders *rev from* The sinner *MS. 134* The sinner *MS. 106 (A)* dost *rev from* doth *MS. 106 (A)* the] thy *rev to* the *MS. 106 (A)* this *rev to* thy *rev to* the *MS. 134*
15 clothe thyself with terrors] execute thy purpose *MS. 106 (A); so MS. 134 rev to text*

Whatever discipline thy Will ordain
For the brief course that must for me remain;
Teach me with quick-eared spirit to rejoice
In admonitions of thy softest voice!
Whate'er the path these mortal feet may trace,
Breathe through my soul the blessing of thy grace,
Glad, through a perfect love, a faith sincere
Drawn from the wisdom that begins with fear;
Glad to expand, and, for a season, free
From finite cares, to rest absorbed in Thee!

VII.

(BY THE SEA-SIDE.)

THE sun is couched, the sea-fowl gone to rest,
And the wild storm hath somewhere found a nest;
Air slumbers—wave with wave no longer strives,
Only a heaving of the deep survives,
A tell-tale motion! soon will it be laid,
And by the tide alone the water swayed.

17–26 Author and life of all things blest are they
Who pacing needfully the worlds broad way
Have learned with quick-eared Spirit to rejoice
In admonitions from thy softest voice
Glad to expand and for a moment free
From finite cares to rest absorbed in thee *MS. 106 (A); so MS. 134 but* moment] season *MS. 128 as MS. 134 but rev in line and again below to text; for nonverbal differences from MS. 106 (A) in MS. 134 see Nonverbal Variants*

18 for] to *MS. 1831JH*

19 quick-eared *rev from* quickened *MSS. 128, 135*

20 In] For *MS. 1831JH*

21–22 *lacking MS. 1831JH*

24 with *rev from* in *MS.* 128_2

25–26 Glad to expand, and for a season free from finite care
To rest absorbed in Thee! *MS. 1831JH*

---

composed probably in late March–early April, 1833
found in DC MSS. 128, 129, 135, 138; CW, Jr., to CW, January 2, 1834; MS. 1835/36
published in *1835, 1836–*
classed Evening Voluntaries *1835, 1836–*
reading text *1835*
title Composed by the sea side after a Storm. *MS. 129* Composed by the Sea-side / At Moresby / After a Storm *MS. 128* Sea side. Moresby *CW, Jr., to CW* By the Sea-side. *WW inserted MS. 135*

Stealthy withdrawings, interminglings mild
Of light with shade in beauty reconciled—
Such is the prospect far as sight can range,
The soothing recompence, the welcome change.
Where now the ships that drove before the blast,
Threatened by angry breakers as they passed;
And by a train of flying clouds bemocked;
Or, in the hollow surge, at anchor rocked
As on a bed of death? Some lodge in peace,
Saved by His care who bade the tempest cease;
And some, too heedless of past danger, court
Fresh gales to waft them to the far-off port;
But near, or hanging sea and sky between,
Not one of all those wingèd Powers is seen,
Seen in her course, nor 'mid this quiet heard;
Yet oh! how gladly would the air be stirred
By some acknowledgment of thanks and praise,
Soft in its temper as those vesper lays
Sung to the Virgin while accordant oars
Urge the slow bark along Calabrian shores;
A sea-born service through the mountains felt
Till into one loved vision all things melt:
Or like those hymns that soothe with graver sound
The gulfy coast of Norway iron-bound;
And, from the wide and open Baltic, rise
With punctual care, Lutherian harmonies.
Hush, not a voice is here! but why repine,
Now when the star of eve comes forth to shine
On British waters with that look benign?
Ye mariners, that plough your onward way,
Or in the haven rest, or sheltering bay,
May *silent* thanks at least to God be given
With a full heart, "our thoughts are heard in heaven!"

13–20 *lacking (cut away) MS. 129*
15 death *rev from illeg word MS. 135* in] at *CW, Jr., to CW*
21–39 *del MS. 129*
23 some acknowledgment] tuneful chaunt or Hymn *rev to* some harmonious strain *rev to text, alt* choral utterance *MS. 129* praise *rev from* praises *MS. 135*
24 Soft in its *alt* Yet soft in *MS. 129* as] as those *CW, Jr., to CW* as *rev from* like *rev from* as *MS. 129*
25 while] where *MS. 129* while *rev in pencil from* where *MS. 128* when *CW, Jr., to CW*
27 service *over illeg word MS. 128*
28 Till *rev in pencil from* While *MS. 128* While *MS. 129; CW, Jr., to CW*
29–32 *lacking MS. 129*
33 but *rev from* w *MS. 135*
35 that *rev from* a *MS. 135*
39 With a *rev from* From the *MS. 129*

VIII. "The sun has long been set"

[Text of MS. 128]

The Labourer wont to rise at break of day
Has closed his door, and from the public way
The sound of hoof or wheel is heard no more
One boat there was, but it has touched the shore
That was the last dip of its slackened oar
The sun has long been set
The stars are out by twos and threes
The little birds are piping yet
Among the bushes and trees
There's a Cuckoo and one or two thrushes
And a far-off wind that rushes
And a noise of waters that gushes
And the Cuckoo's sovereign cry
Fills all the hollow of the sky.

  Who would go parading
In London, and masquerading
On such a night of June
With that beautiful soft half-moon
With what the breathless Lake is feeling
And what the dewy air to peace dismisses
With all that Earth from pensive hearts is stealing
  And Heaven to gladdened eyes revealing,
With all these innocent blisses
  On such a night as this is.

---

composed June 2, 1802, revised 1834–1835
found in DC MS. 128
reading text DC MS. 128

1–2 The Labourer wont to rise with early light
His door is closing for the night *WW's alt MS. 128*

4 but it has touched *MW rev from* soon will it touch *MS. 128*

5/6 *pencil line separates these lines in MS. 128*

6 long *rev from* just so long *MS. 128*

7 The *rev from* That *MS. 128*

9 the *MW inserted MS. 128*

12 noice *alt* sound *MS. 128*

18/19 *Text of ll. 21–24 first entered by MW here then the first two lines del MS. 128*

19 With *rev from* With all *MS. 128*

21–23 *WW's draft:*
With what the still lake vis{i ably bosoms
tremulous as with vital feeling
Of drooping eyelids and of [?of cloying] blisses *MS. 128*

[Text of 1835]

VIII.

[The *former* of the two following Pieces appeared, many years ago, among the Author's poems, from which, in subsequent editions, it was excluded. It is here reprinted, at the request of a friend who was present when the lines were thrown off as an impromptu.

For printing the *latter*, some reason should be given, as not a word of it is original: it is simply a fine stanza of Akenside, connected with a still finer from Beattie, by a couplet of Thomson. This practice, in which the author sometimes indulges, of linking together, in his own mind, favourite passages from different authors, seems in itself unobjectionable: but, as the *publishing* such compilations might lead to confusion in literature, he should deem himself inexcusable in giving this specimen, were it not from a hope that it might open to others a harmless source of *private* gratification.]

THE sun has long been set,
  The stars are out by twos and threes,
The little birds are piping
  Among the bushes and trees;
There's a cuckoo, and one or two thrushes,
And a far-off wind that rushes,
And a sound of water that gushes,
And the Cuckoo's sovereign cry
Fills all the hollow of the sky.

Who would "go parading"
In London, "and masquerading,"
On such a night of June
With that beautiful soft half-moon,
And all these innocent blisses,
On such a night as this is?

---

composed June 8, 1802, revised 1834–1835
found in DC MSS. 41, 44; Longman MS.; DC MSS. 135, 138; MS. 1835/40
published in *1807, 1835, 1836–*
classed Moods of My Own Mind *1807* Evening Voluntaries *1835, 1836–*
reading text *1835*
headnote *rev and moved to precede* "Throned in the Sun's descending car" *1836YR, 1839*

For further variants in headnote and text from 1835 see *Poems, 1800–1807*, pp. 204, 326–329.

IX.

THRONED in the Sun's descending car
What Power unseen diffuses far
This tendernes of mind?
What Genius smiles on yonder flood?
What God in whispers from the wood
Bids every thought be kind?

O ever pleasing Solitude,
Companion of the wise and good,
Thy shades, thy silence, now be mine,
  Thy charms my only theme;
My haunt the hollow cliff whose Pine
  Waves o'er the gloomy stream;
Whence the scared Owl on pinions grey
  Breaks from the rustling boughs,
And down the lone vale sails away
  To more profound repose!

[Alternate Texts of Evening Voluntaries from MS. 128]

[Text 1]

Twilight by the
side of
Grasmere Lake

A twofold slumber the huge hills partake
High in the air and deep in the still lake
Look for the stars—you'll say that there are none
Look up a second time and one by one

---

composed probably assembled in this form in the fall of 1835
found in DC MS. 135, Morgan MS. 5
published in *1835*
classed Evening Voluntaries *1835*
reading text *1835*
headnote *moved from previous poem, para one om, and* latter *ital*] following Piece *1836YR, 1839*
1 in] on *Morgan MS. 5*
5 from] thru' *MS. 135*

---

composed probably around April 1833
found in DC MS. 128 (55^r)
reading text DC MS. 128 (55^r)

For *Twilight by the side of Grasmere Lake,* see the photograph and transcription of DC MS. 128, 55^r on pp. 740–741 and compare Evening Voluntary I, "Calm is the fragrant air, and loth to lose," above.

You see them twinkling out with silver light
And wonder how they could elude your sight
The birds of late so noisy in their bowers
Are hushed and silent as the dim seen flowers
Wheels and the tread of hoofs are heard no more
One boat there was but it will touch the shore
With the next dipping of its slackened oar
A sound that for the gayest of the gay
Might give to serious thought a moment's sway
As the last token of man's toilsome day.

[Text 2]

Twilight

Advancing slowly from the faded west
Sleep treads away prepared for him by rest
Ceased is the rustling on this oak crowned hill
The sky that danced among the leaves is still
Sound is there none at which the faintest heart
Could leap the weakest nerve of fancy start
Save when at intervals the owlet's scream
Pierces the etherial vault; and, in the dream,
From the hushed vales realities transferred
To the still Lake, the imaginative Bird
Seems mid inverted mountains not unheard.
Add all that Earth from human sight is stealing
To all that heaven is at this hour revealing
What does it serve for pleasure or for peace
If he who can alone the Soul release
From bonds, for her deliverance refuse
His signet, or his mercy we abuse.

---

composed probably around April 1833
found in DC MS. 128 (31^v)
reading text DC MS. 128 (31^v)

1, 2 *transposed in rev MS. 128*

15–17 *rev to* If he through whom from bonds our troubles ceas
The Soul for her [The Soul for her *rev to* Do for the Hearts] deliverence refuse
His signet, or his mercy we abuse. *rev to*
If he thro' whom [alone *inserted*] our troubles cease
For the poor hearts deliverence refuse
His signet or his mercy we abuse. *rev to*
Tears vanish [*rev to* Our virtuous] hopes without relapse advance
Come not to speed the Souls deliverance
To the distempered intellect refuse
His gracious help or gives what we abuse. *MS. 128 with final revision transferred to close of* "Alas for them who crave impassioned strife" *(see below)*

[Text 3]

Alas for them who crave impassioned strife
How few the lucid intervals of life
When lonely Natures finer issues hit
The brain's perceptions for the heart are fit
With meekness sensibilities abide
That do but rarely visit stormy pride
Full oft the powers of genius are confined
By chains which round herself she dares to wind
To all that earth from pensive hearts is stealing
And heaven to gladdened eyes is now revealing
And every charm the universe can shew
Through every change its aspects undergo
A respite only can those medicines yield
No perfect cure grows on that bounded field
Vain is the pleasure a false calm the peace
If He thro' whom alone our conflicts cease
Our virtuous hopes without relapse advance
Come not to speed the Soul's deliverance
To the distempered intellect refuse
His gracious help or give what we abuse.

[Text 4]

The dewy evening has withdrawn
The daisies from the shaven lawn
And has restored its tender green
Lost while the sun was up beneath their dazzling sheen
Like office can this sober hour

---

composed probably around April 1833
found in DC MS. 128 (31^v, 35^r)
reading text DC MS. 128 (31^v, 35^r)
10 to *MW rev from* from *MS. 128*
12 Through *MW rev from* To *MS. 128*
15 a *MW rev from* of *MS. 128*
17 Our virtuous *WW rev from* Fears vanish *MS. 128*
18 Soul's] Souls *MS. 128*

---

composed probably around April 1833
found in DC MS. 128 (58^r)
reading text DC MS. 128 (58^r)

With "Alas for them who crave impassioned strife" compare reading texts of Evening Voluntary II, "Not in the lucid intervals of life," and alternate reading text, *Twilight.*

For "The dewy evening has withdrawn" see the photograph and transcription of DC MS. 128, 58^r on pp. 752–753; compare Evening Voluntary IV, "Soft as a cloud is yon blue Ridge—the Mere," ll. 8–19.

Perform for hearts that feel its power
When we, in vain, have wished away
The garish pleasures of broad day
While each stood glittering at his post
Meek even tide shuts up the whole usurping host
And leaves the gentle spirit free
To reassume its own simplicity.

COMPOSED BY THE SEA-SHORE.

WHAT mischief cleaves to unsubdued regret,
How fancy sickens by vague hopes beset;
How baffled projects on the spirit prey,
And fruitless wishes eat the heart away,
The sailor knows; he best whose lot is cast
On the relentless sea that holds him fast
On chance dependent, and the fickle star
Of power, through long and melancholy war.
O sad it is, in sight of foreign shores,
Daily to think on old familiar doors,
Hearths loved in childhood and ancestral floors;
Or, tossed about along a waste of foam,
To ruminate on that delightful home
Which with the dear Betrothèd *was* to come;
Or came and was, and is, yet meets the eye
Never but in the world of memory;
Or in a dream recalled, whose smoothest range
Is crossed by knowledge, or by dread, of change,
And if not so, whose perfect joy makes sleep
A thing too bright for breathing man to keep.
Hail to the virtues which that perilous life
Extracts from Nature's elemental strife;
And welcome glory won in battles fought
As bravely as the foe was keenly sought.
But to each gallant Captain and his crew
A less imperious sympathy is due,
Such as my verse now yields, while moonbeams play
On the mute sea in this unruffled bay;

---

composed Probably late March–early April 1833
found in DC MSS. 143; 151.2; MS. 1836/45 (JC)
published in *1842, 1845–*
classed Evening Voluntaries *1845, 1850*
title, ll. 1–7 *lacking MS. 143 (leaf missing)*
16 world *rev from* range *MS. 151.2*
20 *MW rev from* Too bright for mortal Creature long to keep *MS. 143*

Such as will promptly flow from every breast,
Where good men, disappointed in the quest
Of wealth and power and honours, long for rest;
Or having known the splendours of success,
Sigh for the obscurities of happiness.

TO ——,

UPON THE BIRTH OF HER FIRST-BORN CHILD, MARCH, 1833.

"Tum porro puer, ut sævis projectus ab undis
Navita; nudus humi jacet," &c.—Lucretius.

LIKE a shipwreck'd Sailor tost
By rough waves on a perilous coast,
Lies the Babe, in helplessness
And in tenderest nakedness,
Flung by labouring nature forth
Upon the mercies of the earth.
Can its eyes beseech? no more
Than the hands are free to implore:
Voice but serves for one brief cry,
Plaint was it? or prophecy
Of sorrow that will surely come?
Omen of man's grievous doom!

But, O Mother! by the close
Duly granted to thy throes;
By the silent thanks now tending
Incense-like to Heaven, descending

29 flow *rev from* fall *MS. 151.2*

composed between March 22 and 31, 1833
found in DC MSS. 135; 137 (A) p. 237 (MW), (B) p. 237; MS. 1835/36; MS. 1836/45
published in *1835, 1836–*
classed Sentiment and Reflection *1836–*
reading text *1835*
title To ———/Upon the birth of/Jane Stanley Wordsworth [Jane Stanley Wordsworth *rev to* a first-born Child, *rev to* her first Child,] / March [*illeg numeral del*] 1833. *MS. 135* First-born] First *MS. 137 (A)*
epigraph Tum [Tum *rev from* tum] porro Puer, ut sævis projectus ab undis
Navita [Navita *rev from* Nabi]—' Lucretius *MS. 135; MS. 137 (A) as rev MS. 135 but* Tum *rev from* Tam *and l. 2 rev to text*
3 the *del, reinstated (margin cut away) MS. 137 (A)*
4 tenderest *rev to* tender *rev to* tenderest *MS. 137 (A)*
7 its *rev from* his *MS. 137 (A)* his *MS. 135*
8 the *rev from* his *MS. 137 (A)* his *MS. 135*
12 man's *del, reinstated (margin cut away) MS. 137 (A)*

Now to mingle and to move
With the gush of earthly love,
As a debt to that frail Creature,
Instrument of struggling Nature
For the blissful calm, the peace
Known but to this *one* release;
Can the pitying spirit doubt
That for human-kind springs out
From the penalty a sense
Of more than mortal recompence?

As a floating summer cloud,
Though of gorgeous drapery proud,
To the sun-burnt traveller,
Or the stooping labourer,
Ofttimes makes its bounty known
By its shadow round him thrown;
So, by chequerings of sad cheer,
Heavenly guardians, brooding near,
Of their presence tell—too bright
Haply for corporeal sight!
Ministers of grace divine
Feelingly their brows incline
O'er this seeming Castaway
Breathing, in light of day,
Something like the faintest breath
That has power to baffle death—
Beautiful, while very weakness
Captivates like passive meekness!

And, sweet Mother! under warrant
Of the universal Parent,
Who repays in season due
Them who have, like thee, been true
To the filial chain let down
From his everlasting throne,
Angels hovering round thy couch,
With their softest whispers vouch,
That, whatever griefs may fret,
Cares entangle, sins beset
This thy first-born, and with tears
Stain her cheek in future years,
Heavenly succour, not denied

---

17 Now *rev from* With *MS. 135*
19 that *rev from* this *MS. 135*
37–82 *lacking MS. 137 (A)*
56 her *rev from* his *MS. 135*

To the Babe, whate'er betide,
Will to the Woman be supplied!

Mother! blest be thy calm ease;
Blest the starry promises,
And the firmament benign
Hallowed be it, where they shine!
Yes, for them whose souls have scope
Ample for a wingèd hope,
And can earthward bend an ear
For needful listening, pledge is here,
That, if thy new-born Charge shall tread
In thy footsteps, and be led
By that other Guide, whose light
Of manly virtues, mildly bright,
Gave him first the wished-for part
In thy gentle virgin heart,
Then, amid the storms of life
Presignified by that dread strife
Whence ye have escaped together,
She may look for serene weather;
In all trials sure to find
Comfort for a faithful mind;
Kindlier issues, holier rest,
Than even now await her prest,
Conscious Nursling, to thy breast!

81 await *rev from* awaits *MS. 135*

THE WARNING,

A SEQUEL TO THE FOREGOING.

MARCH, 1833.

LIST, the winds of March are blowing;
Her ground-flowers shrink, afraid of showing
Their meek heads to the nipping air,
Which ye feel not, happy pair!
Sunk into a kindly sleep.
We, meanwhile, our hope will keep;
And if Time leagued with adverse Change
(Too busy fear!) shall cross its range,
Whatsoever check they bring,
Anxious duty hindering,
To like hope our prayers will cling.

Thus, while the ruminating spirit feeds
Upon each home-event as life proceeds,
Affections pure and holy in their source
Gain a fresh impulse, run a livelier course;
Hopes that within the Father's heart prevail,
Are in the experienced Grandsire's slow to fail;
And if the harp pleased his gay youth, it rings
To his grave touch with no unready strings,
While thoughts press on, and feelings overflow,
And quick words round him fall like flakes of snow.

Thanks to the Powers that yet maintain their sway,
And have renewed the tributary Lay.
Truths of the heart flock in with eager pace,
And FANCY greets them with a fond embrace;
Swift as the rising sun his beams extends
She shoots the tidings forth to distant friends;
Their gifts she hails (deemed precious, as they prove
For the unconscious Babe an unbelated love!)

---

composed between about March 22 and 31, 1833

found in DC MSS. 107; 135; 137 (A) pp. 241–247 (MW), (B) pp. 241–247; MS. 1835/36 (MW); MS. 1836/45

published in *1835, 1836–*

classed Sentiment and Reflection *1836–*

reading text *1835*

title Sequel / To the Poem on the birth of a / First born Child March 1833 *rev to* Sequel—to the foregoing [March *inserted*] 1833 (ie [ie *rev to* viz] Lines, to a first born child, &c) *MS. 135* Sequel to the Foregoing. / March, 1833. *MS. 137* March, 1833. *om 1836–, 1839*

10 Each *entered in left margin; line underscored, possibly marked for del MS. 1836/45*

11 like *and* prayers *underscored and* like *alt* that *MS. 1836/45*

13 Upon each home-event] On like events of home *MS. 1835/36* Upon the events of home *1836–, 1839*

29 an unbelated] so prompt to *MS. 1836/45 (in pencil), 1840* so prompt a *1841–*

But from this peaceful centre of delight
Vague sympathies have urged her to take flight.
She rivals the fleet Swallow, making rings
In the smooth lake where'er he dips his wings:
—Rapt into upper regions, like the Bee
That sucks from mountain heath her honey fee;
Or, like the warbling Lark intent to shroud
His head in sunbeams or a bowery cloud,
She soars—and here and there her pinions rest
On proud towers, like this humble cottage, blest
With a new visitant, an infant guest—
Towers where red streamers flout the breezy sky
In pomp foreseen by her creative eye,
When feasts shall crowd the Hall, and steeple bells
Glad proclamation make, and heights and dells
Catch the blithe music as it sinks or swells;
And harboured ships, whose pride is on the sea,
Shall hoist their topmast flags in sign of glee,
Honouring the hope of noble ancestry.

But who (though neither reckoning ills assigned
By Nature, nor reviewing in the mind
The track that was, and is, and must be, worn
With weary feet by all of woman born)—
Shall *now* by such a gift with joy be moved,
Nor feel the fulness of that joy reproved?
Not He, whose last faint memory will command
The truth that Britain was his native land;
Whose infant soul was tutored to confide
In the cleansed faith for which her martyrs died;
Whose boyish ear the voice of her renown
With rapture thrilled; whose Youth revered the crown
Of Saxon liberty that Alfred wore,
Alfred, dear Babe, thy great Progenitor!
—Not He, who from her mellowed practice drew
His social sense of just, and fair, and true;
And saw, thereafter, on the soil of France
Rash Polity begin her maniac dance,
Foundations broken up, the deeps run wild,

---

30 from this peaceful *rev from* Fancy from this *MS. 135*
31 *rev from* Urged by vague sympathies She takes her [her *inserted*] flight *MS. 135*
32–33 *del MS. 1835/36; omitted 1836–, 1836Y, 1839*
32 She *rev from* And *MS. 135*
35 That sucks . . . her *rev from* Sucking . . . his [his *rev from* the] *MS. 135*
45 or] and *MS. 1835/36–, 1839*
49 though neither reckoning ills *rev from* though [?ne'er accoun]ting ills *rev from* omitting ills that are *MS. 135*
50 reviewing *rev from* viewing *rev from* retracing *rev from* reviewing *MS. 135*

Nor grieved to see, (himself not unbeguiled)—
Woke from the dream, the dreamer to upbraid,
And learn how sanguine expectations fade
When novel trusts by folly are betrayed,—
To see presumption, turning pale, refrain
From further havoc, but repent in vain,—
Good aims lie down, and perish in the road
Where guilt had urged them on, with ceaseless goad,
Till undiscriminating Ruin swept
The Land, and Wrong perpetual vigils kept;
With proof before her that on public ends
Domestic virtue vitally depends.

Can such a one, dear Babe! though glad and proud
To welcome Thee, repel the fears that crowd
Into his English breast, and spare to quake
Not for his own, but for thy innocent sake?

76–78 Proofs thickening round her that on public ends *MS. 1836/45 (in pencil), 1840–*
79/80 *pencil insertion:*
That civic strife by hourly calling forth
Mutual despite can turn the happiest hearth
(Thanks for the coming phrase) into a hell on earth *all rev in ink to*
And civic strife, by hourly calling forth
Mutual despite can turn the happiest hearth
Into a rankling sore of self tormented earth
alt in pencil:
That civic strife can turn the happiest hearth
Into a grievous sore of self-tormenting earth. *MS. 1836/45; 1840– as pencil alt*
83 Less for his own, than for thy innocent sake? *MS. 1836/45 (in pencil); so 1840– but no comma*

Too late—or, should the providence of God
Lead, through blind ways by sin and sorrow trod,
Justice and peace to a secure abode,
Too soon—thou com'st into this breathing world;
Ensigns of mimic outrage are unfurled.
Who shall preserve or prop the tottering Realm?
What hand suffice to govern the state-helm?
If, in the aims of men, the surest test
Of good or bad (whate'er be sought for or profest)
Lie in the means required, or ways ordained,
For compassing the end, else never gained;
Yet governors and govern'd both are blind
To this plain truth, or fling it to the wind;
If to expedience principle must bow;
Past, future, shrinking up beneath the incumbent Now;
If cowardly concession still must feed
The thirst for power in men who ne'er concede;
If generous Loyalty must stand in awe
Of subtle Treason, with his mask of law;
Or with bravado insolent and hard,
Provoking punishment, to win reward;
If office help the factious to conspire,
And they who *should* extinguish, fan the fire—
Then, will the sceptre be a straw, the crown
Sit loosely, like the thistle's crest of down;
To be blown off at will, by Power that spares it
In cunning patience, from the head that wears it.

Lost people, trained to theoretic feud;
Lost above all, ye labouring multitude!
Bewildered whether ye, by slanderous tongues

84–91 Too late [thou *del*] or sent too early, for fast bound
In endless cycle good and ill her round
Too late thou com'st into this breathing world
Ensigns of mimic outrage are unfurled;
Who shall preserve or prop the tottering Realm
Who [Who *rev from* Thou] save the good old Ship whose luckless helm
A Pilot grasps [grasps *rev from* ?brave] that plays the Wizards part
Storm raising after storm with treacherous art
If to confound the remnant of the crew
Who yet are sane in mind in spirit true
If in the aims of men the surest test &c *MS. 107*

84–86 Too late, or if from error and abuse
Of man's ambitions to a safe abode
God in his time a blessing shall educe *rev to*
Too late,—the blind and crooked road
Shall lead him, through the righteousness of God, *rev to text MS. 135*

85 Lead, *so 1845–* Lead *1835–1843* blind] dark *MS. 1836/45 (in pencil), 1840–*

100/101 Nor turn aside, unless to shape a way
For domination at some riper day; *MS. 1835/36–, 1836YR, 1839*

102 with] in *1836–, 1836YR, 1839*

Deceived, mistake calamities for wrongs;
And over fancied usurpations brood,
Oft snapping at revenge in sullen mood;
Or, from long stress of real injuries fly
To desperation for a remedy;
In bursts of outrage spread your judgments wide,
And to your wrath cry out, "Be thou our guide;"
Or, bound by oaths, come forth to tread earth's floor
In marshalled thousands, darkening street and moor
With the worst shape mock-patience ever wore;
Or, to the giddy top of self-esteem
By Flatterers carried, mount into a dream
Of boundless suffrage, at whose sage behest
Justice shall rule, disorder be suppress,
And every man sit down as Plenty's Guest!
—O for a bridle bitted with remorse
To stop your Leaders in their headstrong course!
Oh may the Almighty scatter with his grace
These mists, and lead you to a safer place,
By paths no human wisdom can foretrace!
May He pour round you, from worlds far above
Man's feverish passions, his pure light of love,
That quietly restores the natural mien
To hope, and makes truth willing to be seen!
Else shall your blood-stained hands in frenzy reap
Fields gaily sown when promises were cheap.
Why is the Past belied with wicked art,
The Future made to play so false a part,
Among a people famed for strength of mind,
Foremost in freedom, noblest of mankind?
We act as if we joyed in the sad tune
Storms make in rising, valued in the moon
Nought but her changes. Thus, ungrateful Nation!
If thou persist, and, scorning moderation,
Spread for thyself the snares of tribulation,
Whom, then, shall meekness guard? What saving skill
Lie in forbearance, strength in standing still?
—Soon shall the Widow (for the speed of Time
Nought equals when the hours are winged with crime)

---

119 your *rev from* their *MS. 137 (A)* their *MS. 137 (B)*
120 your . . . our] their . . . my *MS. 137 (B); so MS. 137 (A), then rev to text*
130 headstrong *rev from* headlong *MS. 137 (A)* headlong *MS. 137 (B)*
131–132 O may the Almighty, prodigal of Grace,
Lead back your judgementa to some safer place, *MS. 135*
140–142 How is the Past [Past *rev from* past] belied with wicked art,
Why plays Futurity this shameless part,
To cheat a People famed for strength of mind, *rev to text but l. 140* Future *rev from illeg eras MS. 135*

Widow, or Wife, implore on tremulous knee,
From him who judged her Lord, a like decree;
The skies will weep o'er old men desolate:
Ye Little-ones! Earth shudders at your fate,
Outcasts and homeless orphans——

But turn, my Soul, and from the sleeping Pair
Learn thou the beauty of omniscient care!
Be strong in faith, bid anxious thoughts lie still;
Seek for the good and cherish it—the ill
Oppose, or bear with a submissive will.

"He who defers his work from day to day"

He who defers his work from day to day
Does on a river's bank expecting stay,
Till the whole Stream which stopped him shall be gone
Which runs and as it runs for ever will run on.

---

155 will *rev from* shall *MS. 137 (A)* will *MS. 137 (B)*
156 at *rev from* for *MS. 137 (A)* for *MS. 137 (B)*
157–162 Outcasts and homeless. Gracious God
(Is it not sin such misery to forebode?)
How many blooming Girls with laughing eyes
May, e'er youth ends, [ends, *rev from* ?fle] be culled for sacrifice[,*del*]
Or when the expiating blood is spilt
May flee, the scape-goats of their Country's guilt,
Flee to the desart—there to sport and play,
Forgetting want and woe; the blind dismay
Of treacherous night, the ghastly shows of day.
But turn, my Soul, and, from the sleeping Pair
Learn thou the beauty of omniscient care!
Be soothed, be cheered, [?and] reconciled to Ill
Sufficient for the day, with patient will *rev to*
Outcasts and homeless orphans———
But turn, my Soul, and from the sleeping Pair
Learn thou the beauty of Omniscient care!
Give rest to anxious thought, let fear be still,
Sustained by Faith be reconciled to ill *rev to text MS. 135 (A) but l. 162 rev from* [?Restrain] or [?] with submissive will
160 lie *rev from* be *MS. 137 (A)*

---

composed probably on or near April 17, 1833
found in Lutwidge Family MS.
reading text Lutwidge Family MS.

To the Utilitarians.

Avaunt this œconomic rage!
What would it bring?—an iron age,
Where Fact with heartless search explored
Shall be Imagination's Lord,
And sway with absolute controul,
The god-like Functions of the Soul.
Not *thus* can knowledge elevate
Our Nature from her fallen state.
With sober Reason Faith unites
To vindicate the ideal rights
Of Human-kind—the true agreeing
Of objects with internal seeing,
Of effort with the end of Being.—

THE LABOURER'S NOON-DAY HYMN.

Up to the throne of God is borne
The voice of praise at early morn,
And he accepts the punctual hymn
Sung as the light of day grows dim.

Nor will he turn his ear aside
From holy offerings at noontide:
Then here reposing let us raise
A song of gratitude and praise.

What though our burthen be not light
We need not toil from morn to night;
The respite of the mid-day hour
Is in the thankful Creature's power.

Blest are the moments, doubly blest,
That, drawn from this one hour of rest,

---

composed May 5, 1833
found in WW to HCR, May 5, 1833
published in *PW* Knight 1889, vol. 7
reading text WW to HCR, May 5, 1833

---

composed in 1834, probably before mid-July
found in DC MS. 135, MS. 1835/36, MS. 1836/45
published in *1835, 1836–*
classed Sentiment and Reflection *1836–*
reading text *1835*
title *lacking MS. 106*
1 Up *rev from* The *MS. 135*

Are with a ready heart bestowed
Upon the service of our God!

Why should we crave a hallowed spot?
An Altar is in each man's cot,
A Church in every grove that spreads
Its living roof above our heads.

Look up to Heaven! the industrious Sun
Already half his race hath run;
He cannot halt nor go astray,
But our immortal Spirits may.

Lord! since his rising in the East,
If we have faltered or transgressed,
Guide, from thy love's abundant source,
What yet remains of this day's course:

Help with thy grace, through life's short day
Our upward and our downward way;
And glorify for us the west,
When we shall sink to final rest.

Love Lies Bleeding and *Companion to the Foregoing*

Love Lies Bleeding began as a sonnet that Wordsworth wrote in mid-February 1834 (see the first reading text, based on Dora Wordsworth's letter to Edward Quillinan, February 20, 1834). Wordsworth may have been prompted to deepen and broaden the symbolism of the flower's name by an exchange of letters between Dora Wordsworth and Edward Quillinan. In her letter to Quillinan of June 1–2, 1835, she prefaced her transcription of an expanded *Love Lies Bleeding* and its sequel thus: "Father is busy just now turning a sonnet on the flower 'Love lies bleeding' which he composed some time ago and w[ch] by mistake was omitted in the new Vol: [*Yarrow Revisited, and Other Poems*] into two poems[;] they are to make part of a series of 'Morning Voluntaries.'" She continued, "I hope your tender *Saudade* may be the subject of one of them—for nothing can be more poetical and he was much struck with the *meaning* when I read it to him in your first letter wherein that flower was named—." After she transcribed the poem and its sequel she added, "*N.B.* I send you these Poems as specimens from which you must judge whether Father may presume to write on *your* flower[.] *I* think he

---

13 Blest are the moments, *rev from* Blest moments, are they, *MS. 135*
17 Why should *alt* And if *MS. 1836/45* hallowed *rev from* sacred *MS. 135*
Each field is then a hallowed spot, *1845–*
25 rising *rev from* dawning *MS. 135*
32 final *WW rev from illeg word MS. 135*

may—the verses must make amends for this stupid letter[;] that was my hope in transcribing them." Her reference to "your tender *Saudade* . . . *your* flower" is explained by Quillinan's letters to her of March 10 and April 8, 1835. In the first he wrote that "perhaps the most beautiful and the most expressive word in the Portuguese language is *Saudade.* It means tenderness, sorrow, solicitude, longing, and every kind and melancholy thought and wish all blended into one feeling. There is a flower too of the name, an emblem of all this meaning—one word—one flower." In the second letter he translated a Portuguese love poem into English prose and then gave both English and Portuguese verse renditions, calling it "The Flower *Saudade* by Borges de Barros" (WL Letters). In her June 1–2 letter Dora passed on her father's words of praise for the translations—and a few of his suggestions for improvements in the rendering into English verse, indicating a degree of attention that suggests Wordsworth read Quillinan's translations and comments with care.

In any event, by June 1835, Wordsworth had expanded his poem, as yet untitled, to thirty-two lines and appended a sequel *Upon the same subject.* This expansion is represented by the second reading text of *Love Lies Bleeding* and the first of *Companion to the Foregoing,* both based on the copy in Dora's letter to Quillinan, June 1–2, 1835. The final stage of composition of *Love Lies Bleeding* and its companion poem is found in manuscripts preparatory to *Poems, Chiefly of Early and Late Years* (DC MSS. 143 and 151). The first ten lines of the thirty-two-line *Love Lies Bleeding* were revised and employed as an introductory paragraph for *Companion to the Foregoing.* In the opening of the new *Love Lies Bleeding* Wordsworth returned to the colloquial directness of the sonnet, retaining much of its language and its conclusion. The poems were published in *Poems, Chiefly of Early and Late Years* in June 1842; on this publication are based the third reading text of *Love Lies Bleeding* and the second of *Companion to the Foregoing.*

[Text of Dora W to EQ, February 20, 1834]

The Flower
Love lies Bleeding

They call it Love *lies* bleeding rather say
That in this crimson flower Love bleeding *droops*
A Flower how rich in sadness! thus it stoops
With languid head unpropped from day to day
From month to month, life passing not away
Even so the dying Gladiator leans
On Mother-earth and from his patience gleans

---

composed on or shortly before February 20, 1834
found in DC MS. 128; Dora W to EQ, February 20, 1834; Cornell MS. 9
reading text Dora W to EQ, February 20, 1834
title Love lies Bleeding *Cornell MS. 9*
4 languid *rev from* languished *Cornell MS. 9*
7 *rev from* And from his patience tenderest suffering gleans *Cornell MS. 9*

Relics of tenderest thought, regrets that stay
A moment and are gone—O fate bowed flower
Fair as Adonis bathed in sanguine dew
Of his death wound, *that* Lover's heart was true
As heaven, who pierced by scorn in some lone bower
Could press thy semblance of unpitied smart
Into the service of his constant heart.

[Text of Dora W to EQ, June 1–2, 1835]

To the Flower
Love lies bleeding

What keeps this flower reclined upon its bed
With unchanged aspect, when the rose is fled;
And files of stateliest plants have ceased to bloom,
Each in its turn submitting to like doom?
Never enlivened with the liveliest ray
That fosters growth, or checks or cheers decay,
Nor by the heaviest rain drops more depr est,
This lovely One, that once was summer's guest,
Preserves its beauty among falling leaves,
And to its mournful habits fondly cleaves.
You call it "*Love lies bleeding*"—so you may
Though the red Flower, not prostrate, only droops,
As we have seen it here, from day to day
From month to month, life passing not away;
A Flower how rich in sadness! Even thus stoops,
Sentient by Grecian Sculpture's marvellous power,
The dying Gladiator; thus he leans
Alone, with hanging brow, and body bent
Earthward, in uncomplaining languishment,

---

8 tenderest thought,] tenderest thought *Dora W to EQ* tenderest thought *rev from* tender thought *MS. 128* tenderest thoughts *rev to* tender thought *Cornell MS. 9*
11 Of *rev from* From *Cornell MS. 9* death *rev from* [?dear] *Cornell MS. 9*
pierced by scorn in some lone bower
~~slighted~~
scorned
12 As heaven, ~~who flouted by his Paramour~~ *Cornell MS. 9*
14 heart.] heart *Dora W to EQ*

---

composed around June 1, 1835
found in Dora W to EQ, June 1–2, 1835
reading text Dora W to EQ, June 1–2, 1835
1 bed *rev from* [?head] *Dora W to EQ*
3 stateliest] staliest *Dora W to EQ*
8 *no apos Dora W to EQ*

Yet not unblest while he from patience gleans
Reliques of tenderest thought. O fate-bowed flower
So drooped Adonis bathed in sanguine dew
Of his death-wound, while he from innocent air
His softest sweetest respiration drew,
Till Venus in a passion of despair,
Rent, weeping over him, her golden hair.
She suffer'd as Immortals sometimes do;
But keener pangs that gentle Lover knew
Who first, weighed down by scorn, in some lone bower
Did press this Semblance of unpitied smart
Into the service of his constant hea[rt]
And gave, sad Flower, the name that thou wilt ever bear!

[Text of 1842]

LOVE LIES BLEEDING.

YOU call it, "Love lies bleeding,"—so you may,
Though the red Flower, not prostrate, only droops,
As we have seen it here from day to day,
From month to month, life passing not away:
A flower how rich in sadness! Even thus stoops,
(Sentient by Grecian sculpture's marvellous power)
Thus leans, with hanging brow and body bent

31 hea[?rt] *(MS. torn) Dora W to EQ*

composed between June 1835 and March 1842
found in DC MSS. 143, 151.1, 151.2; MS. 1842P (MW)
published in *1842, 1845–*
classed Fancy *1845, 1850; unclassed 1846 (vol. 6)*
reading text *1842*
title *lacking MS. 151.1*
2 Though . . . prostrate] Tho' the red flower, not prostrate *over illeg eras MS. 143*
7 brow and body bent *alt in pencil* brow bent *MS. 143*

Earthward in uncomplaining languishment,
The dying Gladiator. So, sad Flower!
('Tis Fancy guides me willing to be led,
   Though by a slender thread,)
So drooped Adonis bathed in sanguine dew
Of his death-wound, when he from innocent air
The gentlest breath of resignation drew;
While Venus in a passion of despair
Rent, weeping over him, her golden hair
Spangled with drops of that celestial shower.
She suffered, as Immortals sometimes do;
But pangs more lasting far, *that* Lover knew
Who first, weighed down by scorn, in some lone bower
Did press this semblance of unpitied smart
Into the service of his constant heart,
His own dejection, downcast Flower! could share
With thine, and gave the mournful name which thou wilt ever bear.

Companion to the Foregoing

See the headnote to *Love Lies Bleeding* (pp. 262–263).

[Text of Dora W to EQ, January 1–2, 1835]

Upon the same subject

Narcissus cherishing a downcast mien,
The Laurel glittering with immortal green,
The spotted hyacinth, and poplars dank
Sighing in concert on a river's bank;

8–11 Earthward, in uncomplaining languishment;
Yet not unblest while he from patience gleans
Relics of tenderest thought! So, fate-bound flower!
Folllow me, ye who love to tread
Where Fancy leads [leads *rev from* ?flees], (tho' by a Slender [Slender *rev from* slender] Thread) *rev to*
Earthward in uncomplaining languish ment
The dying Gladiator, thus he leans
Along, with hanging brow and body bent *rev to text MS. 143*

10 guides *rev from* guided *MS. 151.1*

16 Rent *rev from* Went *MS. 1842P*

22 his *rev from* his own *MS. 151.2* his own *MS. 151.1*

24 mournful *inserted MS. 151.1*

---

composed around June 1, 1835
found in Dora W to EQ, June 1–2, 1835
reading text Dora W to EQ, June 1–2, 1835
title *rev in pencil by WW from* Continued *Dora W to EQ*

Speak—and remind the Intelligent how free
Were Poets once—how strong in sympathy.
They, touch'd at heart, with lapse of fountain clear,
Unmoved with impulses of viewless air
By bird or beast made vocal, found a cause
To solve the mystery, not in Nature's Laws
But in man's fortunes; hence a thousand tales
Sung to the plaintive lyre in classic Vales:
Nor doubt that something of their spirit swayed
The fancy-smitten Youth, by Hope betrayed,
Who, while he stood companionless, and eyed
This melancholy Flower in crimson dyed,
Thought of a wound that Death is slow to cure;
A fate which has endured and will endure;
And, with the parallel his passion feeding,
Called the dejected Lingerer
"LOVE LIES BLEEDING"

[Text of 1842]

COMPANION TO THE FOREGOING.

NEVER enlivened with the liveliest ray
That fosters growth or checks or cheers decay,
Nor by the heaviest rain-drops more deprest,
This Flower, that first appeared as summer's guest,
Preserved her beauty among summer leaves,
And to her mournful habits fondly cleaves.
When files of stateliest plants have ceased to bloom,
One after one submitting to their doom,
When her coevals each and all are fled,
What keeps her thus reclined upon her lonesome bed?
  The old mythologists, more impress'd than we
Of this late day by character in tree

---

5 Remind the Intelligent how strong how free *rev to*
speak [speak *rev to* Speak]—and remind the Intelligent how free *Dora W to EQ*
6 strong *rev from* bold *Dora W to EQ*

---

composed between June 1835 and March 1842
found in DC MSS. 143, 151.1, 151.2; MS. 1842P
published in *1842, 1845–*
classed Fancy *1845, 1850; unclassed 1846 (vol. 6)*
reading text *1842*
4 This *rev from* That *MS. 151.1*
5 Preserved *rev from* [?Resumed] *MS. 151.1* summer] falling *MS. 143*
Preserves her beauty mid autumnal leaves *1845–1849; so 1850 but* mid] 'mid
10 reclined *rev from* inclined *MS. 143*

Or herb, that claimed peculiar sympathy,
Or by the silent lapse of fountain clear,
Or with the language of the viewless air
By bird or beast made vocal, sought a cause
To solve the mystery, not in Nature's laws
But in Man's fortunes. Hence a thousand tales
Sung to the plaintive lyre in Grecian vales.
Nor doubt that something of their spirit swayed
The fancy-stricken youth or heart-sick maid,
Who, while each stood companionless and eyed
This undeparting Flower in crimson dyed,
Thought of a wound which death is slow to cure,
A fate that has endured and will endure,
And, patience coveting yet passion feeding,
Called the dejected Lingerer, *Love lies bleeding.*

WRITTEN IN AN ALBUM.

SMALL service is true service while it lasts;
  Of Friends, however humble, scorn not one:
The Daisy, by the shadow that it casts,
  Protects the lingering dew-drop from the Sun.

---

13 sympathy *rev from illeg word MS. 143*
21 heart-sick] love sick *rev to* heart sick *MS. 151.1*
22 and eyed *rev from* turned and eyed *MS. 151.2*
27 Lingerer *rev from* Lover *MS. 143* bleeding.] bleeding *1842*

---

composed around but by July 3, 1834
found in Rotha Q's Album; Dora W to Rotha Q, July 19, 1834; Swarthmore MS. 2; Rendell MS.; Berg MS. 6; MS. 1836/45
published in *1835, 1836–*
classed Inscriptions *1836, 1846* Miscellaneous Poems *1845, 1850*
reading text *1835*
title *untitled MSS.* WRITTEN IN THE ALBUM OF A CHILD. *1836, 1839, 1846* TO A CHILD. WRITTEN IN HER ALBUM. *1845, 1850*
2 Of humblest Friends bright Creature, scorn not one *MS. 1836/45*
Of humblest Friends, bright Creature! scorn not one: *1845, 1850*
4/ Rydal Mount / 3^{d} July 1834 *Rotha Q's Album* Wm Wordsworth / Rydal Mount / Jan 1st 1835 *Swarthmore MS. 2* Wm Wordsworth / Rydal Mount / 24th Decr 1835 *Rendell MS.* William Wordsworth / Rydal Mount / 8th June 1846 *Berg MS. 6*

Lines Suggested by a Portrait from the Pencil of F. Stone
and *The Foregoing Subject Resumed*

Wordsworth's composition of *Lines Suggested by a Portrait from the Pencil of F. Stone* and his work on its sequel, *The Foregoing Subject Resumed,* are closely intertwined, and, though the two poems were composed several months apart, they are presented here together to make evident their interrelationship. *Lines Suggested by a Portrait* was probably composed around the time the Wordsworths were preparing copy to send to the printer of *Yarrow Revisited, and Other Poems,* beginning in August 1834, and the latter poem was probably completed around November or December 1834, after the printing had begun. Dora Wordsworth transcribed a keeping copy of the earliest version of *Lines Suggested by a Portrait* (in DC MS. 130) probably at the same time as the copy sent to the printer (MS. 135), and the underlying text in these manuscripts and the uncorrected printed text in the earliest proof stages (MS. 137) show a poem of 120 to 123 lines that ends with a brief address to the portrait (see the *apparatus* below).

After the printer's copy was sent off, Wordsworth altered the poem to include a second part, breaking off the first part with the gnomic ending of the anecdote, "They are in truth the Substance, we the Shadows." Using this line as a subtitle, he turned the original conclusion to *Lines Suggested by a Portrait* into the opening of "Part 2nd," adding the extended simile of the angel at Bethesda's pool and in other ways expanding this portion to a total of forty-one lines. But the two-part state could not have lasted more than a day or two. For on a subsequent set of proofs, in which, however, the printer had not yet incorporated the poem in two parts that the poet had returned with earlier proof pages, Wordsworth revised and expanded *Lines Suggested by a Portrait* to conclude, as it did originally, with the address to the portrait (but now including the Bethesda simile). He then revised and expanded verses he originally added to "Part 2[d]" to form a new separate poem, *The Foregoing Subject Resumed.* A keeping copy of this poem was then made, showing also the revisions to the close of *Lines Suggested by a Portrait,* and this copy was placed with the earlier, unaltered, copy of the latter (all present in MS. 130).

Presentation of reading texts of the original version of *Lines Suggested by a Portrait* and the interim version in two parts has seemed inappropriate for several reasons: the short existence of the works as unique texts, the amount of duplication that would be required, and the nature of the alterations to the first two versions. These early versions can readily be derived from the list of variants reported beneath the reading text of *Lines Suggested by a Portrait.* For a general account of the vexed and complicated exchange of proofs between the Wordsworths and the printer of *Yarrow Revisited, and Other Poems,* see the descriptions of DC MSS. 135, 137, and 138 in the Manuscript Census.

A pencil drawing of a young woman that may be a portrait of Jemima Quillinan, elder daughter of Edward and Jemima Quillinan, survives in the album of her younger sister, Rotha (see Manuscript Census, p. lxxviii). The sketch is signed and dated "F. Stone / 18th Febry 1833." In the Fenwick note, however, referring to the poem's title, Wordsworth remarked that "this portrait" had "hung for many years in our principal sitting room" and comments on its "tone and general effect." He describes it also as being "thinly painted" and in the poem itself he mentions *golden* hair and *azure* eyes. He presumably refers to a painting rather than a pencil sketch. Though passing out of use, the term "pencil," as in Wordsworth's title and in line 74, was still used as late as 1859 to refer to "the smaller kinds of brushes" (*Oxford English Dictionary*). This is apparently the poet's own usage in two sonnets concerned with paintings, *To B. R. Haydon* composed in 1815 ("Or pencil pregnant with etherial hues," l. 3) and *To B. R. Haydon, Esq. On Seeing his Picture of Napoleon Buonaparte on the Island of St. Helena*, composed in 1831 ("thy pencil shown in truth of lines / And charm of colours," ll. 2–3; p. 222).

LINES

SUGGESTED BY A PORTRAIT FROM THE PENCIL OF F. STONE.

BEGUILED into forgetfulness of care
Due to the day's unfinished task, of pen
Or book regardless, and of that fair scene
In Nature's prodigality displayed
Before my window, oftentimes and long
I gaze upon a Portrait whose mild gleam
Of beauty never ceases to enrich
The common light; whose stillness charms the air,
Or seems to charm it, into like repose;
Whose silence, for the pleasure of the ear,
Surpasses sweetest music. There she sits
With emblematic purity attired
In a white vest, white as her marble neck
Is, and the pillar of the throat *would be*
But for the shadow by the drooping chin
Cast into that recess—the tender shade
The shade and light, both there and every where,
And through the very atmosphere she breathes,
Broad, clear, and toned harmoniously, with skill
That might from nature have been learnt in the hour
When the lone Shepherd sees the morning spread
Upon the mountains. Look at her, whoe'er

---

composed Probably between about July 17 and November 1834; revised November–December 1834
found in DC MSS. 130 (A) 1^r–4^r, (B) 5^r; 135; *(the following DC MSS. identified by signature)* 137 (A) M11–12, N1, (B) N1–3 (MW); 138 (A) O8–10, O10a, O11 (MW); 137 (C) O8–10, O10a (MW); 138 (B) O7–9 (MW); Lilly MS. 3, Melbourne MS. (ll. 79–91); MS. 1835/36; MS. 1836/45 (WW and JC)
published in *1835, 1836–*
classed Sentiment and Reflection *1836–*
reading text *1835*
title Stone] Stone Esqr *MS. 135*
subtitle Part 1st *MS. 138 (A)*
15 for *rev from* by *MS. 135*

---

15 In MS. 135 he copyist probably anticipated "by" later in the line.

Thou be, that kindling with a poet's soul
Hast loved the painter's true Promethean craft
Intensely—from Imagination take
The treasure, what mine eyes behold see thou,
Even though the Atlantic Ocean roll between.

A silver line, that runs from brow to crown,
And in the middle parts the braided hair,
Just serves to show how delicate a soil
The golden harvest grows in; and those eyes,
Soft and capacious as a cloudless sky
Whose azure depth their colour emulates,
Must needs be conversant with *upward* looks,
Prayer's voiceless service; but now, seeking nought
And shunning nought, their own peculiar life
Of motion they renounce, and with the head
Partake its inclination towards earth
In humble grace, and quiet pensiveness
Caught at the point where it stops short of sadness.

Offspring of soul-bewitching Art, make me
Thy confidant! say, whence derived that air
Of calm abstraction? Can the ruling thought
Be with some lover far away, or one
Crossed by misfortune, or of doubted faith?
Inapt conjecture! Childhood here, a moon
Crescent in simple loveliness serene,
Has but approached the gates of womanhood,
Not entered them; her heart is yet unpierced
By the blind Archer-god, her fancy free:
The fount of feeling, if unsought elsewhere,
Will not be found.

Her right hand, as it lies
Across the slender wrist of the left arm
Upon her lap reposing, holds—but mark
How slackly, for the absent mind permits
No firmer grasp—a little wild-flower, joined
As in a posy, with a few pale ears
Of yellowing corn, the same that overtopped

23–24 Thou be, that lov'st the Painter's subtle craft *MSS. 130, 135, 137 (A, B); MS. 137 (C) as (A, B) but rev to text except* Painter's *MS. 138 (A) as MS. 137 (A_1 and A_2) but rev to* That kindling with a poet's soul *then rev to text; MS. 138 (A_3) as text but* Poet's *rev to* poet's *and* Painter's

26 The *rev to* This *MSS. 137 (C), 138 (A)* This *rev to* The *MS. 138 (B)*

38 its *rev from* [?in] *rev from* [?in] its *MS. 135*

39 humble grace *rev from* meek content *MS. 135*

46 conjecture *rev from* solution *MS. 135*

51 unsought elsewhere *rev from* elsewhere unsought *MS. 135*

And in their common birthplace sheltered it
'Till they were plucked together; a blue flower
Called by the thrifty husbandman *a weed ;*
But Ceres, in her garland, might have worn
That ornament, unblamed. The floweret, held
In scarcely conscious fingers, was, she knows,
(Her Father told her so) in Youth's gay dawn
Her Mother's favourite; and the orphan Girl,
In her own dawn—a dawn less gay and bright,
Loves it while there in solitary peace
She sits, for that departed Mother's sake.
—Not from a source less sacred is derived
(Surely I do not err) that pensive air
Of calm abstraction through the face diffused
And the whole person.

Words have something told
More than the pencil can, and verily
More than is needed, but the precious Art
Forgives their interference—Art divine,
That both creates and fixes, in despite
Of Death and Time, the marvels it hath wrought.

Strange contrasts have we in this world of ours!
That posture, and the look of filial love
Thinking of past and gone, with what is left
Dearly united, might be swept away
From this fair Portrait's fleshly Archetype,
Even by an innocent fancy's slightest freak
Banished, nor ever, haply, be restored
To their lost place, or meet in harmony
So exquisite; but *here* do they abide,
Enshrined for ages. Is not then the Art
Godlike, a humble branch of the divine,
In visible quest of immortality,
Stretched forth with trembling hope? In every realm,
From high Gibraltar to Siberian plains,
Thousands, in each variety of tongue
That Europe knows, would echo this appeal;
One above all, a Monk who waits on God
In the magnific Convent built of yore

74–76 More than the pencil can; but, precious Art!
Forgive their interference, Art divine, *MS. 135*

83 fleshly] fleshy *1850*

90–94 In visible quest of Immortality, stretched forth
With trembling hope? From every realm
Thousands would echo this appeal, and are, *MS. 135*

To sanctify the Escurial palace. He,
Guiding, from cell to cell and room to room,
A British Painter (eminent for truth
In character, and depth of feeling, shown
By labours that have touched the hearts of kings,
And are endeared to simple cottagers)
Left not unvisited a glorious work,
Our Lord's Last Supper, beautiful as when first
The appropriate Picture, fresh from Titian's hand,
Graced the Refectory: and there, while both
Stood with eyes fixed upon that Masterpiece,
The hoary Father in the Stranger's ear
Breathed out these words:—"Here daily do we sit,
Thanks given to God for daily bread, and here
Pondering the mischiefs of these restless Times,
And thinking of my Brethren, dead, dispersed,
Or changed and changing, I not seldom gaze
Upon this solemn Company unmoved
By shock of circumstance, or lapse of years,
Until I cannot but believe that they—
They are in truth the Substance, we the Shadows."

So spake the mild Jeronymite, his griefs
Melting away within him like a dream
Ere he had ceased to gaze, perhaps to speak:
And I, grown old, but in a happier land,
Domestic Portrait! have to verse consigned
In thy calm presence those heart-moving words:
Words that can soothe, more than they agitate;
Whose spirit, like the angel that went down
Into Bethesda's pool, with healing virtue
Informs the fountain in the human breast
That by the visitation was disturbed.

---

101 hearts *rev from* hearts *MS. 137 (A)*

103 Left not unvisited] Came, in that service, to *1836–, 1839* Came, in that service, to *rev to* Left not unvisited *then reinstated by JC MS. 1836/45*

106–107 Graced the Refectory. There while the eyes
Of both upon that Master-piece were fixed[, *pencil*] *rev to text MS. 130 but see punct variants in nonverbal list; MS. 135 as orig MS. 130 but* Refectory; there *rev from* Refectory; there

117/118 *para and subhead:*
Part 2[d]
"They are in truth the Substance, we the Shadows" *MS. 138 (O10, O10a)*

122 have to verse consigned] do again repeat, *MS. 138 (O10a)*

123 those] his *MS. 138 (O10a)*

124–130 *lacking MSS. 130 (A), 135, 137 (A, B); MS. 137 (C) as MS. 137 (A), then rev to text but l. 129* mute,] mute

128 That] Which *1836–, 1839*

——But why this stealing tear? Companion mute,
On thee I look, not sorrowing; fare thee well,
My Song's Inspirer, once again farewell!

The pile of buildings, composing the palace and convent of San Lorenzo, has, in common usage, lost its proper name in that of the *Escurial*, a village at the foot of the hill upon which the splendid edifice, built by Philip the Second, stands. It need scarcely be added, that Wilkie is the painter alluded to.

THE FOREGOING SUBJECT RESUMED.

AMONG a grave fraternity of Monks,
For One, but surely not for One alone,
Triumphs, in that great work, the Painter's skill,

128/129 While year to year succeeded, man to man,
Thus, mid a grave Fraternity [Fraternity *rev from* fraternity] of Monks,
Has triumphed, through that Work, the Painter's skill,
Humbling the body to exalt the soul;
Or, shall I say? [say? *rev from* say,] exhibiting the warm
And breathing life of flesh, as clothed already
With no mean portion of the inheritance
Reserved for it in future worlds. Thou too,
Though but a simple Object [Object *rev from* object], into light
Called forth by those affections that endear
The private hearth; [hearth; *rev from* heart;] though keeping there thy seat
In singleness, and little tried by time,
Creation as it were of yesterday;
With a congenial function art endured [endured *rev from* endeared]
For each and all of us, together joined,
In course of nature, under this low roof,
By charities [*written over* In course] and duties that proceed
Out of the bosom of a wiser vow. [vow. *rev from* vow;]
To a like Salutary sense of awe,
Or sacred wonder, growing with the power
Of meditation that attempts to weigh,
In faithful scales, things and their opposites,
Can the enduring quiet gently raise
A household small and sensitive—whose love,
Dependent [Dependent *rev from* Dependant] as in part its blessings are
Upon frail ties dissolving or dissolved
On earth, will be reviewed, we trust, in heaven. *MS. 138 (O10a)*

131 And now, my song's Inspirer, fare thee well. [fare thee *rev in pencil to* fare-thee] *MS. 130 (A)* And now, my song's Inspirer fare thee well! *MS. 135; so MS. 137 (A, B) but* song's] Song's Inspirer] Inspirer, *MS. 137 (C) as MS. 137 (A), then rev to text*

---

composed November–December 1834
found in DC MSS. 130; 137 (MW); 138, pp. 307–308, (A) MW's note only, (B) MW's text; MS. 1835/36
published in *1835, 1836–*
classed Sentiment and Reflection *1836–*
reading text *1835*
title RESUMED] resumed *rev from* renewed *MS. 137*

For *The Foregoing Subject Resumed* as "Part 2nd" of *Lines on a Portrait,* see pp. 269 and 273n, above.

Humbling the body, to exalt the soul;
Yet representing, amid wreck and wrong
And dissolution and decay, the warm
And breathing life of flesh, as if already
Clothed with impassive majesty, and graced
With no mean earnest of a heritage
Assigned to it in future worlds. Thou, too,
With thy memorial flower, meek Portraiture!
From whose serene companionship I passed,
Pursued by thoughts that haunt me still; thou also—
Though but a simple object, into light
Called forth by those affections that endear
The private hearth; though keeping thy sole seat
In singleness, and little tried by time,
Creation, as it were, of yesterday—
With a congenial function art endued
For each and all of us, together joined,
In course of nature, under a low roof
By charities and duties that proceed
Out of the bosom of a wiser vow.
To a like salutary sense of awe,
Or sacred wonder, growing with the power
Of meditation that attempts to weigh,
In faithful scales, things and their opposites,
Can thy enduring quiet gently raise
A household small and sensitive,—whose love,
Dependent as in part its blessings are
Upon frail ties dissolving or dissolved
On earth, will be revived, we trust, in heaven.

In the class entitled "Musings," in Mr. Southey's Minor Poems, is one upon his own miniature Picture, taken in childhood, and another upon a landscape painted by Gaspar Poussin. It is possible that every word of the above verses, though similar in subject, might have been written had the author been unacquainted with those beautiful effusions of poetic sentiment. But, for his own satisfaction, he must be allowed thus publicly to acknowledge the pleasure those two poems of his Friend have given him, and the grateful influence they have upon his mind as often as he reads them, or thinks of them.

---

4 *lacking MSS. 130, 137; so MS. 138 (B) but line inserted*
5 Yet *rev from* By *MS. 138 (B)* By *MSS. 130, 137*
8–9 *rev from* Clothed with a portion of the inheritance *MS. 138 (B); MSS. 130, 137 as orig MS. 138 (B)*
11 *line inserted MS. 137* meek *del and reinserted twice MS. 137; inserted MS. 138 (B)*
13 still; thou also—] still *MS. 130*
14 Though but *rev from* Thought [?s] *MS. 137*
15 *rev from* Called forth by that endear *MS. 137*
19 art *rev from* are *MS. 137*
21 a *rev from* the *MS. 137*
32/ *note, first sentence:* entitled *rev from* of *MS. 138 (A)* of his Friend *lacking MS. 138 (B)* *third sentence:* have upon *rev from* have had upon *MS. 138 (B)* reads *rev from* [?looks] on *MS. 138 (B)*

"Desponding Father! mark this altered bough"

DESPONDING Father! mark this altered bough,
So beautiful of late, with sunshine warmed,
Or moist with dews; what more unsightly now,
Its blossoms shrivelled, and its fruit, if formed,
Invisible? yet Spring her genial brow
Knits not o'er that discolouring and decay
As false to expectation. Nor fret thou
At like unlovely process in the May
Of human life: a Stripling's graces blow,
Fade and are shed, that from their timely fall
(Misdeem it not a cankerous change) may grow
Rich mellow bearings, that for thanks shall call;
In *all* men, sinful is it to be slow
To hope—in *Parents,* sinful above all.

LINES

WRITTEN IN THE ALBUM OF THE COUNTESS OF ———.

Nov. 5, 1834.

LADY! a Pen, perhaps, with thy regard,
Among the Favoured, favoured not the least,
Left, 'mid the Records of this Book inscribed,
Deliberate traces, registers of thought
And feeling, suited to the place and time
That gave them birth:—months passed, and still this hand,

---

composed probably between the end of July and around November–December 1834
found in DC MSS. 107; 106; 137 (MW); MS. 1836/45
published in *1835, 1836–, 1838*
classed Miscellaneous Sonnets *1836–, 1838*
reading text *1835*
title Sonnet. *MS. 106*

---

composed probably around but by November 5, 1834
found in DC MSS. 106, 135; MS. 1836/45 (MW)
published in *1835, 1836–*
classed Inscriptions *1836, 1846* Miscellaneous Poems *1845, 1850*
reading text *1835*
title *lacking MS. 106* of———] of Lonsdale *1836–, 1839* Nov. 5, 1834. *so 1836– 1839; date lacking MS. 135* Nov. 5. 1834. *1835, 1836YR*

1 Lady, erewhile a willing Pen by thee, *MS. 106; so MS. 135 but* thee *rev to* Thee *no commas and line rev to text*

See the photographs and transcription of "Desponding Father! mark this altered bough," DC MS. 107, 56v–57r, pp. 758–761.

That had not been too timid to imprint
Words which the virtues of thy Lord inspired,
Was yet not bold enough to write of Thee.
And why that scrupulous reserve? In sooth
The blameless cause lay in the Theme itself.
Flowers are there many that delight to strive
With the sharp wind, and seem to court the shower,
Yet are by nature careless of the sun
Whether he shine on them or not; and some,
Where'er he moves along the unclouded sky,
Turn a broad front full on his flattering beams:
Others do rather from their notice shrink,
Loving the dewy shade,—a humble Band,
Modest and sweet, a Progeny of earth,
Congenial with thy mind and character,
High-born Augusta!

Towers, and stately Groves,
Bear witness for me; thou, too, Mountain-stream!
From thy most secret haunts; and ye Parterres,
Which she is pleased and proud to call her own;
Witness how oft upon my noble Friend
Mute offerings, tribute from an inward sense
Of admiration and respectful love,
Have waited, till the affections could no more
Endure that silence, and broke out in song;
Snatches of music taken up and dropt
Like those self-solacing those under notes
Trilled by the redbreast, when autumnal leaves
Are thin upon the bough. Mine, only mine,
The pleasure was, and no one heard the praise,
Checked, in the moment of its issue checked;
And reprehended by a fancied blush
From the pure qualities that called it forth.

10–11 And why?—the cause lay in the Theme itself. *MS. 106, then rev to text but* that] this
14 by nature *rev from* [?instinctly] *MS. 106*
16 unclouded *inserted MS. 135*
18 their] his *MS. 106*
22 Towers . . . Groves,] Witness Towers, and Groves! *1836–*
23 Mountain-stream *rev from* [?Lowther] Stream *MS. 135* Lowther stream *MS. 106*
And Thou, wild Stream, that giv'st the honoured name
Of Lowther to this ancient Line, bear witness *1836–, 1839*
24–25 *inserted MS. 106*
25 and *rev from* to *MS. 106*
32 those under *rev from* the under *MS. 106* notes *rev from* [?tunes] *MS. 135*

Thus Virtue lives debarred from Virtue's meed;
Thus, Lady, is retiredness a veil
That, while it only spreads a softening charm
O'er features looked at by discerning eyes,
Hides half their beauty from the common gaze;
And thus, even on the exposed and breezy hill
Of lofty station, female goodness walks,
When side by side with lunar gentleness,
As in a cloister. Yet the grateful Poor
(Such the immunities of low estate,
Plain Nature's enviable privilege,
Her sacred recompence for many wants)
Open their hearts before Thee, pouring out
All that they think and feel, with tears of joy;
And benedictions not unheard in Heaven:
And friend in the ear of friend, where speech is free
To follow truth, is eloquent as they.

Then let the Book receive in these prompt lines
A just memorial; and thine eyes consent
To read that they, who mark thy course, behold
A life declining with the golden light
Of summer, in the season of sere leaves;
See cheerfulness undamped by stealing Time;
See studied kindness flow with easy stream,
Illustrated with inborn courtesy;
And an habitual disregard of self
Balanced by vigilance for others' weal.

39–43 *inserted MS. 106*

39 Thus virtue is self-robbed of virtues due; *MS. 106* lives debarred from *rev from* is self robbed of *MS. 135*

41 That while it only spreads *rev from* Which while it overspreads *MS. 106*

42 O'er *rev from* On *MSS. 106, 135*

44 And thus, even *rev from* Thus Lady! *though orig reading not del MS. 106* thus] hence *rev in pencil to* thus *MS. 1836/45*

56 Then shall the Page [Page *rev to* page], before me spread, receive *MS. 106; MS. 135 as orig MS. 106, rev to*

Then let the Book receive and take in charge *rev to text*

56/57 Rich as it is in tokens of esteem *inserted then del MS. 135*

57 A *rev from* This *MS. 135* This *MS. 106*

59 golden *rev from* [?yellow] *MS. 106*

62 See *rev to* And *MS. 135* flow with easy stream,] feelingly allied *alt* flow with easy stream *MS. 106; MS. 135 as orig MS. 106 but rev in pencil and ink to text*

63–64 With inborn courtesy; in every act
And habit utter disregard of Self, *rev to*
Illustrated by [by *rev from* with] inborn courtesy;
See [*rev from* In act] an habitual disregard of Self, *MS. 106; MS. 135 as orig MS. 106 but rev to text*

And shall the verse not tell of lighter gifts
With these ennobling attributes conjoined
And blended, in peculiar harmony,
By Youth's surviving spirit? What agile grace!
A nymph-like liberty, in nymph-like form,
Beheld with wonder; whether floor or path
Thou tread, or on the managed steed art borne,
Fleet as the shadows, over down or field,
Driven by strong winds at play among the clouds.

Yet one word more—one farewell word—a wish
Which came, but it has passed into a prayer,
That, as thy sun in brightness is declining,
So, at an hour yet distant for *their* sakes
Whose tender love, here faltering on the way
Of a diviner love, will be forgiven,—
So may it set in peace, to rise again
For everlasting glory won by faith.

66–70 And shall [?a] verse not tell?—[*dash del*] (surely it may,)
[for mutual pleasure and support *inserted then del*]
Oerlooking else peculiar attributes
Else by the spirit of harmony and grace
Deservedly reproved [reproved *rev from* approved] shall it not tell
Of nymph-like liberty, in nymph-like form, *all above rev to*
And shall the Verse not tell? (surely it may,)
Of lighter gifts and [humbler *inserted*] attributes (with these
Harmoniously conjoined)—of agile grace,
A nymph-like liberty, in nymph-like form, *MS. 106*
And shall the Verse not tell—(surely it may)
Of lighter gifts and humbler attributes
Harmoniously conjoined of agile grace
Of nymph-like liberty, in nymph-like form, *MS. 135, then rev to text but l. 66* verse] Verse *l. 67* conjoined] conjoined, *l. 68* And blended . . . harmony, *rev from* Joined . . . harmony with these,

72 Thou tread, or sweep—borne on the managed steed— *1836–, 1839 but* tread,] tread; *1845–*

73 *rev from* Fleeter than shadows, oer the field and down, *MS. 106*

78–82 God's favour still vouchsafed, so may it set
And be the hour yet distant for our sakes,
To rise again in glory won by Faith! *MS. 106, rev to text but l. 78* So,] —So, *rev to* So— *no ital l. 79* love,] love faltering] faultering on] in *l. 80* love,] love forgiven,—] forgiven
Gods favour still vouchsafed, so may it set,
To rise again in glory won by Faith. *MS. 135, then rev to text but l. 79* faltering *rev from* faultering

"Fairy skill"

Fairy skill,
Fairy's hand,
And a quill
From fairy-land,
Album small!
Are needed all
To write in you;
So adieu
W.W.—

THE REDBREAST.

(SUGGESTED IN A WESTMORELAND COTTAGE.)

DRIVEN in by Autumn's sharpening air,
From half-stripped woods and pastures bare,
Brisk Robin seeks a kindlier home:
Not like a beggar is he come,
But enters as a looked-for guest,
Confiding in his ruddy breast,
As if it were a natural shield

---

composed probably around December 1834 or shortly after
found in Dora Harrison's album *(untraced)*
reading text Catalogue 200 of Dawsons of Pall Mall (1969)

---

composed probably around late December 1834
found in DC MSS. 106; 133; 135; 137 (A) pp. 257–260 (MW), (B) pp. 261–264; 138; MS. 1835/36
published in *1835, 1836–*
classed Affections *1836–*
reading text *1835*
title *lacking MS. 133*
1–70 *WW's draft lines spanning nearly the entire poem:*
And when driven in by nipping air
From leafless [leafless *over illeg wd*] and pastures bare
Bold Robin shews his scarlet breast
No beggar but a parlour guest
[And when the bird with scarlet breast *del*]
[Enter the parlour a bold guest *del*]
Withall [Withall *rev from* With all] a prime ventriloquist
Who seen by glimpses now now missed
Puzzles the Listener with a doubt
If the sweet voice he throws about
Comes from within doors or without
Whether the bird flit here or there
Oer table lilt or perch on chair
Tho [?they] &c *MS. 106*
2 half-stripped woods *rev from* rustling leaves *MS. 133* stripped *over illeg eras MS. 135*
3 Brisk] Bold *alt* Brisk *MS. 133* kindlier] kinder *MS. 133*
4 like] as *MS. 133*

Charged with a blazon on the field,
Due to that good and pious deed
Of which we in the Ballad read.
But pensive fancies putting by,
And wild-wood sorrows, speedily
He plays the expert ventriloquist;
And, caught by glimpses now—now missed,
Puzzles the listener with a doubt
If the soft voice he throws about
Comes from within doors of without!
Was ever such a sweet confusion,
Sustained by delicate illusion?
He's at your elbow—to your feeling
The notes are from the floor or ceiling;
And there's a riddle to be guessed,
'Till you have marked his heaving breast,
Where tiny sinking, and faint swell,
Betray the Elf that loves to dwell
In Robin's bosom, as a chosen cell.

Heart-pleased we smile upon the Bird
If seen, and with like pleasure stirred
Commend him, when he's only heard.
But small and fugitive *our* gain
Compared with *his* who long hath lain,
With languid limbs and patient head,
Reposing on a lone sick-bed;
Where now he daily hears a strain
That cheats him of too busy cares,
Eases his pain, and helps his prayers.
And who but this dear Bird beguiled

---

8 on] in *MS. 133*
11 pensive fancies putting *rev from* putting pensive fancies *MS. 133*
15 listener *WW alt* In-mate *MS. 133*
17–57 Free passage [finds he *inserted*] thro' his ~~humble~~ cot
How happy in his present lot
~~He finds and happy is his lot~~
this bit of sunny weather
And when ~~the sunny time is past~~
That thus brings Man and bird together
~~casement~~
~~The doors close shut the window fast~~
Shall like a pleasant dream be past *MS. 133*
18 confusion *rev from* delusion *MS. 135*
23 'Till you have] Until you've *MSS. 135, 137 (A, B), 138* breast] chest *MS. 1835/36–*
24 And busy throat whose sink and swell, *MS. 1835/36–, 1839*
31 his *ital*] hers *ital 1845–*
34 now he daily] every day he *MS. 135* now she daily *1845–*
35 him] her *1845–*
36 his . . . his] her . . . her *1845–*

The fever of that pale-faced Child?
Now cooling, with his passing wing,
Her forhead, like a breeze of Spring;
Recalling now, with descant soft
Shed round her pillow from aloft,
Sweet thoughts of angels hovering nigh,
And the invisible sympathy
Of "Mathew, Mark, and Luke, and John,
Blessing the bed she lies upon:"*
And sometimes, just as listening ends
In slumber, with the cadence blends
A dream of that low-warbled hymn
Which Old-folk, fondly pleased to trim
Lamps of faith now burning dim,
Say that the Cherubs carved in stone,
When clouds gave way at dead of night,
And the moon filled the church with light,
Used to sing in heavenly tone,
Above and round the sacred places
They guard, with wingèd baby-faces.

* The words—

"Mathew, Mark, and Luke, and John,
Bless the bed that I lie on,"

are part of a child's prayer, still in general use through the northern counties.

39–40 *lacking MSS. 135, 137 (A); so MS. 137 (B), but rev to*
Now cooling, like a breeze of Spring,
Her cheek and brow with passing wing;
39 *rev from* Now cooling like a breeze of spring *MS. 138*
41–42 Recalling, while his descant soft
Fell on her pillow from aloft, *MSS. 135, 137 (A); MS. 138 as MS. 135 but rev to text; MS. 137 (B) as MS. 135 but del and l. 41 rev to text but* now,] now
42 *lacking MS. 137 (B)*
46 *note lacking MSS. 135, 137 (B); inserted MS. 137 (A)*
47–49 Or, haply [haply *rev from* hapily], of that earthly hymn *MS. 135; MS. 137 (B) as MS. 135 rev; MS. 137 (A) as MS. 137 (B) but rev to text*
50–55 Which Old-Folk fond of legends [legends *rev from* legions] dim
Say that the Cherubs carved in stone,
Warble forth with heavenly tone, *MS. 135*
53–54 When stricken by a gleam of light
From the full moon at dead of night *MS. 137 (B); so MS. 137 (A) rev to text but l. 54* And] And,
54 And the ancient church was filled with light, *MS. 1835/36–*
55 sing *rev from* chant *MS. 137 (A)* chant *MS. 137 (B)*

Thrice-happy Creature! in all lands
Nurtured by hospitable hands:
Free entrance to this cot has he,
Entrance and exit both *yet* free;
And, when the keen unruffled weather
That thus brings man and bird together,
Shall with its pleasantness be past,
And casement closed and door made fast,
To keep at bay the howling blast,
He needs not fear the season's rage,
For the whole house is Robin's cage.
Whether the bird flit here or there,
O'er table *lilt,* or perch on chair,
Though some may frown, and make a stir
To scare him as a trespasser,
And he belike will flinch or start,
Good friends he has to take his part;
One chiefly, who with voice and look
Pleads for him from the chimney nook,
Where sits the Dame, and wears away
Her long and vacant holiday;
With images about her heart,
Reflected, from the years gone by,
On human nature's second infancy.

---

58 all lands] every land *MS. 133*

59 Nurtured with [thy *inserted*] hospitable hand *MS. 133*

60 this *rev to* that *MS. 133*

62 And] But *alt* And *MS. 133* the *rev from* this *MS. 133* keen unruffled *rev from* respite of calm *MS. 137 (A)* respite of calm *MSS. 133, 137 (B); MS. 135 as MS. 133 but* calm *rev from* fine

64 with its pleasantness *rev from* like a pleasant dream *MS. 137 (A)* like a pleasant dream *MSS. 133, 135, 137 (B)*

The door clos

65 The casement shut the door made fast *rev to*
And [And *rev to* The] door close shut the casement fast *del MS.* 133_1 casement . . . door *rev from* casements . . . doors *MS.* 133_2

66 *lacking MSS. 133, 135, 137 (B); inserted MS. 137 (A)*

67 needs *rev from* need *MS. 135* need *MS. 133*

71 If some there be that make a stir *rev to*
If some should frown and make a stir *MS. 133, MS. 135 as rev MS. 133 but* frown] frown, *MS. 137 (A) as rev MS. 135*
Though . . . may *rev from* If . . . should *MSS. 137 (B), 138*

73 And *rev from* Though *MSS. 137 (B), 138* Though *MSS. 133, 135, 137 (A)*

74 He wants [wants *rev to* lacks] not friends to take his part *MS. 133*

80 years *rev from* hours *MS. 135* times *MS. 133*

UPON SEEING A COLOURED DRAWING OF THE BIRD OF PARADISE IN AN ALBUM.

WHO rashly strove thy Image to portray?
Thou buoyant minion of the tropic air;
How could he think of the live creature—gay
With a divinity of colours—drest
In all her brightness, from the dancing crest
Far as the last gleam of the filmy train
Extended and extending to sustain
The motions that it graces—and forbear
To drop his pencil! Flowers of every clime
Depicted on these pages smile at time;
And gorgeous insects copied with nice care
Are here, and likenesses of many a shell
Tossed ashore by restless waves,
Or in the diver's grasp fetched up from caves
Where sea-nymphs might be proud to dwell:
But whose rash hand (again I ask) could dare,
'Mid casual tokens and promiscuous shows,
To circumscribe this shape in fixed repose;
Could imitate for indolent survey,
Perhaps for touch profane,
Plumes that might catch, but cannot keep a stain;
And, with cloud-streaks lightest and loftiest, share
The sun's first greeting, his last farewell ray!

Resplendent Wanderer! followed with glad eyes
Where'er her course; mysterious Bird!
To whom, by wondering Fancy stirred,
Eastern Islanders have given
A holy name—the Bird of Heaven!
And even a title higher still,
The Bird of God! whose blessed will
She seems performing as she flies
Over the earth and through the skies
In never-wearied search of Paradise—

---

composed begun June 23, 1835; completed by December 1836
found in Princeton MS. 1; MS. 1836/45 (JC)
published in *1836–, 1839*
classed Sentiment and Reflection *1836–; unclassed 1839*
reading text *1836*
title coloured *inserted Princeton MS. 1*
3 gay] drest *Princeton MS. 1*
4 *omitted Princeton MS. 1*
9 his] the *Princeton MS. 1*
25 her] his *Princeton MS. 1*
31 She . . . she] He . . . he *Princeton MS. 1*

Region that crowns her beauty, with the name
She bears for *us*—for us how blest,
How happy at all seasons, could like aim
Uphold our Spirits urged to kindred flight
On wings that fear no glance of God's pure sight,
No tempest from his breath, their promised rest
Seeking with indefatigable quest
Above a world that deems itself most wise
When most enslaved by gross realities.

AIREY-FORCE VALLEY.

—Not a breath of air
Ruffles the bosom of this leafy glen.
From the brook's margin, wide around, the trees
Are stedfast as the rocks; the brook itself,
Old as the hills that feed it from afar,
Doth rather deepen than disturb the calm
Where all things else are still and motionless.
And yet, even now, a little breeze, perchance
Escaped from boisterous winds that rage without,
Has entered, by the sturdy oaks unfelt;
But to its gentle touch how sensitive
Is the light ash! that, pendent from the brow
Of yon dim cave, in seeming silence makes
A soft eye-music of slow-waving boughs,
Powerful almost as vocal harmony
To stay the wanderer's steps and soothe his thoughts.

---

34 her] his *Princeton MS. 1*
35 She] He *Princeton MS. 1*
38 On *rev from* [?By] *Princeton MS. 1*
42 by *rev from* to *Princeton MS. 1*

---

composed September 28–29, 1835
found in DC MSS. 89, 139, 151.1, 151.2; WW to Joshua Watson, October 5, 1835
published in *1842, 1845–*
classed Imagination *1845, 1850; unclassed 1846 (vol. 6)*
reading text *1842*
title *lacking MS. 139, WW to Joshua Watson*
1 a *inserted MS. 89*
4/5 Following, in patient solitude a course *MS. 89*
5 it] it *illeg word del MS. 151.1*
12 that *alt in pencil* which *MS. 151.2*
15 Powerful] Powerfull *rev from* Powerless *MS. 151.1*

TO THE MOON.

(COMPOSED BY THE SEA-SIDE,—ON THE COAST OF CUMBERLAND.)

WANDERER! that stoop'st so low, and com'st so near
To human life's unsettled atmosphere;
Who lov'st with Night and Silence to partake,
So might it seem, the cares of them that wake;
And, through the cottage-lattice softly peeping,
Dost shield from harm the humblest of the sleeping;
What pleasure once encompassed those sweet names
Which yet in thy behalf the Poet claims,
An idolizing dreamer as of yore!—
I slight them all; and, on this sea-beat shore
Sole-sitting, only can to thoughts attend
That bid me hail thee as the SAILOR'S FRIEND;
So call thee for heaven's grace through thee made known
By confidence supplied and mercy shown,
When not a twinkling star or beacon's light
Abates the perils of a stormy night;
And for less obvious benefits, that find
Their way, with thy pure help, to heart and mind;
Both for the adventurer starting in life's prime;
And veteran ranging round from clime to clime,
Long-baffled hope's slow fever in his veins,
And wounds and weakness oft his labour's sole remains.

The aspiring Mountains and the winding Streams
Empress of Night! are gladdened by thy beams;

---

composed probably around October 1835
found in Dr. Williams's Library MS.; Princeton MS. 2; MS. 1836/45 (MW)
published in *1836–, 1839*
classed Evening Voluntaries *1836–, 1839*
reading text *1836*
title CUMBERLAND.)] Cumberland) / Oct. 1835 *rev to* Cumberland) *Princeton MS. 2*
1 com'st *rev from* comest *Princeton MS. 2*
19 adventurer *rev from* adventurers *Princeton MS. 2*
20 round] [?thus] *rev to* on *Princeton MS. 2*
21 hope's slow] hopes, slow *Princeton MS. 2*
23 winding *JC rev from* aspiring *Princeton MS. 2*

See the photographs and transcriptions of Dr. Williams's Library MS. on pp. 762–765.

A look of thine the wilderness pervades,
And penetrates the forest's inmost shades;
Thou, chequering peaceably the minster's gloom,
Guid'st the pale Mourner to the lost one's tomb;
Canst reach the Prisoner—to his grated cell
Welcome, though silent and intangible!—
And lives there one, of all that come and go
On the great waters toiling to and fro,
One, who has watched thee at some quiet hour
Enthroned aloft in undisputed power,
Or crossed by vapoury streaks and clouds that move
Catching the lustre they in part reprove—
Nor sometimes felt a fitness in thy sway
To call up thoughts that shun the glare of day,
And make the serious happier than the gay?

Yes, lovely Moon! if thou so mildly bright
Dost rouse, yet surely in thy own despite,
To fiercer mood the phrenzy-stricken brain,
Let me a compensating faith maintain;
That there's a sensitive, a tender, part
Which thou canst touch in every human heart,
For healing and composure.—But, as least
And mightiest billows ever have confessed
Thy domination; as the whole vast Sea
Feels through her lowest depths thy sovereignty;
So shines that countenance with especial grace
On them who urge the keel her *plains* to trace
Furrowing its way right onward. The most rude,
Cut off from home and country, may have stood—
Even till long gazing hath bedimmed his eye,
Or the mute rapture ended in a sigh—

---

28 Guid'st *JC rev from* Guides *Princeton MS. 2*
33 has . . . thee at *rev from* have . . . at *Princeton MS. 2*
37 sometimes] sometime *Princeton MS. 2*
46 But] Yet *Princeton MS. 2*
48 domination *rev from* admonition *Princeton MS. 2*

Touched by accordance of thy placid cheer,
With some internal lights to memory dear,
Or fancies stealing forth to soothe the breast
Tired with its daily share of earth's unrest,—
Gentle awakenings, visitations meek;
A kindly influence whereof few will speak,
Though it can wet with tears the hardiest cheek.

And when thy beauty in the shadowy cave
Is hidden, buried in its monthly grave;
Then, while the Sailor, mid an open sea
Swept by a favouring wind that leaves thought free,
Paces the deck—no star perhaps in sight,
And nothing save the moving ship's own light
To cheer the long dark hours of vacant night—
Oft with his musings does thy image blend,
In his mind's eye thy crescent horns ascend,
And thou art still, O Moon, that SAILOR'S FRIEND!

---

49 depths] Depths *rev from* depth *Princeton MS. 2*
56 Touched by] Touched by, *rev from* Touches *Princeton MS. 2*
56–58 *Transcriptions from MS. 1836/45, vol. 5:*
And O dear soother of the pensive breast
Let homelier words without offence attest
How, whereon random topics as they hit
The moment's humour, rough Tars spend their wit
Thy changes, which to wiser Spirits seem
Dark as a riddle prove a favourite theme
Thy motions intricate and manifold
Oft help to make bold fancy's flights more bold
Beget strange therores and to freaks give birth
Of speech as wild as ever heightened mirth. *p. 281, MW's pencil*
And O dear soother of the pensive breast
verse
Let ~~words~~ as true without offence attest
How when these self-taught students of the sky
Turn boon-companionship to jolity
And in bold talk on objects that befit
The humours of the time discharge their wit
Thy aspects, hopeless riddles as they seem
many
To graver heads, oft prove a favourite theme
Thy motions intricate and manifold
Incite each mounting Spirit to uphold
Its own sage theory or to freaks give birth
Of speech as quaint as ever heightened mirth *verso of first endpaper, WW's pencil*
Turn lax enjoyment into *recto of second endpaper, WW's pencil*

TO THE MOON.

(RYDAL.)

QUEEN of the stars!—so gentle, so benign,
That ancient Fable did to thee assign,
When darkness creeping o'er thy silver brow
Warned thee these upper regions to forego,
Alternate empire in the shades below—
A Bard, who, lately near the wide-spread sea
Traversed by gleaming ships, looked up to thee
With grateful thoughts, doth now thy rising hail
From the close confines of a shadowy vale.
Glory of night, conspicuous yet serene,
Nor less attractive when by glimpses seen
Through cloudy umbrage, well might that fair face,
And all those attributes of modest grace,
In days when Fancy wrought unchecked by fear,
Down to the green earth fetch thee from thy sphere,
To sit in leafy woods by fountains clear!

O still belov'd (for thine, meek Power, are charms
That fascinate the very Babe in arms,
While he, uplifted towards thee, laughs outright,
Spreading his little palms in his glad Mother's sight)
O still belov'd, once worshipped! Time, that frowns
In his destructive flight on earthly crowns,
Spares thy mild splendour; still those far-shot beams
Tremble on dancing waves and rippling streams
With stainless touch, as chaste as when thy praise
Was sung by Virgin-choirs in festal lays;
And through dark trials still dost thou explore
Thy way for increase punctual as of yore,
When teeming Matrons—yielding to rude faith
In mysteries of birth and life and death
And painful struggle and deliverance—prayed
Of thee to visit them with lenient aid.

---

composed probably around October 1835
found in Dr. Williams's Library MS., Princeton MS. 3
published in *1836–, 1839*
classed Evening Voluntaries *1836–, 1839*
reading text *1836*
4 thee . . . upper *rev from* that . . . nether *Princeton MS. 3*
14 days *rev from* times *Princeton MS. 3*
16 in *rev from* on *Princeton MS. 3*
17 are *rev from* [?be] *Princeton MS. 3*
25 as *JC inserted Princeton MS. 3*

See the photographs and transcriptions of Dr. Williams's Library MS. on pp. 762–765.

What though the rites be swept away, the fanes
Extinct that echoed to the votive strains;
Yet thy mild aspect does not, cannot cease,
Love to promote and purity and peace;
And Fancy, unreproved, even yet may trace
Faint types of suffering in thy beamless face.

Then, silent Monitress! let us—not blind
To worlds unthought of till the searching mind
Of Science laid them open to mankind—
Told, also, how the voiceless heavens declare
God's glory; and acknowledging thy share
In that blest charge; let us—without offence
To aught of highest, holiest, influence—
Receive whatever good 'tis given thee to dispense.
May sage and simple, catching with one eye
The moral intimations of the sky,
Learn from thy course, where'er their own be taken,
'To look on tempests, and be never shaken;'
To keep with faithful step the appointed way
Eclipsing or eclipsed, by night or day,
And from example of thy monthly range
Gently to brook decline and fatal change;
Meek, patient, stedfast, and with loftier scope,
Than thy revival yields, for gladsome hope!

---

44 *rev from* In that blest change; / Let us without offence *Princeton MS. 3*
46 thee *JC rev from* us *Princeton MS. 3*
51 To keep *rev from* [?] [?help] *Princeton MS. 3*

Poems Written after the Death of Charles Lamb

Three versions of Wordsworth's memorial verses to Charles Lamb are presented below. The first reading text is based on an *Epitaph* that Wordsworth wrote at the request of Mary Lamb, Charles's sister, on November 19, 1835, ten months after Lamb's sudden death at the close of 1834. The text for this earliest version follows Mary Wordsworth's fair copy of "the requested Epitaph" that she transcribed in William's letter to Edward Moxon of November 20, 1835 (*LY*, III, 114–117); Wordsworth hoped it would serve as an inscription for Lamb's grave in Edmonton Church. Appended to this text are the variants found in the November 20 letter to Moxon and the revisions Wordsworth offered in his November 23 letter, also to Moxon (*LY*, III, 119).

The second reading text, then, is based on the thirty-eight-line poem found in Wordsworth's letter to Moxon of November 24. On this date he sent a fresh copy, again transcribed by Mary Wordsworth, incorporating the earlier changes and some further ones (*LY*, III, 120). Moxon must have printed in this form at once. The resulting pamphlet, *Epitaph*, survives in a unique copy in the Ashley Library (BL), and includes the November 23 and 24 revisions. This pamphlet form of the poem arrived at Rydal Mount on November 28 or shortly after (*LY*, III, 126 and 143; the second letter is misdated "[mid-December 1835]" but must surely have followed immediately after the November 28 letter). Wordsworth distributed copies of the pamphlet *Epitaph* to Mary Lamb and other friends in early December (*LY*, III, 130). Appended to the second reading text are the variants from the pamphlet *Epitaph* (which blends readings from the several letters).

However, Mary Lamb objected to the length of Wordsworth's poem as it now stood, as an inscription, and also to the mention in it of Lamb's "troubles" (see the notes to the third reading text—that is, the text of 1836). Only lines 30, 31, and 38 of the second version were eventually used for an inscription inside Edmonton church. (H. F. Cary, Lamb's friend, composed the lines that are actually cut in the stone marking the grave of Charles and Mary Lamb.) The inscription appears on a memorial to William Cowper, John Keats, and Charles Lamb, all three writers having been associated with the village. Beneath a medallion of Lamb is the inscription:

> In Memory of Charles Lamb, the gentle Elia, and author of the Tales from Shakespeare. Born in the Inner Temple 1775, educated at Christ's Hospital, died at Bay Cottage, Edmonton, 1834, and buried beside his sister Mary in the adjoining churchyard—
>
> . . . At the centre of his being lodged
> A soul by resignation sanctified . . .
> O, he was good, if e'er a good Man lived.

Mary Lamb died May 20, 1847 (E. V. Lucas, *The Life of Charles Lamb* [2 vols.; London, 1905; 3d ed., 1906], II, 279–280, 288).

In sending the first set of revisions to Moxon on November 23, Wordsworth had expressed his "regret in not having touched upon the affection of the Brother and Sister for each other" (*LY*, III, 119); and in his letter written the next day, enclosing a fresh copy, he remarked that "if the length makes the above utterly unsuitable, it may be printed with his Works as an effusion by the side of his grave; in this case, in some favorable moment, I might be enabled to add a few Lines upon the friendship of the Brother and Sister" (*LY*, III, 120).

The moment came early in the new year, when Wordsworth began expanding the epitaph form to produce the third version of the poem (see the third reading text—the text of 1836). Crabb Robinson entered in his diary on January 3, 1836, "In the evening Wordsworth read his verses on Charles Lamb—supplemental to the Epitaph. I fear though written with the utmost delicacy that they cannot be printed in Miss Lamb's lifetime" (*HCR Books*, II, 477). The longer monody was certainly under way at this time, if not complete. Wordsworth's letter to Moxon approving a printed form of the poem has been misdated January 4, 1836 (*LY*, III, 147–149), leading one to suppose that Robinson's phrasing was imprecise, and that Wordsworth must have been reading from print, newly arrived, on January 3. But other concerns, some posed by the "January 4" letter itself, make this presumption unnecessary, because the letter in fact dates from March 17. Evidence assuring a date in any case not before early March is found in letters of Robert Southey: Southey's letters show that on February 26 Southey received from Joseph Cottle a packet of manuscript materials toward Cottle's *Recollections*, and that between the time of the arrival of these materials and March 5 he received a copy of Thomas Allsop's two-volume work *Letters, Conversations, and Recollections of S. T. Coleridge* (published anonymously in 1836; see Curry, II, 441–446). Wordsworth's letter of "January 4" states that he has seen Allsop's two volumes "at Mr Southey's two days ago." The letter cannot have been written before early March.

A more precise indication of the date is found in Wordsworth's remark in the "January 4" letter to Moxon that he is pondering questions regarding the format and appearance of a new edition of his poems: "If you see Mr Robinson ask him about this; he complains of the present edition having a shabby appearance . . . . let Mr Robinson have [a copy of the Lamb monody] for Mr S. Cookson, a friend of mine." In a letter to Crabb Robinson (*LY*, III, 149 [misdated "January 4"], 183–184 [March, 17, 1836]) Wordsworth wrote, "Could you call at Moxons that he may talk with you about certain things I have mentioned to him relating to my Poems, in a Letter of this morning, to go by the same parcel as this.—He will furnish you with a copy of my Last Verses [Lamb monody], as an introduction from me to S. Cookson—." The "January 4" letter is plainly the letter written "this morning."

The story of the printing of the long version rather begins with, or at least at the time of, the copy of the concluding portion of the poem written out by Mary Wordsworth and sent to Thomas Noon Talfourd, Lamb's literary executor, who was preparing an edition of Lamb's letters with a biographical memoir, around but by January 13 (the letter being postmarked January 14). Revisions to lines among 90–100 in Mary's autograph copy imply strongly that this copy must have preceded the first printing of the long form of the poem (CL1), and was very likely to have been the copy text. (On January 18, 1836, while HCR was visiting Wordsworth, he noted in his diary "From Talfourd also a letter" [*HCR Books*, II, 482].)

In light of such considerations, Crabb Robinson's phrasing on January 3 looks perfectly apt, and there is no reason to suppose the existence of any Moxon printing of the long form before that represented by CL1, which almost certainly dates after January 14. Some copies of CL1 were bound in a neat wrapper; but none so far has been observed that did not make its way through, or stay within, the Rydal Mount household (these include the Wordsworth Library copy that Dora presented to her cousin John; Edward Quillinan's Ashley Library copy; the copy in the Alexander Turnbull Library; and Robert H. Taylor's copy, now at Princeton University Library). Moxon probably had a few copies bound and sent them to Wordsworth, but waited for Wordsworth's final approval and instructions before preparing and distributing copies in London. Instead, he found himself producing further printings to accommodate Wordsworth's continuing revision.

Wordsworth must have sent some such revisions with or prior to his letter to Moxon of January 30, in which he anticipates early distribution but asks for a revise:

I am glad you like the verses. . . . Do with them what you like as to the number of Copies you will strike off—I wish for 25—. . . . [I]t would not be desirable they should get into the Athenaeum, or any other periodicals, before they come out with the book. . . .

May I beg that you would send me down a Revise, through Mr Robinson who can promise me a Frank; should I think any alterations necessary I will return it immediately. [*LY*, III, 162]

The substance of the revisions sent by January 30 is indicated by second thoughts that Wordsworth expressed in a letter to Moxon of February 8, probably after having received and reflected on the printing represented by the set of proofs (DC1):

Upon reconsidering the Verses, I think the sense in one altered passage is not sufficiently clear if the line

'Otherwise wrought the Will of the most High',

be omitted; therefore let it stand as before, and the line that follows thus—

Yet in all visitations, through all trials,
Still etc—

through instead of *and*, as I think it stood before.

(The poem stands and stood so in the Berg MS. and in CL1.) Still anticipating an almost immediate distribution, Wordsworth added:

Don't send more than 12 Copies of the Verses here; keep the rest for London distribution, and if not too late alter Aptly received etc. thus

Received, *there* may it stand, I trust, unblamed

and print for 'Still were they faithful' 'Still they were faithful.'" [*LY*, III, 164–165]

Wordsworth received a further revise (not surviving) that he apparently had not asked for. It evidently included, with one inadvertent omission, the revisions sent on February 8. He responded to Moxon's revised printing on a Friday, probably February 12—in the letter that is dated, probably by the recipient, "? Feb. 5th," but that cannot have preceded Wordsworth's letter of February 8:

Thanks for the verses, they will be quite correct when you have replaced the line

Otherwise wrought the will of the Most High:
Yet etc.— [*LY*, III, 163]

Apparently assuming that the final printing was at least in the offing, if not yet accomplished, Wordsworth wrote to Samuel Rogers around but by February 17: "Be so good as to say to Moxon that I wish him to present you, as from me, a couple of copies of my verses upon Lamb, one for your Sister. I should have expressed this wish to himself upon the slip on the other side had there been room" (*LY*, III, 173; postmarked February 18, 1836).

No evidence exists that Wordsworth made further changes before his next comments to Moxon, in his letter of March 17:

Thanks for Lamb's Poems, and the Verses—they are now quite correct and I have no wish to alter them further: the only thing which I find amiss in them is the position of the two words By God, in the beginning of a line which gives them the appearance of an oath, but I cannot alter it without weakening the passage. Pray send a Copy to Mrs Marshall 41 upper Grosvenor Street, another for Miss Fenwick 2 lower Seymour Street, Portman Square, and let Mr Robinson have one for Mr S. Cookson, a friend of mine. And pray send 3 Copies enclosed to Joshua Watson Esq. No 6 Park Street Westminster. [*LY*, III, 147]

The printing to which Wordsworth is referring is clearly that represented by the several surviving examples of the pamphlet that we designate as CL2, which was certainly bound carefully in wrappers and distributed to acquaintances outside the Wordsworth family. (Cornell University has a presentation copy "From the author" in Moxon's autograph; copies in the Berg Collection [NYPL] went respectively to Elizabeth Cookson and William Pearson.) Ernest de Selincourt (*PW*, IV) described two states of the privately printed pamphlet, 1836^1 and 1836^2, as represented, respectively, by the Forster copy and all other surviving printed copies, but in fact reversed the order of the states. For this reason we have called the two states CL1 and CL2.

Wordsworth went on distributing copies, and revising, first with a view to presumably impending publication of the lines in Talfourd's book, then with a view to their publication in his own *Poetical Works* (1836–1837), which in the event occurred before the appearance of Talfourd's book (see *LY*, III, 187 [WW to Joshua Watson, around March, 19, 1836]; 192–193 [WW to CW, Jr., late March 1836]; 200 [WW to TNT, April 16, 1836]; 209 [WW to James Spedding, April 28, 1836; 210 [WW to EM, April 28, 1836]; 365 [WW to Robert Shelton Mackenzie, February 23, 1837], and 421 [WW to EM, June 21, 1837]). The third reading text is based on that found in Wordsworth's *Poetical Works* (1836). For additional information concerning the poem's compositional history in correspondence and other sources, see the notes to the text of 1836. For convenience, a summary of the printed texts is provided below.

Summary of the Printed Texts

(1) First form, as British Library copy Ashley 5319: printed by Moxon shortly before November 28, 1835, and received by Wordsworth on that date; 38 lines long, titled

"EPITAPH." There is no imprint in the only surviving example.

(2) Second form, CL1: printed around January 14, 1836, from or duplicating the Talfourd-letter text; stitched in a wrapper—untitled. Copies reached Wordsworth in two states, one with double quotation marks (Taylor copy at Princeton), one with single (Turnbull Library copy). In CL1 p. 6, l. 6 begins "Yet, thro'"; p. 3, l. 8 up, is "'Tis well; and tho' the appropriate bounds have here." Wordsworth received this and revised it, revision including omission of the line "Otherwise wrought..." (p. 6); and he sent off corrections represented in the next printed form, the proof DC1. Wordsworth did not title the now-untitled poem again until his collected edition of 1845.

(3) Third form, DC1: printed shortly before February 8, 1836, and received at Rydal Mount on that date (a revise, and probably the revise that Wordsworth asked for on January 30). A proof, on two bifolia measuring 22.2 by 13.8 of cheap wove paper folded horizontally in three, certainly for mailing. It has on p. 3, eight lines from the foot:

> Tis well; and tho' the record overstepped
> Those narrow bounds, yet, on the printed page
> Aptly received, there it may stand unblamed

The last of these lines was revised by Mary Wordsworth to "Received, there may it stand I trust unblamed"; this last line is substantively the form of the CL2 text, which also has "they were faithful" on p. 6, a reading like that of Mary's revision here in DC1. On p. 6 DC1 omits the line "Otherwise wrought the will of the most High," but the line is written in as a revision by Mary. The next line is printed "And in all visitations, through all trials," and has the first word revised by Mary to "Yet." The next line is printed "Still were they faithful, like two goodly ships" and is revised by Mary to "Still they were [etc]." Following the text is a type signature with place ("44 Dover St."); the address is revised by Mary to "Rydal Mount." These revisions (with confirmation of "through", p. 6, l. 6, as a replacement of CL1 "and") were forwarded to Moxon on February 8 (*LY*, III, 164), the family keeping a copy of DC1 as corrected. The family also brought up to date an available copy of CL1, the Taylor copy at Princeton.

(4) Fourth form (not surviving): printed shortly before February 12 and received at Rydal Mount on that date (*LY*, III, 163); another proof. It included with one exception the revisions that Wordsworth wanted for the poem at that point; the exception is the omission of the line "Otherwise wrought... " that Wordsworth had said on February 8 he wanted restored. If discovered, this revise will probably be found to have as the third line of p. 5, "Not so enriched—not so adorned, to thee," and the fifth line down on p. 6 to commence "Yet, thro...." (Mary sent off some copy of the poem to MMH on February 14 [WL Letters], probably a copy of either CL1 or the fourth form.)

(5) Fifth form, CL2: assumed by Wordsworth to be available for distribution when he wrote to Samuel Rogers a day or two before February 18 (*LY*, III, 173); stitched in a wrapper. This form contains all the revisions, complete with the line commencing "Otherwise wrought." Examples are found in the National Art Library of the Victoria and Albert Museum, the Berg Collection (NYPL), and Cornell University Library. This form has "Otherwise wrought... " as the sixth line down on p. 6, and "Not so enriched—not so adorned, to thee" as p. 5, l. 3. P. 6, l. 6 is "Otherwise wrought...," l. 7 begins "Yet," and l. 8 begins "Still they." Wordsworth went on revising, and forwarding revisions to possessors of the pamphlet, with a view to the form that they would take in Talfourd's book.

(6) Sixth form, that of *Poetical Works* (1836–1837). In preparing this text Wordsworth revised a copy not of CL2 but of CL1, a procedure that resulted in the incorporation in the text of *Poetical Works* of one or more CL1 readings that had been superseded in later forms of the private printing. The spelling "Burnt" in l. 61 is such a case, and the asterisk

sectional division is another. The text of Talfourd's *Letters of Charles Lamb* (1837) derives from this printing.

The following is an outline of the bases of the reading texts and the content of their *apparatus*:

1. First reading text: *Epitaph*, based on Huntington MS. 2 (HM22091) with variants from Huntington MS. 3 (HM6874).
2. Second reading text: *Epitaph written on Charles Lamb by William Wordsworth*, based on Huntington MS. 4 (HM22092) with variants from Huntington MS. 6 (HM22094) and the British Library printed copy (Ashley 5319).
3. Third reading text: the monody "To a good Man of most dear memory," based on *Poetical Works* (1836–1837), with variants from the following:
   Huntington MSS. 7 (HM22098), 8 (HM22088), 9 (HM22095);
   Berg MS. 1: Mary Wordsworth's fair copy of ll. 38–131 (Berg Collection, NYPL);
   WW(a): Wordsworth Library copy of private printing (WW [a] 1836) (CL1);
   Ashley monody: Edward Quillinan's copy (BL, Ashley 4662) of the private printing (CL1);
   RHT MS.: annotations in Princeton Library copy of the private printing (CL1);
   Turnbull: annotations in copy of the private printing (CL1) entered in two main stages (Turnbull 1 and Turnbull 2) for 1836–1837 *Poetical Works*);
   DC1: Wordsworth Library copy of the revise of the first printing, in the form of proofs (CL1, revised);
   Graves MS. (copy): A manuscript "slip" inserted in Robert Perceval Graves's copy, recorded by Edward Dowden, *PW*, 1893; the printed copy (CL2) is in the Berg Collection (NYPL), but the slip of paper is untraced; DW, MW, and WW to CW, Jr., late March 1836, original untraced;
   Letters: *The Letters of Charles Lamb* (1837).

For an account of Wordsworth's friendship with Lamb, including a history of this poem, see Alan G. Hill, "Lamb and Wordsworth; the Story of a Remarkable Friendship," *The Charles Lamb Bulletin, The Journal of the Charles Lamb Society* 37 (January 1982): 85–92.

[Text of Huntington MS. 2]

Epitaph

To the dear memory of a frail good Man
This Stone is sacred. Here he lies apart
From the great City, where he first drew breath,
Was rear'd and taught, and humbly earned his bread,
To the strict labours of the Merchant's desk
By duty chained. Not seldom did those tasks
Teaze, and the thought of time so spent depress,
His spirit, but the recompence was high;
—Firm Independence, Bounty's rightful Sire;
Affections, warm as sunshine, free as air!
And, when the precious hours of leisure came,
Knowledge and wisdom, gained from converse sweet
With books, or while he ranged the crowded streets
With a keen eye, and overflowing heart:
Hence truths poured out in Works by thoughtful love
Inspired,— and potent over smiles and tears.
From the most gentle Creature nursed in fields
Had been derived the Name he bore—a name,
Wherever Christian Altars have been raised,
Hallowed to meekness, and to innocence;
And if in him meekness at times gave way
Provoked out of herself by troubles strange,
Many and strange, that hung about his life;
Or suddenly dislodged by strong rebound
Of animal spirits that had sunk too low,

---

composed around November 19, 1835
found in Huntington MS. 2 (WW to EM, November 20, 1835); Huntington MS. 3 (WW to EM, November 23, 1835)
reading text Huntington MS. 2
title Epitaph *Huntington MS. 3*
15–16 *rev from* Hence truths poured out with [?humble] love, and thought
Inspired,—Works potent over smiles and tears. *Huntington MS. 2*
So Genius [Genius *rev from* genius] triumphed over seeming wrong,
And poured out truth [truth *rev from illeg word rev from* fruit] in works by thoughtful love
Inspired—works potent over smiles and tears. *Huntington MS. 3*
19 *inserted Huntington MS. 2*
21 at times gave way *rev from* did some times fail *Huntington MS. 2*
24–26 *rev from* Nor by wild wit displeased or by quaint views *Huntington MS. 2*
24–25 *canceled Huntington MS. 3*

15–16 In Huntington MS. 3 the copyist, EEH, corrected "fruit" to another word that was then made illegible by WW's revision to "truth."

Or by impetuous fancy, and quaint views
Of domineering humour, overcome—
And if too often, self-reproached, he felt
That innocence belongs not to our Kind—
He had a constant friend in *Charity*;
Her who, among the multitude of sins
That she can cover, left not *his* exposed
To an unforgiving judgment from just Heaven—
O, he was good, if e'er a good Man lived!

[Text of Huntington MS. 4]

Epitaph written on Charles Lamb by
William Wordsworth

To the dear memory of a frail good Man
This stone is sacred.—Here he lies apart
From the great City where he first drew breath,
Was rear'd and taught; and humbly earned his bread
To the strict labours of the Merchant's desk
By duty chained. Not seldom did those tasks
Teaze, and the thought of time so spent depress,
His Spirit, but the recompence was high;
Firm Independence, Bounty's rightful Sire;
Affections, warm as sunshine, free as air!
And, when the precious hours of leisure came
Knowledge and wisdom, gained from converse sweet
With Books, or while he ranged the crowded streets
With a keen eye, and overflowing heart:
So genius triumphed over seeming wrong
And poured out truth in works by thoughtful love
Inspired,—Works potent over smiles and tears.
And as round mountain-tops the light'ning plays,
Thus innocently sported, breaking forth
As from a cloud of some grave sympathy,
Humour and wild instinctive wit, and all
The vivid flashes of his spoken words.—

---

31 who, among the *rev from* that [? ?] *Huntington MS. 2*

---

composed around November 24, 1835
found in Huntington MSS. 4 (WW to EM, November 24, 1835); 6 (WW to EM, mid-December 1835)
printed as *Epitaph* (1835)
reading text Huntington MS. 4
title *added in pencil (MW) Huntington MS. 4*
5 the *rev from* a *(WW) Huntington MS. 4*
18 light'ning *rev from* lightening *Huntington MS. 6* lightning *Epitaph*
20 As *rev from* An *Huntington MS. 4*

From the most gentle Creature nursed in fields
Had been derived the name he bore—a name
Wherever Christian Altars have been raised,
Hallowed to meekness, and to innocence:
And if in him meekness at times gave way
Provoked out of herself by troubles strange,
Many and strange, that hung about his life;
Still, at the centre of his being, lodged
A soul by resignation sanctified:
And if too often self-reproached, he felt
That innocence belongs not to our Kind,
He had a constant friend in *Charity;*
Her who, among the multitude of sins
That she can cover, left not *his* exposed
To an unforgiving judgement from just Heaven.
O, he was good, if e'er a good Man lived!

[Text of 1836]

To a good Man of most dear memory
This Stone is sacred. Here he lies apart
From the great city where he first drew breath,
Was reared and taught; and humbly earned his bread,
To the strict labours of the merchant's desk
By duty chained. Not seldom did those tasks
Tease, and the thought of time so spent depress,
His spirit, but the recompence was high;
Firm Independence, Bounty's rightful sire;
Affections, warm as sunshine, free as air;
And when the precious hours of leisure came,
Knowledge and wisdom, gained from converse sweet
With books, or while he ranged the crowded streets
With a keen eye, and overflowing heart:
So genius triumphed over seeming wrong,

---

composed Late December 1835

found in Berg MS. 1 (MW's ll. 38–131, sent by WW to TNT, around but certainly by January 13, 1836 [postmarked January 14]); Huntington MS. 7 (WW to EM, February 8, 1836 [HM22098]); Huntington MS. 8 (WW to EM, [February 12, 1836] [HM22088]); Huntington MS. 9 (WW to EM, March 17, 1836 [HM22095]); DC1 MS. (MW's revs on proof sheets); RHT MS. (MW's revs in RHT pamphlet); Graves MS. (copy [Dowden's report of revs to ll. 40–47; orig untraced]); DW, MW, and WW to CW, Jr. (late March 1836); Turnbull MSS. 1 and 2 (two stages of JC, MW, and WW's revs in Turnbull pamphlet); MS. 1836/45

printed in pamphlet form CL1; DC1, proof only; CL2 (see the editor's headnote for details)

published in *1836–*, *Lamb Letters* (1837), *1839*

classed Epitaphs *1836–*, *1839*

reading text *1836*

title WRITTEN AFTER THE DEATH OF CHARLES LAMB. *1845–*

1–37 *lacking Berg MS. 1*

1 To the dear memory of a frail good Man *CL1, DC1, CL2; so Turnbull MS. rev to text*

And poured out truth in works by thoughtful love
Inspired—works potent over smiles and tears.
And as round mountain-tops the lightning plays,
Thus innocently sported, breaking forth
As from a cloud of some grave sympathy,
Humour and wild instinctive wit, and all
The vivid flashes of his spoken words.
From the most gentle creature nursed in fields
Had been derived the name he bore—a name,
Wherever christian altars have been raised,
Hallowed to meekness and to innocence;
And if in him meekness at times gave way,
Provoked out of herself by troubles strange,
Many and strange, that hung about his life;
Still, at the centre of his being, lodged
A soul by resignation sanctified:
And if too often, self-reproached, he felt
That innocence belongs not to our kind,
A power that never ceased to abide in him,
Charity, 'mid the multitude of sins
That she can cover, left not his exposed
To an unforgiving judgment from just Heaven.
O, he was good, if e'er a good Man lived!

* * * * *

34–35 He had a constant friend in Charity;
Her who, among the multitude of sins *CL1, DC1, CL2; so Turnbull MS. rev to text*
A Power that never ceased to abide in him
Charity mid a multitude etc. *DW, MW, and WW to CW, Jr.*

38/39 MW entered a row of short rules in Berg MS. 1 to mark the division in the text. The printer supplied asterisks in CL1, but in DC1 and CL2 he omitted the asterisks and marked the division by a drop of six lines.

From a reflecting mind and sorrowing heart
Those simple lines flowed with an earnest wish,
Though but a doubting hope, that they might serve
Fitly to guard the precious dust of him
Whose virtues called them forth. That aim is missed;
For much that truth most urgently required
Had from a faltering pen been asked in vain:
Yet, haply, on the printed page received,
The imperfect record, there, may stand unblamed

40–47 This tribute flowed, with hope that it might guard
The dust of him whose virtues called it forth; [forth; *rev from* forth:]
But 'tis a little space of earth that man,
Stretched out in death, is [is *rev from* if] doomed to occupy;
Still smaller space doth modest custom yield,
On sculptured tomb or tablet, to the claims
Of the deceased, or rights of the bereft.
'Tis well; and, tho' the appropriate bounds have here
Been overstepped, yet may the imprinted [imprinted *rev from* impri[?]] page
Receive the record, there to stand, unblamed, *Berg MS. 1; CL1 as rev Berg MS. 1; DC1 as CL1 but*
'Tis well; and, tho' the record overstepped
Those narrow bounds, yet on the printed page
Aptly received, there it may stand unblamed *DC1*
'Tis well; and, tho' the record overstepped
Those narrow bounds, yet, on the printed page
Received, there may it stand, I trust, unblamed *DC1 MS.; RHT MS. and CL2 as DC1 MS. but* yet,] yet Received] Received *rev from* [?Announced] *RHT MS.; further revs of this passage:*
'Tis well, and if the Record in the strength
And earnestness of feeling, overpass'd
Those narrow limits and so miss'd its aim,
Yet will I trust that on the printed page
Received, it there may keep a place unblamed. *Grave MS. (copy)*
'Tis well, and tho' the record, in the strength
And earnestness of feeling, overpassed
Those narrow limits and so missed its aim
Yet will, I trust, upon the printed page
Received, it there may keep a place unblamed. *DW, MW, and WW to CW, Jr. Turnbull MSS. rev entire passage thus:*
Those [*rev to* These] simple lines flowed with a doubling hope
That, howsoe'er deficient, they might lend
Their humble aid to guard the dust of him
Whose virtues called them forth;—that aim is missed—
For 'tis a little space of earth that man,
Stretched out in death, is doomed to occupy;
Space smaller still doth modest custom yield,
On sculptured tomb or tablet, to the claims
Of the deceased, or rights of the bereft.
'Tis well; and, tho' the appropriate bounds have here
Been overstepped, yet on the printed page
[?Th'] imperfect record, there may stand, unblamed, *Turnbull MS. 1, but last 2 ll. rev to*
Yet may the record on the printed page
Received, there keep, I trust, its place unblamed
Turnbull MS. 2 as text except as noted

43 That] The *Turnbull MS. 2*

47 Received, *there* may it stand, I trust, unblamed *Huntington MS. 7 (see note below)*

As long as verse of mine shall breathe the air
Of memory, or see the light of love.

Thou wert a scorner of the fields, my Friend!
But more in show than truth; and from the fields,
And from the mountains, to thy rural grave
Transported, my soothed spirit hovers o'er
Its green untrodden turf, and blowing flowers;
And taking up a voice shall speak (tho' still
Awed by the theme's peculiar sanctity
Which words less free presumed not even to touch)
Of that fraternal love, whose heaven-lit lamp
From infancy, through manhood, to the last
Of threescore years, and to thy latest hour,
Burnt on with ever-strengthening light, enshrined
Within thy bosom.
'Wonderful' hath been
The love established between man and man,
'Passing the love of women;' and between
Man and his help-mate in fast wedlock joined
Through God, is raised a spirit and soul of love
Without whose blissful influence Paradise
Had been no Paradise; and earth were now
A waste where creatures bearing human form,
Direst of savage beasts, would roam in fear,
Joyless and comfortless. Our days glide on;
And let him grieve who cannot choose but grieve
That he hath been an Elm without his Vine,
And her bright dower of clustering charities,
That, round his trunk and branches, might have clung
Enriching and adorning. Unto thee
Not so enriched, not so adorned, to thee
Was given (say rather thou of later birth
Wert given to her) a Sister—'tis a word
Timidly uttered, for she *lives*, the meek,
The self-restraining, and the ever-kind;
In whom thy reason and intelligent heart
Found—for all interests, hopes, and tender cares,

48–49 As long as verse of mine shall steal from tears
Their bitterness, or live to shed a gleam
Of solace, over one dejected thought. *RHT MS., DC1, CL2*

58 fraternal love *rev from* [?peculiar] sanctity *Berg MS. 1*

61 Burnt on *rev to* Burnt, and *RHT MS.* Burned, and *DC1, CL2*

65 joined *rev from* bound *Berg MS. 1*

66 Through] By *Berg MS. 1, CL1, DC1, CL2, Huntington MS. 9; so Turnbull MS. rev to text* and soul *rev from* of love *Berg MS. 1*

71 glide] pass *Berg MS. 1, CL1, DC1, CL2; so Turnbull MS. rev to text*

74 clustering *rev from* charities *Berg MS. 1*

77 *lacking Berg MS. 1, CL1; added in RHT MS., Turnbull MS.*

All softening, humanising, hallowing powers,
Whether withheld, or for her sake unsought—
More than sufficient recompence!
                                        Her love
(What weakness prompts the voice to tell it here?)
Was as the love of mothers; and when years,
Lifting the boy to man's estate, had called
The long-protected to assume the part
Of a protector, the first filial tie
Was undissolved; and, in or out of sight,
Remained imperishably interwoven
With life itself. Thus, 'mid a shifting world,
Did they together testify of time
And season's difference—a double tree
With two collateral stems sprung from one root;
Such were they—such thro' life they *might* have been
In union, in partition only such;
Otherwise wrought the will of the Most High;
Yet, thro' all visitations and all trials,
Still they were faithful; like two vessels launched
From the same beach one ocean to explore

---

90 assume *rev from* put on *Berg MS. 1*
94 Thus] Yet *Berg MS. 1, CL1, DC1, CL2; so Turnbull MS. rev to text*
95–97 Fix'd—they together [*rev from* Together fixed, they] testified of time
And season's difference, [like *del*] a double tree
With two collateral stems sprung from one root; [root; *rev from* trunk.] *Berg MS. 1*
Fix'd—they together testified of time
And season's difference, a double tree
With two collateral stems sprung from one root; *CL1; so Turnbull MS. rev to text*
Together stood they (witnessing of time
And season's difference) as a double tree
With two collateral stems risen from one root; *DC1, RHT MS., CL2*
98 were they *alt* they were *del RHT MS.*
100 *omitted in proof, restored Huntington MSS. 7, 8*
100–103 [But otherwise *rev to* Otherwise] wrought the will of the most High;
Yet, thro' all visitations, through all trials,
Still were they faithful, like two goodly ships
Launched from the beach one ocean to explore *Berg MS. 1; CL1 as rev Berg MS. 1 but* most] Most *Turnbull MS. as rev Berg MS. 1 but rev to text*
And in all visitations, through all trials,
Still were they faithful, like two goodly ships
Launched from the beach one ocean to explore *DC1*
Otherwise wrought the will of the Most [most *DC1 MS.*] High;
Yet in all visitations, through all trials,
Still they were faithful, like two goodly ships
Launched from the beach one ocean to explore *Huntington MS. 7, DC1 MS.; CL2 as Huntington MS. 7 but* Yet] Yet,
102 they were *rev from* were they *RHT MS.*

With mutual help, and sailing—to their league
True, as inexorable winds, or bars
Floating or fixed of polar ice, allow.

But turn we rather, let my spirit turn
With thine, O silent and invisible Friend!
To those dear intervals, nor rare nor brief,
When reunited, and by choice withdrawn
From miscellaneous converse, ye were taught
That the remembrance of foregone distress,
And the worse fear of future ill (which oft
Doth hang around it, as a sickly child
Upon its mother) may be both alike
Disarmed of power to unsettle present good
So prized, and things inward and outward held
In such an even balance, that the heart
Acknowledges God's grace, his mercy feels,
And in its depth of gratitude is still.

O gift divine of quiet sequestration!
The hermit, exercised in prayer and praise,
And feeding daily on the hope of heaven,
Is happy in his vow, and fondly cleaves
To life-long singleness; but happier far
Was to your souls, and, to the thoughts of others,
A thousand times more beautiful appeared,
Your *dual* loneliness. The sacred tie
Is broken; yet why grieve? for Time but holds
His moiety in trust, till Joy shall lead
To the blest world where parting is unknown.

---

109 rare *rev from* brief *Berg MS. 1*
124 Is *rev from* If *Berg MS. 1*
129–131 Is broken, to become more sacred still. *Berg MS. 1, CL1 as Berg MS. 1 but no comma, DC1, CL2; Turnbull MS. as Berg MS. 1 but rev to text*

EXTEMPORE EFFUSION UPON THE DEATH OF JAMES HOGG.

WHEN first, descending from the moorlands,
I saw the Stream of Yarrow glide
Along a bare and open valley,
The Ettrick Shepherd was my guide.

When last along its banks I wandered,
Through groves that had begun to shed
Their golden leaves upon the pathways,
My steps the border minstrel led.

The mighty Minstrel breathes no longer,
Mid mouldering ruins low he lies;
And death upon the braes of Yarrow,
Has closed the Shepherd-poet's eyes:

Nor has the rolling year twice measured,
From sign to sign, its stedfast course,
Since every mortal power of Coleridge
Was frozen at its marvellous source;

---

composed between November 21 and December 3, 1835

found in Yale MS. 4 (WW to John Hernaman, November 30, 1835); Yale MS. 5 (WW to John Hernaman, December 1, 1835); Huntington MS. 5 (WW to EM, December 6, 1835); Houghton MS. 2 (WW to R. P. Graves, mid-December 1835); Princeton MS. 4; Victoria MS. 2; Berg MS. 2; Southey Album 2; MS. 1836/45

published in *Newcastle Journal*, December 5, 1835 (p. 3); *Atheneum*, December 12, 1835 (No. 424, p. 930); *1836–*, *1839*

classed Epitaphs *1836–*, *1839*

reading text *1836*

title *lacking Victoria MS. 2, Berg MS. 2* Extempore Effusion, upon reading in the Newcastle Journal, the notice of the death of the Poet, James Hogg *Yale MS. 4* Extempore Effusion / on reading in a Newspaper the notice / of the death of the Poet James Hogg) *Houghton MS. 2* Extempore Effusion upon reading in the Newcastle Journal / the notice of the Death of the Poet James Hogg / by W. Wordsworth Decr 1835 *Southey Album 2* THE ETTRICK SHEPHERD. / The following exquisite Verses, which need no comment at our / hands, have been transmitted to us for publication by one / of the most distinguished of England's Bards—one of her / best and most loyal subjects—the poet Wordsworth. We / feel highly flattered by the compliment thus paid to us by / our kind-hearted and excellent friend:— / EXTEMPORE EFFUSION, UPON READING, IN THE NEWCASTLE JOURNAL, THE NOTICE OF THE DEATH OF THE POET, JAMES HOGG. *Newcastle Journal* THE ETTRICK SHEPHERD. / Extempore Effusion, upon reading, in the Newcastle Journal, the notice of the Death of the Poet, James Hogg. *Atheneum (subtitle in ital)*

For a draft stanza, placement uncertain, see l. 44/ below.

1 moorlands] Moorland *Southey Album 2*

3 a *rev from* the *Yale MS. 4*

6 Through *rev from* th *Berg MS. 2*

7 upon] along *Southey Album 2*

13 *rev from* And scarcely twice—the year has measured, *Yale MS. 4* year] Sun *Berg MS. 2*

14 its] his *Victoria MS. 2, Berg MS. 2* its *rev to* his *Yale MS. 4, Houghton MS. 2*

16 at] in *Houghton MS. 2*

The 'rapt One, of the godlike forehead,
The heaven-eyed creature sleeps in earth:
And Lamb, the frolic and the gentle,
Has vanished from his lonely hearth.

Like clouds that rake the mountain-summits,
Or waves that own no curbing hand,
How fast has brother followed brother,
From sunshine to the sunless land!

Yet I, whose lids from infant slumbers
Were earlier raised, remain to hear
A timid voice, that asks in whispers,
"Who next will drop and disappear?"

Our haughty life is crowned with darkness,
Like London with its own black wreath,
On which with thee, O Crabbe! forth-looking,
I gazed from Hampstead's breezy heath.

As if but yesterday departed,
Thou too art gone before; but why,
O'er ripe fruit, seasonably gathered,
Should frail survivors heave a sigh?

Mourn rather for that holy Spirit,
Sweet as the spring, as ocean deep;
For Her who, ere her summer faded,
Has sunk into a breathless sleep.

---

20 hearth *rev from* earth *Victoria MS. 2*
25 infant] infant's *Victoria MS. 2* slumbers] slumber *MS. 1836/45, 1845, 1850*
26 remain] survive *Yale MS. 4* survive *rev to* remain *Yale MS. 5*
28–44 *these lines only in Yale MS. 5; lacking Victoria MS. 2*
28/29 *Houghton MS. 2 inserts ll. 37–40; break between stanzas Huntington MS. 5 (see editor's note)*
29–40, 44 *lacking Yale MS. 4*
30 wreath *rev from* [?veil] *Southey Album 2*
34 but] yet *Yale MS. 5, Southey Album 2, Newcastle Journal, Atheneum*
35 O'er *rev from* For *Huntington MS. 5* For *Yale MS. 5, Southey Album 2, Newcastle Journal, Atheneum* *commas erased Yale MS. 5*
37–40 *lacking Yale MS. 5, Berg MS. 2, Newcastle Journal, Atheneum; placed to follow l. 28 in Houghton MS. 2*
37–39 She, too, a Muse whose holy spirit
Was sweet as Spring as Ocean deep,
She, e'er her Summer yet was faded, *Houghton MS. 2*
37 Mourn *alt in pencil* Grieve *MS. 1836/45*
38 Sweet as the spring *alt in pencil* Pure as the sky *MS. 1836/45*

No more of old romantic sorrows,
For slaughtered Youth or love-lorn Maid!
With sharper grief is Yarrow smitten,
And Ettrick mourns with her their Poet dead.

AT THE GRAVE OF BURNS.

1803.

I SHIVER, Spirit fierce and bold,
At thought of what I now behold:
As vapours breathed from dungeons cold
Strike pleasure dead,
So sadness comes from out the mould
Where Burns is laid.

And have I then thy bones so near,
And thou forbidden to appear?
As if it were thyself that's here,
I shrink with pain;
And both my wishes and my fear
Alike are vain.

Off weight—nor press on weight!—away
Dark thoughts!—they came, but not to stay;

41–43 Away, away ye fancied sorrows
For slaughtered Youth and love-lorn Maid
Thou, too, Crabbe! with whom so lately *three lines del by erasure Yale MS. 4*

42 or] and *Yale MS. 5, Berg MS. 2, Princeton MS. 4, Newcastle Journal, Atheneum*

43 sharper] deeper *Southey Album 2*

44 mourns with her their Poet dead.] mourns with her their Shepherd dead! *rev from* mourns with her their Poet dead! *rev from* mourns thro grove and glade. *Yale MS. 5* mourns her Shepherd dead. *Southey Album 2* with her their Poet *rev in pencil to* her Shepherd Poet *MS. 1836/45* Poet *rev to* Shepherd *with note* quere Poet. *Houghton MS. 2 (WW)* Shepherd *Newcastle Journal, Atheneum*

44/ *additional stanza, placement uncertain:*
I see a lonely mountain Kirkyard
Take shelter, [take *del*] from the [?y *del*] woods & fields
The longest growth for funeral offerings
That desolate November yields *Princeton MS. 4*

---

composed begun between August 18 and early December 1807; completed between November 30 and December 10, 1835

found in DC MSS. 143, 151.1, 151.2; MS. 1842P

published in *1842, 1845–*

classed Miscellaneous Poems *1842* Scotland 1803 *1845, 1850; unclassed 1846 (vol. 6)*

reading text *1842*

title At the Grave of Burns *with* 1803 *MW added MSS. 143, 151.1* AT THE GRAVE OF BURNS. 1803. SEVEN YEARS AFTER HIS DEATH. *1845–*

1 shiver] shudder *MS. 143* shiver *rev from* shudder *MS. 151.1*

3 dungeons *WW rev from* dangerous *MS. 151.1*

5 from out *rev from* out of *MSS. 143, 151.1*

8 thou *rev from* then *MS. 151.1*

With chastened feelings would I pay
The tribute due
To him, and aught that hides his clay
From mortal view.

Fresh as the flower, whose modest worth
He sang, his genius "glinted" forth,
Rose like a star that touching earth,
For so it seems,
Doth glorify its humble birth
With matchless beams.

The piercing eye, the thoughtful brow,
The struggling heart, where be they now?—
Full soon the Aspirant of the plough,
The prompt, the brave,
Slept, with the obscurest, in the low
And silent grave.

Well might I mourn that He was gone
Whose light I hailed when first it shone,
When, breaking forth as nature's own,
It showed my youth
How Verse may build a princely throne
On humble truth.

Alas! where'er the current tends,
Regret pursues and with it blends,—
Huge Criffel's hoary top ascends
By Skiddaw seen,—
Neighbours we were, and loving friends
We might have been;

---

19 whose *rev from* of *MS. 143*
25 thoughtful *rev from* thoughtless *MS. 151.1*
26 struggling] swelling *MS. 143* struggling *rev from* swelling *MS. 151.1* where] what *MS. 143* be *rev from* are *MS. 151.2*
31–36 I mourned with thousands, but as One
More deeply grieved, that [that *rev to* for] he was gone
Whose light I hailed when first it shone
And [And *WW rev to* It] led my Youth
To Poesy that built her throne
On simple truth *MS. 143, with ll. 31–34 rev to text but* as] like *MS. 151.1 as orig MS. 143 but* grieved, that] grieved, for *then WW rev all to text, making these changes in the process:* mourn *rev from* grieve *and* humble *rev from* humblest
I mourned with thousands, but as one
More deeply grieved, for He was gone
Whose light I hailed when first it shone,
And showed my youth *rest as text, 1845–*
37 the] this *MS. 143*
41 loving *rev from* living *MS. 1842P*

True friends though diversely inclined;
But heart with heart and mind with mind,
Where the main fibres are entwined,
Through Nature's skill,
May even by contraries be joined
More closely still.

The tear will start, and let it flow;
Thou "poor Inhabitant below,"
At this dread moment—even so—
Might we together
Have sate and talked where gowans blow,
Or on wild heather.

What treasures would have then been placed
Within my reach; of knowledge graced
By fancy what a rich repast!
But why go on?—
Oh! spare to sweep, thou mournful blast,
His grave grass-grown.

There, too, a Son, his joy and pride,
(Not three weeks past the Stripling died,)
Lies gathered to his Father's side,
Soul-moving sight!
Yet one to which is not denied
Some sad delight.

For *he* is safe, a quiet bed
Hath early found among the dead,
Harboured where none can be misled,
Wronged, or distrest;
And surely here it may be said
That such are blest.

And oh for Thee, by pitying grace
Checked oft-times in a devious race,
May He who halloweth the place
Where Man is laid
Receive thy Spirit in the embrace
For which it prayed!

---

53 sate] sat *MS. 143*
59–60 Do I not hear the whistling blast
And see this [this *rev to* that] stone? *MS. 143; orig MS. 151.1 as rev 143, then rev to text*
62 the *rev from* this *MS. 143*
63 gathered *IF rev to* garnered *MS. 151.2*

Sighing I turned away; but ere
Night fell I heard, or seemed to hear,
Music that sorrow comes not near,
A ritual hymn,
Chaunted in love that casts out fear
By Seraphim.

THOUGHTS

SUGGESTED THE DAY FOLLOWING ON THE BANKS OF NITH, NEAR THE POET'S RESIDENCE.

Too frail to keep the lofty vow
That must have followed when his brow
Was wreathed—"The Vision" tells us how—
With holly spray,
He faultered, drifted to and fro,
And passed away.

Well might such thoughts, dear Sister, throng
Our minds when, lingering all too long,
Over the grave of Burns we hung
In social grief—
Indulged as if it were a wrong
To seek relief.

---

79 but *rev from* and *MSS. 143, 151.1*
80 Night fell *rev from* Nightfall *MS. 1842P*
81 comes If *rev from* [?loves] *MS. 151.2*

---

composed November 30–December 10, 1835; by December 12, 1835
found in DC MSS. 143; 151.1 (A) 34^{v}–35^{v}, 37^{r}, (B) 37^{r}–37^{v}, (C) 38^{r}–38^{v}, (D) 39^{r}–39^{v}; 151.2; Princeton MS. 4; WW to HR, December 23, 1839; MS. 1842P; Laing MS.
published in *1842, 1845–*
classed Scotland 1803 *1845, 1850; unclassed 1846 (vol. 6)*
reading text *1842*
title Composed near / Ellisland / Burn's Farm upon the Banks / of the / Nith. *Laing MS.* Suggested the following day on the banks of the Nith, near the Poet's residence *MS. 143* Suggested the day following on the banks of the Nith, near the Poets residence. *rev to* Thoughts suggested . . . residence *MS. 151.1 (A)*
2 Made, doubtless, after his young brow *Laing MS.*
3 *inserted, MW's ink over WW's pencil MS. 143*
5 He sank—he drifted to and fro, *Laing MS.*
6 And] Then *Laing MS.*
7–12 *lacking Laing MS.*
7 dear *alt* my *MS. 151.1 (A)*
10 In] With *MS. 143* In *rev from* With *MS. 151.1 (A)*

---

79 *At the Grave of Burns. 1803:* In MS. 151.1 WW made an entry that looks like "love bond" above the line and then deleted it.

But, leaving each unquiet theme
Where gentlest judgments may misdeem,
And prompt to welcome every gleam
Of good and fair,
Let us beside this limpid Stream
Breathe hopeful air.

Enough of sorrow, wreck, and blight;
Think rather of those moments bright
When to the consciousness of right
His course was true,
When Wisdom prospered in his sight
And virtue grew.

Yes, freely let our hearts expand,
Freely as in youth's season bland,
When side by side, his Book in hand,
We wont to stray,
Our pleasure varying at command
Of each sweet Lay.

How oft inspired must he have trod
These pathways, yon far-stretching road!
There lurks his home; in that Abode,
With mirth elate,
Or in his nobly-pensive mood,
The Rustic sate.

Proud thoughts that Image overawes,
Before it humbly let us pause,
And ask of Nature, from what cause
And by what rules
She trained her Burns to win applause
That shames the Schools.

---

14 may] might *Laing MS.*
15 prompt] pleased *Laing MS.*
18/19 *Laing MS. introduces ll. 31–35*
19 Enough . . . and] No more . . . or *Laing MS.*
20–23 Think rather of a shining Light;
Think of those moments pure and bright,
And not a few, *Laing MS.*
24 virtue grew] Goodness too *Laing MS.*
25–30 *lacking Laing MS.*
25 Yes,] Yet *MS. 143* Yes, *WW rev from* Yet *MS. 151.1 (A)*
26 Freely *rev from* Free *MS. 1842P*
27 his Book] his Books *inserted MS. 151.2* his Book *rev from* his Books *MS. 1842P*
31 How *rev from* And *MS. 151.1 (A)*
32 yon] these *rev to* this *MS. 143* yon *rev from* this *MS. 151.1 (A)*
35 Or] Or, *rev from* Oft *eras Laing MS.*
37–42 *lacking Laing MS.*

Through busiest street and loneliest glen
Are felt the flashes of his pen;
He rules mid winter snows, and when
Bees fill their hives;
Deep in the general heart of men
His power survives.

What need of fields in some far clime
Where Heroes, Sages, Bards sublime,
And all that fetched the flowing rhyme
From genuine springs,
Shall dwell together till old Time
Folds up his wings?

Sweet Mercy! to the gates of Heaven
This Minstrel lead, his sins forgiven;
The rueful conflict, the heart riven
With vain endeavour,
And memory of Earth's bitter leaven,
Effaced for ever.

But why to Him confine the prayer,
When kindred thoughts and yearnings bear
On the frail heart the purest share
With all that live?—
The best of what we do and are,
Just God, forgive!

---

43 busiest] crowded *Laing MS.* street] Street *rev from* Streets *MS. 151.2* loneliest] lonely *Laing MS.* loliest *MS. 143* loneliest *rev from* loliest *MS. 151.1 (A)*

44 Are] Is *Laing MS.* Are *rev from* All *MS. 151.2* flashes] magic *Laing MS.*

47 Deep in the general] Deep, deep within the *Laing MS.* heart] hearts *Laing MS., MS. 143* heart *rev from* hearts *MS. 151.1 (A)*

49 fields *rev from* field *MS. 151.2* far] bright *Laing MS.*

50 Heroes, Sages, Bards] sages [*rev from* heros] heros bards *MS. 143* Sages, heros, bards *WW rev to* Sages, Heroes, Bards *MS. 151.1 (A); Laing MS. as rev MS. 151.1 (A)*

53 dwell together] dwell *(over illeg eras)* sequester'd— *Laing MS.*

55–56 Thee, Minstrel, to the gates of Heaven,
May Mercy lead:—thy sins forgiv'n [forgiv'n *rev from* forgiven], *Laing MS.*

55 Mercy *rev from* heaven *MS. 151.1 (A)*

56 his *rev from* her *MS. 143*

62 bear *WW rev from* bare *MS. 151.1 (A)*

61–66 *lacking Laing MS.*
Too fondly catching at the bait
Of possibilities in fate
Man heeds [heeds *rev from* heeeds] not in his blind estate
On what a thread
The banners hang that separate
Living and Dead. *Princeton MS. 4, with alts for ll. 64, 66* On what a slender thread *and* The living from the dead

A Night Thought

Wordsworth probably composed the first version of *A Night Thought* shortly before his sojourn in London from early May to early July 1836. First publication, under the title *Stanzas,* was in *The Tribute: A Collection of Miscellaneous Unpublished Poems, by Various Authors,* edited by Lord Northampton (London, 1837; *A Night Thought* is on pp. 3–4). The first reading text is from *The Tribute.* Wordsworth published a shorter version, under the title *A Night Thought,* in 1842 (the second reading text).

[Text of *The Tribute* (1837)]

STANZAS

BY W. WORDSWORTH, Esq.

THE moon that sails along the sky
Moves with a happy destiny,
Oft is she hid from mortal eye
    Or dimly seen;
But when the clouds asunder fly,
    How bright her mien!

Not flagging when the winds all sleep,
Not hurried onward, when they sweep
The bosom of th'æthereal deep,
    Not turned aside
She knows an even course to keep,
    Whate'er betide.

Perverse are we—a froward race;
Thousands, though rich in fortune's grace,
With cherished sullenness of pace
    Their way pursue,
Ingrates, who wear a smile-less face
    The whole year through.

---

composed probably in March or April but by June 12, 1836
found in BL MS. 2, Mary Smith Album
published in *Tribute* (1837), *1842, 1845–*
reading text *Tribute*
title *lacking BL MS. 2* A night-thought *Mary Smith Album*
1 The Moon, slow-sailing up the sky. *Mary Smith Album*
2 happy] favored *Mary Smith Album*
7 when] while *BL MS. 2* winds all] strong winds *Mary Smith Album*
8 onward,] forwards *Mary Smith Album*
10 Not] Nor *BL MS. 2*

If kindred humour e'er should make
My spirit droop for drooping's sake,
From Fancy following in thy wake,
  Bright Ship of Heaven,
A counter-impulse let me take
  And be forgiven.

[Text of 1842]

A NIGHT THOUGHT.

Lo! where the Moon along the sky
Sails with her happy destiny;
Oft is she hid from mortal eye
  Or dimly seen,
But when the clouds asunder fly
  How bright her mien!

Far different we—a froward race,
Thousands though rich in Fortune's grace
With cherished sullenness of pace
  Their way pursue,
Ingrates who wear a smileless face
  The whole year through.

If kindred humours e'er would make
My spirit droop for drooping's sake,
From Fancy following in thy wake,
  Bright ship of heaven!
A counter impulse let me take
  And be forgiven.

---

19 humour e'er] humours ere *BL MS. 2, Mary Smith Album* should] would *Mary Smith Album*

---

composed revised between about February 1841 and February 1842
found in DC MSS. 143, 151.1, 151.2; MS. 1842P; MS. 1836/45 (JC)
published in *1842, 1845–*
classed Sentiment and Reflection *1845, 1850; unclassed 1846 (vol. 6)*
reading text *1842*
title A NIGHT THOUGHT. *rev from* A NIGHT THOUGHT, WHILE IN COMPANY WITH A FRIEND. *MS. 1842P* A Night Thought / while in company with a Friend *MSS. 151.1, 151.2*
3 eye *rev from* [?eyes] *MS. 143*
7 Far different *over illeg eras MS. 143*
11 smileless face *over illeg eras MS. 143*
13 If *over illeg eras MS. 143* e'er *so 1845–* ere *all MSS. and 1842*
14 My Spirit *rev from* Our Spirits *rev from* My Spirits *MS. 151.1*
17 me *rev from* us *rev from* me *MS. 151.1*

On an Event in Col: Evans's redoubted performances in Spain

The Ball whizzed by—it grazed his ear,
  And whispered as it flew,
I only touch—not take—don't fear
For both, my honest Buccaneer!
  Are to the Pillory due.

NOVEMBER, 1836.

EVEN so for me a Vision sanctified
The sway of Death; long ere mine eyes had seen
Thy countenance—the still rapture of thy mien—
When thou, dear Sister! wert become Death's Bride:
No trace of pain or languor could abide
That change:—age on thy brow was smoothed—thy cold
Wan cheek at once was privileged to unfold
A loveliness to living youth denied.
Oh! if within me hope should e'er decline,
The lamp of faith, lost Friend! too faintly burn;
Then may that heaven-revealing smile of thine,
The bright assurance, visibly return:
And let my spirit in that power divine
Rejoice, as, through that power, it ceased to mourn.

The Widow on Windermere Side

The Widow on Windermere Side appears first in a manuscript as a pair of sonnets drafted, then revised, on the versos of three leaves in DC MS. 143 in three versions, A (83^{v}), B (84^{v}), and C (82^{v}). That the poem stood thus at first is confirmed by Wordsworth's statement in the Fenwick note that he adopted the

---

composed between October 28 and 31, or possibily as late as December 18, 1836
found in MW to HCR, November 1 (or December 19), 1836
published in *PW* Knight 1889, vol. 11
reading text MW to HCR, November 1 (or December 19), 1836
title performances *rev from* expedition *MW to HCR*

---

composed November 1836
found in Hoare Album
published in *1836–, 1838*
classed Miscellaneous Sonnets *1836–, 1838*
reading text *1836*
title Sonnet by Mr Wordsworth. *Hoare Album*
4 When those, dear sister! best becomes death's bride; *Hoare Album*
5 trace] race *(mistranscribed) Hoare Album*
9 e'er *so Hoare Album, 1838, 1845–* ere *1836–1843*

sonnet form when he "thought the matter might be included in 28 lines." The first reading text, then, is drawn from the underlying fair copy of version A in MS. 143; the poem's absence from MS. 140 and its presence in MS. 143 suggest a date between August 1837 and November 1841. In the period from December 1841 to about March 1842, when copy was being prepared for *Poems, Chiefly of Early and Late Years*, the two-sonnet version was included among the materials being considered for publication and was soon supplemented by a final sonnet, much revised and recopied by both William and Mary Wordsworth. The earliest, A version of this third sonnet, drawn from MS. 151.1, 99ᵛ, is presented as the second reading text, with variants from the several related manuscripts reported in its *apparatus*. The third reading text is based on the 1842 printing with an *apparatus* of variants found in the remaining manuscript and print forms.

[Text of 143 (A)]

I

Oftimes are carried to the loftiest height
[?In] field, in workshop, within cottage door
The industry and honor of the poor;
One have I reverenced with supreme delight
A Widow left under a heavy weight
Of blameless debt, yet w[o]uld she secure
A just discharge that conscience might be pure
And She with all around her stand upright
In the world's eye. The long day thru She wrought
And far into the night keen vigils kept
With spirit so unremitting that some thought
And said, the noble Creature never slept.
But one by one to the cold grave were brought
Her Children, o how feelingly bewept!

II

Long had she wept nor ceased her tears to flow
Till a winter noonday placed her buried Son
Before her sight—last child of many gone
His raiment of angelic white—and lo

composed between August 1837 and November 1841
found in DC MSS. 143 (A) 83ᵛ, (B) 84ᵛ
reading text MS. 143 (A)
15 Long had [had *rev to* did] she wept *rev to* The mother mourned *MS. 143 (B)*
16 placed *rev in transcription from* [?she saw] *MS. 143 (B)*

See the photographs and transcriptions of DC MS. 143 (A) 83ᵛ on pp. 766–767.

His very feet bright like the dazzling snow
Which they are touching, but far brighter, even
As that which comes or seems to come from heaven
Surpasses aught these elements can show.
Much she rejoiced, as one who from that hour
Should not again be doomed to pine and mourn
But the Transfigured, in and out of season
Appeared, and spiritual Presence gained such power
Over the balances of things, that Reason
Fled, nor will ever to her mind return.

[Text of 151.1 (A)]

But why that prayer? as if to her could come
No good but by the way that leads to bliss
Through Death; so judging you would judge amiss.
Though penury be now her threatened doom
Joy hath not fled but finds with her a home,
And of those Maniacs she is *not* that kiss
The air or laugh upon a precipice,

---

19 like *rev in transcription from* as *MS. 143 (B)*
22 show *rev to* bestow *MS. 143 (B)*
23 as one who *rev to* trusting that *MS. 143 (B)*
24 Should *rev to* Could *MS. 143 (B)* not *rev in transcription from* [?now] *MS. 143 (B)*
line rev to Whateer befel she could not [?mourn] [?mourn *rev to* grieve] or pine *MS. 143 (B)*
25 and *rev in transcription from* or *MS. 143 (B)*
28 *rev to* Fled, O thru heaven above us make her thine. *MS. 143 (B)*

---

composed probably between December 1841 and about March 1842
found in DC MS. 151.1 (A) 99[v], (B) 101[r], (C) 102[r], (D) 103[r]
reading text MS. 151.1 (A)
28 return.] return MS. 143 (B)
29 if *rev to* though *MS. 151.1 (B–D)*
30 by *rev from* through *MS. 151.1 (B, C)*
31 you would] we should *MS. 151.1 (B–D)* amiss. *so MS. 151.1 (C, D)* amiss *MS. 151.1 (A, B)*
32 Though penury be now] No [No *rev to* Tho'] penury is [is *rev to* be] now *rev to* Tho' now with Reason lost *MS. 151.1 (D)* Reason is lost, want now *MS. 151.1 (B)* Reason is lost ~~and~~ want now *alt* Reason hath failed want is *MS. 151.1 (C)*
33 *rev to* Is very want joy hath not left her home *MS. 151.1 (E)*
Joy cannot have with her a settled home *rev to*
But frequent transport mitigates the gloom *rev to*
But frequent transports mitigate her doom [doom *rev to* gloom] *MS. 151.1 (B)*
But frequent transports [*alt* But joy surviving] mitigate the gloom; *MS. 151.1 (C)*
34 And *rev from* While *MS. 151.1 (D)* Nor *MS. 151.1 (B, C)* she is . . . that] she is . . . who *MS. 151.1 (D)* is she one who *MS. 151.1 (B)* is She one that *alt* She is not one who *MS. 151.1 (C)*
35 or] and *MS. 151.1 (B, C)*

See the photograph and transcription of "But why that prayer? as if to her could come," DC MS. 151.1 (A), 99[v], pp. 768–769.

Her transports rise from out the silent tomb.
Her rich reward already is begun;
Oft when black Clouds give way before the breeze,
And light breaks forth she drops upon her knees
Hails with spread arms an Angel in her Son
Descending & in earthly extacies
A Martyr's crown her sufferings have won.

Enrapt smiles as if the tomb
36–42 Tho yet the Sufferer ~~hath not passed~~ the tomb
Unpassd, her brow
{ had
~~She smiles as if a~~ Martyrs crown {[?was] won;
{black [?thick]
Oft when {[?] clouds divide before the breeze
And light beams forth she, fallen upon her knees,
Hails with spread arms in her descending Son
And Angel; and in earthly extacies
Her own angelic glory seems begun *MS. 151.1* (B_1)
Oft when black clouds divide before the breeze
~~rich reward~~
~~Her [?favoured] heaven already is begun;~~
And light beams forth the Sufferer, like a Nun
~~black~~ divide
~~Oft when the clouds give way before the breeze~~,
Enrapt in worship, falls upon her knees
~~And light breaks forth, she drops upon her knees~~
descending
Hails with spread arms ~~an Angel~~ in her ^ Son
~~And spreads her arms for she beholds her Son~~
An Angel earthly
~~her~~
~~Descending~~, and in [~~?those pure~~] extacies
Her own angelic glory seems begun
~~Her suffering~~
~~A martyrs crown her sufferings hath won~~. *MS. 151.1 (D)*
She smiles, as if her sufferings through the tomb
Had passed—her brow a Martyr's crown had won;
Oft when light breaks suddenly thro' waving trees
~~And when thick clouds divide before the breeze~~
With outspread arms and fallen upon her knees
Oft doth she
~~The Mother~~ hail~~s~~ in her descending Son
An Angel and ~~with~~ in earthly extsasies
Her own angelic glory seems begun. *MS. 151.1* (B_2)
like one whose sufferings through the tomb
~~Burthen~~
She smiles ~~as if her suffering~~ {hath
Had passed, whose brows a Martyr's crown {had won;
Oft when light breaks through clouds, or shady trees
Waving on high, She, fallen upon her knees
Hails with spread arms in her descending Son
An Angel and in earthly exstasies
A}
Her own a}ngelic glory seems begun. *MS. 151.1 (C)*
37 While passing through strange suffering [?winds] the doom *alt MS. 151.1 (C)*

[Text of 1842]

THE WIDOW ON WINDERMERE SIDE.

I.

How beautiful, when up a lofty height
Honour ascends among the humblest poor,
And feeling sinks as deep! See there the door
Of One, a Widow, left beneath a weight
Of blameless debt. On evil Fortune's spite
She wasted no complaint, but strove to make
A just repayment, both for conscience-sake
And that herself and hers should stand upright
In the world's eye. Her work when daylight failed
Paused not, and through the depth of night she kept
Such earnest vigils, that belief prevailed
With some, the noble creature never slept;
But, one by one, the hand of death assailed
Her children from her inmost heart bewept.

II.

The Mother mourned, nor ceased her tears to flow,
Till a winter's noon-day placed her buried Son
Before her eyes, last child of many gone—
His raiment of angelic white, and lo!
His very feet bright as the dazzling snow
Which they are touching; yea far brighter, even

---

composed early version around 1837, revised between December 1841 and about March 1842
found in DC MSS. 143 (C) 82^{v}; 151.1 (E) 99^{r}–100^{r}; 151.2 (A) 103^{r}, 103^{v}, (B) 107^{r}
published in *1842, 1845–*
classed Affections *1845; unclassed 1846 (vol. 6)*
reading text *1842*
title *lacking MS. 143 (C)*
1 up] up to *MS. 143 (C)*
2 among *rev from* amongst *MS. 151.2 (A)*
3 Neer without reverence let me pass the door *MS. 143 (C); so MS. 151.1 (E) rev to text*
4 beneath *alt* to bear *MS. 151.1 (E)* beneath *rev from* to bear *MS. 151.2 (A)*
6 complaint] complaints *MS. 143 (C)*
7 conscience-sake] conscience's sake *rev to* conscience sake *MS. 151.1 (E)* conscience' sake *MS. 151.2 (A)*
9 when *rev from* til *MS. 143 (C)*
10 depth] depths *MSS. 143 (C), 151.1 (E)*
14 inmost heart *rev from* heart of hearts *MS. 151.1 (E)* heart of hearts *MS. 143 (C)*
15 her tears to flow *rev from* to mourn *MS. 151.1 (E)*
16 a *rev from* on *MS. 151.1 (E)*
17 Before her eyes *rev from* Stood in her eyes *rev from* Before her sight *MS. 151.1 (E)*
19 His very feet bright as] His very feet bright like *rev to* His feet resplent as *MS. 151.1 (E)* His feet resplendent *rev to text MS. 151.2 (A)*
20 yea *rev from* but *MS. 151.1 (E)*

As that which comes, or seems to come, from heaven,
Surpasses aught these elements can show.
Much she rejoiced, trusting that from that hour
Whate'er befel she could not grieve or pine;
But the Transfigured, in and out of season,
Appeared, and spiritual presence gained a power
Over material forms that mastered reason.
Oh, gracious Heaven, in pity make her thine!

III.

But why that prayer? as if to her could come
No good but by the way that leads to bliss
Through Death,—so judging we should judge amiss.
Since reason failed want is her threatened doom,
Yet frequent transports mitigate the gloom:
Nor of those maniacs is she one that kiss
The air or laugh upon a precipice;
No, passing through strange sufferings toward the tomb,
She smiles as if a martyr's crown were won:
Oft, when light breaks through clouds or waving trees,
With outspread arms and fallen upon her knees
The Mother hails in her descending Son
An Angel, and in earthly ecstacies
Her own angelic glory seems begun.

---

26 a *rev from* such *MS. 151.1 (E)*
27 material forms *rev from* the balances *MS. 151.1 (E)*
27–28 Over the balances of things, that Reason
Fled. O thou Heaven above us, make her Thine! *rev to*
Over material forms of things that mastered Reason
Delay not pitying Heaven oh make her Thine *MS. 151.1 (E), so MS. 151.2 (A) but* Heaven! *then rev to text*
36 No, *rev from* But, *rev from* While, *MS. 151.2 (A)* While *MS. 151.1 (E)*
38 Oft *alt* And *MS. 151.2 (A)* waving] shady *MS. 151.1 (E)*
39–40 Waving on high she fallen upon her knees
Hails with spread arms in her descending Son *MS. 151.1 (E), so MS. 151.2 (A) but* knees] knees,

TO THE PLANET VENUS,

UPON ITS APPROXIMATION (AS AN EVENING STAR) TO THE EARTH, JANUARY 1838.

WHAT strong allurement draws, what spirit guides
Thee, Vesper! brightening still, as if the nearer
Thou com'st to man's abode the spot grew dearer
Night after night? True is it, Nature hides
Her treasures less and less—Man now presides,
In power, where once he trembled in his weakness;
Knowledge advances with gigantic strides;
But are we aught enriched in love and meekness?
Aught dost thou see, bright Star! of pure and wise
More than in humbler times graced human story;
That makes our hearts more apt to sympathise
With heaven, our souls more fit for future glory,
When earth shall vanish from our closing eyes,
Ere we lie down in our last dormitory?

"Wouldst Thou be gathered to Christ's chosen flock"

Wordsworth entered "Wouldst Thou be gathered to Christ's chosen flock" in a small notebook that he had first used as a passport between April 11 and July 28, 1837, on his tour of Italy. The inscription on the rock is still legible; the rock is in Dora's Field, which lies between the bottom of the Rydal Mount front garden and the main road to Ambleside.

Wouldst Thou be gathered to Christ's chosen flock
Shun the broad way too easily explored
And let thy path be hewn out of the rock
The living Rock of God's eternal WORD.
1838

---

composed about January 15–30, 1838
found in Yale Sonnets MS.; DC MS. 151.3 (JC)
published in *1838, 1840, 1842, 1845–*
classed Miscellaneous Sonnets *1838, 1842, 1845–, 1846 (vol. 6); unclassed 1840*
reading text *1838*
1 allurement *rev from* allurements *Yale Sonnets MS.*
7 Knowledge] Science *1845–*

---

composed probably between January and early spring 1838
found in DC MS. 140, Southey Album 2
published in *Memoirs* (1851)
reading text Engraved Rock at Rydal Mount
title Inscription / cut on a Rock at Rydal Mount. *Southey Album 2, lacking elsewhere*
2 way] path *MS. 140*
3–4 And hew thy way from out that living Rock
Established upon Earth, the eternal WORD. *MS. 140*

"Oh what a Wreck! how changed in mien and speech!"

A debilitating illness struck Robert Southey's wife, Edith, in September 1834, depriving her of her mental faculties and leading finally to her death on November 16, 1837. In his consolatory sonnet *To R. S.*, composed shortly after Edith's death, Wordsworth alludes also to his sister Dorothy's mental illness (ll. 11–14), which had made her a mere shadow of her former self since she fell ill in 1835. The sonnet appears with several others concerned with family members and friends in a loose gathering of "Private Memorials" now in the Wordsworth Library (DC MS. 147). This copy forms the basis for the first reading text.

In February or March 1838 Wordsworth asked Dora to "[r]ead the following remodel[ing] of the Sonnet, I addressed to S[outhey]; the personalities are omitted, a few lines only retained," and transcribed for her the sonnet as it stood then (see the photographs and transcriptions of DC MS. 144 and BL MS. 3 on pp. 770–771). He then added:

> The Sonnet as first sent you and S— may be kept, if thought worthy as a private record. The meaning in the passage you object to, is certainly not happily brought out, if you think it better thus, alter it—
>
> Over the sacred Heart—Compassion's Twin,
> The heart that once could feel for every Wretch.

Wordsworth had by this time already sent the unrevised sonnet to the printer for inclusion in *Sonnets* (1838), and, though intending to revise it to conform with this new version, he was concerned that an allusion to Dorothy might still be detected by readers. He wrote to Dora:

> The thought in the Sonnet as it now stands has ever been a consolation to me, almost as far back as I can remember, and hope that thus expressed it may prove so to others makes one wish to print it; but your Mother seems to fear it would be applied at once to your dear Aunt. I own I do not see the force of this objection, but if you and Miss Fenwick and others should be of the same mind, it shall be suppressed. It is already sent to the Press but not as it now stands; if you think it may be printed without *impropriety*, pray be so good as to superintend the Revise, which I shall order the printer to send you—this would save time, for I could not [*illeg words, del*] entrust the revise to the Printer only. [WW to Dora W, February–March 1838; *LY*, III, 524–525]

Wordsworth included the revised poem in his volume of *Sonnets*, 1838, though a printer's error in line 3, surviving in the 1840 printing, was not corrected until 1842, when the sonnet was included in *Poems, Chiefly of Early and Late Years*. The basis for the second reading text is the 1842 printing as corroborated by the corrected proofs of that edition (DC MS. 151.3).

[Text of MS. 147]

To R. S.

God's will ordained that piteous blight should reach
Both mind and aspect; but far, far within
(Tho' warped the brain, tho' clouds appeared to stretch
Their shadow o'er the sacred heart—Love's Twin
For sympathy with every human wretch)
Her's was a holy Being, freed from sin;
And voiceless powers for her did comfort fetch
From heavenly heights that reason may not win.
Such faith was thine—and now to me, dear Friend,
Whose trouble flows from some mysterious source,
While o'er my stricken Sister's couch I bend
Like consolation comes with gentle force
So may remembrance of thy patient course
Long-proved, sustain me till my trials end.

[Text of 1842]

Oh what a Wreck! how changed in mien and speech!
Yet—though dread Powers, that work in mystery, spin
Entanglings of the brain; though shadows stretch
O'er the chilled heart—reflect; far, far within
Hers is a holy Being, freed from Sin.
She is not what she seems, a forlorn wretch,
But delegated Spirits comfort fetch
To Her from heights that Reason may not win.
Like Children, She is privileged to hold
Divine communion; both do live and move,
Whate'er to shallow Faith their ways unfold,

---

composed probably around late November or December 1837
found in DC MS. 147
reading text DC MS. 147

---

composed February–March 1838
found in BL MS. 3; DC MS. 144 (WW to DoraW, February–March 1838); Yale Sonnet MS.; DC MS. 151.3 (IF)
published in *1838, 1840, 1842, 1845–*
classed Miscellaneous Sonnets *1838, 1842, 1845–, 1846 (vol. 6); unclassed 1840*
reading text *1842*
3 of] for *1838, 1840*
10 do] to *Yale Sonnet MS., 1850* do *rev from* to *MS. 151.3*

See the photographs and transcriptions of BL MS. 3 and DC MS. 144, 1r on pp. 770–771.

Inly illumined by Heaven's pitying love;
Love pitying innocence not long to last,
In them—in Her our sins and sorrows past.

VALEDICTORY SONNET.

Serving no haughty Muse, my hands have here
Disposed some cultured Flowerets (drawn from spots
Where they bloomed singly, or in scattered knots)
Each kind in several beds of one parterre;
Both to allure the casual Loiterer,
And that, so placed, my nurslings may requite
Studious regard with opportune delight,
Nor be unthanked, unless I fondly err.
But, metaphor dismissed, and thanks apart,
Reader, farewell! My last words let them be,—
If in this book Fancy and Truth agree;
If simple Nature trained by careful Art
Through It have won a passage to thy heart;
Grant me thy love, I crave no other fee!

"Said red-ribbon'd Evans"

Said red-ribbon'd Evans
'My legions in Spain
Were at sixes and sevens;
Now they're famished or slain:

---

composed probably around March or perhaps as late as June 1838
found in DC MSS. 147; 151.3 (IF)
published in *1838, 1840, 1842, 1845–*
classed Miscellaneous Sonnets *1842, 1845–, 1846 (vol. 6)*
reading text *1838*
title Concluding sonnet— *MS. 147* VALEDICTORY SONNET. / Closing the Volume of Sonnets published in 1838. *MS. 151.3, 1840, 1842, 1845–*

1–2 A lowly Muse's willing Minister
I have disposed these Flowerets (drawn from spots *MS. 147*

1 *alt in pencil at foot* "Serving no haughty Muse *MS. 147*

5–8 That so, before the studious Loiterer,
My little Treasures stand in open sight
With mutual grace, for opportune delight,
Thanks may be due [due *rev from illeg word*] unless I fondly err. *MS. 147*

10 My] my *rev to* thy *MS. 147*

12 If vigorous Nature leagued with thoughtful Art *MS. 147*

14 crave *rev from* ask *MS. 147*

---

composed around but by March 26, 1838
found in WW to HCR, March 26, 1838
published in *PW* Knight 1889, vol. 11
reading text WW to HCR, March 26, 1838

But no fault of mine,
For like brave Philip Sidney
In campaigning I shine,
A true knight of his kidney.
Sound flogging and fighting;
No Chief, on my troth,
Eer took such delight in
As I in them both.
Fontarabbia can tell
How my eyes watched the foe,
Hernani knows well
That our feet were not slow
Our hospitals, too,
Are matchless in story,
Where her thousands fate slew
All panting for glory."
Alas for this Hero
His fame touched the skies,
Then fell below Zero;
Never never to rise!
For him to Westminster
Did Prudence convey,
There safe as a Spinster
The Patriot to play.
But why be so glad on
His feats, or his fall?
He's got his red ribbon
And laughs at us all.—

9–12 *recopied at end of WW to HCR; for first version see below.*

9–14 Sound
[~~?~~]
f } { ;
[?] } logging & fighting { ~~no chief on my troth~~
No Chief on my troth,
{ in
'Ere took such delight { ~~in as I in them both~~
Fontarabbia ~~knows well~~ can tell
~~That my~~ How my eyes watched the foe, *with* That my *del by eras WW to HCR*

18 Are *rev from* The[?y're] *WW to HCR*

"Hark! 'tis the Thrush, undaunted, undeprest"

Hark! 'tis the Thrush, undaunted, undeprest,
By twilight premature of cloud and rain;
Nor does that roaring wind deaden his strain
Who carols thinking of his Love and nest,
And seems, as more incited, still more blest.
Thanks, thou hast snapped a fire-side Prisoner's chain,
Exulting Warbler! eased a fretted brain,
And in a moment charmed my cares to rest.
Yes, I will forth, bold Bird! and front the blast,
That we may sing together, if thou wilt,
So loud, so clear, my Partner through life's day,
Mute in her nest love-chosen, if not love-built
Like thine, shall gladden, as in seasons past,
Thrilled by loose snatches of the social Lay.

Rydal Mount, 1838.

"'Tis He whose yester-evening's high disdain"

'Tis He whose yester-evening's high disdain
Beat back the roaring storm—but how subdued
His day-break note, a sad vicissitude!

---

composed April 8, 1838
found in DC MS. 140; MS. 1838/40; WW to TNT, April 18, 1838; MW to TH & MMH, April 18, 1838; Cornell MS. 10; Yale Sonnets MS.; BL MS. 4; Ransom MS.; DC MS. 151.3 (IF)
published in *1838, 1840, 1842, 1845–*
classed Miscellaneous Sonnets *1842, 1845, 1846 (vol. 6), 1850; unclassed 1838, 1840*
reading text *1838*
title Sonnet *Ransom MS., 1842*

1–3 Hark! tis the thrush the sun low in the west
Struggle with twilight premature in on [?] & rain
Loud roars the wind but smothers not his strain *rev to*
Hark! tis the thrush undaunted unop[op *alt* de]prest
By twilight premature on cloud & rain
Nor does the roaring wind deaden his strain *MS. 140*

3 his *rev from* the *MW to TH & MMH*
6 hast] has *MS. 140, BL MS. 4*
7 Warbler *rev from* Warblers *BL MS. 4*
8 charmed *rev from* eased *BL MS. 4*
9 front] face *WW to TNT, Cornell MS. 10, Ransom MS.*
14 snatches *rev from* notes *MW to TH & MMH* loose] some *WW to TNT*

---

composed on or shortly after April 9, 1838
found in Yale MS. 7, Yale Sonnets MS.
published in *1838, 1840, 1842, 1845–*
classed Miscellaneous Sonnets *1842, 1845–, 1846 (vol. 6); unclassed 1838, 1840*
reading text *1838*

1 high] proud *Yale MS. 7*
2 storm *over illeg eras Yale Sonnets MS.*

Does the hour's drowsy weight his glee restrain?
Or, like the nightingale, her joyous vein
Pleased to renounce, does this dear Thrush attune
His voice to suit the temper of yon Moon
Doubly depressed, setting, and in her wane?
Rise, tardy Sun! and let the Songster prove
(The balance trembling between night and morn
No longer) with what ecstasy upborne
He can pour forth his spirit. In heaven above,
And earth below, they best can serve true gladness
Who meet most feelingly the calls of sadness.

A PLEA FOR AUTHORS. MAY, 1838.

FAILING impartial measure to dispense
To every suitor, Equity is lame;
And social Justice, stript of reverence
For natural rights, a mockery and a shame;
Law but a servile dupe of false pretence,
If, guarding grossest things from common claim
Now and for ever, She, to works that came
From mind and spirit, grudge a short-lived fence.
"What! lengthened privilege, a lineal tie
For *books!*" Yes, heartless Ones, or be it proved
That 'tis a fault in Us to have lived and loved
Like others, with like temporal hopes to die;
No public harm that Genius from her course
Be turned; and streams of truth dried up, even at their source!

---

8 in *rev from* on *Yale Sonnets MS.*
14 calls *rev from illeg word Yale MS. 7*

---

composed May 1838
found in DC MSS. 140 (A) 21^{r}; (B) 20^{v}; (C) 21^{v}–22^{r}; 151.3 (IF); 165; Yale MS. 7; Yale Sonnets MS.
published in *1838, 1840, 1842, 1845–*
classed Miscellaneous Sonnets *1842, 1845–, 1846 (vol. 6); unclassed 1838, 1840*
reading text *1838*
title A [hint *del*] Word or two / from / An Author. *Yale MS. 7*
1 When failing one strict measure to dispense *MS. 140 (C)*
2 every suitor *rev from* all her suitors *MS. 140 (C)* every *rev from* al *Yale MS. 7*
3–4 And social Justice, by fit reverence
Of natural rights unswayed, is but a name; *Yale MS. 7; so MS. 140 (C) but no commas and* name;] name,— *and l. 3 rev to text, l. 4 alt as text*
5 a] the *MS. 140 (C)*
7 Now and *rev from* To work that *MS. 140 (C)* came *rev from* come *MS. 151.3*
8 fence *rev from* chain *Yale Sonnets MS.*
13 her] its *MS. 140 (C)*
14 dried up, even at] dried at *MS. 140 (C)*

See the photographs and transcriptions of *A Plea for Authors. May, 1838,* DC MS. 140 (A) 21^{r} and (B) 20^{v}, pp. 772–773.

PROTEST AGAINST THE BALLOT.
1838.

FORTH rushed, from Envy sprung and Self-conceit,
A Power misnamed the SPIRIT of REFORM,
And through the astonished Island swept in storm,
Threatening to lay all Orders at her feet
That crossed her way. Now stoops she to entreat
License to hide at intervals her head,
Where she may work, safe, undisquieted,
In a close Box, covert for Justice meet.
St. George of England! keep a watchful eye
Fixed on the Suitor; frustrate her request—
Stifle her hope; for, if the State comply,
From such Pandorian gift may come a Pest
Worse than the Dragon that bowed low his crest,
Pierced by the spear in glorious victory.

COMPOSED ON THE SAME MORNING.

LIFE with yon Lambs, like day, is just begun,
Yet Nature seems to them a heavenly guide.
Does joy approach? they meet the coming tide;
And sullenness avoid, as now they shun

---

composed probably around May 1838
found in MS. 1838/40
published in *1838, 1840*
classed Miscellaneous Sonnets *1838; unclassed 1840*
reading text *1838*

---

composed May 1, 1838
found in DC MSS. 140 (A) 17[r]; (B) 16[v], 17[r]; (C) 22[v]; (D) 19[r]; 151.3 (IF); Yale Sonnets MS.; BL MS. 4
published in *1838, 1840, 1842, 1845–*
classed Miscellaneous Sonnets *1842, 1845–; 1846 (vol. 6)*
reading text *1838*
title *lacking MS. 140, BL MS. 4* Composed on the same morning *Yale Sonnets MS.* Composed on a May Morning, 1838. *1845–*

1 Life [Life *rev from eras* Yon] with yon [Mountain *del*] lambs is [like day *inserted*] just begun *MS. 140 (D)* Life with yon [mountain *del*] lambs [lambs *rev to* lambs,] is [like day *inserted*] just begun *BL MS. 4* yon *rev from* young *Yale Sonnet MS.*

See the photograph and transcriptions of *Composed on the Same Morning,* DC MS. 140 (A) 16[v], 17[r], pp. 774–775.

Pale twilight's lingering glooms,—and in the sun
Couch near their dams, with quiet satisfied;
Or gambol—each with his shadow at his side
Varying its shape wherever he may run.
As they from turf yet hoar with sleepy dew
All turn, and court the shining and the green,
Where herbs look up, and opening flowers are seen;
Why to God's goodness cannot We be true,
And so, His gifts and promises between,
Feed to the last on pleasures ever new?

A POET TO HIS GRANDCHILD.

(*Sequel to the foregoing.*)

[Sequel to *A Plea for Authors. May, 1838.*]

"SON of my buried Son, while thus thy hand
"Is clasping mine, it saddens me to think

---

unbrightened
5–6 ~~Hollows enlivened~~ by the rising sun
The lingering gloom of twilight in the sun
~~On slopes to couch with quiet~~ satisfied
To couch with solemn quiet satisfied *MS. 140 (D)*
The lingering glooms of twilight, in the sun
To couch, in the sober quiet satisfied *BL MS. 4*
5–7 In sun
Couch near their dams; or frisk in sportive pride
Each ~~who~~ with his playful shadow at his side *partial draft MS. 140 (C)*
8 wherever] wherever *rev to* where'er *rev to* where ever *MS. 140 (D)*
9–12 with thick and sleepy dew
As they from turf ~~hoary with unsunned dew~~
Yet ~~All~~ whitened oer turn &
~~Turn & do one & all~~ prefer the green,
slopes
To chilly nooks ~~knolls~~ warm with glistening sheen
through life
Why may not we ~~thro' life~~ such course pursue *MS. 140 (D); BL MS. 4 as rev MS. 140 (D) but* oer] o'er, green,] green; sheen] sheen; pursue] pursue,
13 His] God's *MS. 140 (D), BL MS. 4*

---

composed May 23, 1838
found in WW to TNT, June 14, 1838; DC MSS. 140; 165 (A) 2r, (B), 2v; MS. 1838/40
published in *1838, 1840*
reading text *1838*
title *lacking MS. 140*
subtitle *lacking MS. 165 (B)*
1 while thus thy *rev from* whose tiny *MS. 165 (A)* whose tiny *MS. 140*
2 Is clasping *rev from* Thus clings *MS. 165 (A)* Thus clings *MS. 140* saddens *rev from* troubles *MSS. 140, 165 (A)*

"How Want may press thee down, and with thee sink
"Thy Children left unfit, through vain demand
"Of culture, even to feel or understand
"My simplest Lay that to their memory
"May cling;—hard fate! which haply need not be
"Did Justice mould the Statutes of the Land.
"A Book time-cherished and an honoured name
"Are high rewards; but bound they nature's claim
"Or Reasons? No—hopes spun in timid line
"From out the bosom of a modest home
"Extend through unambitious years to come,
"My careless Little-one, for thee and thine!"

May 23rd.

"Come gentle Sleep, Death's image tho' thou art"
[From the Latin of Thomas Warton]

Come gentle Sleep, Death's image tho' thou art
Come share my couch nor speedily depart
How sweet thus living without life to lie
Thus without death how sweet it is to die.

3–4 That thou pressed down by poverty mayst sink
Even till thy Children shall in vain demand *MS. 140; so MS. 165 (A_1)*
How poverty may press thee down and sink
Thy ch *MS. 165 (A_2)*

3 Want *rev from* want *rev from* poverty *MS. 165 (B)*

4 left *rev from* made *MS. 165 (B)* through] by *MS. 165 (B)*

5 Culture,—required to feel and understand *rev to* Culture and neither feel nor understand *MS. 140; MS. 165 (A) as rev MS. 140 but* Culture, *rev to* Culture— and *rev to* nor
Of] For *MS. 165 (B)* or *rev from* and *MS. 165 (B)*

6 *rev from* My least recondite lay that memory *MS. 165 (A) but* Lay] lay

7 *rev from* May keep in trust; hard fate that [that *rev to* which] need not be *MS. 140; MS. 165 (A) as rev MS. 140 but rev to* Perchance may cleave; hard fate which need not be

9 Book time-cherished *rev from* A cherished volume *MS. 140* book time-cherished book *rev from* time-honoured book *MS. 165 (B)*

9–10 *WW to TNT torn, obscuring the last words of each line*

10–11 but bound not Natures [Natures *rev to* Reason's] claim;
No,—hopes, and wishes in a living Line [and . . . Line *rev to* in fond hereditary line] *MS. 140; MS. 165 (A) as rev MS. 140*
These bound not nature's yearnings, reason claim;
Fond hopes and wishes spun in timid line *MS. 165 (B)*

11 Reasons *rev in pencil and ink to* Reason's *MS. 1838/40*

12 From out] Spun from *MSS. 140, 165 (A)*

14/ *date lacking all MSS.*

---

composed perhaps around September 1839
found in MS. 1836/45
reading text MS. 1836/45

1 Death's] Deaths *MS. 1836/45*

3 thus *alt* so *MS. 1836/45*

4 die.] die *MS. 1836/45*

[Two Translations from Michael Angelo]

i. "Grateful is Sleep; more grateful still to be"

Grateful is Sleep; more grateful still to be
Of marble; for while Shameless wrong and woe
Prevail 'tis best to neither hear nor see:
Then, wake me not, I pray you. Hush, speak low.

ii. Michael Angelo in reply to the passage upon his statue of Night sleeping

Night speaks.

Grateful is Sleep, my life in stone bound fast
More grateful still: while wrong and shame shall last
On me can time no happier state bestow
Than to be left unconscious of the woe
Ah then lest you awaken me, speak low.

With a Small Present

A prized memorial this slight work may prove
As bought in Charity and given in Love.

"A sad and lovely face, with upturn'd eyes"

A sad and lovely face, with upturn'd eyes,
Tearless, yet full of grief.—How heavenly fair

---

composed perhaps around September 1839
found in MS. 1836/45
reading texts MS. 1836/45 (EQ)
second poem
1 is *inserted MS. 1836/45*
5 low.] low *MS. 1836/45*

---

composed probably around September 1839
found in DC MSS. 143, 151.1; Betz MS. 2
published in *PW*, IV (1947)
reading text DC MS. 143
title To a female Friend / with a small Present. *Betz MS. 2*

---

composed October 22, 1839
published in *The Home Journal*, October 2, 1847
reading text *The Home Journal*, October 2, 1847

How saintlike is the look those features wear!
Such sorrow is more lovely in its guise
Than joy itself—for underneath it lies
A calmness that betokens strength to bear
Earth's petty grievances—its toil and care:—
A spirit that can look through clouded skies,
And see the blue beyond.—Type of that grace
That lit *Her* holy features, from whose womb
Issued the blest Redeemer of our race—
How little dost thou speak of earthly gloom!
As little as the unblemish'd Queen of Night,
When envious clouds shut out her silver light.

"Lo! where she stands fixed in a saint-like trance"

Lo! where she stands fixed in a saint-like trance,
One upward hand, as if she needed rest
From rapture, lying softly on her breast!
Nor wants her eyeball an ethereal glance;
But not the less—nay more—that countenance,
While thus illumined, tells of painful strife
For a sick heart made weary of this life
By love, long crossed with adverse circumstance.
—Would she were now as when she hoped to pass
At God's appointed hour to them who tread
Heaven's sapphire pavement, yet breathed well content,
Well pleased, her foot should print earth's common grass,
Lived thankful for day's light, for daily bread,
For health, and time in obvious duty spent.

---

composed between about November 1839 and about January 1842; probably around January 1840
found in Yale MS. 6; DC MSS. 143; 147; 151.2; 151.3 (IF)
published in *1842, 1845–*
classed Miscellaneous Sonnets *1842, 1845–; 1846 (vol. 6)*
reading text *1842*

2 she] it *MS. 147*
3 breast *rev from* chest *MS. 151.2* chest *MSS. 143, 147*
4 eyeball] eye-balls *rev to* eye-ball *MS. 147*
7 For] In *MSS. 143, 147*
11 breathed *rev in pencil and ink from* breathe *MS. 143*

See the photographs and transcription of "Lo! where she stands fixed in a saint-like trance," Yale MS. 6, pp. 776–779.

To a Painter and *On the Same Subject*

Edward Quillinan added a note to Dora's copy of *Poems*, 1845: "These two Sonnets [*To a Painter* and *On the Same Subject*], to Margaret Gillies, are on the portrait of M[rs] Wordsworth (the only one for which she ever sat) in which she is painted, on ivory, with her Husband.— Dora's Picture.— W.W.J[r]. had a copy of his Mother's likeness, and Miss Fenwick a daguerrotype copy—but the whole picture has never been copied up to this date. May 24. 1850" (see the Manuscript Census entry for MS. 1845D). Margaret Gillies (1803–1887) specialized in watercolor miniatures on ivory and earned her living as a miniaturist and watercolorist. Raised in Edinburgh, where she became the friend of Scott, Jeffrey, and the Wordsworths, she painted miniatures of Mary, William, and Dora Wordsworth and Isabella Fenwick in October–December 1839 at Rydal Mount. Mary's portrait was completed before the end of the year. After their departure from Rydal together in mid-February Dora gave Isabella Fenwick copies of the two sonnets on the portrait of Mary, remarking that "The Sonnets are most beautiful, most true, most affecting, and Father tells me they were composed almost extempore"; on April 7 Wordsworth wrote to Dora, "your mother tells me she shrinks from Copies being spread of those Sonnets: she does not wish one, on any account, to be given to Miss Gillies, for that, without blame to Miss G., would be like advertising them. I assure you her modesty and humble-mindedness were so much shocked that I doubt if she had more pleasure than pain from these compositions, though I never poured out anything more truly from the heart" (*LY*, III, 756 and note; IV, 59 and note). See also the poems presented as versions of "More may not be by human Art exprest," below.

The first reading text of *On the Same Subject* is drawn from Dora Wordsworth's letter to Isabella Fenwick, mentioned above; the second is that published in *Poems, Chiefly of Early and Late Years* in 1842.

TO A PAINTER.

All praise the Likeness by thy skill portrayed;
But 'tis a fruitless task to paint for me,
Who, yielding not to changes Time has made,
By the habitual light of memory see
Eyes unbedimmed, see bloom that cannot fade,
And smiles that from their birth-place ne'er shall flee

composed between late December 1839 and late March 1840
found in Dora W to IF, April 1, 1840; DC MSS. 143; 147; 151.2 (A) 120[r]; (B) 120[v]; 151.3 (IF)
published in *1842, 1845–*
classed Miscellaneous Sonnets *1842, 1845–; 1846 (vol. 6)*
reading text *1842*
title *lacking Dora W to IF, MSS. 143, 147* On a Portrait *MS. 151.2 (B)* Upon a Portrait *rev to* On A Portrait. *rev to text MS. 151.3* To Miss Gillies. *1846*
1 thy *rev from* the *MS. 151.3* the *MS. 151.2 (A)*
3 changes] change that *Dora W to IF*
5 see] a *Dora W to IF*

Into the land where ghosts and phantoms be;
And, seeing this, own nothing in its stead.
Couldst thou go back into far-distant years,
Or share with me, fond thought! that inward eye,
Then, and then only, Painter! could thy Art
The visual powers of Nature satisfy,
Which hold, whate'er to common sight appears,
Their sovereign empire in a faithful heart.

On the Same Subject

See the headnote to the previous poem.

[Text of Dora W to IF]

With disappointment strange I first beheld
This Portrait, on whose features I so long
Have gazed by new discoveries impelled;
I now can speak as with another tongue;
O my Beloved! I have done thee wrong,
As by this work enlightened, I perceive.
Morn into noon did pass, noon into eve,
And the old day was welcome as the young—
As welcome and as beautiful; in sooth
More beautiful, as being a thing more holy;
Thanks to thy virtues, to the eternal youth
Of all thy goodness, never melancholy—

---

7 phantoms] Phantoms *rev from* [?] *MS. 147*
8 See this, own this, but nothing in its stead. *Dora W to IF*
12 visual powers of Nature] subtle powers of Vision *Dora W to IF*
13 Which] That *Dora W to IF*

---

composed between late December 1839 and late March 1840
found in Dora W to IF [?April 1, 1840]; DC MSS. 143, 147, 151.2
printed in DC MS. 151.3 (uncorrected proof)
reading text Dora W to IF [?April 1, 1840]
title Upon a Portrait *rev to* Continued *MS. 143* Continued. *MS. 151.3*
1–3 Tho' I beheld at first with blank surprize
This [This *rev from* P] Portrait, on its features I so long
Have gazed, allured by new discoveries, *MS. 143; so MS. 147 and MS. 151.2 but* This *so MS. 151.3 but* Though *and* surprise
5 have *rev to* had *MS. 143, MS. 151.2* had *MS. 151.3*
6 this] the *MS. 143, MS. 147, MS. 151.2, MS. 151.3* *line rev to* Of truth too heedless which I now percieve: *MS. 151.3*
9–12 as in sooth
As welcome and ~~more~~ beautiful ~~as being a thing more~~
More beautiful as being a thing more holy holy
~~Thanks to thy goodness never melancholy;~~ *then at foot of page:*
Thanks to thy to the eternal youth
Of all thy goodness never melancholy
To thy *MS. 147*

To thy large heart and humble mind, that cast
Like glory around, future, present, past.

[Text of 1842]

ON THE SAME SUBJECT.

THOUGH I beheld at first with blank surprise
This Work, I now have gazed on it so long
I see its truth with unreluctant eyes;
O, my Belovèd! I have done thee wrong,
Conscious of blessedness, but, whence it sprung,
Ever too heedless, as I now perceive:
Morn into noon did pass, noon into eve,
And the old day was welcome as the young,
As welcome, and as beautiful—in sooth
More beautiful, as being a thing more holy:
Thanks to thy virtues, to the eternal youth
Of all thy goodness, never melancholy;
To thy large heart and humble mind, that cast
Into one vision, future, present, past.

"More may not be by human Art exprest"

Several related drafts of a poem that also pays tribute to a portrait, probably of Isabella Fenwick, were entered in two separate manuscripts. Two occur in a pocket notebook described in 1952 by George Healey (*WPN*). As the manuscript itself has not been seen since Healey examined it, the texts he provided are presented here as the first and second reading texts. A third poem, titled *Upon the sight of the Portrait of a female Friend*, is supplied by Betz MS. 5. The composition of

---

14 Like glory around, *alt* A gracious Spirit round *DoraW to IF* Into one vision, *MS. 143, MSS. 147, 151.3* future,] future *Dora W to IF*

---

composed revised in late 1842, before publication
found in DC MS. 151.3 (A) p. 228 (JC's revision on page); (B) p. 228P1ʳ (JC's copy on pasted-in sheet); MS. 1842P
published in *1842, 1845–*
classed Miscellaneous Sonnets *1842, 1845–; 1846 (vol. 6)*
reading text *1842*
title Continued *del MS. 151.3 (A)*
5 sprung *rev from* came *MS.151.3 (B)*
6 Of truth too heedless which I now perceive *del MS. 151.3 (A)* Ever *WW rev to* Or how *rev to* Or how, *rev to* Ever *MS. 151.3 (A, B)*

these texts probably probably followed shortly after the artist completed the portrait, around October to December 1839. For further discussion of the dating of these various drafts see the note to the reading texts (p. 482). See also Wordsworth's sonnet *Upon a Portrait* (p. 337, and the note on pp. 482–483).

[Text of Pocket Notebook (B)]

More may not be by human Art exprest
But Love, far mightier Power, can add the rest,
Add to the picture which those lines present
All that is wanting for my heart's content:
The braided hair a majesty displays
Of brow that thinks and muses while I gaze,
And O what meekness in those lips that share
A seeming intercourse with vital air,
Such faint sweet sign of life as Nature shows
A sleeping infant or the breathing rose;
And in that eye where others gladly see
Earth's purest light Heaven opens upon me.

[Text of Pocket Notebook (A)]

Art, Nature, Love here claim united praise.
The forehead thinks—it muses while I gaze,
And the light breaking from the eyes to me
For hearts content is all it seems to be,
O that the lips though motionless might share
Some vital intercourse with silent air
Such faint sweet sign of life as Nature shows
The sleeping infant or the breathing rose.—

---

composed probably around January–February 1840
found in Pocket Notebook (B), pp. 28–29
published in *The Seminary Magazine* (1898)
reading text Pocket Notebook (B)
5 The *rev from* Her *Pocket Notebook (B)*
7 *rev from* The lips impart much pleasure as they share *Pocket Notebook (B)*

---

composed probably around January–February 1840
found in Pocket Notebook (A), p. 21
reading text Pocket Notebook (A)
3 to *rev from* from *Pocket Notebook (A)*
5 might *rev from* should *Pocket Notebook (A)*
7 Such *rev from* Some *Pocket Notebook (A)*

[Text of Betz MS. 5]

Upon the sight of the
Portrait of a female Friend.—

Upon those lips, those placid lips, I look,
Nor grieve that they are still and mute as death,
I gaze—I read as in an Angel's Book,
And ask not speech from them, but long for breath.
W[m] Wordsworth—

Ambleside
10th July
1840

Upon a Portrait.

We gaze, not sad to think that we must die
And part; but that the love this Friend hath sown
Within our hearts, the love whose Flower hath blown
Bright as if heaven were ever in its eye
Shall pass so soon from human memory
And not by strangers to our blood alone
But by our best descendants be unknown
Unthought-of this may surely claim a sigh.

---

composed July 10, 1840
found in Betz MS. 5
reading text Betz MS. 3
1 those lips, those *rev from* those those *Betz MS. 3*

---

composed January 1, 1840
found in DC MSS. 143, 147; Trinity MS.
published in *Memoirs* (1851)
reading text DC MS. 147
title Upon a Portrait *rev by WW to* Upon a Portrait of a Friend *MS. 143* Upon the sight of a Portrait of a Female Friend / painted by Margaret Gillies— *Trinity MS.* On a Portrait of I. F., painted by Margaret Gillies. *Memoirs*
1 We gaze—nor grieve to think that we must die, *Trinity MS., Memoirs*
2 sown *rev from* [? shewn] *MS. 147*
But that the precious love this friend hath sown *Memoirs*
3 hearts, . . . hath] breasts— . . . has *Trinity MS.*
5 Shall] Will *Trinity MS., Memoirs*
5–6 *WW's alt* Forgotten—not in Stranger's minds alone
But in the groves [groves *alt* field] and gardens be unknown *MS. 143*
7 *rev to* Where we have wandered—this may claim a sigh *MS. 143*

---

1 In *Upon a Portrait* a mark below "we" in MS. 147 is a modern entry; the ink matches a citation of "1 vol Oxford edn" on the same page.

But blessed Art! we yield not to dejection
Thou against time so feelingly dost strive
Where'er preserved in this most true reflection
The Image of her Soul is kept alive
Some lingering fragrance of the pure affection,
Whose flower with us will vanish, must survive.

"The Star that comes at close of day to shine"

The Star that comes at close of day to shine
More heavenly bright than when it leads the Morn
Is Friendship's Emblem whether the forlorn
She visiteth; or shedding light benign
Thro' shades that solemnize life's calm decline
Doth make the happy happier. This have we
Learnt, Isabel! from thy society
Which now we too unwillingly resign
Tho' for brief absence. But farewell! The page
Glimmers before my sight, thro' thankful tears,
Such as start forth, not seldom to approve
Our truth, when we, old yet unchilled by age
Call Thee, tho' known but for a few fleet years
The heart-affianced Sister of our love.

---

9 *WW rev to* Yet blessed Art! transient is our dejection *alt* Yet transient blessed Art is our dejection *MS. 143* But] Yet, *Memoirs*
11 Where'er] Whereer *rev from* Whateer *MS. 147*
12 The] the *MS. 147* An *Memoirs* kept *rev in pencil and ink from* [?] *MS. 143*
13 pure *rev from* true *MS. 147*

---

composed Around February 8, revised by April 10, 1840
found in Houghton MS. 3; DC MSS. 143, 147; MW to IF, April 10, 1840
published in *Memoirs* (1851)
reading text MS. 147
title To —— / on her departure / from A —— Feb[ry] 1840 *Houghton MS. 3* To I. F. *Memoirs*
1 that] which *Houghton MS. 3, Memoirs*
1–3 Bright is the Star that comes at eve to shine—
More heavenly bright than when it leads [leads *rev from* ?lead] the morn,
And such is friendship; whether the forlorn *MW to IF, so Memoirs but l. 1* star which *and* shine *and l. 3* Friendship, . . . forlorn, *with* Bright . . . at eve . . . And such is Friendship *italicised*
2 More heavenly bright than *over illeg eras MS. 143*
More [brightly still *inserted by IF*] than when it leads [leads *WW rev from* led] the morn, *Houghton MS. 3*
6 This *rev from* Thus *MS. 143*
11 not *rev from* [?f] *Houghton MS. 3*
13 known] knoww *rev to* knowwn *MS. 147* fleet *rev in pencil from* fleeting *MS. 143; so MS. 147 but rev in ink*
14 affianced *rev from* affirmed *MS. 147* love.] love *MS. 147* love! *Houghton MS. 3, Memoirs*

POOR ROBIN*.

Now when the primrose makes a splendid show,
And lilies face the March-winds in full blow,
And humbler growths as moved with one desire
Put on, to welcome spring, their best attire,
Poor Robin is yet flowerless, but how gay
With his red stalks upon this sunny day!
And, as his tuft of leaves he spreads, content
With a hard bed and scanty nourishment,
Mixed with the green some shine, not lacking power
To rival summer's brightest scarlet flower;
And flowers they well might seem to passers-by
If looked at only with a careless eye;
Flowers—or a richer produce (did it suit
The season) sprinklings of ripe strawberry fruit.

  But, while a thousand pleasures come unsought,
Why fix upon his want or wealth a thought?
Is the string touched in prelude to a lay
Of pretty fancies that would round him play
When all the world acknowledged elfin sway?
Or does it suit our humour to commend
Poor Robin as a sure and crafty friend,
Whose practice teaches, spite of names to show
Bright colours whether they deceive or no?—
Nay, we would simply praise the free good-will

* The small wild Geranium, known by that name.

---

composed March 1840
found in DC MSS. 89 (A) 107^{v}, (B) 110^{r}–110^{v}; 143; 151.1 (A) 32^{r}, (B) 96^{r}–96^{v}; 151.2
published in *1842, 1845–*
classed Miscellaneous Poems *1845; unclassed 1846 (vol. 6)*
reading text *1842*
title Ragged Robin (more commonly called Poor Robin) *MS. 89 (A), with paren phrase added*
2 March-winds] March wind *MS. 89 (A)*
4 best] fresh *MW rev to* best *del MS. 89 (B)*
5 Flowerless is [is *rev to* was] ragged [ragged *MW over illeg eras*] Robin! but [but *WW rev to* But] how gay *then WW rev first four words to* Poor Robin still is flowerless *MS. 89 (A)* yet] still *MS. 89 (B)* still *MW rev to* yet *MS. 143, MS. 151.1*
7 tuft] tufts *1845–* leaves *rev from illeg eras MS. 143*
9 lacking *MW rev from* wanting *MS. 89 (B)*
12 looked at] looking *MS. 89 (A)*
14/15 *no break MS. 89 (A, B)*
15 come unsought, *over illeg eras MS. 143*
16 Upon his want or wealth why fix a thought? *MS. 89 (A)* want or wealth *rev from* want of wealth *rev from* want *MS. 89 (B)* wealth or want *1845–*
20 Or would the humour of our verse commend *MS. 89 (A)*
24 we *rev from* why *MS. 89 (B)* free] pure *MS. 89 (A, B)*

With which, though slighted, he, on naked hill
Or in warm valley, seeks his part to fill;
Cheerful alike if bare of flowers as now,
Or when his tiny gems shall deck his brow:
Yet more, we wish that men by men despised,
And such as lift their foreheads overprized,
Should sometimes think, where'er they chance to spy
This child of Nature's own humility,
What recompense is kept in store or left
For all that seem neglected or bereft;
With what nice care equivalents are given,
How just, how bountiful, the hand of Heaven.

March, 1840.

---

25 With which, tho' scorned, he seeks his part to fill; *WW rev to*
With which, though slighted He on furthest hill *MS. 89 (A)*
With which, tho' scorned, He seeks his part to fill *MW rev to*
With which, tho' slighted he on naked hill *MS. 89 (B)*

26 *inserted MS. 89 (A, B)*

28 gems shall deck *MW rev from* wreaths adorn *MS. 89 (B)*

29 despised *over illeg eras MS. 143*

30 foreheads] forehead *MS. 143, MS. 151.1, MS. 151.2*

31–36 Should sometimes think when they this plant espy,
[*inserted* Even though a sleety blast be whirling by,]
With what nice care equivalents are given,
How just, how bountiful, the hand of Heaven. *MS. 89 (A)*
Should sometimes think when they this plant [plant *rev to* Plant] espy
Even tho' a whirling [whirling *rev to* sleety] blast be passing [passing *rev to* whirling] by,
With what nice care equivalents are given,
How just, how bountiful the hand of Heaven. *rev to*
Should sometimes think [think *rev to* pause and think] when they this espy
This Child of Nature's own humility
With what nice care equivalents are given,
How just, how bountiful the hand of Heaven. *MS. 89 (B_1); so MS. 89 (B_2) WW rev to text*

31 Should sometimes think when they this Plant espy, *MS. 89 (A); so MS. 89 (B_1) but* plant *rev to* Plant *and WW rev line to*
Should sometimes think when they this espy *rev to*
Should sometimes pause and think when they this spy [*with* sometimes *WW rev from* someth[?ing]] *MS. 89 (B_2)* *MS. 143 as text but* think, . . . spy *over illeg eras*

32 Even though a sleety blast be whirling by, *WW's inserted MS. 89 (A)*
Even tho' a whirling [whirling *rev to* sleety] blast be passing [passing *rev to* whirling] by *MS. 89 (B_1), WW rev to text but* child] Child *and* humility.] humility

33–34 *lacking MS. 89 (A, B_1)*

33 kept *MW rev from* left *MS. 143*

36/ *date lacking MS. 89 (A)* March 1840 *MS. 89 (B_1), MS. 151.1, MS. 151.2* Mar: 1840 *MS. 143* March, 1840. *1842, 1846–* March 1840 *1845*

The Cuckoo-clock

On receiving the gift of a cuckoo clock from Isabella Fenwick, Wordsworth wrote a poem in two ten-line stanzas, "Stanzas To a simple-minded Lover of Nature and of Art," then altered the title and added a line to each stanza when Mary Wordsworth copied the poem to send to Miss Fenwick on March 24, 1840 (the first reading text). Wordsworth "finished" a four-stanza version on his birthday, April 7, 1840, and later published it in *Poems, Chiefly of Early and Late Years* (1842; the second reading text).

[Text of WW and MW to IF]

Stanzas
Hint to a simple-minded Lover of Nature and of Art.

If thou be wont, when sleep has taken flight,
To crave a voice that softliest will foreshew
How far off yet the gleams of morning light,
And whether wakefulness be wise or no,
Thou need'st not covet a Repeater's stroke
That, answering to thy touch, will tell the hour;
Better provide thee with a Cuckoo-Clock,
For service hung beside thy Chamber door,
And wait, in patience wait. The gentle shock
The double note, as is with living power,
Will teach thee to be blithe as bird in bower.

2

List Cuckoo, Cuckoo! Tho' the tempest howl,
Or nipping frost remind thee trees are bare,
How Cattle pine, and droop the shivering fowl,
Thy spirits will seem to feed on balmy air;
I speak from knowledge. By that sound beguiled
Oft wilt thou greet old memories as they throng
Into thy heart; and fancies running wild,
Beside clear streams and budding groves among

---

composed March 24, 1840
found in WW and MW to IF, March 24, 1840
reading text WW and MW to IF, March 24, 1840
title Hint to *rev from* To *WW and MW to IF*
8 *inserted WW and MW to IF*
11/12 Will teach *entered first then del WW and MW to IF* "2" *added above second stanza in WW and MW to IF*
12 List *rev from* List, *rev from* List! *WW and MW to IF*
14 and *rev from* or *WW and MW to IF*
16 knowledge. *rev to* knowledge, *WW and MW to IF (but capital* B *of* By *unchanged)*

Will make thee happy, happy as a child:
Of sunshine wilt thou think, of flowers and song,
And breathe as in a world where nothing can go wrong.

[Text of 1842]

THE CUCKOO-CLOCK.

WOULDST thou be taught, when sleep has taken flight,
By a sure voice that can most sweetly tell,
How far-off yet a glimpse of morning light,
And if to lure the truant back be well,
Forbear to covet a Repeater's stroke,
That, answering to thy touch, will sound the hour;
Better provide thee with a *Cuckoo-clock,*
For service hung behind thy chamber door;
And in due time the soft spontaneous shock,
The double note, as if with *living* power,
Will to composure lead—or make thee blithe as bird in bower.

List, Cuckoo—Cuckoo!—oft though tempests howl,
Or nipping frost remind thee trees are bare,
How cattle pine, and droop the shivering fowl,
Thy spirits will seem to feed on balmy air;
I speak with knowledge,—by that Voice beguiled,
Thou wilt salute old memories as they throng
Into thy heart; and fancies, running wild

---

19 *inserted WW and MW to IF*
20 child *rev from* Child *WW and MW to IF*

---

composed Between March 26 and April 7, 1840
found in Dora W to IF, April 1, 1840; MW to IF, April 10, 1840; DC MS. 89; Cornell MS. 11 (Dora W); DC MSS. 143 (A) 48^{r}–49^{r}, (B) $47/48I^{r}$, $47/48I^{v}$; 151.2; MS. 1845W; Hoare Album
published in *1842, 1845–*
classed Imagination *1845, 1850; unclassed 1846 (vol. 6)*
reading text *1842*
title *lacking MS. 143 (B), Cornell MS. 11* Lines written upon a Cuckoo Clock / presented by the Author *Hoare Album*
2 can *rev from* canst *MS. 151.2*
3 glimpse *rev from* peep *Dora W to IF*
4 be] were *Cornell MS. 11, Hoare Album*
5 Forbear to *rev from* Thou must not *MS. 151.2* Thou need'st [need'st *rev to* must] not *MS. 89* Thou needst not *Cornell MS. 11, MS. 143 (B), Hoare Album* Thou must not *MS. 143 (A)*
8 For] Its *Hoare Album* behind *rev from* beside *MS. 151.2* beside *MSS. 89, 143, Cornell MS. 11, Hoare Album*
11 Might soothe, or make thee blithe as blithest bird in bower *Dora W to IF* thee *rev from* the *MS. 89*
12 though] the *Hoare Album* tho' *rev from* the *MS. 143 (B)*
13 Or] And *Hoare Album*
15 spirits] Spirit *Cornell MS. 11* spirit *MS. 143 (B)* mind *Hoare Album*

Through fresh green fields, and budding groves among,
Will make thee happy, happy as a child;
Of sunshine wilt thou think, and flowers, and song,
And breathe as in a world where nothing can go wrong.

And know—that, even for him who shuns the day
And nightly tosses on a bed of pain;
Whose joys, from all but memory swept away,
Must come unhoped for, if they come again;
Know—that, for him whose waking thoughts, severe
As his distress is sharp, would scorn my theme,
The mimic notes, striking upon his ear
In sleep, and intermingling with his dream,
Could from sad regions send him to a dear
Delightful land of verdure, shower and gleam,
To mock the *wandering* Voice beside some haunted stream.

O bounty without measure! while the grace
Of Heaven doth in such wise, from humblest springs,
Pour pleasure forth, and solaces that trace
A mazy course along familiar things,
Well may our hearts have faith that blessings come,
Streaming from founts above the starry sky,
With angels when their own untroubled home
They leave, and speed on nightly embassy
To visit earthly chambers,—and for whom?
Yea, both for souls who God's forbearance try,
And those that seek his help, and for his mercy sigh.

---

20 thee happy, happy] thee happy happy *rev from* thee happy *MS. 89*

23 for] from *Hoare Album* shuns the] shrinks from *MSS. 89, 143 (B), Cornell MS. 11, Hoare Album* shrinks the *rev from* shrinks from *MS. 143 (A)* shuns the *rev from* shuns [?from] *MS. 151.2*

24 on *rev from* in *MS. 151.2* in *MS. 89*

28 would scorn my theme] would [*rev from* might] scorn my song *Dora W to IF* my *rev from* thy *MS. 151.2*

30 dream *rev from* dreams *MS. 151.2*

33 Voice *over illeg eras MS. 151.2* some] a *MSS. 89, 143, Cornell MS. 11*

34 while] If *MW to IF; MS. 143 (B), Cornell MS. 11, Hoare Album*

35 doth] do *Cornell MS. 11, MW to IF; MS. 143 (B), Hoare Album* wise *rev from* sort *MW to IF* springs] Springs *rev from* things *MS. 89*

36 pleasure] pleasures *MW to IF; MSS. 89, 143 (A); MS. 1845W*

38 Well may we trust, that richer blessings come *Cornell MS. 11, MS. 143 (B); so Hoare Album but no comma*

39 sky *rev from* skies *Hoare Album*

41 nightly] mighty *MS. 1845W with MW's pencil query* nightly

44 sigh *rev from* cry *MW to IF*

44/ WW. April 7— my 70th birthday. *MS. 89* Wm Wordsworth Finished on the 7th of April 1840 his 70th birthday *Cornell MS. 11* WW April 7th—my 70th birthday *MS. 143 (A)* Finished on the 7th of April 1840. his 70th birthday *MS. 143 (B)* 7th. Apr 1840. My 70th birthday— W.W. *MS. 1845W* WW. *Hoare Album*

34–44 See the photograph on p. 806.

THE NORMAN BOY.

HIGH on a broad unfertile tract of forest-skirted Down,
Nor kept by Nature for herself, nor made by man his own,
From home and company remote and every playful joy,
Served, tending a few sheep and goats, a ragged Norman Boy.

Him never saw I, nor the spot, but from an English Dame,
Stranger to me and yet my friend, a simple notice came,
With suit that I would speak in verse of that sequestered child
Whom, one bleak winter's day, she met upon the dreary Wild.

His flock, along the woodland's edge with relics sprinkled o'er
Of last night's snow, beneath a sky threatening the fall of more,
Where tufts of herbage tempted each, were busy at their feed,
And the poor Boy was busier still, with work of anxious heed.

There *was* he, where of branches rent and withered and decayed,
For covert from the keen north wind, his hands a hut had made.
A tiny tenement, forsooth, and frail, as needs must be
A thing of such materials framed, by a builder such as he.

The hut stood finished by his pains, nor seemingly lacked aught
That skill or means of his could add, but the architect had wrought

---

composed probably around but after May 17, revised between May 22 and 27, 1840

found in WW to EFO, May 22, 1840; DC MS. 143; Betz MS. 4; WL MS. 2; MW to IF, November–early December 1841; DC MS. 151.2

published in *Saturday Magazine* (no. 14, 1842); *1842, 1845–*

classed Childhood *1845, 1850; unclassed 1846 (vol. 6)*

reading text *1842*

title *lacking WW to EFO*

stanza numbers 1 . . . 8 *Betz MS. 4, WL MS. 2*

1 broad] wide *WW to EFO* unfertile tract *rev from* and [? ?] *WW to EFO*

2 Nor kept by Nature for] Not kept by [by *rev from* to] Nature to *WW to EFO; WL MS. as rev WW to EFO*

4 sheep] sheeps *MS. 143*

6 yet my friend] friend of mine *WW to EFO* yet my friend *rev from* friend of mine *WL MS. 2, MW to IF*

7 that] this *WW to EFO, Betz MS. 4*

8 the] that *WW to EFO, WL MS., MS. 151.2, Betz MS. 4*

9–12 *lacking WW to EFO*

9 relics] relicks *rev from* relick *MS. 151.2* sprinkled] speckled *Betz MS. 4*

10 snow *rev from* show *Betz MS. 4*

11 tempted *rev from* threatening *MS. 143* each, *inserted MS. 151.2*

13 withered *rev from illeg word MS. 143*

14 covert] shelter *WW to EFO* the keen *rev from illeg words MS. 143* hut *rev from illeg word Betz MS. 4*

15 A tiny tenement and frail, as needs the Thing must be *WW to EFO*

16 A thing of such materials framed] [?] of such materials framed *rev to* Of such materials there composed *WW to EFO*

17 stood] was *WW to EFO*

18 or means *rev from* of his *MS. 151.2*

Some limber twigs into a Cross, well-shaped with fingers nice,
To be engrafted on the top of his small edifice.

That Cross he now was fastening there, as the surest power and best
For supplying all deficiencies, all wants of the rude nest
In which, from burning heat, or tempest driving far and wide,
The innocent Boy, else shelterless, his lonely head must hide.

That Cross belike he also raised as a standard for the true
And faithful service of his heart in the worst that might ensue
Of hardship and distressful fear, amid the houseless waste
Where he, in his poor self so weak, by Providence was placed.

—— Here, Lady! might I cease; but nay, let *us* before we part
With this dear holy Shepherd-boy breathe a prayer of earnest heart,
That unto him, where'er shall lie his life's appointed way,
The Cross, fixed in his soul, may prove an all-sufficing stay.

SEQUEL TO THE NORMAN BOY.

JUST as those final words were penned, the sun broke out in power,
And gladdened all things; but, as chanced, within that very hour,
Air blackened, thunder growled, fire flashed from clouds that hid the sky,
And, for the Subject of my Verse, I heaved a pensive sigh.

Nor could my heart by second thoughts from heaviness be cleared,
For bodied forth before my eyes the cross-crowned hut appeared;

---

20 Which he was fixing on the top of that small Edifice; *WW to EFO*
21 That . . . fastening] A Cross which he was fixing *WW to EFO*
22 For . . . all] To make up for [for *rev from* from] deficiencies and *WW to EFO*
23–24 And of the melancholy Place where, by all seasons tried,
The lonely Boy, from morn to night, did with his flock abide. *WW to EFO*
25–28 *lacking WW to EFO*
29 —— Here . . . nay] Now, Lady! as thy suit is met *WW to EFO* but nay] nay *WL MS. 2*
30 breathe a *over illeg eras WW to EFO*
31 where'er *rev from* [?which] *Betz MS. 4* lie *rev from* be *WW to EFO*

---

composed Between May 27, 1840, and around November 1841
found in DC MSS. 89, 143, 151.2; Betz MS. 4; WL MS. 2; MW to IF, November–early December 1841; WW to EFO, November 15, 1842
published in *1842, 1845–*
classed Childhood *1845, 1850; unclassed 1846 (vol. 6)*
reading text *1842*
title WW Sequel *Betz MS. 4* The Poets dream Sequel to the Norman Boy. *with* The Poets dream *inserted MS. 143* THE POET'S DREAM, SEQUEL TO THE NORMAN BOY. *1845–; so 1850 but* DREAM.
stanza numbers 1 . . . 19 *Betz MS. 4, WL MS. 2*
1–36 *lacking MS. 89*
5 cleared] cheered *MS. 151.2*
7 it . . . troubling *rev from* [?it's] . . . [?cr] *Betz MS. 4*

And, while around it storm as fierce seemed troubling earth and air,
I saw, within, the Norman Boy kneeling alone in prayer.

The Child, as if the thunder's voice spake with articulate call,
Bowed meekly in submissive fear, before the Lord of All;
His lips were moving; and his eyes, upraised to sue for grace,
With soft illumination cheered the dimness of that place.

How beautiful is holiness!—What wonder if the sight,
Almost as vivid as a dream, produced a dream at night!
It came with sleep and showed the Boy, no cherub, not transformed,
But the poor ragged Thing whose ways my human heart had warmed.

Me had the dream equipped with wings, so I took him in my arms,
And lifted from the grassy floor, stilling his faint alarms,
And bore him high through yielding air my debt of love to pay,
By giving him, for both our sakes, an hour of holiday.

I whispered, "Yet a little while, dear Child! thou art my own,
To show thee some delightful thing, in country or in town.
What shall it be? a mirthful throng, or that holy place and calm
St. Denis, filled with royal tombs, or the Church of Notre Dame?

"St. Ouen's golden Shrine? or choose what else would please thee most
Of any wonder Normandy, or all proud France, can boast!"
"My Mother," said the Boy, "was born near to a blessèd Tree,
The Chapel Oak of Allonville; good Angel, show it me!"

On wings, from broad and steadfast poise let loose by this reply,
For Allonville, o'er down and dale, away then did we fly;
O'er town and tower we flew, and fields in May's fresh verdure drest;
The wings they did not flag; the Child, though grave, was not deprest.

But who shall show, to waking sense, the gleam of light that broke
Forth from his eyes, when first the Boy looked down on that huge oak,
For length of days so much revered, so famous where it stands
For twofold hallowing—Nature's care, and work of human hands?

Strong as an Eagle with my charge I glided round and round
The wide-spread boughs, for view of door, window, and stair that wound
Gracefully up the gnarled trunk; nor left we unsurveyed
The pointed steeple peering forth from the centre of the shade.

---

9 The Child, as *rev from* As *Betz MS. 4*
26 proud] fair *MS. 143, Betz MS. 4*
29 On *rev from* illeg word *Betz MS. 4*
38 stair] stairs, *MS. 89, Betz MS. 4*
40 forth *rev from* up *MS. 89*

I lighted—opened with soft touch a grated iron door,
Past softly, leading in the Boy; and, while from roof to floor
From floor to roof all round his eyes the wondering creature cast,
Pleasure on pleasure crowded in, each livelier than the last.

For, deftly framed with the trunk, a sanctuary showed,
By light of lamp and precious stones, that glimmered here, there glowed,
Shrine, Altar, Image, Offerings hung in sign of gratitude;
And swift as lightning went the time, ere speech I thus renewed:

"Hither the Afflicted come, as thou hast heard thy Mother say,
And, kneeling, supplication make to our Lady de la Paix;
What mournful sighs have here been heard, and, when the voice was stopt
By sudden pangs, what bitter tears have on this pavement dropt!

41–44 I lighted{:— ; opened with soft touch a grated iron door—
Passed softly leading in the Boy, and when from roof to floor
~~the tesselated~~ the tesselated floor
~~Pas{sed t softly{; —and while{, side by side{, we stood on a pav{' e{d floor~~
~~We pressed with conscious feet as the wondering~~
~~Whether around or high or low the wondering~~ ^Creature cast
~~We pressed with conscious feet, where'er the wondering~~^
~~His eyes{, joy seemed to kindle joy{— , each livelier than the last{.~~
From floor to roof, all round, his eyes the wondering Creature cast
Joy kindled other joy, and each seemed lovelier than the last. *MS. 89; MS. 89(P) rev to text but no commas and* all round his eyes *rev from* his eager eyes
I 'lighted;—opened with soft touch a grated iron door—
leading in the boy, & while from roof to
~~Pass'd softly—& while side by side the tesselated floor~~
~~We pressed with conscious feet~~, wherein the wondering
~~Whether around, or high or low, the wondring~~ Creature cast
His eyes, joy seemed to kindle joy—each livelier than the last. *rev to text WL MS. 2*

41 a grated] the chapel's *1845–*

43 wondering creature] Child with wonder *1845–*

45 a] the *1845–*

48 Sight that inspired accordant thoughts; and speech I thus renewed: *1845–*

49 hast] has *MS. 143*

51 heard *rev to* heaved *Betz MS. 4*

51–52 "From body pains or pains of Soul Thou [Thou *rev from* thou] needest no release;
"Thy hours, [hours, *rev from* hours] as they flow on are spent, [spent, *rev from* spent] if not in joy, [joy, *rev from* joy] in peace. *rev to*
Alas what [mournful *inserted*] sighs have here been heaved what bitter tears have dropp'd
Upon that pavement when the voice by sudden pangs was stopped *rev to text MS. 89*
"From body-pains or pains of soul thou needest no release;
"Thy hours as they flow on are spent, if not in joy, in peace. *rev to text WL MS. 2*

51–52, 53–56 In WL MS. 2 MW first transcribed ll. 55–56 after l. 50, deleted them, and inserted the 1842 reading. She then skipped the following stanza (ll. 53–56) to continue with ll. 57–60. The missing stanza was later inserted in another hand, reproducing the text of MW's letter.

"Poor Shepherd of the naked Down, a favoured lot is thine,
Far happier lot, dear Boy, than brings full many to this shrine;
From body pains and pains of soul thou needest no release,
Thy hours as they flow on are spent, if not in joy, in peace.

"Then offer up thy heart to God in thankfulness and praise,
Give to Him prayers, and many thoughts, in thy most busy days;
And in His sight the fragile Cross, on thy small hut, will be
Holy as that which long hath crowned the Chapel of this Tree;

"Holy as that far seen which crowns the sumptuous Church in Rome
Where thousands meet to worship God under a mighty Dome;
He sees the bending multitude, he hears the choral rites,
Yet not the less, in children's hymns and lonely prayer, delights.

"God for his service needeth not proud work of human skill;
They please him best who labour most to do in peace his will:
So let us strive to live, and to our Spirits will be given
Such wings as, when our Saviour calls, shall bear us up to heaven."

53–56 *inserted WL MS. 2*

53–54 Poor Shepherd of the lonely Down a happier lot is thine
[*alt* Poor shepherd Boy another lot and happier far is thine]
Far happier lot dear Boy than brings so many to this shrine *rev to text but no punct MS. 89*

54 dear] poor *WL MS. 2* full *inserted MS. 151.2*

55–56 *inserted MS. 89*

55 needest] needst *MS. 89*

56 flow] pass *WL MS. 2, MW to IF*

59 His *rev from* This *MS. 89*

60 hath] has *Betz MS. 4, WL MS. 2*

61–62 Thou hast been told of that huge Church far far away in Rome,
Where thousands meet to honour God beneath its sumptuous dome *rev to*
"There stands, thou knowest [knowest *rev to* know'st], a marvellous Church far far away in Rome,
Where thousands meet to honour God under its mighty dome; *MS. 89; Betz MS. 4 as rev MS. 89 but* honour] honor dome;] dome: *WL MS. 2 as rev MS. 89 but* stands,] stands Church] Church, Where] "Where God under] God, beneath *rev to* God, under dome] Dome

61 far seen *inserted MS. 143*

62 worship *rev from* [?honour] *MS. 143*

63 *rev from* The bending multitude, he sees, & hears the choral rites; *MS. 89*

64 prayer *rev from* prayers *MS. 89*

65 skill *rev from* hands *MS. 143*

66 best *rev to* most *Betz MS. 4* most, *WL MS. 2*

67 strive to live *rev from illeg eras MS. 89* Spirits *rev from* Spirit *MS. 89*

68 our] our *rev from* the *MS. 89* our *inserted MS. 143* us *rev from* my *MS. 89* calls *rev from* comes *MS. 143*

The Boy no answer made by words, but, so earnest was his look,
Sleep fled, and with it fled the dream—recorded in this book,
Lest all that passed should melt away in silence from my mind,
As visions still more bright have done, and left no trace behind.

And though the dream, to thee, poor Boy! to thee from whom it flowed,
Was nothing, nor e'er can be aught, 'twas bounteously bestowed,
If I may dare to cherish hope that gentle eyes will read
Not loth, and listening Little-ones, heart-touched, their fancies feed.

---

69 made *inserted MS. 143* by *rev from* with *MS. 151.2*

The Boy no answer made by speech {, but so earnest was his look
in

69–72 ~~The Boy no word~~ {in / ~~[?or] answer,~~} {speech / spoke} ~~but so solemn was his look~~
& with it fled ~~the vision; as fast~~ the vision—in the pages of
Sleep fled—{& / ~~what remains? remembrance~~} {is / ~~s?~~} ^ this Book
Set forth in words of simple verse—
~~In which my dream is written down~~ {, that gentle eyes may read
listening Little-ones,
~~Not loth, and Infants hear~~ heart-touched, their fancies feed.
~~while they their fancies feed~~ *rev to*
The Boy no answer made by speech [speech *rev to* words], but so earnest was his look
Sleep fled, & with it fled the dream—recorded in this book
Lest all that passed, should from my mind in silence melt away
As visions still more bright have done, how oft I could not say *rev to*
The Boy no answer made by words, but so earnest was his look
Sleep fled & with it fled the dream—recorded in this book
Should melt away in silence from my mind ~~fade by with lapse of time, as from my mind~~
Lest all that passed ^ ~~should from my mind in silence melt away~~
more
bright~~er oft~~ have done and left no trace behind
~~As~~ Visions still ^ ~~more bright have done, how oft I could not say~~ *MS. 89*

71 *written over illeg eras MS. 143*

72/73 But oh! that Countryman of thine some Bard [some Bard *rev to* dear Boy] whose eye can see
A pledge of endless bliss, in acts of early piety
In verse which to thy seer [seer *rev to* ear] might come would treat this humble [humble *rev to* simple] theme
Nor leave unsung our happy flight dear Boy in that adventurous dream *WW to EFO*
But oh! that Country-man of thine, whose eye, loved Child, can see
A pledge of endless bliss in acts of early piety,
In verse, which to thy ear might come, would treat this simple theme,
Nor leave untold our happy flight in that adventurous dream. *1845–*

73–74 Alas the dream to thee [P *del*] poor Boy! to thee from whom it flowed
Was nothing scarcely can be aught yet 'twas bounteously bestowed *WW to EFO*
Alas the dream, to thee, poor Boy! to thee from whom it flowed,
Was nothing, scarcely can be aught, yet 'twas bounteously bestowed, *1845–*

73–76 And tho' the dream to him from whom, as from its source, it flowed
ere
Was nothing, nor aught ^ can be, 'twas not in vain bestowed
If undeceved I cherish hope that gentle eyes may read
Not loth, & listening Little-ones, heart-touched, their fancies feed *rev to text MS. 89*

73 And though] Alas *1845–* dream, to *rev from* dream for *MS. 151.2*

74 nor e'er . . . 'twas] scarcely . . . yet 'twas *1845–*

75 hope *rev from* hopes *Betz MS. 4*

AT FURNESS ABBEY.

HERE, where, of havoc tired and rash undoing,
Man left this Structure to become Time's prey
A soothing spirit follows in the way
That Nature takes, her counter-work pursuing.
See how her Ivy clasps the sacred Ruin
Fall to prevent or beautify decay;
And, on the mouldered walls, how bright, how gay,
The flowers in pearly dews their bloom renewing!
Thanks to the place, blessings upon the hour;
Even as I speak the rising Sun's first smile
Gleams on the grass-crowned top of yon tall Tower
Whose cawing occupants with joy proclaim
Prescriptive title to the shattered pile
Where, Cavendish, *thine* seems nothing but a name!

---

composed perhaps around July–August 1840; revised around but by August 25, 1843
found in Pocket Notebook; DC MS. 162 (A) 1v, (B) 1r; Victoria MS. 4; MS. 1845W
published in *1845–*
classed Miscellaneous Sonnets *1845–; 1846 (vol. 6)*
reading text *1845*

1–3 Where Man, of yore, tired out with wild undoing
Left [Left *rev from* left] this vast fabric [fabric *rev from* ?abric] to become Time's prey:
The haunt of ruin [*alt* Shattered and rough] pleasant is the way *MS. 162 (A)*

3 Twill soothe our Spirits if we note the way *MS. 162 (B)*

4 her *rev from* a *MS. 162 (A)* a *MS. 162 (B)*

5 Ivy] ivy *rev from* in *MS. 162 (B)*

7 on *rev from* in *alt* see, *Victoria MS. 4* the mouldered] these mouldering *MS. 162 (A)* the mouldered *rev in pencil from* the mouldering *MS. 162 (B)*

8 pearly] morning *MS. 162 (B)* dews] dew *MS. 162 (A), Victoria MS. 4*

9–10 Heart [Heart *rev from* Hart] touch, he knows not how the Regal head
As he goes forth the rising Sun's first smile *MS. 162 (A)*

10 Even as] Even while *Victoria MS. 4*

13 the shattered] this lonely *Victoria MS. 4*

See the transcription of *At Furness Abbey* from Pocket Notebook on p. 830.

ON A PORTRAIT OF THE DUKE OF WELLINGTON, UPON THE FIELD OF WATERLOO, BY HAYDON.

BY Art's bold privilege Warrior and War-horse stand
On ground yet strewn with their last battle's wreck;
Let the Steed glory while his Master's hand
Lies fixed for ages on his conscious neck;
But by the Chieftain's look, though at his side
Hangs that day's treasured sword, how firm a check
Is given to triumph and all human pride!
Yon trophied Mound shrinks to a shadowy speck

---

composed August 31, 1840

found in DC MS. 89; WW to BRH, September 2, 1840; Haydon MS.; Princeton MS. 5; WW to BRH, September 4, 1840; WW to BRH, September 7, 1840; WW to BRH, September 10, 1840; WW to BRH, September 11 (a), 1840; WW to BRH, September 11 (b), 1840; WW to IF, September 14, 1840; WW to HR, September 14, 1840; Berg MS. 5; Huntington MS. 10 (HM12313; in BRH's hand); WW to BRH, September 23, 1840; WW to RMM, September 25, 1840; WW to BRH, October 24, 1840; WW to HCR, October 27, 1840; Rydal Mount MS.; DC MSS. 146; 151.1; 151.2; 151.3 (IF and WW); Monkhouse Album

published in *LG* (September 19, 1840), *1842, 1845–*

classed Miscellaneous Sonnets *1842, 1845–; 1846 (vol. 6)*

reading text *1842*

title *lacking MS. 89, Rydal Mount MS.* On the Ground of Waterloo Painted by Hayden [Hayden *rev from* Haden] *MS. 146,* Upon Hayden's Portrait of The Duke of Wellington. Supposed to be on the field of Waterloo 20 years after the Battle *WW to HR* Sonnet Suggested by Haydon's Picture of the Duke and Copenhagen on the Field at Waterloo 20 years after the battle *Berg MS. 5* Suggested by Haydon's Picture of the Duke and Copenhagen on the Field at Waterloo 20 years after the Battle *Haydon MS.* Sonnet Suggested by Haydon's Picture of the Duke of Wellington and his Horse on the field of Waterloo 20 years after the battle. *Huntington MS. 10* Sonnet / Suggested by Haydon's Picture of the Duke of Wellington / upon the Field of Waterloo 20 y^rs^. after the action *Princeton MS. 5* Suggested by Haydon's Picture of Wellington and his Horse, Copenhagen, on the Field of Waterloo, Twenty Years after the Battle. Painted for St. George's Hall, Liverpool, and now engraving by Lupton. *LG (all in ital)* Sonnet composed by M^r^. Wordsworth on accomplishing the ascent to Helvellyn August 1840, Suggested by Hayden's picture of the Duke of Wellington and his War Horse. *Monkhouse Album* The Picture of the Duke of Wellington, upon the field of Waterloo, painted by Haydon *MS. 151.1* On a Portrait of the Duke of Wellington, upon the field of Waterloo by Haydon *MS. 151.2*

1 By] Through *MS. 89, WW to HR, Monkhouse Album, Huntington MS. 10, LG*

2 yet] still *Berg MS. 5, LG* still *rev to* yet *WW to BRH, October 24, 1840, and WW to RMM* their] the *LG* their *rev from* the *WW to RMM*

3 while] whilst *MS. 89* while *rev from* for *Princeton MS. 5* for *LG*

4 ages *rev from* ever *WW to RMM* ever *Berg MS. 5*

5 Chieftain's] chiefains *rev from* Warrior's *Berg MS. 5* at] by *Berg MS. 5, HM12313, LG*

8 Yon] Yon *rev from* [?Your] *Berg MS. 5* Mound *rev from miscopied* Mount *rev from* [÷] *Huntington MS. 10*

In his calm presence! Him the mighty deed
Elates not, brought far nearer the grave's rest,
As shows that time-worn face, for he such seed
Has sown as yields, we trust, the fruit of fame

9–12 Since that mighty deed
His life is brought far nearer the grave's rest,
As shows that time-worn face. But genuine seed
He sowed that yields, we trust, the fruit of fame *MS. 89*
Since the mighty deed
Life is
His ~~hours have~~ brought far nearer the grave's rest
~~years~~
As shews that time worn face. But he such seed
Hath sown, as yields we trust, the fruit of fame *Haydon MS.*
~~Him~~
Since the mighty deed
~~life is~~ Him years have
{s {brought
Hi{m years have {[?borne] far nearer the grave's rest
~~Him years~~ face ~~face~~ he such
As shews that ~~face~~ time-worn. But ~~genuine~~ seed
{th ~~sown~~ ~~as yields~~
Ha{s ~~sowed that bears~~, we trust, the fruit of fame
Has sowed that bears *Princeton MS. 5*
Since the mighty deed
Him years have brought far nearer the grave's rest,
As shews that time-worn face. But he such seed
i}
Hath sown, as ye} elds, we trust, ~~&c &c~~
the fruit of fame
In Heaven &— *WW to BRH, September 4, 1840*
Him the mighty deed
Elates not brought far nearer the grave's rest
As shows that time-worn face. but he such seed
Hath sown as yields, we trust, &c. *WW to BRH, September 7, 1840; so WW to HCR but* face—but
"Him the mighty deed
Elates not brought far nearer the
grave's rest
As shews that time-worn face; but [but *rev to* But] He
such seed
Hath sown as yields" &c— *WW to BRH, September 10, 1840*

In Heaven; hence no one blushes for thy name,
Conqueror, 'mid some sad thoughts, divinely blest!

9–12 [*cont.*] Him the mighty deed
Elates not{: ,—} neither doth a cloud find rest,
Upon {that his} time-worn face; for He such seed
Hath sown &c. *WW to BRH, September 11(a), 1840*
Since the mighty deed
"His life is brought far nearer the [the *rev from* his] grave's rest,
As shews that time-worn face. But he, such seed
Hath sown, as yields &c— *WW to BRH, September 11(b), 1840*
Him the mighty deed
Elates not brought far nearer the grave's rest
As ~~shows~~ {shows proves} that time-worn face. {But he For} *WW to BRH, September 23, 1840*
Him the mighty deed
Elates not; neither doth a cloud find rest
Upon the [the *rev to* that] time-worn face; For he &c *WW to IF*
Him the mighty deed
Elates not brought far nearer the grave's rest,
As shews that time-worn face. But He such seed
Hath sown as yields, we trust, the fruit of fame *WW to HR*
Him the mighty deed
Elates not, brought far nearer the grave's rest
As shows that Face time-worn—But ~~has~~ such seed
Has sown, as yields we trust the fruit of fame *Berg MS. 5*
{H h}im the mighty deed
Elates not; brought far nearer the grave's rest
As shews that face time-worn; but he such seed
Hath sown, as yields we trust the fruit of of fame *Huntington MS. 10*
Him the mighty deed
Elates not brought far nearer the grave's rest
As shews that timeworn face. But He such seed
Hath sown as yields we trust the fruit of fame *Rydal Mount MS.*
Him, the mighty deed
Elates not: brought far nearer the grave's rest,
As shews that face, time-worn. But he such seed
Hath sown, as yields, we trust, the fruit of fame *LG*

10 the *rev from* his *MS. 151.2* his *MS. 151.1*

11 time-worn face, for he such seed] Face time-worn—But he [has *del*] such seed *Berg MS. 5, so WW to BRH, October 24, 1840 but rev to text* time-worn face] time-worn face *rev from* face, time-worn *WW to RMM* face, for] face; but *Huntington MS. 10* face. But *Princeton MS. 5; Rydal Mount MS.; WW to HR* face; for *MS. 151.1*

12 Has] Hath *Princeton MS. 5; WW to BRH, September 7, 1840; Huntington MS. 10, Berg MS. 5, Rydal Mount MS., MS. 151.1*

14/ *inscription* —WW. *MS. 146* Composed while ascending Helvellyn Monday Aug 31st. 1840 Wm Wordsworth *Princeton MS. 5, so Huntington MS. 10 but* Aug 31st.] Aug—31— *so Berg MS. 5 but* Aug 31st.] Aug 31 *so Haydon MS. but* 1840] 1840. William Wordsworth. Transcribed by the author Wm Wordsworth Novbr 1[?7]th 1840 *Rydal Mount MS.* Composed while ascending Helvellyn. Monday, August 31st, 1840. Wm. Wordsworth. *all but signature in ital, LG; inscription lacking in MS. 89, WW to HR, Monkhouse Album, MSS. 146, 151.1 and 151.2, but* Sonnet composed the other day while I was climbing our Mountain—Helvellyn *introduces transcription of poem in WW to HR*

"Sigh no more Ladies, sigh no more"

Sigh no more Ladies, sigh no more,
Men were deceivers ever!
So says the old Ballad but
Fair Ladies believe it never!

"The Crescent-moon, the Star of Love"

The version of "The Crescent-moon, the Star of Love" that is presented here as the second reading text was published in *Poems, Chiefly of Early and Late Years* in 1842; but it does not appear in the printer's manuscript, which had been submitted by mid-February of that year. Its position in the last dozen pages before the text of *The Borderers* at the end of the volume suggests a late addition. The first reading text is based on an earlier version in DC MS. 143, where the poem is dated "Feb$^{\underline{ry}}$ 25$^{\underline{th}}$ 1841." Wordsworth was making corrections and additions to proof in March and early April and the book appeared in print in mid-April 1842.

[Text of MS. 143]

The Crescent Moon the Star of Love
Bright Pair! with but a span of sky between
Speak one of you my doubt remove
Which is the attendant Page and which the Queen?
Feb$^{\underline{ry}}$ 25$^{\underline{th}}$ 1841

---

composed probably after 1840
found in Victoria MS. 3
4 Fair] fair *Victoria MS. 3*

---

composed February 25, 1841
found in DC MS. 143; DC MS. 151.1
reading text DC MS. 143
1 Crescent *rev from* setting *MS. 143*
4/ 25 *rev from* 24 *MS. 143* Feb^{ry} 25$^{\underline{th}}$ 1841 *MS. 151.1*

[Text of 1842]

THE Crescent-moon, the Star of Love,
Glories of evening, as ye there are seen
With but a span of sky between—
Speak one of you, my doubts remove,
Which is the attendant Page and which the Queen?

"Let more ambitious Poets take the heart"

Let more ambitious Poets take the heart
By storm, my verse would rather win its way
With gentle violence into minds well-pleased
To give it welcome with a prompt return
Of their own sweetness, as March-flowers that shrink
From the sharp wind do readily yield up
Their choicest fragrance to a southern breeze
Ruffling their bosoms with its genial breath.

---

composed in revised form around March or early April 1842
found in DC MS. 151.3; MS. 1836/45 (JC's note only)
published in *1842, 1845–*
classed Evening Voluntaries *1845, 1850; unclassed 1846 (vol. 6)*
reading text *1842*

---

composed possibly early spring 1841
found in DC MS. 143 (A) 4^{v}, (B) 4^{r}, (C) 32^{v}, (D) 32^{v}
published in *PW*, IV (1947)
reading text DC MS. 143 (D)

1 take the heart *rev to* strive to take *MS. 143 (B)* strive to take *rev to text MS. 143 (C)*
2 [By storm *del*] The heart by storm, my verse would win its way *MS. 143 (B)*
The heart by storm, my verse will win its way *rev to text MS. 143 (C)*
3–5 By gentle force into the Mind that yields
With glad [glad *alt* prompt] compliance, as March-flowers that shrink *MS. 143 (B)*
5 *rev from* Of sweetness, as the flowers of March that shrink *MS. 143 (C)*
6 the sharp] a fi[?e]rce *MS. 143 (B)* yield up *rev from* give out *MS. 143 (C)* give out *MS. 143 (B)*
7 choicest] sweetest *MS. 143 (B)*

See the photograph and transcription of "Let more ambitious Poets take the heart," DC MS. 143 (A) 4^{v}, pp. 780–781.

EPITAPH IN THE CHAPEL-YARD OF LANGDALE, WESTMORELAND.

By playful smiles, (alas too oft
A sad heart's sunshine) by a soft
And gentle nature, and a free
Yet modest hand of charity,
Through life was Owen Lloyd endeared
To young and old; and how revered
Had been that pious spirit, a tide
Of humble mourners testified,
When, after pains dispensed to prove
The measure of God's chastening love,
Here, brought from far, his corse found rest,—
Fulfilment of his own request;—
Urged less for this Yew's shade, though he
Planted with such fond hope the tree;
Less for the love of stream and rock,
Dear as they were, than that his Flock,
When they no more their Pastor's voice
Could hear to guide them in their choice
Through good and evil, help might have,
Admonished, from his silent grave,
Of righteousness, of sins forgiven,
For peace on earth and bliss in heaven.

"Though Pulpits and the Desk may fail"

Though Pulpits and the Desk may fail
To reach the hearts of worldly men;

---

composed between April 18 and August 7, 1841
found in Princeton MS. 5; Swarthmore MS. 3; Tombstone (at Chapel Stile, Langdale)
published in *1842, 1845, 1846, 1850*
classed Epitaphs *1845, 1850; unclassed 1846 (vol. 6)*
reading text *1842*
title *lacking Princeton MS. 5* To the Memory of the Rev[d]. Owen Lloyd M.A. nearly 12 years Incumbent of this Chapel. Born at Old Brathay 1803—; Died at Manchester April 18th. 1841. *Swarthmore MS. 3; so Tombstone but* Memory of Owen . . . the Chapel . . . March 31st, 1803, *and* 1841, Aged 38.
1 By smiles of playful glee—too oft *Princeton MS. 5*
3 nature] temper *Princeton MS. 5*
7 spirit] Soul *Princeton MS. 5*
8 humble] Heart-struck *Princeton MS. 5*
15 love] sake *Princeton MS. 5*
19 have, *so 1845–* have *Princeton MS. 5, Swarthmore MS. 3, Tombstone, 1842*

---

composed April 28, 1841
published in *PW*, IV (1947)
reading text *PW*, IV (1947)

Yet may the grace of God prevail
And touch them through the Poet's pen.

WM. WORDSWORTH

BATH, *April* 28*th*, 1841

THE WISHING-GATE DESTROYED

'TIS gone—with old belief and dream
That round it clung, and tempting scheme
Released from fear and doubt;
And the bright landscape too must lie,
By this blank wall, from every eye,
Relentlessly shut out.

Bear witness ye who seldom passed
That opening—but a look ye cast
Upon the lake below,
What spirit-stirring power it gained
From faith which here was entertained,
Though reason might say no.

Blest is that ground, where, o'er the springs
Of history, glory claps her wings,
Fame sheds the exulting tear;
Yet earth is wide, and many a nook
Unheard of is, like this, a book
For modest meanings dear.

It was in sooth a happy thought
That grafted, on so fair a spot,
So confident a token
Of coming good;—the charm is fled;

---

composed probably mid- to late August 1841
found in Yale MS. 8; Huntington MS. 11; DC MSS. 151.1 (A) 79^{r}, 79^{v}, (B) 97^{r}–98^{r}; 151.2 (A) 101^{r}–102^{v}, (B) 125^{r}
published in *1842, 1845—*
classed Imagination *1845, 1850; unclassed 1846 (vol. 6)*
reading text *1842*
title *lacking Yale MS. 8*
headnote see Wishing gate 5th vol authors poems *MS. 151.2 (A)*
stanza numbers 1 to 12 *MS. 151.1 (B)*
1–24, 31–36 *WW ordered stanzas by entering arabic numbers* 1–5 *Yale MS. 8*
7–12 *entered after l. 24, del, then reinstated as second stanza Yale MS. 8*
13 that] the *Yale MS. 8*
15 exulting *rev from* exultion *Huntington MS. 11*
16 Yet *rev from* But *Huntington MS. 11*
17 Unheard *rev from* Unthought *Yale MS. 8*
20 That *rev from* Which *Huntington MS. 11*

Indulgent centuries spun a thread,
  Which one harsh day has broken.

Alas! for him who gave the word;
Could he no sympathy afford,
  Derived from earth or heaven,
To hearts so oft by hope betrayed;
Their very wishes wanted aid
  Which here was freely given?

Where, for the love-lorn maiden's wound,
Will now so readily be found
  A balm of expectation?
Anxious for far-off children, where
Shall mothers breathe a like sweet air
  Of home-felt consolation?

And not unfelt will prove the loss
'Mid trivial care and petty cross
  And each day's shallow grief;
Though the most easily beguiled
Were oft among the first that smiled
  At their own fond belief.

---

24 harsh *rev from* harshd *Yale MS. 8*
25–30 *transposed with* 31–36 *Huntington MS. 11, MS. 151.1 (B); for Yale MS. 8 see notes*
26 Could *rev from* Would *Huntington MS. 11*
31 Where, for the] Ah where for *Yale MS. 8, so Huntington MS. 11 but* Ah!
34 far-off] far off *rev from* absent *Yale MS. 8*
35 like sweet *rev from* softer *Yale MS. 8*
37–42 Where selfish Interest rules, her sway
Fancy and feeling must obey;
But, in this changeful age,
At such mild injuries why repine
When throne and altar tomb and shrine
Have bowed to vulgar rage? *Huntington MS. 11*
Where selfish interest rules—her sway
Fancy and feeling must obey
 But in a sweeping
~~Tis done but in this~~ age
~~At such mild injuries why~~ repine
 Why at a wrong like ours
When throne and altar tomb and shrine
Have bowed to vulgar rage *MS. 151.1 (B)*
Where selfish interest rules—her sway
Fancy and feeling must obey;
But in a sweeping age,
Why at a wrong like ours repine
When throne and altar, tomb and shrine,
Have bowed to vulgar rage. *del MS. 151.2 (A)*
37–66 *lacking Yale MS. 8*

If still the reckless change we mourn,
A reconciling thought may turn
To harm that might lurk here,
Ere judgment prompted from within
Fit aims, with courage to begin,
And strength to persevere.

Not Fortune's slave is man: our state
Enjoins, while firm resolves await
On wishes just and wise,
That strenuous action follow both,
And life be one perpetual growth
Of heaven-ward enterprise.

So taught, so trained, we boldly face
All accidents of time and place;
Whatever props may fail,
Trust in that sovereign law can spread
New glory o'er the mountain's head,
Fresh beauty through the vale.

That truth informing mind and heart,
The simplest cottager may part,
Ungrieved, with charm and spell;
And yet, lost Wishing-gate, to thee
The voice of grateful memory
Shall bid a kind farewell!

SONNET.

THOUGH the bold wings of Poesy affect
The clouds and wheel around the mountain tops
Rejoicing, from her loftiest height she drops

---

43 If *rev to* Yet *MS. 151.2 (A)* change] deed *Huntington MS. 11*
44 reconciling] salutary *Huntington MS. 11* salutary *rev to* reconciling *MS. 151.1 (B), MS. 151.2 (A)*
47 Fit aims *rev from illegible phrase Huntington MS. 11*

---

composed probably around November–December 1841 but by late February 1842
found in DC MS. 143; MS. 1842P; MS. 1838/40 (?JC)
published in *1842, 1845–*
classed Miscellaneous Sonnets *1845–, 1846 (vol. 6)*
reading text *1842*
title *lacking 1845–*
1 affect *rev to* effect *MS. 143*
2 wheel around *rev from* hover round *MS. 1842P* love to sweep *MS. 143*
3 drops] droops *MS. 143*

Well pleased to skim the plain with wild flowers deckt,
Or muse in solemn grove whose shades protect
The lingering dew—there steals along, or stops
Watching the least small bird that round her hops,
Or creeping worm, with sensitive respect.
Her functions are they therefore less divine,
Her thoughts less deep, or void of grave intent
Her simplest fancies? Should that fear be thine,
Aspiring Votary, ere thy hand present
One offering, kneel before her modest shrine,
With brow in penitential sorrow bent!

SUGGESTED BY A PICTURE OF THE BIRD OF PARADISE.

THE gentlest Poet, with free thoughts endowed,
And a true master of the glowing strain,
Might scan the narrow province with disdain
That to the Painter's skill is here allowed.
This, this the Bird of Paradise! disclaim
The daring thought, forget the name;
This the Sun's Bird, whom Glendoveers might own
As no unworthy Partner in their flight
Through seas of ether, where the ruffling sway
Of nether air's rude billows is unknown;
Whom Sylphs, if e'er for casual pastime they
Through India's spicy regions wing their way,
Might bow to as their Lord. What character,
O sovereign Nature! I appeal to thee,
Of all thy feathered progeny
Is so unearthly, and what shape so fair?
So richly decked in variegated down,
Green, sable, shining yellow, shadowy brown,
Tints softly with each other blended,
Hues doubtfully begun and ended;
Or intershooting, and to sight

---

5 in *rev from* on *MS. 143*
10 void *over illeg eras MS. 143*

---

composed probably around November–December 1841 but by late February 1842
found in DC MSS. 143, 151.1, 151.2; MS. 1842P
published in *1842, 1845–*
classed Imagination *1845, 1850; unclassed 1846 (vol. 6)*
reading text *1842*
1–4 *inserted MS. 143*
1 The gentlest Poet *WW added in pencil MS. 143* Poet *rev from* Poets *MS. 151.2*
10 nether *rev from* ne[?]ther *MS. 151.1*
19 blended *rev from* blending *MSS. 143, 151.1*

Lost and recovered, as the rays of light
Glance on the conscious plumes touched here and there?
Full surely, when with such proud gifts of life
Began the pencil's strife,
O'erweening Art was caught as in a snare.

A sense of seemingly presumptuous wrong
Gave the first impulse to the Poet's song;
But, of his scorn repenting soon, he drew
A juster judgment from a calmer view;
And, with a spirit freed from discontent,
Thankfully took an effort that was meant
Not with God's bounty, Nature's love, to vie,
Or made with hope to please that inward eye
Which ever strives in vain itself to satisfy,
But to recal the truth by some faint trace
Of power ethereal and celestial grace,
That in the living Creature find on earth a place.

"Lyre! though such power do in thy magic live"

LYRE! though such power do in thy magic live
  As might from India's farthest plain
  Recal the not unwilling Maid,
        Assist me to detain
        The lovely Fugitive:
Check with thy notes the impulse which, betrayed

---

31 freed *WW rev from* field *MS. 151.1*
35 Which loftiest fiction [fiction *rev in pencil and ink from* picture] cannot satisfy *MS. 143*
Which loftiest [loftiest *rev from* loftest] fiction cannot satisfy
WW's alt Which skill of Angels scarce could satisfy *MS. 151.1*
Which smile of Angels scarce could satisfy, *rev to text MS. 151.2*
36 recal *rev to* recall *MS. 143* recall *MS. 151.1*
38 find *rev from* finds *MS. 1842P* finds *MSS. 143, 151.2*

---

composed probably between late November or early December 1841 through February 1842
found in DC MSS. 89 (A) 95^r–96^v, (B) 104^v–105^r, (C) 119^r; 143; 151.1; MS. 1842P; MS. 1842WC (IF)
published *1842, 1845–*
classed Imagination *1845, 1850; unclassed 1846 (vol. 6)*
reading text *1842*
1 power] Powers *MS. 89 (C), MS. 143*
2 farthest *rev from* farther *MS. 143*
3 not *rev in pencil from* most *MS. 143* Maid *rev from* Fugitive *MS. 151.1*
5 The] My *MS. 89 (C)* The *alt in pencil* My *del MS. 143* The *rev to* My *MS. 151.1* lovely] would-be *MSS. 89 (C), 143, 151.1* *illeg word in pencil left margin MS. 143*
6 the *rev in pencil from* that *MS. 143* that *MS. 89 (C)*

See the photographs and transcriptions of "Lyre! though such power do in thy magic live," DC MS. 89 (A) 95^r–96^v and (B) 104^v–105^r, pp. 782–801.

By her sweet farewell looks, I longed to aid.
Here let me gaze enrapt upon that eye,
The impregnable and awe-inspiring fort
Of contemplation, the calm port
By reason fenced from winds that sigh
Among the restless sails of vanity.
But if no wish be hers that we should part,
A humbler bliss would satisfy my heart.
Where all things are so fair,
Enough by her dear side to breathe the air
Of this Elysian weather;
And, on or in, or near, the brook, espy
Shade upon the sunshine lying
Faint and somewhat pensively;
And downward Image gaily vying
With its upright living tree
Mid silver clouds, and openings of blue sky
As soft almost and deep as her cerulean eye.

Nor less the joy with many a glance
Cast up the Stream or down at her beseeching,
To mark its eddying foam-balls prettily distrest
By ever-changing shape and want of rest;
Or watch, with mutual teaching,
The current as it plays

7/8 No wish were hers that we should part *del MS. 143*
8 that [*alt pencil* her] eye *entered on new line MS. 143*
9 awe-inspiring *rev in ink over pencil from* awful *MS. 143* awful *MS. 89 (C)* fort] port *alt* fort *WW MS. 151.1*
10 port *rev from* fort *MS. 151.1* fort *MS. 143*
11 sigh] try *MS. 89 (C)* try *rev to* sigh *rev to* try *ink over pencil MS. 143* try *rev to* sigh *MS. 151.1*
12 Among the] The *MS. 89 (C)* Among the *rev in pencil to* The *MS. 143*
13 be] were *MS. 89 (C)* were *rev to* be *ink over pencil MS. 143*
14 *rev to* Twould satisfy my heart, *MS. 89*
16 Enough by *rev to* By *MS. 89 (C)*
17 *inserted MS. 89 (C)*
17/18 Shade, sunbeam, substance image, all together;
[F] Freaks of Nature's witchery; *MS. 89 (C)*
18 on or in,] in, or on, *MS. 89 (C)* in or on *rev from* in without *rev from* in or out *MS. 143* in, or on, *MS. 151.1* on or in, *rev from* in or on, *MS. 1842P*
19 the sunshine] still water *MS. 89 (C)* Shade *alt in pencil* Shadow *MS. 143*
20 Faint and somewhat *rev from* Somewhat faint and *MS. 1842P* Somewhat faint and *MSS. 89 (C), 143, 151.1*
21 And downward] Downward *MSS. 89 (C), 143, 151.1* Image *rev from* Images *ink over pencil MS. 143*
22 its *rev from* the *MS. 1842P* the *MSS. 89 (C), 143, 151* upright *rev from* upward *ink over pencil MS. 143*
27 *rev to*
To note in many a nook
Carved by the rapid brook
Its eddying foam-balls prettily distrest *MS. 1842WC*
28 and *over* [?] *ink over pencil over illeg erasure MS. 143*
30 plays *over illeg word MS. 151.1*

In flashing leaps and stealthy creeps
Adown a rocky maze;
Or note (translucent summer's happiest chance!)
In the slope-channel floored with pebbles bright,
Stones of all hues, gem emulous of gem,
So vivid that they take from keenest sight
The liquid veil that seeks not to hide them.

PRELUDE.

In desultory walk through orchard grounds,
Or some deep chestnut grove, oft have I paused
The while a Thrush, urged rather than restrained
By gusts of vernal storm, attuned his song
To his own genial instincts; and was heard
(Though not without some plaintive tones between)
To utter, above showers of blossom swept
From tossing boughs, the promise of a calm,
Which the unsheltered traveller might receive
With thankful spirit. The descant, and the wind
That seemed to play with it in love or scorn,
Encouraged and endeared the strain of words
That haply flowed from me, by fits of silence
Impelled to livelier pace. But now, my Book!
Charged with those lays, and others of like mood,
Or loftier pitch if higher rose the theme,
Go, single—yet aspiring to be joined
With thy Forerunners that through many a year
Have faithfully prepared each other's way—
Go forth upon a mission best fulfilled
When and wherever, in this changeful world,
Power hath been given to please for higher ends
Than pleasure only; gladdening to prepare
For wholesome sadness, troubling to refine,

---

33 summer's happiest *rev in ink over pencil from* summers happy *MS. 143*
35 hues] hue *MS. 89 (C)* hues *rev to* hue *MS. 143*
36 vivid] varied *rev to* vividly *MS. 151.1*
36–37 *lacking (leaf torn out) MS. 143*

---

composed Late November 1841 to March 26, 1842
found in DC MSS. 151.1 (A) 95[r], (B) 95[v]; 151.3 (WW's pencil and ink; JC's corrections)
published in *1842, 1845–*
classed Miscellaneous Poems *1845, 1850; unclassed 1846 (vol. 6)*
reading text *1842*
title PRELUDE, PREFIXED TO THE VOLUME ENTITLED "POEMS CHIEFLY OF EARLY AND LATE YEARS." *1845, 1850*
21–22 *rev from* Where power is given to please for higher ends *MS. 151.3*

Calming to raise; and, by a sapient Art
Diffused through all the mysteries of our Being,
Softening the toils and pains that have not ceased
To cast their shadows on our mother Earth
Since the primeval doom. Such is the grace
Which, though unsued for, fails not to descend
With heavenly inspiration; such the aim
That Reason dictates; and, as even the wish
Has virtue in it, why should hope to me
Be wanting that sometimes, where fancied ills
Harass the mind and strip from off the bowers
Of private life their natural pleasantness,
A Voice devoted to the love whose seeds
Are sown in every human breast, to beauty
Lodged within compass of the humblest sight,
To cheerful intercourse with wood and field,
And sympathy with man's substantial griefs—
Will not be heard in vain? And in those days
When unforeseen distress spreads far and wide
Among a People mournfully cast down,
Or into anger roused by venal words
In recklessness flung out to overturn
The judgment, and divert the general heart
From mutual good—some strain of thine, my Book!
Caught at propitious intervals, may win
Listeners who not unwillingly admit
Kindly emotion tending to console
And reconcile; and both with young and old
Exalt the sense of thoughtful gratitude
For benefits that still survive, by faith
In progress, under laws divine, maintained.

RYDAL MOUNT,
MARCH 26, 1842

---

28 shadows] shadow *MS. 151.3*
29 Such is the *rev from* Such the *MS. 151.3*
37–42 Thy Voice my Book to strains of love and beauty
And morals lurking among woods and fields
And sympathy with [?lov] Man's substantial griefs
[?Devoted] may supplant those wayward moods
at the least if
Or if but heard may not at least be heard
Wholly in vain, *MS. 151.1 (B)*
41–42 Or, at the least, if heard may not be heard
In vain *MS. 151.1 (A)*
43 spreads far and *rev from* is spreading *MS. 151.3*
When distress spreads far and wide *alt MS. 151.3*
49 win *rev from* find *MS. 151.3*
52 And reconcile and in the suffering mind *MS. 151.1 (A)*
54 still *rev from* shall *MS. 151.3* yet *MS. 151.1 (A)*

UPON PERUSING THE FOREGOING EPISTLE THIRTY YEARS AFTER ITS COMPOSITION.

Soon did the Almighty Giver of all rest
Take those dear young Ones to a fearless nest;
And in Death's arms has long reposed the Friend
For whom this simple Register was penned.
Thanks to the moth that spared it for our eyes;
And Strangers even the slighted Scroll may prize,
Moved by the touch of kindred sympathies.
For—save the calm, repentance sheds o'er strife
Raised by remembrances of misused life,
The light from past endeavours purely willed
And by Heaven's favour happily fulfilled;
Save hope that we, yet bound to Earth, may share
The joys of the Departed—what so fair
As blameless pleasure, not without some tears,
Reviewed through Love's transparent veil of years?

Sonnet.

When Severn's sweeping Flood had overthrown
St Mary's Church the Preacher then would cry,

---

composed probably in late 1841 but by December 31
found in DC MSS. 151.1 (A) 45^{v}P1^{v}, (B) 45^{v}; 151.2
published *1842, 1845–*
classed Miscellaneous Poems *1845, 1850; unclassed 1846 (vol. 6)*
reading text *1842*
title Upon perusing the foregoing Epistle 30 years after its composition. *with period deleted MS. 151.1 (B); MS. 151.2 as orig MS. 151.1 (B) but* 30] 30.
4 this *WW rev from* the *MS. 151.1 (B)*
6 slighted *rev from* slightest *MS. 151.1 (B)*
6–7 And Strangers, even haply the [the *rev to* this] Scroll may prize,
For its own sake and kindred sympathies. *rev to*
And Strangers, perchance long-slighted Scroll may prize,
Moved by the touch of kindred sympathies. *MS. 151.1 (B), rev to text except* slightest
8 calm *rev from* blest *MS. 151.1 (B)*
9 misused *rev from* ill used *rev from* misused *MS. 151.1 (B)*
11 favour *rev from* favours *MS. 151.1 (B)*
12 Save *WW rev from* [?] *MS. 151.1 (B)*
13 joys] joy *MS. 151.1 (B)*

---

composed January 23, 1842
found in DC MS. 151.1
published in Cardiff Facsimile (1842), BL pamphlet (Cardiff, 1842)
reading text Cardiff Facsimile (1842)
title *lacking in MS. 151.1, Holland & Everett*
Severns sweeping Flood ~~hath~~ had
1–2 When ~~Cardiffs ancient Church~~ was overthrown
~~sweeping~~ St Marys Church, ~~then~~
By ~~Severns floods~~ the Preachers ~~voice~~ would cry *MS. 151.1*

"Thus, Christian People God his might hath shown
That Ye to Him your love may testify;
Haste, and rebuild the Pile"! But not a stone
Resumed its place. Age after Age went by
And Heaven still lacked its due; though Piety
In secret did, we trust, her loss bemoan.
But now her spirit has put forth its claim
In power, and Poesy would lend her voice
Let the new Work be worthy of its aim,
That in its beauty Cardiff may rejoice!
Oh, in the Past if cause there was for shame
Let not our Times halt in their better choice!
W[m] Wordsworth

Rydal Mount
23[d] Jan[ry] 1842

"*A Poet!*—He hath put his heart to school"

A Poet!—He hath put his heart to school,
Nor dares to move unpropped upon the staff
Which Art hath lodged within his hand—must laugh
By precept only, and shed tears by rule.

3–6 With solemn brow and heaven-uplifted eye,
'Haste and rebuild the pile!' but not a stone
Resumed its place. Age after age went by,
(Each year the mandate uttering solemnly,) *Holland & Everett*

3 To yea oh [oh *rev to* Oh] people God his power has [has *rev to* hath] shewn *rev to text MS. 151.1*

7 *rev from* And the reproach remained. Tho Piety *MS. 151.1 but* its] his

8 In *rev from* W *MS. 151.1* her loss *rev from* the want *MS. 151.1*

9 her spirit] her Spirit *rev from* her genuine Spirit *MS. 151.1* has] hath *MS. 151.1, Holland & Everett* its] her *Holland & Everett*

10 In power, and song [song *rev to* Song] would aid her feeble voice; *rev to text MS. 151.1*

11 Work] church *Holland & Everett*

12 That in its aspect Severn may rejoice; *rev to* that [that *rev to* That] in its beauty Cardiff will [will *rev to* may] rejoice; *MS. 151.1*

O if {d
13 ~~And all good men~~ of the past ha{l ve aught ~~of s~~ inch of shame *MS. 151.1*

14 These Times may say here is a better choice *rev to* Let not these Times [halt *inserted*] in their better choice *rev to text MS. 151.1*

14/ William Wordsworth. / Rydal Mount. Jan. 23. 1842. *BL pamphlet, with date and place in ital; signature, place, date lacking Holland & Everett*

---

composed probably around but by late February 1842
found in DC MSS. 151.1; 151.2; 151.3 (IF and WW); MS. 1842P
published in *1842, 1845–*
classed Miscellaneous Sonnets *1842, 1845–, 1846 (vol. 6)*
reading text *1842*

1 hath] has *MS. 151.1*
2 Nor dares [not *inserted*] a foot unpropped by that dear staff *MS. 151.1*
3 Which art has put into [put into *rev to* lodged within] *MS. 151.1*
4 and shed] shed his *MS. 151.1*

Thy Art be Nature; the live current quaff,
And let the groveller sip his stagnant pool,
In fear that else, when Critics grave and cool
Have killed him, Scorn should write his epitaph.
How does the Meadow-flower its bloom unfold?
Because the lovely little flower is free
Down to its root, and, in that freedom, bold;
And so the grandeur of the Forest-tree
Comes not by casting in a formal mould,
But from its *own* divine vitality.

To a Redbreast—(In Sickness)

Wordsworth stated in the Fenwick note that *To a Redbreast—(In Sicknesss)* represented "almost the only verses by our lamented Sister S. H." but gives no hint as to when Sara Hutchinson wrote them. The poem may have been composed in 1835 during her last illness. Wordsworth reworked the second stanza after the poem had been set in proof for *Poems, Chiefly of Early and Late Years* in February or March 1842. His revisions were recorded by John Carter on the proof page (DC MS. 151.3); in the reading text boldface type signals Wordsworth's contribution.

TO A REDBREAST—(IN SICKNESS).

STAY, little cheerful Robin! stay,
  And at my casement sing,
Though it should prove a farewell lay
  And this our parting spring.

---

6 sip] lap *MS. 151.1* stagnant *rev to* cistern *MS. 151.1*
7 when *rev from* some *MS. 151.1*
8 Have killed him, Scorn will write his epitaph. *rev from* May kill him, and scorn [righteous *del*] epitaph. *MS. 151.1*
9 How *rev from* Whence *MS. 151.1*
10 Because the lovely] In sooth because the *MS. 151.1*
11 From restraint and in her freedom bold *MS. 151.1 (gap not filled)*
12–13 Whence comes the magic of [of *rev from* for] the forest tree
Not from [from *rev from* by] the casting of a formal mold *MS. 151.1*
14 its own] its *MS. 151.1*

---

composed February or March 1842 (WW's revision only)
found in DC MS. 151.3 (JC); MS. 1842P
published in *1842, 1845–*
classed Miscellaneous Poems *1845, 1850; unclassed 1846 (vol. 6)*
reading text *1842*

Though I, alas! may ne'er enjoy
The promise in thy song;
A charm, *that* thought can not destroy,
Doth to thy strain belong.

Methinks that in my dying hour
Thy song would still be dear,
And with a more than earthly power
My passing Spirit cheer.

Then, little Bird, this boon confer,
Come, and my requiem sing,
Nor fail to be the harbinger
Of everlasting Spring.

S. H.

"The most alluring clouds that mount the sky"

THE most alluring clouds that mount the sky
Owe to a troubled element their forms,
Their hues to sunset. If with raptured eye
We watch their splendor, shall we covet storms,
And wish the Lord of day his slow decline
Would hasten, that such pomp may float on high?
Behold, already they forget to shine,
Dissolve—and leave to him who gazed a sigh.
Not loth to thank each moment for its boon

5–8 *rev from*
And I not destined to enjoy
The promise of thy song;
The thought shall not the charms destroy
Which to thy strain belong. *MS. 151.3*

---

composed probably around but by late February 1842
found in DC MSS. 151.1; 151.2 (A) 108r, (B) 111v, (C) 113v; 151.3 (IF and WW); MS. 1842P
published in *1842, 1845–*
classed Miscellaneous Sonnets *1842, 1845–, 1846 (vol. 6)*
reading text *1842*

1 alluring *rev from* bewitching *MS. 151.2 (A, B)* mount] grace *MS. 151.2 (A)* mounts *MS. 151.2 (C)*
3 raptured *rev from* watchful *MS. 151.2 (C)*
4 their splendor, shall we covet] them, shall we therefore covet *rev to* their splendor shall we therefore covet *MS. 151.2 (A); MS. 1842P as rev MS. 151.2 (A), then rev to text*
5 And *rev from* O *MS. 151.2 (A)*
6 *rev from* That such pomp may float on high? *MS. 151.2 (A)*

See the photographs and transcriptions of "The most alluring clouds that mount the sky," DC MS. 151.1, 104r, 104v, pp. 802–805.

Of pure delight, come whencesoe'er it may,
Peace let us seek,—to stedfast things attune
Calm expectations, leaving to the gay
And volatile their love of transient bowers,
The house that cannot pass away be ours.

"Intent on gathering wool from hedge and brake"

Wordsworth first composed a five-line poem ("Text of MS. 143"), recording at least three different versions of it, two in MS. 143 and another, signed and dated at Rydal Mount for Anna Ricketts in March 1842, that was recorded in a Sotheby's catalogue (for a sale on May 6, 1936; item 800). This latter version is reported to be five lines long and begins "Can the World's pomp o'ercome a genuine grief?" The original of this transcription for Anna Ricketts has not been found, but its existence confirms that Wordsworth regarded the poem as "finished" in five lines when he wrote it out for his young friend. But not for long. Within a few weeks he expanded the poem to seven lines ("Text of MS. 151"), and transcribed it in a blank space at the foot of page 214 of the proof pages for the 1842 volume, directing the printer to place it either after his adaptation of *Troilus and Cresida* (p. 214) or, preferably, after "the Epitaph on Owen Lloyd if that sheet be not struck off" (p. 205). His letter to Edward Moxon, with the date "April 1st 1842" added in another hand, in which he asked for the "sheets, following upon those we have, which reach to the 224th page" must have been written before about March 15, since Wordsworth had received all of the proofs by March 23 (*LY*, IV, 313 and 307). Finally, he canceled publication of the seven-line poem and adapted the lines for use in the sestet of a sonnet based on an anecdote of her childhood told to him by Isabella Fenwick. He completed the sonnet sometime between March 15 and the end of the month, in time to insert it on the last page (p. 242) of the final section of sonnets in *Poems, Chiefly of Early and Late Years* ("Text of 1842").

[Text of MS. 143 (A)]

Ambition—can she tame Distress and Grief
And pride keep off affliction at arm's length

---

13 And volatile *rev from* Falsely so called, *MS. 151.2 (A)*

---

composed probably between around February and early March 1842
found in DC MS. 143 (A) 49^{v}, (B) 50^{r}
reading text DC MS. 143 (A)
2 And *rev from* [?Or] *MS. 143 (A)*

See the photograph and transcription of "Ambition—can she tame Distress and Grief," DC MS. 143 (B) 50^{r}, pp. 806–807.

Trust not such aid incompetent as brief
Love from her depth and Duty in her strength
And Faith—these only yield secure relief

[Text of MS. 151.3]

Can drops from flowers of vanity distilled
Sweeten the bitter cup which guilt has filled?
Can Pomp dispel the clouds of heart-born grief?
Pains which the world inflicts, can she requite?
Not for an interval however brief:
Love from on high, and Duty in her might,
And Faith—these only yield secure relief.

[Text of 1842]

INTENT on gathering wool from hedge and brake
Yon busy Little-ones rejoice that soon
A poor old Dame will bless them for the boon:
Great is their glee while flake they add to flake
With rival earnestness; far other strife
Than will hereafter move them, if they make
Pastime their idol, give their day of life
To pleasure snatched for reckless pleasure's sake.
Can pomp and show allay one heart-born grief?
Pains which the World inflicts can she requite?
Not for an interval however brief;
The silent thoughts that search for stedfast light,
Love from on high, and Duty in her might,
And Faith—these only yield secure relief.

MARCH 8*th*, 1842.

---

composed probably early March but by March 15, 1842
found in DC MS. 151.3
reading text DC MS. 151.3

---

composed between March 15 and about March 31, 1842
found in DC MS. 151.1
published in *1842, 1845–*
classed Miscellaneous Sonnets *1845–; 1846 (vol. 6)*
reading text *1842*
13 on high] her depths *1845–*

See the photograph and transcription of "Intent on gathering wool from hedge and brake," DC MS. 151.1, 117[r], pp. 808–809.

The Eagle and the Dove

Shade of Caractacus, if Spirits love
The cause they fought for in their earthly home,
To see the Eagle ruffled by the Dove
May soothe thy memory of the chains of Rome.

These children claim thee for their Sire; the breath
Of thy renown, from Cambrian mountains, fans
A flame within them that despises death,
And glorifies the truant Youth of Vannes.

With thy own scorn of tyrants they advance,
But truth divine has sanctified their rage,
A silver Cross enchased with Flowers of France,
Their badge, attests the holy fight they wage.

The shrill defiance of the young Crusade
Their veteran foes mock as an idle noise
But unto Faith and Loyalty comes aid
From Heaven—gigantic force to beardless Boys.

"What heavenly smiles! O Lady mine"

WHAT heavenly smiles! O Lady mine
Through my very heart they shine;
And, if my brow gives back their light,
Do thou look gladly on the sight;
As the clear Moon with modest pride
  Beholds her own bright beams
Reflected from the mountain's side
  And from the headlong streams.

---

composed probably shortly before but by May 11, 1842
found in WW to AFR, May 11, 1842
published in *Chouannerie* (Paris, 1842)
reading text WW to AFR, May 11, 1842
8 Youth *rev from* Boys *WW to AFR*
12 holy *rev from* faithful *WW to AFR*

---

composed between June 1842 and mid-November 1845, probably May–June 1845
found in MS. 1836/45 (A), end flyleaf of vol. 1; (B), vol. 4, [xii]
published in *1845–*
reading text *1845*
classed Affections *1845–*
1 What . . . mine *rev from* Those . . . thine *MS. 1836/45 (A)*
2 my] this *MS. 1836/45 (B)*
4 Do thou look] Meek wanderer, *MS. 1836/45 (B)*
7 mountain's side] mountain-side *MS. 1836/45*

"Wansfell! this Household has a favoured lot"

Wansfell!* this Household has a favoured lot,
Living with liberty on thee to gaze,
To watch while Morn first crowns thee with her rays,
Or when along thy breast serenely float
Evening's angelic clouds. Yet ne'er a note
Hath sounded (shame upon the Bard!) thy praise
For all that thou, as if from heaven, hast brought
Of glory lavished on our quiet days.
Bountiful Son of Earth! when we are gone
From every object dear to mortal sight,
As soon we shall be, may these words attest
How oft, to elevate our spirits, shone
Thy visionary majesties of light,
How in thy pensive glooms our hearts found rest.
Dec. 24, 1842.

*The Hill that rises to the south-east, above Ambleside.

---

composed December 24, 1842
found in MS. 1838/40 (A) p. [478], (B) p. [xii]; Princeton MS. 6; Houghton MS. 5; Michigan MS.; Trinity MS.
published in *1845–*
classed Miscellaneous Sonnets *1845–; 1846 (vol. 6)*
reading text *1845*

3 while *rev from* when *MS. 1838/40 (A)* Morn] mo[?o]n *Trinity MS.* her] his *Trinity MS.*
4 when *rev from* while *MS. 1838/40 (A), Princeton MS. 6*
9 Bountiful Son of Earth! *rev from* Be what is past forgiven *MS. 1838/40 (A)* Bountiful Son *rev from* B[?eautiful] son *Princeton MS. 6* Beautiful Sun *Trinity MS.*
10 mortal *rev from* human *Princeton MS. 6*
11 these words *rev from* this verse *Houghton MS. 5*
14 pensive *rev from* cl[?] *Princeton MS. 6* thy *rev from* our *MS. 1838/40 (A, B)* glooms *rev from* dreams *MS. 1838/40 (B)*

"Glad sight wherever new with old"

GLAD sight wherever new with old
Is joined through some dear homeborn tie;
The life of all that we behold
Depends upon that mystery.
Vain is the glory of the sky,
The beauty vain of field and grove
Unless, while with admiring eye
We gaze, we also learn to love.

TO A LADY,

IN ANSWER TO A REQUEST THAT I WOULD WRITE HER A POEM UPON SOME DRAWINGS THAT SHE HAD MADE OF FLOWERS IN THE ISLAND OF MADEIRA.

FAIR Lady! can I sing of flowers
  That in Madeira bloom and fade,
I who ne'er sate within their bowers,
  Nor through their sunny lawns have strayed?
How they in sprightly dance are worn

---

composed December 31, 1842, revised around but by November 29, 1843
found in MS. 1838/40, Houghton MS. 4, MS. 1836/45 (MW's fair copy, WW's revs)
published in *1845–*
classed Fancy *1845, 1850; unclassed 1846 (vol. 6)*
reading text *1845*
1–4 *del MS. 1836/45*
Look up, look round, let things unfold,
Far as they may, their mysteries
What profits it if new [and *del*] with old
Unites not by some homeborn ties? *MS. 1838/40*
1 wherever] it is when *Houghton MS. 4* Glad sight wherever] Glad sight it is *rev to* Welcome the sight *MS. 1836/45* with *rev from* and *MS. 1836/45*
2 through *rev from* by *Houghton MS. 4*
3 life] good *MS. 1836/45*
5 sky,] skies *MS. 1838/40, Houghton MS. 4, MS. 1836/45*
7 eye] eyes *MS. 1838/40, Houghton MS. 4, MS. 1836/45*
8 to] *illeg blot MS. 1838/40*

---

composed January 1, 1843
found in MS. 1836/45 (A) front flyleaf of vol. 3; (B) p. [356] (MW); (C) pp. [358–359] (DQ)
published in *Madeira* (1845), *1845–*
classed Sentiment and Reflection *MS. 1836/45* Fancy *1845–; unclassed 1846 (vol. 6)*
reading text *1845*
title Verses Composed at the Request of Jane Wallas Penfold. By William Wordsworth, Esq. Poet Laureate *Madeira*
1 Fair Lady! can] Fair Lady can *rev from* How Lady shall *MS. 1836/45 (C)*
4 Nor *rev from* [?But] *MS. 1836/45 (A)*

By Shepherd-groom or May-day queen,
Or holy festal pomps adorn,
These eyes have never seen.

Yet tho' to me the pencil's art
No like remembrances can give,
Your portraits still may reach the heart
And there for gentle pleasure live;
While Fancy ranging with free scope
Shall on some lovely Alien set
A name with us endeared to hope,
To peace, or fond regret.

Still as we look with nicer care,
Some new resemblance we may trace:
A *Heart's-ease* will perhaps be there,
A *Speedwell* may not want its place.

12–20 *as reading text (with exceptions recorded below), then rev to*
And there in sweet communion live;
Admired for beauty of their own
Loved for the likeness some may bear
To herb or flower by nature sown
To breathe our english air

Thus tempted Fancy with free scope
Will range and on those aliens set
Names among us endeared to hope
To peace or fond regret *MS. 1836/45* (C_1)
draft entered later at foot of opposite page
herb by
In flower ~~or [?plant]~~ to us unkown
[?And] may thine be
~~A Jacobs ladder~~
Jerusalem lace
A touching likeness may be found
To favorite
[~~?To favorite~~] by
To some old favorite of our own
And loved on British ground
To native favorites of our own.
[?and beknownst] of Brit *MS. 1836/45* (C_2)
And there in sweet communion live,
Yet those loved most in which we own
A touching likeness that they bear
To flower or herb by Nature sown
To breathe our English air.
So tempted, Fancy with free scope
May range and those aliens set *MS. 1836/45 (B)*

13 While *rev from* For *MS. 1836/45 (A)*
14 some] each *MS. 1836/45 (C)*
17 Still] Oft *Madeira*
18 Will Fancy widen her embrace; *MS. 1836/45 (C)*
20 may] will *MS. 1845 (C)*

And so may we, with charmèd mind
  Beholding what your skill has wrought,
Another *Star-of-Bethlehem* find,
  A new *Forget-me-not.*

From earth to heaven with motion fleet
  From heaven to earth our thoughts will pass,
A *Holy-thistle* here we meet
  And there a *Shepherd's weather-glass;*
And haply some familiar name
  Shall grace the fairest, sweetest, plant
Whose presence cheers the drooping frame
  Of English Emigrant.

Gazing she feels its power beguile
  Sad thoughts, and breathes with easier breath;
Alas! that meek that tender smile
  Is but a harbinger of death:
And pointing with a feeble hand
  She says, in faint words by sighs broken,
Bear for me to my native land
  This precious Flower, true love's last token.

"While beams of orient light shoot wide and high"

WHILE beams of orient light shoot wide and high,
Deep in the vale a little rural Town*
Breathes forth a cloud-like creature of its own,
That mounts not toward the radiant morning sky,
But, with a less ambitious sympathy,
Hangs o'er its Parent waking to the cares

*Ambleside.

---

24 Nor miss a new Forget me not *MS. 1836/45 (A)*
38 in faint words by] in words, by faint *Madeira*
40/ Rydal Mount, 1st January, 1843 / Wm Wordsworth *Madeira*

---

composed January 1, 1843
found in MS. 1838/40; MS. 1836/45; Princeton MS. 6; Trinity MS.; Houghton MS. 5; Michigan MS.
published in *1845–*
classed Miscellaneous Sonnets *1845–; 1846 (vol. 6)*
reading text *1845*
title Ambleside *Trinity MS., Houghton MS. 5, Michigan MS.*
1 shoot] spread *Trinity MS.*

See the photographs and transcriptions of "While beams of orient light shoot wide and high," MS. 1838/40 and Princeton MS. 6, pp. 810–819.

Troubles and toils that every day prepares.
So Fancy, to the musing Poet's eye,
Endears that Lingerer. And how blest her sway
(Like influence never may my soul reject)
If the calm Heaven, now to its zenith decked
With glorious forms in numberless array,
To the lone shepherd on the hills disclose
Gleams from a world in which the saints repose.
Jan 1, 1843.

GRACE DARLING.

Among the dwellers in the silent fields
The natural heart is touched, and public way
And crowded street resound with ballad strains,
Inspired by ONE whose very name bespeaks
Favour divine, exalting human love;
Whom, since her birth on bleak Northumbria's coast,
Known unto few but prized as far as known,
A single Act endears to high and low
Through the whole land—to Manhood, moved in spite
Of the world's freezing cares—to generous Youth—
To Infancy, that lisps her praise—to Age
Whose eye reflects it, glistening through a tear
Of tremulous admiration. Such true fame
Awaits her *now;* but, verily, good deeds
Do no imperishable record find
Save in the rolls of heaven, where hers may live
A theme for angels, when they celebrate
The high-souled virtues which forgetful earth
Has witness'd. Oh! that winds and waves could speak
Of things which their united power called forth
From the pure depths of her humanity!

---

7 that] which *Houghton MS. 5*
10 The faith how pure and holy in effect *MS. 1836/45*
(Neer may my Soul like influence reject!) *Michigan MS., Houghton MS. 5, both rev to text but* soul] Soul
11 If the calm Heavens, now to their summit decked *MS. 1836/45*
12 With *rev from* In *MS. 1836/45*
14 from *rev from* of *Houghton MS. 5*

---

composed between February 2 and March 1, 1843
found in DC MS. 155, Huntington MS. 12
published in *Darling* (1843); *1845–*
classed Miscellaneous Poems *1845–; unclassed 1846 (vol. 6)*
reading text *1845*
11 to] and *Darling, Huntington MS. 12*

A Maiden gentle, yet, at duty's call,
Firm and unflinching, as the Lighthouse reared
On the Island-rock, her lonely dwelling-place;
Or like the invincible Rock itself that braves,
Age after age, the hostile elements,
As when it guarded holy Cuthbert's cell.

All night the storm had raged, nor ceased, nor paused,
When, as day broke, the Maid, through misty air,
Espies far off a Wreck, amid the surf,
Beating on one of those disastrous isles—
Half of a Vessel, half—no more; the rest
Had vanished, swallowed up with all that there
Had for the common safety striven in vain,
Or thither thronged for refuge. With quick glance
Daughter and Sire through optic-glass discern,
Clinging about the remnant of this Ship,
Creatures—how precious in the Maiden's sight!
For whom, belike, the old Man grieves still more
Than for their fellow-sufferers engulfed
Where every parting agony is hushed,
And hope and fear mix not in further strife.
"But courage, Father! let us out to sea—
A few may yet be saved." The Daughter's words,
Her earnest tone, and look beaming with faith,
Dispel the Father's doubts: nor do they lack
The noble-minded Mother's helping hand
To launch the boat; and with her blessing cheered,
And inwardly sustained by silent prayer,
Together they put forth, Father and Child!
Each grasps an oar, and struggling on they go—
Rivals in effort; and, alike intent
Here to elude and there surmount, they watch

---

whose front ~~exposed~~
25–32 ~~Or as the Rock itself that hath withstood~~
hath braved
~~to~~ to ~~the~~ the hostile elements
{~~hath~~
~~Age after age, the Elements~~ {~~had braved~~
Buffting
~~Their utmost~~ fury.—But thro' misty air
sorrowful objects hath the Maid espied
What ~~hath the Maiden,~~ looking forth, espied
~~Far off?—A shapeless wreck, amid~~ the surf, *MS. 155*

32 —Half [Half *alt* Part] of a vessel split in twain—the rest *MS. 155*

33 Had] Hath *MS. 155*

35 quick] a *MS. 155*

The billows lengthening, mutually crossed
And shattered, and re-gathering their might;
As if the tumult, by the Almighty's will
Were, in the conscious sea, roused and prolonged
That woman's fortitude—so tried, so proved—
May brighten more and more!

True to the mark,
They stem the current of that perilous gorge,
Their arms still strengthening with the strengthening heart,
Though danger, as the Wreck is near'd, becomes
More imminent. Not unseen do they approach;
And rapture, with varieties of fear
Incessantly conflicting, thrills the frames
Of those who, in that dauntless energy,
Foretaste deliverance; but the least perturbed
Can scarcely trust his eyes, when he perceives
That of the pair—tossed on the waves to bring
Hope to the hopeless, to the dying, life—
One is a Woman, a poor earthly sister,
Or, be the Visitant other than she seems,
A guardian Spirit sent from pitying Heaven,
In woman's shape. But why prolong the tale,
Casting weak words amid a host of thoughts
Armed to repel them? Every hazard faced
And difficulty mastered, with resolve
That no one breathing should be left to perish,
This last remainder of the crew are all
Placed in the little boat, then o'er the deep
Are safely borne, landed upon the beach,
And, in fulfilment of God's mercy, lodged
Within the sheltering Lighthouse.—Shout, ye Waves!
Send forth a song of triumph. Waves and Winds,
Exult in this deliverance wrought through faith
In Him whose Providence your rage hath served!
Ye screaming Sea-mews, in the concert join!
And would that some immortal Voice—a Voice
Fitly attuned to all that gratitude
Breathes out from floor or couch, through pallid lips
Of the survivors—to the clouds might bear—

54–55 *beside these lines* [?her] power [?full] *deleted Huntington MS. 12*

56–57 As if the wrath and trouble of the sea
Were by the Almighty's sufferance prolonged, *Darling; so Huntington MS. 12 rev to text*

73–86 *eras pencil in margins, mostly illegible except* Hail the / [?Eighteen] / Through *Huntington MS. 12*

84 Pipe a glad song of triumph, ye fierce Winds! *Darling; so Huntington MS. 2, then rev to text but* Winds,] Winds!

85–86 *lacking Darling; so Huntington MS. 12 rev to text (JC inserted l. 86; see also nonverbal variants)*

Blended with praise of that parental love,
Beneath whose watchful eye the Maiden grew
Pious and pure, modest and yet so brave,
Though young so wise, though meek so resolute—
Might carry to the clouds and to the stars,
Yea, to celestial Choirs, GRACE DARLING's name!

Inscription for a Monument in Crosthwaite Church, in the Vale of Keswick

As he did with his verse memorial to Charles Lamb, Wordsworth took considerable pains with his tribute to Robert Southey, *Inscription for a Monument in Crosthwaite Church, in the Vale of Keswick.* The project seems to have begun with Wordsworth's draft of a prose epitaph (Southey Album 3), containing the "requisites" of an epitaph as he defined them in his first *Essay on Epitaphs.* A revised version was copied by Isabella Fenwick on 48r of DC MS. 89.

Wordsworth's prose draft follows, followed in turn by the copy in MS. 89.

[Sacred *del*] [t *rev to* T]o the Memory of
Robert Southey born at Bristol
died &c.

A man eminent [in Literature *del*] for [g *rev to* G]enius, versatile talents, and habits of the most conscientious industry. Nor [was less *rev to* was he less *in autograph like JC's*] distinguished by strict temperance pure benevolence and warm affections; but his Mind, such are the awful dispensations of Providence, was prematurely and almost totally obscured by a slowly working and inscrutable malady under which he continued to languish untill released by death in the sixty eighth year of his age.

Reader ponder the condition to which [this goo *rev to* this great & good] Man not without merciful alleviations [this great and good *del*] was doomed; and learn from his example to make timely use of thy endowments & opportunities and to walk humbly with thy God.

The revised epitaph, though written in prose, was arranged on the page by Isabella Fenwick to resemble an actual inscription on a stone:

In [In *rev from* To the] Memory
of
Robert Southey,
A Man eminent for genius, vers[?a]tile talents,
Extensive and accurate knowledge,
And habits of the most conscienscious industry.
Nor was He less distinguished for [for *rev from* from] sweet temperance,
Pure benevolence, warm affections and steadfast piety.
But, at a late period of life,
His mental consciousness was gradually obscured
By an inscrutable malady,
Under which He languish'd till the spirit was released from the body,
In the sixty ninth year of His age.—

Reader, ponder this aweful dispensation,
And learn, from His example, to make timely use
Of thy endowments and opportunities,
And to walk humbly with thy God.—

Wordsworth incorporated the sentiment of the opening section in his verse memorial but omitted reference to Southey's "inscrutable malady" and the lesson drawn from it. Wordsworth may have been commenting on a version of the first prose epitaph in his letter to John Taylor Coleridge, December 2, 1843, when he remarked, "'Prematurely' I object to as you do. I used the word with reference to that decay of faculties which is not uncommon in advanced life, and which often leads to Dotage—but the word must not be retained" ("gradually obscured" in the second version replaced "prematurely obscured" in the first; the letter is quoted further below; and see JTC to WW, November 30, 1843; WL MS., A/Coleridge, J.T./9).

Earlier, on June 20, 1843, John Taylor Coleridge had written to Wordsworth (WL MS.; A/Coleridge, J. T./8), inviting him to take part in plans for a monument to Southey at Keswick. Wordsworth responded with a detailed explanation of the history and purpose of the plan in which he was already involved:

In respect to Mr Southey's Monument it was not intended that it should interfere in the least with any testimony that might be paid to his Memory at Westminster Abbey. But as he had chosen the Vale of Keswick for his Residence and had lived there for forty years or upwards, some of the neighbouring Gentry (with whom I conversed) were anxious to erect a Tablet in the Church to express their admiration of the life which he had led and their veneration for his Memory. And it was accordingly intended and I believe still is, that the subscription for this purpose should not extend beyond the surrounding district which he had so long benefited and honoured by his presence.

The project which was suspended by the distressed state of the family and the miserable dissentions that prevailed in it will, I have no doubt now that the Sales [chiefly of RS's books] are over to be resumed forthwith; and for that purpose I shall write to one of the leading Gentlemen of Keswick. Agreeing altogether with you that Monuments to the dead, even in the cases of eminent Men are more touching when connected with local remembrances, I could still wish that Sir. R. Inglis and Mr Wynne would persist in the plan of having a memorial placed in Westminster Abbey. In addition to Southey's claim to be so commemorated for his Genius and attainments, his known attachment to the Anglican Church and the Ability with which he supported it by his Writings and his having been educated in the neighbouring School of Westminster give an especial propriety to his being included among the illustrious dead, who are called to remembrance in that beautiful and sacred Edifice, though their Remains have not been deposited there [a bust of RS was later placed in Poet's Corner]. With regard to the Keswick Monument you shall hear from me again, as soon as any thing is fixed— [June 27, 1843; *LY*, IV, 450–451 and note]

In his diplomatic insistence on a local memorial Wordsworth reiterates his view, expressed in his first *Essay on Epitaphs*, that epitaphs were best positioned near the burial place of the person being honored (see *Prose*, II, 53; for details of some of the intrigue that surrounded the subscription for the monument, see

LY, IV, 523, 540–541).

By mid-November plans for the Keswick memorial were well-advanced. Around this time the prose version was composed and a version sent to John Taylor Coleridge. Mary Wordsworth wrote to James Stanger in mid-November, responding to Stanger's having sent a cutting from the *Examiner* for November 4 in which Walter Savage Landor opened a subscription for a memorial to Southey at Bristol and printed an epitaph Landor had himself composed. Mary wrote, "I have taken the liberty to detain the slip from the Examiner, not wishing Mr Wordsworth to see it until he has expressed what his own mind suggests for the inscription—but it shall be returned to you when you hear again from Rydal" (*LY*, IV, 498–499).

By December 1 Wordsworth had drafted a verse epitaph and on that day he sent a fresh copy, revised, to Stanger, who headed the Keswick "Committee":

I have no objection whatever to the Epitaph being printed and circulated as you propose. The Copy I now send is slightly altered and has the addition of six lines with a view to characterizing his works which seems adviseable as he was distinguished in so many *different* departments of literature. Upon the marble the lines must be engraved in double column and not large letters, which will admit of the Tablet being better proportioned, and make the Inscription appear not quite so long as it is, which will be an advantage. If it be the opinion of the Committee that 'Poet Laureate, L.L.D.' should be added, it will be necessary that the words "He was" should precede the word "born": For my own part I think the bare name is the best upon a monument to be placed in a Church; besides if these Titles be given why not many others? designating the Academies and Societies of which he was a member. He in the Title-page of the last edition of his Poems calls himself Robert Southey. There is also indeed an Engraved title Page with L.L.D. but that was flourish of the Publisher.

It may be as well to mention that the Sculptor may object to so long an epitaph as being likely to hurt the proportions of his Tablet; but this must not be listened to by the Committee if they approve of the Inscription as it stands. [*LY*, IV, 500–501]

The next day Wordsworth wrote again to John Taylor Coleridge, thanking him for taking pains with the inscription for the Keswick memorial and responding to his suggestion in his letter of November 30 that Wordsworth take "some notice of the Lake" in his verses. Wordsworth replied, "There are *two* lakes in the vale of Keswick: both which, along with the lateral Vale of Newlands immediately opposite Southey's study window, will be included in the words, 'Ye vales and hills', by everyone who is familiar with the neighbourhood." The letter continues:

I quite agree with you that the construction of the lines that particularize his writings is rendered awkward, by so many participles passive, and the more so on account of the transitive verb 'informed'. One of these participles may be got rid of, and I think a better Couplet produced, by this alteration— [see ll. 11–12].

As I have entered into particulars as to the character of S's writings, and they are so various, I thought his Historic works ought by no means to be omitted, and therefore, though unwilling to lengthen the Epitaph, I added the following: [see ll. 6–12].

I do not feel with you in respect to the word 'so' [in l. 14 of the *apparatus*]—it refers of course to the preceding line, and as the reference is to the fireside feelings and intimate friends, there appears to me a propriety in an expression inclining to the Colloquial. The Couplet was the dictate of my own feelings, and the construction is accordingly broken and rather dramatic. But too much of this.—If you have any objection to the Couplet as altered be so kind as let me know. [*LY*, IV, 502–503 and notes]

Around December 3 Wordsworth sent the same alteration of lines 11–12 to Stanger and asked him to send a proof of the circular "including of course the Inscription before it is struck off" for correction (*LY*, IV, 504). On December 6 he wrote again to John Taylor Coleridge with further revisions, having decided by this time to follow the latter's wishes in giving notice of the "lakes" (and adding "torrents" for good measure; see the *apparatus* above). And at the same time, or perhaps a few days later, Wordsworth sent alterations to the final two and a half lines (*LY*, IV, 506 and note). The text as it now stood was very closely followed in the circular that Stanger arranged to have printed and distributed as part of the appeal for funds to pay for the memorial.

But Wordsworth was not finished yet. Lady Richardson of Lancrigg, Easedale, recorded in her reminiscences for "the shortest day of the year" that the poet read the epitaph to the company assembled at Lancrigg (including Lady Richardson, her mother, and Isabella Fenwick).

He asked our impression of it. My mother ventured to tell him of one word, or rather two, which she thought might be altered with advantage. They were these: "Wide was his range, but ne'er in human breast / Did private feeling find a holier nest." "Holier nest" were the words she objected to, as not being a correct union of ideas. He took the suggestion most kindly, and said it had been much discussed in his own mind and in his family circle, but that he saw the force of what she said, and that he was aware many others would see it also. He said there was yet time to change it, and that he should consult Judge Coleridge whether the line, as he once had it, "Did private feeling meet in holier rest," would not be more appropriate to the simplicity of an epitaph where you con every word, and where every word is expected to bear an exact meaning. We all thought this was an improvement. [*Prose* (Grosart), III, 438, where the entry is incorrectly dated December 1841]

Two days later, on December 23, Wordsworth began his letter to John Taylor Coleridge by defending his choice of diction in the two new opening lines: "The first line would certainly have more spirit by reading 'your' as you suggest [*that is,* "your rocky steeps"]. I had previously considered *that* [*i.e.* considered using "your"], but decided in favour of 'the', as 'your', I though[t], would clog the sentence in sound, there being 'ye' thrice repeated, and followed by 'you' at the close of the 4th line. I also thought that 'your' would interfere with the application of 'you' at the end of the fourth line to the whole of the particular previous images, as I intended it to do." He then proposed a change in line 14 from "Could private feelings need a holier nest" to " . . . meet in holier rest," but the revision was evidently not passed to Stanger in time to be adopted in the circular, which had probably been printed by this time. In his letter to John Taylor Coleridge he admitted that "meet in holier rest" did "not quite satisfy" him but he felt he "could do no better." He explained further that "the word 'nest' both in itself and in conjunction with 'holier' seems to be somewhat bold and rather startling for marble, particularly in a Church. I should not have thought of my alteration in a merely printed poem, but this makes a difference" (*LY*, IV, 511–512 and note).

Still preoccupied with the propriety of words that were to be carved in marble, he wrote again to James Stanger early in January 1844 to say that "it is thought by some of my friends that the line of Inscription beginning 'Could private feelings' would stand better thus: 'Could private feelings meet in holier rest'," explaining in slightly different terms that "the word 'nest' is deemed too metaphorical, and therefore somewhat startling, for marble—Probably these critics are right; therefore be so good as to let it stand so in the copy sent to the Sculptor" (*LY*, IV, 515–516; for Wordsworth's gentle but firm criticism of an epitaph sent to him around this time by an unknown correspondent, see *LY*, IV, 516–517).

When the circular was being prepared by the printer Wordsworth asked Stanger to send a copy to Chistopher Wordsworth, Jr., and the latter responded with his detailed criticisms. Wordsworth's reply, written on January 16, 1844 (according to CW, Jr.), is equally detailed:

> It is creditable to Mr Southey, and perhaps in some small degree to myself, that the Inscription has given birth to so much minute criticism, and I thank you for taking the pains with it you have done. I question whether there is a couplet in the whole that has not been objected to, by some one or another, and in a way that would surprize you as much, were I to report the instances, as your remarks did me—all but the first, (and a verbal one which I shall notice) viz that referring to the "nest" which for the same reason that induced you to condemn it, I had already altered, tho' not *entirely* to my own satisfaction, thus, "meet in holier rest". As to the 4 concluding lines, what you dwell upon as a defect I deem exactly the contrary; and it may be as well to say—as you appeal to authorities—that 4 intelligent persons who were present when your remarks were read, were of my opinion.
>
> I have no notion of an "ordinary Christian"; a man is a believer with a life conformable to his belief, and if so, all peculiarities of genius, talent and personal character vanish before the sublime position which he occupies with all Brother-Christians, Children of One Father and saved by the One Redeemer. I had sufficiently raised the Subject of the Inscription above ordinary Men, by the first 16 lines, and this being done, all individual distinctions, are in the conclusion merged, as they ought to be, in a condition compared with which every thing else sinks into insignificance.
>
> . . . The ambiguity in the word *calmed* has been, and is likely to be felt by others as well as yourself, the word *was* in the previous line inclining, as I was aware, the reader to expect that *calmed* is united with it as a participle; nevertheless for these awkwardnesses, the language is more in fault than any particular author. I have however altered the passage thus: [see ll. 17–18]
>
> This is thought here an improvement and I thank you dear Chris for having expressed your objection. Nothing seems to be lost by the alteration—the ambiguity is avoided and what I as a writer of verse attach more importance to, than the general reader will, the pause in the sense by being transferred from the 4th to the 6th syllable removes a monotony which before I had always felt in the movement of the verse. [*LY*, IV, 518–519]

Wordsworth sent these latest changes to Stanger on January 21, asking him to forward them to the sculptor, who he hoped had not yet begun his work. He had done so, however, and the changes in lines 17–18 were made on the stone by grinding off the earlier reading and engraving the new one in its place (*LY*, IV, 520). The sculptor was John Graham Lough (1806–1876), originally from Hexham in Northumberland, and a protégé of Benjamin Robert Haydon. Lough completed the monument, a full-length recumbent figure in white marble on a pedestal of Caen stone, in 1846; the inscription is engraved on a white marble tablet on the end of the monument facing the altar in St. Kentigern's Church, Crosthwaite (see *LY*, IV, 342 and note, and 501 and note).

Wordsworth's epitaph was not universally liked. Caroline Bowles Southey, Robert Southey's second wife, said of the lines for the tablet, "Was ever such a miserable failure?—or any thing so utterly heartless & spiritless?" (CBS to Mrs. Huges, December 18,1843; Mark Storey, *Robert Southey, A Life* [Oxford and New York, 1997], p. 344). But few understood Wordsworth's classical aims. He wrote to Henry Crabb Robinson on February 5, 1844, that "It was foolish to print the Epitaph, before it was engraven on the Marble [because of the stir it caused], Lord Ashley [Anthony Ashley Cooper], who is not the wisest of men, thinks it not half encomiastic enough—His letter to Mr Stanger went a *desperate* long way in this strain. How few are there who understand the art of praising either the living or the dead. If you have a copy correct the 2 last lines thus [giving the reading of his letter to CW, Jr.]" (*LY*, IV, 524 and note). Wordsworth altered the text yet again when he published it in 1845.

The broadside circular is found in two states (Broadsides 1a and 1b), with the earlier state reading "own,—" in line 6 and the later omitting the comma. Copies of each state have been examined, including examples of 1a in the British Library and the Wordsworth Library (Southey Album 3) and of 1b in the E. J. Pratt Library (Victoria University Libraries, Toronto). A lithographic printing was also issued (Broadside 2), examples of which are found in the Paul F. Betz Collection and the Wellesley College Library.

INSCRIPTION

FOR A MONUMENT IN CROSTHWAITE CHURCH, IN THE VALE OF KESWICK.

YE vales and hills whose beauty hither drew
The poet's steps, and fixed him here, on you,
His eyes have closed! And ye, lov'd books, no more
Shall Southey feed upon your precious lore,
To works that ne'er shall forfeit their renown,
Adding immortal labours of his own—
Whether he traced historic truth, with zeal
For the State's guidance, or the Church's weal,
Or Fancy, disciplined by studious art,
Inform'd his pen, or wisdom of the heart,
Or judgments sanctioned in the Patriot's mind
By reverence for the rights of all mankind.
Wide were his aims, yet in no human breast
Could private feelings meet for holier rest.
His joys, his griefs, have vanished like a cloud

---

composed November–December 1843, revised in January 1844 and again before November 1845

found in Southey Album 3; DC MS. 89; JTC to WW, November 30, 1843; BL MS. 6 (168, EQ's transcription; four 1843 letters from WW to JTC, 169, December 2; 171, December 6; 174, December 23; 176, December [?]); WW to CW, Jr., January 16, 1844; WW to JS, early January, 1844; WW to HCR, February 5, 1844; Monument (at Crosthwaite Church, Keswick, April 1844)

privately printed the first broadside, around December 20, 1843, the second, a lithograph, probably around February 5, 1844

published in *1845–*

classed Epitaphs *1845, 1850; unclassed 1846 (vol. 6)*

reading text *1845*

title Sacred to the Memory of Robert Southey whose mortal Remains are interred in the adjoining Church-yard. He was born at Bristol October 4th 1774, and died, after a residence of nearly forty years, at Greta Hall in this Parish, March 21st 1843. *BL MS. 6 (168); so Broadside but* Sacred to the Memory *rest all caps and* Southey] Southey, Church-yard] Churchyard Bristol October 4th 1774,] Bristol, October IV. M.DCC.LXXIV. forty years] XL Years Hall] Hall, 21st 1843] XXI. M.DCCC.XLIII

/1 Ye torrents foaming down the rocky steeps,
Ye lakes in which [in which *rev to* wherein] the Spirit of water sleeps, *BL MS. 6 (171); so Broadside as rev but* torrents, / . . . lakes,

7–8 *lacking BL MS. 6 (168)*

9 Or] As *BL MS. 6 (168)*

11 sanctioned . . . the] rooted . . . a *BL MS. 6 (168)*

12 By reverence for] Taught to revere *BL MS. 6 (168)*

13–14 Friends, Family—Ah wherefore touch that string,
In [In *rev to* To] them so fondly did the good man [man *rev to* Man] cling! *BL MS. 6 (168)*
Friends, Family—within no human breast
Could private feelings need a holier nest, *BL MS. 6 (171)*
Large were his aims yet on no human breast
Could private feelings find a holier nest *BL MS. 6 (174)*

14 meet for . . . rest] find a . . . nest *Broadside, Monument* meet in . . . rest *alt BL MS. 6 (174); WW to CW, Jr.; WW to JS*

15 His joys, his griefs, *rev from* His mighty joys, *BL MS. 6 (168)*

The text of the Broadside and the Monument is entirely in capital letters.

From Skiddaw's top; but he to heaven was vowed
Through his industrious life, and Christian faith
Calmed in his soul the fear of change and death.

TO THE REV. CHRISTOPHER WORDSWORTH, D.D.

MASTER OF HARROW SCHOOL,

After the perusal of his Theophilus Anglicanus, recently published.

Enlightened Teacher, gladly from thy hand
Have I received this proof of pains bestowed
By Thee to guide thy Pupils on the road
That, in our native isle, and every land,
The Church, when trusting in divine command
And in her Catholic attributes, hath trod:
O may these lessons be with profit scanned
To thy heart's wish, thy labour blest by God!
So the bright faces of the young and gay
Shall look more bright—the happy, happier still;
Catch, in the pauses of their keenest play,
Motions of thought which elevate the will
And, like the Spire that from your classic Hill
Points heavenward, indicate the end and way.

Rydal Mount, Dec. 11, 1843.

17–18 Through a long life; and calmed by Christian faith,
In his pure Soul, the fear of change and death.— *BL MS. 6 (168); so Broadside but* life, . . . death.
Through a life long and pure; and Christian faith
Calmed in his soul the fear of change and death *BL MS. 6 (176)*
Through a long life and pure, and christian faith
Calmed in his Soul the fear of change and death *WW to CW, Jr.; so WW to HCR and Monument but* Thro . . . Christian *and* soul . . . death. *WW to HCR* pure; and Christian *and* death. *Monument*
18/ This Memorial was erected by Friends of Robert Southey. *BL MS. 6 (168); Broadside*

---

composed December 11, 1843
found in DC MS. 176; WW to CW, Jr., January 16, 1844; Ticknor MS.
published in *Morning Post*, December 15, 1843; *1845–*
classed Miscellaneous Sonnets *1845–; 1846 (vol. 6)*
reading text *1845*
title After] on *MS. 176*
2 Have I received *rev to* Do I receive *WW to CW, Jr.* Do I receive *MS. 176*
8 labour] labours *MS. 176*
12 will] mind *MS. 176*

"So fair, so sweet, withal so sensitive"

The incident described in the poem "So fair, so sweet, withal so sensitive" occurred in July 1844 while Wordsworth was leading visitors on a walk to Loughrigg Tarn over Loughrigg Fell, across the vale from Rydal Mount. The poem was written shortly afterward. The earliest draft suggests that he first conceived the poem as three triplets with beginning and ending couplets (see the transcription of Lilly MS. 4), but by August, when he copied out and dated the poem for Esther Maurice, he had expanded the opening and closing couplets to triplets. The first reading text presents this fifteen-line version and is based on Lilly MS. 5, with an *apparatus* of variant drafts from a working copy made by Edward Quillinan and revised by Wordsworth in MS. 1836/45, where its full title became "To the noontide sun / Suggested at noon on Loughrigg Fell." By November 1845, when he submitted copy to the printer for *Poems,* 1845 (the second reading text), Wordsworth had revised the poem and added two more triplets. For more discussion of the occasion see the note to the reading texts (pp. 501–502).

[Text of Lilly MS. 5]

Suggested upon
Loughrigg Fell.

So fair so sweet, withal so sensitive,
Would that the little Flowers were born to live
Conscious of half the pleasure which they give;

That to this mountain Daisy's Self were known
The beauty of its star-shaped Shadow thrown
On the grey surface of that naked stone!

And what—if hence a bold desire should mount
High as the *Sun*—that he could take account
Of all that issues from his glorious fount;

---

composed July–August 1844
found in MS. 1836/45 (vol. 5, front fly-leaves, EQ, rev by WW); Lilly MS. 4;, Lilly MS. 5; Yale MS. 9
reading text Lilly MS. 5
inscription August 1844 *MS. 1836/45* Transcribed for Esther Morris Augst 1844 *Lilly MS. 5*
title Poem on a Daisy casting its shadow, on Lough Rigg Fell, Aug— *Yale MS. 9* [To the noontide sun. *inserted*] Suggested [at noon *inserted*] on Loughrigg Fell *MS. 1836/45*
1 fair, so] fair and *MS. 1836/45*
4 mountain] mountains *MS. 1836/45*
6 Its sole companion on this naked stone! *MS. 1836/45*

See the photographs and transcription of Lilly MS. 4 on pp. 820–823.

Fond fancies! Wheresoe'er shall range thine eye
Among the Forms and Powers of earth or sky,
Converse with Nature in *pure* sympathy;

A thankful Heart, all lawless wishes quell'd
To joy, to praise and love, alike impelled,
Whatever boon be granted or withheld.

[Text of 1845]

So fair, so sweet, withal so sensitive,
Would that the little Flowers were born to live,
Conscious of half the pleasure which they give;

That to this mountain-daisy's self were known
The beauty of its star-shaped shadow, thrown
On the smooth surface of this naked stone!

And what if hence a bold desire should mount
High as the Sun, that he could take account
Of all that issues from his glorious fount!

So might he ken how by his sovereign aid
These delicate companionships are made;
And how he rules the pomp of light and shade;

And were the Sister-power that shines by night
So privileged, what a countenance of delight
Would through the clouds break forth on human sight!

Fond fancies! wheresoe'er shall turn thine eye
On earth, air, ocean, or the starry sky,
Converse with Nature in pure sympathy;

---

10 range] turn *Yale MS. 9*
10–12 Fond fancies! ~~bred between a smile and sigh~~
~~But learn them and be taught to fix an~~
~~Do thou more wise, where'er thou turnest thi~~ne eye, | stet
~~On holy nature~~
~~Converse with~~ nature in pure sympathy *rev to*
Fond fancies! wheresoer shall range thine eye
Among the forms and powers of earth or sky
Converse with Nature in pure sympathy *MS. 1836/45*
14 praise and . . . impelled] praise, to . . . compelled [compelled *rev to* compell'd] *MS. 1836/45*

---

composed between August 1844 and late November 1845
published in *1845–*
classed Sentiment and Reflection *1845, 1850; unclassed 1846 (vol. 6)*
reading text *1845*

All vain desires, all lawless wishes quelled,
Be Thou to love and praise alike impelled,
Whatever boon is granted or withheld.

SONNET

ON THE PROJECTED KENDAL AND WINDERMERE RAILWAY.

Is then no nook of English ground secure
From rash assault? Schemes of retirement sown
In youth, and mid the busy world kept pure
As when their earliest flowers of hope were blown,
Must perish;—how can they this blight endure?
And must he too the ruthless change bemoan
Who scorns a false utilitarian lure
Mid his paternal fields at random thrown?
Baffle the threat, bright Scene, from Orrest-head
Given to the pausing traveller's rapturous glance:

The degree and kind of attachment which many of the yeomanry feel to their small inheritances can scarcely be over-rated. Near the house of one of them stands a magnificent tree, which a neighbour of the owner advised him to fell for profit's sake. "Fell it," exclaimed the yeoman, "I had rather fall on my knees and worship it." It happens, I believe, that the intended railway would pass through this little property, and I hope that an apology for the answer will not be thought necessary by one who enters into the strength of the feeling. / W.W.

---

composed October 12, 1844

found in Betz MS. 5; Michigan MS.; BL MS. 8; Berg MS. 4; Yale MS. 9; Quaritch MS. (copy); WW to HCR, February 2, 1845; DC MS. 157

published in *Morning Post*, October 16, 1844; *Kendal &* (issues 1 and 2, both January 1845); *1845–*

classed Miscellaneous Sonnets *1845–; 1846 (vol. 6)*

reading text *Kendal & 2*

title *lacking Betz MS. 5, Yale MS. 9* SONNET . . . WINDERMERE RAILWAY] Kendal and Windermere Railway *Michigan MS.* Suggested by the Proposed Kendal and Windermere Railway *BL MS. 8* On the Projected Kendal and Winandermere Rail way. *Berg MS. 4* Sonnet on the Projected Kendal and Winandermere Railway *MP* ON THE PROJECTED KENDAL AND WINDERMERE RAILWAY. *1845–*

note *Berg MS. 4 and MP as Kendal & but* Let not the above be considered as merely a poetical effusion. The degree *etc. and* would] will *and* one] any one *Berg MS. 4, MP, and* thought *rev from* considered *Berg MS. 4* *MS. 157 as Kendal & but* inheritance *1845– as Kendal & but note attached to l. 2 and* †The degree *and* Fell it! *and unsigned; so 1846, 1849, 1850 but* *The

1 Is then no] And is no *BL MS. 8* Is *rev from* Was *WW to HCR* then *rev from* there *MS. 157* there *Berg MS. 4, Yale MS. 9*, *MP*

4 earliest *rev from* [?un] *Betz MS. 5*

5 Must perish *rev from* And [?diminish'd] *Betz MS. 5* Must wither *Michigan MS.*

6 Henceforth must He his old delights disown *rev to* And must he, too his old delights disown *Betz MS. 5 (but* He *is not del)*

And must He too his old delights disown *BL MS. 8, Quaritch MS. (copy); so Michigan MS. but* his old *rev from* [?when]; *Berg MS. 4, MP as BL MS. 8 but* too *rev from* to[?] *Berg* He] he *Yale MS. 9 as BL MS. 8 then rev to text but* he] he

7 false *alt* vain *Betz MS. 5* false *rev from* [?] *Berg*

8 at random *rev from* by Strangers *Betz MS. 5*

9 Orrest *rev from* Orrest's *Yale MS. 9*

10 pausing *rev from* passing *MS. 157*

Plead for thy peace, thou beautiful romance
Of nature; and, if human hearts be dead,
Speak, passing winds; ye torrents, with your strong
And constant voice, protest against the wrong.

WILLIAM WORDSWORTH.

RYDAL MOUNT,
October 12*th,* 1844.

"Proud were ye, Mountains, when, in times of old"

PROUD were ye, Mountains, when, in times of old,
Your patriot sons, to stem invasive war,
Intrenched your brows; ye gloried in each scar:
Now, for your shame, a Power, the Thirst of Gold,
That rules o'er Britain like a baneful star,
Wills that your peace, your beauty, shall be sold,
And clear way made for her triumphal car
Through the beloved retreats your arms enfold!
Heard YE that Whistle? As her long-linked Train
Swept onwards, did the vision cross your view?
Yes, ye were startled;—and, in balance true,
Weighing the mischief with the promised gain,
Mountains, and Vales, and Floods, I call on you
To share the passion of a just disdain.

---

13 your] a *Betz MS. 51*
inscription Fecit indignatio / Wm Wordsworth / Oct^{br} 12th 1844 *Michigan MS.* Wm Wordsworth *BL MS. 8* Wm Wordsworth / Rydal Mount / Oct. 12—1844 *Berg MS. 4* William Wordsworth *Quaritch MS. (copy)* Wm. Wordsworth. Rydal Mount, Oct. 12, 1844 *MP* William Wordsworth / Rydal Mount *MS. 157* Rydal Mount. Oct 12. 1844. *Yale MS. 9* October 12th, 1844. *1845–*

---

composed December 13, 1844
found in MS. 157
published in *Morning Post,* December 20, 1844; *Kendal &* (issues 1 and 2, both January 1845); *1845–*
classed Miscellaneous Sonnets *1845–; 1846 (vol. 6)*
reading text *Kendal & 2*
5 baneful] baleful *MP*

Line 13 of *Sonnet on the Projected Kendal and Windermere Wailway* is entered twice in Betz MS. 5.

THE WESTMORELAND GIRL.

TO MY GRANDCHILDREN.

PART I.

SEEK who will delight in fable
I shall tell you truth. A Lamb
Leapt from this steep bank to follow
'Cross the brook its thoughtless dam.

Far and wide on hill and valley
Rain had fallen, unceasing rain,
And the bleating mother's Young-one
Struggled with the flood in vain:

But, as chanced, a Cottage-maiden
(Ten years scarcely had she told)
Seeing, plunged into the torrent,
Clasped the Lamb and kept her hold.

Whirled adown the rocky channel,
Sinking, rising, on they go,
Peace and rest, as seems, before them
Only in the lake below.

Oh! it was a frightful current
Whose fierce wrath the Girl had braved;
Clap your hands with joy my Hearers,
Shout in triumph, both are saved;

---

composed between perhaps late May, certainly June 6, and July 1, 1845
found in DC MSS. 143, 155; WL MS 1; Cornell MS. 12; WW to HR, July 31, 1845
published in *1845–*
classed Childhood *1845, 1850; unclassed 1846 (vol. 6)*
reading text *1845*
title To my Grandchildren. *MSS. 143, 155* To my Grand children *Cornell MS. 12*
Stanzas
To my Grand-Children. *WL MS. 1*
section PART I.] *lacking MSS. 143, 155, WL MS. 1; Cornell MS. 12*
stanza numbers 1 *to* 21 *WL MS. 1*

4 'Cross] Cross *rev from* Across *MS. 143* thoughtless *rev to* simple *MS. 155* simple *Cornell MS. 12, WL MS. 1*

11 plunged] rushed *MS. 143* plunged *rev from* rushed *MS. 155* torrent *rev from* [?cu]rrent *MS. 143*

15 as *rev from* [?it] *MS. 155*

17 current] torrent *WL MS. 1*

19 Clap your hands my little hearers *rev to* Clap your little hands my hearers *rev to* Clap your hands for joy my hearers *MS. 155* with] for *Cornell MS. 12*

Saved by courage that with danger
Grew, by strength the gift of love,
And belike a guardian angel
Came with succour from above.

PART II.

Now, to a maturer Audience,
Let me speak of this brave Child
Left among her native mountains
With wild Nature to run wild.

So, unwatched by love maternal,
Mother's care no more her guide,
Fared this little bright-eyed Orphan
Even while at her father's side.

Spare your blame,—remembrance makes him
Loth to rule by strict command;
Still upon his cheek are living
Touches of her infant hand,

Dear caresses given in pity,
Sympathy that soothed his grief,
As the dying mother witnessed
To her thankful mind's relief.

---

21 danger] duty *WL MS. 1*
22 by *rev from* and *MS. 143*
23 a *rev from* her *MS. 143*
24/25 PART II.] Second Part. *WL MS.* 2nd Part. *Cornell MS. 12; lacking MS. 143; lacking MS. 155 but two parts divided by two solid ink lines*
25–26 *rev from* Let me twine another chaplet
Round the brow of this brave Child *MS. 143*
27 among *rev from* upon *MS. 143*
29–31 See when Mother's love no longer
Watched her—to restrain & guide
Fared it with this bright-eyed Orphan *rev to*
So when Mother's love no longer
Fared it with this bright-eyed Orphan *MS. 143;*
So, when Mother's love no longer
Watched her an unwearied Guide
Fared it with this bright-eyed Orphan *rev to*
So, from early morn to evening
Mother's love no more her guide
Fared it with this bright-eyed Orphan *rev to text MS. 155*
31 eyed] eye *WL MS. 1*
32 while *inserted MS. 143*
33–40 *lacking MS. 143*
33 And what wonder *rev to* Blame him not *rev to* Spare your blame; remembrance made [made *rev to* makes] him *MS. 155*
34 strict *rev from* stern *MS. 155*
39–40 *rev from* Efforts which by the dying Mother
Witnessed, for her pain's relief *MS. 155*

Time passed on; the Child was happy,
Like a Spirit of air she moved,
Wayward, yet by all who knew her
For her tender heart beloved.

Scarcely less than sacred passions,
Bred in house, in grove, and field,
Link her with the inferior creatures,
Urge her powers their rights to shield.

Anglers, bent on reckless pastime,
Learn how she can feel alike
Both for tiny harmless minnow
And the fierce and sharp-toothed pike.

Merciful protectress, kindling
Into anger or disdain;

41–44 All unshackled as a Spirit
High & low the Daughter moved
Wayward somewhat but submissive
To a law in heaven approved *rev to*
Happy in her aims and errands
Like a Spirit of air she moved
Wayward somewhat but most lively
And in spite of blame beloved *MS. 143, with ll. 43–44 rev to text*

44 her *rev from* a *Cornell MS. 12* her *rev to* a *MS. 155* a *WL MS. 1*

45 T'was in sooth a strong willed passion *rev to*
Passion scarcely less than sacred *MS. 143*
Passions scarcely less than sacred *rev to*
Scarcely less than sacred passion *rev to text MS. 155*

46 That [That *rev to* Did] in every grove and field *MS. 143; MS. 155 as rev MS. 143 but rev to text*

47 Linked [Linked *rev to* Linke] her [her *inserted*] with th'inferior Creatures; *MS. 143*

48 Urge] Urged *MS. 143* Urged *rev to* Urge *MS. 155*

49–52 {s {reckless in their
~~And the~~ Angler{ {in his pastime
Learns how she can feel alike
Nor on Land alone the angler knows
Learns ~~knows how can~~ Both for tiny harmless
~~Knows How she [?could] feel alike~~ minnow
~~Learns how she can~~
~~harmless~~
~~For his prey brown tiny minnow~~
And the ~~fierce the~~ fierce the
~~Upwards to the~~ sharp-toothed, Pike
~~And~~ *MS. 143*

49 bent on reckless *rev from* reckless in their *MS.* 155_1

51–52 For the [For the *rev to* Both for] tiny harmless minnow
And the fierce and sharp-toothed Pike *rev to*
Wanton wrong to harmless minnow
Done—or to the sharp toothed Pike *MS.* 155_1
Wanton wrong to harmless minnow
Done—or to the sharp-toothed pike. *rev to*
Both for little [little *rev to* tiny] harmless minnow
And the fierce and sharp-toothed pike. *MS.* 155_2

53–56 *lacking MSS. 143, 155, WL MS. 1, Cornell MS. 12*

Many a captive hath she rescued,
Others saved from lingering pain.

Listen yet awhile;—with patience
Hear the homely truths I tell,
She in Grasmere's old church-steeple
Tolled this day the passing-bell.

Yes, the wild Girl of the mountains
To their echoes gave the sound,
Notice punctual as the minute,
Warning solemn and profound.

She, fulfilling her sire's office,
Rang alone the far-heard knell,
Tribute, by her hand, in sorrow,
Paid to One who loved her well.

When his spirit was departed
On that service she went forth;
Nor will fail the like to render
When his corse is laid in earth.

What then wants the Child to temper,
In her breast, unruly fire,
To control the froward impulse
And restrain the vague desire?

57–58 Now my little Ones, of duty
Home born [Home born *rev from* Mournful] duty let me tell *MS. 143*

57 with patience *rev from* of Duty *MS.* 155_1 with patience *rev from* with patience hear *MS.* 155_2

58 Hear the homely truths I tell *rev from* The simple truths I tell *MS.* 155_2 Hear the simple truths I tell, *rev from* Home-true duty I would tell, *MS.* 155_1

59 church-steeple] Steeple *rev to* Church Steeple *MS.* 155_2

63 Notice *rev from* Warning *MS. 143*

64 Warning *rev from* Notice *MS. 143*

65–68 *rev from* She fulfilling her Sire's office
Rang alone the far heard knell
All alone, and ~~[?broken] hearted~~ deeply grieving
~~Grieved for One who loved her well~~
For the Friend [?who loved] her well *rev from*
She not [She not *alt* There alone] undisturbed by sorrow
Felt Grief for One that loved her well
She fulfilling her Sire's office
Rang the monitory knell *MS. 143*

69 When his Spirit had departed *rev from* When the [the *rev to* her] Spirit was departing *MS. 143, but* stet *entered in margin*

71 *rev to* And will knoll the mournful summons *MS. 155; WL MS. 1 and Cornell MS. 12 as rev MS. 155*

72 is laid *rev to* must lie *MS. 155; WL MS. 1 and Cornell MS. 12 as rev MS. 155*

73 What *rev from* Where *MS. 155* Child] Girl *alt* Child *MS. 143*

74 her] the *WL MS. 1*

76 restrain] subdue *MSS. 143, 155, WL MS. 1*

Easily a pious training
And a stedfast outward power
Would supplant the weeds and cherish,
In their stead, each opening flower.

Thus the fearless Lamb-deliv'rer,
Woman-grown, meek-hearted, sage,
May become a blest example
For her sex, of every age.

Watchful as a wheeling eagle,
Constant as a soaring lark,
Should the country need a heroine,
She might prove our Maid of Arc.

Leave that thought; and here be uttered
Prayer that Grace divine may raise
Her humane courageous spirit
Up to heaven, thro' peaceful ways.

"Yes! thou art fair, yet be not moved"

YES! thou art fair, yet be not moved
  To scorn the declaration,
That sometimes I in thee have loved
   My fancy's own creation.

Imagination needs must stir;
  Dear Maid, this truth believe,

---

83 May *rev from* Might *rev from* May *MS. 143*
84 For . . . of] To . . . in *Cornell MS. 12*
87 the *alt* our *MS. 143*
88 might] may *MSS. 143, 155, WL MS.; Cornell MS. 12*
89–92 *lacking MSS. 143, 155, WL MS.; Cornell MS. 12*
89 Leave that word—and [?prayer *del*] [here *inserted*] be offer *WW to HR*
90 may] would *WW to HR*
91 Her] This *WW to HR*

---

composed probably between June 2 and November 4, 1845
found in DC MS. 156
published in *1845–*
classed Affections *1845, 1850; unclassed 1846 (vol. 6)*
reading text *1845*

See the photograph and transcription of "Yes! thou art fair, yet be not moved," DC MS. 156, 3^v–4^r, pp. 824–827.

Minds that have nothing to confer
  Find little to perceive.

Be pleased that nature made thee fit
  To feed my heart's devotion,
By laws to which all Forms submit
  In sky, air, earth, and ocean.

"Forth from a jutting ridge, around whose base"

Forth from a jutting ridge, around whose base
Winds our deep Vale, two heath-clad Rocks ascend
In fellowship, the loftiest of the pair
Rising to no ambitious height; yet both,
O'er lake and stream, mountain and flowery mead,
Unfolding prospects fair as human eyes
Ever beheld. Up-led with mutual help,
To one or other brow of those twin Peaks
Were two adventurous Sisters wont to climb,
And took no note of the hour while thence they gazed,
The blooming heath their couch, gazed, side by side,
In speechless admiration. I, a witness
And frequent sharer of their calm delight
With thankful heart, to either Eminence
Gave the baptismal name each Sister bore.
Now are they parted, far as Death's cold hand

---

composed shortly before June 24, 1845
found in MS. 1836/45
published in *1845–*
classed Naming of Places *1845–*
reading text *1845*

2 Winds a [a *alt* our] sequesterd Vale, two Rocks ascend *MS. 1836/45*
2–3 ~~[?This]~~ ~~[? ?]~~ ~~[?headlong]~~ / ~~[? ? ?]~~ W [?W] *pencil interlined MS. 1836/45*
5 lake *alt* [?mere] *MS. 1836/45*
6 Unfolding *rev from* Unfold *MS. 1836/45* eyes] eye *MS. 1836/45*
7 Ever] Eer *MS. 1836/45*
9 two *so MS. 1836/45* too *1845–*
12–16 In speechless admiration. I—a witness
  And frequent sharer of that delight
~~Of that delight which frequently they shared~~
~~With a full heart, in sign of gratitude~~
~~Nor wanting motives for approp~~riated hours
~~Bestowed on either Emminence a Name~~
  With thankful heart to either Eminence
~~The dear~~ Baptismal Name each Sister bore.
  Gave [?D]}
Now are they parted, far as d}eaths cold hand *MS. 1836/45*
alt for l. 16:
True to a common home their early [early *rev from* ch] choice
In this dear Vale the Sisters lived, but long
Have they been parted—far as deaths cold hand *MS. 1836/45*

Hath power to part the Spirits of those who love
As they did love. Ye kindred Pinnacles—
That, while the generations of mankind
Follow each other to their hiding-place
In time's abyss, are privileged to endure
Beautiful in yourselves, and richly graced
With like command of beauty—grant your aid
For Mary's humble, Sarah's silent, claim,
That their pure joy in nature may survive
From age to age in blended memory.

AT FURNESS ABBEY.

WELL have yon Railway Labourers to THIS ground
Withdrawn for noontide rest. They sit, they walk
Among the Ruins, but no idle talk
Is heard; to grave demeanour all are bound;
And from one voice a Hymn with tuneful sound
Hallows once more the long-deserted Quire
And thrills the old sepulchral earth, around.
Others look up, and with fixed eyes admire
That wide-spanned arch, wondering how it was raised,
To keep, so high in air, its strength and grace:
All seem to feel the spirit of the place,
And by the general reverence God is praised:
Profane Despoilers, stand ye not reproved,
While thus these simple-hearted men are moved!
June 21st, 1845.

---

composed June 21, 1845
found in WL MS. 1
published in *1845–*
classed Miscellaneous Sonnets *1845–; 1846 (vol. 6)*
reading text *1845*
title Sonnet / Rail-way Labourers at Furness Abbey— *WL MS. 1*
1 Behold the Labourers in this chosen ground *WL MS. 1*
2 Withdrawn for . . . they] Taking their . . . or *WL MS. 1*
9 That wide-spanned] Yon wide spread *WL MS. 1*
13 ye *rev from* [?you] *WL MS. 1*

"Why should we weep or mourn, Angelic boy"

Why should we weep or mourn, Angelic boy,
For such thou wert ere from our sight removed,
Holy, and ever dutiful—beloved
From day to day with never-ceasing joy,
And hopes as dear as could the heart employ
In aught to earth pertaining? Death has proved
His might, nor less his mercy, as behoved—
Death conscious that he only could destroy
The bodily frame. That beauty is laid low
To moulder in a far-off field of Rome;
But Heaven is now, blest Child, thy Spirit's home:
When such divine communion, which we know,
Is felt, thy Roman-burial place will be
Surely a sweet remembrancer of Thee.

"I know an aged Man constrained to dwell"

I know an aged Man constrained to dwell
In a large house of public charity,
Where he abides, as in a Prisoner's cell,
With numbers near, alas! no company.

---

composed between December 24, 1845 and early January 1846, but by January 10
found in DC MS. 143; MS. 1845W; WW to CW, Jr., around January 10, 1846; WW to HR, January 23, 1846; MS. 1845D; Southey Album 2
published in *1846, 1850*
classed Miscellaneous Sonnets *1846 (vol. 6)* Epitaphs *1850*
reading text *1846*
title On the death of my Grandson: [Chr *del*]
Edward Christopher Wordsworth
who died at Rome 10th Decr 1845 aged 4^{yrs} —8mo *MS. 1845W*
SONNET. *1850*
2 thou *rev from* were *MS. 1845D*
5 heart] thoughts *MS. 1845W*
6 has] hath *WW to CW, Jr., MS. 1845D, Southey Album 2*
12 such] this *MS. 143, MS. 1845W, WW to HR* that *WW to CW, Jr., MS. 1845D*
14 remembrancer *rev from* remembrance *MS. 1845W, MS. 1845D*

---

composed January (but before late February) 1846
found in DC MS. 143 (A) 20^{v}, 21^{v}, (B) 22^{v}, 23^{v}, (C) 25^{v}, 26^{v}, (D) 29^{v}, 31^{v}
published in *1846, 1850*
classed Miscellaneous Poems *1850; unclassed 1846 (vol. 6)*
reading text *1846*
1 know] saw *MS. 143 (D)* dwell *rev from* live *MS. 143 (A)*
3 *rev from* Where he abides, a Prisoner in his cell, *MS. 143 (A)*
4/5 *ll. 25–28 inserted MS. 143 (B)*

When he could creep about, at will, though poor
And forced to live on alms, this old Man fed
A Redbreast, one that to his cottage door
Came not, but in a lane partook his bread.

There, at the root of one particular tree,
An easy seat this worn-out Labourer found
While Robin pecked the crumbs upon his knee
Laid one by one, or scattered on the ground.

Dear intercourse was theirs, day after day;
What signs of mutual gladness when they met!
Think of their common peace, their simple play,
The parting moment and its fond regret.

Months passed in love that failed not to fulfil,
In spite of season's change, its own demand,
By fluttering pinions here and busy bill;
There by caresses from a tremulous hand.

---

5 Whe[Whe *rev to* When] he was free to move about *rev to* Ere while, free then to move about *rev to* While yet he moved about, free then *rev to* While yet he moved [moved *rev from* w] about, free then *MS. 143 (A)* When] While *MS. 143 (C)* creep *rev from* move *MS. 143 (D)* move *MS. 143 (B)*

6 this old Man *rev from* he duly *MS. A*

8 lane] grove *MS. 143 (A, B)* lane *rev to* grove *MS. 143 (C)*

9–12 *lacking MS. 143 (A, B)*
rev from There in broad light, or sheltered by a tree
Or bank this worn-out Labourer might be found,
While Robin peck'd the crumbs, upon his knee,
Laid one by one, or scattered on the ground. *MS. 143 (D) but l. 10* this *rev to* the
There in broad light or sheltered by a tree
While Robin peck'd the crumbs upon His knee
Laid one [one *rev from* ?] by one or scattered on the ground *rev from*
Mid sunshine, or beneath some spreading tree
Oft might the worn out Labourer [Labourer *inserted*] there be found
Seated while Robin peck'd from off his knee
The expected dole of crumbs or from the ground. *MS. 143 (C)*

13 Thither the lone old Man crept, day by day; *rev to*
Thither alone he crept, day after day; *MS. 143 (A)*
Thither [T *rev from* t] alone he crept, day after day; *MS. 143 (B)*
Dear intercourse was theirs day after day; *rev to*
Thither alone he crept day after day; *rev to*
Thither the old Man [ ] day after day; *MS. 143 (C)*

14 What signs of *rev from* Think of their *MS. 143 (C)*

15 Think of their common meal their peace, their play, *rev from* The common meal, the pastime grave or gay, *MS. 143 (A); MS. 143 (B) as rev MS. 143 (A) but* meal] meal,
peace *rev to* meal *rev to* peace *MS. 143 (C)*

17 in love that failed not *rev from* and love failed never *MS. 143 (A)*

18 With the returning light its fresh demand, *MS. 143 (A), so MS. 143 (B) but no comma*

19 pinions] pinions, *MS. 143 (B)* here] there, *MS. 143 (A, B)*

20 There] Here *MS. 143 (A, B)* caresses *rev from* a caressing *MS. 143 (A)* from *alt* with *MS. 143 (B)* tremulous *rev from* trembing *MS. 143 (A)*

Thus in the chosen spot a tie so strong
Was formed between the solitary pair,
That when his fate had housed him mid a throng
The Captive shunned all converse proffered there.

Wife, children, kindred, they were dead and gone;
But, if no evil hap his wishes crossed,
One living Stay was left, and on that one
Some recompense for all that he had lost.

O that the good old Man had power to prove,
By message sent through air or visible token,
That still he loves the Bird, and still must love;
That friendship lasts though fellowship is broken!

TO AN OCTOGENARIAN.

Affections lose their objects; Time brings forth
No successors; and, lodged in memory,
If love exist no longer, it must die,—
Wanting accustomed food must pass from earth,

---

21 Thus in the chosen spot *rev from* Thus in the shady grove *rev from* What wonder then if thus *MS. 143 (C)* Thus in the [the *rev to* that] shady grove *MS. 143 (A); MS. 143 (B) as rev MS. 143 (A)*
22 solitary *rev from* solitry *MS. 143 (C)*
23–24 That when compelled to house amid a throng
The old man shunned all converse that was there *rev to*
That when his fate had housed him mid a throng
The feeble Captive shunned all converse that was there *MS. 143 (A), then rev to text but* all [on *del*]
That when his fate had housed him mid a throng
The Captive shunned all converse proferred there *rev to*
That when the aged Pauper mid a throng
Was housed he shunned all converse proferred there *MS. 143 (B), MS. 143 (C) as MS. 143 (B) rev but rev to* That when the worn out Labourer mid a throng, *rev to* That when his fate had housed him mid a throng / The Captive shunned all converse proffered there.
25–28 *first entered here then moved to ll. 4/5 MS. 143 (B)*
25 they *rev from* all *MS. 143 (C)* all *alt* they *MS. 143 (A)* all *MS. 143 (B_1)*
26 But,] Yet *MS. 143 (A, B)*
27 Stay *rev from* care *MS. 143 (C)* was] is *MS. 143 (B2)* on] in *all MSS.*
28 had] has *MS. 143 (B_2)*

---

composed probably between early January and mid-May 1846
found in DC MS. 143 (A) 2^r (deleted), (B) 27^v
published in *1846, 1850*
classed Miscellaneous Sonnets *1846 (vol. 6)* Miscellaneous Poems *1850*
reading text *1846*
title *lacking MS. 143 (A)* SONNET. (TO AN OCTOGENARIAN.) *1850*
1 Affections lose their objects:] While man's [man's *alt* our] affections perish *MS. 143 (A)* Affections lose their objects; *rev from* While our affections perish *MS. 143 (B)* objects] object *1850*
2 lodged in] in the *MS. 143 (A)*
3 no longer, it must] not it must droop [droop *rev from* drop] *MS. 143 (A)* it *rev from* Love *MS. 143 (B)*

Or never hope to reach a second birth.
This sad belief, the happiest that is left
To thousands, share not Thou; howe'er bereft,
Scorned, or neglected, fear not such a dearth.
Though poor and destitute of friends thou art,
Perhaps the sole survivor of thy race,
One to whom Heaven assigns that mournful part
The utmost solitude of age to face,
Still shall be left some corner of the heart
Where Love for living Thing can find a place.

Written upon a fly leaf in the Copy of the Author's Poems
which was sent to her Majesty Queen Victoria

Deign Sovereign Mistress! to accept a Lay
No Laureate offering of elaborate Art;
But Salutation taking its glad way
From deep recesses of a Loyal heart.

Queen, Wife, and Mother! may all-judging Heaven
Shower with a bounteous hand on Thee and Thine
Felicity, that only can be given
On Earth to goodness, blest by grace divine.

Lady! devoutly honoured and beloved
Thro' every realm confided to thy sway

5–6 Or never hope to gain a second birth.
[This sad belief *inserted*] The happiest that is left. *rev from*
To gain another world a second birth
To this the only consolation left *MS. 143 (A)*
6 *rev to* Wanderer this sad belief the happiest left *MS. 143 (B)*
8 fear *rev from* dread *MS. 143 (B)* dread *MS. 143 (A)*
9 poor and *alt* time may *del MS. 143 (B)*
11 Though heaven [heaven *rev to* Heaven] to Thee assign that mournful part *MS. 143 (A); MS. 143 (B) as rev MS. 143 (A) but rev to text*
13 shall be *rev from* is there *MS. 143 (B)* is there *MS. 143 (A)*
14 Love] love *alt* care *MS. 143 (A)*

---

composed around but by January 9, 1846
found in DC MS. 89; MS. 1845RL; Cornell MS. 13; Yale MS. 10
published in *Prose* (Grosart)
reading text MS. 89
title Author's] Authors *MS. 89* *lacking MS. 1845RL, Cornell MS. 13, Yale MS. 10*
1 Sovereign Mistress] Sovereign Lady *rev to* Royal Mistress *Cornell MS. 13*
3 Salutation] verse spontaneous *Cornell MS. 13*
5 all-judging] all ruling *Cornell MS. 13*
7 Felicity, that] Felicities which *Cornell MS. 13*
8 grace *rev from* Power *Cornell MS. 13*

May'st Thou pursue thy course by God approved
And He will teach thy People to obey.

As Thou art wont thy sovereignty adorn
With Woman's gentleness, yet firm and staid;
So shall that earthly Crown thy brows have worn
Be changed to one whose glory cannot fade:

And now, by duty urged, I lay this Book
Before thy Majesty, in humble trust
That on its simplest pages Thou wilt look
With a benign indulgence, more than just.

Nor wilt Thou blame an aged Poet's prayer
That issuing hence may steal into thy mind
Some solace under weight of Royal care
Or grief, the inheritance of Humankind;

For know we not that from celestial spheres
When Time was young an inspiration came
(O were it mine) to hallow saddest tears,
And help life onward in its noblest aim.

W.W.

Rydal Mount,
9th Jany 1846

---

12 obey.] obey *MS. 89*
14 woman's] woman *Yale MS. 10*
15 have *rev from* [?worn] *MS. 89* thy . . . worn] that [that *rev to* which] thou hast worn *Cornell MS. 13*
16 to] for *MS. 1845RL, Cornell MS. 13* cannot *rev from* shall not *rev from* cannot *Cornell MS. 13*
19 wilt *rev from* mayst *rev from* wilt *rev from* mayst *Cornell MS. 13*
21 Nor wilt Thou blame the Poet's earnest prayer *MS. 1845RL* Thou *rev from* Tow *Cornell MS. 13* blame] slight *Cornell MS. 13* Poet's] Poets *MS. 89*
22 hence] thence *Cornell MS. 13*
23 Some *rev from* Thoughts that may *Cornell MS. 13*
24 grief *added in pencil Yale MS. 10* Humankind.] humankind *rev from* human [?cares] *Cornell MS. 13*
25 from] frome *MS. 89* spheres *rev from* [?spark] *Yale MS. 10*
26 an *rev from* that *Cornell MS. 13*
28/ Your Majesty's / devoted Subject and Servant / William Wordsworth / 9th Jan^ry 1846 *MS. 1845RL* Mary Wordsworth / William Wordsworth / Cloisters Westminster / April 15th 1847 *Cornell MS. 13*

"Who but is pleased to watch the moon on high"

WHO but is pleased to watch the moon on high
Travelling where she from time to time enshrouds
Her head, and nothing loth her Majesty
Renounces, till among the scattered clouds
One with its kindling edge declares that soon
Will reappear before the uplifted eye
A Form as bright, as beautiful a moon,
To glide in open prospect through clear sky.
Pity that such a promise e'er should prove
False in the issue, that yon seeming space
Of sky should be in truth the steadfast face
Of a cloud flat and dense, through which must move
(By transit not unlike man's frequent doom)
The Wanderer lost in more determined gloom!

"How beautiful the Queen of Night, on high"

How beautiful the Queen of Night, on high
Her way pursuing among scattered clouds,
Where, ever and anon, her head she shrouds

---

composed January 10, 1846
found in DC MS. 143 (A) 99^v,(B) 95^v
published in *1846, 1850*
classed Miscellaneous Sonnets *1846 (vol. 6)* Evening Voluntaries *1850*
reading text *1846*
1 Who but is pleased [is pleased *rev from* delights] to watch the moon on high *rev from*
Who but has watched the Queen of night on high *alt*
In [In *rev to* With] calm delight we watch the Moon on *MS. 143 (B)*
2 *rev from* Travelling where oft with gentle grace *rev from*
Travelling where ever and anon she shrouds *MS. 143 (B)*
5 with its] by its [brigh *del*] *MS. 143 (B)*
8 To glide *rev from* Gliding *MS. 143 (B)*
10 in the issue . . . yon *rev from* in the trial . . . a *MS. 143 (B)*
11 should be *rev from* is but *rev from* [?would be] *rev from* should be *MS. 143 (B)*
13–14 *rev from* (Thus symblizing with mans frequent doom
The wanderer lost in more determined gloom *rev from*
The Wanderer lost in more enduring gloom!
Delusive lot; how like Man's frequent doom! *MS. 143 (B)*

---

composed after January 10, 1846, probably between late May 1846 and September 3, 1849
found in MS. 1845W, MS. 1845D
published in *1850*
classed Miscellaneous Poems *1850*
reading text *1850*
3 shrouds *rev from* [?] *MS. 1845W*

See the photograph and transcription of "Who but is pleased to watch the moon on high," DC MS. 143, 99^v, pp. 828–829.

Hidden from view in dense obscurity.
But look, and to the watchful eye
A brightening edge will indicate that soon
We shall behold the struggling Moon
Break forth,—again to walk the clear blue sky.

"Where lies the truth? has Man, in wisdom's creed"

WHERE lies the truth? has Man, in wisdom's creed,
A pitiable doom; for respite brief
A care more anxious, or a heavier grief?
Is he ungrateful, and doth little heed
God's bounty, soon forgotten; or indeed,
Must Man, with labour born, awake to sorrow
When Flowers rejoice and Larks with rival speed
Spring from their nests to bid the Sun good morrow?
They mount for rapture as their songs proclaim
Warbled in hearing both of earth and sky;
But o'er the contrast wherefore heave a sigh?
Like these aspirants let us soar—our aim,
Through life's worst trials, whether shocks or snares,
A happier, brighter, purer Heaven than theirs.

---

6 edge *rev from* end *MS. 1845W*
8 Break *rev from WW's pencil* Walk *MS. 1845W* again to walk *rev from* to walk at ease *MS. 1845W*

---

composed between January 10 and 23, 1846
found in DC MS. 143 (A) 95[r], (B) 94[v]; WW to HR, January 23, 1846
published in *1846, 1850*
classed Miscellaneous Sonnets *1846 (vol. 6)* Evening Voluntaries *1850*
reading text *1846*

2 pitiable] piteous *WW to HR* doom *rev from* lot *MS. 143 (A)*
4 *rev from* Ungrateful is He taking little heed *MS. 143 (A)*
5 God's bounty, *rev from* Of bounties *rev from* Of bounty *MS. 143 (A)*
6 Is Man not man made to mourn? must wake to sorrow *rev to*
Who but must fear that he may wake to sorrow *rev to*
Who that lies down and may not wake to sorrow *rev to*
Is [Is *rev to* does] not man born to trouble [to trouble *rev to* with labour], wakes to sorrow *MS. 143 (A)*
Who but must fear that he may wake to sorrow *rev to*
Who that lies down, and may not wake to sorrow, *WW to HR*
Must *rev from* Doth *MS. 143 (B)*
7 Flowers] flowers *rev from* flower *rev from* plants *MS. 143 (A)*
9 They *rev from* Thy *MS. 143 (B)* rapture as] rapture; this *MS. 143 (A); WW to HR* rapture; this *rev from* raptures this *MS. 143 (B)*
11 But *over illeg word MS. 143 (B)* heave a *rev from* should we *MS. 143 (A)*
12 these] those *MS. 143 (A)*

TO LUCCA GIORDANO.

GIORDANO, verily thy Pencil's skill
Hath here portrayed with Nature's happiest grace
The fair Endymion couched on Latmos-hill;
And Dian gazing on the Shepherd's face
In rapture,—yet suspending her embrace,
As not unconscious with what power the thrill
Of her most timid touch his sleep would chase,
And, with his sleep, that beauty calm and still.
O may this work have found its last retreat
Here in a Mountain-bard's secure abode,
One to whom, yet a School-boy, Cynthia showed
A face of love which he in love would greet,
Fixed, by her smile, upon some rocky seat;
Or lured along where green-wood paths he trod.

RYDAL MOUNT. 1846.

ILLUSTRATED BOOKS AND NEWSPAPERS.

DISCOURSE was deemed Man's noblest attribute,
And written words the glory of his hand;
Then followed Printing with enlarged command
For thought—dominion vast and absolute
For spreading truth, and making love expand.
Now prose and verse sunk into disrepute

---

composed February 11, 1846
found in DC MS. 143; MS. 1845W; MS. 1845D
published in *1846, 1850*
classed Miscellaneous Sonnets *1846 (vol. 6)* Evening Voluntaries *1850*
reading text *1846*
title Upon a Picture brought from Italy by my Son, which, together with its Companions now hangs at Rydal Mount. *inserted over single illeg word MS. 143 lacking MSS. 1845*
4 gazing on] leaning o'er *MS. 1845W, MS. 1845D*
7 Of *and* his sleep would chase *over illeg eras MS. 1845W*
9 O] O *rev to* Here *MS. 143* Here *MS. 1845W, MS. 1845D* its *rev from* a *MS. 1845W*
10 Here in *rev to* Within *(but* Here *not del) MS. 143* Within *MS. 1845W, MS. 1845D*
12 in *rev to* with *MS. 143*
13 seat *rev from* [?road] *MS. 143*
14 lured *rev from* lurd *MS. 143*
14/ Rydal Mount / Feb[ry] 11th 1846 *MS. 143*

---

composed around mid-February but by February 23, 1846
found in DC MS. 143
published in *1846, 1850*
classed Miscellaneous Poems *1846 (vol. 6)* Sentiment and Reflection *1850*
reading text *1846*
3 followed Printing *rev from* Printing followed *MS. 143*
4 For *rev from* Of *MS. 143*

Must lacquey a dumb Art that best can suit
The taste of this once-intellectual Land.
A backward movement surely have we here,
For manhood—back to childhood; for the age—
Back towards caverned life's first rude career.
Avaunt this vile abuse of pictured page!
Must eyes be all in all, the tongue and ear
Nothing? Heaven keep us from a lower stage!

On the Banks of a Rocky Stream

The poem *On the Banks of a Rocky Stream* was probably composed shortly after the 1846 edition had gone to press in April of that year and revised early in 1847 before its appearance in the second stereotype edition of the one-volume *Poetical Works* (starting around April 1847); perhaps the poem was inserted while the printing was in progress, as Moxon did not include the poem's title in the table of contents or the index. The published version shares the main image—and the phrase "eddying balls of foam"—of lines 3–6 with the sonnet *Composed on the Banks of a Rocky Stream* ("Dogmatic Teachers, of the snow-white fur!"), which was first published in 1820. The first reading text is drawn from MS. 143, the second from *Poems,* 1847.

[Text of MS. 143]

Grant me, o blessed Lord a mind
In which my thoughts may have a quiet home
Thoughts which now fret like balls of foam
That in a whirlpool each the other chase
Around and round and neither find
An outlet nor a resting place.—

---

7 that] which *MS. 143*
10 For *rev from* From *MS. 143* From *1850*
11 *rev from* Backward as far as Egypt[?s] oldest [oldest *rev to* darkest] year *MS. 143*

---

composed probably between May and the end of December 1846
found in DC MS. 143
reading text DC MS. 143
3 Thoughts which now fret *rev to* Thither and back as [~~?~~] ~~of~~ *and* like *alt* may *MS. 143*
4 whirlpool] [?reeling *del*] whirlpool *MS. 143*
5 and] & *alt* yet *alt* and *MS. 143*
6 nor *rev from* or *(caret entered to show change but* or *not deleted) MS. 143*

[Text of 1847]

ON THE BANKS OF A ROCKY STREAM

BEHOLD an emblem of our human mind
Crowded with thoughts that need a settled home,
Yet, like to eddying balls of foam
Within this whirlpool, they each other chase
Round and round, and neither find
An outlet nor a resting-place!
Stranger, if such disquietude be thine,
Fall on thy knees and sue for help divine.

Installation Ode

Mary Wordsworth's initialed note on the front endpaper of her own copy of the 1847 London edition of the *Installation Ode*—now at the Wordsworth Library—reads, "The Plan, & composition of this Ode was chiefly prepared by Mr Quillinan, but carefully Revised in M.S. by Mr Wordsworth, who being in a state of deep domestic affliction, could not otherwise have been able to fulfil the engagement with Prince Albert, previously made, in time for the Installation." Preoccupied by his daughter Dora's final illness, Wordsworth had much difficulty with the composition of the ode and expressed deep misgivings about it. Adam Sedgwick in a letter to a Mrs. Malcolm, dated York House, Bath, April 7, 1847, reported that Wordsworth was "hatching an ode for the Installation" but was "get[ting] on badly" (Gordon N. Ray Collection, Pierpont Morgan Library). And Sara Coleridge (Jr.) wrote to Isabella Fenwick at Queen Square, Bath, on April 29, 1847, "You have heard, no doubt, that he has written part of the Installation Ode; Miss F[arrer] says that there is a great deal of thought in it; but he says himself that it is but superficial thought, and that it is not worth much" (*SCML*, II, 112). Though Wordsworth is known to have produced two manuscript versions for his collaborator, the only familial fair copy surviving is in the hand of Edward Quillinan (Cornell MS. 3). Lines of the poem under discussion for revision appear in letters between Wordsworth and the composer of the music, Thomas Attwood Walmisley, Professor of Music at Cambridge (appointed in 1836).

Wordsworth wrote to Walmisley from Bath on March 26, 1847, acceding to

---

composed probably revised in early 1847, but by mid-April
found in MS. 1845W (MW over WW pencil); MS. 1845D (EQ)
published in *1847, 1850*
classed Inscriptions *1847, 1850*
reading text *1847*

3 balls *rev from* bells *MS. 1845W*
4 they *MW rev from* do *MS. 1845W*
5 Round *rev from* round *MS. 1845W* neither *alt in pencil* nowhere *MS. 1845W*
8 help] grace *underlying pencil MS. 1845D*

Prince Albert's request, conveyed by Walmisley, that Wordsworth compose an ode to be set to music by Walmisley.

> I cannot but wish you had a Fellow-labourer more worthy of his office than myself—for it is some time since I ceased to write verse, and gave up the intention of ever resuming the employment—All I can say at present is, that though I have not yet composed a Line, I will endeavour to meet your wish speedily; only be so kind as to let me know, whether you would prefer an irregular style of versification Like Gray's Ode on the Installation of the Duke of Grafton, or a regular form of stanza to be repeated to the conclusion—As soon as I am apprized of this, I shall set about to work in order to comply with your request without delay. [*LY*, IV, 840]

On April 29 Wordsworth enclosed a second version of the *Ode* with his letter to Walmisley (the letter only is in Amherst College Library). Wordsworth wrote: "Here is the promised Ode corrected as well as under distressing domestic circumstances I was able to do it—My nephew Dr Wordsworth gave me hope that it would answer our mutual purpose, that is, that the words would suit your music. . . . I was glad to have been assured by you that you would not shew the Ode to any one till it shall be called into use" (*LY*, IV, 845). Walmisley replied on May 3 to ask that earlier readings—from the copy now lost—be reinstated (as recorded in the *apparatus*, below) and to suggest the addition at the close of another stanza that would "cause the Ode to end more joyously than the present termination, which seems rather sombre" and fulfill Wordsworth's promise in "the argument prefixed to the first copy" that the poem would end with "an acclamation for the Prince & Queen together"—words Walmisley has quoted from the lost copy. He wanted, he said, "a few words added, to which I might write a spirit-stirring Chorus."

In Wordsworth's letter of May 5 (printed by Knight) one change is repeated and others that were later rejected are mentioned:

> I quite agree in most of your remarks. The alterations were made in the notion, mistaken as it seems, that they might better suit your music. Be pleased to understand that you may adopt or reject any alterations as they suit you or not, and whether the note you suggest for the printed Ode may be requisite we will leave to after-consideration. The only alteration that I wish to stand is *lore* instead of *path,* because it is intended to mark her *education,* as a girl, the means by which she acquired a fitting knowledge of the manner in which she was to tread the path of peculiar duty when grown up. The alteration 'past' and 'clarion's blast' was to get rid of the word *trumpet,* which is required near the end of the Ode, but it may be repeated if you like. I will try to supply you with the sort of chorus you wish to conclude with. I felt the need of it, but I was willing to leave the matter where it was, till I was sure that you were desirous of an addition.

Perhaps feeling his own lack of proper attention to the project, and at the same time insisting on his role simply "as a poet" and not as "Laureate," he added,

> The heavy domestic affliction that presses on me, the very dangerous illness of my only daughter, makes it impossible for me to exert myself satisfactorily in this task. . . . P.S.—Do not misunderstand the word *task.* I only feel it one in reference to the great anxiety that I have alluded to, for I was not called on to furnish the *Installation Ode* in my capacity of

Laureate, but simply as a poet to whom His Royal Highness was pleased to apply on the occasion. [*LY*, IV, 846 and note]

The new stanza was not a success, and Walmisley wrote again on May 20 to complain that "words of four syllables" were difficult to put into musical rhythm and to ask again for a closing stanza (not to begin with the word "Albert," the opening word of l. 95 in what is now the penultimate stanza) with "as cheering and joyful a strain as possible." On June 2 he wrote again to express his pleasure in Wordsworth's response; "the concluding stanza which you have sent me will do gloriously" (WL: A/Walmisley/1–4).

The work was performed by soloists, chorus, and orchestra in Senate House, Cambridge, July 6, 1847. An account of the ceremony was supplied by Christopher Wordsworth, Jr., in a letter to his uncle on July 8, 1847 (WL Letters):

I was in the Senate House on Tuesday during the performance of the Installation Ode, and, being on the platform very near Her Majesty, and the Chancellor, and among all the grandees I had the best opportunity of hearing and seeing the affect it produced, and I assure you that nothing could be more gratifying than the manner in which it was received. All seemed to admire the patriotic and moral Spirit of the Ode; and I think it did good to many hearts, as well as gave pleasure to many ears. It has been rehearsed in London at Hanover Square Rooms. It is I hope some comfort to you my dear Uncle in your own private sorrow that you have been affording pleasure to others, and have dignified and sanctified the joy of a great Academic festival.

He added that he was "very graciously" received by the Queen and Prince "for your sake . . . and for my father's" at a reception held the same day at Trinity Lodge. A month later Wordsworth received another, even more effusive account (Adam Sedgwick to WW, August 10, 1847; WL Letters):

During the festivities of our installation one thing only seemed to be wanting, the presence of the venerable poet, who had poured out the stores of his mind to do honour to our Queen's visit and to grace the triumph of her Husband. You would indeed have had a heartfelt greeting and the performance of your Ode was followed by one of the most rapturous manifestations of feeling I have ever had the happiness of witnessing. Nay I do not express myself with sufficient strength, it was the most rapturous, and far beyond any outpouring of the heart I had ever witnessed.

The Cambridge University Press edition of 1847 has been chosen as the basis for the reading text. A limited number of copies were printed by the Press, apparently for distribution to the audience (a copy at Harvard bears pencil notes describing the performance that seem to have been entered at the time). Two other editions by commercial publishers soon followed, one by Metcalfe and Palmer of Cambridge and one by George Bell of London. As well, the text of the poem was reprinted in the poetry column of a Cambridge newspaper on or shortly after July 6, 1847, and in the *Atheneum* for July 10, 1847. Copy for the University Press printing was apparently based on the performed text (Walmisley had suggested a separate "edition"; TAW to WW, May 3, 1847, WL Letters). The Metcalfe and Palmer printing appears to have been based on the one produced by the University Press. The title page of the University Press edition does not identify the author or the composer; that of the Metcalfe and Palmer edition gives equal billing to Wordsworth and to Walmisley; and the Bell edition, an elaborate color production, assigns sole authorship to Wordsworth, "Poet Laureate." A clipping of the unidentified newsprint version survives in the Wordsworth Library. An edition that was "Published for the Author" by Chappell of London in 1849 includes Walmisley's music. Though the editions other than the Cambridge University Press were no doubt published with Wordsworth's permission, it is unlikely that he authorized any of the variant forms of the title and text in any of them. For this reason we have not recorded such variants in the *apparatus* (but for the few verbal differences, see notes, p. 506).

It is fitting, perhaps, that Wordsworth's last poem, or one at least that he helped to produce and refine, should address an audience on the theme of education and its role in the future well-being of the state, echoing in length, aim, and seriousness of purpose his first poem to reach the public ear, his *Lines on the Bicentenary of Hawkshead School,* composed sixty-two years earlier for the celebration of his school's long history and its promise in the years ahead (see *Early Poems, 1785–1797*, pp. 356–361).

---

fly-title

ODE,

PERFORMED IN THE SENATE-HOUSE, CAMBRIDGE,

ON THE SIXTH OF JULY, M.DCCC.XLVII.

AT THE FIRST COMMENCEMENT

AFTER

THE INSTALLATION

OF

HIS ROYAL HIGHNESS THE PRINCE ALBERT,

Chancellor of the University.

INSTALLATION ODE.

INTRODUCTION AND CHORUS.

For thirst of power that Heaven disowns,
For temples, towers, and thrones,
Too long insulted by the Spoiler's shock,
Indignant Europe cast
Her stormy foe at last
To reap the whirlwind on a Libyan rock.

SOLO—Tenor.

War is passion's basest game
Madly played to win a name;
Up starts some tyrant, Earth and Heaven to dare;
The servile million bow;
But will the lightning glance aside to spare
The Despot's laurelled brow?

CHORUS.

War is mercy, glory, fame,
Waged in Freedom's holy cause;
Freedom, such as Man may claim
Under God's restraining laws.
Such is Albion's fame and glory:
Let rescued Europe tell the story.

RECIT. *(Accompanied)*—CONTRALTO.

But, lo, what sudden cloud has darkened all
The land as with a funeral pall?
The Rose of England suffers blight
The flower has drooped, the Isle's delight,
Flower and bud together fall—
A Nation's hopes lie crushed in Claremont's desolate hall.

---

composed (by EQ and WW) between March 26 and April 29, 1847
found in TAW to WW, May 3, 1847; WW to TAW, May 5, 1847; Cornell MS. 3
published in *1847 Cambridge*
reading text *1847 Cambridge*
title Wordsworth's Installation Ode 1847. *Cornell MS. 3*
3 shock *rev from* [?shocks] *Cornell MS. 3*
9 *rev from* Up starts some tyrant in his pride *TAW to WW*

AIR—SOPRANO.

Time a chequered mantle wears;—
Earth awakes from wintry sleep;
Again the Tree a blossom bears,—
Cease, Britannia, cease to weep!
Hark to the peals on this bright May-morn!
They tell that your future Queen is born!

SOPRANO SOLO AND CHORUS.

A Guardian Angel fluttered
Above the Babe, unseen;
One word he softly uttered—
It named the future Queen:
And a joyful cry through the Island rang,
As clear and bold as the trumpet's clang,
As bland as the reed of peace—
"VICTORIA be her name!"
For righteous triumphs are the base
Whereon Britannia rests her peaceful fame.

QUARTETT.

Time, in his mantle's sunniest fold,
Uplifted on his arms the child;
And, while the fearless Infant smiled,
Her happier destiny foretold:—
"Infancy, by Wisdom mild,
"Trained to health and artless beauty;
"Youth, by Pleasure unbeguiled
"From the lore of lofty duty;
"Womanhood in pure renown,
"Seated on her lineal throne:
"Leaves of myrtle in her Crown,
"Fresh with lustre all their own.
"Love, the treasure worth possessing
"More than all the world beside,
"This shall be her choicest blessing,
"Oft to royal hearts denied."

35–36 *WW rev to* And a joyful cry through the Island past
As clear and bold as a clarion's blast *TAW to WW; reading text reinstated WW to TAW*
37 reed *rev from* breath *TAW to WW*
48 lore *rev from* path *WW to TAW*

RECIT. (*Accompanied*)—BASS.

That eve, the Star of Brunswick shone
With stedfast ray benign
On Gotha's ducal roof, and on
The softly flowing Leine;
Nor failed to gild the spires of Bonn,
And glittered on the Rhine.—
Old Camus too on that prophetic night
Was conscious of the ray;
And his willows whispered in its light,
Not to the Zephyr's sway,
But with a Delphic life, in sight
Of this auspicious day:

CHORUS.

This day, when Granta hails her chosen Lord,
And proud of her award,
Confiding in the Star serene
Welcomes the Consort of a happy Queen.

AIR—CONTRALTO.

Prince, in these Collegiate bowers,
Where Science, leagued with holier truth,
Guards the sacred heart of youth,
Solemn monitors are ours.
These reverend aisles, these hallowed towers,
Raised by many a hand august,
Are haunted by majestic Powers,
The memories of the Wise and Just,
Who, faithful to a pious trust,
Here, in the Founder's Spirit, sought
To mould and stamp the ore of thought
In that bold form and impress high
That best betoken patriot loyalty.
Not in vain those Sages taught.—
True disciples, good as great,
Have pondered here their country's weal,
Weighed the Future by the Past,
Learnt how social frames may last,
And how a Land may rule its fate
By constancy inviolate,

60 Leine] Seine *Cornell MS. 3*
69 Granta *rev from* [?Grantas] *Cornell MS. 3*

Though worlds to their foundations reel,
The sport of factious Hate or godless Zeal.

AIR—BASS.

ALBERT, in thy race we cherish
A Nation's strength that will not perish
While England's sceptred Line
True to the King of Kings is found;
Like that Wise* Ancestor of thine
Who threw the Saxon shield o'er Luther's life,
When first, above the yells of bigot strife,
The trumpet of the Living Word
Assumed a voice of deep portentous sound
From gladdened Elbe to startled Tiber heard.

CHORUS.

What shield more sublime
E'er was blazoned or sung?
And the PRINCE whom we greet
From its Hero is sprung.
Resound, resound the strain
That hails him for our own!
Again, again, and yet again;
For the Church, the State, the Throne!—
And that Presence fair and bright,
Ever blest wherever seen,
Who deigns to grace our festal rite,
The pride of the Islands, VICTORIA THE QUEEN!

FINIS.

*Frederick the Wise, Elector of Saxony.

97 *note lacking Cornell MS. 3*

PART II
Notes and Nonverbal Variants

Notes

The notes that Wordsworth dictated to his friend and neighbor Isabella Fenwick in the winter and spring of 1842 and 1843, as recorded by Edward and Dora Quillinan and with occasional comments by others, are cited from *The Fenwick Notes of William Wordsworth* (*FNW*), edited by Jared Curtis (London, 1993).

The notes that Wordsworth appended to the volumes in the lifetime editions of his works (as distinct from notes printed on the page with the poems to which they refer, which accompany the reading texts of the poems) are identified by the year or years of publication. Abbreviations of lifetime printings cited are listed at the end of the Editorial Procedure. Manuscripts are identified in the Manuscript Census.

The evidence by which each poem may be dated is also provided, together with explanatory notes to this edition.

Decay of Piety

"Attendance at church on prayer-days, Wednesdays and Fridays and holidays, received a shock at the revolution. It is now, however, happily reviving. The ancient people described in this Sonnet were among the last of that pious class. May we hope that the practise, now in some degree renewed, will continue to spread." (*FNW*, p. 20.) The earliest version of the poem appears in a notebook (Amherst MS.) used chiefly for sonnets composed largely in 1821–1822 for *ES* (1822); WW seems to have intended *Decay of Piety* for *ES* as well and probably composed it at the same time. The work in the notebook probably dates from 1821, after January 17, though probably by March 12, 1821, or a few weeks later, and certainly by November 24.

3–4 WW's fragment of transcription in MS. 158 (January 1846) combined the two lines in error, no doubt the cause of the copy's being abandoned.

12–14 In MS. 89 these lines were reentered by WW in pencil after part of the leaf was cut away.

Not Love, nor War, nor the tumultuous swell

The earliest version, found in a notebook (Amherst MS.) that WW used for copies of *ES* (1822), can probably be dated in 1821, when he was working on *ES* (see the note to *Decay of Piety*). He probably intended "Not Love, nor War, nor the tumultuous swell" for that series (see the note to ll. 6–14, below), but he instead revised the sonnet by early July 1822, when he sent it with a second sonnet "A volant Tribe of Bards on earth are found," to Joanna Baillie to be included in her *Collection* of 1823. On July 11, 1822, Miss Baillie replied, "I received your letter with the beautiful sonnets yesterday, and I feel very sensibly how good you are in attending to my request at a time when your mind is so painfully occupied [WW had injured his head in a fall from his horse]. . . . The first sonnet [probably "A volant Tribe of Bards"] is full of pleasing and soothing images and is my greatest favorite; but they are both beautiful and will do great honours to my Collection. My packet of contributions is now swelling to a considerable size and I hope to produce an acceptable and rather curious volume" (WL MS., A/Baillie/1).

6–14 The imagery of sky, river, and flower seems to link this poem to the *Introduction* to *ES* (I.i.), ll. 9–14. See Abbie Findlay Potts, *The Ecclesiastical Sonnets of William Wordsworth, A Critical Edition* (New Haven, 1922), p. 36.

12–14 In MS. 89 part of the leaf has been cut away, obliterating the first words of each of these lines.

Recollection of the Portrait of King Henry Eighth, Trinity Lodge, Cambridge.

WW visited CW at Trinity Lodge in March 1821 and again in May 1824; he remarked on Trinity Lodge's complement of "venerable Portraits" after the first visit (*LY*, I, 45), and letters of the period of the second visit show an interest in paintings, though the portrait of Henry VIII is not mentioned (*LY*, I, 266).

Translation of the Sestet of a Sonnet by Tasso

On the half-sheet that is now DC MS. 160 EQ first entered the Italian text of the sonnet by Tasso ("Vasca, le cui felici ardite antenne"); below a solid line he reinscribed the verse in discursive Italian prose and provided his own literal prose translation. On the verso, beneath the end of EQ's translation, is WW's holograph copy of his verse rendition of the sestet. "Wordsworth" is written in pencil below, possibly by EQ but perhaps in a modern hand. Drawing on MS. 160, Richard Garnett printed WW's sestet in *The Academy*, January 2, 1897, along with Garnett's own verse translation of the octet. The full sonnet is reprinted in *PW* Knight 1896, VIII, xxii–xxiii, and Garnett's octet in *PW*, IV, 475. EQ's literal translation of the sonnet follows:

"Vasco whose prosperous (and) bold ship-yards unfurled their sails against the Sun where he brings back the day, and thence returned to where he seems to sink; not more than those through the cruel sea suffered he who did outrage and scorn to the Cyclop; nor he who disturbed the harpies in their dwelling-place, nor gave (either of them) a finer subject for accomplished pens. And now the pen of the accomplished and good Lewis (Camoens) so far extends thy glorious flight that thy tarred (or pitched) ships went less far, so that the fame of thy course reaches [to *del*] him to whom our pole raises itself (over whom our pole-star shines) and him who stands opposite—his antipodes.——"

If EQ entered the text and his translation for WW's benefit, he could not have done so before his meeting with him at Rydal in June 1821, when, as EQ recorded in his diary, they "rambled together for hours; talked of poetry." A likely period for developing their common interest in Tasso may have been what EQ called "so happy and satisfactory a summer" of 1821, when he moved his family to Spring Cottage, Loughrigg, near Rydal Mount (*LY*, I, 701–702).

A volant Tribe of Bards on earth are found

A transcription, apparently by WW, of "A volant Tribe of Bards on earth are found" appears in an album once belonging to Caroline Spencer Churchill. Listed for sale by a London bookseller in the 1950s, the album's present location is unknown. Its text evidently predates that in Joanna Baillie's *Collection* (1823), though variants appear only in the opening three lines. The transcription was signed by WW at Lowther Castle, October 2, 1821. WW probably composed the sonnet, then, toward the end of the period of intense creative activity between March and November 1821, when he was completing the sonnet sequences Ecclesiastical Sketches and Continent 1820 (*LY*, I, 89). The opening lines were altered probably by early July 1822 (see the note to "Not Love, nor War, nor the tumultuous swell," above), but before the sonnet appeared in Baillie's *Collection* (around May 1823). WW revised the poem extensively by the end of January 1827, when he sent copy to the printer for *PW*, 1827.

3 "coignes of vantage" is from *Macbeth*, I.vi.7 (EdeS).

Queen and Negress chaste and fair!

DW, in her letter to CCl, October 24, 1821, remarks on the "lively picture I shaped to myself of the sable Queen sitting with her sable daughters beside you on the sofa in my dear little Parlour at Playford" and copied at the end of her letter "a parody (which I hope will make you laugh) that William and Sara threw off last Sunday afternoon. They had been talking of Mr Clarkson's perserverance in the *African* cause—*especially* of his kindness to every human being and of this last act of kindness to the distressed Negro Widow and her Family. Withal tender thoughts of merriment came with the image of the sable princess by your fire-side. The first stanza of Ben Johnson's [*sic*] poem slipped from W's lips in a parody—and together they finished it with loving fun—Oh! how they laughed. I heard them into my Room upstairs, and wondered what they were about—and when it was finished I claimed the privilege of sending it to you." The "Queen" is Madame Christophe, wife of Henry Christophe, self-declared king and successor to Toussaint l'Ouverture, who ruled the Negro Kingdom in northern Haiti until his death by suicide during the general rebellion against him in 1820. Madame Christophe and her daughters were allowed to leave the island and took refuge with the Thomas Clarksons at Playford Hall (a circumstance much reported in the papers). Not till January 1822 did DW write to apologize for any offence "our joke on poor fallen royalty" may have given to CCl: "Yet still I am sorry that I ever committed [the foolish rhymes] to paper; thinking that, at all events, while those innocent Beings were at your side, who had suffered so much from the Death of Christophe (and perhaps still more from his ungovernable passions) you were little likely to cast off serious thoughts and feelings at once and transport yourself to our fire-side partaking of its half-hour's mirth." See *LY*, I, 30 and note, 87–91 and notes, and 103; and *SHL*, p. 238.

In the manuscript DW separated the stanzas with an ink rule.

1 DW annotated this line: "Ben Johnson's poem begins [']Queen and Huntress chaste and fair'—you *must* know it."

7–12 These lines were entered in the margin at a quarter-turn and labeled "2nd stanza."

13 Wilby's] DW asterisked the word and added in the margin: "Mrs Wilberforce calls her Husband by that pretty diminutive—'Wilby'—you must have heard her."

Epigrams on Byron's *Cain*

WW enclosed the four epigrams in a letter to RS in which he offered the latter advice concerning RS's quarrel with Byron: "The only part of the charge [that Byron made against RS in an appendix to *The Two Foscari*—published with *Cain*] you are any way called upon to notice is that of slander, as this is given with his name, we think it ought to be met. As to the rest—one would never think of it but for the opportunity it gives of chastising the offender." The rest of WW's letter consists of the four epigrams, introduced by the remark, "The Girls [probably RS's daughter EMS and STC's daughter Sara] may be amused" (see Chester L. Shaver, *MLN*, and *LY*, I, 101–102 and notes). Byron's *Cain* (with *The Two Foscari* and a third play) had appeared on December 19, 1821. The first two epigrams appeared in *PW* Knight 1896 and were reprinted in *PW*, IV, 378. Part of the letter and a transcription of the four verses were published in a 1998 sale catalogue (see Manuscript Census, p. 61). The few variants from Shaver's transcription are reported below.

It is not unlikely that SH took part in composing the epigrams (cf. DW to CCl, October 24, 1821). After RS's disclaimer appeared in the *Courier* on January 5, 1822, SH wrote to TM, "I hope you have seen Southeys tickling Letter to Lord Byron—We long to hear of an answer from his lordship, as S. will then let loose upon him a full sail and if he does not bear him down I shall wonder" (*SHL*, p. 237). Byron did not fail to reply—in his raucous parody of RS's *A Vision of Judgment*—in the fall of 1822.

i. "Critics, right honourable Bard! decree"

Variants in the sale catalogue are "thee;" (not "thee," as in Shaver) in l. 2, and an illegible deletion after "Whose" in l. 3.

ii. *On Cain a Mystery dedicated to Sir Walter Scott*

2 "The death of Abel"] In the preface to *Cain*, Byron wrote, "Gesner's *Death of Abel* I have never read since I was eight years of age, at Aberdeen." *Der Tod Abels* by Salomon Gessner was published in 1758 (*LY*, I, 102n); and cf. *Prelude*, VII, 564.

3 "warm-reeking rich"] From Burns's *To a Haggis*, ll. 17–18 (EdeS).

4 Sir Walter's table] Byron's *Cain* (1821) is dedicated thus: "To Sir Walter Scott, Bart. This mystery of Cain is inscribed, by his obliged friend, and faithful servant, The Author." Scott was created a baronet in 1820.

Variants in the sale catalogue are a period after "Scott" in the title, and "cooked" revised to "cook'd" in l. 2.

iii. *After reading a luscious scene of the above—The Wonder explained*

Perhaps the "luscious scene" is the final one in Act III in which the marked Cain bids farewell before setting off "eastward from Eden." Variants in the sale catalogue are "After" revised from "On" and a dash after "explained" in the title.

iv. *On a Nursery piece of the same, by a Scottish Bard—*

6 The first scene of Act III of *Cain* opens with Abel and his wife Adah discussing the future of their son Enoch as he lies asleep beside them.

Variants in the sale catalogue are the deleted word "him" (not "?kick" as in Shaver) in l. 5, and "Ladle!" (not "Ladle.") in l. 6.

Thus far I write to please my Friend

WW's response to a request for his autograph on the date inscribed below the text. The small piece of paper on which the couplet is written may have been clipped from a letter for placement in an album.

By Moscow self-devoted to a blaze

In her letter to HCR, dated in the postscript December 21, 1822, DW wrote, "I will transcribe a Sonnet which [WW] felt himself called upon to write in justification of the Russians whom he felt he had injured; by not having given them *their* share in the overthrow of Buonaparte in conjuction with the elements. Refer to the Political Sonnets for that which is to precede the following," and then transcribed a copy of "By Moscow self-devoted to a blaze" (see *LY*, I, 178–179). The poems referred to are *The French Army in Russia* and *On the Same Occasion* ("Ye Storms, resound the praises of your King!"), which in 1827 and later editions were followed by the sonnet "By Moscow" (see *Poems, 1807–1820*, pp. 206–208).

10 Exalt] lift up.

12–13 He] Moses (Exodus 14–15)

These Vales were saddened with no common gloom

In her letter to EQ, November 29, 1822, MW wrote:

> It is a great satisfaction to me to be able to transmit to you the alterations on [alterations on *rev from* additions to] the other side—which William, without much trouble, made last night—I am certain, on this occasion two heads are better than one—for unless the work had been cast by yourself—W. would have been bewildered, and have found it difficult [found it difficult *rev from* had great difficulty] to satisfy himself—the extreme delicacy and sweetness of the subject, made him fearful of touching upon it.—
>
> (Altered by omission chiefly [chiefly *rev from* only])
>
> [Here follows EQ's lines rev by WW as noted in *apparatus* to poem, p. 27.]
>
> The above is harmonious and tender, but we think it not sufficiently particular; and submit the following additions, and slight alterations [additions . . .

alterations *inserted*] to your judgment, without any opinion of our own.

[Here follows the expanded sixteen-line text.]

We are doubtful of the propriety of dwelling upon personal beauty in an Epitaph, therefore have had less scruple to displace the word 'lovely' [in EQ's sketch]—*patient* being so very appropriate and here quite necessary to bind together the composition. [WL Letters]

MW sent the epitaph to TM on December 3, 1822, asking "What do you think of the following as an Epitaph—the groundwork is Q's own, altered by W. I do not say that it will be adopted. After the usual notice of who she was, etc., these lines [here follows the text of the sixteen-line epitaph] " (*MWL*, p. 95). CW, Jr., reported that "the first six lines" of the epitaph were WW's composition (*Memoir*, I, 444n), but, as EdeS suggested, WW rewrote EQ's draft from beginning to end (*PW*, IV, 477–478).

To the Lady ———. On Seeing the Foundation Preparing for the Erection of ——— Chapel, Westmoreland

"*To The Lady le Fleming* After thanking in prose Lady Fleming for the service she had done to her neighbourhood by erecting this Chapel I have nothing to say beyond the expression of regret that the Architect did not furnish an elevation better suited to the site in a narrow mountain pass and what is of more consequence better constructed in the interior for the purposes of worship—It has no chancel—the Altar is unbecomingly confined, the Pews are so narrow as to preclude the possibility of kneeling—there is no vestry—and what ought to have been first mentioned, the font instead of standing at its proper place at the Entrance is thrust into the farther end of a little Pew—when these defects shall be pointed out to the Munificent Patroness they will it is hoped be corrected—." (*FNW*, pp. 43–44; see also p. 146.)

WW dated the poem 1823 (*MS. 1832/36–*). A version of "80 lines" had been composed by December 21, 1822, when DW mentioned it to HCR as recent work (*LY*, I, 180); WW added to it in the new year but did not publish it until 1827. He sent Lord Lonsdale a copy of the early eight-stanza version on January 24, 1823, describing it as "a short Poem which I have just addressed to Lady le Fleming upon the occasion of erecting a Chapel at Rydal." The following day he wrote again, saying that "On reviewing the Lines which I ventured to send yesterday, they seemed to me in some respect not sufficiently appropriate; I felt also that there was an abruptness in the mode of introducing the 4th Stanza, and that there was a disproportion between the middle and the other parts of the Poem. These several [defects *del*] objections seem in a great measure obviated by the Introduction of a new stanza, as on the opposite page. It follows the third, ending 'To interrupt the deep repose'"; on the page opposite is DW's copy of ll. 20–30, and the first four words of l. 51, to indicate the stanza's placement. Beneath her transcript DW added a note, "A corrected Copy is enclosed, of the whole," but neither this copy nor the one sent the day before has been identified. (See *LY*, I, 183–184.)

WW wrote to Lady B on February 17, 1823, "I hope the verses [*To the Lady* ———] will afford you pleasure. Her ladyship wrote a very proper reply when they were sent to her; but how far they may have power to act as a 'peace-offering' we much doubt, but heartily wish they may. The severe weather has put a stop to all progress with the work. If you or Sir George could send us any hints, or sketch for a chapel that would look well in this situation, it is possible that we could have it made useful—through her agents. We are very anxious that nothing should be done to disfigure the village. They might, good taste directing them, add much to its beauty. The site chosen is the orchard opposite the door leading to the lower waterfall" (*LY*, I, 187). These practical steps in achieving a building suited to the site were not carried through, though in recompense, perhaps, the poet imagined the chapel's future in a new stanza he may have added just before or during construction, "The tower time-stricken, and in shade / Embosomed of coeval trees" (ll. 43–44); WW was not entirely satisfied with the reality, as the IF note shows. The Chapel was opened in December 1824. On April 16, 1828, writing to BF, WW altered these visionary lines (ll. 41–46) to remove the reference to delayed construction and to replace the imagined siting of the building with lines describing the sound of its bells. The one word still referring to the building, "structure," was replaced with "future" in *PW,* 1832.

21–30, 31–40 In MS. 1827/32C MW entered the first two words of the revision, "How fondly &c," to indicate the new placement of the stanza and then numbered the first five stanzas to show the new arrangement.

41–46 In MS. 1827/32C WW first entered revisions in the printed text and then copied the passage below in ink.

81 "'bold bad' men" echoes *Faerie Queene,* I, i, 37 (EdeS).

83 "dark opprobrious den"] From *Paradise Lost,* II, 58 (EdeS).

On the Same Occasion

WW dated the poem 1823 (*MS. 1832/36–*). He probably composed it shortly after completing *To the Lady ———. On Seeing the Foundation Preparing for the Erection of ——— Chapel, Westmoreland* (see the note to the latter poem, above).

4 The mother Church] St. Oswald's, Grasmere.

27 the dayspring from on high] Luke 1:78 (EdeS).

Memory

The IF note to *Written in a Blank Leaf of Macpherson's Ossian* includes mention of *Memory*: "*Lines written in a blank Leaf of Macpherson's Ossian* This Poem should, for variety's sake, take its place among the itinerary Sonnets in one of the Scotch Tours [it was so placed in 1845]. The verses—'or strayed from hope and promise, self betrayed' were, I am sorry to say, suggested from apprehensions of the fate of my Friend H. C. the subject of the verses addressed to H. C. when 6 years old. The piece wh. follows, to 'Memory,' arose out of similar feelings." (*FNW,* p. 43; see also pp. 145–146.) WW assigned the date 1824 to *Written in a Blank Leaf* in editions from 1836, but gave *Memory* the date 1823 in MS. 1832/36 and editions from 1836. Hartley Coleridge, having lost his fellowship at Balliol through bouts of drunkenness and disrespect for authority, was a concern to STC in London, to the Southeys in Keswick, and to the Wordsworths at Rydal. Urged on by his father, though the Southeys and Wordsworths doubted the wisdom of the scheme, Hartley moved north and began teaching in Ambleside under the master Mr. Dawes in the fall of 1822. He was reported to be doing well, though no proper disciplinarian, by DW and WW in correspondence through October 1824 (*LY,* I, *passim*), but was given at intervals, as they had all anticipated, to what the family referred to as "bad behavior." In writing the poem, *Memory,* perhaps within a year of Hartley's arrival, WW seems still to have hoped, against his better judgment, that Hartley's "retirement" to the Lakes would bring him a calm heart and better self-discipline.

In *The Winter's Wreath* (1828) "By W. Wordsworth" is printed beneath the title of the poem and "Rydal Mount" appears below the last line. Unpublished works by WW and his contempories were much sought after by editors of the highly popular annuals, who were keen to increase sales by including well-known authors in their volumes (see Peter J. Manning, "Wordsworth in the *Keepsake, 1829,*" in *Literature in the Marketplace: Nineteenth-century British Publishing and Reading Practices,* ed. John O. Jordan and Robert L. Patten [Cambridge, 1995], pp. 44–73). On February 26, 1828, WW wrote to Allan Cunningham, who had appealed to him for a contribution to *The Anniversary* for 1829, that he was "too late" in his request. He explained by saying, "I have been disagreeably circumstanced—in respect to these Publications" and refused to contribute to them "on the ground that I had never been engaged in any periodical nor meant to be. . . . I have, however, been smuggled into the 'Winter's Wreath' to which I contributed three years ago; it being then intended as a solitary Publication for charitable purposes. (The two pieces of mine [*To a Sky-lark* and *Memory*] which appeared there had some months before been published by myself in the last Edition of the Poems [*i.e.*, *PW*, 1827])" (*LY*, I, 583–584). Joanna Baillie had also solicited a poem from WW for *A Collection of Poems, Chiefly Manuscript, and from Living Authors*, published in 1823.

First Floweret of the year is that which shows

The album from which the reading text is drawn belonged to The Hon. George O'Callaghan (1787–1856). Often meeting him during visits to Lowther Castle, WW—in his letter to Lord Lonsdale on November 9, 1823—mentioned teasing O'Callaghan about his grey head and described him in a letter to Dora W, in 1827, as "your old partner" (*LY*, I, 228 and note, 548). WW signed and dated his entry October 1, 1823, at "Whitehaven Castle," the Lonsdale residence on the Cumberland coast at Whitehaven, where O'Callaghan was evidently a guest and where WW must have visited on that day (DW to Elizabeth Crump, October 10, 1823, mentions that WW left Whitehaven on October 4; *LY*, I, 221). Without noting variants, Helen Darbishire reported the album in her 1958 revision of *PW*, IV (see p. 469).

In her letter to EQ, written in May 1824, after leaving the home of EQ's in-laws at Lee Priory in Kent (where WW, MW, and Dora W had been visiting in April), Dora W introduced WW's poem thus, "I transcribe what my Father wrote in O'Callaghans Album. I did this before at Lee but very stupidly brought it away with me" (WL letters). No other copies of the poem are known to survive.

Mary Moorman and Robert Gittings, in correspondence with Leslie Holden (owner of the O'Callaghan album), both stated unequivocably that O'Callaghan is "Lieut. Col. James O'Callaghan, M. P. for the Cornish borough of Tregony (1806–1820) and living at Heighington, Co. Durham" (thus Gittings). Gittings also noted that O'Callaghan "knew Lowther" (being acquainted with the Lonsdales through Lord Darlington, his patron) and that he was 75 in 1823 (private correspondence).

How rich that forehead's calm expanse!

"Rydal Mount, 1824. Also on M.W." JC added to the IF note printed with the poem in *PW*, 1857, that "Mrs. Wordsworth's impression is that the Poem was written at Coleorton: it was certainly suggested by a Print at Coleorton Hall." (*FNW*, pp. 9, 100–101.) WW gave the same date in MS. 1832/36 and editions from 1836. He and DW spent a month at Coleorton from mid-February to mid-March 1824, while MW remained at Rydal Mount to care for young Willy. WW did not return to Rydal Mount until toward the end of May (*LY*, I, 252–254, 269).

7–8 So looked Cecelia . . . station] Cf. Dryden, *Alexander's Feast*, ll. 161, 170 (EdeS).

A Flower Garden

"*The Flower-Garden.* Planned by my friend Lady Beaumont in connexion with the garden at Coleorton." (*FNW*, p. 11.)

"This garden is made out of Lady Caroline Price's and your own—combining the recommendations [*rev from* advantages] of both." (MW to Lady B, February 25, 1825).

WW dated the poem 1824 in MS. 1832/36 and editions from 1836; he and DW spent a month at Coleorton from around February 15 to around March 17, 1824, before going on to London, where they had arrived by March 23 (*LY*, I, 253–256).

To ——— ("Let other Bards of Angels sing")

"Rydal Mount, 1824. Written on Mary Wordsworth." (*FNW*, p. 9.) WW assigned the same date in MS. 1832/36 and editions from 1836. Perhaps the poem was composed around the same time as "How rich that forehead's calm expanse" and *To* ——— ("Oh dearer far than light and life are dear"; see the notes to these poems). See also the companion poem to "Let other Bards of Angels sing," "Yes! thou art fair, yet be not moved," which was composed in 1845 (p. 395).

To ——— ("Look at the fate of summer Flowers")

"Rydal Mount 1824. Prompted by the undue importance attached to personal beauty by some dear friends of mine." (*FNW*, p. 8.) WW assigned the same date in MS. 1832/36 and editions from 1836. Dora W and her circle of friends may be the "friends" referred to. Dora and her father were in London seeing the "sights" and enjoying the society of London friends in April and May 1824 (*LY*, I, 260). EQ entered the pencil note "S. C." (Sara Coleridge) in the manuscript of the IF notes. Sara and her mother were frequent visitors at Rydal Mount during this period.

20, 22 Cf. Spenser, *Hymne in Honour of Beautie*, ll. 211–215 (EdeS).

To Rotha Q———

"Rotha, the daughter of my Son-in-law Mr. Quillinan." (*FNW*, p. 24; see also p. 125.) The younger daughter of EQ and his first wife, Jemima, was born in Rydal, in Ivy Cottage, beside the river Rotha (or Rothay; see l. 9) in September 1821. Her mother died the following May, at age 28, after suffering injuries in a fire. MW, WW, DW, and Dora W visited EQ from April 23 to 30, 1824, at Lee Priory in Kent, where EQ and his daughters were staying with his late wife's father, Sir Egerton Brydges. Rotha's christening, with WW standing up as her godfather, very probably took place at this time (MW refers to Dora W as godmother to Rotha Q in a letter to TM of June 25, 1824; *MWL*, p. 110). In MS. 1845 (WL) WRH added this note, referring to Rotha Q, below the text: "Died at Loughrigg Holme 1st Feby 1876." Rotha Q was the recipient of WW's *Written in an Album* (see p. 268).

See also the note to *The Infant M—— M——* (pp. 426–427) for DW's comments on the two sonnets.

In a letter to Edwin Hill Handley, October 29, 1835, WW agreed to serve as godfather to Handley's child, while at the same time expressing his reservations and referring Handley to two sonnets in Ecclesiastical Sketches, *Baptism* and *Sponsors*, and to the sonnet *To Rotha Q———*, as explanation of his views on the responsibilities incurred by sponsors (see *SNL*, pp. 219–220).

Composed among the Ruins of a Castle in North Wales

WW toured North Wales with MW and Dora W from August 27 to September 14, 1824. The party visited the ruins of Caenarfon Castle on the morning of August 28 and, after dining at Conwy on September 7, spent three hours in Conwy Castle. They also visited Chirk and Dolbardin Castles, but the evening view of Conwy is the most likely source for the imagery of the sonnet (see *LY*, I, 274–278). Conwy Castle's eight towers in two compact flanks, linked by high curtain walls, form a narrow rectangular enclosure that would make deep pockets of shade in moonlight (ll. 7–8). The walls of the Great Hall still stand, bearing vestiges of stone arches and ornate windows, and the King's apartments in the inner ward are intact, though "roofless" as well (l. 1). Eighteenth- and nineteenth-century engravings and paintings of the castle show it in a more ruinous state ("these wounds," l. 5) than its present restored condition suggests, and depict the curtain walls and towers luxuriantly "wreathed" with greenery (ll. 11–12). WW admired Conwy Castle "amongst many others," when he saw it as a young man (*EY*, p. 484), and around June 6, 1804, he received a gift of two drawings from Sir GB, one of them of Conwy Castle (*Chronology: MY*, p. 262; *EY*, p. 383). Donald E. Hayden has suggested that Caenarfon Castle may be the one depicted in the sonnet, but Conwy Castle makes a better fit; for Hayden's account of this tour see his *Wordsworth's Travels in Wales and Ireland*, University of Tulsa Monograph Series, no. 20 (Tulsa, Okla., 1985), pp. 39–52.

To the Lady E. B. and the Hon. Miss P.

"In this Vale of Meditation my friend Jones resided, having been allowed by his Diocesan to fix himself there without resigning his Living in Oxfordshire. He was with my wife and daughter and me when we visited these celebrated ladies who had retired, as one may say, into notice in this vale. Their cottage lay directly in the road between London and Dublin, and they were of course visited by their Irish Friends as well as innumerable strangers. They took much delight in passing jokes on our friend Jones's plumpness, ruddy cheeks and smiling countenance, as little suited to a hermit living in the Vale of Meditation. We all thought there was ample room for retort on his part, so curious was the appearance of these ladies, so elaborately sentimental about themselves and their *Caro Albergo*, as they named it in an inscription on a tree that stood opposite, the endearing epithet being preceded by the word, *Ecco*! calling upon the Saunterer to look about him. So oddly was one of these ladies attired that we took her, at a little distance, for a Roman Catholic Priest, with a crucifix and relics hung at his neck. They were without caps their hair bushy and white as snow which contributed to the mistake." (*FNW*, p. 24; see also p. 124.)

In his letter to Sir GB of September 20, 1824, WW described the visit to Glyn Myvyr, the Vale of Meditation, thus: "We . . . went down the Dee to Llangollen [where we called] upon the celebrated Recluses, who hoped that you and Lady B. had not forgotten them—they certainly had not forgotten you, and they begged us to say that they retained a lively remembrance of you both. We drank tea and passed a couple of hours with them in the evening, having visited the Aqueduct over the Dee and Chirk Castle in the afternoon. Lady E. has not been well and has suffered much in her eyes, but she is surprisingly lively for her years. Miss P. is apparently in unimpaired health. Next day I sent them the following Sonnet from Ruthin—which was conceived—and in great measure composed in their grounds.—

[Here follows the text of the sonnet.]

The allusion to the Vale of Meditation in the above, would recal to the Ladies minds, as it was meant to do, their own good-natured jokes of the preceding evening upon my friend Mr Jones, who is very rubicund in Complexion and weighs about 17 Stone, and would, as they said, make three good hermits for the Vale of which he is Curate" (WL Letters; *LY*, I, 276–277). See also Donald Hayden's account of the tour and the visit to Glyn Myvyr, cited in the note to *Composed among the Ruins of a Castle in North Wales.*

"Lady Eleanor Butler (1745–1829), sister of the Earl of Ormonde, and the Hon. Miss Ponsonby, cousin of the Earl of Bessborough, retired from society in 1779 and for fifty years lived together, as 'sentimental anchorites' in the vale of Llangollen. Their devotion to each other, and their eccentricities of dress and manner, brought them great notoriety, and they were much visited" (*LY*, I, 274n [EdeS]).

Anna Seward published *Lady Eleanor Butler and Miss Ponsonby* in *MP*, July 8, 1796; the headnote to her poem reads: "The Story of these elegant and accomplished Ladies, is well known. It is now *fifteen* Summers since they have withdrawn themselves from the bustle of the Fashionable World, to lead a life of Philosophic repose in a romantic cottage in *Llangollen-Vale*, in Wales. Miss SEWARD, who has been on a visit to the Young Ladies, lately addressed to them the following beautiful Stanzas. Lady E. BUTLER is Sister to Lord MOUNTGARRAT, of the Kingdom of Ireland; and Miss PONSONBY is a near relation of the eminent Family of that name in Ireland." The apparent discrepancy in these accounts of the two women may be explained by their having both Irish and English relations.

1 A Stream] A tributary of the river Dee (also "Deva," l. 12), which rises in Lake Bala and flows through the vale of Llangollen before turning north to Chester and the Irish Sea.

2 Vale of Meditation] *Glyn Myrvr. *1832–, 1838*

To the Torrent at the Devil's Bridge, North Wales.

WW described the torrent at Devil's Bridge, which he visited with Dora W on September 14, 1824, in his letter to Sir GB of September 20, 1824: "I had seen these things long ago, but either my memory or my powers of observation have not done them justice. It rained heavily in the night, and we saw the waterfalls in perfection. While Dora was attempting to make a sketch from the chasm in the rain, I composed by her side the following address to the torrent:

[Here follows the text of the sonnet.]

If the remembrance of 34 years may be trusted, this chasm bears a strong likeness to that of Viamala in the Grisons, thro' which the Rhine has forced its Way" (*LY*, I, 278–279). In his letter to CW on January 4, 1825, he wrote: "Jones met us at Llanroost, and was our companion during 13 days. We parted at the famous Devil's Bridge. If I find I have room I will send you a Sonnet, which I poured out in the chasm there, during a heavy storm, while Dora was at my side endeavouring to sketch the body of the place, leaving, poor Girl! the soul of it to her Father" (*LY*, I, 297). See also Donald Hayden's account of the tour and the visit to Devil's Bridge, cited in the note to *Composed among the Ruins of a Castle in North Wales.*

4–6 Or hath not Pindus . . . Desperate as thine?] Pindus is a mountain range in Northern Greece. The passage refers to the Greek War of Independence then in progress. Byron had died at Missolonghi the previous April.

7 that young Stream] the Rhine.

8 WW described Viamala, near the source of the Rhine, in *DS* (ll. 160–161); he visited the place with Jones in 1790.

To ——— ("O dearer far than light and life are dear")

"Rydal Mount. 1824. To M.W.—Rydal Mount." (*FNW*, p. 9.) WW assigned the same date in MS. 1832/36 and editions from 1836. The poem was probably written during or shortly after WW's and MW's visit, September 20 to mid-October, 1824, to her brother Thomas's farm at Hindwell, where they found TM (MW's cousin) "in a very alarming state of health"; WW considered TM to be, as he told Sir GB in the same letter, one of his "best friends" (*LY*, I, 279). TM died February 26, 1825.

8 "sober certainties"] Milton's *Comus*, l. 263 (EdeS).

The Contrast

"*The Parrot and the Wren.* The Parrot belonged to M[rs]. Luff while living at Fox-Ghyll. The Wren was one that haunted for many years the Summerhouse between the two terraces at Rydal-Mount." (*FNW*, pp. 11–12; see also p. 106.) WW dated the poem 1825 in MS. 1832/36 and editions from 1836. MW in her letter to EQ on September 27, 1824, remarked, "By the bye Wm. has been writing verses on Mrs. Luff's Birds which I dare say Doro will send you should she fall in with Franks" (*MWL*, p. 117). A copy of the poem, apparently in WW's hand and dated June 3, 1826, was listed as item 475 in a Sotheby catalogue for a sale on December 2, 1942. The original has not been found.

Note that the expansion of the title did not occur until the edition of 1832. Revisions to this poem in MS. 1832/36 are in pencil.

5 The colon after "eyes" in editions of 1843, 1846, and 1849 (see the nonverbal variants) appears to be the result of an imperfect plate.

46 Darkling] Child of darkness.

The Infant M—— M——

Mary Monkhouse (December 21, 1821–1900) was the daughter of TM, MW's cousin. "Nov[r]. 12th 1824"—probably the date of initial composition—is entered below the text in DC MS. 131; the Monkhouse MS. copy is dated "Nov[r] 15th 1824"; revised copies were sent by post on December 13, 1824.

About this sonnet and *To Rotha Q———* DW wrote to HCR (December 13, 1824): "they having been composed only for the love of private Friends; and for the sake of expressing his own peculiar feelings with regard to the two Infants, he is particularly desirous that they should not be spread abroad either by copies—or by being read to any persons but such as may have an interest in the parents or Children" (*LY*, I, 294).

Cenotaph

"*Cenotaph on M^{rs}. Fermor* See the Verses on M^{rs}. F." (*FNW*, p. 75; see also pp. 181–182, and *Elegiac Stanzas. 1824*, edited on pp. 47–48.) Above the title in the first copy she sent to Lady B MW has written, "Say, to the left of the Vista, within the thicket, below the Church-yard wall—M.W" (MW to Lady B [A]).

In Swarthmore MS. 3, which appears to be part of a letter, perhaps that to CW, August 11, 1841, WW introduced his transcription of the poem by saying, "I found the following in the chancel of Coleorton Church—I had almost forgotten that I had written it," and added, "You may have seen these Lines when you were at Coleorton but I send them as a Companion to those upon dear Owen" (the *Epitaph in the Chapel-yard of Langdale, Westmoreland*, copied on the verso). WW revisited Coleorton in July 1841 (*LY*, IV, 216–217). Before the end of the year he included *Cenotaph* among poems sent to the printer for publication in early 1842.

JC's note in MS. 1836/45 directed the printer to include *Cenotaph* among the Epitaphs in the edition of 1845.

7 In her letter of February 25, 1825, MW reported to Lady B that "To fit the lines, intended for an Urn, for a Monument W. has altered the closing stanza—which, (tho' [it *del*] they are not what he would have produced had he first cast them with a view to the Church) he hopes you will not disapprove" (autograph letter in Pierpont Morgan Library; see *LY*, I, 323).

13 WW noted of this line in DC MS. 103: "Words inscribed upon her Tomb at her own request." The quotation is from John 14:6.

Elegiac Stanzas. 1824

"*Elegiac Stanzas* On M^{rs}. Fermor. This lady had been a widow long before I knew her. Her husband was of the family of the Lady celebrated in the Rape of the Lock, and was, I believe, a Roman Catholic. The sorrow which his death caused her was fearful in its character as described in this poem, but was subdued in course of time by the strength of her religious faith. I have been for many weeks at a time an inmate with her at Coleorton Hall as were also Mary and my Sister. The truth in the sketch of her character here given was acknowledged with gratitude by her nearest relatives. She was eloquent in conversation, energetic upon public matters, open in respect to these but slow to communicate her personal feelings, upon these she never touched in her intercourse with me, so that I could not regard myself as her confidential friend and was accordingly surprised when I learnt she had left me a Legacy of £100 as a token of her esteem. See, in further illustration, the second stanzas inscribed upon her Cenotaph in Coleorton Church." (*FNW*, pp. 57–58; see also p. 163.) Lady B's sister, Frances Fermor, died in mid-December 1824. WW probably composed the poem between this date and late January 1825; he sent a copy to the Beaumonts in early February (*LY*, I, 323). WW assigned the poem to 1824 in editions from 1836. Pope's *The Rape of the Lock* (1712), mentioned in the IF note, celebrated Arabella Fermor. See *Cenotaph*, p. 47.

Enclosing the poem in her letter to Lady B, February 25, 1825, MW wrote, "We are all much moved by the manner in which dear Miss Wills [Lady B's sister, Miss Anne Willes] has received the verses—particularly W^{m} who feels himself more than rewarded for the *labour*, I cannot call it, of the composition—for the Tribute was poured forth with a deep stream of fervour that was something beyond labour—and it has required very little correction. In one instance a single word in the 'Address to Sir George' is changed, since we sent the copy—viz 'graciously' for 'courteously' as being a word of more dignity. The additional Stanza *last sent* is intended to close the address . . . " (*LY*, I, 323).

In his letter to Lord Monteagle, December 30, 1839, WW thanked Monteagle for his "touching allusion . . . to a passage in the Excursion," which Monteagle had come to know in the company of his late wife, and transcribed for him ll. 49–54 of *Elegiac Stanzas*: ". . . a stanza in one of my minor poems which you may not be acquainted with. As it often recurs to my memory, in the trials to which grief has subjected me, it will be taken by you, (by which I mean understood and felt,) in its true degree and meaning" (*LY*, III, 754–755 and notes).

Why, Minstrel, these untuneful murmurings—

For the date of composition see the editor's headnote. WW may have indicated a tentative position for this sonnet in its class when he had JC list its first line below the text of "Scorn not the Sonnet; Critic, you have frowned" in MS. 1838/40, probably around the time WW was preparing the one-volume edition of 1845. However, in that edition, and after, he introduced it into "Part I" of Miscellaneous Sonnets.

A Morning Exercise

"Rydal Mount, 1825. I could wish the last five stanzas of this to be read with the poem addressed to the Skylark ['Ethereal Minstrel! pilgrim of the sky']." (*FNW*, p. 11.) Earlier, in his letter to BF, October 24, 1828, WW mentioned the conclusion of *A Morning Exercise* and the "second 'Skylark'" as verses in which he "succeeded . . . in my notice of this bird" (*LY*, I, 644). Finally, in 1845, WW transferred the second stanza of *To a Sky-lark* to *A Morning Exercise.* WW assigned the date 1828 below *A Morning Exercise* in MS. 1832/36 and editions from 1836, influenced perhaps by the date of first publication in 1832, rather than in 1827; but WW's obvious debt in *A Morning Exercise* to a work published in 1825 (see the note to ll. 1–18, below), and the close association of the two poems suggest they were both composed in 1825, as the IF note records (see *PW*, II, 489). See also the note to *To a Sky-lark*, below.

1–18 In his note to l. 16 WW refers to Charles Waterton's *Wanderings in South America, the North-West of the United States, and the Antilles, in the Years 1812, 1816, 1820, and 1824* (London, 1825). WW's argument in the first two stanzas that "Fancy . . Can . . . pervert the evidence of joy," may owe something to Waterton's remark that a bird's song will express sympathy to a listener who is disappointed and "pensive," will "take up the tale of sorrow." But, as Charles Norton Coe has noticed, the more pertinent section is Waterton's description of several species of goatsucker, named for their distinctive songs. Here Waterton observes that one "bids you, 'Work-away, work-work-work-away.' . . . And high up in the country, . . . [another] tells you to 'Whip-poor-Will. Whip-whip-whip-poor Will.'" Coe also pointed out that Waterton's next paragraph clarifies WW's reference to "the Spirit of a toil-worn Slave" in ll. 17–18: "You will never persuade the negro to destroy these birds, or get the Indian to let fly his arrow at them. They are birds of omen, and reverential dread. . . . They are the receptacles for departed souls, who come back again to earth . . . to haunt cruel and hard-hearted masters, and retaliate injuries received from them" (Waterton, *op. cit.*, pp. 14, 141–142; see Coe, "A Note on Wordsworth's 'A Morning Exercise,' 1–18," *Modern Language Notes* 64 [1949]: 36–37).

42/43 Stanza transferred here from *To a Sky-lark* in 1845.

54 singing as they shine] from the last stanza of Addison's *Ode* "The spacious firmament on high" (EdeS).

To a Sky-lark

"*To a Skylark.* Rydal Mount—1825. Ethereal Minstrel!" (*FNW*, p. 16.) WW assigned the date 1825 in MS. 1832/36 and editions from 1836. See also the note to *A Morning Exercise,* above. About the first poem to the skylark, also called *To a Sky-lark* (composed in 1802; see *Poems, 1800–1807*, pp. 117–118), WW wrote to BF, October 24, 1828: "After having succeeded [so well *del*] in the second 'Skylark,' and in the conclusion of the poem entitled 'A Morning Exercise,' in my notice of this Bird, I became indifferent to this poem [the first *To a Sky-lark*], which Coleridge used severely to condemn, and to treat contemptuously. I like however the beginning of it so well, that for the sake of that, I tacked to it the respectably-tame conclusion. I have no objection, as you have been pleased with it, to restore the whole piece. Could you improve it a little?" (BL Add MS. 23801; see *LY*, I, 644). STC condemned the earlier poem for its "*disharmony* in style" (*The Collected Works of Samuel Taylor Coleridge, Biographia Literaria*, ed. James Engell and W. Jackson Bate, [2 vols.; Princeton, 1983], II, 123–124). WW placed *To a Sky-lark* first among "Poems of the Fancy" in all editions from 1832.

In *The Winter's Wreath* (1828) "By W. Wordsworth." is printed beneath the title. For *The Winter's Wreath* see note to *Memory*, above.

1–4 BF, in his "Memoirs of the Life and Poetry of William Wordsworth" (BL), compared Abraham Cowley's poem, "Why dost thou heap up wealth, which thou must quit":

The wise example of the heav'nly lark
 Thy fellow-poet, Cowley, mark;
Above the clouds let thy proud music sound,
 Thy humble nest build on the ground. (Chalmers, V, 212)

7–12 Transferred to *A Morning Exercise* in 1845.

While they, her Playmates once, light-hearted tread

"This is taken from the account given by Miss Jewsbury of the pleasure she derived, when long confined to her bed by sickness, from the inanimate object on which this Sonnet turns." (*FNW*, p. 24; see also pp. 124, 210.) MJJ (1800–1833) first visited the Wordsworths at Rydal Mount on May 23, 1825, and joined the family during their month's holiday at Kent's Bank on Morecambe Bay in July and August. The sonnet was probably written around this time. See also the notes to *The Poet and the Caged Turtledove; Gold and Silver Fishes, in a Vase;* and *Liberty. (Sequel to the Above.)*.

To ——— ("Such age how beautiful! O Lady bright")

"Lady [ ] Fitzgerald as described to me by Lady Beaumont." (*FNW*, p. 24.) MW sent the earliest surviving version to Lady B in her letter December 9, 1825, saying, "I am to send you a corrected copy of the sonnet suggested by you" (see *LY*, I, 413–414). The Lady is perhaps Lady Maria Fitzgerald, first wife of Sir Maurice Fitzgerald who represented Kerry in the Irish and imperial parliaments from 1794 to 1831. She died in 1827.

Ere with cold beads of midnight dew

"Rydal Mount 1826. Suggested by the condition of a friend." (*FNW*, p. 8.) WW assigned the same date in MS. 1832/36 and editions from 1836. EdeS suggested that the "friend" was a suitor for Dora W's hand (see *PW*, II, 473, and *LY*, I, 423–424 and note).

Inscription ("The massy Ways, carried across these Heights")

"The walk is what we call *the far-terrace*, beyond the Summer-house at Rydal Mount. The lines were written when we were afraid of being obliged to quit the place to which we were so much attached." (*FNW*, p. 29.) In MS. 106, DW entered the following note between the title and the first line: "Intended to be placed on the door of the further Gravel Terrace if we had quitted Rydal Mount." Dora W entered a similar note, only a few words of which are legible, in the same position in MS. 135; but this note was later erased. In December 1825 WW learned from Lady le Fleming of her wish to end his lease on Rydal Mount so her aunt could use the house, and by April he had purchased "Dora's Field" as a possible building site. Below the poem in MS. 1832/36 and editions from 1836 WW assigned the date 1826. The inscription was probably composed around this time, but before WW wrote the poem entitled *Composed when a probability existed of our being obliged to quit Rydal Mount as a Residence* sometime in late summer and early fall of 1826 (see *Tuft*, pp. 9–10).

6 The shift in font in the word "Poet's" in 1845 (see the nonverbal variants) is probably WW's emphasis.

Strange visitation! at *Jemima's* lip

"This Sonnet, as Poetry, explains itself, yet the scene of the incident having been a wild wood, it may be doubted, as a point of natural history, whether the bird was aware that his attentions were bestowed upon a human, or even a living, creature. But a Redbreast will perch upon the foot of a gardener at work, and alight on the handle of the spade when his hand is half upon it—this I have seen. And under my own roof I have witnessed affecting instances of the creature's friendly visits to the chambers of sick persons, as described in the Author's poems, vol. i., page 252. One of these welcome intruders used frequently to roost upon a nail in the wall, from which a picture had hung, and was ready, as morning came, to pipe his song in the hearing of the Invalid, who had been long confined to her room. These attachments to a particular person, when marked and continued, used to be reckoned ominous; but the superstition is passing away." WW's note, *1838*. In MS. 1838/40 WW altered "the Author's" to "my" and in editions from 1840 revised the phrasing to read "as described in the verses to the Redbreast," followed by the appropriate reference; *The Redbreast. (Suggested in a Westmoreland Cottage.)* is edited on p. 280.

In the IF note WW refers the reader to the note first published in 1838. The poem was composed after early May 1820 but probably around 1826 to early January 1827, certainly by April 1827. See also "When Philoctetes in the Lemnian Isle" and note.

1 Jemima] Jemima Quillinan, EQ's eldest daughter.

When Philoctetes in the Lemnian Isle

As reported by Knight, the title in the Knight MS. "Suggested by the same Incident" refers to "Strange visitation! at *Jemima's* lip" (see the note to that sonnet, above). If there was a date on the manuscript, Knight did not mention it. However, since the Knight MS. must have contained a copy of "Strange visitation!" for the title of the sonnet "suggested by the same incident" to make any sense, a date of composition of both sonnets around the same time seems most likely, though "When Philoctetes" may have been composed later, perhaps just prior to the publication of *PW*, 1827, in March–April 1827.

1–3 In Greek mythology Philoctetes, who inherited Heracles's "fearful bow," was left by the Greeks on the island of Lemnos, during their expedition to Troy, after he was bitten on the foot by a serpent while leading the Greeks to a holy shrine.

Retirement

EdeS has suggested (*PW*, III, 426) that this sonnet was written in response to HCR's joking charge, in a letter of February 18, 1826, that "some future commentator" on WW might suppose him "to have dyed in the year 1814 as far as life consisted in an active sympathy with the temporary welfare of his fellow creatures" (HCR is perhaps the "patriot Friend" in l. 3). WW replied, on April 6, "Your supposed Biography entertained me much. I could give you the other side" (*LY*, I, 440 and note).

14 Cf. Milton's *Comus*, l. 177, "And thank the gods amiss" (EdeS).

Fair Prime of life! were it enough to gild

"Suggested by observation of the way in which a young friend, whom I do not choose to name, misspent his time and misapplied his talents. He took afterwards a better course, and became an useful member of society, respected, I believe, wherever he has been known." (*FNW*, p. 22; see also p. 121.) The position of the poem in MS. 89, though not conclusive, suggests a date of composition around the time *Retirement* was composed, that is, probably after late February 1826, perhaps around April or May.

7 The "ch" of "chaunt" has been deleted and the letter "u" written above the "a"; perhaps WW's intention was to revise the spelling to "chant" but the alteration went awry.

Go back to antique Ages, if thine eyes

For the dating of this poem see the editor's headnote. Notes to the text of 1827 follow:

5 Tower of Babel] Genesis 11:1–9.

11 mighty Hunter] Nimrod (Genesis 10:8–10).

Just vengeance dost thou crave for rights invaded

EdeS has associated this sonnet, along with *Retirement* and "Go back to antique Ages, if thine eyes," with HCR's letter to DW of February 18, 1826, in which he regretted the lack of any recent poems by WW "dedicated to liberty . . . and public virtue." WW entered copies of *Retirement* and "Go back to Antique ages"—both published in 1827—on the same or nearby pages of MS. 89 with "Just vengeance"; the three sonnets share the theme of liberty (see *PW,* III, 426 and 576).

Text of MS. 89 (A)

2–4 WW alludes to the Greek heroes, Harmodius and Aristogiton. Compare the opening lines of his early translation, *From the Greek,* of the Hymn by Callistratus (as recorded by Atheneus): "And I will bear my vengeful blade / With the myrtle's boughs array'd;" see *Early Poems, 1785–1797,* p. 714; cf. especially the wording of the same passage in the the reading text of MS. 89 (C).

12 Pelayo] See "A few bold Patriots, Reliques of the Fight" (*Poems, 1807–1820,* pp. 49–52, and 498).

13 the Swede] Gustavus I (1496–1560); cf. *Prelude,* I, 211–212: " . . . how Gustavus found / Help at his need in Dalecarlia's Mines."

14 In MS. 89 (B) the letters "as" of "was" were accidentally deleted.

Text of MS. 89 (C)

1, 3, 5 The original l. 1 is underscored in the manuscript and the two revisionary lines written above it. The upper one, "Are States . . . ," is entered in the same color ink as the revisions to ll. 3 and 5, which appear to have been made as adjustments to WW's choice of wording for l. 1.

May Odes

"These two Poems [*Ode, Composed on May Morning* and *To May*] originated in these lines 'How delicate &c—' My daughter and I left Rydal Mount upon a tour through our mountains with Mr. and Mrs. Carr in the month of May 1826. [A]nd as we were going up the Vale of Newlands I was struck with the appearance of the little Chapel gleaming thro' the veil of half opened leaves—and the feeling which was then conveyed to my mind was expressed in the Stanza that follows. As in the cases of 'Liberty' and 'Humanity' mentioned before, my first intention was to write only one Poem; but subsequently I broke it into two making additions to each part so as to produce a consistent and appropriate whole." (*FNW,* p. 46; see also pp. 148–149.)

In MS. 137 WW added "Sept. 24, 1834" below the text of *To May,* perhaps marking the date of revision before publication. In editions from 1836 and in *YR,* 1839, he assigned *Ode, Composed on a May Morning* to 1826 and *To May* to 1826–1834, though in MS. 1835/36 the date to the first poem was entered as 1826 and then corrected to 1834, while the second was assigned the inclusive dates 1826–1834. He wrote to WRH on 26 November 1830, probably speaking of one or both of these poems, that "as I passed through the tame and manufacture-disfigured country of Lancashire I was reminded by the faded leaves of Spring, and threw off a few stanzas of an ode to May" (*LY,* II, 353). Exactly when WW toured the "mountains" with Dora W is not easily established. In May 1826 he was preoccupied with the Westmorland election and with planning the new house he proposed to build if forced to leave Rydal Mount, though it is possible that he and Dora W (and Dr. and Mrs. Thomas Carr of Grasmere) took Dora W's pony-chaise to the

Newlands valley west of Derwentwater at that time. A later date for the excursion seems unlikely, for in 1827, 1828 and 1829 WW was travelling elsewhere in May. A mountain tour was proposed in May of 1830, but Dora W became ill and it was canceled.

Text of MS. 107 (B) ("What month can rival thee sweet May?")

title Note the original title "Vernal Stanzas" in MS. 107 (A). In 1827 WW assigned a similar title, *Vernal Ode*, to a poem first published in 1820 as *Ode.—1817* (see *Poems, 1807–1820*, pp. 237–241).

Text of 1835, *To May*

59–60 "Bring the rathe Primrose that forsaken dies," Milton's *Lycidas*, l. 142 (EdeS).

78–80 EdeS cites WW's *Anacreon*, "The white mist curls on Grasmere's stream" (l. 38; *Early Poems, 1785–1797*, p. 366) and *Prelude* I, 591–593, "drinking in / A pure organic pleasure from the lines / Of curling mist."

89 Cf. Keats, *To Autumn* (1820), "Season of mists and mellow fruitfulness."

Once I could hail (howe'er serene the sky)

"'No faculty yet given me to espy the dusky shape' [ll. 3–4]. Afterwards, when I could not avoid seeing it, I wondered at this and the more so because like most children I had been in the habit of watching the moon thro' all her changes and had often continued to gaze at it while at the full till half blinded." (*FNW*, p. 58.) On July 25, 1826, in his letter to JK in which SH copied the poem, WW remarked that part of the "Verses . . . were written this very morning in the delighful wood that borders our garden on the side towards Rydal Water." He added, "You may be inclined to think from these verses that my tone of mind at present is somewhat melancholy—it is not by any means particularly so except from the shade that has been cast over it recently by poor Southey's afflictions.—I laugh full as much as ever, and of course talk more nonsense; for, be assured that after a certain Period of life old sense slips faster away from one than new can be collected to supply the loss. This is true with all men, and especially true when the eyes fail for the purposes of reading and writing as mine have done" (*LY*, I, pp. 474–475). The tone of the poem, and its epigraph, suggest that WW was recalling STC's *Dejection: an Ode*, composed in 1802, to which WW's *Resolution and Independence* and *Ode. Intimations of Immortality from Recollections of Early Childhood* were in part a response. WW assigned "Once I could hail (howe'er serene the sky" to 1826 in editions from 1836.

epigraph Ll. 1–2 of *Ballad of Sir Patrick Spence.*

The Lady whom you here behold

First published by EdeS in *PW*, IV, 380. See the notes to "Prithee gentle Lady list," below.

To ——— ("Happy the feeling from the bosom thrown")

The poem's absence from manuscripts leading to *PW*, 1827, and its insertion in that edition as a "Dedication" of the Miscellaneous Sonnets—most probably to MW—suggest a date just prior to publication. WW was sending printer's copy between January 8 and 29, 1827, and he received his first published copy May 10.

1–2 "'*Something less than joy, but more than dull content.*' Countess of Winchilsea." WW, *1836–*, *1838*. The quoted line is from *The Shepherd and the Calm* (1713), l. 5. Cf. *Gold and Silver Fishes in a Vase*, ll. 7–8.

3–9 With WW's similes of the "bubble blown" and the stone, found and polished, compare his remarks to Alexander Dyce on the sonnet in his letter to Dyce, around April 22, 1833 (*LY*, II, 604–605): "Instead of looking at [the sonnet] . . . as a piece of architecture, making a whole out of three parts, I have been much in the habit of preferring the image of an orbicular body,—a sphere—or a dew-drop."

To S. H.

SH, in her letter to MMH of December 13, 1826, remarked, "William writing a sonnet last night upon my spinning wheel—but I have not yet heard it—if it really is finished to his own satisfaction you shall have it by way of paying the postage of this Letter"; she included a copy of *To S. H.* in the letter (see *SHL*, p. 354 and facing photograph; the editor of *SHL* has misassigned the letter to 1827, but SH's date, "Wednesday, Decr 13th," is correct for 1826 not for 1827).

Prithee gentle Lady list

A note by Herbert Hill (*m.* Bertha Southey, 1839) in the Southey Family Album (Southey Album 2) suggests the poem was probably composed for EMS and Dora W: "The two Poems above ["Prithee gentle Lady list" and "The Lady whom you here behold"] have the interest [interest *rev from* merit] of being playful effusions of M$^{r.}$ Wordsworth's Muse, they were written for two dolls dressed up by Edith Southey and Dora Wordsworth: the Papers remained [in *del*] as they were originally placed in the arms of the Dolls for some 20 years which accounts for their brown, [brown, *rev from* brownness] or yellow tint. A published poem of M$^{r.}$ W^{s} on a Needlecase in the form of a harp belongs to the same date." Above the note Hill has written "Composed by W$^{m.}$ Wordsworth. / Written by E. M. Southey. / A.D. 18[26 *rev to* 27 *then both numerals eras*]" Another copy, substantially the same poem but lacking the first two lines, was written in the Barlow MS. If the version written to honor Dora W and EMS's dolls was the original version, the probable end date for composition is supplied by a note added below the Barlow copy, "*Composed*, and in part transcribed, for Fanny Barlow, by her affectionate Friend / Wm. Wordsworth. / Rydal Mount, / *Shortest Day*, 1826." It is also possible that the version written for Fanny Barlow was later adapted for EMS and Dora W, and at that time paired with "The Lady whom you here behold," in which case Herbert Hill's revised date is probably correct. See also *PW*, IV, 478.

The copy in the Southey Family Album, transcribed in a tiny hand by EMS, is almost wholly without punctuation. The punctuation in *PW*, IV, 379, is editorial and is not reported here. Knight's transcription of the Barlow MS. (the latter is now untraced) is to be found in *PW* Knight 1896, VIII, 295–296; his punctuation may also be editorial. Fanny Barlow and her mother, of Middlethorpe Hall, Yorkshire, often visited Rydal Mount during this period (*LY*, I, 378 and note).

29–31 The triple rhyme is marked by a brace in the right-hand margin of the manuscript.

Conclusion. To ——— ("If these brief Records, by the Muses' art")

The poem's absence from manuscripts leading to *PW*, 1827, suggests a date just prior to publication. See the note to l. 6 of *To* ——— ("Happy the feeling from the bosom thrown"), above, and "In my mind's eye a Temple, like a cloud," below. In editions from 1845 "If these brief Records, by the Muses' art" concluded Part II of Miscellaneous Sonnets.

3 "*This line alludes to Sonnets which will be found in another Class." WW's note in *1836–, 1838*, in which he refers to the class of Sonnets Dedicated to Liberty.

9–11 Cf. Spenser, *The Fairie Queene*, VII, vi, 1, "the ever-whirling wheel of Change" (EdeS).

Scorn not the Sonnet; Critic, you have frowned

"Composed, almost ex tempore, in a short walk on the western side of Rydal Lake." (*FNW*, p. 22.) The poem could have been composed any time after the publication of *Poems*, 1820, but probably dates from early 1827, when copy was being prepared for the edition of *PW* published in April of that year. See the note to *To* ——— ("Happy the feeling from the bosom thrown"), above.

There is a pleasure in poetic pains

The poem's absence from manuscripts leading to *PW*, 1827, suggests a date just prior to publication. See the note to *To* ——— ("Happy the feeling from the bosom thrown"), above.

1–2 The italicized text is quoted from William Cowper, *The Task*, II, 285 (EdeS).

To the Cuckoo

The poem's absence from manuscripts leading to *PW*, 1827, suggests a date just prior to publication. See the note to *To* ——— ("Happy the feeling from the bosom thrown"), above.

In my mind's eye a Temple, like a cloud

The poem's absence from manuscripts leading to *PW*, 1827, suggests a date just prior to publication but probably after *Conclusion. To* ———, which precedes it in *PW*, 1827. See the note to *To* ——— ("Happy the feeling from the bosom thrown"), above.

On Seeing a Needlecase in the Form of a Harp, the Work of E. M. S.

"*Needle-Case.* 1827." (*FNW*, p. 11.) WW assigned the same date in MS. 1832/36 and editions from 1836. EMS, daughter of RS, was born in 1804; she married Rev. J. J. Warter in 1834. Dora W sent the poem, with the needlecase, as a gift to Mrs. Anne Elliot on April 6, 1827: "My Father's verses addressed to Miss Southey, who for six weeks was a cheering sunshine to my room will make my little Harp better worth your acceptance" (Cornell MS. 4). Mrs. Elliot took over the tenancy of Ivy Cottage in Rydal when EQ left it after his wife's death in 1822.

Her only Pilot the soft breeze the Boat

The copy in MS. 89 was partially cut away and is thus lacking the last few words of every line but l. 2.

The appearance of this fair copy by SH, revised by WW, at the back of MS. 89, along with several sonnets composed in 1821–1822, might suggest an earlier date. But all these sonnets are transcribed on small sheets that were pasted on leaf (219^r), which itself was originally bound in the album, then removed, and recently reattached by means of a sewn-in flap. The pasted sheets were attached after the poems had been copied on them but before being partly cut away; however, the timing of any of this activity, except for the modern restoration, is problematic. On the verso of the bound-in sheet (219^v) WW entered pencil and ink notes on arranging his miscellaneous sonnets into categories that he never actually adopted ("Personal and moral / Personal sonnets / Local"). He rearranged the Miscellaneous Sonnets to some degree at each republication; he made many such changes in the volume of sonnets he published in 1838.

In the absence of other manuscript evidence to confirm an earlier date, it seems probable that this sonnet, in which WW reflects on his having "crowded this small Bark" with "Fancy and the Muse," was a late addition to *PW*, 1827, composed and forwarded to the printer after the main body of the text had been sent. See the note to *To* ——— ("Happy the feeling from the bosom thrown"), above.

Farewell Lines

"These lines were designed as a farewell to Charles Lamb and his Sister who had retired from the throngs of London to comparative solitude in the village of Enfield Hert^{ds}." (*FNW*, p. 66). Notes to the reading text of 1842 follow:

1 "High bliss . . . state"] James Thomson, *To the Rev. Patrick Murdoch*, l. 10 (Knight).

22–28 The text and revisions in MS. 151.1 were entered by MW except for "Their union brought" above l. 25 and l. 28 of the expanded ll. 25–28. In MS. 151.2 the base text is also MW's; the revisions are WW's except for the version of l. 24 in IF's hand at the foot.

Extract from the Strangers book / Station Winandermere / On seeing the above

The same "extract" is given in copy B of the Monkhouse Album.

First published in 1889 (*PW* Knight 1889, X, 373n). Edward Dowden inferred from WW's "wish" to hear the "boatmen of Killarney" that the lines were written before WW's tour of Ireland in September and October of 1829, when he visited Killarney (*Poetical Works of William Wordsworth,* ed. Edward Dowden [7 vols.; London, 1892], V, 202). Lord Darlington is William Harry Vane, first Duke of Cleveland in the second creation and third Earl of Darlington (1766–1842), who married Elizabeth Russell in July 1813. Vane succeeded to the peerage as Earl of Darlington in 1792; he was created Marquis of Cleveland on September 17, 1827, and first Duke of Cleveland on January 15, 1833. The poem was probably composed, then, sometime between mid-September 1827 and September 1829. Of the other members of Lord Darlington's party, Captain Stamp seems to have visited Rydal Mount (with "Five Naval Officers on the Terrace at once") in 1831 (Rydal Mount Visitors Book, WL).

WW described the same site in verse in *Lines left upon a Seat in a Yew-tree,* recalling it before it became a popular viewpoint for tourists; it lies on the hill above the Ferry, opposite Bowness (see WW's *Guide Through the District of the Lakes, Prose,* II, 157, 263, 428–429, and *LB, 1797–1800,* pp. 47–50). The "Strangers Book" itself has not been located.

Four fiery steeds impatient of the rein

"Suggested on the road between Preston and Lancaster where it first gives a view of the Lake Country, and composed on the same day, on the roof of the coach." (*FNW,* p. 23.) WW's visit to Brinsop Court in December 1827, and his return journey at the end of January 1828, are thought to be associated with this sonnet and two others, *St. Catherine of Ledbury* and "Wait, prithee, wait." WW intended the poem for *The Keepsake* (1829), edited by FMR, but it did not appear there and he later withdrew it (*LY,* II, 14 and note; see the note to *St. Catherine of Ledbury,* below).

Roman Antiquities Discovered, At Bishopstone, Herefordshire

WW probably conceived and perhaps composed this sonnet while on a visit to Brinsop Court, Herefordshire, from December 11, 1827, to around January 24, 1828. He probably included it among the sonnets sent to FMR for publication in *The Keepsake* (1829), but it did not appear there (see the note to *St. Catherine of Ledbury*).

St. Catherine of Ledbury

"Written on a journey from Brinsop Court Herefordshire." (*FNW,* p. 23.) The sonnet was composed between December 11, 1827, when WW left Birmingham for Brinsop Court, the home of MW's brother TH, and January 25, 1828, when he had arrived at Liverpool on his way from Brinsop Court to Rydal Mount (*LY,* I, 561, 575). The earliest version, in MS. 89, is presented in transcription and photograph (pp. 664–665).

This sonnet and three others, "Four fiery steeds impatient of the rein," *Roman Antiquities Discovered, At Bishopstone, Herefordshire,* and *To* ——— ("'Wait, prithee, wait!' this answer Lesbie threw"), were intended for *The Keepsake,* but were rejected by the compiler, FMR; WW withdrew them and did not contribute to *The Keepsake* again (WW to FMR, January 27, 1829; *LY,* II, 14). WW wrote to CW, Jr., that "The word Anchoress is no doubt a coinage—tho' I rather think not originally of mine—Anchoritess, the proper term, is unmanageable in that Place, and neither Hermitess nor Votaress, both allowable words, exactly suit my purpose. If you cannot stomach Anchoress take the latter" (October 23, 1835; *LY,* III, 107).

To ——— ("'Wait, prithee, wait!' this answer Lesbia threw")

"The fate of this poor dove, as described, was told to me at Brinsop Court, by the Young Lady to whom I have given the name of Lesbia." (*FNW,* p. 24.)

As a young man WW had composed an imitation of Catullus' *Carmina* V, *Lesbia,* probably in 1787, perhaps during his first months at Cambridge, and later turned it over to STC, who published it in *MP* for April 11, 1798 (see *Early Poems, 1785–1797,* pp. 375–377).

For the date of composition see the editor's headnote.

Filial Piety

"Filial Piety This was also communicated to me by a coachman in the same way. In the course [*corr in error to* courses] of my many coach rambles and journeys which, during the daytime always, and often in the night, were taken on the outside of the coach, I had good and frequent opportunities of learning the character of this class of men. One remark I made that is worth recording, that whenever I had occasion especially to notice their well-ordered, respectful and kind behaviour to women, of whatever age, I found them, I may say almost always, to be married men." (*FNW,* p. 25.)

In MS. 89 this sonnet shares with *A Tradition of Darley Dale, Derbyshire* the canceled title "Stagecoach Inspirations by an Outside Passenger"; the facing leaf is torn out but may have contained other such "inspirations." The poem was composed during WW's visit to Brinsop Court, December 13, 1827, to January 9, 1828 (*LY,* I, 561–570); the earliest copy is dated at Brinsop Court, January 1828. The sonnet was first published as *The Peat Stack* in *The Casket* in December 1828. "Thomas Scarisbrick was killed by a flash of lightning whilst building a turf-stack in 1779. His son James Scarisbrick, who was then thirty years old, completed the stack, and ever after during his life reverently kept it in repair as a memorial to his father. James died in 1824, consequently for forty-five years he had tended this rude monument, and to further perpetuate the remembrance of it he left to his grandchildren sets of goblets and decanters, on each of which are incised his own and his wife's monogram and a representation of the turf-stack between two trees . . . . [The farm was located] about a mile north of Ormskirk, and abutted to the Preston highway . . . . The turf-stack stood between two large sycamore trees . . . . [It] was pulled down and its turf used for field drainage on the farm within six years after the death of James Scarisbrick in 1824" (James Bromley, "The Story of a Sonnet," *The Atheneum,* May 17, 1890, p. 641).

A Grave-stone upon the Floor in the Cloisters of Worcester Cathedral

"*Miserrimus.* Many conjectures have been formed as to the person who lies under this Stone. Nothing appears to be known for a certainty. ? —The Revd M^r^. Morris, a Non-Conformist, a sufferer for conscience-sake; a worthy man, who having been deprived of his benefice after the accession of William 3^d^. lived to an old age in extreme destitution, on the alms of charitable Jacobites.—" (*FNW,* p. 24). EQ penciled parentheses around "?—The Revd . . . Jacobites.—" and added opposite, "See Hist of Monuments from which Mr Q. has an extract—" (the book has not been identified). Thomas Morris (1660–1748) is the probable author of the inscription.

WW's sonnet was first published with four other poems—*The Country Girl* (*i.e., The Gleaner*), *The Triad, The Wishing-gate,* and *A Tradition of Darley Dale, Derbyshire*—in *The Keepsake* in December 1828. The date of composition assigned to the poem in Cornell MS. 5—January 1828—seems accurate. WW and MW were staying with the Beaumonts at Coleorton in Leicestershire in November 1827, and around December 10 they traveled to Brinsop Court in Herefordshire, where Dora W and her friend EMS were spending the winter. Their route took them via Birmingham and Worcester, where WW must have visited the Cathedral. They left Brinsop Court on January 9, 1828, returning to Rydal Mount by way of Chester and Liverpool (*LY,* I, 552, 560, 561, 569–570, 575). By this time WW had already sent a copy of the sonnet to Rydal Mount, for SH wrote to EQ on January 27 that "Mr W. has written a Sonnet (*Occasion*) upon seeing a Tombstone in Worcester Cathedral without any inscription except the word *Miserrimus*—and one upon the same arrived here today from the Bp of Chester written by a Gent to whom Mr W. had mentioned the inscription at Chester—They both have the same view of the subject and both are very good" (*SHL*, pp. 358–359). Besides meeting the Bishop of Chester on his way to Liverpool, around January 23, WW "accidently met with" his "old Friend Archdeacon Wrangham at Chester" (*LY*, I, 575–576). It seems likely that Francis Wrangham is the "Gent" who turned his hand to a sonnet on the same subject.

The Wishing-gate

"Rydal Mount 1828. See also 'Wishing-Gate Destroyed.'" (*FNW*, p. 16; see also p. 115.) WW assigned the same date in MS. 1832/36 and editions from 1836. In his letter to MW and Dora W of early March 1828, WW mentions several poems, recently composed, which he might offer for publication in *The Keepsake* for 1829, including *The Wishing-gate* in "82 lines" and the "same stanza as Ruth" (*LY*, I, 590). Published in *The Keepsake* with four other poems (see the note to *A Grave-stone upon the Floor in the Cloisters of Worcester Cathedral*, above). The earliest extant version (Victoria MS. 1) is in thirteen stanzas, or 78 lines.

In MS. 1832/36 MW entered a note to the printer, "after, and *next* to the Mad [Mother]"—the original title of "Her eyes are wild, her head is bare"—which followed *The Triad* in 1832; "Her eyes are wild" was moved in 1836 from Imagination to Affections and *The Wishing-gate* took its place after *The Triad.* In the edition of 1845 *The Wishing-gate Destroyed* and *The Wishing-gate* were made to look alike, with indented third and sixth lines in each stanza. The gate, located between White Moss Common and Town End on the old carriage road between Rydal and Grasmere, was also known to the Wordsworths as "Sara's gate" (Dorothy Wordsworth, *The Grasmere Journals*, ed. Pamela Woof [Oxford, 1991], p. 133; October 31, 1802; see Grevel Lindop, *A Literary Guide to the Lake District* [London, 1993], p. 76).

A Tradition of Darley Dale, Derbyshire

"This pleasing tradition was told me by the coachman at whose side I sate while he drove down the dale, he pointing to the trees on the hill as he related the story." (*FNW*, p. 25; see also p. 126.) The date of composition was probably close to early March 1828, when WW had sent off the poem with four others to FMR to be printed in *The Keepsake* (see *LY*, I, 590; see the note to *A Grave-stone upon the Floor in the Cloisters of Worcester Cathedral*, above). MW's copy in EMS's album is dated 1828 at Brinsop Court. WW and MW joined Dora W (and her friend, EMS) at Brinsop Court from early December 1827 to January 24, 1828, MW and Dora W staying on until mid-March 1828(*LY*, I, 544, 554, 581); WW's coach journey from Rydal to Coleorton, where he met MW before continuing to Brinsop Court, is the likely occasion of his hearing the story. In his letter to DW of November 8, 1830, WW described a more recent journey, this one on horseback, through Darley Dale: "A mile below [Darley churchyard], upon an eminence to the right I recognized the two Trees that gave occasion to my Sonnet on the parting of the two Brothers—I could not hear of any such tradition from the people whom I questioned, but a little Boy told me that the trees, two sycamores, were called Wm Shore's trees from the name of the man who had planted them above 200 years ago; and that a woman had been buried near them" (*LY*, II, 340).

The unremitting voice of nightly streams

For the dating of this poem see the editor's headnote.

8 Against WW's indications to the contrary in the surviving manuscript copies, all printed forms of this line are flush with the left margin.

The Gleaner. (Suggested by a Picture.)

"This Poem was first printed in the Annual called the 'Keepsake'—the Painter's name I am not sure of, but I think it was Holmes." (*FNW*, p. 44.) James Holmes (1777–1860) was a painter and water colourist of genre, portraits, and miniatures. Some of his genre pictures were engraved for publications, such as *The Amulet, The Literary Souvenir,* and *The Keepsake.* His untitled painting of a country girl holding a sheaf of corn was engraved by Charles Heath (1785–1848) for *The Keepsake* (1829) and appeared opposite WW's poem. WW wrote to MW and Dora W in early March 1828, "I have written one little piece, 34 lines, on the Picture of a beautiful Peasant Girl bearing a Sheaf of Corn. The Person I had in my mind lives near the Blue Bell, Tillington—a sweet Creature, we saw her when going to Hereford" (*LY,* I, 590). In MS. 1832/36 and editions from 1836 WW dated the poem 1828.

"The Country Girl," the title of the poem in *The Keepsake,* appears in what is probably FMR's hand at the top of the page in the copy WW sent to him (Huntington MS. 1). Below it, and obviously entered first, is WW's note, "Title to be supplied by Mr. Reynolds." In the letter cited above, WW mentioned *The Gleaner, The Wishing-gate,* and *The Triad* as poems he was sending FMR to "fulfill [his] engagement"). Besides these three poems, *A Grave-stone upon the Floor in the Cloisters of Worcester Cathedral* and *A Tradition of Darley Dale, Derbyshire* also appeared there.

The Triad

"*Rydal Mount. 1828.* The girls Edith May Southey, my daughter Dora and Sara Coleridge." (*FNW,* p. 16, see also p. 115.) WW assigned the same date in editions from 1836. The poem was probably composed early in 1828, certainly by early March, when WW sent revisions of an early version (which does not survive) to MW and Dora W (*LY,* I, 590–591). WW wrote to BF, December 20, 1828, "I am truly glad you liked the Triad—I think [?a] great part of it is as elegant and spirited as any thing I have written—but I was afraid to trust my judgement as the aery Figures are all sketched from living originals that are Dear to me" (Houghton MS., bMS Eng 327 [18]; *LY,* I, 695). And in a letter to George Huntley Gordon of December 15, 1828, WW reacted in surprise to a query about his title: "How strange that any one should be puzzled with the name, Triad, *after* reading the Poem. I have turned to D[r] Johnson, and there find, *'Triad, three united;'* and not one word more, as nothing more was needed. I should have been rather mortified, if *you* had not liked this Piece, as I think it contains some of the happiest verses I ever wrote. It had been promised several years to two of the Party—before a fancy fit for the performance struck me—it was then thrown off rapidly—and afterwards revised with care" (*LY,* I, 689).

In DC MS. 89 (94[r]), alongside lines for *On Power of Sound* and "The unremitting voice of nightly streams," WW has entered a passage which may be rejected lines for *The Triad*:

Advance [*rev from* ?As] like that harmonious Sisterhood
Or in fix'd prayers, mid this grove, unite
Like those three Angel Visitants that stood,
Furling their wings before their patriarch-host,
In beauty not unwilling to be lost
For sweet recovery, in each other's sight.

(See the editor's headnote to "The unremitting voice of nightly streams," p. 101.)

In the Keswick MS., WW's explanatory headnote was added in the margin. In the same manuscript a further note justifying changes WW had made in *The Triad* was squeezed into the available space below the end of *The Wishing-gate* and then deleted. The last part was rendered illegible; the part that can be read is as follows (cut away letters are supplied in brackets): "The line 'shooting star' [l. 90, *apparatus criticus*] &c was changed as anticipating 'Swift as a Thracian'—and the change has introduced a trail of characters.—'All things intermingle &c' [ll. 136–137, *apparatus criticus*] was altered both for brevi[ty] and to substitute something thought better— 'The Vision of the Wes[t'] [l. 176] was infinite trouble but it is now to our mind and I hope to yours. My sister muse has had more to do with this Poem than I am willing to let out upon paper— [here follow eight lines, about 60 words, of heavily deleted and illegible prose] Take care of this copy and destroy the *others.*" As the manuscript is among RS's papers, it is presumed to have been addressed and sent to him by the Wordsworths. RS—two of whose poems also appear in *The Keepsake* for 1829—must then have sent the manuscript on to the editor of *The Keepsake*, FMR, whose printer made an annotation on one of its pages. The text of the Keswick MS. for *The Triad* resembles most closely the text found in *The Keepsake.* It is not known precisely what part was played by DW ("my sister muse") in the composition of the poem.

In MS. 1832/36 WW added a note to the printer: "This Poem does not come in here, / Keep back the leaf." On the next page, presumably sent later, MW added "*To follow the Haunted tree* / The former Part of the following is in the Printers hands)."

36–79 "Lucida" is EMS.

40 the hermit's long-forsaken cell] Perhaps a reference to St. Herbert's Island, Derwentwater, near the Southeys' home (JOH).

89–170 "The youngest" is Dora W.

116 FLOWER OF THE WINDS] the anemone.

129–134 According to Sara Coleridge the passage is an allusion to Dora's supposed likeness in contour of face to the "great Memnon head in the British Museum, with its overflowing lips and width of mouth, which seems to be typical of the ocean" (*SCML*, II, 410).

171–208 The "eldest born" is Sara Coleridge, STC's daughter, who many years later wrote to the Rev. Henry Moore on August 4, 1847, that *The Triad* "contains a poetical glorification of Edith Southey (now W[arter]) of Dora, and myself. There is *truth* in the sketch of Dora, poetic truth, though such as none but a poet-father would have seen"; she wrote to HR on May 19, 1851, that the poem "is, to my mind, *artificial* and *unreal.* There is no truth in it as a whole, although bits of truth, glazed and magnified, are embodied in it . . . . The poem always strikes me as a mongrel—an amphibious thing, neither portrait nor ideal, but an ambiguous cross between the two" (*SCML*, II, 126, 410).

177 anxious hope] Explained by Sara Coleridge's daughter Edith (the editor of *SCML*) as an allusion to her mother's anticipated marriage to her cousin Henry Nelson Coleridge (*SCML*, I, 37).

180–183 Explained by Edith Coleridge as an allusion to her mother's classical attainments—at age twenty she published her translation from Latin of a work by Martin Dobrizhoffer on the people of Paraguay, where he had been a missionary (*SCML*, I, 35–36).

On the Power of Sound

"*On the power of sound.* Rydal Mount. 1828. I have often regretted that my tour in Ireland, chiefly performed in the short days of October in a carriage and four, (I was with M[r]. Marshall) supplied my memory with so few images that were new, and with so little motive to write. The lines however in this poem, 'Thou too be heard, lone eagle!' &c. [ll. 199–202] were suggested near the Giants' Causeway, or rather at the promontory of Fairhead where a pair of eagles wheeled above our heads and darted off as if to hide themselves in a blaze of sky made by the setting sun." (*FNW* p. 17; see also p. 116.) WW assigned the poem to 1828 in editions from 1836. In his letter to George Huntly Gordon of December 15, 1828 (see note *The Triad*, above), WW said of *On the Power of Sound*, "During the last week I wrote some stanzas on the Power of Sound which ought to find a place in my larger work—if aught should ever come of that" (*LY*, I, 689). He must be speaking here of the earliest complete version of the poem, that found in MS. 131, begun perhaps as early as March and concluded in the second week of December 1828. In his remark about the poem's finding "a place in [his] larger work" he compares *On the Power of Sound* to "any detached Poem that [he] is now writing" that he does not consider his "own." Though there are very few published poems that WW did not find a "place" for in his "larger work" (the body of his poetry organized into classes), he seems to mean that *Sound* belongs among those written in a "higher strain" (*Paulo majora canamus*, the original epigraph to *Ode: Intimations of Immortality* and provisionally so employed in early manuscripts of *Sound*). His placement of the poem at the close of Imagination in editions from 1836 bears out this ranking, as he himself pointed out in a letter to Alexander Dyce (December 23, 1837; *LY*, III, 502; see also *Poems, 1800–1807*, pp. 270–271).

Text of 1835

fly-title and title WW dropped the separate title page, or fly-title, in 1836, resolving the anomaly of the variant titles in 1835, "Stanzas on the Power of Sound" on the fly-title and "On the Power of Sound" above the first stanza. Oddly, an early form of the title "The Power of Sound" is preserved in the 1835 printing in the running heads (but not retained in this edition). The running heads were dropped in 1836.

WW's note to printer in MS. 137 (A): "The volume to end with this Poem" (thus revising its position, in the manuscript and this proof stage, where it stood after *Lines Suggested by a Portrait from the Pencil of F. Stone* and before *The Somnambulist*).

14 Knight compares Thomas Gray, *Elegy Written in a Country Church Yard*, ll. 39–40: "Where thro' the long-drawn isle and fretted vault / The pealing anthem swells the note of praise."

50 In some copies of *Yarrow Revisited*, 1835, the semicolon after "mirth" looks like a colon, apparently a result of defective type.

76 Lydian airs] Milton, *L'Allegro*, l. 136 (EdeS). Of this line WW wrote to CW (September 26, 1835): "Tell [JW_3] . . . I have altered the passages which he found obscure; all but the last, in *the power of Sound*. 'Even She'—that is obscure solely on account of the omission of a note of Interrogation immediately preceding the words, 'Even She', viz. the Power of sound, or, in this place, of harmony" (*LY*, III, 96).

93 uplifted arm of Suicide] Cf. WW's early depiction of "Suicide": "Dire was the prospect [ ] of lifted arms," *Suicide and Despair*, in *Early Poems, 1785–1797*, p. 537.

134–136 EdeS compares *A Midsummer-Night's Dream*, II.i.150–151: "And heard a mermaid, on a dolphin's back, / Uttering such dulcet and harmonious breath."

150–151 Knight compares Thomas Gray, *The Progress of Poesy*, l. 34, "To brisk notes in cadence beating."

158 knell;] The use of a comma in the manuscripts clearly indicates that the final couplet in the stanza was meant as the last in the series of fabled sounds described in ll. 156–160. WW replaced the period after "knell"—the reading from 1835 through the various stereotype editions of 1836—with a semicolon in 1845, thus confirming the rhetorical link with what follows.

177–180 Pythagoras and his followers (the "Sages") proposed a numerical basis for reality (the "one pervading Spirit . . . that mystery old"); see WW's "Argument" to the poem. See Brennan O'Donnell, *The Passion of Meter, A Study of Wordsworth's Metrical Art* (Kent, Ohio, and London, 1995), for a discussion of WW's use in this poem of "Pythagorean theory" and "imaginations consonant with such a theory" (pp. 238–243).

181–192 Cf. the transcription of *The Triad* from MS. 108 on pp. 680–683.

199–202 See the IF note, above.

204–205 Deep to Deep . . . calls] Psalms 42:7 (EdeS).

217–218 These lines echo ll. 157–158 of *Ode: Intimations of Immortality*:

Our noisy years seem moments in the being
Of the eternal Silence.

EdeS and Helen Darbishire (*PW*, II, 526–527, 532–534) note the similarity of both passages to lines in *Address to Silence* (published over the initials "W. C." in the *Weekly Entertainer*, March 6, 1797).

The Egyptian Maid; or, The Romance of the Water Lily

"*The Egyptian Maid.* In addition to the short notice prefixed to this poem it may be worth while here to say that it rose out of a few words casually used in conversation by my nephew Henry Hutchinson. He was describing with great spirit the appearance and movement of a vessel which he seemed to admire more than any other he had ever seen, and said her name was the Water-Lily. This plant has been my delight from my boyhood, as I have seen it floating on the Lake; and that conversation put me upon constructing and composing the poem. Had I not heard those words it would never have been written. The form of the stanza is new, and is nothing but a repetition of the first five lines as they were thrown off, and is perhaps not well suited to narrative, and certainly would not have been trusted to had I thought at the beginning that the poem would have gone to such a length." (*FNW*, p. 30.) WW assigned the poem to 1830 in editions from 1836 and in *YR*, 1839. However, the poem was probably composed between November 18 and 25, 1828; WW told George Huntly Gordon on the latter date that he had "just concluded a kind of romance"; in a letter written the same day or shortly after MW told EQ that it was written "within the last 8 days" and WW added that "it rose out of my mind like an exhalation" (*LY*, I, 663, 665, 667). On December 19, 1828, WW remarked to FMR, "I am rather rich, having produced 730 verses during the last month—after a long fallow—In the list are two stories—and three incidents" (*LY*, I, 692). One of the "stories" must be *The Egyptian Maid; or, The Romance of the Water Lily*, reported in WW's letter to HCR on November 28 as "360 verses" thrown off "at a heat" (*LY*, I, 675). The other is probably *The Somnambulist* (162 ll.). The "incidents," which must have been composed between November 29 and December 19, 1828, are *A Jewish Family. (In a small valley opposite St. Goar, upon the Rhine.)* (48 ll.), *The Poet and the Caged Turtledove* (24 ll.; see below, pp. 442, 443), and *Incident at Bruges* (40 ll.). Approximately 100 lines of WW's "730" remain unaccounted for, but perhaps WW included the 96 lines of the early form of *On the Power of Sound* in the total.

The source that WW mentions in the headnote to the poem is *The History of the Renowned Prince Arthur, King of Great Britain; with his Life and Death, and All his Glorious Battles. Likewise, the Noble Acts and Heroic Deeds of his Valiant Knights of the Round Table* (2 vols.; London: printed for Walker and Edwards; J. Richardson [*et al*], 1816).

Comparison of variants suggests that the copy of *The Egyptian Maid* in MS. 134 derives from the copy in MS. 106; in MS. 137 the corrected proofs of this poem contain only ll. 31–386.

Text of 1835

11 In MS 1835B the capital "A" of "As" was not altered when "Became" was added. WW entered numbers 1 through 12 (with some omissions) in the margins of MS. 107 (A), perhaps to indicate the order of revisions.

47–48 EdeS has pointed out (*PW*, III, 502) that this passage was drawn from a description of a storm by Sir Thomas Herbert in *Description of the Persian Monarchy* (1634; p. 7), a book WW owned.

94 Lady of the Lake] Dora W supplied a mocking note in her copy in DC MS. 109: "not Rydal Lake."

247–252 Three notes in MS. 109 direct the copyist to "ask Dora"—presumably for the latest version of this much revised stanza.

258 cloud emerging,] Confusion over the correction of this line in MS. 137 led to the printer producing two states of this page. WW's intentions were established with respect to l. 258 in the second state (1835_2), but commas at the ends of ll. 261 and 263 fell out when the printer loosened the forme to alter l. 258. In the reading text we follow the second state of 1835 only in l. 258.

265 At this point in MS. 109, after the third "ask Dora" note, the two following stanzas are renumbered from "1" and subsequent stanzas follow suit, with several revisions of these numbers to accommodate insertions, deletions, and rearrangement of stanzas. It may have been WW's intention to split the poem into two parts, though this would have broken the narrative in an awkward place and the two parts would have been markedly uneven in length. A more likely explanation is that the contents and order of the remaining portion of the poem were still unsettled when Dora W left off at l. 264. When the

copying recommenced stanza numbers were omitted, and when revision began—it seems to have occurred almost simultaneously with the copying—the numbers (starting with 1) were probably added to keep track of the changes.

270/271 In MS. 109 there is a foreshortened version of the "trial" (see the *apparatus*) in which only Gawaine, Launcelot, and "Gallehad" stepped forward to touch the Egyptian Maid. This version appears to have been only briefly considered, however, for the two summary stanzas were struck out and Dora W proceeded with a fuller version that introduced additional "suitors" (ll. 271–300), and the stanzas were renumbered to reflect the new order. A second expansion followed, elaborating Sir Gawaine's vision and past glories (ll. 301–318), and requiring a further renumbering of stanzas to the end of the poem.

316 the PERILOUS SEAT] Sir Galahad's display of inherent strength against a powerful spell matches the Egyptian Maid's passive endurance of Merlin's necromancy. In the 1816 edition of Malory (see p. 441, above) that WW cites in his headnote, the scene in which the seat is created is in vol. I, p. 86 (Caxton's bk. III, chap. 4), and the key episode of Sir Galahad and the "seige perilous" occurs in vol. II, pp. 208–213 (bk. XIII, chap. 2–4).

355–386 As suggested by the variant in MS. 109 for l. 354, there were at one time seven stanzas of the Angels' Chorus: in fact, the first version in MS. 109 is in six stanzas (see the alternate text, based on MS. 109_1, which appears below the 1835 text, and the changes as reported in the *apparatus criticus*). After some revision of this version in pencil by WW, Dora W entered a new version of stanzas 1–5 on the first page of the manuscript (MS. 109_2) and added numbers to the stanzas that include the last two stanzas of the first version, still undeleted; at this point l. 354 was revised to "these seven verses." WW then revised this seven-stanza Chorus and subsequently Dora W recopied a revised third and fifth stanzas and added a new fourth on a slip (MS. 109_4) that she pasted over the intermediate version (MS. 109_2), renumbering the stanzas to a total of eight. L. 354 was then further revised to accommodate the change (see the *apparatus criticus*). A draft of ll. 367–370 (MS. 109_3) was entered in the margin and then deleted when the paste-over was inserted.

Text of MS. 109, Chorus only

3 To God] The erased words "Who hopes" must have been entered and erased before the whole of line 3 was entered; in any case "Who hopes proclaims defiance" does not quite make sense. For this reason the revised reading is adopted in the reading text.

A Jewish Family. (In a small valley opposite St. Goar, upon the Rhine.)

"Coleridge and my daughter and I, in 1828, passed a fortnight upon the banks of the Rhine, principally under the hospitable roof of M^r^. Aders at Gotesburg, but two days of the time were spent at S^t^. Goa or in rambles among the neighbouring vallies. It was at St. Goa that I saw the Jewish family here described. Though exceedingly poor, and in rags, they were not less beautiful than I have endeavoured to make them appear. We had taken a little dinner with us in a basket, and invited them to partake of it, which the mother refused to do, both for herself and her children, saying it was with them a fast day; adding, diffidently, that whether such observances were right or wrong, she felt it her duty to keep them strictly. The Jews, who are numerous in this part of the Rhine, greatly surpass the German peasantry in the beauty of their features, and in the intelligence of their countenance. But the lower classes of the German peasantry have, here at least, the air of people grievously opprest. Nursing mothers, at the age of seven or eight and twenty, often look haggard and far more decayed and withered than women of Cumberland and Westmoreland twice their age. This comes from being underfed, and overworked in their vineyards in a hot and glaring sun." (*FNW*, p. 17; see also pp. 115–116.) WW assigned the poem to 1828 in MS. 1835/36 and editions from 1836.

DW added a note to her transcription for Lady B of *A Jewish Family* and the only other poem composed during this tour, *Incident at Brugès*: "The two following poems are taken from two incidents recorded in Dora's journal of her Tour with her Father and S. T. Coleridge. As I well recollect, she has related the Incidents very pleasingly, and I hope you will agree with me in thinking that the Poet has made good use of them" (Morgan MS. 2).

The date of composition of *A Jewish Family* is fixed by WW's remark to FMR in a letter of December 19, 1828 (see the note to *The Egyptian Maid; or, The Romance of the Water Lily*, end of the first paragraph). *A Jewish Family* may be the poem WW referred to in his letter to George Huntly Gordon on December 15, 1828: "The remainder of this Page shall receive a few stanzas to which you must be indulgent as they were *strictly* extempore—and no older than yesterday evening" (*LY*, I, 689 and note). If the "few stanzas" were included, they are no longer with the letter.

The tour took place between July 22 and August 6. EQ added a pencil note to the IF note: "the three went from my house in Bryanstone Street London"; the trip was suddenly agreed upon in London between STC and WW in June 1828, the first lengthy reunion between them since the rupture of their friendship in 1810 (*LY*, I, 614–615). Dora's journal of the tour gives a detailed account (WL, DC MS. 110) and is generously quoted in Donald E. Hayden, *Wordsworth's Travels in Europe II*, University of Tulsa Monograph Series, no. 23 (Tulsa, Okla., 1988), pp. 22–48. Of the encounter with the family of the poem she wrote, "When Mr. Coleridge told this Rachel how much he admired her Child—'Yes, said she, she is beautiful,' (adding with a sigh) 'but see these rags and misery'—pointing to its frock which was made up of a thousand patches" (*op. cit.*, p. 37). St. Goar is between seventeen and eighteen miles downstream from Bingen, which was the southernmost point of their tour (roughly sixty miles upstream from Bad Godesburg).

The Poet and the Caged Turtledove

"Rydal Mount, 1830. This Dove was one of a pair that had been given to my daughter by our excellent friend Miss Jewsbury, who went to India with her husband, M^r^. Fletcher, where she died of cholera. The Dove survived its mate many years, and was killed to our great sorrow by a neighbour's cat that got in at the window and dragged it partly out of the cage. These verses were composed ex tempore, to the letter, in the Terrace Summer House before spoken of. It was the habit of the bird to begin cooing and murmuring whenever it heard me making my verses." (*FNW*, p. 12; see also p. 107.) MJJ (1800–1833), was a poet and a friend of the Wordsworths, especially Dora W; she dedicated her *Phantasmagoria, or Sketches of Life and Literature* (London, 1825) to WW ('O long unrecked, and unseen/Hast thou my spirit's father been'). She died in India a year after her marriage to Rev. W. K. Fletcher, a chaplain in the East India Company. See the notes to "While they, her Playmates once, light-hearted tread," *Gold and Silver Fishes, in a Vase;* and *Liberty*.

WW assigned the date 1830 below the poem in MS. 1835/36 and editions from 1836 and affirmed this date in his IF note, but evidence for the date of composition is provided by his letter to FMR of December 19, 1828 (see the note to *The Egyptian Maid; or, The Romance of the Water Lily*, toward the end of the first paragraph). On June 16, 1829, WW sent the poem with others to George Huntly Gordon to be submitted to FMR for the 1830 issue of *The Keepsake* (*LY*, II, 86; *Letters of Dora Wordsworth*, ed. Howard P. Vincent [Chicago, 1944], p. 57), but FMR did not include it, and, after many requests by WW and his friends, the manuscripts were eventually returned to him in late October 1829 (*LY*, II, 165). Interestingly, WRH corrected the date below the poem to 1829 in the copy of *Poems*, 1845 now in WL (MS. 1845W), and added a note in which he states that "This poem . . . was repeated by W Wordsworth to me at the Observatory, Dublin, in 1829." WW stayed with the Hamiltons during the first few days of September of that year before setting off with the Marshalls on a tour of southern Ireland (*LY*, II, 117). However, the title in one of the manuscripts dates the poem "at the beginning of December," confirming the evidence in WW's letter to FMR for a December 1828 date. Several later fair copies were made, one dated 1829 and another "21st Jan^ry^ 1832"; the poem was published in 1835.

Written in Mrs. Field's Album

The album belonging to Mrs. Field has not been located. BF asked WW to write in Mrs. Field's album in his letter of December 24, 1828; two months later he wrote: "Mrs. Field thanks you for writing in her Album, and my Brother is very proud of your praise" (WL Letters).

EdeS reported that underneath WW's lines in the Album BF wrote:

> Words inky! They're worth more than that,
> I can't let that go forth;
> The line that would detract from words
> Itself shews a Word's-worth." (*PW*, IV, 479)

Presumably on the occasion of returning the album, WW wrote to BF ("an unknown correspondent" in *LY*, II, 6) on January 19, 1829, "I was much pleased with a little drawing by Mr Edmund Field—exceedingly so, and I wrote opposite it two stanzas which I hope he and Mrs Field will pardon, as I have taken a liberty with his name. The drawing is admirably done, and of just such a scene as I delight in, and my favourite rivers, the Duddon, Lowther, Derwent, etc. abound in . . . " (the fragment breaks off).

The Russian Fugitive

"*The Russian Fugitive* Early in life this story had interested me and I often thought it would make a pleasing subject for an opera or Musical drama." (*FNW*, p. 51.) In his letter to George Huntly Gordon of November 25, 1828, WW mentioned having composed a "kind of romance"—that is, *The Egyptian Maid*—but said nothing of *The Russian Fugitive* (*LY*, I, 663); two months later, on January 29, 1829, WW wrote again to Gordon, remarking that he "lately wrote a Tale (350) verses the Scene of which is laid in Russia, though it is not even tinged with Russian imagery" (*LY*, II, 26). In MS. 1835/36, collected editions from 1836 and in *YR*, 1839, WW assigned the poem to 1830.

WW's main source, mentioned in his note, was *Memoirs of Peter Henry Bruce, Esq., a Military Officer, In the Services of Prussia, Russia and Great Britain. Containing An Account of his Travels in Germany, Russia, Tartary, Turkey, the West Indies, &c. As Also Several very interesting private Anecdotes of the Czar, Peter I. of Russia.* (London, 1782). The anecdote, which WW presumably read "early in life" though probably referred to it again at the time of composition, is from Book III (pp. 91–94) and reads as follows:

"The czar was some time after smitten with the charms of another beautiful young lady, the daughter of a foreign merchant in this city: he first saw her in her father's house, where he dined one day; he was so much taken with her appearance, that he offered her any terms she pleased, if she would live with him; which this virtuous young woman modestly refused, but dreading the effects of his authority, she put on a resolution, and left Moscow in the night, without communicating her design even to her parents. Having provided a little money for her support, she travelled on foot several miles into the country, till she arrived at a small village where her nurse lived with her husband and their daughter, the young lady's foster-sister, to whom she discovered her intention of concealing herself in the wood near that village: and to prevent any discovery, she set out the same night, accompanied by the husband and daughter. The husband, being a timberman by trade, and well acquainted with the wood, conducted her to a little dry spot in the middle of a morass, and there he built a hut for habitation. She had deposited her money with her nurse to procure little necessaries for her support, which were faithfully conveyed to her at night by the nurse or her daughter, by one of whom she was constantly attended in the nighttime.

"The next day after her flight, the czar called at her father's to see her, and finding the parents in anxious concern for their daughter, and himself disappointed, fancied it a plan of their own concerting. He became angry; and began to threaten them with the effects of his displeasure, if she was not produced: nothing was left to the parents but the most solemn protestations with tears of real sorrow running down their cheeks, to convince him of their innocence and ignorance what was become of her, assuring him of their fears that some fatal disaster must have befallen her, as nothing belonging to her was missing, except what she had on at the time. The czar, satisfied of their sincerity, ordered great search to be made for her, with the offer of a considerable reward to the person who should discover what was become of her, but to no purpose: the parents and relations, apprehending she was no more, went into mourning for her.

"Above a year after this she was discovered by an accident. A colonel who had come from the army to see his friends, going a hunting into that wood, and following his game through the morass, he came to the hut, and looking into it saw a pretty young woman in a mean dress. After enquiring of her who she was, and how she came to live in so solitary a place, he found out at last that she was the lady whose disappearance had made so great a noise: in the utmost confusion, and with the most fervent intreaties, she prayed him on her knees that he would not betray her; to which he replied, that he thought her danger was now past, as the czar was then otherways engaged, and that she might with safety discover herself, at least to her parents, with whom he would consult how matters should be managed. The lady agreed to his proposal, and he sat [*sic*] out immediately and overjoyed her parents with the happy discovery: the issue of their deliberations was to consult Madam Catherine (as she was then called) in what manner the affair should be opened to the czar. The colonel went also upon this business, and was advised by madam to come next morning, and she would introduce him to his majesty, when he might make the discovery and claim the promised reward. He went according to appointment, and being introduced, told the accident by which he had discovered the lady, and represented the miserable situation in which he found her, and what she must have suffered by being so long shut up in such a dismal place, from the delicacy of her sex. The czar shewed a great deal of concern that he should have been the cause of all her sufferings, declaring, that he would endeavour to make her amends. Here Madam Catherine suggested, that she thought the best amends his majesty could make was to give her a handsome fortune and the colonel for a husband, who had the best right, having caught her in pursuit of his game. The czar, agreeing perfectly with Madam Catherine's sentiments, ordered one of his favourites to go with the colonel, and bring the young lady home; where she arrived, to the inexpressible joy of her family and relations, who had all been in mourning for her. The marriage was under the direction, and at the expence of the czar, who himself gave the bride to the bridegroom; saying, that he presented him with one of the most virtuous of women; and accompanied his declaration with very valuable presents, besides settling on her and her heirs, three thousand rubles a year. This lady lived highly esteemed by the czar, and every one who knew her. Besides the concurring reports of other people, I had this her story from her own mouth." For comparisons of this source with the poem see Charles Norton Coe, "Wordsworth's 'The Russian Fugitive,'" *Modern Language Notes* 64 (1949): 31–36, and Patrick Waddington, *From The Russian Fugitive to The Ballad of Bulgare* (Oxford, and Providence, R.I., 1997), pp. 32–59. Waddington also suggests other possible sources.

A leaf, probably bearing the separate internal title page, or fly-title, and the headnote on its verso, is missing from the first corrected proofs (MS. 137).

fly-title and parts The fly-title, appeared only in *Yarrow Revisited* (1835, 1836, and 1839). In the printer's copy (MS. 135) MW added "The Russian Fugitive" as a running head to each page of the text; instead, in the published version, the title was repeated at the beginning of each part, a format that may have been suggested by MW's insertion of the running head at mid-page at the beginning of the fourth part. In subsequent editions the title was not repeated above each part.

180 The footnote is lacking in all manuscripts except MS. 135, deleted in MS. 1835/36, and omitted from *1836–*, *1839*; in MS. 135 the variants are: From . . . work.] From Golding . . . [the *del*] Ovids Metamorphosis See . . . dedicatory . . . work

EdeS points out (*PW,* IV, 441) that WW refers to *Metamorphoses,* I:

There was not any wheare
As yet a Bay; by meanes whereof was Phebus faine to weare
The leaves of every pleasant tree about his goolden heare;

and Golding's *Epistle to the Earle of Leycester.*

As for example, in the tale of Daphnee turned to Bay
A myrror of virginitee appeare unto us may,
Which yielding neither unto feare, nor force, nor flatterye,
Doth purchace everlasting fame and immortalitye.

206–216 This passage on icons was added in pencil to the underlying version in MS. 107.

211–212 "Not a Russian house, Bruce tells us, was at this time without a picture of the Virgin." WW's note in MS. 116. Waddington (*op. cit.,* p. 56) has pointed out that Bruce describes (correctly) the use as icons in Russian houses only images of saints, not images of the Virgin Mary, and he suggests that WW may here be following Guy Miege's *A Relation of the Embassies from his Sacred Majestic Charles II to the Great Duke of Muscovie . . . in the Years 1663 and 1664* (London, 1669), which does mention the icon of the Virgin Mary over the city gates of Moscow. WW may simply have chosen the more familiar figure.

249 belovèd] In the margin beside the correction from "beloved" in MS. 1835/36 WW has added "here vital"; that is, the meter requires the extra syllable.

364–376 A leaf is missing from MS. 107 (B).

The Primrose of the Rock

"*The Primrose of the Rock.* Rydal Mount, 1831. It stands on the right hand a little way leading up the vale from Grasmere to Rydal. We have been in the habit of calling it the glow-worm rock from the number of glow-worms we have often seen hanging on it as described. The tuft of primrose has, I fear, been washed away by heavy rains." (*FNW,* pp. 16–17.) The rock is actually on the left (north) side of the the old carriage road to Rydal, about 100 yards before it rejoins the main road (Grevel Lindop, *A Literary Guide to the Lake District* [London, 1993], p. 75), as the IF note says, "a little way leading up the vale." In WW's note "Grasmere" and "Rydal" seem to be reversed.

Text of 1835

MW added a note above the poem in MS. 137 (proof pages): "In *short* pieces the Printer is requested not to insert numbers" (for stanzas).

25/26 MW's note in MS. 137 corrects the setting of part two as a separate poem: "The following piece not being a separate Poem, but a *continuation* of the foregoing—let the asterisks and another stanz[a] be printed upon this page—"

The Armenian Lady's Love

"Rydal Mount, 1830" (*FNW,* p. 10). WW assigned the date 1830 (revised from 1829) in MS. 1835/36 and in editions from 1836.

In his headnote to the poem WW acknowledged his debt to *Orlandus,* by his "friend, Kenelm Henry Digby" (1800–1880). *Orlandus* is the fourth book of Digby's study of medieval chivalry, *The Broad Stone of Honour: The True Sense and Practice of Chivalry* (4 vols.; London, 1826 and 1828–1829). This work was Digby's revision, carried out after his conversion to Catholicism, of his earlier book *The Broad Stone of Honour: Or, Rules for the Gentlemen of England,* which had been published anonymously in 1822. In March 1829 WW received a gift of *Orlandus* through a mutual friend, the Reverend William Whewell. In his letter to Whewell WW praised Digby's writing and found in it "as much truth as there can be in Pictures where only one side is looked at" (*LY,* II, 47). It seems likely the poem was composed shortly after March 13, 1829, but perhaps as late as 1830, the date when WW assigned to it both in the IF note and in editions from 1836. WW and Digby met at Cambridge in November 1830, evidently at Digby's request (*LY*, II, 354; *Letters of Dora Wordsworth*, ed. Howard P. Vincent [Chicago, 1944], p. 78). WW moved the location of the knight's castle from Erfurt to Stolberg and changed the Egyptian lady for an Armenian one, adding her open declaration of love for the knight, but in the main features of his story he followed Digby's account closely (quoted from *Orlandus* [London, 1829; vol. 4 of the edition cited above, pp. 385–386]):

> In an ancient church at Erfurt, I saw the tomb of a knight, in the attitude of a crusader, placed between the figures of his two wives: that on his right bearing the coronet of a German countess; that on his left the insignia of a princess of Egypt. . . . In the wars with the Saracens he had been taken prisoner, and was conducted to Egypt. Here, after a long time, his skill in gardening obtained for him the charge of superintending the gardens of the Sultan, whose daughter determined secretly to enable him to escape, though she was aware that he had a wife in Germany, to whom he had vowed a constant fidelity. The plan succeeded, and the knight and the princess escaped and sailed for Venice. Upon landing on the pier, the knight instantly recognized an old servant, who came up and embraced him with transports of joy: he had been sent to Venice by the countess in search of news respecting her husband. The knight immediately dispatched him to his castle, to acquaint his wife with the circumstances of his escape, and to assure her, that while he owed his freedom to the princess of Egypt, his affection for his faithful wife was the same as ever. This good lady overjoyed at his return, hastened to assure him that the woman who had saved her lord should ever be dear to her as a sister, and the worthy knight is said to have returned to his castle in company with the fair Egyptian. I do not know how the truth may be, but there they are all three represented on his tomb.

WW had earlier considered an "India Piece": in a letter of December 19, 1828, BF had written to WW, "By the bye, all your travellers 'step westward'. You have no oriental poem. I wish you would write me one, as unlike 'Lalla Rookh' as possible" (*Lalla Rookh*, a series of oriental tales in verse by Thomas Moore, published in 1817); in reply, on December 20, WW wrote "I should like to write a *short* India Piece, if you would furnish me with a story—Southey mentioned one to me in Forbes's travels in India. . . . He has it not—it is of a Hindoo Girl—who applied to a Bramin to recover a faithless Lover, an Englishman.—The Bramin furnished her with an Unguent with which she was to anoint his Chest while sleeping—and the Deserter would be won back." He asked BF to consult a copy of the book and let him know "whether . . . any thing can be made of it" (*LY*, I, 695–696, and note). WW turned to the story from Digby instead.

In the versions in DC MSS. 107 (A and B), 106, and 134 the last two lines of each stanza are divided into four lines, in each pair a pentameter line followed by a dimeter, with appropriate initial capitals; for example, the end of the first stanza in these manuscripts is arranged thus:

How she loved a Christian Slave,
    And told her pain
By word, look, deed, with hope that he
    Might love again.

The same is true of MS. 135, the printer's copy, but MW appended a note to the printer pointing out the "mistake," arising apparently from the copyist's having to accommodate the narrow page, and altered the final lines of each stanza to reflect the six-line structure. In the *apparatus* (see pp. 173ff.) each pentameter and dimeter pair of lines in MSS. 107, 106, and 134 has been treated as one line in order to maintain correspondence with reading-text lines and to avoid unduly complicating the record of variants. The dimeter line always begins with a capital letter in these manuscripts, and this detail must be assumed by the reader, for it is not reported in the nonverbal list. MW's alterations in MS.

135 that convert four lines to two are omitted from the *apparatus*, except where a variant occurs between the original wording and the revision.

Rural Illusions

"Rydal Mount 1832. Observed a hundred times in the grounds at Rydal Mount." (*FNW*, p. 12; see also p. 107.) WW assigned the same date in MS. 1835/36 and editions from 1836, but on August 5, 1829, he sent a copy of the poem to DW, who was lying ill at the home of WW's son John in Whitwick: "I send you three little copies of verses, which may perhaps amuse you at a distance; if read at home with your heart so full as it will be then I hope of pleasant things, they would scarcely have told" (*LY*, II, 104).

The two versions of the poem in MS. 107 (for MS. 107 [A] see photographs and transcription, pp. 718–719), both predating all the others, contain lines which eventually found their place in two other poems composed around the same time in a similar metrical form, *The Primrose of the Rock* and "This Lawn, a carpet all alive." The A version in MS. 101A is divided into four six-line stanzas; a fifth stanza, copied on the verso of the next leaf, has been marked for insertion between stanzas 3 and 4. The B version in the same manuscript includes the new stanza, in its place, but lacks the fifth stanza, probably because the leaf on which it was copied was removed for use elsewhere. Both versions, including all but a few pencil revisions by WW, are in DW's hand. A fragmentary copy, also in DW's hand, is on the pasted-down side of a bifolium added to the printer's copy (MS. 135) to supply a text of "This Lawn, a carpet all alive." This copy is also in six-line stanzas and the fair-copy portion comes to five stanzas. The six lines beginning "Not such the World's illusive shows" were entered in pencil by WW, who then numbered the stanzas to indicate three twelve-line stanzas. A version in MS. 106 has the three "double stanzas" of twelve lines each, the form in which the poem was finally published.

This Lawn, &c.

"This lawn is the sloping one approaching the kitchen garden and was made out of it. Hundreds of times have I here watched the dancing of shadows amid a press of sunshine; and other beautiful appearances of light and shade, flowers and shrubs. What a contrast between this and the Cabbages and Onions and Carrots that used to grow there on a piece of ugly shaped unsightly ground! No reflexion however either upon Cabbages or Onions—the latter we know were worshipped by the Egyptians and he must have a poor eye for beauty who has not observed how much of it there is in the form and colour which cabbages and plants of that genus exhibit through the various stages of their growth and decay. A richer display of colour in vegetable nature can scarcely be conceived than Coleridge my Sister and I saw in a bed of Potatoe plants in blossom near a hut upon the moor between Inversneyd and Loch Katrine. These blossoms were of such extraordinary beauty and richness that no one could have passed them without notice: but the sense must be cultivated through the mind before we can perceive these inexhaustible treasures of Nature for such they truly are without the least necessary reference to the utility of her productions, or even to the laws whereupon, as we learn by research, they are dependent. Some are of opinion that the habit of analysing decomposing, and anatomizing is inevitably unfavorable to the perception of beauty. People are led into this mistake by overlooking the fact that such processes being to a certain extent within the reach of a limited intellect we are apt to ascribe to them that insensibility of which they are in truth the effect and not the cause. Admiration and love, to which all knowledge truly vital must tend, are felt by men of real genius in proportion as their discoveries in Natural Philosophy are enlarged; and the beauty in form of a plant or an animal is not made less but more apparent as a whole by more accurate insight into its constituent properties and powers—A Savant who is not also a Poet in soul and a religionist in heart is a feeble and unhappy Creature." (*FNW*, pp. 44–45; see also pp. 147–148.) For the date of composition see the editor's headnote.

Text of MS. 107 (A)

11 The word "knights" was inadvertently omitted in the original line.

Text of 1835

6 strenuous idleness] Cf. *Prelude,* IV, 378 (*14-Bk Prelude,* p. 89 and note).

Presentiments

"Rydal Mount, 1830." (*FNW,* p. 17.) WW assigned the same date in editions from 1836. For the date of composition see the editor's headnote.

Gold and Silver Fishes, in a Vase

"*Gold and Silver Fishes.* They were a present from Miss Jewsbury of whom mention is made in the note at the end of the next Poem. The fish were healthy to all appearance in their confinement for a long time but at last, for some cause we could not make out, they languished and one of them being all but dead they were taken to the pool under the old Pollard Oak—the apparently dying one lay on its side unable to move. I used to watch it and about the tenth day it began to right itself, and in a few days more was able to swim about with its companions—for many months they continued to prosper in their new place of abode—but one night by an unusually great flood they were swept out of the pool and perished to our great regret." (*FNW,* p. 44.) In MS. 1835/36 and editions from 1836 the poem is dated 1829. The copy in MS. 113 is inscribed "W[m] Wordsworth / Rydal Mount / Nov[b] 1829" (DW apparently prepared it to be sent to WW, Jr., at Bremen) and on WW's behalf Dora W sent ll. 17–23 (omitting l. 24) to MJJ in November or December 1829, as "a third stanza to his Poem." According to notes left by John A. Finch, Dora W made another copy, dated December 1829, to send to WW, Jr. The fish were a gift to Dora W from MJJ.

In her letter to EQ, December 19, 1829, Dora W wrote, "I am sorry to say Father has not yet heard from Longman—Aunt and I are exceedingly anxious something were done towards forwarding the printing of these small Poems, for till they are out of the way we feel convinced, his great work will never be touched[;] every day he finds something to alter or new stanzas to add—or a fresh sonnet—or a fresh Poem growing out of one just finished—which he always promises shall be the last—Two or three stanzas are added to the Ode on Sound—'After thoughts' to the Rock and Primrose Poem and so on—I send quite a new Poem which I hope will please you as much as it pleases the Poet's Ladies" (WL Letters): then follows *Gold and Silver Fishes, in a Vase.*

1–2 Lark . . . at Heaven's gate] From the song in *Cymbeline,* II, iii, 19 (EdeS).

7–8 something "more than dull content / Though haply less than joy"] Adapted from the Countess of Winchelsea; see WW's note to *To* ——— ("Happy the feeling from the bosom thrown"), above.

To a Friend

For the date of composition, see the headnote.

40/41 In MS. 106 a solid line across the page divides the first verse paragraph from the second and MW's note in similar ink reads, "From this pass to, 'While here I sit'" (*i.e.,* l. 103, "While, musing, here I sit," where there is a similar note).

41–62 In MS. 114 MW took over as copyist from Dora W, who resumed her transcription at l. 63.

41 In MS. 135 (A_1) two thumbnail-sized fragments of a paste-over covering ll. 41–43 show, surprisingly, that ll. 189–191 were entered here. The paste-over was removed, mostly, and ll. 41–43 were deleted.

103 MW's solid line marks off the preceding section and her note reads, "The above from 'Field for thee' does not belong to this Poem" (*i.e.,* from l. 41 through l. 102). See the IF notes to *Liberty* and *Humanity,* below.

Liberty. (Sequel to the Above.)

"*Liberty Sequel to the above* The connection of this with the preceding Poem is sufficiently obvious." (*FNW*, p. 44; see also p. 147.) WW assigned the poem to 1829 in MS. 1835/36 and editions from 1836. See the note to *To a Friend*, above. WW explained his division of *To a Friend* in the IF note to *Humanity. (Written in the Year 1829.)* given below. See also the editor's headnote and notes to *To a Friend* and *Liberty. (Sequel to the Above.)*.

2 Anna] Maria Jane (Jewsbury) Fletcher.

8 living Well] From Spenser, *Fairie Queene*, I, ii, 43 (EdeS).

60–66 These lines refer to *The Squire's Tale*, ll. 610–620 (EdeS).

91–110 See WW's early translations and adaptations of Horace's verse, *Septimi, Gades* and *Bandusian Ode* (*Early Poems, 1785–1797*, pp. 760–769, and *Evening Walk*, ed. James Averill [Ithaca, 1984], pp. 202–203). See also *Musings at Aquapendente*, ll. 255–262.

111–119 EdeS compares Abraham Cowley's *The Complaint*, ll. 1–7:

In a deep vision's intellectual scene,
Beneath a bower for sorrow made,
Th'uncomfortable shade
Of the black yew's unlucky green,
Mixt with the mourning willow's careful grey,
Where reverend Cham cuts out his famous way,
The melancholy Cowley lay. (Chalmers, V, 96)

Humanity. (Written in the Year 1829.)

"*Humanity* These Verses and the preceding ones entitled 'Liberty' were composed as one piece which M[rs]. W.— complained of as unwieldly and ill proportioned; and accordingly it was divided into two on her judicious recommendation." (*FNW*, p. 45; see also p. 148.) WW omitted the subtitle and added the date 1829 below the poem in MS. 1835/36 and editions from 1836. See also the editor's headnote and notes to *To a Friend* and *Liberty*, above.

33 In his note to this line WW refers to Kenelm Henry Digby (see note to *The Armenian Lady's Love*). In editions from 1836 the note was moved to the end of the volume and in the editions of 1845 and 1850 altered to read "I am indebted . . . ."

70–95 Around May 1833, WW wrote to Mary Ann Rawson to turn down her request for his contribution to a volume of anti-slavery writings (*The Bow and the Cloud*, 1834): "Your Letter which I lose no time in replying to, has placed me under some embarrassment, as I happen to possess some Mss verses of my own upon the subject to which you solicit my attention. But I frankly own to you, that neither with respect to this subject, nor to the kindred one, the slavery of the children in the Factories, which is adverted to in the same Poem, am I prepared to add to the excitement already existing in the public mind upon these, and so many other points of legislation and government. Poetry, if good for anything, must appeal forcibly to the Imagination and the feelings; but what at this period we want above every thing, is patient examination and sober judgement. It can scarcely be necessary to add that my mind revolts as strongly as anyone's can, from the law that permits one human being to sell another. It is in principle monstrous, but it is not the worst thing in human nature. Let precipitate advocates for its destruction bear this in mind. But I will not enter farther into the question than to say, that here are three parties—the Slave—the Slave owner, and the imperial Parliament, or rather the people of the British Islands, acting through that organ. Surely the course at present pursued is hasty, intemperate, and likely to lead to gross injustice. Who in fact are most to blame? the people—who, by their legislature, have sanctioned not to say encouraged, slavery. But now we are turning round at once upon the planters, and heaping upon them indignation without measure, as if we wished that the Slaves should believe that their Masters alone were culpable—and they alone fit objects of complaint and resentment" (see *LY*, II, 614–615 and notes).

78–95 Cf. *Excursion,* VIII and IX, 113–128 (EdeS).

79 Stone-walls a Prisoner make] Lovelace, *To Althea from Prison,* l. 25 (EdeS).

84 "Slaves cannot breathe in England"] From Cowper, *The Task,* II, 40 (EdeS).

90–91 Idol, falsely called "the Wealth of Nations"] A reference to Adam Smith's *Inquiry into the Nature and Causes of the Wealth of Nations* (1776). Cf. *Prelude,* XIII, 77–78.

Why art thou silent! Is thy love a plant

"In the month of January, [ ], when Dora and I were walking from Town End Grasmere across the vale, snow being on the ground, she espied in the thick though leafless hedge, a bird's nest half filled with snow. Out of this comfortless appearance arose this Sonnet, which was in fact written without the least reference to any individual object, but merely to prove to myself that I could, if I thought fit, write in a strain that poets have been fond of. On the 14th. of Feb[y]. in the same year, my daughter, in a sportive mood, sent it as a Valentine under a fictitious name to her Cousin C.W.—" (*FNW,* pp. 25–26.) For the date of composition see the editor's headnote.

Inscription Intended for a Stone in the Grounds of Rydal Mount

For IF note and the date of composition see the editor's headnote.

WW's transcription for Mr. and Mrs. William Bennett of the *Inscription Intended for a Stone in the Grounds of Rydal Mount,* dated at Rydal Mount, November 12, 1846, is without significant variants; the original manuscript is untraced. Mr. Bennett left an account of his conversations with the poet during his visits to Rydal Mount in September and November 1846 (see *LY,* IV, 822n).

Elegiac Musings in the Grounds of Coleorton Hall, the Seat of the Late Sir George Beaumont, Bart.

"*Elegaic Musings* These verses were in fact composed on horseback during a storm whilst I was on my way from Coleorton to Cambridge—they were alluded to elsewhere—." (*FNW,* p. 58.) In the IF note "elsewhere" refers to the note to the sonnet "Chatsworth! thy stately mansion, and the pride" (see below). DQ added to the entry in the IF note for this poem: "(My Father was on my poney w[h]. he rode all the way from Rydal to Cambridge that I might have the comfort and pleasure of a horse at Cambridge—the storm of wind and rain on this day was so violent that the coach in which my Mother and I travelled the same road was all but blown over and had the coachman drawn up as he attempted to do at one of his halting places we must have been upset. My Father and his poney were several times entirely blown out of the road. D.Q.)." WW assigned the poem to November 1830 in MS. 1835/36 and editions from 1836.

MW wrote to Lady B on December 21, 1830, that "Mr W. sends a revised copy of the verses, with which it gave him pleasure to find Sir Geo. and you had been pleased. Dora and myself were very much affected when he poured them out to us on his arrival—we were affected by the verses for their own sake, thinking them characteristic of our lamented friend—and not a little from the consideration of their having been composed thro' such a storm—on a day when our great comfort for his sake had been 'that the weather was so bad no one could think of venturing out on horseback'. We are all apprehensive that the composition will be found too long for an inscription—but do not see how it could be shortened. I do not like to mention the subject to Mr W. at present—but I should rather wish him to recast something shorter, than attempt to reduce the verses which, as they stand, appear to me to be so happy" (*LY,* II, 357). In some of its readings the abbreviated version of the poem in DW's Commonplace Book (DC MS. 120) seems contemporary with the earliest version found in Lilly MS. 2, but in others it is later—how much later is impossible to tell. Given its title—not "Supposed to be written in the grounds of Coleorton" but "For a Monument to be placed in the grounds"—DW's version may represent an effort to compress the poem to make it more suitable for being inscribed. It was, however, not inscribed.

"N.B. These verses were repeated to the Archbishop of Canterbury by their Author on the memorable evening of the [first] of March 1831—and a few minutes after he and his Family had learned the Heads of the Bill [for reform in parliament *inserted*] brought into the House by Lord John Russel[l]. 'Let us turn,' said the Archbishop in his mild manner [']from this unhappy subject to something that will soothe us,' and accordingly at his request, this Tribute to the memory of his departed Friend, which he had heard before, was again recited" (DW's note in MS. 107 beneath the last line of the poem). WW dined with Archbishop Howley in London on the first of March (the date left blank by DW). The first reading of the Reform Bill in the House of Commons took place that evening (see *LY*, II, 370n, 379n).

epigraph Beneath her copy of the poem in her Commonplace Book DW added a note that echoes the epigraph of the other versions and supplies additional details: "Sir G. B ordered that no Inscription but the common one of Name, age, time of decease &c—should be placed over his tomb; but desired that the following words might be inscribed on his coffin

'Enter not into judgment with thy Servant, O Lord!'" (DC MS. 120).

See *Epitaph* ("By a blest Husband guided, Mary came," edited on p. 223) for speculation that draft lines leading to ll. 13–18 of that poem may have originated as an addition to *Elegiac Musings in the Grounds of Coleorton Hall, the Seat of the Late Sir George Beaumont, Bart.*

15 WW added "Qy" in the margin opposite the alternate reading "fine" in Lilly MS. 2.

40–41 From Edward Fairfax's translation from Tasso, *Godfrey of Bullogne* (1600), II, xviii, "The Rose within herself her sweetness closed" (EdeS).

Chatsworth! thy stately mansion, and the pride

"Rose early—rode down the valley, with Haddon Hall in view, and at the point where Wey and Derwent unite, turned up towards Chatsworth—rode a mile, and leaving my Pony to bait, walked up the valley and through Chatsworth Park to the House—[a house *del*] splendid and large but growing larger every year. The trees in this valley are still in many places clothed with rich variegated foliage—and so I found many all the way almost to Derby.—My feelings at Chatsworth, as contrasted with those which had moved me in the higher part of the Peak Country will be best given in the following, for which as [warm *del*] fresh from the brain, make such allowance as you can—" (WW to DW, November 8, 1830; WL Letters and *LY*, II, 339–340).

"Chatsworth. I have reason to remember the day that gave rise to this Sonnet, the 6th. of Novbr. 1830. Having undertaken, a great feat for me, to ride my daughter's pony from Westmoreland to Cambridge, that she might have the use of it—while on a visit to her Uncle at Trinity Lodge, on my way from Bakewell to Matlock I turned aside to Chatsworth, and had scarcely gratified my curiosity by the sight of that celebrated place before there came on a severe storm of wind and rain, which continued till I reached Derby, both man and pony in a pitiable plight. For myself I went to bed at noonday. In the course of that journey I had to encounter a storm worse if possible in which the pony could (or would) only make his way slant-wise. I mention this merely to add that, notwithstanding this battering, I composed, on pony-back, the lines to the memory of Sir George Beaumont, suggested during my recent visit to Coleorton." (*FNW*, p. 25.) For *Elegiac Musings in the Grounds of Coleorton Hall, the Seat of the Late Sir George Beaumont, Bart.*, see p. 218. Having spent the night in Manchester, WW continued his journey through Derbyshire, spent the night in Bakewell on November 5, 1830, visited Chatsworth on the sixth, and reached Coleorton the following day.

WW entered drafts of this sonnet on a sheet in MS. 107 that was first used for *Elegiac*

Musings in the Grounds of Coleorton Hall, the Seat of the Late Sir George Beaumont, Bart. and later for *This Lawn, &c*

To B. R. Haydon, Esq. on seeing his Picture of Napoleon Buonaparte on the Island of St. Helena

"This Sonnet, though said to be written on seeing the portrait of Napoleon was in fact composed some time after, extempore, in the wood at Rydal Mount.—" (*FNW*, pp. 26.) Composed around June 11, 1831 (*LY*, II, 396). WW saw the painting two months earlier while visiting the painter's studio in London (April 12, 1831). WW's IF note is followed by a heavily deleted and only partially legible paragraph in ink: "(I omit [?mention of another] recollection that I have of the [*eight or ten illegible words*] M[r]. Haydon's [?execution in] the picture." EQ then inserted his own pencil note referring to the thought expressed in the sonnet: "but it was said in prose in Haydon's studio for I was present—relate the facts and why it was versified—." (*FNW*, p. 127; EQ had hoped to write WW's "memoirs" but the task was assigned to CW, Jr., instead.)

WW sent another copy of the sonnet to WRH and his sister Eliza Hamilton in a letter dated June 13, 1831, but the original letter is untraced (see *LY*, II, 398–400; an illustrated 1983 sale catalogue gives reduced detail of the leaf bearing DW's copy of the sonnet, at the beginning of DW's portion of the letter; it begins "Sonnet / To R. B Haydon Esq[r]" but the copy is otherwise illegible).

In a loose folio notebook containing "Sonnets addressed to and one Written by B. R Haydon — From 1817 to 1841 — Twenty Four Years — copies for Fun — 1844," BRH has copied, on 6[v], WW's two sonnets, *To B. R. Haydon, Esq. on seeing his Picture of Napoleon Buonaparte on the Island of St. Helena* and *On a Portrait of the Duke of Wellington, upon the Field of Waterloo, by Haydon.* The former is dated June 11, 1831, and the latter Monday, August 31, 1840. The authority of these copies is suspect and their variants have not been recorded in the *apparatus.* Their readings may derive from lost correspondence between WW and BRH, but they are without corroboration from any known authorial copies. Substantive variants in the copy of *To B. R. Haydon* are: *l. 3* colours] Color those signs *rev from* the thought *l.* 7 laboured *rev from* tried the World *l. 8* bare hill *rev from* bleak rock (Pierpont Morgan Library, MS. MA2987). Another copy of *To B. R. Haydon* is certainly without authority; it is thought to be in Sir Robert Peel's hand (so Houghton Library autograph file). The one substantive variant is in l. 10, which for "we" has "one," a possible slip by the copyist when transcribing from a published version (Robert Peel Collection, Houghton Library).

Epitaph ("By a blest Husband guided, Mary came")

"This Lady was named Carleton, she, along with a sister, was brought up in the neighbourhood of Ambleside. The Epitaph, a part of it at least, is in the church at Bromsgrove where she resided after her marriage." (*FNW*, p. 57.) For the dating of this poem see the editor's headnote.

The "church at Bromsgrove" mentioned by WW is St. Mary's Church in the village of Shrawley, near Bromsgrove, Worcestershire (the name of the village is misprinted "Sprawley" in an account of the inscription by "Cuthbert Bede," a pseudonym for the novelist Edward Bradley, in *Notes and Queries*, 8, no. 205 [October 1, 1853]: 315). The verbal differences from the published text do not appear in any surviving manuscript, though WW clearly knew at least that some text was omitted when he dictated the IF note. The version of the poem on the tablet shifts the emphasis on the husband's grief to the loss felt by a wider group of mourners. WW may well have been sympathetic to the impulse for making such changes; for in 1810, in his third *Essay on Epitaphs,* he spoke of epitaphs in "our Country Church-Yards" that name the deceased in association with members of the same family, adding the reflection that "Such a frail memorial . . . is not without its tendency to keep families together" (*Prose*, II, 92–93). It is unlikely, however, that the alterations were authorial. The tablet is headed, "SACRED TO THE MEMORY OF / MARY ELIZABETH VERNON WIFE OF GEORGE CROFT VERNON ESQ[R] / OF BROMSGROVE IN THIS COUNTY / AND SECOND DAUGHTER OF JOHN CARLETON ESQ[R] / OF HIGH PARK COUNTY OF DUBLIN / SHE DIED AT HANBURY ON THE XII DAY OF JUNE MDCCCXXXI / AGED XXVIII YEARS." The epitaph itself begins "She came, though meek of soul, in seemly pride," omitting WW's two opening lines, and except for a "which" for "that" in l. 8, follows WW's text through l. 11. The next two lines of the tablet appear thus:

Its sister-twin survives, whose smiles impart
A trembling solace to her father's heart.

The following lines coincide with WW's text until the last two couplets, which in the tablet read,

Bear with those—judge those gently who make known
Their bitter loss by monumental stone;
And pray that in their faithful breasts the grace
Of resignation find a hallowed place.

17 Five leaves are missing from MS. 135 so that Dora W's fair copy on 25[v] breaks off at this point.

Devotional Incitements

"Rydal Mount. 1832" (*FNW*, p. 17). WW assigned the same date in editions from 1836. For the date of composition see the editor's headnote. Notes to the reading text of 1835 follow:

epigraph From *Paradise Lost*, V, 77–80:

Taste this, and be henceforth among the Gods
Thy self a Goddess, not to Earth confin'd,
But somtimes in the Air, as wee, somtimes
Ascend to Heav'n. (EdS)

26–37 In his letter to JK, December 31, 1833, WW introduced these lines by saying, "To shew you how *great wits jump*, I will transcribe a few lines from a little M.S. poem of my own, written about 18 months ago which you may be sure was called to my mind when I read your excellent line 'And incense breathes at once thro sense and Soul'—and what immediately follows." He refers to JK's poem, *A Rhymed Plea for Tolerance*, published earlier in the year and sent to WW a few days before his reply (see *LY*, II, 658 and note, 673–674).

72 not by bread alone we live] Luke 4:4.

To the Author's Portrait

"To the Author's portrait. The six last lines of this sonnet are not written for poetical effect but as a matter of fact, which in more than one instance, could not escape my notice in the servants of the house." (*FNW*, pp. 25, 126–127.) The sestet describes the response to the chalk portrait that Pickersgill made at Rydal Mount to take back to his London studio, where he painted the oil portrait. The poem was completed soon after the chalk portrait was done (WW to TA, September 19, 1832; see the Manuscript Census). Of the portrait WW told TA, "We have had Mr Pickersgill with us who has done all that was needful on the spot and in my presence, towards completing a Portrait of me, for St John's Coll. The Likeness is said to be admirable, and every one is pleased w[it]h [it]. It will be engraved, if as we presume the College has no objection." In the letter from WW to JSmith, November 28, 1832, a note has been added at the top of the page in an unknown hand: "S[t]. John's College Cambridge requested a Portrait of M[r]. Wordsworth, and sent the Painter (whom he chose to name) into Westmorland to obtain it" (Lilly MS. 1). A reproduction of the finished portrait appears in Halliday, p. 113.

2 Margaret] Lady Margaret Beaufort, mother of Henry VII, was the foundress of St. John's College (JOH).

6–7 These lines allude to the Reform Bill of 1832; the alteration from the gentler "breath of Change" to the more apocalyptic vision implicit in "torn up by the roots" may have been WW's delayed reaction to TA's more liberal views (see Cecil Lang's notes on WW to TA, September 19, 1832 in *The Arnoldian*, 15, no. 3 [1989–1990], 63–64). In his letter to TA in which he enclosed the sonnet, WW wrote, "Since your departure I have carefully read your Letters printed in the Sheffield paper. With a great portion of their Contents I can clearly agree, but there are points seeming to me material, on which you are pushing change farther than I am prepared to go," and then added, "I hope it will not be disagreeable to you and Mrs Arnold if I fill the remainder of this Sheet with a Sonnet called forth by the Pickersgill Picture.—" (*ibid.*, p. 5).

10 tear] In an unknown hand in the letter from WW to JSmith: "The picture was painted at the Poet's House in the midst of his Family, who shed tears of delight at the pleasing strong resemblance."

Poems Written in Response to the Reform Movement, December 1832

In WW, DW, and Dora W to JW_3, December 5, 1832, WW introduced the first epigram, "For Lubbock vote—no legislative hack": "Here follows an Epigram for you, allusive to [allusive to *rev from* Upon] the testimonials of the Astronomical Professor [in favor of J. Lubbock Esqr as a Candidate to represent the University of Cambridge in Parliament. *del*]" (see *LY*, II, 568 and note). In WW to JW_3, December 7, 1832, he prefaced the three "squibs" ("If this great world" is omitted): "I see that the Speaker [Charles Manners-Sutton, who was opposed by Lubbock, a Whig banker, astronomer, and mathematician] stands for Cambridge University—I hope with every prospect of success—The last of the Squibs on the other side, was composed on horseback yesterday [*Question and Answer*]—you may burn them or [burn them or *inserted*] do what you like with them, only don't let be known that I wrote them" (see the Manuscript Census and *LY*, II, 572 and note).

ii. If this great world of joy and pain

Introduced by WW thus: "Should [Should *rev from* If] the Epigram gives [*sic*] you no pleasure—the following which I threw off this morning may perhaps make a little amends." DW added in the margin: "If you please, you may print this in the Chronicle immediately after the Epigram" (WW, DW, and Dora W to JW_3, December 5, 1832; see *LY*, II, 570). In MS. 1835/36 WW dated the poem 1833.

title In the letter to JW_3, WW could have intended a pun on "lunatics" by addressing his poem to "Revolunists"; but he has squeezed the title in as an afterthought and may have unwittingly elided the fourth syllable of "Revolutionists."

iii. Now that Astrology is out of date

In his letter of December 7, 1832, WW asked JW_3 "Is the name of the french astronomer spelt right, I have no means of ascertaining, and rather think not" (WW, DW, and Dora W to JW_3, December 5, 1832). The astronomer, Jean Sylvain Bailly, held prominent posts during the French Revolution but fell out with those in power and was guillotined (see *LY*, II, 573n).

iv. Question and Answer

6 "Mouvement" may be a triple pun, playing on celestial movement, political movement, and possibly the mechanical "movement" of the guillotine.

Thought on the Seasons

"Written at Rydal Mount 1829." (*FNW*, p. 45.) WW assigned the same date in MS. 1835/36 and editions from1836. In his letter to JW_3 on December 7, 1832, WW included this poem, noting it was composed "in the Summer house at the end of the Terrace, whe[n the *MS. torn*] wind was blowing high the other evening" (see *LY*, II, 573).

title In MSS. 137 and 138 (A), both reflecting an early stage of proof, the title *Rural Illusions* included three poems, each assigned a Roman numeral, "Sylph was it? or a Bird more bright" (I), "This Lawn, a carpet all alive" (II), and "Flattered with promise of escape" (III). Both examples of this stage of proof were then revised to the arrangement of the printed text, with each poem standing independently beneath its own title. The printer may have added the Roman numerals himself when he found two untitled poems following *Rural Illusions* in MS. 135 (the printer's copy). MS. 138 (B) is postmarked December 29, 1834.

A Wren's Nest

"1833. Rydal Mount. This nest was built, as described, in a tree that grows near the pool in Dora's field next the Rydal Mount Garden.—" (*FNW*, p. 12; see also p. 107.) WW assigned the same date in MS. 1835/36 and editions from 1836.

Evening Voluntaries, I. Calm is the fragrant air, and loth to lose

WW assigned the poem to 1832 in MS. 1835/36 and editions from 1836.

II. Not in the lucid intervals of life

"The lines following 'Nor do words' were written with L. Byron's character as a Poet before me and that of others among his contemporaries who wrote under like influences." (*FNW*, p. 55.)

7–15 The lines on Byron are lacking in the earliest manuscript version. Byron died in 1824; his letters were published in 1830 and 1832. WW assigned the poem to 1834 in MS. 1835/36 and editions from 1836.

17–23 O Nature . . . pensive hearts . . . every charm] EdeS notes WW's reminscence of Burns, *To W. S*****n, Ochiltree*, ll. 73–80.

III. (By the Side of Rydal Mere.)

WW assigned the poem to 1834 in MS. 1835/36 and editions from 1836.

IV. Soft as a cloud is yon blue Ridge—the Mere

WW assigned the poem to 1834 in MS. 1835/36 and editions from 1836.

V. The leaves that rustled on this oak-crowned hill

"Composed by the side of Grasmere Lake. The mountains that enclose the vale, especially towards Easedale, are most favorable to the reverberation of sound: there is a passage in the Excursion towards the close of the 4th. Book where the voice of the Raven in flight is traced thro' the modifications it undergoes as I have often heard it in that Vale and others of this district." (*FNW*, p. 55.) In the manuscript of the IF notes EQ penciled in the passage from *The Excursion* about the Raven's flight (IV, 1175–1178). WW assigned the poem to 1834 in MS. 1835/36 and editions from 1836.

14–34 MW entered these lines on 15[v] and 16[r] in MS. 128, perhaps by dictation, and, though the "grave creature" is not identified until the eighth line from the end, the verses may have been intended as an independent poem.

27 headless Owl] WW refers to the headless "aspect" of an owl in silhouette; he may be playing upon Puck's promise of mischievous shape shifting in *A Midsummer Night's Dream*, "some time a horse I'll be, sometime . . . a headless bear" (III.i.109). The printer's "heedless" in proof (MS. 137), which WW corrected to "headless," is clearly an error.

VI. The Sun, that seemed so mildly to retire

"The lines were composed on the road between Moresby and Whitehaven while I was on a visit to my Son then Rector of that place. This succession of Voluntaries with the exception of the 8th. and 9th., originated in the concluding lines of the last paragraph of this Poem. With this coast I have been familiar from my earliest childhood and remember being struck for the first time by the town and port of Whitehaven and the white waves breaking against its quays and piers as the whole came into view from the top of the high ground down which the road,—which has since been altered, then descended abruptly. My Sister when she first heard the voice of the sea from this point and beheld the scene spread before her burst into tears. Our family then lived at Cockermouth and this fact was often mentioned among us as indicating the sensibility for which she was so remarkable." (*FNW*, pp. 55–56, 160–161.) In MS. 128 WW's inscription, added below the revision of ll. 17–26, is "(7th April 1833—6[3][d] birthday)." In MS. 134 the poem is inscribed by the copyist "April 7th Easter Sunday and my sixty third birthday. WW." In *MS.* 1835/36, probably before he revised the title to include the date, WW wrote "Easter Sunday April 7th 1833 / the Author's 63rd birth-/day" below the final line of the poem; the printer reduced this addendum to 1833—the date given in editions from 1836.

WW visited his son John, who was Rector of Moresby, at the end of March through April 7, 1833. For the "8th and 9th" poems in the sequence, as it stood in 1843, when WW composed the IF note, see "The sun has long been set" (above) and *Ode, Composed upon an Evening of Extraordinary Splendor and Beauty,* written in 1817 (*Poems, 1807–1820*, pp. 258–260).

The poem appears as number XIII in the sequence of poems entered in MS. 128, labeled on the cover, "Tour. 1833."

VII. (By the Sea-side.)

WW assigned the poem to 1833 in MS. 1835/36 and editions from 1836. He visited his son John at Moresby (see the title given the poem in MS. 128) in late March and early April 1833 (*LY*, II, 599).

16 who bade the tempest cease] Matthew 8:26.

39 From Young's *Night Thoughts*, II, 95. The full line is quoted by CW, Jr., as a note to this line in his copy of the poem in CW, Jr., to CW, January 2, 1834 (but "thy thought").

VIII. The sun has long been set

"Reprinted at the request of my Sister in whose presence the lines were thrown off." (*FNW*, pp. 55–56.) See the entry for June 8, 1802, in *The Grasmere Journals*, edited by Pamela Woof (Oxford, 1991), p. 107. WW assigned the poem to 1804 in MS. 1835/36 and editions from 1836.

The first reading text is based on the version in MS. 128. MW entered a fair copy of the first stanza, with a few of her corrections, on 53[r], beginning with l. 1 and continuing on the recto with the second stanza, ending with the final couplet following l. 18. WW then added two couplets and reentered the final couplet below, but without deleting MW's final couplet.

See *Poems, 1800–1807*, pp. 204–205, 326–329, for WW's first printing, a record of early manuscripts and photographs and transcriptions showing this later expansion of this poem in MS. 128. In the end, however, WW adopted the early, briefer, version for the Evening Voluntaries with a headnote explaining its return to print in 1835.

IX. Throned in the Sun's descending car

WW's headnote to Evening Voluntaries VIII and IX appears in MS. 135, with the following verbal variants from the text given above VIII:

para one: The former of the *rev from* The here *inserted* the lines *rev from* it was

para two: latter, *rev from* latter here, sometimes] often in his own mind *inserted* in itself *inserted* a harmless *rev from* a Love of

WW's combined headnote for VIII and IX was divided in *YR*, 1836, 1839, with each poem assigned its own headnote. He did not reprint the cento or its headnote in any of the collected editions from 1836. The stanza from Akenside, Thomson's *Hymn on Solitude*, and the passage from Beattie's *Retirement* all appear in *Poems and Extracts chosen by William Wordsworth for an Album Presented to Lady Mary Lowther Christmas, 1819* (edited by Harold Littledale from a manuscript then owned by J. Rogers Rees and published by Henry Frowde, London, 1905; see pp. 58, 45, and 47).

1–6 Mark Akenside, *Ode V, Against Suspicion* (1745), ll. 43–48.

7–8 James Thomson, *Hymn on Solitude* (1725), ll. 1–2. WW has altered the first line from "Hail, ever-pleasing Solitude." In Lady Lowther's Album the line reads "Hail, mildly-pleasing Solitude," suggesting that WW was working from memory.

9–16 James Beattie, *Retirement* (1758), ll. 49–56.

Alternate Texts, Text 1: Twilight by the side of Grasmere Lake

This sonnet, in MW's hand, was first revised by WW in pencil and then added to in pencil and ink.

Text 2: Twilight

See Evening Voluntaries II, "Not in the lucid intervals of life" and V, "The leaves that rustled on this oak-crowned hill" and alternate text "Alas for them who crave impassioned strife."

1–4 These lines were rearranged in MS. 128 by the insertion of numbers above each line.

Text 3: Alas for them who crave impassioned strife

1–16 Entered by MW on the recto (35^r^) facing the text of *Twilight* (on 31^v^), the intervening leaves having been torn out. There is no direction at line 16, but it seems apparent that WW then revised the last four lines of *Twilight* at the foot of 31^v^ as the ending of "Alas for them who crave impassioned strife."

17–20 For the earlier versions of these lines see *Twilight* ("Advancing slowly from the faded west").

Text 4: The dewy evening has withdrawn

Dora W entered a fair copy of this poem, made up of two stanzas and a couplet, on 58^r^ of MS. 128. WW then developed this material in pentameter couplets on 57^v^ and 58^v^; much of this, then, became *(By the Side of Rydal Mere.)*.

Composed by the Sea-shore

"These lines were suggested during my residence under my Son's roof at Moresby on the coast near Whitehaven, at the time when I was composing those verses among the Evening Voluntaries that have reference to the Sea. In some future edition I purpose to place it among that Class of Poems. It was in that neighbourhood I first became acquainted with the ocean and its appearances and movements. My Infancy and early childhood were passed at Cockermouth about eight miles from the coast, and I well remember that mysterious awe with which I used to listen to anything said about storms and shipwrecks. Sea-shells of many descriptions were common in the town, and I was not a little surprised when I heard M^r^. Landor had denounced me as a Plagiarist from himself for having described a boy applying a sea shell to his ear and listening to it for intimations of what was going on in its native element: This I had done myself scores of times and it was a belief among us that we could know from the sound whether the tide was ebbing or flowing." (*FNW*, p. 74.) WW's remark on seashells refers to *Excursion*, IV, 1132–1147 (see *FNW*, p. 180).

Probably composed, with "The Sun, that seemed so mildly to retire" and (*By the Sea-side.*), in late March or early April 1833, while WW was visiting his son John at Moresby; he wrote to his family at Rydal Mount, "I have walked and ridden a great deal . . . , and one day with another, I have scarcely walked less than 12 miles. The sea is a delightful companion and nothing can be more charming, especially for a sequestered Mountaineer, than to cast eyes over its boundless surface, and hear as I have done almost from the brow of the steep in the Church field at Moresby, the waves chafing and murmuring in a variety of tones below, as a kind of base of harmony to the shrill yet liquid music of the larks above" (*LY*, II, 600). A year later, however, when WW and MW spent a fortnight with John and his family at the end of March 1834, WW "took a long and most delightful walk, following from Whitehaven, along the top of the Cliffs the indentings of the Coast, as far as the Monastry of St. Bees" (*LY*, II, 697). *Composed by the Sea-shore* was placed among the Evening Voluntaries in editions of 1845 and 1849–1850 (WW's instructions for this placement, in JC's hand, appear in MS. 1836/45).

To ———, Upon the Birth of her First-Born Child, March, 1833.

"*To I —— W —— on the birth of her first Child* written at Moresby near Whitehaven 1833, when I was on a visit to my Son then Incumbent of that small living. While I am dictating these notes to my Friend Miss Fenwick Jany. 24th. 1843. the Child upon whose birth these verses were written is under my roof and is of a disposition so promising that the wishes and prayers and prophecies, w^{h}. I then breathed forth in Verse are thro' God's mercy likely to be realized." (*FNW*, p. 45; see also p. 148.) Isabella (Curwen) Wordsworth, wife of WW's son John, gave birth to Jane Stanley (1833–1912) at Moresby in May.

WW wrote to his family at Rydal on April 1, 1833, from Moresby, "I have composed since I came here the promised Poem upon the birth of the Baby, and thrown off yesterday and today, in the course of a ride to Arlecdon (Mr Wilkinson's), a sober and sorrowful sequel to it which I fear none of you will like. They are neither yet fairly written out but I hope to send them for your impressions in this parcel" (*LY*, II, 600–601). The "promise" was evidently extracted by Dora W. For the "sequel" see *The Warning.*

epigraph From *De Rerum Natura,* V, 222–223: "Then, furthermore, a child, like a sailor thrown up by the fierce waves, lies on the ground naked. . . ."

The Warning, a Sequel to the Foregoing. March, 1833

"These lines were composed during the fever spread thro' the Nation by the reform bill. As the motives which led to this measure and the good or evil which has attended or has risen from it, will be duly appreciated by future Historians, there is no call for dwelling on the subject in this place. I will content myself with saying that the then condition of the people's mind is not, in these verses, exaggerated." (*FNW*, p. 45.) Though the Reform Bill was passed in June 1832, it remained a subject of heated debate through 1833. WW assigned the poem to 1833 in MS. 1835/36 and editions from 1836.

"Aware that expressions of regret for the past, are seldom of much use as a preventive of future evils, the Author has not admitted without reluctance the above into a Collection of Poems so different from it in character. But it was poured out in sincerity of heart—and the heart of a Poet may in some cases be trusted, where the opinion of a practical Statesman is er[r]oneous: at all events, the verses, however profitless or insignificant they may appear to many, could not have been suppressed, without shrinking, from what the Writer felt (and he hopes without presumption) to be a duty to his Country in the present peril of her social Inst[it]utions." WW's note, in MW's hand, in the printer's copy (MS. 135, 112^{v}P3); the note was not set in proof and was never printed by WW. MW made the following alterations in this copy of the note:

expressions *rev from* the expressions past, are *rev from* past, however well founded, are seldom *rev from* [?rarely] use as a *rev from* consequence Writer *rev from* Author

The words "erroneous" and "Institutions" are corrected from miswritings. Of an earlier version (on 113^{r}) the first part is missing except for a few fragments, and the last part is heavily deleted; what survives reads, " . . . [judgment *rev to*] opinion of a practical Statesman [may present *rev to*] is erroneous however profitless and insignificant they may appear to many; at all events the verses could not have been suppressed, without shrinking from what the Author felt (and he hopes without presumption) to be a duty to his Country in the present peril of her social institutions."

The two sets of proof pages in MS. 137 present a confusing picture at first glance. WW first received, corrected, and returned MS. 137 (A); before the printer entered these corrections he sent WW another set (B) which WW returned without correcting the text but with a note referring to his earlier instructions. Thus, though B is later than A, it reflects a state of the text earlier than the corrected A.

20–21 WW is quoted in *Memoirs* (II, 476): "Many of my poems have been influenced by my own circumstances when I was writing them. *The Warning, A Sequel to the Foregoing* was composed on horseback, while I was riding from Moresby in a snow-storm. Hence the simile in that poem, "'While thoughts press on and feelings overflow, / And quick words round him fall like *flakes of snow.*'"

23 In MS. 1836/45 WW added a note to this line, "See page"—intended to refer to *To ———, Upon the Birth of her First-Born Child, March, 1833.*

Lay.] Despite Nowell C. Smith's conjecture, and EdeS's concurrence with it (*PW*, IV, 427), that the line should end with a comma not a period, we retain the reading of all manuscripts and printed texts. WW's pencil annotation to this line in MS. 1836/45, mentioned above, and revisions of the punctuation in ll. 29 and 34 on the same page, without any change in punctuation indicated in l. 23, suggest that the original reading is what the poet intended.

He who defers his work from day to day

The only evidence for the date is the inscription in the Lutwidge Family MS., "Wm Wordsworth / Rydal Mount / 17 April 1833" (see Manuscript Census).

To the Utilitarians

In his undated letter to HCR, which HCR has endorsed "5th May 1833," WW wrote, "To fill up the Paper a[ccept?] these verses composed or rather thrown off this morning," and, after transcribing the poem, added, "Is the above intelligible—I fear not—I know however my own meaning—and thats enough [On] Manuscripts" (*LY*, II, 610; Morley's reading, "On" rather than "for" is probably correct; *HCR Correspondence*, I, 238). WW may be alluding to John Stuart Mill, whom HCR had met the year before. Mill's Utilitarian Society met during 1823–1826 and in 1825 he edited Bentham's "Treatise upon Evidence." His obituary article on Bentham, published anonymously, appeared in the *Examiner*, June 10, 1832.

7–8 On the May 18, 1833, WW wrote to HCR again and remarked, "In the extempore lines I filled up the corner of my paper with were two execrably bad, mere stop gaps, in which the word 'elevate' was used improperly" (*LY*, II, 622).

The Labourer's Noon-day Hymn

"Bishop Ken's Morn[g] and Ev[g]. Hymns are as they deserve to be familiarly known. Many other hymns have also been written on the same subjects but not being aware of any being designed for Noon-day I was induced to compose these verses. Often one has occasion to observe Cottage children carrying in their baskets dinner to their Fathers engaged with their daily labours in the fields and woods. How gratifying would it be to me could I be assured that any portion of these Stanzas had been sung by such a domestic concert under such circumstances. A friend of mine has told me that she introduced this Hymn into a Village school which she superintended—and the Stanzas in succession furnished her with texts to comment upon in a way which without difficulty was made intelligible to the Children and in which they obviously took delight; and they were taught to sing it to the tune of the *old 100th* Psalm." (*FNW*, pp. 45–46, 148.) WW assigned the poem to 1834 in MS. 1835/36 and editions from 1836; it was certainly composed by mid-July, when he was sending the printer the last sheets of copy for *Yarrow Revisited*, which was published in January 1835.

"The 4th, 6th, 7th, and 8th, Stanzas of the above have been given to a religious Society for the use of their Schools"; WW's note (MW's hand) in MS. 135, deleted.

17–20 In letters of February 28 and March 6, 1844, WW, in giving permission to editors (respectively Henry Alford and perhaps John Mason Neale) to reprint the poem, asked each in turn to alter the first line of the fifth stanza to "Each field is then a hallowed spot" or else to omit the stanza altogether. The stanza was omitted from the *Select Pieces from the Poems of William Wordsworth* printed by James Burns (London, 1843), perhaps on the poet's direction; and WW took this step himself in the next authorized edition of his poem, Moxon's one-volume edition of 1845 (Mark L. Reed, "Wordsworth's Surprisingly Pictured Page: *Select Pieces*," *Book Collector* 46 [1997]: 74–75).

Love Lies Bleeding

In her June 1–2 letter to EQ, in which she enclosed the first expansion of the poem, Dora W referred to an intended group of "Morning Voluntaries," and her reference is explained by the IF note to Evening Voluntaries (dictated in 1843): here WW mentioned "that among the miscellaneous Sonnets are a few alluding to morning impressions which might be read with mutual benefit in connection with these Evening Voluntaries"; though he included the class of poems among some notes for revisions in a copy of *PW*, 1840 (DC MS. 154), while preparing for the 1845 edition, the series of "Morning Voluntaries" never materialized.

Text of 1835

"It has been said that the English, though their Country has produced so many great Poets, is now the most unpoetical nation in Europe. It is probably true; for they have more temptation to become so than any other European people. Trade, commerce, and manufactures, physical science and mechanic arts, out of which so much wealth has arisen, have made our country men infinitely less sensible to movements of imagination and fancy than were our Forefathers in their simple state of society. How touching and beautiful were in most instances the names they gave to our indigenous flowers or any other they were familiarly acquainted with! Every month for many years have we been importing plants and flowers from all quarters of the globe many of which are spread thro' our gardens and some perhaps likely to be met with on the few commons which we have left. Will their botanical names ever be displaced by plain English appellations which will bring them home to our hearts by connection with our joys and sorrows? It can never be, unless society treads back her steps towards those simplicities which have been banished by the undue influence of Towns spreading and spreading in every direction so that city life with every generation takes more and more the lead of rural. Among the Ancients, Villages were reckoned the seats of barbarism. Refinement, for the most part false, increases the desire to accumulate wealth; and while theories of political economy are boastfully pleading for the practise, inhumanity pervades all our dealings in buying and selling. This selfishness wars against disinterested imagination in all directions, and, evils coming round in a circle, barbarism spreads in every quarter of our Island. Oh for the reign of justice, and then the humblest man among us would have more power and dignity in and about him than the highest have now!" (*FNW*, pp. 66–67.)

5 A flower] Either the crossbar of the letter "A" has been reinforced in MS. 151.2—or the "A" was deleted when "flower" was altered to "Flower." Whether or not WW intended deletion, he never made the change in print.

Companion to the Foregoing

See the note to *Love Lies Bleeding*.

Written in an Album

"*Written in the Album of a Child.* This quatrain was extempore on observing this image, as I had often done, on the lawn of Rydal Mount. It was first written down in the Album of my God-daughter Rotha Quillinan." (*FNW*, p. 30.) The quatrain was probably composed around the date WW added below his inscription in Rotha Q's Album. Dora W, in her letter to Rotha Q (July 19, 1834) spoke of WW's composing the quatrain, "a little good moral advice," as his second entry in Rotha's album, which Dora had in her keeping at Rydal Mount. The lines, "which he [WW] threw off the other morning whilst basking on the grass plot below the mount" (WL Letters), were put to use on later occasions in three other albums (Swarthmore MS. 2, Berg MS. 6, and Rendell MS.). See also WW's IF note to *To Rotha Q———.*

Lines Suggested by a Portrait from the Pencil of F. Stone

"*Lines suggested by a Portrait / Subject resumed* This Portrait has hung for many years in our principal sitting room and represents J.Q. as she was when a girl—The picture, tho' it is somewhat thinly painted, has much merit in tone and general effect—it is chiefly valuable however from the sentiment that pervades it. The Anecdote of the saying of the Monk in sight of Titian's Picture was told in this house by Mr. Wilkie, and was, I believe, first communicated to the Public in this Poem the former portion of wh. I was composing at the time. Southey heard the story from Miss Hutchinson and transferred it to the Dr.—but it is not easy to explain how my friend Mr. Rogers in a note subsequently added to his 'Italy' was led to speak of the same remarkable words having many years before been spoken in his hearing by a monk or Priest in front of a picture of the Last Supper placed over a refectory-table in a Convent at Padua." (*FNW*, p. 46.) WW assigned the poem to 1834 in MS. 1835/36 and editions from 1836. "J. Q." is Jemima Quillinan (1819–1891), EQ's elder daughter. Frank Stone, R. A. (1800–1859), probably did Jemima's portrait early in 1833 (see the editor's headnote, pp. 269–270); he became widely known as a portrait painter in the 1840s and 50s. David Wilkie (1785–1841), painter and friend of BRH and Sir GB, visited Rydal Mount in September 1834 (Rydal Mount Visitor's Book, WL). For discussion of Samuel Rogers's use of the same anecdote see *FNW*, pp. 149–150. The "principal sitting room" was also the library; William Westall's print of the Rydal Mount library shows a picture which may be Jemima's portrait (the print is reproduced in Blanshard, plate 21).

In the first set of proofs, MS. 137 (A), *Lines Suggested by a Portrait* followed *The Redbreast. (Suggested in a Westmoreland Cottage.)*, which followed *Humanity.* MW's note in MS. 137 (A)—and her similar note under the title in MS. 138—correct this placement: "This Poem to follow Humanity and to precede the Power of Sound."

16ff. In this poem only, copies of what is apparently a second issue of *PW*, 1841, reveal a few minor differences from the first issue (see the entries identified as "1841*" in the list of Nonverbal Variants).

79–91 These lines—ending at the phrase "trembling hope?"—were transcribed by WW and dated "Rydal Mount / 22 Febry- 1836" on a single sheet of paper, now in the State Library of Victoria, Melbourne, Australia (see the entry for Melbourne MS. in the Manuscript Census). Geoffrey Little has speculated that these lines were intended by WW to stand as a separate poem, citing WW's habit, early in his career, of excerpting passages from longer unpublished poems to be published as freestanding poems (see "Wordsworth in Melbourne: a 'New' Poem?" *The Bibliographical Society of Australia and New Zealand Bulletin* 10 [1986]: 134–138). However, as attractive as this suggestion may be, it is offset by WW's much more common practice in his later years of copying out excerpts from his poems, published ones more often than not, to give to visitors and friends. It seems probable that the Melbourne MS. is one such example (compare Lilly MS. 3 of the same poem, but see also the Manuscript Census, above, for many other examples). The Rydal Mount Visitor's Book (WL MS.) lists seven visitors for February 1836, including WW's sons, William and John. Either son might be presumed to have expressed interest in the portrait of Jemima Quillinan, who with her sister Rotha was often part of the Wordsworth family circle after their mother's death in 1822. Little's suggestion that John W's fourth son Charles, who emigrated to Australia in 1863, brought with him this portion of his grandfather's poem, is an ingenious one. But a Sotheby sale catalogue entry, dated "Wed., 22nd June, 1955," describes lot 697 as "Holograph Manuscript Poetry, 13 lines beginning 'Strange contrasts have we in this world of ours!' [extract from his *Lines Suggested by a Portrait from the Pencil of F. Stone*], 1p., 4to, *signed and dated 'Rydal Mount, 22 February, 1836', framed and glazed.*" Records show that lot 697 was purchased by L. V. Smithe, who has not otherwise been identified.

89–90 Geoffrey Little (p. 135 of the article cited above) supposed that a mark in the printer's copy (DC MS. 135) was WW's own mark showing a new verse paragraph at l. 89, but the bracket at l. 90, which is connected by a hand-drawn line to a notation at the top of the manuscript page, is a printer's mark indicating the beginning of a new gathering ("N"). At a later stage WW added to this poem and rearranged others, thus positioning the revised text of *Lines* in a subsequent gathering.

95–117 "Wilkie was the painter to whom this affecting incident occurred (I know it is not proper to say *incident occurred* but I know not what other word to use—) and he told it to us when at Rydal the other day" (MW's pencil note in MS. 130).

118 Jeronymite] A hermit of one of the orders of St. Jerome.

125–126 like the angel . . . Bethesda's pool] Cf. John 5:2–4.

On surviving proof pages (MS. 138, O10 and O10a), WW instructed the printer to present a single poem in two parts, and to transfer the note sent earlier with *Lines* (now "Part 1st") to the end of "Part 2[d]" and "add the note that follows on the next page" (*i.e.*, the note eventually attached to *The Foregoing Subject Resumed*; see below, and the editor's headnote to both poems on p. 269).

The Foregoing Subject Resumed

See the note to *Lines Suggested by a Portrait from the Pencil of F. Stone.* WW assigned the poem to 1834 in MS. 1835/36 and editions from 1836.

32 In *PW*, 1850, the last line ends with a closing quotation mark, but no matching mark appears in that text.

The poems by RS referred to in WW's note are *On My Own Miniature Picture, Taken at Two Years of Age* (1796) and *On a Landscape of Gaspar Poussin* (1795) published among "Occasional Pieces" in his "Juvenile and Minor Poems" (*Poetical Works* [10 vols., London, 1843], II, 229, 221).

Desponding Father! mark this altered bough

The poem does not appear in surviving printer's copy (MS. 135) or in the two holograph collections (DC MSS. 133 and 134) that preceded it in the preparation of materials for *YR*, 1835. MW's fair copy, which both she and WW extensively revised, does appear in MS. 107, originally a set of fair copies but evolved by 1834 into WW's workbook for new materials or for extensive revision of old (see photographs and transcriptions, pp. 760–761). There is also a fair copy approximating the published text in MS. 106. These details suggest that the poem was composed after printer's copy had been sent off, that is, toward the end of July 1834, and before printing was well under way, around November–December 1834. However, the many delays in printing left opportunity for change and addition as late as February or March 1835.

Lines Written in the Album of the Countess of ——. Nov. 5, 1834

"*Lines in Lady Lonsdale's Album.* This is a faithful picture of that amiable Lady as she then was. The youthfulness of figure and demeanour and habits, which she retained in almost unprecedented degree, departed a very few years after and she died without violent disease by gradual decay before she reached the period of old age." (*FNW*, p. 30; see also p. 134.)

Both manuscripts reveal shorter versions beneath the revisions. These early versions ended with the lines given in the *apparatus* for ll. 78–82. Both fair copies seem to have been corrected almost immediately to the full text of the published version, thus making an alternate reading text of either shorter version unjustified. The copy of this poem in Lady Lonsdale's album may have revealed an early state but the album is untraced.

8 See *To the Earl of Lonsdale* in the sequence Tour 1833.

Fairy skill

The poem appears in a small autograph album, presented to "Dora Harrison, Wordsworth's cousin from her friend Mary Dickinson, December 1834." Dora Harrison was the daughter of Dorothy (Wordsworth) Benson, WW's cousin, who lived near Ambleside. The original manuscript has not been found. Apart from its reproduction in the catalogue issued by Dawsons of Pall Mall in 1969, the poem has not been published before.

The Redbreast. (Suggested in a Westmoreland Cottage.)

"*The Redbreast,* Rydal Mount, 1834. Our cats having been banished the house, it was soon frequented by Red-breasts. Two or three of them, when the window was open, would come in, particularly when Mary was breakfasting alone, and hop about the table picking up the crumbs. My Sister being then confined to her room by sickness, as, dear creature, she still is, had one that, without being caged, took up its abode with her, and at night used to perch upon a nail from which a picture had hung. It used to sing and fan her face with its wings in a manner that was very touching." (*FNW*, p. 10.) WW assigned the same date in editions from 1836. In a letter to Jane Marshall on December 27, 1834, MW gave a similar account of DW and her companionable robin (*MWL*, pp. 135–136). See also WW's "Strange visitation! at *Jemima's* lip" (later titled *In the Woods of Rydal*) on p. 58, and his published note to that sonnet on p. 429.

Instructions to the printer of *YR*, 1835, in MW's hand, in MS. 135 place *The Redbreast. (Suggested in a Westmoreland Cottage.)* "*after* the Lines intitled '*Humanity*' and to be *followed* by the address to the Portrait—which precedes the concluding Poem to the Power of Sound"; but these instructions were supplanted by later ones that direct the printer to introduce "Any smaller pieces that have not yet been printed" (MS. 137 [B]; see Appendix I for the arrangement of poems in *YR*, 1835).

10 Ballad] *The Children in the Wood* (ll. 125–128).

47–64 In MS. 137 (B) MW corrected this page simply by adding a note referring the printer to "altered sheet before sent"—that is, MS. 137 (A), in which several substantive changes were made.

70 "lilt" in Northern dialect means "move with a lively action" (*Oxford English Dictionary*).

Upon Seeing a Coloured Drawing of the Bird of Paradise in an Album

"*Bird of Paradise* I cannot forbear to record that the last seven lines of this Poem were composed in bed during the night on the day on w^{h}. my Sister S. H. died about *6.P.M* and it was the thought of her innocent and beautiful life that, through faith, prompted the words 'On wings that fear no glance of God's pure sight, no tempest from his breath.' The reader will find two poems on pictures of this bird among my Poems. I will here observe that in a far greater number of instances than have been mentioned in these notes one Poem has as in this case grown out of another either because I felt the subject had been inadequately treated or that the thoughts and images suggested in course of composition have been such as I found interfered with the unity indispensable to every work of Art however humble in character." (*FNW,* pp. 46–47, 150.) SH died at Rydal Mount on June 23, 1835. WW assigned the poem to 1835 in editions from 1836. The second of the "two poems" mentioned in the IF note is *Suggested by a Picture of the Bird of Paradise*; see below, pp. 360–361.

25–33 A pencil line along the left margin and an "X" beside it suggest an intended deletion or alteration of these lines in MS. 1836/45. No change was made.

35–42 This passage contains the "seven lines" first composed by WW (see IF note, above).

Airey-Force Valley

WW toured along the shores of Ullswater in September 1835 with Joshua Watson and his daughter; a short time later, on October 5, he sent Watson a copy of the poem, remarking, "My walk from Lyulph's Tower to Hallsteads was beguiled by throwing into blank verse a description of the scene which struck Miss Watson and me at the same moment" (*LY,* III, 104). Aira Force, also the scene of *The Somnambulist,* is on the west side of Ullswater, about halfway up the lake.

To the Moon. (Composed by the Sea-side,—on the Coast of Cumberland.)

This and the following poem, *To the Moon. (Rydal.),* were added to Evening Voluntaries in the edition of 1836, where WW dated them 1835; the title in Princeton MS. 2 originally included the date "Oct. 1835."

10–11 on this sea-beat shore / Sole-sitting] Cf. Naming of Places, iv. 38: "Sole-sitting by the shores of old romance" (EdeS).

To the Moon. (Rydal.)

The poem was probably composed at the same time as *To the Moon. (Composed by the Sea-side,—On the Coast of Cumberland.),* which in Princeton MS. 2 is subtitled, before revision, "Oct. 1835." Both poems were added to Evening Voluntaries in the edition of 1836, where WW dated them 1835.

49 'To look on tempests, and be never shaken'] Shakespeare, *Sonnets,* cxvi. 6 (EdeS).

Poems Written after the Death of Charles Lamb

Text of Huntington MS. 2, ***Epitaph***

WW wrote to EM about *Epitaph,* the earliest form of the poem: "On the other page you have the requested Epitaph, it was composed yesterday—and, by sending it immediately, I have prepared the way, I believe, for a speedy repentance—as I dont know that I ever wrote so many lines without some retouching being afterwards necessary. If these verses should be wholly unsuitable to the end Miss L. had in view, I shall find no difficulty in reconciling myself to the thought of their not being made use of, tho' it would have given me great, *very* great pleasure to fulfil, in all points, her wishes.

"The first objection that will strike you, and every one, is its extreme length, especially compared with epitaphs as they are now written—but this objection might in part be obviated by engraving the lines in double column, and not in capitals.

"Chiabrera has been here my model—tho' I am aware that Italian Churches, both on account of their size and the climate of Italy, are more favourable to long inscriptions than ours—His Epitaphs are characteristic and circumstantial—so have I endeavoured to make this of mine—but I have not ventured to touch upon the most striking feature of our departed friend's character and the most affecting circumstance of his life, viz, his faithful and intense love of his Sister. Had I been pouring out an Elegy or Monody, this would and must have been done. But for seeing and feeling the sanctity of that relation as it ought to be seen and felt, lights are required which could scarcely be furnished by an

Epitaph, unless it were to touch on little or nothing else.—The omission, therefore, in my view of the case was unavoidable: and I regret it the less, you yourself having already treated in verse the subject with genuine tenderness and beauty" (WW to EM, November 20, 1835; *LY*, III, 114–115). The impetus for WW to overcome his reluctance to perform this task came from MW. On February 14 MW sent MMH a copy of the long form of the poem, presumably a printed copy in the form printed by EM between DC1 and CL1, but perhaps a handwritten one, neither of which survives. She wrote, "I send you a copy of verses which W[m] wrote in consequence of Miss Lamb having expressed a wish that he should write her B[rs] Epitaph—which he shrank from till I proposed that he might take it up after the manner of those he translated from Chiabrera—and he began and as you will see wrote the first part, but found that it was too long, yet did not express the most important characteristic part of his life—so the idea of the Epitaph was relinquished—and he has given the verses to be printed with his memoir and letters, which his Executors are preparing" (WL Letters). The Chiabrera translations were done in late 1809 and all but three appeared in STC's *The Friend* in 1809 and 1810; "True is it that Ambrosio Salinero," "Weep not, beloved Friends! nor let the air," and "O flower of all that springs from gentle blood" did not see print until *PW,* 1836, along with the verses on Lamb. In WW's translation of "True is it that Ambrosio Salinero," the latter's "frank courageous heart / And buoyant spirit triumphed over pain" (ll. 6–7; *Poems, 1807–1820,* p. 60).

14/15 and 24–25 "It has been in respect to the Epitaph as I foretold; I have been tempted to retouch it, and beg that after the word 'overflowing heart' you would read thus: [see the revision in the *apparatus* to *Epitaph,* Text of Huntington MS. 2]

"The composition is by this alteration a little inspirited, but at the cost of an add[l] line—for which room may be made by striking out the two that follow, some lines below—viz [ll. 24–25 canceled] and indeed these two lines may easily be spared. Again I cannot help expressing a wish that Miss L.'s purpose had been better carried into effect. Suppose M[r] Talfourd or yourself were to try? I cannot *put* aside my regret in not having touched upon the affection of the Brother and Sister for each other" (WW to EM, November 23, 1835; *LY,* III, 119).

34 Below "if e'er" MW "made a stroke to signify the lines were finished" (Huntington MS. 4), leading the printer to set up the phrase in italic type (see the second reading text, l. 38, and the note to ll. 34, 36, and 38, below).

Text of Huntington MS. 4, *Epitaph written on Charles Lamb by William Wordsworth*

"I have sent you the Epitaph again revized; yesterday I sent through a frank a few alterations, those which the present sheet contains being added, I send the whole repenned. [For the alterations see *apparatus* to *Epitaph written on Charles Lamb by William Wordsworth,* Text of Huntington MS. 4.]

"I hope the changes will be approved of, at all events, they better answer my purpose. The lines, as they now stand, preserve better the balance of delicate delineation, the weaknesses are not so prominent, and the virtues placed in a stronger light; and I hope nothing is said that is not characteristic. Of this you and Mrs Moxon will be more competent judges than myself, as I never saw my poor Friend, when his afflictions were lying most heavily upon him. . . . [Here follows MW's fair copy of *Epitaph written on Charles Lamb by William Wordsworth*; see the second reading text.]

"If the length makes the above utterly unsuitable, it may be printed with his Works as an effusion by the side of his grave; in this case, in some favorable moment, I might be enabled to add a few Lines upon the friendship of the Brother and Sister" (WW to EM, November 24, 1835; *LY,* III, 120).

"As to the lines sent—the more I think of them, the more do I feel that their number renders it little less than impossible that they should be used as an Epitaph—so convinced am I of this, that I feel strongly impelled, as I hinted to Moxon in my yesterday's letter, containing a revised copy of the lines, to convert them into a Meditation supposed to be uttered by his Graveside; which would give me an opportunity of endeavouring to do some little justice to a part of the subject, which no one can treat *adequately*—viz—the sacred friendship which bound the Brother and sister together, under circumstances so affecting. Entertaining this view, I have *hoped* rather than expected that I might be able to put into ten or twelve couplets, a thought or feeling which might not be wholly unworthy of being inscribed upon a stone—consecrated to his memory and placed near his remains. Having however thrown off my first feeling already, in a shape so different—I wish that some one else, Mr Talfourd, Mr Moxon, Mr Southey, or any other of his friends accustomed to write verse would write the Epitaph.—Miss L. herself, if the state of her mind did not disqualify her for the undertaking.—*She* might probably do it better than any of us" (WW to HCR, November 25, 1835; *LY*, III, 122).

34, 36, 38 "I have not mentioned Lamb's epitaph, having said all I have to say on that subject to Mr Moxon and Mr Robinson. Let me, however, be excused for adding that I was sorry to see the italics at the close of the printed copy sent me down to-day. Mrs Wordsworth takes to them all, except those in the last line. That upon the word 'her' is the only one I approve of, or wish to have retained" (WW to TNT, November 28, 1835; *LY*, III, 126).

"Thanks for the printed Copy [of *Epitaph written on Charles Lamb by William Wordsworth*], which, tho' a line longer than I supposed, *looks* at least a good deal shorter than in M.S.—The *italics* at the close must all be struck out except in the word *her*—Mrs W accounts for the *if e'er* being in italics, by the supposition of her having made a stroke to signify the lines were finished—The rest she marked designedly. The only thing I am *anxious* about is, that the lines should be approved of by Miss L. as a not unworthy tribute, as far as they go, to her dear Brother's memory" (WW to EM, November 28, 1835, or shortly after; *LY*, III, 143).

Though EdeS and Alan G. Hill speculate that a word like "exception" has dropped out after "Mrs Wordsworth takes" in the November 28 letter to TNT, it is apparent from the italics in the Ashley copy of *Epitaph written on Charles Lamb by William Wordsworth* and WW's subsequent letter to EM that she deliberately marked all but "if e'er" in the final line. The letter to EM has been dated "mid-December" in *LY*, but WW is thanking EM for the "printed Copy" which, as he told TNT on November 28, had been "sent . . . down today."

WW's appeal to friends to compose additional epitaphs bore fruit in one by Owen Lloyd, "the Son of [Lamb's] old friend Charles Lloyd"; he had shown Lloyd his own "Verses observing that they were unfit on acc[t] of their length." He "did the same to Mr Hartley Coleridge and *asked* him to try his powers"; he continues, "Now as he is very ready, and has *great* powers, and retains a grateful affection for our deceased Friend, we expect something good and appropriate and suitable. Not that it is our wish that any thing from this quarter should take [the] place of what may be produced by Mr Talfourd, yourself, or any other London friend. Mr Owen Ll.'s verses are not without merit, and would be read with pleasure in many a church, or ch. yd, but they are scarcely good or characteristic for the Subject" (WW to EM, December 6, 1835; *LY*, III, 130).

On December 8, 1835, EM wrote to WW that Mary Lamb "feels greatly obliged to you for the lines on her brother [*Epitaph*], and would be very glad to see them printed with his Letters, as verses written by the side of his grave, but she is afraid that they are too long to be used as an Epitaph. She has also an objection to the allusion to her brother's troubles, which she herself brought upon him, and which she would rather should not be inquired into by those who may visit his grave. But she would not object to the allusion in a distinct Poem." EM added, "I am sorry that we have given you so much trouble, but the verses are too good to be entirely lost. Should you at your leisure add to them, I shall feel obliged by your sending me a perfect copy" (WL MS.). In reply WW wrote, "that the more I have thought about the lines I sent you, the more I am convinced of their unfitness for an Epitaph—therefore say to dear Miss L., with my love, how much I am pleased that her determination coincides with my own. My taking up the subject again will depend upon impulses concerning which I can only vaguely conjecture. I should like to know, however, what time your publication is likely to come out" (WW to EM, December 10, 1835; *LY*, III, 135 and note).

On December 22 EM wrote again to say that Mary Lamb was pleased with Owen Lloyd's verses and "will be very glad to have Mr. Hartley Coleridge's, and tho' she should not use either, yet she will attach a great value to both, as so many tributes to the memory of her brother." He added in a postscript that "Miss Lamb requested I would send her love to you and best thanks for the verses"(WL MSS.). Throughout this letter, "verses" refers to the *Epitaph* as first printed in thirty-eight lines; it is not likely that EM means the expanded poem, which WW would hardly have had time to compose and send to Mary Lamb by this time.

Text of 1836, ("To a good Man of most dear memory")

"To a good Man of most dear Memory. Light will be thrown upon the tragic circumstance alluded to in this Poem when after the death of Charles Lamb's Sister, his biographer Mr. Sergeant Talfourd shall be at Liberty to relate particulars which could not at the time when his memoir was written be given to the public. Mary Lamb was ten years older than her brother and has survived him as long a time. Were I to give way to my own feelings I should dwell not only on her genius and intellectual powers but upon the delicacy and refinement of manner which she maintained inviolable under most trying circumstances. She was loved and honored by all her brother's friends—and others—some of them strange characters, whom his philanthropic peculiarities induced him to countenance. The death of C. Lamb himself was doubtless hastened by his sorrow for that of Coleridge to whom he had been attached from the time of their being school-fellows at Christ's Hospital. Lamb was a good Latin scholar and probably would have gone to college upon one of the school foundations if it had not been for the impediment in his speech. Had such been his lot he would have probably been preserved from the indulgences of social humours and fancies which were often injurious to himself and causes of severe regret to his friends without really benefiting the object of his misapplied kindness." (*FNW*, pp. 58, 164–165.) WW dated the poem 1835 in 1836 and subsequent editions.

MW's sending the text to TNT around but by January 13, 1836, probably indicates that by this time an agreement had been made with TNT to include WW's monody in an edition of CL's letters that he was then preparing for publication by EM. *Letters of Charles Lamb*, containing the monody, eventually appeared in 1837. WW wrote to TNT in April 1836, "I wrote twice to Mr Moxon not long ago, through a sort of private channel and am not sure as I have not heard from him since that my last Letter has reached him. One of them contained corrections of the Verses upon Lamb, which I wished to be looked to when the Lines were printed in your Work. They are a written down on the other leaf" (WW to TNT, April 16, 1836, *LY*, III, 200). The "other leaf" has been detached and has not been traced.

23 "This way of indicating the *name* of my lamented friend has been found fault with, [with; *1845–*] perhaps rightly so; but I may say in justification of the double sense of the word, that similar allusions are not uncommon in epitaphs. One of the best in our language in verse, I ever read, was upon a person who bore the name of Pilgrim, [Palmer, *MS. 1836/45 (in pencil), 1840–1843* Palmer; *1845–*] and the course of the thought, throughout, turned upon the Life of the Departed, considered as a pilgrimage. Nor can I think that the objection in the present case will have much force with any one who remembers Charles Lamb's beautiful sonnet addressed to his own name, and ending—

'No deed of mine shall shame thee, gentle name!'" *1836–, but no single close quot in last line 1839, 1841–1843, 1846, 1849*

Knight (*PW*, VIII, 19 [1896]) cites a fifteenth-century epitaph from a transcription by John Weever (1576–1632), *Epigrams in the Oldest Cut* (1599):

Palmers all our faders were;
I, a *Palmer* livyd here
And travyld still till worne with age,
I endyd this world's pylgramage,
On the blyst assention day
In the cherful month of May;
A thousand wyth fowre hundryd seven,
And took my jorney hense to heven.

Also noticed by HR in a modernized form (*The Complete Poetical Works of William Wordsworth*, ed. Henry Reed [Philadelphia, 1852], p. 467).

46–47 WW's letter to EM, February 8, 1836, cites only the first words of the original line, "Aptly received etc." and does not show how l. 46 stood at this stage.

50 scorner of the fields] EdeS (*PW*, IV, 459) notes Lamb's letter to WW (January 30, 1801) in which he declined WW's invitation to visit Grasmere; Lamb wrote, "separate from the pleasure of your company, I don't much care if I never see a mountain in my life" (*The Letters of Charles Lamb to which are added those of his sister Mary Lamb*, ed. E. V. Lucas [3 vols.; London, 1835], I, 241).

56 peculiar sanctity] A phrase used in *Excursion*, VII, 479 (EdeS).

62–64 The quoted words are from II Samuel 1:26.

100–102 WW first deleted l. 100 then restored a revised version of these lines in his letters to EM around February 5 and on February 8, 1836 (*LY*, III, 163–165). In the first letter he asked EM to "replace" the lines (*i.e.*, "restore" them). In the letter of February 8, in again asking that the lines be restored, WW indicated he wanted l. 101 to read "through" not "and," a change he later rescinded by further revision (see the verbal variants to the reading text, above). He explained the change from "Still were they" to "Still they were" by his wishing to avoid repeating "the previous *inversion* of 'were they'" in l. 98 (*LY*, III, 165).

128 *dual* loneliness] Cf. Lamb, *Mackery End*: "We house together, old bachelor and maid, in a sort of double singleness" (EdeS).

131/ WW affixed various forms of his signature to several texts: W. Wordsworth *Berg MS. 1* W. WORDSWORTH / 14 DOVER STREET *DC1* W. WORDSWORTH / Rydal Mount *DC1 MS.* W. WORDSWORTH *CL1, CL2* W. WORDSWORTH *del Turnbull MS.*

Extempore Effusion upon the Death of James Hogg

WW's note, first published in 1836:

Walter Scott died	21st Sept. 1832.
S. T. Coleridge	25th July, 1834.
Charles Lamb	27th Dec. 1834.
Geo. Crabbe	3rd Feb. 1832.
Felicia Hemans	16th May, 1835.

so 1836–, but Sept., Dec., Feb., *1845, 1850 and* S. T.] ST *1843 only*

In the *YR* reissue of 1839 WW presented the note thus: "*Walter Scott died 21st of Sept. 1832; S. T. Coleridge, 25th July, 1834; Charles Lamb, 27th Dec. 1834; George Crabbe, 3rd Feb. 1832; Felicia Hemans, 16th May, 1835."

James Hogg died November 21, 1835. WW sent a version of the poem in seven stanzas to John Hernaman, editor of the *Newcastle Journal*, commenting, "I send you these verses on the other page, a parting tribute of my respect, for the manner in which your journal is conducted and the great variety of solid information that it contains. . . . If you print the Verses let them by all means appear in your *next* number, and *printed correctly*, which the haste unavoidable in the bringing out of newspapers often prevents being done." The next day he wrote again, sending the three additional stanzas with instructions to print them as the conclusion to the poem: "By yesterday's post I forwarded to you a copy of Extempory verses (which thro' inadvertence were dated Dec[r] 1st instead of Nov[r] 30th) and which I will beg you, if not too late, to correct—as well as the word '*survive*', in the 7th Stanza for which pray substitute remain [remain *rev from underscored* remain]. And add to the poem the following 3 stanzas—*which were cast,* but unfinished *yesterday*; and I did not wait, not knowing if I should turn to it again in time for your next publication. If this alteration does not suit your convenience for this week, I should rather the Poem were kept back till the week following—both for the fact above stated, and because without the concluding stanz: the verses scarcely do justice to the occasion that called them forth" (Yale MS. 5). For a record of various signatures and dates see the note to l. 44/, below. WW dated the poem "Nov. 1835" in *PW,* 1836, and subsequent editions.

Herbert Hill's copy in the Southey Family Album (Southey Album 2) might be expected to derive from one of the newspaper printings, but its independent readings suggest that it was transcribed from an authorial manuscript now untraced. A copy of the poem in the hand of BF in the Berg Collection, NYPL, is addressed to "Mrs. Hughes" (the sister of WW's friend, Robert Jones) and postmarked January 30, 1837. It is without independent authority.

1, 5 When first . . . When last] See *Yarrow Visited,* recording WW's first visit to Yarrow in September, 1814, and *Yarrow Revisited,* commemorating WW's return visit there with Sir Walter Scott in the fall of 1831.

21 In the December 1 letter to Hernaman WW added a note after the signature and date below the poem: "*note*— In the above, is an expression borrowed from a Sonnet by Mr [Mr *rev from* G] G. Bell, the author of a small vol: of Poems lately printed in Penrith. Speaking of Skiddaw, he says—'yon dark cloud *rakes* and [and *rev from* to] shrouds its noble brow.' These Poems, tho' incorrect often in expression and metre do [great *del*] honour to their unpretending Author; and may be added to the number of proofs, daily occurring, that a finer perception of appearances of Nature is spreading thro' the humbler classes of Society.—"

"*Note.*— In the above is an expression borrowed from a Sonnet by Mr. G. Bell, the Author of a small volume of Poems lately printed at Penrith. Speaking of Skiddaw, he says, 'Yon dark cloud *rakes* and shrouds its noble brow.' these Poems [poems *Atheneum*], though incorrect often in expression and metre, do honour to their unpretending Author; and may be added to the number of proofs daily occurring, that a finer perception of the appearances of Nature is spreading through the humbler Classes of Society [classes of society *Atheneum*]." *Newcastle Journal, Atheneum.*

29–32 In a letter to EM (December 6, 1835; Huntington MS. 2) WW suggested that it "might be a question for criticism whether the Stanza beginning 'Our haughty life' should not be separated from the foregoing either by asterisks or a break, as if it were the beginning of [a] 2^{d} Fit or Part of the same lyric effusion" (*LY,* III, 131).

31 WW introduced a version of this line in the canceled draft of the final stanza in Yale MS. 4 (see the verbal variants to ll. 41–43 of the reading text).

37–40 In his letter to Robert Percival Graves, enclosing the poem, WW wrote, "To save you the trouble of hunting for the verse, I have sent them transcribed, with the stanza given to the memory of our lamented Friend." Opposite this stanza in his copy, Herbert Hill noted: "Mrs Hemans is meant" (Southey Family Album).

44 Note WW's entry beneath the last line in Houghton MS. 2, "quere Poet." Either his revision of "Poet" to "Shepherd" in this manuscript followed his query, or he contemplated changing back to "Poet." In Yale MS. 5 WW rewrote the last line (see the *apparatus*), as he said, "to prevent a mistake." Beneath the text in editions from 1836 WW inserted a reference to the note at the back of the volume ("*See Note.").

44/ WW affixed various forms of his signature and date to several texts: Wm Wordsworth / Rydal Mount / Novr 1st 1835 *Yale MS. 4* Wm Wordsworth / Rydal Mount / Novr 30th *Yale MS. 5* Rydal Mount, Nov. 30, 1835. WM. WORDSWORTH. *Newcastle Journal* Wm. Wordsworth. / Rydal Mount, Nov. 30, 1835. *Atheneum* Park street May 29th —36 Wm Wordsworth *Berg MS. 2*

At the Grave of Burns. 1803

"*At the grave of Burns* To be printed among the poems relating to my first tour in Scotland. For illustration see my Sister's journal. It may be proper to add that the second of these pieces tho' *felt* at the time was not composed till many years after." (*FNW*, p. 63; see also pp. 169–170.)

WW conceived the poem while visiting Burns's grave on August 18, 1803, during his tour of Scotland with DW, or shortly thereafter, and completed it in a three-stanza version between late March 1804 and early 1807. He titled it "Ejaculation at the Grave of Burns" and included it in the sequence Scotland 1803 in a copy he was preparing for the printer of his *Poems, in Two Volumes*, 1807, but deleted it before sending off the manuscript. Many years later, as he explained in a letter to EM, December 10, 1835, "The verses upon dear Lamb ["To a good Man of most dear memory," pp. 291–305], threw my mind into that train of melancholy reflexion which produced several things in some respects of the same character, such as those lines upon Hogg and some others brought forth with more reflexion and pains—for on turning over an old vol: of Mss, I met with some verses that expressed my feelings at the Grave of Burns 32 years ago. These I was tempted to retouch, and not only added to them, but threw off another piece, which is a record of what passed in my mind when I was in sight of his residence on the banks of the Nith, at the same period. So that I have to the best of my power done my duty to that great, but like many of his Brother Bards, unhappy man" (WW to EM, December 10, 1835; *LY*, III, 135 and note). A year later he considered adding this poem and its sequel, *Thoughts Suggested the Day Following on the Banks of the Nith, Near the Poet's Residence*, to his other poems associated with the tour that DW had incorporated in her *Recollections of a Tour Made in Scotland*, and invited EM to prepare estimates for printing his sister's journal, thus augmented. But as he told HCR in December 1837, he saw no hope that her taking part in seeing it through the press would be "a *profitable* stirring of her mind, at all," and as this hope was his "only inducement to undertake the experiment" he abandoned the plan (*LY*, III, 495 and 496n).

The first, second and penultimate stanzas of the augmented *At the Grave of Burns. 1803* are based on the earlier *Ejaculation*. For that earlier version, and its less conventional view of the grave as a place "of silent peace, and 'friendly aid,'" see *Poems, 1800–1807*, pp. 534–535. Since the printer's copy sent to Longman, the publisher of *Poems, in Two Volumes*, was never again in WW's possession, the "old vol: of Mss" that he perused in 1835, if it still survives, is one that has not been identified. See the headnote and notes to the sequel, *Thoughts Suggested the Day Following on the Banks of the Nith, Near the Poet's Residence*, also presumably conceived in 1803 but wholly composed at the later time.

1–12, 73–78 An early version of these three stanzas was entered in the printer's copy for *Poems, in Two Volumes*, 1807 (the Longman MS.), under the title "Ejaculation at the Grave of Burns." It was deleted before the manuscript was sent off (see *Poems, 1800–1807*, pp. 534–535, 534n, 548, and 553).

20 "glinted" forth] EdeS identified the allusion to Burns, *To a Mountain Daisy*, l. 15:

Yet cheerfully thou glinted forth
Amid the storm.

39 Mount Criffel (in Dumfries) is the "Scruffel" of Drayton's lines quoted in WW's note to *Thoughts Suggested the Day Following on the Banks of Nith, Near the Poet's Residence*, given below.

40 Neighbours we were] Cf. WW quotation from DW's journal of the tour in his note to *Thoughts Suggested the Day Following* (given below).

50 "poor Inhabitant below"] From Burns, *A Bard's Epitaph*, l. 19 (EdeS).

62 Refers to the period when WW and DW stood beside Burns's grave (see WW's note to *Thoughts Suggested the Day Following*).

77–78 Receive thy Spirit in the embrace / For which it prayed!] Below analogous lines in the copy of the three stanzas that appear in the Longman MS. is the note "See in his poem *The Ode to Ruin*." WW refers to ll. 15–28 of *To Ruin*, in which the poet prays to the "grim Pow'r" to "close this scene of care," when there will be

No fear more, no tear more,
To stain my lifeless face,
Enclasped, and grasped,
Within thy cold embrace!

Thoughts Suggested the Day Following on the Banks of Nith, Near the Poet's Residence

For the idea for the poem, conceived on August 18, 1803, and its date of composition, see the note to *At the Grave of Burns. 1803*, above. See also the entry for Princeton MS. 4 in the Manuscript Census, p. lxxvi. For poems composed in the same "train of melancholy reflection" (*LY*, III, 135), see *At the Grave of Burns. 1803* (see also the note to this poem, above) and the two elegies, "To a good Man of most dear memory" (*Written After the Death of Charles Lamb*) and *Extempore Effusion upon the Death of James Hogg*.

"The following is extracted from the journal of my fellow-traveller, to which, as persons acquainted with my poems will know, I have been obliged on other occasions:—

'Dumfries, August 1803.

'On our way to the church-yard where Burns is buried, we were accompanied by a bookseller, who showed us the outside of Burns's house, where he had lived the last three years of his life, and where he died. It has a mean appearance, and is in a bye situation; the front whitewashed; dirty about the doors, as most Scotch houses are; flowering plants in the window. Went to visit his grave; he lies in a corner of the churchyard, and his second son, Francis Wallace, beside him. There is no stone to mark the spot; but a hundred guineas have been collected to be expended upon some sort of monument. "There," said the bookseller, pointing to a pompous monument, "lies Mr.—(I have forgotten the name)—a remarkably clever man; he was an attorney, and scarcely ever lost a cause he undertook. Burns made many a lampoon upon him, and there they rest as you see." We looked at Burns's grave with melancholy and painful reflections, repeating to each other his own poet's epitaph:—

"Is there a man, &c.

'The churchyard is full of grave-stones and expensive monuments, in all sorts of fantastic shapes—obelisk-wise, pillar-wise, &c. When our guide had left us we turned again to Burns's grave, and afterwards went to his house, wishing to inquire after Mrs. Burns, who was gone to spend some time by the sea-shore with her children. We spoke to the maid-servant at the door, who invited us forward, and we sate down in the parlour. The walls were coloured with a blue wash; on one side of the fire was a mahogany desk; opposite the window a clock, which Burns mentions in one of his letters having received as a present. The house was cleanly and neat in the inside, the stairs of stone scoured white, the kitchen on the right side of the passage, the parlour on the left. In the room above the parlour the poet died, and his son very lately, in the same room. The servant told us she had lived four years with Mrs. Burns, who was now in great sorrow for the death of Wallace. She said that Mrs. B.'s youngest son was now at Christ's Hospital. We were glad to leave Dumfries, where we could think of little but poor Burns, and his moving about on that unpoetic ground. In our road to Brownhill, the next stage, we passed Ellisland, at a little distance on our right—his farm-house. Our pleasure in looking round would have been still greater, if the road had led us nearer the spot.

* * * * * *

'I cannot take leave of this country which we passed through to-day, without mentioning that we saw the Cumberland mountains within half-a-mile of Ellisland, Burns's house, the last view we had of them. Drayton has prettily described the connexion which this neighbourhood has with ours, when he makes Skiddaw say,—

"Scruffel, from the sky

> That Annandale doth crown, with a most amorous eye
> Salutes me every day, or at my pride looks grim,
> Oft threatening me with clouds, as I oft threaten him."

'These lines came to my brother's memory, as well as the Cumberland saying,—

> "If Skiddaw hath a cap,
> Scruffell wots well of that."

'We talked of Burns, and of the prospect he must have had, perhaps from his own door, of Skiddaw and his companions, indulging ourselves in the fancy that we might have been personally known to each other, and he have looked upon those objects with more pleasure for our sakes.'" *PELY.*

The notation "MS." in the variants that are listed below indicates MW's corrected copy in DC MS. 151.2 (123^{r}–124^{r}), the printer's copy for *PELY.*

l. 2 persons] Persons *MS.* know,] know *1849P* occasions:—] occasions. *MS.* *l. 4* Dumfries Aug 1803— *MS.* *ital 1850* August] August, *1845–* *l. 5* our *rev from* Our *MS.* church-yard] Church yeard *MS.* churchyard *1850* *l. 6* bookseller,] bookseller *MS.* *l. 8* situation;] situation, *MS.* doors,] doors *MS.* *l. 10* son, Francis Wallace,] son Francis Wallace *MS.* him. There] him; there *MS.* *l. 11* upon *rev from* on *MS.* There,] There *MS.* *l. 13* man; he] man. He *MS.* *l. 14* attorney,] attorney *MS.* *l. 16* own poet's epitaph:—] own verses *rev to* own Poets Epitaph *MS.* *l. 17* Is there a Man &c *MS.* &c.] &c." *1850* *l. 18* monuments,] monuments *MS.* *l. 19* shapes—] shapes, *MS.* *l. 20* grave,] grave; *MS.* wishing to inquire after *inserted MS.* *l. 23* wash;] wash, *MS.* *l. 24* desk;] desk, *MS.* mentions in one of his letters] mentions, . . . letters, *MS., 1845–* *l. 28* servant] Servant *MS.* *l. 29* son] Son *MS.* *ll. 33–34 last sentence rev from* We might there have had more pleasure in looking round if we had been nearer the spot *MS.* *l. 35* through to-day,] thro' to day *MS.* *l. 36* half-a-mile] half a mile *MS.* *l. 41* grim,] grim *MS.* *l. 47* companions,] companions; *1845–1849* companions: *1850* we *rev from* he *MS.* sakes.] sakes! *MS.*

To MS. 151.1 WW added a long note—in three versions, C, D, and E—that, in the end, he did not publish. He evidently first intended this note to the two tributes to Burns to be printed immediately below the text of *Thoughts Suggested the Day Following*. . . (see the note to ll. 55–66, below). As the original version C differs substantially from the next full version D, a transcription of C is given first, followed by a clean reading text of D with all its variants and the verbal variants of the incomplete version E recorded in the *apparatus* attached to it.

[recto]
In connection with the two preceding Poems the
Reader may be referred to the "Address to the
Sons of Burns, after visiting their Father's Grave.
(see Wordsworth's Poems vol)
I became acquainted
almost
with the Poems of Burns ^ immediately upon the
appearance of the vol: printed at Kilmarnock
1796. Their effect upon my mind has been

[verso]
{expressed {. ~~M~~} F}
sufficiently {spoken above {, ~~& m y~~ f} amiliarity
with the dialect of the border counties of Cumb^{d}
& West^{d} made it easy for me not only to un-
derstand/ but to feel them. It was not so with

his contemporary or rather his Predecessor
Cowper; ~~this is to be regretted,~~ as appears from
this is to be regretted ~~since~~ for
L} {. {the
one of his l} etters{, ^ the simplicity {& truth ~~of Burns~~ &
notwithstanding occasional coarseness
would have strongly recommended him ^ to the sympathies
& the vigour of Burns of Cowper &
~~judgement of his distinguished Contemporary~~ and
insured the approval of his judgement
~~rather Predecessor, for the Task appeared earlier~~
~~than the poems of Burns.~~ It gives me pleasure
venial I trust to acknowledge, [?~~there~~]
~~pardonable, I trust~~ ^ at this late day, my obliga-
whose writings
tions to these two great Authors ^ in conjunction
with Percy's Reliques, powerfully counteracted
influence
the mischievous ~~effect~~ of Darwin's dazzling mann[ ]
extravagance of Schiller's
y
& the ^ earl~~ier productions of Schiller~~ & other
dramas
up
German writers, ^ on my taste & natural tendencies.
M}
~~&~~ m} ay these few words serve as a warning
are in danger
of {ing {enticed
to Youthful Poets who ~~may~~ be{ {carried
away by the inundation of foreign literature
own
from which our ~~native genius~~ is at present
suffering so much, both in style & points of far
greater moment. True it is that in the poems of Burns himself,
as now collected, are too many reprehensible passages; but their
immorality is rather the ebulition of natural temperament & a humour
of levity than a studied thing: whereas in those foreign writers against
others in our ~~English~~
which I ~~here~~ protest, & in ~~an~~ eminent ~~deceased~~ ^ ~~Poet of~~ our own
age the evil, whether of impiety or licentiousness, is courted upon system [?&]
& country
therefore it is greater, & less pardonable.—

In the last sentence of this version (ll. 48–56) WW probably contrasts Burns with Byron (no doubt the poet described as "an eminent deceased English Poet of our own age," among others. Before revision he acknowledged Thomas Percy's *Reliques of Ancient English Poetry* (3 vols.; London, 1765), with Burns's poems (*Poems, Chiefly in the Scottish Dialect* [Kilmarnock, 1786]), as having "powerfully counteracted the mischievous influence" of Erasmus Darwin and Schiller. The revised version D reads as follows:

"In connection with the two preceding Poems the Reader may be referred to the 'Address to the Sons of Burns, after visiting their Father's Grave.' (See Wordsworth's Poems Vol [ ])

"With the Poems of Burns I became acquainted almost immediately upon their first appearance in the volume printed at Kilmarnock in 17[8]6. Their effect upon my mind has been sufficiently expressed above. Familiarlity with the dialect of the border Counties of Cumb^{d} and West^{d} made it easy for me not only to understand but to feel them. It was not so with his Contemporary or rather his Predecessor Cowper,—as appears from one of his letters. This is to be regretted; for the simplicity the truth and the vigour of Burns would have strongly recommended him, notwithstanding occasional coarseness, to the sympathies of Cowper, and ensured the approval of his judgement. It gives me pleasure, venial I trust, to acknowledge at this late day, my obligations to these two great Authors, both then and at a later period, when my taste and natural tendencies were under an injurious influence from the dazzling manner of Darw[i]n, and the extravagance of the earlier Dramas of Schiller and that of other German Writers. May these few words serve as a warning to youthful Poets who are in danger of being carried away by the inundation of foreign Literature, from which our own is at present suffering so much, both in style and points of far greater moment. True it is that in the poems of Burns, as now collected, are too many reprehensible passages; but their immorality is rather the ebulition of natural temperament and a humour of levity, than a studied thing: whereas in those foreign Writers, and in some of our own Country not long deceased, the evil, whether of voluptuousness, impiety, or licentiousness, is courted upon system, and therefore it is greater, and less pardonable."

l. 2 Grave.'] Grave. *D* their *rev from* the *D* *l.* 5 first *inserted D* in *rev from* of *D* 1796 *for* 1786 *D* Their *rev from* their *D* *l.* 8 It was not so with [Cowper, *del by JC*] *D* Cowper,— *inserted by JC D* *E, which is incomplete, begins* for the Task appeared earlier than the poems of Burns. *l.* 9 letters. This *rev from* letters, this *D* regretted; *rev from* regretted, *D* simplicity [*comma deleted*] *D* *l.* 12 venial . . . acknowledge] pardonable I trust at this late day to acknowledge *rev to* pardonable I trust to acknowledge at this late day *E* *ll.* 13–16 both . . . Writers. *rev by JC (through* Schiller*) and MW from* whose writings, in conjunction with Percy's Reliques, powerfully counter-acted the mischievous influence of Darwin's dazzling manner, and the extavagance of Schiller's dramas and other German Writers upon my taste and natural tendencies. *D* whose work in conjunction with Percy's Reliques powerfully counteracted the mischievous effect of Darwin's dazzling manner [Darwin's . . . manner *rev from* Darwin], and the early productions of Schiller and other German writers on my taste and natural tendencies *E* *l.* 15 Darw[i]n] Darwen *D* *l.* 16 Writers. May] tendencies—and may *E* few words *over illegible word or words D* *l.* 17 in danger of being] may be *E* *l.* 18 from *rev from* to *E* our own] natural genius *inserted after* own *then del E* is at present *rev from* is *E* points *rev from* matters *E* *l.* 19 that in [*with* in *inserted*] *D* poems] Poems *rev from* writings *E* as *rev to* namely as *E* *l.* 20 reprehensible *inserted E* passages] passages [favorable to the indulgence of per-[?eril] *del*] *E* *l.* 21 temperament] character *alt* temperament *E* and a humour of levity, *lacking E* thing: whereas in] thing. In *rev to* thing. Whereas in *E* *l.* 22 Writers . . . the evil,] Writers whom I want to guard against in one [? ?] at least or two [?] of our own the immorality *rev to* Writers Against whom I here protest and in an eminent deceased Poet of our own age the evil *E* Country *rev to* Age *rev to* Country *D* *ll.* 22–23 whether of . . . or] whether of the nature of impiety or licenciousness *E* *l.* 23 voluptuousness, *inserted D* *ll.* 23–24 system . . . pardonable.] system *E*

5 faultered] An old spelling kept through all lifetime editions.

25–30 WW and DW had read Burns's *Poems, chiefly in the Scottish Dialect* (Kilmarnock, 1786) by December 1787 (*EY*, p. 13).

39–42 WW may allude to ll. 61–64, 73–78 of Burns's *Epistle to J. L[aprai]k, An Old Scotch Bard* (EdeS).

55–66 In his letter to HR, December 23, 1839, WW included these lines, remarking that "The other day I chanced to be looking over a MS poem belonging to the year 1803—tho' not actually composed till many years afterwards. It was suggested by visiting the neighbourhood of Dumfries, in which Burns had resided and where he died; it concluded thus [ll. 55–60]. Here the verses closed, but I instantly added the other day [ll. 61–66]. The more I reflect upon this last exclamation, the more I feel and perhaps it may in some degree be the same with you, justified in attaching comparatively small importance to any literary monument that I [have been, or *del*] may be enabled to leave behind. It is well however I am convinced that men think otherwise in the earlier part of their lives, and why it is so is a point I need not touch upon in writing to you" (WL Letters; *LY*, III, 751–752).

61–66 WW did not add the final stanza to the poem until around but by December 23, 1839, when he sent a copy of it to HR (*LY*, III, 752; see note to ll. 55–66). Along the inner margin opposite l. 64 in MS. 151.1 (A), MW has written "And of some not long deceased," which is probably her own commentary (referring to the recent deaths of CL, STC, Sir Walter Scott, James Hogg, George Crabbe, and Felicia Hemans; see the note to *Extempore Effusion on the Death of James Hogg*, p. 469) but may be the first (or second or fifth) line of another stanza left unfinished.

61–66 The fragmentary Princeton MS. 4 was cut from a larger sheet as a gift for a visitor to Rydal Mount. At the top edge are ll. 59–60 followed by a heavily drawn line, suggesting that the poem ended at that point. Below the line, also in WW's hand but in different ink, is the draft of an additional stanza and a recasting of the two dimiter lines in trimeter (recorded in the *apparatus*).

66/ A date is affixed to several forms of the text: 1803 *MSS. 143, 151.1 (A, C) but del in 151.1 (A)* 1803 *del MS. 151.2* Rydal Mount/ 12th Dec[r] 1835. *Laing MS.*

In MS. 151.2 "See Notes at the end of the Volume." appears below the text. In MS. 1842P "Notes" was revised to "Note" and *PELY* printed the revised MS. 1842P text. In editions from 1845 the annotation became simply "See note."

A Night Thought

"These verses were thrown off extempore upon leaving M[rs]. Luff's house at Fox Ghyll one evening. The good woman is not disposed to look at the bright side of things, and there happened to be present certain ladies who had reached the point of life where *youth* is ended and who seemed to contend with each other in expressing their dislike of the country and the climate. One of them had been heard to say she could not endure a country where there was 'neither sunshine nor Cavaliers.'" (*FNW*, p. 66; see also p. 173.)

In MS. 1836/45 JC instructed the printer to insert this poem among the Evening Voluntaries, after *Composed by the Sea-shore* ("What mischief cleaves to unsubdued regret"), and then deleted his note. In 1845 it appeared in Sentiment and Reflection.

In two manuscripts the poem was inscribed thus: W[m] Wordsworth / Upper Grosvenor Sreet / 12 June 1836 *BL MS. 2* W[m] Wordsworth / Rydal Mount / Sept 3[d]—1836 *Mary Smith Album*

On an Event in Col: Evans's redoubted performances in Spain

HCR wrote to MW (October 27, 1836), "By the bye, could you answer me a question that has been put to me more than once? Did the author of *The Excursion* ever write an Epigram?" MW replied on November 1 (or possibly on December 19), "To show you that *we* can write an Epigram—we do not say a good one," and after transcribing the epigram, she added, "The Producer thinks it not amiss as being murmured between sleep and awake over the fire while thinking of you last night!" (*LY*, III, 317, 330; and see 317n and *PW*, IV, 479–480). Colonel George de Lacy Evans (1787–1870) was awarded the red ribbon of the K.C.B. for his service in Spain in August 1837. See also "Said red-ribboned Evans," below.

November, 1836 ("Even so for me a Vision sanctified")

November, 1836 was paired with "Methought I saw the footsteps of a throne" in editions from 1836, with each sonnet assigned a Roman numeral in its heading. SH fell seriously ill in May 1835 and died June 23, 1835. The IF note to "Methought I saw the footsteps of a throne" reads "The latter part of the first of these was a great favourite with my Sister Sara Hutchinson. When I saw her lying in death I could not resist the impulse to compose the Sonnet that follows." (*FNW*, p. 21.) It seems probable that the sonnet was conceived and perhaps begun at the time of her death; it was completed in November 1836, when WW was preparing copy for volume III of the 1836 collected edition (published one volume per month starting in October). Beneath the text in Hoare Album, in Sarah Hoare's hand, are the initials "SH." and the note "(Nov. 1836 Published Wks)."

1 Even so] That is, like the vision of the paired sonnet, "Methought I saw the footsteps of a throne" (see *Poems, 1800–1807*, pp. 148–149).

4 The Hoare Album reading makes sense if "becomes" is taken as a mistranscription of "become": "those" refers back to "countenance" and "mien" in l. 3.

The Widow on Windermere Side

"*The Widow on Winandermere side.* The facts recorded in this Poem were given me and the Character of the person described by my highly esteemed friend the Rev[d] R. P. Graves who has long officiated as Curate at Bowness to the great benefit of the parish and neighbourhood. The individual was well known to him. She died before these verses were composed. It is scarcely worth while to notice that the Stanzas are written in the Sonnet-form which was adopted when I thought the matter might be included in 28 lines." (*FNW*, p. 75.) "Winandermere" is an old form of "Windermere" (see *Prelude*, II, 138, and *The Eclipse of the Sun, 1820*, l. 75). Notes to the reading text of 1842 follow:

19 The variant from MS. 151.1 (F)—"resplent"—is a miswriting of "resplendent."

41 ecstacies] WW consistently spelled the word thus.

To the Planet Venus, upon its Approximation (as an Evening Star) to the Earth, January 1838

Though visible on the southern horizon through most of December 1837, in January 1838 Venus was a prominent object in the evening sky, by this date setting later than the sun and thus growing in brightness with each passing day ("brightening still," l. 2). Watching the sky over successive evenings in January, WW observed the Evening Star's "approximation to the Earth" as its orbit swung the planet closer and closer to the earth (ll. 2–3). The date of composition, then, is probably mid to late January 1838.

Wouldst Thou be gathered to Christ's chosen flock

For the probable date of composition, see the headnote to the poem. WW left the poem untitled; the now familiar title *Inscription on a Rock at Rydal Mount* was supplied by EdeS (*PW*, IV, 389).

Oh what a Wreck! how changed in mien and speech!

The personal reading "for her brain" in l. 3 of the manuscript became "for the brain" in 1838–1840 and finally a more generalized "of the brain" when WW reprinted the sonnet in 1842.

Valedictory Sonnet ("Serving no haughty Muse, my hands have here")

In MS. 147, which is labeled "*Private* Memorials / not to be *printed*," a version of this poem, titled "Concluding Sonnet," occupies the final position; below the last line the copyist has entered "The End" (see the Manuscript Census). The earliest sonnet in the collection was composed in 1834, the latest in February 1840. *Valedictory Sonnet* was probably composed specifically to close the volume of sonnets published in 1838. Six sonnets follow it in that volume, "composed," WW reported in a note, "as this Volume was going through the Press, but too late for insertion in the class of miscellaneous ones, to which they belong" (*Sonnets*, 1838). However, *Valedictory Sonnet* is printed in the same signature with them and was probably composed at the same time and sent with them to the printer while the printing was in process, perhaps as late as June 1838, before WW set off for a tour (*LY*, III, 618), but probably sometime in April or May (see Appendix II). The *Publisher's Circular* of August 1, 1838, lists WW's *Sonnets* among works published July 16–31.

A copy of *Poems*, 1845, was listed by David L. O'Neal, Antiquarian Booksellers, Inc., 263 Elm Hill Rd., Peterborough, New Hampshire 03458, in Catalog 38, March 1981 (item 143). The entry notes that lines 11–14 are inscribed on the endpaper in WW's hand, and signed, "William Wordsworth/Rydal Mount/1st Febry 1847" with no verbal variants. The volume has not been traced.

Said red-ribbon'd Evans

For Evans see *On an Event in Col: Evans's redoubted performances in Spain.* Evans raised WW's ire as a radical member of Parliament since 1833, and a strong supporter of the Reform Bill. WW prefaced his transcription of the poem by saying "You know of old my partiality for Evans the Squib below I let off immediately upon reading his modest self-defence speech the other day," and added after the copy, "One memorable stanza of the above is rather difficult to decypher, here you have it again—" (followed by ll. 9–12 recopied; see *LY*, III, 543 and note). As EdeS and Helen Darbishire have pointed out, WW's unjust attacks on Evans, here and in *On an Event in Col: Evans's redoubted performances in Spain*, were motivated by political prejudice (*PW*, IV, 480).

13, 15 Fontarabbia . . . Hernani] Evans and his forces were defeated at these locations in late 1836. He recaptured both in May 1837.

Hark! 'tis the Thrush, undaunted, undeprest

WW wrote to TNT on April 18, 1838, "I send you a sonnet which I threw off last Sunday evening almost extempore"; in the same letter he asked TNT to "shew the above, with my best regards, to Mrs Talfourd. It will be printed in the Volume now going through the press, consisting of all the sonnets I have written" (*LY*, III, 555). On the same day MW wrote to the Hutchinsons: "I will transcribe a sonnet which W^m^ after being in a poorly uncomfortable way all the day—(the day on which I forwarded my last to Dora) composed, almost extempore—some of the expressions he softened—otherwise it was not the labor of more than an hour, if so much—A proof I think that age is not making the havoc with him as he seems to apprehend" (WL MS.; see *MWL*, p. 209). MW refers to a letter to Dora W that she began on April 4 and completed on Easter Sunday, April 8 (*MWL*, p. 204–208). In WW's letter to TNT quoted above, by "last Sunday evening" he means what we would now call "the Sunday before last." This surmise is confirmed by the several transcriptions of the sonnet, which are variously inscribed: WW. Easter Sunday *WW to TNT* Wm Wordsworth / Rydal Mount, / Easter Sunday 1838 *Cornell MS. 10* Rydal Mount Easter / Monday Evening / 1838 *BL MS. 4* William Wordsworth / Rydal Mount / Easter Sunday Evening / 1838 *Ransom MS.* Rydal Mount, 1838 *Yale Sonnets MS.*

"Hark! 'tis the Thrush, undaunted, undeprest" is one of the six sonnets printed after *Valedictory Sonnet* in *Sonnets* (1838); see the note to *Valedictory Sonnet*, above. For WW's unrealized plan to include this sonnet, with other poems, in a set of "Morning Voluntaries," see his IF note to *Composed upon an Evening of Extraordinary Splendour and Beauty*, one of the Evening Voluntaries (*FNW*, p. 56). See also the note to *Composed on the Same Morning*, p. 480, below.

'Tis He whose yester-evening's high disdain

One of the sonnets printed after *Valedictory Sonnet* in *Sonnets*, 1838, "'Tis He whose yester-evening's high disdain" was probably composed between about April 9 and mid-

May (see the notes to *Valedictory Sonnet* and "Hark! 'tis the Thrush, undaunted, undeprest," above).

A Plea for Authors, May, 1838

The date of composition is probably that given in the title. WW was in correspondence with TNT concerning the progress through Parliament of his new Copyright Bill, written November 22, 1837. He provided TNT with "notices" in its favor and wrote "scarcely less than 50 letters" in support to Members of Parliament and others during the early part of 1838. On April 12 of that year the *Kendal Mercury* published WW's letter to the editor in support of the Copyright Bill, and on April 18 WW sent TNT a letter "in favour of [the Bill's] principles" that TNT then published in *MP* on April 23 (*LY,* III, 498, 553, 556–558; *Prose,* III, 309–314; for WW's renewed interest in *MP* and its editorial views at this time, see Alan G. Hill, "Wordsworth, William Johnston, and the Table Talker of the *Morning Post*: an Unpublished Wordsworth Letter," *RES,* n.s., 3 [1997]: 205–210). The Copyright Act was passed in 1842.

A Plea for Authors is one of the six sonnets printed after *Valedictory Sonnets* in *Sonnets* (1838); see the note to *Valedictory Sonnet,* above.

Protest Against the Ballot. 1838

In Yale MS. 7 *Protest Against the Ballot. 1838* is inscribed "May 1838." WW published the sonnet and a note to it at the end of Miscellaneous Sonnets in *Sonnets,* 1838. The note contained a second sonnet, "Said Secrecy to Cowardice and Fraud." *Protest Against the Ballot* was included, with its note, in the appendix to *PW,* 1840 (see Appendix II). WW did not reprint *Protest Against the Ballot* again, but he later included "Said Secrecy to Cowardice and Fraud" in the sonnet sequence Liberty and Order first published in 1845. The 1838 note, with printed variants through 1840, is reported below.

"Having in this notice alluded only in general terms to the mischief which, in my opinion, the Ballot would bring along with it, without especially branding its immoral and anti-social tendency, (for which no political advantages, were they a thousand times greater than those presumed upon, could be a compensation,) I have been impelled to subjoin a reprobation of it upon that score. In no part of my writings have I mentioned the name of any co[n]temporary, that of Buonaparte only excepted, but for the purpose of eulogy; and therefore, as in the concluding verse of what follows, there is a deviation from this rule (for the blank will be easily filled up) I have excluded the Sonnet from the body of the collection, and placed it here as a public record of my detestation, both as a man and a citizen, of the proposed contrivance:—

Said Secrecy to Cowardice and Fraud,
Falsehood and Treachery, in close council met,
Deep under ground, in Pluto's cabinet,
'The frost of England's pride will soon be thawed;
'Hooded the open brow that overawed
'Our schemes; the faith and honour, never yet
'By us with hope encountered, be upset;—
'For once I burst my bands, and cry, applaud!'
Then whispered she, 'The Bill is carrying out!'
They heard, and, starting up, the Brood of Night
Clapped hands, and shook with glee their matted locks;
All Powers and Places that abhor the light
Joined in the transport, echoed back their shout,
Hurrah for ———, hugging his Ballot-box!"

The sonnet appeared thus in *1838, 1840.* In *MS. 1838/40* WW revised "proposed contrivance" to "skulking contrivance"; *1840* corrected "contemporary" from misprinted "cotemporary" (*Sonnets,* 1838). "Said Secrecy" was composed around February or March

1838, but by March 10, when WW sent a copy to his nephew John with these remarks, "I have sent you a sonnet which I shall not print in my collection, because my poems are wholly as I wish them to continue, without *personalities* of a vituperative character" (*LY*, III, 530). He offered the sonnet to John to send it to the *Cantabridge Chronicle* "without a name," but it did not appear there. George Grote (1794–1871), a well-known advocate of the ballot, is the target of the last line of the sonnet (so identified in another copy that WW sent to Dora W in February–March 1838; see *LY*, III, 525 and note).

Composed on the Same Morning

In BL MS. 4 the poem is inscribed "May-morn[g] 1838."

First published among the six sonnets printed after *Valedictory Sonnet* in *Sonnets*, 1838, where it was paired with *Composed on May-Morning, 1838* ("If with old love of you, dear Hills! I share"), *Composed on the Same Morning* ("Life with yon Lambs") was included (with "If with old love") among Miscellaneous Sonnets in *PELY* (1842). In 1843 at the end of his IF note to Evening Voluntaries WW added, "In concluding my notices of this class of Poems it may be as well to observe that among the Miscellaneous Sonnets are a few alluding to morning impressions which might be read with mutual benefit in connection with these Evening Voluntaries. See for example that one on Westminster Bridge—that 1st on May, 2[d]. on the song of the Thrush and the one beginning 'While beams of orient light'." (*FNW*, p. 56.) The "1st on May" appears to refer to *Composed on May-Morning, 1838* ("If with old love") and perhaps by implication, *Composed on the Same Morning* ("Life with yon Lambs"). However, "Life with yon Lambs" found its place alone, under the title *Composed on a May-Morning, 1838*, in the Miscellaneous Sonnets in the collected works in 1845 and 1850, while the similarly titled "If with old love," a reminiscence of WW's visit to Italy the previous spring, was placed in Italy 1837 as *Composed at Rydal on May Morning, 1838* in 1845 and 1850. See also the notes to "Hark! 'tis the Thrush, undaunted, undeprest" and *Valedictory Sonnet*, above, and Appendix II, below.

1–14 The base text in MS. 140 (19[r]) is in MW's hand; revisions are in WW's hand.

A Poet to His Grandchild. (Sequel to the foregoing.)

WW included the poem, immediately following *A Plea for Authors. May, 1838*, among the six sonnets printed after *Valedictory Sonnet* in *Sonnets*, 1838, and in the appendix in volume five of *PW*, 1840, in support of TNT's copyright bill, which was twice defeated. A bill protecting copyright was finally passed by Parliament in 1842; WW did not reprint *A Poet to His Grandchild. (Sequel to the Foregoing.)*. See also the notes to *Valedictory Sonnet* and "Hark! 'tis the Thrush, undaunted, undeprest," above.

4 "The author of an animated article, printed in the Law Magazine, in favour of the principle of Sergeant Talfourd's Copyright Bill, precedes me in the public expression of this feeling; which had been forced too often upon my own mind, by remembering how few descendants of men eminent in literature are even known to exist." *1838, 1840.*

Come gentle Sleep

WW's translation from the Latin of Thomas Warton, "Come gentle Sleep, Death's image tho' thou art," is written in his own hand on the second flyleaf of volume one of MS. 1836/45, WW's copy of *PW*, 1836, which he used for entering revisions for later editions. The entry was probably made before the translations from Michael Angelo transcribed below it and on the facing page, perhaps as early as September 1839 (see the note to *Two Translations from Michael Angelo*, below).

Warton's Latin text is as follows:

Somne veni! quamvis placidissima Mortis imago es,
  Consortem cupio te tamen esse tori;
Huc ades, haud abiture citò! nam sic sine vita
  Vivere quam suave est, sic sine morte mori!

The source is "Ad Somnum," quoted, and attributed to Thomas Warton the Younger, in Robert Anderson's *Complete Edition of the Poets of Great Britain* (1795), XI, 1102. WW's poem, with its Latin source, was first published by Edward Dowden in 1893 (*Poetical Works of William Wordsworth,* ed. Edward Dowden [7 vols.; London, 1893], V, 205).

Two Translations from Michael Angelo

WW transcribed these two translations of the same passage from Michael Angelo on the first and second flyleaves of volume one of MS. 1836/45, the copy of *PW,* 1836, that he used for entering revisions for later editions. Beneath the second translation WW inscribed his initials. A stanza from George Herbert's *Elixir* is transcribed on the following half title page and signed "Rydal M[t]. A.F.R. 1839."—probably Alexis Francois Rio, editor of *La Petite Chouannerie ou Histoire d'un College Breton sous l'Empire,* to which WW contributed a poem. Rio's earliest recorded meeting with WW took place at Samuel Rogers's on June 7, 1841 (*HCR Books,* II, 595), but the Rydal Mount Visitors Book records a visit from RMM in September 1839; RMM also contributed to Rio's anthology and may have introduced Rio to WW at this time. See the note to *The Eagle and the Dove.*

First published by Edward Dowden in 1893 (*Poetical Works of William Wordsworth,* ed. Edward Dowden [7 vols.; London, 1893], V, 206).

With a Small Present

EdeS suggested that *With a Small Present* was written at the same time as "The Crescent Moon, the Star of Love," which appears on the same page of MS. 151 and is dated February 25, 1841. But the autograph manuscript (Betz MS. 2) supplies the correct date in its inscription: "Wm Wordsworth / Ambleside Sept[br] 1839."

A sad and lovely face, with upturn'd eyes

On its publication in *The Home Journal,* October 2, 1847, the poem was headed, "ORIGINAL SONNET BY WORDSWORTH / A valuable correspondent sends us the following exquisite sonnet, to a picture by Luca Giordano, in the Museo Borbonico, at Naples which he says he has reason to believe was never before published." Under the poem is "WILLIAM WORDSWORTH, *Rydal Mount, Westmorland, Oct.* 22, 1839." WW's tour of Italy in 1837 was the subject of his sequence Italy 1837, first published in *PELY* in 1842. The sonnets were for the most part composed between late November 1838 and February 8, 1842. It seems likely this sonnet on Lucca Giordano's painting was among them, though no manuscript copy of the poem has been found and WW never included it in the sequence.

Lo! where she stands fixed in a saint-like trance

The sonnet describes WW's response to Margaret Gillies's portrait of Dora W. During the painter's extended stay at Rydal Mount, October through December 1839, she completed portraits of MW, WW, Dora W, and IF. See *To a Painter* ("All praise the Likeness by thy skill portrayed") and *On the Same Subject* ("Though I beheld at first with blank surprise"), both on MW's portrait, and *Upon a Portrait* ("We gaze, not sad to think that we must die"), on IF's portrait. It seems probable that all four sonnets were composed soon after the portraits were completed. Copies of these sonnets and three others appear in DC MS. 147, titled on the first leaf, "*Private* Memorials / not to be *printed*"; the ones on MW's portrait were certainly composed by April 1840, when DW sent copies to IF. See the note to *Valedictory Sonnet,* above, and the headnote to *To a Painter,* and *On the Same Subject.*

The portrait of Dora W, on ivory, is in the Dove Cottage Trust collection, Grasmere. A reproduction appears in Blanshard, plate 47, and in Halliday, p. 117.

To a Painter

"*To a Painter* The picture which gave occasion to this and the following Sonnet was from the pencil of Miss M. Gillies, who resided for several weeks under our roof at Rydal

Mount." (*FNW*, pp. 76–77.) For "the following Sonnet" see *On the Same Subject* ("Though I beheld at first with blank surprise"). For the dating of this sonnet, and other related matters see the headnote to *To a Painter* and *On the Same Subject*. A reproduction of the painting of William and Mary appears in Blanshard, plate 17; one of the painting of Mary alone appears in Halliday, p. 127. The portraits, both on ivory, are in the Dove CottageTrust collection, Grasmere.

On the Same Subject

For the IF note, the dating of this sonnet, and other related matters see the headnote and notes to the reading texts of *To a Painter* and *On the Same Subject*. Notes on the reading text of 1842 follow:

2–6 *On the Same Subject* appears on p. 228 of the proofs of *PELY* (DC MS. 151.3). JC has entered corrections on the proof page in two stages, first altering l. 6 and then rewriting ll. 2–6. He then copied over the first six lines on a separate sheet (228P1; the sheet is of wove stock measuring 12.4 by 15.6 cm.) that was folded and pasted to p. 228 (it is now loose). JC wrote "Please send a Revise. WW" on the front of the printed gathering.

More may not be by human Art exprest

The "Pocket Notebook" has not been located. George H. Healey, who saw the notebook in the early 1940s, dated WW's verse entries between the spring of 1839 and the spring of 1840 (*WPN*, p. 2) and identified the subject as Margaret Gillies's portrait of IF (*WPN*, p. 94), painted at Rydal Mount along with portraits of MW and Dora W around October–December 1839. Healey suggests that these two sets of verses were composed at the same time as two other poems, one on Margaret Gillies's portrait of IF, *Upon a Portrait,* and the other on IF's imminent departure, "The star which comes at close of day to shine" (see pp. 337, 338), which are dated, respectively, New Year's Day, 1840, and February, 1840 (*WPN*, pp. 91–95). A copy of the portrait is held by the Dove Cottage Trust.

Healey provides a physical description of the notebook (*WPN*, pp. 1–2), and one photograph (of text A, p. ii); his edition is our only modern record. Earlier accounts of it were published by its then owner, Richard Hall, in "An unpublished Poem of William Wordsworth," in *The Seminary Magazine* 12 (December, 1898): 113–116, and in "Items, Hitherto Unpublished from a Note Book of William Wordsworth," in *The Chimes*, [Rome, Ga.] 40 (December 1927): 5–9 (including a photograph of the outside of the notebook).

In 1945 Helen Darbishire (*PW*, III, 575) recorded the text of *Upon the sight of the Portrait of a Female Friend* "from a MS." (now in the possession of Paul F. Betz) and suggested that the "female friend" is IF, and the portrait the one painted by Gillies. See the notes to *To a Painter* ("All praise the Likeness by thy skill portrayed"), *On the Same Subject* ("Though I beheld at first with blank surprise"), and *Upon a Portrait* ("We gaze—nor grieve to think that we must die").

Upon a Portrait

The subject of this sonnet, like the earlier poem in couplets, "More may not be by human Art exprest," and the later quatrain, "Upon those lips, those placid lips, I look," is the portrait of IF by Margaret Gillies and was evidently composed January 1, 1840, though the portrait was painted in November or early December 1839. The reading text of *Upon a Portrait* is taken from DC MS. 147, a notebook transcribed by MW and labelled "*Private* Memorials / not to be *printed*" (see the note to *Valedictory Sonnet*, above). The "Memorials" include sonnets on portraits of Dora W and MW, on Edith Southey's illness (addressed to her husband, RS), and the *Valedictory Sonnet* that closed the volume of *Sonnets* published in 1838. Though most of the seven sonnets were composed in time for their inclusion in the 1838 volume, "The Star that comes at close of day to shine" and *Upon a Portrait* were first printed by CW, Jr., in *Memoirs* in 1851 (I, 21n, 22n), where the latter bears an inscription "William Wordsworth. Rydal Mount" with the probable date of composition, "New

Year's Day, 1840." However, the manuscript from which the editor of *Memoirs* printed his text has not been traced.

For a description of the "Private Memorials" and the arrangement of the sonnets, see the entry for DC MS. 147 in the Manuscript Census. See also "The Star that comes at close of day to shine," below, and the two sonnets on Margaret Gillies's portrait of MW *To a Painter* and *On the Same Subject.*

The Star that comes at close of day to shine

"The former part of the Sonnet to you W^m^ wishes you to read thus" MW to IF, April 10, 1840. (WL Letters.) The inscriptions below the text read, "Wm Wordsworth / Rydal Mount / Feb^ry^" (Houghton MS. 3) and "William Wordsworth. Rydal Mount, Feb. 1840" (*Memoirs*).

The sonnet records WW's feelings on IF's departure from Ambleside in February 1840 (see the inscriptions in Houghton MS. 3 and *Memoirs*). She and Dora W left for London on February 12, and, after a short period in the city and a stay of some months in Somerset, both women returned at the end of April, Dora W to Rydal Mount and IF to her residence in Ambleside. Before their return MW sent IF the revised first three lines of the poem (MW to IF, April 10, 1840).

The reading text is taken from DC MS. 147 ("*Private* Memorials"; see the note to *Valedictory Sonnet*). "The Star that comes at close of day to shine" was composed in February 1840, probably shortly before February 12. This sonnet and *Upon a Portrait* were first printed by CW, Jr., in *Memoirs* (I, 21n, 22n), where he somewhat freely adapted his text for "The Star that comes" from the manuscript now in the Houghton Library and, as an addendum, included the revised version of the first three lines from MW's letter.

For a description of the "Private Memorials" and the arrangement of the sonnets see the entry for DC MS. 147 in the Manuscript Census.

Poor Robin

"*Poor Robin* I often ask myself what will become of Rydal Mount after our day—will the old walls and steps remain in front of the house and about the grounds, or will they be swept away with all the beautiful mosses and Ferns and Wild Geraniums and other flowers which their rude construction suffered and encouraged to grow among them? This little wild flower 'Poor Robin' is here constantly courting my attention and exciting what may be called a domestic interest with the varying aspects of its stalks and leaves and flowers. Strangely do the tastes of men differ according to their employment and habits of life. 'What a nice well would that be' said a labouring man to me one day, 'if all that rubbish was cleared off.' The '*rubbish*' was some of the most beautiful mosses and lichens and ferns, and other wild growths, as could possibly be seen. Defend us from the tyranny of trimness and neatness showing itself in this way! Chatterton says of freedom 'Upon her head wild weeds were spread,' and depend upon it if 'the marvellous boy' had undertaken to give Flora a garland, he would have preferred what we are apt to call weeds to garden-flowers. True taste has an eye for both. Weeds have been called flowers out of place. I fear the place most people would assign to them is too limited. Let them come near to our abodes, as surely they may without impropriety or disorder." (*FNW*, p. 75.) "The marvellous boy"—a phrase from *Resolution and Independence* (l. 43)—is Thomas Chatterton (1752–1770); the line by Chatterton is from his verse play, *Goddwyn. A Tragedie*:

Whan Freedom dreste, yn blodde steyned veste,
 To everie Knighte her Warre Song sunge;
Uponne her hedde, wylde Wedes were spredde,
 A gorie Anlace by her honge. (ll. 196–199)

In a letter to the Rev. Charles Alexander Johns (1811–1874), thanking him for sending a copy of his *Flora Sacra; or, the knowledge of the works of Nature conducive to the knowledge of the God of Nature* (1840), WW told Johns of "a little plant the small common Geranium, called with us 'Poor Robin', that is an especial favorite with me, so much so that I was tempted last March to describe its characteristics in verse and to moralize upon it in a way which perhaps will give you pleasure, when the Verses see the light, which they will probably next Spring" (August 5, 1841; *LY*, IV, 220). By "last March" WW means March 1840.

In all but one of its manuscript copies, as well in the first published form, the poem is dated "March 1840," its probable date of composition. MW entered two fair copies in DC MS. 89, the one on 110^{r}–110^{v} apparently transcribed from that on 107^{v}, but each copy was then revised independently, with some revisions in WW's hand in each case, though the copy last revised was certainly the one on 110^{r}–110^{v}, from which the later ones derive.

The Cuckoo-clock

"Of this clock I have nothing further to say than what the Poem expresses except that it must be here recorded that it was a present from the dear friend for whose sake these notes were chiefly undertaken and who has written them from my dictation." (*FNW*, p. 75.)

IF, before leaving Ambleside for Bath in February 1840, presented the Wordsworths with a cuckoo clock. MW reported on March 24, 1840, that "W^{m} is ashamed to tell you because you will be sorry to hear it, that he could find no better employment for this morn^{g}, than composing" what she then transcribed, "Stanzas, Hint to a simple-minded Lover of Nature and of Art" (*LY*, IV, 52–53). A third stanza was added by March 26, when WW wrote to IF again, remarking that "After I had sent off my Cuckoo verses I felt as if they wanted something of solidity, and am now tempted, my beloved Friend, to send you, in Joanna's writing, a copy slightly revised, with an additional stanza toiled at unsuccessfully yesterday evening, but thrown off in a few minutes this morning." He added, "We all like it and hope you and Dora will do the same. But it is too lately born for sound judgment, and I never sent to any one verses immediately after they were composed without some cause for regret I had been so hasty" (*LY*, IV, 56). There was thus a brief stage when the poem was in three stanzas, but JH's copy, sent in WW's letter to IF on March 26, has not been traced. The revisions that Dora W sent to IF from Hampstead Heath (probably on Wednesday, April 1) could reflect this intermediate version, since she offers no revisions to the fourth stanza (WL MS.). As is recorded on several of the copies of the four-stanza poem, WW "finished" it on his birthday, April 7, 1840—until publication seemingly a fact regarded as germane to a reading of the poem (see the *apparatus*, l. 44/)—and at that time titled it *The Cuckoo-clock.* On April 10, MW sent a copy of the fourth stanza to IF for "the Cuckoo," assuming no doubt that IF had received only the three-stanza version.

Text of 1842

5 Repeater's stroke] The chime of a watch or clock with a pressure-activated mechanism that strikes the hour; the repeater was a popular timepiece in the nineteenth century.

32–33 Dora W sent IF these lines (?April 1840) as a correction of the original reading, but the lines do not survive in any known manuscript; probably she is correcting these lines in the three-stanza version copied by JH, now untraced.

33 *wandering* Voice] An echo of l. 4 of *To the Cuckoo* (note the quotation marks in the manuscript copies).

34–44 In MW's letter to IF, April 10, 1840 (*MWL*, pp. 241–242), in which she supplied her fair copy, corrected by WW, of the last stanza of *The Cuckoo-clock*, she also copied out the sonnet "John the Baptist" (*Before the Picture of the Baptist, by Raphael, in the Gallery at Florence*, published in the sequence Italy 1837), which poem, MW remarks, has "a covert connection with" *The Cuckoo-clock* "thro' the Poem written at Laverna" (*Cuckoo at Laverna*, also published in Italy 1837); the link between the three poems is the image of the "voice" calling from the desert, a symbol of mercy or "grace" (l. 34 of *The Cuckoo-clock*).

44/ In MS. 151.2 the foot of the leaf is torn away, perhaps to remove the inscription concerning the poet's completion of the poem on his seventieth birthday.

The Norman Boy

"*The Norman Boy.* The subject of this Poem was sent me by M[rs]. Ogle, to whom I was personally unknown, with a hope on her part that I might be induced to relate the incident in Verse, and I do not regret that I took the trouble, for not improbably the fact is illustrative of the boy's early piety and may concur with my other little pieces on Children to produce profitable reflection among my youthful readers. This is said however with an absolute conviction that Children will derive most benefit from books which are not unworthy the perusal of persons of any age. I protest with my whole heart against those productions so abundant in the present day, in which the doings of children are dwelt upon as if they were incapable of being interested in anything else. On this subject I have dwelt at length in the poem on the growth of my own Mind." (*FNW*, pp. 74–75; see also p. 180; for the relevant discussion in "the poem on the growth of my own Mind" see *14-Bk Prelude*, V, 225–247.)

See also WW's note to *Sequel to The Norman Boy*.

EFO wrote to WW in May 1840 (the postmark indicates the letter had been received on or shortly after May 16, 1840): "An earnest and grateful admirer of Mr. Wordsworth's hopes to be pardoned for intruding upon him, having no better plea than the following. On reading the two beautiful little poems; one 'Composed in one of the Catholic Cantons of Switzerland', the other to 'Our Lady of the Snow'; she was forcibly reminded of an incident to which she was witness several years ago, and which seemed to her to demand a pen like Mr. Wordsworth's, a spirit like that which pervades the two beautiful pieces before referred to. And not having the happiness of knowing any friend of Mr. Wordsworth's thro' whom the suggestion might be made, she has ventured to have recourse to this mode of making known to him a circumstance, trifling indeed to some, but whose simple beauty she is persuaded will not be uninteresting to him, and which she should rejoice were it ever to be recorded by a Pen that will make it live for ever.—— It was in Normandy, and on one of those bare uninclosed downs skirted by a wood (dignified by the name of forest) which are the characteristic scenery of that part of the country. The day was bitter cold, towards the end of December; a little snow had fallen in the night, and the sky seemed charged with more. Under the shelter of the wood, a few miserable sheep and goats were cropping the tufts of grass where the snow did not lie; and tending them, was a little boy, a ragged urchin, who had succeeded in forming for himself a tiny hut, composed of the decayed branches of the trees, to shelter him from the cold north wind that blew directly across the downs—a frail tenement it may be believed, materials and builder considered. The hut was finished; and the little boy had shaped a *wooden cross* (of twisted twigs) and this he was now fixing on the top of his construction—as the best means of supplying all deficiencies—!"

EFO ended her story here, a narrative that WW followed very closely in the first version of the poem, which he dated "Rydal Mount / May 20th 1840" and sent to EFO on May 22 (see entries for "WW to EFO" in the *apparatus*). She then added a personal account of her acquaintance with WW's poetry that may suggest why he responded so promptly, by composing and sending her the poem within a very few days of receiving her letter. She begins by expressing her wish to acknowledge "the debt of gratitude which she is conscious of owing" him, and, continuing to speak in the third person, proceeds with this account of her acquaintance with his "writings": "at a time when, wearied with painful excitement and worn with inward conflict, her mind greatly needed the benefit of such a restorative, such a strengthening, yet calm giving balm. And here she found it—here she first began to draw those waters of peace, of comfort, of quiet yet earnest joy, which (with reverence be it spoken) she has found nowhere else in such rich abundance, excepting at the Fount of Life itself. Here she gladly learned the 'cheerful faith, that all which we behold is full of blessing'; a faith from which she hopes never again to depart. Here she learned so many lessons of truth, of wisdom, of happiness, of humility, yet of confidence, of lofty piety and endearing charity—that, tho' to enumerate them might be tedious, yet to acknowledge is most grateful to her feelings.—— Of Mr. Wordsworth's merits as a Poet it is not for her to speak, but of his power as a Teacher she can render undoubting testimony, evidenced by the deep and enduring influence he has obtained over her habits of mind and feeling." The two poems EFO mentioned in the first part of her letter are from the sequence Continent 1820, the quotation in the second part is from *Lines written a few miles above Tintern Abbey, on revisiting the Banks of the Wye, during a Tour, July 13, 1798* (ll. 133–134). In her reply to WW's letter she explained that it was her "*Mother* who witnessed the incident of which I wrote—two and twenty years ago, when I was but an infant; and it was only the other night, when, in the fulness of my heart, I carried to her (as I always do) the poems I had just been reading, that she might share with me the delight they gave me, that she for the first time mentioned the little incident, which has now become to me one of such importance. Having expressed to her how much I wished it could be made known to Mr. Wordsworth, she gave me permission to make the attempt, but so little encouragement that when I ventured to send my little story—I feared it was such a forlorn hope, that I did not even attempt to separate the personages, and, for the sake of brevity, related to you the circumstance as if I had myself been the witness of it" (EFO to WW, May 26, 1840; WL Letters, A/Ogle/2). Two days later she wrote to thank WW for the "receipt of yr letter this morning" in which he sent some revisions and additional (and "very beautiful") stanzas (A/Ogle/ 3). See *LY*, IV, 73–75 and 73n (Hill dated the letter May 20, 1840).

Sequel to The Norman Boy

WW's note appears below the last line of the text of the sequel in 1842; in editions from 1845 he added "See note" below the last line of the sequel and printed the note with the endnotes. None of the manuscripts of the poem contain the note.

"NOTE TO THE NORMAN BOY.

'Among ancient Trees there are few, I believe, at least in France, so worthy of attention as an Oak which may be seen in the "Pays de Caux," about a league from Yvetot, close to the church, and in the burial-ground of Allonville.

'The height of this Tree does not answer to its girth; the trunk, from the roots to the summit, forms a complete cone; and the inside of this cone is hollow throughout the whole of its height.

'Such is the Oak of Allonville, in its state of nature. The hand of Man, however, has endeavoured to impress upon it a character still more interesting, by adding a religious feeling to the respect which its age naturally inspires.

'The lower part of its hollow trunk has been transformed into a Chapel of six or seven feet in diameter, carefully wainscotted and paved, and an open iron gate guards the humble Sanctuary.

'Leading to it there is a staircase, which twists round the body of the Tree. At certain seasons of the year divine service is performed in this Chapel.

'The summit has been broken off many years, but there is a surface at the top of the trunk, of the diameter of a very large tree, and from it rises a pointed roof, covered with slates, in the form of a steeple, which is surmounted with an iron Cross, that rises in a picturesque manner from the middle of the leaves, like an ancient Hermitage above the surrounding Wood.

'Over the entrance to the Chapel an Inscription appears, which informs us it was erected by the Abbé du Détroit, Curate of Allonville in the year 1696; and over a door is another, dedicating it "To Our Lady of Peace."' *Vide* 14 *No. Saturday Magazine.*"

1842, 1845; so 1845– but l. 1 "The Norman Boy"*; 1850 as 1845 but l. 8* Oak of Allonville] oak of Allonville *and l. 23* 14 No.] No. 14

Variants found in DC MS. 151.2: *l. 2* Trees] Trees, *l. 4* church] Church burial-ground] burial ground *l. 14* body of the Tree.— *rev from* body of the Chapel.— *l. 16* surface] surface, *l. 17* large *rev from* long *l. 20* Hermitage] Hermitage, *l. 21* entrance to *rev from* entrance of *l. 22* erected by *inserted* Curate of Allonville] Curate of Allonville, *l. 23* Peace."] Peace'. *ellipses follow the final word in paragraphs one through four and six*

In his printed note WW quotes several paragraphs from an article, "The Chapel Oak of Allonville," which appeared in the September 22 issue of *The Saturday Magazine* (1.14 [1832]: 109–110), "translated and abridged from the original memoir by Professor Marquis, of the Botanic Garden, Rouen."

MW's copies of *The Norman Boy* and *Sequel to The Norman Boy* accompany her letter to IF, dated only "Sunday" but probably close to the time when printer's copy was being prepared for *PELY* in late November and early December 1841; in her letter MW wrote, "Mr Wordsworth was much gratified to find by your kind letter,—for which pray accept my best thanks, hastily given,—that you had been so much pleased with his little Norman Boy, and he has desired me to send you a correction—made in the 2[d] Stanza and also an alteration which introduces an additional one into the Sequel—one of your nieces will be kind enough to save you the trouble by transcribing these changes into your copy—as the Author thinks the Poem improved by them" (see the Census entries for the letter and for WL MS. 2).

28 *note* See the Print, and account of the tree [tree *rev from* Oak] of Allonville in the first vol of the Penny Magazine— *Betz MS. 4* [a mistake for "Gentleman's Magazine"]

28–48 WW's description is based closely on the print depicting the exterior of the tree and chapel which accompanied the article in *Gentleman's Magazine.*

49–52 The pilgrimage of "the afflicted" to the chapel is WW's invention, though the article mentions the "reverence of the villagers" and their vigorous opposition to efforts to destroy it at the time of the French Revolution.

61 Church in Rome] St. Peter's Basilica.

72/73 In his letter to EFO, November 15, 1842, WW commented, "To obviate in part one objection to the sequel of the Norman Boy which you have been so well natured as to be pleased with, I have added a stanza near the Conclusion as follows [see the six-line addition in the *apparatus*]. This addition connects, however faintly, the Boy at least with a knowledge of the dream in which he bears a leading part" (Uncatalogued Beinecke Library manuscript; see *LY*, IV, 722, where it is incorrectly dated 1845—the postmark reads November, 15 1842). The revision was printed in 1845.

In the inserted stanza the "verse" of "that Countryman of thine" was identified by Émile Legouis as the poem *Solitude* by Hippolyte de la Morvonais, as an admirer of WW (the passage is quoted by EdeS, *PW*, I, 365–366).

The sequel was probably begun shortly after WW completed *The Norman Boy*. The first sign of its existence, however, appears in his letter to EFO, written November 15, 1842, in which he sent her revisions of a copy of the poem that he had apparently sent her only a short while before (see also the notes to *The Norman Boy*).

At Furness Abbey ("Here, where, of havoc tired and rash undoing")

In an annotated copy of the 1845 *Poems* at WL (MS. 1845W) WRH has supplied the date 1832 in ink beside this poem; but so early a date seems unlikely. In his own note, inscribed below his fair copy (Victoria MS. 4), WW described the poem as "Retouched, or rather rewritten Aug[st] 25th 1843." While the sonnet was very probably rewritten around this time, it may have been composed as early as July 1840, when, as George H. Healey points out in *WPN* (pp. 90–91), WW revisited Furness Abbey with "a party of seven." This "Tour of seven days, Keswick, Buttermere, &c. Ennerdale, Calder Abbey, Wastdale, Eskdale, Duddon, Broughton, Furness Abbey, Coniston" was undertaken by "Mary, Dora, Miss

Fenwick, a Niece of hers, Mr Quillinan and his elder Daughter" (WW to CW, Jr., July 31, 1840; *LY*, IV, 98).

6 Fall to prevent] *i.e.*, to prevent a fall.

14 Cavendish] "Furness Abbey was the property of the Duke of Devonshire, the head of the Cavendish Family. The railway runs alongside the abbey"(EdeS).

On a Portrait of the Duke of Wellington, upon the Field of Waterloo, by Haydon

"*Duke of Wellington* This was composed while I was ascending Helvellyn in company with my daughter and her husband. She was on horseback and rode to the very top of the hill without once dismounting—a feat which it was scarcely possible to perform except during a season of dry weather and a guide with whom we fell in on the mountain told us he believed it had *never* been accomplished before by any one." (*FNW*, p. 76.)

Composed August 31, 1840. WW reported to HCR, September 4, 1840, that "Haydon has just sent me a spirited Etching of his Portrait of the Duke of Wellington taken 20 years after the Battle of Waterloo, from the Life. He is represented in the field; but no more of the Picture—take my Sonnet which it suggested the other day. The lines were composed while I was climbing Helvellyn" (*LY*, IV, 106). WW had great difficulty satisfying both BRH and himself in the phrasing of this sonnet. On September 2, 1840, in return for a copy of the engraving by Thomas Lupton of BRH's picture that BRH had sent to him, WW sent the poem to BRH (*LY*, IV, 100–101). In the letter accompanying the poem WW requested that the sonnet "may not be put into circulation for some little time, as it is warm from the brain, and may require, in consequence, some little retouching," and repeated the request on September 11, "as that would afford an opportunity of paying a Compliment here and there by sending it in Mss as you design to do to the Queen Dowager" (*LY*, IV, 111–112). Judging from the several copies that survive in BRH's autograph, he apparently did send out manuscript copies. But by mid-month he had also sent it to several newspapers and journals, including the *Literary Gazette and Journal of Belles Lettres, Arts, Sciences, &c.* (London) where it appeared on September 19, 1840 (p. 614), probably its latest such appearance. The lengthy exchange of letters between poet and painter, and between poet and several other friends, both before and after the sonnet's appearance in the press, show the poet trying to rescue his text from error and to accommodate both his own and the artist's wishes. Variously worded titles and inscriptions appeared with the sonnet in its many copies, perhaps as demanded by the occasion of making each copy (see the *apparatus criticus* to the poem).

More than twenty holograph copies of the poem have been identified, though some of these manuscripts have not been traced, and nearly all of those examined have substantive variants from the version WW himself published in 1842 in *PELY*. In October 1841, still rankled by his experience with BRH and the press, he told EM, when writing to learn the expense of printing a hundred copies of his *Sonnets Upon the Punishment of Death*, that, because of the "gross typografical blunders" in the newspaper and journal versions of his sonnet on BRH's painting of the Duke of Wellington, he "resolved nothing of mine shall make its first appearance in that way again" (*LY*, IV, 246; WW to EM, October 2, 1841). For other relevant correspondence see the entries for this poem in the Manuscript Census and *LY*, IV, 100–101, 105, 107, 108, 115, 117, 120–121, 126, 131, 133.

Above the verses transcribed in the letter from WW to BRH (September 2, 1840) at Princeton is a note in BRH's hand, "*Final reading*"—BRH's indication that he had entered WW's subsequent revisions on this holograph copy from WW.

A copy of the sonnet in an unidentified hand in the Senate House Library, University of London (MS. 282), is titled "Sonnet Suggested by *Haydon's* Picture of the Duke of Wellington upon the Field of Waterloo, 20 years after the battle. (painted for St. George's Hall Liverpool.)" and is inscribed "Composed while ascending Helvellyn—Monday Aug 31st. 1840." A note in the same hand—"Private / at / Present / [?Time] "—appears on the bottom left hand of the sheet. The text in this copy appears to derive from WW to BRH, September 4 and September 11, 1840, and is without independent authority. Variants of note are: *l. 7* triumph *rev from* human pride *(unique to this manuscript)* *l. 9* Him *rev from* Since *l. 10* Elates not *rev from* Him years have *l. 11* face, for] face. But

A copy in Pierpont Morgan Library of *On a Portrait of the Duke of Wellington, upon the Field of Waterloo, by Haydon* in the hand of BRH appears in the same manuscript (MA2987) with a copy of *To B. R. Haydon, Esq. on seeing his Picture of Napoleon Buonaparte on the Island of St. Helena*; both are without independent authority (see the note to *To B. R. Haydon*). The unique readings appear to be BRH's own alterations: *title* Sonnet To Haydon, on his Painting of the Hero and His Horse on the Field of Waterloo 20 years after the battle (painted for Liverpool) *l. 2* their] the *l. 10* Elates] Affects *ll. 11* As shows that care worn face, but he such seed *inscription* Monday Aug 31, 1840. composed while ascending Helvellyn / Wm Wordsworth

1, 5 In his letter to BRH on September 10, 1840, WW wrote, "By is certainly a better word than through, but I fear it cannot be employed on account of the subsequent line, 'But, by the Chieftain's look'. To me the two 'bys' clash both to the ear and understanding, and it was on that account I changed the word. I have also a slight objection to the alliteration 'By bold' occurring so soon" (*LY*, IV, 108).

9–12 In his letter to BRH, September 4, 1840, WW explained his revision of ll. 11–12 thus: "You will see the reason of this alteration it applies now to his life in general and not that particular act as before." He also told BRH at this time that he could "print the Son. where and when you like, if you think it will serve you—only it may be as well that I should hear from you first, as you may have something to suggest, either as to the title, or the lines" (see *LY*, IV, 105). On September 7, 1840, he sent a revision of ll. 9–12, explaining, "I am quite ashamed to trouble you again but after considering and reconsidering, changing and rechanging, it has been resolved that the troublesome passage shall stand thus" (see the *apparatus*). On September 10 WW wrote, "I am glad you like Elates not, as the passage first stood, 'Since the mighty deed' there was a transfer of the thought from the picture to the living Man—which divided the Sonnet into two parts—the presence of the Portrait is now carried thro', till the last line where the Man is taken up. To prevent the possibility of a mistake I will repeat the passage as last sent and in which state I consider it finished—and you will do what you like with it" (*LY*, IV, 108). The next day WW wrote twice (*LY*, IV, 110–112), first in reply to an earlier letter from BRH, saying "Your remarks are just and had passed thro' Mrs W's mind and my own—nevertheless I could not otherwise get rid of the prosaic declaration of the matter of fact that the Hero was so much older: You will recollect that it at first stood "Since the mighty deed / Him years &c"—I know not what to do with the passage, if it be not well corrected as follows" (see the *apparatus*). WW also noted that, in compliance with BRH's request, he had sent the sonnet "as before corrected" to Matthew D. Lowndes, the Liverpool attorney who had purchased the picture. Later the same day, after receiving a letter from BRH, WW wrote that he had "this morn^g^ sent off an imperfect correction" and enclosed a reading which in part reverts to an earlier reading (see the *apparatus*). On September 23 WW wrote, "The unlucky Sonnet I have not yet seen in print—The reading— [see the *apparatus*] is most liked by the best judges, especially by Mr Rogers who is now writing at the same table with me" (*LY*, IV, 121). WW sent the final reading of these lines to HCR on October 27, remarking, "The Sonnet upon the Duke's Picture was printed very incorrectly, in all the newspapers in which I saw it. It was in one passage altered by myself after I sent it to you, thus. [ll. 9–11, through "face.—"] Haydon tells me that it is Altered" (*LY*, IV, 133–134). The earlier copy sent to HCR has not been found.

The portrait of Wellington was one of BRH's most successful paintings and was copied and sold by him many times. Geoffrey Jackson, who owns an engraving of the original painting, describes it thus: "This picture of the Duke of Wellington upon the field of Waterloo, by B. R. Haydon (1786–1846), is one of the few personal effects mentioned in

Christopher Wordsworth's *Memoirs of William Wordsworth* (1851) as having been at Rydal Mount when the poet lived there. It is described as hanging on the staircase, opposite the picture celebrated in the sonnet 'Giordano, verily thy pencil's skill,' and Christopher Wordsworth states that Haydon's picture was commemorated in another sonnet. The relationship of picture and sonnet is, in fact, rather more complicated. Haydon's original painting (now in St. George's Hall, Liverpool) was finished on November 30, 1839. The following year Haydon made an etching of the picture, and sent a copy to Wordsworth. This copy, inscribed 'B. R. Haydon to William Wordsworth 1840 with affection and gratitude,' and now the property of the Rydal Mount Trust, was clearly the inspiration of the sonnet. Wordsworth sent his poem to Haydon on September 2, 1840, together with criticism of the picture: 'The outline of the face we all think too faint.' A correspondence ensued in which Haydon in his turn criticized the sonnet, and Wordsworth made a number of alterations. The engraving [owned by Jackson] is a print by the well-known engraver Thomas Goff Lupton (1791–1873). Haydon wrote to Wordsworth on March 30, 1843: 'Your Print will come by Coach and Train directly a very fair Impression, which I hope you will keep and have framed in Maple-wood, with your own immortal Sonnet on the back of it.' In his reply of April 6, Wordsworth agreed that it was 'an excellent Impression, and the whole effect a great improvement upon the first sketch.' The picture was framed as Haydon suggested, but Wordsworth failed to inscribe the sonnet on the back. Now hanging in Rydal Mount are the original 'sketch'—the first etching, presumably by Haydon, the sonnet, separately framed, and several pictures—in the staircase—with 'Maple-wood' frames which match the one on the engraving of Wellington" (private document).

Sigh no more Ladies, sigh no more

1–2 The opening lines of the song sung by Balthasar in *Much Ado About Nothing* (II.iii).

Probably composed after 1840, when WW began to be much in demand as a contributor of verses to ladies's albums.

The Crescent-moon, the Star of Love

For the date of composition see the headnote.

In MS. 1836/45 JC instructed the printer to add three poems, first published in the 1842 volume, to Evening Voluntaries. "The Crescent-Moon" (the second reading text) was to follow *Composed by the Sea-shore* and *A Night Thought*; but the note is deleted. In 1845 "Crescent-moon" followed *Composed by the Sea-shore* in Evening Voluntaries while *A Night Thought* was placed in Sentiment and Reflection.

1 Star of Love] The planet Venus; see *To the Planet Venus, upon its approximation (as an evening star) to the earth, January 1838* (p. 321).

Let more ambitious Poets take the heart

The poem may have been intended to introduce *PELY*, the collection WW published in April 1842 and for which he was preparing copy in December 1841. DC MS. 143, a collection from which many *PELY* poems were drawn, is the only manuscript to contain this eight-line *envoi.* In version B in MS. 143 the poem is entered on the same page with what is apparently an entry to mark the beginning of a series of sonnets: "Sonnets / — / Suggested by the first view of Lancaster Castle / approached from the South." The sonnet so titled (probably one of the *Sonnets on the Punishment of Death*) was not entered, however, and WW used the blank space below the entry to draft "Let more ambitious Poets take the heart," while deleting only the word "Sonnets" from the title on the page. Geoffrey Jackson suggests (in his forthcoming edition of WW's *Sonnet Series and Itinerary Poems, 1819–1850*) that the probable occasion of WW's "view of Lancaster Castle . . . from the South" was his return to Rydal on June 15, 1839, after a trip to London and Oxford.

Epitaph in the Chapel-yard of Langdale, Westmoreland

"*Epitaph in Langdale Church yard.* Owen Lloyd, the subject of this Epitaph, was born at Old Brathay [*rev from* Brathey] n^{r}. Ambleside and was the son of Charles Lloyd and his wife Sophia (née Pemberton) both of Birmingham who came to reside in this country soon after their marriage. They had many children, both sons and daughters, of whom the most remarkable was the subject of this Epitaph. He was educated under Mr. Dawes of Ambleside, Dr. Butler of Shrewsbury, and lastly at Trin: Col. Cambridge where he would have been greatly distinguished as a Scholar, but for inherited infirmities of bodily constitution which from early childhood affected his mind. His love for the neighbourhood in which he was born and his sympathy with the habits and characters of the mountain yeomanry, in conjunction with irregular spirits that unfitted him for facing duties in situations to which he was unaccustomed, induced him to accept the retired Curacy of Langdale. How much he was beloved and honored there, and with what feelings he discharged his duty under the oppression of severe malady is set forth tho' imperfectly in this Epitaph." (*FNW*, p. 76.)

JC's note in MS. 1836/45 directed the printer to include *Epitaph in the Chapel-yard of Langdale, Westmoreland* among the Epitaphs in the edition of 1845.

WW sent a copy of the epitaph to his brother Christopher on or around August 11, agreed to have the poem privately printed at Kendal around but by November 5, 1841 (*LY*, IV, 225, 257), and published it himself in *PELY* in 1842. Owen Lloyd (1803–1841), who suffered throughout his life from epilepsy, took up the curacy in Langdale in 1829 and died in early spring 1841. His tombstone in the chapel-yard at Chapel Stile, Langdale, bears WW's epitaph as inscription; the stone is now "sinking into, and gently inclining towards, the earth," as WW said of a tombstone sighted in a country churchyard in his note to the sonnet *A Parsonage in Oxfordshire* (in *ES*, 1822). Owen's father, Charles Lloyd (1775–1839), who had published *Poems* jointly with STC and CL in 1797, was a student and friend, for a time, of STC, and around 1800 came to live in the hamlet of Clappersgate, near Ambleside, at Old Brathay.

Mr. Dawes and Dr. Butler, mentioned in the IF note, were, respectively, the Rev. John Dawes, who also taught Hartley and Derwent Coleridge, Basil Montagu's second son Algernon, and WW's son John (*MY*, I, 282, 402 and notes; *MY*, II, 123, 246), and the Rev. Samuel Butler, D.D. (1774–1839), who was a contemporary of STC at Cambridge and headmaster of the school at Shrewsbury from 1798–1836 (*LY*, I, 371n).

On November 5, 1841, WW sent CW, Jr., "a Copy of poor Owen's Epitaph, struck off at Kendal, upon the suggestion of Thomas Troughton, the Ambleside Chapel Clerk, and Bookseller" (*LY*, IV, 257). No example of this private printing has been found. CW, Jr., was married to Priscilla Lloyd, Owen Lloyd's sister.

The reading text is based on the 1842 printing.

Though Pulpits and the Desk may fail

"From a bookseller's Catalogue. Mr. Gordon Wordsworth inspected the Manuscript, and guaranteed its genuineness. W. was at Bath on the date recorded on the Manuscript" (*PW*, IV, 480). Gordon Graham Wordsworth was WW's grandson. Neither the manuscript nor the catalogue has been found; the reading text is from *PW*, IV, 390, which is based on the unnamed catalogue. See *LY*, IV, 194, for WW's presence in Bath at this date.

The Wishing-gate Destroyed

"*The wishing-gate destroyed* See printed note upon this." (*FNW*, p. 75.) WW refers to the end-of-volume note, below. In the IF note to *The Sailor's Mother* the gate is located "on the high-road that then led from Grasmere to Ambleside" (*FNW*, p. 9); it is on the south side of the road.

"See 'The Wishing-Gate,' Vol. II. page 200, of the Author's Poems." Note below title in 1842.

"'In the Vale of Grasmere, by the side of the old highway leading to Ambleside, is a gate which, time out of mind, has been called the "Wishing-gate."'—*Notice prefixed to a Poem,* page 200, 2nd Vol. *of my Poems.*

"Having been told, upon what I thought good authority, that this gate had been destroyed, and the opening where it hung walled up, I gave vent immediately to my feelings in these stanzas. But going to the place some time after I found, with much delight, my old favourite unmolested."

End-of-volume note to *The Wishing-gate Destroyed* in 1842.

variants in the end-of-volume note in DC MS. 151.2 (B) *l. 1* Vale] vale highway] high-way *l. 2* Notice *rev from* note *l. 3* page . . . *Poems*] Page 200 2^{d} Vol of my Poems *l. 4* gate *rev to* Gate *l. 6* to the place *rev from* immediately *ll. 6–7* found, . . . delight,] found . . . delight *l. 7* unmolested.] unmolested.—

variants in 1845– *l. 2* "Wishing-gate"] Wishing-gate *ll. 2–3* —Notice prefixed . . . my Poems. *lacking* *l. 5* opening . . . hung] opening, . . . hung, *l. 6* after] after,

After l. 66 in 1842 the following direction appeared: "See Note at the end of this Volume." Editions from 1845 follow 1842, but print "the" for "this"; the note is lacking from all manuscripts except for MS. 151.2 (A), where it reads "see note—at the end of this vol." On the verso of the leaf (in DC MS. 151.1 [B]) on which the last four stanzas of this poem are copied is the start of what may have been an early version of WW's note: "By happy chance" (30^{v}).

The Huntington manuscript of *The Wishing-gate Destroyed,* in WW's hand, is signed and dated "Wm Wordsworth / Rydal Mount / August 29th — —"; the year is omitted but must be 1841. For the most part the version in this manuscript shows the earliest readings, but in some it postdates that in DC MS. 151.1 (B). The poem has the same stanza form as *The Wishing-gate,* composed in 1828 (see the reading text and notes to that poem, above).

25–30 In Yale MS. 8 WW entered only l. 25, indicating the commencement of what was to be the sixth stanza, without writing out the remainder.

Sonnet ("Though the bold wings of Poesy affect")

The poem was probably composed as WW was preparing copy for *PELY* for the printer in November and December 1841; it must have been among the first sheets sent off to the printer after *Guilt and Sorrow,* probably some time in mid- to late-December 1841, though no text of the sonnet is found among the surviving printer's copy (MS. 151.2). The title "SONNET" was introduced perhaps because the poem stands first in a miscellaneous group of poems after the text of *Guilt and Sorrow* in the 1842 volume. Later WW may have indicated a tentative position for this sonnet in its class when he had JC list its first line below the text of "Scorn not the Sonnet; Critic, you have frowned," in MS. 1838/40, probably around the time WW was preparing the one-volume edition of 1845. However, in that edition, and after, he used it to introduce a new "Part III" of Miscellaneous Sonnets.

Suggested by a Picture of the Bird of Paradise

"*The Bird of Paradise* This subject has been treated of before (see a former note) I will here only by way of comment direct attention to the fact that pictures of animals and other productions of nature as seen in conservatories, menageries and museums etc—would do little for the national mind, nay they would be rather injurious to it, if the imagination were excluded by the presence of the object, more or less out of a state of nature; If it were not that we learn to talk and think of the Lion and the Eagle, the Palm tree and even the Cedar from the impassioned introduction of them so frequently into Holy Scripture and by Great Poets, and Divines who write as Poets, the spiritual part of our nature and therefore the higher part of it would derive no benefit from such intercourse with such [objects]." (*FNW,* pp. 67, 203.) See the earlier poem, *Upon Seeing a*

Coloured Drawing of the Bird of Paradise in an Album, pp. 284–285, and WW's note, p. 464.

The rationale for dating this poem is the same as for *Sonnet* ("Though the bold wings of Poesy affect"; see the note, above). In addition to the copy in MS. 143, two autograph copies of the poem appear in DC MS. 151, among the preparatory copies (151.1) and in the copy sent to the printer (151.2). The copies in MS. 151 seem more or less contemporary, while that in MS. 143, a notebook of keeping copies, may be slightly earlier.

In MS. 143, the earliest extant version, the poem began with l. 5 and the opening quatrain was added on the facing page beneath WW's pencil entry of the first three words of l. 1.

7–9 Glendoveers . . . seas of ether] Sprites so named make such a journey in RS's *The Curse of Kehama* (1810), Bk. VII.

Lyre! though such power do in thy magic live

WW's IF note to *The Forsaken* mainly concerns "Lyre! though such power do in thy magic live": "This [*The Forsaken*] was an overflow from the affliction of Margaret, and excluded as superfluous there, but preserved in the faint hope that it may turn to account by restoring a shy Lover to some forsaken Damsel. My poetry having been complained of as deficient in interests of this sort, a charge w[h]. the next piece beginning "*Lyre! tho' such power do in thy magic live*" will scarcely tend to obviate. The natural imagery of these verses [*i.e.*, "Lyre! though such power do in thy magic live"] was supplied by frequent, I might say intense, observation of the Rydal torrent. What an animating contrast is the ever changing aspect of that and indeed of every one of our mountain brooks to the monotonous tone and unmitigated fury of such streams among the Alps as are fed all the summer long by Glaciers and melting snows. A Traveller observing the exquisite purity of the great rivers such as the Rhone at Geneva and the Aare at Lucerne when they issue out of their respective Lakes might fancy for a moment that some power in nature produced this beautiful change with a view to make amends for those Alpine sullyings which the waters exhibit near their fountain heads: but alas! how soon does that purity depart before the influx of tributary waters that have flowed thro' cultivated Plains and the crowded abodes of Men." (*FNW*, p. 63.)

Probably composed in 1841, perhaps while materials were being assembled for *PELY* from late November or early December through February 1842. The close resemblance between what appear to be the latest versions in the various drafts in MS. 89 and the fair copies in MSS. 143 and 151 suggests that the drafts and copies were made at about the same time (see also the note to *Suggested by a Picture of the Bird of Paradise*, above). The image of eddying foam balls in a turbulent current of water appeared first in the sonnet, *Composed on the Banks of a Rocky Stream* ("Dogmatic Teachers, of the snow-white fur"), composed possibly in 1820 (before May, when WW left Rydal Mount for his tour of the continent) and published in the four-volume *Miscellaneous Poems* in July of the same year (*MWL*, p. 65 and note; see also *Poems, 1807–1820*, pp. 278, 549). WW used the image again in *On the Banks of a Rocky Stream* ("Behold an emblem of our human mind"), an inscription published for the first time in the edition of 1849–1850 (see the latter poem edited below).

2 An alternate to this line, "Couldst call my Emma back, beloved Maid" (see the transcription of 96[r] of DC MS. 89 on p. 791, below), probably refers to DW, WW's "sister muse"; see WW's several early poems in which he refers to her as "Emma" and "Emmeline" ("It was an April morning: fresh and clear" in *LB, 1797–1800*, pp. 243; "Among all lovely things my Love had been," *To a Butterfly, The Sparrow's Nest,* and "There is a little unpretending Rill," in *Poems, 1800–1807*, pp. 102–103, 203–204, 212–213, and 531; see also his deleted note to *The Triad* on p. 438, above). DW fell seriously ill in 1835 and did not fully recover her mental faculties. Jeffrey C. Robinson in "A Late Poem by Wordsworth to 'Emma'," *Philological Quarterly*, 64 (1985), 406–415, presents evidence for identifying "Emma" with Dorothy and with Emmeline Fisher, "a young prodigy poetess brought to

the attention of Wordsworth in 1837," deciding finally that the poem "was written with [Emmeline Fisher] in mind but that Wordsworth easily associated to the first Emma, his sister Dorothy" (p. 412). As a caution against precise identification, however, it should be remembered that in the note he dictated to IF shortly after writing the poem, WW treated the "Lover" and "Damsel" as fictions imagined by the speaker of the poem, while in notes to other poems he routinely identified living subjects wherever appropriate. It is worth remembering, too, that he used and reused names that he liked the sound of, regardless of association (for example, the names "Mary" and "Lucy").

Prelude ("In desultory walk through orchard grounds")

"*Prelude to the Last Vol.* These verses were begun while I was on a visit to my son John at Brigham and finished at Rydal. As the contents of this Vol to which they are now prefixed will be assigned to their respective Classes when my Poems shall be collected in one Vol: I should be at a loss where with propriety to place this Prelude being too restricted in its bearing to serve as a Preface for the Whole. The lines towards the conclusion allude to the discontents then fomented thro' the country by the Agitators of the Anti-Corn Law league: the particular causes of such troubles are transitory but disposition to excite and liability to be excited are nevertheless permanent and therefore proper objects for the Poet's regard." (*FNW*, p. 62; see also pp. 166–167.)

WW spent "only one day" with John at his Brigham Rectory at the end of November 1841 before going on to Lowther Castle for a week (*LY*, IV, 269). He wrote to IF from Lowther on December 2, 1841, that "the best news I have of myself is my having done I trust with that most troublesome prefatory Poem; never was I so hampered with anything, the chief difficulty rising out of the simultaneous actions of both the Bird and the Poet being engaged in singing, and the word 'while' [*l. 3*] not being manageable for both—that having done this to my own mind and Mary's and having improved, I cannot but think, the little I now send, I trust I shall not write another line while I am here" (*LY*, IV, 268; the "little" sent with this letter consisted of four stanzas of *At Vallombrosa*). The date WW printed below the poem in 1842 must signal his (and perhaps Mary's) later dissatisfaction with the poem and further substantial revision "at Rydal" before its publication in *PELY*, 1842. The reading text is based on the 1842 printing.

The poem, printed in italics, remained as "Prelude" in the rearrangement and reprinting of most of the contents of *PELY* in the sixth volume of the multivolumed stereotype editions of 1846 and 1849; but it was folded into the class of Miscellaneous Poems (where it appeared wholly in roman type) in the newly set editions of 1845, its stereotypes of 1847 and 1849, and the six-volume small octavo edition of 1849–1850.

42–48 The Anti-Corn Law League, mentioned by WW in his IF note, above, was formed in 1839 of local associations opposed to legislation that kept the price of grain artificially high and was supported by wealthy manufacturers who wanted free trade in general. The League launched a propaganda campaign to discredit rich landlords and greedy farmers. Pressure was intense and sustained, linking up with more revolutionary movements at times (like Chartism in 1842), eventually resulting in the repeal of the protectionist Corn Laws in 1846. In the IF note to "Feel for the wrongs to universal ken" WW recommended this sonnet "to the perusal of the Anti Corn Law Leaguers, the Political Economists, and of all those who consider that the Evils under which we groan are to be removed or palliated by measures ungoverned by moral and religious principles." (*FNW*, p. 76.)

Upon Perusing the Foregoing Epistle Thirty Years after its Composition

In the IF note to *Epistle to Sir George Beaumont, Bart. From the South-west Coast of Cumberland.—1811.* WW remarked that the *Epistle* was thoroughly revised, probably in late 1841, in preparation for its first publication in the 1842 volume (see *FNW*, p. 66); *Upon Perusing the Foregoing Epistle* was probably composed in response to this revisionary work but before the end of December, when printer's copy was being sent off.

For the text of the *Epistle* and commentary see *Poems, 1807–1820*, pp. 78–95, 514–517.

Sonnet ("When Severn's sweeping Flood had overthrown")

In their *Memoirs of the Life and Writings of James Montgomery* (7 vols.; London, 1854–1856) John Holland and James Everett state: "In the earlier part of this year [1842], a number of ladies at Cardiff, in South Wales, determined to get up a bazaar in aid of a fund for the erection of a church in that place, on the site of one which had been washed away, in the year 1607, by a flood of the river Severn, which caused a great influx of water into the Bristol Channel. Mr. John Dix, author of the 'Life of Chatterton,' and at this period editor of the 'Merthyr Guardian' Newspaper, wrote to Wordsworth and Montgomery, soliciting from each a poetical offering for the bazaar. Both poets complied with the request: the former, by contributing what Mr. Dix, in his letter to Montgomery, called at the time a 'noble sonnet'. . . . The bazaar was held in Cardiff Castle, on the 5th and 6th of October, this year; on which occasion these compositions, along with two other poetical pieces—one by T. W. Booker, Esq., of Cardiff, and the other by Mr. Dix himself,—were printed in an elegant style, and sold to the visitors. Mr. Dix soon afterwards went to America, and while there republished the two leading compositions in a Boston newspaper . . . " (pp. 105–106). WW's sonnet, at least, was published in facsimile as a broadsheet from a holograph manuscript. A pamphlet containing all four sonnets, reset in type, was printed after the bazaar had taken place.

After reprinting the newspaper version of WW's sonnet, Holland and Everett then quote Dix's note, published with the sonnet in the same newspaper: "In this slight production, which is, however, quite unworthy of the present laureate, and only interesting as a recent effort of his pen, much pains was [*sic*] taken; for, after the sonnet was forwarded, Mr. W. sent six or seven notes requesting alterations in words and lines, so that, as printed, it is almost entirely different from the original copy. This may show how laboriously Mr. W. polishes his poems" (pp. 106–107). The altered octet of this version (ll. 3–6) may reflect WW's "requests" to Dix, though the odd rhyme scheme is further strained; the verbal variants from the reading text are given in the *apparatus* (the nonverbal variants, probably the work of Dix or the newspaper editor, are not reported).

As for the facsimile the hand is undoubtedly WW's, as is the transcription of the sonnet without indenting lines to reflect the rhyme scheme, a style he rejected. Paul F. Betz obtained his copy in 1973 from the great-granddaughter of the woman who purchased it in 1842 "at £1–05" at the Cardiff Bazaar held in aid of St. Mary's Restoration Fund. Dix went to America about 1846 and, after an attack on him as a literary forger in the *Athenaeum* (December 5, 1857, and January 23, 1858), published a reply in *Saturday Evening Gazette* of Boston. In *Notes and Queries* of July 20, 1872, a correspondent stated that Dix died in America about seven years previously (*Dictionary of National Biography*, ed. Leslie Stephen and Sidney Lee [63 vols.; London, 1885–1900]).

The only known copy of the pamphlet is in the British Library; the title page reads: POEMS ON THE LOSS AND RE-BUILDING OF ST. MARY'S CHURCH, CARDIFF. BY WILLIAM WORDSWORTH. JAMES MONTGOMERY. THOMAS WILLIAM BOOKER. JOHN DIX. CARDIFF: W. BIRD. 1842 (BL 11645 de 22). A note on the third page of the pamphlet reads: "The following Poems were written by their respective Authors for the purpose of adding something to the Fund for rebuilding the New Church of Saint Mary, Cardiff. But a limited number were struck off, and numerous applications having been made for them, they are now printed for the first time in a collected form." What was "struck off" was, in WW's case at least, a lithographic facsimile, certainly taken from an original holograph copy of the poem. This facsimile is the basis for the reading text (two examples have been identified; see the entry for "Cardiff Facsimile" in the Manuscript Census). Other "facsimiles" were produced later in autotype (a collotype process of reproduction), by the Rev. R. Wilkins

Rees, but the known examples (one at Trinity College, Dublin, the other at WL but now missing and surviving only in a photographic record) are of a manuscript not in WW's hand and do not appear to have been authorized by him. Another copy, not facsimile but an original autograph, is at the Bodleian Library. The hand of both it and the autotype copies is imitative of WW's and in both cases is probably forgery by Dix, who gained a reputation for such activities. Variants in these later productions are slight and can be attributed to errors and the copyist's preferences in capitalization, punctuation, and style of indentation; they are without authority.

A Poet!—He hath put his heart to school

"*Sonnet A Poet &—* I was impelled to write this Sonnet by the disgusting frequency with which the word *artistical*, imported with other impertinencies from the Germans, is employed by writers of the present day, for artistical let them substitute artificial and the Poetry written on this system both at home and abroad will be for the most part much better characterised." (*FNW*, p. 76; see also p. 182.)

The sonnet appears in a manuscript of draft material prepared for the volume of 1842, in the same section (DC MS. 151.1) with a version of the sonnet "Well worthy to be magnified are they" (published as *Pilgrim Fathers*, later included in Ecclesiastical Sonnets) which can be dated around February 1842 by WW's letter to HR written on March 1 (*LY*, IV, 297).

The poem is the first in the group of "Miscellaneous Sonnets" in *PELY*. In MS. 1842P this heading was printed as "Sonnets" and then revised to "Miscellaneous Sonnets."

1 Above her copy of the poem in MS. 151.2 MW's note reads "(To the Printer. Herewith I send a recorrected copy of 3 Sonnets you have already had — also an additional one intended to stand first in the same collection)" and below the poem is her copy of the first three and a half lines of "The most alluring clouds that mount the sky" (see the note to that poem, below); the two poems are numbered 1 and 2, the order followed in the section of Miscellaneous Sonnets in 1842.

To a Redbreast—(In Sickness)

SH contracted rheumatic fever in May 1835; she died of the illness on June 23, 1835 (*MWL*, 147). In the headnote to *Floating Island*, a poem by DW that followed *To a Redbreast—(In Sickness)* in *PELY*, WW explained "These lines are by the Author of the Address to the Wind, &c. published heretofore along with my Poems. Those to a Redbreast are by a deceased female Relative." For the date of WW's revisions see the headnote.

The most alluring clouds that mount the sky

"Sonnet 'The most *alluring clouds*' &c—Hundreds of times have I seen hanging about and above the Vale of Rydal clouds that might have given birth to this Sonnet which was thrown off on the impulse of the moment one evening when I was returning home from the favorite walk of ours along the Rotha under Loughrigg." (*FNW*, p. 76.)

Like "*A Poet!*—He hath put his heart to school," the poem seems to have been drafted and revised shortly before publication. For the position of this sonnet in *PELY*, 1842, see the note to "*A Poet!*—He hath put his heart to school," above.

1 MW's note beside her copy of ll. 1–4 on leaf 108^r in MS. 151.2 reads "(the first line being altered)" and must refer to the original line, "The most bewitching clouds that grace the sky," on 4^r of the same manuscript.

Intent on gathering wool from hedge and brake

WW's note in MS. 151.3 reads, "These lines to be presented here [on the last page of WW's modernization of *Troilus and Cresida*] unless there be a better place in some sheet not struck off. They would stand better than [ever *del*] here after the [the *del*] Epitaph on Owen Lloyd if that sheet be not struck off."

Text of 1842

"*Intent on gathering Wool* Suggested by a conversation with Miss F— who along with her Sister had during their childhood found much delight in such gatherings for the purpose here alluded to." (*FNW*, p. 77.) "Miss F—" is Isabella Fenwick.

The date assigned the poem in *PELY*, March 8, 1842, must refer to WW's construction of the sonnet from the earlier fragments. No full manuscript of the sonnet version has been found.

The Eagle and the Dove

WW was invited to contribute a poem to *La Petite Chouannerie, ou Histoire d'un Collège breton sous l'Empire*, by its compiler, Alexis François Rio, who had explained the subject conveyed by the book's title as the "revolt of the schoolboys of the college of Vannes in 1815 against the soldiers of the French republic" (*LY*, IV, 335–336n; see the same note for Alan Hill's account of Rio and his acquaintance and correspondence with WW). The manuscript at Cornell is in MW's hand, signed by WW; it was enclosed in WW's letter to EM of May 11, 1842 (also at Cornell), and was duly addressed by EM to Rio and sent on the same day. *La Petite Chouannerie* (Paris: Olivier Fulgence, Libraire) was published later in 1842; WW's poem appeared above his name "W. Wordsworth" on pp. 64–65. Other poems in English printed in the volume are by Caroline Norton, Walter Savage Landor, and RMM. WW did not reprint the poem.

1 Caractacus] Caradoc, the king of the Silures in the west of Britain during the reign of Claudius, was defeated by the Romans, captured, and taken to Rome in AD 51, where the emperor pardoned him out of respect for his noble spirit.

What heavenly smiles! O Lady mine

WW entered a draft of this poem on the closing flyleaf of the first volume of MS. 1836/45, his copy of *PW*, 1836, that he used to prepare the editions of 1840 and 1845. The entry was probably made between the late spring of 1842, when it was too late to include the poem in *PELY*, and mid-November 1845, when *Poems* (1845) appeared. The poem's presence only in MS. 1836/45 before first publication in 1845 suggests a date of composition near that time, probably around May–June of that year, when copy was being sent to the printer.

Wansfell! this Household has a favoured lot

The on-page note was retained in editions from 1845, with the variant "south east" for "south-east" in 1849; asterisks and note are lacking in all manuscripts. Copies of the sonnet in several manuscripts are inscribed thus below the text: Rydal Mount / Chistmas Eve / 1842 *MS. 1838/40 (A)* Dec[r]. 24th 1842 [42 *rev from* 38] *MS. 1838/40 (B)* W[m] Wordsworth—/ Dec. 24. 1842 *Trinity MS.* December 24, 1842 *1845* W[m] Wordsworth / 25th Dec[r]. 1842. *Princeton MS. 6*

1 this Household] IF's residence in Ambleside.

Glad sight wherever new with old

The earliest version, beginning "Look up, look round, let things unfold," was composed on New Year's Eve, 1842, as indicated by the inscription below the poem in MS. 1838/40, "31st Dec[br] / 1842."

To a Lady, in answer to a request that I would write her a poem upon some drawings that she had made of flowers in the Island of Madeira

The poem was published in JWP's *Madeira Flowers, Fruits and Ferns* (London, 1845) and appeared in the same year in WW's *Poems*. In the *Madeira* volume WW included the date of composition, January 1, 1843, below the text of the poem. The reading text is based on WW's *Poems*, 1845.

The nature of WW's connection with JWP is not known. Perhaps one of WW's sons, John or William, Jr., met her in Madeira. JWP's daughter, Mrs. Augusta J. Robley, published a similar book, *A Selection of Madeira Flowers,* but neither book mentions the other or clarifies the connection with WW. The books are relatively rare; there is a copy of JWP's book in the WL and one of each in the Victoria and Albert Museum.

Not relevant to the history of WW's text is Thomas J. Wise's "brochure," "the only example known to exist" (with Wise's description are three stanzas of WW's poem; *Two Lake Poets* [London, 1927]); the brochure makes little sense as a publication separate from the volume of colored prints. These pages are identical in typeface, design, and text to their equivalent in the *Madeira* volume and must be an offprint or proof from the original run.

12–20 In version A in MS. 1836/45 WW entered the pencil note "Sentiment and Reflection" between the lines of draft at the foot of p. [356], but he assigned *To a Lady* to the class of Fancy when he published it in 1845.

While beams of orient light shoot wide and high

In the IF note to one of the Evening Voluntaries WW listed this sonnet, with others, as poems "alluding to morning impressions which might be read with mutual benefit in connection with these Evening Voluntaries" (see the note to "'Tis He whose yester-evening's high disdain").

The date inscribed on four of the surviving manuscripts of this sonnet is January 1, 1843. WW's dating of several drafts of the poem January 1 and January 5, 1843, in MS. 1838/40 suggest that at least these entries in the manuscript date from the beginning of January 1843.

2 Town*] The note below the text, "Ambleside," was retained in editions from 1845; the note is lacking in all manuscripts, though the word appears as title of the sonnet in three transcriptions, one from 1843 and two from 1844. Apparently at the time of printing WW transformed the title into a note to l. 2.

Grace Darling

WW told Richard Parkinson on March 17, 1843, that he composed the poem "two or three weeks ago" (*LY,* IV, 401 and note). Two weeks earlier he was in Carlisle seeing to the printing of the pamphlet form of the poem, between March 1 and 7 (*LY,* IV, 399). It was printed by Charles Thurnam (see Healey, nos. 121–124). In editions from 1845 WW assigned the poem to 1842.

On September 7, 1838, Grace Darling (1815–1842) and her father William, keeper of the Longstone lighthouse on the Farne Islands, rescued nine survivors of the wreck of the Forfarshire steamboat. In the years after the open-boat rescue she gained widespread renown for her heroism; she died October 20, 1842. A contemporary account of the wreck and dramatic rescue, which was published as a broadsheet or in the newspaper, is preserved at WL and is excerpted below:

WRECK OF THE FORFARSHIRE STEAMER. LOSS OF NEARLY FIFTY LIVES.

> We have this week to place on record the mournful details of one of the most calamitous events that has ever occurred in connexion with transit by Steam on this difficult and dangerous coast. Early on Saturday, the intelligence reached us that the Forfarshire Steamer, from Hull to Dundee, had been wrecked on the Fern [*i.e.,* Farne] Islands, and that nearly the whole of the passengers on board had perished. The account produced the deepest sensation in the town, but beyond this melancholy fact few particulars could be obtained. From inquires *made on the spot,* we are now enabled to publish the following authentic account of the sad and mournful event.

> The Forfarshire Steamer, a vessel of about 300 tons burden, under the command of Mr. John Humble, formerly master of the Neptune of this port, sailed from Hull, on her voyage to Dundee, on the evening of Wednesday the 5th instant, about half-past six o'clock, along with the Pegasus and Innisfail for Leith. Previous to leaving Hull the boilers had been examined and a small leak closed up; but when off Flambro' Head the leakage re-appeared, and continued for about six hours, not however to much extent, as the pumps were able to keep the vessel quite dry. The engineman, Allan Stewart, who furnished these particulars, also states that he had frequently seen the boiler as bad as it was on this occasion. The fireman, Daniel Donovan, however represents the leakage as considerable, so much so that two of the fires were extinguished, but they were re-lighted after the boilers had been partially repaired. [more follows on the state of the boilers, etc.]
>
> In this inefficient state the vessel, with about sixty individuals on board, was sent out on her voyage. Forth they went from the kind embraces of relatives and friends—"the glorious main expanding e'er the view"—and in a few short hours the gurgling waters rolled over their frail bark and swept them to a grave "unknelled, uncoffined, and unknown."

An account of the wreck follows, progressing to the vessel's splitting up on the rocks of Farne Islands, leaving the fore section on the rocks and sending the stern section spinning through a current called the "Piper Gut."

> The situation of the few passengers who remained on the fore part of the vessel was perilous in the extreme. Placed on a small rock surrounded by the sea which threatened to engulph them, and their companions having but just before been swept away from them, they were clinging to life whilst all hope of relief was sinking within them, and crying for help whilst the tempestuous billows drowned their feeble shrieks, and defied their puny efforts to escape. Their cries, however, were not unheard. Their shouts of distress fell upon the ear of Miss Grace Horsley Darling, who with her father Mr. Wm. Darling, occupies the outer Fern Light-house [on Longstone Island]. She awakened her parent, and at day-break he launched his boat and prepared to proceed to their rescue. The state of the tide and of the weather was such as to render any attempt to reach the wreck extremely dangerous; and the old man who had never before known the quailings of fear was loath in such a tremendous gale to rush as he considered on certain death. After watching the wreck for some time, they discovered, from some movement, that living beings were still clinging to it, and the gallant female, who partook of her father's generous sympathy, as she acknowledged the relationship of flesh and blood, with matchless intrepidity seized the oar and entered the boat. This was enough, the noble parent followed, and with the assistance of the fair sailor, conducted the frail skiff over the foaming billows to the spot where the wreck appeared. By a dangerous and desperate effort the father was landed on the rock, and to preserve the frail coble from being dashed to pieces, was rapidly rowed back among the awful abyss of waters, and kept afloat by the skilfulness and dexterity of this noble-minded young woman. At length the whole of the survivors, consisting of five of the crew and four of the deck passengers, were taken from the wreck, and conveyed to the light-house, where the same tender hand administered to their wants, and anxiously for three days and three nights waited on the sufferers, and soothed their afflictions. By the assistance of the crew, they were enabled to bring the coble and its burthen to the Long-stone Island. It is impossible to speak in too high terms of this unparalleled act of humanity, bravery and disinterestedness. The clouds of evening would to some have precluded the remotest hope of rendering assistance if ever so inclined; and the breaking forth of morning over the ocean foam, tossed high in wild confusion, whilst the elements in fierce contention rolled their tempest[u]ous fury over land and sea, would have presented a barrier apparently

> insurmountable by human energy. There was no hope of reward to stimulate to brave exertion—no encouraging plaudit to awaken emulation. Danger presented itself in a thousand forms on every hand—the current running with fearful impetuosity, or the eddy whirling and engulphing all within its reach—mountains of water bursting in wild confusion, or the tempest sweeping the spray from the billow as it rolled along. From her isolated abode this intrepid woman rushed forth under the promptings of humanity, and hastened through the scene of desolation and danger, regardless of her own life in order that she might save the life of others. This perilous achievement—unexampled in the feats of female fortitude—was witnessed by the survivors in silent wonder—and down the weather-beaten cheek of one old seaman stole the big round tear when he beheld from the wreck the noble exertions of a young female of slender appearance, buffetting the storm, and periling her life for their preservation. The main land could not be reached, from the state of the weather, till Sunday, and during the whole of this time the attentions of the heroine were indefatigable. Mr. Darling has lived on the Island for some years, and has on many occasions been instrumental in saving life and property when precautionary measures were unavailable.

The article continues with an account of rescue attempts from the mainland, none successful in saving further lives; details of the inquest, held on the following Tuesday in Bamburgh Castle; lists of known survivors, and other matters. Several words and phrases in WW's poem (1843 version) suggest that he read this article.

WW wrote of the poem to HR, March 27, 1843, "I threw it off two or three weeks ago, being in a great measure impelled to it by the desire I felt to do justice to the memory of a heroine, whose conduct presented some time ago a striking contrast to the inhumanity with which our Countrymen shipwrecked lately upon the French coast have been treated" (*LY*, IV, 416).

Among letters from EFO to WW is a transcription in an unidentified hand of verses from *Grace Darling*. It seems likely that the copy was taken from the pamphlet published in 1843. It is on two bifolia of creamy wove stock measuring 27.5 by 18.5 cm., the same type of paper used by EFO for letters sent to WW in 1840–1842. The text is virtually the same as the 1843 pamphlet including the two verbal variants from the 1845 text in ll. 56–57 and 84, and two missing lines at ll. 85–86. The transcription probably has no independent authority. (WL, Letters, A/Ogle/4.)

27 holy Cuthbert's cell] St. Cuthbert, a monk of the monastery of Melrose, was made prior of Lindisfarne in 684; seeking solitude just before his death he retired to the small island of Farne, where he died in his cell on March 20, 687. His body was said to have remained uncorrupted for several years and was removed from the island only when the monks were driven from Lindisfarne by the Danes.

85–86 In Huntington MS. 12 WW first entered the new lines in very light pencil and retraced them in ink. He then entered l. 85 and the revision of l. 84 between the printed lines and JC recopied l. 86 in the margin.

Inscription for a Monument in Crosthwaite Church, in the Vale of Keswick

For the dating of this poem see the headnote.

Pages 191–192 of Hoare Album contain the epitaph in the autograph of Sarah Hoare. It is quite clearly a transcript of the first broadside, with the omission of some punctuation, and without independent textual authority.

To the Rev. Christopher Wordsworth, D.D. Master of Harrow School

In his letter to EM of December 4, 1843, WW inquired whether CW, Jr., had forwarded a copy of his *Theophilus Anglicanus*, an exposition of the Anglican *via media* in the form of a dialogue (*LY*, IV, 505 and note). On December 20 WW wrote to his brother, CW, that he had read "Chris's Work both with profit and pleasure" and commented, "I have not thanked him for it yet, except through the medium of the Morning Post, in a Sonnet printed in that journal, friday or Saturday last" (*LY*, IV, 510 and note). The poem appeared in *MP* on December 15, 1843; there are no verbal differences between the *MP* text and that of *Poems*, 1845; as the many variants in punctuation and capitalization in *MP* are not likely to be authorial, we do not report them.

In 1845 WW assigned December 11, 1843, as the date of composition, as does Dora W beneath her copy in DC MS. 176. WW transcribed the sonnet on the flyleaf of at least two copies of CW, Jr.'s book: his entry in one that was on display at Rydal Mount in the 1980s probably dates from around January 16, 1844. Verbal variants in the copy are the title, *To the Author*, and the correction in l. 2, probably by CW, Jr., of "Have I received" to "Do I receive" (as directed by WW in his letter to CW, Jr., January 16, 1844; (*LY*, IV, 519). The copy once belonged to CW, Jr.; it was on display at Rydal Mount in the 1980s, but it is now untraced. MW's copy in the Ticknor MS. (see the Manuscript Census) was probably entered sometime in the latter half of 1845.

So fair, so sweet, withal so sensitive

WW wrote to Julius Charles Hare, in late August 1844, that "a few days after our delightful walk upon Loughrigg Fell I threw off the verses which I enclose, with a view to their being inserted in the Copy of my poems which you presented to Miss Morris [*i.e.*, Maurice]" (*LY*, IV, 589–590). Alan Hill notes that Esther Maurice, the sister of Frederick Denison Maurice, was with Hare, his widowed sister-in-law, and her son, when they visited the Arnolds at Fox How in July. In August Hare became engaged to Esther Maurice (*LY*, IV, 589n). She was in the party, with Hare, William Archer Butler, Sir William R. Hamilton, and R. P. Graves, which made the excursion led by WW over Loughrigg Fell to Loughrigg Tarn. Hare, Butler and Graves were all clergymen. Graves gave the following account (in a letter published in the introductory memoir of the Rev. William Archer Butler in Butler's *Sermons Doctrinal and Practical*, [ed. Thomas Woodward; Dublin, 1849], pp. xxviii–xix):

> The party consisted of Mr. Wordsworth, Archdeacon Hare, Sir William R. Hamilton, Professor Butler, and two ladies, both by name and mental qualities worthy of the association, besides myself. The day was brilliant, and continued so throughout, as we ascended one of the ravines of Loughrigg Fell, opposite to Rydal, crossed over the Fell, descended to the margin of Loughrigg Tarn, and returned to the social circle of Rydal Mount by the western side of Grasmere and Rydal Lakes, enjoying the perfect view of the former lake to be seen from the green terrace of Loughrigg, and the equally advantageous aspect of Rydal Mere and Nab Scar, which this route presents. . . . The day was additionally memorable as giving birth to an interesting minor poem of Mr. Wordsworth's. When we reached the side of Loughrigg Tarn . . . , the loveliness of the scene arrested our steps and fixed our gaze. The splendour of a July noon surrounded us and lit up the landscape, with the Langdale Pikes soaring above, and the bright tarn shining beneath; and when the poet's eyes were satisfied with their feast on the beauty familiar to them, they sought relief in the search, to them a happy vital habit, for new beauty in the flower-enamelled turf at his feet. There his attention was attracted by a fair, smooth stone, of the size of an ostrich's egg, seeming to imbed at its centre, and, at the same time, to display a dark star-shaped fossil of most distinct outline. Upon closer inspection this proved to be the shadow of a daisy projected upon it with extraordinary precision by the intense light of an almost vertical sun. The poet drew the attention of the rest of the party to the minute, but beautiful phenomenon, and gave expression at the time to thoughts suggested by it, and which so interested our friend, Professor Butler, that he plucked the tiny flower, and, saying 'that it should be not only the theme but the memorial of the thoughts they had heard,' bestowed it somewhere, carefully, for preservation. The little poem, in which some of those thoughts were afterwards crystallized, commences with the stanza,

So fair, so sweet, withal sensitive,
Would that the little flowers were born to live,
Conscious of half the pleasure that they give.

Hare replied to WW's August letter on September 14, 1844, remarking that "nor shall we [*i.e.*, Hare and Esther Maurice] ever forget your stopping and drawing our attention to the exquisitely pencilled shadow which the daisy cast on the neighbouring stone. I remember saying at the time, 'We shall have a sonnet upon it'; and this prophecy has been fulfilled, I rejoice to learn, save that, instead of the sonnet, you have adopted a new form of verse, that is, new, I believe, in your writings, in composing the beautiful triplets" (WL Letters; quoted in part in *PW*, IV, 430). Lilly MS. 5 is inscribed "W[m] Wordsworth / Trin: Lodge / Cambridge Nov[r] 4th 1844"; WW stopped to see CW at Cambridge on his way back to Rydal from Leamington (*LY*, IV, 618–621).

An "autograph of a poem" (perhaps Lilly MS. 4 or 5) was sent to Robert Perceval Graves by Thomas H. Hutchinson in 1869, prompting Graves to describe the poem as one "which has indeed a very peculiar interest for me as having been conceived during that walk on Loughrigg which joined in elevated pleasure men so above their fellows as your illustrious uncle [by marriage] Sir W. R. Hamilton, Professor Archer Butler, and Archdeacon Hare. I have a few Wordsworth autographs, but this I assure you will be amongst the most prized of them, being the most precious record of that to me very memorable day" (R. P. Graves to T. H. Hutchinson, June 10, 1869; WL Letters).

Sonnet on the Projected Kendal and Windermere Railway

A copy of this sonnet in an unidentified hand is in the Cornell University Library (Healey, 2292). The sheet on which the poem is copied was used first as a cover to send something else in the post. But as the ink of the transcription flows into the tear made by the seal, the poem must have been copied, apparently, from *MP*—the two texts are identical—after the sheet had been posted and received. The title was added at the foot, below WW's name and date, but the manuscript cannot claim any authority.

For the text of the pamphlet and an account of WW's tenacious but futile opposition to parliamentary approval of the construction of a railway line from Kendal to Windermere see *Prose*, III, 331–366. Approval was granted in April 1845; the line from Oxenholme to Kendal was opened on September 22, 1846, and from Kendal to Windermere on April 21, 1847. The reading text is based on WW's revised second issue of the pamphlet, published in London soon after February 2, 1845.

1 WW revised "was" to "is" on the advice of HCR, "Your suggestion of *is* for *was* &c will be attended to" (*LY*, IV, 658).

13 This line was entered twice in Betz MS. 5.

Proud were ye, Mountains, when, in times of old

In her letter to IF on December 14, 1844, MW said she had been "writing for W[m] at a cold window, the day being too dark to see elsewhere, all the morning. You must look to the Morn[g] Post for his labours. If you have not seen it, refer to last Wednesday's number—for the long-promised letter on the Rail-way, and in a few days you may see its sequel, with another Sonnet thrown off yesterday morning" (*LY*, IV, 638). WW ended his second published letter "On the Kendal and Windermere Railway" (which MW was probably "writing" on December 14) with "Proud were ye, Mountains, when, in times of old," having first concluded that his motive in opposing the construction of the railway was selfish only "If gratitude for what repose and quiet in a district hitherto, for the most part, not disfigured but beautified by human hands, have done for me through the course of a long life, and hope that others might hereafter be benefited in the same manner and in the same country, *be* selfishness" and adding that he was not protesting against it "on account of the inhabitants of the district *merely*, but . . . for the sake of every one, however humble his condition, who coming hither shall bring with him an eye to perceive, and a heart to feel and worthily enjoy" (*Prose*, III, 355).

In the second *MP* letter and the proofs for the pamphlet (MS. 157; the original holograph letter does not survive) a note follows WW's name: "Note.—If any one, from the perusal of these letters, should suppose that I am blind to the power by which railways have been produced and the good that may be expected from them in their *legitimate* application, let him take the trouble, if he think it worth while, to read a sonnet of mine, published some years ago, entitled 'Steamboats, Viaducts, and Railways.' W.W." (with "Rydal Mount, Dec. 17, 1844," added in *MP*). In the revised pamphlet the sonnet, *Steamboats and Railways* (so titled), and a concise version of WW's note were incorporated into the main text just preceding "Proud were ye." See the notes to *Sonnet on the Projected Kendal and Windermere Railway*.

The reading text is based on WW's revised second issue of the pamphlet, published in London on February 2, 1845.

The Westmoreland Girl. To My Grandchildren

WW sent a copy of the earlier version of the poem to HR on July 1, 1845 (*LY*, IV, 688), saying that it was written "the other day." Below a copy of this same version that she entered in her Portuguese Sketchbook (WL GRMDC: B52), DQ added the annotation "K:S M:S Received from Rydal Mount at The Foz: July 2. 1845." Several manuscript copies of this version are inscribed: "Rydal May 1845" (MS. 143), "W.W. / June / 45" (WL MS.), and "Wm Wordsworth / Rydal Mount / June 6th 1845" (Cornell MS. 12).

In his letter to HR of July 31, 1845, WW sent two additional stanzas with the comment: "The little Poem which I ventured to send you lately I thought might interest you on account of the fact as exhibiting what sort of characters our mountains breed. It is truth to the Letter"; he added, after copying out the new concluding stanza, "It was thought by some of my Friends that the other conclusion took the mind too much away from the subject" (*LY*, IV, 694).

57 In MS. 155_1 a dot midway between "while" and "of" may represent hesitant punctuation in the base text (see the nonverbal variants for this line).

Yes! thou art fair, yet be not moved

WW probably composed the poem between early June and early November 1845, while preparing copy and revisions for the one-volume *Poems*. The only known holograph copy of the poem is found in MS. 156: revisions for other poems entered in the same manuscript were adopted in the edition of 1845. In the stereotype editions of 1846 and 1849 WW included "Yes! thou art fair" in the miscellaneous group of poems in the new "sixth volume"—that is, the 1842 volume, *PELY*, with its contents rearranged and fitted out with a new title page, and a binding uniform with the rest of the set. But WW intended the poem to follow—and to comment upon—*To* ——— " ("Let other Bards of Angels sing"; see above, pp. 38, 423), and so placed it in all editions except 1846. Both poems are addressed to MW.

Forth from a jutting ridge, around whose base

In a letter to George Huntley Gordon, June 24, 1845, WW politely declined taking Gordon's suggestion about a subject for a poem. "The Extract which [you] have sent me is very pleasing, but I do not feel I could make any thing of it in a poem, as you recommend. Besides, there is some thing wayward in matters of this kind. When a subject was proposed to Gainsborough for a picture, if he liked it he used to say, 'What a pity I did not think of it myself'." He illustrated his point by referring to the composition of "Forth from a jutting ridge, around whose base": "My own practise is odd even in respect to subjects of my own chusing. It was only a few days ago that I was able to put into Verse the Matter of a short Poem which had been in my mind with a determination and a strong desire to write upon it for more than thirty years; nor is this the first time when the like has occurred" (*LY*, IV, 680).

WW entered a draft of the poem at the end of Naming of Places in MS. 1836/45, probably very near the time of publication. Beneath his draft of the poem he added the note "28 lines" and immediately corrected the number to 26. In editions from 1845 he dated the poem 1845.

2–3 The words interlined in pencil, as noted in the variants, probably refer to "Forth from a jutting Ridge," but may be jottings, entered first but not erased, for "When, to the attractions of the busy world," the final lines of which (and its note) appear at the top of p. 302 in vol. 2.

8–9 twin . . . two] The reading "To one or other brow of those twin Peaks / Were too adventurous Sisters wont to climb" is present in all printed forms of the text, but the one manuscript version, MS. 1836/45, reads "twin . . . two," the point of the passage having to do with two sisters and two peaks. Although the Wordsworths read proof for the 1845 edition, "too" appears to be an undetected printer's error that was not caught in subsequent editions.

16 Now are they parted] SH died on June 23, 1835.

24 Mary and Sarah Point, the twin rock formation, is in Bainriggs, the wood that lies between the old road from Grasmere to Rydal and the foot of Grasmere Lake. The viewpoint from the two rocks at the top of Bainriggs was long a favorite with MW and SH, who liked its prospect of Rydal and Grasmere (*LY*, IV, 680 and note).

At Furness Abbey ("WELL have yon Railway Labourers to THIS ground")

MW wrote to HCR on June 21, 1845: "Miss Fenwick with Kate Southey returned last night to R[ydal] M[ount] from a 2 days Excursion to Newby Bridge and Furness Abbey with the Miss Arnolds—they had the pain (tho it was a picturesque appearance) of seeing the Old Abbey occupied by the 'Navys' at their meal, who are carrying a rail-way, so near to the East window that from it Persons might shake hands with the Passengers!!" (*LY*, IV, 679). WW composed the sonnet later on the same day. A fortnight later, in Portugal, Dora W added a note beneath her transcript of this poem in her Portuguese Sketchbook (WL): "sent to me by him to the Foz: July 2^{d}. 1845. N.B. *True* as witnessed by Miss Fenwick Miss Southey and *others* Transcribed again. 3^{d}" Her notation "Transcribed again. 3^{d}" probably means she made a copy of the sonnet for someone else the day after receiving the copy from WW.

8–10 At the time of his own visit to Furness Abbey in July 1840, WW recorded in his pocket notebook the approximate dimensions of the great arch between the transepts and choir of the church: "30 feet from Centre to / Centre / 70 feet hight / to Keystone" (*WPN*, p. 30).

Why should we weep or mourn, Angelic boy

WW received word "on Christmas Eve" from Isabella, wife of his son John, that their son Edward (b. April 1841) had died of fever in Rome; he told Elizabeth Fisher on January 2, 1846, that "the child . . . was one of the noblest Creatures both in mind and body I ever saw" (*LY*, IV, 740–741). Around January 10 he enclosed his sonnet in a letter to CW, Jr. (*LY*, IV, 746), and on January 23 he sent it, with a copy of "Where lies the truth," in his letter to HR (*LY*, IV, 752). The copy in the Southey Family Album (Southey Album 2) is annotated by Herbert Hill as having been "written January 1846." WW dated the poem 1846 in *PW* of 1846, 1849, and 1850. See also the note to "Where lies the truth? has Man, in wisdom's creed."

I know an aged Man constrained to dwell

Three of WW's four copies in MS. 143 are dated "Jan^{ry} 1846," too late for inclusion in the one-volume edition published in December 1845 but early enough to be slipped into the revised stereotype seven-volume edition in late February 1846 (*LY*, IV, 760–761; the new edition was published by early July). WW added the poem to a miscellaneous grouping in the new sixth volume printed from revised plates of the 1842 volume, *PELY.* In the editions of 1846, 1849, and 1850 WW dated the poem 1846.

In his 1843 IF note to *The Old Cumberland Beggar, a Description* (published in 1798), WW discussed the earlier poem in relation to the present condition of the poor in the aftermath of what he called the "AMENDED poor-law bill" of 1834: the "inhumanity that prevails in this measure is somewhat disguised by the profession that one of its objects is to throw the poor upon the voluntary donations of their beighbours, that is, if rightly interpreted, to force them into a condition between relief in the union poor House and Alms robbed of their Christian grace and spirit. . . ." (*FNW,* p. 56; see also WW's Postscript to *Yarrow Revisited,* 1835 [*Prose,* III, 240–248, 261–267, and the editors' commentary on pp. 233–234], and *LB, 1797–1800,* pp. 393–394). In "I know and aged Man constrained to dwell" WW has shifted the focus away from the loss to the community of its opportunity for natural generosity and placed it instead on the poignancy of old man's loss *of* community, his kinship or "tie" (l. 21) with the redbreast.

To an Octogenarian

In a note above version B of the poem in MS. 143, WW wrote, "This Sonnet to precede the last Poem"; "last Poem" refers to *Poor Robin.* Version A in MS. 143 is deleted with a large ink cross.

The poem was first published in *PW,* 1846, which was in preparation in January 1846, after *Poems,* 1845, had been printed and distributed, and went to press in May of 1845. The presence of two copies in MS. 143, for the most part a collection of poems published in *PELY,* 1842, might suggest a date of composition as early as March 1840, but the later date seems more likely. WW assigned the poem to 1846 in the edition of 1846, its stereotype of 1849, and the final edition of 1850.

Written upon a fly leaf in the Copy of the Author's Poems which was sent to her Majesty Queen Victoria

MW's fair copy of "Deign Sovereign Mistress" is entered, along with its descriptive title, in DC MS. 89. WW probably composed the poem very near the date he inscribed below the copy presented to the Queen (MS. 1845RL), the same date that MW added to her copy, January 9, 1846. The poem, never published by WW, first appeared in print in *Prose* (Grosart), I, [vi], in 1876.

5 Queen Victoria was twenty-seven in 1846 and was the mother of four children by this date; she married Prince Albert of Saxe-Coburg-Gotha in 1840.

Who but is pleased to watch the moon on high

WW has dated the second copy in MS. 143 "Jan 10th 1846." WW assigned the poem to 1846 in *PW,* 1846, its stereotype of 1849, and the final edition of 1850. Another version of these lines in two quatrains, edited below as "How beautiful the Queen of Night, on high," was first published in 1850.

How beautiful the Queen of Night, on high

This set of quatrains seems to derive from WW's sonnet "Who but is pleased to watch the moon on high," which was composed on January 10, 1846, according to WW's note in MS. 143. But he did not insert the poem into volume six of the 1846 edition, which was published in June, as he did the sonnet and a number of other "miscellaneous" poems composed in the first few months of the year. EQ dated the copy of "How beautiful the Queen of Night" that he entered in MS. 1845D, September 3, 1849.

Where lies the truth? has Man in wisdom's creed

In his letter to HR on January 23, 1846, WW enclosed this sonnet and "Why should we weep or mourn, Angelic boy." Commenting first on the death of his grandson in Rome and the "alarming state of health" of his "only surviving Brother" (CW) and the "mortal illness" of his brother Richard's son, he added, "These sad occurrences with others of like kind have thrown my mind into a state of feeling which the other day vented itself in the two Sonnets which Mrs W. will transcribe as the best acknowledgement she can make for Mrs Reed's and your kindness" (*LY*, IV, 752). "Why should we weep" was composed by January 10, when it was enclosed in WW's letter to CW, Jr.; news of CW's illness seems to have reached WW after his letter to CW, Jr., was sent (*LY*, IV, 745–746).

WW assigned the poem to 1846 in the edition of 1846, its stereotype of 1849, and the final edition of 1850.

7–8 Cf. *L'Allegro*, ll. 41, 46: "To hear the Lark begin his flight, . . . / And at my window bid good morrow" (EdeS).

To Lucca Giordano

Lucca Giordano (1632–1705) of Naples, an artist. CW, Jr., reported that the picture was displayed on the staircase at Rydal Mount and was brought "with some others by the author's eldest son from Italy" (*Memoirs*, I, 28). WW assigned the poem to 1846 in the edition of 1846, its stereotype of 1849, and the final edition of 1850.

Illustrated Books and Newspapers

On February 23, 1846, WW told EM he would "send you soon as they can be transcribed 6 Sonnets and 2 other small Poems to be inserted in the last Vol." *Illustrated Books and Newspapers* was one of six sonnets added to volume six in the edition of 1846. By April 2, 1846, a title page had been printed for this new volume (made up primarily from the contents of *PELY*). (See *LY*, IV, 760 and note, and 768).

WW assigned the poem to 1846 in the edition of 1846, its stereotype of 1849, and the final edition of 1850.

10 For manhood—] JC may have been responsible for the change to "From" in 1850, which was probably set up from the 1846 text. But WW clearly intended "For," having traced over MW's "From" in MS. 143 to establish a parallel construction with "for the Age—" at the end of the same line.

On the Banks of a Rocky Stream

For date of composition see the headnote.

Installation Ode

1, 3, 11 These lines were altered in the intermediate version and then restored, apparently at TAW's request, but the rejected revision does not survive (TAW to WW, May 3, 1847).

3, 6 Spoiler . . . Libyan rock] Napoleon, exiled to the island of Elba in the Mediterranean.

9, 11 "and" replaces "to" in *1847 Bell.*

22 the Isle's delight] Princess Charlotte Augusta, only child of George IV, died in childbirth in 1817.

36 "bold and clear" replaces "clear and bold" in *1847 Bell.*

38 Victoria] Queen Victoria, daughter of the Duke of Kent, was born in 1819.

59–61 Gotha's ducal roof . . . spires of Bonn] Prince Albert was born at Gotha and studied at Bonn. The river Leine is 60 miles north of Gotha near Goslar, where WW and DW spent the winter of 1799.

63 Camus] The river Cam, also called Granta (l. 69), flows through Cambridge.

94 "faction's" replaces "factious" in *1847 Bell.*

99 The note is lacking in *1847 Bell.*

Nonverbal Variants

The nonverbal differences from reading texts listed here include variants in spelling, punctuation, and capitalization found in authorially influenced manuscripts and in lifetime editions, except for (1) those that appear in manuscripts presented in photographs and transcriptions, (2) those that are integral parts of verbal changes, and (3) those identified among verbal variants as part of a distinctive phase of authorial or editorial revision of a complex manuscript. Also not recorded are ampersands, single-letter overwritings (corrected by the copyist), and reinforcements of punctuation marks when no change is made. Poems not listed here either lack nonverbal variants or appear in transcription.

Abbreviations of lifetime printings cited are listed at the end of the Editorial Procedure. Manuscripts are identified in the Manuscript Census.

Decay of Piety

title *no punct all MSS. except MS. 158*

1 seen, *rev from* seen *MS. 89* ploughed] plowed *MSS. 89, 131*

2 Sires—] Sires, *MS. 131* Sires. *Amherst MS.* Sires— *rev from* Sires, *MS. 158* who, *rev from* who *MS. 89* who *Amherst MS., MS. 131*

3 Church,] Church *Amherst MS., MS. 131* Fast or Festival] fast or festival *Amherst MS., 1836–, 1838* Festival, *MS. 131*

4 Through] Thro' *MSS. 89, 131* Prayer] prayer, *Amherst MS.* seek:] seek *Amherst MS., 1849* seek, *rev to* seek. *MS. 89* seek, *MS. 131*

6 winds,] winds *MS. 131* *no commas Amherst MS.* Hut] hut *Cornell MS., Amherst MS., 1836–, 1838* Hall] hall *1836–, 1838*

7 came *rev to* came— *MS. 89* Stall,] stall *Amherst MS., MS. 131* stall, *1836–, 1838*

8 fervour] fervor *MS. 131* meek: *rev to* meek— *MS. 131*

9 places] Places *Amherst MS.* *no comma Amherst MS.*

10 ask, *rev from* ask *MS. 89* *no commas Amherst MS.*

11 ancient] antient *Amherst MS.* Piety] piety *Amherst MS.*

12 Alas!] Alas *Amherst MS.* seemed] seemed, *alt MS. 89*

13 That,] That *MS. 89, Amherst MS.* through] thro' *MSS. 89, 131* sky,] sky[ ] *MS. 89* sky *Amherst MS.*

14 sun!] sun. *MS. 131* sun *Amherst MS.*

Not Love, nor War, nor the tumultuous swell

Cornell MS. 2 and MS. 89 unpunct except as shown below.

1 Love . . . War] love . . . war *Baillie* *commas present MS. 89*

3 Duty] duty *MS. 89, Cornell MS. 2, Baillie* strange,] strange— *1836–, 1838*

4 alone] alone *ital 1836–, 1838*

6 Muse] muse *Baillie* range, *MS. 89*

8 Skyward] Sky-ward *MS. 89*

9 her,] her *Baillie*

10 content,] content *Baillie*

11 river,] river— *1836–, 1838*

12 Diaphanous,] Diaphanous *1836–, 1838* slowly;] slowly: *Baillie*

13 ever;] ever, *Baillie*

Recollection of the Portrait of King Henry Eighth, Trinity Lodge, Cambridge.

8 far descried] far-descried *1836–, 1838*

10 Mid . . . King!] 'Mid . . . King, *1832–, 1838* worthies] Worthies *1836–, 1838*

14 check,] check *1836–, 1838* abate.] abate! *1832–, 1838*

A volant Tribe of Bards on earth are found

MS. 89 unpunct except as noted

1 Tribe of Bards] tribe of bards *Baillie*

2 flattering] flatt'ring zephyrs *Baillie*

3 *no quots MS. 89, single quots 1836–, 1838* clay;] clay, *MS. 89* clay. *Baillie*

4 aery *rev from* [?airry] *MS. 89* unbound,] unbound! *1834*

5 oblivion! To *rev from* oblivion! to *MS. 89* *accidental mark between* solid *and* ground *MS. 89*
7 Convinced] Convinc'd *MS. 89*
8 round,] round *MS. 89*
10 eye] eye, *MS. 89*
12 Angel's] Angels *MS. 89* angel's *Baillie*

By Moscow self-devoted to a blaze

2 sacrifice;] sacrifice— *DW to HCR*
3 hardihood;] hardihood— *DW to HCR*
4 Elements] elements *DW to HCR*
5 Human-nature] human nature *DW to HCR* praise] praise. *DW to HCR*
7 deliverance . . . pure] deliverance, . . . pure; *DW to HCR*
9 Most] most *DW to HCR*
10 Voice;—] voice, *DW to HCR* voice;— *1836–, 1838*
11 Power . . . Ally] power . . . ally *1836–, 1838*
12 He] He, *1836–, 1838*
14 Finish . . . Victory!] "Finish . . . victory!" *1836–, 1838*

These Vales were saddened with no common gloom

1–16 *entire text on Tablet in small and large capitals*
2 bloom;] bloom *Mary Smith Album* bloom: *Tablet*
3 When (such . . . heaven)] When, . . . heaven, *Tablet* heaven] Heaven *MW to EQ, MS. 131, Mary Smith Album*
4 fire-side.] fire-side.— *MS. 131* fire-side! *Mary Smith Album* fire side. *Tablet*
5 Earth] earth *MS. 131*
6 know, . . . heart;] know; . . . heart— *Mary Smith Album* know, . . . heart: *Tablet*
7 she] She *MS. 131, MW to EQ, MW to TM*
8 speak; *rev to* speak: *MW to TM* speak, *Mary Smith Album*
9 tell] tell, *MW to EQ, Tablet* record,] record *Mary Smith Album*
10 deplored,] deplored *Mary Smith Album*
11 grief's] griefs *Mary Smith Album* adorn'd,] adorn'd *MS. 131* adorned, *MW to EQ* adorned *MW to TM, Mary Smith Album, Tablet*
12 mourn'd;] mourned; *MS. 131, MW to EQ, MW to TM* mourned. *Mary Smith Album* mourned: *Tablet*
13 virtues] Virtues *MS. 131* life,] life *Mary Smith Album, Tablet*
14 Wife,] wife— *Mary Smith Album*
15 cheerful] chearful *MS. 131* shone:] shone; *MW to TM* shone *Mary Smith Album* shone— *Tablet*
16 light] Light *MS. 131, Mary Smith Album* past] passed *MS. 131, Mary Smith Album* pass'd *MW to EQ* done!] done. *Tablet*

To the Lady ———. On Seeing the Foundation Preparing for the Erection of ——— Chapel, Westmoreland

1 Isle—] Isle, *Cornell MS. 1* Land;] Land, *MSS. 100, 131, Cornell MSS. 1, 3* Land, *rev from* land, *MW to Lady B*
2 battlement . . . gate] Battlement . . . Gate *Cornell MS. 1*
4 Time] time *Cornell MS. 1* Time *rev from* time *Cornell MS. 3*
6 wreaths, *rev from* wreathes, *Cornell MS. 3* wreaths *Cornell MS. 1*
7 rampart's] ramparts *Cornell MS. 3, MS. 131* require; *MSS. 100, 131, MW to Lady B, Cornell MSS. 1, 3*
8 heaven-directed] heav'n-directed *MW to Lady B, Cornell MS. 3* Spire] spire *MS. 1832/36–*
9 steeple] Steeple *Cornell MS. 1* Tower] tower *Cornell MS. 1, MS. 1832/36–*
10 Far heard] Far-heard *1845–* —our] our *Cornell MS. 1* Citadels.] Citadels! *MS. 100* citadels. *MW to Lady B, Cornell MS. 1, MS. 1832/36–*
11 O Lady!] Oh Lady, *Cornell MS. 1*
12 Chieftains] Chieftans *MS. 131* chieftains *MS. 1832/36–*
13 spear] Spear *MW to Lady B, Cornell MSS. 1, 3, MS. 131* works] Works *MW to Lady B, Cornell MS. 1, MS. 131*
14 *no comma Cornell MS. 1*
15 Dell] dell *Cornell MS. 3*
16 Nightshade*] Night Shade *Cornell MS. 1* tell)] tell;) *MS. 1832/36–*
note to l. 16 Abbey,] Abbey *1845, 1850*
18 build,] build *Cornell MS. 1* Vale] vale *MS. 1832/36–*
19 Him *rev from* him *MW to Lady B, Cornell MS. 3*
20 rests.] rests! *MSS. 100, 131, MW to Lady B, Cornell MS. 3*
21 Villagers] villagers *MS. 1832/36–*
23 voice *rev to* Voice *MS. 131* Voice *WW to Lord Lonsdale, MW to Lady B, Cornell MS. 1*
24 praise;] praise: *WW to Lord Lonsdale, MW to Lady B, Cornell MSS. 1, 3, MS. 131*
25 wild-wandering] wild wandering

Cornell MS. 1, 1836– Youth] youth, *Cornell MS. 1*

26 receive] recieve *WW to Lord Lonsdale* curb of sacred] Curb of Sacred *Cornell MS. 1* truth,] truth; *WW to Lord Lonsdale, MW to Lady B, Cornell MS. 1* Truth, *MS. 131*

28 Promise,] Promise *Cornell MS. 1, MS. 131* ear;] ear, *MW to Lady B, Cornell MS. 1, MS. 131*

29 all] all *rev to* All *WW to Lord Lonsdale* all *MW to Lady B, Cornell MS. 1, MS. 131*

30 Sabbath-day.] sabbath-day. *MS. 1832/36–* Sabbath day *MW to Lady B* Sabbath day. *rev to* Sabbath day— *Cornell MS. 1* Sabbath day. *Cornell MS. 3* Sabbath Day. *MS. 131*

32 *no comma Cornell MS. 3*

34 recess] Recess *MS. 100, MW to Lady B, Cornell MS. 3, MS. 131* fair;] fair! *MSS. 100, 131, MW to Lady B, Cornell MS. 1*

35 hour;] hour *MSS. 100, 131, Cornell MSS. 1, 3* hour, *MW to Lady B*

36 it,] it *Cornell MSS. 1, 3, 1836–*

37 Sacrifice] Sacrifice *double underscore MW to Lady B, Cornell MSS. 1, 3, MS. 131* *no comma MW to Lady B, Cornell MSS. 1, 3, MS. 131*

38 soil] Soil *Cornell MS. 1*

47 evening] Evening *WW to BF*

48 Death] death *MS. 1832/36–*

49 Generations] generations *MS. 1832/36–*

50 Eternity] eternity *MS. 1832/36–*

51 Man] man *Cornell MS. 1, MS. 1832/36–*

52 pomp] pomp, *MS. 100, MW to Lady B, Cornell MS. 1* noise,] noise *Cornell MS. 1*

54 enjoys?] enjoys; *MSS. 100, 131, MW to Lady B, Cornell MSS. 1, 3*

55 dream] dream, *Cornell MS. 1*

56–57 *no punct Cornell MS. 1*

56 murmur *rev from* murmer *MS to Lady B*

57 aught *rev from* ought *WW to Lord Lonsdale, Cornell MS. 1*

58 verdure *rev from* [?verture] *MS. 100* fields;] fields *Cornell MS. 1*

60 Sun] sun *1832–* Setting *Cornell MS. 1* shrouds.] shrouds? *MSS. 100, 131* shrouds! *MW to Lady B*

61 Soul] soul *MW to Lady B, MS. 1832/36–*

61–64 *no commas Cornell MS. 1*

63 scorn] Scorn *Cornell MS. 1*

64 pride,] Pride, *Cornell MS. 1* pride *Cornell MS. 3, MS. 131* pride; *1836–*

65 unblest—] unblest, *Cornell MS. 1*

64–65 *no punct MS. 131*

67 scope *rev from* Scope *MW to Lady B* Scope *Cornell MS. 1*

68 faith and Christian] Faith and Christian *Cornell MS. 1* faith—and christian *MW to Lady B* faith and christian *Cornell MS. 3, MS. 131, MS. 1832/36–* *no punct Cornell MS. 1*

69 shipwrecked] shipwreck'd *1845–*

72 Britain's] Britains *Cornell MS. 1* ground!] ground; *MSS. 100, 131, MW to Lady B, Cornell MSS. 1, 3*

74 wound] wound, *MSS. 100, 131, Cornell MS. 3*

78 defy,] defy; *MSS. 100, 131, MW to Lady B, Cornell MSS. 1, 3*

79 *ital canceled MS. 1832/36, no ital 1836–*

80 extremity!] extremity. *MSS. 100, 131, MW to Lady B, Cornell MS. 1* extremity, *Cornell MS. 3*

81 "bold bad" men;] "bold bad men" *Cornell MS. 1* "bold bad Men;" *Cornell MS. 3* "bold bad Men"! *MW to Lady B; so MS. 131 but* men *rev to* Men men] Men *MS. 100*

82 *no comma MSS. 100, 131, Cornell MS. 1, MW to Lady B* *no exclam Cornell MS. 1*

83 *no comma MS. 100, Cornell MS. 1, MW to Lady B*

84 Thee *rev from* thee *Cornell MS. 1* tread.] tread:— *MS. 100, MW to Lady B, Cornell MS. 3* tread;— *MS. 131*

86 Through] Thro' *MW to Lady B, Cornell MS. 1*

87 tenour] tenor *Cornell MSS. 1, 3, MS. 131, MS. 1832/36–* Song *MS. 100, MW to Lady B, Cornell MS. 1*

88 Charity] charity *MS. 1832/36–*

90 days *Cornell MS. 1* work,] Work, *MS. 100* Work *MW to Lady B* work *Cornell MS. 1, MS. 131*

91 peace,] peace *MW to Lady B, MS. 131* *no commas Cornell MS. 1*

92 hope,] hope *MS. 100* consolation,] consolation *MS. 100, MW to Lady B, Cornell MSS. 1, 3* fall,] fall *MS. 131*

93 its] it's *MS. 131* influence,] influence *MS. 131*

94 all;] all— *MSS. 100, 131, Cornell MS. 3* all, *MW to Lady B, Cornell MS. 1*

95 who,] who *MW to Lady B, Cornell MS. 1* Fane,] Fane *MS. 131*

96 domain] Domain *MS. 100, Cornell MS. 3* domain *rev to* Domain *MW to*

Lady B, MS. 131 *no punct Cornell MS. 1*

97 Thee,] Thee *rev from* thee *Cornell MS. 1* Thee *double underscore MW to Lady B, MS. 131* pure,] pure *MS. 100, Cornell MS. 1, MW to Lady B, MS. 131*

98 ordinance,] ordinance *MSS. 100, 131, Cornell MS. 1, MW to Lady B* endure,] endure *Cornell MS. 1*

100 *no comma MS. 100, Cornell MS. 1, MW to Lady B*

On the Same Occasion

title OCCASION] Occasion *with first* "c" *rev from illeg letter MS. 89* *no punct MSS. 89, 131*

epigraph

2 requires;] requires, *1849*

4 Sires] sires *1836–*

headnote, first sentence due] due *ital 1832–* Saint] saint *1832–*

second sentence Ancestors] ancestors *1836–*

1 age] Age *MS. 131*

2 clothed] cloathed *MS. 131*

3 Ministers] ministers *MS. 1832/36–, 1847M* *no comma MSS. 89, 131*

4 mother] Mother *1845, 1847M, 1850* Church] church *MS. 1832/36, 1836–1843* vale;] Vale. *MSS. 89, 131*

5 Then,] Then *MS. 131* Saint] Saint, *MS. 89*

6 *no comma MS. 89*

7 Through] Thro' *MSS. 89, 131*

8 Till] 'Till *MS. 131*

10 They] They, *1845—, 1847M*

11 work's *rev to* Work's *MS. 131* Work's *MS. 89*

12 high] High *MS. 89* Altar] altar *MS. 1832/36–, 1847M* its] it's *MS. 131* place;] place. *MS. 89* place *MS. 131*

14 lived, . . . cross . . . life resigned,] lived . . . Cross . . . Life resigned *revised MS. 89* lived . . . Cross . . . Life resigned; *MS. 131*

15 Morn] morn *MS. 1832/36–, 1847M* *no punct MS. 131*

16 Mankind] mankind *MS. 131, MS. 1832/36–, 1847M*

17 *no ital MSS. 89, 131* creed;— *rev from* creed— *MS. 89* Creed— *MS. 131* *no comma MS. 131*

18 Mid] 'Mid *1832–, 1847M* *no comma MS. 131*

19 die] die, *1832–, 1847M*

20 Sun] sun *MS. 1832/36–, 1847M*

22 men] Men *MSS. 89, 131* days,] days *MS. 89, 1840–, 1847M*

23 Christian Altar] christian altar *MS. 1832/36–, 1847M* East,] East *MS. 131* east, *MS. 1832/36–, 1847M*

24 window *rev from* Window *MS. 89* Window *MS. 131* rays;] rays. *MS. 131*

26 devotion,] devotion *MSS. 89, 131*

27 dayspring] day-spring *MS. 89, 1836–, 1847M* Day-spring *MS. 131* *no comma MS. 131*

28 o'er] oer *rev from* [?ore] *MS. 89* grave] Grave *MS. 131*

Memory

2 wards;] wards *Winter's Wreath*

4 Bards] bards *Winter's Wreath*

9 smooths] smoothes *Winter's Wreath, 1836–* distress,] distress— *Winter's Wreath*

12 hues:] hues; *1836–*

13 Fancy] fancy *Winter's Wreath*

14 Spectres] spectres *Winter's Wreath*

15 Conscience,] conscience *Winter's Wreath*

17 O!] O, *Winter's Wreath*

18 such,] such *Winter's Wreath*

22 scene,] scene; *Winter's Wreath*

23 nook,] nook *Winter's Wreath, 1840–*

24 serene;] serene, *Winter's Wreath*

25 Lakes] lakes *MS. 1832/36–, Winter's Wreath* sleep,] sleep *Winter's Wreath*

27 Rivers] rivers *MS. 1832/36–, Winter's Wreath*

29 listening.] listening! *Winter's Wreath*

First Floweret of the year is that which shows

3 company of heaven] Company of Heaven *Dora W to EQ*

4 first] first, *Dora W to EQ*

6 diadem] Diadem *Dora W to EQ*

7 *no commas Dora W to EQ*

8 station . . . page,] Station . . . page? *Dora W to EQ*

11 call'd] called *Dora W to EQ*

12 Dear words, for memory "characters of light"? *Dora W to EQ*

13 enraptur'd Fancy] enraptured fancy *Dora W to EQ*

14 image?—] Image! *Dora W to EQ*

16 on,] on *Dora W to EQ*

How rich that forehead's calm expanse!

2 Heaven-directed] heav'n-directed *Reed MS.* heaven-directed *MS. 1832/36–*

3 —Waft] Waft *Reed MS.* Glory] glory *Reed MS., MS. 1832/36–*

Powers,] Powers! *Reed MS.*
4 Sorrow] sorrow *Reed MS., MS. 1832/36–* renewed,] renew'd; *Reed MS.*
6 mood!] mood; *Reed MS.*
9 looked—] look'd *Reed MS.* looked; *MS. 1832/36–*
10 adoration!] adoration. *Reed MS.*
12 *no ital Reed MS.*
13 birth;—] birth: *MS. 1832/36–*
15 lies—] lies, *Reed MS.*
16 rise,] rise *Reed MS.*
19 *no comma Reed MS.*
20 eyes] eyes, *1832–*
21 revealing!] revealing. *Reed MS.*

A Flower Garden

1 me, ye Zephyrs! that] me ye Zephyrs that *MW to Lady B* me Ye Zephyrs That *Morgan MS. 1*
2 Recess] recess *Morgan MS. 1*
3 fanned . . . mould] fann'd . . . mold *MW to Lady B, Morgan MS. 1*
4 wilderness] Wilderness *Morgan MS. 1*
5 Hours] hours *rev from (mistaken)* flowers *MW to Lady B* hours *MS. 1832/36–*
6 flowers] Flowers *Morgan MS. 1*
7 *no ital Morgan MS. 1* Creatures] creatures *Morgan MS. 1, MS. 1832/36–* saw] saw, *Morgan MS. 1*
10 Growths] growths *MS.1832/36–*
11 Fawn . . . Kid] fawn . . . kid *MW to Lady B, Morgan MS. 1, MS. 1832/36–*
12 Rose . . . Lily] rose . . . Lily *Morgan MS. 1* rose . . . lily *MS. 1832/36– no hyphen Morgan MS. 1*
13 peeped] peep'd *MW to Lady B, Morgan MS. 1*
16 Sun] sun *MS. 1832/36–*
18 bud or bloom.] Bud or Bloom— *Morgan MS. 1*
19 Summer long] summer long *MW to Lady B* summer-long *MS. 1832/36–*
20 Spot her flowers] spot her flow'rs *Morgan MS. 1*
21 e'er, . . . fancy,] eer . . . fancy *MW to Lady B* e'er . . . fancy *Morgan MS. 1*
23 Things] things *Morgan MS. 1, MS. 1832/36–* Fate] fate *Morgan MS. 1*
24 great.] great— *Morgan MS. 1*
25 Fence] fence *MW to Lady B, Morgan MS. 1, MS. 1832/36–*
26 subtly] subt'ly *Morgan MS. 1*
27 Bound] bound *MW to Lady B, Morgan MS. 1, MS. 1832/36–*
29 semblance—crost] semblance, crossd *MW to Lady B, Morgan MS. 1*
31 though] tho' *MW to Lady B*
32 prest] press'd *Morgan MS. 1*
33 never-sullied] never sullied *MW to Lady B* dews,] dews; *Morgan MS. 1*
34 breezes . . . West,] Breezes . . . west! *MW to Lady B* breezes . . . west! *Morgan MS.* 1 breezes . . . west, *MS. 1832/36–*
35 ministers] Ministers *MW to Lady B* Hope,] hope, *Morgan MS. 1, MS. 1832/36* Hope, *MW to Lady B* hope *1836–*
36 slope!] slope. *MW to Lady B, Morgan MS. 1*
37 Birds] birds *Morgan MS. 1, MS. 1832/36–* resort;] resort, *Morgan MS. 1*
40 guests;] guests, *MW to Lady B, Morgan MS. 1*
41 Hare . . . Leveret] hare . . . leveret *MS. 1832/36–*
42 *no ital MW to Lady B, Morgan MS. 1*
43 emblem (for . . . pride)] emblem, for . . . pride, *MW to Lady B* Emblem, for . . . Pride, *Morgan MS. 1*
44 Enclosure] enclosure *Morgan MS. 1* shows] shews *Morgan MS. 1, MW to Lady B*
45 kindness,] kindness *MW to Lady B* hide,] hide *Morgan MS. 1*
46 bestows;] bestows, *MW to Lady B*
48 Ensuring] Insuring *Morgan MS. 1, MW to Lady B* Innocence *Morgan MS. 1*
49 Muse—] Muse, *MW to Lady B*
52 heart;] heart, *MW to Lady B*
53 old] Old *Morgan MS. 1* Age] age *1832–*
54 Page;] Page, *MW to Lady B, Morgan MS. 1*
56 Shade.] Shade *MW to Lady B* Shade— *Morgan MS. 1*

To ——— ("Let other Bards of Angels sing")

title no period 1836–
1 Bards of Angels] bards of angels *MS. 1832/36–*
2 Suns] suns *MS. 1832/36–*
3 Thing;] Thing: *1832* thing: *MS. 1832/36–*
7 Fancy] fancy *MS. 1832/36–1843* do,] do? *1832–1843*
8 Feelings] feelings *MS. 1832/36–1843*
13 beauty] Beauty *1832* *no comma BL MS. 7, Catalogue Facsimile*
14 unremoved] unremov'd *Catalogue Facsimile*
15 Till] 'Till *BL MS. 7*
16 Lover] lover *BL MS. 7, MS. 1832/36–* beloved.] belov'd! *Catalogue Facsimile*

To ——— ("Look at the fate of summer Flowers")

title *no period 1836–*

1 Flowers,] flowers, *MS. 1832/36–* floweres *MS. 159*

2 daybreak, . . . evensong;] day-break, . . . evensong, *MS. 159*

3–4 *no punct MS. 159*

5 that trembling] that, trembling, *1832–*

6 long!] long. *MS. 159*

8 Flower] flower *MS. 1832/36–*

10 Beauty] beauty *MS. 1832/36–*

11 Rose] rose *MS. 1832/36–*

14 Lovers] lovers *MS. 1832/36–*

19 Love] love *MS. 1832/36–*

20 draw] draw, *1832–* Object] object *MS. 1832/36–*

21 Thee] thee *MS. 1832/36–*

To Rotha Q———

title Q———] Q———. *1832–, 1834, 1838*

1 Rotha,] Rotha! *Rotha Q's Album* Spiritual] spiritual *MS. 131, Rotha Q's Album* Child!] Child, *DW to HCR* Child *Rotha Q's Album* grey] grey, *Monkhouse MS. (copy)*

2 Font for Thee] font for thee *1836–, 1838* stood;] stood, *MS. 131, WW to TBB, DW to HCR*

4 stay:] stay! *MS. 131* Stay. *DW to HCR* stay; *Monkhouse MS. (copy)*

5 late,] late *Monkhouse MS. (copy)* feel,] feel *Rotha Q's Album, Monkhouse MS. (copy)* Orphan!] Orphan, *WW to TBB, DW to HCR* orphan! *Rotha Q's Album*

6 stedfast] steadfast *MS. 131, 1831* contract *rev to* Contract *WW to TBB*

7 blessing] Blessing *WW to TBB* o'er] oer *Rotha Q's Album* still,] still *MS. 131* still; *Monkhouse MS. (copy)*

8 *no comma DW to HCR, Rotha Q's Album*

9 Stream*] Stream, *MS. 131* Stream *WW to TBB, Rotha Q's Album* stream, *rev to* Stream, *DW to HCR*

note to l. 9 River] river *1845–*

10 soothed] sooth'd *MS. 131, Monkhouse MS. (copy)* Mother's] mother's *MS. 131*

12 theme] Theme *Rotha Q's Album*

13 others;] Others, *rev to* Others; *MS. 131* Others, *WW to TBB, DW to HCR* others, *Monkhouse MS. (copy)* self] Self *DW to HCR* self, *1836–, 1838*

14 fancies] <u>fancies</u> *MS. 131, WW to TBB, Monkhouse MS. (copy)* Time's] time's *Monkhouse MS. (copy)* cell.] Cell! *MS. 131* cell! *WW to TBB*

Composed among the Ruins of a Castle in North Wales

4 He] he *1836–, 1838*

6 falls,] falls *1838*

7 Towers and Walls] towers and walls *1836–, 1838*

9 Wars] wars *1832–, 1838*

10 Stars] stars *1832–, 1838*

14 recompense] recompence *1836–* Thine] thine *1836–, 1838*

To the Lady E. B. and the Hon. Miss P.

title LLANGOLLIN] LLANGOLLEN *1836–, 1838*

1 Stream,] Stream— *WW to Sir GB*

2 MEDITATION] MEDITATION* *1832–, 1838*

3 pleased] pleas'd *WW to Sir GB*

4 repose;] repose, *WW to Sir GB*

5 Hermit] hermit *1836–, 1838*

6 die,] die *WW to Sir GB* heaven *1836–, 1838*

7 sequestered] sequester'd *WW to Sir GB*

8 name. *rev from* name, *WW to Sir GB*

9 *no small caps indicated WW to Sir GB*

10 ours] our's *WW to Sir GB* ours, *1836–, 1838* spot] Spot *WW to Sir GB* Vale of Friendship *ital*] Vale of Friendship *WW to Sir GB* VALE OF FRIENDSHIP *1836–, 1838*

11 named; . . . Cot,] named— . . . Cot *WW to Sir GB*

12 banks, ye] banks <u>ye</u> *WW to Sir GB*

13 love—] love, *1836–, 1838*

14 Earth] earth *1836–, 1838* Time!] Time!— *WW to Sir GB*

To the Torrent at the Devil's Bridge, North Wales.

1 thou *rev to* Thou *WW to Sir GB* land] Land, *WW to Sir GB* land? *WW to CW* land, *1850*

2 height,] Height, *WW to Sir GB* height *WW to CW*

3 waters] Waters *WW to Sir GB* source,] source? *WW to CW* or hath *entered at end of line, then del WW to Sir GB*

4 Thee,] thee, *rev in pencil to* thee? *WW to Sir GB* thee?— *WW to CW* thee, *1836–, 1838* band] Band *WW to Sir GB*

5 scoop *rev from* scopp *WW to Sir GB* out,] out *WW to Sir GB, WW to CW*

6 thine? *rev to* thine— *WW to CW*
7 Stream,] Stream *WW to Sir GB, WW to CW*
8 Viamala? *rev from* Viamala *WW to CW* There] There *WW to Sir GB* stand,] stand *WW to CW*
9 Life's] life's *1836–, 1838* Morn;] morn, *WW to Sir GB* morn; *1836–, 1838*
10 woods] woods, *1832–, 1838*
11 not, . . . snows,] not; . . . snows; *1832–, 1838*
12 repose;] repose. *WW to CW*
13 Family] family *WW to Sir GB, 1836–, 1838* floods *rev to* Floods *WW to Sir GB*
14 Poets,] Poets *WW to CW*

To ——— ("O dearer far than light and life are dear")

title *no period 1845, 1850*
10 offend,] offend; *1836–*
12 march;] march: *1832–*
13 Intellect] intellect *MS. 1832/36–*
14 Love] love *1832* love *rev to* Love *MS. 1832/36*
15 seek;] seek: *1836–*
16 creed] Creed *1845–*

The Contrast

5 eyes;] eyes: *1843, 1846, 1849*
9 Mantle's] mantle's *MS. 1832/36–*
17 Bowers] bowers *MS. 1832/36 (in pencil)* bowers *1836–*
25 Bird] bird *MS. 1832/36–*
29 This moss-lined] THIS MOSS-LINED *MS. 1832/36–*
33 unendeared] unendeared, *1836–*
39 Hermitess] hermitess *MS. 1832/36–*
41 me] me, *1836–* Moon] moon *MS. 1832/36–*
43 Bird . . . Saloon] bird . . . saloon *MS. 1832/36–*
44 Lady fingers] lady-fingers *MS. 1832/ 36–*
46 Shed] shed *MS. 1832/36–*

The Infant M—— M——

title M——.] M—— *1850*
1 Childhood] childhood *Monkhouse MS. (copy)* special] 'special *MS. 131*
3 its] it's *MS. 131*
4 chase,] chase *WW to TBB, MS. 131, Monkhouse MS. (copy), DW to HCR* chace *Monkhouse Album (copy)*
5 nought *rev from* naught *Monkhouse Album (copy)* naught *DW to HCR* voice;] voice, *DW to HCR*
7 *no hyphen WW to TBB* meek] meek; *Monkhouse MS. (copy)* meek— *Monkhouse Album (copy)*
8 one] one *rev to* One *WW to TBB* One *MS. 131* enrapt] enwrapt *MS. 131* face,] face *WW to TBB, Monkhouse Album (copy), 1832–, 1838*
9–10 *no parens WW to TBB, Monkhouse MS. (copy), Monkhouse Album (copy), MS. 131, DW to HCR*
9 Death] death *Monkhouse Album (copy), MS. 131, 1836–, 1838*
10 make more] make more *WW to TBB, Monkhouse MS. (copy), MS. 131* placid] plcid *Monkhouse MS. (copy)* Heaven] heaven *WW to TBB, Monkhouse Album (copy), MS. 131, 1836–, 1838* bright,] bright *Monkhouse Album (copy), 1832–, 1838*
11 picture,] picture *MS. 131, Monkhouse MS. (copy), DW to HCR* faith,] faith *Monkhouse MS. (copy)* Faith *DW to HCR*
12 Virgin] Virgin *MS. 131, Monkhouse MS. (copy)* light;] light *WW to TBB* light: *Monkhouse Album (copy)* light, *MS. 131, Monkhouse MS. (copy), DW to HCR*
13 Nursling] nursling *1836–, 1838* couched] couch'd *Monkhouse Album (copy), DW to HCR* Mother's] mother's *Monkhouse Album (copy), 1836–, 1838* knee,] knee *WW to TBB, Monkhouse Album (copy), MS. 131, DW to HCR* Knee *Monkhouse MS. (copy)*
14 Palm] palm *MS. 131, 1836–, 1838* Galilee.] Galilee! *WW to TBB*

Cenotaph

headnote variants in MS. 103: Fermor, whose] Fermor. Whose Worcester, this] Worcester. This by] By wife] Wife Bart.,] Bart. who] Who deceased, commends] Deceased, Commends to] To in] In
1 unenthralled,] unenthrall'd *MW to Lady B*
2 called] called, *MS. 103*
3 eye,] eye; *MW to Lady B*
3, 6, 9, 12 *indented MS. 103, MW to Lady B*
4 nun] Nun *MW to Lady B (A)*
5 feared] fear'd *MW to Lady B (A)* sun] Sun *MW to Lady B (B)*
6 Fermor live] Fermor live, *MW to Lady B, with* ermor *of* Fermor *double-underscored to mark small capitals*
8 heart-relieving] heart relieving *MW to*

Lady B (A) claim;] claim, *MS. 103*
10 choice,] choice *MS. 103*
11 spirit] Spirit *MW to Lady B* voice] Voice *MS. 103*
12 tomb!] Tomb. *MW to Lady B (A)* tomb *MW to Lady B (B)*
13 *no period MW to Lady B (A)*

Elegiac Stanzas. 1824

1 dirge! But] Dirge— but *MW to Lady B*
2 triumphal] Triumphal *MW to Lady B* strain] Strain *MW to Lady B (A)*
3–54 *third and sixth lines of each stanza indented, WW to Lady B*
4 boughts] boughs, *MW to Lady B*
5 *no comma MW to Lady B*
6 work] Work *MW to Lady B*
9 votive] Votive *MW to Lady B* lay] Lay *MW to Lady B (A)*
13–14 *no commas MW to Lady B*
15 bear:] bear; *MW to Lady B (A)* bear! *MW to Lady B (B), 1840–*
16 hers—] hers; *MW to Lady B* to think] to think— *MW to Lady B (A)*
18 despair!] despair. *MW to Lady B*
19 nature] Nature *MW to Lady B (A)*
20 Faith] faith *MW to Lady B (B)* refined,] refined; *1836–*
21 given;] given, *MW to Lady B* given: *1832–*
22 dew-drop's,] Dew-drop's, *MW to Lady B (A)* Dew-drops,— *MW to Lady B (B)*
23 breeze-fanned] breeze-fann'd *MW to Lady B*
24 heaven.] heaven.— *MW to Lady B (A)* Heaven. *1836–*
26 —that] that *MW to Lady B (B)*
28 *no dash MW to Lady B*
29 love *rev to* Love *MW to Lady B (A)* Love *MW to Lady B (B)*
30 restless,] restless— *MW to Lady B (A)*
31 hue;] hue, *MW to Lady B* mortal] Mortal *WW to Lady B (B)*
33 wrong,—] wrong, *MW to Lady B*
34 wound;] wound;— *MW to Lady B*
35 *no comma WW to Lady B (A)*
37 hushed] hush'd *MW to Lady B (A)*
38 things;] things, *MW to Lady B (A)* things! *MW to Lady B (B)*
40 feet,] feet *MW to Lady B (B)*
41 violet] violet, *MW to Lady B, 1832–* sweet,] sweet; *MW to Lady B*
42 jasmine] jas'mine *MW to Lady B (B)* pure;—] pure; *MW to Lady B* pure— *1836–*
43 infant's grave,] Infant's grave; *MW to Lady B*
46 Vesper, ere] vesper, e're *MW to Lady B (A)* vesper, 'ere *MW to Lady B (B)*
47 mountain top] mountain-top *MW to Lady B (A)*
49 *no punct BL MS. 5* *no comma MW to Lady B (B), WW to Lord Monteagle, Fleming Album*
50 perisheth] perishet[ ] *WW to Lord Monteagle (writing runs off page)*
51 more;] more— *BL MS. 5* more. *Fleming Album*
52 *no punct Fleming Album*
54 adore.] adore! *MW to Lady B (B)* adore!! *WW to Lord Monteagle* adore—. *BL MS. 5*

Why, Minstrel, these untuneful murmurings—, Text of MS. 89

1–2 *no quots MS. 89 (B)*
4 wander,] wander *MS. 89 (B)*
5 *exclam inserted MS. 89 (A)*
9 Innocence *rev from* innocence *MS. 89 (A)*
10 axe—] axe, *MS. 89 (B), Cornell MS. 3*
12 mourner's] Mourner's *MS. 89 (B)* pen;] Pen; *MS. 89 (B), Cornell MS. 3 (B)* Pen: *Cornell MS. 3 (C)*

Why, Minstrel, these untuneful murmurings—, Text of 1827

4 Country] country *1836–, 1838*
5 answer] Answer *1832*
7 that *ital 1832–, 1838*
8 Things] things *1836–, 1838*
9 Men] men *1836–, 1838*
11 Moon . . . Stars] moon . . . stars *1836–, 1838* *no commas Cornell MS. 3* (B_2)
12 sympathy; what] Sympathy—What *Cornell MS. 3* (B_2)
14 Fields] fields *1836–, 1838*

A Morning Exercise

6 Man's] man's *1845–*
7 Ravens . . . Owl] ravens . . . owl *MS. 1832/36–*
10 mishap,] mishap *1836–*
15 Task-master] task-master *MS. 1832/36–*
16 Will*,] Will*! *1845–*
17 Spirit . . . Slave] spirit . . . slave *MS. 1832/36–*
18 grave!] grave. *1845–*
21 Messenger] messenger *MS. 1832/36–*
22 Swallow] swallow *MS. 1832/36–1843*
23 Lark] lark *MS. 1832/36–1843*
30 Bird] bird *MS. 1832/36–*
33 Halcyon] halcyon *MS. 1832/36–*
36 Bird of Paradise] bird of paradise *MS. 1832/36–*
37 Dove] dove *MS. 1832/36–*
40 aerial] aërial *1836–*

42 voice!] voice. *1845–*
43 Ocean] ocean *in pencil with note* stet *MS. 1832/36*
44 Sailors] sailors *MS. 1832/36–*
49 Heaven] heaven *MS. 1832/36–*
54 them] them, *1836–*

To a Sky-lark

title *no hyphen Winter's Wreath*
1 Minstrel!] Minstrel, *Lonsdale Album* minstrel! *1836–* Pilgrim] pilgrim *1836–*
2 earth] Earth, *Lonsdale Album*
4 ground?] ground, *Lonsdale Album*
5 will,] will; *Winter's Wreath*
6 compos'd, . . . still? [still? *rev from* still,] *Lonsdale Album*
8 Warbler!] warbler! *Winter's Wreath* warbler!— *1836–1843* that] That *Lonsdale Album* strain,] strain *rev from* strain, *Lonsdale Album* strain *Winter's Wreath, 1831*
9 ('Twixt thee] '('Twixt ['('Twixt *rev from* 'Twixt] Thee *Lonsdale Album*
10 plain:] plain; *Lonsdale Album, Winter's Wreath*
11 privilege! *rev from* priviledge! *Lonsdale Album*
12 spring.] Spring! *Lonsdale Album*
13 Nightingale] nightingale *Winter's Wreath, 1836–* wood;] wood, *Lonsdale Album*
14 thine;] thine, *Lonsdale Album*
16 harmony,] harmony *Lonsdale Album*
17 wise who soar, . . . roam;] wise, who soar. . . roam, *Lonsdale Album* wise who soar— . . . roam, *Winter's Wreath*
18 Home!] Home. *Winter's Wreath*

While they, her Playmates once, light-hearted tread

6 Charge] charge *1836–, 1838*
8 Friends] friends *1836–, 1838*
13 shout,] shout; *1832–, 1838*

To ——— ("Such age how beautiful! O Lady bright"), **Text of MW to Lady B, December 9, 1825**

8 Time *rev from* time *MW to Lady B*

To ——— ("Such age how beautiful! O Lady bright"), **Text of 1827**

title TO ———. *1831*
10 Child of Winter] child of winter *1836–, 1838*

Ere with cold beads of midnight dew

8 Oriental] oriental *1832–* Chain] chain *MS. 1832/36–*
13 Rivulet] rivulet *MS. 1832/36–*
15 Lake] lake *MS. 1832/36–*

Inscription ("The massy Ways, carried across these Heights")

1 *no comma MS. 106* Heights] heights *1836–*
2 Perseverance,] Perseverance *MS. 106* perseverance, *1836–*
3 *no period MS. 106*
5 Walk?] Walk! *1836YR*
6 Poet's] POET'S *1845–*
7 Bard,] Bard— *1836–* fro] fro, *MS. 106*
8 skies,] skies *MS. 106, 1836–*
9 year,] year *MSS. 106, 135, 137* year— *1836–*
11–12 *no commas MS. 135*
13 he *rev to* He *MS. 135*
14 *no comma MS. 106*
15 *no comma MS. 106*
17 gathered! *rev from* gathered. *MS. 135* gathered.— *MS. 106* *no comma MS. 106* Power] power *1836YR*
18 yearning] yearning, *MS. 106* yearning— *1836–* favoured] favored *MS. 135*
20 regrets,] regrets— *1836–*
22 Minds] minds *MSS. 106, 135* *no period MS. 106 (page cut away), MS. 135*

Strange visitation! at *Jemima's* lip

5 grey,] grey *1832*
9 His, *so 1827, 1838, MS. 1836/45* His *1832–*

When Philoctetes in the Lemnian Isle

1 Isle] isle *1836–, 1838*
4 settle,] settle *1832–, 1838*
12 Wretchedness] wretchedness *1836–, 1838*
14 Man for Brother Man] man for brother man *1836–, 1838*

Retirement

1 *no comma MS. 89*
2 blend] blend, *1831*
3 action, . . . Friend!] action . . . Friend *MS. 89*
4 *no punct MS. 89*
6 *no punct MS. 89* Being,] Being *1832–, 1838*
8 mischief] mischief, *MS. 89*
9 bliss;] bliss: *1836–, 1838*
10 Here, . . . stream . . . slake,] Here . . . Stream . . . slake *MS. 89*
11 rustling *rev from miscopied* rusting *MS. 89* *no comma MS. 89*

12 breathe;] breathe *MS. 89* Mind,] Mind *1849P*
13 assign'd *MS. 89*
14 Natures,] Natures *MS. 89* natures, *1831* Heaven amiss.] heav'n [heav'n *rev to* Heav'n] amiss *MS. 89*

Fair Prime of life! were it enough to gild

1 life! . . . gild] Life . . . guild *MS. 89*
2 shower;] shower *MS. 89* shower, *1838*
3 And,] And *MS. 89*
5 errands,— . . . half-tilled] errands; . . . half-till'd, *MS. 89*
6 flower,] flower *MS. 89*
7 Minions . . . chant] minions . . . chaunt *MS. 89*
8 stilled] still'd *MS. 89*
9 show . . . honours] shew . . . honors *MS. 89* due;] due: *1834*
10 Life!] Life *MS. 89* life! *1836–, 1838* heart;] heart, *MS. 89*
12 aim;] aim, *MS. 89*
13 *no comma MS. 89*
14 joy] Joy *MS. 89*

Go back to early ages if thou prize, Text of MS. 89 (A)

8 immortalise. *rev from* immortalise; *MS. 89 (A)*

Go back to antique Ages, if thine eyes, Text of 1827

1 Ages,] ages *MS. 89 (B)* ages *rev to* Ages *MS. 89 (C)*
3 place,] place *MS. 89 (B, C)*
4 World's] world's *MS. 89 (B)* world's *1836–, 1838* vanities!] vanities *MSS. 89 (B, C)*
5 See,] See! *MS. 89 (C)* rise;] rise, *MS. 89 (C)*
6 Pyramid] pyramid *1836–, 1838* *no comma MSS. 89 (B, C)*
7 short-lived] shortliv'd *MS. 89 (B)* short lived *MS. 89 (C)* *no comma MSS. 89 (B, C)*
8 *no punct MS. 89 (B)*
9 There,] There *MS. 89 (B2)*
10 *no comma MSS. 89 (B_2, C)*
11 brute] Brute *MSS. 89 (B_2, C)* brute— *1832–, 1838*
12 *no comma MS. 89 (B_2)* men *rev to* Men *MS. 89 (B_2)* packed] packd *MS. 89 (B_2)* pack'd *MS. 89 (C)*
13 field-pastime,] field-Pastime *MS. 89 (B_2)* field-pastime *MS. 89 (C), 1836–, 1838* absolute,] absolute *MS. 89 (B_2)*
14 While,] While *MSS. B_2, C* game,] game, *rev to* game *MS. 89 (B_2)* game *rev to* Game *MS. 89 (C)* cities] Cities *MS. 89 (C)* sacked!] sack'd *MS. 89 (B_2)* sack'd. *MS. 89 (C)*

Just vengeance dost thou crave for rights invaded, Text of MS. 89 (A)

1 invaded,] invaded? *MS. 89 (B)*
2 Lo] Lo! *MS. 89 (B)*
3 Tyrants . . . Snake] Tyrants, . . . Snake, *MS. 89 (B)*
4 Sword . . . mirtles braided,] sword . . . myrtles braided! *MS. 89 (B)*
6 hush'd] husdd *rev to* hushd *MS. 89 (A)* hushed *MS. 89 (B)* partake,] partake *MS. 89 (B)*
8 couch, . . . oershaded, *MS. 89 (B)*
9 starts— . . . carabine! *MS. 89 (B)*
11 Liberty, *MS. 89 (B)*
12 illustrious mountain; *rev to* <u>Illustrious Mountain</u>; *MS. 89 (B)*

May Odes:

What month can rival thee sweet May? Text of MS. 107 (B)

1 thee . . . May?] thee, . . . May, *MSS. 101A, 112*
2 extremes] extremes; *rev from* extremes? *MS. 112* extremes, *MS. 101A*
3 noon-day] noon day, *MS. 101A*
4 gleams] gleams; *MSS. 107 (A), 112* gleams, *MS. 101A*
5 trill] trill, *MSS. 107 (A), 112*
6 excite] excite, *MSS. 107 (A), 112, 101A*
7 air—] air, *MS. 101A*
8 delight.] delight; *alt* delight. *MS. 107* (A) delight! *rev from* delight; *MS. 101A*
9 streams] Streams *MS. 112*
11 water-break] water-break, *MSS. 112* water-break, *rev from* water-Break, *MS. 101A*
12 pool] pool; *MS. 112* pool. *MS. 101A*
13 only,] only *MS. 101A*
15 unconfirmed] unconfirm'd *MS. 112*
17 Veil] veil, *MS. 112* veil *MS. 101A*
18 house of God] House of God, *MS. 112* House of God *MS. 101*
19 thou] Thou *MS. 112* renew'd] renewed *MS. 101A* dale] Dale *rev from* dale *MS. 107 (B)* dale *rev from* dale, *MS. 101A*
20 Shepherds] shepherds *MSS. 112, 101A* trod] trod; *MS. 101A*
21 huts,] Huts *MS. 112*

23 wreaths] wreath's *MS. 112*
24 forth] forth, *MS. 101A* admired.] admired! *MS. 112*
25 fancy] fancy, *MS. 101A* hope] hope! *MS. 107* (A) hope, *MS. 101A*
26 not] not, *MS. 112* hour] hour, *MSS. 107 (A), 112*
27 blossom] Blossom *MS. 112* drop] drop, *MSS. 107 (A), 112, 101A*
28 flower] flower; *MSS. 107 (A), 112* flower! *rev from* flower, *MS. 101A*
30 art] art, *MSS. 107 (A), 101A* art; *MS. 112*
31 much] much, *MSS. 107 (A), 112, 101A*
32 Part seen,] Part seen— *MS. 112* —Part seen— *MS. 101A* imagined *rev from* imagin'd *MS. 112* part.] part! *MSS. 107 (A), 112*

Ode to May, Text of MS. 107 (D)

4 gleams,] gleams; *MS. 106*
10 away] away; *rev to* away. *MS. 106*
11 Oh] Oh! *MS. 106*
12 return— *rev from* return! *MS. 106*
16 Winter's] winter's *MS. 106*
19 express] express, *MS. 106*
26 pay] pay, *MS. 106*
28 Thee] thee *MS. 106*
30 drest *rev in pencil to* drest, *MS. 106*
35 forth] forth, *MS. 106*
36 solemnize.] solemnize, *MS. 106*
37 *no comma MS. 106*
38 Untouch'd] Untouched *MS. 106*
39 Spirit . . . o'er . . . Slight:] spirit . . . oe'r [oe'r *rev from* oer] . . . slight: *MS. 106*
40 changes] changes, *MS. 106*
43 Warm'd] Warmed *MS. 106*
44 joy.] joy *MS. 107 (C)* joy; *MS. 106*
46 roves] roves, *MS. 106*
47 serv'd] served *MS. 106*
48 groves] groves. *MS. 106*
52 pool;] pool: *MS. 106*
55 unconfirm'd] unconfirmed *MS. 106*
56 side.] side, *MS. 106*
59 mid] 'mid *MS. 106* *no comma MS. 106*
61 huts . . . Ways] huts, . . . Ways, *MS. 106*
65 hope,] hope *MS. 106*
67 *no comma MS. 106*
72 seen] seen, *MS. 106*
73 Lyre] lyre! *MS. 106*
74 prolong] prolong; *MS. 106*
75 *no comma MS. 106*
76 unfinish'd song] unfinished song; *MS. 106*

Ode, Composed on May Morning, Text of 1835

1 east *rev from* East *MS. 137*
2 Star] star *MS. 1835/36–, 1839* dawn] lawn *(printer's error) MS. 137*
4 lawn *rev (in error) to* dawn *MS. 137*
8 shower. *rev from* Shower. *MS. 137*
10 Tempers . . . years *rev from* Temper's . . . year's *MS. 137*
11 *comma added MS. 137*
13 *second comma added MS. 137*
17 Power! *rev from* Power *MS. 137* youths and maids *MS. 1835/36–, 1839*
27 Things] things *1836YR, 1836–, 1839*
29 Plant *rev to* plant *rev to* Plant *MS. 137* plant *MS. 1835/36–, 1836YR, 1839*
30 Deer] deer *MS. 1835/36–, 1836YR, 1839*
31 Fishes] fishes *MS. 1835/36–, 1836YR, 1839*
33 *hyphen added MS. 137* Peak, . . . Heath,] peak . . . heath *1836YR* peak, . . . heath, *MS. 1835/36–, 1839*
35 Cave] cave *MS. 1835/36–, 1836YR, 1839*
36 Thee] Thee *rev from* thee *MS. 137* thee *MS. 1835/36–, 1839*
37 Cities] cities *MS. 1835/36–, 1836YR, 1839*
39 Flower] flower *MS. 1835/36–, 1836YR, 1839* Flower-pot-nursling *rev from* Flower-pot nursling *MS. 137*
42 Pole] pole *MS. 1835/36–, 1839*
44 game,] game; *1836–, 1839*
45 vow *rev from* vow, *MS. 137*
48 love *rev from* Love *MS. 137*
53 One *rev from* one *MS. 137* one *MS. 1835/36–, 1839*
55 ocean-tide] ocean-tide *rev from* Ocean tide *MS. 137*
57 *rev from* Hush feeble Lyre! weak Words! refuse *MS. 137* words,] words *1836–, 1839*
58 prolong! *rev from* prolong, *MS. 137*
59 Thrush] thrush *MS. 1835/36–, 1839*
60 Intrusts *rev from* Entrusts *MS. 137* Entrusts *MS. 1835/36–, 1839*
61 chant] chaunt *MS. 137*
63 Star] star *MS. 1835/36–, 1836YR, 1839*

To May, Text of 1835

2 born,] born; *1836YR only*
4 scorn; *rev from* scorn, *MS. 137*
17 Sea] sea *MS. 1835/36–*
20 Heavens] heavens *MS. 1835/36–, 1839*

39 Mother *rev from* mother *MS. 137*
41 Weed] weed *MS. 1835/36–, 1836YR, 1839*
43 Cliff] cliff *MS. 1835/36–1836YR, 1839*
51 Choose] "Choose *1836–, 1839*
52 The] "The *1836–, 1839*
53 Heaven's] "Heaven's *1836–, 1839*
54 From] "From *1836–, 1839*
55 Drops] "Drops *1836–, 1839*
56 And] "And *1836–, 1839*
74 rule;] rule: *MS. 137*
76 pool: *rev from* pool. *MS. 137*
78 Mists *rev from* mists *MS. 137* mists *MS. 1835/36–, 1836YR, 1839*
82 House] house *MS. 1835/36–, 1839*
83 Gleams 'mid *rev to* Gleams mid *MS. 137*
85 Huts] huts *MS. 1835/36–, 1839*
88 forth,] forth *1836YR only*
90 hour] hour, *1836–, 1839*
92 flower! *rev from* flower; *MS. 137*
93 May, *rev from* May! *MS. 137*

Once I could hail (howe'er serene the sky)

2 Moon *rev from* moon *MW and WW to JK*
4 Shape . . . imbound] shape . . . embound *MW and WW to JK*
6 Ghost] ghost *MW and WW to JK, MS. 1832/36–*
7 Young,] Young *MW and WW to JK*
8 dim; *rev to* dim: *MW and WW to JK*
16 Its . . . splendour] It's . . . splendor *MW and WW to JK*
20 me?] me?— *1832–*
21 Fairies love,] fairies love; *MW and WW to JK*
22 Cynthia,] Cynthia— *MW and WW to JK*
25 spectral Shape] spectral Shape, *rev from* spectral shape, *MW and WW to JK* Spectral-shape *1832* spectral Shape *rev from* Spectral-shape *MS. 1832/36*
26 Moon] moon *MW and WW to JK*
28 Life's] life's *MW and WW to JK, MS. 1832/36–* Prime,] prime— *MW and WW to JK*
31 glance,] glance *MW and WW to JK*
34 stern;] stern, *MW and WW to JK*
35 bliss, or phantoms] bliss; or phantoms— *MW and WW to JK* that] that, *1845–*
36 lustre] lustre, *1845–* vain.] vain *MW and WW to JK*
37 Life] life *MW and WW to JK*
38 Reason] reason *MW and WW to JK*
41 Domain] domain *MS. 1832/36–*
42 perfect,] perfect— *MS. 1832/36–*

To —— ("Happy the feeling from the bosom thrown")

2 shape whose] shape, whose *1832, 1836* shape (whose *MS. 1836/45, 1838, 1840–*
3 it,] it) *MS. 1836/45, 1838, 1840–*
13 Thou] thou *1832–, 1838*

To S. H.

3 Wheel] wheel *SH to MMH*
4 *no ital SH to MMH* shrink,—tho' near,] shrink—tho' near *SH to MMH*
5 Dorhawk's . . . ear,] Dor-hawk's . . . ear— *with dash eras SH to MMH*
6 head.] head: *1838*
7 feigned *alt* feign'd *SH to MMH*
8 Lady!] Lady, *SH to MMH*
10 Poor] poor *1838*
11 Its] It's *SH to MMH*
13 Intellect] intellect *1836–, 1838*
14 man's] Man's *SH to MMH*

Conclusion. To —— ("If these brief Records, by the Muses' art")

title TO ——] TO ——. *1832–, 1834, 1838, but 1845, 1850 as 1827*
3 life] life* *1836–, 1838*
6 tears,] tears; *1838, 1840–, MS. 1836/45*
7 not: but] not. But *1836–, 1838* soul] Soul *1838*
12 zeal;] zeal! *1836–, 1838*
13 heal,] heal *1832*
14 senseless] senseles *1832*

Scorn not the Sonnet; Critic, you have frowned

1 Critic,] Critic! *1838* you] You *Montague MS. no commas Montague MS.*
2 honours;—] honors; *Montague MS.* honours; *1832–, 1838* Key] key *1836–, 1838*
3 Shakespeare unlocked] Shakespear unlock'd *Montague MS.*
4 Lute] lute *1834, 1836–, 1838* wound; *rev from* wound— *Montague MS.*
5 Pipe] pipe *1836–, 1838*
6 Exile's] exile's *1836–, 1838*
7 Leaf] leaf *Montague MS., 1836–, 1838*
9 brow:] brow; *Montague MS.* glow-worm Lamp,] Glowworm-lamp *Montague* glow-worm lamp, *1836–, 1838*
10 cheered . . . Spenser,] cheered . . . Spenser *Montague MS.*
11 and] and, *Montague MS., 1832–,*

1838 damp] Damp *Montague MS.*
13 Trumpet,] trumpet; *1836–, 1838*
14 strains—] strains; *rev to* Strains; *Montague MS.* few!] few *1831* few. *1834*

There is a pleasure in poetic pains
2 'twas] 't was *1836–, 1838*
5 Strains,] strains *1836–, 1838*
9 clear] clear, *1832–, 1838*
10 last . . . hindrance] last, . . . hinderance *1832–1843, 1838* last, . . . hindrance *1845–*
11 Star . . . Morn] star . . . morn *1836–, 1838*
12 speckless] speckless, *1832–, 1838*
13 Virgin's] virgin's *1836–, 1838*
14 Thorn] thorn *1836–, 1838*

To the Cuckoo
4 paired.] paired, *1834*
5 Captive,] Captive *1832* captive *1836–, 1838*
9 Eagle-race] eagle-race *1836–, 1838*
11 Lion] lion *1836–, 1838*
12 Cock] cock *1836–, 1838*

In my mind's eye a Temple, like a cloud
3 still,] still; *1836–, 1838*
6 virtues] Virtues *1832–, 1838*
8 loud,] loud. *1836* loud *MS. 1836/45*
14 Hell-gates . . . build.] "Hell-gates . . . build." *1836–, 1838*

On Seeing a Needlecase in the Form of a Harp, the Work of E. M. S.
title ON SEEING A *raised to full capitals 1836–* on seeing a *Cornell MS. 4, Morgan MS. 3, Monkhouse Album* Needlecase] Needle-case *Cornell MS. 4* needle case *Morgan MS. 3* needle-case *Monkhouse Album* Harp,] Harp. *1845–* Work] work *Morgan MS. 3, Monkhouse Album* *no punct Cornell MS. 4, Morgan MS. 3*
1 Muse's] Muses *Monkhouse Album* *no comma Cornell MS. 4*
2 *no comma Cornell MS. 4*
3 mimickry *rev from* mimicry *Monkhouse Album* mimicry *1836–*
6 gradation!] gradation. *Cornell MS. 4*
9 Needle] needle *MS. 1832/36–* *no ital Morgan MS. 3*
10 spirit] Spirit *Cornell MS. 4*
11 Though] Tho' *Cornell MS. 4* *no comma Morgan MS. 3*
12 *no punct Cornell MS. 4*
13 this, too,] this too *Morgan MS. 3* this too, *Monkhouse Album* Laureate's] Laureates *Monkhouse Album* Child,] Child *Cornell MS. 4* child, *Morgan MS. 3* Child! *rev to* Child, *Monkhouse Album*
14 Lord] lord *MS. 1832/36–* melody] Melody *Cornell MS. 4*
17 spake,] spake *Monkhouse Album* whispered] whisperd *Cornell MS. 4*
18 Bard!] Bard *Monkhouse Album* ire;] ire *Cornell MS. 4* ire, *Monkhouse Album* ire: *1841, 1843, 1846, 1849*
19–40 *no opening quots 1836–*
20 Lyre] lyre *MS. 1832/36–*
21 Pygmean] Pigmæan *Monkhouse MS.*
22 Dwarf] Dwarf, *Morgan MS. 3*
23 shells] Shells *Cornell MS. 4*
24 lays.] Lays. *Cornell MS. 4* lays; *Monkhouse Album*
25 Some,] Some *Cornell MS. 4, Morgan MS. 3, Monkhouse Album* ear,] ear *Monkhouse Album*
26 lutes] Lutes *Cornell MS. 4, Monkhouse Album*
27 framework] frame-work *Cornell MS. 4, Morgan MS. 3, Monkhouse Album* *no comma Morgan MS. 3, Monkhouse Album*
28 *no period Cornell MS. 4*
29 Sylphs] Sylps *Monkhouse Album* Miniature] Minature *1832* minature *MS. 1832/36* miniature *Morgan MS. 3, Monkhouse Album, 1836–*
30 *no comma Monkhouse Album*
32 Around] Arond *Monkhouse Album* strings;] strings. *Cornell MS. 4, Morgan MS. 3* strings *Monkhouse Album*
33 Maiden *alt* maiden *MS. 1832/36* maiden *1836–*
34 Bower] bower *Morgan MS. 3, MS. 1832/36–*
35 cheer,] cheer *Cornell MS. 4* chear *Monkhouse Album*
37 Trust,] Trust *Cornell MS. 4, Monkhouse Album* Sprite] sprite *Morgan MS. 3*
38 deplores;] deplores, *Cornell MS. 4*
39 Though . . . stars] Tho . . . Stars *Cornell MS. 4* Tho' . . . Stars *Monkhouse Album* mid] 'mid *Monkhouse Album, 1845–* *no comma Morgan MS. 3, Monkhouse Album*
40 *no ital Cornell MS. 4, Monkhouse Album* soars."] soars!—" *Cornell MS. 4* soars" *Morgan MS. 3*

Her only Pilot the soft breeze the Boat
1 Pilot *rev to* Pilot, *MS. 89* pilot *1836–, 1838* breeze] breeze, *1832–, 1838* Boat] boat *1836–, 1838*

6 along; *rev from* along, *MS. 89*
7 Heavens] heavens *1836–, 1838* smile,] smile *MS. 89*
10 Bark] bark *1836–, 1838*
11 Ideal Crew] ideal crew *1836–, 1838*
12 One *rev from* one *MS. 89*

Farewell Lines, Text of 1842

1 *para 1850*
2 But,] But *MS. 151.1*
9 friend,] Friend *MS. 151.1* Friend, *MS. 151.2, 1845–*
10 city] City *MS. 151.2*
11 deep,] deep *MS. 151.1*
12 content.] content: *MS. 151.1*
13 So,] So *MS. 151.1, 1845–*
14 herons] Herons *MS. 151.1* oft-times *rev from* ofttimes *MS. 1842P* ofttimes *MS. 151.2*
15 side,] side *MS. 151.1*
16 ease;] ease[?] *MS. 151.1*
17 *no commas MS. 151.1*
18 glowworms] glow worms *rev to* Glow worms, *MS. 151.2* glow-worms *1845– no comma MS. 151.1*
19 seemed] seemed *rev to* seem'd *MS. 151.1* *no commas MS. 151.1*
20 ground, *rev to* ground *MS. 151.2* ground *MS. 151.1*
21 He *rev from* he *MS. 151.2* repose.] repose.— *1845–*
26 will *rev from* well *MS. 1842P*
27 you, *rev from* you *MS. 1842P*
28 Friends! *rev from* friends! *MS. 1842P*

Extract from the Strangers book / Station Winandermere / On seeing the above

subtitle above] above. *MS. B*
1 Darlington] Darlington, *MS. B*
2 tone] tone, *MS. B*
3 Vane] Vane, *MS. B*
4 pain] pain, *MS. B* moment's] moments *MSS. A, B*
5 Stamp] Stamp, *MS. B*
6 *no ital MS. B* cramp] cramp; *MS. B*
10 Ketterine] Ketterine, *MS. B*
12 Lomond's . . . discuss] Lomonds . . . discuss, *MS. B*
13 wish'd] wished *MS. B*
14 boatmen of Killarney] Boatmen of Killarney, *MS. B*
16 Zurcih . . . Genêve] Zurich, . . . Geneve, *MS. B* *no quots MS. B*
17 bow'd] bowed *MS. B*
18 Como, *MS. B*
19 Simplon's] Simplons *MS. B*
20 Reclinèd] Reclined *MS. B*
22 breast] breast,— *MS. B*
23 *no comma MS. B* Heaven] heaven *MS. B*
24–26 *no commas MS. B*
24 charms . . . station] Charms . . . Station *MS. B*
25 Cap^{n}] Captain *MS. B*
28 Hyperbole—!] Hyperbole! *MS. B*

Four fiery steeds impatient of the rein

1 steeds] Steeds *MSS. 107, 106*
2 Whirled *rev from* Whirl'd *MS. 107* o'er] oer *MS. 107* ground] ground, *MS. 106 (B)*
3 when,] when *MSS. 106, 107* Plain,] plain *MSS. 106 (A), 107* Plain *MS. 106 (B)* plain, *1836–, 1838, 1839*
4 Mountains] mountains *MSS. 106, 107, 1836–, 1838, 1839* *no comma MSS. 106 (A), 107*
5 *no comma MSS. 106, 107*
6 lustre.] lustre— *MS. 106 (A)* lustre.— *MSS. 106 (B), 135*
7 Yes,] Yes *MSS. 106, 107* One;— *rev from* one;— *MS. 106 (B)* One— *MSS. 106 (A), 107* one;— *1838* One,] one *MS. 107* One *rev from* one *MS. 106 (A)* One *MS. 106 (B)* one, *1838*
8 ethereal] etherial *MS. 135* *no punct MSS. 106 (A), 107*
9 out,] out *MSS. 106 (A), 107* field,] field *MSS. 107, 106 (A)* field. *1849*
10 Home; *rev from* home; *MS. 135* home; *MSS. 106, 107*
12 wield] wield, *MS. 106 (B)*
14 moon] moon, *MS. 106 (B)* revealed. *rev from* revealed *MS. 138*

Roman Antiqities Discovered, At Bishopstone, Herefordshire

title ANTIQUITIES DISCOVERED, / AT] ANTIQUITIES / DISCOVERED AT *1836–, 1838*
1 Antiquarians *MW rev from* antiquarians *MS. 137* ground *rev from* ground, *MS. 135* ground, *MS. 106*
2 Bard and Seer, *MW rev from* bard and seer, *MS. 137* Bard and Seer *MS. 106*
3 The] the *MSS. 107, 106, 135* reappear] re-appear *1836YR*
4 girt,] girt; *MS. 106* gowned,] gowned; *MS. 106, 1836–, 1838* gown'd; *rev from* gowned; *MS. 107* gowned, *MW rev from* gown'd, *MS. 137* gown'd, *Betz MS. 1*
5 couches,] couches *MS. 107*

myrtle- *MW rev from* myrtle *MS. 137* crowned, *MW rev from* crown'd, *MS. 137* crown'd *rev from* crowned *MS. 107* crown'd *Betz MS. 1*

6 glee:] glee:— *MSS. 107, 106, 135* not? *rev from* not, *MS. 107* For] for *MS. 107, Betz MS. 1* clear,] clear *MSS. 107, 106, 135, Betz MS. 1*

7 year,] year *MSS. 107, 106, Betz MS. 1*

8 pavement.] pavement— *Betz MS. 1* mound] Mound *MS. 135*

9 Maximins,] Maximins *MS. 106*

10 warlike] war like *MS. 107* toil:] toil. *MS. 106, Betz MS. 1* toil, *MS. 107*

11 impress] Impress *MSS. 107, 106, 135, Betz MS. 1*

12 tenderness—] tenderness, *Betz MS. 1* Wolf, *rev from* wolf, *MS. 137* Wolf *MS. 106* Wolfe *MS. 107* Wolf— *Betz MS. 1* Twins *rev from* twins *MS. 107, MS. 137*

13 unlettered] unletter'd *MS. 107, Betz MS. 1* Ploughboy] Plough-boy *MSS. 107, 135, Betz MS. 1* Plough boy *MS. 106* Plough-boy *MW rev from* plough-boy *MS. 137* ploughboy *1836–, 1838* pities] pities, *MS. 107, Betz MS. 1*

14 furrowed *MW rev from* furrow'd *MS. 137* furrow'd *MS. 107*

St. Catherine of Ledbury

title St Catharine of Lethbyry [Lethbyry *rev to* Ledbury *MS. 107 (B)* ST.] St *MSS. 107, 106* S^{t} *MS. 1835*

1 touch, as monkish books attest,] touch (as monkish Books attest) *MS. 107 (A); so 1836–, 1838 but* books *no punct MS. 107 (B)* attest,] attest *MSS. 106, 135*

2 Nor was applied nor could be,] Nor <u>was</u> applied nor <u>could</u> be, *MS. 107 (A)* Nor was applied nor could be; *MS. 107 (B)* Nor was applied, nor could be, *MSS. 106, 135* applied *rev from* applied, *MS. 137* bells] Bells *MS. 106*

3 concert *rev from* concert, *MS. 137* concert, *MSS. 106, 135*

4 upward,] upward *MS. 107 (B)* crest; *rev from* crest, *MS. 137* crest *rev from* crest, *rev from* crest; *MS. 135*

5 tones,] tones!— *MS. 107 (A)* Lady] lady— *rev to* Lady— *MS. 107 (B)* Lady, *MS. 106* Lady— *rev in pencil to* Lady *MS. 135* lady *rev to* Lady *MS. 137*

6 rapture!] rapture;— *MS. 107 (A)* rapture: *MSS. 107 (B), 106* rapture: *rev to* rapture! *MS. 135* listened] listen'd *MS. 107 (A, B)*

7 loved] lov'd *MS. 107 (A, B)* Mistress:] Mistress— *MS. 107 (A)* mistress *rev to* Mistress *MS. 137* mistress *1845–* music died,] Music died *MS. 107 (A, B)* music died *MS. 106*

8 Catherine] Catherine *rev to* Katherine *MS 107 (A)* Catharine *MS. 107 (B)* said,] said *MS. 107 (A)* "Here . . . rest."] "Here ["Here *rev from* "here] . . . rest. *MS. 107 (B)* "*Here . . . rest." 1836YR* **Here I set up my rest.** *1836–, 1838*

9 Warned] Warnd *MS. 107 (A, B)* dream,] dream *MSS. 107 (A, B), 106, 135* Wanderer *rev from* wanderer *MS. 137*

10 home *rev to* Home *MS. 107 (B)* Home, *MS. 106* home, *MS. 135* home, *rev to* home *MS. 137*

11 revealed:—] reveal'd: *MS. 107 (A)* revealed— *MS. 107 (B)* now,] now; *MS. 107 (A)* now— *MS. 107 (B)* now *rev to* now, *MS. 137*

12 The] Thee *MS. 107 (B)* *no punct MS. 107 (A, B)*

13 there,] there *MS. 107 (A, B)* Anchoress] anchoress *rev to* Anchoress *MS. 137* Anchoress, *1836–, 1838*

14 heaven] heav'n *MS. 107 (A)* Heaven *MSS. 106, 135* *no punct MS. 137*

To ——— ("'Wait, prithee, wait!' this answer Lesbia threw"), **Text of MS. 89**

1 "Wait, prithee wait!"] "<u>Wait prithee wait</u>"! *Betz MS. 1*

4 Harp,] Harp *Houghton MS. 1, Betz MS. 1* soul-engrossing] soul engrossing *Betz MS. 1* speed; *rev from* speed *MS. 89* speed. *Houghton MS. 1, Betz MS. 1*

6 rose] rose, *Houghton MS. 1, Betz MS. 1*

7 Tow'rd] Towa'rd *Betz MS. 1* casement,] casement *Houghton MS. 1, Betz MS. 1* Favorite,] Favorite *Houghton MS. 1*

8 affections] affections, *Betz MS. 1*

9 O] O! *Betz MS. 1*

10 voice,] voice *rev to* Voice *Houghton MS. 1* voice *Betz MS. 1*

11 harmony attuned] Harmony attuned *rev to* Harmony attun'd *Houghton MS. 1* harmony attun'd *Betz MS. 1*

12 self-reproach] self reproach *Houghton MS. 1* kite] Kite, *Houghton MS. 1* Kite *Betz MS. 1*

13 Pounced, and] Pounc'd and *Betz MS. 1* Dove,] Dove *Houghton MS.*

1, Betz MS. 1 beak] beak, *Houghton MS. 1*

To ——— ("'Wait, prithee, wait!' this answer Lesbia threw"), Text of 1835

title *no period 1845, 1850*
epigraph *placed above the title MS. 106* *no brackets MSS. 106, 135* *l. 1* occasion;] occasion: *1836–, 1838* *l. 2* subtile] subtle *1850* Time, *rev from* time, *MS. 135* *l. 3* moment's putting-off *rev from* moments putting-off, *MS. 138*
1 prithee,] prithee *MSS. 106, 135*
2 heed;] heed *1840–1849* heed. *1850*
4 harp] Harp *MS. 106* soul-engrossing] soul engrossing *1845–* speed;] speed, *rev to* speed. *MS. 106*
5 bondage *rev from* Bondage *MS. 135*
7 Favorite] Favourite *MS. 106, 1845, 1850*
11 harmony!— *rev from* harmony:— *MS. 135*
12 self-reproach!— *rev from* selfreproach *MS. 138* self-reproach! *MSS. 106, 135, 1836–, 1838* for, . . . Kite] for . . . kite *MS. 106*
13 Pounced,] Pounced,— *1836–, 1838*
14 sight!] sight— *rev to* sight. *MS. 106*

Filial Piety

1 Untouched *rev to* Untouch'd *Southey Album 1* Untouch'd *Houghton MS. 1, Casket, Betz MS. 1* through] thro' *MS. 106* cold,] cold; *Houghton MS. 1, Betz MS. 1, 1836–, 1838* cold *MS. 107*
2 Inviolate, whate'er] In violate whateer *rev to* Inviolate, whateer *Houghton MS. 1* cottage] Cottage *Houghton MS. 1, Southey Album 1, Betz MS. 1* hearth] Hearth *Houghton MS. 1*
3 comfort,] comfort *Houghton MS. 1, Southey Album 1, Betz MS. 1, Casket* mirth,] mirth. *MS. 107* mirth; *1836–, 1838*
4 Pile] pile, *Casket* Turf] turf *MS. 89, Casket* old: *rev from* old. *Houghton MS. 1*
5 Yes,] Yes *Houghton MS. 1, Southey Album 1, MS. 89, Casket, Betz MS. 1* Traveller! *rev from* traveller! *Houghton MS. 1* traveller, *Casket*
6 dart of death] Dart of Death *MS. 89*
7 raised it,—] rais'd, it, *Houghton MS. 1, Casket* raised it, *Southey Album 1, MSS. 89, 107, Betz MS. 1* rais'd it, *Casket* earth; *rev from* earth. *Houghton MS. 1* earth. *MS. 106* earth: *1836–, 1838*
11 waste.—Though] waste; though *Houghton MS. 1, Southey Album 1* waste;—tho' *MS. 89, Betz MS. 1* waste;— though *rev to* waste: Though *MS. 107* waste,— Though *rev to* waste.—Though *MS. 106* waste, though *Casket* air,] air *Houghton MS. 1, Southey Album 1, Betz MS. 1* air. *MSS. 89, 107, Casket*
12 stands—] stands; *Houghton MS. 1, Southey Album 1, Betz MS. 1* stands: *MSS. 89, 107, 106, Casket*
13 Mausoleum] mausoleum *MS. 107, Casket* Mausoleum *rev from* mausoleum *MS. 106* wrens] Wrens *Houghton MS. 1, Betz MS. 1* there,] there *Houghton MS. 1, Southey Album 1, MSS. 89, 107, Betz MS. 1*
14 red-breasts] Red-breasts *Houghton MS. 1* red-breasts *rev from* red-breast *MS. 89* redbreasts *Southey Album 1, MS. 107, Casket* Red breasts *Betz MS. 1* rare.] rare *Houghton MS. 1, Southey Album 1*

A Grave-stone upon the Floor in the Cloisters of Worcester Cathedral

title GRAVE-STONE] Grave Stone *Cornell MS. 5, Southey Album 1* Grave stone *Betz MS. 1* FLOOR] floor *Cornell MS. 5, Southey Album 1, Betz MS. 1* CATHEDRAL] Cath[l] *Betz MS. 1* *no punct Cornell MS. 5, Southey Album 1, Betz MS. 1*
1 *Miserrimus!*"] Miserrimus!" *MS. 106, Keepsake* Miserrimus"! *Cornell MS. 5, Southey Album 1* name] name, *Cornell MS. 5, Southey Album 1, Betz MS. 1* date,] date *Yale MS. 1, Cornell MS. 5, Southey Album 1, Betz MS. 1*
2 text,] text *Betz MS. 1* symbol,] symbol *MS. 106* graven] grav'n *Yale MS. 1, Cornell MS. 5, Southey Album 1, Betz MS. 1, Keepsake* stone;] Stone, *MS. 106*
3 Nought *rev from* Naught *MS. 106* assigned] assign'd *Cornell MS. 5, Southey Album 1, Betz MS. 1, Keepsake* unknown] Unknown *MS. 106* *no comma Cornell MS. 5, Southey Album 1, Betz MS. 1*
6 beneath.] beneath.— *Yale MS. 1,*

Southey Album 1, Betz MS. 1 beneath— *Cornell MS. 5* one,] ONE *Yale* One, *Keepsake* one! *Cornell MS. 5, Southey Album 1, Betz MS. 1* One! *MS. 106*

7 Who *ital*] Who *Yale MS. 1, Cornell MS. 5, Southey Album 1, Betz MS. 1, MS. 106, Keepsake* Epitaph] epitaph *Yale MS. 1, MS. 106, Keepsake, 1845–* Himself] Himself *Yale MS. 1, Cornell MS. 5, Southey Album 1, Betz MS. 1* —Himself *1836–, 1838*

8 dared] dar'd *Yale MS. 1, Betz MS. 1* *no comma Yale MS. 1*

9 crown;] crown. *Yale MS. 1, Cornell MS. 5, Southey Album 1, Betz MS. 1, MS. 106, Keepsake*

10 He] he *Cornell MS. 5, Southey Album 1, MS. 106, Keepsake* marked] mark'd *Cornell MS. 5, Southey Album 1, Betz MS. 1, Keepsake* own,] own *Yale MS. 1, Cornell MS. 5, 1836–, 1838*

11 steps] steps, *Betz MS. 1* burial-place] burial place *Cornell MS. 5, Southey Album 1, Betz MS. 1*

11–12 *no commas Yale MS. 1, Cornell MS. 5, Southey Album 1*

12 *no comma Betz MS. 1*

13 vileness.] vileness— *Cornell MS. 5, Southey Album 1, Betz MS. 1* Stranger,] Stranger! *Yale MS. 1, Cornell MS. 5, Southey Album 1, Betz MS. 1*

14 Softly!—] Softly;— *Yale MS. 1, Cornell MS. 5, Southey Album 1, Betz MS. 1* To] to *Yale MS. 1, Cornell MS. 5, MS. 106, Betz MS. 1, Keepsake* contrite,] Contrite *Yale MS. 1, Cornell MS. 5, Southey Album 1, Betz MS. 1, MS. 106* bled.] bled.— *Yale MS. 1, Southey Album 1, Betz MS. 1*

The Wishing-gate

title WISHING-GATE] Wishing Gate *MSS. 108, 131* Wishing Gate *rev to* Wishing-gate *Keswick MS.* Wishing-gate *Victoria MS. 1*

indentation ll. 3 and 6 of each stanza, Victoria MS. 1, MS. 131, Keepsake, 1845–

headnote vale] Vale *Keswick MS.* gate,] Gate *Keswick MS., Keepsake* mind,] mind *Keswick MS.* wishing-gate] Wishing-gate *Keepsake, 1836–* favourable] favorable *Keswick MS.*

1 *para Keepsake* green:] green *Victoria MS. 1* green; *MS. 108, Keswick MS.* green. *MS. 131, Keepsake*

2 powers *rev to* Powers *Victoria MS. 1* Powers *MS. 108, Keswick MS.* bright-eyed] bright-ey'd *Victoria MS. 1* Queen] Queen, *Victoria MS. 1, MS. 108, Keswick MS.* queen *MS. 131, Keepsake*

4 disappear;] disappear: *MS. 131, Keepsake*

5 near,] near *Victoria MS. 1, MS. 108*

6 Fancy *rev from* fancy *Victoria MS. 1* smooths] smooth's *Victoria MS. 1* *no punct MS. 108*

7 land *rev to* Land *Victoria MS. 1* Land *MS. 108, Keswick MS.* wishes] Wishes *MS. 131, Keepsake, 1836–*

8 fruitless] fruit-less *MS. 131* day-dreams] Day-dreams *Victoria MS. 1, MS. 108, Keswick MS.* prayer] Prayer *Victoria MS. 1, MS. 108, Keswick MS.*

9 thoughts *rev to* Thoughts *Victoria MS. 1* Thoughts *Keswick MS., MS. 131, Keepsake* things] Things *Victoria MS. 1, Keswick MS., MS. 131, Keepsake* *no punct Victoria MS. 1*

10 forlorn] forlorn, *Victoria MS. 1, MSS. 108, 131, Keswick MS., Keepsake, 1836–* ye *ital*] Ye *Victoria MS. 1* depart,] depart *Victoria MS. 1, MS. 108, Keswick MS., MS. 1832/36–*

11 superstitions] Superstitions *Victoria MS. 1* heart; *ital*] Heart, *Victoria MS. 1* Heart; *MS. 108, Keswick MS.*

12 poor] poor— *Victoria MS. 1* poor, *Keswick MS., MS. 131, Keepsake, 1836–* life!] life. *Victoria MS. 1*

13 lore abjured] Lore abjur'd *Victoria MS. 1* *no comma Victoria MS. 1, MS. 131*

14 *no comma Victoria MS. 1*

16 symbol] Symbol *Victoria MS. 1, MS. 108* symbol *rev to* Symbol *Keswick MS.*

18 Wishing-gate!] Wishing-gate. *Victoria MS. 1, Keepsake* Wishing Gate. *MS. 108* Wishing-Gate! *Keswick MS.* Wishing-gate *MS. 131*

19 Inquire] Enquire *Keswick MS.* faery race] Fairy-race *Victoria MS. 1* Faery-race, *MS. 108* Faery race *Keswick MS.* fairy race *MS. 131, Keepsake*

20 *no comma Victoria MS. 1*

21 Ere *rev from* Eere *Keswick MS.* retired] retir'd *Victoria MS. 1*

22 warrior . . . spell] Warrior . . . Spell *Victoria MS. 1, MS. 108, Keswick MS.*

23 glory] Glory *Victoria MS. 1, MS. 108* fell;] fell, *Victoria MS. 1*

24 saint] Saint *Victoria MS. 1, MSS. 108, 131, Keswick MS.* expired.]

expired? *MS. 108*

25 is *rev from miswritten* if *Victoria MS. 1* fair,] fair; *MS. 108, Keswick MS.*

27 love;] love, *Victoria MS. 1* love— *1836–*

28 content,] content *MS. 108, Keswick MS.* content— *1836–*

30 *no punct Victoria MS. 1*

31 even] ev'n *Victoria MS. 1* Stranger] stranger *Keepsake, 1836–1843* afar,] afar *Victoria MS. 1, MS. 131*

32 *no comma Victoria MS. 1*

33 Unknowing,] Unknowing *Victoria MS. 1, MSS. 108, 131, Keepsake* unknown,] unknown *Victoria MS. 1*

34 partakes,] partakes *Victoria MS. 1* partakes— *MS. 108* partakes, *rev to* partakes— *Keswick MS.*

35 Belov'd—] Belov'd *Victoria MS. 1* Beloved, *MS. 108* Beloved, *rev to* Belov'd, *Keswick MS.* Belov'd— *rev from* Beloved— *MS. 131* Beloved— *1841, 1843, 1846, 1849*

37 conscious] conscious *Victoria MS. 1* Spirits] spirits *MSS. 108, 131, Keepsake* fear] fear, *MS. 108*

38 stirrings] Stirrings *MS. 108, Keswick MS.*

39 ancient] antient *Victoria MS. 1*

40 Genius *rev from* genius *Victoria MS. 1* genius *MS. 108* ne'er] neer *Victoria MS. 1*

44 some,] some *MS. 131* outworn] out-worn *Victoria MS. 1*

47 vow,] vow *Victoria MS. 1* true,] true *Victoria MS. 1, MS. 108*

48 firmer,] firmer *Victoria MS. 1, MS. 108, Keswick MS.*

49 *no comma Victoria MS. 1, MS. 108*

51 penitent] Penitent *Victoria MS. 1, MS. 108, Keswick MS., 1845–* sincere] sincere, *MS. 108*

52 *no comma Victoria MS. 1, MSS. 108, 131*

54 tear.] tear! *MS. 108*

55 Worldling,] Wordling *(miscopied) Victoria MS. 1* worldling, *MS. 131, Keepsake, 1836–1843*

57 fate *rev from miswritten* gate *MS. 108*

58 favoured] favored *MS. 108* favourd *Victoria MS. 1, MS. 131, Keepsake* *no comma Victoria MS. 1, Keswick MS.*

60 Wishing-gate.] Wishing-gate, *Victoria MS. 1* Wishing Gate. *MS. 108, Keswick MS.*

61 Sage,] Sage *Victoria MS. 1, MS. 108* Sage *rev to* Sage— *Keswick MS.* sage, *MS. 131, Keepsake* blind,] blind *MS. 108, Keswick MS.* weak *rev from* weak, *Victoria MS. 1*

62 man] Man *MS. 108* loth] loth *MS. 131* *no final comma MS. 108*

63 pause,] pause *Victoria MS. 1* *no commas MS. 108*

65 *no comma Victoria MS. 1*

66 withdraws;] withdraws. *MS. 108*

67 church-clock's] Church-clocks *Victoria MS. 1* Church-clock's *MSS. 108, 131, Keswick MS.* profound] profound, *MS. 108*

69 midnight] midnight, *MS. 131, Keepsake* reply;] reply *Victoria MS. 1* reply, *MS. 108*

70 on] on, *Keswick MS., MS. 131* crest,] crest *Victoria MS. 1, MS. 108* Crest *MS. 151.1*

72 eternity!] eternity. *Victoria MS. 1, MS. 108, 1850* Eternity *MS. 151.1* eternity *1845*

A Tradition of Darley Dale, Derbyshire

title DARLEY DALE] Darley-dale *MS. 89, Betz MS. 1* *no period MS. 89, no comma MS. 106, no punct MS. 134, Betz MS. 1*

2 Brothers] brothers *Keepsake* clomb,] clomb; *MSS. 106, 134, Southey Album 1, Betz MS. 1* clomb— *1838* and,] and *MSS. 89, 134, Betz MS. 1*

3 exchanging,] exchanging— *MS. 89, Southey Album 1, Betz MS. 1* still] still, *MSS. 89, 106*

5 Tree; *rev from* tree; *MS. 89* Tree: *MS. 106* Tree. *MS. 134* tree. *Southey Album 1, Betz MS. 1* tree; *Keepsake* then] Then *MS. 134, Southey Album 1, Betz MS. 1* *no comma MS. 89, Southey Album 1*

6 new-born] newborn *Keepsake* rivers] Rivers *MS. 89*

8 far-seen] far seen *MS. 89* mount.] Mount. *MSS. 89, 106* mount:— *Betz MS. 1* No] no *Betz MS. 1*

9 memorial;—] memorial— *MS. 89, Keepsake* Memorial. *Southey Album 1* memorial. *Betz MS. 1* the] The *Southey Album 1, Betz MS. 1* trees] Trees *MSS. 89, 106, 134* grew; *MS. 89*

10 arms;] arms, *MS. 89, Keepsake*

11 those *rev from* Those *MS. 106* Brothers] brothers *Betz MS. 1, Keepsake* earth's] Earth's *Betz MS. 1* plain;] plain, *MSS. 89, 106, 134, Southey Album 1, Betz MS. 1, Keepsake*

12 knew] knew, *Keepsake*
13 spirits] Spirits *Southey Album 1* sea] Sea *MS. 89, Southey Album 1, Betz MS. 1*
14 all—] all, *1836–, 1838* Eternity.] Eternity *MS. 134* Eternity! *Southey Album 1, Betz MS. 1*

The unremitting voice of nightly streams, Text of 1846

4 grass, . . . bowers,] grass . . . bowers *MS. 143 (C)*
5 flowers,—] flowers *MS. 143 (C)*
8 *deeply indented MS. 143 (C)*
11 breast,] breast *MS. 143 (C)*
13 issues—] issues,— *MS. 143 (C)*
14 brooks] brooks, *MS. 143 (C)*
15 day, . . . swains] day . . . Swains *MS. 143 (C)*
17 water-breaks,] water-breaks *MS. 143 (C)*

The Gleaner. (Suggested by a Picture.)

1 *no comma MS. 108*
2 summer's] Summer's *MS. 131, Huntington MS. 1, Keepsake* *no comma Huntington MS. 1*
3, 6 *no indent Huntington MS. 1*
3 shed;] shed *MS. 108* shed, *Huntington MS. 1*
4 cheek— *rev from* cheek, *MS. 108* cheek— *rev from* cheek *Huntington MS. 1* kindling] kind'ling *Huntington MS. 1*
5 lip— *rev from* lip *Huntington MS. 1* rose-bud] rosebud *MS. 108* thorn, *rev from* throrn, *MS. 131*
6 saw;—] saw— *MS. 108* saw,— *rev from* saw; *Huntington MS. 1* saw; *MS. 131, Keepsake, MS. 1832/36–* Fancy *rev from* fancy *MS. 108*
7 through] thro' *MS. 131* *no commas MS. 108*
8 care,] care; *MS. 131, Huntington MS. 1, Keepsake*
9 flies—] flies, *MS. 108*
10 How] (How *MS. 1832/36–* it *rev from* it, *rev from* it? *Huntington MS. 1* dies?] dies; *MS. 108* dies? *rev from* dies, *Huntington MS. 1* dies?) *MS. 1832/36–*
11 Of *rev from* of *Huntington MS. 1* *no comma MS. 108*
13 pity,] Pity *MS. 108, Huntington MS. 1, Keepsake* conveyed] convey'd *Keepsake*
14 pleasure,] pleasure *MS. 131, Huntington MS. 1, Keepsake* shade] shade, *Huntington MS. 1, Keepsake*
15 Time] time *MS. 131, Keepsake* Grandsire] grandsire *MS. 131, Huntington MS. 1, Keepsake, MS. 1832/36–*
16 smoothly-gliding] smoothly gliding *1845–*
16/17 *page break 1832; stanza break MS. 1832/36–*
17 *para MSS. 108, 131, Huntington MS. 1, MS. 1832/36–* form, . . . face,] Form . . . Face *MS. 108* form, . . . face *1845–*
18 *no commas MS. 108, Huntington MS. 1*
19 colours,] colours *MSS. 108, 131, Huntington MS. 1, Keepsake*
20 feed;] feed— *MS. 108* feed? *MS. 131, Huntington MS. 1, Keepsake*
21 For] For, *MS. 131, Huntington MS. 1, Keepsake* flowers,] flowers *MSS. 108, 131*
22 Damsel,] Damsel! *MS. 108, 1836–* damsel, *Keepsake* o'er . . . mind,] oer . . . mind *Huntington MS. 1*
24 'Mid] Mid *Huntington MS. 1* bowers,] bowers *MS. 108*
25 hung, for hours.] hung for hours! *MSS. 108, 131, Huntington MS. 1, Keepsake*
25/26 *no stanza break MS. 131*
26 —Thanks] Thanks *with para MS. 108, MS. 1832/36–* *no para MS. 131, Huntington MS. 1, Keepsake* corn,] corn *MS. 108, Huntington MS. 1*
28 share] share, *MS. 131, Keepsake*
29 *no comma MS. 108*
30 rise,] rise *MS. 108* rise *rev from* rise; *Huntington MS. 1* head,] head *MS. 108*
32 Heaven] heaven *MSS. 108, 131, Huntington MS. 1, Keepsake* *no ital MSS. 108, 131, Huntington MS. 1, Keepsake* repeat,] repeat *MSS. 108, Huntington MS. 1*
33 prayer] Prayer *MS. 131*

The Triad

1 Show . . . time,] Shew . . . time *MS. 108, Keswick MS.*
2 fancy] Fancy *Keswick MS.*
3 *no comma Keswick MS., Keepsake*
4 Returned . . . Consort] Return'd . . . consort *Keswick MS., Keepsake*
6 star] Star *Keepsake* *no comma MS. 108*

7 mate . . . him] "mate . . . him" *Keswick MS., Keepsake* blissfully.] blissfully! *MS. 108, Keswick MS., Keepsake*

9 power)] power), *Keepsake*

10 leaf-crowned] leaf-crown'd *Keepsake*

11 Sea-nymph] Sea Nymph *MS. 108* bower;] bower— *MS. 108, Keswick MS.* bower;— *Keepsake*

12 Mortals] mortals *MS. 108* Mortals, *Keswick MS., Keepsake* still,] still *MS. 108*

15 *para 1836–* "Appear!—] Appear! *MS. 108* Appear!— *Keswick MS.* lyre's] Lyre's *MS. 108, Keswick MS.*

18 Sisters] sisters *Keepsake*

21 They] they *MS. 108, Keswick MS., Keepsake*

22 spheres] spheres, *Keepsake*

23 union] union, *1836–* above."—] above." *MS. 1832/36–* *no quot MS. 108, Keswick MS.*

24 vain,] vain; *1836–* hushed] hush'd *Keepsake* waving:] waving *MS. 108, so Keswick MS. but MS. cut away* waving. *Keepsake*

27 *no comma MS. 108, Keepsake*

28 And,] And *MS. 108*

29 Occupants] occupants *MS. 108, Keswick MS., Keepsake, MS. 1832/36–* hide:—] hide— *MS. 108* hide.— *Keswick MS., Keepsake*

32 Beings] beings *Keepsake* one by] one, by *MS. 108, Keswick MS* one,] one; *1836–*

34 *para 1836–* *quot added in pencil MS. 108, no quot Keswick MS.* measure!] measure, *MS. 108*

36 Lucida] Lucida *double underscored MS. 108, Keswick MS.* LUCIDA *Keepsake* *no comma MS. 108*

38 *no comma MS. 108*

39 *no comma MS. 108, Keswick MS.*

40 hermit's] Hermit's *Keswick MS.* *punct added in pencil MS. 108, no quot Keswick MS.*

41 —She] She *MS. 1832/36*

42 Figure] figure *Keepsake* ship] Ship *Keswick MS.* *no comma MS. 108, Keswick MS.*

43 draws— . . . veil—] draws; . . . veil; *MS. 1832/36–*

45 gale] gale, *Keswick MS.*

46 mould] mold *1836–* mould *in pencil MS. 1836/45*

48 splendour,] splendor, *MS. 108, Keswick MS.* splendour— *1836–*

49 train] train, *MS. 108, Keswick MS.*

50 governed] govern'd *Keepsake*

51 music,] music *Keepsake* alone.—] alone— *MS. 108, Keswick MS., Keepsake* alone. *1836–*

51/52 *stanza break MS. 1832/36–*

52 *para 1836–* O Lady,] —O Lady! *MS. 108, Keswick MS., Keepsake* "O Lady, *MS. 1832/36–* throne!] throne *MS. 108* throne, *Keswick MS., Keepsake*

55 queen] Queen *MS. 108, Keswick MS.* unknown;] unknown! *MS. 108*

56 Man *MS. 108, WW to MW & Dora W*

57 malice,] malice *MS. 108* thou] Thou *1836–* near,] near *MS. 108, Keswick MS.*

58 lily stem] Lily stem *MS. 108, Keswick MS.* lily-stem *1836–* sceptre *rev to* Sceptre *Keswick MS.*

60 too] too, *MS. 108*

61 —Queen] Queen *WW to MW & Dora W*—Queen, *MS. 1832/36–, Keepsake* handmaid] Handmaid *MS. 108, Keswick MS.* Handmaid *rev to* handmaid *WW to MW & Dora W*

62 day] Day *MS. 108* *no comma MS. 108*

64 invents] invents, *MS. 108*

65 thou,] Thou *MS. 108, Keswick MS.* Thou, *1836–* lip,] lip *MS. 108* smile,] smile *Keswick MS., Keepsake, 1836–*

68 Nursling] nursling *Keepsake* palace] Palace *MS. 108, Keswick MS.*

69 hawthorn roof] hawthorn-roof *1836–*

70 archer] Archer *MS. 108, Keswick MS., 1836–* caves] Caves *MS. 108*

72 a] a̲ *MS. 108* glimpse *ital*] g̲l̲i̲m̲p̲s̲e̲ *MS. 108* day? *rev from* day, *MS. 108*

73 *no comma MS. 108, Keswick MS., Keepsake*

75 Majesty] majesty *MS. 108, Keswick MS., Keepsake, MS. 1832/36–*

76 deer] Deer *MS. 108, Keswick MS.*

77 here;)] here) *MS. 108, Keswick MS.* here); *Keepsake*

78 *no comma MS. 108, Keswick MS.*

79 smoothed] smooth'd *Keepsake*

82 strive,] strive *MS. 108, Keswick MS.*

83 out,] out *MS. 108, Keswick MS.*

84 rainbow's] Rainbows *MS. 108* Rainbow's *in pencil MS. 1836/45* *no comma MS. 108, Keswick MS.*

85 shrine;—] shrine— *MS. 108, Keswick MS.*

86 lyre] Lyre *MS. 108, Keswick MS.*

88/89 *stanza break 1836–*

88 shades] Shades *Keswick MS.* Nymph] nymph *Keepsake* call,] call *MS. 108*

89 Three.—] Three— *MS. 108, Keswick MS.*
90 *no quot Keswick MS.* pierce;] pierce, *Keswick MS.*
91 verse,] verse. *MS. 108* verse *Keswick MS.*
92 thee!"] Thee. *MS. 108* Thee! *Keswick MS.*
93 —I sang;] —I sang *alt* I sang! *MS. 108* —I sang; *rev from* —I sang— *Keswick MS.* virginal] virginal, *MS. 108*
95 elements.] elements; *MS. 108, Keswick MS.*
96 sheen,] sheen *MS. 108* sheen: *Keepsake* sheen; *1836–*
97 *no punct MS. 108* green! *rev from* green, *Keswick MS.*
99 charm] Charm *in pencil MS. 1836/45* Charm *1845, 1850*
100 stringèd] stringed *Keswick MS., Keepsake* lute] Lute *MS. 108, Keswick MS.*
101 cheered] cheer'd *Keepsake* trellised] trelliced *MS. 108, Keswick MS.* trellis'd *Keepsake* arbour's] Arbour's *MS. 108*
102 raftered] rafter'd *Keepsake* hall.] hall *MS. 108* Hall— *Keswick MS.*
103 air! *rev from* air, *Keswick MS.*
104 tripped] tripp'd *Keepsake* Muse,] Muse *MS. 108, Keswick MS., Keepsake*
105 Euphrosyne!] Euphrosyne *MS. 108* Euphrosine! *Keswick MS.*
106 head] head, *Keepsake*
109 shepherdess] Shepherdess *MS. 108, Keswick MS.*
111 breathed,] breathed; *Keswick MS.*
112 in] in, *Keswick MS., Keepsake*
113 rose] Rose *MS. 108*
115 floweret] floweret, *Keepsake* forlorn)] forlorn!) *MS. 108, Keswick MS., Keepsake*
116 worn;] worn *MS. 108* worn, *Keswick MS.* worn— *1836–* *no small caps MS. 108*
118 Open,] Open *MS. 108, Keswick MS.* thickets] Thickets *Keswick MS.*
119 Nymph] Nymph, *Keswick MS.* nymph, *Keepsake*
120 She,] She *Keswick MS.* she, *Keepsake* Her] her *MS. 108, Keswick MS., 1836–* her, *Keepsake, 1845–*
121 Stranger's] stranger's *Keepsake*
123 *no comma MS. 108*
124 Turning . . . out] "Turning . . . out" *MS. 108, Keepsake* audacity.] audacity! *MS. 108*
124/125 *no stanza break 1845–*
125 show] shew *MS. 108, Keswick MS.*
128 go!] go— *MS. 108* go!— *Keswick MS., Keepsake*
129 fastened] fasten'd *Keepsake* rivulet's] rivulets *MS. 108*
130 there (while] there, while *MS. 108, Keepsake* there—while *Keswick MS.* mien,] mien *MS. 108*
131 waters] waters, *Keswick MS., Keepsake*
132 birth-place] birthplace *Keepsake* cleft] cleft, *MS. 108, Keepsake*
133 bends)] bends, *MS. 108, Keswick MS., Keepsake*
134 *no comma Keswick MS.*
136 countenance . . . soul] Countenance . . . Soul *MS. 108* truth,] Truth, *MS. 108* truth; *1836–*
137 youth!] youth. *MS. 108*
138 sea] Sea *MS. 108, Keswick MS.* Sea *in pencil MS. 1836/45*
140 presides;] presides, *MS. 108, Keswick MS., Keepsake*
141 Maiden] maiden *Keepsake* he.—] he. *MS. 108, 1836–*
142 heaven *rev to* Heaven *Keswick MS.* *no comma MS. 108*
143 ether] Ether *Keswick MS.* good-will,] good-will; *1836–*
144 And,] And *MS. 108*
145 rill;] rill: *1836–*
146 star] star, *MS. 108* Star *Keswick MS.*
149 *no commas MS. 108* is,] is *Keswick MS.*
150 faces.] faces.— *MS. 108*
151 *no comma MS. 108, Keswick MS.*
153 If] If, *Keepsake* do,] do *MSS. 108, 107, Keswick MS.*
155 unfit,] unfit *MS. 108* unfit; *1836–*
156–157, 159 *no punct MS. 107*
157 self-forgetfulness] Self-forgetfulness *MS. 107*
159 tutored] tutord *MS. 107*
160 Her's] Hers *MS. 108* Her's *ital Keswick MS., Keepsake* *no comma MS. 108*
161 joy-flushes—] joyflushes *MS. 108* joy-flushes; *1836–*
164 gaiety] gaiety *rev from* gaeity *Keswick MS.* gayety *Keepsake* *no comma MS. 108*
165 wit—] wit; *MS. 108* wit— *rev from* wit; *Keswick MS.*
166 Daughter] daughter *Keepsake* mountains] Mountains *MS. 108, Keswick MS.* free] free, *Keepsake*
167 Faery] fairy *Keepsake*
168 crossed] cross'd *Keepsake* vagary] vaguery *Keswick MS.*
169 bands] bands, *MS. 108, Keswick MS.*
170 triumph] triumph, *MS. 108*

hands.] hands *MS. 108* hands! *Keswick MS., Keepsake*
171 *para 1836–* "Last] Last *MS. 108, Keswick MS.* born,] born *MS. 108* born! *Keepsake*
172 morn,] morn *MS. 108* Morn *Keswick MS., 1836–*
173 Touched] Touch'd *Keepsake* skylark's] Skylarks *MS. 108, Keswick MS.*
174 afloat.] afloat; *MS. 108, Keswick MS.*
175 semblance] Semblance *Keswick MS.*
176 dawn—or eve,] Dawn,—or Eve, *MS. 108, Keswick MS.* Dawn—or Eve, *1836–* dawn, or eve— *Keepsake* west,] West, *MS. 108* west. *1840–1843, 1846–1849*
178 woman's] Woman's *Keswick MS.*
179 grief, . . . meekness,] grief . . . meekness *MS. 108, Keswick MS., Keepsake* rest.] rest— *rev to* rest! *Keswick MS.* rest! *Keepsake*
180 high-wrought] high wrought *MS. 108*
181 hand] hand, *Keswick MS.*
182 spirit] Spirit *MS. 108, Keswick MS.* stand] stand, *Keswick MS.*
183 age."] Age— *MS. 108* age.— *Keswick MS.* age."— *Keepsake*
183/184 *no stanza break MS. 108, Keswick MS., Keepsake*
184 —Her] Her *1836–* opened] open'd *Keepsake* *no comma MS. 108*
185 hair;] hair— *MS. 108* hair,— *Keswick MS.*
186 *no comma MS. 108, Keswick MS.*
187 groves.] groves— *MS. 108* groves.— *Keswick MS., Keepsake*
188 —Tenderest] Tenderest *1836–* cheek;] cheek *MS. 108* cheek, *Keswick MS.*
189 streak— *rev to* streak; *Keswick MS.* streak, *Keepsake* streak; *1836–*
190 eye;] eye *MS. 108*
191 love,] love *Keswick MS.* field] field, *MS. 108*
193 purity.—] purity. *Keepsake, 1836–*
194 What] —What *Keswick MS.* would'st] wouldst *MS. 108, Keswick MS.* glade] glade, *Keswick MS., 1836–*
195 *no comma MS. 108*
197 angels mused?] Angels mused! *MS. 108, Keswick MS.*
198 *no comma MS. 108, Keswick MS.*
199 dew-drops,] dew-drops *MS. 108* dew-drops— *Keswick MS., 1836–*
200 *no apos MS. 108, Keswick MS.* breast;] breast, *MS. 108*
201 flowers] Flowers *Keswick MS.* hue,] hue *MS. 108*
203 listening;] listening— *1836–*
204 And] And, *Keswick MS.*
205 wisely—] wisely; *1836–*
206 shepherd] Shepherd *MS. 108, Keswick MS.* *no comma MS. 108*
207 on,] on *MS. 108* on— *1836–*
207/208 *stanza break Keswick MS.*
208 cropped] cropp'd *Keepsake*
209 charm] Charm *MS. 1836/45, 1840–* phantoms] Phantoms *Keswick MS., MS. 1836/45 1840–* phantom's *(printer's error) 1836* over; . . . gone,] over, . . . gone *MS. 108*
210 not,] not *Keswick MS.* favoured Youth;] favored Youth! *MS. 108, Keswick MS.* favour'd Youth! *Keepsake*
211 apparition] Apparition *MS. 108, Keswick MS.*
212 Obeyed] Obey'd *Keepsake* truth.] truth; *MS. 108, Keswick MS.*
214 tried,] tried; *MS. 108, Keswick MS.*
215 Bride!] bride! *Keswick MS., Keepsake* Bride. *1836–*

On the Power of Sound, Text of MS. 131

1 Spirit,] Spirit *MSS. 89 (A, B)* spirit, *MS. 115*
2 controll'd,] controlled *MS. 89 (A)* controlled; *MSS. 89 (B), 115*
3 glorious *rev from* glorrow *MS. 89 (B)* privilege] privelege *MS. 89 (B)*
4 *no punct MS. 89 (A)*
5 Heavens *rev to* Heav'ns *MS. 89 (B)* *no comma MS. 89 (A)*
6 be] be, *MS. 89 (B)*
9 Headlands] headlands, *MS. 89 (B)* headlands *MS. 115* crown'd *rev from* crowned *MS. 115* mist,] mist *MS. 115*
11 harmonist:—] harmonist; *rev to* Harmonist; *MS. 89 (A)* harmonist: *MS. 89 (B)*
12 pinions] pinions, *MS. 89 (B)* Air! *rev from* air! *MS. 89 (B)* Air *MS. 89 (A)*
13 *no punct MS. 89 (A)*
14 harmony] Harmony *MS. 89 (A)* Harmony, *MS. 89 (B)*
15 *no punct MS. 89 (A)*
16 winter] Winter *MS. 89 (A) (B)* sound.] sound— *MS. 89 (A)*
18 day, *rev to* day *MS. 89 (B)* powers,] powers; *MS. 89 (B)*
19 Tent,] tent *MS. 89 (B)*
20 *no commas MS. 89 (B)* ten-thousand] ten thousand *MS.*

89 (B)

21 roar— *rev from* roar, *MS. 89 (B)* *no quot MS. 89 (B)*

22 fearful . . . Desart] fearfull . . . desart *MS. 89 (B)*

23 bleat,] bleat— *MS. 89 (B)* *no commas MS. 89 (B)*

24 Straggler] straggler *MS. 89 (B)*

25 Cuckoo! *rev from* Cockoo *MS. 89 (B)*

26 thee] the *(copyist's slip) MS. 89 (B)*

27 Bell-Bird] Bell-bird *MS. 89 (B)* Bell-Bird *rev from* bell-Bird *MS. 131*

29 Mercy . . . throne] Mercy, . . . throne, *MS. 89 (B)*

30 soft sigh] soft-sigh *MS. 89 (B)* *no comma MS. 89 (B)*

31 sailor's] Sailors *MS. 89 (B)* darkening] dark'ning *MS. 89 (B)*

32 widow's cottage] Widow's Cottage *MS. 89 (B)*

33 *no commas MS. 89 (B)*

34 images] Images *MS. 89 (B)*

35 woods] words *(copyist's slip) MS. 89 (B)* *no commas MSS. 89 (B)*

37 *punct added MS. 89 (B)*

40 bridal] Bridal *MS. 89 (B)*

66 Vast] vast *MS. 131*

67 Babe's] Babes *rev from* babes *MS. 131*

81–96 *see transcription of MS. 89 (B)*

91 tears *rev from* tears, *MS. 131*

94 Bond slave] Bondslave *MS. 89 (B)*

On the Power of Sound, Text of 1835

argument *no caps, no punct MS. 135*

1 Ear *rev from* ear *MS. 135*

2 individual, *rev from* individual *MS. 137 (C)* individual *MSS. 135, 137 (A, B), 138 (A)* harmony.—] harmony— *MS. 135* Sources] Sources, *MS. 135*

3 —The] The *MS. 135*

5 —The] The *MS. 135*

6 severally. *WW rev to* severally: *MS. 135* Stanza] Stanz: *MS. 135*

9 contemplation.— . . . The] contemplation— . . . the *MS. 135* 12th.)] 12th) *MS. 135* 12th). *1836–*

10 universe] Universe *MS. 135*

11 (in 11th Stanza)] (in 11th Stan:) *rev from* (in (11th Stan:) *MS. 135* realised,] realized *MS. 135*

12 degree,] degree *MS. 135*

13 Last Stanza] Last Stanz: *rev from dash MS. 135* Last Stanza *rev from* Last Stanza. *MS. 137 (C)* the] The *MSS. 135, 137 (A, B), 138 (A)* the *rev from* The *MS. 137 (C)*

14 harmony,] harmony *MS. 135*

15 Holy Writ] holy writ *rev to* holy Writ *MS. 135*

stanza numbers *no punct MSS. 107, 135; so MS. 134 except* 6. 7. *and* 10. 11. 12. 13.

1 etherial,] etherial *MSS. 107, 106, 134, comma del and reentered MS. 135* ethereal *1836–, 1839*

2 Mind] Mind *rev from* mind *MS. 107* mind *Cornell MS. 6, MS. 1835/36–*

3 Vision] vision *MS. 107, 1836–* And *rev from* and *MS. 135* and *MSS. 107, 106, 134* Spirit] spirit *MSS. 107, Cornell MS. 6* aerial] aërial *1836YR, 1836–, 1839*

4 hearing] Hearing *1836–, 1839*

5 labyrinth,] labyrinth! *MSS. 107, Cornell MS. 6, MS. 137 (A)* labyrinth *MSS. 106, 134* labyrinth! *rev from* labyrinth— *MS. 135* labyrinth! *MS. 137(B) so MS. 137 (A) rev to* labyrinth, dread] dread, *rev to* dread— *MS. 106* thought] Thought *MSS. 107, 106, Cornell MS. 6, MSS. 134, 135, 137, 138*

6 enter] enter, *MS. 106* cave] Cave *MSS. 107, 106, Cornell MS. 6, MSS. 134, 135*

7 passage, *rev from* passage! *MSS. 135, 137 (A* passage *MSS. 107, 106, 134)* passage! *MS. 137 (B)* through] thro' *MSS. 106, 134, 135* brought,] brought *MS. 134*

8 whispers,] whispers *1836–, 1839* heart] Heart *MS. 107, Cornell MS. 6* slave] slave *rev from* Slave *Cornell MS. 6*

9 shrieks,] shrieks *MSS. 107, 106, Cornell MS. 6, MS. 134, 135*

10 air] Air *MSS. 107, 106, 134, Cornell MS. 6, MS. 135*

13 despair;] Despair; *MSS. 107, 106, Cornell MS. 6* despair *MS. 134*

14 long-drawn aisle,] long drawn aisle *MS. 134*

15 answered *alt* answer'd *MS. 107* answer'd *Cornell MS. 6*

16 retreats!] retreats. *MS. 107, Cornell MS. 6; rev in pencil to text MS. 107*

17 Streams and Fountains *rev in pencil from* streams and fountains *MS. 107* streams and fountains *Cornell MS. 6, MS. 1835/36–, 1839*

18 Thee,] thee, *MSS. 107, 106, Cornell MS. 6, 1839* Thee *MS. 134* Invisible] invisible *1836–* Spirit, *rev from* Spirit! *MS. 137 (A)* Spirit! *MSS. 107, 106, Cornell MS. 6, MSS. 134, 135, 137 (B)* Spirit *1839* powers;] powers *MSS. 107, 106,*

Cornell MS. 6, MS. 134

19 Cheering] Chearing *MSS. 107, 106, Cornell MS. 6, MS. 134* Tent] tent *MS. 1835/36–, 1839* mountains,] Mountains *MS. 107, Cornell MS. 6* mountains *MSS. 106, 134, 135*

20 lull perchance] lull, perchance, *MS. 106* lull perchance, *MS. 134* flowers.] flowers *MSS. Cornell MS. 6, MS. 134*

21 That *(ital)* roar,] That Roar— *MSS. 106* That roar— *MS. 134* That Roar— *MS. 107* That Roar— *rev to* That Roar— *Cornell MS. 6* That roar— *MS. 135* Lion's] lion's *MS. 1835/36–* Here I am, *ital rev from* Here I am! *MS. 137 (A)* here I am *MSS. 107, 106, Cornell MS. 6, MS. 134* here I am— *MS. 135* Here I am! *MS. 137 (B)*

22 desert] desart *MSS. 107, 106, Cornell MS. 6, MSS. 134, 135* *no punct MS. 134*

23 bleat, *rev to* Bleat, *MS. 107* Bleat— *MS. 106* Bleat, *Cornell MS. 6* bleat— *MS. 134* tender! *rev from* tender *MS. 137 (A)* tender *MSS. 134, 135, 137 (B)* Dam] Dam; *MS. 106* dam *MS. 1835/36–, 1839*

24 straggler] Straggler *MSS. 106, 135* side. *rev from* side! *MS. 138(B)* side! *MSS. 107, 106, Cornell MS. 6, MSS. 135, 137, 138(A)* side *MS. 134*

25 Shout, *rev from* Shout *MS. 135* Shout *MSS. 107, 106, Cornell MS. 6, MS. 134* Cuckoo!] Cuckoo *MS. 134* cuckoo! *MS. 1835/36* cuckoo!— *1836–, 1839*

26 zone;] zone! *MSS. 107, 106, Cornell MS. 6* zone *MS. 134*

27 Bell-bird, *rev from* Bell-bird *MSS. 135, 137 (A)* Bell-bird *MS. 134* Bill-bird, *(printer's error) MS. 137 (B)* bell-bird, *MS. 1835/36–, 1839* toll!] toll *MSS. 107, 106, Cornell MS. 6, MS. 134, 1850*

28 Mercy] mercy *MS. 107, Cornell MS. 6* Mercy *rev from* mercy *MSS. 106, 135* *no punct MS. 134*

30 Nun's] nun's *MS. 107, Cornell MS. 6, MS. 1835/36–, 1839* Nun's *rev from* nun's *MS. 106* *no comma MS. 134*

31 Sailor's] sailor's *Cornell MS. 6, MS. 1835/36–, 1839* Sailors *MS. 134* sea,] Sea, *MS. 107* sea *MSS. 106, 134*

32 Widow's] widow's *MS. 107, Cornell MS. 6, MS. 1835/36–, 1839* Widows *MS. 134* cottage lullaby.] cottage lullaby *MS. 106* cottage-lullaby. *1836–, 1839* *no punct MS. 134*

33 Shadows,] Shadows *MS. 134, 1836YR, 1845, 1850* Shadows *in pencil MS. 1836/45*

34 Images] images *Cornell MS. 6* Image's *MS. 134*

35 rock-bestudded] rock bestudded *MS. 134*

36 and, . . . caves, *rev from* and . . . caves *MS. 137 (A)* and . . . caves *MSS. 134, 135, 137 (B)* reborn,] reborn *MS. 134* reborn— *1836–, 1839*

37 with *written twice MS. 107* pastime! *rev from* pastime, *MS. 135* pastime, *MSS. 106, 134* till] 'till *MS. 135* church-tower] Church-tower *MSS. 107, 106, 134, 135*

38 *no ital MSS. 106, 134, 1845, 1850*

40 symphony.] symphony! *MS. 106* symphony *MS. 134, 1839*

41 Then,] Then *MS. 134*

44 *no comma MS. 134*

45 Milk-maids] milk-maids *MS. 1835/36–, 1839* one] one, *MS. 106*

46 ditty *rev from* ditty, *MS. 135* desire,] desire *MS. 107*

47 Art,] art, *MSS. 107, 106* Art *MS. 134*

48 heart.] heart! *MSS. 107, 106* heart *MS. 134*

49 Blest *rev from* Blessed *MS. 134* Bless'd *MS. 106*

50 blind] Blind *MS. 137* Man's] mans *MS. 107, MS. 1835/36–, 1839* Mans *MS. 134* Man's *rev to* -man's *MS. 137 (A)* gloom,] gloom *MS. 134* Veteran's] Veterans *MSS. 107, 134* veteran's *MS. 1835/36–, 1839* mirth;] mirth, *MSS. 107, 106, 134*

51 Peasant's *rev from* Pheasant's *(copyist's slip) MS. 135* Peasants *MS. 107* peasant's *1836–, 1839* breath,] breath *MSS. 107, 106, 134, 135*

52 earth.] earth! *MSS. 107, 106* earth *MS. 134*

53 Slave,] Slave *MS. 107* slave, *MS. 1835/36–, 1839* Song *rev from* song *MS. 135* *no commas MS. 134*

54 fall, *rev from* fall— *MS. 135* fall— *MSS. 107, 106, 134*

56 *no punct MS. 134*

57 Pilgrims] pilgrims *MS. 1835/36–, 1839* see— *rev from* see *MS. 137 (A)* see! *MSS. 107, 106* see *MS. 134* see, *MSS. 135* see, *alt* see! *MS. 137 (B)*

58 move; *rev from* move, *MS. 137 (A)* move, *MSS. 107, 135, 137 (B)* move *MS. 134*

59 Ave Marie *ital*] ave marie *MSS. 107, 106* beguile,] beguile *MSS. 107, 134*

61 ray:] ray; *MSS. 106, 134, 135* ray. *rev to* ray; *MS. 107*
62 He,] He *MS. 107* he, *1836–, 1839* Prisoner . . . Mind] prisoner . . . mine *MS. 1835/36–, 1839*
64 draw,] draw *MS. 107* draw; *MS. 106*
66 kingdom,] Kingdom *MSS. 107, 134* Kingdom, *MSS. 106, 135*
67 Inspiration *rev from* inspiration *MS. 135* inspiration *MSS. 107, 106, 134*
68 tune,] tune *MSS. 106, 134* blast *rev from* blast, *MS. 137 (A)* blast, *MSS. 106, 137 (B)*
69 through] thro' *MSS. 107, 106, 134* thro *MS. 135*
70 Sluggard, *rev from* sluggard, *MS. 135* Sluggard *MS. 107* sluggard, *MSS. 106, 134, MS. 1835/36–, 1839*
71 Freedom,] freedom *MS. 107* Freedom *rev from* freedom *MS. 106* Freedom *MS. 134*
72 promises,] promises— *MSS. 107, 106, 134* shrill, wild,] shrill wild *MSS. 107, 134, 135* sweet!] sweet *MS. 134*
73 Who, *rev from* Who *MS. 135* —Who *rev from* Who *MS. 106* Who *MSS. 107, 134* pageant, *ital*] <u>pageant</u> *MS. 107* pageant *MSS. 106, 134*
74 battle-day, *rev from* battle-day *MS. 137 (A)* battle day, *MS. 106* battle day *MSS. 107, 134* battle-day *MSS. 135, 137 (B)*
75 unweaponed *rev from* unweapened *MS. 106* heads; *rev to* heads? *MS. 106* heads *MS. 134* heads! *rev from* head? *rev from* heads, *MS. 135* heads? *1836YR* heads?— *MS. 1835/36–, 1839*
76 She *rev from* she *MS. 137 (A)* she *MS. 137 (B)*
77 striving,] striving *MS. 107*
78 desire] desire, *MS. 106*
79 Graces,] Graces *rev from* graces *MS. 107*
80 Love. *rev from* Love; *MS. 135* Love— *MS. 107*
81 *no comma MS. 134*
82 Sound, *rev from* Sound; *MS. 135* Sound! *MSS. 107, 106* Sound *MS. 134* sound, *MS. 137 (B)* sound, *rev to* Sound! *MS. 137 (A)* sound, *MS. 1835/36–, 1839* dangerous] <u>dangerous</u> *ink over pencil underscore MS. 106* Passions *rev from* passions *MS. 137 (A)* passions *MSS. 107, 106, 135* passions *MS. 137 (B)* trod! *rev in pencil from* trod *MS. 107* trod *MS. 134* trod! *rev from* trod, *MS. 135*
83 through *rev from* thro *MS. 135* thro' *MSS. 107, 106, 134* Temple] temple *MS. 1835/36–, 1839* *no commas MS. 134*
84 *no comma MS. 134*
86 Votaries,] Votaries— *rev from* Votaries— *MS. 107* Votaries— *MSS. 106, 134* Votaries *MS. 135* votaries, *MS. 1835/36–, 1839* resigned] resign'd *MS. 106*
88 better] better, *1845–* *no punct MS. 134*
90 *no punct MS. 134*
91 Virtuous *rev from* virtuous *MS. 134* virtuous *MS. 1835/36–, 1839* *no commas MSS. 107, 106, 134*
92 patience,—] patience— *MSS. 107, 106, 134*
93 Suicide; *rev from* suicide; *MS. 135* Suicide *MS. 134*
95 *no comma MS. 134*
96 Martyr . . . Patriot] martyr . . . patriot *MS. 1835/36–, 1839* bleeds!] bleeds *MSS. 106, 134*
97 Conscience,] Conscience *MSS. 107, 106, Cornell MS. 6, MS. 134* Connscience, *MS. 135* centre] Centre *Cornell MS. 6*
98 Being,] being *MS. 107, Cornell MS. 6* Being *MSS. 106, 134* being, *MS. 1835/36–, 1839* pain, *rev in pencil from* pain *MS. 107* pain *Cornell MS. 6, MS. 134* pain; *1836–1840* pain *1845–*
99 cadence,] cadence *MS. 107* Cadence *Cornell MS. 6*
100 Idiot's] Idiots *MS. 107* idiot's *MS. 1835/36–, 1839* brain,] brain *MSS. 107, 134, 135*
101 wretch] Wretch *rev from* wretch *MS. 107* Wretch *MSS. 106, 134* hurled—] hurled, *rev from* hurl'd, *MS. 106* hurl'd, *MS. 107* hurled *MS. 134* hurled, *MSS. 135, 137 (B)* hurled,— *rev from* hurled— *MS. 137 (A)*
102 Convulsed *rev from* Convulsied *MS. 135* Convulsied *MS. 134* din; *rev in pencil from* din, *MS. 107* din; *rev from* din *MS. 106*
104 in *rev from* in[?] *MS. 106*
106 soul! *rev from* soul, *MS. 137 (A)* soul *MS. 107* soul; *rev from* soul *MS. 106* soul; *rev in pencil from* soul *MS. 134* soul, *MSS. 135, 137 (B)*
107 Or, awed *rev from* Or awed, *MS. 137* Or awed *MS. 107* Or awed, *MSS. 134, 135, 137 (B)* weeps,] weeps *MS. 107* dismay.] dismay *MS. 134* dismay, *1836YR*
108 Art] art *MSS. 107, 106, 134* art *WW*

rev to Art *MS. 135*

109 pole;] pole? *MSS. 107, 106, 134*

111 divine] Divine *MSS. 137, 138* Love, *rev from* love, *MS. 135* Wisdom, Beauty, Truth *rev from* wisdom, beauty, truth *MS. 135*; *MS. 107 as orig MS. 135* wisdom, beauty, truth, *MS. 106* wisdom beauty truth *MS. 134* Truth] Truth, *1836YR, 1839*

112 Order *rev from* order *MS. 134* order *MS. 107* dwell,] dwell *MSS. 107, 106, 134* youth? *rev from* youth. *MS. 137* Youth. *MSS. 106, 134* youth. *MS. 107*

114 Miser,] Miser *MSS. 107, 106, 134* miser, *MS. 1835/36–, 1839* Time. *rev from* Time; *MS. 137 (A)* Time; *MSS. 107, 106, 135, MS. 137 (B)* Time *MS. 134* Time: *1836YR*

115 Insight! *rev from* Insight, *MS. 135* Insight *MS. 107* Insight, *MSS. 106, 134* Truth's] truth's *MS. 1835/36–, 1839* Lover,] Lover *rev from* lover *MS. 107* Lover *MS. 134* lover, *MS. 1835/36–, 1839*

116 tutored] tutor'd *MS. 107* climb,] climb *MSS. 107, 134*

117 deigned *rev from* degned *MS. 107*

118 enfold, *rev from* enfold *MS. 137 (A)* enfold *MSS. 107, 134, MS. 137 (B)* enfold; *MS. 106* enfold *WW rev from* infold *MS. 135*

119 Voice *rev from* voice *MS. 134* voice *MS. 107, MS. 1835/36–, 1839* shell *MS. 107, MS. 1835/36–, 1839*

120 Nature's] nature's *MS. 107* self] Self *MS. 106* *no punct MS. 134*

121 strenuous *rev from* srenuous *MS. 137* strennuous *MS. 107* infant] Infant *1836YR, 1839* Age: *rev from* Age; *MS. 138* age; *MS. 107* Age, *rev from* age, *MS. 106* Age *MS. 134* Age; *MSS. 135, 137 (B)*

122 *commas ink over pencil MS. 107* *no commas MS. 134*

123 Stirred *rev to* Stirr'd *MS. 106* Stirr'd *MSS. 107, 134, 135* nowhere] no where *MSS. 107, 106*

125 weal:] weal *MS. 107* weal; *MSS. 106, 134*

126 Hell *rev from* He'll *MS. 137* low;] low *MS. 107* arch] Arch *MSS. 106, 134, 135*

129 King] king *MS. 1835/36–, 1839* Amphion] Amphion, *MS. 106*

130 city] City *MSS. 107, 106, 134*

131 dream;] dream: *MSS. 107, 134, 135* dream:— *1836–, 1839* skill,] skill *MSS. 106, 134* skill, *pencil over ink MS. 107* Arion!] Arion *MS. 134*

132 humanise] humanize *MS. 107* creatures] Creatures *MSS. 106, 134, 135* sea] Sea *MSS. 107, 106, 134, 135*

133 craves,] craves *MS. 134*

134 chant] chaunt *MSS. 107, 106, 134, 135* sound] sound— *MS. 134*

135 waves,] waves *MS. 107*

136 Dolphins] dolphins *MS. 107, MS. 1835/36–, 1839* round. *rev from* round, *MS. 135* round; *MSS. 107, 106, 134*

137 Self-cast, *rev in pencil from* Self-cast *MS. 107*

138 'Mid] Mid *MSS. 134, 135* audience,] audience *MSS. 107, 106, 134*

139 One] one, *MS. 106* One, *MS. 107* One, *rev in pencil from* one, *MS. 134* horse;] horse *MSS. 107, 134*

141 Master *rev from* master *MS. 137 (A)* master *MS. 137 (B)* *no semicolon MS. 134*

143 Preserver, *rev from* preserver *MS. 134* preserver *MSS. 107, MS. 1835/36–, 1839* preserver, *MS. 106* star-bright] star bright *MSS. 134, 135* *no commas MS. 107*

144 memory,] memory *MSS. 107, 106, 134* night.] night *MS. 134*

145 pipe *rev from* Pipe *MS. 137 (A)* Pipe *MSS. 107, 106, 134, 135, 137 (B)* Pan,] Pan *MSS. 107, 106, 134* Shepherds] shepherds *MS. 107, MS. 1835/36–, 1839*

146 Menalian] Mænalian *1836–, 1839* Pines,] Pines *MSS. 107, 106, 134* pines, *MS. 1835/36–, 1839*

147 sweet; *rev from* sweet! *MS. 138* sweet! *MSS. 107, 106, 134, 135, 137* eyeballs] eye balls *MS. 106* eye-balls *MSS. 134, 135* Leopards,] Leopards *MSS. 107, 134* leopards, *MS. 1835/36–, 1839*

148 triumph] triump *MS. 134* vines, *rev from* Vines *MS. 137 (A)* Vines *MSS. 107, 134* Vines, *MSS. 106, 135, 137 (B)*

150 Fauns] Fawns *MSS. 106, 134, 135*

151 cadence,—] cadence— *MSS. 106, 134*

152 wild-flowers] wild flowers *MSS. 106, 134* crowned.] crown'd. *MS. 106* crowned *MS. 134*

153 life *ital*] life *MSS. 107, 106, 134, 135, 137 (B)* LIFE *ital added MS. 137 (A)* *no comma MS. 107* Ear: *rev from*

Ear:— *rev from* Ear! *MS. 137 (A)* ear: *MSS. 107, 106, MS. 1835/36–, 1839* ear *MS. 134* Ear! *rev from* ear *MS. 135* Ear! *MS. 137 (B)*

154 Ye] Ye, *MS. 106*

155 Fable] fable *MS. 1835/36–, 1839* though] tho' *MS. 135* truth] Truth *MSS. 106, 134*

156 earth] earth, *MSS. 106, 134*

157 coffin lid;] coffin-lid; *1836–* coffin lid: *1839*

158 Convict's] Convicts *MS. 107* convict's *MS. 1835/36–, 1839*

159 "The vain distress-gun,"] The vain distress gun *MSS. 106, 134* The vain distress-gun, *MSS. 107, 135, 137 (B); so MS. 137 (A) but* gun, *rev to* gun,* *and so MS. 138 but* gun*, *rev to* gun, shore,] shore *MSS. 107, 106, 134, 135*

160 Repeated—heard,] Repeated—heard— *MS. 107* Repeated,—heard— *MSS. 106, 134*

161 pity,] pity *MSS. 107, 106, 134*

162 compass, *rev from* compass *MS. 135* compass *1836–* notes:] notes; *MSS. 107, 106, 134*

163 Babe's] babe's *MS. 1835/36–, 1839* City, *rev from* city, *MS. 137 (A)* city, *MSS. 107, 137 (B), MS. 1835/36–, 1839* City *MS. 134*

164 bass,] Bass *MSS. 107, 106, 134* bass *MS. 135*

166 Songstress] songstress *MS. 1835/36–, 1839*

167 Angel] angel *MS. 107, 1836–, 1839* descend,] descend *MSS. 107, 106, 134*

168 *no period MS. 134*

169 O *rev from* Oh *MSS. 135, 137 (A)* Oh! *MS. 106* Oh *MSS. 134, 137 (B)*

170 *no ital MS. 107, underscore added in pencil MS. 106*

172 memory!] memory? *1836–, 1839* O *rev from* Oh *MS. 135* Oh, *MSS. 106, 134* O *rev from* Oh *rev from* O *MS. 137 (A)*

173 Chains,] Chains— *MSS. 107, 106, 134*

174 laboured *rev from* labored *MS. 135* labored *MS. 134* through] thro' *MSS. 107, 135*

175 O *rev from* O *MSS. 135, 137 (A)* Oh, *MSS. 106, 134* Oh *MS. 137 (B)*

176 Unsubstantial, *rev from* insubstantial, *MS. 135* unsubstantial, *MSS. 106, 134, MS. 137 (B)* unsubstantial *MS. 107* Unsubstantial, *rev from* unsubstantial, *MS. 137 (A)*

pondered *rev to* ponder'd *MS. 107* ponder'd *MS. 106*

177 Spirit] spirit *MS. 1835/36–, 1839*

178 controlled,] controlled *MSS. 107, 134* controll'd, *MS. 106*

179 Sages] sages *MS. 1835/36–, 1839* taught,] taught *MS. 107*

180 old.] old *MSS. 106, 134*

181 Heavens] heavens *MS. 107, MS. 1835/36–, 1839*

182 *no ital MS. 107, 1845, 1850; underscore added in pencil MS. 106 no comma MS. 134*

184 harmony;] harmony *MS. 134*

185 Headlands,] Head-lands *MS. 107* headlands, *MS. 1835/36–, 1839* crowned] crown'd *MS. 107* mist, *rev in pencil from* mist *MS. 107* mist *MS. 134* mist— *MS. 106*

186 billows, *rev in pencil from* billows *MS. 107* billows— *MSS. 106, 134*

188 pinions,] pinions *MS. 107* Air,] Air *MS. 134*

189 fro,] fro *MSS. 107, 106, 134, 135*

190 harmony] Harmony *MSS. 106, 134*

191 Seasons *rev from* seasons *MS. 138* seasons *MSS. 107, 106, 134, 135, 137 (B)* round; *rev in pencil from* round *MS. 107* round;— *MS. 106* round; *WW rev from* round[?] *(page worn) MS. 135*

192 Winter *rev from* winter *MS. 135* winter *MS. 107*

193 thanksgiving,] thanksgiving *MSS. 107, 134, 135*

194 Instruments] instruments *MS. 1835/36–* chords;] chords *MS. 134* chords; *rev to* chords! *MS. 135*

195 *no commas MS. 134*

196 *no punct MS. 134*

197 *no comma MSS. 107, 134*

198 noon;] noon! *MSS. 107, 106* noon *MS. 134*

199 Thou too] Thou, too, *MS. 106* heard,] heard— *MS. 107* heard *MS. 134* Eagle!] Eagle, *MSS. 107, 106* Eagle *rev in pencil to* Eagle— *MS. 134* eagle! *1836–, 1839*

200 peak] peak, *MS. 106* *no comma MS. 134*

201 hymn *rev from* Hymn *MS. 137 (A)* Hymn *MSS. 107, 106, 134, 135, 137 (B)*

202 joy,] joy *MS. 107*

203 six-days' *rev from* six-day's *MS. 137 (A)* six days *MS. 107* six-day's *MSS. 134, 135, 137 (B), 1839* Work, *rev from* work, *MS. 138* work *WW rev in pencil to* Work *MS. 107* Work *MSS. 106, 134,*

1839 work, *MS. 137, 1836YR* Seraphim, *rev from* seraphim, *MS. 138* Seraphim *MSS. 107, 106, 134, 1840–* seraphim, *MS. 137*

205 Shouting *rev from* Sho[?o]ting *MS. 107* Shouting, *MSS. 106, 134* through] thro' *MS. 107* valley *rev from* Valley *MS. 138* Valley *MSS. 135, 137* calls, *rev from* calls *MS. 137 (A)* calls *MSS. 134, 135, 137 (B)*

206 worlds,] worlds *MS. 107* natures,] natures *MSS. 107, 106, 134*

207 praise *rev from* praise, *MS. 137 (A)* praise, *MSS. 107, 106, 134, 135, 137 (B)* gratulation,] gratulation *MSS. 107, 106, 134* poured] pour'd *MS. 106*

208 God, . . . Lord! *rev in pencil from* God . . . Lord. *MS. 107* *no punct MS. 134*

209 Light *rev from* light *MSS. 107, 134* Being;] being, *MS. 107* Being, *MS. 106* Being *MS. 134*

210 earth-born *rev from* earth-born *MS. 137* Chronicler;] chronicler; *1836–* Chronicler *MS. 134*

211 Voice *rev from* voice *MS. 135* voice *MS. 134* *no comma MS. 134*

212 stir;] stir, *MS. 107* Stir: *MS. 106* Stir *MS. 134*

213 Trumpet] Trumpet— *MSS. 106, 134* trumpet *1836–, 1839* *no commas MSS. 107, 106, 134, 135*

214 deadly *rev from* dedly *MS. 135* wars] wars, *MS. 137 (B), comma del MS. 137 (A)*

215 archangelic] arch-angelic *MSS. 107, 106, 134* *no comma MS. 134*

216 *no punct MS. 134* stars] Stars *MS. 107*

217 Man's *rev from* man's *MS. 135* mans *MS. 134* *no punct MS. 134*

219 Queen] queen *MS. 1835/36–, 1839* *no commas MS.134*

221 *no comma MS. 134*

222 Bond-slave . . . Earth] bond-slave . . . earth *MS. 1835/36–, 1839* No! *rev from* No *MS. 135* No; *MSS. 107, 106, 135* No *MS. 134* though *rev from* tho' *MS. 135* tho *MS. 107* tho' *MSS. 106, 134*

223 though *rev from* tho' *MS. 135* tho' *MSS. 107, 106, 134* Heavens] heavens *MS. 1835/36–, 1839* stay] Stay *MSS. 107, 106, 135* *no commas MS. 134*

224 *no comma MSS. 107, 106* *no punct MS. 134*

The Egyptian Maid; or, The Romance of the Water Lily

title *no punct except* LILY] Lily— *MS. 107 (A); no punct MSS. 107 (C), 135 del; no comma or period MS. 106; no punct except* Lily. *MS. 109* MAID; . . . WATER LILY.] Maid, . . . Water-Lily *MS. 131* OR,] Or *MS. 131* OR. *1840–1843, 1846, 1849 (imperfect plate)*

headnote, l. 1 persons . . . poem, . . . "History] Persons . . . Poem . . . History *MS. 135*
l. 2 Arthur . . . Table;"] Arthur, . . . Table: *MS. 135*
l. 3 add, . . . Lotus, . . . goddess]add . . . Lotus . . . Goddess, *MS. 135* goddess] Goddess *1836YR, 1836–, 1839*
l. 5 art, . . . Museum.] art . . . Museum *MS. 135*

1 sands,] sands *MSS. 107 (A), 134* Sands, *MSS. 106, 109, 131*

2 *no hyphen MS. 131* toward] tow'rd *MSS. 107 (A), 106, 131, 134* toward *rev to* tow'rd *MS. 109* Rocks] rocks *MS. 107 (A), 1836–, 1839* Scilly,] Scilly *MS. 134*

4 Ship] ship *MS. 107 (A)* Ship, *MS. 106* air,] air; *MSS. 107 (A, C), 106* air *MS. 134*

5 hands,] hands *MSS. 107 (A), 131, 134* hands; *MS. 106*

6 men] Men *MSS. 107 (A, C), 106, 134* name—The] name the *MSS. 107 (A), 134* name, the *MSS. 107 (C), 106, 109* name, The *MS. 131* WATER LILY] Water Lily *MSS. 107 (A), 106, 109* Water-lily *MS. 131* *no period MSS. 107 (A), 109, 134*

7 wind,] wind *MSS. 107 (C), 106, 131, 134* blew;] blew, *MSS. 107 (A, C), 106, 109, 131* blew *MS. 134*

8 And,] And *MSS. 131, 134* Moon,] moon *MSS. 107 (A, C), 109, 131, 134* moon, *MS. 106* o'er] oer *MS. 131* ascendant,] ascendant *MSS. 107 (A, C), 109, 134* ascendant— *MS. 131*

10 Pinnace] pinnace *MS. 131* bright,] bright *MSS. 131, 134, 1836–, 1839*

11 Coast] coast *MSS. 107 (A, C), 109, 131, 1836YR, 1836–, 1839* drew,] drew *MSS. 131, 134*

12 *no comma MSS. 107 (C), 134* sail and pendant] Sail and Pendant *MSS. 107 (C), 106* sail [sail *rev to* Sail] and Pendant *MS. 109* *no period MSS. 131, 134*

13 Shape] shape *MS. 107 (A)*

14 admiration:] admiration *MSS. 107 (A, C), 131, 134* admiration; *MS. 106*

15 *no commas MSS. 107 (A), 134*

16 Aught *rev from* Awght *MS. 134* shown] shewn *MSS. 107 (A, C), 106, 131* glass;] glass *MSS. 107 (A, C), 134* glass, *MSS. 106, 109, 131*

17 built] built, *MS. 131* care;] care *MSS. 107 (A, C), 134* care, *MSS. 106, 131* care; *rev to* care, *MS. 1835Col*

18 *no commas MSS. 107 (A, C), 106, 131, 134* *no period MSS. 107 (A), 131, 134* wondrous *rev in pencil from* wonderous *MS. 106*

19 though] tho' *MSS. 131, 134* Mechanist,] Mechanist— *MSS. 107 (B), 131* *no commas MSS. 107 (C), 106, 131, 134*

20 science *rev to* Science *MS. 106* *no comma MSS. 107 (C), 134*

21 (and *rev to* —and *MS. 107 (B)* —and *MSS. 107 (C), 106, 134*

22 lore)] lore— *MSS. 107 (C), 106, 134*

23 will] Will *MSS. 106, 134*

24 thoughts,] thoughts *MSS. 107 (B, C), 131, 134* defiance.] defiance *MSS. 107 (B, C), 134*

25 *no comma MS. 107 (C)*

27 *no commas MSS. 107 (C), 134* cried,] cried *MSS. 106, 134*

28 pride—"] pride"! *MS. 107 (A)* pride!" *MSS. 107 (C), 106* pride," *MS. 109* pride." *MS. 131* pride *rev in pencil to* pride' *MS. 134*

29 blast,] blast; *MSS. 106, 131* blast *MS. 134*

30 rose,] rose— *MS. 131* rose *MS. 134* danger.] danger; *MSS. 107 (A, C)* danger *MS. 134*

31 *no comma MSS. 107 (C), 106, 131, 134*

32 beach, *rev from* Beach, *MS. 137* beach *MSS. 107 (A, C)* Beach, *MSS. 106, 135* Beach *MS. 134* urges;] urges *MSS. 107 (A), 134* urges, *MS. 106*

33 *no comma MSS. 107 (A, C), 106, 134*

34 Fiends *rev from* fiends *MS. 137* fiends *MSS. 107 (A, C), 106, 131, 134, 135* vanish,] vanish *MS. 134* vanish— *MS. 135* crossed] crost *MSS. 107 (A, C), 131*

35 Fiends *rev from* fiends *MS. 137* fiends *MSS. 107 (A, C), 106, 131, 134, 135* malign; *rev from* malign, *MS. 137* malign *MSS. 107 (A, C)* malign, *MSS. 106, 131, 134, 135*

36 roused] rouzed *MS. 134* Deep] deep *MSS. 107 (A, C)* *no punct MSS. 107 (A), 134*

37 she] She *MS. 106*

38 Sea-flower, *rev in pencil from* sea-flower, *MS. 107 (C)* sea-flower, *MSS. 107 (A), 109, 134* Galley; *rev from* galley; *MS. 109* galley; *MSS. 107 (A, C), 106* Galley, *MS. 131* galley *MS. 134*

39 loveliness] loveliness, *MSS. 107 (A), 109*

41 o'er] oer *MS. 106* *no comma MS. 107 (A)*

42 flood] flood, *MSS. 106, 134* roughened] roughen'd *MSS. 107 (A), 109* valley. *rev from* valley, *MS. 109* valley.— *MSS. 107 (A, C), 131* valley *MS. 134*

43 *no comma MSS. 107 (A, C), 106, 109, 131, 134, 135*

44 Wizard's] wizards *rev to* Wizards *MS. 107 (C)* Wizards *MSS. 131, 134* confounding:] confounding!— *MS. 107 (A)* confounding— *MS. 107 (C)* confounding! *MSS. 106, 131* confounding; *rev to* counfounding! *MS. 109* confounding *MS. 134*

45 Ocean] ocean *MSS. 107 (C), 109*

46 young, *rev to* young; *MS. 106* young; *MS. 107 (A)* young *MS. 134*

47 sea-flashes, *rev from* sea-flashes *MS. 137* sea flashes *MSS. 107 (A), 109* sea-flashes *MSS. 107 (C), 106, 131, 134* waves *rev from* waves, *MS. 137* waves, *MS. 135*

48 Top-gallant] Top gallant *MSS. 107 (C), 131* high, rebounding] high rebounding, *MSS. 107 (A, C), 106, 109* high rebounding *MS. 134* *no exclam MS. 134*

49 *no comma MSS. 107 (C)*

50 Thing] thing *MS. 131* cherished:] cherish'd; *MSS. 107 (A), 106, 109* cherished; *MSS. 107 (C), 131* cherished *MS. 134*

51 Ah!] Ah *MS. 131* She] she *MSS. 107 (A), 109, 131, 1836–, 1839* *no comma MS. 134*

52 Luminous,] Luminous; *MS. 106* debonair? *rev from* debonnair? *MS. 137* *no punct MS. 134*

53 storm *rev from* Storm *MS. 137* Storm *MS. 107 (C)* Storm *rev from* storm *MS. 135* stripped] stripp'd *MSS. 107 (A), 109* leaves;] leaves, *MSS. 107 (A, C), 106, 109, 131* leaves *MS. 134*

54 Lily *rev to* Lilly *MS. 109* longer!—] longer— *MSS. 107 (A, C), 109, 134, 135* longer.— *MS. 106* longer: *MS. 131* longer— *rev from* longer;— *MS. 137* perished. *rev to*

perished! *MS. 137* perish'd. *MSS. 107 (A), 106, 109* perished *MS. 134*

55 her,—] her— *MSS. 107 (A, C), 106, 109, 134* her— *MS. 131* her, *1850* She *rev from* she *MS. 135* she *MSS. 107 (A, C), 106, 109, 131, 134, 1836YR, 1836–, 1839* less;] less *MSS. 107 (A, C), 109, 134* less, *MSS. 106, 131*

56 like, . . . unlike,] like— . . . unlike— *MSS. 107 (C), 106, 134* Creature! *rev from* Creature; *MS. 107 (C)* creature! *MS. 106* Creature *MS. 134*

57 brain;] brain *MS. 134*

58 Though] Tho' *MS. 131* loved,] loved *MSS. 107 (A, C), 109, 131, 134* again;] again, *MSS. 107 (A, C), 106, 109* again *MS. 134*

59 Though] Tho' *MS. 131* pitied,] pitied *MSS. 107 (A, C), 109, 131, 134* *no ital MSS. 107 (A, C), 106, 131, 134, 135* distress;] distress, *MSS. 107 (A, C), 106, 109* distress *MSS. 131, 134*

60 us, *rev to* us *MS. 135* us *MSS. 107 (A, C), 131* us— *MS. 109* Nature.] nature. *MSS. 107 (A, C), 106, 109* nature *MS. 134*

61 tears;] tears *MSS. 107 (A, C), 109, 131, 134* tears, *MS. 106*

62 Galley *rev from* galley *MS. 109* laden;] laden *MS. 134* laden, *1836–, 1839, but* laden; *1849*

63 Herself] herself *MSS. 107 (A, C), 106, 109, 131, 134, 1836–, 1839* bore,] bore *MSS. 106, 134*

64 And,] And *MSS. 107 (A, C), 106, 109, 131, 134* struggles,] struggles *MSS. 107 (C), 131, 134* ashore;] ashore, *MSS. 107 (A, C), 106, 109, 131* ashore *MS. 134*

65 One,] One *MSS. 107 (A, C)* One *rev from* one *MS. 109* one *MS. 131*

66 wave—] wave[?] *MS. 107 (A)* wave, *MSS. 109, 131* guileless] guiless *MS. 109* Maiden.] Maiden.—[?] *MS. 107 (A)* Maiden *MSS. 109, 134*

67 cave *rev to* Cave *MS. 135* cave *rev from* Cave *MS. 137* Cave *MSS. 106, 134* fled] fled, *MSS. 107 (A, C)*

68 *no comma MSS. 107 (A, C), 106, 109, 131, 134* muttered; *rev from* muttered, *MS. 137* mutter'd; *MS. 107 (A)* mutter'd *MS. 106* muttered *MS. 134* muttered, *1836YR*

69 And,] And *MSS. 107 (A, C), 106, 109, 131, 134, 1836–, 1839* while] while, *MSS. 106, 134, 1836–, 1839* late,] late *MSS. 107 (A, C), 109, 131, 134*

70 sate,] sate *MSS. 106, 109, 131, 134*

71 voice, *rev to* voice *MS. 135* voice *MSS. 107 (A), 109, 134* saw, . . . head,] saw . . . head *MSS. 107 (A, C), 106, 109, 131, 134* half-raised] half rais'd *MS. 107 (A)* half-rais'd *MS. 107 (C)* half raised *MS. 134*

72 Visitant *rev from* Visitant, *MS. 135* visitant *MSS. 107 (A), 109* Visitant, *MSS. 106, 134* uttered:] utter'd— *MS. 107 (A)* utter'd. *MS. 106* uttered *rev to* utter'd *MS. 109* uttered *MS. 134* uttered; *MS. 135, 1836–, 1839*

73 "On] On *MS. 134*

74 Sailed" (hear me, Merlin!) "under] Sailed, hear me Merlin, under *MS. 107 (C)* Sailed, (hear me, Merlin) under *with parens added MS. 106* Sailed (hear me Merlin) under *MS. 134* Sailed (hear me, Merlin!) under *1836YR* me,] me *MS. 135* *no final comma MSS. 107 (C), 106, 134*

75 heathen *rev from* Heathen *MS. 137* Heathen *MS. 135*

76 carved— *rev from* carved,— *MS. 135* carved *MS. 107 (C)* carved, *MSS. 106, 134* Goddess] Goddess, *MS. 134* flower,] flower *MSS. 107 (C), 134*

77 Egyptian's] Egyptians *MS. 107 (C)* Egyptians' *MS. 106*

78 immortal] immortal, *MS. 106* *no punct MS. 134*

79–92 *opening quots MS. 107 (A)*

79 "Her] Her *MSS. 107 (C), 106, 131, 134, 135, 1836–, 1839* strand, *rev to* Strand, *MS. 106* Strand, *MSS. 107 (A), 109, 131* Strand *MS. 134* strand, *1836–, 1839*

80–84 *opening quots MS. 109*

80 freight] Freight *MS. 135* freight, *1836–, 1839* Damsel] damsel *MS. 109, 1836–1843, 1839* peerless;] peerless. *MSS. 107 (A, C), 106* peerless, *MS. 109* peerless *MS. 134*

81 above,] above; *MSS. 106, 134* above *MSS. 109, 131* strong] strong, *MSS. 107 (A, C), 109*

82 wrong] Wrong *MS. 135*

83 Princess,] Princess *MSS. 107 (A, C), 106, 109, 131, 134* Land *rev from* land, *MS. 109* Land, *MSS. 107 (A, C), 106* land *MS. 134*

84 left,] left; *MS. 131* left *MS. 134* though] tho' *MSS. 107 (A), 109, 131, 134, 135* sad *rev from* sad, *MS. 107 (C)* sad— *MS. 107 (A)* sad, *MS. 106* *no period MS. 134*

85 "And] And *MSS. 106, 134, 135, 1836–, 1839* Caerleon's *rev from* Caerlion's *MS. 137* Caerlions *MS. 134* Caerlion's *MS. 135* tower] Tower *MS. 131*

86–90 *opening quots MS. 109*

86 Knights] knights *MSS. 106, 109* Table *rev from* table *MS. 135* table *MSS. 107 (A, C), 109*

87 send;] send, *MSS. 106, 134*

88 attend,] attend *MSS. 107 (A, C), 106, 109, 131, 134*

89 Stranger's] Strangers *MS. 134* hour, *rev from* hour *MS. 137* hour *MSS. 106, 131, 134, 135*

90 sea] Sea *MSS. 106, 131* made *rev from* made, *MS. 137* unnavigable.] unnavigable *MSS. 107 (C), 134*

91 "Shame!] "Shame *MSS. 107 (A), 109* Shame *MSS. 107 (C), 131, 134* Shame, *MS. 106* Shame! *1836–, 1839* Royal] royal *MS. 131, 1836YR, 1836–, 1839* Line] line *MSS. 107 (A, C), 109, 131, 1836–, 1839*

92 Die] "Die *MS. 109* through] thro' *MS. 131* malice:"] malice"! *MS. 107 (A)* malice!" *MSS. 107 (C), 131* malice! *MS. 106* malice!" *rev from* malice." *MS. 109* malice *MS. 134* malice;" *MS. 135* malice?" *1840–*

94 Lady *rev from* lady *MS. 109* Lake,] Lake; *MSS. 107 (A, C)* Lake;* *MS. 109* Lake *MS. 134*

95 Sorceress,] Sorceress *MSS. 107 (A, C), 106, 131, 134, 135* benign,] benign *MSS. 131, 134*

96 embittered] embitter'd *MS. 107 (A)* man's] Man's *MSS. 107 (A), 131* chalice] Chalice *MS. 107 (A)* *no period MSS. 106, 134, 135*

97–114 *opening quots MS. 107 (A)*

97 "What] What *MSS. 131, 134* boots," . . . "to] boots, . . . to *MSS. 107 (A), 109, 131* boots . . . to *MS. 134* boots" . . . "to *MS. 135* she,] She, *MS. 131* she *MS. 134, 135* mourn? *rev in pencil from* mourn *MS. 106* mourn *MS. 134*

98–99 *opening quot MS. 109*

98 sin] Sin *MSS. 107 (C), 131* sin *rev to* sin, *MS. 106* endeavour! *rev from* endeavour *MS. 106* endeavour; *MSS. 107 (A, C), 109, 131* endeavour *MS. 134* endeavour: *1836–, 1839*

99 isle] Isle *MSS. 107 (A, C), 106, 109, 131, 134* *no comma MSS. 107 (A, C), 109, 131, 134, 135*

100 art, *rev from* Art, *MS. 135* art *rev from* Art *MS. 107 (C)* Art, *MSS. 106, 134*

101 borne] borne, *MSS. 107 (C), 106*

102 life] Life *MS. 131* *no comma MSS. 134, 135, 137*

103–204 *lacking MS. 135*

103 "My] My *MSS. 106, 134, 1836–, 1839* pearly *rev from* Pearly *MS. 107 (C)* Boat, *rev from* boat, *MS. 137* boat *MS. 107 (A, C)* Boat *rev from* boat *MS. 109* Boat *MS. 134* shining] Shining *MS. 131* Light,] light *MSS. 107 (A, C), 109, 131, 134* light, *rev from* Light, *rev in pencil from* light, *MS. 106*

104–108 *opening quot MS. 109*

104 *no comma MS. 134*

105 wave,] wave: *MS. 131* wave *MS.134*

106 back] back, *MS. 109* her] her, *MSS. 107 (A, C), 106, 109, 134* sea-cave;] sea cave; *MSS. 107 (A, C)* sea cave; *rev to* sea cave, *MS. 109* sea-cave: *MS. 131* sea cave, *MS. 134* sea-cave;— *1836–, 1839*

107 Then] Then, *1836YR, 1839* Merlin! *rev from* Merlin, *MS. 109* Merlin, *MS. 131*

108 Through] Thro' *MS. 131* air] air, *MSS. 107 (A, C), 106, 1836–, 1839* charge] Charge *MSS. 107 (A, C), 109, 1836–, 1839* charge *rev to* Charge *MS. 106* *no period MSS. 131, 134*

109 "The] The *MSS. 107 (C), 106, 131, 134, 1836–, 1839* Cars] cars *MSS. 107 (A, C), 106, 109, 134, 1836–, 1839*

110–114 *opening quot MS. 109*

110 Must,] Must *MS. 134* ready;] ready, *MS. 107 (A)* ready *MSS. 107 (C), 109, 134*

111 Meanwhile,] Meanwhile *MSS. 107, 131 (A, C)* Mean-while *MS. 109* guidance,] guidance *MSS. 107 (A, C), 106, 109, 131, 134*

112 book; *rev from* book, *MS. 137* Book *MS. 131* book *MS. 134*

113 And, . . . fail,] And . . . fail *MS. 131* And . . . fail, *MS. 134* Stars] stars *MSS. 107 (A, C), 106, 109*

114 course; farewell!] course,—farewell— *MS. 107 (A)* course—farewell *MS. 107 (C)* course:—farewell, *MS. 106* course—farewell— *MS. 109* course—farewell! *MS. 131* course, farewell, *MS. 134* prompt] prompt, *MSS. 107 (A), 106, 109* steady."] steady. *MSS. 107 (A, C), 106* steady *MSS. 109, 134* steady" *MS. 131*

115 *no comma MSS. 107 (A, C), 109, 131, 134*

116 Shallop, *rev from* shallop, *MS. 137* Shallop; *MSS. 107 (A, C)* Shallop; *rev to* shallop; *MS. 109* Shallop *MS. 131, 134* shallop, *1836–, 1839*
117 That, *rev from* That *MS. 137* That *MSS. 106, 134* o'er] oer *MS. 131* yet-distempered] yet distemper'd *MS. 107 (A)* yet distempered *MSS. 107 (C), 106, 109, 134* Deep,] deep, *MSS. 107,* 109_1 Deep *MSS. 106, 131, 134*
118 sweep, *rev from* sweap, *MS. 109* Sweep, *MS. 106* sweep; *MS. 131* sweep *MS. 134*
119 steed,] steed *MSS. 107 (A, C), 106, 109, 134* Steed *MS. 131* rein,] rein *MSS. 107 (A, C), 109, 131, 134*
120 Urged] Urg'd *MS. 107 (A)* o'er] oer *MS. 131* *no period MSS. 131, 134*
122 Isle *rev from* isle *MS. 137* haven;] haven *MS. 134*
123 sought,] sought? *MSS. 107 (A, C), 106, 109, 131* sought *MS. 134* she] She *MS. 131*
124 aught *rev from* aught, *MS. 137* aught *rev from miscopied* ag *MS. 131*
125 carved] carv'd *MS. 107 (A)* shore *rev from* shore, *MS. 137*
126 waves, *rev from* waves *MS. 137*
127 relique, *rev in pencil from* relique! *MS. 106* relique! *MSS. 107 (A, C), 131* relique *MS. 134* while!] while *MS. 134*
128 For *rev in pencil to* For, *MS. 106* gently] gently, *MSS. 107 (A),* 109_2*, 131, 1836YR*
129 curve,] curve *MS. 134* revealed *rev to* reveal'd *MS.* 109_2 reveal'd *MSS. 107 (A), 106* <u>revealed</u> *MS. 131*
130 bosom] bosom, *MS. 131* half,] half *MSS. 107 (A, C),* 109_2*, 131, 134* half— *MS.* 109_1 concealed,] conceal'd *MSS. 107 (A),* 109_1 conceal'd, *106* concealed *rev to* conceal'd *MS.* 109_2 concealed *MS. 134*
131 *no comma MSS. 107 (A), 109, 131, 134*
132 Nina] Nina, *MS. 131, 1836–, 1839* passed,] pass'd, *MS. 107 (A)* passed *MSS. 107 (C),* 109_1*, 134* greeting.] greeting *MS.* 109_1*, 134*
133 hers] her's *MS. 131* *no comma MSS. 107 (C), 106, 134*
134 tortured] tortur'd *MS. 107 (A)* hope] hope, *MS. 131* shaken;] shaken: *MS. 131, 1836YR* shaken *MS. 134*
135 bay, *rev from* Bay, *MS. 137* bay *MSS. 107 (A), 109, 131* Bay, *MS. 106* Bay *MS. 134*
136 Cast-away, *rev from* cast-away, *MS. 109* Castaway, *MSS. 107 (C), 106, 109* Castaway *MSS. 131, 134*
137 Unmarred, unstripped] Unmarr'd, unstripp'd *MS. 107 (A)* Unmarr'd, unstripped *MS. 107 (C)* Unmarred unstripped *MS. 134* attire,] attire; *MSS. 107 (C), 106, 109* attire *MS. 134*
138 eyes,—] eyes, *MSS. 107 (A, C), 106, 109, 131* eyes *MS. 134* *no period MSS. 131, 134*
139 Nina,] Nina *MSS. 107 (A, C), 106, 109* down,] down *MSS. 107 (A, C), 106, 109, 131* embraced,] embraced *MSS. 107 (A, C), 106, 131, 134* embraced *rev to* embrac'd *MS. 109*
140 *no comma MSS. 107 (A, C), 106, 131, 134*
141 Damsel, *WW rev from* damsel, *MS. 109* Damsel *MSS. 107 (A, C), 109, 131, 1836YR* trance] Trance *MS. 131* embound;] embound *MS. 134*
142 And,] And *MSS. 107 (C), 131, 134* ground,] ground *MSS. 107 (A, C), 106, 109, 134*
143 shallop] Shallop *MSS. 107 (A, C), 106, 131* placed,] plac'd *MS. 107 (A)* placed *MSS. 107 (C), 106, 134* placed, *rev to* plac'd, *MS. 109*
144 air,] air; *MS. 107 (A)* air *MSS. 107 (C), 131* stilled] still'd *MS. 107 (A)* ocean.] Ocean *MSS. 107 (A), 134* Ocean. *MSS. 107 (C), 131*
145 *no comma MSS. 107 (A), 131*
146 opened,] opened— *MS. 131*
147 fragrance,] fragrance *MSS. 107 (B, C), 106, 131, 134, 1836YR* earth,] earth *MSS. 107 (B, C), 106, 134* Earth *MS. 131*
148 Sun] sun *MSS. 107 (B, C), 106, 134, 1836–, 1839* *no comma MSS. 107 (B, C), 131, 134*
150 Angels] angels *MS. 106* make,] make *MSS. 107 (B, C), 131* love] Love *MS. 131* *no period MSS. 107 (B), 131, 134*
152 Flower] flower *MSS. 107 (A, C), 109, 1836–, 1839* spoken:] spoken, *MSS. 107 (A, C), 106* spoken; *MS. 131* spoken *MS. 134*
153 *no quot MSS. 107 (A, C), 106, 109, 134* achieved,] atchieved, *MS. 107 (C)* achieved *MS. 134*
154 done;] done *MSS. 131, 134*
155 Go,] Go *MS. 109* "Go *MS. 131* enterprise] enterprize *MS. 131*

rejoice!] rejoice, *MSS. 107 (A, C), 109* rejoice: *MS. 106* rejoice *MSS. 131, 134*
156 sky,] sky *MSS. 107 (A, C)* heaven, *rev from* heaven *MSS. 107 (A, C)* heaven *134* betoken."] betoken. *MSS. 107 (A, C), 106* betoken *MS. 134*
157 cheered] cheered, *MSS. 106, 134, 1836–, 1839* bleak,] bleak *MSS. 107 (C), 134*
158 rock] Rock *MSS. 106, 134* cluster;] cluster *MSS. 107 (A, C), 134* cluster, *MS. 106* Cluster, *MS. 131*
159 And,] And *MSS. 107 (A, C)* traversed *alt* travers'd *MSS. 107 (C), 106* travers'd *MS. 107 (A)* brine, *rev from* Brine, *MS. 137* brine *MSS. 107 (C), 134*
160 self-illumined] self-illumin'd *MSS. 107 (A), 109* Brigantine *rev from* brigantine *MS. 109*
161 *no comma MSS. 107 (A, C), 106, 109, 131, 134* Slumberer's *rev from* slumberer's *MS. 137* Slumberers *MS. 131*
162 *no comma MSS. 109, 131; no period MSS. 131, 134*
163 course, and] course—and, *MSS. 107 (A), 109* course—and *MSS. 107 (C), 106, 134*
164 cavern, *rev from* Cavern, *MS. 137* cavern *MSS. 107 (A, C), 109, 131* river] River *MS. 131*
165 *no hyphen MSS. 107 (A, C), 109, 131* flood,] flood *MS. 131*
166 fixed] fix'd *MS. 107 (A)* *no commas MS. 134*
167 Dame:] Dame, *MSS. 107 (A, C), 106, 109* Dame; *MS. 131, 1836–, 1839* Dame *MS. 134*
168 "Behold] "Behold, *MSS. 106, 131* Behold *rev in pencil to* Behold! *MS. 109* Behold *MS. 134* Charge *rev from* charge *MSS. 106, 137* charge *MS. 107 (C)* deliver!] deliver." *MS. 106* deliver!" *rev from* deliver." *MS. 109* deliver *MS. 134* deliver!" *1836YR*
169 "But] But *MSS. 107 (C), 106$_2$, 134, 1836–, 1839* chariot—where?"] Chariot where *MSS. 107 (C), 134* Chariot? Where— *MS. 106$_1$* Chariot; [Chariot; *rev to* Chariot?] where? *MS. 106$_2$* chariot—where?"— *1836–, 1839*
170 Merlin, "Even] Merlin "even *MS. 107 (C)* Merlin, "even *MSS. 106$_1$, 109* Merlin, even *MS. 106$_2$* Merlin even *MS. 134* bidden,] bidden *MSS. 107 (C), 106, 109, 131, 134*
171 *no punct MS. 134* barge] Barge *MSS. 106, 134*
172 vehicle] Vehicle *MS. 134* prove—] prove: *MS. 106* prove. *MS. 106$_2$* prove *MS. 134* Charge! *rev from* charge! *MS. 137* Charge *MS. 134*
173 death,] death *MS. 106$_2$* *no punct MS. 134*
174 books] Books *MS. 106$_2$* *no punct, no quot MS. 134*
175 spake,] spake: *MS. 131* spake; *1836–, 1839* and] and, *MSS. 107 (A, C), 106, 109, 134* view] view, *MS. 106*
176 grotto's] Grotto's *MSS. 107 (A, C), 106, 109, 131* Grottos *MS. 134* dimmest *rev from* dimest *MS. 109* chamber] chamber, *MSS. 107 (A, C), 109*
177 Swans,] swans *MS. 107 (A)* Swans *MSS. 107 (C), 109, 131*
178 Changed, as *rev from* Changed; as *MS. 107 (A)* Changed, as *rev to* Changed (as *MSS. 109, 131* pair *rev from* Pair *MS. 137* Pair *MSS. 106, 134* approached] approach'd *MSS. 107 (A, C)* light,] light *MSS. 107 (A, C), 106, 109, 131, 134*
179 car, *rev from* Car; *MS. 107 (A)* Car, *MS. 107 (C)* Car) *MS. 109* Car *MS. 131* car, *rev from* Car,*MS. 137* hue *rev from* hue, *MS. 137* hue, *MSS. 107 (A, C), 106, 131, 134*
180 (Like] Like *MSS. 107 (C), 131* sunset) sunset—) *MS. 107 (C)* sunset, *MS. 131* amber. *rev from* ambre. *MS. 109* amber *MS. 134*
182 *no comma MSS. 109, 131, 134$_1$* changes:] changes; *MSS. 107 (A, C), 106, 109, 131* changes *MS. 134*
183 car,] Car, *MSS. 107 (A, C), 106, 131, 134* Car *rev to* Car) *MS. 109* her;] her: *MSS. 107 (A, C), 109* her, *MS. 134$_1$* her *MS. 134$_2$* her;—*1836–, 1839* up-went] up went *MSS. 106, 109, 131, 134*
184 ethereal] etherial *MSS. 107 (A, C), 131, 134* ætherial *MS. 109* element *rev from* Element *MS. 137*
185 Birds *rev from* birds *MS. 109*
186 thought, *rev from* thought— *MS. 109* through] thro' *MSS. 107 (A, C), 106, 109, 134$_1$* ranges.] ranges, *MS. 106* ranges *MS. 134$_2$*
187 *no commas MSS. 107 (A, C), 109, 131, 134$_1$; no apos MS. 131* side,] side *MS. 134$_2$*
188 measure;] measure *MSS. 107 (A), 134*

measure, *MSS. 107 (C), 109, 131*

189 Caerleon's *rev from* Caerlion's *MS. 137* Caerlion's *MS. 134* towers *rev from* Towers *MS. 137* Towers *MSS. 106, 134* appeared,] appear'd, *MS. 107 (A)* appear'd *MS. 106* appeared *MSS. 109, 134*

191 pavilions] Pavilions *MSS. 107 (A, C), 106, 134* pavillions *MS. 131* spreading *rev from* spreding *MS. 109* *no comma MSS. 107 (C), 106, 131, 134*

192 *no hyphen, no period MS. 134*

193 Dames] Dames, *MS. 107 (C)* Dames— *MS.* 109_2

194 car *rev from* Car *MS. 137* Car *MSS. 107 (A, C), 106, 134* car *rev to* Car *MS.* 109_2 *no punct MS. 134*

195 past] past *rev from* passed *MS.* 109_2 pass'd *MS. 106* passed *MS. 131* *no comma MS. 134*

197 *no comma MSS. 107 (A, C),* 109_2*, 131*

198 pride,] pride *MS. 106* pride; *1836–, 1839* blighted.] blighted— *MS. 107 (C)* blighted *MS. 134*

199 Said] "Said *MS. 109* Merlin, "Mighty *rev from* Merlin, "mighty *MS. 109* Merlin "mighty *MSS. 106, 134* King] king *MS. 109* Lords,] Lords *MS. 131* *no commas MS. 134*

200–211 *opening quots begin line MS. 107 (A)*

200–204 *opening quots begin line MS. 131*

200 Away] "Away *MS. 109* feast] feast, *MSS. 107 (A, C), 106* tilt] tilt, *MS. 106* tourney!] Tourney! *MS. 109* tourney *MS. 134*

201 saw,] saw *MSS. 107 (C), 106, 134* Royal House,] royal house, *MSS. 107 (A, C), 109, 131* Royal House *MS. 134* royal House, *1836–, 1839*

202 heard,] heard *MSS. 107 (C), 106, 109, 134*

203 turrets] turrets *rev from* Turrets *MS. 137* Turrets *MSS. 107 (C), 106, 134*

204 *no period MS. 134*

205 "Lo!] Lo! *MSS. 107 (C), 106, 134, 135, 1836–, 1839* Lo!— *MS. 131*

206 *no comma MSS. 107,* 109_1*, 134 (C); no semicolon MSS.* 109_1*, 134* turned] turn'd *MS. 107 (A)* sorrow;] sorrow. *MS.* 109_2 sorrow *MSS. 131, 134*

207 wished-for] wish'd for *MS. 107 (A)* wish'd-for *MS. 107 (C)* wished for *MS. 134* Bride, the Maid] Bride, The Maid *rev from* bride, the maid *MS.* 109_2 Bride the Maid *MS. 134*

208 Egypt,] Egypt *MSS.* 109_1*, 131* conveyed] convey'd. *MS. 107 (A)* conveyed, *MSS. 107 (C),* 109_2 convey'd, *MS. 106* conveyed *MS.* 109_1

209 shipwreck] Shipwreck *MS.* 109_1 thrown;] thrown, *MS. 109* thrown *MS. 134*

210 sight!] sight *MS.* 109_1 morrow."] morrow. *MSS. 107 (A), 106,* 109_2 morrow."— *MS. 107 (C)*

211 "Though] Though *MSS. 107 (C), 134* power,] power *MSS. 107 (A, C), 131, 134* weak,"] weak" *MSS. 107 (A, C), 106, 131* weak *MS. 134* weak,' *1849*

212 *no punct, no quot MS. 134*

213–268 *opening quots begin line MS. 107 (A)*

213–216 *opening quots begin line MSS. 109, 131*

213 Child!] Child, *MSS. 107 (A, C), 106, 109, 131, 1836–, 1836YR, 1839* Child *MS. 134* hard!] hard *MS. 134*

214 reward?] reward *MS. 134* reward?— *MS. 135*

215 Those] —Those *MS. 131* cheek!] cheek *MSS. 107 (A, C), 106, 134* cheek! *rev to* cheek, *MS. 109*

216 O winds *rev from* Oh winds *MS. 109* remorse!] remorse, *MSS. 107 (A, C), 106, 109, 135* remorse *MS. 134* O shore] o shore *rev from* oh shore *MS. 109* ungrateful!] ungrateful *MS. 134*

217 "Rich] Rich *MSS. 107 (C), 106, 109, 134, 1836–, 1839* moth;] moth, *MS. 131* moth *MS. 134*

218–222 *opening quots begin line MS. 131*

218 temples, *rev to* Temples, *MS. 107 (A)* Temples, *MS. 107 (C)* temples *MS. 106* Temples *MS. 131* *no punct MS. 134*

219 *no commas MSS. 107 (C), 131, 134*

221 troth;] troth *MSS. 106, 134*

222 burn,] burn *MSS. 107 (C), 134* *no period MS. 134*

223 "Alas!] "Alas, *MS. 107 (A)* Alas, *MSS. 107 (C), 106, 109* Alas *MS. 134* Alas! *1836–, 1839* woe;] woe! *MSS. 107 (A, C), 109* woe *MS. 134*

224–228 *opening quots begin line MS. 131*

224 For, *rev from* For *MS. 135 (comma added in pencil), MS. 137* For *MSS. 107 (C), 106, 131, 134* Neighbours *rev from* neighbours *MS. 135* neighbours *MSS. 107 (A, C), 106, 109, 131, 134*

225 Realm,] realm, *MSS. 107 (A, C)* realm, *rev from* relm, *MS. 109* realm *MS. 131*

226 Christ] Christ, *MS. 106* Lord,] Lord; *MSS. 107 (A, C), 106, 131* lord; *MS. 109* Lord *MS. 134*

227 Knight] knight *MS. 106* bestow] bestow, *MSS. 106, 134*

228 choose] chuse *MSS. 107 (C), 106, 134, 135* labours.] labours *MS. 134, 1849*

229 "Her] Her *MSS. 107 (C), 131, 134, 1836–, 1839* birth] Birth *MS. 131* heathen, *rev from* Heathen, *MS. 137* heathen; *MS. 106, 1836–, 1839* Heathen, *MS. 135*

230 hovered;] hover'd: *MSS. 107 (A), 106* hovered: *MS. 107 (C), 1836–, 1839* hovered: *rev to* hover'd: *MS. 109* hovered *MS. 134*

231 court] court, *MSS. 107 (A, C), 109* Court, *MS. 106* Court *MS. 135*

232 fair,] fair *MSS. 107 (C), 134* report *rev from* report, *MS. 106*

233 seemed] seem'd *MSS. 107 (A), 131* *no comma MS. 134*

234 kingdoms] Kingdoms *MS. 131* recovered.] recover'd. *MSS. 107 (A), 106* recovered *rev to* recover'd *MS. 109* recovered *MS. 134*

235 "Ask] Ask *MSS. 106, 109, 134, 1836–, 1839* whom,] whom *MS. 134* champions] Champions *MSS. 106, 134, 1836–* true!] true *MSS. 107 (C), 134* true, *MS. 106*

236–240 *opening quots begin line MS. 131*

236 reserved] reserv'd *MSS. 107 (A), 109 (pencil version)* me] me, *MSS. 106, 131* life's *rev from* Life's *MS. 137* Life's *MSS. 107 (A, C), 135* betrayer;] betrayer. *MS. 131* betrayer *MS. 134*

237 bride *rev from* Bride *MS. 137* Bride *MSS. 107 (A, C), 106, 131, 134, 135*

238 corse;] Corse; *MSS. 107 (C), 135* corse *MS. 134* corse: *1836–, 1839*

239 thoughts,] thoughts; *MS. 131* thoughts *MS. 134* ye,] ye *MSS. 107 (C), 106, 134*

240 rites] Rites *MSS. 107 (A, C)* Rites *rev from* rights *MS. 109 (copyist's slip)* *no comma MS. 134* her."] her. *MSS. 106, 134*

241–386 *lacking MS. 135*

241 *no quots, no commas MS. 134* tomb] Tomb *MS. 131* Merlin," *rev from* Merlin[?] *MS. 109*

242–246 *opening quots begin line MS. 131*

242 beauty;] beauty. *MSS. 107 (A, C), 106, 109, 131* *no punct MS. 134*

243 will] Will *MSS. 106, 134* will, *MS. 131*

244 me,] me *MSS. 107 (C), 131, 134* Liege!] Liege, *MS. 106* Liege *MS. 134* I,] I *MSS. 107 (A), 106, 131, 134*

245 Wafted *rev from* wafted *MS. 109* *no comma MS. 134*

246 *no period MS. 134*

247 "My] My *MSS. 107 (C), 106, 109, 134, 1836–, 1839* bare] bare, *MS. 106*

248–252 *opening quots begin line MS. 131*

248 thou] Thou *MS. 107 (C)* keeping; *rev from* keeping, *MS. 137* keeping. *MSS. 107 (A, C), 106, 131* keeping *MSS. 109_1, 134* keeping: *1836–, 1839*

249 *no comma MSS. 107 (C), 106, 109_2, 131, 134*

250 *ital added MS. 137, no ital MSS. 107 (A, C), 106, 131, 134* ordained] ordain'd *MSS. 107 (A, C)* Heaven; *rev from* heaven; *MS. 137* Heaven *MSS. 107 (A), 134* heaven *MS. 107 (C)* Heaven, *MSS. 106, 131* heaven. *MS. 109_2* Heaven: *1836–*

251 glass] Glass, *MS. 106* Glass *MS. 134* significants] Significants *MS. 131*

252 may *rev from* my *(copyist's slip) MS. 109_2* *no period MS. 134*

253 "For] For *MSS. 106, 109, 134, 1836–, 1839* this,] this *MSS. 109_1, 131, 134* approaching,] approaching *MSS. 107 (A, C), 106, 109, 131, 134* One by One,] one by one *MSS. 107 (A, C), 109, 134* one by one; *MS. 106* one by one, *MS. 131*

254–258 *opening quots begin line MS. 131*

254 Knights] knights *MSS. 106, 109_2* Virgin;] virgin *MSS. 107 (A), 109_1* Virgin *MSS. 107 (C), 134* Virgin: *MS. 106* Virgin, *rev from* virgin, *MS. 109_2*

255 So,] So *MSS. 107 (A, C)* favoured] favor'd *MSS. 107 (A, C)* One,] One *MSS. 107 (A, C), 134* Flower] flower *MSS. 107 (A, C)*

256 more;] more, *MSS. 107 (A, C)* more: *MS. 106, 1836–, 1839* more *MS. 134* but, *rev from* but *MS. 137* but *MSS. 107 (A, C), 106, 134* doom,] doom *MSS. 107 (C), 106, 134*

257 *no comma MSS. 107 (C), 134*

258 assurance,] assurance *MSS. 107 (A, C), 134*

259 loss; *rev from* loss, *MS. 137* loss *MSS. 107 (A, C), 134* loss, *MS. 106*

260–264 *opening quot begins each line MS. 131*

260 *no commas MSS. 107 (A, C), 106, 109, 131, 134* rises] rises, *MS. 106*

261 melts;] melts, *MSS. 107 (A, C), 109*

melts *MS. 134* endure,] endure *MSS. 107 (A, C), 106, 109, 134,* 1835_2

263 purposes] purposes, *MS. 106* cross,] cross *MSS. 107 (A, C), 106, 109, 134,* 1835_2

264 hopes] hopes, *MSS. 106, 131* enterprises."] enterprizes *MS. 107 (C)* enterprizes. *MS. 109* enterprizes! *MS. 131* enterprises *MS. 134* enterprises. *1840–1843*

265 "So] So *MSS. 109, 134* it,"] it" *MSS. 107 (A, C)* it *MSS. 109, 134* King;— *rev from* king;— *MS. 137* King— *MSS. 107 (A, C), 109* King,— *MS. 106* King.— *MS. 131* King *MS. 134* "anon,] "anon *MSS. 107 (A, C), 106* anon *MSS. 109, 134* Anon *MS. 131*

266 Here,] Here *MSS. 131, 134* lies,] lies; *MS. 109* lies *MSS. 131, 134* trial;] trial, *MSS. 107 (A), 106* trial *MS. 134*

267 Knights] Knights! *MSS. 107 (A, C), 106, 109, 131* stand] stand, *MS. 109*

268 forth."] forth:" *MS. 107 (A)* forth" *MSS. 106, 131* forth: *MS. 109* forth *MS. 134* —To] —to *MSS. 107, 109* To *MSS. 106, 134*

269 advanced;] advanced;— *MSS. 107 (A, C), 109, 131* advanced:— *MS. 106* advanced *MS. 134*

270 Heaven] heaven *MSS. 107 (C), 109* Earth;—] Earth— *MSS. 107 (A), 131, 134* earth— *MSS. 107 (C), 109* Earth:— *MS. 106* earth;— *1845–* *no period MS. 134*

271 Abashed,] Abashed *MS. 131* turned *rev to* turn'd *MS. 109* away;] away. *MS. 131* away *MS. 134*

272 Percival] Percevale *MS. 109* disclosure;] disclosure *MSS. 107 (A, C), 134* disclosure, *MSS. 106, 131* disclosure! *1839*

273 Though] Tho' *MSS. 107 (A), 109, 131* Tho *MS. 107 (C)* Champions,] champions, *MSS. 107 (A, C), 109* Champions *MS. 134* ere] e're *MS. 107 (A)*

274 car,] car— *MSS. 107 (A, C), 109* Car— *MS. 106* Car, *MS. 131* Car *MS. 134*

275 Whereon . . . snow the Damsel] Whereon, . . . snow, the damsel [damsel *rev to* Damsel] *MS. 109; MS. 131 as rev MS. 109* *no comma MS. 134*

276 crossed] cross'd *MS. 109* himself] himself, *MS. 107 (C)* *no period MS. 134*

277 (but . . . can?)] —but . . . can *MS. 107 (A)* (but — [(but — *rev to* but,] . . . can!) *with punct added in pencil MS. 107 (C)* —(but . . . can!) *MS. 106* but . . . can *MS. 134* Saints!] Saints *MSS. 107 (A), 134* saints, *MS. 106*

278 trembled;] trembled *MSS. 107 (A, C), 134* trembled, *MS. 106* trembled— *1836–, 1839*

279 wishes,] wishes *MSS. 107 (A), 134* despites *rev from* despites, *MS. 106*

280 Knights;] knights *rev to* Knights *MS. 107 (A)* Knights *MSS. 107 (C), 106, 134* Knights: *1836YR*

282 time] time, *MS. 106* *no period MS. 134*

283–284 *no punct MS. 134*

284 there] there, *MS. 106*

285 While] While, *MSS. 107 (C), 106, 109* toward] tow'rd *MSS. 107 (A), 106, 134* tow'ard *MS. 107 (C)* Car] Car, *MS. 106* car *1836–, 1839* Car Sir Gawaine *rev from* Sir Gawaine Car *MS. 137* Gawaine, mailed] Gawaine mailed, *MS. 107 (A)* Gawaine mailed *MSS. 107 (C), 134* Gawaine mail'd *MS. 106* Gawaine, mail'd *rev from* Gawen mail'd *MS. 109* Gawaine mail'd *rev from* Gawaine mailed *MS. 131*

286 tournament,] tournament *MS. 134* Beaver] beaver *MSS. 131, 1836–, 1839* vailed,] vail'd *MS. 107 (A)* vailed *MSS. 107 (C), 134* vail'd, *MS. 106* vail'd— *MS. 109*

287 touched;] touch'd; *MSS. 107 (A), 109* touched *MSS. 107 (C), 134* touched, *MS. 131* but,] but *MSS. 107 (A, C), 109, 134* —but *MS. 131*

288 *no comma MSS. 107 (A), 109; no period MS. 134*

289 Next,] Next *MSS. 107 (C), 134* harp, *rev from* Harp, *MS. 137* harp *MS. 107 (C)* Harp, *MS. 106* Harp *MS. 134*

290 *no commas MS. 134* brother, *rev from* Brother, *MS. 137*

291 proof,] proof— *MS. 107 (C)* proof; *MS. 106* proof *MS. 134*

292 change;—] change— *MS. 107 (C)* change:— *MS. 106* change *MS. 134* Izonda] Isonda *MSS. 107 (C), 106* Izonda *rev from* Isonde *MS. 134*

293 true,] true *MS. 134* sharp,] sharp *MSS. 106, 134*

294 *no punct MS. 134*

295 Launcelot;—] Launcelot— *MSS. 107 (A, C), 109, 131* Launcelot:—

MS. 106 Launcelot— *rev in pencil from* Launcelot *MS. 134* Heaven's] Heav'n's *MS. 107 (A)* heavens *rev to* heav'ns *MS. 109*

296 craved, *rev from* craved, *MS. 107 (C)* crav'd, *MS. 107 (A)* craved, *MS. 106* craved, *rev in pencil from* craved *MS. 134* slave *rev from* Slave *MS. 137* contrition; *rev from* contrision *MS. 109* contrition, *MS. 107 (A)* contrition *MS. 134*

298 failed.] failed; *MSS. 107 (C), 106* failed *MS. 134* Next] next *MSS. 107 (C), 106, 134* Galahad;] Galahad, *MS. 107 (C)* Galahad *MS. 134*

299 paused,] paused,— *MSS. 107 (C), 106* paused *MS. 134* face] face, *MS. 106*

300 in] in:[?] *MS. 107 (A)* noontide] noon-tide *MS. 131* *no period MS. 134*

301 *no comma MSS. 107 (C), 134*

302 'mid] mid *MSS. 107 (A), 109, 134* arbour *rev from* Arbour *MS. 137* shady,] shady *MSS. 106, 109, 134*

303 *no commas MSS. 107 (C),* 109_2*, 134*

304 bed;] bed, *MSS. 107 (A, C), 106, 131* bed *MSS. 109, 134*

305 *no commas MSS. 107 (A, C), 109, 131, 134*

306 sense] sense, *MS. 107 (A)* *no period MSS. 109, 134*

307 Now,] Now *MSS. 107 (C), 131* bright-haired] bright-hair'd *MSS. 107 (A), 109* bright haired *MS. 134* bowed,] bowed *MSS. 107 (A, C), 109, 131, 134* bow'd, *MS. 106*

308 stood,] stood *MSS. 131, 134* far-kenned *rev from* far kenned *MS. 137* far-kenn'd *MSS. 107 (A, C)* far kenn'd *MS. 109* far-kenned *alt* far-kenn'd *MS. 131* mantle] Mantle *MS. 106* furred] furr'd *MSS. 107 (A), 109, 131* ermine,] ermine *MSS. 107 (C), 109, 134*

309 o'er *rev from* oer *MS. 106* oer *MS. 131* Body] body *MSS. 107 (A, C), 109, 131*

310 enrapt,] enrapt *MSS. 106, 134*

312 he] He *MS. 131* *no period MSS. 107 (C), 109, 134*

313 strange;] strange: *MSS. 107 (A, C), 106* strange *MS. 134*

314 glory,] glory *MSS. 107 (A, C), 109, 134* glory; *MS. 131*

315 achieved] achiev'd *MS. 107 (A)* atchieved *MS. 107 (C), 134* *no comma MSS. 107 (C), 134*

316 Perilous Seat,] Perilous-Seat, *MS. 107 (A)* "Perilous-Seat" *MS. 107 (C)* "Perilous Seat," *MS. 106* Perilous-Seat. *rev from* perilous-seat. *MS. 109* "Perilous Seat" *MS. 131* perilous Seat *MS. 134*

317 approached] approach'd *MS. 107 (C)* *no comma MSS. 107 (C), 134*

318 King . . . Knight] King, . . . Knight, *MSS. 107 (A, C)* King, . . . knight, *MS. 106* King . . . Knight, *MS. 134* story.] story *MSS. 106, 134*

319 touched] touch'd *MSS. 107 (A), 109* hand,] hand; *MS. 106* hand *MSS.* 109_1*, 131, 134* hand— *MS.* 109_2*, 1836–, 1839*

320 Birds, *rev from* Birds *MS. 137* birds *MS. 107 (A)* Birds *MSS. 107 (C), 106, 134* birds, *rev to* birds *MS. 109* far-famed] far famed *MS.* 109_2 far-fam'd *MS. 131* through] thro' *MSS. 107 (A, C), 106, 109, 131* Love's] loves *MSS. 107 (A),* 109_2 love's *MS.* 109_1 dominions,] dominions *MSS. 107 (C),* 109_1*, 134, 1836YR*

321 Swans, *rev from* Swans *MS. 137* Swans *MS.* 109_1 triumph *rev from* triump *MS. 107 (A)* wings; *rev from* wings, *MS. 137* wings, *MSS. 107 (A, C), 106, 109* wings *MSS.* 109_1*, 131, 134*

322 play,] play *MSS. 107 (A, C), 109, 131, 134* rings,] rings *MSS. 106,* 109_1*, 131, 134*

323 snakes] Snakes *MS.* 109_1 land;—] land. *MS. 107 (A)* land, *MSS. 107 (C), 109* Land, *MS. 106* land *MS.* 109_1 land; *MS. 131* Land *MS. 134* land— *rev from* land, *MS. 137*

324 *no quots MSS.* 109_1*, 134* she,] she *MSS. 107 (A), 109, 134* She! *MS. 107 (C)* she! *rev from* she— *MS. 106* Knight;—] Knight— *MSS. 107 (A, C), 106* Knight *MSS.* 109_1*, 134* Knight— *rev from* Knight, *MS.* 109_2 clapped] clapp'd *MSS. 107 (A), 109* pinions.] pinions! *MSS. 107 (A, C)* pinions *MSS.* 109_1*, 134* pinions. *rev to* pinions! *MS.* 109_2

325 "Mine] Mine *MS. 134* she—] she, *MS. 107 (A)* She— *MS. 107 (C)* She— *rev from* She—" *MS. 131* she *MS. 134* she is,] She is *MS. 131* she is *MSS. 107 (C), 134, 1836YR* though] tho' *MS. 131* dead,] dead; *MS. 107 (C)* dead; *MSS. 106, 109* dead *MS. 134*

326 And] "And *MSS. 107 (A), 131* name] Name *MSS. 107 (A, C)* name *rev to* Name *MS. 109* soul *rev from* Soul *MS. 109* Soul *MS. 107 (A)* sorrow;" *rev to* sorrow" *MS. 109* sorrow:"— *MS. 106* sorrow—" *MS. 131* sorrow *MS. 134*

327 *no comma MSS. 107 (A, C), 106, 131, 134*

328 colour] color *MSS. 107 (A), 109, 131* Damsel's *rev from* damsel's *MS. 109* dawned] dawn'd *MS. 131* cheek;] cheek *MSS. 107 (A, C), 134* cheek, *MSS. 106, 109, 131*

329 *no commas MSS. 107 (A, C), 131, 134*

330 Seemed] Seemed *alt* Seem'd *MS. 107 (C)* *no punct MSS. 107 (A), 134*

331 awe,] awe— *MS. 131* high,] high *MSS. 107 (A, C), 106, 109, 131, 134*

332 love *rev from* Love *MS. 137* Love *MSS. 107 (C), 106, 109, 131, 134* emboldened] embolden'd *MS. 107 (A)* hope] Hope *MS. 131* *no final comma MS. 131; no commas MS. 134*

333 *no commas MSS. 107 (A, C), 109, 131* Death] death *MSS. 107 (A), 109*

334 Allowed] Allow'd *MSS. 107 (A, C)* *no comma MSS. 107 (A, C), 109, 134*

335 Precursor *rev from* Precurssor *MS. 109* *no comma MSS. 107 (C), 134*

336 eyelids] eye-lids *MS. 109* *no comma MSS. 107 (C), 109, 134; no period MS. 134*

338 tarry, *rev from* torry, *MS. 109* tarry *MSS. 131, 134*

339 watched] watch'd *MSS. 107 (A), 109*

340 Nature] nature *MSS. 107 (C), 106, 109, 131, 134* life;] life, *MSS. 107 (A), 106, 109* life *MS. 107 (C), 131, 134*

341 Soul] soul *MSS. 106, 134, 1836–*

342 God,] God *MSS. 107 (A), 106, 109* Queen—]Queen, *MSS. 107 (A), 106, 109, 131* Queen *MSS. 107 (C), 134* *no period MS. 134*

343 he,] he— *MS. 131* he *MS. 134* "Take *rev from* "take *MS. 109* Take *MS. 134* heart] heart, *1836YR, 1836–, 1839*

344–348 *opening quots begin each line MSS. 107 (A), 131*

344 Galahad!] Galahad, *MSS. 107 (A, C), 106, 109, 131* Galahad *MS. 134* treasure] treasure, *1836–, 1839* giveth, *rev from* giveth— *MS. 137* giveth *MS. 134*

345 indissoluble] indissolubile *MS. 109*

346 Through] Thro' *MS. 131* change] change, *MS. 131* immortality;] immortality. *MS. 106* immortality *MS. 134*

347 happy] happy, *MSS. 107 (A, C), 106, 109, 134* unenvied, *rev from* unenvied *MS. 137*

348 Knight *rev from* knight *MS. 109* knight *MS. 106* Peer] Peer— *MS. 109* peer *MS. 131, 1836–, 1839* liveth!"] liveth! *MSS. 107 (A), 109* liveth." *MS. 106* liveth *MS. 134*

349 Nuptials *rev from* nuptuals *MS. 137* nuptials *MSS. 107 (A, C), 1836YR, 1839* delayed;] delay'd; *MS. 107 (A)* delayed *alt* delay'd *MS. 131* delayed *MS. 134*

350 sage] Sage *MS. 131* tradition] Tradition *MSS. 106, 131, 134*

351 pomp *rev from* pomp, *MS. 137* pomp, *MSS. 107 (A, C), 106, 109, 134, 1850* glory *rev from* glory, *MS. 137* glory, *MSS. 107 (A), 109* hour *rev from* hour, *MS. 137*

352 toward] tow'rd *MSS. 107 (A), 106, 134* toward *rev to* tow'rd *MS. 109* Altar *rev from* altar *MS. 137* altar *MSS. 109, 131, 1836YR, 1836–, 1839* bower *rev from* bower, *MS. 137*

353 led *rev from* lead *MS. 109* Maid, *rev from* Maid *MS. 137* Maid *MS. 134*

354 Angels *rev from* angels *MS. 137* carolled] carol'd *MSS. 107 (A, C)* carrol'd *rev to* carol'd *MS. 109* far-echoed] far echoed *MSS. 107 (A, C), 131* verses;— *rev from* verses:— *MS. 137* verses— *MSS. 107 (A, C)* verses. *MSS. 106, 131* verses *MSS. 109, 134*

354/355 *stanza break inserted MS. 137*

356 Powers, *rev from* powers, *MS. 109_2* Powers *MSS. 107 (C), 134*

357 *no comma MSS. 107 (C), 106, 131, 134*

358 *no period MS. 131, 134*

359 Ship . . . devoted] Ship, . . . devoted, *MSS. 107 (A), 109_2*

360 Land] land *MSS. 107 (A, C)* *no punct MSS. 107 (C), 106, 131, 134*

361 Alas!] Alas *MS. 109_2* floated,] floated *MSS. 107 (A, C), 106, 109_2, 134* floated— *MS. 131*

362 An] —An *MS. 131* Prow. *rev from* Prow *MS. 109_2* Prow *MS. 134* prow. *1836–*

363 *no comma MSS. 131, 134*

364 Heaven-permitted] heaven-permitted *MS. 131* vent *rev from* vent, *MS. 109_4*

365 *no comma MSS. 107 (C), 106, 131, 134*

366 *no period MS. 134*

367 Flower, *rev from* flower, *MS.* 109_4 Flower *MS.* 109_3 Flower, *rev from* Flowe, *MS. 137* Form *rev from* form *MS.* 109_4 it,] it *MSS. 106,* 109_3*, 131, 134*

368 need?] need *MS.* 109_3*, 134*

369 port *rev from* Port *MS. 137* Port *MS. 106* *no comma MSS. 107 (C), 134*

370 *no period MSS.* 109_3*,134*

371 tempest] Tempest *MSS. 107 (C), 106,* 109_4*, 131, 134* her,] her *MSS.* 109_2*, 134*

372 more;] more *MSS.* 109_2*, 131, 134*

373 gently gently] gently, gently *MSS. 107 (A, C), 106,* 109_4*, 131, 1836YR, 1836–, 1839* her,] her— *MSS. 107 (A, C), 106, MS.* 109_4*, 1836–, 1839* her *MSS.* 109_2*, 131, 134*

374 ashore.] shore *MS.* 109_2*, 134*

375 hearkened,] hearken'd, *MSS. 107 (A), 106* harken'd *MS. 107 (C)* harkened, *rev to* harken'd, *MS.* 109_2 hearknd *MS. 131* hearkened *MS. 134*

376 him] Him *MSS. 107 (C), 106, 131, 134* *no comma MS. 134*

377 Till] 'Till *MSS. 107 (C), 131* death] Death *MS. 107 (C)* darkened] darken'd *MSS. 107 (A), 106* darkened *rev to* darken'd *MS.* 109_2 *no comma MSS. 131, 134*

378 sleep] Sleep *MS. 107 (C)* sleep, *MS. 106* death.] Death. *MS. 107 (C)* death *MS. 134*

380 watch,] watch *MS. 134* band;] band *MSS. 107 (A, C)* Band, *MS. 106* Band *MS. 134*

381 And,] And *MSS. 107 (C), 106, 134* billow *rev from* billow, *MS. 106* favouring] favoring *MSS. 107 (C), 134* billow,] billow *MS. 134*

382 strand. *rev from* Strand. *MS. 137* Strand. *MS. 106* Strand *MS. 134*

383 Pair!] pair! *MS. 107 (A)* Pair, *MS. 131* befall] befal *MSS. 106, 137, 1836–, 1839* you,] you *MSS. 131, 134*

384 faith *rev to* Faith *MS. 107 (A)* Faith *MSS. 107 (C), 106* Him] him *MSS. 107 (A), 131, 134* approve] approve, *MS. 106, 1836YR*

385 earth *rev from* Earth *MS. 137* Earth *MSS. 107 (C), 131* *no comma MSS. 107 (A), 131, 134, 1836YR, 1836–, 1839*

386 bowers *rev from* Bowers *MS. 137* Bowers *MSS. 106, 134* love!] Love. *MSS. 107 (A, C), 106, 131* Love *MS. 134*

A Jewish Family. (In a small valley opposite St. Goar, upon the Rhine.)

title FAMILY.] Family *MSS. 107 (A), 134*

1 Raphael!] Raphael *MSS. 107, 134* Raphael, *MSS. 106, 115*

2 glen,] glen *MS. 107* Glen *MSS. 106, 134* Glen, *Morgan MS. 2, MS. 115*

4 dear] dear, *MS. 106, Morgan MS. 2* pen,] pen *MSS. 107 (B), 134, 150*

5 wouldst] would'st *MS. 106, Morgan MS. 2, MSS. 115, 131, 150, 1836–* *no comma MSS. 107, 106, Morgan MS. 2, MSS. 131, 134, 150*

6 *no punct MSS. 107 (B), 134* majesty, *rev to* majesty— *MS. 150* majesty— *1836–*

8 O'er] Oer *MS. 150* family.] Family *Morgan MS. 2* family *MS. 107* Family. *MSS. 106, 115, 131, 134*

9 Mother— *rev from* mother— *MS. 137* thou] Thou *MS. 150* *no comma Morgan MS. 2, MSS. 107, 106, 115, 131, 134*

10 *no comma MSS. 106, 134* came *rev from* came, *MS. 137*

11 between,] between[?] *MS. 107* between; *Morgan MS. 2* between *MS. 134*

12 *no punct MS. 134*

13 image,] Image, *MSS. 107 (B), 106* Image *MSS. 131, 134* too,] too *MSS. 131, 134* Boy, *rev from* boy, *MS. 137* Boy *MSS. 107, 106, Morgan MS. 2, MSS. 115, 134, 150*

14 give:] give; *rev from* give, *MS. 107* give; *MS. 106* give, *Morgan MS. 2, MSS. 115, 131* give *MS. 134* give— *MS. 150, 1836–*

15 joy,] joy *MS. 106, Morgan MS. 2, MS. 115* joy— *MS. 131* *no commas MSS. 107, 131, 134, 150*

16 Predestined] Predestin'd *Morgan MS. 2, MS. 131* live.] live *MSS. 107 (B), 134*

17 *no comma MSS. 107, 115, 131, 134*

18 *no comma MSS. 107, 106, 134*

20 skies!] skies!— *MS. 115* *no punct MS. 134*

21 beguiled; *rev from* beguiled *MS. 137* beguiled *MSS. 107, 134* beguiled: *MSS. 106, 115* beguiled:— *Morgan MS. 2*

22 gone,] gone; *MSS. 107, 106, Morgan MS. 2, MSS. 115, 131* gone *MS. 134*

23 *no comma MSS. 106, 134* Child, *rev from* child, *MS. 137*

24 Saint] St *MS. 107, Morgan MS. 2, MSS. 115, 131* John.] John *MSS. 107 (B), 134* John! *MSS. 115, 131*

25 dark brown] dark-brown *MSS. 107 (A), 106, 115, 131, 1836–* curls,] curls *MSS. 107, 134* curls— *Morgan MS. 2* brow,] brow *MSS. 107, 106, 134* brow— *Morgan MS. 2, MS. 115*
26 *no comma MSS. 107, 106, 134*
27 *no comma MSS. 107, 106, 115, 131, 134* show] shew *MSS. 107 (B), 106, Morgan MS. 2, MSS. 115, 134*
28 within;] within: *MSS. 107, 106, Morgan MS. 2, MSS. 115, 131* within *MS. 134*
29 Infancy] infancy *MSS. 107, 106, Morgan MS. 2, MSS. 115, 131, 134, 150*
30 untamed; *rev from* untamed, *MS. 137* untamed, *MS. 107 (A), Morgan MS. 2* untamed, *alt* untamed. *MS. 106* untamed *MS. 134*
31 Age *rev from* Age, *MS. 137* mother's] Mother's *MSS. 107, 106, Morgan MS. 2, MSS. 115, 131, 134, 150* *no comma MSS. 107, 134*
32 *no punct MSS. 107 (B), 134*
33 Sisters, *rev from* sisters, *MS. 137* Sisters *MS. 134*
34 side;] side *MSS. 107 (B), 134*
36 pride: *rev from* pride. *MS. 137* pride; *MSS. 107 (A), 106, 150, Morgan MS. 2* pride *MSS. 107 (B), 134*
37 poured] pour'd *MSS. 107, 106, Morgan MS. 2, MSS. 115, 131*
38 them] them, *MSS. 106, 134, 150* forlorn,] forlorn *MS. 107 (B), Morgan MS. 2, MSS. 115, 134* forlorn; *MS. 150*
39 Though] Tho' *MS. 131* abhorred] abhorr'd *MSS. 107 (A), 106, Morgan MS. 2, MS. 115* *no comma MSS. 107, 134*
40 redeemed] redeem'd *MS. 107 (A), Morgan MS. 2, MSS. 115, 131* *no punct MS. 107 (B), Morgan MS. 2, MS. 134*
41 safeguard,] safe-guard *MSS. 107 (B), MS. 134* safeguard— *MS. 106* safeguard! *Morgan MS. 2, MS. 115* safeguard!— *MS. 131* that,] that *MSS. 107 (A), 106, 134*
42 poverty] Poverty *MS. 107 (B)* *no comma MSS. 107, 106, Morgan MS. 2, MS. 134*
43 *no punct MSS. 107, 106, Morgan MS. 2, MSS. 115, 131, 134*
44 sprung;] sprung, *MSS. 107, 106, 115* sprung *Morgan MS. 2, MS. 134*
45 group to cast] Group to cast, *MS. 115*
46 dell] Dell *MSS. 107, 106, Morgan MS. 2, MSS. 131, 134, 150* dell, *MS. 115*
47 Palestine,] Palestine— *MSS. 107, 106, Morgan MS. 2, MS. 115* Palestine.— *MS. 131* Palestine *MS. 134* past,] past *MSS. 107, 106, 134*
48 Jerusalem!] Jerusalem. *MSS. 107 (A), 106, Morgan MS. 2, MSS. 115, 134* Jerusalem *MS. 107 (B)* Jerusalem.— *MS. 131*
48/ *two illeg lines, eras MS. 107 (A)*

The Poet and the Caged Turtledove

title CAGED] caged *MS. 134* Turtledove] Turtle Dove *MSS. 106, 134* TURTLE-DOVE *1836YR, 1839*
2 half-formed *rev from* half-form'd *MS. 137* half-form'd *MSS. 107 (A), 115, Morgan MS. 4, Cornell MS. 7, Fitzwilliam MS.* *no comma MSS. 107, 106, 115, 131, 134, Morgan MS. 4*
3 Straight *rev from* Strait *Cornell MS. 7* Straight, *comma del MS. 135* Strait *MSS. 107, Fitzwilliam MS., Coatalen MS.* *no comma MSS. 107, 106, 115, 116, 131, 134, Morgan MS. 4, Coatalen MS.*
4 Turtledove *rev from* turtledove *MS. 137* Turtle Dove *MS. 107* Turtle-dove *MS. 106, 115, 116, 131, 134, Morgan MS. 4, Coatalen MS.* Turtle-dove *rev from* Turtle-Dove *MS. 135, Fitzwilliam MS.* Turtle-Dove *Cornell MS. 7* replies:] replies *MSS. 107, 134* replies. *MSS. 106, Morgan MS. 4, Coatalen MS.* replies; *MSS. 116, 131, Fitzwilliam MS.*
5 Though] Tho' *MSS. 107, 131* *no comma MSS. 107, 106, 116, 134, Coatalen MS.*
6 captive] Captive *MSS. 107, 106, 115, 116, 131, 134, 135, Morgan MS. 4, Cornell MS. 7, Fitzwilliam MS., Coatalen MS.* coos;] coos: *rev from* cous: *Morgan MS. 4* *no punct MSS. 107, 134*
7 Is] —Is *MS. 115* *no comma MSS. 107, 115, 134, Coatalen MS.*
8 Muse] Muse *rev from* muse *MS. 137, Coatalen MS.* muse *MSS. 107, 106, 116, 134, Cornell MS. 7* *no punct MSS. 107, 106, Coatalen MS.*
9 Dove *rev from* dove *MS. 137* *no comma MSS. 107, 106, 115, 116, 131, 134, Morgan MS. 4*
10 murmuring *rev from* murm'ring *MS. 137* *no comma MSS. 107, 134*
11 Displeased] Displeas'd *MS. 107 (A), Cornell MS. 7* Lays of Love *MS.*

131

12 dared] dar'd *MSS. 107 (A), Cornell MS. 7* aloof;] aloof *MS. 107 (A)* aloof. *MS. 107 (B)* aloof, *MSS. 106, 134* aloof— *MS. 131, Morgan MS. 4*

13 I,] I *MS. 107, 116, 131, Fitzwilliam MS., Coatalen MS.* Bard *rev from* bard *MS. 135* bard *MS. 107 (B)* Hill *Cornell MS. 7* dale, *rev from* Dale, *MS. 135* dale *MSS. 107, 106, 115, 116, 134, Fitzwilliam MS., Coatalen MS.* Dale *MS. 131* Dale, *Cornell MS. 7*

14 caroll'd,] carolled, *MSS. 106, 134, 135* carol'd *MS. 131, 1850–* carol'd, *Morgan MS. 4* caroll'd *MSS. 107 (A), Cornell MS. 7, Fitzwilliam MS.* carolled *MSS. 107 (B), 116* fancy free,] fancy-free *MS. 107* fancy-free, *MSS. 106, 115, 116, 131, 134, Morgan MS. 4, Cornell MS. 7, Fitzwilliam MS.* Fancy-free, *MS. 135, Coatalen MS.*

15 dove,] Dove *MSS. 107, 106, 116, 131, 134, 135, Morgan MS. 4, Cornell MS. 7, Fitzwilliam MS., Coatalen MS.* Dove, *MS. 115* dove *1836–* nightingale] Nightingale *MS. 107, 106, 115, 116, 131, 134, 135, Morgan MS. 4, Cornell MS. 7, Fitzwilliam MS., Coatalen MS.* *no commas MSS. 107, 106, 116, 131, 134, 135, Morgan MS. 4, Coatalen MS.* *no final comma MS. 115*

16 *no punct MSS. 107 (A), 106*

17 meaning,] meaning *MS. 115, 131* O] O, *rev from* Oh *MS. 106* O, *MSS. 134, 135, Coatalen MS.* Oh, *MS. 115* O, *rev from* o, *Fitzwilliam MS.* *no commas MS. 107* *no final comma MSS. 116, 134, Cornell MS. 7, Coatalen MS.*

18 Bird! *rev to* Bird, *MS. 106*, Bird, *MS. 131, 134* Bird! *MS. 116* Bird *Fitzwilliam MS.* wrong;] wrong *MSS. 107, 134* wrong! *MS. 131*

19 blessed] blessêd *MS. 116* blessèd *Morgan MS. 4* Love, is] Love is *MSS. 106, 131, 134, 135* love is *Morgan MS. 4* every where] everywhere *MSS. 131* every-where *Cornell MS. 7* *no commas MSS. 107, Coatalen MS.*

20 spirit *rev to* Spirit *MS. 106* Spirit *MSS. 116, 131, 134, Fitzwilliam MS.* song:] song, *rev to* Song, *MS. 115* Song, *MS. 115* song; *MS. 116* Song;— *MSS. 131* song;— *rev from* song, *Morgan MS. 4* Song:— *Cornell MS. 7* Song: *Coatalen MS.* *no punct MSS. 107, 134*

21 'Mid] Mid *MSS. 107 (B), 116, 131, 134, 135, 137, Morgan MS. 4, Cornell MS. 7, Fitzwilliam MS., Coatalen MS.* fireside] fire-side *MSS. 107, 116, 131, 137, Cornell MS. 7, Fitzwilliam MS., Coatalen MS.* fireside:— *Morgan MS. 4* *no commas MSS. 107, 106, 116, 134, Fitzwilliam MS., Coatalen MS.* *no final comma MS. 115, 131*

22 lyre;] Lyre *MS. 107* lyre— *MS. 106, 1836–* Lyre— *MS. 116, Fitzwilliam MS.* Lyre; *MS. 131* lyre *MS. 134* Lyre; *MS. 135, Cornell MS. 7* Lyre: *Coatalen MS.*

23 —That *MSS. 106, 115, 134, 135, Morgan MS. 4* coo] Coo *MS. 115, Morgan MS. 4, Coatalen MS.* again!—] again— *MS. 107* again! *rev from* again— *MS. 116, Coatalen MS.* chide,] chide, *MS. 115* chide *MSS. 107, 134*

24 feel,] feel— *MSS. 107, 134, Coatalen MS.* feel,— *MS. 106* feel— *rev to* feel, *MS. 116* feel,— *rev to* feel, *Cornell MS. 7* feel,— *Fitzwilliam MS.* inspire. *rev from* inspire! *MS. 135* inspire *MSS. 107 (B), 134* inspire. *MS. 115* inspire! *MS. 137* inspire.—— *Morgan MS. 4*

The Russian Fugitive

fly-title *no punct MS. 116* FUGITIVE.] Fugitive *MS. 134* *roman capitals MS. 107 (B)*

title *no punct MSS. 134, 135*

headnote *no surrounding square brackets MSS. 107, 106, 116, 1839, 1845, 1850* *para 1* Bruce,] Bruce *MS. 107* Memoirs] memoirs *MSS. 107, 106, 116* Tale,] Tale; *MS. 107* affirms,] affirms *MSS. 106, 116, 1845, 1850* that,] that *MS. 107 (A)* Lady's] lady's *1845, 1850* *para 2* Lady Catherine,] Lady Catharine *MS. 107 (A)* Lady Catherine *MSS. 106, 116* famous Catherine,] famous Catharine *MS. 107 (A)* famous Catherine *MSS. 107 (B), 106* Wife] wife *MSS. 107, 116* Great.] Great *alt in pencil* Great— *MS. 107 (A)*

1 rose-bud] rose bud *MSS. 107 (A), 116* rosebud *MS. 131* lips,] lips *MS. 107 (A), 131*

2–7 *no punct MS. 134*

2 dew,] dew; *MS. 116*

3 cheek] Cheek *MSS. 107, 116* carnation] Carnation *MS. 107*

4 hue;] hue, MS. 107 hue. *rev to* hue! MS. 106

6 flowers; *rev from* flowers, MS. 137 flowers, MSS. 106, 116, 135 flowers: MS. 131

7 Yea,] Yea MSS. 106, 116, 135, 1836YR

8–16 *lacking (page cut away)* MS. 134

8 hours.] Hours. MS. 107 (A) hours MS. 107 (B)

9 Through] Thro' MS. 107 gates,] gates MS. 107 Gates, MS. 135 unbarred, *rev from* unbarr'd MS. 137 unbarr'd MSS. 107, 106, 131 unbarred MS. 116 unbarr'd, MS. 135

10 Stepped] Stepp'd MS. 107 one] One MSS. 107, 106, 116, 135, 1836–, 1839 One, MS. 131 night,] night MSS. 107, 106

12 blight;] blight: MSS. 107, 106, 131 blight. MS. 116

13 passed,] pass'd, MSS. 107 (A), 106 passed MS. 107 (B) past, MS. 131

14 fawn, *rev from* faun, MS. 107 (B) faun, MS. 107 (A) fawn; MS. 135, 1836YR

15 stopped,] stopp'd, MS. 107 (A) stopped MSS. 106, 131 stopped— MS. 135 east] East MSS. 106, 135

16 Appeared] Appear'd MS. 107 (A) dawn.] dawn MS. 107

17–23 *no punct* MS. 134

17 lurked] lurk'd MS. 107 field,] field MS. 107

18 renewed,] renew'd, MS. 106 renewed MS. 107 (B) renew'd MS. 131

19 scrip] Scrip MSS. 106, 134 s<u>crip</u> MS. 131 yield,] yield MS. 107

20 wood;] wood: MSS. 107 (B), 106, 131 wood. MS. 116

21 length,] length MSS. 107, 106, 116, 131, 135 on,] on MSS. 107, 131, 135 on, *rev from* on; MS. 106

22 shut,] shut MSS. 107, 131

23 hope] hope, MS. 107 (A) won,] won MS. 107

24 Foster-mother's] foster Mother's MS. 107 foster-mother's MS. 116 Foster mother's MS. 135 hut.] hut MS. 107 hut. *rev to* Hut. MS. 135

25–52 *no punct* MS. 134

25 proof] proof" MSS. 107 (A), 135

26 I come,] "I come MSS. 107, 116 she,] she MS. 107 (A) far;] far." MS. 107 (A) far MSS. 107 (B), 106 far, MSS. 116, 131

27 For] "For MSS. 107, 116 Father's *rev from* father's MS. 137 Fathers MS. 134 roof,] roof MSS. 107, 106, 131

28 In] "In MSS. 107, 116 Czar."] Czar"; MS. 107 Czar;—" MS. 131

29 Matron] matron MS. 116 give,] give MS. 107 (B), 1836YR

30 cast;] cast, MSS. 107 (B), 106, 131, 1836–

31 Fugitive, *rev from* fugitive, MS. 137 Fugitive MS. 107 (B)

32 Embracing] Embracing, MS. 107 (A) *no period* MS. 107 (B)

34 glimmering *rev to* glimm'ring MS. 107 glimmering *rev from* glimmring MS. 116 fire,] fire MSS. 107 (B), 106

35 Bathed] Bath'd MS. 107 (A) wayworn] way-worn MSS. 107, 106, 116, 131, 134, 135

36 desire:] desire; MSS. 107, 106, 116, 131, 135 desire:— MS. 1835/36–, 1839

37 chirped,] chirp'd— MS. 107 chirped— MSS. 106, 116, 131 house-dog *rev from* house dog MS. 137 house dog MS. 107 (B) dozed,] doz'd, MS. 107 (A) dozed,— MSS. 107 (B), 106 dozed; MS. 131

38 bed,] bed MSS. 107, 106, 116

39 Where] Where, MS. 106 reposed,] repos'd MS. 107 (A) reposed MSS. 106, 116

41 she,] she MSS. 107, 106 She MS. 131 She, MS. 135 sod,] sod MSS. 107 (B), 106

42 curtain] curtain, MSS. 107, 106, 1836–, 1839 pine or thorn,] Pine or Thorn, MS. 107 (A) Pine, or thorn, MS. 107 (B) pine or thorn MS. 106

43 God,] God MSS. 107, 106, 116, 131, 135

44 forlorn;] forlorn: MS. 107 (A) Forlorn: MS. 106 Forlorn MS. 134

45 Matron] matron MS. 116 bent] bent, MSS. 107, 106

46 sealed] seal'd MS. 107 (A) eyes,] eyes MS. 107 (B)

47 spent,] spent MSS. 107, 106, 116

49 Refreshed,] Refresh'd, MS. 107 (A) Refreshed MSS. 116, 131 morn,] morn; MS. 134 morn MS. 107 (B), 1836YR

50 again *rev from* against *(copyist's slip)* MS. 116 dight] dight, MS. 107 (A)

51 vestments] vestments, MS. 106

52 Through] Thro MS. 107 (A) Thro' MS. 131 flight;] flight. MS. 116

53 And] And, MSS. 106, 116 Nurse," *rev from* nurse," MS. 137 Nurse"! MS. 107 (A) nurse"! *rev to* Nurse"! MS. 107 (B) Nurse MSS. 106, 134 nurse"! MS. 116 said,] said MSS. 107, 134

55–88 *opening quot MSS. 107 (A), 116*
55–61 *no punct MS. 134*
55 Have] "Have *MS. 107 (B)* Heaven *rev from* [?h]eaven *MS. 131* You *rev from* you *MS. 137* you *MSS. 107 (B), 106, 116, 131, 134, 135* paid:] paid *MSS. 107, 106* paid, *MSS. 116, 131* paid; *MS. 135*
56 fears!] fears." *MSS. 107 (A), 116* fears. *MS. 106* fears. *MS. 131*
57 "Have] Have *MSS. 106, 131, MS. 1836/45* forgot"—] forgot" *MS. 107* forg[o]t?" *MS. 106* forgot," *MSS. 116, 135* forgot,"— *MS. 131* smiled—] smiled, *MSS. 107, 106, 116, 131, 135* smiled,— *MS. 137*
58 "The] The *MS. 106* flatteries] flatteries, *MSS. 107, 116*
59–88 *opening quots MS. 107 (B)*
59 lavished] lavish'd *MS. 107 (A)* child] Child *MSS. 107, 116, 131, 134, 135* Child, *MS. 106*
60 knees? *rev from* knees, *MS. 135*
61 I] —I *MS. 106* lambkin,] Lambkin, *MSS. 107, 116* lambkin *MS. 106* bird, *rev from* Bird, *MS. 107 (B)* bird *MS. 131*
62 star *rev to* Star *MS. 107 (B)* flower;] flower *MSS. 107 (A), 134* flower,— *MS. 106* flower— *MS. 131* Flower, *MS. 107 (B)*
63–71 *no punct MS. 134*
63 *no comma MSS. 107, 106, 131* more . . . heard *MS. 131*
64 hour!] hour *MS. 107* hour. *MSS. 106, 131*
65 "The] The *MS. 131* praised] prais'd *MS. 107 (A)* praised, *MS. 135*
66 *no punct MSS. 107 (B), 106*
67 One *rev from* one *MS. 137* gazed;] gazed, *MSS. 107 (A), 106* gazed *MS. 107 (B)*
68 suit, *rev in pencil from* suit; *MS. 106* suit; *MSS. 107, 131* suit: *MS. 116*
69 wrath:] wrath; *MSS. 107 (A), 135* wrath *MS. 107 (B)* wrath— *MSS. 116, 131*
70 dear,] dear *MSS. 107 (B), 131*
71 path;] path *MS. 107 (B)* path, *MS. 106*
72 here!] here. *MSS. 107 (A), 106, 116, 134* here *MS. 107 (B)* here." *MS. 131*
74–86 *no punct MS. 134*
74 fidelity."—] fidelity"— *MSS. 107 (A), 116* fidelity" *MSS. 107 (B), 106* fidelity;"— *MS. 135*
75 Child, *rev from* child, *MS. 137* Child! *MS. 107 (B)* child! *rev to* child, *MS. 116* Mistress, *rev from* mistress, *MS. 137* Mistress! *MS. 107* mistress! *MS. 116* so!] so; *MS. 107 (A)* so *MS. 107 (B)* so, *MS. 106*
76 die."] die" *MS. 107 (B), 106* die! *MS. 116*
77 "Nay] —"Nay *MS. 135* nay,] nay— *MSS. 107, 106, 116* feigned] feign'd *MS. 107 (A)* feign'd *rev from* feigned *MS. 106*
78 embrowned] embrown'd *MS. 107 (A)* art;] Art, *MS. 107 (A)* Art *MS. 107 (B)* Art, *rev to* art, *MS. 116* art, *MS. 106*
79 Yet,] Yet *MS. 107* unstained,] unstain'd *MSS. 107 (A), 106* unstained *MS. 107 (B)*
81 "But] —"But *MS. 135* whither *rev from miscopied* wither *MS. 107 (B)* would you,] would you *MS. 107 (B)* could you,] could you *MSS. 107, 106, 116*
82 A] —A *MS. 106* Man's *rev from* man's *MS. 137* man's *MS. 116*
83 Holy] holy *MSS. 107, 106, 116, 135*
85 Rest] Rest, *MS. 106, MS. 1835/36–, 1839* grace;] grace *MS. 107* grace, *MSS. 106, 116, MS. 1835/36–, 1839*
87 abiding-place, *rev from* abiding place, *MS. 137* abiding-place *MSS. 107, 106, 116, 134*
88 tread."] tread". *MS. 107 (A)* tread" *MS. 107 (B)* tread *MS. 134*
89 Dwelling *rev from* dwelling *MSS. 116, 137* dwelling *MS. 1835/36–, 1839* pair] Pair *MSS. 107, 106, 131, 134, 135*
90 village] Village *MSS. 106, 131, 134* stood,] stood; *MSS. 107 (A), 116, 131* stood *MS. 134*
91 One *rev from* one *MS. 137* one *MS. 131*
92 *no punct MS. 134*
93 wide around] wide-around *MS. 131* forest ground] forest-ground *MSS. 106, 134, 135* forest-ground, *MS. 131*
94 blind;] blind *MS. 107 (B)* blind, *MS. 106*
95 pine-trees] pine trees *MSS. 107, 106, 116, 134, 135* shade] shade, *MS. 106*
96–104 *no punct MS. 134*
96 *no period MSS. 107 (A), 131*
97 *no commas MSS. 107, 116*
98 *no comma MSS. 107, 106, 116*
99 noonday] noon day *MS. 107* noon-day *MSS. 106, 135* light] light, *MS. 106*
100 lamp;] lamp *MS. 107* lamp, *MS. 106*

lamp. *MS. 116*

101 And] And, *MS. 135* midway] mid-way *MSS. 107, 116* morass,] morass *MSS. 107, 116*

102 rose] rose, *MS. 131*

103 ground,] ground *MSS. 107, 116, 131* healthful] heathful *(copyist's slip) MS. 107 (A)* grass] grass, *MS. 131*

104 Adorned,] Adorn'd, *MS. 107 (A) no punct MS. 107; no comma MS. 116*

105 Woodman *rev from italic* woodman *MS. 137* Woodman *MSS. 106, 131, 134, 135* woodman *MS. 116* knew, for] knew (for *MSS. 107, 106, 116, 131, 134, 135*

106 Vassal *rev from* vassal *MS. 137* vassal *MS. 1835/36–, 1839* plied,] plied *MS. 107 (A)* plied) *MSS. 107 (B), 106, 116, 131, 134, 135*

107 fowler's] Fowler's *MSS. 107, 134, 135* Fowlers *MS. 131* gun, *rev by eras to* gun *MS. 116* gun *MS. 134*

108 archer,] Archer, *MSS. 107, 135* archer, *rev by eras to* archer *MS. 116* Archer *MSS. 131, 134* tried;] tried *MSS. 107, 134* tried: *MS. 106* tried. *MS. 116*

109 sanctuary] Sanctuary *MSS. 134, 135* spot] Spot *MS. 135*

110 instrusion *rev to* Intrusion *MS. 134* free; *rev from* free, *MS. 137* free *MS. 107* free, *MSS. 106, 116, 134*

111 planned] plann'd *MS. 107 (A)* Cot *rev from* cot *MS. 137* cot *MS. 116*

112 secrecy, *rev from* secresy, *MS. 135 no punct MSS. 107, 134*

113–123 *no punct MS. 134*

113 pains] pains, *MSS. 106, 135* unchecked] uncheck'd *MS. 107 (A)*

114 Power's] Powers *MSS. 107, 116 no hyphen MSS. 107 (A), 134; no comma MSS. 107, 116*

115 Man *rev from* man *MS. 137* labour] labor *MSS. 107 (B), 131*

116 nature's] Nature's *MSS. 106, 116, 131, 134, 135* command;] command, *MS. 106*

117 Heart-soothed,] Heart-sooth'd *MS. 107 (A)* Heart-soothed *MSS. 107 (B), 131* wren,] Wren *MS. 107 (A)* wren *MSS. 107 (B), 116, 131* wren *rev to* Wren *MS. 135*

118 *no commas MSS. 107, 106, 116, 131, 135*

119 sight-eluding *rev from* sight eluding *MS. 137* sight eluding *MSS. 107 (A), 116* den] den, *MSS. 107 (A), 106*

120 *no punct MS. 107*

121 *no comma MS. 107*

122 twain *rev from* Twain *MS. 135* Twain, *MS. 106* Twain *MSS. 107, 134* day] day, *MS. 106*

123 forth,] forth *MS. 107* and through] and, thro' *MS. 106* and thro' *MSS. 107 (B), 135* forest] Forest *MS. 106* wind] wind, *1839*

124 Their] "Their *MS. 131* way;] way *MS. 107* way. *MSS. 106, 116, 134* way:" *MS. 131* way: *MS. 135*

125 speak,] speak *MSS. 107 (B), 134* speak; *MS. 106*

126 *no comma MSS. 107, 116, 131, 134*

127 crossed] cross'd *MS. 107 (A)* marsh] Marsh *MSS. 106, 134, 135 no comma MSS. 107, 116, 131, 134*

128 reached] reach'd *MS. 107 (A) no punct MS. 107*

129–166 *no punct MS. 134*

129 sun] Sun *MSS. 107 (A), 116 no hyphen MSS. 107 (B), 106, 116, 131, 134* showed] shewed *MSS. 107 (A), 106, 116, 131, 134, 135*

130 cheerful] chearful *MSS. 106, 131* face;] face *MS. 107* face, *MSS. 106, 116, 131*

131 looked] look'd *MS. 107 (A)* abode, *rev to* Abode, *MS. 135 no comma MSS. 107, 106*

132 promised] promis'd *MS. 107 (A)* hiding-place;] hiding-place *MS. 107* hiding-place. *MS. 106* hiding-place, *MS. 116* hiding place. *MS. 131* hiding place *MS. 134* hiding-place; *rev to* Hiding-place; *MS. 135*

133 vain,] vain; *MS. 106* vain *rev to* vain— *MS. 116* vain;— *MS. 131* vain,— *MS. 135* Woodman *rev from* woodman *MS. 137* smiled;] smiled *MS. 107*

134 seen,] seen *MS. 107* seen; *MS. 131*

135 roof,] roof *MS. 107 (B)* window;] window, *MS. 107 (A)* window: *MS. 106* window *rev to* window— *MS. 116* window— *MS. 131* window;— *MS. 1835/36–, 1839* seemed] seem'd *MS. 107 (A)*

136 been.] been *MS. 107 (B)* been; *MS. 131*

137 Advancing, you] Advancing—you *MSS. 107 (B), 106* Advancing—"you *MS. 116* hour,] hour *MSS. 107, 106* hour" *MS. 116*

138 The] (The *MSS. 107, 106, 116*

139 masked,] masked!) *MS. 107 (A)* masked) *MSS. 107 (B), 106, 116* "if] if *MSS. 107, 106, 135, 137* bower,"] bower; *MS. 107 (A)* bower, *MSS. 107 (B), 106, 135, 137* bower." *1836YR*

140 are;] are. *MSS. 107 (A), 106, 116, 131* are *MS. 107 (B)*

141 roof] roof, *MS. 131*

142 intertwined, *rev from* interwtined, *MS. 137* intertwined *MSS. 107, 116, 131* intertwined; *MS. 106*

143 within,] within— *MSS. 107, 106* air-proof,] air proof *MS. 107 (A)* air proof *rev in pencil to* air-proof *MS. 107 (B)*

144 lined.] lined: *MS. 1835/36–, 1839*

145 *no commas MSS. 107 (B), 131*

147 wish] wish, *MS. 116*

148 repose;] repose. *MSS. 107, 106, 116, 131*

153 Queen] queen *MS. 116, MS. 1835/36–, 1839* *no commas MSS. 107, 106* crowd,] crowd *MS. 131*

154 bridal] Bridal *MS. 135* *no comma MSS. 107, 106, 116*

155 E'er *rev from* E're *MS. 107 (B)* E'er *rev from* Ere *MS. 135* E're *MS. 107 (A)* Ere *MS. 116* *no comma MS. 107*

156 palace gate;] palace gate *MS. 107 (B)* palace gate— *MS. 131* Palace gate; *MS. 135*

157 Rejoiced] —Rejoiced *MSS. 106, 135* world] World *MS. 107 (A)* *no comma MSS. 107, 116*

158 Anchoress] anchoress *MS. 116, MS. 1835/36–, 1839*

159 E'er *rev from* Ere *MSS. 116, 135* E're *MS. 107 (A)* E're *rev to* Ee'er *MS. 107 (B)* cell] Cell *MSS. 107, 106, 131, 134, 135*

160 *no punct MS. 107*

161 all,] all! *MSS. 107 (A), 116* All! *MSS. 107 (B), 106, 131* All *MS. 134* All; *MS. 135*

162–163 *opening quots MSS. 107, 116*

162 *no punct MSS. 107, 131*

163 thou *rev to* Thou *MS. 106* Thou *MSS. 107 (A), 116, 131, 134* safeguard!"—] Safe-guard." *MS. 107 (A)* safe-guard"— *MS. 107 (B)* safeguard:" *rev to* Safeguard:" *MS. 106* safeguard" *rev to* safeguard"— *MS. 116* safe-guard *MS. 134* Safe-guard!" *MS. 135* such] Such *MS. 135* prayer] Prayer *MS. 131*

164 alone, *rev from* alone; *MS. 116* alone *MS. 107 (B)*

165 wilderness] Wilderness *MS. 107 (B)*

166 passed] pass'd *MS. 107 (A)* *no comma MS. 107 (B)*

167 smiles,] smiles— *MSS. 107 (B), 134, 135* distress] distress, *MS. 131*

168–191 *no punct MS. 134*

169 prayer *rev from* Prayer *MS. 137* Prayer *MSS. 107 (B), 134, 135* heard,] heard *MS. 107 (B)* heard: *MS. 106* heard; *MSS. 116, 135* heard— *MS. 131* Saints *rev from* saints *MS. 137* saints *MSS. 107 (B), 116* seen,] seen *MSS. 107 (B), 106, 116* *first three words miscopied at l. 170 then del MS. 106*

170 through] thro' *MS. 135* face,] face *MSS. 107, 131*

171 serene; *rev in pencil from* serene, *rev in pencil from* serene *MS. 107 (A)* serene, *rev in pencil from* serene *MS. 107 (B)* serene, *MS. 106* serene *MSS. 116, 131*

174 Reason] reason *MS. 131* control;] controul *MS. 107 (A)* control *MSS. 107 (B), 131* control, *MSS. 106, 116*

175 shows *rev to* shews *MS. 107 (B)* shews *MSS. 106, 131, 134, 135*

176 statue] Statue *MSS. 134, 135* soul.] Soul *MSS. 107 (A), 106, 134* soul *MS. 107 (B)* Soul. *MSS. 131, 135*

177 sung] sung, *MSS. 107, 116* minstrelsy] minstrelsy, *MSS. 107, 106, 116*

179 "The] The *MSS. 107, 106, 116, 131, 1836–, 1839* any] <u>any</u> *MS. 131*

180 hair,"*] hair—; *MS. 1835/36* hair; *MS. 107, 1836—, 1839* hair; *MS. 106* hair, *MSS. 116, 131*

181 Till] 'Till *MS. 131* *no comma MSS. 107 (B), 116*

182 love, *rev from* love *MS. 106*

183 transformed] transform'd *MS. 107 (A)* root,] root *MS. 135*

184 laurel] Laurel *MSS. 107, 131, 134, 135* Laurel, *MS. 106* grove.] grove *MS. 107 (B)* Grove. *MSS. 106, 131, 134, 135*

185 Penitent *rev from* penitent *MS. 116*

186 laurel] Laurel *MSS. 106, 131* green;] green *MS. 107* green, *MSS. 106, 116*

187 And] And, *MS. 135* 'mid] mid *MSS. 107, 116, 131, 134, 135* locks] locks, *MSS. 106, 131* shorn *rev from* shorn, *MS. 137* shorn, *MSS. 131, 135*

189 Poets] Poet's *MS. 107 (B)* poets *MS. 116, MS. 1835/36–, 1839* sage,] sage *MSS. 107 (A), 116* through] thro' *MSS. 131, 134, 135* age,] age *MSS. 107, 106, 116, 131*

191 bay,] Bay, *MSS. 107 (A), 106, 134, 135* Bay, *MS. 107 (B)* bay: *MS. 131* Conquerors *rev from* Conquerers *MS. 135* conquerors *MS. 116, MS. 1835/36–, 1839* thanked] thank'd

MSS. 107 (A), 131 Gods,] Gods *MSS. 107, 131, 135* gods, *MS. 116*

192 chaplets] Chaplets *MSS. 106, 134, 135* crowned.] crown'd *MS. 107 (A)* crowned *MS. 107 (B)* crown'd. *MS. 106*

193–256 *no punct MS. 134*

193 Time] time *MSS. 107, 116, 131* Time; *MS. 106*

195 Beauty,] beauty *MSS. 107, 116, 131, 134, 135* beauty, *MS. 106*

196 ways;] ways, *MSS. 106, 131*

197 temptation;] temptation, *MSS. 107, 106, 116, 131* defies] defies, *MSS. 116, 131*

198 not;] not, *MSS. 107, 106, 131*

200 *no punct MS. 107 (B)*

201 fair] Fair *MS. 131* Votaress,] Votaress *MSS. 107, 131, 135* votaress *MS. 116*

202 Heaven] heaven *MSS. 116, 131* ordain] ordain, *MSS. 107 (A), 116*

203 Island] island *MS. 131* desolate; *rev from* desolate *MS. 107 (B in pencil)*

204 *no commas MSS. 107, 106, 116, 135*

205 *no comma MSS. 107, 106, 116, 135*

206 *no punct MSS. 107, 106*

207 birds] Birds *MSS. 107 (B), 106, 134, 135* tamed,] tamed; *MSS. 107, 106, 116* tamed— *MS. 131*

208 forth] forth, *MS. 107 (A)* cheer.] chear *MS. 107 (A)* chear. *MS. 131*

209 *no commas MSS. 107, 106, 116, 135* Presence] presence *MS. 107 (A, pencil)*

210 soothed] sooth'd *MS. 107 (A, ink)* clung,] clung *MS. 107*

211 picture] Picture *MSS. 107 (A, pencil; B), 106, 134, 135* Cabin] cabin *MSS. 107 (A, pencil), 116, MS. 1835/36–, 1839*

212 hung— *rev from* hung, *MS. 135* hung *MS. 107* hung, *MSS. 106, 116*

213 Mother-maid, *rev from* mother-maid, *MSS. 116, 137* Mother Maid— *MS. 107 (A, pencil)* Mother Maid *MS. 107 (A, ink)* Mother Maid *rev in pencil to* Mother-Maid *MS. 107 (B)* mother-maid *MS. 106* Mother-maid, *rev from* Mother Maid, *MS. 135*

214 love *rev from* love, *MS. 137* Love, *MS. 107 (A, pencil)* love, *MS. 116* abridged] abridg'd *MS. 107 (A)* day;] day *MS. 107* day, *MSS. 106, 116*

215 And,] And *MS. 106* *no commas MS. 107 (A, pencil; B)* with] with, *MSS. 107 (A), 106* with *rev by eras from* with, *MS. 116*

216 Chased] Chas'd *MS. 107 (A)* away.] away! *MS. 107 (A, pencil)* away *MS. 107 (A, ink)*

217 oft,] oft *MS. 131* came,] came; *MS. 107 (B)*

218 retreat] Retreat *MS. 131*

219 common . . . shame,] common . . . shame *MS. 131*

221 Recluse,] Recluse— *MS. 131* whate'er *WW rev from* what e'er *MS. 116* what e'er *MSS. 107, 134*

222 brought,] brought *MS. 107 (A)* brought— *MS. 131*

224 spring] Spring *MS. 131*

225 Parents] Parent's *MS. 107 (A)* *no commas MSS. 107, 106, 116, 131*

226 bear;] bear *MS. 107 (B)* bear, *MS. 106*

227 And,] And *MS. 131* enwrought,] enwrought *MS. 107 (A)* enwrought; *MS. 131* *no commas MSS. 107 (B), 106*

228 near. *rev from* near: *MS. 135* near *MSS. 107, 106*

230 prove,] prove; *MSS. 107 (A), 116, 131* prove *MSS. 107 (B), 106*

231 Daughter *rev from* daughter *MS. 137* daughter *1839* feared] fear'd *MSS. 107 (A), 106*

232 love.] Love *MS. 107 (A)*

233 Past *rev from* past *MS. 135* past *MSS. 107 (A), 116, 131, MS. 1835/36–, 1839* them,] them; *MSS. 107 (B), 106, 131* them; *rev from* them, *MS. 116*

234 Future] future *MSS. 107, 116, 131, MS. 1835/36–, 1839* *no comma MSS. 107, 106, 116*

235 Till] 'Till *MS. 131* Saints] saints *MS. 116* bark] Bark *MSS. 135, 137*

236 sea— *rev from* sea; *MS. 135* Sea; *MS. 107 (A)* sea; *MSS. 107 (B), 106, 116, 131* Sea— *MS. 137*

237 Nature *rev from* nature *MS. 106* nature *MS. 116* *no comma MSS. 107, 106, 116, 131*

238 Spirit] spirit *MSS. 107, 106, 116, 131, 135* free] free, *MS. 137*

239 altar *rev from* Altar *MS. 137* Altar *MSS. 107 (A), 116, 134, 135* *no comma MSS. 107, 106, 116, 131*

240 *no punct MS. 107*

241 Yet,] Yet *MSS. 107, 106, 131* forest-glooms] forest glooms *MSS. 107, 106, 116, 134*

242 white swans] White Swans *MS. 107 (A)* white Swans *MS. 131* passed,] pass'd, *MS. 107 (A)* passed *MS. 107 (B)* pass'd *MS. 106*

244 fancy] Fancy *MS. 107* blast;] blast

MSS. 107, 106 blast, *MS. 131*

245 tow'rd] toward *MS. 1835/36–, 1839* fields] Fields *MSS. 106, 134, 135* France,] France *MS. 107, 1847, 1849P*

246 Father's *rev from* father's *MS. 137* land,] Land *MSS. 107 (A), 106, 134* land *MS. 107 (B)* land— *MS. 116* Land, *MSS. 131, 135*

247 *no comma MS. 107*

248 band!] band. *MS. 107 (A)* band *MS. 107 (B)* Band. *MS. 106* Band *MS. 134* Band! *MSS. 131, 135*

249 fields *rev from* fields, *MS. 137*

250 Father *rev from* father *MS. 137* tell] tell, *MSS. 107 (A), 116, 131*

251 phrase *rev in pencil from* Phrase *MS. 107 (B)*

252 Cell; *rev from* cell; *MS. 137* cell: *MSS. 107 (A), 131* Cell *MSS. 107 (B), 106* cell; *MS. 116, MS. 1835/36–, 1839*

253 hereditary *rev from* heriditary *MS. 107 (B)*

254 *no punct MS. 107*

255 towers *rev from* towers, *MS. 137* Towers *MSS. 106, 134*

256 dream!] dream *MS. 107* dream. *MSS. 106, 116, 131*

257–376 *no punct MS. 134*

257 *hyphen added in pencil MS. 107 (B)* Moon] moon *MSS. 107 (B), 106, 116, 131, 134, 135*

258 *no comma MS. 107 (B)*

259 through] thro' *MSS. 107 (B), 131, 135* Waste] waste *MSS. 107 (A), 116, 137*

261 sent] sent, *MS. 107* one *rev to* One *MS. 135* chased] chas'd *MS. 107 (A)* chaced *MS. 131*

262 Deer, *rev from* deer, *MSS. 135, 137* deer, *MSS. 107 (B), 116, 134, MS. 1835/36–, 1839*

263 through] thro' *MS. 107* interlaced,] interlac'd, *MS. 107 (A)* interlaced *MSS. 107 (B), 131*

264 *no punct MS. 107* *no closing quot 1840–1843*

265 Creature *rev from* creature *MS. 137* creature *MS. 116, MS. 1835/36–, 1839* marsh,] Marsh, *MSS. 106* Marsh *MSS. 134, 135*

266 toward] tow'rd *MSS. 107, 106, 131, 134* Island *rev from* island *MS. 137* island *MSS. 107 (B), 116* *no comma MS. 107 (B)*

267 plovers] Plovers *MSS. 107, 134, 135* screamed *rev from* screamed, *MS. 137* scream'd *MSS. 107 (A), 131* screamed, *MS. 135* harsh *rev from* harsh, *MS. 137* harsh, *MS. 135*

268 head;] head: *MSS. 107, 106, 116, 131*

269 This,] This *MSS. 107, 106, 116, 131* saw; and,] saw and *MS. 107 (A)* saw, and *MSS. 107 (B), 116* fear,] fear *MSS. 107, 116, 1836YR*

270 citadel;] Citadel *MS. 107 (A)* Citadel *rev in pencil to* Citadel; *MS. 107 (B)* Citadel: *MS. 106*

271 Deer *rev from* deer *MS. 137* deer *MSS. 106, 116, MS. 1835/36–, 1839* rushed] rush'd *MS. 107 (A)* *no comma MS. 107*

272 covert] Covert *MSS. 107, 135* *no punct MS. 107 (A), MS. 106*

273 marsh] Marsh *MSS. 107 (A), 134, 135*

274 Hunter *rev from* hunter *MS. 137* hunter *MS. 116* followed] follow'd *MS. 107 (A)* *no comma MSS. 107 (B), 131*

275 paused,] paus'd *MS. 107 (A)* paused *MSS. 107 (B), 106, 116* paused, *rev to* paused— *MS. 135* Stag *rev from* stag *MS. 137* stag *MS. 116, MS. 1835/36–, 1839*

276 *hyphen added in pencil MS. 107 (B)*

277 Then,] Then *MSS. 107, 106, 116* mind,] mind *MS. 106*

278 Maid] maid *MSS. 107 (B), 116*

279 Behold,"] Behold" *MS. 107 (A)* "Behold" *MS. 107 (B)* "Behold"! *MS. 116* Behold,"— *MS. 131* said,] said— *MS. 131* Hind *rev from* hind *MS. 137* Hind" *MS. 107 (B)* Hind *rev from* hind *MS. 106*

280 destiny!] destiny." *MSS. 107, 116* destiny. *MS. 106*

281 deportment,] deportment *MS. 135* Sir! *rev from* sir! *MS. 137* Sir, *MSS. 107, 106, 116, 131*

282–320 *opening quots MSS. 107, 116*

282 sword,] sword *MSS. 107 (B), 131*

283 esteem *rev from* esteem, *MS. 137*

284 woman's] Woman's *MSS. 107, 106, 134* word;] word. *MSS. 107 (A), 106, 116* word *MS. 107 (B)* word— *MS. 131*

285 covert,] Covert, *MSS. 107, 135* covert; *MS. 131* there] there, *MSS. 106, 131* perchance] perchance, *MS. 131*

286 concealed,] concealed *MS. 107 (B)* conceal'd, *MS. 106*

287 *no comma MS. 107 (B)*

288 you *rev from* You *MS. 135* *no punct MS. 107 (B)*

289–320 *lacking MS. 137*

289 might] <u>might</u> *MSS. 107 (B), 116* shed,] shed; *MS. 131* pray,] pray *MS. 134*

290 *no comma MS. 107*
291 to day,] today *MSS. 107, 106, 116, 131, 134* to day *MS. 135*
292 *no punct MSS. 107, 106*
293 not] <u>not</u> *MSS. 107, 106, 116, 134, 135*
294 to adore *rev to* t' adore *MS. 107 (A)*
295 heaven;—] Heav'n: *MSS. 107, 116* Heaven: *MS. 106* heaven:— *MS. 131* Heaven *MS. 134* attend,] attend *MSS. 107 (B), 106* just:] just, *MS. 107 (A), 135* just *MS. 107 (B)* just; *MSS. 106, 131, 1836–, 1839*
296 I,] I *MS. 107 (B)* more!] more *MS. 107* more. *MSS. 106, 116, 131*
297 winter's] Winter's *MS. 107 (A)* *no comma MSS. 107, 106, 116, 135*
298 exchanged] exchang'd *MS. 107 (A)* *no comma MSS. 107, 106, 116, 131*
299 lodged] lodg'd *MS. 107 (A)* hold,] hold *MSS. 107 (B), 106* Hold *MS. 131* hold *rev to* Hold *MS. 135*
300 estranged;] estrang'd; *MS. 107 (A)* estranged *MS. 107 (B), 131* estranged;— *MS. 106*
301 alarms:] alarms, *MS. 107 (A)* alarms *MSS. 107 (B), 106* alarms; *MSS. 116, 131, 135*
302 Heaven] heaven *MS. 116* defence;] defence *MS. 107 (B)* defence, *MS. 135*
303 season *rev to* Season *MS. 135*
304 Innocence. *rev from* innocence. *MS. 135* Innocence *MS. 107* innocence. *MSS. 106, 116* innocence *MSS. 131, 134*
305 Wilderness] wilderness *MSS. 106, 116, 134*
306 come,] come *MS. 107 (B), 131* come; *MS. 116*
307 harbourless,] harbourless *MS. 107 (A), 131* harborless *MSS. 107 (B)*
308 honour] Honor *MS. 107 (A)* honor *MSS. 107 (B), 116, 131, 134* home;] home *MS. 107 (B)* home, *MS. 106*
309 *no comma MSS. 107, 106*
311 life] Life *MS. 107 (A)* here] here, *MSS. 107 (A), 106, 131* Deer, *rev from* deer,*MS. 135* deer, *MSS. 116, 134, MS. 1835/36–, 1839* Deer *MS. 107 (B), 131*
312 Lamb *rev from* lamb *MS. 135* lamb *MSS. 107 (B), 106, 116, 134, MS. 1835/36–, 1839* hill."] hill" *MS. 107 (A)* hill."— *MS. 135*
313 "Are] Are *MS. 131* Maid,"] Maid" *MS. 107 (B)* Maid?" *MS. 135* Stranger] stranger *MS. 116* cried,] cried *MSS. 107 (B), 106, 135*
314 "From] From *MSS. 106, 135* Parents] parents *MSS. 116, 134, MS. 1835/36–, 1839* *no comma MSS. 107, 106, 131*
315 rumoured] rumour'd *MS. 107 (A)* rumored *MSS. 107 (B), 116, 131, 134* *no comma MSS. 107 (B), 131*
316 tongue;] tongue! *MSS. 107, 106, 131* tongue? *MS. 116*
317 quest?] quest *MS. 107 (B)* quest, *MS. 106* quest— *MS. 116*
318 You,] You *MS. 107 (B)* Lady, *rev from* Lady! *MS. 116* lady *MS. 107 (B)*
319 *no comma MS. 107 (B)*
320 lair!" *rev from* lair?" *MS. 135* lair. *rev in pencil to* lair! *MS. 107 (B)* lair. *MS. 106*
321 But] But, *MS. 131* quelled;] quelled *MS. 107 (A)* quell'd; *MS. 106* quelled, *MS. 116* quell'd *MS. 131* *no punct MS. 107 (B)*
323 soul's] Soul's *MS. 135* beheld] beheld, *MS. 116*
324 between: *rev to* between; *MS. 135* between; *MSS. 107 (A), 116, 131* between *MS. 107 (B)*
325 loved,] lov'd, *MS. 107 (A)* loved *MS. 107 (B)* hoped,—] hop'd; *MS. 107 (A)* hoped; *MSS. 107 (B), 106, 116* hoped: *MS. 131*
326 'mid] mid *MSS. 107, 116, 131*
328 *no punct MS. 107 (B)*
329 chance,] Chance *MS. 107 (B)* chance *MS. 131*
330 Exclaimed] Exclaim'd *MSS. 107 (A), 131* he;] he, *MSS. 107, 116, 131* Heaven,] Heaven *MS. 107 (B)*
331–340 *opening quots MSS. 107, 116*
331 *no comma MS. 107*
332 me *rev from* Me *MS. 137* me *rev to* Me *MS. 135* given.] giv'n *MS. 107 (A)* given *MS. 107 (B)* given: *MS. 106* given— *MS. 131* given; *MS. 135*
333 Czar full oft] Czar, full oft, *MS. 106*
334 self-willed;] self-willed *MS. 107* self-will'd; *MS. 106* self-will'd *MS. 131*
335 *no commas MSS. 107, 106, 116, 131*
336 stilled.] stilled *MS. 107 (B)* still'd. *MS. 106*
337 wish] wish, *MS. 106* course,] course *MSS. 107, 116*
338 *no punct MSS. 107, 106, 131*
339 heavenly *rev to* heav'nly *MS. 116* heav'nly *MS. 107* *no comma MSS. 107, 106, 116, 131, 135*
340 Good,] Good *MS. 107 (B)* good, . . . flow.] good . . . flow *MS. 107* good . . . flow"— *MS. 131*
341 given] giv'n *MSS. 107, 116* *no*

comma MS. 107
342 *no comma MS. 107 (B)*
343 Though] Tho' *MS. 107 (B)*
344 Maiden's] Maidens *MS. 134*
345 step,— *rev from* step, *MS. 135* step; *MSS. 107 (A), 116* step: *MSS. 107 (B), 106* step, *MS. 131* hopes, more light,] hopes more light *MSS. 107, 116*
346 desires;] desires, *MS. 131*
348 Moscow's] Moscows *MSS. 107 (B), 134* spires. *rev from* spires; *MS. 135* Spires. *MS. 107*
349 sued:—] sued— *MS. 131* heart-mitten *rev from* Heart-smitten *MS. 137* wrong,] wrong *MSS. 107, 106*
350 Fugitive] Fugitive, *MS. 106* fugitive *MS. 116*
352 *no punct MS. 107*
353 O] O, *MS. 106* Oh! *MS. 131* change! *rev from* change, *MS. 135* If *rev from* if *MS. 135* if *MSS. 107, 106, 116, 131, 134*
354 *no comma MSS. 107 (B), 131*
355 over-joy *rev from* over joy *MS. 135* overjoy *MS. 107 (B)* over joy *MS. 134*
356 vain,] vain *MSS. 107 (B), 106* vain; *1836–*
357 Parents, *rev from* parents, *MS. 137* Parents *MS. 107 (B)* parents, *MSS. 106, 116, 1836YR* mourned] mourn'd *MSS. 107, 131*
358 lost . . . dead,] Lost . . . Dead, *MSS. 107 (A), 131* Lost . . . Dead *MS. 107 (B)* Lost, . . . Dead *MS. 106* Lost . . . dead *MS. 134* Lost . . . dead, *MS. 135*
359 Child *rev from* child *MS. 137* child *MS. 116* returned,] return'd *MSS. 107 (A), 106* returned *MS. 107 (B)*
362 Maiden's] Maidens *MSS. 131, 134* breast:] breast; *MSS. 107 (A), 116, 135* breast *MSS. 107 (B), 106* breast, *MS. 131*
363 Delivered] Delivered, *MS. 107 (B)* Deliverer *rev to* Deliv'rer *MS. 137* Deliverer, *MS. 106* deliverer *MS. 116*
364 drest;] drest: *MS. 131*
364–376 *lacking MS. 107 (B)*
366 dower;] dower *MS. 131*
367 shared] shar'd *MS. 107 (A)*
369–372 *no punct MS. 107 (A_2)*
369 strewed] strew'd *MS. 107 (A_2)*
370 state;] state, *MS. 106*
371 there,] there *MS. 116* 'mid] mid *MSS. 107 (A_2), 116, 134, 135* Guest, *rev from* guest, *MS. 135* guest *MSS. 107 (A_2), 106, 116, 134* guest, *MS. 1835/36–, 1839*
372 Foster-parents *rev from* Foster-Parents *MS. 137* foster parents *in pencil MSS. 107 (A_2), 116* foster Parents *MS. 107 (A_3)* sate;] sate: *MS. 106*
373 by *rev from* bp *(printer's error) MS. 137* *no comma MSS. 116, 135* imperial] Imperial *MSS. 106, 131, 134, 1836YR* eye] Eye *MS. 131*
374 shade;] shade: *MS. 106*
375 bliss,] bliss,— *MS. 106* bliss— *MSS. 107 (A), 116* honour] honor *MSS. 131, 134, 135*
376 paid!] paid *MS. 107 (A)* paid. *MSS. 106, 116* paid— *MS. 131*

The Primrose of the Rock, Text of 1835

1–32 *no punct MS. 107 (F)*
1 Rock *rev from* rock *MS. 135*
2 Traveller *rev from* Trav'ller *MS. 137* traveller *1836–, 1839* slights;] slights, *MS. 106* slights *MS. 134*
3 Glow-worms] Glow worms *MS. 107 (F), hyphen inserted MS. 137* glow-worms *1836–, 1839* lamps,] lamps *MSS. 106, 134, 135*
4 *no punct MSS. 106, 134*
5 Rock] rock *MSS. 107 (F), 106, 134, 135*
6 *no punct MS. 134*
7–8 *no punct MSS. 106, 134*
8 kingdoms] Kingdoms *MS. 134*
9 *no hypen MSS. 107 (F), 106, 134* tuft] tuft, *MS. 106*
10 marked] mark'd *MS. 137* own;] own, *MS. 106* own *MS. 134*
11 Nature's] natures *MS. 107 (F)* nature's *MSS. 106, 134, 135*
12 Heaven] heaven *MSS. 107 (F), 106, 134, 135, 137, 1836–, 1839* *no punct MS. 134*
13 Flowers, *rev from* flowers, *MS. 135* flowers, *MSS. 107 (F), 106, 134, 1836–, 1839* Flowers *MS. 106, 134* stems,] stems *MS. 106, 134*
14–30 *no punct MS. 134*
15 stems] stems, *MS. 135*
16 view; *rev from* view, *MS. 106*
17 adheres] adheres, *MS. 106*
18 every *rev from* ev'ry *MS. 137*
20 Though] Tho' *MS. 107 (F)* fall; *rev from* fall, *MS. 137* fall, *MS. 106, 135*
21 sphere; *rev from* sphere, *MS. 137* sphere, *MSS. 106, 135*
22 all: *rev from* all; *MS. 137* all. *MS. 106* all; *MS. 135*
23 lonely *rev from* lovely *MS. 137*

Plant,] plant *alt in pencil* Plant *MS. 107 (F)* Plant; *MS. 106*

24/25 *broken line or asterisks dividing first and second parts present in all manuscripts but MSS. 107 (B–E)*

25 Strain; *rev from* strain; *MS. 137* strain, *MS. 106* strain *MS. 134* strain; *rev from* strain, *rev from* strain. *MS. 135* strain; *MS. 1835/36–, 1839*

26 day,] day; *MS. 106*

27 *no hyphen MSS. 107 (F), 106, 134* cheered,] cheer'd, *MS. 106* cheered *1849 imperfect plate*

28 sunny] Sunny *1836YR* looked *rev from* look'd *MS. 137* gay;] gay, *MS. 106*

30 after-lay. *rev from* after-Lay. *MS. 137* after Lay *MSS. 107 (F), 134* after Lay. *MS. 106* after-Lay. *MS. 135*

31 sang, Let] sang let *MS. 107 (F)* sang, "Let *rev from* sang, "let *MS. 106* sang—"Let *rev from* sang—"let *MS. 134* sang, "Let *MS. 135, 1836YR* sang—Let *1836–, 1839* flowers, *rev from* flowers *MS. 137* flowers *MSS. 134, 135*

32 Thee, *rev from* thee, *MS. 137* grove] grove, *MS. 135* grove *rev from* grove, *MS. 137*

33 unenvied,— *rev from* unenvied, *MS. 137* unenvied; *rev in pencil from* unenvied *MS. 107 (F)* unenvied; *MS. 106* unenvied *MS. 134* unenvied, *MS. 135* unenvied;— *1836–, 1839* far] far, *1836–*

35 hope] hope, *MS. 135, 1836–*

36–42 *no punct MS. 107 (F)*

36 God's] Gods *MS. 107 (F)* love: *rev from* love. *MS. 137* Love. *MS. 107 (F)* love; *rev in pencil from* love *MS. 106* love *MS. 134* love. *MS. 135* love; *MS. 1835/36–, 1836YR, 1839*

37 changed,] changed *MSS. 106, 134* changed— *MS. 1835/36–, 1839* disease, *rev from* disease *MS. 106* disease *MS. 134*

38 bent] bent— *MS. 106*

39 O'er] Oer *MS. 107 (F)* withered *rev from* wither'd *MS. 137* age, *rev in pencil from* age *MS. 106* age *MS. 134* age— *MS. 1835/36–, 1839*

40 element,] element; *rev in pencil from* element *MS. 106*

41 thistles *rev from* Thistles *MS. 137* Thistles *MSS. 107 (F), 106, 134, 135*

42–52 *no punct MS. 134*

42 *no punct MS. 106*

43 Sin] "Sin *1836YR* *hyphen added in pencil MS. 107 (F)* too,] too *MS. 107 (F)*

44 Sons *rev from* sons *MS. 135* sons *MSS. 107 (F), 106, 134* Men, *rev from* Men; *MS. 137* men *MSS. 107 (F), 134* men, *MS. 106* men; *rev to* Men; *MS. 135*

45 called *rev from* call'd *MS. 137* call'd *MS. 106*

46 rise,] rise *MSS. 107 (F), 106* again;] again. *rev from* again! *MS. 107 (F)* again, *MS. 106*

48–52 *no punct MS. 107 (F)*

48 threescore] three score *MSS. 107 (F), 135*

49 To] "To *1836YR*

50 high,] high *MS. 106*

51 Just,] just *MS. 107 (F)* Just *MS. 106* just, *MS. 1835/36–, 1839*

52 Before] Before, *MSS. 106, 134* die;] die, *MS. 106* die: *1849 (possibly an imperfect plate)*

53 heaven, *rev from* Heaven,— *MS. 137* Heavn *MS. 107 (F)* Heaven, *MSS. 106, 135* Heaven *MS. 134*

54 court] Court *MSS. 107 (F), 106, 134, 135* Deity.] Diety." *1836YR*

The Armenian Lady's Love

title *no punct MS. 107 (A)*

headnote Digby;] Digby: *1836–*

stanza numbers *no punct MSS. 107 (A), 106, 131, 135, so 134 but* 14. *roman numerals, MS. 107 (A), 1836–; roman numeral for first stanza only is lacking MSS. 107 (B), 131, 134*

1–156 *no quots MS. 134*

1 "a] a *MS. 131* Lady *rev from* Lady" *MS. 137* Lady" *MSS. 134, 135*

2 Man;"* *rev from* Man;* *MS. 137* Man;" *MS. 107* Man" *MS. 106* man; *MS. 131* Man *MS. 134* Man";* *MS. 135* man;"* *MS. 1835/36* man*;' *1836–, 1839*

3 *no comma MSS. 107, 134*

4 Soldàn; *rev from* Soldan; *MS. 137* Soldàn, *MSS. 107 (A), 135* Soldàn *MSS. 107 (B), 106, 131, 134*

5 loved] lov'd *MSS. 107 (A), 131* Christian] Xtian *MSS. 107, 134 (B)* Slave, *rev from* slave, *MS. 137* Slave *MSS. 107, 106, 131, 134*

6 again.] again *MS. 107 (B)*

7 "Pluck *rev to* 'Pluck *MS. 131* rose,] rose— *MSS. 107, 106, 131* rose *MSS. 134, 135* liking,"] liking" *MSS. 107, 134* liking", *rev to* liking', *MS. 131*

8 veil;] veil, *MSS. 107, 106, 131, 135*

9–53 *no punct MS. 134*

9 "Pluck] 'Pluck *MS. 107 (A)* "Pluck *rev*

to 'Pluck *MS. 131* me,] me *MS. 107* Gardener,] Gardener *MS. 107 (A)* Gardener! *MS. 131* gardener, *MS. 1835/36–, 1839*

10 Ere] 'Ere *MS. 131* pale."] pale!' *MS. 107 (A)* pale"! *MS. 107 (B)* pale!" *MS. 106* pale—" *rev to* pale—' *MS. 131*

11 "Princess] 'Princess *MS. 107 (B)* fair,] fair *MSS. 107 (A), 131* fair! *MS. 107 (B)* ground,] ground *MSS. 106, 131* but] 'But *MS. 107 (B)* take] take, *MS. 107*

12 From] "From *MS. 107 (A)* 'From *MS. 107 (B)* flower,] Flower *MS. 107 (A)* flower *MSS. 107 (B), 106, 131* sake.] sake! *MS. 107 (B), MS. 1835/36–*

13 "Grieved *rev to* 'Grieved *MS. 131* 'Griev'd *MS. 107 (A)* I,] I *MSS. 107 (B), 135* Christian! *rev from* Christian, *MS. 137* Christian *MS. 107 (B)* Christian, *MSS. 106, 131, 135* Xtian *MS. 134*

14 To] 'To *MS. 131* captive] Captive *MSS. 107 (B), 134* state;] state *MS. 106*

15 Women,] Women *MSS. 107, 106, 134* 'Women *MS. 131* land,] land *MS. 107* Land *MSS. 106, 131* pity *rev from* pity, *MS. 135* pity, *MSS. 107 (B), 131*

16 May] 'May *MS. 131* not? *rev from* not, *MS. 131* not *MS. 107 (B)* unfortunate."] unfortunate;' *MS. 107 (A)* unfortunate; *MS. 107 (B)* unfortunate" *MS. 106* unfortunate.' *MS. 131* Unfortunate *MS. 134* Unfortunate;" *MS. 135*

17 "Yes,] 'Yes *MS. 107 (B)* "Yes *MS. 131* Lady! *rev from* Lady, *MS. 137* Lady, *MSS. 107, 106* Lady *MS. 131* Man] man *MS. 131, MS. 1835/36–, 1839*

18 Life,] Life *MSS. 107, 106, 131* is] 'Is *MS. 107 (B)* care."] care *MS. 134*

19 "Worse] 'Worse *MSS. 107 (A), 131*

20–24 *opening quots eras MS. 107 (B)*

20 If] 'If *MS. 131* sighs;] sighs, *MSS. 107 (A), 131* sighs *MSS. 107 (B), 106*

21 Thee] 'Thee *MS. 131* rescue] rescue, *MSS. 107 (A), 106*

22 And] 'And *MS. 131* indignities;] indignities. *MS. 107 (A)* indignities *MS. 107 (B)* indignities, *MS. 106* indignities: *MS. 131*

23 Nurtured, *rev from* Nurtured *MS. 137* 'Nutured *MS. 131* Nurtured *MS. 135* bespeaks, *rev from* bespeaks *MS. 137* bespeakes, *MS. 107 (B)* bespeaks *MS. 135* degree.] degree *MSS. 107 (B), 131*

24 Look] 'Look *MS. 131* up— *rev from* up *MS. 137* up *MSS. 107, 106, 131, 135* free."] free! *MS. 107 (A)* free!" *MSS. 107 (B), 106* free.' *MS. 131*

25 "Lady,] "—Lady *MS. 107* —"Lady *MS. 131* "Lady! *MS. 1835/36–, 1839*

26–30 *opening quots eras MS. 107 (B)*

26 In] "In *MS. 131* engage;] engage, *MSS. 107, 131*

27 Think] "Think *MS. 131*

28 Your] "Your *MS. 131* Father's] father's *MS. 1835/36–, 1839* rage:] rage *MSS. 107, 106* rage— *MS. 131*

29 Sad] "Sad *MS. 131* be,] be *MSS. 107, 106, 131, 135* shame,] shame *MSS. 107, 131*

30 Should] "Should *MS. 131* came."] came.' *MS. 107 (B)*

31 "Generous] Generous *MS. 107 (A)* 'Generous *MS. 131* Frank! *rev from* Frank: *MS. 135* Frank, *MSS. 107, 106, 131*

32–36 *opening quots eras MS. 107 (B)*

32 Are] 'Are *MS. 131* secure;] secure *MSS. 107, 131* secure *rev in pencil to* secure, *MS. 106* secure: *1836–, 1839*

33 Hardships] 'Hardships *MS. 131* brave] Brave *MSS. 106, 134, 135, 137* encountered,] encounter'd *MSS. 107 (A), 106* encountered *MSS. 107 (B), 131, 135* encounter'd, *MS. 137*

34 Even] 'Even *MS. 131* endure:] endure *MS. 107 (B)* endure *rev in pencil to* endure; *MS. 106*

35 If] 'If *MS. 131* Almighty Grace *rev from* Almighty Grace, *MS. 135* almighty grace *MSS. 107 (A_2), 107 (B), MS. 1835/36–, 1839* me *rev from* me, *MS. 135* unbind, *rev from* unbind *MS. 106* unbind *MS. 107, 1840–*

36 My] 'My *MS. 131* Father] Father, *MS. 106* father *MS. 1835/36–, 1839* slave's] Slave's *MSS. 107 (A), 134, 135* slaves *MS. 107 (B)* Slaves *MS. 131* slave] Slave *MSS. 106, 131, 134, 135* mind." *rev to* mind.' *MS. 131* mind. *MS. 107 (A)* mind" *MS. 107 (B)*

37 "Princess,] "Princess *MS. 107 (A)* 'Princess *MS. 107 (B)* Princess, *MS. 106* goodness,] goodness *MSS. 107, 106, 131, 135*

38 My *rev from* “My *MS. 107 (B)* “My *MS. 131* long-frozen *rev from* long frozen *MS. 137* long frozen *MSS. 131, 134, 135* warm!”] warm,” *MS. 107 (A)* warm’ *MS. 107 (B)* warm *rev in pencil to* warm”— *MS. 106* warm—” *MS. 131* warm.” *MSS. 135, 137*

39 “Yet *rev in pencil from* Yet *MS. 106* ‘Yet *MS. 131* *no comma MSS. 107, 106, 131, 135*

40 Me *rev from* “Me *MS. 107 (B)* harm:] harm’ *MS. 107 (A)* harm” *MS. 107 (B)* harm.” *MS. 106* harm *MS. 131* harm; *MS. 137*

41–42 *opening quot del MS. 107 (B)*

41 Leading] “Leading *MS. 106* ‘Leading *MS. 131* Companion] Companion, *MS. 107 (A)* companion *MS. 1835/36–, 1839* I] I, *MSS. 107 (A), 106, 131* that] That *rev from* “That *MS. 107 (B)* Dome,] Dome *MSS. 107, 135* dome *MS. 131* dome, *MS. 1835/36–, 1839*

42 Minarets, *rev to* Minarets *MS. 135* Minarets *MS. 107 (A)* minarets *rev to* Minarets *MS. 106* minerets *MS. 107 (B)* minarets, *MS. 131, MS. 1835/36–, 1839* for] “For *rev to* For *MS. 107 (B)* home.”] home.’ *MS. 107 (A)* home. *MS. 107 (B)* home” *MS. 106* home’. *MS. 131*

43 “Feeling] ‘Feeling *MS. 107 (B)* your] y^{r} *MS. 135* voice,] voice *MSS. 107, 131* Princess!] Princess *MSS. 107, 131* Princess, *MSS. 106, 135, 137*

44–46 *opening quots eras MS. 107 (B)*

44 And] “And *MS. 131* *no comma MS. 107*

45 Else] “Else *MS. 131* would] w$^{d.}$ *MS. 135* mockery,] mock’ry *MS. 107* mockery *MSS. 106, 131*

46 Sharper] “Sharper *MS. 131* thorn.”] thorn.’ *rev from* thorn. *MS. 107 (B)* thorn!” *MS. 106* thorn” *MS. 131*

47 “Whence] ‘Whence *MSS. 107 (A), 131* undeserved] underserv’d *MS. 107 (A)* mistrust? Too *rev from* mistrust too *MS. 135*

48 Our] ‘Our *MS. 131* been,— *rev from* been. *MS. 135* been, *MS. 107 (B)* been; *MS. 106* been— *MS. 131* O *rev in pencil from* Oh! *MS. 106* heart!”] heart!’ *MS. 107 (A)* heart” *MS. 107 (B)* heart *MS. 131*

49 “Tempt] ‘Tempt *MS. 107 (B)* *no comma MSS. 107 (B), 135* pray; *rev in pencil from* pray, *MS. 106* pray, *MS. 131* pray; *rev from* pray,— *MS. 135* pray; *rev from* pray, *MS. 137*

50–56 *opening quots eras MS. 107 (B)*

50 These] “These *MS. 131* implements *rev to* Implements *MS. 131* Implements *MS. 107* wield;] wield, *MSS. 107 (A), 131* wield *MS. 107 (B)* wield *rev in pencil to* wield—, *with comma eras MS. 106*

51 Rusty] “Rusty *MS. 131* Lance,] lance, *MS. 107 (A), MS. 1835/36–, 1836YR, 1839* lance *MS. 107 (B)* thee,] thee *MSS. 107 (B), 131*

52 Ne’er] “Ne’er *MS. 131* assoil *rev from* assail *MS. 137* cobwebb’d *rev from* cobweb’d *rev from* cobwebb’d *MS. 137* cobweb’d *MS. 107* cobwebbed *MSS. 131, 134, 135* shield! *rev from* shield; *MS. 137* shield; *MSS. 107 (A), 135* shield *MSS. 107 (B), 131* Shield *rev in pencil to* Shield; *MS. 106* Shield *MS. 134*

53 Never] “Never *MS. 131* land,] Land, *MSS. 107 (A), 131, 135* land *MS. 107 (B)* Land *MSS. 106, 134* castle] Castle *MS. 107* towers,] towers *MS. 107* Towers *MS. 131*

54 Nor] “Nor *MS. 131* Her *rev from* her *MS. 137* her *MSS. 107 (B), 134, 134* widowed *rev from* widow’d *MSS. 107 (A), 137* hours.”] hours’ *MS. 107 (B)* hours. *MS. 106*

55–57 *no punct MS. 134*

55 “Prisoner! *rev from* “Prisoner, *MS. 137* ‘Prisoner, *MSS. 107 (A), 131* “Prisoner *MS. 107 (B)* “Prisoner, *MSS. 106, 135* fancies; *rev from* fancies, *MS. 137* fancies *MS. 107* fancies— *MSS. 106, 131* fancies, *MS. 135*

56–59 *opening quots eras MS. 107 (B)*

56 Wedded? *rev from* Wedded— *MS. 135* Wedded?— *MSS. 107, 106* ‘Wedded?— *MS. 131* If] if *MS. 131* *no ital MSS. 107, 106, 131, 134* no!—] no; *MSS. 107, 106, 131* no! *1836–*

57 Blessed] ‘Blessed *MS. 131* is and be] is, and be, *MS. 107* is, and be *MS. 106* Consort; *rev from* consort; *MS. 137* Consort, *MSS. 107, 131* Consort! *MS. 106* consort; *1836–, 1839*

58 Hopes] —Hopes *MSS. 106, 134* ‘Hopes *MS. 131* cherished] cherish’d,— *MS. 107 (A)* cherished— *MSS. 107 (B), 106, 131, MS. 1835/36–, 1839* cherish’d *MS. 137* go!] go. *MSS. 107, 106, 131* go *MS. 134*

59–95 *no punct MS. 134*

59 Handmaid’s] Handmaids *MS. 107*

'Handmaids *MS. 131* *no comma MSS. 107, 106, 131*

60 Without] 'Without *MS. 131* felicity." *rev from* Felicity. *MS. 135* Felicity.' *MS. 107 (A)* "Felicity." *MS. 107 (B)* Felicity." *MS. 106* felicity'. *MS. 131* Felicity *MS. 134*

61 love] Love *MSS. 107, 131* Christians,] Christians *MSS. 107 (A), 131* Xtians *MSS. 107 (B), 134*

62–64 *opening quots eras MS. 107 (B)*

62 Lady,] Lady! *MS. 107* "Lady! *MS. 131* mystery *rev from* myst'ry *MS. 137* rare; *rev from* rare, *MS. 137* rare *rev in pencil to* rare, *MS. 106* rare, *MS. 131*

63 Body, *rev to* Body *MS. 135* Body *MS. 107 (B)* "Body *MS. 131* heart,] heart *MSS. 107, 131, 135* union,] union *MSS. 107, 106, 131, 135*

64 Make] "Make *MS. 131* being] Being *MSS. 107 (A), 106, 131, 134, 135* pair."] pair!" *MSS. 107, 106* Pair!"— *MS. 131*

65 "Humble] 'Humble *MS. 131* love] Love *MS. 131* for] "For *rev to* For *MS. 107 (B)* return,] return *MSS. 107, 131 (B)* return; *MS. 106*

66 Soft] "Soft *MS. 107 (B)* 'Soft *MS. 131* star] Star *MSS. 107 (A), 134, 135* cheers,] cheers *MSS. 131, 135* burn."] burn! *MS. 107 (A)* burn' *MS. 131*

67 "Gracious] 'Gracious *MS. 107 (B)* Allah] Alla *MS. 131*

68–72 *opening quots del MS. 107 (B)*

68–69 *no comma MS. 107 (B)*

68 Do] "Do *MS. 131* God,] God *MS. 131*

69 Him] "Him *MS. 131* spirit,] Spirit *MS. 131*

70 Flower] "Flower *MS. 131* sod!] sod *MS. 107 (B)* sod; *MS. 106*

71 Or] "Or *MS. 131* wings] wings, *MS. 106* heaven] heav'n *MS. 107 (A)* wear?] wear *MS. 131*

72 What] "What *MS. 131* seen,] seen *MSS. 107, 131* heard,] heard *MS. 107 (B)* dreamt?] dreamt, *MSS. 107 (A), 131, 135, 137* dreamt *MS. 107 (B)* I?] I, *MSS. 107 (A), 131* I *MS. 107 (B)* where?" *rev from* where!" *MS. 131* where?' *MSS. 107 (B), 106, 1836_1, 1840* where?' *with a second inverted comma added 1836_2*

73 dangerous *rev from* dang'rous *MS. 137* converse: *rev in pencil from* converse *MS. 106* Converse— *MS. 107 (A)* converse *MS. 107 (B)* converse;— *MS. 131*

74 impassioned] impassion'd *MS. 107 (A)*

75 Pair] pair *MSS. 107 (B), 131, MS. 1835/36–, 1839* *no comma MSS. 107 (B), 131*

76 *no comma MSS. 107 (B), 131*

77 heart] heart, *MSS. 106, 131* Father's *rev from* father's *MS. 137* father's *MS. 1835/36–, 1839* door,] door *MSS. 107, 131, 135*

78 world,] world *MSS. 107, 106, 131, 135* passed *rev from* pass'd *MS. 137* pass'd *MSS. 107 (A), 106* past *MSS. 134, 135* evermore.] evermore.? *1836YR*

79 *no commas MSS. 107 (A_4), 107 (B)*

80 Urged] Urgd *MS. 107 (A_4)* *no punct MS. 107 (A_4)* trust] trust *MS. 106*

82 Woman's *rev from* Womans *MS. 107 (B)* Womans *MSS. 107 (A_2), 134* birthright] Birthright *MS. 107 (A_4)* *no punct MSS. 107 (A_4), 107 (B)*

83 then, *rev from* then *MSS. 107 (A_4), in pencil 106* none, *rev in pencil from* none *MS. 106* none *MSS. 107 (A_4), 107 (B)*

84 Maid, *rev from* maid, *MS. 137* Maid *rev in pencil from* maid *MS. 107 (B)* Maid *MS. 107 (A_{1-3})* maid *MS. 107 (A_4)* *no period MS. 107*

85 Fugitives *rev from* fugitives *MS. 107 (A)* knowledge:] knowledge *MSS. 107 (B), 106* knowledge; *MS. 131* knowledge, *MS. 135*

86 days] days, *MSS. 107 (A), 131* days: *MS. 106*

87 soul's] Souls *MS. 107 (A)* Soul's *MS. 131* commandments *rev from* commandments, *MS. 134*

88 restrain, *rev from* restrain *MS. 107 (A)* restrain *MS. 131* raise.] raise; *MSS. 107 (A), 106, 131* raise *MS. 107 (B)*

89 path,] path *MS. 107 (B)* near,] near; *MSS. 107, 106* near *MSS. 131, 137*

90 selves] Selves *MS. 131* *no punct MS. 107 (B)*

91 *no apos MS. 107 (A), no comma MSS. 107 (B), 131*

92 desert] desart *MSS. 107, 106, 131, 134, 135*

93 *no comma MS. 107 (B)*

94 Forest-fruit *rev from* Forest fruit *MS. 137* Forest fruit *MSS. 107, 106, 131, 135* hands; *rev from* hands, *MS.*

137 hands *MS. 107 (B)* hands, *MS. 106*
96 heads,] heads *MSS. 131, 135, 137*
97 reposing *rev from* reposing, *MSS. 135, 137* reposing, *MS. 106*
98–136 *no punct MS. 134*
98 They at length] They, at length, *MS. 106* steer;] steer *MS. 107*
99 There, *rev from* There *MS. 107 (A)* There *MS. 107 (B)* voyage,] voyage *MS. 107*
100 *no comma MS. 107* Pier] pier *MS. 106, MS. 1835/36–, 1839*
101 Watched *rev from* Watch'd *MS. 137* Watch'd *MS. 107 (A)* East,] East *MS. 107 (A)* east *MS. 107 (B)* Lord,] Lord *MSS. 107 (B), 135*
102 down] down, *MS. 106* clasped] clasp'd *MSS. 107 (A), 137* *no comma MS. 107* word.] word *MS. 107 (B)*
103–106 *no punct MS. 107 (B)*
103 transport;] transport, *MS. 106*
105 moment,] moment *MS. 131*
106 last;] last *MS. 106* last! *1836YR*
107 "Hie] Hie *MS. 106* Countess,] Countess *MSS. 131, 135* Friend! *rev from* Friend, *MS. 137* Friend— *MSS. 107 (A), 131* Friend, *rev to* Friend— *MS. 107 (B)* Friend *MS. 106* Friend, *MS. 135* friend! *MS. 1835/36–, 1839* return] "Return *rev to* Return *MS. 107 (B)* speed,] speed *MSS. 107 (B), 135*
108 And *rev from* "And *MS. 107 (B)* "And *MS. 131* speak] speak, *MSS. 107, 106* her] Her *alt* her *del* Her *MS. 135* Her *rev from* "Her *MS. 107 (B)* Lord] lord *MS. 107 (B), 1836–, 1839* freed.] freed." *MSS. 107 (B), 106* freed *1849*
109 "Say *rev from* Say *MS. 107 (B)* Say *MS. 107 (A), 1836–, 1839* I,] I *MS. 131* languished, *rev from* languish'd, *MS. 137* languish'd *MS. 107 (A)* languish'd, *MS. 106* languished *MS. 131*
110–119 *opening quots del MS. 107 (B)*
110 Drooped *rev from* Droop'd *MS. 137* Droop'd, *MS. 107 (A)* Drooped, *MS. 107 (B)* "Drooped *MS. 131* pined] pin'd *MS. 107 (A)* pine'd *MS. 131*
111 Now] "Now *MS. 131* gates] Gates *MSS. 106, 134*
112 My] "My *MS. 131* Deliverer *rev from* Deliv'rer *MS. 137* present] present— *MS. 107 (A)*
113 For] "For *MS. 131* recompence,] recompense *MS. 107 (B)* recompense, *1836–*
114 Of] "Of *MS. 131* place." *rev in pencil from* place" *MS. 106* place" *MS. 107 (B)* place *rev in pencil to* place" *MS. 107 (B)*
115 "Make] Make *MSS. 107 (A), 106, 1836–, 1839*
116–120 *opening quots del MS. 107 (B)*
116 Is] "Is *MS. 131* Eastern] eastern *MS. 1835/36–, 1839* blood,] blood; *MSS. 107, 106, 131, 135*
117 Thirsting *rev from* Thursting *MS. 135* "Thirsting *MS. 131* *no comma MSS. 107 (B), 131*
118 Innocent] "Innocent *MS. 131* *no commas MSS. 107 (B), 131, 135* good,] good *rev in pencil to* good; *MS. 106* good; *MS. 135*
119 Though] "Though *MS. 131* misbelievers] Misbelievers *MSS. 107, 106, 135* bred;] bred *MSS. 107, 106* bred, *MSS. 131, 135*
120 Will] "Will *MS. 131* Holy] holy *MSS. 107, 106, 131, MS. 1835/36–, 1839* Gospel Light."] Gospel light." *MS. 107* Gospel Light. *MS. 106* gospel light." *MS. 131* gospel-light." *MS. 1835/36–, 1839*
121 grey-haired] grey-hair'd *MSS. 107, 137* Servant, *rev from* servant, *MS. 137* servant *MS. 107 (B)* Servant; *MSS. 106, 131, 135*
122 returned *rev from* return'd *MS. 137* return'd *MS. 107 (A)* Page] Page, *MSS. 107 (A), 106* page, *MS. 131*
123 Charged] Charg'd *MS. 107 (A)* benedictions,] benedictions *MS. 131*
124 praises,] praises— *MSS. 107, 106, 131*
125 cheer] chear *MS. 107 (A)* Stranger's *rev from* stranger's *MS. 137* Strangers *MS. 107* way,] way *MS. 131*
126 *no comma MS. 107 (B)*
127 while, *rev from* while *MS. 137* while *MSS. 107, 106, 131, 135*
128 walls, *rev to* walls *MS. 135* walls *MS. 107*
129 Deafening *rev from* Deaf'ning *MS. 137* Deafning *MS. 107 (B)* *no comma MSS. 107, 131*
130 Trumpets,] Trumpets *MS. 131* Drums,] drums, *MS. 107* Drums *MSS. 131, 137* Atabals,)] Atabals) *MSS. 107, 131* atrabals) *rev in pencil to* atabals) *MS. 106* *commas del MS. 135*
131 fell *rev from* fell, *MS. 137*

132 farewell.] farewell *MS. 107 (B)* farewell! *MS. 131*
133 Through] Thro' *MSS. 107, 131* nature, *rev to* nature *MS. 135* nature *MSS. 107, 106, 131*
134 *no comma MSS. 107, 106, 131, 135*
135 Looked . . . Deliverer *rev from* Look'd . . . Deliv'rer *MS. 137*
136 sight,] sight *MSS. 107 (B), 131* sight; *MS. 106*
137 strayed,] stray'd *MSS. 107 (A),106* strayed *MSS. 107 (B), 131, 135* stray'd *rev to* strayed *MS. 137*
138 *no punct MSS. 107 (B), 131, 135*
139–156 *no punct MS. 134*
140 Knelt,] Knelt *MS. 107 (B)* kissed *rev from* kiss'd *MS. 137* kiss'd *MS. 107 (A)* Stranger's *rev from* stranger's *MS. 137* Strangers *MS. 134* hand;] hand *MSS. 107, 131* hand, *MS. 106*
141 *no comma MS. 107*
142 band:] band *MS. 107* band; *MS. 131*
143 *no comma MSS. 107, 106*
144 *no commas MSS. 107, 106, 131; no period MS. 107 (B)* crowd] Crowd *MSS. 106, 134*
145 *no comma MSS. 107, 131, 135*
146 moved, *rev from* moved *MS. 137* mov'd *MS. 107 (A)* moved *MSS. 107 (B), 135* moved: *MS. 106* moved; *MS. 131*
147 Spirit *rev from* spirit, *MS. 137* spirit *MS. 107 (B), MS. 1835/36–, 1839*
148 Reverenced,] Reverenc'd *MS. 107 (A)* Sister, *rev from* sister *MS. 137* Sister *MSS. 107 (A), 106, 131* sister *MS. 107 (B)* sister, *MS. 1835/36–, 1839* loved.] lov'd *MS. 107 (A)* loved *MSS. 107 (B), 131*
149 Christian] Xtian *MSS. 107 (B), 134* life,] life *MSS. 107 (B), 106* life; *MS. 135*
150 *no punct MS. 107 (A)*
151 Memento *rev from* momento *MS. 137* memento *MSS. 107, 106, 134, 135, MS. 1835/36–, 1839* union *rev from* Union *MS. 137* Union *MSS. 107, 131, 134, 135* Union, *MS. 106*
152 Church] church *MS. 1835/36–, 1839* *no comma MSS. 107 (B), 135*
153 cross-legged] crosslegged *MS. 107 (B)* cross-legg'd *rev to* cross-leggd *MS. 137* Knight *rev from* knight *MS. 137* knight *MSS. 131, 134* sculptured] sculptur'd *MS. 107 (A)*
154 Wives— *rev from* wives— *MS. 137* wives; *MS. 107 (A)* Wives; *MSS. 107 (B), 106, 131* wives— *MS. 135*
155 *no comma MSS. 107 (B), 131*
156 Pilgrims] pilgrims *MS. 1835/36–, 1839* earth.] Earth. *MS. 107 (A)* earth *MS. 107 (B)*

Rural Illusions

1 it? *rev from* it! *rev from* it, *MS. 135 (B)* it *MS. 107 (B)* it, *MSS. 101A, 106, 134*
2 stock?] stock *MS. 134*
3 by;—and lo! *rev from* by; and lo! *MS. 106* by & lo *MS. 107 (B)* by—and lo! *MS. 112* by and lo *MS. 134*
4 flock,] flock *MSS. 107 (B), 134*
5 bough] bough, *MS. 112*
6 rock.] rock *MSS. 107 (B), 134*
7–8 *no punct MS. 134*
9 Strangers, *rev from* strangers, *MS. 135 (B)* strangers *MSS. 107 (B), 101A, 134* strangers, *MS. 106* Strangers *MS. 112* strangers, *MS. 1835/36–* hailed *rev to* hail'd *MSS. 107 (B)* hail'd *112*
10 trees,] trees *MSS. 107 (B), 101A, 106, 134*
11 Proved] Prov'd *MS. 112* last year's] last years *MS. 107 (B)* last-year's *MSS. 101A* leaves,] leaves *MSS. 107 (B), 101A, 106, 134* pushed] push'd *MS. 107 (B)* push'd *rev from* pus'd *MS. 112*
12 breeze.] breeze *1835 only*
13 Flora! *rev from* Flora, *MS. 135 (B)* Flora *MSS. 107 (B), 101A, 134* Flora, *MS. 106* show] shew *MSS. 107 (B), 101A, 106, 112, 134, 135 (B)* face,] face *MSS. 107 (B), 106 (A), 112, 134*
14 seen] seen, *MS. 112, 1836–*
16 That,] That *MSS. 107 (B), 101A (B), 134* green,] green *MSS. 107 (B), 101A* Green *MSS. 106, 134*
17 root (so . . . it)] root, so . . . it, *MS. 112*
18 honour] honor *MSS. 107 (B), 112, 134* Queen.] queen *MS. 107 (B)* Queen *MSS. 101A (B), 134*
19 Yet,] Yet *MSS. 107 (B), 101A (B), 135 (A)* sooth,] sooth *MS. 101 (B)* specks,] specks *MSS. 107 (B), 101A (B), 112, 134, 135 (A)*
20 That . . . vain] That, . . . vain, *MS. 112* aspired *rev from* aspired, *MS. 106* aspir'd *MS. 112*
21 growths,] growths *MSS. 107 (B), 101A, 106, 134, 135 (A)* growths *rev to* Growths *MS. 112*
22 dainty,] dainty *MS. 107 (B), 134* admired,] admired *MSS. 107 (B), 101A (A), 134* admired. *MS. 135 (A)*
23 dropped] dropp'd *MS. 112*

24 tired.] tired *MS. 107 (B)* tir'd. *MS. 112*

25 World's *rev from* world's *MS. 135 (B)* world's *MSS. 106, 134* World's *MS. 112* shows;] shows;— *MS. 107 (B_2)* shows: *MS. 106* shows *rev to* Shows, *MS. 112* shows *MSS. 134, 135 (A)* shows, *rev to* shows: *MS. 135 (B)*

26 *no ital MSS. 107 (B_2), 135 (A); ital added MS. 135 (B)* flutterings, *rev from* flutterings; *MS. 135 (B)* flutterings *MS. 134* flutterings; *MS. 135 (A)*

27 *no commas MSS. 107 (B_2), 112, 134, 135 (A)*

28 Floweret *rev from* Floweret, *MS. 135 (B)* Floweret, *MS. 106* floweret *MS. 1835/36* floweret, *1836–* springs,] springs *MSS. 112, 134, 135 (A)*

29 Undeceived,] undeceiv'd, *MS. 107 (B_2)* Undeceiv'd, *MS. 112* undeceived *MSS. 134, 135 (A)* undeceived, *MS. 1835/36–* may,] may *MSS. 134, 135 (A)*

30 things:] things! —— *MS. 107 (B_2)* things. *MS. 112* things *MSS. 134, 135 (A)*

31 Nature *rev to* nature *MS. 135 (A)*

32 wiles,] wiles *MSS. 107 (B), 101A (A), 134*

33 transient *rev from* transcient *MS. 107 (B)*

34 reconciles,] reconciles *MSS. 107 (B), 101A (A), 106 , 134, 135 (A)*

35 Idlers *rev from* idlers *MS. 135 (B)* idlers *MSS. 101A, 106, 135 (A)* pleased] pleased, *MS. 106* pleas'd *MS. 112*

36 beguiles.] beguiles.— *rev from* beguiles *MSS. 107 (B), 134*

This Lawn, &c., Text of 1835

1–6 *no punct MS. 134*

1 Lawn, *rev from* Lawn— *MS. 135* lawn— *MS. 107 (B)* Lawn— *MSS. 107 (C), 106, 112, MS. 1835/36*

3 dance, amid] dance amid *MSS. 107 (B), 106, 112, 135* dance a mid *MS. 107 (C)*

4 sunshine— *rev from* sunshine, *MS. 135* sunshine, *MSS. 107 (B, C), 106, 112, 1836–, 1839*

6 idleness; *rev from* idleness. *MS. 135* idleness— *MS. 107 (B)* idleness; *rev to* idleness: *MS. 107 (C)* idleness. *MSS. 106, 112* idleness: *1836YR, 1839*

8 *no comma MSS. 107 (C), 134*

9 moment's] moments *MSS. 107 (C, E)* rest;] rest *MS. 134*

10 boreal] Boreal *MS. 107 (C), 106* Lights *rev from* lights *MS. 135* lights *MSS. 106, 134*

11 fro] fro, *MS. 1835/36–, 1839* aery] aëry *1839* Sprites *rev from* sprites *MS. 135* sprites *MSS. 106, 134*

12 addrest! *rev from* addrest *MS. 135* addrest. *MSS. 107 (C), 106* addrest— *MS. 107 (E)* addrest *MS. 134*

13–18 *no punct MS. 134*

13 Yet, *rev from* Yet *MS. 135* Yet *MSS. 107 (C), 107 (D), 112* strife,] strife *MSS. 107 (C), 107 (D)*

14 play, *rev from* play *MS. 135* play *MS. 107 (C)*

15 steadfast] stedfast *1836–1849, 1839* hours, *rev from* hours *MSS. 135, 137* hours *MSS. 107 (C, D)*

16 *no comma MSS. 107 (C), 112*

17 *no comma MS. 107 (C)*

18 flowers.— *MS. 112*

Presentiments, Text of MS. 107 (A)

1 Presentiments! *rev in pencil to* Presentiments!— *MS. 107 (A)*

7–13 *no punct MS. 89*

7 misdeem'd] misdeemd *MS. 89*

8 Faith] faith *MS. 89*

9 Castles,] castles *rev from* catles *MS. 89 comma added in pencil MS. 107 (A)*

10 Will *rev from* will *MS. 107 (A)*

12 *no period MS. 89*

13 Foes] foes *MS. 89*

14 blood] blood, *MS. 89*

19 Man] man *MS. 89*

20 *no comma MS. 89*

24 Alchemy] alchemy *MS. 89*

Presentiments, Text of 1835

title *no punct MSS. 107 (B), 107 (D), 106*

1 Presentiments!] Presentiments!— *MS. 107 (B)* Presentiments *MS. 133*

3 shame;] shame *MSS. 107 (B, D, E), 133* shame. *MS. 107 (C)* shame: *MS. 106*

4 heaven-born *ital*] heaven-born *MSS. 107 (B, D)* heaven born *MS. 107 (E)* Instincts *rev from* instincts *MS. 135* instincts *MSS. 107 (B, C, D, E), 133*

5 vulgar *rev from* Vulgar *MS. 107 (B)* sense,] sense *MS. 133* sense,— *1836–, 1839* and,] and *MSS. 106, 135*

6 ye] Ye *MSS. 107 (C), 106, 133* claim.] claim *MSS. 107 (B, C), 133*

claim— *MS. 107 (E)*
7 guess, *rev from* guess; *MS. 137* guess *MSS. 107 (B, D, E), 133* guess; *MS. 135*
8 seemed *rev from* seem'd *MS. 137* seem'd *MSS. 107 (C, D)* fatherless, *rev from* fatherless *MS. 137* fatherless *MSS. 107 (B, C, D, E), 106, 133, 135*
9 days;] days, *MS. 107 (B)* days *MSS. 107 (D, E), 133*
10 now,] now *MS. 107 (E), 133* Time *rev from* time *MS. 137* time *MS. 135, MS. 1835/36–, 1839*
11 Fancy] fancy *MSS. 107 (B, C, E), MS. 1835/36–, 1839* heart,] heart *MSS. 106, 133*
12 praise.] praise *MSS. 107 (B, D, E), 133*
13–18 *no punct MS. 107 (B)*
13–30 *no punct MS. 133*
13 Foes *rev from* foes *MS. 135* foes *MSS. 107 (D), 106, 133, MS. 1835/36–, 1839* good,] good *MS. 107 (D)*
14 *no comma MS. 107 (D)*
15 you,] you— *1836–, 1839*
16 infuse,] infuse *MS. 107 (C, D)* infuse; *1836–, 1839*
17 Muse] muse *MSS. 107 (B, C)*
19 you,] you *MS. 107 (B)* You, *MS. 135* derided *rev from* divided *(printer's error) MS. 137* Powers!] Powers *MSS. 107 (B), 106*
20 Faith] faith, *MS. 107 (B)*
21 castles] Castles *MS. 135* air;] air, *MSS. 107 (B, D)* air! *MS. 106* air: *MS. 1835/36–, 1839*
22 unsanctioned] unsanction'd *MSS. 107 (C, D)* will *rev to* Will *MSS. 107 (B, C)* Will *MSS. 107 (D), 106, 133, 135*
23 *no comma MSS. 107 (B, C, D), 106*
25 bosom-weight,] bosom-weight *MS. 107 (B)* bosom weight, *MSS. 107 (C, D), 106* bosom weight *MS. 133* gift,] gift *MSS. 107 (C, D), 106*
26 *no comma MSS. 107 (B, C, D), 106*
27 vanish,] vanish *MS. 107 (D)* please,] please *MS. 107 (C, D)*
28 and, . . . lay,] and . . . lay *MSS. 107 (B, C, D), 106* mist;] mist: *1836–, 1839*
29 spirits *rev from* spirits, *MS. 137* Spirits, *MS. 107 (B)* spirits, *MSS. 107 (D), 106, 135* bidding *rev from* bidding,*MS. 137* bidding, *MSS. 107 (B, D), 106, 135*
30 ease.] ease *MSS. 107 (C, D)*
31 Contemplations *rev from* contemplations *MS. 135* contemplations *MS. 133, MS. 1835/36–, 1839*
32 Through *rev from* Thro' *MS. 135* Thro' *MS. 133* though] tho' *rev from* thr *MS. 133*
33 rule;] rule? *MSS. 107 (D), 106*
34 Wild, *rev from* wild, *MS. 137* wild, *MS. 1835/36–, 1839* *no comma MSS. 107 (D), 133*
35 And haply, too,] And, haply too, *MSS. 107 (D), 106* And, haply too *MS. 133* And haply too *MS. 135* Child,] Child *MSS. 107 (D), 133* Child *rev from* child *MSS. 106, 137*
36–48 *no punct MS. 133*
36 school.] school *MS. 107 (D)* school; *MS. 135*
38 instruments? *rev from* instruments— *MS. 107 (C)*
39 rainbow,] Rainbow— *MS. 107 (C)* Rainbow— *MSS. 107 (D), 106* Rainbow *MSS. 133, 135* Rainbow, *rev to* rainbow, *MS. 137* sunbeam,] Sun-beam— *MSS. 107 (D), 106* Sun-beam *MS. 133*
40 unbinds, *rev from* unbinds— *MS. 107 (C)* Spring *rev from* spring, *MS. 137* spring *MSS. 107 (B), 135*
41 winds, *rev from* winds— *MS. 107 (C)* winds *MSS. 107 (B, D)*
42 echo,] echo— *MSS. 107 (C, D), 106*
43 Christmas *rev from* christmas *MS. 107 (C)* Xmas *MSS. 133, 135*
44 *hyphen added in pencil MS. 107 (B), no hyphen MS. 135*
45 reprove;] reprove, *rev in pencil from* reprove *MS. 107 (B)* reprove *MS. 107 (C, D)*
46 *no commas MSS. 107 (B, C, D), 106*
50–64 *no punct MS. 134*
50 Nation's] Nations *MS. 107 (C_1), MS. 134* Nation's *MS. 107 (D)* hope, *rev in pencil from* hope *MS. 106* hope *MS. 107 (C_1, D)*
51 startled] startled, *MS. 107 (C)* Oft, *rev from* Oft *MS. 137*
52 interpretings,] Interpretings *MS. 107 (C)* interpretings *MS. 107 (D)*
53 simply-meek *rev to* Simply-meek *MS. 107 (D), 106* Simply-meek *MS. 135* springs] Springs *MSS. 107 (C, D), 106*
55 War,] war, *MS. 107 (C), MS. 1835/36–, 1839* War *MS. 107 (D)*
56 Ocean] Ocean,— *rev to* Ocean!— *MS. 107 (B)* ocean— *MSS. 107 (C, D), 106* ocean *MS. 1835/36–, 1839*
57 sail] Sail *MSS. 107 (C, D), 135* unfurled; *rev from* unfurl'd; *MS. 137*

unfurled;— *MS. 107 (B)* unfurl'd; *MSS. 107 (C), 106* unfurl'd *MS. 107 (D)*

58 Dancers *rev in pencil from* dancers *MS. 106* dancers *MS. 1835/36–, 1839* hall] Hall *MSS. 106, 134, 135*

59 Partners] partners *MS. 107 (D), MS. 1835/36–, 1839*

60 Fetched *rev from* Fetch'd *MS. 137* Fetch'd *MS. 107 (D)* world!] world *1840–1843, 1846, 1849* world. *1845, 1850*

61 *no apos MS. 135* said,] said *MSS. 107 (C, D)* dispense,] dispense *MSS. 107 (D), 135*

62 Emboldened *rev from* Embolden'd *MS. 137* Embolden'd *MSS. 107 (C, D)* sense;] sense, *MSS. 107 (D), 106*

63 lived] livd *alt* liv'd*MS. 107 (B)* *no comma MSS. 107 (B, C, D), 106*

64 *no comma MSS. 107 (B, C), 106*

66 *no punct MS. 107 (B)*

67 Insight! Yet] Insight!—yet *MSS. 107 (C, D), 106* Insight yet *MS. 134* Insight! yet *MS. 135* insight! Yet *MS. 1835/36–, 1839*

68–78 *no punct MS. 134*

68 mystery *rev to* Mystery *MS. 107 (C)* Mystery *MS. 107 (D)* bare,] bare *MS. 107 (D)*

69 shews *MSS. 107 (C, D), 106, 135* face,] face *MS. 107 (D)* face; *in pencil MS. 1836/45*

70 While] While, *MS. 135* Isthmus] isthmus *MS. 1835/36–, 1839*

71 councils] Councils *MSS. 107 (D), 106, 134* worlds] worlds, *MSS. 107 (C), 135, 1836–, 1839* stands,] stands *MSS. 107 (D), 135*

72 Spirits! *rev from* spirits! *MS. 137* Spirits, *MSS. 107 (C), 106* grace. *rev in pencil from* grace *MS. 106*

73 *no comma MSS. 107 (B, C), 106* Brutes *rev from* brutes *MS. 107 (D)* brutes *MSS. 107 (B, C), MS. 1835/36–, 1839*

74 *no comma MSS. 107 (B, D)*

75 fixed *rev from MS. 137* fix'd fix'd *MSS. 107 (C, D)*

76 Natures] Natures *rev from* natures *MS. 107 (D)* natures *MS. 106, MS. 1835/36–, 1839* *no comma MSS. 107 (B)*

77 humbler,] humbler *MSS. 107 (C, D), 106* guides,] guides *MSS. 107 (B, D), 106, 135* Guides *MS. 107 (C)*

78 Reason *rev from* Reason, *MS. 135* reason *MS. 107 (B), MS. 1835/36–, 1839* fail.] fail *MS. 107 (B)*

Gold and Silver Fishes, in a Vase

title Gold and Silver Fishes in a Vase. *BL MS. 1* GOLD AND SILVER FISHES IN A VASE. *1836–*

1 Lark] lark *MSS. 107, 106, BL MS. 1, WW and MW to EQ, 1836–, 1839* Lark! *MS. 113, Dora W to EQ*

2 Heaven's] heaven's *MS. 113, Dora W to EQ, 1836–, 1839* Heaven's *rev to* heaven's *BL MS. 1*

3 roving] roaving *WW and MW to EQ* Bee] bee *MSS. 107, 106, 113, Dora W to EQ, BL MS. 1, WW and MW to EQ, 1836–, 1839*

4 Her] Her *MS. 113, Dora W to EQ* flight] flight; *MS. 106* wings;] wings, *MSS. 107, 106, WW and MW to EQ*

5 Ye] ye *MS. 113, Dora W to EQ, Monkhouse MS. (copy)*

7–8 *quots lacking MSS. 107, 113, Dora W to EQ, BL MS. 1, WW and MW to EQ, 1836–; quots added in pencil MS. 106, added in ink BL MS. 1*

7 content] content, *MS. 113, Dora W to EQ, WW and MW to EQ, BL MS. 1, 1836–*

8 Though] Tho' *MS. 113, Dora W to EQ, Monkhouse MS. (copy)* joy.] joy *MS. 107, Dora W to EQ* joy! *MS. 135*

10 known,] known; *MS. 113, Dora W to EQ, Monkhouse MS. (copy)*

11 flash] flash, *MS. 106*

13 While,] While *MSS. 107, 106, 113, WW and MW to EQ, Monkhouse MS. (copy)* about,] about *MSS. 107, 106, 113, WW and MW to EQ*

14 Elves!] Elves, *MSS. 107, 106, WW and MW to EQ* Elves *MS. 113, Dora W to EQ, Monkhouse MS. (copy)*

15 weave—] weave,— *MS. 113* without,] without *MS. 113, WW and MW to EQ*

16 yourselves.] yourselves! *MS. 113, Dora W to EQ, Monkhouse MS. (copy)*

18 Cell;] Cell, *MSS. 107, 106, WW and MW to EQ* cell *MS. 113, Dora W to MJJ* Cell *Dora W to EQ, Monkhouse MS. (copy)* cell; *MS. 1835/36–, 1839*

19 Fear] fear *MS. 113, Dora W to MJJ, Dora W to EQ* Guest, *rev from* guest, *MS. 135* guest *MSS. 107, 113, Dora W to EQ, Dora W to MJJ, WW and MW to EQ* guest, *MS. 106, Monkhouse MS. (copy), MS. 1835/36–, 1839*

20 Humours *rev from* humours *MS. 135* humours *MS. 107, Monkhouse MS. (copy), WW and MW to EQ, 1836YR* humors *MS. 113, Dora W to EQ,*

Dora W to MJJ dwell;] dwell, *MS. 106* dwell *Dora W to MJJ*

21 *no comma MSS. 107, 113, 135, Dora W to EQ, Dora W to MJJ, Monkhouse MS. (copy), WW and MW to EQ*

22 sea,] sea *MS. 107, Dora W to MJJ, Monkhouse MS. (copy), WW and MW to EQ* sea. *Dora W to EQ*

24 loan] loan, *Dora W to EQ* *no period MS. 107*

25 beautiful! *rev by erasure to* beautiful, *MS. 107* beautiful, *MS. 106* beautiful— *Monkhouse MS. (copy)* beautiful!— *1836–, 1839* Yet] yet *WW and MW to EQ, MS. 135* why] why, *MS. 107, WW and MW to EQ*

26 *no hyphen MS. 113, Dora W to EQ* change,] change! *MSS. 107, 106, WW and MW to EQ*

27 Renewed—] Renewed,— *MS. 106* incessantly—] incessantly *MSS. 107, 106, 113, Dora W to EQ, Monkhouse MS. (copy), WW and MW to EQ* incessantly— *rev from* incessantly, *MS. 137*

28 range.] range: *MS. 106* range; *Dora W to EQ, Monkhouse MS. (copy)*

29 Is] —Is *MSS. 106, 135* ye] ye, *MSS. 107, 106, WW and MW to EQ*

30 glide;] glide, *MS. 113, Dora W to EQ, WW and MW to EQ, Monkhouse MS. (copy)*

31 sometimes,] sometimes *Dora W to EQ* your] y[r] *MS. 113* will,] will *MS. 113, Dora W to EQ, Monkhouse MS. (copy)*

32 dwarfed] dwarf'd *MS. 107, WW and MW to EQ*

33 Fays—] Fays, *MS. 113, Dora W to EQ, MS. 1835/36–, 1839* size—] size *MSS. 107, 106, WW and MW to EQ* size, *MS. 113* size; *Dora W to EQ, Monkhouse MS. (copy)* size! *MS. 1835/36–, 1839*

34 now,] now *MS. 107, WW and MW to EQ* dim, *rev in pencil from* dim *MS. 106* dim *MS. 107, WW and MW to EQ*

35 Eyes *rev from* eyes *MS. 137* eyes, *MS. 107, MS. 1835/36–, 1839* eyes *MSS. 106, 135, WW and MW to EQ*

36 Cherubim, *rev from* cherubim, *MS. 137* cherubim, *MSS. 107, 106, 135* Cherubim *MS. 113, Dora W to EQ, Monkhouse MS. (copy)*

37 glare:] glare; *MSS. 113, 135, Dora W to EQ, Monkhouse MS. (copy)* glare;— *1836–*

38 forms] Forms *MS. 135* *no comma MSS. 107, 113, WW and MW to EQ*

39 Whate'er] What e'er *MS. 107* are,] are *MSS. 107, 113, WW and MW to EQ* are— *MS. 1835/36–*

40 *no punct MS. 113*

41 be,] be *MS. 135, Dora W to EQ* pure;] pure, *WW and MW to EQ*

43 kinds *rev from* Kinds *MS. 135* kinds *rev to* Kinds *WW and MW to EQ*

44 Through] Thro' *Dora W to EQ, Monkhouse MS. (copy)* tyranny] Tyranny *MS. 107, WW and MW to EQ* sense. *rev from* sense; *MS. 135* sense: *Dora W to EQ, Monkhouse MS. (copy)*

45 Ah!] Ah *WW and MW to EQ* colours] colors *MS. 135, Dora W to EQ*

46 Ye *rev from* ye *MS. 135, WW and MW to EQ* ye *Dora W to EQ, Monkhouse MS. (copy)* Heaven] heaven *MS. 1835/36–, 1839* allied,] allied *MSS. 107, 106, Dora W to EQ, WW and MW to EQ* allied,— *Monkhouse MS. (copy)*

47 When,] When *MSS. 107, 106, Dora W to EQ, WW and MW to EQ* Forms] forms *Dora W to EQ, Monkhouse MS. (copy)* light,] light *MSS. 107, 106, WW and MW to EQ*

48 *no punct Dora W to EQ, no comma Monkhouse MS. (copy)*

49 *no hyphen MS. 113, Dora W to EQ* e're] ere *MS. 113* beguiled] beguiled, *MS. 106*

50 Day-thoughts *ital*] Day-thoughts *MS. 113, Monkhouse MS. (copy)* *no ital MSS. 107, 106, MS. 1835/36–, 1839; no ital or hypen Dora W to EQ* repose;] repose, *MSS. 107, 106, WW and MW to EQ* repose *MS. 113*

51 mild] mild, *MSS. 107, 106, Dora W to EQ, WW and MW to EQ, 1836–*

52 gift,] gift— *Dora W to EQ, Monkhouse MS. (copy)* close;] close, *MSS. 107, 106, WW and MW to EQ* close— *MS. 1835/36–, 1839*

53 Captives!] Captives, *MSS. 107, 106, Dora W to EQ, Monkhouse MS. (copy), WW and MW to EQ* Captives *MS. 113* praise;] praise, *MS. 113, WW and MW to EQ* praise. *Dora W to EQ*

56 Delight] Delight, *MS. 113* love. *rev by eras from* love! *MS. 107* love! *MS. 106, WW and MW to EQ*

To a Friend

2, 4 *parens added in pencil and ink MS. 114*

4 spots] spots, *MS. 106* thing *rev from* thing: *MS. 114*

8 Well *rev in pencil to* Well, *MS. 114*

Well, *MS. 106*

9 opaque *rev in pencil to* opaque, *MS. 114*

10 make *rev in pencil to* make, *MS. 114* make, *MS. 106*

13 Hailstones,] Hailstones *MS. 106* shower: *rev in pencil from* shower. *MS. 106*

14 There] <u>There</u> *MS. 106* swims, but . . . obscured! *rev to* swims (but . . . obscured!) *MS. 114; MS. 106 as rev MS. 114* golden *no ital MS. 106*

16 unsurpass'd *rev in pencil to* unsurpass'd; *MS. 114* unsurpass'd; *MS. 106*

20 eyes. *rev in pencil to* eyes! *MS. 114* eyes! *MS. 106*

21 perhaps, . . . languished—] perhaps; . . . languished *MS. 106*

22 And] And, *MS. 106*

23 place,] place *MS. 106*

24 disgrace?] disgrace; *rev in pencil to* disgrace? *MS. 114* disgrace *MS. 106*

25 But, . . . then,] But . . . then *MS. 106*

26 gain. *rev in pencil to* gain! *MS. 114*

33 on] on, *MS. 106*

34 independence . . . Deep! *rev from* independance . . . Deep. *MS. 114*

35 sail, *rev in pencil to* sail; *MS. 114* Sail, *MS. 106*

36 Dive] Dive, *MS. 106*

39 width *rev in pencil to* width, *MS. 114*

40 thee *rev in pencil to* thee! *MS. 114* thee! *MS. 106*

43 Power! *rev from* Power, *MS. 114*

47 *no commas MS. 135 (*A_2*)*

49 Oracles, *rev from* oracles, *MS. 114* wingèd Auguries,] winged Auguries *MSS. 106, 135 (*A_2*)*

50 ancient] antient *MS. 106* Wise.] Wise *MS. 135 (*A_2*)*

51 ways, *rev in pencil to* ways; *MS. 114* ways; *MS. 106* ways *MS. 135 (*A_2*)*

52 *no comma MS. 135 (*A_2*)*

53 blessèd] blessed *MS. 106* spirits] Spirits *MS. 106* *no punct MS. 135 (*A_2*)*

56 fade *rev in pencil to* fade, *MS. 114*

57 palm *rev in pencil to* palm, *MS. 114* Palm *MS. 135 (*A_2*)*

58 altar] Altar *MS. 135 (*A_2*)* calm; *rev to* Calm; *MS. 106* *no punct MS. 135 (*A_2*)*

60 Press'd, . . . love,] Pressed, . . . love *MSS. 106, 135 (*A_2*)*

61 bosoms.— *from* bosoms: *MS. 114*

62 climbing,] climbing *MS. 135 (*A_2*)*

67 angels] Angels *MS. 106*

68 Patriarch; . . . flight *rev in pencil to* Patriarch, . . . flight; *MS. 114*

70 Messengers] Messengers, *MS. 106*

78 *no commas MSS. 114 (*2^v*P), 106* providence] Providence *MSS. 114 (*2^v*P), 106*

80 dust! *rev from* dust; *MS. 114*

83 flow] flow, *MS. 114 (*2^v*P)* caprice; *rev in pencil from* caprice, *MS. 106*

84 harsh Tyranny] harsh tyranny *MSS. 114 (*2^v*P)* <u>harsh tyranny</u> *MS. 106*

86 qualified *underscored in pencil MS. 106*

88 respect *rev in pencil to* respect, *MS. 114*

91 Slave] Slave, *MS. 106*

92 forlorn: *rev in pencil to* forlorn; *MS. 114* forlorn! *MS. 106*

95 Alas!] —Alas, *alt in pencil* Alas, *MS. 106* Isles *rev in pencil to* Isles, *MS. 114* Isles, *MS. 106*

96 day] Day *MS. 106*

98 (As . . . mounts) . . . fanned] As . . . mounts, . . . fann'd *MS. 106*

99 land . . . seats] Land . . . Seats *MS. 106*

100 Council] Council, *MS. 114 (*3^r*P5)* council *MS. 106* green Vales—] green vales *MS. 114 (*3^r*P5)* green <u>vales</u>— *with dash added MS. 106*

101 there,] there *MSS. 114 (*3^r*P5), 106*

103 While, musing,] While musing *MS. 106*

106 Companions, *rev from* companions, *MS. 114*

107 luxuries *rev in pencil to* luxuries, *MS. 114* luxuries, *MS. 106* luxuries *MS. 135 (*A_3*)*

108 them (like . . . spell *rev from* them, like. . . spell, *MS. 114*

109 Cell *rev in pencil to* Cell, *MS. 114* Cell, *MS. 106*

110–112 *no commas MS. 135 (*A_3*)*

111 bound.] bound *MS. 135 (*A_3*)*

112 marr'd, *rev from* marred, *MS. 114* marr'd; *MS. 106*

113 jarr'd;] jarr'd: *MS. 106* jarred *MS. 135 (*A_3*)*

114–118 *no punct MS. 135 (*A_3*)*

119 beams. *rev in pencil to* beams! *MS. 114* beams! *MS. 106*

120 fared *rev in pencil to* fared, *MS. 114* fared, *MS. 106*

121 *no punct MS. 135 (*A_3*)*

127 mistress . . . land] Mistress . . . Land *MS. 106*

130 through] thro' *MS. 106*

132 worst,] worst *MS. 106*

133 track, *rev in pencil to* track; *MS. 114*

134 back, *rev in pencil to* back; *MS. 114* back; *MS. 106*

137 same,— *rev in pencil to* same, *MS. 114* same, *MS. 106*
138 All] —All *MS. 106* ranks— *rev in pencil to* ranks!— *MS. 114* ranks!— *rev to* Ranks!— *MS. 106* name *rev in pencil to* name, *MS. 114* name, *MS. 106*
141 shew *rev in pencil to* show *MS. 114* Show *MS. 106*
144 Philomel] philomel *MS. 107* *(A_2)* *no commas MS. 107* *(A_2)*
147 meal, *rev in pencil to* meal,— *MS. 114*
148 business *rev in pencil to* business, *MS. 114*
151 grandeur] grandeur, *MS. 106*
153 stealth] stealth, *MS. 106*
155 overcome] overcome, *MS. 106*
156 wearisome] wearisome, *MS. 106*
159 lyre] lyre, *MS. 106*
160 distress *rev from* distress, *MS. 106*
162 *dash del MS. 106*
165 farm] Farm *MS. 106*
167 ear,] ear— *MS. 106*
172 Ruler,] Ruler *MS. 106*
173 scene,] scene *MS. 106*
178 Man and Muse] man and muse *MS. 114 (5^rP1)* wrong *rev in pencil to* wrong, *MS. 114* wrong, *MS. 114 (5^rP1)* wrong; *MS. 106*
179 Cam's] Cams *MS. 114 (5^r)*
180 high,] high—, *MS. 114 (5^rP1)* high— *MS. 106*
181 privacy. *rev in pencil to* privacy! *MS. 114* privacy! *MSS. 114 (5^rP1), 106*
183 Court, *rev from* court, *MS. 114*
184 wishes,] wishes; *MSS. 114 (5^rP1), 106*
185 true *rev in pencil to* true, *MS. 114 (5^rP1)* true, *MS. 106*
186 best *rev in pencil to* best, *MS. 114 (5^rP1)*
187 Muses, *rev from* muses, *MS. 114* Books, Fields, Liberty, *MS. 106* rest. *rev in pencil to* rest! *MS. 114* rest! *MS. 114 (5^rP1)* Rest! *MS. 106*
189 fame,] fame *MS. 114 (5^rP1)*
191 course;] course— *in pencil MS. 114 (5^r)* course, *MSS. 114 (5^rP2), 106* aspire;] aspire *in pencil MS. 114 (5^r)* aspire *MS. 114 (5^rP1–P2)* aspire, *MSS. 114 (5^r, in pencil), 106*
192 *no ital MS. 106*
194 Being's god-like] being's godlike *MS. 114 (5^rP1–P2)* mate.] mate! *MS. 106*
196 forfeit . . . vow;] forfeit, . . . vow *MS. 106*
197 what e'er] whate'er *MS. 106*
198 wingèd *rev in pencil from* winged *MS. 106* mind *rev in pencil to* mind; *MS. 114* mind; *MS. 106*
202 page. *rev in pencil from* page *MS. 114*

Liberty. (Sequel to the Above.)

headnote Friend . . . Gold . . . Silver Fishes] friend . . . gold . . . silver fishes *1850*
epigraph *quots lacking MS. 137* *first sentence* liberty . . . people . . . laws] Liberty . . . People . . . Laws *second sentence* private man, . . . master . . . laws . . . country . . . discourse.] Private Man . . . Master . . . Laws . . . Country . . . discourse *MS. 137*
1 Tokens *rev from* tokens *MS. 135*
3 *no comma MS. 135, 1836–, 1839*
4 thing;) *rev from* thing) *MS. 137* thing) *MS. 135*
6 need, *rev from* need *MS. 137*
7 Removed *rev from* —Removed *MS. 135*
8 Well;] Well— *1845–*
10 make,] make; *MS. 135*
13 *no ital MS. 137, ital added MS. 138*
16 unsurpast; *rev from* unsurpassed; *MS. 135*
21 They] —They *MS. 135*
22 gone] gone, *MSS. 137, 138*
23 lost,] lost *MSS. 135, 137, 138*
24 Creature *rev from* creature *MS. 135* creature *MS. 1835/36–, 1839* disgrace? *rev from* disgrace *MS. 135* disgrace *1850*
25 *para del MS. 135*
28 Lark] lark *MS. 1835/36–, 1839*
30 privilege! No *rev from* privilege, no *MS. 135* privilege!—No *1836–, 1839*
33 Whales] whales *MS. 1835/36–, 1839*
35 Nautilus] nautilus *MS. 1835/36–, 1839*
36 gale! *rev from* gale *MS. 135* gale! *rev from* gale. *MS. 137*
37 Eagle] eagle *MS. 1835/36–, 1839*
39 Ocean's *rev from* oceans, *MS. 137* ocean's *MS. 1835/36–, 1839*
41 *para added MS. 137*
42 pool, *rev to* pool *rev to* pool, *MS. 137*
43 Among . . . trees,] (Among . . . trees) *MS. 1835/36–, 1839*
44 caught— *rev from* caught, *rev from* caught *MS. 137* caught *MS. 135* caught, *MS. 1835/36* ease—] ease, *MSS. 135, 137, 138, MS. 1835/36–, 1839*
47 Cell] Cell *rev from* cell *MS. 137* cell *MS. 1835/36–, 1839*
49 bound. *rev to* bound! *MS. 135* bound. *rev from* bound, *MSS. 137, 138*
50 Their *rev from* Their *ital MS. 138* <u>Their</u> *MS. 135* Their *ital MS. 137*

marred] marr'd *MSS. 135, 137, 138*
51 jarred] jarr'd *MSS. 135, 137, 138*
52 dart,] dart *MS. 135* fear? *rev from* fear! *MS. 137* fear, *rev to* fear! *MS. 135*
53 stone,] stone *MS. 135*
54 the *rev from* tho *MS. 137* room,] room *MSS. 135, 137*
59 ours] our's *MS. 135*
60 Is] —Is *MS. 135* Bird] bird *MS. 1835/36–, 1839*
61 from] form *(printer's error) 1836YR* brow)—] brow) *MSS. 135, 137* brow) *rev from* brow), *MS. 138*
62 Fondling] fondling *MS. 1835/36–, 1839*
65 Mistress] mistress *MS. 1835/36–, 1839* land, *rev from* Land, *MS. 137*
66 would] w^{d} *MS. 135*
68 captive] Captive *MS. 135*
71 Beetle *rev from* beetle *MS. 135* beetle *MS. 1835/36–, 1839*
72 Snail *rev from* snail *MS. 135* snail *MS. 1835/36–, 1839* back:] back; *1836–, 1839*
73 Worm *rev from* worm *MS. 135* worm *MS. 1835/36–, 1839* would] w^{d} *MS. 135*
75 instinct;] instinct, *rev to* instinct! *MS. 135* Kinds] kinds *rev to* Kinds, *MS. 135* kinds *MS. 1835/36–, 1836YR, 1839*
76 Ranks] ranks *MS. 1835/36–, 1839* What *rev from* what *MS. 135* Sovereign] sovereign *MS. 1835/36*
81 *para rev from no para MS. 135*
85 meal— *rev from* meal, *MS. 135* Nature's *rev from* nature's *MS. 135*
86 Time, place, and business,] Time place and business— *MS. 135* command!] command!— *1836–, 1839*
88 prize, *rev from* prize *MS. 138*
89 grandeur, *rev to* grandeur *MSS. 137, 138* grandeur *MS. 135*
90 lost?] lost; *MS. 135*
91 life— *rev from* life *MS. 138* life *MSS. 135, 137* stealth,] stealth— *MS. 1835/36–, 1839*
92 health;] health, *MSS. 135, 137, 138*
94 noise,] noise *1836–, 1839*
95 Rome?] Rome?— *MS. 1835/36–, 1839*
96 Let *rev to* —Let *MS. 135*
97 lyre,] lyre *MS. 135*
98 verse *rev from* verse, *MS. 137* that] that, *MS. 1835/36–, 1839* Distress] distress *MS. 135*
99 garlands] garlands, *MS. 1835/36–, 1839* cheats *rev from* cheats, *MS. 135* happiness; *rev from* happiness, *MS. 137* happiness, *MS. 135*
100 *para del MS. 135*
102 chance sunbeam] chance-sunbeam *1836–, 1839*
103 Farm] farm *MS. 1835/36–*
104 Bandusia's] Blandusia's *MS. 1835/36–, 1839*
105 listening—] listening! *MSS. 135, 137, 138*
109 favour] favor *MS. 135*
110 World's] world's *MS. 1835/36–, 1839* honoured] honored *MS. 135*
113 Cowley,] Cowley *MS. 135*
116 Man *rev from* man *MS. 138* man *MSS. 135, 137* Muse] muse *MS. 135*
118 Towers] towers *MS. 1835/36–, 1839*
121 Servant *rev from* servant *MS. 137*
122 You] you *MS. 135, MS. 1835/36–, 1839*
123 *no ital 1845–*
125 Books, Fields, Liberty, and Rest] books, fields, liberty, and rest *MS. 1835/36–, 1839*
126 *para MS. 137, 1836–, 1839; para del MS. 138* they] they— *MS. 135*
128 *no ital MSS. 135, 137, 1845–; ital added MS. 138*
132 godlike mate] god-like-mate *MS. 135*
133 *no para MS. 137, para added MS. 138* Friend] Friend* *MSS. 135, 137*
134 Woman *rev from* woman *MS. 137* woman *MS. 1835/36–, 1839*
136 mind! *rev from* mind, *MS. 137* mind, *MS. 135*
138 thought,] thought *MS. 135*
139 unclosed,] unclosed *MS. 135*
140 page.*] page. *MSS. 135, 137* page*. *1836–, 1839*
note to l. 140, para one anticipation, *rev from* anticipation *MS. 138* anticipation *MSS. 135, 137* Individual *rev from* individual *MS. 137* Rev. Wm. Fletcher,] Revd Wm Fletcher *MS. 135* cholera,] Cholera *MS. 135* thirty-two or thirty-three years,] 32 or 33 years [of age *del*] *MS. 135* Shalapore *rev from* Shatapore *MSS. 135, 137*
para two enthusiasm] Enthusiasm *MS. 135* steadfast] stedfast *MS. 1836/45* maiden] Maiden *MS. 135* and, indeed,] and indeed *MS. 135* merits; *rev from* merits, *MS. 138* merits, *MSS. 135, 137* those] those, *MS. 135* powers] powers, *1836–, 1839* viz.] viz *MS. 135* author's]

Author's *MS. 135, 1836–, 1839*

Humanity. (Written in the Year 1829.)

headnote, l. 1 Rocking-stones,] rocking Stones *rev to* Rocking-Stones *MS. 135* *l. 3* found, . . . day,] found . . . day— *rev to* found . . . day *MS. 135*

2 Man] man *MS. 135, MS. 1835/36–, 1839*

3 Or] Or, *MS. 135* Judge's *rev from* "Judge's *MS. 135*

4 STONE OF POWER] Stone of Power *MS. 135*

5 Block,] Block *rev from* block" *MS. 135*

7 groves, *rev to* Groves, *MS. 135* groves *1836YR, 1839*

8 Druid-priest] Druid Priest *MS. 135*

9 Yet,] Yet *MS. 135*$_{1}$

10 offices!] offices; *MS. 135*$_{1}$

11 dwells,] dwells *MS. 135*$_{1}$

12 That,] That *MS. 135*$_{1}$ listen, *rev in ink over pencil from* listen *MS. 135*$_{1\text{-}2}$

13 heart,] heart *MS. 135*$_{1}$

14 wingèd *rev from* winged *MS. 138 (A)* winged *MS. 135*$_{1\text{-}2}$ Auguries,] Auguries *MS. 135*$_{1}$

15 Science *rev from* Sience *MS. 135* science *MS. 135*$_{1}$ wise.] Wise *MS. 135*$_{1}$

16 ways;] ways— *MS. 135*$_{1}$

17 praise— *rev in pencil from* praise *MS. 135*$_{2}$ praise *MS. 135*$_{1}$

18 hear;] hear *MS. 135*$_{1}$

19 Man *rev from* man *MS. 135*$_{2}$ man *MS. 1835/36–, 1839*

21 things!] things: *rev from* things. *MS. 135*$_{2}$ things *MS. 135*$_{1}$

22 Christian] christian *1836–, 1839* portrayed,] portrayed *MS. 135*$_{1}$

23 That, . . . fade,] That . . . fade *MS. 135*$_{1}$

24 Lily . . . Palm] lily . . . palm *1836–, 1839*

25 Altar] altar *1836–, 1839* calm;] calm *MS. 135*$_{1}$

26 Lamb . . . Dove] lamb . . . dove *1836–, 1839*

27 love] Love *MS. 135*$_{2}$

28 bosoms!—] bosoms.— *MS. 135*$_{1}$

29 Affections,] Affections *rev to* affections *MS. 135* affections, *MS. 135*$_{1}$ affections *MS. 1835/36–, 1839*

30 life,] life *MS. 135*$_{1}$

32 High; *rev from* High— *MS. 135*

33 charity;*] charity; *rev to* charity: *MS. 135* charity*; *1836YR* charity; *1836–, 1839*

note to l. 33 author] Author *MS. 135* works.] Works *MS. 135*

35–36 *in pencil, but no commas and* pendent] pendant *MS. 106*

35 Field] field *MS. 1835/36–, 1839* sight;] sight *1845, 1850*

36 All, *rev from* All *MS. 135*

37 Messengers] messengers *MS. 1835/36–, 1839*

38–39 *commas in pencil MS. 135*

42 *para added in revision MS. 135* World] world *MSS. 135, 137, 138 (A), MS. 1835/36–, 1839* Verse *rev from* verse *MS. 135* verse *MS. 1835/36–, 1839*

45 Vision,—] Vision— *rev to* Vision, *MS. 135* faith *rev from* Faith *MS. 135* Providence;] Providence, *MS. 135*

47 *semicolon added in revision MS. 135*

48 And, . . . decrees,] And . . . decrees *MS. 135*

53 *semicolon in pencil MS. 135* Minds *rev from* minds *MS. 135* minds *MS. 1835/36–, 1839*

55 *Comma in pencil MS. 135*

56 Pride] pride *MS. 135*

59 <u>harsh tyranny</u> *with instruction* boldface *in pencil MS. 135* tyranny *rev to* Tyranny *MS. 138 (A)* Tyranny *MS. 137*

61 *comma in pencil MS. 135* *no ital MS. 1835/36–, 1839* oppression, *rev from* Oppression, *MS. 138 (A)* Oppression, *MS. 137*

62 *semicolon in ink over pencil MS. 135*

63 respect] respect, *MS. 1836/45*

64 *comma in pencil* effect. *written over* eff[?][?]t. *MS. 135*

67 *semicolon in pencil MS. 135*

68 Or,] Or *MS. 135*

69 *exclam pt in ink over pencil MS. 135* gratitude!] gratitude? *MS. 138 (A)*

70 Alas *rev in pencil from* Alas, . . . Isles, *rev in pencil from* Isles *MS. 135*

71 *punct in pencil MS. 135*

72 land] Land *MS. 135, MS. 137, MS. 138 (A, B)* *comma in pencil MS. 135*

73 *semicolon in pencil MS. 135*

74 seats *rev to* Seats *MS. 135*

75 vales,] vales *MS. 138 (A)* vales— *dash in pencil MS. 135* Retreats *rev from* retreats *MS. 135* retreats *MS. 138 (A), MS. 1835/36–, 1839*

76 Shades . . . Heroes, *rev from* shades . . . heroes *MS. 135* Shades . . . heroes, *MS. 1835/36* shades . . . heroes, *1836–, 1839* *comma in pencil MS. 135*

79 Stone-walls *rev in pencil from* Stone walls *MS. 135* Stone walls *MSS. 137, 138 (A)* Prisoner . . . Slave *rev in*

ink over pencil from prisoner . . . slave *MS. 135* prisoner . . . slave *MS. 1835/36–, 1839* Slave.] Slave, *MS. 135*

80 Man . . . Man? *rev in ink over pencil from* man . . . man? *MS. 135* man . . . man? *MS. 1835/36–, 1839*

81 Will] will *MS. 1835/36–, 1839*

84 "Slaves . . . England"—] "Slaves . . . England—" *hyphen in pencil MS. 135* 'Slaves . . . England'— *1836–, 1839* boast!] boast *with alt* boast! *MS. 135* boast *1836–, 1836YR, 1839*

85 *comma in pencil MS. 135*

86 *period in pencil, rev to comma in pencil MS. 135*

87 *no comma MS. 135*

89 schools,] Schools, *with comma in pencil MS. 135*

90–91 "the . . . / Of Nations,"] "the . . . / Of Nations," *comma in pencil and quots del in pencil MS. 135* 'the . . . / Of Nations,' *1836–, 1839* 'the . . . / Of Nations,' *rev to* 'the . . . / Of Nation's,' *rev to* 'the . . . / Of Nations,' *MS. 1836/45* *end punct in pencil MS. 135*

92 *semicolon in ink over pencil MS. 135*

94 *comma in ink over pencil MS. 135*

95 *period in ink over pencil MS. 135*

96 *first comma in pencil; end punct in ink over pencil MS. 135*

99 human kind] human-kind *MS. 135* *end punct in ink over pencil MS. 135*

102 There] —There *MS. 135* grove,] grove *Mary Smith Album, WW to Sarah Coles Stevenson, 1836YR, 1839*

103 *semicolon in ink over pencil MS. 135*

105 flower] Flower *WW to Sarah Coles Stevenson* possesses *rev from* possess *MS. 135*

106 fugitive,] fugitive *MS. 135*

107 Infinite] infinite *WW to Sarah Coles Stevenson* could *rev from* c^d *MS. 135*

Why art thou silent! Is thy love a plant, Text of 1835

1–14 *no punct MS. 107 (B)*

1 silent!] silent, *MS. 106* silent! *rev to* silent? *MS. 135* silent? *Cornell MS. 8, 1836YR, 1838, 1839* Is] is *MS. 106 Dora W to ?* love] Love *Cornell MS. 8, Dora W to ?*

4 there *rev from* their *MS. 107 (B)*

5 thee] Thee *Cornell MS. 8* vigilant] vigilant, *MS. 106, Dora W to ?, Cornell MS. 8* vigilant— *1845–*

6 (As . . . been) *rev from* As . . . been *MS. 135* As . . . been, *MS. 106, Dora W to ?, Cornell MS. 8* (As . . . been) *rev from* (As . . . been), *MS. 137* care,] care; *MS. 106*

7 mind's *rev to* Mind's *MS. 135* minds *Cornell MS. 8* mendicant] Mendicant *Cornell MS. 8*

8 could] c^d *MS. 107 (B)*

9 Speak,] Speak— *1836–, 1838, 1839* tho' *MS. 107 (B), Dora W to ?, Cornell MS. 8*

10 pleasures, . . . mine,] pleasures— . . . mine— *MS. 106* pleasures . . . mine, *Dora W to ?, Cornell MS. 8*

11 desolate, *rev from* desolate *rev from* desolate, *MS. 135* desolate *Cornell MS. 8* cold] cold, *1838*

12 snow] snow, *Dora W to ?, Cornell MS. 8*

13 eglantine;] eglantine, *MSS. 106, 135, 137* Eglantine *MS. 107 (B)* Eglantine, *Dora W to ?, Cornell MS. 8* eglantine; *rev from* eglantine, *MS. 138* eglantine— *1836–, 1838, 1839*

14 Speak,] Speak *MS. 106, Cornell MS. 8* Speak— *Dora W to ?* know!] know. *MS. 106*

Inscription Intended for a Stone in the Grounds of Rydal Mount, Text of MS. 120 (B)

1 Vale] Vale *rev from* vale *MS. 107 (A)* tree *MS. 120 (A)*

2 spared:] spared *MSS. 120 (A), 107 (A)* *no apos MS. 107 (A)*

3 builder . . . STONE—] Builder . . . stone *MS. 120 (A)*

5 —and] and *MSS. 120 (A), 107 (A)* *no commas MS. 107 (A)*

6 good and tender-hearted] good and tenderhearted *rev to* Good and Tenderhearted *MS. 107 (A)*

7 *no punct MSS. 120 (A), 107 (A)*

Inscription Intended for a Stone in the Grounds of Rydal Mount, Text of 1835

1 Vales] Vales, *WW to JK* vales *Rydal Mount Stone, 1836–, 1836YR, 1839*

3 Builder's] builder's *Rydal Mount Stone, 1836–, 1836YR, 1839*

5 Bard:] Bard; *WW to JK*

6 rest,—] rest; *Rydal Mount Stone, 1836–, 1836YR, 1839*

7 tender-hearted *rev from* Tender-hearted *MS. 137*

8 sigh] sigh, *WW to JK* him,] him *MSS. 106, 134, WW to JK*

9 one] One *WW to JK* departed.] departed. *rev from* Departed. *MS. 137* Departed. *MSS. 106, 114, 134, WW to JK* departed *MS. 134*

Elegiac Musings in the Grounds of Coleorton Hall, the Seat of the Late Sir George Beaumont, Bart.

title MUSINGS] MUSINGS. *1850*

headnote, l. 1 grounds] Grounds *MSS. 107, 106* Church,] Church *MSS. 106, 135* monument,] Monument, *MSS. 107, 106, 135* *l. 2* which,] which *MS. 107* deceased] Deceased *MSS. 107, 106, 135* *l. 3* name *rev to* Name *MS. 135* words:—] words— *MSS. 107, 106* words. *MS. 135* words: *1839* servant,] Servant *MSS. 107, 106* Lord!] Lord. *MSS. 107, 107, 135*

1 rhyme] rime *rev to* rhime *Lilly MS. 2* rhyme, *MS. 107*

2 tomb] tomb, *Lilly MS. 2, MSS. 107, 106* Tomb *MS. 120* Time,] time *MS. 107* time; *MS. 120*

3 *no comma MS. 135*

4 man] Man *Lilly MS. 2, MSS. 107, 106, 135* dies:] dies. *Lilly MS. 2, MSS. 107, 106* dies *1850*

5 dreaded] dreaded, *MS. 107* dreaded; *rev to* dreaded, *MS. 106* forbade,] forbade *MS. 107* forbad *Lilly MS. 2*

6 spirit] Spirit *Lilly MS. 2, MSS. 107, 106, 135* meek] meek, *MSS. 107, 106, 120* clad.] clad; *MSS. 107, 106* clad *MS. 120*

7 here *ital*] here, *rev to* here *MS. 106* here *Lilly MS. 2, MS. 107* here, *ital rev to* here *ital MS. 137* least,] least *MS. 120* though few] tho' Few *MSS. 107, 106, 135* (though few *MS. 120* numbered] number'd *MS. 107*

8 shunned] shunn'd *MS. 107* praise,] praise *Lilly MS. 2, MS. 107* praise) *MS. 120*

9 *no comma Lilly MS. 2, MS. 107*

10 would] w[d] *MS. 135* play,] play *MSS. 107, 135* play. *Lilly MS. 2*

12 reserve;] reserve, *MSS. 107, 106* reserve, *rev to* reserve: *Lilly MS. 2*

13 sense— *rev from* Sense— *MS. 137* sense *Lilly MS. 2* sense, *MSS. 107, 106, MS. 1835/36–, 1836YR, 1839* Sense— *rev from* sense *MS. 135* bland *rev from miscopied* blind *MS. 106* life] life, *1836–, 1836YR, 1839*

14 checked] check'd *MS. 107, MS. 120* warmed] warm'd *Lilly MS. 2, MS. 120* strife;] strife, *Lilly MS. 2, MSS. 107, 106, 120*

15 accomplishments,] accomplishments *MSS. 107, 106, 120* powers,] Powers *Lilly MS. 2* powers *MSS. 106, 120*

16 record] record, *Lilly MS. 2* sylvan *rev from* silvan *MS. 106* [?]lvan *MS. 120* bowers.] bowers *MSS. 107, 106*

17 —Oh,] Oh *MS. 107* —Oh *MS. 135* Oh, *MS. 1835/36–, 1836YR, 1839* vanished] vanish'd *MS. 107* blast] blast, *MS. 106*

18 passed; *rev from* pass'd; *MS. 137* passed, *Lilly MS. 2* pass'd; *MS. 107* pass'd, *MS. 106* pass'd! *MS. 120* pass'd *rev from* past— *MS. 135* passed;— *1836–, 1839*

19 sea,] sea *MS. 107* earth, air, sea, and sky,] earth air sea and sky *Lilly MS. 2, so MS. 135 but* sky,

20 *no comma Lilly MS. 2, MSS. 107, 106, 135*

21 Painter's] painters *Lilly MS. 2* painter's *MSS. 107, 106, MS. 1835/36–* *no comma Lilly MS. 2, MS. 135*

22 Poet's] poets *Lilly MS. 2* poet's *MSS. 107, 106, MS. 1835/36–* Poets *MS. 135* heart;] heart;— *Lilly MS. 2* and,] and *MSS. 107, 106*

23 Portrayed] Pourtrayd *Lilly MS. 2* Pourtray'd *MS. 107* Pourtrayed *MSS. 106, 135* pencil, *rev from* pencil— *MS. 137* pencil *Lilly MS. 2* pencil— *rev from* pencil, *MS. 135*

24 recognitions *rev from* recognitions, *MS. 137* recognitions, *Lilly MS. 2, MSS. 107, 106, 120*

25 Flowed] Flow'd *MS. 107* divine— *rev from* divine,— *MS. 137* divine; *Lilly MS. 2, MS. 1835/36* divine.— *MS. 106* divine. *MS. 120* divine;— *1836–, 1839*

26 severed] sever'd *MS. 107* severed, *1836–, 1839* abruptly] abruptly, *1836–, 1839*

27 seasons] Seasons *MS. 135* rights— *rev from* rights; *MS. 137* rights, *Lilly MS. 2* rights!— *MS. 107* rights— *rev from* rights *MS. 135* rights; *MS. 120* rights;— *1836–, 1839*

28 Rapt] Rapt, *Lilly MS. 2* age,] Age, *MS. 106* Age *MS. 135* age *MS. 120*

29 soul-felt] soulfelt *Lilly MS. 2* music,] music *Lilly MS. 2, MSS. 107, 106, 120* page,] page *Lilly MS. 2, MSS. 106, 135, 1836–, 1839*

30 loved *rev from* I loved *miscopied MS. 106*

31 honoured] honourd *Lilly MS. 2* honor'd *MS. 107* honored *MS. 135*

head,] head *rev in pencil to* head— *MS. 107* head *MS. 106* head; *1836–, 1839*

32 Friends *rev from* friends *MS. 135* mien,] mien *Lilly MS. 2, MSS. 107, 106, 120, 135*

33 Shakspeare's] Shakespear's *MS. 120* scene— *rev from* scene *MSS. 106, 135* scene *Lilly MS. 2, MS. 107* scene— *rev from* scene, *MS. 137* scene, *MS. 120* scene;— *1836–, 1839*

34 not!—The] not.—the *Lilly MS. 2* mandate] Mandate *MSS. 107, 106, 135* obeyed] obey'd *MS. 106*

35 "Let *rev from* let *MS. 135* "let *Lilly MS. 2, MSS. 107, 106* laid;" *rev from* laid"; *MS. 135* laid", *Lilly MS. 2* laid *MS. 107* laid; *MS. 106*

36 *no comma Lilly MS. 2, MSS. 107, 106*

37 Marble,] marble *Lilly MS. 2* Marble *MSS. 107, 106* marble, *1836–, 1839* dust;] dust, *Lilly MS. 2, MS. 106* dust *MS. 107*

40 abashed] abash'd, *MS. 107* abashed, *MS. 106* Name *rev from* name *MS. 135* Rose *rev from* rose *MS. 135* rose *MSS. 107, 106, MS. 1835/36–, 1839*

41 *no quots Lilly MS. 2; no quots, no punct MSS. 107, 106*

42 Daisy *rev from* daisy *MS. 135* daisy *MSS. 107, 106, MS. 1835/36–, 1839*

43 which] w^h *MS. 135* up.] up *MS. 106*

44 Groves,] Groves *MS. 107* groves, *MS. 1835/36–*

45 Past,] past, *MS. 107* past *MS. 106* Past, *rev to* Past *MS. 135* sigh,] sigh *MSS. 107, 106*

47 Thee! *rev from* Thee. *MS. 137* Thee. *MSS. 107, 106, 135*

49 Recall] Recal *MSS. 107, 106, 135, 1836–* Tomb,] tomb, *MS. 107* tomb *MS. 106*

50 ivy,] ivy *1836–* cheerful] chearful *MSS. 107, 106* earth,] earth *MSS. 107, 106*

51 lettered] letter'd *MS. 107* stone;] Stone; *MSS. 107, 135* Stone, *MS. 106* forth,] forth *MSS. 107, 106*

52 *no commas MSS. 107, 106*

53 wound; *rev from* wound, *MS. 137* wound, *MS. 135*

54 fulfil,] fulfil *MS. 107* fulfil— *MS. 135*

55 skill,] skill *MSS. 107, 106*

56 concealed] conceal'd *MS. 107* Thou] thou *MS. 135* known;] known. *MSS. 107, 106*

57 He *ital* . . . He *ital*] He . . . He *MS. 107* He . . . He *both words double-underscored MS. 106* He *ital* . . . He *no ital MS. 1835/36–* judge,] judge *MS. 135* alone,] alone— *MS. 107* alone, *ital 1836YR*

Chatsworth! thy stately mansion, and the pride

1 Chatsworth!] Chatsworth *MS. 107 (A)* Chatsworth, *MS. 107 (B)* mansion,] Mansion *MSS. 107 (A), MS. 106*

2 domain,] Domain *MSS. 107, 106* contrast] Contrast *MS. 107 (A)*

3 House *MS. 107 (A)* rent *rev to* Rent *MS. 106*

4 Peak; *rev from* peak; *MS. 137* Peak *MS. 107 (B)* Peak, *MS. 120* new-born] newborn *MS. 107 (A)* glide] glide, *MS. 107 (B)*

5 fields] fieds *MS. 106* fields *rev from* fields, *MS. 137* Occupants *rev from* occupants *MS. 137* occupants *MSS. 107 (A), 120, 1836–, 1838*

6 banishment,] banishment; *WW to DW, MS. 107 (A)* banishment *MSS. 107 (B), 120*

7 every *rev from* evr'y *MS. 137* semblance] semblance *MS. 107 (A)* content; *rev from* content, *MS. 137* content *MS. 107 (B)* content: *MS. 106* content, *MS. 120*

8 Nature,] Nature *MS. 107 (A)* Nature *rev from* nature *MS. 106* nature *MS. 120* tried! *rev from* tried; *MS. 137* tried. *MSS. 107 (A), 106*

9 He *rev from* he *MS. 137* he *WW to DW, MSS. 107 (B), 120*

10 dales,] dales *WW to DW, MSS. 107 (B), 120* Dales *MS. 107 (A)* thin set] thin-set *WW to DW, MSS. 107, 106, 120, 1836–, 1838* farms,] Farms, *WW to DW* farms *MSS. 107, 106* Farms *MS. 120*

11 judgement *rev to* judgment *MS. 137* judgment *1836–, 1838* growth,] growth *MSS. 107, 106*

12 That, *rev in pencil from* That *MS. 106* That *WW to DW, MS. 107* Fancy *rev from* fancy *MS. 137* only, *rev from* only *MS. 107 (A)* only *WW to DW* pomp] Pomp *WW to DW, MSS. 107, MS. 106, 120* charms;] charms *MSS. 107, 106*

13 And,] And *MSS. 107 (A), 106*

14 favoured] favour'd *WW to DW* favord *rev to* favor'd *MS. 107 (A)* favor'd

MS. 107 (B) favored *MSS. 106, 120* honour both.] honor both.— *WW to DW* honor both *MS. 107 (A)*

To B. R. Haydon, Esq. on seeing his Picture of Napoleon Buonaparte on the Island of St. Helena

1 judges] Judges *Yale MS. 3*
2 shown] shewn *MSS. 107, 135, Yale MS. 3* lines] lines, *WW to BRH*
3 colours; *rev from* colours: *MS. 107* colours, *Yale MS. 3* *no ital Yale MS. 3*
4 thought,] thought— *Yale MS. 3* poetic] poetic *ital NMM* thrill;] thrill,— *WW to BRH, NMM*
5 unencumbered] unincumbered *MSS. 107, 135* unincumbered *rev to* unincumber'd *MS. 114, Yale MS. 3, NMM as rev MS. 114* whole] Whole *MS. 107, WW to BRH, MSS. 114, 135, Yale MS. 3, NMM* still,] still; *MS. 107, Yale MS. 3* still— *WW to BRH, MS. 135, NMM*
6 wave;] wave, *MSS. 114, 135* wave— *NMM* *no punct Yale MS. 3*
7 Man] Man, *WW to BRH, MS. 114* laboured] labour'd *MS. 107, Yale MS. 3, NMM* labored *MS. 135*
8 World, *rev from* world, *MS. 135* world *Yale MS. 3* sole-standing] sole standing *NMM* the] the *Morgan MS. 6* hill—] hill *MS. 135* hill; *Yale MS. 3* hill, *WW to BRH, NMM*
9 turned,] turnd *MS. 107* turn'd, *MS. 114* turned— *MS. 135* turn'd *Yale MS. 3* turn'd— *NMM* folded,] folded *MS. 107, Yale MS. 3* folded— *MS. 135, NMM*
10 Tinged, we may fancy,] Tinged, (we may fancy), *with parens added MS. 107* Tinged (we may fancy) *WW to BRH, MSS. 114, 135, NMM* Tinged (we may fancy), *Yale MS. 3*
11 sun] sun, *Yale MS. 3* Sun *MS. 107, WW to BRH, MSS. 114, 135, NMM, 1838*
12 Set] Set *rev from miswritten* Let *MS. 107* Set— *WW to BRH, NMM* Set, *1836–, 1838* fortunes;] fortunes, *Yale MS. 3* fortunes! *WW to BRH, NMM* fortunes— *MS. 114*
13 them. The] them. The *WW to BRH, NMM ital* them—the *Yale MS. 3,* them: the *1838* way,] way; *MS. 107* way *MS. 114*
14 him] Him *WW to BRH, Yale MS. 3, NMM* *no ital MS. 114, Yale MS. 3* *no punct MSS. 114, 135*

Epitaph ("By a blest Husband guided, Mary came")

title *no punct MS. 135*
2 kindred, . . . name;] kindred— . . . name [name *rev to* Name] *MS. 106*
5 so,] so *MS. 106*
7 through] thro' *MS. 135*
8 Heaven: *rev in pencil from* Heaven. *MS. 106*
9 Babes *rev from* babes *MS. 135*
10 third] Third *MS. 106*
11 Sister-twin *rev from* sister twin *MS. 137*
12/13 *no stanza break MS. 106*
13 Reader!] —Reader, *MS. 106*
16 Time] Time, *MS. 106*
17 Mourner's *rev from* mourner's *MS. 135* mourner's *MS. 106, MS. 1835/36–, 1839*
18 cannot,] cannot *MS. 106*
19 Him *ital*] him *no ital MS. 106* him *ital 1836YR*
20 Stone; *rev from* stone; *MS. 135*

Devotional Incitements, Text of MS. 133

5 wholly *rev from* wholy *MS. 133*
11 sanctities *rev from* scantities *MS. 133*
27 Poor *rev from* poor *MS. 133*

Devotional Incitements, Text of 1835

epigraph *quots del in pencil MS. 1835/36*
1 stop, *rev from* stop *MS. 137* Powers; *rev from* powers; *MS. 137*
2 Spirits *rev from* spirits *MS. 137*
7 humble] humble, *MS. 1835Col* violet *rev to* Violet *MS. 135* violet, *MS. 1835/36* violet— *1836–, 1839* thyme *rev from* thyme, *MS. 137* thyme— *1836–, 1839*
8 Exhaled, *rev from* Exhaled *MS. 137* climb,] climb *MS. 135*
10 satisfy: *rev from* satisfy; *MS. 137*
13 *hyphen added MS. 137*
16 *no commas MS. 135*
17 Birds *rev from* birds *MS. 137* birds *MS. 1835/36–, 1839*
18 throats,] throats— *1836–, 1839*
26 earth;] earth, *WW to JK* aspire! aspire! *rev from* aspire, aspire, *MS. 137* aspire, aspire, *WW to JK*
27 Town's Cathedral *WW to JK* choir,] quire *over illeg eras WW to JK* quire, *1845, 1850* quire *1846, 1849*
28 height *rev from* height. *MS. 137*
29 flight;] flight *WW to JK*
30 altar] Altar *WW to JK* breathes *rev from* breathes, *MS. 137*
31 wreaths; *rev from* wreaths, *MS. 137* wreaths, *WW to JK*

32 Or, . . . censer] Or . . . Censor *WW to JK*
33 taper lights] taper-lights *1836–, 1839*
34 Forms, *rev from* forms, *MS. 137* forms, *WW to JK*
35 painter's skill,] Painter's skill *WW to JK*
36 wait] wait, *WW to JK*
37 moment,] moment *WW to JK* moment, *rev from* moment *MS. 137* revealed.] revealed *WW to JK* revealed *1849P*
41 imagery? *rev from* imagery. *MS. 137* imagery— *1836–, 1839*
47 mind, *rev from* mind *MS. 137*
53 dust: *rev from* dust. *MS. 137*
55 vicissitude *rev from* vicissitude, *MS. 137*
58 Nature *rev from* nature *MS. 137*
62 fresh cloven] fresh-cloven *1836–, 1839*
67 head;] head— *1836–, 1839*
69 almighty Will, *rev from* Almighty will, *MS. 137*
75 heart;] heart: *1836–, 1839*
77 eve, *rev from* eve *MS. 137*

To the Author's Portrait

1 Portrait! *rev from* Portrait *MS. 106*
2 saintly *rev from* Saintly *MS. 135* Saintly *MS. 134* place] Place *WW to TA*
3 colours] Colors *MS. 106, WW to TA* colors *MS. 134* Colors *St. John's MS.* *no comma MS. 134, WW to TA, Dora W to EQ, Lilly MS. 5, WW to JSmith, St. John's MS.*
4 work *rev to* Work *MS. 134* Work *MS. 106, Dora W to EQ, Coatalen MS., Lilly MS. 5, WW to JSmith, MS. 135* skill] Skill *WW to JSmith* *no comma Dora W to EQ, St. John's MS.*
5 reclined] reclin'd *Coatalen MS.* though] tho' *MS. 106, WW to TA, Dora W to EQ* tho *St. John's MS., MS. 135* Kingdoms *rev from* kingdoms *MS. 138* kingdoms *MSS. 135, 137, 1836–, 1838, 1839*
6 States] states *1836–, 1838, 1839*
7 peace,] peace *Dora W to EQ, Lilly MS. 5* peace—*WW to JSmith* stream,] Stream, *MS. 134, Coatalen MS., St. John's MS., MS. 135* Stream— *Lilly MS. 5, WW to JSmith*
8 think] think— *MSS. 106, 134, WW to TA, Coatalen MS., Lilly MS. 5, WW to JSmith* feel] feel— *WW to JSmith* felt.] felt *St. John's MS.*
9 Whate'er] Whateer *MS. 106, WW to TA, Coatalen MS., WW to JSmith* features] Features *Coatalen MS.*
10 Unrecognized *MSS. 106, 134, WW to TA, Coatalen MS., Lilly MS. 5, WW to JSmith, St. John's MS., 1838* through] thro' *MSS. 106, 134, WW to TA, Dora W to EQ, St. John's MS.* tear,] tear *MSS. 106, 134, WW to TA, Dora W to EQ, Coatalen MS., Lilly MS. 5, WW to JSmith, St. John's MS., MS. 135, 1836–, 1838, 1839*
11 prompt . . . fall *rev from* prompt, . . . fall, *MS. 137* prompt, . . . fall, *MSS. 106, 134, WW to TA, Dora W to EQ, St. John's MS., MS. 135* prompt— . . . fall *Coatalen MS., Lilly MS. 5* prompt, . . . fall *1836–, 1836YR, 1839* prompt . . . fall *MS. 1836/45* glad] glad, *1840–, MS. 1836/45*
12 morning *rev to* Morning *Coatalen MS., Lilly MS. 5, WW to JSmith* Morning *MSS. 106, 134, WW to TA, Dora W to EQ, St. John's MS.* flower] Flower *WW to JSmith* half blown;] half-blown; *MS. 106, WW to TA, Dora W to EQ, 1836–, 1838, 1839* half-blown, *Coatalen MS., Lilly MS. 5, MS. 134, WW to JSmith, St. John's MS., MS. 135*
13 delight,] delight *MS. 106, WW to TA, Dora W to EQ, Coatalen MS., Lilly MS. 5, WW to JSmith, St. John's MS.*
14 life *rev to* Life *MS. 135* Life *MSS. 106, 134, WW to TA, Coatalen MS., Dora W to EQ, St. John's MS.* though] Thou *Coatalen MS., Lilly MS. 5, WW to JSmith* truth,] truth *MS. 134, Dora W to EQ, WW to JSmith* dear!] dear. *Coatalen MS.*

Poems Written in Response to the Reform Movement, December 1832

i. "For Lubbock vote—no legislative Hack"

Text of WW, DW, and Dora W to JW3, December 5, 1832

2 History— *rev from* history— *WW, DW, and Dora W to* JW_3

Text of WW to JW3, December 7, 1832

5 He'll *rev from* he'll *WW to* JW_3

ii. If this great world of joy and pain

1 world] World *WW, DW, and Dora W to* JW_3*, Gluck MS.*
2–8 *even numbered lines not indented Gluck MS.*
2 track;] track *MS. 133* track, *WW, DW, and Dora W to* JW_3
3 Freedom,] freedom *MS. 135* freedom, *Gluck MS., MS. 1835/36–, 1839*

4 Virtue,] Virtue *MS. 135* virtue, *Gluck MS., MS. 1835/36–, 1839* back; *rev from* back *MS. 137 (A)* back *MS. 137 (B)*
6 day's] days *WW, DW, and Dora W to* JW_3 care;] care, *WW, DW, and Dora W to* JW_3 care; *rev to* care, *MS. 135*
6–8 *no punct MS. 133*
8 bear,] bear *WW, DW, and Dora W to* JW_3 forbear!] forbear!— *WW, DW, and Dora W to* JW_3 forbear. *Gluck MS.*

iii. "Now that Astrology is out of date"
4 Friends *rev from* friends *WW to* JW_3

iv. Question and Answer
title Answer. *rev from* answer. *WW to* JW_3
4 Guillotine: *rev from* Gyillotine: *WW to* JW_3

Thought on the Seasons
1 Flattered] Flatter'd *WW to* JW_3
3 O *rev from* o *WW to* JW_3, *MS. 135* shape,] shape *MS. 135*
4 last.] last! *WW to* JW_3
5 summer] Summer *WW to* JW_3
11 And] And, *WW to* JW_3
12 bough,] bough; *MS. 1835/36–, 1839*
13 *no comma WW to* JW_3
14 she] She *WW to* JW_3
15 winter] Winter *WW to* JW_3, *MS. 135* in,] in— *WW to* JW_3
16 emblematic *rev from* emblamatic *MS. 135*
19 touch, *rev to* touch *WW to* JW_3 touch *MS. 135*
20 Through] Thro' *MS. 135* heaven-born] heav'n-born *WW to* JW_3 end! *rev to* end. *WW to* JW_3 end! *rev to* End! *MS. 135* end! *rev from* End! *MS. 138 (A)*

A Wren's Nest
1 dwellings . . . birds] Dwellings . . . Birds *MS. 135*
2 forest *rev from* forest, *MS. 135*
5 tenement *rev to* Tenement *MS. 135*
6 laboured *rev from* labored *MS. 135*
7 sun] Sun *MS. 135*
8 Impervious] Impervious, *MS. 135, MS. 1835/36–*
9 withal, *rev to* withal *MS. 135*
11 Kind *rev from* kind *MS. 135*
13 And . . . abodes] And, . . . Abodes *MS. 135*
15 Hermit] hermit *MS. 1835/36–*
17 Abbey walls] abbey-walls *MS. 1835/36–*
21 Bird] bird *MS. 1835/36–* Mate] Mate, *MS. 135* mate *MS. 1835/36–*
23 Streamlet] streamlet *MS. 1835/36–* both *rev from* both, *MS. 138*
24 to . . . long. *rev from* to, . . . long: [long: *rev from* long;] *MS. 135*
26 Bird's *rev from* Bird s *MS. 138* bird's *MS. 1835/36–*
28 urn] Urn *MS. 135*
32 rest; *rev to* rest: *MS. 135*
33 Builders] builders *1836–*
34 covert, *rev from* Covert, *MS. 138* Covert, *MS. 135* where, *rev from illeg punct MS. 135*
35 oak,] oak *rev to* Oak *MS. 135* Oak, *rev to* oak, *MS. 138*
36 antlers] Antlers *MS. 135* sprout; *rev from* sprout, *MS. 138* sprout. *MS. 135*
37 She *rev from* she *MS. 135* Lodge] lodge *MS. 1835/36–*
41 brow,] brow *MS. 135*
43 nest *rev to* Nest *MS. 135* nest, *1836YR, 1839*
45 treasure *rev from* Treasure *MS. 138* Treasure *MS. 135* show] shew *MS. 135*
47 things,] things; *1836–*
48 vain: *rev from* vain. *MS. 138* vain. *MS. 135*
49 Spoiler's] spoiler's *MS. 1835/36–* prey,] prey *MS. 135*
50 beauty, love,] beauty love *MS. 135*
51 it) *rev from* it, *MS. 135*
54 light] light, *1836YR* moss-built] moss built *MS. 135*
55 mouth,] mouth; *1836–*
57 Primrose . . . spread] Primrose, . . . spread, *MS. 135*
60 Flower *rev from* flower *MS. 135* flower *MS. 1835/36–*
63 eyes *rev from* eyes, *MS. 135*
65 mother-bird] Mother-Bird *MS. 135* Mother-bird *MS. 1835/36–*
66 and] and, *MS. 135*
67 flower] Flower *MS. 135, 1836–*
70 grove] grove, *1836YR*
71 primrose tuft] Primrose-tuft *MS. 1835/36–*
72 love] Love *MS. 135*

Evening Voluntaries

I. Calm is the fragrant air, and loth to lose
series number 1 *MS. 135*
2 tho'] though *MS. 1831JH* dews: *rev from* dews; *MS. 135*
3 stars, *rev to* stars— *MS. 135*
4 and, . . . one,] and . . . one *MS. 1831JH*

6 sight.] sight *MS. 1831JH* sight! *MS. 1835/36–, 1839*
7 birds,] birds *MS. 1831JH* Birds, *MS. 135*
8 a while *rev from* awhile *MS. 138* awhile *MS. 1831JH, MSS. 135, 137*
9 dim-seen *rev from* dim seen *MS. 135* dim seen *MS. 1831JH*
10 Village] village *MS. 1831JH, MS. 1835/36–, 1839* Chruch-clock's] church-clock's *MS. 1831JH*
12 bound *rev from* bonnd *MS. 137*
13 sequence;] sequence, *rev to* sequence: *rev to* sequence— *MS. 135* sequence— *MS. 1835/36–, 1839*
14 *no commas MS. 1831JH*
15 fireside] fire-side *MS. 135* Listeners] Listeners *rev from* listeners *MS. 138* listeners *MSS. 135, 137, MS. 1835/36–, 1839* hear! *rev from* hear. *MS. 135*
16 Shepherd] shepherd *MS. 1835/36–, 1839*
19 Children] children *MS. 135* Children *rev from* children *MS. 137* children *MS. 1835/36–, 1839*
20 Bat] bat *MS. 1835/36–, 1839*
21 reflits] reflits *MS. 135* arcade; *rev from* arcade: *MS. 135* arcade. *MS. 1831JH*
22 Far-heard] Far heard *MS. 1831JH, MSS. 135, 137, 138* Dor-hawk] dorhawk *MS. 1831JH* dor-hawk *MS. 1835/36–, 1839* Moth *rev from* moth, *MS. 135* moth *MS. 1835/36–, 1839*
23 Industry and Sloth] industry and sloth *MS. 1831JH*
25 more; *rev from* more, *MS. 135*
26 Boat *rev from* boat *MS. 137* boat *MS. 135, 1835/36–, 1839*
30 Man's] man's *MS. 1835/36–, 1839*

II. Not in the lucid intervals of life

series number 2 *MS. 135*

2 curse *rev from* corse *(printer's error) MS. 137* Party-strife; *rev from* party-strife; *MS. 135* party-strife; *MS. 1835/36–, 1839*
3 Pleasure *rev from* pleasure *MS. 135*
5 Slave] slave *MS. 1831JH, MS. 1835/36–, 1839*
6 Mammon's] mammon's *MS. 1831JH* cave, *rev from* cave *MS. 137* cave *MS. 135* cave— *MS. 1835/36–, 1839*
7 Nature] nature *1836–1843,1839* words, *rev from* words *MS. 137*
8 Talent] talent *MS. 1835/36–, 1839*
12 Genius,] genius *MS. 1831JH* Genius *MS. 135* take] take, *MS. 1831JH*
13 passion *rev from* Passion *MS. 137* Passion *MS. 135* passion's] passions *MS. 135*
15 Great . . . Innocent] great . . . innocent *MS. 1835/36–, 1839*
15/16 *stanza break 1836–, 1839*
16 *para 1836–, 1839* innocent? By] innocent—by *MS. 1831JH*
17 O Nature!] oh! nature, *MS. 1831JH*
18 Through] Thro' *MS. 135*
21 gladdened *rev from* gladden'd *MS. 137*
22 show] shew *MS. 135*
23 Through] Thro' *MS. 135* undergo,] undergo— *MS. 1835/36–, 1839*
24 repealed;] repealed. *MS. 1831JH* repealed: *MS. 135*
27 through] thro' *MS. 135*
29 Soul's] Souls *MS. 1831JH* soul's *MS. 135*
30 Intellect *rev from* intellect *MS. 137* intellect *MSS. 1831JH, 135*

III. (By the Side of Rydal Mere)

series number 3 *MS. 135*

1 Linnet's] linnet's *MS. 1835/36–, 1839*
2 Thrush] thrush *MS. 1835/36–, 1839*
3 Thrush] thrush *MS. 1835/36–, 1839* heedless, *rev from* heedless; *MS. 135*
4 Monitor] monitor *MS. 1835/36–, 1839*
7 Star *rev from* star *MS. 138* star *MS. 1835/36–, 1839*
8 Rooks] rooks *MS. 1835/36–, 1839*
11 grove) . . . noise *rev from* grove,) . . . noise, *MS. 138*
12/13 *stanza break 1836–, 1839*
13 *para 1836–, 1839* Who *rev from* who *MS. 135*
14 moved, *rev to* moved *MS. 135* strong *rev from* strong, *MS. 138*
15 cheated] cheated, *MSS. 135, 138*
16 thee *rev to* Thee *MS. 135* thee *rev from* tree *(printer's error) MS. 138*
17 lands,] lands *MS. 135*
19 would] w^{d} *MS. 135* be,] be *MSS. 135, 138, 1836–, 1839*
21 Lays . . . night;] lays . . . Night; *MS. 1835/36* lays . . . Night: *1836–, 1839* dawn *rev from* dawn *ital MS. 138* dawn *MS. 135*
22 dawn *ital rev from* dawn *MS. 138* dawn *MS. 135*
23 light; *1836–*
24 led,] led *MS. 135*

26 king . . . peasant] King . . . Peasant *MS. 135*
27 Soldiers] soldiers *MS. 135*
28 thou *rev to* Thou *MS. 135*
29 nightingale] Nightingale, *MS. 135*
30 on] on, *MS. 135, MS. 1835/36–, 1839*
34 happiest,] happiest *MS. 138*
36 goodness] goodness, *MS. 135* goodness— *1845–*

IV. Soft as a cloud is yon blue Ridge—the Mere

series number 4 *MS. 135*
1 Ridge—the Mere *rev from* ridge—the mere *MS. 135*
3 motionless; and,] motionless; and *rev to* motionless—and, *MS. 135*
4 Ocean, *rev from* Ocean; *MS. 135* ocean, *MS. 1835/36–, 1839*
8 Twilight *rev from* twilight *MS. 135*
12 this *rev from* this, *MS. 138* Hour *rev from* hour *MS. 135*
13 minds *rev to* Minds *MS. 135*
16 Eve] eve *1845–*
18 free *rev from* free, *MS. 138*
19/20 *stanza break 1836–, 1839*
20 *para 1836–, 1839* 'Tis] 'T is *1835* Tis *MS. 135*
21 Wisdom . . . Nature's *MSS. 135, 138*
22 thoughts *rev to* Thoughts *MS. 135* Thoughts *Monkhouse Album (copy)* descend,] descend *Monkhouse Album (copy)*
23 Angels *rev from* angels *MS. 135* bowers] bower's *Monkhouse Album (copy)*
24 To-morrow] Tomorrow *rev from* tomorrow *MS. 135* Tomorrow *Monkhouse Album (copy)* say,] say *Monkhouse Album (copy)*
26 vanities] Vanities *Monkhouse Album (copy)* yesterday?" *rev from* yesterday? *MS. 138* yesterday? *MS. 135*

V. The leaves that rustled on this oak-crowned hill

series number 5 *MS. 135*
1–2 *no punct MS. 128*
1 oak-crowned] oak crowned *MS. 128* hill,] hill *MS. 135*
2 still;] still: *MS. 135*
5 eyelid] eye-lid *MS. 135*
5, 7 *no punct MS. 128*
6 which] w^h *MS. 135*
9 and 'mid] and, mid *MS. 135* and (mid *1836–1849* and ('mid *MS. 1835/36, 1839, 1850*
10 imagery—] imagery, *1836–, 1839*
11 vale's *rev from* Vale's *MS. 138* Vale's *MS. 135* *no punct MS. 128*
12 lake, *rev from* Lake *MS. 138* Lake, *MSS. 128, 135* lake) *MS. 1835/36–, 1839*
13 'mid] mid *MSS. 128, 135* mountains] mountains *rev from* Mountains *MS. 138* Mountains *MS. 135* *no commas MS. 128*
14 Creature!] Creature!— *MS. 1835/36–, 1839* moon] Moon *MS. 128* *no punct MS. 128*
15 opened] open'd *MS. 128* *no comma MS. 128*
16 *no comma MS. 128*
17 Lady's] lady's *MS. 1835/36–, 1839* bower:] bower; *MS. 135, MS. 1835/36–, 1839, but* bower: *1843* bower *1846* bower, *rev to* bower; *MS. 138* *no punct MS. 128*
18 Or *rev from* Or, *rev from* Or *MS. 138* Or, *MS. 135* thou] Thou *MS. 128*
19 churchyard yew] Church yard Yew *MS. 135*
19–29 *no punct MS. 128*
23 whereabout; *rev from* whereabout. *MS. 138* whereabout— *1836–, 1839*
23/24 *stanza break rev to text MS. 138*
24 *para MS. 135; para rev to text MS. 138* seen,] seen *MS. 135*
25/26 *stanza break 1836–, 1839*
26 *para 1836–, 1839* men] Men *MS. 135*
27 headless *rev from* heedless *MS. 138* Owl] Owl *rev from* owl *MS. 135* owl *MS. 128*
30 Eagle's] Eagles *MS. 135*
31 Fate] fate *MS. 128*
31–32 *no punct MS. 128*
32 Thou, too,] Thou too *MS. 135* side—] side:— *1836–1849, 1839* side: *1850*
33 Hark *rev from* Hark! *MS. 135* larum! *rev from* larum *MS. 135* larum!— *MS. 1835/36–, 1839*
35 *no comma MS. 128*

VI. The Sun, that seemed so mildly to retire

series number 6 *MS. 135*
1 Sun,] Sun *MS. 106 (A)* sun, *MS. 128* retire,] retire *MS. 106 (A)*
2 fire,] fire; *MS. 106 (A)* fire *MS. 128*
3 gleams,] gleams *MS. 106 (A)*
4 *no apos MSS. 106 (A), 134* dreams.] dreams; *MS. 106 (A)* dreams! *MS. 135*

5 round;—] round, *MS. 106 (A)* moving;] moving *MS. 106 (A), MS. 1831JH* moving, *MS. 128*
6 *no apos MS. 106 (A)* *no commas MS. 106 (A)* loving.] loving: *MSS. 134, 128*
7 *no commas MSS. 106 (A), 128, 134* stedfast] steadfast *1836YR, 1839*
8 lie:—] lie, *MS. 106 (A)* lie;— *MS. 134*
9 *no apos MS. 106 (A)*
10 headland] Headland *MSS. 128, 135* shore!] shore *MSS. 106 (A), 128, MS. 1831JH* shore? *MSS. 134, 135, MS. 1835/36–, 1836YR, 1839*
11 sea,] sea *MS. 106 (A)* Sea *MS. 128* sea *rev to* Sea *MS. 134*
12 can *(ital)* be!] can be? *MS. 106 (A)* can be *MS. 1831JH*
12/13 *no stanza break MS. 134; no stanza break MSS. 128, 135*
13 *no para MS. 128; para added MS. 135* supreme!] supreme *MS. 128*
14 Offenders,] Offenders *MS. 128* *no commas MS. 106 (A)*
15 flood *rev from* flood, *MS. 138*
16 ocean] Ocean *MSS. 134, 128, 135* roused] rouzed *MS. 106 (A)* mood,] mood *MS. 106 (A)* mood! *MSS. 134, 128*
17 Will *rev from* will *MS. 135* will *MS.* 128_2
17–26 *variants from version in MS. 106 (A) reported in apparatus:*
[17] life . . . things] Life . . . things! *MSS. 134, 128*
[18] Who . . . worlds . . . way] Who, . . . worlds . . . way, *MS. 134* Who, . . . world's . . . way *MS. 128*
[19] Spirit] spirit *MSS. 134, 128*
[20] voice] voice; *MS. 134* voice. *MS. 128*
[21] Glad *rev from* Gr *MS. 128* expand and] expand, and, *MSS. 134* expand, and *MS. 128*
[22] cares . . .thee] cares, . . . Thee! *MSS. 134, 128*
18 remain;] remain *MS.* 128_2 remain, *MS. 135*
19 quick-eared] quick eared *MS.* 128_2
20 voice!] voice *MS.* 128_2, *MS. 1831JH* voice; *MS. 135*
21 *no apos MS. 128*
22 through] thro' *MSS.* 128_2, *135*
23 Glad,] Glad *MS. 1831JH* through] thro' *MSS.* 128_2, *135*
24 fear; *rev from* fear, *MS. 138* fear, *MSS.* 128_2, *135, 1836–, 1839*
25 expand,] expand; *1836–* *no commas MS.* 128_2
26 Thee!] Thee. *MS. 128*

VII. (By the Sea-side.)

series number 7 *MS. 135*
1 sun *rev to* Sun *MS. 135* Sun *MSS. 129; 128; CW, Jr., to CW* sea-fowl *rev to* Sea-fowl *MS. 135* Sea-fowl *MS. 129* *no commas MS. 129*
2 storm *rev to* Storm *MS. 135* Storm *MS. 129* somewhere] some where *CW, Jr., to CW* nest;] nest. *MS. 129; CW, Jr., to CW* nest *MS. 128*
3 slumbers—] slumbers, *CW, Jr., to CW* wave] Wave *CW, Jr., to CW* *no comma MSS. 129, 128*
4 deep] Deep *MSS. 129, 135* survives,] survives. *MS. 128*
5 motion!] motion— *MSS. 129; 128; CW, Jr., to CW* *no comma MSS. 129; 128; CW, Jr., to CW*
6 swayed.] swayed; *CW, Jr., to CW* swayed *MS. 128*
9 prospect] prospect, *CW, Jr., to CW* range,] range *MS. 128; CW, Jr., to CW*
10 *no comma MSS. 129; 128; CW, Jr., to CW* change.] change; *CW, Jr., to CW*
11 *para MS. 129* ships *rev to* Ships *MS. 135* Ships *MS. 129* blast,] Blast, *MS. 129* blast *MSS. 129; 128; CW, Jr., to CW*
12 breakers] Breakers *MSS. 129, 128, 135* passed;] passed, *MS. 129* past *MS. 128; CW, Jr., to CW*
13 clouds *rev to* Clouds *MS. 135*
13–14 *no punct MS. 128; CW, Jr., to CW*
15 Some] some *CW, Jr., to CW* peace,] peace *MS. 128; CW, Jr., to CW* peace; *MS. 135*
16 His *rev from* his *CW, Jr., to CW* his *MSS. 128, 135* bade *rev in pencil from* bad *MS. 128* cease;] cease, *MS. 128; CW, Jr., to CW*
17 *no commas MS. 128* heedless] heed less *CW, Jr., to CW*
18 far-off] far off *MS. 128* port;] Port *MS. 128* port. *CW, Jr., to CW* Port: *MS. 135*
19 *no commas MS. 128*
20 one *rev to* One *MS. 135* wingèd *rev from* winged *MS. 128* winged *CW, Jr., to CW* Powers] powers *MS. 1835/36–, 1839* seen,] seen *MS. 128*
21 nor 'mid] nor, mid *MSS. 129, 128, 135; CW, Jr., to CW* quiet *rev in pencil to* quiet, *MS. 128* quiet, *MSS. 129; 135; CW, Jr., to CW* heard;]

heard *rev in pencil to* heard. *MS. 128* heard. *CW, Jr., to CW*

22 Yet] Yet, *CW, Jr., to CW* oh!] oh *MSS. 129; 128; CW, Jr., to CW* air *rev to* Air *MS. 135*

23 acknowledgment] acknowledgement *CW, Jr., to CW* praise,] praise. *MS. 129* praise *MS. 128*

24 vesper lays *rev to* Vesper Lays *MS. 129* Vesper lays [lays *rev to* Lays] *MS. 128* Vesper Lays *MS. 135; CW, Jr., to CW*

25 Virgin] Virgin, *CW, Jr., to CW*

26 bark] Bark *MSS. 129, 128* Bark *rev from* [?Hart] *MS. 135* shore;] shores, *MS. 129* shores *MS. 128* shores— *MS. 135* shores. *CW, Jr., to CW*

27 service *rev from* service, *CW, Jr., to CW* through] thro' *MSS. 128, 135* thro *CW, Jr., to CW* mountains felt] Mountains felt, *CW, Jr., to CW*

28 melt:] melt. *MS. 129; CW, Jr., to CW* melt *MS. 128* melt; *MSS. 128, 135*

30 gulfy] gulphy *MSS. 128; 135; CW, Jr., to CW* iron-bound;] iron bound *MS. 128* iron-bound, *CW, Jr., to CW*

31 *no commas MS. 128; CW, Jr., to CW*

32 harmonies.] harmonies! *CW, Jr., to CW* *no punct MS. 128*

33 Hush, *rev from* Hush! *MS. 135* Hush!— *MSS. 129, 128* Hush! *CW, Jr., to CW* here! . . . repine,] here!— . . . repine *MS. 129* here!— . . . repine *MS. 128* here, . . . repine *CW, Jr., to CW*

34 star of eve] Star of Eve *MSS. 129, 128* star of Eve *CW, Jr., to CW; MS. 135*

35 waters] waters, *CW, Jr., to CW* benign?] benign. *MSS. 129, 128*

36 *para CW, Jr., to CW* mariners] Mariners *MSS. 129; 128; 135; CW, Jr., to CW* *no commas MSS. 129, 128*

37 rest,] rest *MSS. 129; 128; 135; CW, Jr., to CW* bay,] bay *MSS. 129, 128*

38 *no ital MS. 129; MS. 1835/36–, 1839*

39 heart,] heart— *MSS. 129; 128; CW, Jr., to CW* heart *rev to* heart,— *MS. 135* heart; *1836–* heard] heard *ital MS. 1835/36–, 1839* "our . . . heaven!"] our . . . heaven! *MS. 129* our . . . heaven *MS. 128* our . . . Heaven. *CW, Jr., to CW* our . . . heaven! *rev to* "our . . . heaven!" *MS. 135*

VIII. The sun has long been set, Text of 1835

series number 8 *MS. 135*

headnote, para two, second sentence unobjectionable:] unobjectionable; *1836YR, 1839*

IX. Throned in the Sun's descending car

series number 9 *MS. 135*

1 car] Car *MS. 135*

3 mind? *rev from* mind, *Morgan MS. 5*

4 Genius *rev from* genius *MS. 135*

7 ever pleasing] ever-pleasing *1836YR, 1839*

9 shades . . . silence] Shades . . . Silence *MS. 135*

10 charms] Charms *MS. 135*

11 cliff] Cliff *MS. 135*

15 vale] Vale *MS. 135*

Composed by the Sea-shore

title SEA-SHORE] Sea Shore *MS. 151.2*

3 prey,] prey *MS. 151.2*

5 sailor] Sailor *MS. 151.2, 1845–* best] best, *1845–*

6 sea] Sea *MS. 151.2*

7 dependent *rev to* dependant *MS. 151.2*

8 power, through . . . war. *rev from* Power thro . . . War *MS. 143* Power, thro . . . War *MS. 151.2*

9–12 *no punct MS. 143*

11 childhood] Childhood *MSS. 143, 151.2* childhood, *1845–*

14 Betrothèd] Betrothed *MSS. 143, 151.2*

15 was,] was *1845–* *no commas MS. 143*

16–20 *no punct MS. 143*

16 memory;] memory, *MS. 151.2*

18 change,] change; *MS. 151.2*

23 glory] Glory *MS. 143*

24 *no punct MS. 143*

25 crew] Crew *MS. 143*

26 due,] due. *MS. 143*

27 yields, . . . moonbeams] yields . . . moon-beams *MS. 143*

28 sea . . . bay] Sea . . . Bay *MSS. 143, 151.2* *no punct MS. 143*

29 *no comma MSS. 143, 151.2*

31 honours] honors *MSS. 143, 151.2* *no punct MS. 143*

32 Or, *MS. 151.2, 1845–* splendours] splendors *MS. 143* *no comma MS. 143*

To ———, Upon the Birth of her First-Born Child, March, 1833.

title TO ——,] TO ——. *MS. 137, 1836–* 1833.] 1833 *1836* 1833. *in pencil MS. 1836/45*

epigraph Navita;] Navita, *1836YR, 1836–, 1839* jacet," &c.] jacet," etc. *MS. 137 (A)* jacet, &c.' *1836–*
5 labouring *rev from* laboring *MS. 135*
6 earth.] earth: *rev to* Earth. *MS. 135*
7 beseech?] beseech?— *MS. 135, MS. 1835/36–, 1839*
9 cry,] cry— *MS. 135* cry; *MS. 1835/36–, 1839*
11 come? *rev from* come, *MS. 135*
12 doom! *rev to* doom *rev to* doom! *MS. 137 (A)*
15 thanks now] thanks, now, *MS. 135* thanks, now *MS. 1835/36–, 1839*
16 descending] descending, *MS. 135*
17 Now] Now, *MS. 135*
19 debt] Debt *MS. 135* debt *ital 1836YR* Creature, *rev from* creature, *MS. 137 (A)* Creature; *MS. 135*
22 *ital added MS. 137 (A)* release;] release— *MS. 1835/36–, 1839*
24 human-kind *rev to* Human-kind *MS. 135*
29 sun-burnt] sun burnt *rev to* sunburnt *MS. 137 (A)* sunburnt *MS. 137 (B)* traveller] Traveller *MS. 135*
30 labourer] Laborer *rev to* Labourer *MS. 135*
31 Ofttimes] Oftimes *MS. 135* Oft-times *MS. 1835/36–, 1839*
33 So, . . . chequerings *rev from* So . . . checkerings *MS. 135*
34 guardians] Guardians *MS. 135, MS. 1835/36–, 1839*
36 sight! *rev from* sight *MS. 135*
39 Castaway] Cast-away *MS. 135*
44 meekness!] meekness. *1836–*
48 thee] Thee *MS. 135*
51 Angels . . . thy] Angels, . . . thy *MS. 135*
53 That,] That— *1836–, 1839*
54 beset] beset, *1836–, 1839*
55 first-born] First-born *MS. 135, MS. 1835/36–, 1839*
56 years,] years— *1836–, 1839*
58 Babe] babe *MS. 1835/36–, 1839*
59 Woman] woman *MS. 135, MS. 1835/36–, 1839*
61 promises,] promises; *MS. 135* promises,— *1836–, 1839*
64 souls] Souls *MS. 135*
65 wingèd *rev from* winged *MS. 137 (B)* winged *MS. 135*
67 here,] here *MS. 135*
68 new-born] new born *MS. 135* Charge] charge *MS. 137 (B)*
70 light] Light *MS. 135*
71 virtues] Virtues *MS. 135*
73 heart,] heart; *1836–, 1839*
78 trials] trials, *MS. 135*
80 rest, *rev to* rest *MS. 135*
81 her *rev from* her, *MS. 137 (B)*

The Warning, a Sequel to the Foregoing. March, 1833

title WARNING,] WARNING. *1845–*
7 Change] change *MS. 137*
8 range,] range *1836YR*
11 prayers *underscored MS. 1836/45, 1836YR*
13 home-event *rev from* home event *MS. 137 (A)* home event *MS. 137 (B)*
29 love!)] love!)— *MS. 1836/45 (in pencil), 1840–*
30 But] —But *MSS. 135, 137*
31 flight. *rev from* flight! *MS. 135* flight: *MS. 1836/45 (in pencil), 1840–*
32 Swallow, *rev to* swallow, *MS. 137 (A)*
34 —Rapt] Rapt *MS. 1836/45 (in pencil), 1840–* Bee] bee *MS. 1835/36–, 1839*
35 fee;] fee *1850*
36 Or, *rev from* Or *MS. 137 (A)* Lark] lark *MS. 1835/36–, 1839*
39 towers, *rev from* Towers, *MS. 137 (A)* Towers, *MS. 137 (B)*
43 Hall] hall *MS. 1835/36–, 1839*
45 swells;] swells *1840–1843* swells, *1845–*
53 *no ital MS. 137 (B), ital added MS. 137 (A)*
56 truth *rev from* Truth *MS. 137 (A)* Truth *MS. 137 (A)*
57 tutored *rev from* tutor'd *MS. 137 (A)* tutor'd *MS. 137 (B)*
58 died;] died, *MS. 137*
60 thrilled;] thrilled, *MS. 137*
68 see,] see *1836–, 1839*
72 presumption] Presumption *MS. 1835/36–, 1836YR, 1839*
75 guilt *rev from* Guilt *MS. 137 (A)* Guilt *MS. 137 (B)* on,] on *in pencil MS. 1836/45* on *1840–*
77 kept;] kept— *in pencil MS. 1836/45*
79 depends.] depends, *in pencil MS. 1836/45* depends, *1840–*
80 one] One *MS. 1835/36–, 1839*
81 Thee] thee *MS. 1835/36–, 1839*
83 own,] own *1840–*
87 soon—] soon, *rev from* soon, *rev from* soon, *MS. 137 (A)* soon, *MS. 137 (B)*
90 state-helm? *rev from* state helm? *MS. 137 (A)* state helm? *MS. 137 (B)*
100 concede;] concede *1836YR*
102 law;] law, *1845–*
104 reward] reward *ital MS. 137*
107 sceptre *rev from* Sceptre *MS. 137 (A)*

Sceptre *MS. 137 (B)*
109 Power] power *1836YR*
111 feud; *rev from* feud, *rev from* feud! *MS. 137 (A)* feud! *MS. 137 (B)* feud! *MS. 1835/36–, 1839*
114 wrongs;] wrongs, *1836YR, 1839*
117 Or,] Or *in pencil MS. 1836/45*
122 marshalled] marshall'd *MS. 137*
128 Guest! *rev from* Guest. *MS. 137 (A)* Guest. *MS. 137 (B)*
129 —O *rev from* —O! *MS. 137 (A)* —O! *MS. 137 (B)*
131 Oh . . . Almighty . . . grace *rev from* O! . . . Almighty, . . grace, *MS. 137 (A); MS. 137 (B) as orig MS. 137 (A)*
139 cheap.] cheap.— *1836–, 1839*
149 meekness *rev from* Meekness *MS. 137 (A)* Meekness *MS. 137 (B)*
151 Widow] widow *MS. 1835/36–, 1839*
153 Widow] widow *MS. 1835/36* Wife] wife *MS. 1835/36–*
154 Lord] lord *MS. 1835/36–*
156 Little-ones] little-ones *rev from* little ones *MS. 137 (A)* little ones *MS. 137 (B)* little-ones *MS. 1835/36–*
158 Soul] soul *MS. 137* Pair] pair *MS. 1835/36–, 1839*
159 omniscient] Omniscient *MS. 137*
160 still; *rev from* still, *MS. 137 (A)* still, *MS. 137 (B)*

To the Utilitarians

11 Human-kind— *rev from* human-kind— *WW to HCR*

The Labourer's Noon-day Hymn

title LABOURER'S *rev from* LABORER'S *MS. 135* *no punct MS. 135*
2–32 *even-numbered lines are indented MS. 135*
6 noontide:] noon-tide; *MS. 135* noontide. *1840–*
9 though] tho' *MS. 135*
10 night; *rev from* night[?] *MS. 135*
18 Altar] altar *MS. 1835/36–* man's cot] Man's Cot *MS. 135*
19 Church] church *MS. 1835/36–* grove] Grove *MS. 135*
21 Heaven!] Heaven!— *MS. 135*
24 immortal] Immortal *MS. 135*
26 faltered] faultered *MS. 135*
27 love's] Love's *MS. 135*
28 course:] course! *MS. 135*
29 grace . . . through . . . life's] Grace . . . thro' . . . Life's *MS. 135* day] day, *MS. 135, 1836–*
31 west,] West *MS. 135*

Love Lies Bleeding, Text of Dora W to EQ, February 20, 1834

1 bleeding] bleeding! *Cornell MS. 9*
3 Flower] flower *MS. 128, Cornell MS. 9*
7 Mother-earth] Mother earth *MS. 128, Cornell MS. 9*
8 regrets] regrets— *Cornell MS. 9*
9 flower] flower! *Cornell MS. 9*

Love Lies Bleeding, Text of Dora W to EQ, January 1–2, 1835

12 Flower, *rev from* flower, *Dora W to EQ*

Love Lies Bleeding, Text of 1842

1 it,] it *MS. 143* "Love lies bleeding,"—] Love lies bleeding! *MS. 143* "Love lies bleeding"! *MS. 151.1* "Love lies bleeding"— *MS. 151.2* may,] may *MSS. 143, 151.1*
2 Though] Tho' *MSS. 143, 151* Flower] Flower *rev from* flower *MS. 151.2, MS. 1842P* flower *MSS. 143, 151.1*
3 day,] day *MSS. 143, 151.1*
4 away:] away; *MSS. 143, 151.1*
5 flower *rev to* Flower *MS. 151.2* Flower *MS. 1842P* sadness!] sadness!— *rev from* sadness? *MS. 151.2*
6 *parens lacking MS. 143* sculpture's] Supltures *MS. 143* Scuplture's *MS. 151.1, MS. 1842P* Scupltures *rev from* Sculptor's *(copyist's slip) MS. 151.2*
7 leans,] leans *MSS. 143, 151.1* brow] brow, *MS. 151.1* bent] bent— *MS. 143*
8 *no comma MS. 151.1*
9 Flower! *rev from* flower! *MS. 151.1* Flower! *rev from* Flower? *MS. 1842P*
10 'Tis . . . led,] Tis . . . led *MS. 151*
11 *no para 1845–* Though] Tho *MS. 151* *no comma MS. 151.1*
12 sanguine] Sanguine *MS. 143* dew *rev from* due *(copyist's slip) MS. 151.1*
13 *no hyphen MS. 151, MS. 1842P*
16 Rent, *rev from* Went, *(printer's error) MS. 1842P*
18 do;] do, *MSS. 143, 151.1*
19 far,] far *MS. 143*
20 first,] first *MSS. 143, 151.1* bower] bower, *MS. 143*
21 semblance] Semblance *MS. 151.1*
22 heart,] heart *MSS. 143, 151.1*
23 dejection,] dejection *MSS. 143, 151.1* downcast Flower] down-cast-flower *MS. 143* Flower] Flower *rev from* flower *MS. 151.2* flower *MS. 151.1*
24 bear.] bear! *MS. 143* bear *MS. 151.1*

Companion to the Foregoing, Text of 1842

title *no punct MSS. 143, 151.1*

2 growth] growth, *MS. 151.1* cheers] chears *MS. 143* decay,] decay *MSS. 143, 151.1*

3 deprest,] depressed *MS. 143* deprest *MS. 151.1*

4 Flower, *rev from* flower, *MS. 151.2* flower *MSS. 143, 151.1* summer's] summers *MS. 143* Summer's *MS. 151* guest,] guest *MSS. 143, 151.1*

5 summer] Summer *MS. 151.2* leaves,] leaves *MSS. 143, 151.1*

7 bloom,] bloom *MSS. 143, 151.1*

8 doom,] doom *MSS. 143, 151.1*

9 coevals *rev to* Coevals *MS. 151.2* coevals *rev from* co-evals *MS. 1842P* fled,] fled *MSS. 143, 151.1*

10 bed?] bed *MSS. 143, 151.1*

10/11 *stanza break 1845–*

11 *no comma MSS. 143, 151.1* impress'd] impressed *MS. 151.1* impressed, *rev to* impressed *MS. 151.2*

12 day *rev from* day, *MS. 151.2, MS. 1842P* day, *MS. 151.1*

13 herb,] herb *MS. 143*

17 *no comma MSS. 143, 151.1*

18 Man's] Mans *MS. 143* man's *MS. 151.2* Man's *rev from* man's *MS. 1842P*

19 lyre] Lyre *MS. 151*

21 youth . . . maid,] Youth . . . Maid *MS. 143* youth, . . . Maid *MS. 151.1* youth . . . maid *rev to* Youth . . . Maid *MS. 151.2* Youth . . . Maid, *1845–*

22 *no comma MSS. 143, 151.1* companionless] companionless, *MS. 151.1*

23 Flower *rev from* flower *MS. 151.2* flower *MSS. 143, 151.1* dyed,] dyed *rev from* died *MS. 143* dyed *MS. 151.1*

24–26 *no commas MSS. 143, 151.1*

24 cure,] cure *1849*

27 *no comma MS. 151.1* Lingerer, *rev from* lingerer, *MS. 1842P* "Love lies bleeding." *MS. 143* Love lies Bleeding. *MS. 151*

Written in an Album

1 lasts;] lasts: *Berg MS. 6, 1845, 1850* lasts, *1846*

2, 4 *no indent 1845–*

2 *no commas Rotha Q's Album, Dora W to RQ, Swarthmore MS. 2, Rendell MS., 1836YR, Berg MS. 6* Friends] Friend's *Dora W to RQ* however] hower *Berg MS. 6* one:] One; *Rotha Q's Album* One; *rev from* one; *Dora W to RQ* one; *Swarthmore MS. 2, Rendell MS., Berg MS. 6* one. *1846*

3 Daisy] daisy *Swarthmore MS. 2, Rendell MS., Berg MS. 6* shadow] Shadow *Rotha Q's Album, Dora W to RQ* *no commas Berg MS. 6*

4 dew-drop] dew drop *rev to* Dew drop *Rotha Q's Album* Dew-drop *Dora W to RQ* dew drop *Swarthmore MS. 2, Berg MS. 6* dewdrop *Rendell MS.* Sun] sun *Rendell MS., Berg MS. 6*

Lines Suggested by a Portrait from the Pencil of F. Stone

title STONE. *rev from* STONE, ESQ. *MS. 137 (A)*

2 task,] task; *1836–, 1839*

5 oftentimes] —oftentimes *Lilly MS. 3*

6 Portrait *rev from* portrait *MS. 137 (A)* portrait *MS. 137 (B)*

8 light;] light, *MS. 130* air, *rev in pencil from* air *MS. 130*

10 ear,] ear *Lilly MS. 3*

14 *no ital MS. 1835/36–, 1839*

16 shade] shade, *MSS. 130, 137, 138 (A), 1841**

20 nature] Nature *MS. 130*

21 Shepherd *rev from* shepherd *MS. 137 (A)* shepherd *MSS. 130, 137 (B), MS. 1835/36–*

22 whoe'er] who e'er *MS. 130*

23 be, that . . . soul] be, that . . . soul, *MS. 1835/36* be that, . . . soul, *1836–, 1839*

26 treasure, *rev in pencil to* treasure; *MS. 130* treasure,— *MS. 1835/36–* treasure— *1839* behold] behold, *MS. 130*

27 though] tho' *MS. 130* Ocean] ocean *MS. 1835/36–, 1839, but* Ocean *1841**

28 crown,] crown *1836–, 1839*

30 show] shew *MS. 130*

34 *no ital 1841*, 1845–*

35 nought] nought, *1836YR*

38 earth *rev in pencil to* earth, *MS. 130*

41 soul . . . Art,] Soul . . . Art *MS. 130*

42 confidant] Confidant *MS. 130*

43 abstraction? *rev from* abstration? *MS. 130*

44 lover] Lover *MS. 130*

48 womanhood] womanhood *rev from* Womanhood *MS. 137 (C)* Womanhood *MSS. 130, 137 (A, B), 138 (A)*

50 Archer-god, *rev from* Archer-God, *MS. 137 (A)* archer God, *MS. 130* Archer-god; *1836–, 1839* fancy] Fancy *MS. 130*

52 hand, . . . lies] hand . . . lies *rev in*

pencil to hand . . . lies, *MS. 130*
53 arm *rev in pencil to* arm, *MS. 130*
54 holds—] holds, *MS. 130*
56 grasp—] grasp, *MS. 130* wild-flower, joined] wild-flower joined *rev in pencil to* wild-flower, joined, *MS. 130*
57 posy] Posey *rev from* Possy *MS. 130*
58 corn,] corn *1836YR*
60 'Till *rev from* Till *MSS. 137 (C), 138 (B)* Till *MSS. 130, 137 (A), 138 (A), 1836YR* together;] together: *rev in pencil to* together;— *MS. 130*
61 weed; *ital rev in pencil from* weed *ital MS. 130* *no ital 1845–*
62 Ceres, *rev from* Ceres *MS. 137 (A)* Ceres *MS. 137 (B)* garland, *rev from* garland *MS. 137 (C)* garland *MSS. 130, 137 (A, B), 138 (A)*
63 ornament, *rev from* ornament *MS. 137 (A)*
64 knows, *rev from* knows *MS. 137 (A)* knows *MS. 137 (B)*
65 (Her] Her *MS. 130* so) *rev from* so), *MS. 137 (A)* so, *MS. 130* so), *MS. 137 (B)* Youth's] youth's *MS. 130, MS. 1835/36–, 1839*
67 dawn—] dawn, *MS. 130*
68 it] it, *in pencil MS. 1836/45* it, *1840–*
72 through] thro' *MS. 130*
75 needed, *rev in pencil to* needed; *MS. 130*
76 interference—] interference, *MS. 130*
79 ours!] ours!. *Victoria MS.*
80 love *rev from* love, *MS. 137 (A)* love, *MS. 137 (B)*
83 Archetype, *rev in pencil from* Archetype *MS. 130*
84 freak *rev in pencil to* freak, *MS. 130*
85 ever, haply,] ever haply *Victoria MS.*
87 here *no ital Victoria MS.* abide,] abide *MSS. 130, 137, 138, Victoria MS.*
89 Godlike . . . divine] God-like . . . Divine *MS. 130*
90 immortality,] Immortality *MS. 130* immortality *Victoria MS.*
91 Stretched *rev from* Sretched *MS. 137 (A, B)* Stretch'd *Victoria MS.* hope? *rev in pencil to* hope?— *MS. 130* hope?— *MS. 1835/36–, 1839* realm, *rev in pencil from* realm *MS. 130*
92 plains, *rev in pencil from* plains *MS. 130*
94 appeal; *rev in pencil to* appeal;— *MS. 130*
95 God *rev from* God, *MS. 137 (A)* God, *MS. 137 (B)*
96 Convent *rev from* Convent, *MS. 137 (A)* Convent, *MS. 137 (B)*
97 Escurial palace. *rev in pencil to* Escurial-palace. *MS. 130* He,] He— *MS. 1835/36–, 1839*
98 Guiding, *rev from* Guiding *MS. 137 (A)* Guiding *MSS. 130, 137 (B)* to cell] to cell, *MS. 130*
100 shown] shewn *MS. 130*
101 kings, *rev from* Kings, *MS. 137 (A)* Kings *MS. 130* Kings, *MS. 137 (B)*
102 endeared *rev from* endear'd *MS. 137 (A)* endear'd *MS. 137 (B)* cottagers)] Cottagers) *MS. 130* cottagers)— *MS. 1835/36–, 1839*
104 Last] last *MS. 130*
105 *no commas MS. 130*
106 Refectory: and there,] Refectory. And There *MS. 130*
107 Masterpiece] Master-piece *MS. 130* masterpiece *MS. 1835/36–, 1839*
108 Stranger's *rev from* stranger's *MS. 137 (A)* stranger's *MS. 137 (B)*
109 words:—] words. *MS. 130* sit, *rev in pencil from* sit *MS. 130*
110 here *rev in pencil to* here, *MS. 130*
111 Times] times *MS. 1835/36–, 1839*
116 they—] they *MS. 130*
117 They are, in truth, the Substance we the Shadows." *MS. 130* They . . . we *rev from* They . . . we *ital MS. 137 (C), MS. 138 (A)* They . . . we *ital MS. 137 (A, B)*
118 *no para MS. 137 (A, B); para reinstated MS. 137 (C)* Jeronymite, *rev from* Jeronimite, *MS. 137 (C)* Jeronimite *MS. 137 (A, B)* Jeronymite— *MS. 138 (O10-a)*
122 consigned *rev in pencil to* consigned, *MS. 130*
123 presence . . . words:] presence . . . words, *rev in pencil to* presence, . . . words, *MS. 130* presence, . . . words; *MS. 138 (O10-a)*
125 *no comma MS. 130 (B)* angel] Angel *MS. 130 (B)*
129 tear? *rev from* tear— *MS. 138 (O10a)* mute,] mute *MSS. 130 (B), 138 (O10a)*
131 farewell!] farewell!* *1845* farewell*! *1850*
note to l. 131 The pile] *The pile *1850* added,] added *1850*

The Foregoing Subject Resumed

title *no punct MS. 130*
3 Triumphs, *rev from* Triumps, *MS. 130* skill,] skill; *MSS. 137, 130* skill. *1840*

6 dissolution] dissolution, *MS. 138 (B_2)*
10 Thou,] Thou *MSS. 137, 130*
11 flower,] flower *MS. 130*
12 passed,] passed *1836–*
14 object] Object *MSS. 137, 130*
17 time, *rev from* time,— *MS. 138 (B)*
18 Creation,] Creation *MSS. 137, 130* yesterday— *rev from* yesterday, *MS. 137* yesterday— *rev from* yesterday,— *MS. 138 (B)* yesterday *MS. 130*
20 joined,] joined *1836–*
21 nature,] Nature, *MSS. 137, 130* nature *1836–* roof] roof, *MS. 130*
24 awe,] awe *1836–*
29 sensitive,—] sensitive, *rev to* sensitive— *MS. 137* sensitive, *MS. 130*
32 *no punct MS. 130* heaven.] heaven.* *1845* heaven.*" *1850*
note to l. 32, first sentence Musings,] Musings *MS. 137* Mr.] Mr *MS. 138 (A)* childhood] child-hood *1836–, 1839* another] another, *MS. 138 (A)* landscape] Landscape *MS. 138 (A)* Poussin. It] Poussin; it *MSS. 138 (A), 137 (B)*
second sentence author] Author *MS. 138 (A)*
third sentence But, . . . satisfaction,] But . . . satisfaction *MS. 137 (B)* poems] Poems *MS. 138 (A), 1836–* Poems, *MSS. 137, 138 (B)* Friend] friend, *MSS. 137, 138 (B)*

Desponding Father! mark this altered bough

1 Father!] Father, *MS. 106* altered *rev from* alter'd *MS. 137* bough,] bough *MS. 106*
2 warmed, *rev from* warm'd, *MS. 137* warm'd, *MS. 106*
3 dews;] dews,— *MS. 106*
4 shrivelled, *rev from* shrivell'd, *MS. 137* formed, *rev from* form'd, *MS. 137* form'd *MS. 106*
5 yet] Yet *MS. 106*
9 Stripling's *rev from* stripling's *MS. 137*
10 Fade] Fade, *MS. 106* shed,] shed— *1838, MS. 1836/45* fall] Fall *MS. 106*
11 cankerous *rev from* cank'rous *MS. 137*
12 bearings,] bearings *MS. 106* call;] call *MS. 106* call: *1836–, 1838, 1839*
13 *no ital 1836YR, 1845–*
14 Parents *ital*] Parents *ital rev from* parents *ital MS. 137* Parents *1836–, 1838, 1839* hope—] hope; *MS. 106* above] above *ital 1836–1843, 1838, 1839*

Lines Written in the Album of the Countess of ———. Nov. 5, 1834

1 Pen, perhaps,] Pen (perhaps *1836YR, 1836–, 1839*
2 Favoured, *rev from* favoured, *MS. 106* least,] least) *1836YR, 1836–, 1839*
3 Left, *rev in pencil to* Left *MS. 135* Left *1836YR* 'mid] mid *MSS. 106, 135* Records . . . Book] records . . . book *MS. 106* inscribed,] inscribed *1836YR, 1839*
5 feeling,] feeling *MSS. 106, 135*
6 birth:—] birth: *MS. 106* months *rev from* Months *MSS. 106, 135* passed,] past, *rev to* pass'd— *MS. 106* pass'd— *MS. 135*
12 *para MS. 135* Flowers] —Flowers *MS. 106*
16 Where'er] Whereer *MS. 106*
17 beams:] beams; *MS. 106, 1836YR*
18 shrink,] shrink *1836YR*
19 shade,—] shade, *MS. 106* Band,] Band *MSS. 106, 135* band, *1836–, 1839*
20 Progeny] progeny *1836–, 1839* earth,] earth *MSS. 106, 135*
22 Groves] groves, *MSS. 106, 135*
23 thou, too,] thou too *MSS. 106, 135* stream! *rev from* stream; *MS. 106*
24 ye] Ye *MS. 106* Parterres,] partee *rev to* parterres *MS. 106* Parterres *MS. 135*
25 she] She *1836–* own;] own, *MS. 106, 1845–* own *1836–1843*
27 offerings, *rev from* offerings,— *MS. 106* *no ital MS. 106*
29 waited,] waited; *rev to* waited— *MS. 106* waited— *1836–, 1839*
30 song;] song, *1836–*
32 self-solacing *rev from* self-solacing, *MS. 106* self-solacing, *1836YR, 1836–, 1839* self-solacing— *MS. 135* self-solacing *MS. 1836/45* under notes] under-notes *1836, 1839* under, notes *MS. 1836/45, 1840–*
33 redbreast] red-breast *MSS. 106, 135*
36 issue checked;] issue, checked *1836–, 1839*
37 reprehended] reprehended, *1836–, 1839*
44 *para, rev to no para MS. 106*
45 station, *rev from* Station, *MS. 106*
47 cloister. Yet *rev from* cloister; yet *MS. 106*
49 Nature's] nature's *MS. 106*
53 Heaven: *rev from* Heaven; *MS. 106* heaven: *1836–, 1839*
55 truth] Truth *MS. 135*
57 thine *rev to* Thine *MS. 106*

58 they, *rev from* They, *MS. 135* they *MS. 106*
61 Time;] Time— *MSS. 106, 135*
65 vigilance *rev from* vigilence *MS. 106* others' *rev from* Other's *MS. 106*
66 verse] Verse *1836–*
72 steed] Steed *MS. 106, 1839* borne,] borne *MSS. 106, 135*
75 Yet] —Yet *MS. 106*
76 passed] pass'd *MS. 135* prayer,] prayer— *1836–, 1839*
77 That,] That *MS. 106* sun] Sun *MSS. 106, 135*
78 So,] So— *1836–, 1839*
80 forgiven,—] forgiven— *1836–, 1839*
81 So] —So *MS. 106*

The Redbreast. (Suggested in a Westmoreland Cottage.)

1–13 *no punct MS. 133*
1 *no comma MS. 135, 1845–*
2 half-stripped woods] half-stripped-woods *MS. 135*
3 home:] home; *MS. 135*
5 *no comma MS. 135*
10 Ballad *rev from* ballad *MS. 137 (A)* ballad *MSS. 135, 137 (B), 1839*
11 But] But, *MS. 135, 1836YR* by,] by *MS. 135, 1836YR*
12 sorrows] sorrrows *MS. 133* Sorrows *MS. 135*
14 now— . . . missed,] now, . . . missed *MS. 133* *dash added MS. 135*
15–81 *no punct MS. 133*
15 listener] Listener *MS. 135*
18 Was *rev to* —Was *MS. 135*
19 illusion? *rev from* illusion! *MS. 135*
21 ceiling;] cieling; *MS. 135* ceiling: *1836YR*
22 *no comma MS. 135*
23 'Till] Till *1836YR, 1839*
24 *no commas MS. 135*
27 Bird *rev from* bird *MS. 135*
28 and . . . stirred *rev from* and, . . . stirred, *MS. 137 (A)* and, . . . stirred, *MS. 137 (B)*
30 *no ital 1836–, 1836YR, 1839*
32 *no comma 1840–*
33 sick-bed; *rev from* sick-bed, *MS. 137 (A)* sick-bed, *MSS. 135, 137 (B)*
37 And who] —And who, *MS. 135* Bird *rev from* Bird, *MS. 137 (A)* Bird, *rev from* bird, *MS. 135* Bird, *MS. 137 (B)* bird *rev from* Bird *MS. 138* bird *MS. 1835/36*
38 Child?] Child *rev from* Child, *MS. 135* child? *rev from* child; *MS. 137 (A)* Child? *rev from* child? *MSS. 137 (B), 138* child? *MS. 1835/36* Child; *1836–, 1839*
39 *no commas MS. 138*
40 Spring;] Spring, *MS. 138* Spring: *1836–, 1839*
43 angels] Angels *MS. 135*
45 "Matthew *rev from* Matthew *MS. 137 (A)* Matthew *MSS. 135, 137 (B)*
46 upon:"* *rev from* upon; *MS. 137 (A)* upon; *MSS. 135, 137 (B)* upon*; *1836–1843* upon'*; *1839* upon*?' *1845–*
note to l. 46 words—] words, *MS. 137 (A)* Luke,] Luke *MS. 137 (A)* on,] on *MS. 137 (A)* child's] Child's countries] Countries *MS. 137 (A)*
50 Old-folk] old folk *MS. 1835/36–* old-folk *1839*
51 faith] faith, *1836–, 1839*
53 night,] night *1836–*
57 wingèd] winged *1836–, 1839*
58 Thrice-happy] Thrice happy *MS. 135* Creature! *rev from* creature! *MS. 137 (A)* creature! *MS. 137 (B)*
59 hands: *rev from* hands; *MS. 135*
60 cot] Cot *MS. 135*
61 exit *rev from* exit: *MS. 135* *no ital MS. 133*
65 closed] closed, *MS. 135*
67 *no ital MS. 133*
68 Robin's] Robins *MS. 133*
69 bird *rev to* Bird *MS. 135* Bird *MS. 133*
70 O'er] Oer *MS. 133* *no ital MS. 133*
71 frown,] frown *1836–* stir] stir, *1836–, 1839*
76 chimney nook,] chimney nook *1836YR* chimney-nook, *1836–*
77 Dame, *rev from* dame, *MS. 137 (A)* dame, *MS. 137 (B)*
80 Reflected,] Reflected *1836–, 1839*

Upon Seeing a Coloured Drawing of the Bird of Paradise in an Album

title Bird of Paradise *and* Album *underscored, all other words lower case except* Upon *and* The *Princeton MS. 1*
1 Image] image *1839* portray? *rev from* pourtray? *Princeton MS. 1*
2 minion] Minion *Princeton MS. 1*
3 creature—] creature, *MS. 1836/45*
4 colours—] colours; *MS. 1836/45* colours, *1845–*
9 *para break after* pencil! *Princeton MS. 1*
10 time; *rev to* Time; *Princeton MS. 1*
11 insects] Insects *Princeton MS. 1*
13 *para Princeton MS. 1*
14 Diver's *Princeton MS. 1*
17 'Mid . . . shows,] Mid . . . shows *Princeton MS. 1*

18 shape] Shape *1845–*
21 keep] keep, *MS. 1836/45, 1840–* stain;] stain, *Princeton MS. 1*
23 sun's] Sun's *Princeton MS. 1*
26 stirred,] stirred; *Princeton MS. 1*
30 Bird of God] Bird of God *underscored Princeton MS. 1*
34 beauty,] beauty *MS. 1836/45, 1840–*
42 realities.] realities! *MS. 1836/45, 1840–*

Airey-Force Valley

title Airay Force valley *MS. 89*
1 —Not] Not *MSS. 89, 139, 151 (A), WW to Joshua Watson* ———Not *1845–*
2 glen.] glen *MS. 151 (A)* glen, *WW to Joshua Watson*
3 brook's] brooks *MS. 151 (A, B)* margin,] margin *WW to Joshua Watson*
4 stedfast] steadfast *1850*
7 motionless. *rev from* motionless, *MS. 89*
8 breeze,] breeze
10 unfelt;] unfelt, *MSS. 89 ,151 (A), 1845–*
11 its] it's *MS. 139* touch] touch, *MSS. 89, 139, WW to Joshua Watson*
12 ash!] Ash, *rev to* Ash! *MS. 89* ash, *MS. 139, WW to Joshua Watson* Ash! *MS. 151 (A)* ash! *rev to* Ash! *MS. 151 (B)* that,] that *MSS. 139, 151 (A)*
13 cave, *rev from* Cave, *MS. 151 (B)* Cave *MS. 151 (A)* cave, *rev to* Cave, *WW to Joshua Watson* silence *rev from* silence, *MS. 89*
14 slow-waving boughs,] slow waving boughs; *MS. 139* slow waving boughs *WW to Joshua Watson*
15 Powerful almost] Powerful, almost, *MSS. 89, 139* Powerfull, almost *MS. 151 (A)*
16 wanderer's *rev to* Wanderer's *MS. 89* Wanderer's *MSS. 139, 151 (A, B), WW to Joshua Watson* steps] steps, *MSS. 89, 139*

To the Moon. (Composed by the Sea-side,—on the Coast of Cumberland.)

3 Night and Silence *rev from* night and silence *(JC) Princeton MS. 2, MS. 138*
5 *no commas Princeton MS. 2* cottage-lattice *rev from* Cottage-lattice *Princeton MS. 2*
12 thee *rev from* Thee *Princeton MS. 2*
14 shown] shown *JC rev from* shewn *Princeton MS. 2*
22 weakness] weakness, *Princeton MS. 2*
23 *para added Princeton MS. 2* Mountains *JC rev from* mountains *Princeton MS. 2* Streams *JC rev from* streams *Princeton MS. 2* Streams, *1845, 1849, 1850*
27 minster's] Minster's *Princeton MS. 2*
29 Canst . . . Prisoner] Can'st . . . prisoner *Princeton MS. 2*
33 One, *rev from* One— *Princeton MS. 2*
40 Moon! *rev from* moon! *Princeton MS. 2* bright] brigh *(printer's error) 1850*
41 rouse] rouze *Princeton MS. 2*
48 Sea *rev from* sea *Princeton MS. 2*
49 depths *underscored Princeton MS. 2*
56 Touched] Touched, *Princeton MS. 2*
59 *no end dash Princeton MS. 2*
61 *no comma Princeton MS. 2*
65 mid] 'mid *1839, 1850*

To the Moon. (Rydal.)

title no periods Princeton MS. 3
1 *dash inserted Princeton MS. 3*
3 o'er] oer *Princeton MS. 3*
4 forego, *rev from* forgo, *Princeton MS. 3*
5 below— *rev from* below, *Princeton MS. 3*
6 who,] who *Princeton MS. 3* wide-spread *rev from* widespread *Princeton MS. 3*
7 thee *rev to* Thee *Princeton MS. 3*
17 belov'd (for *rev from* beloved—for *Princeton MS. 3*
18 fascinate *rev from* facinate *Princeton MS. 3*
19 outright,] outright *Princeton MS. 3*
20 Mother's *rev from* mother's *Princeton MS. 3* sight) *rev from* sight *Princeton MS. 3*
21 still] Still *1839* worshipped!] worshipped, *Princeton MS. 3* Time, *rev from* time, *Princeton MS. 3*
23 splendour; still] splendour!—Still *Princeton MS. 3*
26 Virgin-choirs] virgin choirs *Princeton MS. 3*
28 increase] encrease *Princeton MS. 3* yore,] yore *Princeton MS. 3*
29 Matrons— *rev from* Matrons, *Princeton MS. 3*
31 deliverance— *JC rev from* deliverance, *Princeton MS. 3*
35 cannot cease,] cannot, cease *1845, 1849, 1850*
37 Fancy, *rev from* fancy, *Princeton MS. 3*
41 Science] science *Princeton MS. 3* mankind—] mankind; *Princeton MS. 3*
50 *quot lacking Princeton MS. 3*
52 eclipsed, *rev from* eclipsed; *Princeton MS. 3*
54 change;] change, *Princeton MS. 3*

55 Meek, patient, stedfast,] Meek patient steadfast *Princeton MS. 3*

Epitaph, Text of Huntington MS. 2

9 Independence, *rev from* independence, *Huntington MS.* 2

17 *no para rev from no para Huntington MS.* 2

29 Kind— *rev from* Kind; *Huntington MS.* 2

31 Her *rev from* Th *(false start of line below) Huntington MS. 3*

Epitaph written on Charles Lamb by William Wordsworth, Text of Huntington MS. 4

2 —Here] Here *Epitaph*

3 City] city *Epitaph*

4 rear'd *rev from* reared *Huntington MS. 4* taught; *with colon over eras Huntington MS. 4* bread] bread, *Epitaph*

5 Merchant's] merchant's *Epitaph*

6 By *rev from* by *Huntington MS. 4*

7 Teaze] Tease *Epitaph*

8 Spirit] spirit *Epitaph*

9 Independence, *rev from* independence, *Huntington MS. 4*

11 And, . . . came] And . . . came, *Epitaph*

13 Books] books *Epitaph*

15 wrong] wrong, *Epitaph*

17 Inspired,—Works] Inspired—works *Epitaph*

22 words.—] words. *Epitaph*

23 *no para Epitaph* Creature] creature *Epitaph*

24 a name *rev from* a name, *Huntington MS. 5* a name, *Epitaph*

26 meekness,] meekness *Epitaph* *colon rev from comma Huntington MS. 4*

27 way] way, *Epitaph*

32 often] often, *Epitaph*

33 Kind] kind *Epitaph*

37 judgement] judgment *Epitaph*

38 if e'er *rev from* if e'er *ital Huntington MS. 6* if e'er *ital Epitaph*

To a good Man of most dear memory, Text of 1836

2 Stone] stone *Lamb Letters*

4 reared . . . earned *rev from* rear'd . . . earn'd *Turnbull MS.* rear'd . . . earn'd *CL1, DC1, CL2*

7 Tease, . . . depress, *rev to* Tease . . . depress *Turnbull MS. 1* Teaze . . . depress *Lamb Letters*

8 high;] high,— *Turnbull MS. 1*

9 sire] Sire *Lamb Letters, YR1839*

10 air; *rev from* air! *Turnbull MS. 1* air! *CL1, DC1, CL2*

11 And] And, *DC1, CL2*

25 christian altars] Christian Altars *CL1, DC1, CL2, Turnbull* Christian altars *Lamb Letters*

38 e'er] ere *Berg MS. 1* Man] man *Lamb Letters*

38/39 *line of dashes Berg MS. 1; 3-line space but no asterisks DC1, CL2*

43 missed;] missed, *Turnbull MS. 2* missed *Lamb Letters, 1846, 1849*

44 For] For, *Turnbull MS. 2*

50 scorner] Scorner *Berg MS. 1* Friend!] Friend *1840–1843* Friend, *1845–*

51 show] shew *Berg MS. 1, CL1, DC1, CL2* truth;] truth, *CL1* truth, *rev to* truth; *Turnbull MS. 1* truth! *Lamb Letters*

53 spirit] Spirit *DC1, CL2*

56 sanctity] sanctity, *Lamb Letters*

58 love,] love *Berg MS. 1*

59 through] thro' *CL1, DC1, CL2*

62 *no para Berg MS. 1, CL1, DC1, CL2 para inserted Turnbull MS. 1*

62, 64 *double quots Berg MS. 1, CL1, DC1, CL2*

72 choose] chuse *Berg MS. 1*

76 thee] thee, *1845, 1850*

77 enriched,] enriched— *RHT MS., DC1, CL2* enriched,— *Turnbull MS. 1* adorned,] adorned,— *Turnbull MS. 1*

81 ever-kind] ever kind *DC1, CL2*

83 Found—for *rev from* Found for *Turnbull MS. 1* Found for *Berg MS. 1, CL1, DC1, CL2*

84 humanising] humanizing *Berg MS. 1*

85 unsought— *rev from* unsought, *Turnbull MS. 1* unsought, *Berg MS. 1, CL1, DC1, CL2*

91 protector] Protector *rev from* Proctector *Berg MS. 1*

94 'mid] mid *Berg MS. 1*

99 such; *rev from* such: *Turnbull MS. 1*

108 Friend] Friend *rev from* friend *Turnbull MS. 1* friend *Berg MS. 1, CL1*

115 mother)] mother,) *CL1*

122 hermit] hermit *rev from* Hermit *Turnbull MS. 1* Hermit *Berg MS. 1, CL1, DC1, CL2*

124 vow, *rev to* vow *Berg MS. 1*

126 souls,] souls; *Berg MS. 1, CL1, DC1, CL2*

127 appeared,] appeared *Berg MS. 1, CL1, DC1, CL2*

Extempore Effusion upon the Death of James Hogg

1 first,] first *Southey Album 2*

moorlands,] Moorlands, *Victoria MS. 2, Newcastle Journal, Atheneum* moorlands *Yale MS. 4*

2 Stream] stream *Houghton MS. 2, Southey Album 2, Newcastle Journal, Atheneum* glide] glide, *Houghton MS. 2*

3 valley,] Valley *Houghton MS. 2, Berg MS. 2, Southey Album 2* Valley, *Newcastle Journal*

4 guide.] guide; *Berg MS. 2* Guide. *Southey Album 2* guide, *Newcastle Journal*

5 wandered,] wander'd, *Victoria MS. 2* wandered *Houghton MS. 2, Berg MS. 2* wander'd *Southey Album 2*

6 Through] Thro' *Yale MS. 4, Houghton MS. 2, Southey Album 2, Newcastle Journal, Atheneum*

7 pathways,] Pathways, *Victoria MS. 2* pathways *Berg MS. 2* Pathways *Southey Album 2*

8 border minstrel] border Minstrel *Yale MS. 4, Houghton MS. 2, Berg MS. 2* Border Minstrel *Victoria MS. 2, Southey Album 2, Newcastle Journal, Atheneum* Border-minstrel *1845, 1850* led. *rev from* led: *Houghton MS. 2*

9 *no comma Southey Album 2*

10 Mid] 'Mid *Victoria MS. 2, Newcastle Journal, Atheneum* lies;] lies, *Southey Album 2*

11 death] death, *Victoria MS. 2, Berg MS. 2* Death *Southey Album 2* braes] Braes *Southey Album 2, Newcastle Journal, Atheneum* *no final comma Yale MS. 4, Houghton MS. 2, Southey Album 2, Newcastle Journal, Atheneum*

12 closed *rev to* clos'd *Victoria MS. 2* Shepherd-poet's eyes:] Shepherd-poet's eyes: *rev to* Shepherd-poet's eyes. *Houghton MS. 2* Shepherd-Poet's eyes. *Victoria MS. 2* Shepherd Poet's eyes. *Berg MS. 2, Southey Album 2*

13 year *rev to* Year *Yale MS. 4* Year *Newcastle Journal* measured, *rev to* measur'd, *Victoria MS. 2* measured *Yale MS. 4, Houghton MS. 2, Southey Album 2*

14 sign,] sign *Victoria MS. 2, Southey Album 2* stedfast] steadfast *Berg MS. 2, Southey Album 2*

15 mortal *rev from* Mortal *Huntington MS. 5* Mortal *Houghton MS. 2, Newcastle Journal, Atheneum* power] Power *Yale MS. 4, Newcastle Journal, Atheneum*

16 source;] source;— *Victoria MS. 2*

17 'rapt One,] rapt One *rev from* rapt one *Yale MS. 4* rapt One, *Houghton MS. 2* rapt One *Newcastle Journal, Atheneum* rapt one, *Berg MS. 2, Victoria MS. 2* rapt one *Southey Album 2* rapt One, *1850* godlike *rev from* Godlike *Huntington MS. 5* Godlike *Southey Album 2, Newcastle Journal, Atheneum* forehead,] forehead,— *Berg MS. 2*

18 heaven-eyed] heaveneyed *Southey Album 2* creature] creature, *rev to* Creature, *Yale MS. 4* Creature, *Houghton MS. 2, Newcastle Journal, Atheneum* Creature *Berg MS. 2* creature, *Southey Album 2* earth:] earth; *Victoria MS. 2, Berg MS. 2, Newcastle Journal, Atheneum* Earth: *Southey Album 2*

19 *no commas Southey Album 2*

20 vanished *rev to* vanish'd *Victoria MS. 2* vanish'd *Southey Album 2* hearth.] hearth; *Southey Album 2*

21 mountain-summits] mountain summits *Victoria MS. 2, Berg MS. 2* Mountain Summits *Southey Album 2*

23 brother . . . brother,] Brother . . . Brother *Yale MS. 4, Houghton MS. 2, Berg MS. 2, Southey Album 2, Newcastle Journal, Atheneum* followed *rev to* follow'd *Victoria MS. 2* follow'd *Southey Album 2* *no comma Victoria MS. 2, Southey Album 2*

24 sunshine] Sunshine *Victoria MS. 2, Southey Album 2*

25–26 *no commas Southey Album 2*

26 raised, *rev to* rais'd, *Victoria MS. 2, Berg MS. 2*

27 voice,] voice *Southey Album 2* whispers,] whispers *Houghton* *no commas Berg MS. 2*

28 "Who] Who *Berg MS. 2* disappear?"] disappear"? *Yale MS. 4* disappear. *Berg MS. 2*

29 darkness,] Darkness *Berg MS. 2, Southey Album 2*

31 which] which, *Yale MS. 5, Newcastle Journal, Atheneum* thee, *rev from* thee *Yale MS. 5* thee *Berg MS. 2* O *rev from* o *Houghton MS. 2* Crabbe!] Crabbe, *Yale MS. 5, Southey Album 2, Newcastle Journal, Atheneum* forth-looking] forth looking *Houghton MS. 2, Southey Album 2* *no final comma Yale MS. 5, Houghton MS. 2, Southey Album 2, Newcastle Journal, Atheneum*

32 Hampstead's] Hampsteads *Berg MS. 2* heath.] heath; *Yale MS. 5, Southey Album 2, Newcastle Journal, Atheneum*

33–35 *no commas Houghton MS. 2, Southey Album 2*

35 *no apos, no commas Berg MS. 2; no commas Yale MS. 5*

36 Survivors *Berg MS. 2, Houghton MS. 2, Southey Album 2*

37 Spirit,] Spirit *Southey Album 2*

38 spring, as ocean deep;] spring as Ocean deep, *Southey Album 2*

39 Her] her *Southey Album 2* *no commas Southey Album 2*

41 *no comma Yale MS. 5, Houghton MS. 2, Princeton MS. 4, Berg MS. 2, Southey Album 2, Newcastle Journal, Atheneum*

42 slaughtered] slaughter'd *Berg MS. 2, Southey Album 2* Youth *rev from* youth *Yale MS. 5* youth *Houghton MS. 2, Newcastle Journal, Atheneum* love-lorn] lovelorn *Princeton MS. 4* love lorn *Berg MS. 2* Maid!] Maid *(sheet cut away) Princeton MS. 4* Maid, *rev from* maid, *Yale MS. 5, Berg MS. 2, Newcastle Journal, Atheneum* maid; *Houghton MS. 2* maid, *Southey Album 2*

43 smitten,] smitten *Princeton MS. 4, Houghton MSS.* smitten; *Berg MS. 2*

44 Ettrick] Etterick *Berg MS. 2* dead.] dead! *Yale MS. 4, Newcastle Journal, Atheneum* dead *Houghton MS. 2* dead *Berg MS. 2, Princeton MS. 4 (sheet cut away)* dead*. *1836–*

At the Grave of Burns. 1803

1, 4 *no commas MS. 143*

6 *no period MS. 143*

7 *no comma MSS. 143, 151.1, 151.2*

8–10 *no punct MS. 143*

8 appear? *rev from* appear, *MS. 151.1*

9 *no comma MSS. 151.1, 151.2, 1845–*

12 vain. *rev from* vain— *MS. 151.1*

13 weight!—] weight— *MS. 143* weight! *rev from* weight— *MS. 151.1*

14 thoughts!— *rev from* thoughts — *MS. 151.1* stay;] stay! *MS. 143* stay; *rev from* stay! *MS. 151.1*

17 *no comma MS. 143*

19 *no comma MSS. 143, 151.1*

20 *no commas MS. 143* forth,] forth; *MS. 151.1*

21–22 *no commas MS. 143*

24 beams. *rev from* beams.— *MS. 151.2*

25 brow,] brow *MS. 143*

26 *no punct MSS. 143* now?—] now? *rev from* now *MS. 151.1*

27 plough,] Plough *MS. 143* plough, *rev from* Plough *MS. 151.1*

28 brave,] brave *MS. 143*

29 Slept,] Slept *MS. 143* obscurest, *rev from* Obscurest, *MS. 151.1*

30 And . . . grave.] —And . . . grave *MS. 143*

31 He *rev from* he *MS. 151.2*

32 *no punct MSS. 143, 151.1*

33 When, *rev from* When *MS. 1842P* forth *rev from* forth, *MS. 143* *no commas MSS. 151.1, 151.2* nature's] Nature's *MSS. 143, 151.1*

34 youth *rev to* Youth *MS. 151.1* youth *rev from* Youth *MS. 1842P*

35 Verse] verse *MS. 151.1* Verse *rev from* verse *MS. 151.2*

36 *no period MS. 151.1*

37 Alas! where'er] Alas whereer *MS. 143* Alas! where'er *rev from* Alas where'er *MS. 151.1* *no comma MSS. 143, 151.1, 151.2*

38 blends,—] blends; *MS. 143* blends *MS. 151.1* blends; *rev from* blends *MS. 151.2*

39 Criffel's] Criffels *MSS. 143, 151.1*

40 seen,—] seen *MS. 143* seen; *MS. 151.1*

41 friends *rev to* Friends *MS. 151.1*

43 friends] friends, *MS. 143* though] tho' *MSS. 143, 151.1, 151.2* *no semicolon MS. 143*

45 fibres *rev from* fibers *MS. 151.2* entwined,] intwined *rev from* int[?]ined *MS. 143* entwined, *rev from* entwined *MS. 151.2*

46 Through] Thro' *MSS. 143, 151.1, 151.2* *no comma MSS. 143, 151.1, 151.2*

49 *no punct MS. 143* start, . . . flow;] start— . . . flow: *rev from* start . . . flow *MS. 151.1*

50 *no quot MS. 143* *no comma MSS. 143, 151.1*

53 *no comma MS. 143*

54, 56 *no punct MS. 143*

56 reach; *rev from* reach, *MS. 151.1*

57 fancy] Fancy *MS. 143* Fancy, *rev to* Fancy *MS. 151.1* repast! *rev from* repast; *MS. 151.2*

58 But *rev to* But, *MS. 151.1* on?—] on? *rev from* on, *rev from* on *MS. 151.1* *no punct MS. 143*

59 Oh!] Oh *MS. 151.1*

60 grass-grown.] grass-grown! *MS. 151.1*

61 *no punct MS. 143* Son,] Son *MS. 151.1* pride, *rev to* pride *MS. 151.1*

62 Stripling *rev from* stripling *MS. 151.1* died,)] died) *MSS. 143, 151.1*

63–64 *no punct MS. 143*

64 soul moving *MS. 143*

66 *no punct MS. 143*

67 he *ital*] he *MS. 143*
67–68 *no comma MS. 143*
69–70 *no commas MSS. 143, 151.1, 151.2*
72–73 *no punct MS. 143*
73 oh] Oh *MS. 143* Thee] thee *MSS. 143, 151.1* Thee *rev from* thee *MS. 151.2*
74 oft-times] ofttimes *rev from* oftimes *MS. 143,* ofttimes *MS. 151.1* oft-times *rev from* ofttimes *MS. 1842P* *no punct MS. 143*
75 He] he *MSS. 143, 151.1* He *rev from* he *MS. 151.2*
78 prayed!] prayed *MS. 143* prayed! *rev from* prayed!— *MS. 151.2*
79 away; *rev from* away— *MS. 151.1* *no punct MS. 143*
80 *no commas MSS. 143, 151.1, 151.2*
81 sorrow] Sorrow *MS. 143*
82 *no comma MSS. 143, 151.1*
83 Chaunted] Chanted *1850*
84 Seraphim.] Seraphim.— *MS. 151.2*

Thoughts Suggested the Day Following on the Banks of Nith, near the Poet's Residence

title FOLLOWING] FOLLOWING, *1845, 1850* POET'S] Poets *MS. 151.2*
1 vow] Vow *MS. 151.1 (A)*
3 wreathed—"The Vision"] wreath'd (the Vision *Laing MS.* wreathed, the Vision *MS. 143* how—] how) *Laing MS.* how *MS. 143* how, *MS. 151.1 (A)*
4 holly spray,] holly-spray, *Laing MS.* holly spray *MS. 143*
5 fro, *rev from* fro *MS. 151.2* fro *MS. 143*
6 *no period MS. 143*
7 Sister,] Sister; *rev to* Sister! *MS. 151.1 (A)* *no commas MS. 143*
8 when, lingering . . . long,] when lingering, . . . long *MS. 143* when lingering . . . long, *comma del MS. 151.1 (A)*
10 grief—] grief, *MS. 151.1 (A)* grief *MSS. 143, 151.2*
13 But,] But *MSS. 143, 151.1 (A), Laing MS.*
14 judgments] judgements *Laing MS.*
14, 16 *no comma MS. 143*
17 us] us, *Laing MS.* Stream] Stream, *Laing MS.* Stream *rev from* stream *MS. 151.2*
18 air. *rev from* air *MS. 151.2* air *MS. 143* air— *MS. 151.1 (A)*
19 *no commas MSS. 143, 151.1 (A), 151.2*
22 *no comma MS. 143*
23 Wisdom] wisdom *MSS. 143, 151.1 (A)* prospered] prosper'd *Laing MS.* sight] sight, *Laing MS., MS. 151.1 (A)*
24 *no period MS. 143*
25 *no commas MS. 143*
26 *no comma MSS. 143, 151.1 (A)*
27 side *rev to* side, *MS. 151.2* book *MS. 151.1 (A)* *no commas MS. 143*
30 Lay. *rev from* lay. *MS. 151.2*
31 oft inspired] oft, inspired, *Laing MS., MSS. 143, 151.1 (A)*
32 pathways, . . . road!] pathways, . . . road; *Laing MS.* pathways . . . road; *MS. 143*
33 home; . . . Abode,] Home! . . . Abode, *Laing MS.* home, . . . Abode *MS. 143* home, . . . abode, *MS. 151.1 (A)* Abode, *rev from* abode, *MS. 151.2*
34 *no comma MSS. 143, 151.2*
35 nobly-pensive *rev from* nobly pensive *MS. 1842P* nobly pensive *MSS. 143, 151.1 (A)* mood,] mood *MS. 143*
36 Rustic *rev from* rustic *MSS. 143, 151.2*
37 overawes,] overawes; *MSS. 143, 151.1 (A)*
38 pause,] pause; *MS. 151.1 (A)*
39 *no comma MS. 151.1 (A)*
43 Through] Thro' *MSS. 143, 151.1 (A), 151.2* glen] Glen *Laing MS.*
44 pen] Pen *Laing MS.*
45 mid] 'mid *1850* winter snows,] winter-snows *MS. 143*
47 men *rev from* Men *MS. 151.1 (A)* Men *MS. 143*
49 fields . . . clime] Fields, . . . clime, *Laing MS.*
50 Heroes] Heros *MS. 151.2* *no commas MS. 143*
52 springs,] Springs *Laing MS., MS. 143*
53 till] 'till *Laing MS.*
54 wings?] wings. *MSS. 143, 151.1 (A)* Wings. *MS. 151.2*
55 Mercy! *rev from* mercy! *MS. 143* mercy *WW to HR* Heaven] heaven *WW to HR*
56 lead,] lead *MS. 143* forgiven;] forgiven, *MSS. 143, 151.1 (A), WW to HR*
57 *no comma MS. 143, WW to HR* riven] riv'n *Laing MS.*
58 *no comma MS. 143*
59 Earth's *rev from* earth *MS. 151.2* earths *MS. 143* earth's *Laing MS., MS. 151.1 (A), WW to HR* *no comma Laing MS., MS. 143, WW to HR*
60 ever.] ever!— *Laing MS.*
61 Him] him *MSS. 143, 151.1 (A)* Him *rev from* him *MS. 151.2* *no comma MSS. 143, 151.1 (A, C), 151.2*
64 live?—] live *MS. 143* live? *MS. 151.1 (A, C), WW to HR* live? *rev from* live: *MS. 151.2*

65 *no comma MS. 143*
66 forgive!] forgive!* *1845, 1846–1849* forgive*! *1850* *no comma MS. 143*

A Night Thought, Text of *The Tribute* (1837)
1 moon] Moon *BL MS. 2* sky] sky, *Mary Smith Album*
2 destiny,] destiny; *BL MS. 2* destiny: *Mary Smith Album*
4 *no punct BL MS. 2*
5 But] But, *BL MS. 2*
8 *no comma BL MS. 2*
9 th'æthereal] the etherial *all MSS.*
10 turned aside] turn'd aside, *BL MS. 2*
11 *no comma Mary Smith Album*
12 *no apos Mary Smith Album*
13 we . . . race;] We . . . race! *Mary Smith Album*
14 fortune's] Fortune's *BL MS. 2*
15 cherished] cherish'd *BL MS. 2*
16 pursue,] pursue; *BL MS. 2*
17 Ingrates,] Ingrates *BL MS. 2* Ingrates! *Mary Smith Album* smile-less] smileless *all MSS.*
21 Fancy . . . wake,] fancy . . . wake *all MSS.*
22 Heaven] heaven *all MSS.*
23 counter-impulse] counter impulse *Mary Smith Album* take] take, *BL MS. 2*
24 forgiven.] forgiv'n! *Mary Smith Album*

A Night Thought, Text of 1842
title A night thought *MS. 143*
1 *no punct MS. 143*
2 destiny; *rev from* destiny, *MS. 1842 P* destiny *MSS. 143, 151.1* destiny, *MS. 151.2*
3 mortal *rev from* Mortal *MS. 151.2* mortal *MSS. 143, 151.1*
4 *no comma MSS. 143, 151.1*
5 fly] fly, *MSS. 143, 151.1*
7 we] We *MS. 151.1* race,] race *MS. 143* Race *MS. 151.1* Race, *MS. 151.2*
8 though] tho' *MSS. 143, 151.1, 151.2* Fortune's] fortune's *MS. 143*
10 *no comma MSS. 143, 151.1*
12 through.] through— *MS. 143* thro'. *MSS. 151.1, 151.2*
14 spirit] Spirit *MS. 151.2* *no comma MSS. 143, 151.1*
15 *no comma MSS. 143, 151.1*
16 heaven! *rev from* Heaven! *MS. 151.2* heaven, *MSS. 143, 151.1*

On an Event in Col: Evans's redoubted performances in Spain
1 by— *rev from* by, *MW to HCR*

November, 1836 ("Even so for me a Vision sanctified")
series number II. *1836–, 1838*
1 Vision] vision *Hoare Album*
2 Death; . . . ere] death . . . 'ere *Hoare Album*
3 *no punct Hoare Album*
4 Sister! . . . Bride:] sister! . . . death's bride; *Hoare Album*
6 change:—] change— *Hoare Album*
9 decline,] decline *Hoare Album*
10 burn;] burn. *Hoare Album*
12 *no punct Hoare Album*
14 as, through that power,] as thro' that power *Hoare Album*

The Widow on Windermere Side, Text of 151.1 (A)
29 prayer?] prayer?— *MS. 151 (B)*
31 Through Death;] Thro death;— *MS. 151.1 (D)* Through death; *MS. 151.1 (B, C)*
33 fled] fled, *MS. 151.1 (D)*
35 air] air, *MS. 151.1 (D)* precipice,] precipice; *MS. 151.1 (B–D)*
38 breeze,] breeze *MS. 151.1 (B)*
39 knees] knees, *MS. 151.1 (B)*

The Widow on Windermere side, Text of 1842
title SIDE] side *MS. 151.1 (E)*
1 *no comma MS. 143 (C), 1845–*
2 Honour] Honor *MSS. 143 (C), 151.1 (E)* poor,] poor! *MS. 143 (C)* Poor! *MS. 151.1 (E), MS. 151.2 (A)*
3 deep!] deep. *MS. 151.1 (E), MS. 151.2 (A)*
4 One, a Widow,] One—a Widow *MS. 143 (C)* One, a Widow *MS. 151.1 (E)*
6 *no comma MSS. 143 (C), 151.1 (E)*
7 *no hyphen MSS. 143 (C), 151.1 (E), MS. 151.2 (A)*
8 herself *rev to* Herself *MSS. 143 (C), 151.2 (A)* Herself *MS. 151.1 (E)* hers *rev from miswritten* hears *MS. 143 (C)* hers *rev to* Hers *MS. 151.2 (A)*
9 world's] World's *MSS. 143 (C), 151.1 (E), 151.2 (A)* daylight] day-light *MS. 151.1 (E)*
10 through] thro' *MSS. 151.1 (E), 151.2 (A)* she] She *MS. 143 (C)*
11 vigils,] vigils *MSS. 143 (C), 151.1 (E)* prevailed] prevailed, *MSS. 143 (C), 151.1 (E)*
12 Creature *MSS. 143 (C), 151.1 (E), 151.2 (A), 1845–* slept; *rev from* slept, *MS. 151.1 (E)* slept *MS. 143 (C)*
13 one by one] One by One *MS. 151.1 (E), 151.2 (A)*

no commas MSS. 143 (C), 151.1 (E) death *rev from* Death *MS. 143 (C)* Death *MSS. 151.1 (E), 151.2 (A)*

14 children *rev to* Children *MS. 143 (C)* Children *MSS. 151.1 (E)* Children— *MSS. 151.1 (E), 151.2 (A)* from] —from *MS. 151.1 (E)*

15 *no commas MS. 151.1 (E)*

17 last *rev to* Last *MS. 151.1 (E)* child *rev to* Child *MS. 151.2 (A)*

18 angelic *rev from* Angelic *MS. 151.1 (E)*

20 touching; yea] touching, yea, *MS. 151.1 (E)*

21 heaven,] heaven *MSS. 151.1 (E), 151.2 (A)*

23 *no comma MS. 151.1 (E)*

24 Whate'er] Whateer *MS. 151.1 (E)*

25 season,] season *MS. 151.1 (E)*

26 presence] Presence *MSS. 151.1 (E), 151.2 (A)*

31 Death,—] Death— *MS. 151.1 (E)* amiss.] amiss *MS. 151.1 (E)*

32 *no comma MS. 151.1 (E)*

33 *no punct MS. 151.1 (E)*

34 maniacs] Maniacs *MS. 151.1 (E)*

35 *no punct MS. 151.1 (E)*

36 through] thro' *MSS. 151.1 (E), 151.2 (A)* tomb,] tomb *MS. 151.1 (E), 1849P*

37 Martyr's *MS. 151.1 (E)* *no punct MS. 151.1 (E)*

38 through] thro' *MSS. 151.1 (E), 151.2 (A, B)* *no punct MS. 151.1 (E), MS. 151.2 (A, B)*

41 Angel,] Angel *MS. 151.1 (E)* ecstacies] extacies *MSS. 151.1 (E), 151.2 (A)*

42 *no punct MS. 151.1 (E)*

To the Planet Venus, upon its Approximation (as an Evening Star) to the Earth, January 1838

title VENUS,] VENUS. *1845–* EARTH,] earth *Yale Sonnets MS.* 1838.] 1838 *Yale Sonnets MS.* JANUARY] JAN. *1845–*

1 guides *rev to* guides, *MS. 151.3* guides, *1842, 1845–*

4 it,] it *Yale Sonnets MS., MS. 151.3, 1842, 1845–*

5 less—] less.— *MS. 151.3, 1842, 1845–* presides,] presides *Yale Sonnets MS., MS. 151.3, 1842, 1845–*

8 meekness? *rev from* meekness; *Yale Sonnets MS., MS. 151.3*

Wouldst Thou be gathered to Christ's chosen flock

1 Thou] thou *MS. 140* gathered] gather'd *Southey Album 2* flock] Flock *MS. 140* flock, *Southey Album 2*

2 explored] explored, *MS. 140* explored; *Southey Album 2*

3 rock] Rock, *Southey Album 2*

4 WORD] word *Southey Album 2*

Oh what a Wreck! how changed in mien and speech! Text of 1842

1 OH *rev to* Oh *MS. 151.3* Wreck] wreck *1838, 1840*

4 within] within, *1838, 1840*

5 Sin] sin *1838, 1840*

6 wretch,] wretch *Yale Sonnet MS.* wretch; *1838, 1840*

12 love;] love *Yale Sonnet MS.* love; *rev from* love, *MS. 151.3*

Valedictory Sonnet ("Serving no haughty Muse, my hands have here")

1–14 *set in roman type 1840, 1842, 1845–*

3 *no comma MS. 147* knots)] knotts) *MS. 147* knots), *MS. 151.3, 1842, 1845–*

4 parterre;] parterre.— *MS. 147*

6 nurslings *rev to* Nurslings *MS. 151.3* Nurslings *1842, 1845–*

9 But,] But *MS. 151.3, 1842, 1845–*

10 be,—] be, *MS. 147* be, *rev to* be— *MS. 151.3* be— *1842, 1845–*

11 book] Book *MS. 147* agree;] agree, *MS. 147*

13 It *rev from* it *MS. 151.3* it *MS. 147* heart;] heart, *MS. 147*

14 love,] love,— *MS. 147* fee!] fee. *MS. 147*

Said red-ribbon'd Evans

23 Zero; *rev from* zero; *WW to HCR*

26 Prudence *rev from* prudence *WW to HCR*

30 His feats, *rev from* His, feats *WW to HCR*

Hark! 'tis the Thrush, undaunted, undeprest

1 Hark!] Hark, *Cornell MS. 10, Ransom MS.* 'tis] tis *Cornell MS. 10, BL MS. 4, Ransom MS.* Thrush,] Thrush— *rev from* thrush— *WW to TNT* Thrush— *MW to TH & MMH, Ransom MS.* Thrush! *Cornell MS. 10* undaunted,] undaunted *Ransom MS.* undeprest,] undepressed, *MW to TH & MMH* undeprest *Cornell MS. 10, Ransom MS.* undeprest *rev from* undepressed *BL MS. 4*

2 premature *rev from* premature, *BL MS. 4* rain; *rev from* rain— *MW to*

TH & MMH rain! *rev from* rain; *Cornell MS. 10* rain— *BL MS. 4* rain! *Ransom MS.*

4 nest,] nest *MS. 140* Nest, *WW to TNT* nest; *Ransom MS.*

5 blest.] blest: *BL MS. 4* *no punct MS. 140*

6 Thanks,] Thanks! *MS. 140, WW to TNT, MW to TH & MMH, Cornell MS. 10, BL MS. 4* Thanks; *Yale Sonnets MS., MS. 151.3, 1842, 1845, 1850* Thanks— *1840* thou] Thou *Ransom MS.* snapped] snapt *MS. 140, Cornell MS. 10* fire-side] fireside *Ransom MS.* chain,] chain *MS. 140, MW to TH & MMH, Cornell MS. 10, BL MS. 4, Ransom MS.* chain, *rev to* chain *WW to TNT*

7 Warbler!] Warbler *MS. 140* Warbler, *WW to TNT, Cornell MS. 10,* Warbler! *rev to* Warbler, *MW to TH & MMH* brain,] brain *MS. 140*

9 Yes,] Yes *MS. 140, MW to TH & MMH, Cornell MS. 10* Yes, *rev to* Yes! *Ransom MS.* forth,] forth *MS. 140* Bird!] bird, *MS. 140, Cornell MS. 10, BL MS. 4* Bird! *rev from* Bird, *MW to TH & MMH* blast,] blast *MS. 140, MW to TH & MMH, Cornell MS. 10, Ransom MS.* blast. *BL MS. 4* *no commas but end of last word under wax seal WW to TNT*

10 *no commas MS. 140, WW to TNT, MW to TH & MMH*

11 through] thro' *MS. 140, MW to TH & MMH, Cornell MS. 10, BL MS. 4* life's] lifes *MS. 140* day,] day *MW to TH & MMH, Cornell MS. 10* day; *Yale Sonnets MS.* *no commas MS. 140*

12 nest *rev from* nest,— *Cornell MS. 10* nest, *BL MS. 4* love-chosen,] love-chosen *MS. 140* love-chosen, *rev in pencil to* love-chosen *MS. 1838/40* love chosen, *WW to TNT*

13 thine, *rev from* thine,— *Cornell MS. 10* *no commas MS. 140*

14 Thrilled] Thrill'd *WW to TNT, Ransom MS.* social] Social *MS. 140* Lay.] Lay! *MW to TH & MMH, BL MS. 4, Ransom MS.*

'Tis He whose yester-evening's high disdain

1 He . . . yester-] He, . . . yester *Yale MS. 7*

2 storm—] storm,— *Yale MS. 7*

5 nightingale,] Nightingale *Yale MS. 7* nightengale, *Yale Sonnet MS.*

8 depressed] deprest *Yale MS.* wane] wain *Yale MS. 7*

9 prove] prove, *Yale MS. 7*

11 ecstasy] ecstacy *Yale Sonnet MS., 1842*

13 gladness *rev from* gladness, *Yale MS. 7*

A Plea for Authors. May, 1838

title *no punct Yale Sonnets MS.* AUTHORS. MAY,] AUTHORS, MAY *MS. 151.3, 1842, 1845–*

2 suitor, Equity] Suitor, equity *Yale MS. 7* *no punct MS. 140 (C)*

3 Justice,] justice *MS. 140 (C)* justice, *MS. 151.3, 1842*

4 *no punct MS. 140 (C), no comma MS. 165*

5–6 *no commas MS. 140 (C), Yale MS. 7*

7 She,] She *MS. 140 (C)* works *rev to* Works *MS. 140 (C), Yale MS. 7*

8 *no comma MS. 140 (C)* short-lived] short lived *MS. 140 (C)*

9 "What! *rev from* "What, *MS. 140 (C)* tie *rev to* tie, *MS. 151.3* tie, *1842, 1845–*

10 books! *ital*] Books! *MS. 140 (C), Yale MS. 7* Books! *ital Yale Sonnets MS., MS. 151.3, 1842, 1845–* Ones,] ones, *rev to* ones! *Yale MS. 7*

11 'tis] tis *MS. 140 (C)* Us] us *MS. 140 (C), Yale MS. 7*

14 turned; . . . source!] turn'd, . . . source. *MS. 140 (C)* turned, . . . source.— *Yale MS. 7*

Composed on the Same Morning

title Composed on the same morning *Yale Sonnets MS.*

1 day,] day *Yale Sonnets MS.*

2 Yet] Yet, *Yale Sonnets MS.* Nature *rev from* nature *BL MS. 4* guide.] guide; *BL MS. 4*

3 approach?] approach?— *Yale Sonnets MS.* tide;] tide *MS. 140 (D)* tide, *BL MS. 4*

4 *no comma MS. 140 (D)*

7 gambol—] gambol *MS. 140 (D)* gambol, *BL MS. 4* side] side, *MS. 151.3, 1842, 1845–*

12 God's goodness . . . We] Gods Goodness . . . we *MS. 140 (C)* *no comma MS. 140 (C)*

13 His] his *MS. 140 (C)* between,] between *MS. 140 (C)*

14 new?] new.? *MS. 140 (D)* new?— *Yale Sonnets MS.*

A Poet to His Grandchild. (Sequel to the foregoing.)

title *no punct MS. 165 (A)*

subtitle *no ital, no parens MS. 165 (A)*

1–14 *no quots MSS. 140, 165, WW to TNT*
1–8 *lacking WW to TNT (sheet missing)*
1 Son of *rev from* Son, of *MS. 140*
2 *no comma MS. 165*
7 cling;—] cling; *MS. 165 (B)*
8 Justice] justice *MS. 165 (B)* Statutes] statutes *MSS. 140, 165 (A)*
9 Book] book *MSS. 140, 165 (A)* time-cherished] time-cherished, *MS. 165 (A)* name] name— *MS. 165 (B)*
10 rewards;] rewards, *MS. 140* rewards *MS. 165 (A)*
12 home] home, *MS. 140, WW to TNT*
13 through] thro *MS. 140* come,] come *MS. 165 (A)*
14 *no comma MS. 165 (A), WW to TNT* thine!] thine. *MS. 165 (A)*

With a Small Present

title Small] small *MS. 151.1*
1 memorial . . . work . . . prove] Memorial . . . Work . . . prove, *Betz MS. 2* Memorial . . . work . . . prove *MS. 151.1*
2 Charity . . . Love.] charity . . . love. *Betz MS. 2* Charity, . . . Love! *MS. 151.1*

Lo! where she stands fixed in a saint-like trance

1 she] She *MSS. 143, 151.2* stands] stands, *MS. 147* saint-like] Saint-like *MS. 147* trance,] trance *MSS. 143, 147, 151.2*
2 *no comma MSS. 143, 147*
3 *no comma MSS. 143, 147*
4 ethereal] etherial *MSS. 147, 151.2* glance;] glance. *MS. 143* glance *MS. 147*
5–6 *no commas MSS. 143, 147*
8 love, *rev to* love *MS. 147* long crossed] long–crossed *MS. 147* *no period MSS. 143, 147*
9 she] She *MS. 143, 1845–* now] now, *MSS. 143, 147* pass] pass, *MS. 147*
10 appointed] appointed *MSS. 143, 147* hour] hour, *MS. 147*
11 sapphire] Sapphire *MS. 151.2* content,] content *MS. 143*
12 *no commas MS. 143*
13 bread,] bread *MS. 143*
14 health,] heath *rev to* health *MS. 143*

To a Painter

1 Likeness] Likeness *Dora W to IF, MS. 143* portrayed;] pourtrayed, *Dora W to IF* pourtrayed; *MS. 151.2 (A)* pourtrayed *MSS. 143, 147*
2 'tis] tis *MS. 147* me,] me *Dora W to IF, MSS. 143, 147*
3 Time *rev from* time *MS. 147* made,] made *Dora W to IF, MSS. 143, 147*
5 fade,] fade *Dora W to IF, MSS. 143, 147*
6 birth-place ne'er] birth place neer *Dora W to IF*
7 ghosts *rev from* ghost *(printer's error) MS. 151.3* Ghosts *MS. 151.2 (A)* be; *rev from* be, *MS. 151.3* be— *Dora W to IF* be. *MS. 147* be *MSS. 143, 151.2 (A)*
8 *no commas MS. 143* And,] And *MS. 147*
9 far-distant] far distant *Dora W to IF* years,] years *MSS. 143, 147*
10 me, fond thought!] me (fond thought) *MS. 147* eye,] eye *Dora W to IF*
11 only,] only *MSS. 143, 147*
12 satisfy,] satisfy *MSS. 143, 147*
13 whate'er] whateer *MS. 143* appears,] appears *MSS. 143, 147, 151.2 (A)*

On the Same Subject, Text of Dora W to IF

4 tongue;] tongue *MSS. 143, 147, 151.2* tongue. *MS. 151.3*
5 wrong,] wrong *MSS. 143, 147, 151.2*
6 As] As, *MS. 151.2* work *rev to* Work *MS. 151.2* enlightened,] enlightened *MS. 147* perceive.] perceive: *MSS. 143, 147*
7 pass,] pass *MS. 143*
8 young—] young; *MSS. 143, 147* young, *MSS. 151.2, 151.3*
9 welcome and as beautiful;] welcome, and, as beautiful— *MS. 143* welcome, and as beautiful,— [beautiful,— *rev to* beautiful—] *MS. 151.2, MS. 151.3 as rev MS. 151.2*
10 beautiful,] beautiful *MS. 143*
12 goodness,] goodness *MSS. 143, 151.2* melancholy—] melancholy;— *MS. 143* melancholy; *MSS. 151.2, 151.3*

On the Same Subject, Text of 1842

title On the same subject. *ital MS. 151.3 (B)*
4 O, *rev from* Oh, *MS. 151.3 (B)* Belovèd! *rev from* Beloved! *MS. 151.3 (A), MS. 1842P*
5 but,] but *MS. 151.3 (A, B)* but, *rev from* but *MS. 1842P*

6 perceive:] percieve. *MS. 151.3 (B)*
10 holy: *rev from* holy; *MS. 151.3 (A)*

More may not be by human Art exprest [Text of Pocket Notebook (A)]

1 Nature, *rev from* nature, *Pocket Notebook (A)*

Upon a Portrait

2 part; . . . Friend] part:— . . . friend *Trinity MS.*
3 hearts,] hearts— *MS. 143* Flower] flower *Memoirs*
4 eye] eye— *Trinity MS.* eye, *Memoirs*
5 memory *rev to* memory, *MS. 143* memory, *Trinity MS.* memory; *Memoirs*
6 strangers] Strangers *MS. 143* alone] alone, *Memoirs*
7 unknown] unknown, *Memoirs*
8 Unthought-of] Unthought of— *MS. 143, Memoirs* Unthought of *Trinity MS.* *no period Trinity MS.*
9 Art! . . . dejection] Art, . . . dejection; *Memoirs*
10 time] Time *MS. 143, Memoirs* strive] strive. *Trinity MS.* strive: *Memoirs*
11 Where'er *rev from* Wheerer *MS. 143* Where'er, *Memoirs* reflection] reflection, *Memoirs*
12 image . . . soul *Memoirs* alive] alive, *Trinity MS., Memoirs*
13 affection,] affection *MS. 143*
14 flower] Flower *MS. 143, Trinity MS.* must] must *MS. 143* survive.] survive *MSS. 143, 147*

The Star that comes at close of day to shine

1 Star] star *Memoirs*
2 Morn] morn, *Houghton MS. 3, Memoirs*
3 Emblem] emblem; *Houghton MS. 3* emblem, *Memoirs*
4 visiteth; or] visiteth, or, *Houghton MS. 3, Memoirs*
5 Thro' . . . decline] Through . . . decline, *Houghton MS. 3, Memoirs* solemnize] solemnise Life's *Memoirs*
7 Learnt, *rev from* Learn't, *Houghton MS. 3* Learnt *MS. 143* Isabel! *rev from* Isabel, *Houghton MS. 3* Isabel, *MS. 143, Memoirs* society] society, *Houghton MS. 3, Memoirs*
8 now *rev from* now, *Houghton MS. 3* resign] resign, *Houghton MS. 3*
9 Tho'] Though *Houghton MS. 3, Memoirs* The *rev from* the *Memoirs*
10 sight,] sight *MS. 143, Houghton MS. 3, Memoirs* thro'] through *Houghton MS. 3, Memoirs* thankful *rev from* thanful *Houghton MS. 3*
11 forth, not *rev from* fourth, not *MS. 143* forth not *rev to* forth (not *Houghton MS. 3* seldom] seldom) *Houghton MS. 3* seldom, *Memoirs*
12 unchilled by age] unchill'd by age, *Houghton MS. 3, Memoirs*
13 Thee] Thee *rev from* thee *MS. 147* thee *Memoirs* tho' . . . years] though . . . years, *Houghton MS. 3, Memoirs* known *rev to* knowwn *MS. 147*
14 Sister] sister *Memoirs*

Poor Robin

title *no asterisk, no period MS. 89 (B)* ROBIN*.] Robin *MS. 89 (B)* ROBIN.* *1845, 1849* ROBIN.† *1850*
note to title *The] †The *1850* Geranium,] Geranium *1845–*
1 Now] Now, *MS. 89 (A)* primrose] Primrose *MS. 151.1* show, *rev from* shew, *MS. 89 (A)* shew *MS. 89 (B), MS. 143, MS. 151.1*
2 March-winds] March winds *MS. 89 (B), MS. 143, MS. 151.2* March winds, *MS. 151.1* *no comma MS. 89 (B), MS. 143, MS. 151.1*
3 growths . . . desire] growths, . . . desire, *MS. 89 (A)*
4 spring,] Spring, *MS. 89 (A, B), MS. 151.2* Spring *MS. 143, MS. 151.1* attire,] attire *MS. 143, MS. 151.1*
5 flowerless,] flowerless; *1845–*
6 day!] day *MSS. 89 (B), 143, 151.1* day, *MS. 151.2*
7 And,] And *MSS. 89 (B), 143, 151.1*
9 green] green, *1845–* shine,] shine *MS. 89 (A), 1845–*
10 summer's] summers *MS. 151.1* Summer's *MS. 151.2* flower;] flower: *MS. 89 (B)* flower *MSS. 143, 151.1* flower, *MS. 151.2*
11 flower] flowers *MS. 89 (B)* passers-by] Passers-by *MSS. 89 (B), 143, 151.1*
12 *no punct MSS. 143, 151.1*
13 Flowers—] Flowers, *MS. 89 (A)* produce (did] produce, did *MS. 89 (A)* produce, (did *MS. 89 (B)*
14 season)] season, *MS. 89 (A)* fruit. *rev from* fruit; *MS. 89 (B)* fruit *MSS. 143, 151.1*
15 But, while] —But while *MS. 89 (B)* But while *MSS. 143, 151.1, 1845–*
17 lay] Lay *MSS. 89 (B), 143, 151.1, 151.2*

19 elfin] Elfin *MSS. 89 (A, B), 143, 151.2* Elfin *MW rev from* Elpin *MS. 151.1*

21 Robin . . . friend,] Robin, [*comma del*] . . . friend *MS. 89 (A)*

22 names, to shew *MS. 89 (A, B)* names to shew *MSS. 143, 151.1, 151.2*

23 colours] colors, *MS. 89 (A)* no?—] no? *MSS. 89 (A, B), 143, 151.1*

24 Nay,] Nay— *MS. 89 (A)* good-will] good will *MSS. 89 (A, B), 143, 151.1, 151.2*

25 which, though slighted, he,] which tho' slighted he, *MS. 143* which tho' slighted, he *MSS. 151.1, 151.2*

26 *no punct MSS. 89 (A, B), 143, 151.1*

27 Cheerful] Chearful *MS. 89 (A, B), MS. 143* flowers] flowers, *MS. 89 (B)*

28 brow:] brow, *MSS. 89 (A, B), 143* brow. *MS. 151.1*

29 more,] more; *MS. 89 (A)* men by men] Men by Men *MSS. 89 (B), 143* despised,] despised *MSS. 143, 151.1*

30 foreheads] foreheads, *MS. 89 (A) no punct MS. 143*

31 *no comma MSS. 89 (B), 151.1*

32 child] Child *MSS. 143, 151.1, 151.2* Nature's] natures *MS. 89 (B_2)* humility] humility *rev from* humity *MS. 89 (B_2) no punct MSS. 143, 151.1*

34 bereft;] bereft *MSS. 89 (B), 143, MS. 151.1*

35 *no comma MSS. 89 (B_2), 143, 151.1*

36 bountiful,] bountiful *MS. 89 (B)* Heaven.] Heaven *MS. 151.1*

The Cuckoo-clock, Text of 1842

title The Cuckoo Clock *MSS. 89, 143 (A), 151.2*

1 taught,] taught *MSS. 89, 143 (A), Cornell MS. 11* sleep] Sleep *MSS. 89, 143 (B), 151.2, Cornell MS. 11* <u>Sleep</u> *MS. 143 (A)* flight,] flight *Cornell MS. 11, MS. 143 (B), Hoare Album*

2 voice] voice— *MS. 89* Voice— *MS. 143 (A)* Voice, *Cornell MS. 11, MSS. 143 (B), 151.2 no comma Hoare Album*

3 far-off] far off *Cornell MS. 11, MS. 143 (B), Hoare Album no comma Hoare Album*

4 truant] Truant *MSS. 89, 143, 151.2, Cornell MS. 11* well,] well; *Cornell MS. 11, MSS. 143 (B), 151.2* well *Hoare Album*

5 Repeater's] Repeaters *MS. 143 (B), Hoare Album* stroke,] stroke *MSS. 89, 143 (A)* stroke; *Hoare Album*

6 That,] That *MSS. 89, Cornell MS. 11, Hoare Album* hour;] hour *MS. 89, Hoare Album* hour: *MS. 151.2 no punct MS. 143 (A)*

7 Cuckoo-clock,] Cuckoo Clock *MSS. 89, 143 (A, B), Cornell MS. 11* Cuckoo clock *Hoare Album* Cuckoo Clock, *MS. 151.2* Cuckoo-clock *1845– no ital MSS. 89, 143 (B), 151.2, Cornell MS. 11, Hoare Album, 1845–*

8 chamber door;] chamber door *MS. 89, Hoare Album* Chamber door *MS. 143 (A)* Chamber door; *MS. 151.2* chamber-door; *1845–*

9 shock,] shock *MSS. 89, 143 (A), Hoare Album*

10 *no ital MSS. 89, 143, Cornell MS. 11, Hoare Album, 1845–* power,] power *Cornell MS. 11, Hoare Album*

11 lead—] lead, *MS. 89* thee] the *Hoare Album*Thee *MS. 143 (B)* Bird *MSS. 89, 151.2* bower.] bower *Cornell MS. 11, Hoare Album* bower. *rev from* Bower. *MS. 143 (A)*

12 List,] List *Cornell MS. 11, Hoare Album* Cuckoo—] Cuckoo, *MSS. 89, 143, Cornell MS. 11* Cuckoo *Hoare Album* Cuckoo!—] Cuckoo! *Cornell MS. 11, MS. 143* Cuckoo, *Hoare Album* oft] Oft, *MS. 89* oft, *MSS. 143, 151.2* 'oft *Hoare Album* though] tho' *MSS. 89, 143 (A), 151.2, Cornell MS. 11,1845–*

13 bare,] bare; *MSS. 89, 143 (A)* bare *Hoare Album*

14 cattle] Cattle *MSS. 89, 143, 151.2* pine,] pine *Cornell MS. 11* shivering fowl] shiv'ring Fowl *MSS. 143 (A), 151.2*

15 spirits] Spirits *MSS. 89, 143 (A), 151.2* air;] air: *1845–*

16 knowledge,—] knowledge: *MSS. 89, 143 (A), Hoare Album* knowledge;— *Cornell MS. 11, MS. 143 (B)* Voice] voice *MS. 89, Cornell MS. 11, Hoare Album* beguiled,] beguiled *MS. 89, MS. 143 (A)*

18 heart;] heart;— *Cornell MS. 11, MS. 143 (B)* fancies,] fancies *MS. 89*

19 Through] Thro' *MSS. 89, 143, 151.2, Cornell MS. 11, Hoare Album* fields,] fields *Cornell MS. 11, MS. 143 (B), Hoare Album* among,] among *MSS. 89, 143 (A), Hoare Album*

20 child] Child *MSS. 89, 143, 151.2, Cornell MS. 11*

21 think, . . . song,] think . . . song *MS. 89, 143 (A)* *no commas Cornell MS. 11, MS. 143 (B), Hoare Album*

22 *no punct Hoare Album*

23 know—] know *MSS. 89, 143, Cornell MS. 11, Hoare Album* that,] that *Cornell MS. 11, MSS. 89, 143, Hoare Album* him] him *rev to* Him *MS. 89* Him *MSS. 143, 151.2, Cornell MS. 11* day] day, *MSS. 89, 143 (B), Cornell MS. 11*

24 pain;] pain, *Cornell MS. 11, MS. 143 (B)* pain *Hoare Album*

25 joys,] joys *Cornell MS. 11, MS. 143* memory . . . away,] memory, . . . away *MSS. 89, 143 (A)* *no punct Hoare Album*

26 unhoped] un-hoped *MS. 151.2* for,] for *Cornell MS. 11, Hoare Album* again;] again, *Hoare Album*

27 —that,] that *MSS. 89, 143, Cornell MS. 11, Hoare Album* him] Him, *MS. 89* him, *MSS. 143 (A), 151.2* thoughts,] thoughts *Hoare Album* severe] serene *(mistranscription) Hoare Album*

28 theme,] theme *MSS. 89, 143 (A)*

29 notes,] notes *Cornell MS. 11, MS. 143 (B), Hoare Album*

30 dream,] dream *MSS. 89, 143 (A)* dream— *Cornell MS. 11* dream;— *MS. 143 (B)* dream; *Hoare Album*

32 Land *Cornell MS. 11, MS. 143 (B)* gleam,] gleam *MSS. 89, 143, Cornell MS. 11* *no commas Hoare Album*

33 wandering *(ital)* Voice] "wandering Voice" *MS. 143 (B), Cornell MS. 11* "wandering voice" *Hoare Album* Voice *rev from* voice *MS. 151.2* stream.] Stream. *MS. 143 (A)* stream *MS. 143 (B), Hoare Album*

34 bounty] Bounty *Hoare Album* measure!] measure, *MSS. 89, 143 (A), MS. 1845W* grace] Grace *MSS. 143 (A), 151.2* Grace, *MS. 1845W*

35 Heaven] heaven *MS. 143 (B)* doth . . . wise,] doth . . . wise *MS. 89* doth, . . . wise *MS. 151.2* springs] Springs *MS. 143 (A), MS. 1845W* *no commas Cornell MS. 11, MW to IF, MSS. 89, 143, Hoare Album, MS. 1845W*

36 forth, *rev to* forth *MW to IF* solaces] solaces, *Cornell MS. 11, MS. 143 (B)*

37 things,] things *MS. 89* things; *Cornell MS. 11, MS. 143 (B), Hoare Album* things *MSS. 89, 143 (A), MS. 1845W*

38 come, *rev to* come *MW to IF*

39 founts] Founts *MS. 143 (B)* *no comma Cornell MS. 11, MW to IF, MS. 143 (B)*

40 angels] Angels— *Cornell MS. 11, MS. 143 (B)* Angels, *MW to IF* Angels *MSS. 89, 143 (A), 151.2, Hoare Album , MS. 1845W*

41 embassy] embassy, *MW to IF*

42 chambers,—] chambers— *Cornell MS. 11, MW to IF, MSS. 89, 143, MS. 1845W* chambers *Hoare Album*

43 souls] Souls *Cornell MS. 11, MW to IF, MSS. 89, 143, 151.2, MS. 1845W* God's *rev from* god's *MW to IF, MS. 151.2* Gods *MS. 89, MS. 1845W* *no commas Hoare Album*

44 help,] help *MS. 89, Cornell MS. 11, Hoare Album* mercy] Mercy *MS. 89, 143 (A), 151.2* sigh.] sigh! *MS. 89* sigh *Cornell MS. 11, MS. 143 (B), Hoare Album*

The Norman Boy

title *lacking WW to EFO* BOY.] Boy *MS. 143, Betz MS. 4, WL MS. 2*

1 tract *rev from miswritten* track *Betz MS. 4* forest-skirted *rev from* forest skirted *WW to EFO* *no comma WW to EFO*

2 herself,] herself *WL MS. 2* man] Man *WW to EFO, Betz MS. 4, WL MS. 2*

3 remote] remote, *MS. 143, Betz MS. 4, WL MS. 2, comma erased MS. 151.2*

4 Boy] boy *WW to EFO, WL MS. 2*

5 spot,] spot; *WW to EFO, WL MS. 2, 1850* Spot, *MSS. 143, 151.2* Spot; *Betz MS. 4* English Dame,] english Dame *WW to EFO*

6 me] me, *Betz MS. 4, MW to IF* friend, *rev from miswritten* friendly, *WW to EFO* came,] came *MSS. 143, 151.2*

7 speak in verse] speak, in verse, *MS. 151.2* child] Child, *WW to EFO* Child *MS. 143, Betz MS. 4, WL MS. 2*

8 winter's *rev to* Winter's *MS. 143* day,] day *MS. 143* Wild] wild *WW to EFO, Betz MS. 4*

9 flock,] flock *MS. 143, Betz MS. 4* flock— *WL MS. 2* relics] reliques *MS. 143, Betz MS. 4, WL MS. 2* o'er] oer *MS. 151.2*

10 night's *rev from* nights *MS. 151.2* snow,] snow *MS. 143, Betz MS. 4, WL MS. 2*

11 each, . . . feed,] each . . . feed; *MS. 143* each— . . . feed; *Betz MS. 4, WL MS. 2*

12 *comma erased MS. 151.2*

13 *no ital WW to EFO, Betz MS. 4, WL MS. 2* he,] he *WW to EFO* He, *WL MS. 2* where] where, *MS. 151.2* rent] rent, *MS. 143*
14 made.] made; *WW to EFO* made, *MSS. 143, 151.2, Betz MS. 4*
15 tenement,] tenement *Betz MS. 4, WL MS. 2* tenement, *rev from* tenemant, *MS. 151.2* forsooth,] forsooth *MSS. 143, 151.2* frail,] frail,— *MS. 143*
16 framed,] framed *MS. 143, WL MS. 2* builder] Builder *MSS. 143, 151.2* he] He *rev from* he *WW to EFO*
17 hut] Hut *MSS. 143, 151.2, Betz MS. 4, WL MS. 2* *no comma WL MS. 2*
18 add,] add; *WW to EFO, Betz MS. 4, WL MS. 2* add *MS. 143* architect] Architect *WW to EFO, MSS. 143, 151.2, Betz MS. 4, WL MS. 2*
19 Cross, *rev from* cross, *MS. 151.2* Cross *WW to EFO* well-shaped] (well shaped *WW to EFO* well shaped *MS. 143, Betz MS. 4* nice,] nice) *WW to EFO*
20 edifice] Edifice *rev from* edifice *WW to EFO* Edifice *MSS. 143, 151.2, Betz MS. 4, WL MS. 2*
21 there,] there *WW to EFO* power] Power *Betz MS. 4*
22 deficiencies,] deficiencies— *MS. 143, Betz MS. 4, WL MS. 2* wants] wants, *MS. 151.2* nest] nest, *WW to EFO*
23 which,] which *Betz MS. 4, WL MS. 2*
24 Boy,] Boy *MS. 143, Betz MS. 4* boy, *MS. 151.2* shelterless,] shelterless— *MS. 143*
25 Cross belike] Cross, belike, *MS. 143* raised] raised, *MS. 151.2* standard] Standard *MSS. 143, 151.2, Betz MS. 4, WL MS. 2*
26 heart] heart, *Betz MS. 4*
27 hardship] hardship, *MS. 143* waste] Waste *MS. 143, WL MS. 2*
28 self *rev from* Self *MS. 151.2* Self *MS. 143* placed.] placed.— *WL MS. 2* *no commas WL MS. 2*
29 ——Here,] Here *MSS. 143, 151.2, Betz MS. 4, WL MS. 2* cease;] cease— *MS. 143* cease! *Betz MS. 4* cease? *WL MS. 2* but *rev from miswritten* by *MS. 143* nay,] nay; *Betz MS. 4* nay *WL MS. 2* us *ital*] us, *no ital WW to EFO* us, *WL MS. 2*
30 Shepherd-boy] Shepherd-boy, *WW to EFO, WL MS. 2* Shepherd-boy *with pencil comma added Betz MS. 4* shepherd-boy *1845–* heart,] heart *WW to EFO, MS. 143, WL MS. 2*
31 where'er] whereer *MS. 151.2* lie] lie, *WW to EFO*
32 soul] Soul *WW to EFO, MSS. 143, 151.2, Betz MS. 4, WL MS. 2* stay] Stay *MS. 143, WL MS. 2* *no period 1849*

Sequel to The Norman Boy

title BOY] boy *MS. 151.2*
1 penned,] penned *Betz MS. 4, WL MS. 2* power,] power *MSS. 143, 151.2, WL MS. 2*
2 *no commas Betz MS. 4, MS. 143, WL MS. 2*
3 sky,] sky; *Betz MS. 4, MS. 143, WL MS. 2*
4 And,] And *Betz MS. 4, MS. 143, WL MS. 2* Subject] subject *MS. 143* Verse,] verse *MS. 143, WL MS. 2*
5 thoughts] thoughts, *Betz MS. 4, MS. 143* cleared,] cleared; *MS. 143*
6 bodied forth] bodied-forth *MS. 143* hut] Hut *Betz MS. 4, WL MS. 2*
7 And,] And *Betz MS. 4, MS. 143* air,] air *Betz MS. 4, MS. 143*
8 *no commas MS. 143* saw,] saw *Betz MS. 4* Boy] boy *WL MS. 2*
9 *no commas MS. 143* call,] call *Betz MS. 4*
10 fear,] fear *Betz MS. 4, WL MS. 2* All;] all *Betz MS. 4* all; *WL MS. 2*
11 eyes,] eyes *MS. 143, WL MS. 2*
12 cheered] cheered *MSS. 143, 151.2*
13 —What] What *Betz MS. 4, MS. 143, WL MS. 2* —what *1845, 1850* *no comma WL MS. 2*
14 night!] night; *Betz MS. 4, MSS. 143, 151.2, WL MS. 2*
15 showed] shewed *Betz MS. 4, MSS. 143, 151.2, WL MS. 2* Boy] boy *MS. 151.2* Cherub *WL MS. 2* transformed,] transformed *MS. 151.2*
16 Thing *rev from* thing *MS. 151.2*
17 dream] Dream *WL MS. 2* wings,] wings; *MS. 143, Betz MS. 4, WL MS. 2* arms,] arms *MSS. 143, 151.2, WL MS. 2*
18 alarms,] alarms; *Betz MS. 4, WL MS. 2* alarms *MS. 143*
19 through] thro' *Betz MS. 4, MSS. 143, 151.2, WL MS. 2* air] air, *Betz MS. 4* pay,] pay *Betz MS. 4, WL MS. 2*
20 holiday.] holiday *Betz MS. 4*
21 Yet] yet *MS. 151.2* while,] while

Betz MS. 4, MSS. 143, 151.2, WL MS. 2

22–28 *lines begin with dbl quot Betz MS. 4, MSS. 143, 151.2, WL MS. 2*

22 show] shew *Betz MS. 4, MSS. 143, 151.2, WL MS. 2* thing,] thing *Betz MS. 4* country] Country *WL MS. 2* town.] town: *rev from* Town: *Betz MS. 4* town:— *MSS. 143, 151.2* Town; *WL MS. 2*

23 be?] be, *WL MS. 2* throng,] throng? *Betz MS. 4, MS. 143, WL MS. 2, 1845–*

24 St. Denis,] St Denis *Betz MS. 4* St Denis *MSS. 143, 151.2, WL MS. 2* tombs,] tombs? *MS. 151.2, Betz MS. 4* tombs, *rev to* tombs? *WL MS. 2* Dame] dame *MS. 151.2*

25 St.] St *MSS. 143, 151.2, Betz MS. 4, WL MS. 2* Ouen's *rev from* Ouens' *Betz MS. 4* Ouens *MS. 143* or] Or *Betz MS. 4, 1845–* choose] chuse *Betz MS. 4, WL MS. 2*

26 France,] France *WL MS. 2* boast!] boast!? *Betz MS. 4* boast!— *MS. 151.2* boast. *WL MS. 2*

27 *para MS. 151.2* Mother,] Mother *MS. 143* Boy,] boy *WL MS. 2* "was *rev from* was *Betz MS. 4* 'was *MS. 143* blessèd] blessed *Betz MS. 4, MSS. 143, 151.2, WL MS. 2* Tree, *rev from* tree, *Betz MS. 4*

28 Chapel-Oak *WL MS. 2* Allonville;] Alonville; *rev to* Allonville, *Betz MS. 4* Allonville, *MS. 143, WL MS. 2* Angel,] Angel *Betz MS. 4* show] shew *Betz MS. 4, MSS. 143, 151.2, WL MS. 2* me!"] me!' *MS. 143*

29 wings, . . . poise] wings . . . poise, *MS. 143, WL MS. 2* wings . . . poize, *Betz MS. 4* steadfast] stedfast *MSS. 143, 151.2, WL MS. 2, 1845–* reply,] reply; *MS. 143, WL MS. 2*

30 Allonville, *rev from* Alonville, *Betz MS. 4* Allonville *MSS. 143, 151.2, WL MS. 2* o'er] oer *MSS. 143, 151.2, WL MS. 2* down and dale] Down and Dale *Betz MS. 4*

31 O'er] Oer *Betz MS. 4, MSS. 143, 151.2, WL MS. 2* drest;] drest *Betz MS. 4, MS. 143* drest, *WL MS. 2*

32 *no commas MS. 143* Child,] Child *Betz MS. 4* though] tho' *Betz MS. 4, MSS. 143, 151.2, WL MS. 2*

33 show,] shew *Betz MS. 4, MS. 143, WL MS. 2* *no commas WL MS. 2*

34 eyes,] eyes *Betz MS. 4, MSS. 143, 151.2, WL MS. 2* oak,] Oak— *Betz MS. 4* Oak *WL MS. 2*

36 hands?] hands. *Betz MS. 4, MS. 143, WL MS. 2*

37 Eagle] Eagle, *MS. 89, WL MS. 2* charge] Charge *MS. 89, Betz MS. 4* Charge, *MS. 143* charge, *WL MS. 2*

38 wide-spread] wide spread *MS. 151.2* boughs,] boughs *MSS. 89, 143, Betz MS. 4, WL MS. 2* window,] window *MS. 143, WL MS. 2*

39 gnarled] knarled *Betz MS. 4*

40 steeple] Steeple *MS. 143* forth] forth, *Betz MS. 4* shade.] shade, *WL MS. 2*

41 lighted—] lighted, *Betz MS. 4* door,] door *Betz MS. 4, MS. 143, WL MS. 2, MW to IF*

42 Past] Passed *Betz MS. 4* Boy;] Boy, *MS. 151.2, Betz MS. 4, WL MS. 2 (B), MW to IF* and,] and *Betz MS. 4, MS. 143, WL MS. 2 (B), MW to IF*

43 roof] roof, *WL MS. 2 (B), MW to IF* round] round, *Betz MS. 4* creature] Creature *Betz MS. 4, MW to IF* cast,] cast *Betz MS. 4, MS. 143, WL MS. 2 (B), MW to IF*

44 crowded in] crowded-in *Betz MS. 4* *no punct MS. 143, Betz MS. 4*

45 For,] For *MSS. 89, 143* framed *rev to* framed, *MS. 89* framed, *Betz MS. 4, WL MS. 2* trunk,] trunck, *rev from* trunck *MS. 89* trunk *MS. 143* sanctuary] Sanctuary *Betz MS. 4* showed,] showed, *rev from* shewed *MS. 89* shewed *Betz MS. 4, MS. 143* shewed, *MS. 151.2, WL MS. 2*

46 stones,] stones *MSS. 89, 143, Betz MS. 4* here,] here *MS. 143*

47 gratitude; *rev from* gratitude. *MS. 89*

48 lightning] Lightening *MS. 89* lightening *MSS. 143, 151.2, WL MS. 2* time,] time *MS. 89, Betz MS. 4, WL MS. 2* renewed:] renewed; *Betz MS. 4* renewed *MS. 89* renewed. *MSS. 143, 151.2, WL MS. 2*

49–68 *dble quots Betz MS. 4, MS. 151.2, WL MS. 2 (A)*

49–56 *no quots WL MS. 2 (B), MW to IF*

49, 53, 57, 61, 65 *no quots MS. 143*

50 And,] And *MSS. 143, 151.2, WL MS. 2 (B), MW to IF* kneeling,] kneeling *MS. 151.2, WL MS. 2 (B), MW to IF*

51 and,] and *Betz MS. 4, MS. 143, WL MS. 2, MW to IF*

52 pangs,] pangs; *1845–* dropt!] dropt *MSS. 89, 143* dropt. *MS. 151.2, WL MS. 2 (B), MW to IF*

53 Down, *rev from* down, *WL MS. 2* thine,] thine *Betz MS. 4, MS. 143, WL*

MS. 2, MW to IF

54 lot,] lot *rev from* [?lost] *MS. 143* lot, *rev from* lot *MS. 151.2* lot *Betz MS. 4, WL MS. 2, MW to IF* Boy, . . . shrine;] Boy . . . shrine *MS. 143* Boy! . . . Shrine *Betz MS. 4* boy . . . shrine *WL MS. 2 (A)* Boy . . . Shrine, *WL MS. 2 (B), MW to IF*

55 body pains] body-pains, *WL MS. 2 (A)* needest *rev from* needst *Betz MS. 4* release,] release *MS. 89, MS. 143, WL MS. 2, MW to IF*

56 hours] hours, *Betz MS. 4* on] on, *Betz MS. 4* spent,] spent *MS. 89, Betz MS. 4, WL MS. 2 (B), MW to IF* joy,] joy *MS. 89, Betz MS. 4, 1850* peace.] peace *MS. 89, WL MS. 2 (A)* peace— *WL MS. 2 (B), MW to IF*

57 God] God, *MS. 143, WL MS. 2* praise,] praise; *rev from* praise, *MS. 89* praise; *Betz MS. 4, MS. 143, WL MS. 2*

58 Him *rev from* him *MSS. 143, 151.2* him *Betz MS. 4, WL MS. 2* thoughts,] thoughts *MSS. 89, 143, Betz MS. 4, WL MS. 2* days;] days, *MSS. 89, 143, Betz MS. 4, WL MS. 2*

59 His *rev from* his *MSS. 89, 143, Betz MS. 4, WL MS. 2* sight *rev in pencil to* sight, *MS. 89* Cross,] Cross *MS. 89, Betz MS. 4, WL MS. 2* cross *rev to* Cross *MS. 143* hut,] hut *MSS. 89, 143, Betz MS. 4, WL MS. 2*

60 Tree;] Tree. *MS. 89, Betz MS. 4* Tree, *MS. 143* Tree.— *WL MS. 2*

62 Dome;] Dome *MS. 143*

63 he *rev to* He *WL MS. 2* rites, *rev by erasure from* rites; *MS. 151.2* rites; *MS. 143*

64 children's] Children's *MSS. 143, 151.2* hymns] Hymns *MS. 89* hymns, *Betz MS. 4* prayer,] prayer *MS. 89, Betz MS. 4* delights. *rev by erasure from* delights: *MS. 151.2* *no punct MS. 143*

65 skill; *rev from* skill. *MS. 89* skill *MS. 143*

66 him] Him *MS. 89* will:] will; *rev from* will. *MS. 89* will; *Betz MS. 4, WL MS. 2* will *MS. 143*

67 us] <u>us</u> *MSS. 89, 143, Betz MS. 4, WL MS. 2* live,] live; *MS. 143, WL MS. 2*

68 wings as,] wings as *Betz MS. 4, WL MS. 2* wings, as *MS. 143* heaven."] heaven. *MS. 143* Heaven." *WL MS. 2*

69 but,] but *Betz MS. 4, MS. 143, WL MS. 2* look,] look *Betz MS. 4, MS. 143, WL MS. 2*

70 dream—] Dream *Betz MS. 4* Dream— *WL MS. 2* book,] book *Betz MS. 4, MS. 143, WL MS. 2* book, *rev by erasure to* book *MS. 151.2*

71 mind,] mind *Betz MS. 4, MS. 143, WL MS. 2*

72 visions] Visions *Betz MS. 4* done,] done *MS. 143*

73 though] tho' *MSS. 89, 151.2, WL MS. 2* tho *MS. 143* dream,] dream *Betz MS. 4* Dream *MS. 143* thee,] thee *MSS. 143, 151.2, WL MS. 2* flowed,] flowed *Betz MS. 4, MS. 143, WL MS. 2*

74 e'er] e'er *rev from* eer *Betz MS. 4* eer *MS. 151.2* bestowed,] bestowed *MS. 143, WL MS. 2*

76 loth,] loth *MS. 143* Little-ones] Little Ones *WL MS. 2* heart-touched] heart touched *Betz MS. 4, WL MS. 2* feed.] feed *MS. 143* feed.* *1845–*

At Furness Abbey ("Here, where, of havoc tired and rash undoing")

1 where,] where *MS. 162 (B), Victoria MS. 4* undoing,] undoing *MS. 162 (B)*

2 prey] prey, *MS. 162 (B), Victoria MS. 4*

3 spirit *rev to* Spirit *Victoria MS. 4*

4 *no comma MS. 162 (B)* counter-work] counterwork *MS. 162 (A)*

5 Ivy] ivy *MS. 162*

6 prevent] prevent, *Victoria MS. 4* decay;] decay! *MS. 162 (A)* decay *MS. 162 (B)*

7 mouldered] moulder'd *Victoria MS. 4* *no commas MS. 162*

8 flowers] Flowers *MS. 162, Victoria MS. 4* renewing!] renewing *MS. 162 (A)* renewing. *MS. 162 (B)*

9 place . . . hour] Place . . . Hour *Victoria MS. 4*

11 grass-crowned . . . Tower] grass-crown'd . . . tower; *Victoria MS. 4*

12 occupants] Occupants *Victoria MS. 4*

13 pile] Pile, *Victoria MS. 4*

14 thine *ital*] thine *Victoria MS. 4*

On a Portrait of the Duke of Wellington, upon the Field of Waterloo, by Haydon

title WELLINGTON,] WELLINGTON *1845–*

1 Art's] Arts *Monkhouse Album, University of London MS., Huntington MS. 10, MS. 151.2* privilege] privilege; *MS. 89* privilege, *WW to HR, Haydon MS., Princeton MS. 5,*

Huntington MS. 10 Warrior and War-horse] warrior and war horse *MS. 89* Warrior and Warhorse *Rydal Mount MS.* Warrior and War Horse *Monkhouse Album, Haydon MS.* Warrior and War horse *MS. 151.1* warrior and War-Horse *LG*

2 battle's] Battle's *MS. 89* battles *Haydon MS., MS. 151.1* battles *MS. 151.2* wreck; *rev from* wreck *MS. 151.2* wreck. *MS. 89, WW to HR, Monkhouse Album, Haydon MS., Huntington MS. 10, Berg MS. 5, Rydal Mount MS., Princeton MS. 5, LG* wreck *MS. 151.1*

3 Steed] stead *rev to* steed *MS. 89* steed *Haydon MS., Berg MS. 5, LG* glory] glory, *MS. 89, WW to HR, Monkhouse Album, Princeton MS. 5, MS. 151.1, LG* Master's] Masters *Monkhouse Album* master's *Berg MS. 5, Huntington MS. 10*

4 Lies . . . ages] Lies, . . . ages, *MS. 89, WW to HR, Rydal Mount MS., Princeton MS. 5* Lies, . . . Ages *Monkhouse Album* Lies . . . ages, *Haydon MS.* Lies . . . Ages *MS. 151.1* neck; *rev from* neck *MS. 151.2* neck. *MS. 89, WW to HR, Monkhouse Album, Haydon MS., Berg MS. 5, Huntington MS. 10, Princeton MS. 5* neck *MS. 151.1, LG*

5 But] But, *MS. 89, WW to HR, Monkhouse Album, Princeton MS. 5* Chieftain's] Chieftains *MS. 89, Rydal Mount MS., Monkhouse Album, Haydon MS., MS. 151.1* though] tho' *Princeton MS. 5, MSS. 146, 151.1, 151.2*

6 sword,] sword *MS. 146* sword *rev to* Sword, *MS. 151.1*

7 triumph *rev from* triumph, *MS. 151.2* triumph, *Haydon MS., Princeton MS. 5, LG* pride!] pride. *MS. 89, Monkhouse Album* pride *MS. 151.1* pride, *rev to* pride! *MS. 151.2*

8 trophied] tro[?p]hied *MS. 146* Mound] mound *Haydon MS., Berg MS. 5, LG*

9 presence!] presence. *MS. 89, WW to BRH, September 2 and September 7, 1840; Huntington MS. 10; WW to HR; Monkhouse Album; WW to HCR; MS. 151.1; LG* presence.— *Berg MS. 5* presence, *rev to* presence; *MS. 151.2* Him] Him, *Berg MS. 5*

10 not, *rev from* not, *WW to HCR* not *WW to BRH, September 7, 1840; Rydal Mount MS.* not, *rev from* not,— *MS. 151.2* grave's] graves *MS. 151.1* rest, *rev from* rest *MS. 151.2* rest *WW to HCR, Rydal Mount MS., MS. 151.1*

11 shows] shews *Rydal Mount MS., Berg MS. 5, WW to HCR, MSS. 151.1, 151.2* time-worn] timeworn *Rydal Mount MS.* face,] face; *MSS. 151.1, 151.2* he] He *Rydal Mount MS.*

12 sown] sown, *WW to BRH, September 4, 1840; Berg MS. 5* yields, we trust,] yields we trust *WW to BRH, September 4, 1840; Rydal Mount MS.; Huntington MS. 10; Berg MS. 5*

13 Heaven;] Heaven: *MS. 89, Monkhouse Album, LG* Heaven— *Berg MS. 5* heaven; *WW to HR, Rydal Mount MS.* Heaven, *MS. 151.1* Heaven. *MS. 151.2* thy name,] thy name *WW to HR, Monkhouse Album* thy name, *Berg MS. 5* thy name *Haydon MS., Princeton MS. 5* name,] name *MSS. 89, 151.1, 151.2, Rydal Mount MS., Huntington MS. 10*

14 Conqueror, *rev from* Conqueror! *MS. 151.2* Conqueror! *Haydon MS.* Conqueror! *MS. 89, Huntington MS. 10, Princeton MS. 5, LG, MS. 151.1* Conqueror!— *Berg MS. 5* 'mid] mid *all MSS., LG, 1845* thoughts, *rev from* thoughts *MS. 151.2* thoughts *Berg MS. 5, Monkhouse Album, MS. 151.1* blest!] blest. *MS. 89, Haydon MS., Berg MS. 5, Princeton MS. 5, MS. 146, LG, MS. 151.1*

Sigh no more Ladies, sigh no more

4 believe *rev from* beleve *Victoria MS. 3*

The Crescent-moon, the Star of Love, Text of MS. 143

1 Moon *rev from* moon *MSS. 143, 151.1*

3 you] you! *MS. 151.1*

The Crescent-moon, the Star of Love, Text of 1842

1 *no para 1845, 1850* Crescent-moon, *rev from* Crescent moon, *MS. 151.3* Crescent-Moon, *MS. 1836/45*

Epitaph in the Chapel-yard of Langdale, Westmoreland

1 smiles, (alas] smiles—alas! *Swarthmore MS. 3* smiles, alas *Tombstone* smiles, (alas! *1845–*

2 sunshine)] sunshine— *Princeton MS. 5, Swarthmore MS. 3* sunshine *Tombstone*

4 charity] Charity *Swarthmore MS. 3, Tombstone*

5 Through] Thro' *Swarthmore MS. 3*
6 young and old;] Young and Old;— *Princeton MS. 5* Young and Old; *Swarthmore MS. 3, Tombstone*
7 spirit] Spirit *Swarthmore MS. 3*
8 mourners] Mourners *Princeton MS. 5, Swarthmore MS. 3*
9 When,] When *Tombstone*
11 corse . . . rest,—] Corse . . . rest;— *Princeton MS. 5* Corse [Corse *rev from* Course] . . . rest— *Swarthmore MS. 3* Corse . . . rest *Tombstone*
12 request;—] request— *Princeton MS. 5* request *Swarthmore MS. 3, Tombstone*
13 Yew's *rev from* Yew-tree's *Swarthmore MS. 3 (copyist's slip)* shade,] shade *Princeton MS. 5* shade— *Swarthmore MS. 3* though] tho' *Swarthmore MS. 3* he] He *Swarthmore MS. 3, Tombstone*
14 Planted . . . hope] Planted, . . . hope, *Swarthmore MS. 3* tree;] Tree, *Princeton MS. 5, Swarthmore MS. 3* Tree; *Tombstone*
15 stream] Stream *Tombstone* rock,] rock *Princeton MS. 5, Swarthmore MS. 3* Rock *Tombstone*
16 than *rev from* that *Swarthmore MS. 3 (copyist's slip)* *no punct Tombstone*
17 Pastor's *rev from* pastor's *Princeton MS. 5* voice] Voice *Swarthmore MS. 3, Tombstone*
18 choice] Choice *Tombstone*
19 Through] Thro' *Swarthmore MS. 3* evil,] evil *Tombstone*
20 grave,] grave *Tombstone*
22 earth . . . heaven.] Earth, . . . Heaven *Swarthmore MS. 3* Earth . . . Heaven. *Tombstone*

The Wishing-gate Destroyed

1 'Tis] Tis *Yale MS. 8, Huntington MS. 11, MS. 151.1 (B)*
2 clubg,] clung— *Huntington MS. 11*
4 landscape] Landscape *Yale MS. 8, Huntington MS. 11* lie,] lie *MS. 151.2 (A)*
5 wall,] wall *Yale MS. 8* Wall, *Huntington MS. 11* eye,] eye *Yale MS. 8, Huntington MS. 11, MS. 151.1 (B)*
6 out.] out! *Huntington MS. 11*
7 ye] Ye *Huntington MS. 11* passed] pass'd *Yale MS. 8, MSS. 151.1 (B), 151.2 (A)*
8 opening—] opening *Yale MS. 8* opening *rev to* Opening *Huntington MS. 11* ye] Ye *Huntington MS. 11*
9 lake] Lake *Huntington MS. 11* below,] below *Yale MS. 8, MS. 151.1 (B)*
10 spirit-stirring] Spirit-stirring *Huntington MS. 11*
11 *no comma Yale MS. 8, Huntington MS. 11, MS. 151.1 (B)*
12 Though] Tho' *MS. 151.2 (A)* reason] Reason *Yale MS. 8, MS. 151.1 (B), Huntington MS. 11* say no] say, No *MS. 151.1 (B), Huntington MS. 11*
13 ground,] ground *Yale MS. 8, Huntington MS. 11* where,] where *Yale MS. 8, MS. 151.1 (B)* o'er] oer *Yale MS. 8, Huntington MS. 11, MS. 151.1 (B)*
14 history, *rev from* History, *Huntington MS. 11* glory] Glory *Yale MS. 8, 1845–* *no commas Yale MS. 8, Huntington MS. 11, MS. 151.1 (B)*
15 *no punct Yale MS. 8*
16 wide,] wide,— *Huntington MS. 11*
17 of *rev from* of, *MS. 151.2 (A)* is,] is *Yale MS. 8, MS. 151.1 (B)* this,] this *Yale MS. 8, MSS. 151.1 (B), 151.2 (A)*
18 *no punct Yale MS. 8*
20 grafted,] grafted *Yale MS. 8, MS. 151.1 (B)* spot,] spot *Yale MS. 8* Spot *Huntington MS. 11, MS. 151.1 (B)*
21 token] Token *Huntington MS. 11*
22 good;—] good— *Yale MS. 8* good:— *Huntington MS. 11, MSS. 151.1 (B), 151.2 (A)* fled;] fled *Yale MS. 8, MS. 151.1 (B)* fled: *Huntington MS. 11*
23 centuries] Centuries *Yale MS. 8, Huntington MS. 11* thread,] thread *Yale MS. 8, Huntington MS. 11, MS. 151.1 (B)*
24 day *rev to* Day *Huntington MS. 11* broken.] broken *MS. 151.1 (B)*
25 Alas! . . . him] Alas . . . Him *Huntington MS. 11* word;] word! *Huntington MS. 11* word *MS. 151.1 (B)* *no punct Yale MS. 8*
26–30 *no punct MS. 151.1 (B)*
27 heaven] Heaven *MS. 151.1 (B)*
28 hearts . . . hope . . . betrayed;] Hearts . . . Hope . . . betrayed *Huntington MS. 11*
30 given?] given. *MS. 151.2 (A)*
31 love-lorn] love lorn *Yale MS. 8* maiden's wound,] Maiden's wound *Yale MS. 8, Huntington MS. 11* maidens wound *MS. 151.1 (B)*
33 expectation?] expectation *Yale MS. 8* expectation; *MS. 151.2 (A)*
33–34 *no punct MS. 151.1 (B)*
34 far-off] far off *MS. 151.1 (B)* *no comma Yale MS. 8*

35 mothers] Mothers *Yale MS. 8, Huntington MS. 11* air] air, *MS. 151.1 (B)*
36 home-felt] homefelt *Yale MS. 8* home felt *Huntington MS. 11* consolation?] consolation *MS. 151.1 (B)* consolation. *Yale MS. 8, MS. 151.2 (A)*
38 'Mid] Mid *MSS. 151.1 (B), 151.2 (A)*
39 day's] days *MSS. 151.1 (B), 151.2 (A)* grief;] grief *MS. 151.1 (B)*
42 belief.] belief *MS. 151.1 (B)*
43 reckless *rev from* wreckless *MS. 151.2 (A)* mourn,] mourn *MSS. 151.1 (B), 151.2 (A), Huntington MS. 11*
45 here,] here *MS. 151.1 (B)*
46 judgment] Judgment *Huntington MS. 11*
47 aims,] aims— *Huntington MS.* begin,] begin *MS. 151.1 (B), MS. 151.2 (A)*
49 Fortune's *rev from* fortune's *MS. 151.2 (A)* fortunes *MS. 151.1 (B)* man:] man; *MSS. 151.1 (B), 151.2 (A)* Man:— *Huntington MS. 11* Man: *1845–*
50–52 *no punct MS. 151.1 (B)*
52 both,] both *MS. 151.2 (A)*
54 heaven-ward] Heavenward *MS. 151.1 (B)* Heaven-ward *MS. 151.2 (A)* enterprise.] enterprise *MS. 151.1 (B)* enterprize. *MS. 151.2 (A)*
59 o'er] oer *Huntington MS. 11* mountain's head,] mountains head *MS. 151.1 (B)* mountain's head *MS. 151.2 (A)*
60 vale.] vale *MS. 151.1 (B)* vale; *Huntington MS. 11*
61 heart,] heart *MS. 151.1 (B), Huntington MS. 11*
62 cottager] Cottager *MSS. 151.1 (B), 151.2 (A), Huntington MS. 11* part,] part *MSS. 151.1 (B), 151.2 (A)*
63 Ungrieved,] Ungrieved *MSS. 151.1 (B), 151.2 (A)*
64 yet,] yet *MS. 151.1 (B)* Wishing-gate,] Wishing gate *MS. 151.1 (B)* Wishing-gate! *rev from* wishing-gate *Huntington MS. 11*
66 farewell!] farewell *MS. 151.1 (B)* farewell. *Huntington MS. 11, MS. 151.2 (A)*

Sonnet ("Though the bold wings of Poesy affect")

1 Though] Tho' *MS. 143*
2 clouds] clouds, *1845–*
6 dew—] dew, *MS. 143*
8 respect.] respect, *MS. 143*
9 *no comma MS. 143*

Suggested by a Picture of the Bird of Paradise

1 Poet,] Poet *MSS. 143, 151.1* endowed,] endowed *MSS. 143, 151.1, 151.2*
2 master . . . strain,] Master . . . strain: *MSS. 143, 151.1* Master . . . strain, *MS. 1842P*
3 disdain] dis-dain *MS. 151.2*
4 allowed.] allowed *MS. 143*
6 name;] name *MSS. 143, 151.1*
7 Bird,] bird *MS. 143*
9 Through] Thro *MSS. 151.1* Thro' *MS. 143, MS. 151.2* *no comma MSS. 143, 151.1, 151.2*
10 air's] airs *MSS. 143, 151.1* unknown; *rev from* unknown, *MS. 1842P* unknown *MSS. 143, 151.1* unknown, *MS. 151.2*
11 *no comma MSS. 143, 151.1* e'er] eer *MSS. 143, 151.1*
12 Through] Thro' *MSS. 143, 151.1, 151.2* *no comma MSS. 143, 151.1*
14 *no punct MSS. 143, 151.1*
15 progeny] Progeny *MS. 143*
16 shape] Shape *MS. 143*
17 *no comma MSS. 143, 151.1*
19 blended,] blended *MS. 143*
23 there?] there. *MS. 143* there, *MS. 151.1*
24 proud *rev from* prouds *(printer's error) MS. 1842P*
24–25 *no commas MSS. 143, 151.1*
25 Began *rev from* Begun *MS. 1842P*
26 *no punct, no apos MSS. 143, 151.1*
26/27 *no stanza break MSS. 143, 151.1*
27 *para 1845–*
28 Poet's] Poets *MS. 143* song;] song, *MSS. 143, 151.1* Song; *MS. 151.2, MS. 1842P*
29 *no commas MSS. 143, 151.1*
30 view;] view, *MSS. 143, 151.1*
31 And,] And *MS. 143* discontent,] discontent *MSS. 143, 151.1*
33 love, . . . vie,] love . . . vie *MSS. 143, 151.1*
37 ethereal] etherial *MSS. 143, 151.1* *no comma MSS. 143, 151.1*
38 *no punct MS. 151.1*

Lyre! though such power do in thy magic live

1 power] Power *MS. 151.1*
3 Recal *rev from* Recall *MS. 1842P* Recall *MSS. 89 (C), 143, 151.1*

Maid, *rev from* maid, *MS. 89 (C), MS. 1842P*

5 Fugitive:] Fugitive; *MS. 89 (C)* Fugitive *MSS. 143, 151.1*

6–10 *no punct MSS. 143, 151.1*

8 enrapt] enwrapt *MS. 151.1*

13 *no comma MSS. 89 (C), 143, 151* hers] her's *MS. 151.1*

15 *no comma MSS. 143, 151.1*

18 And,] And *MS. 89 (C)* near, the brook,] near the Brook *MS. 89 (C)* near the brook *MSS. 143, 151.1*

20 pensively;] pensively, *MS. 89 (C)* pensively *MSS. 143, 151.1*

22 tree] tree, *MS. 89 (C)*

23 Mid] 'Mid *1850* *no comma MSS. 89 (C), 143, 151.1*

24 almost *rev from* almost, *MS. 1842P* almost, *MS. 151* eye.] eye *MSS. 143, 151.1*

25 joy] joy, *MS. 89 (C)*

26 Stream] stream *MS. 89 (C)* down] down, *MS. 89 (C)*

28 rest;] rest *MSS. 143, 151.1*

29 *no commas MSS. 143, 151.1; commas added MS. 1842P*

32 *no punct MSS. 143, 151.1*

33 *no parens MSS. 143, 151.1*

34–35 *no commas MSS. 143, 151*

37 *no punct MS. 151.1*

Prelude ("In desultory walk through orchard grounds")

1–55 *set in roman type 1845, 1850*

3 Thrush, *rev from* thrush, *MS. 151.3*

5 heard *rev from* heard, *MS. 151.3*

16 loftier *rev from* lofter *MS. 151.3*

19 way— *rev from* way.— *MS. 151.3*

25 raise; and, *rev from* raise, and *MS. 151.3* Art *rev from* art *MS. 151.3*

31 inspiration; *rev from* inspiration, *MS. 151.3*

32 and, *rev from* and *MS. 151.3*

34 wanting *rev from* wanting, *but marked* stet *in pencil, probably by printer, MS. 151.3*

37 Voice] voice *MS. 151.3* Voice— *1845, 1850*

41 griefs— *rev from* griefs *MS. 151.3*

50 Listeners *rev from* Listeners, *MS. 151.3*

51 emotion] emotion, *MS. 151.1 (A)*

54 survive,] survive *MS. 151.1 (A)*

55 maintained.] maintained *MS. 151.1 (A)*

Upon Perusing the Foregoing Epistle Thirty Years after its Composition

2 young Ones *rev from* Young Ones *rev from* young-ones *MS. 151.2* Young-ones *MS. 151.1 (B)* Young Ones *MS. 151.1 (A)* nest;] nest *MS. 151.1 (A)*

4 penned.] penned; *MS. 151.1 (B)*

5 moth] Moth *MS. 151.2*

6–7 *no punct MS. 151.1 (B)*

7 sympathies. *rev from* sympathys. *MS. 151.2*

8 For— *rev from* For *MS. 151.2* For, *rev from* for, *MS. 151.1 (B)* o'er] oer *MSS. 151.1, 151.2*

9 life,] life; *MS. 151.1 (B)*

10 The . . . willed *rev from* —The . . . willed, *MS. 151.1 (B)*

11 Heaven's *rev from* heaven's *MS. 151.1 (B)*

13 Departed—] Departed; *MS. 151.1 (B)*

14 tears, *rev from* tears *MS. 151.1 (B)*

15 through] thro' *MSS. 151.1, 151.2* Love's *rev from* loves's *MS. 151.1 (B)*

Sonnet ("When Severn's sweeping Flood had overthrown")

2 St Mary's] St Marys *MS. 151.1* St. Mary's *BL pamphlet* Church] Church, *BL pamphlet*

3 "Thus, . . . shown] Thus, . . . shewn *MS. 151.1* Thus . . . shown *BL pamphlet* People] people *MS. 151.1* cry,] cry,, *Cardiff Facsimile*

4 Him . . . testify;] him . . . testify: *MS. 151.1*

5 *no comma MS. 151.1, BL pamphlet* Pile"!] Pile *rev to* Pile! *MS. 151.1* Pile." *BL pamphlet* But *rev from* but *MS. 151.1*

6 place— *BL pamphlet* Age after Age *rev from* Age after age *MS. 151.1* age after age *BL pamphlet* by] by, *BL pamphlet*

7 Heaven . . . lacked . . . due; though] heaven . . . lack'd . . . due. Tho *MS. 151.1*

8 secret *rev from* secred *MS. 151.1* *no period MS. 151.1*

10 voice] voice— *BL pamphlet*

11 *no comma MS. 151.1*

13 Oh, . . . shame] Oh! . . . shame, *BL pamphlet*

14 choice!] choice *MS. 151.1*

***A Poet!* —He hath put his heart to school**

1 Poet!— *rev from* Poet— *MS. 151.1* Poet!— *rev to* Poet! *MS. 151.2* He *rev from* he *MS. 151.2* he *MS. 151.1*

3 hand—] hand, *MS. 151.1*

4 rule.] rule *MS. 151.1*

5 Art be Nature; . . . quaff,] art be

nature! . . . quaff *MS. 151.1*

6 *no comma MS. 151.1*

7 *no comma MS. 151.1* Critics *rev from* critics *MS. 151.1*

9 Meadow-flower *rev from* meadow-flower *MS. 1842P* meadow-flower *MS. 151.2* *no punct MS. 151.1*

14 *no punct MS. 151.1* *no ital MS. 151.1*

To a Redbreast—(In Sickness)

title TO A REDBREAST—(IN SICKNESS.) *1850*

4 spring. *rev from* spring; *MS. 151.3*

7 that *ital* . . . can not *rev from* that *no ital* . . . cannot *MS. 1842P*

The most alluring clouds that mount the sky

1 clouds] Clouds *MS. 151.2 (A)*

2 forms,] forms *rev from* formes *MS. 151.2 (C)*

3 sunset. If] sunset; if *MS. 151.2 (A)*

4 splendor,] splendor *MS. 151.2 (C)*

8 Dissolve— *rev from* Disolve— *MS. 151.2 (A)*

10 whencesoe'er] whensoe'er *1850*

12 gay] gay, *MS. 151.2 (A)* gay *rev from* gay, *MS. 1842 P*

13 volatile *rev from* volatile, *MS. 1842 P*

The Eagle and the Dove

1 Spirits] spirits *Chouannerie*

5 Sire] sire *Chouannerie*

8 Youth] youth *Chouannerie*

11 Cross] cross *Chouannerie*

13 Crusade] crusade *Chouannerie*

16 Heaven—gigantic *rev from* Heaven, gigantic *WW to AFR* Boys] boys *Chouannerie*

What heavenly smiles! O Lady mine

1 smiles!] smiles, *MS. 1836/45 (B)*

2 shine;] shine *MS. 1836/45 (B)*

3–8 *no punct MS. 1836/45 (A)*

3 light,] light. *1849*

4 thou] Thou *MS. 1836/45 (A)* sight;] sight, *MS. 1836/45 (B)*

5 Moon *rev from* moon *MS. 1836/45 (B)*

8 streams.] streams *1849*

Wansfell! this Household has a favoured lot

1 Household] household *MS. 1838/40 (A), Trinity MS.* Household *rev from* household *MS. 1838/40 (B)* favoured] favor'd *Michigan MS.* favored *MS. 1838/40, Houghton MS. 5, Princeton MS. 6, Trinity MS.* *no comma Michigan MS., Houghton MS. 5, Trinity MS.*

2 thee] Thee *Princeton MS. 6, Houghton MS. 5, Michigan MS.* gaze,] gaze— *MS. 1838/40 (A)* gaze; *MS. 1838/40 (B), Michigan MS., Houghton MS. 5* gaze *Trinity MS.*

3 Morn] morn *MS. 1838/40 (A, B), Trinity MS.* thee] Thee *Princeton MS. 6* rays,] rays *MS. 1838/40 (A), Trinity MS., 1849*

5 Evening's] Evenings *Houghton MS. 5* clouds. *rev from* clouds: *MS. 1838/40* Clouds. *Princeton MS. 6* ne'er] neer *Houghton MS. 5*

6 sounded (shame . . . Bard!)] sounded—Shame . . . Bard!— *MS. 1838/40 (A)* sounded, shame . . . Bard! *MS. 1838/40 (B)* sounded, Shame . . . Bard! *Trinity MS.*

7 thou,] Thou, *Princeton MS. 6, Houghton MS. 5, Michigan MS.* thou *Trinity MS.* heaven,] Heaven, *MS. 1838/40 (A)* heaven *Trinity MS.*

8 glory] Glory *Trinity MS.* *no punct Trinity MS.*

9 Earth!] Earth *MS. 1838/40 (A)* Earth *rev from* earth *Princeton MS. 6* when *rev from* When *Princeton MS. 6*

10 sight,] sight *MS. 1838/40 (A), Trinity MS.*

12 spirits] Spirits *Princeton MS. 6, Houghton MS. 5, Michigan MS.* *no commas Trinity MS.*

13 light,] Light *Trinity MS.*

14 rest.] rest *MS. 1838/40 (A)*

Glad sight wherever new with old

2 through] thro' *MS. 1836/45₁* homeborn tie;] home-born tie *MS. 1836/45₁* homeborn tie, *MS. 1836/45₂* home-born tie; *Houghton MS. 4*

3 behold] behold, *MS. 1836/45₂*

4 mystery.] mystery *MS. 1836/45* mystery: *Houghton MS. 4*

6 grove] grove, *Houghton MS. 4*

7 Unless,] Unless *MS. 1838/40, Houghton MS. 4, MS. 1836/45*

8 gaze,] gaze *MS. 1838/40, MS. 1836/45* love.] love *MS. 1836/45*

To a Lady, in answer to a request that I would write her a poem upon some drawings that she had made of flowers in the Island of Madeira

1 I] I *ital Madeira* flowers *rev from* Flowers *MS. 1836/45 (C)*

2 fade,] fade; *MS. 1835/45 (C)*
3 I] I, *Madeira* bowers,] bowers *MS. 1836/45 (C)*
4 through] thro' *MS. 1836/45 (C)* strayed?] strayed *MS. 1836/45 (C)*
6 Shepherd-groom] shepherd-groom *Madeira* queen] Queen *MS. 1836/45 (C), Madeira*
9 tho'] though *MS. 1836/45 (C), Madeira*
11 portraits] Portraits *MS. 1836/45 (C), MS. 1836/45 (A)*
12 there . . . pleasure] there, . . . pleasure, *MS. 1836/45 (A)* live;] live *MS. 1836/45 (A)* live, *Madeira*
13 scope] scope, *Madeira*
17 care,] care *MS. 1836/45 (C), Madeira*
19 Heart's-ease] Heart's-Ease *Madeira* there,] there *MS. 1836/45 (C)*
20 Speedwell *ital*] Speedwell *MS. 1836/45 (C)* Speed-well *ital Madeira* place.] place *MS. 1836/45 (C)* place: *Madeira*
21 charmèd mind] charmèd mind, *MS. 1836/45 (C)* charmed mind, *Madeira*
22 your] yr. *MS. 1836/45 (C)*
23 Star-of-Bethlehem *ital*] Star of Bethlehem *MS. 1836/45 (C)* Star of Bethlehem *ital Madeira*
24 Forget me not *MS. 1836/45 (C)*
25 heaven . . . fleet] Heaven . . . fleet, *MS. 1836/45 (C), Madeira*
26 heaven] Heaven *MS. 1836/45 (C), Madeira*
27–28 *no ital MS. 1836/45 (C)*
27 Holy-thistle *ital*] Holy Thistle *MS. 1836/45 (C)* meet] meet, *MS. 1836/45 (C), Madeira*
28 weather-glass *ital*] weather glass *MS. 1836/45 (C)* Weather-glass *ital Madeira*
30 fairest, sweetest, plant] fairest sweetest plant *MS. 1836/45 (C)* fairest sweetest plant, *Madeira*
32 Emigrant.] Emigrant; *rev to* Emigrant— *MS. 1836/45 (C)* Emigrant:— *Madeira*
34 breath;] breath, *Madeira* breath *1849*
35 meek] meek, *Madeira*
36 death:] death; *Madeira*
39 Bear] "Bear *Madeira* native land] native-land *MS. 1836/45 (C)*
40 Flower . . . token.] flower . . . token! *MS. 1836/45 (C)* flower . . . token!" *Madeira*

While beams of orient light shoot wide and high

1 high,] high *Trinity MS.*
2 vale] Vale *Trinity MS., Michigan MS., Houghton MS. 5* Town*] town *Trinity MS.* Town *Michigan MS., Houghton MS. 5*
3 cloud-like] cloudlike *Michigan MS.* creature] Creature *all MSS.* *no comma Trinity MS., Michigan MS.*
4 toward] tow'rd *Houghton MS. 5* *no comma Trinity MS., Houghton MS. 5*
5 *no commas Trinity MS., Michigan MS., Houghton MS. 5*
6 o'er] oer *Michigan MS., Houghton MS. 5* Parent] parent *Trinity MS.*
7 *no punct Trinity MS.*
8 Fancy, . . . Poet's] fancy . . . poets *Trinity MS.* eye,] eye *Trinity MS., Michigan MS., Houghton MS. 5*
9 Lingerer. And] lingerer and *Trinity MS.* blest] bles't *Trinity MS.* sway] sway, *Michigan MS., Houghton MS. 5*
11 calm Heaven,] Calm Heaven *Trinity MS.* decked] deck't *Trinity MS., Houghton MS. 5* deck't *rev to* deck'd *Michigan MS.*
12 forms] Forms *MS. 1836/45, Michigan MS., Houghton MS. 5* array,] array *MS. 1836/45, Houghton MS. 5, Trinity MS.*
13 lone] Lone *MS. 1836/45* shepherd] Shepherd *MS. 1836/45, Michigan MS., Houghton MS. 5*
14 saints] Saints *Trinity MS., Michigan MS., Houghton MS. 5* saints *rev to* Saints *MS. 1836/45* repose.] repose *MS. 1836/45, Trinity MS.*
14/ Jan^{ry} 1st. 1843. *Michigan MS.* Jan] Jan. *1846, 1849, 1850*

Grace Darling

22 Maiden] maiden *1846, 1849*
31 isles] Isles *MS. 155*
34 vain,] vain *MS. 155*
36 optic-glass discern,] optic glass discern *MS. 155*
84 Winds,] Winds! *Huntington MS. 12*
86 Him *rev from* him *Huntington MS. 12* served!] served. *Huntington MS. 12*
88 Voice—] Voice, *Darling, Huntington MS. 12*
91 survivors— . . . bear—] survivors, . . . bear, *Darling, Huntington MS. 12*
92 Blended] (Blended *Darling, Huntington MS. 12*
95 resolute—] resolute,) *Darling, Huntington MS. 12*

Inscription for a Monument in Crosthwaite Church, in the Vale of Keswick

All text in Broadsides 1 and 2 and on Monument is in capital letters.

1 vales] Vales *BL MS. 6 (168)* hills] Hills, *BL MS. 6 (168)* hills, *Broadside, Monument*

2 poet's] Poet's *BL MS. 6 (168)* steps,] steps *Monument* him *rev to* Him *BL MS. 6 (168)* you,] you *BL MS. 6 (168), Broadside*

3 closed! And ye] closed; and Ye *BL MS. 6 (168)* loved *BL MS. 6 (168), Broadside, Monument* books] Books *BL MS. 6 (168)*

5 works . . . forfeit *rev from* Works . . . forfet *BL MS. 6 (168)* *no comma BL MS. 6 (168), Broadside, Monument*

6 own—] own, *BL MS. 6 (168, 169)* own,— *Broadside 1a*

7 *no comma BL MS. 6 (169)*

8 guidance,] guidance *BL MS. 6 (169), Monument*

9 Fancy, *rev from* fancy, *BL MS. 6 (169)* studious art] Studious Art *BL MS. 6 (168)* studious Art *BL MS. 6 (169–170)* *no commas BL MS. 6 (168)*

10 Inform'd] Informed *BL MS. 6 (fols. 168, 169–170), Broadside, Monument* wisdom] Wisdom *BL MS. 6 (168)*

11 judgments] Judgments *BL MS. 6 (168)* judgements *BL MS. 6 (169, 171)*

12 mankind] Mankind *BL MS. 6 (168)* mankind *BL MS. 6 (169)*

15 cloud] Cloud *BL MS. 6 (168)*

16 he to heaven] He to Heaven *BL MS. 6 (168)* —He to Heaven *BL MS. 6 (176)*

To the Rev. Christopher Wordsworth, D.D. Master of Harrow School

title To the Rev^{d} . . . Wordsworth D. D. / Master . . . School . . . perusal . . . "Theophilus Anglicanus" recently published. *MS. 176* To . . . Wordsworth. / Master . . . School.— / after the Perusal . . . Anglicanus *Ticknor MS.* D. D.] D. D., *1850*

1 Teacher,] Teacher! *MS. 176*

3 Thee . . . Pupils] thee, . . . pupils *MS. 176*

4 That, . . . native isle] That . . . Native Isle *MS. 176* land,] land *MS. 176*

5 divine command] Divine Command *MS. 176*

6 trod:] trod. *MS. 176*

8 God!] God. *1849*

10 happy,] happy *MS. 176* still;] still, *MS. 176* still *Ticknor MS.*

12 thought] thought, *MS. 176* will] will, *rev to* Will, *Ticknor MS.*

13 Spire] spire *Ticknor MS.* classic] Classic *MS. 176*

14 heavenward,] heavenward *MS. 176*

So fair, so sweet, withal so sensitive, Text of Lilly MS. 5

1–15 *no stanza breaks MS. 1836/45*

2 Flowers . . . live] flowers . . . live, *MS. 1836/45*

3 give;] give! *Yale MS. 9*

4 mountain] mountain, *Yale MS. 9* Daisy's] daisys *MS. 1836/45*

5 star-shaped] Star shaped *MS. 1836/45* Shadow] shadow *Yale MS. 9, MS. 1836/45*

7 what—] what *Yale MS. 9, MS. 1836/45*

8 Sun— *ital*] Sun, *Yale MS. 9* sun,— *MS. 1836/45*

9 his . . . fount;] His . . . Fount, *Yale MS. 9*

10 Wheresoe'er . . . eye] Wheresoe're . . . Eye *Yale MS. 9*

11 Forms and Powers *rev from* forms and powers *Lilly MS. 5* forms and powers *Yale MS. 9* *no comma Yale MS. 9*

12 Nature *rev from* nature *Lilly MS. 5* sympathy;] Sympathy, *Yale MS. 9*

13 Heart] heart *MS. 1836/45* quell'd] quelled, *Yale MS. 9* quell'd, *rev from* quelled, *MS. 1836/45*

14 praise] praise, *Yale MS. 9* love,] love *Yale MS. 9, MS. 1836/45*

15 Boon . . . withheld!— *Yale MS. 9*

So fair, so sweet, withal so sensitive, Text of 1845

6 stone!] stone *1846, 1849*

Sonnet on the Projected Kendal and Windermere Railway

2 assault?] assault?† *1845*– assault?* *1846, 1849, 1850*

3 mid] 'mid *Michigan MS., BL MS. 8*

4 flowers] Flowers *Michigan MS.* hope] Hope *BL MS. 8* *no comma Betz MS. 5*

5 perish;—how *rev from* perish? How *MS. 157* perish how *Betz MS. 5* perish: how *Berg MS. 4, Yale MS. 9, MP* perish!—how *Quaritch MS. (copy)* endure?] endure?— *Betz MS. 5*

6 he] he *Quaritch MS. (copy)*

7 lure] lure, *BL MS. 8*

8 Mid] 'Mid *Michigan MS.* fields, *BL MS. 8* thrown?] thrown. *Betz MS. 5*

9 threat,] threat! *Quaritch MS. (copy)* Scene, *rev from* scene, *MS. 157* scene *Yale MS. 9, MP* Orrest-head] Orrest-head, *Michigan MS.* ORREST-HEAD *BL MS. 8* Orest-head *Quaritch MS. (copy)* *no commas Betz MS. 5*

10 Given *rev from* Civin *MS. 157* traveller's] Travellers *Betz MS. 5* Traveller's *Michigan MS., BL MS. 8, Berg MS. 4* glance:] glance; *BL MS. 8* glance! *Michigan MS., Berg MS. 4, Yale MS. 9, MP* glance *Betz MS. 5* glance, *Quaritch MS. (copy)*

11 peace,] peace *Betz MS. 5, BL MS. 8, Quaritch MS. (copy)* romance] Romance *Betz MS. 5, Michigan MS., BL MS. 8, Berg MS. 4*

12 nature;] Nature *Betz MS. 5, BL MS. 8* Nature; *Michigan MS., Berg MS. 4* and,] and *Quaritch MS. (copy)* *no punct Betz MS. 5, no commas Yale MS. 9*

13 Speak,] Speak *Betz MS.* 5_1, *Berg MS. 4, MP* winds;] winds, *Yale MS. 9, Berg MS. 4, MP* winds;] winds! *Betz MS. 5* ye] Ye *Betz MS.* 5_1, torrents,] Torrents, *Betz MS.* 5_1, Torrents, *Michigan MS., BL MS. 8* torrents *Quaritch MS. (copy)*

14 *no comma Betz MS. 5* wrong! *BL MS. 8, Berg MS. 4, Yale MS. 9, Quaritch MS. (copy), MP*

Proud were ye, Mountains, when, in times of old

4 Power] power *MS. 157*

11 startled;—] startled; *MP, MS. 157*

The Westmoreland Girl. To My Grandchildren

1 will] will, *WL MS. 1* fable] Fable *MS. 143, WL MS. 1* fable, *Cornell MS. 12*

2 truth. A] truth;—a *MS. 143* Truth. A *WL MS. 1*

3 Leapt . . . bank] Leap't . . . bank, *MS. 143*

4 'Cross the brook] Cross the Brook *WL MS. 1* dam.] Dam *MS. 143* Dam. *WL MS. 1, Cornell MS. 12*

5 hill] Hill *Cornell MS. 12* valley] Valley *WL MS. 1, Cornell MS. 12*

6 fallen,] fallen— *MSS. 143, 155, WL MS. 1, Cornell MS. 12* rain,] rain *MSS. 143, 155*

7 mother's] Mother's *MS. 143, WL MS. 1, Cornell MS. 12* Young-one] Young-One *rev from* young-One *Cornell MS. 12* young one *WL MS. 1*

8 vain:] vain *MSS. 143, 155, WL MS. 1* vain. *Cornell MS. 12*

9 But, as chance,] But as chanced *MSS. 143, 155, WL MS. 1* Cottage-maiden] Cottage Maiden *MSS. 143, 155, Cornell MS. 12* Cottage Maiden, *WL MS. 1*

10 (Ten . . . told)] Ten . . . told, *WL MS. 1*

11 Seeing, *rev from* Seeing— *Cornell MS.* Seeing— *WL MS. 1 12* torrent,] Torrent *WL MS. 1*

12 Clasped] Clasp't *WL MS. 1* Lamb] Lamb, *Cornell MS. 12* *no punct MSS. 143, 155*

13 *no punct MSS. 143, 155, WL MS. 1*

14 rising,] rising *WL MS. 1* go,] go *MSS. 143, 155* go; *Cornell MS. 12*

16 lake] Lake *MSS. 143, 155, WL MS. 1, Cornell MS. 12* *no punct MS. 155*

17 Oh!] Oh *MS. 155*

18 Girl] girl *WL MS. 1* braved;] braved— *MS. 143* braved *MS. 155* braved! *WL MS. 1* braved, *rev to* braved— *Cornell MS. 12*

19 joy] joy, *Cornell MS. 12* Hearers,] Hearers *MS. 143* hearers, *MS. 155* hearers! *WL MS. 1* hearers, *rev to* Hearers, *Cornell MS. 12*

20 triumph, . . . saved;] triumph . . . saved. *MS. 143* triumph; . . . saved! *WL MS. 1* triumph— . . . saved! *rev from* triumph— . . . saved.) *Cornell MS. 12* *no punct MS. 155*

22 love,] love *MS. 143* Love; *WL MS. 1* love; *Cornell MS. 12* *no punct MS. 155*

23 And belike] And, belike, *Cornell MS. 12* guardian angel] gaurdian [gaurdian *rev to* guardian] Angel *MS. 143* guardian Angel *MS. 155* Guardian Angel *WL MS. 1, Cornell MS. 12*

24 *no punct MSS. 143, 155*

25 Audience] audience *MS. 143* Audience *rev from* audience *MS. 155* *no commas MS. 143, WL MS. 1*

26 Child] Child, *Cornell MS. 12*

27 mountains] Mountains *MS. 155, Cornell MS. 12*

28 Nature] nature *MS. 143, WL MS. 1*

29 Love *Cornell MS. 12* *no commas WL MS. 1*

31 Orphan] orphan *WL MS. 1* Orphan, *Cornell MS. 12*

32 father's] Father's *MS. 155, WL MS. 1,*

Cornell MS. 12 *no period MS. 155, WL MS. 1*

33 blame,—] blame; *WL MS. 1, Cornell MS. 12*

34 command;] command *MS. 155* command, *WL MS. 1*

36 *no comma WL MS. 1*

37 *no comma MS. 155*

38 *no comma MS. 155, WL MS. 1*

39 mother] Mother *WL MS. 1, Cornell MS. 12* witnessed] witnessed, *Cornell MS. 12*

40 *no apos MS. 155, Cornell MS. 12; no period MS. 155*

41 happy,] happy *MS. 155* happy; *Cornell MS. 12*

42 air] Air *WL MS. 1, Cornell MS. 12* *no comma MS. 155, WL MS. 1*

44 *no punct MS. 143*

45 passions,] Passions *WL MS. 1, Cornell MS. 12*

46 *no punct MS. 155*

47 creatures,] Creatures, *WL MS. 1, Cornell MS. 12* Creatures *MS. 155*

48 powers] powers, *WL MS. 1* shield.] shield; *MS. 143* shield *MS. 155*

49 *no commas MS. 155, WL MS. 1*

51 minnow *rev from* minow *WL MS. 1* minnow, *Cornell MS. 12*

52 pike] Pike *Cornell MS. 12*

53 protectress] Protectress *WW to HR*

54 disdain;] disdain, *WW to HR*

55 captive] Captive *WW to HR*

56 pain.] pain *1846, 1849, WW to HR*

57 awhile:—] awhile *WL MS. 1* a while— *rev from* a while *MS. 155*$_1$ a while;— *MS. 155*$_1$ awhile:— *Cornell MS. 12* patience] patience, *WL MS. 1*

58 tell,] tell: *WL MS. 1* tell! *Cornell MS. 12*

59 old] Old *Cornell MS. 12* church-steeple] Church steeple *MS. 143* Church Steeple *MS. 155*$_1$*, WL MS. 1* Church-Steeple *Cornell MS. 12*

60 Tolled] Toll'd *MSS. 143, 155, Cornell MS. 12* passing-bell] passing bell *MSS. 143, 155* Passing Bell *WL MS. 1* passing-Bell *rev to* Passing-bell *Cornell MS. 12*

61 Girl] girl *WL MS. 1* mountains] Mountains *MS. 155, WL MS. 1, Cornell*

62–63 *no punct MS. 143*

63–64 *no punct WL MS. 1*

65 sire's] Sire's *MS. 155, Cornell MS. 12* office,] office *MS. 155* Office, *WL MS. 1*

66 alone] alone, *WL MS. 1*

67 Tribute,] Tribute *WL MS. 1, Cornell MS. 12* sorrow,] sorrow *MS. 143, WL MS. 1, 1849*

68 One] one *MS. 155, Cornell MS. 12* *no punct MS. 155, WL MS. 1*

69 spirit] Spirit *MS. 155, WL MS. 1, Cornell MS. 12* departed] departed, *Cornell MS. 12*

70–76 *no punct MS. 143*

70 *no punct MS. 155*

72 corse] Corse *Cornell MS. 12* *no punct MS. 155*

73 *no comma MS. 155, WL MS. 1, Cornell MS. 12*

74 breast,] breast *WL MS. 1, Cornell MS. 12* *no punct MS. 155*

75 control] controul *MS. 143, WL MS. 1* impulse] impulse, *WL MS. 1, Cornell MS. 12*

77 training] training, *WL MS. 1, Cornell MS. 12*

78 power] power, *MS. 155, WL MS. 1, Cornell MS. 12*

79 weeds . . . cherish,] weeds, . . . cherish, *MS. 155* weeds, . . . cherish *MS. 143, WL MS. 1, Cornell MS. 12*

80 *no comma WL MS. 1* flower] Flower *WL MS. 1* *no punct MS. 143*

81 Lamb-deliv'rer,] Lamb-deliverer *MS. 143* Lamb-deliverer, *MS. 155, Cornell MS. 12* Lamb-Deliverer *WL MS. 1*

84 sex,] sex *MSS. 143, 155* age.] age *MS. 143*

85 eagle] Eagle *MSS. 143, 155, WL MS. 1, Cornell MS. 12*

86 lark,] Lark— *MS. 143* Lark, *MS. 155, WL MS. 1* Lark, *alt* Lark; *Cornell MS. 12*

87 country] Country *MSS. 143, 155, WL MS. 1, Cornell MS. 12* heroine] Heroine *MS. 143, WL MS. 1, Cornell MS. 12* *no comma WL MS. 1, Cornell MS. 12*

88 Maid of Arc] <u>Maid of Arc</u> *MS. 155, WL MS. 1*

91 spirit] Spirit *WW to HR*

92 thro'] through *WW to HR*

Forth from a jutting ridge, around whose base

1 ridge,] Ridge *MS. 1836/45*

2 Rocks *rev from* [?r]ocks *MS. 1836/45*

4 height; yet both,] height, yet both

5 O'er . . . mead,] Oer . . . mead *MS. 1836/45*

7 Up-led] Up led, *MS. 1836/45*

8 Peaks *rev from* peaks *MS. 1836/45*

9 *no comma MS. 1836/45*

10 gazed,] gaz'd *MS. 1836/45*
11 The . . . couch, gazed, side by side,] (The . . . couch) gazed side by side *MS. 1836/45*
12 I,] I— *MS. 1836/45*
14 heart,] heart *MS. 1836/45*
18 Pinnacles—] Pinnacles *MS. 1836/45*
19 That,] That *MS. 1836/45*
20 hiding-place] hiding place *MS. 1836/45*
21 abyss,] abyss *MS. 1836/45*
22 yourselves,] yourselves *MS. 1836/45*
23 beauty—] beauty, *MS. 1836/45*
24 *no apos MS. 1836/45* claim,] claim *MS. 1836/45*
25 survive] survive, *MS. 1836/45*
26 to age] to age, *MS. 1836/45*

At Furness Abbey ("Well have yon Railway Labourers to this ground")
2 rest.] rest! *WL MS.* sit,] sit *WL MS. 1*
3 Ruins, *rev from* ruins, *WL MS. 1*
6 long-deserted Quire] long deserted quire, *WL MS. 1*
7 earth,] earth *WL MS. 1*
8 *no comma WL MS. 1*
9 raised,] rais'd *WL MS. 1*
10 *no commas WL MS. 1* grace:] grace. *WL MS.*
11 spirit . . . place] Spirit . . . Place *WL MS. 1*
12 praised:] praised. *WL MS. 1*
14 men *rev to* Men *WL MS. 1* moved!] moved. *WL MS. 1*

Why should we weep or mourn, Angelic boy
1 mourn,] mourn— *MS. 143, MS. 1845W, WW to HR* mourn, *rev to* mourn! *WW to CW, Jr.* mourn! *Southey Album 2* Angelic] angelic *MS. 1845D, Southey Album 2* boy,] Boy *MS. 143, WW to HR* Boy! *MS. 1845W, MS. 1845D* Boy, *WW to CW, Jr., Southey Album 2*
2 wert] wert, *MS. 1845W, WW to HR* removed,] removed *MS. 143, MS. 1845W* removed; *WW to CW, Jr., MS. 1845D, Southey Album 2*
3 *no comma MS. 1845W, WW to CW, Jr., WW to HR, Southey Album 2*
4 *no comma MS. 143, WW to HR, Southey Album 2*
6 earth] Earth *MS. 1845W, WW to CW, Jr., MS. 1845D, Southey Album 2* pertaining. *MS. 143, MS. 1845W, MS. 1845D, Southey Album 2*
7 might,] might— *MS. 1845W* mercy,] mercy— *MS. 143, MS. 1845W, WW to CW, Jr., MS. 1845D, Southey Album 2* behoved—] behoved. *MS. 143* behoved, *MS. 1845W, WW to CW, Jr., MS. 1845D, Southey Album 2* behoved; *WW to HR*
8 Death] Death, *WW to CW, Jr., MS. 1845D, Southey Album 2* he] He *MS. 1845W, WW to HR*
9 frame.] Frame— *MS. 1845W* Frame. *MS. 143, WW to HR* That] that *MS. 1845W*
10 *no punct MS. 143, MS. 1845W*
11 now,] now *MS. 143, MS. 1845W, WW to CW, Jr., WW to HR, MS. 1845D* Child,] Child! *MS. 143, WW to CW, Jr., WW to HR, MS. 1845D* Child, *MS. 1845W* Spirit's] Spirits *MS. 143, WW to CW, Jr.* home:] home *MS. 143, WW to HR* home. *MS. 1845W* home; *WW to CW, Jr.* home, *MS. 1845D*
13 felt,] felt,— *WW to CW, Jr.* felt, *rev to* felt— *MS. 1845D* Roman-burial place] Roman-burial-place *MS. 143* Roman burial-place *MS. 1845W, WW to CW, Jr., WW to HR, Southey Album 2*
14 Thee.] thee. *WW to HR* Thee.— *rev from* thee.— *Southey Album 2* *no punct MS. 143*

I know an aged Man constrained to dwell
2 house] House *MS. 143* *no comma MS. 143 (A, C)*
3 he] He *MS. 143 (B)* Prisoner's] prisoner's *MS. 143 (B, C)* *no commas MS. 143 (C, D)*
4 near,] —near *MS. 143 (B)* alas!] alas, *MS. 143 (A)* *no period MS. 143 (D)*
5 about,] about *MS. 143 (B, C, D)*
6 forced] forc'd *MS. 143 (B)*
7 cottage door] cottage-door *MS. 143 (A, B, C)*
8 *no period MS. 143 (C)*
9 *no commas MS. 143 (D)*
10 found] found, *MS. 143 (D)*
11 pecked . . . crumbs . . . knee] peck'd . . . crumbs, . . . knee, *MS. 143 (D)*
14 met!] met *MS. 143 (D)*
16 moment] moment, *MS. 143 (B)*
17 *no comma MS. 143 (B, C, D)*
18 *no commas MS. 143 (C)* demand,] demand *MS. 143 (D)*
19 *no punct MS. 143 (C)* pinions] pinions, *MS. 143 (D)*
20 There] There, *MS. 143 (D)* hand.] hand *MS. 143 (A)*
22 pair,] pair *MS. 143 (A, B, C)*
24 proffered] proffer'd *MS. 143 (B, C, D)*

no punct MS. 143 (B)

25 *no punct MS. 143 (A)* children,] children *MS. 143 (B_1)* kindred,] kindred *MS. 143 (B_2, C)* gone;] gone *MS. 143 (B_1, C)* gone, *MS. 143 (B_2, D)*

26 *no punct MS. 143 (A, B_1, C)* crossed] cross'd *MS. 143 (A, B_2, C, D)*

27 *no punct MS. 143 (A, B)*

28 He *MS. 143 (A)* *no punct MS. 143 (B_1)*

29 *no punct MS. 143*

30 *no punct MS. 143 (A, B, C)*

31 *no punct MS. 143 (A, C)* Bird,] Bird *MS. 143 (B, C)*

32 broken!] broken. *MS. 143 (A, C, D)* broken— *MS. 143 (B)*

To an Octogenarian

2 successors;] successors, *rev to* Successors, *MS. 143 (B)* and,] and *MS. 143 (B)* memory,] memory *MS. 143*

3 die,—] die *MS. 143 (A)*

4 *no comma MS. 143 (A)*

7 *no commas MS. 143* Thou;] Thou— *MS. 143 (A)* howe'er] howeer *MS. 143*

8 Scorned *alt* Scorn'd *del MS. 143 (A)* *no commas MS. 143* dearth.] dearth *MS. 143 (A)*

9 Though] Thoug *MS. 143 (A)* friends] Friends *MS. 143* *no comma MS. 143*

10 *no comma MS. 143*

12 *no comma MS. 143*

14 Love] love *MS. 143 (B)* Thing] thing *MS. 143* place.] place *MS. 143*

Written upon a fly leaf in the Copy of the Author's Poems which was sent to her Majesty Queen Victoria

1 Deign] Deign, *Yale MS. 10*

2 Laureate offering] laureate Offering *MS. 1845RL* Art;] art; *MS. 1845RL* Art *Cornell MS. 13* art *Yale MS. 10*

3 Salutation] salutation *MS. 1845RL, Yale MS. 10* its] it's *Yale MS. 10*

4 Loyal] loyal *MS. 1845RL, Cornell MS. 13, Yale MS. 10* heart.] heart *Cornell MS. 13, Yale MS. 10*

5 Queen,] Queen *Yale MS. 10* Wife,] Wife *Cornell MS. 13, Yale MS. 10* all-judging] all judging *Yale MS. 10* Heaven] heaven *Cornell MS. 13*

6 Thee *rev from* thee *MS. 89* thee *Yale MS. 10* Thine] thine *Yale MS. 10*

7 Felicity,] Felicity *MS. 1845RL, Yale MS. 10*

8 Earth] Earth, *Cornell MS. 13* earth *MS. 1845RL, Yale MS. 10* goodness,] goodness *MS. 1845RL, Yale MS. 10* grace] Grace *MS. 1845RL* devine.] divine *Cornell MS. 13, Yale MS. 10*

9 Lady! *rev from* Lady, *MS. 89* Lady *Cornell MS. 13* honoured] honored *MS. 1845RL, Cornell MS. 13*

10 Thro'] Through *MS. 1845RL, Yale MS. 10* realm] Realm *Cornell MS*

11 May'st] mayst *Cornell MS. 13* Thou *rev from* thou *MS. 89* thou *Yale MS. 10* thou *Cornell MS. 13* approved] approved, *MS. 1845RL*

12 He] <u>He</u> *Cornell MS. 13* People] people *MS. 1845RL, Yale MS. 10* obey.] obey; *MS. 1845RL* obey *Yale MS. 10*

13 Thou] thou *Yale MS. 10* thy *rev from* they *(copyist's slip) MS. 89* wont . . . sovereignty] wont, . . . Sovereignty *MS. 1845RL, Cornell MS. 13*

14 Woman's] woman's *Yale MS. 10* gentleness,] gentleness *Yale MS. 10* staid;] staid *Cornell MS. 13, Yale MS. 10*

15 Crown] crown *MS. 1845RL, Yale MS. 10*

16 changed] chang'd *MS. 1845RL* *no punct Yale MS. 10*

17 now, . . . urged,]now— . . . urged *Cornell MS. 13* now . . . urged *Yale MS. 10* Book] book *Yale MS. 10*

18 Majesty, . . . trust] Majesty . . . Trust *Cornell MS. 13* Majesty . . . trust *Yale MS. 10*

19 Thou *rev from* thou *MS. 89, MS. 1845RL* thou *Yale MS. 10*

20 indulgence,] indulgence *MS. 1845RL, Cornell MS. 13, Yale MS. 10* just:] just. *MS. 1845RL* just *Cornell MS. 13, Yale MS. 10*

21 Thou . . . Poet's] thou . . . poets *Yale MS. 10*

22 mind *rev from miswritten* ming *Cornell MS. 13*

23 Royal] royal *all other MSS.* care] care, *MS. 1845RL*

24 grief, . . . Humankind] grief— . . . human Kind *MS. 1845RL* grief . . . Human kind *Yale MS. 10*

25 spheres] spheres, *MS. 1845RL*

26 Time] time *Yale MS. 10* young] young, *MS. 1845RL*

27 (O were it mine)] (Oh! were it mine) *MS. 1845RL* O! were it mine *Cornell MS. 13* *no comma Cornell MS. 13, Yale MS. 10*
28 life] Life *MS. 1845RL, Cornell MS. 13* *no punct Yale MS. 10*

Who but is pleased to watch the moon on high

3 loth . . . Majesty] loth, . . . majesty *MS. 143 (B)*
4 till . . . clouds] 'til . . . Clouds *MS. 143 (B)*
5 One] One, *MS. 143 (B)*
7 bright,] bright *MS. 143 (B)* moon] Moon *MS. 143 (B)*
8 through] thro' *MS. 143 (B)*
9 e'er] e're *MS. 143 (B)*
11 steadfast] stedfast *MS. 143 (B), 1850*
13 *no parens MS. 143 (B)*
14 gloom!] gloom *1850*

How beautiful the Queen of Night, on high

2–3 *no punct MSS. 1845W, 1845D*
4 obscurity.] obscurity, *MS. 1845W* obscurity: *MS. 1845D*
7 Moon *rev from* moon *MS. 1845D*

Where lies the truth? has Man in wisdom's creed

1 Man] Man *rev from* man *MS. 143 (A)* *no comma MS. 143 (A), WW to HR*
2 doom; *rev from* doom[?] *WW to HR* doom, *MS. 143 (A)*
3 *no comma WW to HR* *no punct MS. 143 (B)*
4 *no comma MS. 143 (B), WW to HR*
5 God's] Gods *MS. 143 (B)* forgotten;] forgotten? *WW to HR* indeed,] indeed *MS. 143 (B)* *no commas WW to HR*
7 Flowers] flowers *MS. 143 (B), WW to HR* rejoice] rejoice, *WW to HR* Larks] larks *MS. 143 (A), WW to HR*
8 morrow?] morrow. *MS. 143 (A), WW to HR*
11 o'er] oer *MS. 143, WW to HR* *no punct WW to HR*
12 aspirants] Aspirants *WW to HR* *no comma MS. 143 (A)*
13 life's] lifes *MS. 143 (A)* Life's *MS. 143 (B)* trials, *rev in pencil from* trials *WW to HR* snares,] snares *MS. 143 (B)* *no commas MS. 143 (A)*
14 purer] purer, *MS. 143 (B)* Heaven] heaven *MS. 143, WW to HR* theirs.] theirs! *MS. 143 (B)* theirs *WW to HR*

To Lucca Giordano

1 Giordano,] Giordano! *all MSS.* Pencil's] pencils *rev to* Pencils *MS. 1845D* pencil's *MS. 1845W*
2 portrayed] pourtrayed *all MSS.* Nature's] nature's *MS. 143*
3 Latomos-hill;] Latmos-hill, *MS. 143* Latmos hill; *MS. 1845W, MS. 1845D*
3–4 *over illeg pencil eras MS. 145*
5 —yet] yet *MS. 1845W, MS. 1845D* embrace,] embrace *MS. 1845W, MS. 1845D*
7 chase] chace *MS. 143* *no comma MS. 1845W, MS. 1845D*
8 *no punct MS. 1845W* *no commas MS. 1845D*
9 work] Work *MS. 1845W, MS. 1845D*
10 Mountain-bard's] mountain-Bard's *rev to* Mountain-Bard's *MS. 143* Mountain Bard's *MS. 1845W* mountain bard's *MS. 1845D* abode] Abode *MS. 143*
11 *no commas MS. 1845W, MS. 1845D*
12 he *rev to* He *MS. 143* *no comma MS. 143, MS. 1845W*
13 *no punct MS. 1845W, MS. 1845D*
14 green-wood] greenwood *MS. 1845W, MS. 1845D*

Illustrated Books and Newspapers

1 *no comma MS. 143*
2 *no punct (leaf damaged) MS. 143*
3 Printing *rev to* Printing— *MS. 143*
4 thought—] thought, *rev to* thought; *MS. 143*
5 truth, . . . love expand.] Truth . . . love expand.] Love expand; *MS. 143*
7 lacquey . . . Art] lackey . . . art *MS. 143*
9 *no comma MS. 143*
10 age] Age *MS. 143*
11 caverned life's] cavern'd . . . Lifes *MS. 143* *no punct MS. 143*
12–13 *no punct MS. 143*
14 Nothing? . . . stage!] Nothing?— . . . stage— *MS. 143*

On the Banks of a Rocky Stream, Text of 1847

title On the banks of a rocky Stream *MS. 1845D* On the Banks of rocky Stream *MS. 1845W, MS. 1845D*
7 thine,] thine *MS. 1845W*

Installation Ode

part assignments *Cornell MS. 3 lacks abbreviations, dashes, and occasional final periods*
1 disowns,] disowns *Cornell MS. 3*

2 thrones,] thrones. *Cornell MS. 3*
3 *no comma Cornell MS. 3*
7 game] game, *Cornell MS. 3*
9 Earth and Heaven] earth and heaven *Cornell MS. 3*
12 Despot's] despot's *Cornell MS. 3*
14 Freedom's . . . cause;] freedom's . . . cause *Cornell MS. 3*
15 Freedom, . . . Man] Freedom . . . man *Cornell MS. 3*
17 glory:] glory; *Cornell MS. 3*
19 lo,] lo! *Cornell MS. 3*
24 Nation's] nation's *Cornell MS. 3*
25 wears;—] wears, *Cornell MS. 3*
26 sleep;] sleep: *Cornell MS. 3*
27 Tree] tree *Cornell MS. 3* bears,—] bears— *Cornell MS. 3*
28 *no commas Cornell MS. 3*
31 Guardian Angel] guardian angel *Cornell MS. 3*
32 Babe] babe *Cornell MS. 3*
unseen;] unseen, *Cornell MS. 3*
35 through] thro' *Cornell MS. 3*
38 name!"] name"! *Cornell MS. 3*
43 And,] And *Cornell MS. 3*
45 Wisdom] wisdom *Cornell MS. 3*
46–56 *opening quots lacking Cornell MS. 3*
47 *no comma Cornell MS. 3* Pleasure] pleasure *Cornell MS. 3*
49 Womanhood] Womanhood, *Cornell MS. 3*
50 throne:] throne; *Cornell MS. 3*
51 Crown] crown *Cornell MS. 3*,
56 royal] Royal *Cornell MS. 3*
57, 59 *no commas Cornell MS. 3*
62 Rhine.—] Reine. *Cornell MS. 3*
63 Camus too] Camus, too, *Cornell MS. 3*
65 *no comma Cornell MS. 3*
66 Zephyr's] zephyr's *Cornell MS. 3*
68 day:] day. *Cornell MS. 3*
71 Star] star *Cornell MS. 3*
73 Collegiate] collegiate *Cornell MS. 3*
74 Science] science *Cornell MS. 3*
79 Powers,] powers *Cornell MS. 3*
80 Wise and Just] wise and just *Cornell MS. 3*
86 Sages] sages *Cornell MS. 3*
taught.—] taught— *Cornell MS. 3*
87 disciples,] disciples *Cornell MS. 3*
89 Future . . . Past] future . . . past *Cornell MS. 3*
91 Land] land *Cornell MS. 3*
93 Though] Tho' *Cornell MS. 3*
94 Hate . . . Zeal] hate . . . zeal *Cornell MS. 3*
95 *no comma Cornell MS. 3*
96 Nation's strength] nation's strength, *Cornell MS. 3*
97 Line] line *Cornell MS. 3*
98 found;] found: *Cornell MS. 3*
99 Wise* Ancestor] wise ancester *Cornell MS. 3*
101 first,] first *Cornell MS. 3*
108 Hero] hero *Cornell MS. 3*
109 resound] Resound *Cornell MS. 3*
112 Throne!—] Throne— *Cornell MS. 3*
113 Presence] presence *Cornell MS. 3*
115 rite,] rite— *Cornell MS. 3*
note below text FINIS. *lacking Cornell MS. 3*

PART III

Selected Transcriptions and Photographic Reproductions

Transcriptions

Each of the manuscripts transcribed here is described in the Manuscript Census. Manuscript transcriptions are presented in accordance with the principles outlined in the Editorial Procedure. We selected materials for this treatment for their degree of difficulty and intrinsic interest. In scope they range from a portion of a single page that could not easily be represented in an *apparatus* beneath the reading text to substantial pieces of transcription and draft that differ markedly from the reading text but could not themselves be fairly reduced to an alternate reading text or an *apparatus.* A manuscript identification, with leaf number, appears above each photograph. The title of the poem appears in brackets at the top of each page of transcription. Line numbers to the left of the transcriptions are assigned serially to the base text; the numbers that sometimes appear to the right refer to lines of reading texts (notes provide further details). Any extraneous material not transcribed is identified in the notes. Editorial conventions used in transcriptions are summarized below.

roman type	=	in Wordsworth's hand
italic type	=	in the hand of a copyist (identified, whenever possible, in the notes)
boldface type	=	printed text beneath autograph revisions
reduced type	=	a revision of, or entry made later than, the base text
screened text	=	revised entry over an illegible erasure
~~deleted text~~	=	words deleted by a single line (but when a large block of text is crossed out and a photograph faces it, no deletion lines appear in the transcription)

["Go back to antique Ages, if thine eyes"]

[1–12]

~~Nor lack high [?purpose] with this hour~~
{See
{The the first mighty Hunter in pursuit
Of men, by armies of his fellows back'd
whos while
See those by whom the elements are rackd
With spell & clamorous ritual better
Hope from the sickly tur

1 Go back to antient ages, ere disguise
2 Was thought of—ere a mask conceald the face
her
3 Of the rash spirit that still holds ~~a~~ place
4 Prompting
Others behold who cast in midnight hours
Black
Their expectation upon weird powers
Dark
5 Others behold who cast in midnight hours
[?Outrageous]
{Their
{[?] murky hopes upon infernal
6 Their expectations upon weird powers
{ (}
Others behold{—}not lacking & this hour
{Some
{All Successor who cast on weird power
A hope that while the element are rackd
Which

For readings from the version entered above the one transcribed here, see pp. 61–62. Related draft lines entered along the top right margin are not visible in the photograph:

like craving after power
Others behold—(~~such wasting to this hour~~)
~~Survive past punishment for misus'd power~~
Punish the weak & wicked to this hour

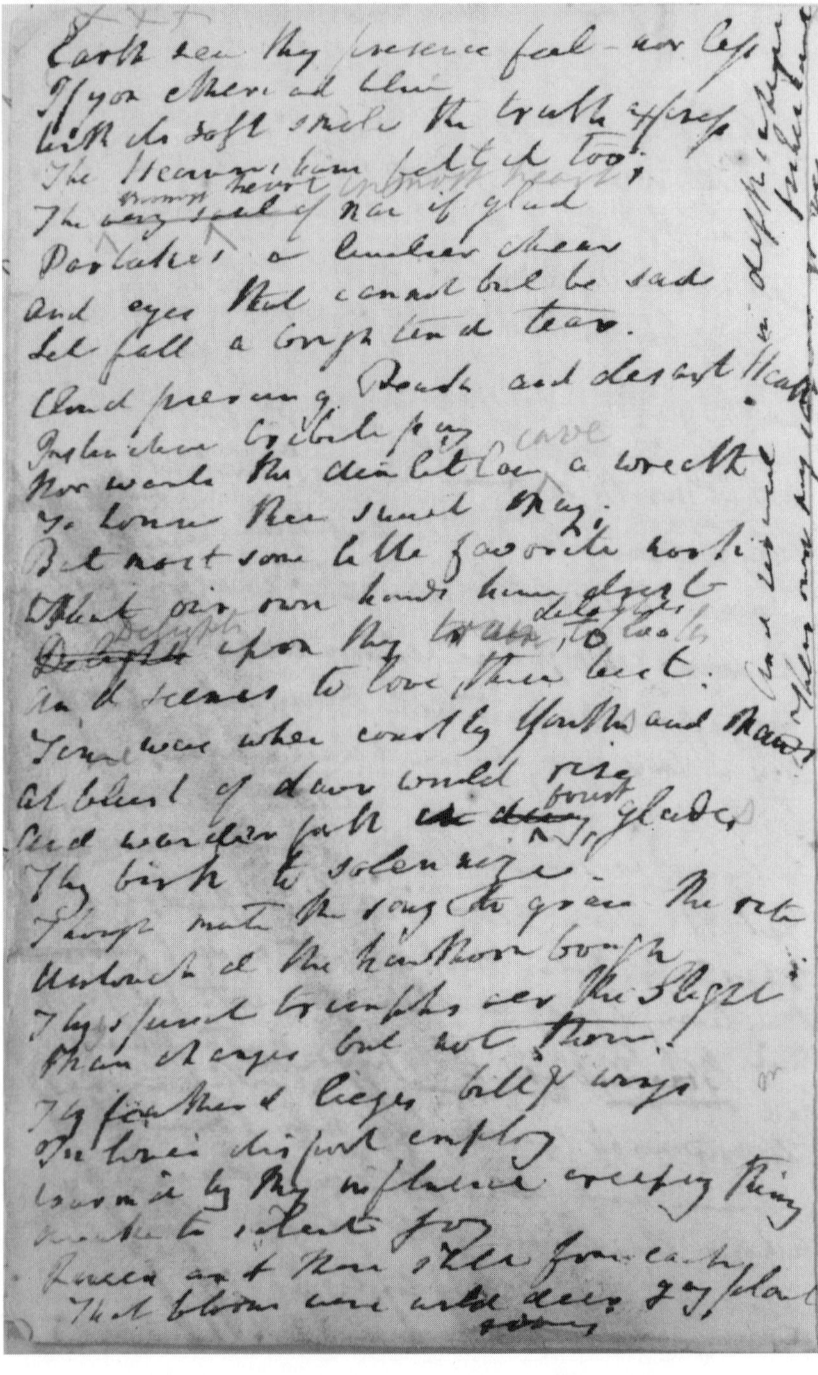

Earth sees thy presence feel—nor less
Of yon ethereal blue
With its soft smile the truth express
The Heavens have felt it too;
The ~~very soul~~ inmost heart of man if glad
Partakes a livelier cheer
And eyes that cannot but be sad
Let fall a brighten'd tear.
Cloud piercing Peaks and desert Heath
Instinctive tribute pay
Nor wants the dim lit ~~lane~~ cave a wreath
To honour thee sweet May;
But most some little favorite nook
That our own hands have dressed
~~Delights~~ Delights upon thy train ~~to~~ delights to look
And seems to love thee best.
Time was when courtly Youths and Maids
At blush of dawn would rise
And wander forth ~~in the dewy~~ in forest glades
Thy birth to solemnize.
Though mute the song to grace the rite
Untouched the hawthorn bough
Thy spirit triumphs over the slight
Man changes but not thou.
Thy feathered lieges bill & wings
In love's disport employ
Warmed by thy influence creeping things
Awake to silent joy
Queen art thou still for each gay plant
That blooms were wild dews ~~lay~~ are laid

[*To May* and *Ode to May*]

X X X
17 Earth sea thy presence feel—nor less
18 If yon etherial blue
19 With its soft smile the truth express
20 The Heavns have felt it too;
inmost heart inmost heart
21 The ^ ~~very soul~~ of man if glad
22 Part^akes ^a livelier chear
23 And eyes that cannot but be sad
24 Let fall a brightend tear.
25 Cloud piercing Peak and desart Heath
26 Instinctive tribute pay
cave
27 Nor wants the dim lit Cae ^ a wreath
28 To honour thee sweet May;
29 But most some little favorite nook
That}
30 Whic} our own hands have drest
Delights {train delights
31 ~~Delight~~ upon thy {train, to look
32 And seems to love thee best:
e} s}
33 Tim } was when courtly Youth } and Maids
34 At blush of dawn would rise
{in forest s}
35 And wander forth {[?oer] ~~dewy~~ glade }
^
36 Thy birth to solemnize.

37 Though mute the song to grace the rite
38 Untouchd the hawthorn bough
{y S}
39 Th{e spirit triumphs oer the s} light
40 Man changes but not thou.
41 Thy featherd lieges bill & wings
42 In love's disport employ
43 Warm'd by thy influence creeping thing
44 Awake to silent Joy
45 Queen art thou still for each
gay plant
46 That blooms were wild deer
roves

47 And served in depths where
fishes haunt
48 There own mysterious groves

Line numbers on the left correspond to those of the reading text of "D" in MS. 107, pp. 69–71.

17 The "Xs" above the line are in pencil.

21 The deletion, the carets, and the right-hand revision above the line are all in pencil.

27 The caret below the line and "cave" above are in pencil.

31 Above the line the first "Delights" is in pencil; "train" is overwritten in pencil.

33 The "e" of "Time" and the "s" of "Youths" were added in pencil.

35 The "s" has been added in pencil.

39 The "e" of "The" was revised to "y" in pencil and in ink.

45–46 WW entered a variant of these two lines at the foot of 81[r]:
Queen art thou still for each gay plant
Where the slim wild deer roves

46 The "h" was omitted from the word "where."

47–48 Lacking room at the foot, WW squeezed the final two lines in the right margin; l. 48 runs over onto the recto of the next stub.

Ode Composed on May-Morning

While from the purpling east departs
The Star that led the dawn
Blithe Flora from her couch upstarts
For May is on the lawn
A quickening hope a freshening glee
Foreran the expected Power
Whose first drawn breath from bush & tree
Shakes off that pearly shower

~~#9~~ 8 — the joyous ye

Earth sea ~~thy~~ presence feel. nor less
If ~~yon~~ etherial blue
With its soft smile the truth express
The Heavens have felt it too
The inmost heart of man if glad
Partakes a livelier cheer
And eyes that cannot but be sad
Let fall a brightened tear

~~Hea[illegible]~~

[*Ode to May*]

Ode { *Composed on May-Morning* / *to May* }

\- - - - - -

I

While from the purpling east departs [*Ode*, 1–8]
The Star that { *led* / *leads the dawn* }
Blithe Flora from her couch upstarts
For May is on the Lawn
A quickening hope { *a* / *& freshening* } { *glee* / [*?cheer*] }
Foreran the expected Power
Whose first drawn breath from bush & tree
Shakes off that pearly shower
—the joyous year [*Ode*, 56]

{ 8 / 2 } { 8 / 6 }

Earth sea { thy / T / ~~her~~ } *presence* ~~*feels*~~ *nor less* [*To May*, 17–24]
If { yon / [?] } *etherial blue*
With its soft smile the truth express
The Heavens have felt it too
The inmost heart of man if glad
Partakes a livelier cheer
And eyes that cannot but be sad
Let fall a brightened tear

~~9~~
~~*Hush feeble* [*?word*]~~ [*Ode*, 57]

Fair copy of *Ode to May* in DC MS. 133 is in Dora W's hand.

9–16 WW's vertical bar marks the stanza for deletion here. (See 22^{v}P1^{v} where it is reinserted.)

9 Revision in pencil (including the stanza number "8"). The "s" of "feels" was deleted by erasure.

~~3~~ 2

All Nature welcomes her whose sway
Tempers the years extremes
And scattereth lustres o'er noon-day
Like mornings dewy gleams
While mellow warble sprightly trill
The tremulous heart excite
And hums the balmy air to still
The balance of delight

Blest Power when
Time was ~~when~~ ~~courtly~~ Youths & Maids
At peep of dawn would rise
And wander forth, ~~blest Power~~! in forest glades
Thy birth to solemnize.
Though mute the song—to grace the rite
Untouched the hawthorn bough
Thy spirit triumphs o'er the slight
Man changes but not thou

~~5~~ 4

Thy feathered Lieges bill & wings
In love's disport employ,
Warmed by thy influence creeping Things
Awake to silent joy

[*Ode to May*]

~~3~~ 2

All Nature welcomes her whose sway [*Ode*, 9–16]
Tempers the years extremes
And scattereth lustres o'er noon day
Like mornings dewy gleams
While mellow warble sprightly trill
The tremulous heart excite
And hums the balmy air to still
The balance of delight
~~Earth sea her pres~~

~~4~~ 3

blest Power when
Time was ~~when courtly~~ Youths & Maids [*Ode*, 17–24]
At peep of dawn would rise
P ! forest
And wander forth, ~~blest p~~ ~~ower~~ , in^ glades
Thy birth to solemnize.
Though mute the song—to grace the rite
Untouched the hawthorn bough
Thy spirit triumphs o'er the slight
Man changes but not thou

~~5~~ 4

Thy feathered Lieges bill & wings [*Ode*, 25–32]
,
In love's disport employ
Warmed by thy influence creeping Things
Awake to silent joy

8/9 "Earth sea" etc. was entered to indicate the stanza that follows but the entry was rubbed out.
9 The phrase "blest Power when" is written over and through the stanza numbers.

Queen art thou still for each gay plan[t] (18

Where the slim wild deer roves

And served in depths where fishes haunt

Their own mysterious groves.

5 Trackless

Cloud-piercing Peak & ~~dizzy~~ Heath

Instinctive homage pay

Nor wants the dim-lit cave a wreath

To honor thee, sweet May!

Where Cities fanned by thy brisk airs

Behold a smokeless sky

Their puniest Flower-pot-nursling dares

To open a bright eye

4 thus 6 natal

And ~~what~~ if on thy ~~birth-day~~ morn

The Pole from which thy name

Hath not departed stands forlorn

Of song & dance & game

Still from the village green a vow

Aspires to thee addrest

Wherever peace is on the brow,

Or Love within the breast.

7

~~Hast Public~~

Yes! where Love nestles

[*Ode to May*]

Queen art thou still for each gay plant
Where the slim wild deer roves
And served in depths where fishes haunt
Their own mysterious groves.

~~6~~ 5

trackless
Cloud-piercing Peak & ~~desart~~ Heath [*Ode*, 33–40]
Instinctive homage pay
-
Nor wants the dim {lit cave a wreath
{e, {!
To honor the{ sweet May{
C
Where c{ities fanned by thy brisk airs
Behold a smokeless sky
{F
Their puniest {flower-pot-nursling dares
To open a bright eye

{6
~~7~~ {7
this natal
And ~~what~~ if on ^ thy ~~birth-day~~ morn [*Ode*, 41–48]
{P
The {pole from which thy name
{s
Hath not departed stand{ forlorn
Of song & dance & game
Still from the village green a vow
Aspires to thee addrest
{,
Wherever peace is on the brow{
{.
Or Love within the breast{

7
~~Hush feeble Lyre [?]~~ [*Ode*, 57, 49]
Yes where Love nestles

13 Deletion of "what" and entry of "this" are in pencil.
21–22 WW's initial entry and its replacement point to the next stanza and express two different arrangements of stanzas.

8

Hush feeble Lyre weak words refuse
The service to prolong
To yon exulting thrush the muse
Entrusts the imperfect song
His voice shall chaunt in accents clear
Throughout the livelong day
Till the first silver star appear
The sovereignty of May.
------------ End

7

Yes! where Love nestles thou canst teach
The soul to love the more
Hearts also shall thy lessons reach
That never loved before
Stript is the haughty one ~~are stripped~~ of pride
The bashful freed from fear
While rising like the Ocean tide
In flows the joyous year

Earth sea

Earth

The Lyre of Seasons cast old Time

[*Ode to May*]

~~9~~ 8

Hush feeble Lyre weak words refuse [*Ode*, 57–64]
The service to prolong
To yon exulting thrush the muse
Entrusts the imperfect song
His voice shall chaunt in accents clear
Throughout the livelong day
Till the first silver star appear
The sovereignty of May.
------------ End

When orient day attends
{More
{So eagerly on [?whom] the bright
Morn lovingly descends

~~8~~ 7

Yes! where Love nestles thou canst teach [*Ode*, 49–56]
The soul to love the more
Hearts also {*shall* / *can* *thy lessons reach*
That never loved before
Stript is
~~*The*~~ *haughty One*~~*s*~~ ~~*are stripped*~~ *of pride*
The bashful freed from fear
While rising like the Ocean tide
In{- *flows the joyous year*
Earth, sea &c [*To May*, 17–18]
The Lord of Seasons least old Time Earth
Should te{ll [?may] / ac of his long race
Teach from some ethereal clime
As thee ~~fair daughter of the~~ Prime
~~Hush feeble Lyre~~ To animate his pace [*Ode*, 57]
And not a foe hath cold Despite

The draft in the margin has no counterpart in any of the reading texts.

8/ "End" is a late addition, after WW made *Ode to May* into two poems.

13 The "s" of "Ones" was deleted by erasure.

16/ "Earth, sea &c" in pencil (to indicate the next stanza).

2

18(a)

All Nature welcomes thee whose sway
Tempers the year's extremes;
~~And~~ Who Scattereth lustres o'er noon-day
Like morning's dewy gleams;
While mellow warble, sprightly trill
The tremulous heart excite;
And hums the balmy air ~~#~~ to still
The balance of delight.

Thy feathered Lieges bills & wings
In love's disport employ;
Warmed by thy influence, creeping Things
Awake to silent joy:
Queen art thou still for each gay Plant
Where the slim wild Deer roves;
And served in depths where Fishes haunt
Their own mysterious groves.

[*Ode to May*]

[?*off*] [?*pearly*]
2
{*H*
All Nature welcomes {*her whose sway* [*Ode*, 9–16]
Tempers the year's extremes;
Who {*s*
~~*And*~~ ^ {*Scattereth lustres o'er noon-day*
Like morning's dewy gleams;
While mellow warble, sprightly trill
The tremulous heart excite;
{~~t~~
And hums the balmy air { *to still*
The balance of delight.

Thy feathered Lieges bill & wings [*Ode*, 25–32]
In love's disport employ;
Warmed by thy influence, creeping Things
Awake to silent joy: P
Queen art thou still for each gay ~~*p*~~*lant*
{D
Where the slim wild {*deer roves;*
{F
And served in depths where {*fishes haunt*
Their own mysterious groves.

On the folio 17^r–18^v (the lower half of a full sheet) are copies of stanzas 2, 4, 6, and 8; the missing half no doubt bore copies of stanzas 1, 3, 5, and 7.

1 Above the line the down-strokes of "off" and "pearly" of the missing stanza are visible.

18(b)

And if, on this thy natal morn,
The Pole, from which thy name
Hath not departed, stands forlorn
Of song and dance and game,
Still from the village-green a vow
Aspires to thee addrest,
Wherever peace is on the brow,
Or Love within the breast.

Hush feeble Lyre! weak words, refuse
    The service to prolong!
To yon exulting thrush the Muse
    Entrusts the imperfect song;
His voice shall chaunt, in accents clear,
    Throughout the livelong day
Till the first silver star appear,
    The sovereignty of May.

[*Ode to May*]

And if, on this thy natal morn, [*Ode*, 41–48]
The Pole, from which thy name
Hath not departed, stands forlorn
Of song and dance and game ,
Still from the village-green a vow
Aspires to thee addrest,
Wherever peace is on the brow,
Or Love within the breast.

Hush feeble Lyre! weak {W / *words!*} *refuse* [*Ode*, 57–64]
The service to prolong {*!* / ;}
To yon exulting {T / *thrush*} *the Muse*
Entrusts the imperfect song;
His voice shall chaunt, in accents clear,
Throughout the livelong {*day* / [? *may*]}
Till the first silver Star appear,
The sovereignty of May.
– – – – – –

4 Original punctuation after "game" has been erased.

Ode to May

All nature welcomes thee, blithe May
Tempering the year's extremes
And scattering lustres o'er noonday
Like morning's pearly gleams
While mellow warble sprightly trill
The tremulous heart excite
And hums the balmy air to still
The balance of delight!

Delicious odours music sweet
Too sweet to pass away
Oh for a deathless song to meet
~~This blest return~~ a Day
The souls desire
That when a thousand years are told
Should praise thee genial Power
Through summer heat autumnal [illegible]
And winter's dreariest hour
~~The [illegible]~~

[*Ode to May*]

Ode to May

\- - - - - - - - -

All nature welcomes thee, blithe May [*Ode*, 9–16]
Tempering the year's extremes
And scattering lustres o'er noonday
Like morning's pearly gleams
While mellow warble sprightly trill
The tremulous heart excite
And hums the balmy air to still
The balance of delight!

Delicious odoûrs music sweet [*To May*, 9–16]
Too sweet to pass away
m
Oh for a deathless song to {*gr*} *eet*
L
~~*This blest return*~~ *a* {*l*} *ay*
The Souls desire
That when a thousand years are told
Should praise thee genial Power
{rou}
Th{*orou*}*gh summer heat autumnal cold*
And winter's dreariest hour!
~~The Lord of Seasons least old~~ Time

1–8 Canceled by a paste-over (P1[r]); see the next photograph and transcription, pp. 636–637.
9–16 The number "2" for this stanza appears at the foot of the paste-over.
9 The mark over the "u" of "odours" probably queries, or cancels, the letter.
16/ WW's canceled tag refers to the stanza drafted on 18[v].

To May

~~Twelve bright Suns~~ 1

Tho' many Suns have risen & set
Since thou blithe May wert born
And bards who hailed thee may forget
Thy gifts, thy beauty scorn
There are who to a natal birth-day strain
Confine not harp & voice
But ever more throughout thy reign
Are grateful & rejoice

2

Delicious odours music sweet
Too sweet to pass away
Oh for a deathless song to meet
~~This blest return~~ The souls desire a Day
That when a thousand years are told
Should praise thee genial Power
Through summer heat autumnal cold
The wild winter's dreariest hour
~~The[illegible] old time~~

[*Ode to May*]

To May

\- - - - -

~~*twelve bright Suns*~~

1 *Tho' many suns have risen & set* [*To May*, 1–8]
2 *Since thou blithe May wert born*
3 *And bards who hailed thee may forget*
4 *Thy gifts, thy beauty scorn*
birth-day
5 *There are who to a natal* ^ *strain*
6 *Confine not harp & voice*
7 *But ever more throughout thy reign*
8 *Are grateful & rejoice*
2

9 The e
10 Sh

The paste-over covers the top half of the page; for the text on the lower half see the previous transcription. The "2" below l. 8 goes with the stanza below the paste-over.

9–10 These fragments appear on two surviving segments of a paste-over that was once attached to the foot of 19^r^ (P2 on the left and P3 on the right); cf. WW's draft at the foot of 16^v^, "The Lord of Seasons least old Time / Should teac[h] of his long race," and his deletion at the foot of 19^r^.

Earth sea thy presence feel—nor less
In yon etherial blue
With its soft smile the truth express
The heavens have felt it too
The inmost heart of man is glad
Partakes a livelier cheer
And eyes that cannot but be sad
Let fall a brightened tear

4

Cloud piercing Peak & desert Heath
Instinctive tribute pay
For whom the dew-lit gave a wreath
To honor thee sweet May
But most some little favorite nook
That our own hands have drest
Upon thy train delights to look
And seems to love thee best
Her mother ... free to taste
Earth's sweetness in thy breath

[*Ode to May*]

Since thy return, through days & weeks [*To May*, 25]
Earth Sea thy presence feel—nor less [*To May*, 17]
that grew by
Of hope [?by] by stealth [*To May*, 26]
If yon etherial blue [*To May*, 18]
How many wan and faded cheeks [*To May*, 27]
With its soft smile the truth express [*To May*, 19]
Have kindled into health [*To May*, 28]
The Heavens have felt it too [*To May*, 20]
The inmost heart of man if glad [*To May*, 21]
The old by thee revived have said [*To May*, 29]
Partakes a livelier cheer [*To May*, 22]
Another year is ours [*To May*, 30]
And eyes that cannot but be sad [*To May*, 31]
Perhaps the poor Man wanting bread [*To May*, 31]
Let fall a brightened tear [*To May*, 24]
Has smiled upon thy flowers [*To May*, 32]

4
~~*Cloud piercing Peak & desart Heath*~~ [*Ode*, 33]
tripping
Who ~~runs and~~ lisps a merry song [*To May*, 33]
Instinctive tribute pay [*Ode*, 34]
Amid his playful peers [*To May*, 34]
Nor wants the dim-lit cave a wreath [*Ode*, 35]
C} Infant was
The Winter ~~c}hild~~ who ~~hath been~~ long [*To May*, 35]
To honor thee sweet May [*Ode*, 36]
A prisoner of fond fears, [*To May*, 36]
But most some little favorite nook [*Ode*, 29]
But now when every sharp edge blast [*To May*, 37]
That our own hands have drest [*Ode*, 30]
Is quiet in its sheath [*To May*, 38]
Upon thy train delights to look [*Ode*, 31]
And seems to love thee best [*Ode*, 32]
leaves
His mother ~~sets~~ him free to taste [*To May*, 39]
Earths sweetness in thy breath [*To May*, 40]

After Dora W entered two stanzas in ink, WW interlined two new stanzas, the first in pencil, the second in ink. The page was canceled by the two paste-overs that follow (19^vP1^r and 19^vP2^r).

Earth sea thy presence feel her less
Since thy return thro' days & weeks
Of hope that grew by stealth
How many wan & faded cheeks
Have kindled into health
The Old by thee revived have said
Another year is ours
And many a poor man wanting bread
Has smiled upon thy flowers

Who tripping
Who ~~tripping~~ lisps a merry song
Amid his playful peers?
The tender Infant who was long
A prisoner of fond fears;
But now when every sharp-edged blast
Is quiet in its sheath,
His Mother leaves him free to taste
Earth's sweetness in thy breath

run of lifes

[*Ode to May*]

3
Earth Sea thy presence feel nor less [*To May*, 17]
3

4
Since thy return thro' days & weeks [*To May*, 25–32]
~~dawned~~
Of hope that grew by stealth
How many wan & faded cheeks
Have kindled into health
The Old by thee revived have said
Another year is ours
And many a
~~Perhaps the~~ poor man wanting bread
Has smiled upon thy flowers

{5
{*4*
who tripping merry
~~runs &~~ {[?pret]
~~Who tripping~~ lisps a {*~~merry~~ song* [*To May*, 33–40]
stet ~~The merry infant~~
Amid his playful peers?
e ~~that~~
Th~~at~~ tender Infant who was long
A prisoner of fond fears;
But now when every sharp-edged blast
Is quiet in its sheath,
His Mother leaves him free to taste
Earth's sweetness in thy breath

run — & lisp

16/ WW's entry "run—& lisp" revises l. 9 above.

6

Thy help is with the weed that creeps
Along the humblest ground
No cliff so bare but on its steeps
Thy favors may be found
But most on some peculiar nook
That our own hands have drest
Thou & thy train are proud to look
And seem to love it best

7

And yet how pleased we wander forth
When May is whispering, "Come!
"Choose from the bowers of virgin earth
" The happiest for your home;
"Heaven's bounteous love thro' me is spread
" From sunshine clouds winds waves;
"Drops on the mouldering turrets head
" And on your turf-clad graves!"

We hear Thee nor can [illegible]

[*Ode to May*]

{6
{4 6

Thy help is with the weed that creeps [*To May*, 41–48]
Along the humblest ground
No cliff so bare but on its steeps
Thy favors may be found
But most on some peculiar nook
That our own hands have drest
Thou & thy train are proud to look
And seem to love it best

{7
{5 7

And yet how pleased we wander forth [*To May*, 49–56]
{*When* *is* {*C*
{*If May* ~~*be*~~ *whispering,* "{*come!*
"Chuse from the {s
~~*In every*~~ *bower*{ *of virgin earth*
" *The happiest for your*
~~*Is but a happy*~~ *home;*
"}
}*Heaven's bounteous love thro' me is spread*
"}
}*From sunshine clouds winds waves;*
"}
}*Drops on the mouldering turrets head*
"} {*!*
}*And on your turft-clad graves*{. "
~~who carroll'd thus~~
~~When May Who thus called forth~~
We hear thee nor can mark with

For lilies that must fade
Or the rathe primrose as it dies
Forsak[en] in the shade.
Vernal fruitions and desires
Are link[ed] in endless chase
While as one kindly growth retires
Another takes its place
And if thy sweet May ...
Mishap ... of worm or blight
If expectations newly blown
Have perished in thy sight;
If loves and joys, while up they sprung,
Were caught as in a snare;
Such is the lot of all the young
However bright and fair.
Lo streams that April

If promises while yet half blown

[*Ode to May*]

8

This greeting heard away with sighs [*To May*, 57–64]

{ shall

~~how [?unciva]lly~~ { ~~will~~ we

~~For lilies~~

{ ~~Thus~~ ~~summoned who~~

1 { ~~*Who heard thee & can mark with sighs*~~

Who hears thee &

{ ies

2 For ~~*The lil*~~ { ~~*y*~~ *that must fade*

~~This greeting heard away with sighs~~

3 *Or the rathe primrose as it dies*

4 *Forsaken in the shade*

Vernal fruitions

5 ~~*Complacencies too bl*~~*and desires*

~~*Are linked*~~ ~~*eager*~~

~~*Succeed* [*?in*] *fitful chase*~~

6 *Are linked in endless chase*

ki }

7 *While as one* [*?fo*] } *ndly growth retires* [*To May*, 65–72]

8 *Another takes its place*

& gracious [?scenes] if thou hast known

And, ~~if thy Sweet May thy~~ [?hopes]

have known

9 ~~Lo! Streams that April [?did]~~

~~[?may] offspring, sweet~~

10 ~~Nor will we grieve if thou hast known~~

Mishap ~~by from~~ by or

11 ~~The checks of~~ worm ~~and~~ blight

newly

12 If expectations ~~but~~ ^ ~~half~~ blown

13 Have perished in thy sight;

14 If loves and joys, while up they sprung,

15 Were caught as in a snare;

of

16 Such is the lot ~~for~~ all the Young,

However bright and fair

17 ~~The doom for all the fair.~~—

18 Lo Streams that April [*To May*, 73]

[left margin, vertical:] fragrant
If promises while yet half-blown

---

9 An aborted beginning to the stanza that follows.

12 WW entered an alternate to this line along the left margin.

18 The opening words of the next stanza (on 21[v]).

20(b)

Time was when courtly Youths & Maids
At blush of dawn would rise
And wander forth in forest glades
Thy birth to solemnize
Though mute the song—to grace the rite
Untouched the hawthorn bough,
Thy spirit triumphs o'er the slight
Man changes, but not thou.

Thy feathered Lieges bill and wing
In love's disport employ
Warmed by thy influence, creeping things
Awake to silent joy
Queen art thou still for each gay plant
Where the slim wild deer roves
And served in depths where fishes haunt
Their own mysterious groves

[*Ode to May*]

Time was when courtly Youths & Maids [*Ode*, 16-24]
At blush of dawn would rise
And wander forth, in forest glades
Thy birth to solemnize
Though mute the song—to grace the rite
Untouched the hawthorn bough,
Thy spirit triumphs o'er the slight
Man changes, but not thou.

Th{y/*e feathered* {*L*/*lieges bill and wing*{s [*Ode*, 25-32]
In love's disport employ
Warmed by th{y/*e influence, creeping* {T/*things*
Awake to silent joy
Queen art thou still for each gay plant
Where the slim wild deer roves
And served in depths where fishes haunt
Their own mysterious groves

---

9 The "y" of "Thy" is in pencil.
11 The revisions are in pencil.

10

So streams that April could not check
Are patient of thy rule
Gurgling in foamy water-break
Loitering in glassy pool
By thee, thee only could be sent
Such gentle mists as glide
Curling with unconfirmed intent
On that green mountain's side

11

How delicate the leafy veil
Through which ~~the~~ yon House of God
Gleams mid the peace of this deep dale
By few but shepherds trod
And lowliest huts near beaten ways
No sooner stand attired
In thy fresh wreaths than they for praise
Peep forth, and are admired

[*Ode to May*]

~~7~~ 10

Lo! Streams that April could not check [*To May*, 73–80]
Are patient of thy rule
Gurgling in foamy water-break
Loitering in glassy pool
By thee, thee only could be sent
Such gentle mists as glide
Curling with unconfirmed intent
On that green mountain's side

{~~9~~ / ~~8~~} 11

How delicate the leafy veil [*To May*, 81–88]
yon
Through which ~~*the*~~ *House of God*
Gleams mid the peace of this deep dale
By few but shepherds trod
{*y*
And lowl{~~*iest*~~ *huts near beaten Ways*
No sooner stand attired
In thy fresh wreaths than they for praise
Peep forth, and are admired

12

Season of fancy and of hope
Permit not for one hour
A blossom from thy crown to drop
Nor add to it a flower
Of self-restraining art
The modest charm of not too much
Part seen imagined part.

End

Hush feeble lyre weak words refuse
The service to prolong
To yon exulting Thrush the Muse
Intrusts the unfinished song
His voice shall chaunt in accent clear
Throughout the live long day,
Till the first silver star appear
The sovereignty of May.

[*Ode to May*]

12 ~~11~~
~~9~~ ~~10~~

Season of fancy and of hope [*To May*, 89–96]
Permit not for one hour
A blossom from thy crown to drop
Nor add to it a flower
~~For perfect now is that fine~~ ~~like the touch~~
~~*So perfect now is that finest touch*~~
~~For perfect now as if by touch~~ is [?I]
Of self-restraining art
~~Is now the~~ The modest
~~*The modest*~~^ *charm of not too much*
~~Is the fine~~^^
Part seen imagined part.
End

– – – – – – – – – – – –

Keep lovely May as if by touch
Of self-restraining art

Hush feeble lyre weak words refuse [*Ode*, 57–64]
The service to prolong
To yon exulting Thrush the Muse
Entrusts the unfinished song
His voice shall chaunt in accent clear
Throughout the live long day,
Till the first silver star appear
The sovereignty of May
Glad Spirit keep as with the touch
Keep yet awhile as if by touch
Of self restraining art
perfect charm
This ~~modest charm &c~~ This

Leaf 13 DC MS. 134 was transferred from its position in DC MS. 133 (leaf 25) in a reorganization of these manuscripts in 1995 (the penciled page number "21" was a modern addition while the leaf was still in MS. 133).

To May

9

And what, Sweet May, if thou hast known
Mishap by worm & blight;
If expectations newly blown
Have perished in thy sight;
If loves and joys, while up they sprung,
Were caught ~~[illegible]~~ as in a snare;
Such is the lot of all the Young,
However bright and fair.

10

Lo! Streams that April could not check
Are patient of thy rule;
Gurgling in foamy water-break,
Loitering in glassy pool.
By thee, thee only, could be sent
Such gentle mists as glide,
Curling with unconfirmed intent,
On that green mountain's side.

[*Ode to May*]

To May 56

9

And what sweet May {! *if thou, hast known* [*To May*, 65–72]
2 1
Mis {- *hap by worm & blight;*
If expectations newly blown
Have perished in the sight;
If loves and joys, while up they sprung,
as in
Were caught ~~within~~ a snare;
Such is the lot of ^all^ the Young,
However bright and fair.

10

{*S*
Lo! {*streams that April could not check* [*To May*, 73–80]
Are patient of thy rule;
Gurgling in foamy water-break,
Loitering in glassy pool.
{*T* {*T*
By {*thee,* {*thee only, could be sent*
Such gentle mists as glide,
Curling with unconfirmed intent,
On that green mountain's side.

The drafts at the foot and in the left margin revise ll. 5–8.

Leaf 23 of DC MS. 135 was transferred from DC MS. 133 (leaf 21) in a reorganization of these manuscripts in 1995. The page number "56" was added in ink by MW; the penciled "19" is modern. The fair copy is in the hand of Dora W; the running head, "To May," was entered by MW.

57. to May
11

How delicate the leafy veil
Through which yon House of God
Gleams mid the peace of this deep dale
By few but shepherds trod!
And lowly Huts, near beaten ways,
No sooner stand attired
In thy fresh wreaths than they for praise
Peep forth, and are admired.

12.

Season of fancy and of hope
Permit not for one hour
A blossom from thy crown to drop,
Nor add to it a flower;
Keep, lovely May! as if by touch
Of self-restraining art,
This modest charm of not too much,
Part seen, imagined part!

[*Ode to May*]

57 *To May*

II

How delicate the leafy veil [*To May*, 81–85]
Through which yon House of God
Gleams mid the peace of this deep dale
By few but shepherds trod!
{*H*
And lowly {*huts, near beaten ways*
No sooner stand attired
In thy fresh wreaths than they for praise
Peep forth, and are admired.

I2.

Seasons of fancy and of hope [*To May*, 89–96]
Permit not for one hour
A blossom from thy crown to drop,
Nor add to it a flower;
Keep, lovely May, as if by touch
Of self-restraining art,
{*is*
Th{*e modest charm of not too much,*
Part seen, imagined part!

– – – – – – – – – –

Leaf 23 of DC MS. 135 was transferred from DC MS. 133 (leaf 2[r]) in a reorganization of these manuscripts in 1995. The page number "57"was added in ink by MW. The fair copy is in the hand of Dora W; the running head, "To May," was entered by MW.

15

"High bliss is only for a higher state,"
But surely, if severe affliction borne
With patience merit the reward of peace
Peace ye deserve; & may the good ~~which~~ loved
Beneath your lowly cottage roof
accorded ~~never~~, never be withdrawn,
Be for the ~~life's~~ worlds best promises renounced.
Most soothing was it for a welcome Friend
Fresh from the crowded City, to ~~behold~~ forget
Noise hurry & distraction in the sight
~~That~~ lonely union, privacy so deep
Of such calm employments, such entire content
So, when the rain is over, the storm laid
A pair of Herons ~~sometimes~~ oft times ~~may be seen~~ seen
have I seen
Upon a rocky islet, side by side
Drying their feathers in the sun, at ease;

19 5

[*Farewell Lines*]

1 *"High bliss is only for a higher state,"* [1–16]
2 *But surely, if severe affliction borne*
3 *With patience merit the reward of peace —*
ye *solid*
4 *Peace they deserve; & may the good ~~which here~~*
To you { b
{ *Beneath your lowly cottage roof*
5 *~~Has been accorded,~~ never be withdrawn,* far less
Accorded ~~never,~~
{ *Be* { *the*
6 { *Nor for* { *our ~~life's~~ best promises renounced.*
worlds
7 *Most soothing was it for a welcome Friend*
forget
8 *Fresh from the crowded City, to ~~behold~~*
Noise hurry & distraction in the sight
9 *~~That~~ lonely union, privacy so deep*
Of
10 *Such calm employments, such entire content!*
11 *So, when the rain is over, the storm laid*
oft times ~~have I may be~~
have I
12 *A pair of Herons ~~sometimes may be~~ seen,*
have I seen
13 *Upon a rocky islet, side by side*
14 *Drying their feathers in the sun, at ease;*

The fair copy here and its continuation on 19[v] are in MW's hand. The line numbers on the left match those of the reading text drawn from this manuscript; the bracketed ones on the right correspond to lines in the text of 1835. What appears to be a large cross through the text is ink offset from the facing page.

and when to tell and fathe

Farewell dear Friends ~~and Well & Heston~~

Beloved I greet again those happy Creatures

Roused by their own free choice ~~spirit~~ or Natures will

~~To Lake & Mountains I great behold~~

by their own or ~~Natures~~ will

Those ~~happy Creatures those by Natures power~~

~~Roused~~

~~Even~~ as your presence led my thoughts to them

They in their several ~~spirit~~ hearts, tho', of such power

unconscious, will not fail to pay the debt

And, mid a thousand images of peace

Honour & love on Earth or sky ~~Heaven or Earth~~

Will send a thankful spirit back to you perceived

Farewell dear Friends and when to Hall I

Beloved, ~~again~~ I greet again those happy Creat

Roused by their own or Natures will

[*Farewell Lines*]

and when to hill and Lake [23–27]
Farewell dear Friends, ~~farewell & when~~
Returned I greet again those happy Creatures
~~Natures~~
Paired by their own free choice or Nature's will
~~shall greet~~
15 ~~*In Lake & Mountain I again behold*~~
~~by their own or Natures~~ will
16 *Those ~~happy Creatures thus by Nature paired~~*
~~Paired~~
17 ~~*Even*~~ *as your presence led my thoughts to*
several *them*
18 *They in their ~~quiet~~ haunts, tho', of such power*
19 *Unconscious, will not fail to pay the debt,*
20 *And, mid a thousand Images of peace*
Earth or sky
21 *Concord & love in* ^ ~~*Heaven or Earth*~~
perceived,,
22 *Will send a thankful spirit back to you.*
30 {H
Farewell dear Friend! and when to {hill & Lake
again
Returned, ~~again~~ I greet those happy Creatures
Paird by their own or natures will

22 WW or MW entered the number "30" beneath the end of this line, perhaps, as elsewhere in this manuscript, to record the line count, though it is here inaccurate. WW wrote through it in revising.

537/3p.

Two glowworms, in such nearness that they share
As seemed their soft self-satisfying light
Each with the other, on the dewy ground
Where He that made them blesses their repose
The peace which others seek they find
The heaviest storms not longest last
Heaven grants even to the guilty mind
An amnesty for what is past
When will my sentence be reversed
I only pray to know the worst
And wish as if my heart would burst.

O weary struggle! silent years
Tell seemingly no doubtful tale
And yet they leave it short & fears
And hopes are strong, & will prevail
My calmest faith escapes not pain
And feeling that my hopes are vain
I think that he will come again

[*Farewell Lines*]

Two glowworms, in such nearness that they shared [18–27]
As seeme’d their soft self-satisfying light
Each with the other, on the dewy ground
Where He that made them blesses their repose.
When I ~~behold~~ once more to Lake and hill returned
Shall see
~~Returned,~~ those Creatures thus by Nature paired
Even as your ~~presence~~ happy presence to my mind ~~19~~ 24
~~Brought them~~ will they ~~dear friends~~ repay the debt
And send a thankful Spirit back to you. 24

Their union brought

will
~~Will~~ Brought them, even so shall they repay the
With mutually endearing promptitude *debt*
Will send a thankful spirit back to you.
With hope dear friends that we may meet
again

Fair copy and most of the revisionary lines are in MW’s hand. The lines written in the margins expand the revised conclusion of the poem. MW’s figure—“19” corrected to “24”—may be a line total for this version of the poem.

Below the solid line MW’s fair copy of *The Forsaken* (two stanzas) occupies the lower half of the page.

Where He that made them blesses their repose.

When wandering among lakes & hills I note,

Once more, those Creatures thus by nature paired

Even, as your happy presence to my mind

Their union brought, will they repay the debt

And send a thankful spirit back to you

With hope that we, dear Friends! shall meet again

And guarded in their tranquil state of life

[*Farewell Lines*]

H}
Where h }*e that made them blesses their repose* [21–28]
~~more~~
~~*When I once again to Lake & Hill returned*~~
wandering I note,
When ~~*I*~~ ^ *among* ~~*my*~~ *Lakes & Hills* ~~*shall see*~~
~~one~~
Once more, those Creatures thus by Nature paired
× | ~~And guarded in their course of tranqu~~il life; ~~[?]~~
Even, as your happy presence to my mind
Their union brought, will they repay the *debt*
~~*debt*~~
{d
And sen { *t a thankful Spirit back to you*
dear Friends! shall
With hope~~/~~ ~~*dear friends*~~ *that we,* ~~*may*~~ *meet again.*
~~*again* [?]~~.
× |
And guarded in their tranquil state of life
~~*An*~~

Fair copy is in MW's hand. The words "one" above l. 4 and "An" beneath the last draft line were deleted by smudging the wet ink.

St Katherine of Ledbury.

When human touch as monkish Books attest
Nor was applied nor could be, Ledbury bells
Broke forth in concert — flung adown the Dells
And upward high as Malvern's cloudy crest,
Sweet tones — and caught by one who listened
To rapture — Mabel listened by the side
Of her loved Mistress — soon the Music died
And Katharine said, Here I set up my rest.
Warned in a dream, the Wanderer long had sought
A Home that by such miracle of sound
Must be revealed — she heard it now, or felt
The deep deep joy of a confiding thought
And there a saintly Anchoress she dwelt
Till she exchanged for heaven that happy ground

[*St. Catherine of Ledbury*]

St. Kathine of Ledbury.

When human touch as monkis Books attest
Nor was applied nor could be, Lethbury bells
~~Angel Guest~~
~~Was it the rushing Wind—or from the crest~~
Broke forth in concert—flung adown the Dells
~~Of earth (for human touch as Story tells~~
{ ,
And upward { —high as Malvern's cloudy crest;
~~Was wanting that awaken'd Ledbury Bells~~
~~A supernatural influence to attest?~~
Sweet tones—and caught by one who listend blest
A ~~Wanderer caught the tones—and listen'd,—blest~~
To rapture—Mabel listened by the side
Of her loved Mistress—soon the Music died
{H set
And Katharine said, "{here I ~~take~~ up my rest."
Wanderer
Warned in a dream the ~~Lady~~ long had sought
that by such miracle of sound
A Home ~~which only by that wondrous~~ sound
~~Must~~ Must
~~Could~~ be revealed—she heard it now, or felt
The deep deep joy of a confiding thought
~~sacred~~ a sainted anchoress
And there a ~~holy Hermitess~~ she dwelt
Till she exchanged for heaven that happy ground.

The photograph is cropped to show only the relevant text on 118[r].

3 The closing parenthesis after "wanting" was omitted by mistake.

The photographs of 91v and 92r show the opening in DC MS. 89 where WW entered several drafts of "The unremitting voice of nightly streams," as well as a stanza of *On the Power of Sound* and some lines related to *The Triad.* Photographs of selected segments of these pages follow with facing transcriptions.

["The unremitting voice of nightly streams"]

The unsuspended Voce of mountain streams
Where Nature seems to work with wasted powers
The small birds [?haply] feel in their bowers
    that   may
And tones perchance soothe the drowsy flowers
         {as
Who   h{ave been know to mix with
That ~~penetrate the caves of human sleep~~
And regulate the ~~notion~~ motion of a dream
In concert with affection dear & deep
         strange
To what ~~sad~~ issues sometimes he full well
Had learned who scoopd into a Hermits cell
             {wed
This low bro{ad rock that he therein might dwell
     {r}
To {o} ever bound
To one deep   solemn thought-controuling sound
    {!   {—
Why{ let these words to simple listeners tell{.

The unsuspended Voice of mountain streams
Where Nature seems to work with wasted power
If neither soothing to the Worm that gleams
Through   nor small birds in thier bowers
No unto silent leaves & and drowsy flowers
Has yet been known to enter human sleep
                                    our   {s
And regulate the notions of a dream{
~~And~~ Once for how strange an issue he full well
Had learnd who scoopd into a cell
This}
[?A]} rock impending from the shaggy steep
   {at
Th{en He in hermits weeds therein might dwell
        For ever bound
To one deep solemn ~~[?hope]~~ thought-controuling sound
                                        Why? let these words

Draft A and the following draft B on 92r are probably the earliest versions of this poem.

10 WW began to write "To o[ne]" (cf. l. 11) and then revised to "For ever" but without converting the "T" to an "F" by crossing its stem.

The lines along the inner margin may belong to an early draft of *The Triad*, ll. 15–23 (see above, p. 105).

Advance like [?those] harmonius Sister Loves
Or in fix'd presence, mid this grove, unite,
Like those three Angel visitants that stood,
Furling their wings before their patriarch-host,
In beauty not unwilling to be lost
For sweet recovery, in each other's sight.

["The unremitting voice of nightly streams"]

✳ The unsuspended voice of mountain streams [1–5, 9–10]
Tires not the day nor wastes on night its powers
That voice ~~perch~~ (which ~~be~~ soothes perchance the worm that gleams
hush'd in
Through summer grass and small birds ~~in their~~ bowers
And lulls at dewy eve the shutting flowers)
Sl
I has been known to mingle with the sl}eep
Of human kind & regulate our dreams
Once for event how strange

The Hermits Cell
nr. Knaresboro

Calls on the breeze to modulate ~~ist~~ powers

The lines in the center of 91v (E), flagged with an asterisk, appear to be nearly immediate revisions of draft C at the top of this page, while the marginal entry D must have preceded E. For a record of the variants in the draft at the top of 91v see the notes to text C.

5 at dewy eve the shutting flowers] Cf. *Paradise Lost,* IX, 278, "at shut of evening flowers" (EdeS).

5–8 For an explanation of the notation to the right of these lines see the editor's headnote, pp. 99–100.

["The unremitting voice of nightly streams"]

[1–17]

In unremitting {ed
The unsuspend{ing Voice of mountain streams
That morning, noon & night
Where Nature works ~~with~~, we think, with wasted powers
If neither soothing to the worm that gleams
dusky
Throgh dewy grass nor small birds in their bowers
Nor unto ~~lea~~ silent leaves & drowsy flowers
{shall
Yet who what <u>is</u> {[?can] measure from what seems
to be or not to be
Or tax high heaven with prodigality
That voce is known to enter human sleep
it has been known to mix with dull sleep
And regulate the motions of ~~dreams~~ our dreams;
fu}
for event how strange a Knight we}ll
Once ~~to~~ how strange an issue ~~he full~~ well
H}
h}ad learnd who scoop'd into a cell
This rock impending from the shaggy steep
The ~~Knigh who [?carvd]~~
H} {might
That he ~~That h}e~~ in Hermits weeds ~~therein~~ {~~[?stayd!]~~ dwell
~~The Knight who~~
For ever bound
{one
To {[?a] deep solemn thought-controuling sound
Why, let these words to simple listeners tell.

That voice it has been known to mix with sleep
Once for event how strange—a knight full well
Had learnd who scooped into a cell
This}
The}rock impending oer the shaggy steep
That he in Hermits weeds might dwell
For ever bound

The draft of ll. 9–15 entered along the left margin of D appears to revise draft C beside it.

Introduction to the Somnambulist

The unremitting voice of mountain streams
That wastes so oft, we think, its tuneful powers
Is neither soothing to the worm that gleams
Thro' dewy grass nor small birds hushed in bowers
Nor unto silent leaves & drowsy flowers
Yet who, what is, shall measure by what seems
To be or not to be
Or tax high heaven with prodigality
That voice is known with healing power to creep
Into the human heart and mix with sleep
[illegible] regulate the motion of our dreams
For kindly issues as a Knight could tell
Was taught who stooped into a votive cell
Upon Rock impending from the shaggy steep
That clothed in Hermit's weeds he here might dwell
For ever bound [illegible]
In the lone lover's heart-controlling sound
Why? let these lines to courteous listeners tell.
That voice by night with healing power can creep
Into the human heart or mix with sleep

["The unremitting voice of nightly streams"]

Introduction to the
Somnambulist

1 *The unremitting voice of mountain streams* [1–17]

tuneful

2 *That wastes so oft, we think, its*^*powers*

3 *If neither soothing to the worm that gleams*

dewy

4 *Thro'* { *gra grass nor small birds hushed in*
bowers

5 *Nor unto silent leaves & drowsy flowers*

7 *(Yet who, what is, shall measure by what seems*

T

8 *t* } *o be or not to be*

9 stet *Or tax high heaven with prodigality—*

is with healing power to creep

10 *That voice*^*known to mix with human sleep*

voice { has

11 Th~~at vo~~ ~~ices po~~wer. Into the human heart and

(~~in vain~~ mix with sleep

12 ~~*And*~~ *regulate the motion of our dreams*

And ~~so thus~~ could tell

13 *For ki~~ndly~~ issues as a Knight ~~too well~~*

was taught c

14 ~~*Had learne*~~*d who scooped into a votive C* } *ell*

Yon

~~at~~ the

15 ~~*Th*~~ { ~~*e*~~ *rock impending from* { *a shaggy steep*

clothed He ~~here th~~ he there

16 *That ~~he~~ in Hermits weeds*^*might dwell*

~~[?Within] the [?Cumbrian] M~~

17 *For ever bound ~~to the lone river's heart-controlling~~*

spirit-soothing ~~*sound.*~~

16 *To the lone river's heart-controlling sound*

?

19 *Why* { *, let these lines to courteous Listeners tell*

stet That voice by night with healing power can creep
Into the human heart or ~~might~~ mix with sleep.

The base text is in MW's hand.

5–7 Beneath these lines is a penciled sum in WW's hand—"8 x 27 = 216"—probably a line count, but for what poem or poems is not certain. No poem in the notebook matches the count, but on 1[v] and 2[r] WW entered several sums that he identified as line counts for *PELY*.

8–10 The brace beside "stet" was probably drawn by WW, perhaps to reinforce the verbal direction to restore what had been deleted.

10–12 The brace may indicate replacement by the revision at the foot of the page.

As lower of yore the hermit in his cell 38
[illegible] out from rocky sleep
[illegible] [illegible] can tell

The Norman Boy

[illegible] all this day [illegible] [illegible] [illegible] [illegible]

High on a broad unfertile tract of forest-skirted Down,
Nor kept by Nature for herself, nor made by man his own,
From home & company remote, & every playful joy,
Served, tending a few sheep & goats, a ragged Norman Boy.

Him never saw I, nor the spot, but from an English Dame,
Stranger to me & yet my friend, a simple notice came,
With suit that I would speak in verse of that sequestered Child
Whom one bleak Winter's day she met upon that dreary Wild.

His flock along the woodland's edge with relics sprinkled o'er
Of last night's snow beneath a sky threatening the fall of more,
Where tufts of herbage ~~threatening~~ tempted each were busy at their feed,
And the poor Boy was busier still, with work of anxious heed.

There was he, where of branches rent, & withered & decayed,
For covert from the keen north wind, his hands a Hut had made,
A tiny tenement forsooth, & frail, as needs must be
A thing of such materials framed by a Builder such as he.

["The unremitting voice of nightly streams"]

As knew of yore the hermit in his cell
    Scooped out from rocky steep
As all with gratitude can tell
Who at this day ~~amon~~ mid ~~Cumbrian~~ mountains dwell

WW entered this version of ll. 13–16 above MW's fair copy of *The Norman Boy* (for the latter poem see pp. 344–345).

The unremitting voice of ~~mountain~~ nightly streams
That wastes so oft we think its ~~soothing~~ tongue powers
If neither soothing to the worm that gleams
~~Mind~~ Through dewy grass nor small birds hushed in bowers
Nor unto silent leaves and drowsy flowers
That voice of unrelenting [illegible]
(~~The~~ who what [illegible] measure [illegible] what seems
Tors To be, or not to be;
Or tang[illegible] high [illegible] with [illegible]
[illegible] a [illegible] which [illegible]
That voices ~~[illegible]~~ with ~~healing power~~ to creep
Into the [illegible] breast and ~~[illegible]~~ with sleep
To regulate the motion of our dreams,
For [illegible]; as through dewy [illegible]
Was felt [illegible] earliest
As at this day the [illegible] sentinels [illegible]
Where torrents [illegible] or [illegible] the ~~[illegible]~~ [illegible]
~~[illegible]~~
Of water-breaks with ~~[illegible]~~ [illegible] tells
grateful heart could tell

["The unremitting voice of nightly streams"]

nightly
1 The unremitting voice of ~~mountain~~ streams [1–17]
tuneful
2 That wastes so oft we think its ~~soothing~~ powers
3 If neither soothing to the worm that gleams
4 ~~Mid~~ Through dewy grass, nor small birds hushed
in bowers
5 Nor unto silent leaves and drowsy flowers
{ That voice of unpretending harmony
6 { (~~Yet~~ who what is shall measure by what seems
{ For,
7 To be, or not to be;
8 Or tax high heaven with prodigality?)
{which
Wants not a healing influence {t can quiet
influence can
9 — That voice is ~~known~~ with ~~healing power~~ to creep
breast and
{and
10 Into the human ~~heart~~ {or mix with sleep
11 To regulate the motion of our dreams,
d} is } through
12 For king }ly [?] } sues; as ~~in~~ every clime
in
13 Was felt near murmuring brooks ~~from~~ earliest
time
simplest who dwell
14 As at this day the rudest swains ~~could tell~~
Where torrents roar
{~~By~~ tinkling knell
15 {~~Near murmuring brooks~~ or hear the ~~tinkling~~
~~[?]~~ ~~knell~~
could
16 Of water-breaks with ~~gratitude might tell~~
tell
grateful heart could tell

6 The purpose of WW's brace is not clear.

His soul with but a glimpse of heavenly day.
Who that hath loved thee but would lay
His strong hand on the wind, if it were bent
To take thee in thy majesty away!
— Pass onward (even the glancing deer
Till we depart intrude not here)
That mossy slope o'er which the woodbine thro[ws]
A canopy, is smoothed for thy repose. +

There is a Universe of Spirit
Which all who truly live inherit
There is a
~~A wondrous~~ world together bound
By sights dependant upon sound
A world where passion is the tie
Though mans degraded ear & eye
Do ill perceive that mystery.
rapture
By ~~passion~~ moved the vernal throng
Of warblers in full concert strong
Strive, & not vainly strive, to rout

[*The Triad*]
[*On the Power of Sound*]

His soul with but a glimpse of heavenly day { ? , [*Triad*, 72–79]
Who that hath loved thee but would lay
His strong hand on the wind, if it were bent
To take thee in thy majesty away?
——Pass onward (even the glancing deer
Till we depart intrude not here)
That mossy slope o'er which the woodbine throws
A canopy, is smoothed for thy repose. ×

There is a universe of Spirit 20 [*Sound*, 1–7]
Which all who truly live inherit
There is a
~~*A wondrous*~~ *world together bound*
By sight dependant upon sound
A world where passion is the tie
Though mans degraded ear & eye
Do ill perceive that mystery.
rapture
By ~~*passion*~~ *moved the vernal throng* [*Triad*, 80–82]
Of warblers in full concert strong
Strive, & not vainly strive, to rout

In her fair copy of *The Triad* (here called *The Promise*) in DC MS. 108, SH first entered the seven lines on 3^r beginning "There is a universe of Spirit" as a continuation of the text of *The Triad* meant to flowed into the lines that follow; WW revised l. 11 and l. 16 and later expanded the seven lines to sixteen, which SH then copied on a new sheet that she pasted over the original lines (3^rP1^r; see the next page). At a later point, on 3^rP1^r, WW revised l. 80 again at the foot of the page and deleted the sixteen-line insertion. SH then added plus signs and the tag line (completed by WW) in the right margin to show the new configuration of *The Triad*. WW subsequently used a version of the deleted lines as the opening stanza to the first version of *On the Power of Sound* (line numbers in brackets on the right). The insertion itself corresponds to ll. 181–192 of the 1835 text of *On the Power of Sound*.

9 SH entered the figure "20" here and at twenty-line intervals throughout the poem.

His soul with but a glimpse of heavenly day,
Who that hath loved thee but would lay
His strong hand on the wind, if it were bent
To take thee in thy majesty away?
— Pass onward (even the glancing deer
Till we depart intrude not here)
That mossy slope o'er which the woodbine thro
A canopy, is smoothed for thy repose. +

Initiation in that mystery old;
The Heavens whole aspect makes our mind as still
As they themselves appear to be
Innumerable voices fill
With everlasting harmony.
The towering headlands crowned with mist,
Their feet among the billows, know
That Ocean is a mighty harmonist.
Thy pinions universal Air,
For ever sweeping to & fro,
Are delegates of harmony & bear
~~Accent~~ Strains that ~~they~~ support the seasons in their round —
Even winter loves a dirge like sound —
~~With rapturous notice the full throng~~
Glad moment is it when the
Of warblers in full concert strong
Strive, & not vainly strive to rout

This is a world of spirit
Whose motions by the breath are unfolded
And closed to it the visions of its needs

+ Glad moment is it when the throng

[*The Triad*]
[*On the Power of Sound*]

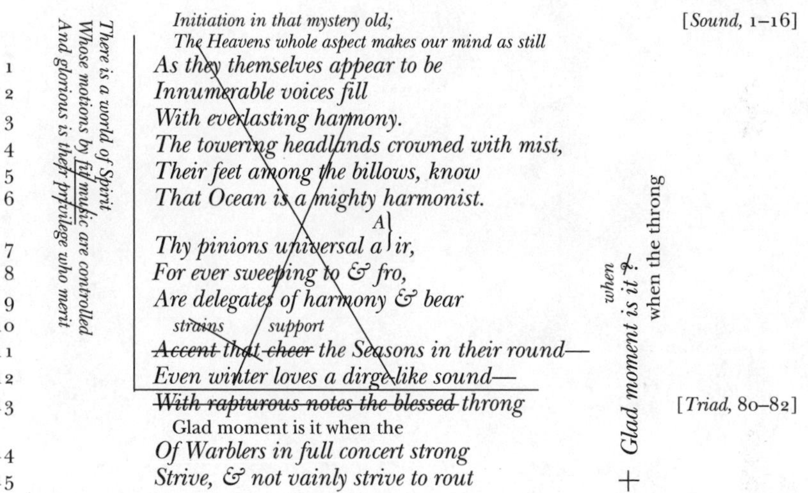

There is a world of Spirit
Whose motions by fit music are controlled
And glorious is their privilege who merit

Initiation in that mystery old; [*Sound*, 1–16]
The Heavens whole aspect makes our mind as still
As they themselves appear to be
Innumerable voices fill
With everlasting harmony.
The towering headlands crowned with mist,
Their feet among the billows, know
That Ocean is a mighty harmonist.
A
Thy pinions universal a ir,
For ever sweeping to & fro,
Are delegates of harmony & bear
strains support
~~*Accent*~~ *that* ~~*cheer*~~ *the Seasons in their round—*
Even winter loves a dirge-like sound—
~~*With rapturous notes the blessed*~~ *throng* [*Triad*, 80–82]
Glad moment is it when the
Of Warblers in full concert strong
Strive, & not vainly strive to rout

\+ *Glad moment is it* ~~?~~ *when*
when the throng

See the note to the transcription of 3[r], p. 681. SH inserted five lines (along the margin and above l. 1) after entering ll. 1–15 on the smaller sheet that was trimmed to fit over the original lines on the page. The line in the left margin and above l. 18 was drawn after the deletion to connect l. 8 on 3[r] to l. 13 (l. 80 of *The Triad*) on the paste-over in order to show how the text of *The Triad* continues from the previous page.

13 The line written up the right margin was probably entered as a tag, after WW's revision.

[*On the Power of Sound*]

Of mor[?] [170–176]
Those viewless [?]
O that [?] thou wan[?] taught to bear
Chains—such precious chains of sight
As laboured melodies thrugh ages wear.
O for a balance fit the truth to tell
Of the unsubstantial pondered well

All things are ruled by Spirit [177–180]
The universe is guided & controll'd
through
~~By~~ tuneful numbers, as they learn who merit
Initiation in that mystery old
more
~~O wo~~ndrous Labyrinth for Mind ~~more~~ [5–8]
Thy [?courses]
{O
To enter the {oracular cave
H}
h}ome to chaste whispers sighs are brought
{S}
{Of}trong fetter of the heart their slave

Along the inner margin of the remains of leaf 103[r] (now a stub; not photographed) WW entered text, two lines of which survive: "With her smooth ~~tones~~ tones and discords just" (l. 220) and "[? ?] skill divine a [?skill] [?]" (cf. l. 91 of the text of MS. 131 and l. 131 of text of 1835).

On its verso are pencil fragments at the foot—"e" and "d"—that are probably associated with the pencil draft on the facing leaf.

The tear in 104[r] defaced parts of the first three lines. The numbers to the right of the transcriptions are keyed to the text of 1835.

10 The deletion of "By" and the entry "through" are in pencil.

11–15 The final lines are all in pencil (see text of 1835).

Fragments of line endings in WW's hand on the verso of 104[v] are as follows: "d / ial / med / dread / of [*rev to* for] [?thoug] / d / — / [?nloose] / d beguile / re [?brought] / [?Slave] / [?]" (see ll. 2–14 of the transcription on 105[v]).

Thy functions are ethereal
As if within thee dwelt a glancing mind
Organ of vision — and a Spirit aerial
Informs the cell of hearing dark & blind,

Pervade [illegible]

Organ of sight and Shrouded like a Hard
Hollow the functions of [illegible]
To which the [illegible],
Intricate Labyrinth more dread for thought
To enter than oracular cave;
Strict passage through which sighs are brought,
And whispers, for the Heart, their slave;
And shrieks that revel in the abuse
Of shivering Flesh, and blanch the hair;
And artful concerts that the chains unloose
Of Phrenzy and entice a smile
Into the ambush of despair
[illegible]
[illegible]
[illegible]
[illegible]
[illegible]

The headlong streams and fountains
Serve thee Invisible Spirit with untired Powers;
Cheering the wakeful Tent on Syrian mountains
They lull perchance ten thousand thousand Flowers.
That Roar — the hungry Lion's here I am,
How fearful to the desert wide!
That bleat how tender of the Dam
Calling a Straggler to her side!
Shout, Cuckoo! Let the vernal Soul
Go with thee to the frozen Zone!
Toll, from thy highest perch, lone Bell-bird, toll!
At the still hour to Mercy dear,
Mercy listening from her throne,
To Nun's faint sob of holy fear
To Sailor's prayer breathed from a darkening sea
Or widow's cottage lullaby

3

[*On the Power of Sound*]

Thy functions are ethereal [1–18]
As if within thee dwelt a glancing Mind
~~On the power~~ of sound
Organ of Vision—and a Spirit aerial
~~functions are~~
Pervade Informs the cell of hearing dark & blind,
1 ~~Thy virtue is ethereal~~
~~Spiritual life and~~
2 ~~Organ of sight—and no inferior Mi~~nd
3 ~~Hallows the functions of that cell material~~
4 ~~To which the world of hearing is confined~~;
5 Intricate Labyrinth! more dread for Thought
6 To enter than oracular cave {! ;
Strict
7 ~~Blind~~ passage through which Sighs are brought,
8 And Whispers, {for to the Heart, their Slave {; !
9 And shrieks that revel in ~~the~~ abuse
10 Of shivering Flesh, and blanch the hair;
And concords
11 ~~Or~~ artful ~~measures~~ that the chains unloose
and
12 Of Phrenzy ~~or~~ entice a smile
13 Into the ambush of despair
the light in triumph of their speech beguile
14 Or ~~caught from far do of their speech beguile~~
And ~~Or~~ sway the dance where in smooth eddies move
15 ~~The Wood nymphs — or those eddies sway where move~~
~~Or sway those eddys of the dance where move~~
16 ~~The dancing Graces fann'd by hovering Love.~~—
~~The~~ The Graces fanned by hovering {L love.
2
headlong
~~headlong~~
17 The ^ streams and ~~headlong~~ fountains
18 Serve thee Invisible Spirit! with untir'd Powers;

The numbers to the left of the reading text are keyed to those of the text of MS. 131. The numbers in brackets on the right indicate the corresponding lines of the text of 1835.

The title appears in pencil underneath the draft lines at the top of the page.

15 "Wood" is deleted in pencil and ink; "smooth" is in pencil, written over in ink.

[*On the Power of Sound*]

[19–32]

They {at cheer / chearing / cheering} the wakeful {T / t}ent on Syrian mountains
~~And lull~~ They lull perchance ten thousand thousand Flowers.
<u>That</u> <u>{R / r}oar</u>—the hungry Lions here I am,
How fearful to the desart wi{de / [?ld]}!
That bleat—how tender of the Dam
Calling a Straggler to her side!
Shout, Cuckoo! let the ve{rn / neal} Soul
Go with thee to the frozen Zone{! / ;}
Toll from thy loftiest perch, lone Bell-bird, toll!
At the still hour to Mercy dear,
Mercy listening from her throne,
To {N / nun}'s faint sob of holy fear
To Sailor's pray'r breath'd from a darkening sea
Or widows cottage lullaby

---

19 The revision "chearing" is in pencil, written over in ink.

20 WW deleted "And" in pencil; he wrote "They" first in pencil and reinforced it in ink.

21 The underscore beneath "Roar" may be deleted.

25 WW first wrote "veneal" then made the second "e" into an "n" and let the original "n" stand for "r."

On stub 106[r] this fragment survives:

Betray not by the c
manly
Embattle every [?]
{To / I} tra

The first line is in pencil; all is in WW's hand. In the reading texts cf. l. 53 of the Text of MS. 131 and l. 85 of the Text of 1835.

On the verso of stub 106, at the foot of the page, are endings to two lines in WW's hand, "their round;" and "sound."

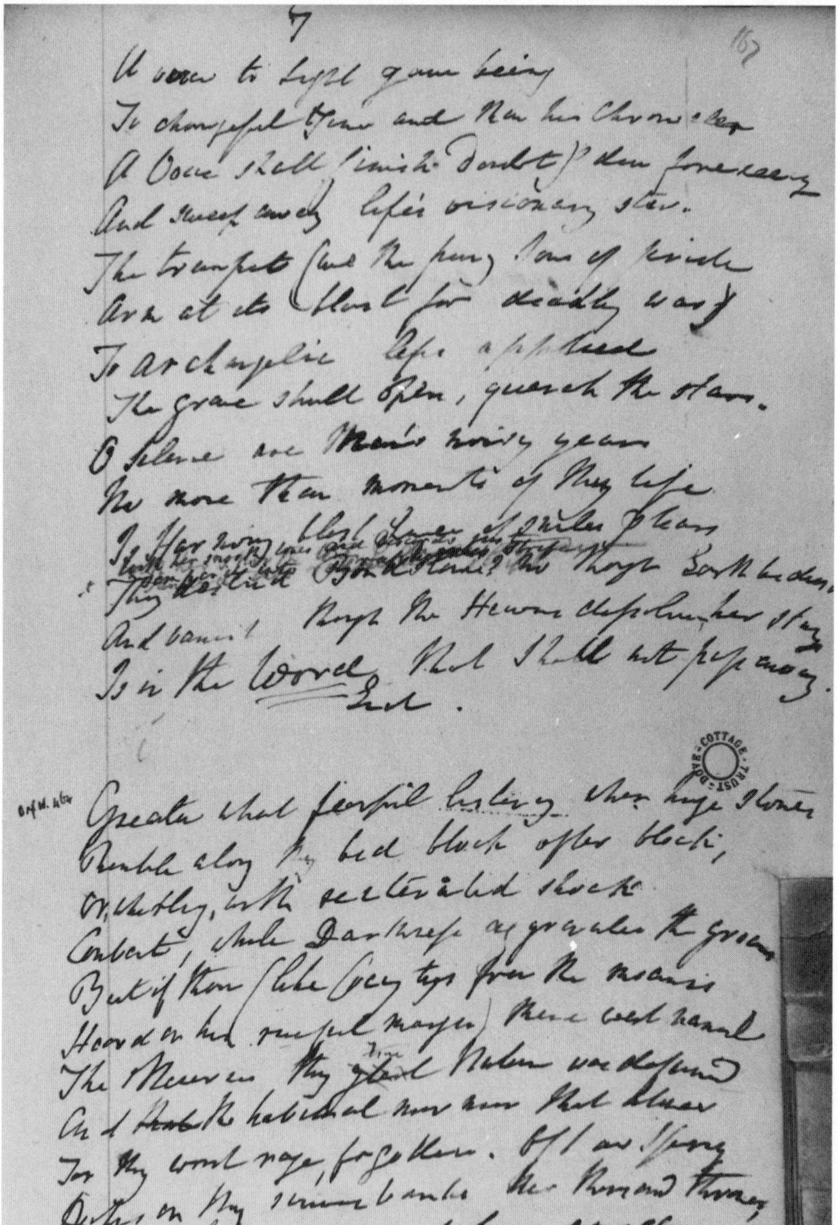
7
107
A voice to light gave being
To changeful Time and then his Chronicler
A Voice shall (finish doubt & dim foreseeing)
And sweep away life's visionary stir.
The trumpet (we the perjury sons of pride
Arm at its blast for deadly wars)
To archangelic lips applied
The grave shall open, quench the stars.
O Silence are Man's noisy years
No more than moments of thy life
Is Harmony [illegible]
Thy [illegible] though Earth be dust
And vanish though the Heavens dissolve her stay
Is in the Word, that shall not pass away.
God.

Greater than fearful history, when huge stones
Rumble along thy bed block after block,
Or whirling, with reiterated shock
Combat, while Darkness aggravates the groans
But if thou (like Cocytus from the moans
Heard on his rueful margin) thence wert named
The Mourner, thy true nature was defamed
And the habitual murmur that atones
For thy worst rage, forgotten. Oft as Spring
Decks on thy sinuous banks her thousand thrones,
Seats of glad instinct and loves carolling
The concert, for the happy, then may vie
With lustiest peal of [illegible] [illegible]
To a grieved heart the notes are benign.

[*On the Power of Sound*]

{7
6}

A voice to Light gave being [209–224]
To changeful Time and Man his Chronicler
A Voice shall finish doubt & dim foreseeing
And sweep away life's visionary stir.
The trumpet (we the puny Sons of pride
Arm at its blast for deadly war{) s}
To archangelic lips applied
The grave shall open, quench the stars.
O Silence are Man's noisy years
No more than moments of th{y is} life
Is Harmony blest Queen of smiles & tears
With her smooth tones and discords just
Temper'd into rapturous strife
Thy destin'd Bondslave? no though Earth be dust
And vanish though the Heavens dissolve{, —}her stay
Is in the Word that shall not pass away.
End.

92–93 WW's ink over pencil; "Temperd" is the reading in the second pencil line.
Below the end of *On the Power of Sound* is WW's copy of *To the River Greta, near Keswick,* published in Tour 1833.

3

Ye Voices, and ye Shadows &
And Images of voice — to hound and horn
~~From rocky Steep &~~ rock-besprinkled meadow
~~[illegible] from the woods the meadow~~
the sky's blue caves reborn
Flung back, & in ~~a crystal sky reborn~~
On with your pastime, till the Church-tower bells
A greeting give of measured glee;
And milder echoes from their cells
Repeat the bridal symphony!
Then, or far earlier, let us rove
Some pastoral hill, of mists be gone,

3

Ye Voices, and ye Shadows
And Images of voice to hound and horn
~~lake and woodland~~
From rocky Steep & ~~rock besprinkled~~ meadow
Flung back, & in the sky's blue caves reborn

On with your pastime, till the Church-tower be

[*On the Power of Sound*]

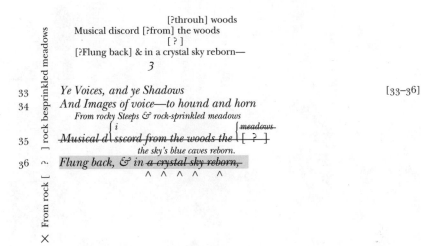

[?throuh] woods
Musical discord [?from] the woods
[?]
[?Flung back] & in a crystal sky reborn—

3

33 *Ye Voices, and ye Shadows* [33–36]
34 *And Images of voice—to hound and horn*
From rocky Steeps & rock-sprinkled meadows
i *~~meadows~~*
35 *~~Musical d{sscord from the woods the~~ {~~[?]~~*
the sky's blue caves reborn.
36 *Flung back, & in ~~a crystal sky reborn,~~*
^ ^ ^ ^ ^

× From rock [?] rock besprinkled meadows

[*On the Power of Sound*]

3
from winds & cliff & Lake, & rocky sh
v [?plain]
33 *Ye {Voices, and ye Shadows* [33–36]
34 *And Images of voice—to hound and horn*
lake and woods and
35 *From rocky Steep & ~~rock besprinkled~~ meadows*
36 *Flung, back, & in the sky's blue caves reborn*

WW's entries on 10[v] (see photograph at top) are in pencil; those entered above DW's text are erased. See the notes to ll. 35–36 of the text of 1835 for a related entry on the facing page of the manuscript. The line in pencil written along the inner margin was entered before the paste-over was applied and is not fully legible. WW's entry at the top edge of the paste-over is also in pencil.

[illegible]

A Rock there is whose homely front
The passing traveller slights
Yet there the glowworms hang their lamps
Like stars, at various heights
And one coy Primrose to that Rock
The vernal breeze invites.

What hideous warfare hath been wag'd
What kingdoms overthrown.
Since first I spied that Primrose tuft
And mark'd it for my own
A lasting link in Nature's chain
From highest Heaven let down

The flowers still faithful to the stem
Their fellowship renew
The stems are faithful to the root
That worketh out of view
And to the rock the root adheres
In every fibre true.

[*The Primrose of the Rock*]

S   reveald
[?]ymbdols of ~~a quie~~t hope—
                                     for we

A Rock there is whose homely front
The passing Traveller slights
Yet there the Glowworms hang their lamps
Like stars, at various heights
And one coy Primrose to that Rock
The vernal breeze invites.

What hideous warfare hath been wag'd
What kingdoms overthrown
Since first I spied that Primrose tuft
And mark'd it for my own
A lasting link in Nature's chain
From highest Heaven let down

The flowers still faithful to the stems
Their fellowship renew
The stems are faithful to the root
That worketh out of view
And to the rock the root adheres
In every fibre true.

The fair copy for version A is in MW's hand. WW's entry above l. 1 is in pencil.
8 The mark after "overthrown" is random or an offset from the facing page.

Close clings to earth the living rock
Tho' threatening still to fall
The earth is constant to her sphere
And God upholds them all
So blooms this lonely plant, nor dreads
Her annual funeral —
[illegible]
We also earth's most noble growth
The reasoning Sons of Men
From one oblivious winter call'd
Shall rise & breathe again
And for eternal summer change
Our threescore years & ten;
[illegible]
Deep as the roots of Being
That faith [illegible] the just & good
Before & when they die
Hath made each soul a separate heaven
A court for Deity
[illegible]

[*The Primrose of the Rock*]

just
All, symbols of sweet hope for we
[?to]
19 *Close clings to earth the living rock*
20 *Tho' threatening still to fall*
21 *The earth is constant to her sphere*
22 *And God upholds them all*
23 *So blooms this lonely plant, nor dreads*
{—
24 *Her annual funeral* {
All, symbols of sweet hope—
After thought {for
Symbols of hope— {[?] we have
too

25 *We also Earth's most noble growth*
26 [?] *The reasoning Sons of Men*
{*rom* *call'd*
27 *T* {*o one oblivious winter* ~~*doom'*~~*d*
28 *Shall rise & breathe again*
29 *And for eternal summer change*
30 *Our threescore years & ten*
{old
Bold speech yet more b{d than words
{From lips that cannot lie
{Those [? ? ? ?]
31 ~~*Else why was foresight givn with*~~ *love*
&
32 *Deep as the roots of Being?*~~,~~ *why*
{which, in
The {that in kind
33 *That faith* ~~*among*~~ *the just &* ~~*good*~~ [?kind]
34 *Before, & when they die,*
~~*Doth*~~ Hath made
35 ~~*That*~~ *make*~~*s*~~ *each Soul a separate heav'n*
36 *A court for Deity*
Bold speech yet not more bold than
words
From lips that cannot lie
Words whence the just derive a faith

The unplaced lines above l. 19 and between ll. 24, 25, are in pencil. WW entered further pencil drafting for this passage in pencil above MW's fair copy of *The Egyptian Maid; or The Romance of the Water Lily* on 4[r] of MS. 107 (see also the line in pencil above l. 1 on 3[r], pp. 694–695). Only the first of four lines is legible: "All symbols of sweet hope—for we."

24 The dash and the draft lines below the line are in pencil.

30/31 Some of the phrases in these drafted lines appear also in *Rural Illusions.* See pp. 720–721 (MS. 107, 57[r]).

31 The revision of this line, "From lips that cannot lie," was written over mainly illegible pencil.

33 "good" is deleted in pencil; "The" and "[?kind]" (twice) are in pencil.

[*The Primrose of the Rock*]

pendant earth
And let the pendant revolve [31–33]
~~And Let~~
Let flowers in field & grove
Renew their bloom

And let the earth revolve; and
Flowers
When quicken breeze move
Renew their bloom,

1 gods redeeming love 2 [35]

s
He came and lifted S} orrow, grief,
And mortal accident,
And slow decay, and wither'd age,
Above the first intent
Of some dread doom—and filld the
world

With types beneficent. [42]
We also shall revive, &c [43]

In versions B through G the numbers in brackets on the right indicate the corresponding lines in the text of 1835. The significance of the ink numerals "1" and "2" is not clear. The four lines in pencil along the left margin may be draftings for *Excursion,* I:

We sought the House
To shun the garden and as we approach'd
The silent door the afflicted [afflicted *rev from* wretched] One replied
If I had any [?hope]

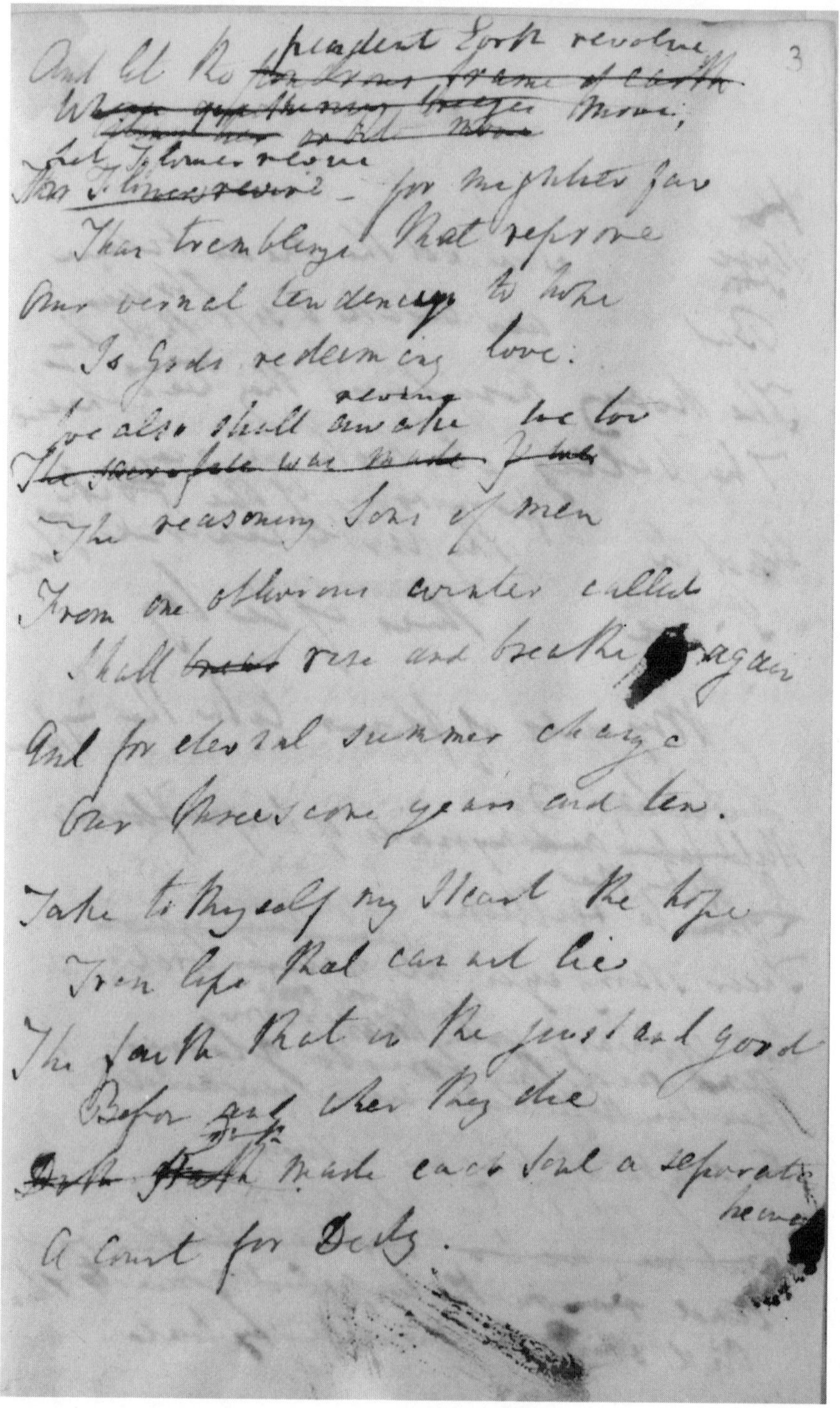

And let the pendent Earth revolve
Whom ... breezes move;
Let Flowers revive — for mightier far
Than tremblings that reprove
Our vernal tendency to hope
Is God's redeeming love:

We also shall awake alive we too
The reasoning Sons of men
From one oblivious winter called
Shall rise and breathe again
And for eternal summer change
Our threescore years and ten.

Take to thyself my Heart the hope
From life that cannot lie
The faith that in the just and good
Before and when they die
Hath made each soul a separate heaven
A Court for Deity.

[*The Primrose of the Rock*]

pendent Earth revolve
And let the ~~pondrous frame of earth~~ [31]
~~When quickening breezes move;~~
~~Along her orbit m~~ove—
{The Let Flower revive
{Her ~~Flowers revive—~~for mightier far
Than tremblings that reprove
{ y }
Our vernal tendenc{ ies} to hope
Is Gods redeeming love. [36]
revive
We also shall awake we too
~~The sacrifice was made & we~~ [43]
The reasoning Sons of men
From one oblivious winter called
Shall ~~breat~~ rise and breathe ~~[?]~~ again
And for eternal summer change
Our threescore years and ten. [48]

Take to thy self my Heart the hope
From life that can not lie
The faith that in the just and good [51]
Before and when they die
Doth
{~~Hath~~
~~Doth~~ {~~[?]~~ made each Soul a separate
heaven
A Court for Deity. [54]

The base text is in MW's hand.

[*The Primrose of the Rock*]

~~[?Her]~~
Here   {s {ed
~~This~~   clo{se{d the meditative [25]
strain
But air breathd soft that day
were
The hoary mountains they wer cheerd
The Valley it looked gay
primrose of the rock
And to   the little central Flower
And to the primrose
I gave this after Lay [30]

Myriads of flowers like the [?]
And thus   Thee
~~Like her~~ do
~~Mild fate! and~~ myriads of bright flowers [31]
Like thee
~~Expire~~ to reillume
in gardens [?doze]
~~when Spring returns~~
Their starry eyes at natures torch;
[?] [?]
to   Man'}
Sad contrast ~~with~~ man}s doom
And mid the forests gloom
~~When the departed were bewail'd~~
Or on the turf-clad grave to [?shew]
~~In~~ depth of pagan gloom
And [?raisd] the mouldering tomb
~~But we, we too earths noblest~~ growth
And ~~raise~~ on the turf clad grave to [?shew]
{ing
And [?raise]~~d~~ the moulder{t tomb

Pencil draft interlined with the first five lines is only partly legible; it appears to be unrelated to *The Primrose of the Rock.*

5 The alternate reading below the line is in pencil.
7 "And thus" is in pencil; "Like her" is deleted in pencil.
9 "in gardens [?doze]" is in pencil; the phrase below is deleted in pencil.
10 The illegible words are in pencil.
11 The revision is in pencil, overwritten in ink.
12 The revision is in pencil.
13 The revision is in pencil.

To 5

On humbleness of heart descends
That prescience from on high,
The faith that elevates the just
Before & when they die;
And makes each Soul a separate Heaven
A court for Deity &c—
Inter

B

That love which changed for wan disease
For sorrow that had bent
O'er hopeless dust, for withered age,
Their moral element;
And turned the thistles of a curse
To types beneficent.

Sin blighted though we are—we too.

[*The Primrose of the Rock*]

{ 5
{ 4

To
1 ~~On~~ humbleness of heart descends [49]
{ is prescience
2 Th{ at ~~wisdom on~~ from on high, [50]
{ at faith that
3 Th{ [?is] faith ~~which~~ elevates the
just
4 Before & when they die.
5 And makes each Soul a separate Heavn
6 A court for Deity ⁄— —
End

3
7 That love which changd for wan disease [55]
8 For sorrow that had bent
9 Oer hopeless dust, for withered age,
10 Their moral element;
11 And turn'd the Thistles of a
curse
12 To types beneficent [60]

13 Sin-blighted though we are—we too

39

2nd part

1

~~Thus~~ Here closed the meditative strain

But air breathed soft that day—

The hoary mountains ~~they were~~ heights were cheer

Tho sunny vale looked gay

And to the ~~little tentmate flower~~ Primrose of the rock

I gave this after lay.

2

I sang let myriads of bright flowers

Like thee in field and grove

Revive unenvied;—mightier far

Than tremblings that reprove

Our vernal tendencies to hope

Is God's redeeming love.

~~3~~ 4

Sin-blighted though we are, we too

The reasoning Sons of Men

From our oblivious winter call'd

Shall ~~breathe~~ rise and ~~rise~~ breathe again

And ~~for~~ in eternal summer ~~[illegible]~~ lose

Our threescore years and ten.

[*The Primrose of the Rock*]

2nd part

1

Here
{~~Here~~
{~~Thus~~ closed the meditative strain [25]
that
But air breathed soft day—
heights
The hoary mountains ~~they were~~ were chee[?rd]
The sunny Vale lookd gay
Primrose of the rock
And to the ~~little central Flower~~
{gave L}
I {[?] this after l} ay.

2

I sang let myriads of bright flowers [31]
T}
Like t} hee in field and grove
Revive unenvi'd;—mightier far
Than tremblings that reprove
Our vernal tendencies to hope [35]
Is Gods redeeming love.

{4
{3

Sin-blighted through we are, we too [43]
M}
The reasoning Sons of m} en
From one oblivious winter call'd
rise breathe
Shall ~~breathe~~ and ~~rise~~ again
in lose
And ~~for~~ eternal summer ~~change~~
Our threescore years and ten. [48]

1

~~Here~~ Thus closed the meditative strain
But air breathed soft that day
The hoary mountains they were cheer'd
The valley it look'd gay
And to the little central Flower
I gave this after lay;

2

I sang — let myriads of bright flowers
Like thee in field & grove
Revive unenvied — mightier far
Than tremblings that reprove
Our vernal tendencies to hope
Is God's redeem[ing] love;

3

From humbleness of heart proceeds
Divine Philosophy;
That faith which in the just & pure
Before & when they die
Doth make each soul a separate Heaven
A court for Deity

[illegible] blighted as we are

[*The Primrose of the Rock*]

Thus
1
Here closed the meditative strain [25]
But air breathed soft that day
The hoary mountains they were cheerd
The valley it look'd gay
And to the little central Flower
I gave this after lay.

2
I sang—let myriads of bright flowers [31]
Like thee in field & grove
Revive unenvied—mightier far
Than tremblings that reprove
Our vernal tendencies to hope
Is Gods redeeming love.

3
From humbleness of heart proceeds [49]
Divine Philosophy,
That faith which in the just & pure
Before & when they die
Both make each soul a separate
{for Heaven
A court {o Diety [54]

Sin-blighted as we are [43]

Draft for ll. 31–36, 43–48 appears on 59ʳ of MS. 107, with draft for *Rural Illusions* (see pp. 720–721).

41

And so ~~all~~ let myriads of bright flowers
Strewn on field and grove
Unmoved—a far mightier power
Than trembling, that reprove
Our vernal tendencies to hope
To God's redeeming love.

4

Sin-blighted as we are we too,
The reasoning Sons of Men
From one oblivious winter called
Shall ~~breathe~~ rise and breathe again
And for eternal summer change
Our threescore years and ten.

From humble tops of heart proceeds my soul the hope
Faith to taught Philosopher
Divine ~~that faith the voice~~
~~And on that faith the voice~~
That faith which in the first of ...
Before and when they die
Doth make each soul a separate heaven
A court for Deity.

[*The Primrose of the Rock*]

let
And so ~~do~~ myrads of bright Flowers [25]
Revive on field and grove
Unenvied—a far mightier power
Than tremblings that reprove
Our vernal tendencies to hope
G
Is g}od's redeeming love.

4
Sin-blighted as we are we too, [43]
The reasoning Sons of men
From one oblivious winter called
rise
Shall ~~breathe~~ and breathe again
And for eternal summer change
Our threescore years and ten. [48]

From humbleness of heart proceeds
Take to thyself the my Soul the hope, [49]
Divine Philosphy
~~And on that faith relie~~
That faith which in the just & pure
Before and when they die
Doth make each Soul a separate heaven
A court for Deity. [54]

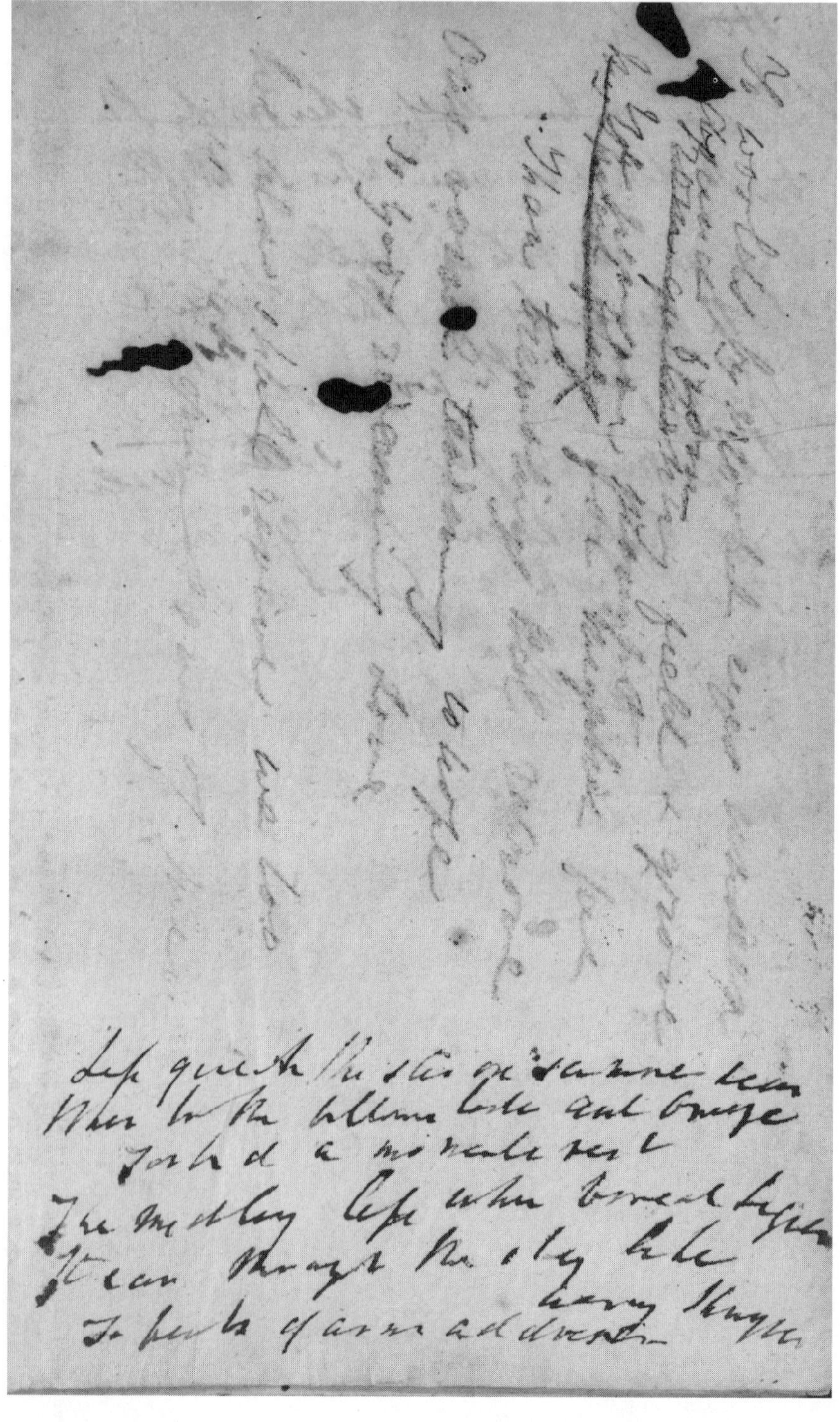

[*The Primrose of the Rock*]

To worlds by mortal eyes unseen [31]
    Ascend from
  ~~From quicke~~ning field & grove
  Ye pensive thought
~~My spirit [?fly]~~ ^ for mightier far
  Than tremblings that reprove
Our vernal tendency to hope
  Is Gods redeeming Love [36]

We also shall revive—we too [43]
    [? ?]
  The reasoning sons of men
    [? ?]

Entirely in pencil. The ink lines at the foot of the page are from *This Lawn, &c.*, ll. 7–12 (see pp. 184–185).

[*The Primrose of the Rock*]

1 Here paused the meditative [25]
mind
[~~? ? ? ? ?~~]
2 But for the primrose of the
rock
[? ? ? ? ?]
[? ? ? ? ?]

3 Here paused the meditative [25]
{mind
{[?]
4 But air breathed soft that
day
5 And life was sweet & down the vale
6 As I pursu d my way
The [?lingering] of my
7 Rememb~~rance of the primrose~~
~~[?Inspired this]~~
Linger around the primrose

The draft for *The Primrose of the Rock* is in pencil. The lines in ink, probably entered first, are draftings for the opening stanza of *The Somnambulist,* composed in 1833.

[*The Primrose of the Rock*]

1 Here paused the meditative [25]
2 The air breath fre that day
Th }
3 [?] } e image of the primrose tuft
4 When I had turnd awyay
5 Reviv d me ~~& my sound~~
~~broke forth~~
6 Into a [?heartfelt] Lay

7 Here paused the meditative
mind [25]
8 ~~When I had turned away~~
9 ~~The [?memory] of the primrose~~
tuft
heaving brine
~~They skimmed the sea the~~
10 And here might [?close the day]
11 [?] [?] but through [?the] [?]
12 As I pursued my way

Entirely in pencil. Between ll. 9 and 10 is a line drafted for *The Egyptian Maid* (l. 159) with the sheet turned 180 degrees. The fragment reads, "They skimmed the sea / the heaving brine."

Innocent Illusions

Sylph was it or a dazzling bird
Sprung from a foreign stock?
A brighter darted by, & lo!
Another of the flock
Through Sunshine flitting from the bough
To nestle in the rock

~~The pride~~
Soon was the pride of fancy tamed
Conjecture set at ease
The ~~dazzling~~ brilliant strangers hail'd with joy
Among the budding trees
Proved last years leaves pushed from the spray
~~pushed off~~ To frolic on the breeze.

Maternal Flora shew thy face
~~And let thy~~ hand be seen
Here sprinkling softly full-blown flowers
Bespangling earth with " .
That as they touch the green
Take root ~~when the breeze~~
as seems with life & grace
Well worthy of their queen.

[*Rural Illusions*]

Innocent Illusions

1 *Sylph was it or a dazzling bird*
2 *Sprung from a foreign stock?*
3 *A brighter darted by, & lo!*
4 *Another of the flock*
Through
5 ~~*In*~~ *sunshine flitting from the bough*
6 *To nestle in the rock*

~~*The pride*~~
7 *Soon was the pride of fancy tamed*
8 *Conjecture set at ease*
brilliant
9 *The* ~~*dazzling*~~ *Strangers hail'd with joy*
10 *Among the budding trees*
~~*only*~~ ~~*leaves pushed up*~~
11 ~~*More withered last years withered leaves*~~
Proved last years leaves push'd from the spray
{*T*
12 ~~*Pushed up*~~ {*to frolic on the breeze*

shew thy face
13 *Maternal Flora* ~~*I exclaimed*~~
And let that *be*
14 ~~*Why is thy*~~ *hand* ~~*un*~~*seen*
Here sprinkling softly
15 ~~*So swiftly scattering*~~ *full-blown flowers*
Bespangling earth with "
16 ~~*Of various hue & mien*~~
~~*as they fall, at thy command*~~ ~~*fall*~~
17 ~~*That fall thro' air & as they drop*~~
That as they touch the green
18 *Take root* ~~*upon the green*~~
as seems with life & grace
Well worthy of their queen.

The fair copy is in MW's hand. The line running vertically through the text is in pencil.
18 "em" of "seems" has been retraced in darker ink.

[*Rural Illusions*]

[*The Primrose of the Rock*]

sooth those starry specks
1 *Bold words yet ~~those small flowers in sooth~~*
2 *That not in vain aspired*
3 *To be confounded with live growths*
Most dainty
4 *~~By flora~~, most admired*
5 *Were only blossoms dropt from shrubs*
~~Shrubs of their mother~~ ~~tired~~
6 *~~That of their hues were tired~~*
Of their own offspring tired.
~~And let the~~ pendant earth revolve
And ~~[?ever]~~ also shall revive {— A / . a} scend!
7 ~~To worlds, by mortal eyes~~ unseen
8 Ascend from field and grove
9 Ye pensive Thoughts!— for mightier far
10 Tha{n / t} tremblings that reprove
11 Our vernal tendencies to hope
12 Is gods redeeming love.

13 We also shall revive—we too
14 The reasoning Sons of men
15 From one oblivious winter called
16 Shall breathe and rise again
17 And for eternal summer change
18 Our {fourscore / yea} years & ten.

Bold {w / y} ords ~~—yet why should Man repine~~

1–6 The fair copy of *Rural Illusions* is in MW's hand (version A).

7–18 A version of these draft lines appeared in *The Primrose of the Rock* (see version E, p. 172, ll. 31–36, 43–48). The underlining in l. 7 may be poorly drawn deletion lines.

91d

Remov'd, in kindness from their ~~crystal~~ glassy cell
To the fresh waters of a living well;
Diffused into an elfin pool opaque
Of which close boughs a glimmering mirror make
On whose smooth breast in dimpled light and shade
The flying wither'd leaf or blossom falls
Whirlwind, and big drops of the thunder
Heavy as hail — there swims the golden Prince
That from his bauble-prison used to cast
Gleams by the richest jewel unsurpast
And there — a dazzling Gnome sullen & pale
The silver Tenant of the crystal globe
Both now sequestered from the wildness
Of hue & altering shape that charmed all eyes
The World, sole-standing high on the bare hill
Arms knit — Back turned — the unapparent Face
Tinged (we may fancy) in this dream place
With light &c.

They pined perhaps & languished while they shone
But not to that mutton beauty then gone
And admiration lost by change of place
That brings to the inward creature no disgrace
Is there a brilliant fondling of the cage
Though a sun of pleasure on his costly stage
But gladly would escape. and if need were
Scatter his colours on the woods that bear
The emancipated Captive, though to be dear

[*To a Friend, Liberty,* and *Humanity*]

glassy
1 Removd, in kindness from the~~ir crustal~~ [7]
cell
2 To the fresh waters of a living well, [8]
Di }
3 In } ffus'd into an elfin pool opake [9]
4 Of which close boughs a glimmering mirror [10]
make
5 On whos smooth breast in dimples light and [11]
small
or
6 The Fly may settle, leaf ~~&~~ blossom fall, [12]
7 Hailstones, and big drops of the thunder shower, [13]
8 Heavy as hail—there swims the golden Power [14]
9 That from his bauble-prison used to cast [15]
10 Gleams by the richest jewel unsurpast; [16]
in
11 And there—a darkling Gnome ~~of~~ sullen robe [17]
12 The Silver Tenant of the crystal globe [18]
13 Both here sequesterd from the wilderness
14 Of hue & altering shape that charmd all eyes [20]

languishd
15 They pin'd perhaps & ~~sicken'd~~ while they [21]
shone
16 But if not so what matters beauty gone [22]
B
17 And admiration lost by change of place [23]
{B
{b
18 That brings to the inward Creature no disgrace [24]
brilliant {ing
19 Is there a gaudy fondl{ y of the cage [124]
20 Though sure of ~~his~~ plaudits on his costly [125]
stage
21 But gladly would escape; and if need were [128]
Scatter his colours on the winds that bear[?ed] [129]
emancipated
23 The ~~liberated~~ ^ Captive, through blithe air, [130]

Numbers in brackets on the right correspond to the reading text of *To a Friend.*

14/15 Between these lines are ll. 8–11 of *To B. R. Haydon, Esq. on seeing his Picture of Napoleon Buonaparte on the Island of St. Helena* (see p. 222), which were entered first on the page.

17 The purpose of the letter "B" above and beneath this line is unclear, though the first may be a false start for "But" of l. 16.

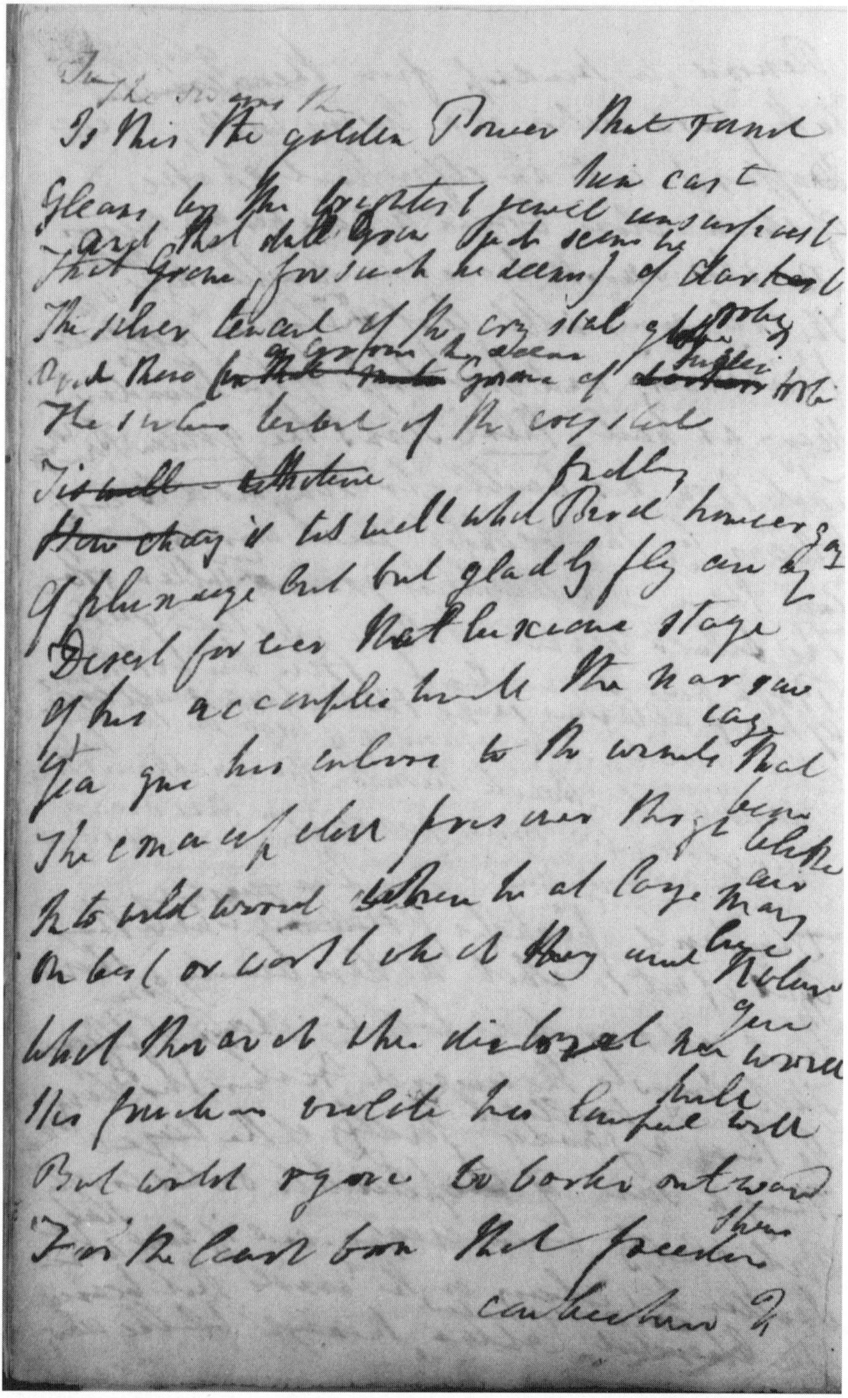

[*To a Friend, Liberty,* and *Humanity*]

Tis
The swims the
Is this the golden Power that round [14–15]
him cast
Gleams by the brightest jewel unsurpast [16]
And that dull Gnome such seems he
~~That Gn~~ome, for such he seems) of dar~~kest~~ [17]
{obe? robe
The silver tenant of the crystal gl{b [18]
a Gnome he seems sullen
And there (~~in that mute~~ Gnome of ~~darkest~~ robe [17]
The silver tenant of the crystal [18]
~~Tis well—whateve~~
fondling
~~How chang~~'d tis well what Bird however gay
Of plumage but but gladly fly away [128]
{that
Desert for ever {th[?] luscious stage [126]
Of his accomplishments the narrow [125]
\+ cage
Yea give his colours to the winds that [129]
bear
The emancipated prisoner thrgh blithe [130]
air
Into wild wood where he at large may [131]
live
On best or worst which they and Nature [132]
give
What Monarch when disloyal ner would [140]
kill
His function violate his lawful will [139]
But would rejoice to barter outward [141]
show
For the least boon that freedom [142]
can bestow?

11/12 The plus sign may mark the insertion of lines on 53[v] (version E; see the note to l. 18/19 of the transcription on p. 729 below).

[*To a Friend, Liberty,* and *Humanity*]

Or admiration lost by
~~Tis well~~
Tis well
1 What matters [?b]f ~~oppress~~ by change of place [23]
2 That brings to the inward Creature [24]
no disgrace
3 What fondled Bird of plume however gay
4 But from his cage would gladly flee away [128]
Scatter
5 ~~And~~ shed his colours on the winds that bear [129]
6 ~~Tis well they pined & sickend while~~ [21]
tis well what matter beauty gone
7 [22]
8 They pined perhaps & sikend while they [21]
shone
9 ~~For humblest change what matters beauty gone~~ [22]
10 And if not so what matters beauty [22]
11 And admiration lost by change of place [23]
12 That brings to the inward Creature no [24]
disgrace
13 What fondled Bird of plumage however
14 ~~Is~~ there a fondled Bird however gay [124]
wd
15 Of plumage but gladly flee away [128]
~~Yea Lay~~
16 — on his luxurious cage & [?of nest] [125]
17 Is there a bird of plumage howeer gay [124]
18 That
part his
19 Yea quit for ever ~~that~~ luxurious stage [125]
~~Of dainties~~
~~[?Cast]~~ the dainties of his cage
20 That would not gladly from his cage take [124]
flight
21 ~~And fling~~ dainties
~~Cast~~
Cast all da and [?] so he might
22 Scatter and if need were

[*To a Friend, Liberty,* and *Humanity*]

By this dull pool robbd of there [?gorgeous]
cell [109]
That like enchantment wrought a [?spe] [108]

1 There swims the golden Power that round
him cast [14–15]
Gleams richest
2 ~~Gleams~~ by the brightest jewel unsurpass'd [16]
darkling in
3 And there (a Gnome ~~he seems of~~ sullen robe) [17]
4 The silver Tenant of the crystal Globe. [18]
{y
5 The{ pined perhaps and sickend while they
shone [21]
6 And if not so—what matters beauty gone [22]
7 And admiration lost by change of place [23]
8 That brings to the inward Creature no disgrace [24]
9 Is there a gaudy Fondling of the cage [124]
{narrow
10 Though sure of plaudits on his {[?glamorous] stage [125]
11 But gladly would escape and if need were [128]
{on from the plumes
12 Scatter {his colours ~~to the winds~~ that bear [129]
13 The emancipated Prisoner/ through blithe
air, [130]
strange
13 Into ~~wild~~ woods where he at large may live [131]
14 On best or worst which they and Nature
give [132]
Sovern
15 What Monarch if disloyal thus would kill [138, 140]
16 His functions, violalate his lawful will [139]
B}
17 Th}at would rejoice to barter outward show [141]
18 For the least boon that Freedom may
air [?&c] can bestow? [142]

---

19 Into strange woods where he at large may
live [131]
20 On best or worst which they and nature give. [132]
21 The beetle loves his unpretending track [133]
22 The snail the house he carries on his back [134]
The farfetched worm disown
23 ~~The lowly~~ worm with pleasure would ~~disown~~ [135]
farfetchd disown
The moth or worm

---

16 A mark after "will" is probably random.

17 The "a" of "That" was made to serve as "u" in the revision to "But."

18/19 Above the solid line the word "air" and what is perhaps "&c" point back to l. 13 above; note also the plus sign near an earlier draft of the same passage in version C (p. 725 above). For a later entry of a line from *Liberty* see the following photograph and transcription.

[*Epitaph* ("By a blest Husband guided, Mary came")]

~~releasd to~~
1 If from ~~the the day the Inhabitant~~
[?]
some pure divine
2 Hat~~h [?soared] to some celestial scene~~
3 ~~The Soul~~
4 If from the day releasd to some [?pure]
shrine
some [?mounted] to some [?sphere]
5 The soul hath passd to some cherishd [?sphe]
reachd some sphere
6 That to her calm Intelligence
mortal care
7 The hollowness of earth & human care
8 [?Retreat]

fits
1 ~~And~~ in {[?mind] revive the wholesome pain
tender
2 Of ~~thoughts truant~~ thoughts, once combated
in vain
3 Of tears— & thoughts once combated in vain
5 Or in [?fitful] mood the wholesome pain
from
5 Of tears ~~&~~ thoughts once combated in
vain

[*Liberty. (Sequel to the Above.)*]

82 Lark of the dawn & philomel of night
~~[?Can] [?trans]~~

The entry for *Liberty* on 40[r] postdates the entry of *To a Friend* on 52[r]–53[v].

No door the Tenement requires
Nor needs the [illegible] roof
Yet [illegible] baffled is the fiercest sun [illegible]
[illegible] tempest-proof

But there may be where general share
Is good, a better and a best
Is good, we find a better & a best
And among fairest objects [illegible]

And what a Structure Sites they chuse!
The world-renouncing [illegible]
They [illegible] has no finer eye
For shadowy quietness

Some darkling flitting to and fro,
Betray that their Abodes are nigh
But watch the Owners in and out
Else vainly shall you pry

Some in an abbey ivied wall
Find for their nests a sheltering nook
Others are penthoused by a brae
That overhangs a brook
There to the brooding Bird her Mate
Thence chaunts by fits his slender song
And by the busy Streamlet both
Are sung to all day long.

[*A Wren's Nest*]

\+ No door the Tenament requires [5–8]
workman
Nor need the ~~Builder~~ raise a roof
baffled is the fiercest Sun
Yet ~~not [?one] Structure fears the Sun~~
The Dwellers
~~And each is~~ tempest-proof

But there may be where general choice [31–32]
Is good, a better and a best
Is good, we find a better & a best
And among fairest objects some are
fairer than the rest

\+ And what attractive Sites they chuse! [13–24]
The
~~No~~ world-renouncing Votaress
The no
~~Nor~~ Hermit has ~~a~~ finer eye
For shadowy quietness
, darkling,
Some ~~by their~~ flitting to and fro,
Betray that their Abodes are nigh
But watch the owners in and out
Else
~~Else~~ vainly shall you pry

Some in an Abbeys ivied wall
nook
Find for their nests a sheltering ~~roof~~
~~cave~~
Others
~~And some~~ are penthous'd by a brae
That overhangs a brook
To
{~~Then~~
{~~To~~ chear the Brooding Bird her Mate
{ts
There chaunts by fi{ [?] his slender song
And by the busy Streamlet both
Are sung to all day long.

The stanzas on the inside front cover were entered as additions to or revisions of the text in MW's hand that begins on 1r. WW's pencil jottings (not transcribed), entered with the notebook at a quarter-turn, appear to be associated with several sonnets published in Tour 1833.

1, 8 The asterisks mark each stanza for insertion in the text on the facing page, where there are corresponding marks (see the photograph on p. 734).

7 Two lines are written out as one.

Of all the mansions framed built by Birds
In grove or woodland with nice care
Is none that with the little Wren's
In snugness may compare

+ So warm so beautiful withal
Thro' perfect fitness to its aim
That to the Kind by special grace
Their instinct surely came
But where judgments all are good
There is a better and a best
Among the good is found a best
And among fairest objects some
Are fairer than the rest
This one of those small Builders shewn
And this to me was proved by one
Of those small Builders where from out
In a green covert
The forehead of a pollard Oak
The leafy antlers sprout

For she who planned the mossy lodge
Mistrusting her evasive skill
Had to a Primrose looked for aid
Her wishes to fulfill

[*A Wren's Nest*]

Among the Mansions
~~Of all the Dwellings~~
~~Of all the Mansions~~ ~~framed~~
~~Among the Mansions~~ built by Birds [1–12]
~~Among the~~ field or forest with
In ~~grove or woodland with~~ nice care
~~to~~
Is none that ~~with~~ the little wren's
In snugness may compare

\+ *So warm so beautiful withal*
Thro' perfect fitness to its aim
That to the Kind by special grace
The{ir instinct surely came

×
still ~~the~~
But ~~still~~ where ~~gen~~eral choice is good
all have been
But ~~oft~~ where judgments ~~all are~~ good [29–40]
^
There is a better and a best { *a*
~~Among the good~~ is found { *the best*
~~Amid The~~ And among
~~And among~~ fairest objects some
Are fairer than the rest;

As} showed
Th} is one of those small Builder ~~provd~~
~~And this to me was proved by one~~
~~small~~
~~Of those Builders~~ where from out
In a green covert
{ *lared*
The forehead of a pol { *lard oak*
The leafy antlers sprout

For
~~But~~ She who planned the mossy lodge
Mistrusting her evasive skill
Had to a primrose looked for aid
Her wishes to fulfill

The fair copy is in MW's hand.
2 MW's "with" is masked by offset ink from the blot on the inside front cover.
3 The deletion of "to" (by smudging) restores the deleted "with."

High on the trunks projecting brow,
And fixed three fingers breadth above
The yellowing buds, peeped forth the nest
The prettiest of the grove
To some who
Or little things without disdain
I pointed out the nest, but once
love
looked for it in vain
And so I pointed out the nest
To some whose ...
Tis gone ...
Who heeds not beauty, love or song
Tis gone—so seem'd it—& I grieved
Indignant at the wrong

Just
Three days after, passing by
In clearer light, the moss-built cell
I saw—espied its shaded mouth
And felt that all was well

The largest of her ... leaves
Bless ... the ...
By which a flower deceives.
Hid her awhile from friends that
...

[*A Wren's Nest*]

1 *High on the trunk's projecting brow,* [41–62]
2 *And fixed three fingers breadth above*
3 *The yellowing buds, peeped forth the nest*
4 *The prettiest of the grove*

whose genial m
whose ~~ample minds make way~~
To some ~~who have a/ mind that turns~~
{ r
5 ~~*But|as I/once approached the t hee*~~
For}
In } little things without disdain
6 ~~*My greeting was a shock of pain*~~
I pointed out the nest but once
that
7 ~~*When for my treasure I looked up*~~
We But once up
8 ~~*But*~~ ^*looked*^ *for it in vain*
And so I pointed out the nest
To some whose minds without disdain

spoilers prey
9 *Tis gone said I some* ~~*ruthless hand*~~
Can turn to little Things but once
10 *Who heeds not beauty, love, or song*
we
11 *Tis gone—so seem'd it—& ~~I~~ grieved*
12 *Indignant at the wrong*

Just
13 ~~*But*~~ *three days after, passing by*
{- {*cell*
14 *In clearer light, the moss*{ *built* {[?]
15 *I saw—espied its shaded mouth*
16 *And felt that all was well*

How shaded? by the primrose spreading
~~spreading~~
17 ~~*The primrose for a veil had spread*~~
~~Had spread~~
her
18 *The largest of ~~its upright~~ leaves*
~~for the Creatures~~ for the ~~Creatures~~ sake the
Inmates bold
19 *Bless ~~happy Bird~~ the ~~simple~~ course*
20 *By which a flower deceives.*
F}
21 Hid her awhile from f }riends ~~who~~ that
marred
22 Her quiet with no ill intents

The fair copy is in MW's hand.

5 The "n" of "an" in the revisionary line was deleted by erasure.

and saves her [illegible] from evil eyes have taken
and hands or mischief [illegible]
~~And when thy young ones shall take flight~~
Rest happy Bird! & when thy Young
~~[illegible] free & flowery~~ to roam
Are fledg'd & thou art free to roam
~~And~~ withered is the guardian flower,
When
And empty thy late home,

Think how ye prospered thou & thine,
Within the unviolated grove
Housed near the growing primrose tuft
In foresight or in love.

~~I pointed out thy~~
To some whose thoughts without disdain
They the darlings of little things, [illegible] from friends that shared
~~Not less~~ from ~~[illegible]~~ who [illegible]
marred
Thy quiet with no ill intent
And saves thee [illegible] from [illegible]
And hands or mischief [illegible]

Rest happy Bird & when thy Young
Are fledged and thou art free to roam
To some whose genial minds can turn
To little things without disdain
I pointed out the nest, but once
Looked up for it in vain

[*A Wren's Nest*]

And saves her still from evil eyes [63–72]
And hands on mischief bent
~~*And when thy young ones shall take*~~ *flight*
Rest happy bird & when thy Young
when
~~*And thou art free & pleased*~~ *to roam*
{thou {t
Are fled, [?yo] & {thee ar{e free to roam
~~*And*~~ *withered is the guardian flower,*
When
And empty thy late home,

Think how ye prospered, thou & thine,
Within the unviolated grove
growing
Housed near the ~~*spreading*~~ *primrose tuft*
{*or*
In foresight {*& in love.*
I pointed out the [46–47]
M}
To some whose m} inds without disdain
Can turn to little things, but once
Hid the awhile from friends that marred
us
~~Hid thee~~ from ~~earth~~ who haply [61–66]
marred
Thy quiet with no ill intent
And saves thee still from evil
[?] [? eyes]
And hands on mischief bent
Then when the Young have [?taken]
flight
Rest happy Bird & when thy Young
Are fledged and thou art free to roam
To some whose genial Minds can turn [46–48]
To little Things without disdain
I pointed out the nest, but once
Looked up for it in vain

The fair copy in ll. 1–8 is in MW's hand.

12–16 The base text is in pencil, apparently entered in a gap left between the ink drafts; "earth" in l. 12 is deleted in pencil.

17–22 These ink lines were overlapped by the pencil lines; l. 17 appears above l. 16 in the photograph but is transposed here for the sake of clarity.

104

Twilight by the
side of
Grasmere Lake

A twofold ~~slumber the huge~~ Steep the mountain hills partake
High in the air & deep in the ~~still~~ within lake
Look for the Stars—you'll say that there are none
Look up a second time & one by one
You ~~see~~ mark them twinkling out with silver light
And wonder how they could elude y^r. sight
The birds of late so noisy in their bowers
Are ~~hushed~~ all for now & silent as the dim seen flowers
Wheels & the tread of hoofs are heard no more
One boat there was but it will touch the shore
With the next dipping of its slackened oar
~~A~~ Faint sound that for the gayest of the gay
Might give to serious thought a moments sway
~~To the~~ a last token of man's toilsome day.
The Shepherd bent on rising with the sun
Has closed his door the Bat her flight
that flutters begun
Through ~~the dim~~ air ~~of evening~~ slow to lose
Its grateful warmth though moist with falling dews
The Church-clock strikes nor this does
The ~~quiet~~ Season's calm soothes its own tone
influence
Numbers declared to teach [illegible]
other [illegible]

[*Evening Voluntaries*]

Twilight by the
side of
Grasmere Lake

sleep the mountain tops
A twofold ~~slumber the huge hills~~ partake
within
High in the air & deep in the ~~still~~ lake
Look for the Stars—you'll say that there [*I*, 3–9]
are none
Look up a second time & one by one
mark
You ~~see~~ them twinkling out with silver light
~~the~~
And wonder how they could elude yr. sight
The birds { *of* / *so late so noisy in their bowers*
~~all as~~ now
Are ~~hushed~~ & silent as the dim seen flowers
Wheels & the tread of hoofs are heard no more [*I*, 25–30]
One boat there was but it will touch the shore
With the next dipping of its slackened oar
Faint
~~A~~ sound that for the gayest of the gay
Might give to serious thought a moments
a *sway*
As ~~the~~ ^ *last token of man's toilsome day.*
The Shepherd bent on rising with the sun
The { Shepherd / Peasant bent on rising with the sun [*I*, 16–17]
Has closed his door the Bat her flight
Has closed his door the Bat her flight
begun
begun
slowly
that changed
Through ~~the dim~~ air ~~at eve~~ning slow to lose [*I*, 1–2]
Its grateful warmth though moist with
falling dews
The Church-clock strikes nor ~~its~~ does
its iron tone [*I*, 10–12]
seasons
The night-calm's soothing influence disown
Nine beats disinctly to each
other bound

1–14 MW's hand. WW's deletions and revisions are in pencil.
15–16 Base lines, with on-line revision, are in pencil.

103

The Chantry of St Bees

Cruel of heart were they bloody of hand
Who in these wilds then struggled for command
The strong were merciless without hope the weak
Till this bright Stranger came, fair as ~~a streak~~ day break
~~Of dawn or cresset~~ a standing that gives out its length
Or as a cresset
Of beamy lustre from a tower of strength
~~Guiding~~ Guide for the Mariner thro' troubled seas
And cheering oft his peaceful reveries
Like the fixed light ~~which~~ that crowns the
headland of St Bees

To aid the votaress

In drowsy sequence how unlike the sound
That in rough winter oft inflicted a fear
On fireside listeners doubling
what they hear

[*Evening Voluntaries*]

1 In drowsy sequence how unlike the
sound [*I*, 13–15]
2 That in rough winter oft inflicts a fear
3 On fireside Listeners doubting
what they hear

Above the lines transcribed is a stanza from *Stanzas suggested in a Steamboat off Saint Bees' Heads, on the Coast of Cumberland* (published in 1835 and later incorporated into Tour 1833).

The Shepherd bent on rising with the Sun
Has closed his door — the Bat his flight begun
Between the pollard trees that overshade
The dusty high-way with a low arcade
[illegible] [illegible]
Over the vale, and oer the mountain heads
That seem a twofold stature to partake
Up in the air & deep within the Lake
~~Look forth the [illegible]~~
The Church clock strikes now [illegible]
iron tone
The tones of seasons influence [illegible]
[illegible] [illegible] distinctly to each other bear
In drawy sequence [illegible] [illegible] the
sound
That in some [illegible] winter oft inspired a fear
On fireside listeners doubly what they hear
Look

the Owl her chaunt began
lured forth where trees
The Bat ~~where pollard~~ Oaks the lane oershade
Flits & reflits along the close arcade,
While the Rooks homeward bend — compact yet
spread
Like a large cloud they cross the mountain head,
That seems a twofold
The Shepherd bent on rising with the sun
Has closed his door
And the [illegible] by [illegible] began

[*Evening Voluntaries*]

{S
1 The {shepherd bent on rising with the Sun [*I*, 16–17]
2 Has closed his door—the Bat his flight begun
{ose
3 Between th{e pollard trees that overshade [*I*, 20–21]
4 The dusty high-way with a low arcade
~~Thridding~~
~~Of the~~
~~[?Flitting]~~
5 Over the vale, and oer the mountain heads
6 That seem a twofold slumber to partake
7 High in the air & deep within the Lake
8 ~~Look for the stars~~
9 The church clock strikes nor doth ~~its i~~ron [*I*, 10–15]
iron tone
10 The time's & season's influence disown
11 Nine beats distinctly to each other bound
12 In drowsy sequence how unlike the
sound
13 That in rough winter oft inflicts a fear
14 On fireside Listeners doubting what they
hear
15 Look [*I*, 3]

16 the Owl her chaunt begun
lured forth where Trees
17 The Bat ~~where pollard~~ Oaks the Lane oershade
18 Flits & reflits along the close arcade,
19 While the Rooks homeward wend;—compact yet
spread
20 Like a large cloud they cross the mountains head,
21 That seems a twofold
The Shepherd bent on rising with the sun
Has closed his door
And the moth hunting Nightjars chase
begun

Calm ~~as~~ is the fragrant air & loth to lose
Day's grateful warmth, tho' moist with falling ~~dews~~;
~~The Shepherd bent on rising with the Sun~~
The Birds of late so noisy in their bowers
~~Are warbling now with~~
Warbled awhile with faint & fainter powers,
And now are silent as the dim-seen flowers;
Nor does the striking village Church-clock's iron tone
The time's & season's influence disown;
Nine beats distinctly to each other bound
In drowsy sequence; how unlike the sound
That in rough winter oft inflicts a fear
On fireside listeners doubting what they hear!
The Shepherd bent on rising with the Sun
Has closed his door the Owl her ~~[illegible]~~ changed bower
~~The Bat when~~ pollard Oaks the lane o'ershade
~~The flitting Bat here finds a close~~ arcade
Flits & reflits along the close arcade
Of pollard oaks with ~~tempted~~ by ~~that~~ shade
While the Rooks homeward wend; compact yet
Gloomier ~~than stealthy evening~~ ~~yet has spread~~
Like a large cloud they cross
~~Over the Vale, or on~~ the Mountain's head

[*Evening Voluntaries*]

is
Calm ~~as~~ the fragrant air & loth to lose [*I*, 1–21]
Day's grateful warmth, tho' moist with { *dews*
falling { [?]
~~*The Shepherd bent on rising with the Sun*~~
T
t } *he Birds of late so noisy in their bowers*
~~*Are warbling now with*~~
Warbled awhile with faint & fainter powers,
And now are silent as the dim-seen flowers;
~~*striking*~~ village
Nor does the ^ *Church-clock's iron tone*
The time's & season's influence disown;
Nine beats distinctly to each other bound
In drowsy sequence; how unlike the sound
That in rough winter oft inflicts a fear
On fire-side listeners doubting what they hear!
The Shepherd bent on rising with the Sun
chaunt
Has closed his door, the owl her ~~flight~~ begun
✳ Bat where pollard oaks the lane oer shade
The ~~flitting Bat here~~ thrids a close arcade
Flits & reflits along the close arcade
its
Of pollard oaks forth tempted by ~~that~~ shade
{ While
{ Th the Rooks homeward wend; compact yet
~~*Gloomier than stealthy evening yet ha*~~*s spread*
Like a large cloud they ~~[?]~~ cross
~~*Over the vale; or on t*~~*he Mountain's head*

Fair copy is in MW's hand.

7 The caret and the deletion above the line are in pencil.

15 The asterisk may mark WW's acceptance of the revision.

That seems a twofold slumber to partake,
High in the air & deep within the Lake:
Wheels & the tread of hoofs are heard no more;
One Boat there was, but it will touch the shore
With the next dipping of its slackened oar,
Sound that for the gayest of the gay ~~tripping elves & [illegible]~~ gay
Might give to serious thought a moment's sway
As a last token of Man's toilsome day.

The Ploughman ~~Shepherd~~ bent on rising with the [illegible]
Hath closed his door, ~~the long~~ [illegible]
And with a thankful heart to bed doth creep,
And join his little Children in their sleep
The Bat lured forth [illegible]
Lists to the ~~night~~ hawk chasing the grey moth
~~The grey moth with the barring note~~
With barring note which ~~that~~ industry & sloth
Might both be pleased with for it suits them both

Ls. last mark of reference
to the Notes in Sonnets

[*Evening Voluntaries*]

That seems a twofold slumber to partake,
High in the air & deep within the Lake:
Wheels & the tread of hoofs are heard no more, [*I*, 25–30]
One Boat there was, but it will touch the
shore
With the next dipping of its slackened oar,
A faint the gayest of the gay
Sound that for ~~tripping elves & goblins~~ gay
Might give to serious thought a moment's
sway
As a last token of Man's toilsome day.

Peas
The ~~Shep~~herd bent on rising with the sun [*I*, 16–24]
~~[?Had cl]~~ was
before the day is
~~Has~~ [?s] closed his door, ~~the long-days labors~~
And now don,
And with a thankful heart to bed doth creep
And joins his little Children in their
sleep
The Bat lured Dor while
List tis the ~~night~~ Hawk chasing the grey moth
~~The grey moth with burring note~~
which
With burring note ~~that~~ industry & sloth
Might both be pleased with for it suits them
both

1–8, 13–16 MW's hand.

2/3 The carets may signal insertion of the revisionary lines on the facing page, where there is a matching caret.

9–13 Interlined entries are in pencil, except for "before . . . don," and "Dor."

WW's note at foot of page bears on the sonnet sequence eventually published in 1835 as Tour 1833.

^ Look for the Stars, you'll say that there
are none;
Look up a second time, &, one by one,
You mark them twinkling out with silvery
light
And wonder how they could elude the sight.
seems
Wheels No cloud ~~at~~ softer than yon ~~[illegible]~~ blue hill
The gleaming waters how profoundly still
O Nightingale whoever heard thy song
Might here be moved till fancy grows so strong
That listening sense is pardonably cheated
In Vales that by thy voice were never greeted
Surely if Nature from most favored lands
Held not some favor back with jealous hands
This hour of gathering shadows here w.d be
As a fresh morning for new harmony
Heart-thrilling Bird 'mid Eastern roses bred
empire
For ~~[illegible]~~ deeply felt as widely spread
To King to Peasant & rough Sailor dear
And to the Soldier's wearied trumpet ear
Whether thou givest or withhold'st thy lay
~~Be still~~ Be ours to walk content with Nature's way
~~[illegible]~~
~~While~~ at all times & seasons ~~when~~ we miss
Wise if the gravest thought of what
~~Temper~~ in the fullness of a loving bliss
~~Be with thee~~ kindly office satisfied
~~And~~ unrepining sadness is allied
While
In thankful bosoms ~~with~~ judicious pride
To [illegible]

[*Evening Voluntaries*]

1 ∧ *Look for the Stars, you'll say that there* [*I*, 3–6]
3 *are none;*
2 *Look up a second time, &, one by one,*
3 *You mark them twinkling out with silvery*
light
4 *And wonder how they could elude the sight.*
seems { pale
5 *Wheels* *No cloud ~~is~~ softer than yon* [?*pure*] *blue hill* [*V*, 1–2]
The gleaming waters how profoundly still

6 *O Nightingale whoever heard thy song* [*III*, 13–41]
7 *Might here be moved till fancy grows so strong*
8 *That listening sense is pardonably cheated*
9 *In Vales that by thy voice were never greeted*
10 *Surely if Nature from most favored lands*
11 *Held not some favor back with jealous hands*
12 *This hour of gathering shadows here w.^d be*
13 *As a fresh morning for new harmony*
14 *Heart-thrilling Bird 'mid Eastern roses bred*
empire
15 *For ~~sway as~~ deeply felt as widely spread*
16 *To King to Peasant & rough Sailor dear*
17 *And to the Soldier's wearied/trumpet ear*
18 *Whether thou givest or withold'st thy lay*
{ *ours*
19 *~~We still~~ Be* { *mine to walk content with Nature's way*
~~Ours to rejoice without her while~~
20 *~~While at all times~~ & ~~seasons what~~ we miss*
Wise if the gravest thought of what
{ *ing*
21 *Temper* { *s* *the fullness of a loving bliss*
Be with that kindly office satisfied
22 *~~And~~ unrepining sadness is allied*
While *to*
23 *In thankful bosoms ~~with~~ judicious pride*
To jo with what we [?miss]

Fair copy and all entry not by WW is in MW's hand. WW's entry at 19/20 is written over illegible pencil.

1 For comment on the caret see note to l. 2/3 on p. 749.
20 The first four words are deleted in pencil.

Small service is true service while it lasts
Of Friends however humble scorn not one
The Daisy by the Shadow that it casts
Protects the lingering dewdrop from the Sun

The dewy evening has withdrawn
The daisies from the shaven lawn
And reinstates its verdant leaves green
Lost while the sun was up beneath
their dazzling sheen
Like office can this sober hour
Perform for hearts that feel its power
Which in vain, have wished away
The garish pleasures of broad day
That each stood glittering at his post
Meek even tide shuts up the whole usurping host
And leaves the humble spirit free
To reassume its own simplicity.

[*Evening Voluntaries*]

[*IV*, 8–19]

1 *The dewy evening has withdrawn*
2 *The daisies from the shaven lawn*
reinstates ~~natural~~ tender
3 *And ~~has restored~~ its ~~tender~~ green*
And gives to view its [?natur]
4 *Lost while the sun was up beneath*
their dazzling sheen
5 *Like office can this sober hour*
6 *Perform for hearts that feel its power*
Oft when ~~we~~ we
7 *~~When we~~, in vain, have wished away*
8 *The garish pleasures of broad day*
That each
9 *~~While each~~ stood glittering at his post*
10 *Meek even tide shuts up the whole usurping*
host
tender
~~thankful~~ gentle
~~humble~~
11 *And leaves the ~~gentle~~ spirit free*
its ~~her~~
12 *To reassume ~~its~~ own simplicity.*

At the top of the page is MW's copy of *Written in an Album* (see p. 268 above). Dora W entered "The dewy evening has withdrawn" below it.

The Linnet's warble ~~[illegible]~~ sinking towards a clo[se]
Hints to the Thrush 'tis time for their repose
The shrill voiced Thrush is heedless & again
The Monitor revives his own sweet strain
But a few minutes more of fading light will
~~Will~~ Leave the whole copse voiceless silent ere the nigh[t]
By some commanding Star ~~[illegible]~~ dismiss to rest
~~The multitude~~ ~~[illegible]~~ that now from bough or rest
~~[illegible] of the grove disturb with cawing noise~~
~~The liquid music's sweet equipoise.~~
After a home-bound flight on earnest wings
And a quaint game of mazy hoverings
In their appropriate grove with cawing noise
Disturb the liquid music's equipoise.
But mark how dewy twilight has withdrawn
The throng of daisies from the shaven lawn
And has restored to view its tender green
Lost while the sun was safe beneath their dazzling sheen
Like office can this sober shadowy hour
Perform for hearts disposed to feel its power
Not seldom when in vain we have wished away
The petty pleasures of the garish day
[illegible] always each glitters at his post
Meek eventide shuts up the whole usurping host
And leaves the groundwork of our nature free
To resume its own simplicity.

Though good and evil [illegible]
Of [illegible]

[*Evening Voluntaries*]

sinking ,
The Linnet's warble ~~waning~~ towards a close [*III*, 1–12]
Hints to the Thrush 'tis time for their repose
The shrill voiced Thrush is heedless & again
The Monitor revives his own sweet strain
But a few minutes more of fading light
S } [?Shall] silent ~~the~~ will
W} ill leave the whole copse voiceless ere ~~the~~ night
dismiss to
By some commanding star ~~to silent~~ rest
The multitudes ^ bough
~~Dismiss the rooks~~ that now from twig or nest
yon ^
~~In yon old grove disturb with cawing noise~~
~~The liquid music's easy equipoise.~~
After a home bound flight on earnest wings
And a quaint game of mazy hoverings
In their appropriate grove with cawing noise
Disturb the liquid music's equipoise +
But mark how dewy twilight has withdrawn [*IV*, 8–19]
The throng of daisies from the shaven lawn
And has restored to view its tender green
Lost while the sun was up beneath their
dazzling sheen
Like office can this sober shadowy hour
Perform for hearts disposed to feel its power
Not seldom when in vain we have wished away
The petty pleasures of the garish day
Unbashful dwarfs each glitters at his post
Meek eventide shuts up the whole usurping host
And leaves the groundwork of our nature free
To reassume its own simplicity.
Through good and evil there in [*II*, 18–19]
just degree
Of rational & manly sympathy

The fair copy is in Dora W's hand. "[?Shall]" at l. 6 is in pencil. WW's two lines at the foot are a continuation from the facing inside back cover (see pp. 755–756).

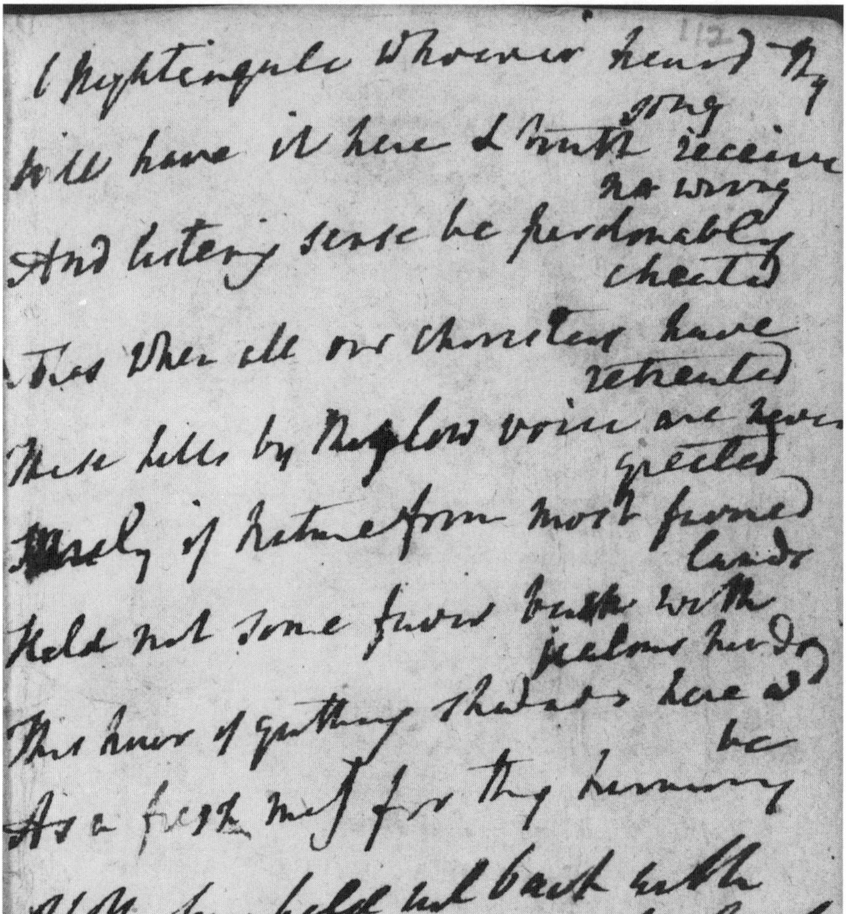

[*Evening Voluntaries*]

1 *O Nightingale whoever heard thy song* [*III*, 13–20]
2 *Will have it here & truth receive no wrong*
3 *And listening sense be pardonably cheated*
4 *Alas when all our choristers have retreated*
5 *These hills by th*{y / *e*} *low voice are never greeted*
6 {*Surely* / [?*From*]} *if nature from most favored lands*
7 *Held not some favor back with jealous hands*
8 *This hour of gathering shadows here w*[d] *be*
9 *As a fresh mng for thy harmony*

10 If Nature held not back with jealous hands [*III*, 17–18]
11 Some first-rate favord from most favord land.

12 But from the picture in that still retreat [*IV*, 6–7]
13 Turn to the humbler objects changes about

14 But who is innocent by grace divine [*II*, 16–18]
15 Not otherwise O Nature are we thine
16 Through good and evil ~~there in~~ just

1–9 MW's hand.
16 WW completed this line and added another at the foot of the facing page (58[v]; see p. 755).

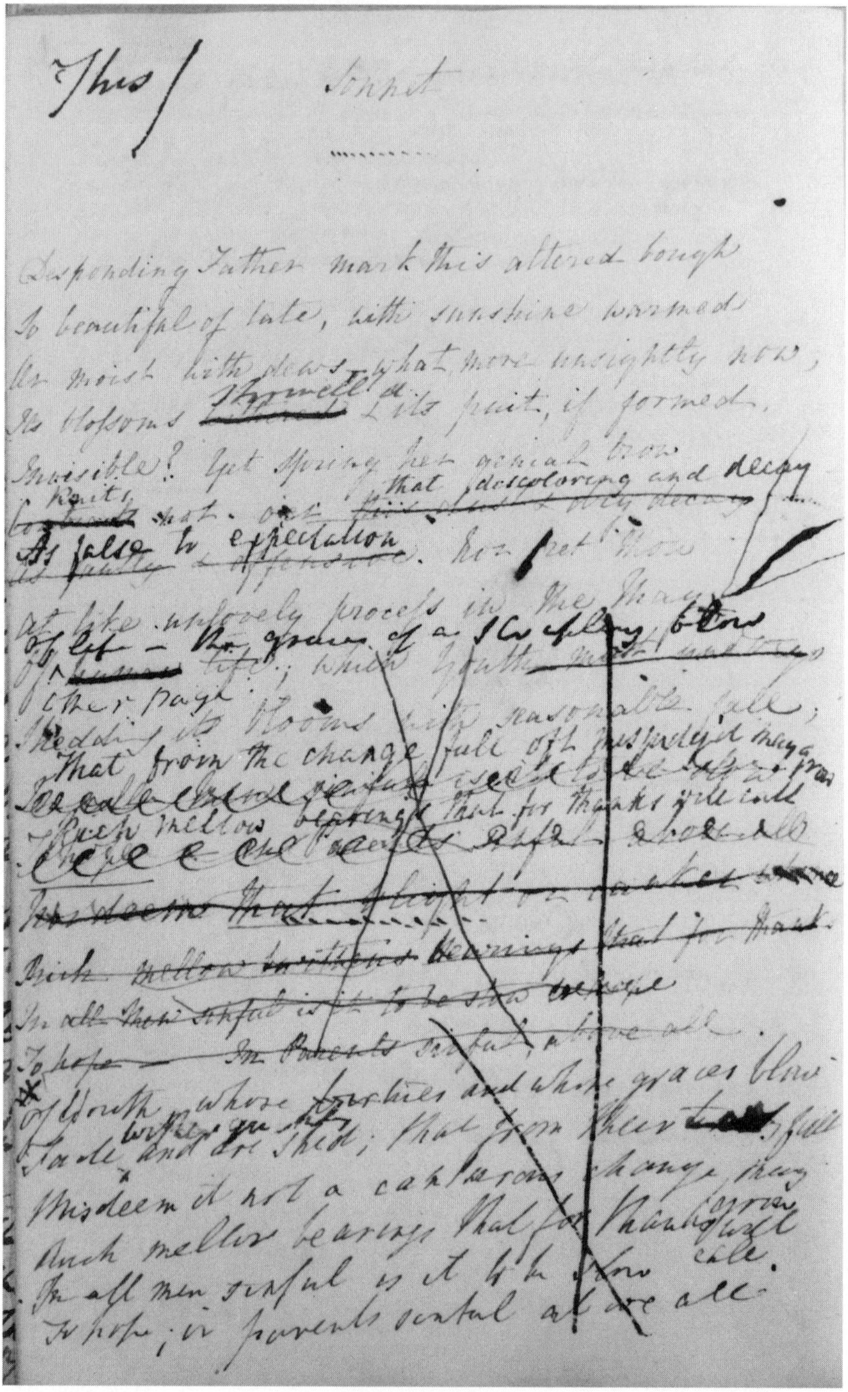

["Desponding Father! mark this altered bough"]

Sonnet

. . . .

1 *Desponding Father mark this altered bough*
2 *So beautiful of late, with sunshine warmed*
3 *Or moist with dews—what, more unsightly now;*
shrivell'd
4 *Its blossoms ~~withered~~ & its fruit, if formed,*
5 *Invisible? Yet Spring her genial brow*
Knits *that discoloring and decay*
6 *~~Contracts~~ not o'er ~~this dust & dry decay~~*
As false to expectation
7 *~~As faulty & offensive~~. Nor fret thou*
8 *At like unlovely process in the May* ✳
Of life—tho graces of a Stripling blow
9 *Of^ ~~human~~ ~~life~~; which Youth ~~must undergo~~*
other page
10 *Shedding its blooms with seasonable fall;*
That from the change full oft misjudg'd may grow [11]
11 *~~In all men sinful is it to be slow~~*
Rich mellow bearings that for thanks will call [12]
12 *~~To hope—in Parents sinful above all~~*

———

13 *~~Nor deem that blight or canker [?whence]~~ shall ~~grow~~*
will
14 *~~Rich mellow burthens bearings that for thanks shall~~ call.*
~~In all Men sinful is it to be slow to hope~~ ^ [13]
~~To hope—In Parents sinful, above all.~~ [14]

✳ Of y{Y}outh whose Virtues and whose graces blow [9–14]
wither quickly
Fade^and are shed; that from their ~~timely~~ fall

Misdeem it not a cankerous change may grow
Rich mellow bearings that for thanks will call.

In all men sinful is it to be slow
To hope; in parents sinful above all

The word "This" at the top of the page appears to be WW's mark to indicate the poems in MS. 107 that he wanted recopied elsewhere. The fair copy is in MW's hand.

9–14 Between the original ll. 9 and 10 WW wrote "other page" to direct the copyist to his revision on 57^r and drew an arrow on that page across to the end of l. 8 on 56^v. Other marks suggest similar, if provisional, instructions or reminders: broken rules between original ll. 13 and 14; a shorter broken rule below the second l. 14 (appearing to delete the word "Virtues" in WW's revision); and an asterisk below the end of l. 8 pointing to another such mark at the beginning of WW's revised l. 9 below. WW crossed out just these lines when he entered the revised version below. The revision was then deleted by a cross when he used the facing page to revise the lines again.

11–12 The two words and the end of each line were written on the facing leaf (see the photograph of 57^r on the next page).

["Desponding Father! mark this altered bough"]

life a stripling
Of ~~Youth~~—the graces of thy Offspring blow, [9]
Fade & are shed that from their
timely fall. [10]

Fade & are shed a striplings
graces blow

Of human life; a Stripling's graces blow [9]
that
—Fade and are shed^from their timely fall [10]
(Misdeem'd not a <u>cankerous</u> change) may grow [11]
Rich mellow bearings that for thanks will
call [12]
In all men sinful is it to be slow [13]
To hope—in parents sinful above all. [14]

~~Nor cankerous deem a change from wh shall grow~~ [11]
shall ~~grow~~
will
~~shall~~ call.
^

And fade—that from their withering and
their fall [10]

Draft lines below the first l. 10 are in pencil. The deleted l. 11 is in MW's hand.

WW's revision of ll. 9–14 appears to be deleted but the marks were offset from those on the facing page. WW's arrow points from the second l. 9 on this page to the asterisk below the end of MW's revised l. 8 on the facing page. The slashes beside the two lines at the top and the pencil revision appear to mark their deletion.

What fond affections on the name attend
Which calls thee, gentle Moon! the Sailor's Friend!
So call'd thee not alone for what the sky
Through mist or cloud permits thee to supply
As from a moving watchtower of war light
To guide his Bark through perils of the night;
But for thy private bounties, for that meek
And ~~tender~~ influence of which few will speak
Though it can wet with tears the hardest cheek.
Say is there one
Queen of the Stars, as bright as when of yore
Whilst nations thought thy presence to adore
Thee to whom Fable gave (Truth loved thee so)
When thou ~~[illegible]~~ doomed thine regions to forego
Alternate empire in the shades below,
Say breathes there
Breathes ~~there a Man~~ of all whose business lies
On the great ~~waters~~ deep cut off from household ties,
A Man endowed with human sympathies,
Who has not felt the [illegible] of thy sway
To cherish thoughts that shun the blaze of day,
The ~~tone~~ soft accordance of thy bland cheer
With all that fancy the memory holds most dear
Or fancy pictures forth to soothe the breast
[illegible]

[*To the Moon. (Composed by the Sea-side,—on the Coast of Cumberland.)* and *To the Moon. (Rydal.)*]

What fond affections on the name atten[ ] [*Cumberland*, 11–12]
Which calls thee, gentle Moon! the Sailor's Friend!
So calls thee not alone for what the sky
Through mist or cloud permits thee to supply
(As from a moving watchtower) of wan light [*Cumberland*, 15–16, 68–69]
To guide his Bark through perils of the night;
But for thy private bounties; for that meek [*Cumberland*, 6–62]
And [?~~kinder~~] influence of which few will speak
Though it can wet with tears the hardiest cheek.
Say is there one
{ Queen of the Stars, as bright as when of yore [*Rydal*, 1–5]
While nations knelt thy presence to adore;
Thou to whom Fable gave (Truth loved the ~~S~~ so)
When thou ~~doom~~ doomed these regions to forego
~~Alternate~~ empire in the shades below,
Say is there one,
Breathes ~~there a Man~~, of all whose business lies [*Cumberland*, 31–38]
O deep cut off
I }n the great ~~waters~~ far from household ties,
A Man endowed with human sympathies,
{e
Who has not felt th{y fulness of thy sway
To cherish thoughts that shun the blaze of day,
soft
The ~~true~~ accordance of thy placid chear [*Cumberland*, 56–59]
With all that pensive memory holds most dear
Or Fancy pictures forth to soothe a breast
~~That asks not happiness but longs for~~ [ ]
Tired with its daily share of ear[ ]

Edith J. Morley gave an account of this manuscript, including a reproduction and her transcription, in "A Manuscript Poem of Wordsworth," *Modern Language Review* 19 (1924): 211–214, and *HCR Correspondence*, II, 875–877. WW used lines from this draft in *To the Moon. (Composed by the Sea-side,—on the Coast of Cumberland.)* and *To the Moon. (Rydal.)*. The abbreviated title and line numbers in brackets on the right indicate placement in those poems.

1 The manuscript is torn; the final word was probably "attend."

23 Another tear affects the base line and its revision; the final word of the base line was probably "rest" while the last words of the revision were probably "earth's unrest."

[*To the Moon. (Composed by the Sea-side,—on the Coast of Cumberland.)* and *To the Moon. (Rydal.)*]

[ ] the Helmsman above the seas [*Cumberland*, 65–66]
along on
And [ ] the life long wanderer oer the seas
Steers his [ ]nt ship
~~Runs a smooth course~~ before a steady breeze
While he keep watch in some far distant clime
Dull darkness
~~Thy absence~~ adding to the weight of time [*Cumberland*, 70, 72]
Oft does thy image with his musings blend
And thou art Still, O moon, the ~~Poet~~ Sailors friend.

has marked watched [*Cumberland*, 31–38]
Who ~~while he marks~~ thee bright as when of yore
While nations knelt thy presence to adore
crossed
Beholds the girt by clouds that slowly move
Catching the lustre they in part reprove,
Nor felt the fitness of thy modest sway
To cherish the thought that shuns the blaze of day

---

24 The manuscript is torn; the obliterated word in the base line was probably "when."
25 The word in the revision that is obliterated by the tear may have been "errant."
29 Though the six lines entered below this line look continuous with it, they clearly revise ll. 15–19 on the other side of the sheet (see p. 763).

Never without reverence let me pass the door
Of one, a Widow left beneath a weight
Of blameless debt. On evil fortune's spite
She wasted no complaint, but strove to make
Just repayment, both for conscience' sake
And that herself & hers should stand upright
In the world's eye. Her work when daylight failed
Paused not & through the depths of night she kept
So unremittingly that some thought
And said, the noble Creature never slept.
But one by one to the cold grave were brought
Her Children, out of her heart's heart bewailed.

[*The Widow on Windermere Side.*]

up
How beautiful when to a lofty height
{ ~~how~~
~~Yes doubt it not~~ { ~~[?why] to the loftiest height~~
Honor ascends among [?the] humblest poor
~~Can rise the sense of honor in the Poor~~
Neer without reverence let me pass the door
Of one, a Widow left beneath a weight
1 ~~Oftimes are carried to the loftiest height~~
~~A field~~ of blameless debt. On evil fortune's spite
{ ~~A~~
{ ~~The~~
2 { ~~[?In] field, in workshop, within cottage door~~
She wasted no complaint but strove to make
3 ~~The industry and honor of the poor;~~
Just ~~restitution~~ both for consciences sake
^ repayment
4 ~~One have I reverenced with supreme delight~~
~~Of just repayment~~
~~beneath~~ {er
5 ~~A Widow left under a heavy~~ { ~~weight~~
~~Of debt than tender conscience could endure~~
6 ~~Of blameless debt, yet wuld she secure~~
~~Hence endless toil just payment to secure~~
{ that
7 ~~A just discharge~~ { ~~[?and] conscience might be~~
~~From stain and~~ ~~pure~~
8 ~~And She with all around her stand upright~~
should
And that herself & her's ~~might~~ stand upright
9 In the world's eyes ~~The long day thr She wrought~~
{ when
Her work { till day light failed
Paused not & thro the depths of night she kept
10 ~~And far into the night keen vigils kept~~
vigils ~~so un~~
11 ~~With spirit~~ so unremitting that some thought
12 And said, the noble Creature never slept.
13 But one by one to the cold grave were brought
~~with what agony~~
14 Her Children, ~~o how feelingly bewept!~~
bewailed
out of her hearts heart ~~bewept~~

But why that prayer? as if to her could come
No good but by the way that leads to bliss
Through Death; so judging we should judge amiss
Though ... was her threatened doom
Its ... joy has not left her home
Joy hath not fled but finds ... her a home,
And of those maniacs she is not one who kiss
The air or laugh upon a precipice;
Her transports rise from out the silent tomb.
Her rich reward already is begun;
Oft when ... before the breeze
And light ... forth ... upon her knees
Hails with spread arms an Angel in her descending Son
An Angel & in earthly ecstacies
Her own angelic glory seems begun.
Oft when ... before the breeze
... she fallen upon her knees
Hails with spread arms in her descending Son
An Angel & in earthly ecstacies
Her own angelic glory seems begun

[*The Widow on Windermere Side*]

Since reason failed want is till
~~With reason lost want is her~~ threatened doom
frequent transports mitigate Her gloom
Yet ~~was not joy a stranger to her home~~
1 *But why that prayer? as if to her could come* [29–42]
y
2 *No good but by the way that leads to bliss*
we should
3 *Through Death; so judging ~~you would~~ judge*
amiss
With reason lost want is her
~~now with Reason lost~~
4 *~~Though penury be now her~~* threatened *doom*
Yet, reason lost
~~Is very want~~ joy has not left her home
5 *~~Joy hath not fled but finds with her a home,~~*
is she one
× Nor of {who
6 *~~And of~~ those Maniacs she is* not {*~~that~~ kiss*
7 *The air or laugh upon a precipice,*
~~Tho' yet she hath not passed the silent tomb,~~
8 *~~Her transports rise from out the silent tomb.~~*
~~A martyrs crown her sufferings hath won~~
9 *~~Her rich reward already is begun;~~*
While passing thro strange sufferings toward the tomb
divide
10 *~~Oft when black Clouds give way before the~~ breeze,*
{ on
She smiles as of a Martyrs she falling { [?to] her knees
~~sufferer like a nun~~
beams *S* } crown were won
11 *And light ~~breaks~~ forth ~~s~~ ~~he drops upon her knees~~*
{*~~Enrapt~~*
{[?] *~~in worship falls upon her knees descending~~*
12 *Hails with spread arms ~~an Angel in her Son~~*
^
in her descending Son
An Angel
13 *~~Descending~~ & in earthly extacies*
~~Her own angelic glory seems begun~~
in A Martyrs crown her suffering hath won
14 *~~A Martyrs crown her sufferings hath won.~~*
light breaks thro' clouds or shady trees
Oft when ~~black clouds~~ divide before the breeze
waving on high
~~And light beams forth~~ she fallen upon her knees
Hails with spread arms in her descending Son
An Angel & in earthly extacies
Her own angelic glory seems begun

The third sonnet (ll. 29–42), in MW's hand with a few revisions by WW, was entered on the verso of the page (99[r]) that bears MW's fair copy, corrected by WW, of the first and second sonnets. Four additional copies in various hands follow in this manuscript (see the *apparatus* for the second reading text: version A in MS. 151.1).

Oh, what a wreck! how changed in mien and speech
Yet though dread Powers, that work in mystery, spin
Entanglings for her brain; though shadows stretch
O'er the chilled Heart — reflect! far, far within
Hers is a holy Being, freed from sin:
She is not what she seems a forlorn wretch;
But delegated Spirits comfort fetch
To her from heavenly heights that Reason may not win.

d move,
Whate'er to shallow unfold
Truly illumined by Heaven's pitying love,
Love pitying innocence not long to last,
In them — in Her, our sins and sorrows past.

["Oh what a Wreck! how changed in mien and speech!"]

Oh, what a wreck!—how changed in mien and speech!
Yet~~;~~ though dread Powers, that work in ~~[?secr]~~ mystery, spin
~~her~~
~~Entanglings for the brain; though~~
~~Nets for her brain; though chill shadows stretch~~
Entanglings for her brain; though shadows stretch
~~Over the sacred Heart — far far within~~
O'er the chill'd Heart—reflect! far, far within
Hers is a holy Being, freed from sin:
She is not what she seems a forlorn wretch;
But delegated
~~To her attendant~~ ^ Spirits comfort fetch
To her, from may
~~From heavenly~~ ^ heights that Reason ~~can~~ not win.
[ ] [?privi]leged to hold

[ ] [?a]nd move,
Whateer to shallow [ ] [?wa]ys unfold,
Heaven's
Inly illumined by ~~a~~ pitying love,
Love pitying innocence not long to last,
In them{—, in h{H er, our sins and sorrows past.

1–9 From BL MS. 3.

4–6 In the letter containing the sonnet (see the editor's headnote on p. 322) WW sent an alternative to lines to which Dora W had objected:

Over the sacred Heart—Compassion's Twin,
The heart that once could feel for every Wretch

Presumably l. 5 as above was to follow the second line of revision.

10–14 From DC MS. 144, the piece separated from BL MS. 3; parts of ll. 9 and 10 are missing, this portion of the letter having been excised, probably to preserve a signature.

[*A Plea for Authors. May, 1838*]

When impartial
~~F~~ failing one strict measure to dispense
every
To all her suitors Equity is lame
And social justice by fit reverence
Of natural right unswayed is but a name
And Law the servile dupe of false pretence
If guarding grossest things from common claim
Now & for ever, she for work that came
From mind and spirit grudge a short lived fence.
our
But no ~~the~~ Sages join in banded force
That may
With books by right or wrong ~~to~~ glad the Isle;
would future should our
Say, can this serve the people ~~if~~ the course
Of pure domestic hopes be checked the
Of ~~prejudice be less approved the while,~~
Though
~~If~~ toil-worn Genius want a cheering smile
And streams of Truth be dried up at their source

impartial
~~If~~ failing ~~all her~~ one strict measure to dispense
To all her suitors, Equity is lame
And social Justice by fit reverence
Justice ~~unswayed~~, unmoved by reverence
of ~~what is she but a name~~
~~For~~ natural right ~~is but an empty name~~
unswayed is but a
{L ~~is~~
~~And~~ {law the servile dupe of False-pretence—
If
When, guarding grossest things from common claim
Now & for ever, she to work that came
From mind & spirit grudge
Out of the mind grudges a short-lived fence.
But no—the Sages in banded force
~~And now preposterous Sages is your course~~
~~[?wail]~~ with ~~cheap books a [?sad] excuse~~
~~Who cry give~~ books ~~free passage thru~~ the isle
Say can this serve the people if the course
~~By right or wrong, for better or for worse~~
y}
~~Friends to the~~ people what care w} e the while
Tho toil-worn Genius want a cheering smile
And far-fetched truth be dried up at her Source

WW entered text with the notebook turned. This and the next photograph show full openings. The draft on 20v was entered after that on the facing page, 21r.

20v, l. 2 What looks like underlining is ink offset from the facing page.

[*Composed on the Same Morning.*]

1 Yon mountain Lambs whose life is just begun
2 Sure guidance know to Mans grave years denied
3 Does joy approach? they meet the coming tide
4 And sulleness avoid as now they shun
{by rising
5 Hollows unbrightened {[?] the morning sun
6 On slopes to couch with quiet satisfied
7 Or gambol, each with his shadow at his side
{wherever
8 Varying its shape {[?wheresoere] he may run
9 As they from turf hoary with unsunned dew
All {r}
10 Turn, {ar} ound do one & all prefer the green
11 To chilly nooks knowlls cheered with glistening [?sheen]
12 Why may not we a ~~kindred~~ course pursue
through lifes
13 And so, God's gifts & promises between

11 To dull cold nooks
{*Yon* *whose life is*
1 ~~*Your lives,*~~ {*ye Mountain Lambs* ~~*tho*~~ ^ *just begun*
Sure *our best*
2 ~~*A*~~ *guidance know to* ~~*Man's grave*~~ *years denied;*
Does joy approach? they meet the coming tide
3 ~~*O that by nature we were prompt the tide*~~
they *now*
4 ~~*Of joy to meet as ye are who there*~~ *shun*
And sullenness avoid as now they shun
5 *Hollows unbrightened by the rising sun*
On slopes to couch with quiet satisfied,
6 ~~*To couch on slopes where he his beams has tried*~~
Or gambol, each with his shadow at his side
7 ~~*Sporting & running wheresoeer ye run*~~
Running in sport wherever he may run.
8 *As from dull turf hoary with unsunned dew*
They
9 ~~*Ye*~~ *turn, & one & all prefer the green*
10 *To chilly nooks, knowlls cheered with glistening sheen*
11 *Why may not we a kindred course pursue*
13 *And so, heaven's gifts & promises between,*
14 *Feed to the last on pleasures ever new.*
To chilly nooks knowlls warm with glistening
sheen

MW made a fair copy on 17^r first, entering the revisions herself (except for a few entries by WW); WW then entered a version incorporating much of this revision on 16^v but omitting the last line (the two leaves transcribed above). Subsequently MW copied a newly revised version on 19^r that was much altered by WW, who then entered further revisions of ll. 6–7 and 12–13 on 22^v (see the *apparatus* on pp. 328–329).

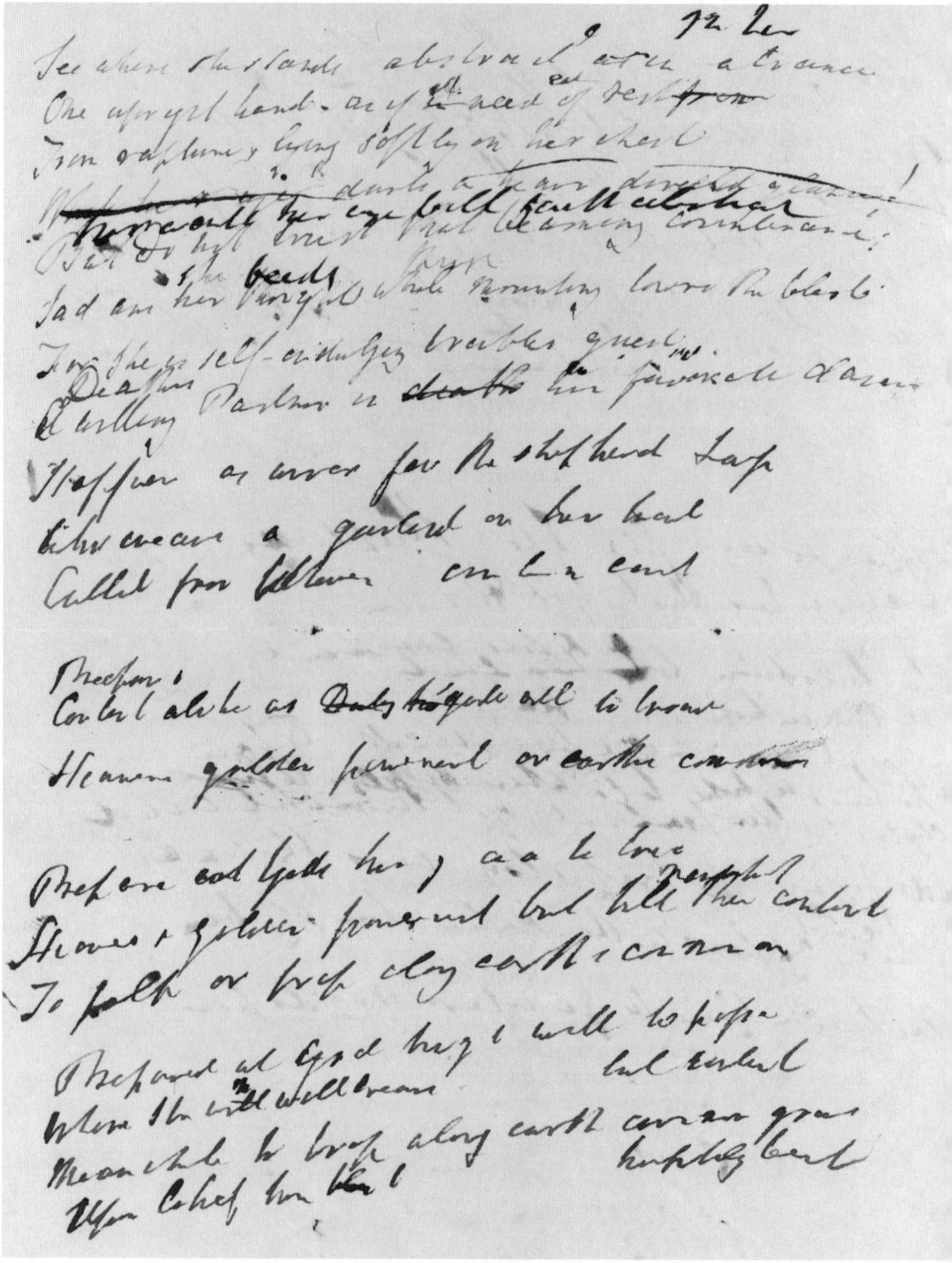

["Lo! where she stands fixed in a saint-like trance"]

& In her
See where she stands abstract ~~as~~ in a trance
it ed
One upright hand—as if ~~in~~ need of rest ~~from~~
From rapture, lying softly on her chest
[?]
~~While her eye~~ darts ~~a heavn directed glance!~~
Nor wants her eye ball faith celestial
But do not trust that beaming countenance;
she [?feeds] though
Sad are her thought while mounting towrd the blest
For She is self-endulging troubles guest,^
Deathes in u
A willing Partner in ~~death~~ his favorite dance
Happier as wiser far the shepherd Lass
Who wears a garland on her head
W
Culled from w hever [?convenient]

[?Preepar d]
Content alike as ~~Duty [?bid]~~ god's will to tread
Heavens golden pavement or earths common

at
Prepare in Gods [?hig] [?care] to trea
meanwhile
Heavens golden pavement but till then content
To [?halt] or press along earths common

Prepared at God high will to pass
[?be]
Where she ~~will~~ will [?tread] but content
Meanwhile to press along earth common gras
[?Upon belief how blest] happly bent

---

4 The entry above "eye" may be a random mark.

7–8 The comma after "guest" and the "u" above "favorite" actually appear side-by-side, separated by a tiny caret (shown here at the end of l. 7).

["Lo! where she stands fixed in a saint-like trance"]

Happier as wiser far the Shepherd-Lass
[?becomes] [?ou spent]
Whose tuft of youthful flower ~~[? is out spent]~~
Before its time, who lives prepared to pass
as clouds upon a [?descent]
[?Preap ar] at Gods ~~[?hig]~~ all ruling will to pass
{but
Where she will tread heavens pavement, {and content
{ip
Meanwhile to tr{[?ead] along earths common grass
On obvious cares & duties [?in] ~~du~~ ~~duties~~
On simple cares and ~~[?humble] pleasures~~ bent.

happier as wiser far the Shephe[?rd]
Whichever hour that God his [?tim]
[?at time convenient]
Whose [?] lo~~t her short~~
Who lives in hope, pace
Prepared when summed by Gods will to pace
{angels
Who lives in hope to go where {she will [?tread]
Heavens golden pavement, yet meanwhile content
And please to trip along earth common
[?eart]
On her appointed du duties humbly ben
Who lives in hope to go where angels pa

"Wm Wordsworth" was written in an unidentified hand up the page in the lower center panel that was created by the fold.

["Let more ambitious Poets take the heart"]

1 Listeners not unwilling,
if approached
2 By kindly visitation, to disclose
3 Their sweetness gently as the flowers of
March
4 That from sharp winds & pattering hail shrink up [5]
fragrance
5 Will give out ~~sweetness~~ to a soft warm breeze [7]
6 Ruffling their bosoms.— [8]

7 Reader no wish is mine to take thy [1]
heart
~~take the heart as if by storm~~
8 By storm, the verse would gently win its way [2]
~~Reader to seize upon thy he~~art by storm
9 ~~Listener! I seek not to assail~~ thy heart
~~violence~~ ~~will the verse~~
10 ~~With a rude force, gentle is my approach~~
I seek ~~[?rest]~~, gently would the verse approach
11 And to ~~the~~ visitation do Thou yield
{ing
A correspond {ent sweetness
12 With sympathizing spirit as March-flowers, [5–6]
p } pattering
13 That from sharp winds & b } attering hail shrink up,
G } their
14 ~~Yet~~ g } ive out fragrance to a soft warm breeze [7]
15 Ruffling their bosoms.:—— [?etc] [8]

16 Reader ~~I seek not~~ to assail thy heart [1]
B } storm
17 [?W] } y ~~force~~; the verse gently would win its way [2]
18 And to its visitation do Thou yield
Flowers
19 With answering sweetness as the ~~winds~~ of March

Numbers on the right correspond to reading-text lines. WW seems to have made three separate attempts at this passage, ll. 1–6, 7–15 and 16–19, though the order of entry is not certain.

["Lyre! though such power do in thy magic live"]

O could I gaze elsewhere
O then what bliss with her
this
What bliss with ~~her~~ to sit in sunny weather Or if she stoop
this
Aloft, and in a brook below espy [18]
Substance & shade and image all together
Freaks of nature's witchery
on
[~~?Chan~~] [?Shadow] in the rivulet lying [19–22]
Somewhat faint & pensively
{y
And Downward image gaily v{iing
With its type the living tree,
Or up the stream to cast a glance [25–26]
translucent
And note—(fantastic summer's luckiest chance!) [33–37]
The sloping channel floored with pebble bright
Stones of all tint gem emulous of gem
vivid
So beset that they take from keenest sight
{ei {not
The liquid v{iel that seeks {but to hide them.—

Lyre that from Indias farthest plain [1–2]
By powers that in thy magic live
detain
Coulds' call her back assist me to [?strain]
{is {Fugitive—
Th{e would-be {Fug [5–7]
Check with thy notes the impulse which betrayed
sweet
By her look, I longed to aid.—

Numbers on the right correspond to reading-text lines. Transcription of 95^r continues on p. 785.

["Lyre! though such power do in thy magic live"]

that eye the fort [8–9]
Of contemplation the still port [10]
Reason
Which guards from gales that try [11]
The restless sails of vanity
all the [?vague]
Where even divine affections lie
With their sails furled in modesty

Let the Halcyon chant with plumes
Seen and hidden at her will
The mocking bird in forest glooms
{d
Deep as mi{nnight from her skill

Still yes
~~Let me [?] St Still~~ let me gaze, enrapt, upon that eye [8–12]
So oft
~~That eye~~ the impregnable and awful port
Of contemplation the calm port
Which reason guards from gales that try
The restless sails of vanity
{~~light~~ vague
~~Which reason guards, where all {vag meanings lie~~
Where all ~~the vague~~ affections lie
With their sails furled in modesty

30–34/ Entered in a lighter ink, probably later than the lines above.
30 By "yes" WW may have intended "yet."
33–34 The vertical marks in the left margin suggest WW's preference for the revised lines below.

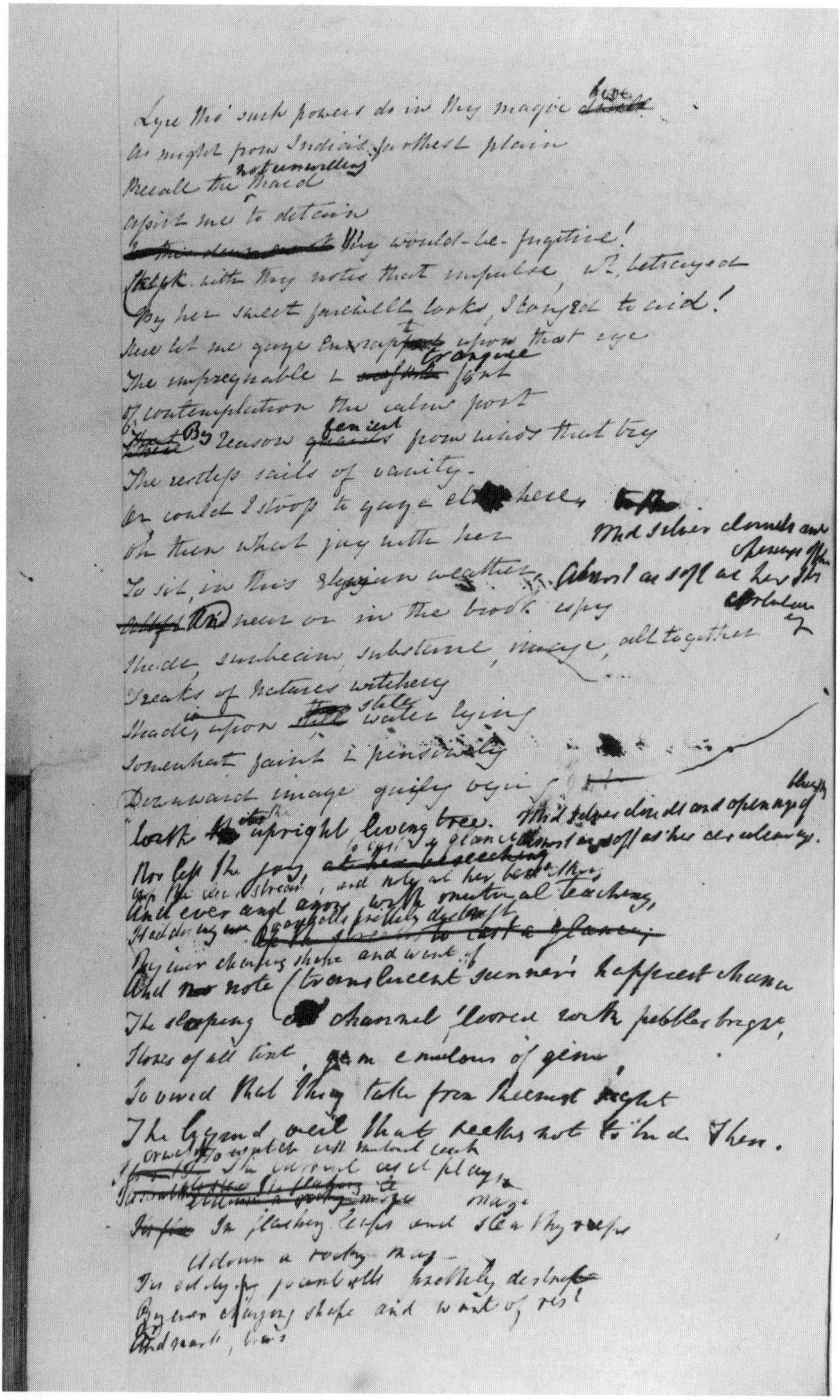

["Lyre! though such power do in thy magic live"]

live
Lyre tho' such powers do in thy magic ~~*dwell*~~ [1–21]
As might from India's farthest plain
not unwilling
Recall the^ *maid*
Assist me to detain
M}
~~*In this dear nook*~~ *m*} *y would-be-fugitive!*
{*Check*
{*Stay with thy notes that impulse, w*[h] *betrayed*
{e}
By her sweet farewell looks, I long{'}*d to aid!*
t
Here let me gaze en~~*w*~~*rap*~~*ped*~~ *upon that eye*
tranquil
The impregnable & ~~*awful*~~ *fort*
Of contemplation the calm port
~~*That*~~ By fenced
~~*Where*~~ *reason* ~~*guards*~~ *from winds that try*
The restless sails of vanity.
Or could I stoop to gaze elsewhere,
Oh then what joy with her
{i
To sit, in this Elys{*yan weather,*
{ And
~~*Aloft*~~ {*&* *near or in the brook espy*
Shade, sunbeam, substance, image, all together
Freaks of Natures witchery
~~in~~ ~~the~~ still
Shade, upon ~~*still*~~ *water lying*
Somewhat faint & pensively
{i
Downward image ga{*yly vying*

[right margin:]
~~to the~~
Mid silver clouds and
openings of blue
sky
Almost as soft as her
cer[?l]ulean
eye

Transcription of 95[r] continues on p. 789.

1–21 Fair copy is in MW's hand.

In the right margin WW has entered a version of ll. 23–24 (repeated below; see the continuation).

["Lyre! though such power do in thy magic live"]

~~its~~ the blue sky
22 With ~~the~~ upright living tree. Mid silver clouds and openings of [22]
to cast a glance Almost as soft as her cerulean eye
23 Nor less the joy, ~~at her beseeching~~ [25–28]
Up the clear stream, and note at her beseeching
24 And ever and anon with mutual teaching,
It eddying ~~[?w]~~ foamballs prettily distrest
25 ~~Up the stream to cast a glance;~~
Thy ever changing shape and want of
26 And ~~no~~ note (translucent summer's happiest chance [33–37]
27 The sl{o / ee}ping ~~ch~~ channel floored with pebbles bright,
28 Stones of all tint, gem emulous of gem,
29 So vivid that they take from keenest sight
30 The liquid veil that seeks not to hide Them.
Or watch To watch with mutual teach [29–32]
31 ~~Its s t I[?s]~~ The current as it plays~~,~~
~~its stea~~
~~Its stealthy~~ ~~In flashing le~~
~~Adown a rocky maze~~ maze
32 ~~In fla~~ In flashing leaps and steathy seeps
33 Adown a ro^c^ky maze
Its eddying foamballs prettily distres{t / sd} [27–28]
By ever changing shape and want of rest
Or
~~And~~ mark, trans

In the right margin WW has entered another version of ll. 23–24. WW's arrow above it points to the end of l. 22 and leads from the same passage on facing leaf 96r (see pp. 790–791).

["Lyre! though such power do in thy magic live"]

Lyre! that from Indias farthest plain
for such powers doth
Couldst, (~~by such powers that~~ in thy magic live)
as
Recall my own beloved Maid
Assist me to detain
The would be Fugitive

my Emma
Couldst call ~~her~~ back,
beloved Maid,
Assist me to detain

1 *Lyre, that from India's farthest plain* [1–22]
2 ~~*By Powers that in thy magic live*~~
Couldst by the powers that in thy magic live
H
3 ~~*Couldst call h*~~*}* ~~*er back, assist me to detain*~~
Recall my own beloved Maid, assist me to detain
Assist me to detain
4 *The would-be fugitive—*
{at
5 *Check with thy notes th*{*e impulse, which betrayed*
farewell {, at first
6 *By her sweet*^ *looks*{ ~~*at first*~~ *I longed*^ *to aid.*
7 *Here let me gaze enwrapped upon that eye*
f}
8 *So oft* *The impregnable and awful p*} *ort*
9 *Of contemplation, the calm port*
10 *That reason guards from winds that try*
11 *The restless sails of vanity*
12 *Or could I stoop to gaze elsewhere*
13 *Oh then what joy with her*
Thro hour
{*Thro this mild* {hour noontide
14 *To sit* {*In* ~~*this soft*~~ {*time of sunny weather*
near ~~or~~ in the
15 *Aloft, and in the brook* ~~*below*~~ *espy*
all to seen
16 *Substance, & shade, & image,* ~~*al*~~*together*
17 *Freaks of nature's witchery—* shade, sunbeam, substance
{e *up*} still water image, all together
18 *Shad*{*es* }*on* ~~*the rivulet*~~ *lying*
19 *Somewhat faint & pensively*
20 ~~And~~ *Downward Image gaily vying*
th upright
21 *With* ~~*its Type*~~ *the living Tree,*

Fair copy is in Dora W's hand. Transcription of 96[r] continues on p. 793.

2 For commentary on the alternate to this line, "Couldst call my Emma back, beloved Maid," see the note to "Lyre! though such power do in thy magic live" on p. 493, above.

15 The revision "or" is obscured, probably deleted, by a heavy blot.

21 The solid line points across the gutter to the facing leaf (see pp. 788–789).

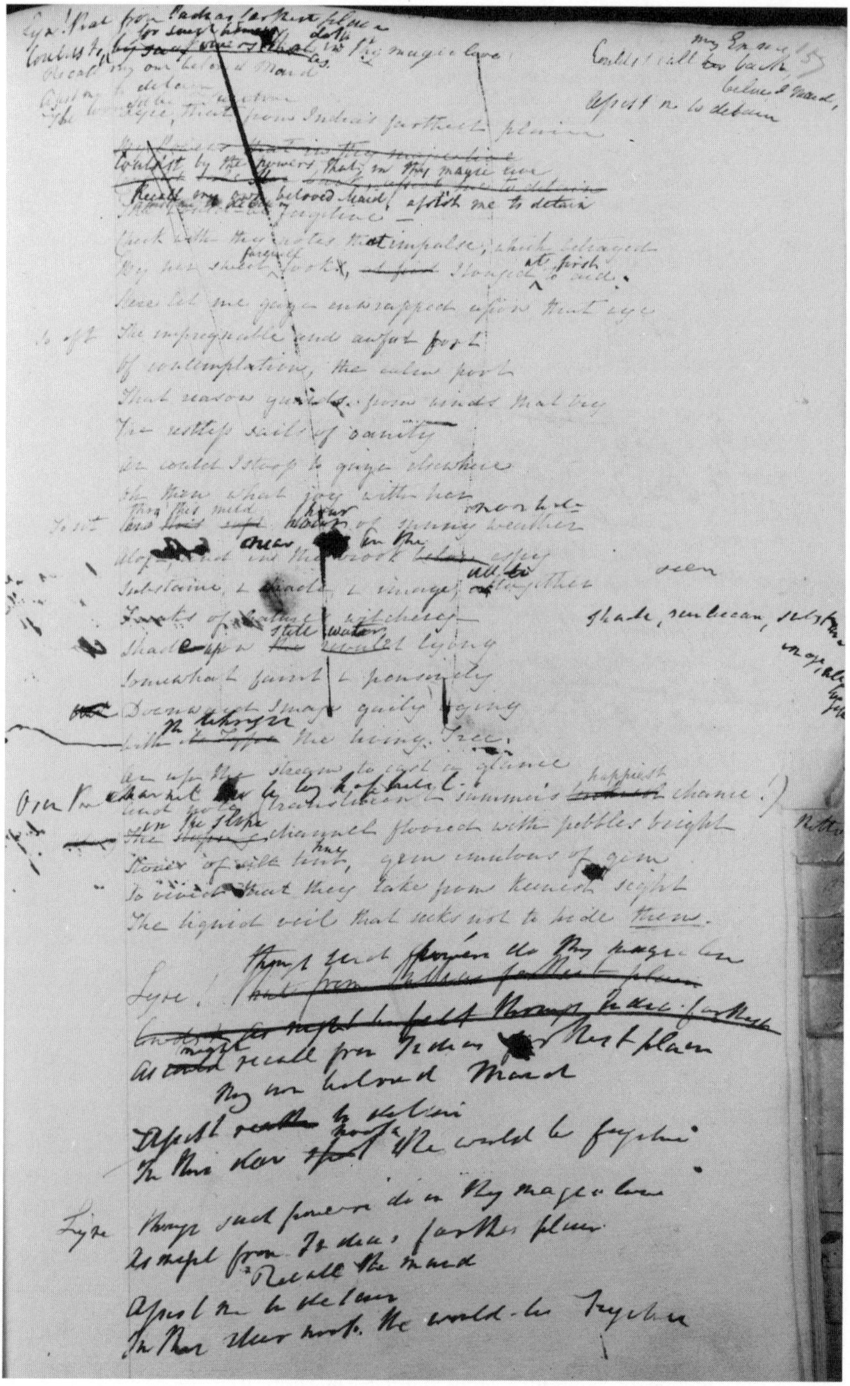

["Lyre! though such power do in thy magic live"]

22 *Or up the stream to cast a glance* [25–26, 33–37]
Or in the channel note by happiest *happiest*
23 *And note (translucent summer's ~~luckiest~~ chance!)*
in the slope
24 ~~Along~~ *~~The sloping~~ channel floored with pebbles bright*
hue
25 *Stones of all tint, gem emulous of gem*
26 *So vivid that they take from keenest sight*
27 *The liquid veil that seeks not to hide them.*

though such powers do in thy magic live
28 Lyre! ~~that from Indias farthest plain~~ [1–5]
29 ~~Coudst as might be felt through Indias farthest~~
might
30 As ~~could~~ recall from Indias farthest plain
31 My own beloved Maid
A}
32 T} ssist ~~recall~~ to detain
nook
33 In this dear ~~spot~~ the would be fugitive

34 Lyre though such powers do in thy magic live [1–5]
35 As might from Indias farther plain
36 Recall the maid
37 Assist me to detain
38 In this dear nook the would-be Fugitive

22–27 Fair copy is in Dora W's hand.

["Lyre! though such power do in thy magic live"]

With the upright living tree [22–33]
to stray, and
Nor less the joy to cast a glance
~~note~~ mark { se
Up the clear stream and ~~mark~~ at her be { [?]eching
Its eddying foam balls prettily distrest
By ever changing shape and want of rest
Or with mutual teaching
~~And~~ watch, th~~e current as it plays~~
The current as it plays
In flashing leaps and stealthy creeps
Adown a rocky maze;
{ r
O { er note, translucent summers happiest chance

cerulean eye
~~with many~~ to cast
Nor less the joy ~~to stray, and cast a g~~lance [25–37]
clear
~~Cast~~ up the stream or down at her beseeching
And its eddying
To mark ~~the~~ ^ foamballs, prettily distrest
By ever changing shape and want of rest,
Or watch, with mutual teaching
The current as it plays
In flashing leaps & stealthy creeps
Adown a rocky maze
~~[?St]~~ ~~Or note~~ Or note, (translucent summers happiest chance!)
~~Or in the channel note~~ by happiest chance;
{ o } In the slope channel
~~The sl { ee } ping channel~~ floored with pebbles bright,
hue
Stones of all tint gem emulous of gem
So vivid that they take from keenest sight
{ ei { not
The liquid v { iel that seeks { [?but] to hide them.

["Lyre! though such power do in thy magic live"]

Lyre! though such Powers do in thy magic live [1–18]
I
As might from i ndia's farthest plain
Recall the not unwilling Maid
Assist me to detain
nook The F
In this ~~dear~~ My would-be f ugitive
Check with thy notes that impulse—which betrayed
By her sweet farewell looks I longed to aid.
O ~~soothe her into full content~~
With ~~what this place and hour present~~
in Here ~~Here let me~~ gaze, enrapt, upon that eye
~~and let the~~ let me awful her
The impregnable and ~~tranquil~~ fort Soothe my verse into
Of contemplation—the calm port entire content
By reason fenced from winds that try With what this place and
✱ The restless sails of vanity: ~~!~~! but if hour present
Soothe her my verse into entire content And let me look the while
~~Or could I stoop to gaze elsewhere~~ upon that eye
e
With what th is place and hour present
Oh the~~n what bliss with her~~
~~sit in~~ stray or stir us
Here let us ~~In this To sit~~ in this elysian weather ✱
‡ And in or near the Brook espy
Shade sunbeam substance image all together
Freaks of Natures witchery.
Shade upon

Only the lower portion of the page is shown in the photograph.

12, 15 The asterisks to the left and right of these lines may refer to revisions on the facing recto (see the *apparatus* for this poem).

16 The mark in the left margin is linked by the angular line to the upper marginal entry on the facing recto (see the following transcription).

18/ "Shade upon" is evidently a tag pointing to the first words on the next page (pp. 798–799).

["Lyre! though such power do in thy magic live"]

Shade upon still water lying [19–37]
Somewhat faint and pensively;
I}
Downward i}mage gayly ~~with~~ vying
With the upright living Tree
Mid silver clouds and openings of blue sky
as
As soft almost and deep her cerulean eye.

Nor less the joy, with many a glance
Cast up the stream or down at her beseeching
{ly
To mark its eddying foam balls pretty{ distrest
{and
By everchanging shape {[?or] want of rest
Or watch, with mutual teaching;
The current as it ~~strays~~ plays
In flashing leaps and stealthy creeps
{z}
Adown a rocky ma{iz}e;
{(
Or note{, translucent summers happiest chance!)
In the ~~slope~~ slope channel floored with pebble bright,
S}
T}tones of all hue gem emulous of gem
So vivid that they take from keenest sight
The liquid veil that seeks not to hide them.

✳ But if no wish were her{s/e} that we should part
A humbler bliss could satisfy my heart.
Where all things are so fair
Enough by her dear side to breathe the air
of this Elysian weather
And in or on or near the Brook espy
Shade &c&c

WW entered a version of reading-text ll. 14–18 in the left margin and repeated them farther down the same margin (see the continuation of the transcription of 105r on p. 801). The asterisk signals their placement after l. 12 on the facing page. The ink line seems to serve a similar purpose, but points to ll. 16–18 farther down the facing page (see pp. 796–797).

["Lyre! though such power do in thy magic live"]

Soothe her my verse into entire content
With what the place and hour present
Me the while it well might sastify
~~O then what joy in this elysian weather~~ [14–19]
A humbler wish in this might satisfy
In this elysian weather
Within upon or near the brook to spy
sun } {e
Shade sub} shine substance imag{ge all togeth

[?]
Or ~~note a~~ humbler ~~wish~~ might satisfy [14–18]
Couldst have been In this elysian weather
Within upon or near the brook to spy

[?] Or humbler bliss my heart would satisfy; [14–18]
Where all things are so fair
Enough by her dear side to breathe the air
Of this elysian weather,
And in, or on, or near, the brook espy

no wish be hers that we should
Or if she wish not that we twain should part
A humbler bliss would satisfy my heart.
Where all things are so fair
Enough by her dear side the breathe the air
Of this elysian weather
And in or on or near the brook espy

27, 30 The two illegible marks (above deleted "wish" and before the second "Or humbler") may signal WW's choice of the lower set of revisions. He also transcribed a version of reading-text ll. 14–18 in the left-hand margin (see the transcription of the top half of the page, p. 799).

["The most alluring clouds that mount the sky"]

gentl }
bright } est cloud
The clouds ~~here~~ fixd and floating there on high [1–14]
Look a
~~Owe~~ to ~~the~~ a troubled element their forms
if { ra
Their hues to sunset ~~while~~ with { [?]ptured
{ m therefor
We watch the { ir ~~beauty~~ shall we ~~then~~ covet storms
And wish the sun could hasten his decline
That they may spread their pomp
~~That such a [?]~~ a pomp might fill the sky
Behold they break away and faintly shine
And soon will leave to us a fruitless sight

That faint regret more faintly soon must dim
And leave to him who gazed a fruitless sigh
Behold already they forget to shine,
Dissolve & leave to him who gazed a sigh

Or
Wish that the Lord of Day his slow decline
such
Would hasten that ~~their~~ pomp may fill the sky

Not loth to thank for innocent delight
such transient bowers
Each passing moment let ~~us leave~~ to [?build]
~~For [?love]~~ but let us build
On firm [?] found —
[?Then let] the ground be [?seen]
Too fond [?] sense with [?mortal] flowers

Tis not for us to dwell in transient bowers
A House of firm foundations [?may be]
[?one gives]
[?For friends] [?] [?with]

The drafting in the margin, corresponding to reading-text ll. 13–14, is a continuation of ll. 16–20.

["The most alluring clouds that mount the sky"]

fairest ~~deck the sky~~
1 The brigh clouds that ~~float on high~~ deck the sky [1–14]
e
2 Owe to a troubled element th{[?]ir forms
3 Their hues to sunset; if with raptured eye
w
4 We {[?]atch their beauty shall we covet storms
5 Or wish the Lord of Day his slow decline
6 Would hasten that such Pomp may ~~fill~~ float on high
7 Behold already they forget to ~~sh~~ shine
im
8 Dissolve—and leave to h{[?e] who gazed a sigh.
~~Applaud~~ Not loth to
9 ~~Not censuring those~~ who take the moments gift
10 Of innocent delight come when it may
Peace to our ~~wish~~ hope [?our wish] [?come]
11 ~~Our hope or wish~~ — let us to [?lift]
Regard a dwelling place in
12 ~~Abode~~ ~~of~~ transient bower
13 Our [?wish] of finer trust
14 be filled

15 Why should we crave abodes in transient [9–14]
16 [?For quite divine] [?] will [?impartial] flow
17 There is a House that need not fear [?]
18 ~~The abode of all the~~
19 Heavns
boon
20 Not loth to thank each moment for its ~~gift~~
21 Of pure delight come whensoeer it may
~~Peace be our [?]~~
22 ~~Our~~ Peace let us seek to steadfast things attune
23 ~~Or~~ calm expectations leaving to the gay
in love
24 Falling to each the choice of a transient
25 The House that cannot ~~melt~~ pass away be ours

Up the center panel of the sheet someone, perhaps MW, has written "Mr Driver's letter"—possibly a reference to Henry Austen Driver, the champion of Lord Byron's reputation after his death (see *LY*, III, 659–660 and note). The sheet was otherwise blank when WW used it for drafting his poem.

46

O bounty without measure, while the Grace
Of Heaven doth in such wise from humblest springs
Pour pleasures forth, & solaces that trace
A mazy course along familiar things
Well may our hearts have faith that blessings come,
Streaming from founts above the starry sky,
With Angels when their own untroubled home
They leave, & speed on nightly embassy
To visit earthly chambers — & for whom?
Yea, both for souls who God's forbearance try,
And those that seek his help, & for his Mercy sigh.

WW April 7th

Ambition can it conquer pain & grief my 70th birthday
Or Pride keep off the assailants at arms length
Can worldly pleasure

~~worldly~~ Pleasure battle
Not Can pleasure still the sighs of genuine grief
Not ~~Shut off~~ distress and ~~trouble~~ at arms length?
~~Ambition keep off anguish~~
Trust ~~Seek~~ not ~~their~~ such help, incompetent as brief,
Love from her depths & duty in her strength
And faith ~~from~~ these only ~~yield~~ secure relief.

59 35

["Intent on gathering wool from hedge and brake"]

Ambition can she conquer pain & grief
Or Pride keep off the Assailants at arm's length
Can worldly pleasure

~~wordly~~ Pleasure baffle
Stet *Can pleasure still the sighs of genuine grief*
~~Keep off~~ distress and tr~~ouble~~
Stet *~~Ambition keep off anguish~~ at arms length?*
Trust such
~~Seek~~ not ~~their~~ help, incompetent as brief;
{from
Love {*in* *her depths & duty in her strength,*
Faith {yield
And ~~prayer~~—these only {*seek secure relief.*

At the top of the page is MW's copy of ll. 34–44 of *The Cuckoo-clock* (see p. 343).
4–8 Fair copy is in MW's hand.

With a Small Present

A prized memorial this slight work may prove
As bought in Charity, & given in Love!

The Crescent Moon, the Star of Love
Bright Pair! with but a span of sky between
Speak one of you! my doubts remove
Which is the attendant Page & which the Queen

Feby 25th 1841

Can the worlds pleasures cope with genuine grief
Its pride keep off affection at arms length?
Not for an instant however brief
Love from her depths, & Duty in her strength,
And Faith, these only yield secure relief.

Can sport & pleasure heal distress or grief
The pains the world afflicts can the degenerate
Not for an interval however brief
Love from her depths and Duty and the might
Of Faith these only yield secure relief

["Intent on gathering wool from hedge and brake"]

cope with genuine
the world's pleasure ~~quell the pangs of~~

1 *Can^ ~~pleasure still the sighs of genuine~~ grief*
Her pride keep off affliction

2 *~~Ambition keep off anguish~~ at arms length?*
Not for an interval however brief.

3 *~~Trust not their help incompetent as brief~~*

4 *Love from her depths, & Duty in her strength,*

5 *And Faith,—these only yield secure relief.*

Can pomp & pleasure heal distress or grief
The pains the World inflicts can She requite
Not for an interval however brief
Love from her depths and Duty and the might
Of Faith these only yield secure relief

For *With a Small Present* and "The Crescent Moon, the Star of Love" see pp. 331 and 354, above. Fair copy on this page is in MW's hand.

["While beams of orient light shoot wide and high"]

Rydal Mount Jan^{ry} 5th 1843

1 While beams of orient light shoot wide
and high,
2 Deep in the Vale a little rural Town
{in
{of
C}
3 Breathes forth a cloud-like c}reature of its own
4 That mounts not toward the radiant morning
sky
But with a less ambitious sympathy
5 But to a Parent cleaves in sympathy,
~~As she awakes to meet the heavy cares~~
6 ~~(So might it seem) with dull & heavy care,~~
At this still hour when she awakes to cares
7 Troubles and toils which every day prepares,
S}
8 And feeds till s}leep shall close the weary eye
^ So Fancy whispers nor reject ~~the thought~~
9 ~~Once more. Be this conceit though sad or~~
Once more ^ ~~chast'ning~~
The thought tho' sad & blessed is
10 ~~And unreproved let Fancy hold~~ her sway
11 If the calm Heaven now to its zenith, deckd
Forms
12 With glorious ~~Shapes~~ in numberless array
lone Shepherd on the hills
13 To the ~~poor Peasant in the fields~~ disclose
from a world
14 Gleams ~~of that bliss~~ in which the Saints
repose

But with a less ambitious sympathy [5–9]
To share its splendor; but in sympathy
prepares
Cleaves to its Parent waking
to the cares
And feeds till sleep once more the
weary eye
Shall close; so Fancy whispers nor
reject
The thought tho' sad, & blessed is her
sway

The order of composition of the several drafts is MS. 1838/40, pp. iv and 2, Princeton MS. 7, MS. 1838/40, pp. 3 and 1. The hand is WW's, except for MW's fair copy and JC's alteration of l. 11 on p. 2 of MS. 1838/40.

The first base line of the revision at the foot is written through l. 14, so that "repose" appears below "sympathy."

CLASS FIRST.

MISCELLANEOUS SONNETS.

PART I.

["While beams of orient light shoot wide and high"]

1 every day prepare [7–14]
2 So Fancy, to the musing Poets eye
3 Endears that Lingerer. And how blest her
sway
Like influence never may my Soul
4 (~~Ne'er may my Soul like influence~~ ^ reject)
5 If the calm Heaven, now to its zenith deckt
6 With glorious Forms in numberless array
7 To the lone Shepherd on the Hills disclose
8 Gleams from a world in which the Saints
repose
For the beginning
of the above, see overleaf.– —

WW's note at the foot directs the reader to p. 2 of the manuscript.

While beams of orient light shoot wide
& high,
Deep in the Vale a little rural Town
Breathes forth a cloud-like Creature of
its own,
That mounts not toward the radiant morning
sky,
But, with a less ambitious sympathy,
Hangs o'er its Parent waking to the cares
Troubles & toils that every day prepares.
So Fancy whispers;
How soothing, how benign, & sweet,
If the calm Heaven, now to its zenith decked
With glorious Forms in numberless array,
To the lone Shepherd on the hills disclose
Gleams from a world in which the Saints
repose. —

Jany 1st 1843

["While beams of orient light shoot wide and high"]

1 *While beams of orient light shoot wide*
& high,
2 *Deep in the Vale a little rural Town*
3 *Breathes forth a cloud-like Creature of*
its own,
4 *That mounts not toward the radiant morning*
sky,
a
5 *But, with ^ less ambitious sympathy,*
6 *Hangs o'er its Parent waking to the cares*
{toils {;
7 *Troubles & {cares that every day prepares*{
So to the Poet musing pensively
8 ~~*And feeds till Sleep once more the weary*~~
eye
Doth Fancy whisper & ~~nor~~ her sway
9 ~~*Shall close. So Fancy whispers; nor reject*~~
~~timely thought~~ ~~and her sway~~
10 ~~*The thought tho' Sad, & blessed be her sway*~~
~~with~~ the
How soothing, how benign, ~~in its~~ effect,
the
11 *If the calm Heaven, now, to ~~its~~ Zenith deckt*
12 *With glorious Forms in numberless array*
13 *To the lone Shepherd on the hills disclose*
14 *Gleams from a world in which the Saints*
repose.—
Jan^ry^ 1st 1843

prepares
~~which every day~~ [7–10]
~~So to the Poet musing pensively~~
~~Doth Fancy whisper. And how blest~~
her sway
~~For other hearts, how precious its effect~~

Fair copy is in MW's hand.

DEDICATION.

Happy the feeling from the bosom thrown
In perfect shape (whose beauty Time shall spare
Though a breath made it) like a bubble blown
For summer pastime into wanton air;
Happy the thought best likened to a stone
Of the sea-beach, when, polished with nice care,
Veins it discovers exquisite and rare,
Which for the loss of those moist gleams atone
That tempted first to gather it. If here,
O Friend! such feelings sometimes I present
To thy regard, with thoughts so fortunate,
Then let a hope spring up my heart to cheer
That thou, if not with partial joy elate,
Wilt smile upon this Gift with more than mild content!

["While beams of orient light shoot wide and high"]

1 prepares [7–11]
2 So Fancy, to the musing Poets eye
~~Image~~ Lingerer
3 Endears that ~~Object~~. And how ~~belss'd~~
blest her sway
4 (O, Never may my soul the like reject)
5 If the calm heaven now to its zėnith
deck

6 So Fancy charms the musing Poets eye
7 Fixd on that Lingerer.

8 prepares [7–12]
9 So Fancy, to the musing Poet's eye,
10 Endears that Lingerer. And how blest
her sway
Neer may my Soul the the intercourse reject
11 (~~O never may my Soul the like reject~~!)
now
12 If the calm Heaven [?was] to its zenith deckt
F
13 With glorious f orms &c

RHT

While beams of orient light shoot wide and high,
Deep in the vale a little rural Town
Breathes forth a cloud-like Creature of its own
That mounts not toward the radiant morning sky,
But, with a less ambitious sympathy,
Hangs oer its Parent waking to the cares
Troubles and toils that every day prepares;
So Fancy to the musing Poets eye
Endears that Lingerer. And how blest her sway;
[illegible]
Never may my soul like influence reject and her sway
[illegible]
[illegible] and blessed be her sway
[illegible]
[illegible]
If the calm Heaven & now to its zenith decked
With glorious forms in numberless array
To the lone Shepherd on the Hills disclose
Gleams from a world in which the Saints repose
W Wordsworth

Front of Rydal Mount
Jany 1st 1843.
every day prepares;
every day prepares
To Fancy to the musing Poets eye,
Endears that Lingerer. And how blest her sway;
(Like influence never may my soul reject!)
Never may my soul like influence
If the calm Heaven, now to its zenith decked
With glorious forms in numberless array,
To the lone Shepherd on the hills disclose
Gleams of a world in which the Saints repose

[While beams of orient light shoot wide and high]

1 While beams of orient light shoot wide and high,
2 Deep in the vale a little rural Town
3 Breathes forth a cloud-like Creature of its own
4 That mounts not tow'rd the radiant morning sky,
5 But, with a less ambitious sympathy,
6 Hangs o'er its Parent waking to the cares
7 Troubles and toils that every day prepares{ : ,
So Fancy to the musing Poet's eye,
Endears that Lingerer: and how blest her sway,
8 ~~And feeds till Sleep once more the weary eye~~
Neer may my Soul like influence reject
and her sway
9 ~~Shall close. So Fancy whispers,— nor reject~~
10 T~~he thought — though sad,~~ and blessed be her sway
~~How soothing, how benign in its effect~~
11 ~~If the calm Heavn, now to the zenith decked~~
If the calm Heaven, now to its zenith deckt
12 With glorious Forms in numberless array,
13 To the lone Shepherd on the Hills disclose
14 Gleams from a world in which the Saints repose
Wm Wordsworth
Front of Rydal Mount
Jan^ry 1st 1843.

every day prepares, [7–14]
every day prepares
So Fancy, to the musing Poets eye,
Endears that Lingerer. And how blesst her sway;
Like influence never may my Soul
~~Neer may my Soul like influence~~ reject!)
If the calm Heaven, now to its zenith deckt
With glorious Forms in numberless array
To the lone Shepherd on the hills disclose
Gleams of a world in which the Saints repose

The manuscript was folded as for an enclosure and "Mrs Arnold" was written in an unknown hand on the outer panel, across the revisionary lines at the foot of the sheet.

2.

Suggested upon [illegible]

Would that the little Flowers were born to live
Conscious of half the pleasure which they give
That to this mountain daisy's self were known
The beauty of its star-shaped shadow thrown
On the grey surface of this naked stone
[illegible]
[illegible]
[illegible]
And in his love, who sees and governs all
With one paternal care for great and small
[illegible]
[illegible]
[illegible]
[illegible]
[illegible]
[illegible]
[illegible]
[illegible]

["So fair, so sweet, withal so sensitive"]

Suggested upon Loughrigg Fell

Would that the little Flowers were born to live
Conscious of half the pleasures which they give
That ~~th~~ to this mountain daisys self were known
The beauty of its star-shaped shadow thrown
On the grey surface of this naked stone
O fondly thus to heave a fruitless sigh
Rarther rejoice werhereer [?thou] turns thine eye
In Natures boundless prodigality.——
And in his love, who sees and governs all
With one paternal care for great and small

second
A wiser thought reprove that fruitless sigh, [6–8]
{nd
A{ whisperd wheresoeer thou turnst thine eye
Rejoice in natures prodigality

Whispering, again whereer thou turns thine eye
In nature
When had thus been
Thus inwardly my heart ~~was~~ moved
A second thought the fruitless soft reprove
Whispering [?reproof]

Above the first revisionary line "second" is entered in pencil.

["So fair, so sweet, withal so sensitive"]

in this sort my fancy had been moved
When inwardly my heart had thus been moved [6–10]
A second thought the fruitless sigh reproved
Whispering, rejoice whereer thoug turnst thine eye
In natures boundless prodigality.
And in his love who sees & governs all
paternal
With one ~~familial~~ care for great & small

6/ "amen"—written several times below the text with the sheet reversed—is a word often used by the Wordsworths in pen trials.

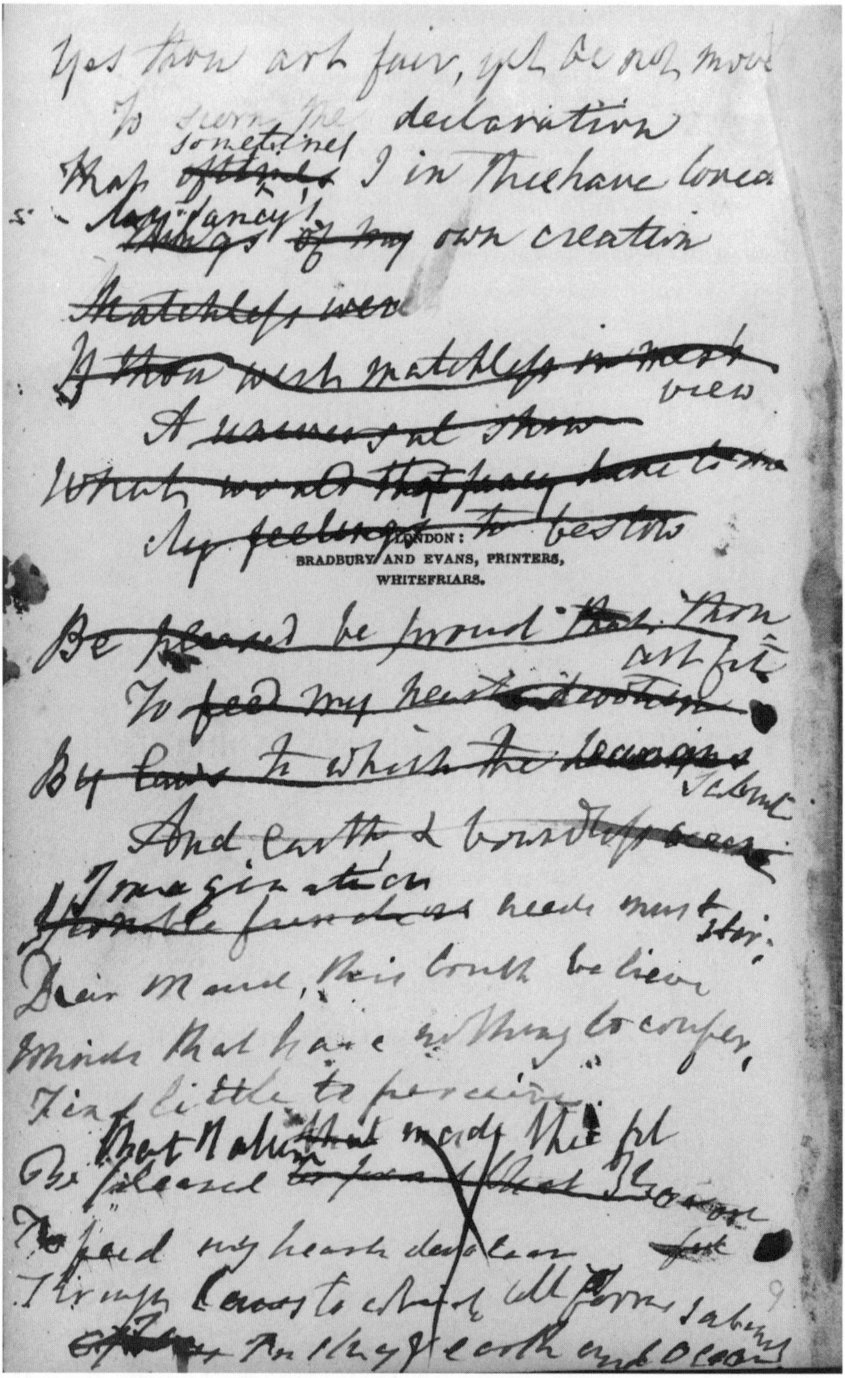
LONDON:
BRADBURY AND EVANS, PRINTERS,
WHITEFRIARS.

["Yes! thou art fair, yet be not moved"]

Yes thou art fair, yet be not moved [1–4]
To scorn the declaration
sometimes
That ~~ofttimes~~ I in thee have loved
My fancy's^
~~Things of my~~ own creation
~~Matchless weret~~
~~If thou wert matchless in men's~~
view
A ~~universal show~~
{at
~~What would th~~{ *~~y fancy have to do~~*
~~My feelings to bestow~~

~~Be pleased be proud that thou~~ [9–12]
art fit
To ~~feed my heart's devotion~~
{*~~heavens~~*
By ~~laws to which the~~{~~[?]~~
submit
~~And earth, & boundless ocean~~
Imagination
~~Humble function~~ needs must stir; [5–12]
Dear Maid, this truth believe
Minds that have nothing to confer,
Find little to perceive.
that Nature ~~that~~ made thee fit
Be pleased ~~be proud that Th~~ou art
fit
To feed my hearts devotion
Through laws to which all forms submit
~~[?Of Laws]~~ In sky & earth and ocean

1–12 The fair copy is in MW's hand.

41

For the Sun is in her harbour
weary —

44

While Youth's roses are thy crown

75

There an Old Man an older measure

270

His brother swooning by the Body
lay

Be pleased that Nature made thee fit
To feed my heart's devotion
By ~~laws~~ to which all Forms submit
In sky, ~~and~~ air, earth, and ocean.

22

Motto

Pretium ocm istam; falsa enim
dicam si ~~coges~~ coges.

Eusebius

["Yes! thou art fair, yet be not moved"]

Be pleased that Nature made Thee [9–12]
fit
To feed my heart's devot~~ed~~
~~[?tenets]~~ ion
By laws to which all Forms submit
air,
In sky, ~~and~~ earth, and ocean—
^

WW's entries above and below the four lines transcribed are unrelated to "Yes! thou art fair, yet be not moved." The first two entries are from *The Longest Day* (1820; ll. 3, 68); the third is l. 147 of *Descriptive Sketches;* the fourth is l. 174 of *The Prioress' Tale;* the "Motto" in Latin below, from Eusebius, was used by WW as the epigraph for *Anecdote for Fathers* that he added in 1845 (see *LB, 1797–1800,* pp. 71, 347). The figures, all apparently in WW's hand, seem to be line counts of several unidentified poems.

Who but delights to watch the Moon on her
Travelling where ever and anon she shrouds
~~Who but has watched the Queen of night on her~~
Her head and nothing loth, her Majesty
~~Enthroned or~~ travelling where her head she shrouds
Who but has watched the Queen of night on her
Travelling, where, ever & anon she shrouds
~~And nothing loth her [illegible]~~
Her head and nothing loth her majesty
Renounces, till among the scattered clouds

One by its kindling edge declares that soon

Will reappear before the uplifted eye
A form as bright ~~[illegible]~~ as beautiful a moon
To glide in open ~~[illegible]~~ prospect thro' clear sky
Pity that such a promise ere should prove
False on the trial, that a seeming space
Of dark pure blue sky should be in truth the face
~~The face~~ Of a deceitful cloud thro' which
much more
The Wanderer look in more determined gloom
Muse on her lot so like Man's frequent doom
frequent
Delusive lot, [illegible] Who must [illegible] dream

["Who but is pleased to watch the moon on high"]

Who but delights to watch the Moon on high
Travelling where ever and anon she shrouds
1 *~~Who but has watched the Queen of night on high~~*
her Head—and nothing loth, her majesty
2 *~~Enthroned, or~~ travelling where her head she shrouds*
Who but has watched the Queen of night on high
Travelling, where, ever & anon she shrouds
3 *~~And nothing loth her native majesty~~ renounces*
Her head, and nothing loth her majesty
4 *Renounces, till among the scattered clouds,*

5 *One by its kindling edge declares that soon*

6 *Will reappear before the uplifted eye*
7 *A form as bright as beautiful a moon*
~~prospect~~
8 *To glide in open ~~view~~ thro'^clear sky*
prospect
9 *Pity that such a promise ere should prove*
o}
10 *False i}n the trial, that a seeming space*
pure
11 *Of dark blue sky should be in truth the*
O} *face*
12 *~~The face~~ o}f a deceitful cloud thro' which*
must move
13 *The Wanderer lost in more determined gloom.*
{m
14 *Muse on her lot so like Man's frequent doo{n*
frequent
{frequent
Delusive lot, how like mans {[?present] doom

The ink lines in the margin connect the revised ll. 1–2 with "Her head . . . " below l. 3.

3 "renounces" has been partially erased.

8 The caret may mark the insertion of l. 7. The word "prospect" had already been entered above, was then deleted, and reentered below.

[*At Furness Abbey* ("Here, where, of havoc tired and rash undoing")]

[9r]

this
1 Caught by ~~yon~~ Tower where busiest joy prevails
hence
2 For ~~thence~~ the cawing brood new-waked proclaim [12]
3 Prescriptive title to the lonely pile; [13]
4 While thine O Cavendish is but a name [14]
and often good
5 Nor seldom pleased & at [?]
6 Now [?] perchance [?]
7 The peasant

[9v]

1 While Man delights in shattering & undoing [1–4]
2 His noblest works or leaves them to decay
3 Nature puts forth her gentle powers to stay
4 And to adorn where there is no renewing
5 Her ivy props this venerable ~~Ruin~~ [5]
6 In beauteous of her kind intent
7 And where are sweeter flowers than over
rent
8 Tottering or prostrate here her hand is
in shewing
9 The Peasant ~~from~~ the rising suns first smile [10]
~~the~~
10 Caught by yon tower ~~a~~ gladder promise hails
11 That morning yields—The Rook The daws tell
tales

[10r]

1 Then [~~—?—~~] morning yields the rooks
2 Tell tales merry & loud & with the daw
3 Proclaim presumptive to this lonely pile [13]
4 While thine O Cavendish is but a name [14]
[~~—? ? ? ?—~~]
5 Pleasant to hear and loudly they proclaim [12]
6 Presumptive to this lonely Ruin [13]

This transcription is adapted from that printed by George Harris Healey in *WPN* (pp. 25–27) and, for 9v–10r, Dr. Richard Hall's facsimile reproduction of an opening of the notebook in his "Items, Hitherto Unpublished, From A Note Book of William Wordsworth," *The Chimes* (Rome, GA) 40 (December 1927), between pp. 8 and 9. See also Healey's commentary, *WPN,* pp. 86–91; the original manuscript has not been located.

9r, l. 3 Prescriptive] So Healey's transcription (following Hall's), but the word is probably "Presumptive" as in ll. 3 and 6 on 10r.

9v, l. 2 The line was squeezed between ll. 1 and 3, although clearly part of the octet being drafted rather than a revision of the line above or the one below.

APPENDIXES

Appendix I

Contents of *Yarrow Revisited, and Other Poems* (1835, 1836, 1839) and *Poems, Chiefly of Early and Late Years* (1842)

Many of the poems composed between 1820 and 1850 first appeared in the collections of 1835 and 1842. *Yarrow Revisited, and Other Poems* (1835) was revised and reissued in one volume in 1836 and 1839, though Wordsworth distributed the contents among the classes of *Poetical Works,* beginning with the edition of 1836. *Poems, Chiefly of Early and Late Years* (1842) was also reissued, without the volume title and with some rearrangement of contents, as an additional volume in the multivolume *Poetical Works* in 1846 and 1849. However, Wordsworth redistributed the poems in his one-volume *Poems* in 1845 and in the final edition of his *Poetical Works* in 1849–1850. The lists below provide an overview of these single-volume works, through their several reissues. Significant rearrangements, additions, and omissions are recorded in notes; sequences of poems and individual poems that are edited elsewhere in The Cornell Wordsworth are so identified in the notes. The titles of groups of poems have been set in large and small capitals to distinguish them from titles of poems ("SONNETS," for example). To avoid any confusion, the wording of the title or first line is cited from the page on which the poem appears in each volume rather than from the contents list, which is often at variance with the text itself.

A. Contents of *Yarrow Revisited, and Other Poems* (1835)

- YARROW REVISITED, AND OTHER POEMS, COMPOSED DURING A TOUR IN SCOTLAND, AND ON THE ENGLISH BORDER, IN THE AUTUMN OF 1831[1]
- The Egyptian Maid; or, the Romance of the Water Lily
- Ode, Composed on May Morning
- To May
- Inscription ("The massy Ways, carried across these Heights")

---

[1]Individual poems in this sequence and subsequent changes in its makeup are not detailed here; they will appear in Geoffrey Jackson's forthcoming edition in The Cornell Wordsworth series, *Sonnet Series and Itinerary Poems, 1819–1850.*

Elegiac Musings in the Grounds of Coleorton Hall, the Seat of the late Sir George Beaumont, Bart.
Epitaph ("By a blest Husband guided, Mary came")
Inscription Intended for a Stone in the Grounds of Rydal Mount
Written in an Album
Incident at Brugès[2]
A Jewish Family. (In a Small Valley opposite St. Goar, upon the Rhine.)
Devotional Incitements
The Armenian Lady's Love
The Primrose of the Rock
Presentiments
The Poet and the Caged Turtledove
Sonnets
Chatsworth! thy stately mansion, and the pride
Desponding Father! mark this altered bough
Roman Antiquities Discovered, at Bishopstone, Herefordshire
St. Catherine of Ledbury
The Russian Fugitive
Sonnets
Why art thou silent! Is thy love a plant
Four fiery steeds impatient of the rein
To the Author's Portrait
Gold and Silver Fishes, in a Vase
Liberty. (Sequel to the Above.)
Evening Voluntaries
Calm is the fragrant air, and loth to lose
Not in the lucid intervals of life
(By the Side of Rydal Mere.)
Soft as a cloud is yon blue Ridge—the Mere
The leaves that rustled on this oak-crowned hill
The Sun, that seemed so mildly to retire[3]
(By the Sea-side.)
The sun has long been set
Throned in the Sun's descending car
The Labourer's Noon-day Hymn
A Wren's Nest
Sonnets, 1833, Composed or Suggested during a Tour in Scotland, in the Summer of 1833[4]
Lines Written in the Album of the Countess of ———. Nov. 5. 1834
The Somnambulist[5]
To ———, upon the Birth of her first-born Child, March, 1833
The Warning, a Sequel to the Foregoing. March, 1833
If this great world of joy and pain
Sonnet, Composed after reading a Newspaper of the Day[6]

---

[2]Transferred to Sentiment and Reflection in *1836* and to Continent 1820 in *1845*.
[3]Titled *On a high part of the coast of Cumberland* in *1836–*.
[4]See note 1.
[5]Transferred to the end of Tour 1833 in *1836YR* and *1839*.
[6]Present in *1836YR*, *1839*, as VIII in the sequence Yarrow Revisited. A note in *1835* states that it was mistakenly omitted from its proper place following VII in the series.

Loving and Liking: Irregular Verses addressed to a Child[7]
Stanzas Suggested in a Steam-boat off St. Bees' Heads, on the Coast of Cumberland [St. Bees, Suggested in a Steam-boat off St. Bees' Heads][8]
SONNETS[9]
Deplorable his lot who tills the ground
The Vaudois
Praised be the Rivers, from their mountain-springs
The Redbreast (Suggested in a Westmoreland Cottage.)
To ——— ("'Wait, prithee, wait!' this answer Lesbia threw")
Rural Illusions
This Lawn, &c.
Thought on the Seasons
Humanity. (Written in the Year 1829.)
Lines Suggested by a Portrait from the Pencil of F. Stone
The Foregoing Subject resumed
Stanzas on the Power of Sound [On the Power of Sound]

B. Contents of *Yarrow Revisited, and Other Poems* (1836) [Only additions are listed.]
EVENING VOLUNTARIES
Had this effulgence disappeared[10]

C. Contents of *Yarrow Revisited, and other Poems* (1839) [Only additions are listed.]
SONNETS
What if our numbers barely could defy[11]
Even so for me a Vision sanctified[12]
Coldly we spake. The Saxons, overpowered[13]
EVENING VOLUNTARIES[14]
To the Moon. Composed by the Sea-side, on the Coast of Cumberland
To the Moon. (Rydal)
Upon Seeing a Coloured Drawing of the Bird of Paradise in an Album
Epitaphs Translated from Chiabrera[15]
Six months to six years added he remained[16]
To a good Man of most dear memory
Extempore Effusion upon the Death of James Hogg

D. Contents of *Poems, Chiefly of Early and Late Years* (1842)
Prelude
Guilt and Sorrow; or, Incidents upon Salisbury Plain[17]
Sonnet ("Though the bold wings of Poesy affect")[18]

---

[7]By DW.
[8]Moved to Tour 1833 in *1845*.
[9]The three sonnets were moved to Ecclesiastical Sonnets in *1836*.
[10]*Ode, Composed upon an Evening of Extraordinary Splendour and Beauty*, first published 1820; see *Poems, 1807–1820*, pp. 255–260.
[11]Composed in 1803, first published in Liberty in *1836;* see *Poems, 1800–1807*, pp, 584–585.
[12]First published in Miscellaneous Sonnets in *1836*.
[13]First published in Ecclesiastical Sonnets in *1836*.
[14]Both poems were first published in *1836*.
[15]Composed in 1809 or 1810; see *Poems, 1807–1820*, pp. 60–68.
[16]Composed in 1812 or 1813; see *Poems, 1807–1820*, p. 123.
[17]Moved to Poems Written in Youth in *1845* and *1846;* see *SPP*.
[18]Moved to Miscellaneous Sonnets in *1845* and *1846* (vol. VI).

The Forsaken[19]
Lyre! though such power do in thy magic live
Address to the Scholars of the Village School of ——. 1798.[20]
Lines on the Expected Invasion. 1803[21]
At the Grave of Burns. 1803
Thoughts Suggested the Day Following on the Banks of Nith, near the Poet's Residence
Elegiac Verses in Memory of my Brother John Wordsworth[22]
At Applethwaite, near Keswick. 1804[23]
Epistle to Sir George Howland Beaumont, Bart.[24]
Upon Perusing the Foregoing Epistle Thirty Years after its Composition
Airey-Force Valley
A Night Thought
Farewell Lines
Love Lies Bleeding
Companion to the Foregoing
Address to the Clouds[25]
Suggested by a Picture of the Bird of Paradise
Maternal Grief[26]
MEMORIALS OF A TOUR IN ITALY. 1837[27]
The Cuckoo and the Nightingale. (From Chaucer.)[28]
SONNETS UPON THE PUNISHMENT OF DEATH. IN SERIES[29]
Composed by the Sea-shore
The Norman Boy
Sequel to The Norman Boy
Poor Robin
The Cuckoo-clock
The Wishing-gate Destroyed
The Widow on Windermere Side
Cenotaph
Epitaph in the Chapel-yard of Langdale, Westmoreland
Troilus and Cresida. (Extract from Chaucer.)[30]
MISCELLANEOUS SONNETS
  A Poet!—He hath put his heart to school
  The most alluring clouds that mount the sky
  Feel for the wrongs to universal ken[31]

---

[19]See *Poems, 1800–1807*, pp. 571–572.
[20]See *LB, 1797–1800*, pp. 808–811.
[21]See *Poems, 1800–1807*, pp. 598–599.
[22]See *Poems, 1800–1807*, pp. 614–616.
[23]See *Poems, 1800–1807*, pp. 532–533.
[24]See *Poems, 1807–1820*, pp. 78–95.
[25]See *Tuft*, pp. 61–71.
[26]See *Poems, 1807–1820*, pp. 119–122.
[27]See note 1.
[28]See *Translations*, pp. 45–55.
[29]See note 1.
[30]Moved to follow *The Cuckoo and the Nightingale* in *1845* and *1846*. See *Translations*, pp. 56–60.
[31]Transferred to Liberty and Order in *1845*.

ASPECTS OF CHRISTIANITY IN AMERICA
I. The Pilgrim Fathers[32]
II. Continued
III. Concluded.—American Episcopacy
On a Portrait of the Duke of Wellington, upon the Field of Waterloo, by Haydon
In allusion to Various Recent Histories and Notices of the French Revolution[33]
Continued
Concluded
Men of the Western World! in Fate's dark book
Lo! where she stands fixed in a saint-like trance
To a Painter
On the Same Subject
To a Redbreast—(in Sickness)[34]
Floating Island[35]
The Crescent-moon, the Star of Love
SONNETS[36]
Blest Statesman He, whose Mind's unselfish will[37]
Composed on a May Morning, 1838[38]
Composed on the Same Morning
At Dover[39]
To the Planet Venus, Upon its Approximation (as an Evening Star) to the Earth, January, 1838
Hark! 'tis the Thrush, undaunted, undeprest
'Tis He whose yester-evening's high disdain
Oh what a Wreck! how changed in mien and speech
A Plea for Authors, May, 1838
Valedictory Sonnet. Closing the Volume of Sonnets published in 1838
Intent on gathering wool from hedge and brake
The Borderers. A Tragedy[40]

E. Contents of Volume 6 of *Poetical Works* (1846, 1849). [Only additions are listed.]
The Simplon Pass[41]
Inscription for a Monument in Crosthwaite Church, in the Vale of Keswick
MISCELLANEOUS SONNETS
To the Rev. Christopher Wordsworth, D.D. Master of Harrow School, After the perusal of his Theophilus Anglicanus, recently published.
Wansfell! this Household has a favoured lot

---

[32]This and the two following sonnets were transferred to Ecclesiastical Sonnets in *1845*.

[33]This and the three following sonnets were transferred to Liberty and Order in *1845*.

[34]By SH, revised by WW. This poem and the next two were moved in *1845* to follow *The Gleaner* in Miscellaneous Poems and in *1846* (vol. VI) to follow *Inscription for a Monument in Crosthwaite Church, in the Vale of Keswick.*

[35]By DW.

[36]Contents were included, with some rearrangement, in Miscellaneous Sonnets (originating in *PELY*) in *1846* (vol. VI).

[37]Transferred to Liberty and Order in *1845*.

[38]Transferred to Italy 1837 in *1845*.

[39]Transferred to Continent 1820 in *1845*.

[40]See *Borderers* (Osborn).

[41]From *Prelude*, VI, 622–641; first published in *Kendal and Windermere Railway* (1845), added to Imagination in *1845*, and inserted after *Airey-Force Valley* in volume six of *1846* and *1849*.

On the projected Kendal and Windermere Railway
Proud were ye, Mountains, when, in times of old
At Furness Abbey ("Here, where, of havoc tired and rash undoing")
At Furness Abbey ("Well have yon Railway Labourers to THIS ground")
Said Secrecy to Cowardice and Fraud[42]
To the Pennsylvanians[43]
Young England—what is then become of Old
To Lucca Giordano
To an Octogenarian
Who but is pleased to watch the moon on high
Where lies the truth? has Man, in wisdom's creed
Why should we weep or mourn, Angelic boy

---

[42]Appeared first in *1838*, then in the appendix of *1840;* transferred to Liberty and Order in *1845*.
[43]*To the Pennsylvanians* and "Young England" first appeared in *1845*, in Liberty and Order.

Appendix II

Late Additions to *Sonnets* (1838) and *Poetical Works* (1840)

In the volume of Wordsworth's *Sonnets* published by Moxon in 1838 the last signature of poetic text is taken up with the final eight pages of Ecclesiastical Sonnets, followed by *Valedictory Sonnet* and a group of six sonnets that Wordsworth introduced with the statement, "The six Sonnets annexed were composed as this Volume was going through the Press, but too late for insertion in the class of miscellaneous ones, to which they belong." The sonnets are the following:

I. *Composed on May-Morning, 1838.*[1] ("If with old love of you, dear Hills! I share")
II. *Composed on the Same Morning.* ("Life with yon Lambs, like day, is just begun")
III. "Hark! 'tis the Thrush, undaunted, undepress"
IV. "'Tis He whose yester-evening's high disdain"
V. *A Plea for Authors. May, 1838.*
VI. *A Poet to His Grandchild. (Sequel to the foregoing.)*

In addition to these six, a seventh sonnet, "Said Secrecy to Cowardice and Fraud," appeared in the note to *Protest Against the Ballot. 1838.*

In his *Poetical Works* of 1840 Wordsworth added an "Appendix" to the fifth volume in the final signature of poetic text. Again the insertion must have come late in the printing process, for the poems included in the appendix are not listed in the Contents or in the Indexes in volume five. Facing the first poem is the following "Advertisement":

Since the first impression of this stereotyped edition was taken, a collection of the Sonnets was published separately, which contained also twelve sonnets composed while that volume was going through the press. It has been thought proper to annex them here; and for my own satisfaction, and in the hope I acknowledge, of gratifying some readers, I have added Latin Translations, by a near relative of mine, of the two Odes to May, and also of the Somnambulist; with an account, by the Translator, in an Elegiac epistle to a friend, of

[1]The title of "If with old love" in *Sonnets* and the Appendix to *PW*, 1840, is without the article, a narrowing of the date to May 1 that WW maintained in *Poems,* 1845, where he retitled the sonnet *Composed at Rydal on May Morning, 1838,* to distinguish it from the retitled *Composed on the Same Morning.* Briefly, in *PELY,* 1842, the title of "If with old love" was *Composed on a May Morning, 1838.*

the circumstances under which the Translations were made.
RYDAL MOUNT,
Nov. 20th, 1839

The apparent discrepancy between the "twelve sonnets" of 1840 and the six that were "annexed" to the volume of *Sonnets* in 1838 can be explained by Wordsworth's inclusion in the *Sonnets* volume of *Valedictory Sonnet* as the concluding sonnet, just preceding the annexed group, his addition of four sonnets (sonnets I through IV below) to the end of Miscellaneous Sonnets, and his placement of *At Dover* as the final sonnet in "Itinerary Sonnets. First Series. Selected from Memorials of a Tour on the Continent. 1820." Each of these six new sonnets, except for *At Dover*, was marked with an asterisk in the contents list to show it was one of the "new Sonnets." Listed below are the poems in the appendix to volume five of *Poetical Works* (1840).

I. *Protest Against the Ballot. 1838.* [with a note containing another sonnet, "Said Secrecy to Cowardice and Fraud"]
II. "Blest Statesman He, whose Mind's unselfish will"[2]
III. *To the Planet Venus, upon its approximation (as an Evening Star) to the Earth, January 1838.*
IV. "Oh what a wreck! how changed in mien and speech!"
V. *At Dover.*[3] ("From the Pier's head, musing—and with increase")
VI. *Composed on May-Morning, 1838.*[4] ("If with old love of you, dear Hills! I share")
VII. *Composed on the Same Morning.* ("Life with yon Lambs, like day, is just begun")
VIII. "Hark! 'tis the Thrush, undaunted, undepress"
IX. "'Tis He whose yester-evening's high disdain"
X. *A Plea for Authors. May, 1838.*
XI. *A Poet to His Grandchild. (Sequel to the foregoing.)*
XII. *Valedictory Sonnet, at the Close of the Volume of Sonnets.*
Notes.
Epistola ad amicum clericum scriptori ægrotanti itineris socium per ripas sequanæ, cum carminibus rydalii vatis sonnullis latine redditis.
Carmen maiis calendis compositum.
Carmen ad maium mensem.
Somnivaga.

The appendix was also printed off for independent private distribution, with pages numbered from 1 up. It was not reprinted as an appendix in subsequent stereotype editions. Instead, in 1842, Wordsworth included all but two of the new sonnets in his *Poems, Chiefly of Early and Late Years* (see Appendix I above). The sonnets excluded are *A Poet to His Grandchild. (Sequel to the foregoing.)* and *Protest Against the Ballot. 1838*, though the sonnet appended to the latter, "Said Secrecy to Cowardice and Fraud," was placed among the Sonnets Dedicated to Liberty and Order in the edition of 1845. The Latin poems, written by John Wordsworth, Wordsworth's son (*LY*, III, 738–739), were not reprinted.

---

[2]Transferred to Liberty and Order in *1845*.
[3]Transferred to Continent 1820 in *1845*.
[4]See note 1, above.

Appendix III

The Contents and Arrangement of Evening Voluntaries in *Poetical Works* (1849–1850).

Wordsworth added to and rearranged the series of Evening Voluntaries through all collective editions after their first appearance in 1835 in *Yarrow Revisited, and Other Poems.* Listed below are the titles or first lines of the poems as they appeared in the final lifetime edition of 1849–1850.

I. "Calm is the fragrant air, and loth to lose"
II. *On a High Part of the Coast of Cumberland.* ("The Sun, that seemed so mildly to retire")
III. *(By the Sea-side.)*
IV. "Not in the lucid intervals of life"
V. *(By the Side of Rydal Mere.)*
VI. "Soft as a cloud is yon blue Ridge—the Mere"
VII. "The leaves that rustled on this oak-crowned hill"
VIII. "The sun has long been set"
IX. *Composed upon an Evening of Extraordinary Splendour and Beauty.*
X. *Composed by the Sea-shore.*
XI. "The Crescent-moon, the Star of Love"
XII. *To the Moon. (Composed by the Sea-side,—on the Coast of Cumberland.)*
XIII. *To the Moon. (Rydal.)*
XIV. *To Lucca Giordano.*
XV. "Who but is pleased to watch the moon on high"
XIV. "Where lies the truth? has Man, in wisdom's creed."

Index of Titles and First Lines

Entries are alphabetized by word. Titles beginning with "A," "An," or "The" are alphabetized by their second word, first lines by their first word. Words in brackets clarify the reference, usually by identifying the authors of poems not written by Wordsworth. Page numbers of reading texts are in **boldface**. Page numbers of transcriptions are in *italics*. References to the notes in Part II, which include rationales for the dating of poems and discussions of related poems, are identifiable by their occurrences within pages 417–506; references to the lists of nonverbal variants for the poems fall within pages 507–614.